"Media anthropology, just like the media itself, is a fast-moving field of enquiry, especially in the light of new digital technologies. What makes this volume essential is the way it effectively brings the reader up to date with some of the most exciting and insightful developments as well as new approaches. It also provides a very effective balance between the depth one associates with ethnographically based studies and the breadth that is required in encompassing a field that ranges from infrastructure and practice to materiality and inequality."

Daniel Miller, *Professor, UCL Department of Anthropology, London*

"This rich and engaging volume successfully redefines the field of media anthropology for a digital world, while respecting and building upon the pioneering work that established the field. Over 40 ethnographers explore contemporary phenomena and the cultural practices around them – from gaming to YouTube, fashion to tourism – while interrogating the global realities of inequality, injustice, and surveillance. Especially timely is the focus on the role of media in the rise of extremism and the crisis of truth, offering a stark warning for the future."

Elizabeth Bird, *Professor Emerita, Department of Anthropology, University of South Florida*

"This important collection brings together many of the world's significant and emerging voices in media studies, digital research, and anthropology. It offers a comprehensive overview of where media anthropology has come from, how it has developed, and where it is going. Contributions include reflections on key moments in the development of media anthropology, consideration of the methodological, theoretical, and political opportunities that media anthropology has brought to academic research, and a vision of the near future that media anthropology offers new generations of students and scholars. The transregional and multigenerational scope demonstrates how media anthropology has developed and evolved, both within and beyond the disciplines from which it began."

Anna Cristina Pertierra, *Professor, School of Design, University of Technology Sydney*

THE ROUTLEDGE COMPANION TO MEDIA ANTHROPOLOGY

The Routledge Companion to Media Anthropology provides a broad overview of the widening and flourishing area of media anthropology, and outlines key themes, debates, and emerging directions.

The Routledge Companion to Media Anthropology draws together the work of scholars from across the globe, with rich ethnographic studies that address a wide range of media practices and forms. Comprising 41 chapters by a team of international contributors, the Companion is divided into three parts:

- Histories
- Approaches
- Thematic Considerations.

The chapters offer wide-ranging explorations of how forms of mediation influence communication, social relationships, cultural practices, participation, and social change, as well as production and access to information and knowledge. This volume considers new developments, and highlights the ways in which anthropology can contribute to the study of the human condition and the social processes in which media are entangled.

This is an indispensable teaching resource for advanced undergraduate and postgraduate students and an essential text for scholars working across the areas that media anthropology engages with, including anthropology, sociology, media and cultural studies, internet and communication studies, and science and technology studies.

Elisabetta Costa is Assistant Professor in Media Studies at the University of Groningen, the Netherlands.

Patricia G. Lange is Associate Professor and Chair of Critical Studies at California College of the Arts, USA.

Nell Haynes is a faculty member in the Department of Global Studies at Saint Mary's College, USA.

Jolynna Sinanan is a Lecturer in Social and Digital Anthropology at the University of Manchester, UK.

Routledge Anthropology Handbooks

The Routledge Handbook of Anthropology and Reproduction
Edited by Sallie Han and Cecília Tomori

The Routledge Companion to Contemporary Anthropology
Edited by Simon Coleman, Susan B. Hyatt and Ann Kingsolver

The Routledge Handbook of Anthropology and the City
Edited by Setha Low

The Routledge Handbook of Medical Anthropology
Edited by Lenore Manderson, Elizabeth Cartwright and Anita Hardon

The Routledge Handbook of the Anthropology of Labor
Edited by Sharryn Kasmir and Lesley Gill

The Routledge Companion to Media Anthropology
Edited by Elisabetta Costa, Patricia G. Lange, Nell Haynes, and Jolynna Sinanan

www.routledge.com/Routledge-Anthropology-Handbooks/book-series/RANTHBK

THE ROUTLEDGE COMPANION TO MEDIA ANTHROPOLOGY

*Edited by Elisabetta Costa, Patricia G. Lange,
Nell Haynes, and Jolynna Sinanan*

LONDON AND NEW YORK

Cover image: arda savaşcıoğulları / Alamy Stock Photo

First published 2023
by Routledge
4 Park Square, Milton Park, Abingdon, Oxon OX14 4RN

and by Routledge
605 Third Avenue, New York, NY 10158

Routledge is an imprint of the Taylor & Francis Group, an informa business

© 2023 selection and editorial matter, Elisabetta Costa, Patricia G. Lange, Nell Haynes and Jolynna Sinanan; individual chapters, the contributors

The right of Elisabetta Costa, Patricia G. Lange, Nell Haynes and Jolynna Sinanan to be identified as the authors of the editorial material, and of the authors for their individual chapters, has been asserted in accordance with sections 77 and 78 of the Copyright, Designs and Patents Act 1988.

With the exception of Chapters 6, 7, 12 and 15 no part of this book may be reprinted or reproduced or utilised in any form or by any electronic, mechanical, or other means, now known or hereafter invented, including photocopying and recording, or in any information storage or retrieval system, without permission in writing from the publishers.

Chapter 6 of this book is available for free in PDF format as Open Access at www.taylorfrancis.com. It has been made available under a Creative Commons Attribution-No Derivatives 4.0 (CC-BY-ND) International license.

Chapters 7, 12 and 15 of this book is available for free in PDF format as Open Access from the individual product page at www.routledge.com. It has been made available under a Creative Commons Attribution-Non Commercial-No Derivatives 4.0 license.

Trademark notice: Product or corporate names may be trademarks or registered trademarks, and are used only for identification and explanation without intent to infringe.

British Library Cataloguing-in-Publication Data
A catalogue record for this book is available from the British Library

Library of Congress Cataloging-in-Publication Data
Names: Costa, Elisabetta (Anthropologist), editor.
Title: The Routledge companion to media anthropology /
edited by Elisabetta Costa [and others].
Description: Milton Park, Abingdon, Oxon ; New York : Routledge, 2023. |
Series: Routledge anthropology handbooks |
Includes bibliographical references and index. | Identifiers: LCCN 2022010937 (print) |
LCCN 2022010938 (ebook) | ISBN 9781032007762 (hardback) |
ISBN 9781032007786 (paperback) | ISBN 9781003175605 (ebook)
Subjects: LCSH: Mass media and anthropology. |
Mass media and culture. | Anthropological ethics.
Classification: LCC P96.A56 R68 2023 (print) |
LCC P96.A56 (ebook) | DDC 302.23–dc23/eng/20220523
LC record available at https://lccn.loc.gov/2022010937
LC ebook record available at https://lccn.loc.gov/2022010938

ISBN: 978-1-032-00776-2 (hbk)
ISBN: 978-1-032-00778-6 (pbk)
ISBN: 978-1-003-17560-5 (ebk)

DOI: 10.4324/9781003175605

Typeset in Bembo
by Newgen Publishing UK

The OA version of Chapter 6 was funded by Patricia G. Lange
The OA version of Chapter 7 was funded by University of Wisconsin
The OA version of Chapter 12 was funded by University of Tübingen
The OA version of Chapter 15 was funded by University of Exeter

CONTENTS

List of Figures   *xiii*
List of Contributors   *xv*
Acknowledgements   *xxv*

Introduction   1
Elisabetta Costa, Patricia G. Lange, Nell Haynes, and Jolynna Sinanan

PART I
Histories   **15**

1 Media Anthropology and the Digital Challenge   17
   Mark Allen Peterson

2 Indigenous Media: Anthropological Perspectives and Historical Notes   33
   Philipp Budka

3 A Longitudinal Study of Media in Brazil   47
   Conrad Phillip Kottak and Richard Pace

Contents

PART II
Approaches   **61**

A
Media as Infrastructure   **63**

4   "Here, Listen to My CD-R": Music Transactions and Infrastructures in Underground Hip-Hop Touring   65
Anthony Kwame Harrison

5   "Technology is Wonderful Until It Isn't": Community-Based Research and the Precarity of Digital Infrastructure   77
Jerome Crowder, Peggy Determeyer, and Sara Rogers

6   Media Migration   89
Patricia G. Lange

7   The Digitally Natural: Hypomediacy and the "Really Real" in Game Design   103
Thomas M. Malaby

B
Media as Practice   **117**

8   Media Practices and Their Social Effects   119
John Postill

9   Television is Not a Democracy: The Limits of Interactive Broadcast in Japan   132
Elizabeth A. Rodwell

10   Producing Place through Play: An Ethnography of Location-based Gaming   145
Kyle Moore

11   PhotoMedia as Anthropology: Towards a Speculative Research Method   157
Edgar Gómez Cruz

12   Content-as-Practice: Studying Digital Content with a Media Practice Approach   171
Christoph Bareither

C
Media as Materiality — 183

13 The Materiality of the Virtual in Urban Space — 185
Jordan Kraemer

14 Anthropology and Digital Media: Multivocal Materialities of Video Meetings and Deafness — 200
Rebekah Cupitt

15 Cloudwork: Data Centre Labour and the Maintenance of Media Infrastructure — 213
A.R.E. Taylor

16 Media Anthropology and Emerging Technologies: Re-working Media Presence — 229
Sarah Pink, Yolande Strengers, Melisa Duque, Larissa Nichols, and Rex Martin

D
Media as Representation — 243

17 #Everest: Visual Economies of Leisure and Labour in the Tourist Encounter — 245
Jolynna Sinanan

18 Postcolonial Digital Collections: Instruments, Mirrors, Agents — 258
Haidy Geismar and Katja Müller

19 Ethnographies of the Digitally Dispossessed — 272
Heather Ford

PART III
Thematic Considerations — 285

A
Relationships — 287

20 "Friends from WeChat Groups": The Practice of Friendship via Social Media among Older People in China — 289
Xinyuan Wang

21	Mediated Money and Social Relationships among Hong Kong Cross-boundary Students *Tom McDonald, Holy Hoi Ki Shum and Kwok Cheung Wong*	301
22	Narratives of Digital Intimacy: Romanian Migration and Mediated Transnational Life *Donya Alinejad and Laura Candidatu*	314

B
Social Inequality and Marginalisation — 329

23	Mediating Hopes: Social Media and Crisis in Northern Italy *Elisabetta Costa*	331
24	Digital Inequality and Relatedness in India after Access *Sirpa Tenhunen*	343
25	In This Together: Black Women, Collective Screening Experiences, and Space-Making as Meaning-Making *Marlaina Martin*	355
26	Black Gamer's Refuge: Finding Community within the Magic Circle of Whiteness *Akil Fletcher*	368

C
Identities and Social Change — 379

27	Inking Identity: Indigenous Nationalism in Bolivian Tattoo Art *Nell Haynes*	381
28	Being Known and Becoming Famous in Kampala, Uganda *Brooke Schwartz Bocast*	395
29	The Hall of Mirrors: Negotiating Gender on Chilean Social Media *Baird Campbell*	410

D
Political Conservatism — 425

30	Media Anthropology and the Crisis of Facts *Peter Hervik*	427

31	Conspiracy Media Ecologies and the Case for Guerilla Anthropology *Leighton C. Peterson and Jeb J. Card*	441
32	Researching Political Trolls as Instruments of Political Conservatism in Turkey: A Historical Framework and Methodological Reflections on a Discourse Community *Erkan Saka*	454
33	Performing Conservatism: A Study of Emerging Political Mobilisations in Latin America using "Social Media Drama" Analysis *Raúl Castro-Pérez*	465

E
Surveillance 479

34	Algorithmic Violence in Everyday Life and the Role of Media Anthropology *Veronica Barassi*	481
35	Queer and Muslim? Social Surveillance and Islamic Sexual Ethics on Twitter *Benjamin Ale-Ebrahim*	492
36	Queer Sousveillance: Publics, Politics, and Social Media in South Korea *Alex Wolff*	505

F
Emerging Technologies and Contemporary Challenges: Data, AI and VR 517

37	The Algorithmic Silhouette: New Technologies and the Fashionable Body *Heather A. Horst and Sheba Mohammid*	519
38	Unlocking Heritage *In Situ*: Tourist Places and Augmented Reality in Estonia *Christian S. Ritter*	532
39	Precarity, Discrimination and (In)Visibility: An Ethnography of "The Algorithm" in the YouTube Influencer Industry *Zoë Glatt*	544

Contents

40 AI Design and Everyday Logics in the Kalahari   557
   Nicola J. Bidwell, Helen Arnold, Alan F. Blackwell, Charlie Nqeisji,
   |Kun Kunta, and Martin Ujakpa

41 Ethnography of/and Virtual Reality   570
   Lisa Messeri

   Afterword   581
   Eric W. Rothenbuhler

Appendix   *586*
Index   *596*

FIGURES

7.1	A screenshot of Persuasive Games' *Take Back Illinois* (medical malpractice version)	107
9.1	The Nico Nico Douga broadcast runs longer than the TV broadcast, and though they overlap at times, each involves different kinds of interaction	133
11.1	Discarded facemasks in Sydney, Australia	158
11.2	Discarded facemask in Sydney, Australia	162
11.3	Discarded facemask covered in leaves	165
13.1	Cozy café in Kreuzberg, 2015	189
13.2	Laptop and projector streaming the World Cup 2010 final match on the sidewalk in Kreuzberg	192
13.3	JusticeforGeorgeNYC Instagram page, June 2020	194
13.4	Screenshot of the chat window from a mutual aid group Zoom call, August 2020. One member's poor sound quality garnered more discussion in the chat than was typical	195
14.1	(a) Louisa signing to René and Anna that she only sees half of René; (b) A view similar to the one that Louisa would see of René and Anna was shown on a secondary monitor in the Falun meeting room; (c) Louisa's image as seen by those in Falun and taken from the view of the anthropologist	205
14.2	(a) The image Axel sees from his Stockholm meeting room. Note how Rickard is only half visible on the right-hand side of the screen; (b) Rickard leaning forward and waving to make sure he is visible before he picks up the remote and starts moving the camera angle	208
15.1	One of the server rooms in GigaTech's East London facility	214
15.2	"The Cloud is a Lie", James Bridle (2011)	219
15.3	A technician running diagnostic tests to ensure equipment is correctly functioning	220

Figures

15.4	LinkedIn's service disruption error screen visualises data centre server maintenance, providing users with a momentary hint of the labour and infrastructure that otherwise remains distant and unseen behind the screen	223
16.1	Edna participating in the video tour of her home during the first stage of our research with Sarah and Melisa	232
16.2	Bob, Edna's husband participating in the online ethnography during the final stage of our research with Sarah and Melisa	233
17.1	A screen advertising NCell data SIM cards featuring Mount Everest in the baggage claim area of Tribhuvan Airport, Kathmandu	250
17.2	A trekking guide taking a photo of a group of trekkers	253
18.1	Digitizing in an Indian museum	261
18.2	Screenshot of Jatan's frontend	263
20.1	WeChat groups can be broken down into three types, based on three interpersonal ties. This chart is adapted from the original chart called 'a theoretical model of face and favor in Chinese society'	295
27.1	Tattoo of ñatita with chullo and coca leaves	389
27.2	Tattoo of swallow with aguayo textile design	390
28.1	An example of the *Red Pepper*'s coverage of female university students	396
28.2	A4L mural on Makerere University Campus	397
28.3	Juxtaposition of tabloid and public health representations of female university students	402
29.1	This photo, posted to Alexa's Instagram in December 2016, appears with the (translated) caption: "We can all be what we want to be. In the first photo I was 7 and dreamed of being a girl. Now, at 24, I can say that I am definitely a woman"	413
29.2	A post from Alexa from October 2020	416
33.1	Portrait of the event "A Minute of Silence": religious leaders and parliamentarians at the closing ceremony of the Pro-Life march, held in Lima on 5 May 2018	471
33.2	Young people participating at the concert of Lima's Pro-Life march on 5 May 2018	473

CONTRIBUTORS

Benjamin Ale-Ebrahim is a sociocultural and linguistic anthropologist researching digital media, communication, religion, gender, and sexuality in the Middle East and North America. He is a PhD candidate in the Department of Anthropology at Indiana University, Bloomington in the United States. He is currently completing his doctoral dissertation, an ethnographic analysis of online communication practices among LGBTQ+ Muslims and Middle Eastern people living in the United States.

Donya Alinejad has a PhD in anthropology and is Assistant Professor in Digital Media Studies at Utrecht University's Media and Culture Department. Her work has focused on the role of social media platforms in people's experiences of spatial mobility, cultural identity formation, and emotional care. More recently, she has been involved in research investigating the significance of social media in processes of science communication on publicly controversial topics.

Helen Arnold is a freelance mathematics tutor, based in Cambridge in the UK. She has degrees in mathematics and in education, and has worked as a secondary school mathematics teacher in New Zealand. She also has extensive experience as a software developer in the finance and consulting sectors. Her interests in mathematics education research have included advisory contributions to Cambridge Mathematics, and a postgraduate certificate in mathematics education research from the Open University.

Veronica Barassi is a social anthropologist and Professor of Media and Communication Studies in the School of Humanities and Social Sciences as well as Chair of Media and Culture of the MCM Institute at the University of St. Gallen. Her research focuses on the impact of data technologies and artificial intelligence on human rights and democracy. She is the author of three books: *Activism on the Web: Everyday Struggles Against Digital Capitalism* (Routledge 2015); *Child Data Citizen: How Tech Companies are Profiling Us from before Birth* (MIT Press 2020) and *I Figli dell'Algoritmo: Sorvegliati, Tracciati e Profilati dalla Nascita* (Children of the Algorithm: Surveilled, Tracked and Profiled from Birth) (in Italian, LUISS University Press 2021).

Contributors

Christoph Bareither is Professor of Historical and Cultural Anthropology at the Ludwig Uhland Institute (LUI) at the University of Tübingen. His research is concerned with the transformations of everyday practices and experiences enabled by digital technologies. He is especially interested in the fields of media and digital anthropology, museum and heritage studies, popular culture and game studies, digital methods, ethnographic data analysis and the ethnography of emotions.

Nicola J. Bidwell is Research Group Head of Techno-Anthropology and Participation in Aalborg University's Technical Faculty of IT and Design, in Denmark, and Adjunct Professor at International University of Management, Namibia. Her research in Human-computer-interaction (HCI) focuses on contexts that are marginalized by techno-geopolitics including those of indigenous and rural people, such as in southern Africa where she has lived for 14 years. Nic's ethnographically informed participatory technology research has informed policy debate and received awards for contributions to social and economic development.

Alan F. Blackwell is Professor of Interdisciplinary Design at the University of Cambridge Department of Computer Science and Technology. He is a founder and Co-Director of Cambridge Global Challenges, a cross-disciplinary initiative responsible for developing research collaborations that address the Sustainable Development Goals with partners in low- and middle-income countries. He has developed an undergraduate software design curriculum for Cambridge, drawing on his professional experience as a consulting engineer, and qualifications in engineering, computer science and psychology.

Brooke Schwartz Bocast is Assistant Professor of Anthropology at Montana State University. She is the author of *"If Books Fail, Try Beauty": Educated Womanhood in the New East Africa* (forthcoming, Oxford University Press). She writes and teaches at the intersection of anthropology, gender and sexuality studies, and African studies.

Philipp Budka is a researcher and Lecturer at the Department of Social and Cultural Anthropology of the University of Vienna. He has been researching media, technologies and infrastructures in the Americas and Europe. Currently, Philipp is exploring transport and digital infrastructures in the North American Arctic.

Baird Campbell holds a PhD in Sociocultural Anthropology from Rice University and an MA in Latin American Studies from Tulane University, New Orleans. His research engages queer activism in post-dictatorship Chile through the lenses of critical archival studies and science and technology studies. He is currently Postdoctoral Instructor in Rice University's Program in Writing and Communication in Houston, Texas.

Laura Candidatu is Lecturer in the Gender Graduate Program, Media and Culture Studies Department at Utrecht University. Her areas of expertise are gender studies, diaspora studies, media and migration studies, and digital ethnography. She has published research on feminist approaches to researching digital media, digital diaspora, and the role of motherhood in migration and diasporic processes.

Jeb J. Card is Assistant Teaching Professor in Anthropology at Miami University. His work includes study of colonial transformations in Central America, such as the *Archeology of Hybrid Material Culture* (SIU Press 2013) and the history of archaeology in light of broader public and intellectual interests in the past with *Lost City, Found Pyramid* (University of Alabama Press 2016) and *Spooky Archaeology* (University of New Mexico Press 2018).

Raúl Castro-Pérez is Dean of the Human Sciences Faculty at the Universidad Científica del Sur, in Lima, Peru, and Director of its Communication and Advertising program and its Master's program in Political Communication and Innovative Media. He holds an MA in Communication, Culture and Society from Goldsmiths University of London and is currently a PhD candidate in Anthropology at Pontificia Universidad Católica del Perú. He writes social science features with a focus on Latin America for the journal *Desde El Sur*.

Elisabetta Costa is a social anthropologist and media scholar researching social media, personal relationships, politics, gender, and social inequality in the Middle East and Europe. She is Assistant Professor at the Department of Media and Journalism Studies at the University of Groningen, the Netherlands. She is the author of *Social Media in Southeast Turkey* (UCL Press 2016) and co-author of *How the World Changed Social Media* (UCL Press 2016).

Jerome Crowder is a visual and medical anthropologist who conducts community-engaged research in the Texas Gulf coast as well as in the Bolivian and Peruvian highlands. He is Clinical Associate Professor in the Department of Behavioral and Social Science at the University of Houston, College of Medicine (Houston, Texas, USA). He is currently the past-president of the Society for Visual Anthropology and the co-editor for the Photo Essay Section in the journal *Medicine Anthropology Theory*.

Rebekah Cupitt is a Lecturer in Digital Design at the Department of Film, Media and Cultural Studies at Birkbeck, University of London and Co-Director of Birkbeck's Centre for Interdisciplinary Research on Media and Culture (BIRMaC). Rebekah's research examines the ways in which human and non-human technologies intertwine. Through taking a post-human and anti-normative approach to techno-utopias, Rebekah highlights how socially-embedded assumptions about what is and is not human underpin our everyday interactions with technology.

Peggy Determeyer received her PhD in Medical Humanities from the University of Texas Medical Branch – Galveston, and serves as Director of the Community Bioethics and Aging Center (CBAC) and McGee Fellow at the Hope and Healing Center & Institute (HHCI). Her research interests include end-of-life planning, health literacy, nurse empowerment, and physician-patient communications.

Melisa Duque is Research Fellow of the Emerging Technologies Research Lab, where she leads the Future Health and Wellbeing research program and co-leads the Sustainability research theme. She is a full-time member based at the Department of Design MADA. Her latest projects explore healthcare and wellbeing design ethnography with ageing people in the contexts of the home, the hospital and residential aged care. She is a co-author of the recent book *Design Ethnography: Research, Responsibilities and Futures* (Routledge 2022), and currently working on her book *Designing Homeliness: Everyday Practices of Care* (Routledge).

Akil Fletcher is a PhD candidate at the University of California, Irvine, researching Black online gaming communities. Funded by the National Science Foundation, his research seeks to understand how Black gamers form community and selfhood in online gaming environments.

Contributors

Heather Ford is a digital ethnographer and is currently Head of Discipline for Digital and Social Media at the University of Technology Sydney's School of Communication in Australia. She has a background working for global technology corporations and non-profits in Kenya, South Africa, the United Kingdom, and the United States.

Haidy Geismar is Professor of Anthropology at University College London. She has research interests in intellectual and cultural property, indigenous rights, new forms of cultural representation, the anthropology of art, critical museology and the South Pacific, especially Vanuatu and New Zealand. Her books include *Museum Object Lessons for the Digital Age* (UCL Press 2018) and *Treasured Possessions: Indigenous Interventions into Cultural and Intellectual Property* (Duke University Press 2013).

Zoë Glatt is a PhD candidate in the Department of Media and Communications at the London School of Economics and Political Science (LSE). She is conducting an ethnographic study of the London influencer industry, interrogating the platformisation of creative labour and the sociocultural, economic, and technological structures of power and barriers to entry for marginalised creators. She is the Co-Founder of the LSE Digital Ethnography Collective and served as Managing Editor of the ICA journal *Communication, Culture & Critique* (2018–2021). As an expert on influencer culture and social media, she has been featured in many journalistic outlets, including *Wired*, *The Guardian*, *The Washington Post* and *Vice*.

Edgar Gómez Cruz is an interdisciplinary scholar researching material visual practices, innovative methods, and algorithmic cultures. He is Associate Professor at the School of Information at the University of Texas at Austin. He is the author of *Vital Technologies: Thinking Digital Cultures from Latin America* (Puerta Abierta/Universidad Panamericana, 2022), From Kodak Culture to Networked Images: An ethnography of digital photography (UOC, 2012), and co-editor of *Refiguring Techniques in Visual Digital Research* (Palgrave Macmillan 2017) and *Digital Photography and Everyday Life: Empirical Studies in Material Visual Practices* (Routledge 2016).

Anthony Kwame Harrison is a cultural anthropologist whose research focuses on popular music, race, and social constructions of space. He is the Edward S. Diggs Professor in Humanities at Virginia Tech. He is the author of *Hip Hop Underground* (Temple University Press 2009) and *Ethnography* (Oxford University Press 2018).

Nell Haynes is a cultural and linguistic anthropologist researching gender, indigeneity, media, and performance in Latin America. She is faculty in the Department of Global Studies at Saint Mary's College. She is author of *Social Media in Northern Chile* (UCL Press 2016) and co-author of *How the World Changed Social Media* (UCL Press 2016).

Peter Hervik is an anthropologist and migration scholar affiliated with the Free University of Copenhagen and the Network of Independent Scholars of Education.

Heather A. Horst is Director of the Institute for Culture and Society at Western Sydney University. A sociocultural anthropologist by training, Professor Horst researches material culture and the mediation of social relations through digital media and technology. Her regional focus includes Fiji, Papua New Guinea and Jamaica. Her books include *The Cell Phone: An Anthropology of Communication* (Horst and Miller, Berg 2006), *Hanging Around, Messing Around* *and Geeking Out: Kids Living and Learning with New Media* (Ito et al., MIT Press 2010), *Digital Anthropology* (Horst and Miller, eds., Routledge 2012), *Digital Ethnography: Principles and Practices* (Pink, Horst et al., SAGE 2015), *The Routledge Companion to Digital Ethnography* (Hjorth, Horst, Galloway and Bell, eds., Routledge 2016), *The Moral Economy of Mobile Phones: Pacific Island Perspectives* (Foster and Horst, eds., ANU Press 2018) and *Location Technologies in International Context* (Wilken, Goggin and Horst, eds., Routledge 2019).

Conrad Phillip Kottak (A.B. Columbia College, PhD Columbia University) is the Julian H. Steward Collegiate Professor Emeritus of Anthropology at the University of Michigan, where he served as Anthropology Department Chair from 1996 to 2006. A sociocultural anthropologist whose field research encompasses Brazil, Madagascar, and the United States, he is an elected member of the American Academy of Arts and Sciences and the National Academy of Sciences, where he chaired Section 51, Anthropology from 2010 to 2013.

Jordan Kraemer is Visiting Scholar of Anthropology at New York University. She is an anthropologist of media and technology, studying how social and mobile media reshape everyday experiences of place. She is currently completing a book on media practices among urban middle classes in Berlin, and developing new research on technology design, urban transformation, and the "sharing" economy. Previously, she taught at Wesleyan University, where she was a Mellon Fellow from 2014–15, and teaches in New York at the Brooklyn Institute for Social Research. Her work has been supported by the Mellon Foundation, the DAAD, Intel, and the Institute for European Studies at UC Berkeley. Her forthcoming book is entitled *Mobile Berlin: Transnationalism, Design, and Social Media*, to be published by University of Pennsylvania Press.

|Kun Kunta was born, raised, and works in the North Eastern Kalahari of Namibia. He has acted as local video editor, tech supporter and trainer in various research and technology deployment projects over the past five years. This includes running workshops about Cybertracker software for conservancy staff and coordinating deployments across 40 remote villages in in!huin!om community network project.

Patricia G. Lange is Associate Professor and Chair of Critical Studies at California College of the Arts (San Francisco). She is an anthropologist studying sociality of video, social media, and technical identities. She is the author of *Kids on YouTube: Technical Identities and Digital Literacies* (Routledge 2014), and director of the ethnographic film, *Hey Watch This! Sharing the Self Through Media* (2020). Her book, *Thanks for Watching: An Anthropological Study of Video Sharing on YouTube* (University Press of Colorado 2019), received the Franklyn S. Haiman Award for Distinguished Scholarship in Freedom of Expression.

Thomas M. Malaby is a sociocultural anthropologist who studies the ever-changing relationships among institutions, indeterminacy, and technology, especially as they are realized through games and game-like processes. He is Professor and Chair of Anthropology at the University of Wisconsin-Milwaukee, where he co-directs the Digital Cultures Collaboratory with Professor Stuart Moulthrop. He has published numerous works on play and games in human experience. His two books are *Gambling Life: Dealing in Contingency in a Greek City* (Illinois University Press 2003) and *Making Virtual Worlds: Linden Lab and Second Life* (Cornell University Press 2009).

Contributors

Marlaina Martin earned her Anthropology PhD from Rutgers University in May 2019. Her research interests span critical race, gender, media, Black feminist, and embodiment studies. Her book-in-progress examines New York City-based Black women media-makers' production pathways. Currently, she is an Anthropology Presidential Postdoctoral Fellow at University of Maryland, College Park.

Rex Martin is a PhD candidate at Monash University's Emerging Technologies Research Lab. His PhD project investigates the social and sensory experiences of households using rooftop solar PV and battery storage. Rex's research examines how everyday people understand and use generation and storage technologies, and negotiate the weather-dependent nature of renewable generation. By exploring and accounting for lay understandings and experiences, his research seeks to promote the integration of intermittent and decentralised forms of renewable energy generation and storage. His research interests include: theories of social practice, (domestic energy) consumption, smart grids, renewable energy, batteries and energy storage, and lay understandings of energy.

Tom McDonald is an anthropologist based at the Department of Sociology, The University of Hong Kong. His current research examines novel formations of digital money and credit in China. He has published articles in numerous academic journals, including *American Anthropologist*, *China Quarterly*, and the *Journal of Cultural Economy*.

Lisa Messeri is Assistant Professor of Anthropology at Yale University. She is researching new developments in virtual reality in a study supported by an NSF Scholars Award. Drawing on ethnographic fieldwork in Los Angeles, the project analyzes the mix of entertainment, academic research, and industry developments that shape VR and its community. Her research links knowledge about VR as a technology of immersion—which promises to transport us to existing and fictitious places—to conversations in science and technology studies, media studies, cultural geography, and environmental humanities. Previously, she studied influences of contemporary science and technology on place and place-making in scientific work in her book, *Placing Outer Space: An Earthly Ethnography of Other Worlds* (Duke University Press 2016).

Sheba Mohammid a Research Fellow at University College London. She has over 15 years experience in national and global policy, engagement and research. Her research focuses on bringing diverse global perspectives to discourse on emerging technology through ethnographic approaches. Her recent work has included multi-sited research projects in the United States, Australia and the Caribbean on artificial intelligence, creativity, fashion and automated decision making; and digital media and learning. Dr Mohammid's applied work has included leadership roles in managing national development projects and serving as ICT policy specialist for the Government of Trinidad and Tobago, a director on the Global Social Media Impact Study and Internet Governance expert for the Internet Society.

Kyle Moore researches playful and playable digital media. He is Lecturer in Digital Media at Swinburne University of Technology. He has published research on location-based games, young people's gaming habits, and mobile technology.

Katja Müller is Privatdozentin for social anthropology at Halle University. Her research interests are visual anthropology, material culture, museum anthropology, digital anthropology, and energy and environmental anthropology. Her latest book is Digital Archives and Collections: Creating Online Access to Cultural Heritage (Berghahn 2021).

Larissa Nichols is a social scientist and Adjunct Senior Research Fellow in the Emerging Technologies Research Lab at Monash University. Her human-computer interaction research focuses on the smart home, distributed electricity generation, and other digital technologies. Over the past 10 years, Larissa has investigated energy demand, technology, and pricing issues with early adopters of smart homes, participants in demand management programs, and vulnerable or disadvantaged households.

Charlie Nqeisji was born, raised, and works in the North Eastern Kalahari of Namibia and has translated, interpreted, and transcribed the local Ju|'hoansi language for over 20 years. As he speaks many Namibian and European languages, he has been involved with a wide range of international research projects, from technology to medicine and social sciences. Charlie has helped edit the indigenous language in textbooks and journals on various topics from customary law to traditional stories. He has also served as Manager of Nyae Nyae Conservancy and Community Forest.

Richard Pace is Professor of Anthropology at Middle Tennessee State University. His research interests are in media anthropology with a focus on Brazil, particularly the Amazon. His books include *Amazon Town TV: An Audience Ethnography in Gurupá, Brazil* (University of Texas Press 2013) with Brian Hinote, and *The Struggle for Amazon Town: Gurupá Revisited* (Lynne Rienner Publishers 1998). His articles have appeared in *American Anthropologist, American Ethnologist, Boletim do Museu Goeldi, Current Anthropology, Ethnology, Journal of Anthropological Research, Luso-Brazilian Review,* and *Reviews in Anthropology.*

Leighton C. Peterson, PhD is Associate Professor of Anthropology at Miami University. A linguistic and media anthropologist, he has published numerous works on emergent practices in Native media, indigenous film, and Navajo language use in media. As a public television producer, his works include *Weaving Worlds* (2008), *Columbus Day Legacy* (2011), and *Metal Road* (2017).

Mark Allen Peterson is Professor of Anthropology and International Studies at Miami University. His work focuses on media anthropology, and global flows of culture, including news and entertainment media, marketing and consumption. He has conducted fieldwork in Egypt, India and the U.S. He is the author of the books *Anthropology and Mass Communication: Myth and Media in the New Millennium* (Berghahn 2003) and *Connected in Cairo: Growing Up Cosmopolitan in the Modern Middle East* (Indiana University Press 2011), and co-author of *International Studies: An Interdisciplinary Approach to Global Issues* (Westview 2014). He is co-editor of Berghahn Books' Media Anthropology book series with Sahana Udapa.

Sarah Pink is Professor and Director of the Emerging Technologies Research Lab and Associate Director of the Monash Energy Institute at Monash University. She also co-leads the People Programme, and leads the Transport Mobilities Focus Area of the Australian Research Council Centre of Excellence for Automated Decision Making and Society. She is also an advocate of Design Anthropological Filmmaking, and her latest films are *Smart Homes for Seniors* (2021) and *Digital Energy Futures* (2022). Her recent books include the co-authored *Design*

Ethnography (Routledge 2022), co-edited *Everyday Automation* (Routledge 2022), and her new sole authored book *Emerging Technologies: Life at the Edge of the Future* (Routledge 2022).

John Postill gained a PhD in Anthropology from University College London in 2000. He researches media and sociopolitical change and has done fieldwork in Malaysia, Indonesia, and Spain, as well as online in the Anglosphere. He is currently Senior Lecturer at the School of Media and Communication, RMIT University, Melbourne, where he was previously Vice-Chancellor's Research Fellow. His publications include *The Rise of Nerd Politics* (Pluto 2018), *Localising the Internet* (Berghahn 2011), *Theorising Media and Practice* (Berghahn 2010), and *Media and Nation Building* (Berghahn 2006).

Christian S. Ritter Senior Lecturer in the Department of Geography, Media and Communication at Karlstad University, Sweden. His prime research interests include locative media, contemporary mobilities, expertise, tourism and the cultures of influencers. Christian held research fellowships at the Centre of Excellence in Media Innovation and Digital Culture, Tallinn University, and in the Department of Social Anthropology, Norwegian University of Science and Technology. He received his PhD from Ulster University, UK. In the past decade, he has conducted long-term ethnographic fieldwork in Estonia, Ireland, Norway, Singapore, Turkey and the UK. His latest research, which was funded by the Estonian Research Council between 2018–2020, assesses the emergence of travel influencers as a professional group in the global tourism industry. He has been a board member of the working group Digital Ethnology and Folklore of the International Society for Ethnology and Folklore (SIEF) since 2019. His work has been published in journals including Qualitative Research, Anthropology of the Middle East, Civilisations and Cultural Analysis.

Elizabeth A. Rodwell is Assistant Professor of Digital Media at the University of Houston, Texas. She is an anthropologist of media and technology currently studying conversational user experience (UX). Her manuscript, *Push the Button: Interactive Television and Collaborative Journalism in Japan* is forthcoming from Duke University Press.

Sara Rogers is a clinical specialist researching patient values, ethical priorities, and access to personalized medicine. She is Clinical Assistant Professor at the Department of Pharmacy Practice at the Texas A&M College of Pharmacy.

Eric W. Rothenbuhler is Dean of the School of Communications and Professor at Webster University. He was previously Associate Dean of the Scripps College of Communication and Professor of Media Arts and Studies at Ohio University (2010–2012), Director of the Media Studies MA Program at New School University (2001–2004), and a faculty member at University of Iowa (1985–2001) and Texas A&M University (2004–2010). He is author or co-editor of three books and a four-volume encyclopedia and author of over 70 articles, chapters, essays, and reviews on media, ritual, community, media industries, popular music, and communication theory.

Erkan Saka is Associate Professor of Media and Journalism Studies at the School of Communication at Istanbul Bilgi University. He is currently Head of the Media Department. His recent and current research topics include social life of disinformation, citizen journalism and social movements, digital web archiving and internet histories, and ethnography of cryptocurrency circles in Turkey. He is the author of *Social Media and Politics in Turkey. A Journey* *through Citizen Journalism, Political Trolling, and Fake News* (Lexington Books 2019) and "Big data and gender-biased algorithms" in *The International Encyclopedia of Gender, Media, and Communication*. (Wiley Blackwell 2020).

Holy Hoi Ki Shum is a PhD candidate at the Department of Sociology, The University of Hong Kong. Her PhD research is about new technologies and their impact on the transformation of creative industry and creative labour. She is also interested in popular culture. She conducted an ethnographic study about non-mainstream music in Hong Kong, Shenzhen, and Taiwan at her Master's research project.

Jolynna Sinanan is Lecturer in Social and Digital Anthropology at the University of Manchester. She has an interdisciplinary background in anthropology and development studies and her research focuses on digital media practices in relation to regionally comparative mobilities, family relationships, work, and gender. Her current region of focus is Nepal and she has previously contributed ethnographic studies on Trinidad, Australia, and Cambodia. Her books include *Digital Media Practices in Households* (Hjorth et al., Amsterdam University Press 2020), *Social Media in Trinidad* (UCL Press 2017), *Visualising Facebook* (Miller and Sinanan, UCL Press 2017), *Webcam* (Miller and Sinanan, Polity 2014), and *How the World Changed Social Media* (Miller et al., UCL Press 2016).

Yolande Strengers is a digital sociologist and human–computer interaction design scholar investigating the gender, wellbeing, and sustainability impacts of smart and emerging technologies in our homes and lives. She is Associate Professor of Digital Technology and Society in the Emerging Technologies Research Lab at Monash University, where she leads the Energy Futures research program. Co-authored books and edited collections include *Design Ethnography: Research, Responsibilities and Futures* (Routledge 2022), *The Smart Wife* (MIT Press 2020), and *Social Practices and Dynamic Non-Humans* (Palgrave Macmillan 2018).

A.R.E. Taylor is a Lecturer in Communications at the University of Exeter and Marconi Fellow in the History and Science of Wireless Communication at the University of Oxford. He works at the intersection of social anthropology, science and technology studies, and media and communication studies. His research concentrates on the material infrastructure and labour that underpin digital services, with a focus on data storage. His publications have predominantly focused on data centre security, the environmental impact of cloud computing, and the failure and breakdown of internet infrastructure. He is an Editor of the Journal of Extreme Anthropology and co-founder of the Cambridge Infrastructure Resilience Group, a network of researchers exploring critical infrastructure protection in relation to global catastrophic risks.

Sirpa Tenhunen leads a Finnish Academy-funded research project, "Sustainable Livelihoods and Politics at the Margins: Environmental Displacement in South Asia." She is the author of *A Village Goes Mobile: Telephony, Mediation and Social Change in Rural India* (Oxford University Press 2018).

Martin Ujakpa became Head of Department and Senior Lecturer at Ghana Communication Technology University's Department of Computer Science, after being Faculty Dean at the International University of Management, Namibia. Martin's doctoral research focused on social relationships around technology acceptance in Africa, informed by insights about tools to support co-teaching, co-researching, and co-learning that he gained while teaching, supervising over 70 students and researching in 17 international projects in four African universities.

Xinyuan Wang is a digital anthropologist from the UCL Department of Anthropology. Wang received her PhD and MSc degrees from the UCL Department of Anthropology. She was one of the researchers of the "Why We Post – Global social media impact study" ERC project. Currently, Wang is one of the post-doc researchers of the "Anthropology of Smartphone and Smart Ageing" ERC project. Wang is the author of the book *Social Media in Industrial China* (UCL Press 2016), and the co-author of the books *How the World Changed Social Media* (UCL Press 2016), and *The Global Smartphone: Beyond a Youth Technology* (UCL Press 2021).

Alex Wolff is a PhD candidate in the Department of Anthropology at the University of California, Irvine. Their research examines intersections among economics, temporality, gender and sexuality, through a focus on the lives and politics of queer young adults in South Korea.

Kwok Cheung Wong is Research Assistant at the Department of Sociology, The University of Hong Kong. His previous research has explored gender performativity through visual dialogue. He also holds a degree in business administration and management and has a long career history in various business sectors.

ACKNOWLEDGEMENTS

The editors would like to thank all the chapter contributors for their impressively varied and insightful work on media anthropology. We deeply appreciate their hard work in helping us realize our vision for the volume. We wish to thank and acknowledge the work of our intellectual forebears who were pioneers in the field of media anthropology. We are grateful that they laid the foundation for thinking through a vast range of media concepts and ideas in ethnographic and anthropological terms. We look forward to continuing conversations beyond this volume. We also wish to acknowledge our institutions, the University of Groningen, California College of the Arts, Saint Mary's College, the University of Manchester and Western Sydney University, for their support of this project. The editors also wish to thank the entire Routledge team, especially Katherine Ong, Meagan Simpson, Eleanor Simmons Catchpole, Amy Doffegnies, Emma Yuan, and all the staff for helping to shepherd this volume into its final form.

INTRODUCTION

Elisabetta Costa, Patricia G. Lange, Nell Haynes, and Jolynna Sinanan

The *Routledge Companion to Media Anthropology* defines the widening and flourishing area of media anthropology, and outlines key themes, debates, and emerging directions. Developed at the junction of several disciplines such as media studies, cultural studies, communication, and science and technologies studies (STS), media anthropology has achieved significant insights about human life as it is conducted through media. This field has answered enduring questions about the sociocultural implications of media technologies in our world. Amid the diffusion of new technologies and media infrastructures, shifting social and political configurations, and changing theoretical frameworks and debates, media anthropology has now been growing for more than 20 years. The *Companion* showcases the most relevant developments in the field, draws together the work of scholars from across the globe who have carried out influential studies, provides an overview of past and contemporary research, and brings different approaches into dialogue with each other. With this introduction, we demonstrate the relevance, urgency, and scope of this volume, and outline its structure and content.

At the turn of the millennium, four volumes contributed to establish the field of media anthropology and outline the state of-the-art of this research area: *Media Worlds* (Ginsburg, Abu-Lughod, and Larkin 2002), *Anthropology of Media: A Reader* (Askew and Wilk 2002), *Anthropology and Mass Communication: Media and Myth in the New Millennium* (Peterson 2003), and *Media Anthropology* (Rothenbulher and Coman 2005). These earlier volumes engaged in conversations about mass media and explored the very early genres of digital and internet culture. Since then, communication technologies have significantly changed and diversified. This heterogeneity has yielded a broad range of analytical approaches and different types of social and cultural anthropology. For example, questions of representation and interpretation that dominated the study of mass media and broadcast communication have been followed by questions about technology and materiality that characterize the study of digital media and cultures. We believe that differences between media and their related conceptual categories should not lead to further sub-disciplinary divisions. We instead think that multiple anthropological trajectories and traditions might benefit from more cross-fertilization. For instance, issues of representations, imagination, and meaning-making are central aspects of contemporary digital cultures, as well as matters important to technologies and materiality that lie at the core of broadcasting and media production.

DOI: 10.4324/9781003175605-1

New media do not make old media obsolete. Media history is rather characterized by processes such as "remediation" (Bolter and Grusin 1999), integration, and convergence. The latest technological and media industry developments are making it even more apparent that old and new media are integrated into each other. Older mass media continue to persist through the assimilation of digital forms, and new media integrate older technologies. For example, TV streaming services such as Netflix contribute to processes of datafication. Spotify radio is a form of social media, and YouTube, initially designed as a social media platform, has been increasingly used as a broadcasting channel to communicate with larger audiences. Processes of remediation and integration have characterized the development of new media throughout the last two decades. Artificial intelligence systems use algorithms that adopt features from previous forms of computing. Social media have incorporated elements of both earlier one-to-one phone communications and broadcast media, and thereby, processes of "production" and "reception," traditionally at the core of mass media anthropology, are often entangled with practices of "participation" or "exchange." In this volume, we have ensured that different scholarships and approaches are brought into dialogue with each other to make sense of increasingly complex media ecologies. We also connect the study of broader socio-political processes and social changes to rapid technological transformations as well as continuities.

Media anthropology is a messy and open field characterized by its major developments and directions. This field not only has developed at the intersection of other disciplines, but also at the junction of broader debates in anthropology, such as those around inequality, social change, identity, migration, mobility, relationships, and politics. In the last two decades, technologically-mediated practices have become part of many more aspects of people's everyday lives, and the study of media has become an unavoidable part of many anthropological research projects whose primary analytical focus is not media. We want to make the theoretical horizons and the tools of media anthropology available to the larger community of anthropologists who are approaching media for the first time. The lack of a broad-based media anthropology journal has made this Companion even more relevant within the entire discipline of anthropology.

In the last two decades, media anthropology has been rapidly growing worldwide, with conferences, publications, and graduate programs in this field taking place across Europe, North and South America, East Asia, and Australia, as well as in Africa, where the Anthropology of Communications often includes foci on media. As a result, media anthropology has been playing a more important role in the interdisciplinary field of media and cultural studies. Ethnographic methods, as well as anthropology's conceptual tools and lenses, have shaped dialogues and debates outside the discipline. Digital ethnography has developed into a prominent methodological approach in interdisciplinary contexts (Pink et al. 2016; Hjorth et al. 2017), and during the years of the COVID-19 lockdown, has become even more popular among media scholars working under mobility restrictions. Anthropology has refined and enriched media studies' conceptual tools, such as the concept of affordances (Costa 2018), mediatization (Madianou 2014), media practices (Brauchler and Postill 2010), ritual (Couldry 2003), and myth (Coman 2005). Interdisciplinary cross-fertilization prompts the need to redefine the specifics of anthropological perspectives on media.

For all these reasons, we felt the urgency to compile a *Companion* that explores prior and emerging developments, and that deems media anthropology as an inclusive research field encompassing a variety of analytical perspectives and different media technologies. Our conceptualization of media includes technologies that produce and shape content, and that provide connections between people, and between people and technologies. Our definition is intentionally broad to facilitate wide-ranging explorations of how forms of mediation influence communication, social relationships, cultural practices, participation, and social change, as well as production and access to information and knowledge. This inclusive and comprehensive definition of media also fits within anthropology's main goal, which is the comparative study of context-specific cultural forms and practices.

Media Anthropologies

We have selected chapters that present a rich variety of ethnographic studies from all over the world and that cover different approaches and disparate media technologies, such as TV, radio, newspaper, gaming, social media, artificial intelligence (AI), and virtual reality. The *Companion* reflects the diversity of populations that use media in the contemporary world. First, chapters draw from ethnographic studies carried out in six continents, and cover the study of a large array of social, ethnic, and generational groups. The studies here focus on ordinary populations and sometimes on marginalized communities with attention to the ways that they have asserted agency or dismantled power in relation to media. We have also included chapters that "study up" (Nader 1969), such as examining the workings of authoritarianism and other repressive forces through a lens of media.

Second, the *Companion* includes contributions written by senior and emerging authors affiliated with a wide range of academic institutions across Asia, Australia, Europe, Latin America, and North America, and come from different geographic, cultural, and racial backgrounds. We have prioritized the inclusion of voices from different identity categories and from across the globe. We do this in recognition of the "colonial baggage" (Harrison 1997) of anthropology as a discipline, as well as how media studies have privileged the idea of media production in "global centres" carrying messages unidirectionally to the "global periphery." Instead we orient this volume around the interplay of centre and periphery, and even question the clear distinction between the two. We also aim to counteract some of the most prominent aspects of anthropology that have historically justified its representation as the handmaiden of colonialism. Key amongst these problematic traditions is the centring of "Western" perspectives, understandings of what constitutes knowledge and its sources, and legitimation of certain aesthetics and forms of academic work at the exclusion of others. As such we have been mindful in our inclusion of authors who were born in, have spent parts of their careers in, and/or currently write from globally marginalized places. Their work reflects approaches to methods, analysis, argumentation, and writing conventions that decentre perspectives from those commonly used in Global North academic writing. Calls for "decolonization" in anthropology are right to focus on methodology, citational practices, pedagogy, and community involvement (see for instance McGranahan and Rizvi 2016). But above all, we recognize that anthropology will never shed its association with colonialism if it does not substantively include the works of people from all global subject positions. This must go beyond inclusion of only the "diverse" voices who are able to conform to the recognized Western modes of academic discourse. Instead we must embrace new ways of seeing, critiquing, and knowing.

Third, the *Companion* brings together chapters that are fundamentally rooted in anthropological and ethnographic methods, and at the same time emerge from creative and multi-method approaches that include digital methods, interviews, participant-observation, diaries, and analyses of artifacts. As the diversity of chapters across the entire volume illustrate, methods vary according to the aims of research within media encounters and are intimately informed by the relationship between research questions and cultural contexts. All chapters give a brief background to the methods the author employed and to the novelty of their current interventions. As such, the volume is not intended to have an extended section on methods or be a handbook of methods as there are now several widely available (see for instance Boellstorff et al. 2012; Harrison 2018; Kozinets 2020; Sanjek and Tratner 2016).

Fourth, all chapters make new interventions, either building on original ethnographic data or drawing from prior material. Some contributions are more explicitly theoretical than others, but all engage with important current debates. We grouped the contributions in three parts, named "History," "Approaches," and "Thematic Considerations." The part on "History" traces foundational scholarship in media anthropology as well as the history of senior scholars' works and their impact on the development of the field. The second part, "Approaches," provides an overview of the main perspectives in media anthropology, including "materiality," "representation," "infrastructure," and "practice." These do not constitute four discrete categories, but rather offer four different foci that stand in dialectical relations with one another. "Materiality" and "Representation" stress two opposite aspects of mediation processes, which are always to some extent connected and intertwined. Representations are materially shaped, and material forms are embedded in symbols and meanings. In a similar manner, "Infrastructure" and "Practice" highlight two complementary motives. The first stresses the role of larger systems and structures, while the second foregrounds situated micro media practices. The third part, "Thematic Considerations," includes six sections that reflect current research and relevant topics in media anthropology in the early 21st century: "Relationships," "Social Inequality and Marginalization," "Identities and Social Change," "Political Conservatism," "Surveillance," and "Emerging Technologies." We provide further details on each of the sections below.

Histories

The first section reflects on the interplay between the changing and enduring nature of media anthropology. It analyzes how the field started and developed in conversation with long-standing discussions in anthropology and the interdisciplinary study of media. The three chapters in this section shed light on different aspects of the linkages between media technologies, the global socio-political context in which they are situated, and the theoretical horizons used to make sense of media-related cultural processes. They reflect upon the ways in which theoretical and methodological approaches have transformed in relation to social and technical changes. Mark Allen Peterson offers an excellent account of the history of media anthropology. He first explores the origins of the subfield as entangled in an historic moment characterized by the presence of radial and broadcast media that privileged a focus on production, circulation, and consumption of symbolic content and configurations. The chapter then considers the more recent theoretical developments that emerged in response to the challenges that digital technologies posed to the pre-existing conceptual tools and frameworks in media anthropology. Philipp Budka traces the history of the anthropological studies of indigenous media, which played an important role in consolidating the field of media anthropology during the 1990s. His chapter critically discusses the cultural activist approach to the study of indigenous media, and advocates paying more attention to technical constraints and infrastructure of communication, as well as to the everyday ordinary media use of indigenous people. Conrad Phillip Kottak and Richard Pace retrace the trajectories of Kottak's long-term foundational research project on the effect of television and new media in small towns and villages in Brazil. The chapter stresses the importance of longitudinal research to study media and social change, and social histories of local communities. It engages with issues of media power, influence, and effects, which balance and complement Peterson's engagement with symbolic and interpretive anthropology. These three contributions together reflect upon the past and help map out the future of media anthropology. They engage with lively sets of conversations, debates, and theoretical perspectives, and

Introduction

all show how new questions tied to diffusion of digital media and cultures are better answered by taking into account the multiple conceptualizations of media-related processes that have been developing over the last decades. These three chapters contribute to our call for an anthropology of media that is plural and engages with long-standing debates developing at the intersection of numerous anthropological and interdisciplinary traditions.

Approaches

The volume's second part foregrounds approaches to thinking about what media is and does, in addition to how media can be used to understand aspects of social life. Depending upon one's perspective, media may play dramatically different roles in supporting human sociality, self-expression, and creativity. This second part explores specific dimensions, complications, and opportunities for engagement that revolve around media as infrastructure, media as practice, media as materiality, and media as representation. Approaches naturally intersect and rarely can be contained in singular categories. Nevertheless, taking a deeper dive into specific approaches reveals insight about the process of mediation in terms of what they offer, and at times, what they fail to do. Taking the literal meaning of approach as "to come nearer to something," the chapters in this part work towards getting closer to understanding what media does and what it means to particular groups operating within disparate cultural contexts.

The first set of chapters, included in the "Media as Infrastructure" section, illustrate how, seen in a certain light, media may act as infrastructures that support human interaction. They support exchange of ideas and communicative acts. In "Media as Practice," the second set of chapters explores how media facilitate and indeed embody forms of practice. The day-to-day individual actions that are accomplished with and through media add up to much larger worldviews and understandings of how media impact human behaviour. In the third set of chapters, titled "Media as Materiality," the authors show that despite discourses emphasizing ephemerality, media has tangible, physical dimensions through which sociality is conducted and sensorially experienced. Finally, the fourth set of chapters underscores the importance of perspectives that conceive of "Media as Representation." Representational media do not merely reflect, but also create human subjects. Media offer proposals for how humans are perceived and reconstituted through them. Each series of chapters offers a scholarly conversation that provides insight into how to approach the study of media.

Media as Infrastructure

The concept of infrastructure is viewed along numerous, nuanced dimensions in this section of the volume. Hardly a neutral substrate, infrastructures may deeply influence what is possible when accomplishing interaction and knowledge exchange. Infrastructures involve much more than technical platforms; they can be conceptualized, for instance, in terms of emotional infrastructures that help individuals and groups to self-actualize and accomplish goals. Infrastructures can mistakenly be seen as taken-for-granted backdrops for action, when in fact, infrastructures play a crucial role supporting, and sometimes failing, the needs of media participants. Anthony Kwame Harrison's chapter leads off the section by taking us back in time to the world of hip hop in the United States, in an era when older forms of media, specifically CD-Rs, were used for demo purposes to promote musicians. He explains how circulation of music instantiated soft infrastructures of emotions, aesthetics, and feelings of collective belonging in hip hop communities. He shows that studying these infrastructures reveals how social collectivities form. The chapter by Jerome Crowder, Peggy Determeyer, and Sara Rogers examines an array of old and new media to discuss the challenges and even struggles of using a variety of digital technologies to promote medical literacies amid community dialogues. The authors trace why infrastructures around technologies of information dissemination, such as networked digital files, failed older populations of participants. They provide lessons learned for moving forward with promoting academic and community partnerships and attend closely to supporting digital inclusiveness when disseminating medical information. In her chapter, Patricia G. Lange examines the platform of YouTube as an infrastructure for supporting video exchange and commensurate sociality. The chapter traces how socially motivated vloggers from the U.S. ultimately left the site for other social media such as Twitter to deepen social exchange that they felt was not being adequately supported by YouTube. The chapter ultimately seeks to broaden conversation about what media migration means, by examining its similarities and differences to traditional, physical migration in the anthropological record. Thomas M. Malaby's chapter engages with infrastructure as defined by the design and implementation of material technologies and protocols that may be appropriated across contexts to influence a wide range of interactions. He concludes this section by exploring how rituals in gaming underwrite what is considered real through continued performances. Malaby analyses the role of "hypomediacy" in which practices of game remediation are denied, with implications for how institutions use gaming infrastructures to make claims about reality. All the chapters in the section explore various ways in which infrastructures may be viewed, as well as their influences in shaping social worlds.

Media as Practice

Practice theory as applied to media anthropology served an important role in expanding the field beyond textual and audience consideration, which remain important, but constitute only part of the human mediation saga. Scholarship in practice theory has explored an astonishing range of everyday mediated practices and social processes. A key aspect in practice theory is that everyday interactions and practices may seem small, but often add up to quite serious consequences that influence larger societal concerns. John Postill sets the stage with a provocative chapter that calls for recognition that many media anthropological studies are essentially about understanding media effects – despite this concept's past connotations and uncertain position in media anthropology. He urges moving beyond aversion to this topic based on effects theories of the past, and instead invites anthropologists to acknowledge the many ways that media have demonstrably impacted people's social worlds. The chapter by Elizabeth A. Rodwell explores past visions of future television that promised interactivity for a broadcast medium. Examining a grand experiment of combined television and web-based interactive practices on Japanese social media, she concludes that the promise of democratization of television has yet to be fully realized, given media industry structures and their consistent dependence on governmental approval for broadcast practices. Kyle Moore's chapter examines everyday practices in location-based gaming to explore how games shape representations and understanding of place amid urban mobility. Analysing gaming communities in Australia, Moore shows how map-making practices in gaming expose how mobilities become unequally distributed, such that spaces and their uses become contested. The final two chapters in this section offer fascinating approaches to method, expanding the ethnographer's toolkit while also drawing on new methods to provide insight into subjects such as how human bodies connect to media, memory, and specific mediated affordances. In his chapter, Gómez Cruz reformulates modes of anthropological observation by orienting away from the ethnographic practice of assessing the past and instead inviting photographic practices that look toward a speculative future. He proposes a photomedia method to illustrate how images and imagination serve as anthropological practice, and how media production itself is anthropology. By photographing discarded COVID masks in Australia – a result of everyday mask-wearing – he illustrates how photography as anthropology exhibits multiple functions simultaneously, including serving as object, method, and intervention or visual activism. Finally, the chapter by Christoph Bareither examines tourist media practices at Berlin's Memorial to the Murdered Jews of Europe, including images that are posted to social media. He contributes to both media anthropology and practice theory by advocating a content-as-practice approach that examines how practices of media creators live on through digital content, thus outlining a new perspective for conducting ethnographic research through images.

Media as Materiality

The chapters in this section draw attention to media as part of socio-material entanglements. They emphasize the ways in which aspects of social and cultural life are manifested through media and digital technologies. The first chapter by Jordan Kraemer presents a comparative study of how digital platforms shape the material environments of urban life within the context of new social and spatial mobilities. Kraemer considers the impacts of restrictions imposed due to the COVID-19 pandemic in Brooklyn and reflects on earlier fieldwork conducted in Berlin to compare and contrast how digital platforms restructure encounters with friends and neighbours. The materiality of media reveals public experiences of care and contestations over social inequalities in places that have been shaped by precarity and displacement. Rebekah Cupitt reflects on how deafness is framed in mainstream discourse as a disability, but it also creates a shared visual culture mediated through technologies. Through an investigation of the Swedish television's team for programming in Swedish Sign Language, Cupitt illustrates that technological mediation not only enhances the effects of Sign Language, it becomes a critical part of the repertoire for the embodiment and performative enactments of deaf identities. Following Cupitt's chapter, Alex Taylor provides a fine-grained study of the materiality of the cloud through an ethnographic exploration of data centres and the labour involved with data storage. The complexity of large-scale technological systems and the human actors that are part of cloud infrastructure in the form of labour, financial corporations, and institutions draw attention to the invisibility of the multiple working parts behind the seeming ubiquity of cloud storage and its maintenance. The final chapter by Sarah Pink, Yolande Strengers, Melisa Duque, Larissa Nichols, and Rex Martin establish approaching media as emerging technologies: digital technologies that produce, use, and share data as part of new configurations with larger automated systems. Building on the well-established trajectory in media and digital anthropology that has focused on situated practices of digital devices, Pink and her colleagues argue that the crucial element of connections with third parties represents a new moment in media materiality and mediated communication. They establish the theme that is picked up in the closing section of the book that media anthropology is creating a substantial body of research into the relationship between emerging technologies and everyday life.

Media as Representation

The section on representation highlights the symbolic and material consequences of who, what, and how representation (or lack thereof) takes place in relation to various forms of media. Jolynna Sinanan explores the production of images of Mount Everest through digital technologies and how they shape the ways in which Everest is imagined and experienced in Nepal. Her focus on the mobile workforce (tour operators, guides, and porters) highlights how they are active producers in the visual economy of Everest within locally bound and global networks and how "visual work" is intertwined with making a livelihood. From this focus on images and the meanings they generate within different socialities, we then shift to concern with the lingering effects of colonial representation. Haidy Geismar and Katja Müller connect a critical history of digital technologies in museums to media anthropology, in order to emphasize their relationship to former practices of collection and display. They situate a study of top-down and bottom-up processes of display and archiving in museums in India in discussion with postcolonial and decolonial theories of representation. In their discussion, they challenge key power relations that are inherent within museum projects in relation to storage, collection, and display. The section concludes with a chapter that focuses on a lack of representation and efforts to reverse this erasure. Heather Ford shows both the ways in which some knowledge is marginalized and erased in online spaces and the efforts of individuals to abate inequalities that are a product of media structures. Her chapter on the legitimacy of oral citations on Wikipedia focuses on the Indian game of surr, demonstrating how regimes of power/knowledge remain connected to the legacy of colonial ideology. Together, these chapters explore both positive and negative effects of representation, and the ways in which politics – whether local or global – are always implicated.

Thematic Considerations

We have chosen six areas of thematic consideration which reflect a breadth of topics that are fundamental to understanding societies of the early 21st century. By looking at how these themes intersect with media from an anthropological perspective, we demonstrate the importance of anthropology's methods and theory to understanding the impact of media on social and personal life in the present era. First, we turn our attention to the classic anthropological topic of relationships, with chapters discussing media as diverse as digital currency, text and video-based forms of interpersonal communication, and more outward-facing forms of social media. They focus on the ways media have had a hand in shaping relationships – sometimes in local areas, and other times across borders. In the second section, we highlight the contributions of media anthropology to the study of inequality and marginalization. As the discipline of anthropology has become more aware of inequalities related to race, gender, religion, socio-economic status, and (post)colonial global dynamics, media anthropology has taken up these considerations as well. Here we highlight the ways different forms of online media have reinforced inequality, been used by activists to decrease marginalization, and in many cases, both simultaneously. Following this focus, the third section on identities and social change explores how media has both fostered and hindered a proliferation of identity-making practices against a backdrop of social inequalities. They discuss the ways media function to constrain or recast identification practices, as well as how people's uses of media are key to their own understandings and representations of selfhood. The fourth section switches perspective, concentrating on political conservatism. It investigates the ways in which different media have been used to serve the purposes of conservative political forces, movements, and institutions across different countries. In the fifth section, the thorny topic of surveillance is tackled from a variety of perspectives that include concerns about objectification and oppression, but also spur a disciplinary conversation about creative ways to re-appropriate the act of surveillance to achieve political ends and fight for LGBTQ+ rights. The sixth section highlights the contribution that anthropology brings to the study of emerging technologies and how they generate new media-related forms and practices. It focuses both on the appropriation of these technologies into people's everyday life,

Introduction

and on processes of design and their imaginative components. Together, the various sections within "Thematic Considerations" thus demonstrate the importance of media anthropology for understanding the most pressing issues and anthropological concerns of the 21st century.

Relationships

The section on relationships focuses on the role of different media technologies in shaping personal and family ties, as well as group interactions and socialities. While social relationships have always been mediated, as shown by extensive anthropological studies, in the last two decades, the role of media industries and technologies has been unprecedented in molding the ways people meet, fall in love, communicate with relatives, and create and maintain friendships. The three chapters in this section investigate different media technologies and types of relationships. Xinyuan Wang describes the ways in which the massive usage of the Chinese social media platform, WeChat, has led to the formation of a new typology of friendship among older middle-class adults in Shangai, the "friends from WeChat group." Wang shows how the interactions between Confucian and Communist legacies and the possibilities afforded by digital media have not only shifted pre-existing social norms and everyday practices of friendships, but have also generated a new social category of friend. Tom McDonald, Holy Hoi Ki Shum, and Kwok Cheung Wong look at how monetary practices of Hong Kong cross-boundary students shape kin relations. Their chapter proposes treating money as social media, and stresses how communication and exchange are two inseparable aspects of payment and media practices as well. Donya Alinejad and Laura Candidatu explore mediated family lives in the context of migration and diaspora. They build on the study of intra-European migration from Romania to show the ways in which the subjective experience of long-distance mediated communication is embedded in narratives and imaginaries of migration. Unlike the two previous chapters, which privileged the study of media practices, this one focuses on the analysis of social discourses, narratives, and meaning-making around social media use in the context of migration.

Social Inequality and Marginalization

The section on social inequality and marginalization takes on the important subject of the ways media may reinforce social inequality or foster cultural changes that mitigate marginalization, as related to race, colonialism, and economic and educational disparities. It begins with Elisabetta Costa's exploration of how social media works as a source of hope for Italians still experiencing the fallout of the 2008 global economic crisis. She argues that while social media does little to improve job prospects, they are central to surviving structural inequalities at the same time as reproducing precarious workers' subordinations. Following this, Sirpa Tenhunen explores the contours of who has access to online spaces, in what ways, and under what circumstances, in her chapter on "digital relatedness." Concentrating on low-income and little-educated people in India, she demonstrates how digital media use is embedded in social relationships, and may serve to refashion hierarchies. Similarly taking up the themes of social relationships and inequality, Marlaina Martin discusses Black feminist film screenings as spaces for creating community and challenging power relations in the United States. She argues that the physical presence of viewers at these events is central to understanding their interpretations and sense of belonging. Relating these screenings to the co-presence in protest actions, she argues for their revolutionary potential. Conversely, Akil Fletcher discusses a disembodied form of racial marginalization and resistance through his research on Black online gaming groups. He illustrates the ways Black people must remain protective of their own online spaces in order to mitigate what he calls the "magic circle of whiteness." In one of the two groups of focus in his chapter, Black space was quickly co-opted by white play and pleasure. Members of the second group he highlights were able to build community and joy, reinforcing his approach which eschews media determinism for a more contextual approach. Together, these chapters show that media – including gaming platforms, film screenings, smartphone browsers, and social media – are neither sources nor salvations of inequality. Rather, they may reinforce already existing forms of marginalization when uncritically left to reproduce social relations, or may be employed as tools of change when individuals and communities focus energy on social transformation.

Identities and Social Change

The chapters exploring identities and social change approach the ways media has become central to individuals' crafting of identity within larger social formations, often both reinforcing them and cultivating subtle forms of social change along the way. Nell Haynes discusses the emerging practice of tattooing Indigenous symbolism in Bolivia as a form of identity making. Yet, she cautions that rather than this being a wholly affirmative celebration of Indigenous Andean peoples, it is complicated by the ways indigeneity in Bolivia has been absorbed into nationalist projects which do not always benefit Indigenous communities. She demonstrates how tattooing, like other forms of media, draws from and contributes to ideological transformation of the quotidian to the political. Brooke Bocast discusses female university students' bodies as spaces of contestation within media related to public health. Global health NGOs target students in HIV awareness campaigns while at the same time tabloid newspapers circulate sexually explicit images of female students. She argues that despite their vast differences, these two forms of media do violence to young women's claims to personhood by constructing them as promiscuous and immoral. Finally, Baird Campbell writes about social media as a key mode of self-making for transgender people in Chile. Taking into consideration competing aims of visibility, security, and social change, he demonstrates, through a focused story of a transgender woman, that media are part of a larger socio-technical sphere in which individuals are able to enact "authentic" selves, while simultaneously foreclosing and reducing the range of available models of gender expression and identity. Campbell argues that this contributes to discussions of social media as technology that may be understood as spaces of both homogenization and transgression. Together these chapters draw from a range of anthropological discussions on identity and selfhood, showing how a wide variety of media are intimately connected to self-making and self presentation projects in contexts of inequality related to race, gender, and colonial histories.

Political Conservatism

Whereas other thematic sections in this volume engage with topics and concepts that have been at the core of the anthropological endeavor for many years, this section explores what we consider now to be a fundamental theme in the anthropological study of media, which is political conservatism. While during the 1990s and the first decade of the 21st century the ethnographic study of the interplay between media and politics has prioritized the investigation of progressive social movements and revolutionary politics, in the last decade, a growing scholarship has explored media-political relations in the context of groups and institutions that aim at promoting traditional values and ideas. Peter Hervik builds on the findings of his previous research projects on racialized discourses and exclusionary reasoning in Denmark to explore the work of strategic ignorance, which is ignorance that is actively produced to serve specific

Introduction

ends. He calls for a media anthropology that focuses on the crisis of facts and engages with the epistemology of ignorance production. Similarly the chapter by Leighton Peterson and Jeb Card engages with the crisis of facts. They explore the production and circulation of pseudo-science and conspiracy discourses of the US-based QAnon and Q-aligned social networks within a media ecology made of old and new media, and characterized by spreadability, circulation, and bricolage of content and symbols. Erkan Saka's chapter describes almost a decade of pro-government political trolling in Turkey, and reflects on the methodological challenges of doing research on trolling at different historical moments. The chapter also argues that political trolling in Turkey forms a discursive community that functions on a voluntary basis. Raul Castro investigates pro-life mobilizations in Latin America as representative of larger trends of morality-centered politics. By building on Turner's notion of "social drama," he formulates the concept of "social media drama" to account for the media practice of filming public assemblies, live-streaming them on social media platforms, and watching and re-experiencing them again. Castro shows that these cultural performances reinforce activists' own values and ideas, while also serving educational purposes. These four ethnographically grounded studies offer new ways of thinking about new and old questions on the intersection between media and conservative politics in the early 21st century.

Surveillance

The topic of surveillance and the oppressiveness of being watched has long been a societal concern. Given the complex and embedded apparatus of surveillance in contemporary society, we have sailed past Orwell's dystopian fears which are now our reality. Surveillance is imbricated in social life in ways even he could not have imagined. Rather than solely human entities who might be held accountable for their oppressive watching, it is now algorithms or complex formulas that are being deployed to surveill and make decisions that profoundly shape human worldviews, interactions, and subjectivity. The chapters in this section tackle this complex subject in nuanced ways. Veronica Barassi urges consideration of understanding how technical surveillance in everyday life in the U.K. and the U.S. has produced algorithmic profiling in which people are reduced to qualities that facilitate commercialism in ways that are profoundly objectifying and belittling. People feel the effects of surveillance in the form of algorithmic violence, and she draws on the anthropology of bureaucracy to deepen understanding of individual impacts of surveillance in everyday life. In his chapter, Benjamin Ale-Ebrahim examines surveillance from a very different perspective, exploring forms of lateral surveillance in Islamic culture. Contrary to the idea that surveillance is always a negative practice, Ale-Ebrahim notes that promoting ethical behaviour by encouraging it among observed peers is part of foundational Islamic practice. Queer Muslims have used the platform of Twitter to engage in lateral moral surveillance. As an important practice, social media participants do not protest surveillance per se, but rather call out the behaviour of those who hypocritically condemn queer Muslims while they themselves engage in questionable practices that violate Islamic principles. Queer Muslims counter-surveill homophobic and transphobic detractors in ways that reveal important dynamics in interpersonal surveillance that are not part of any governmental apparatus. Finally, Alex Wolff also takes up surveillance in the context of LGTBQ+ rights in their fieldsite of South Korea. Long denied a political existence, young queer and trans activists post anonymous images of people at group meetings and gatherings on social media such as Facebook and Twitter. Using anonymity strategically, they enumerate their existence by showing, contrary to governmental claims, that queer populations exist and demand social, legal, economic, and political recognition. While avoiding traceable identities, their demands to be seen constitute powerful and creative ways of claiming existence and protecting their survivability. Taken together, these chapters demonstrate the complexities of surveillance, and how the practice must always be considered in political terms.

Emerging Technologies

From the perspective of technological disciplines and industries, emerging technologies are those that have not fully become integrated into everyday life, are not fully realized in terms of the markets they are intended to reach, or have not had their intended impacts on society, as envisaged by design. A growing area of scholarship in the social sciences is taking a more critical view as to what design processes might imagine and how emerging technologies could be met, challenged, recreated, and reimagined according to different populations. For example, popular keywords associated with AI in countries in the Global North are "innovation," "inclusion," and "ethics," whereas keywords that are related to challenges and opportunities of AI in countries considered to be located in the Global South are "sovereignty," "rights," "justice," "postcolonial," and "decolonial." The chapters in this section present recent studies of the implications of emerging technologies in a variety of contexts. Heather Horst and Sheba Mohammid argue that machine learning in the form of wardrobe assistants reinforce ideas of normative style according to ideals of predominantly Western countries in the Global North. Their study of Amazon Echo Look in the Caribbean island of Trinidad reveals how aesthetics of colour and femininity are shaped by regionally inflected concepts of style and fashion. The next chapter by Christian Ritter continues the theme of the ways that emerging technologies can draw or deflect attention of the gaze by examining the design and uptake of augmented reality apps that can be downloaded onto camera phones. These apps in Tallinn, Estonia are contributing to urban tourism and a renewed appreciation of heritage sites. Zoë Glatt's chapter considers how algorithms in YouTube's recommender systems might be felt and experienced, as explored through an ethnography of content creators. Her chapter draws attention to the ways in which algorithms might be designed as a series of code and numbers, but remain a different, elusive beast to the people whose content and data contribute to the scale and complexity of algorithmic systems that are ultimately in the control of large, technological corporations and not users. Nicola J. Bidwell, Helen Arnold, Alan F. Blackwell, Charlie Nqeisji, |Kun Kunta and Martin Ujakpa build upon critical, regional studies on emerging technologies in Africa and argue that combining ethnographic research with computational expertise can contribute to meeting the ideal of making AI more inclusive and explainable. They explore the stories of the Ju|'hoansi people in Namibia to reveal the experiences, livelihoods, and knowledge practices of such marginalized groups. Finally, the closing chapter by Lisa Messeri explores the ways in which both ethnographic and virtual reality (VR) practices and promises seek to create an experience of "being there." She critically examines the definition of immersion between these two areas and how anthropological thinking might contribute to a critique of immersion according to VR industries. These chapters present a recent showcase of the intersection between anthropology and ostensibly the newest media in the form of emerging technologies.

References

Askew, K. M. and Wilk, R. R. (eds) (2002). *Anthropology of Media: A Reader*. Hoboken: Blackwell Publishing.
Bolter, J. D. and Grusin, R. (1999). *Understanding New Media*. Cambridge: MIT Press.
Bräuchler, B. and Postill, J. (eds) (2010). *Theorising Media and Practice*. New York.: Berghahn.

Introduction

Boellstorff, T., Nardi, B., Pearce, C., and Taylor, T. L. (2012). *Ethnography and Virtual Worlds: A Handbook of Method*. Princeton: Princeton University Press.

Costa, E. (2018). "Affordances-in-practice: An ethnographic critique of social media logic and context collapse." *New Media & Society* 20(10): 3641–3656. doi:10.1177/1461444818756290

Coman, M. (2005). "News stories and myth – the impossible reunion?" In Rothenbulher, E. and Coman, M. (eds), *Media Anthropology*. London: Sage, pp. 111–120.

Couldry, N. (2005). *Media rituals: A Critical Approach*. London: Routledge.

Ginsburg, F. D., Abu-Lughod, L. and Larkin, B. (eds) (2002). *Media Worlds: Anthropology on New Terrain*. Berkeley: University of California Press.

Harrison, A. K. (2018). *Ethnography*. Oxford: Oxford University Press.

Harrison, F. V. (ed) (1997). *Decolonizing Anthropology*. Arlington: American Anthropological Association.

Hjorth, L., Horst, H., Galloway, A., and Bell, G. (eds) (2017). *The Routledge Companion to Digital Ethnography*. London: Routledge.

Kozinets, R. V. (2020 [2009]). *Netnography: The Essential Guide to Qualitative Social Media Research, Third Edition*. London: Sage.

Madianou, M. (2014). "Polymedia communication and mediatized migration: an ethnographic approach." In K. Lundby (ed), *Mediatization of Communication*. Berlin: De Gruyter, pp. 323–348.

McGranahan, C. and Rizvi, Uzma Z. (2016). "Decolonizing anthropology." Savage Minds blog. April 19. https://savageminds.org/2016/04/19/decolonizing-anthropology/

Nader, L. (1969) "Up the anthropologist: Perspectives gained from 'studying up'." In Hymes D. (ed), *Reinventing Anthropology*. New York: Random House, pp. 284–311.

Pink, S., Horst, H., Postill, J., Hjorth, L., Lewis, T., and Tacchi, J. (2012). *Digital Ethnography: Principles and Practices*. London: Sage.

Peterson, M. A. (2003). *Anthropology and Mass Communication: Media and Myth in the New Millennium*. New York: Berghahn.

Rothenbulher, E. and Coman, M. (eds) (2005). *Media Anthropology*. London: Sage.

Sanjek, R. and S. W. Tratner (eds) (2016). *eFieldnotes*. Philadelphia: University of Pennsylvania Press.

PART I

Histories

1
MEDIA ANTHROPOLOGY AND THE DIGITAL CHALLENGE

Mark Allen Peterson

From pictographs on clay tablets to acoustical structures designed to aid speaking, to newspapers, film and television, to social media, humans have developed a vast array of mediational spaces, artifacts and practices that use technology to fix, extend and elaborate on human communication. In every era, and within every community, these tools and the practices associated with them entered into every aspect of human life and transformed those lives. Each new technology for symbolic communication led to new social institutions and new ways of sharing cultural models of social and cosmological orders. Media, therefore, are fundamental elements in human life and a necessary subject for anthropological inquiry.

The anthropology of media emerged in a particular historical moment, and developed theories and methods primarily to study a range of physical and electronic media technologies such as the printing press, phonographs and broadcast communications. As a result, early work in the anthropology of media tended to be focused on the creation, circulation and consumption of fixed texts in an environment of radial media. The emergence of social media, web-based media and digital gaming has created a variety of fascinating challenges for media anthropologists as texts give way to new semiotic practices and processes involving entextualization, collective narrative construction, spreadability and decentered agency that requires new ways of conceiving media practices. At the same time, ethnographic methods, comparative approaches and holistic perspectives continue to offer promising ways forward for the anthropology of media. In this chapter, I trace the history of media anthropology and identify five challenges social media poses to the paradigms and methods that have been used to analyze print and electronic media.

Functionalist Foundations

Serious anthropological interest in media arose in the 1930s with the emergence of ethnographic studies of contemporary US cities, such as Robert and Helen Lynd's Middletown studies (Lynd and Lynd 1929, Lynd 1937) and William Lloyd Warner's Yankee City project (Warner and Lunt 1941, Warner 1959). The Lynds focused on how print media, and later radio, introduced new ideas into Middletown (a pseudonym for Muncie, Indiana) and how these ideas were incorporated into local social formations or led to social change. In his decades-long study of a New England town, Warner initially saw media as serving informational functions but later

DOI: 10.4324/9781003175605-3

came to view media as primarily symbolic and expressive of dominant local cultural norms and values. Although important, and influential at the time they were produced, these works introduced an unfortunate tendency into ethnography: while print, film and electronic media were included in most studies of Western European and North American societies, they were largely ignored among non-Western societies (one exception being Powdermaker's *Coppertown* in 1962).

Written within the structural-functionalist paradigm that dominated social theory at the time, most early works by anthropologists on media were concerned with how media enabled and constrained the flow of information within a social structure, how media content expressed (and shaped) cultural norms and values, and how people incorporated ideas and practices from media into their lives. Social structures were seen as essentially coherent and stable, and the primary function of media was to integrate people successfully into that structure. Perhaps the most widely read of these early works was Hortense Powdermaker's *Hollywood: The Dream Factory* (1950), a substantive anthropological study of the US film industry.

Over time these studies also became interested in changing media mobilities, such as the emergence of portable radios, and the ways media content broadcast into the community from outside changed peoples' awareness of the world outside the civic community. These interests coincided with critiques of the functionalist insistence on circumscribing communities as integrated aggregates of social institutions whose interconnections created a complete and bounded whole.

Amidst a growing awareness of urbanization and "modernization" trends globally, anthropologists began asking what roles media played in facilitating social change. Modernization studies, which sought to describe and explain the cultural relationships and potential for innovation created by movements of people between cities and "traditional" villages, became an increasingly interesting project of study. In a series of influential works, Robert Redfield and Milton Singer proposed an "urban-folk" continuum, arguing that urban intellectuals—including media professionals but also religious leaders, political propagandists, educators and many others—drew on "folk" symbols, which were appropriated, rationalized and incorporated into "Great Traditions"— cultural discourses at a national level. In turn, new ideas, cosmologies and social practices from these national cultures made their way back into local communities and were incorporated into everyday life. In this model, local communities served as sources of authenticity, creativity and innovation, while urban centers served to fuse local traditions into a shared civilizational culture that could serve as a basis for national identity without seeming too alien (Redfield and Singer 1954, Singer 1960).

National Culture

The Second World War disrupted most ongoing anthropological research in the US and cut ethnographers off from their field areas. Drawing on the Boasian notion that cultures could be conceptualized as coherently patterned and bounded units, a large school of anthropologists emerged which sought to analyze 'culture at a distance' (Mead and Metraux 1954).

The primary method was to understand mass media texts as expressive of the national cultures that produced them, in the same ways that rituals, art, folktales and mythologies were studied by anthropologists as expressive of the cultures of smaller-scale societies (Bateson 1980: 21). A core theoretical assumption was that culture could be treated as the "personality" of the society, and personality as the "culture" of the individual (Sapir 1985a). The primary technique was to read novels, newspapers and essays, view movies, listen to music and radio, and then to discuss these with informants from the communities under study, variously constituted by refugees, immigrants, or even first- or second-generation descendants of immigrants living in the US or UK. Anthropologists often worked together in small groups, meeting and discussing the interviews and the ongoing research. They labeled their technique "cultural analysis," seeing it as analogous to the psychoanalysis of individuals. The goal was to elicit high-order "themes," propositions about what constitutes moral behavior or the goals of human existence, and which recur in multiple cultural expressions across a range of materials and which could be clustered to offer broad assessments of "national cultures." One of the most sophisticated studies was Bateson's analysis of the film *Hitlerjunge Quex* (1932), in which he examines how Nazi filmmakers used psychologically relevant symbols from German national culture to influence German audiences in order to create Nazis (Bateson 1980).

While always subject to criticism within anthropology (even by its practitioners) for both its theoretical assumptions and methods, this network of scholars produced a significant body of work, perhaps the most notable of which was Ruth Benedict's *The Chrysanthemum and the Sword* (1946), a description of Japanese national culture that influenced US post-war policies toward Japan.

The fundamental criticisms of the project were twofold: whether it made sense to use "nations" as cultural units, and the extent to which culture can be viewed as "patterned." Margaret Mead readily acknowledged that the nation was not a natural unit, but an artifact of the method which could be applicable to units of any scale, "including families, clans, ethnic groups, gender groups, socioeconomic classes, or castes" (Beeman 2000: xxii). Nonetheless, the generalizability of the holistic statements that anthropologists abstract from their data continued to be widely questioned. The project declined within a decade after the war, and was moribund by the mid-1960s.

Development Communications

During the Cold War between the US and USSR, US anthropologists were often enlisted in efforts to "develop" non-Western societies. Many development theories were rooted in a teleological model of social evolution that assumed all societies passed through a series of stages from "primitive" (indicated by kin-based social organization and dominated by non-market systems of exchange) to "advanced" (marked by industrialization and market economies). Traditional cultures become, in this model, impediments to advancement. Development theorists advocated using print, radio, film, television and other media to promote new values and norms that would assist societies in adapting to industrialization, wage labor, market exchange, commodification, bureaucratic systems of government and other forms of modernity. Anthropologists were often employed not only to develop culturally appropriate forms of symbolic content for such media, but also to assist in creating culturally appropriate modes of media communication—for example, should men and women watch films together? Were separate screenings necessary for different age sets (Carael and Stanbury 1984)?

Modernization theories had introduced the notion that media played a significant role in fusing authentic local traditions with innovation to make modernization palatable. This served as one of several theoretical bases for the creation of development communication. Anthropologists were recruited to assist in creating soap operas in which pro-development messages were embodied in sympathetic characters while supposedly backward-looking characteristics were embodied in unsympathetic characters (Singhal and Rodgers 1989). Others helped encode development messages into popular genres of media, such as family planning music videos in Mexico (Coleman 1986).

Ultimately, efforts to harness media as a "magic bullet" to transform societies failed to yield the kinds of results development projects sought. In addition, most development theories of the time came under severe criticism by anthropologists (Portes 1976, Frank 1969), as did the linear transmission model of media they utilized (Singer 1966, 1972).

Media as Symbolic Systems

In the 1960s, media anthropology began to increasingly focus on media content as forms of expressive culture in industrialized, technological societies. It was strongly influenced by the structural anthropology of Claude Levi-Strauss, and the symbolic and interpretive anthropological approaches advanced by Mary Douglas, Victor and Edith Turner and Clifford Geertz. Anthropologists primarily focused on how cultural messages, especially value systems, moral codes and cosmological orders, were encoded in media.

One unfortunate peculiarity of this movement was a tendency by anthropologists to focus on the media of their own societies. Susan Bean, a renowned Tamil linguist, analyzed American soap operas, rather than exploring the large and vibrant Tamil media industry (Bean 1981). Ivan Karp, an expert on African ideological systems, wrote on the Marx Brothers (Karp 1981). John L. Caughey, a specialist on the Truk, studied how Americans interact with media figures in their imaginations (1984). South Asianist Peter Claus offered a structural analysis of *Star Trek* (1982). Non-western scholars followed a similar pattern. Pakistan-born anthropologist Akbar Ahmed wrote about press coverage of a religious mass suicide in Pakistan (1986) and about Indian films (1991); Indian anthropologist Veena Das examined the structure of kinship in Pakistani romance novels (1973), and Indian anthropologist T.N. Madan examined Hindi, Kannada, Marathi and Tamil novels to explore Hindu concepts of morality and suffering (1987). Exceptions include William O. Beeman on Iranian media (1982), Susan Rodgers on Indonesian cassette culture (1986) and Conrad Kottak on Brazilian television (1990). An additional trend explored encounters and intersections between Western media and local non-Western practices (Granzberg 1982, Augé 1986, Abu-Lughod 1989).

Interpretive and symbolic approaches to media received a significant boost with the advent of the field of cultural studies in the UK during the 1970s which added an important focus on power. Cultural studies dealt with such traditional anthropological foci as class structures, national formations, race and gender, but asked how popular media might express, reinforce or contest ideologies that support inequalities within these social forms. Cultural studies drew attention to the ways social forms and identities were represented in popular culture forms—primarily media texts—and asked how consuming such media created opportunities for media consumers to reinforce, negotiate or resist their own identities and social formations. Several anthropologists published nuanced readings of American films in mainstream anthropology journals, and many anthropologists studying media found ideas in the cultural studies literature about polysemic readings of texts within the contexts of political economy far more useful than earlier forms of symbolic anthropology. Elizabeth Traube's *Dreaming Identities* (1992) and Steven Caton's *Lawrence of Arabia: A Film's Anthropology* (1999) are notable examples.

Although influenced by its attention to power and inequality, few media anthropologists fully embraced the cultural studies movement for a number of reasons. First, cultural studies primarily focused on analyzing social positions inscribed in texts rather than ethnographically engaging with actual text consumers occupying those social positions. Second, although much of the theory in cultural studies was predicated on a critical stance toward capitalist culture industries, there was little interest in ethnographic research into actual practices of media production. Third, the strong emphasis in cultural studies on how media consumption is inflected by race, gender and class produced what was for many anthropologists an ethnocentric bias toward North American and European cultural categories, giving little attention to categories like caste, religious community, language community, age set, or other identity distinctions that may be equally or more salient in non-Western settings. Work like Purnima Mankekar's *Screening Culture* (1999) demonstrates the power of ethnographic engagement with text consumers within an approach influenced by cultural studies, while Barry Dornfeld's *Producing Public Television, Producing Public Culture* (1998) and William Mazzarella's *Shoveling Smoke* (2003) demonstrate the necessity of more nuanced approaches to cultural production both in North America and elsewhere in the world.

The Emergence of Media Anthropology

An upsurge in anthropological attention to media began in the 1990s, driven largely by a recognition that radio, film, television, news and magazines were globally ubiquitous and anthropology could not ignore their presence as part of the everyday lives of the peoples they studied. The launch of the journal *Public Culture* in 1985, the Media Anthropology Workshop at the University of Hamburg in 1999, the founding of the Media Anthropology Network within the European Association of Social Anthropologists (EASA) in 2003, and the establishment of media anthropology degree programs at universities such as the Free University of Berlin, Harvard, New York University, and SOAS, University of London, as well as the inclusion of media topics in many cultural anthropology textbooks, attested to the growing institutionalization of media anthropology within the broader discipline. Within the first five years of the millennium, four book-length efforts to summarize this rising domain of research emerged (Askew and Wilk 2002, Ginsburg, Abu-Lughod and Larkin 2002, Peterson 2003, Rothenbuehler and Comans 2005).

This emergent anthropology of media took as its foci the construction of difference, media production outside the industrialized West and attention to the role of mass media in the construction of identities. Theoretically eclectic, the anthropology of media freely borrowed concepts and theoretical language from communication studies, British cultural studies and literary criticism, as well as from theoretically sympathetic strands of social theory and political science. It built on the turn in media studies toward audience analysis, but introduced into it the reflexivity that had become increasingly central to ethnography in anthropology.

Media anthropologists also focused on the study of media and global cultural flows (Appadurai 1996). The notion of "globalization" draws our attention to the ways media is distributed, and to understand distribution as a cultural process, a system of exchange and a way of generating social networks. Media play a central role in the processes through which capital, goods, people, images and ideas move around the world. Media serve as both vehicles for the flow of images and discourses, and shape the content of that flow. Information and communication technologies—press, radio, film, television, computers, cell phones and their many hybrids—move through the world and become incorporated into local media systems—dynamic, complex assemblages in any given social field in which media technologies interact with each other and with other social and cultural systems. This interaction occurs both at the levels of media technologies—their authorization, ownership and infrastructure—but also at the level of media content. Because media technologies are always tools for the production, distribution and consumption of texts and messages, the structural and infrastructural interrelationships shape the production, circulation, transformation and consumption of images, texts and information within this system. It is possible to discern in the work from this period a dynamic model of media in which public symbolic configurations are selectively appropriated by various culture industries, that is, social organizations and institutions that control the technology, skills and knowledge needed for media production. These culture industries, large and small, transform these symbolic configurations and return them to public circulation in new, textualized and commodified (or otherwise objectified) forms.

This production process is mirrored by the consumption process. Audiences selectively appropriate symbols from the sets of media texts available to them and employ these in their practices of social formation. The circuit is completed as the culture industries become aware of and evaluate consumer choices through various means of surveillance (not the least of which are the observations and intuitions of producers who, after all, are also media consumers). Through this circuit, not only content but processes of selection and transformation may themselves be selectively transformed. This process scales at various local, national, regional and global levels.

The Anthropology of News and Journalism

One of the most significant and prolific areas of research in media anthropology is the anthropology of news and journalism, which explores the creation, circulation and consumptions of news as a discourse about selected contemporary events. News in this sense is a locus of "interpretive practices" (Beeman and Peterson, 2001) through which people reflect on everything from "morality, to religion, to race" (Bird, 2010: 35) to the nation-state to the state of the world. News provided a new way for members of states to envision themselves as members of large-scale communities but is also significant in the emergence of new modes of translocal social experience including those of refugees and labor immigrants, as well as mobile, cosmopolitan professional groups.

Assessments of news as semiotic systems are complicated by the fact that news stories make truth claims. "Truth" is a defining feature of news discourse and understanding what truth means to journalists, viewers, state actors and other users of news in particular social contexts becomes a central project. Multiple "regimes of truth" may exist in a particular social field and different news stories may root themselves in different kinds of truth claims that can be related to other social, economic and political contexts. News may be a particularly potent tool for encoding, articulating, reinforcing or resisting ideologies because of people's tendency to believe in news as a straightforward account of objective realities happening "out there" in the phenomenal world.

The anthropology of news and journalism is thus situated within a tension between a folk understanding of news as a form of rational modern representation of the world through which information circulates in order to provide the knowledge required for the functioning of civil society, and recognition by ethnographers that news is always articulated in narratives that express cultural values, key symbols and ideologies.

There has been a strong focus in the anthropology of journalism on the ethnography of newsmaking as opposed to studies of news texts or their consumption. Ethnographers situate themselves within the spaces in which news is produced in order to describe the everyday practices and social networks through which news is created. As well, anthropologists attend to the ways news is circulated and remediated—spoken of in everyday life, tweeted, parodied, trolled, denied and reinterpreted in myriad ways. News easily moves from print to audio to television to digital in both patterned and unexpected ways. News is at once big business, produced by gigantic corporations through myriad high-tech newsrooms, and deeply personal, exchanged by individuals as part of everyday micro interactions.

Anthropologists have described and analyzed the similarities and differences between the world's journalisms. Anthropological work on world journalism so far has demonstrated that although there are some formal similarities in newswriting throughout the world that derive predominantly from Western norms, there are also fundamental differences—local inflections—in style, truth claims, ascription of authority, modes of legitimizing content and other practices. This kind of ethnography often exposes the ineffectiveness of Western folk models that frame press-state relations using such elementary categories as "free," "not free," and "partially free," revealing instead much more complex relationships (Roudekova 2017, Nyiri 2017). But some anthropologists also study news at a global level by examining the interactions of newsmakers and journalists as they work with and alongside one another in multiple locales (Hannerz 2005), including the ways Western news organizations incorporate the work of local journalists into their own news processes (Bishari 2013). This is a central area within media anthropology in which transformations wrought by the emergence of new media technologies and practices is especially salient (Boyer 2013).

Indigenous and Activist Media

Another flourishing domain within the larger anthropology of media that is especially affected by new forms of digital media is the study of the ways indigenous and marginalized peoples make use of media in ways that parallel, counter, resist and evade mainstream media circuits. The term *indigenous media* refers to "that work produced by indigenous peoples, sometimes called the 'Fourth World,' whose societies have been dominated by encompassing states, such as the United States, Canada and Australia" (Ginsburg 1991: 107). Indigenous media production always exists in a dialogical relationship with other media industries. As early as the late 1970s, Gary Granzberg and his colleagues reported on the appropriation of television characters into Cree tales (Granzberg 1982). The appropriation of media technologies of production by indigenous communities has primarily been seen as a mode of resistance against such processes through a reassertion of cultural forms.

The study of indigenous media production begins with the seminal work of Eric Michaels, who examined the ways Aboriginal cultural orders organized the rules of media production within the Warlpiri community (Michaels 1994). Since then, ethnographers have described work by filmmakers among the Warlpiri, Kayapo, Waipai, Inuit, Mapuche, Navajo, Saami, Yolngu, Oaxacans and others (Wilson and Stewart 2008).

Media is "indigenous" only in relation to a non-indigenous encompassing state, so the term invokes relationships of power predicated on the mutual recognition of difference. Studies of indigenous media initially described the use of media production as a form of cultural assertion against alternative cultural forms being imposed on indigenous communities. "When other forms are no longer effective, indigenous media offers a possible means—social, cultural, political—for reproducing and transforming cultural identity among people who have experienced massive political, geographic and economic disruption" (Ginsburg 1994: 94). As more and more anthropologists worked with indigenous media producers, it became clear that indigenous media production is often organized around a "Faustian contract" (Ginsburg 1991) or "double-edged sword" (Jhappan 1990) between self-assertion and the risk of becoming exoticized. Although indigenous media projects are often non-commercial, many involve the assistance of state institutions, NGOs and non-indigenous media professionals (Turner 2002, Peterson 2014).

The boundaries of indigenous media spill over into other forms of activist media, especially when cultural assertion extends into large-scale political activism such as the Zapatista movement or the popular politics that propelled Evo Morales into the Bolivian presidency (Himpele 2008, Stephen 2012), or the boundaries between indigenous assertion of identity and demands for cultural and linguistic reassertion through media production by Basque, Catalan, Walloons and Welsh activists in Europe (Cotter 1999, Buszard-Welcher 2018).

Indigenous media thus necessarily overlaps with efforts by activists within social movements who use media in an attempt to gain greater control over their social and cultural futures. This activist imaginary in media production includes media services through which Tibetan Buddhist activists seek to speak to and through the world's press services (McLagen 1996); the production of alternative media in the United States to construct alternatives to dominant ideological positions (Pedelty 1993); rival political parties in India using cassette tapes to spread election messages in the face of ruling-party control of electronic media (Manuel 1993); efforts of political dissidents in foreign countries to use cassettes, faxes, and other "small media" to build revolutionary movements at home in Iran (Sreberny-Mohammadi and Mohammadi 1994) or Quechua revolutionaries smuggling texts and images to computer users who upload them to websites abroad to pursue international attention (Cleaver 1998), and efforts by citizens to establish civil society media spaces outside the structures of corporate-dominated markets and state media (Stein, Kidd and Rodríguez2009, Rodríguez, Kidd and Stein 2010).

Digital Challenges

The history of media anthropology has been primarily a history of human practices and engagements with radial media, in which media produced in a particular place by those who control the means of production is circulated or broadcast to various publics to be read, listened to or viewed and interpreted within the networks and contexts of their everyday social lives. While the idea that there exist some forms of media in which to own the means of consumption is also to own the means of production and distribution dates back at least 50 years (Enzenberger 1970), until recently little attention was paid to such technologies. An exception is studies of the capacity of cassette players to also rapidly reproduce cassettes, allowing them to be utilized by small scale producers for local music markets (Manuel 1993) or by revolutionaries seeking to evade state censorship (Sreberny-Mohammadi and Mohammadi 1994).

The emergence of social media, and the personalization of convergent technologies like personal computers, cell phones and tablets, significantly expanded interest in media anthropology. Anthropologists began to explore 3D virtual environments (Boellstorff 2008, Malaby 2009, Nardi 2010), blogging (Doostdar 2004), geek/hacker cultures (Coleman 2013), mobile media (Tenhunen 2018), social media (Gershon 2010, Miller et al. 2016), webcams (Miller and Sinanan 2013), as well as practices like trolling and hate speech (Udupa and Pohjonen 2019). Meanwhile, anthropology is transforming its own practices with digital methodologies (Pink et al. 2016, Hjorth et al. 2019), open publishing platforms and new multimedia transnational scholarship projects such as For Digital Dignity (www.fordigitaldignity.com) and Why We Post (www.ucl.ac.uk/why-we-post).

While coherent media texts continue to be produced by professional news and entertainment industries, the ways in which texts are produced and circulated, and the ways consumers engage with these texts has changed significantly. As a result, any sharp distinction between producers and consumers has also collapsed, with terms like "produsers" (Bruns 2008) and "prosumers" (Toffler 1980) emerging among media scholars to emphasize this change. It may now be more useful to explore practices of "entextualization" (Briggs and Bauman 1992)—the processes by which speech and ideas become mediated units that can be shared—than continue the metaphors of production and consumption. In what follows, I want to describe five challenges posed by these emerging new digital technologies of representation and interaction.

These are challenges to theory and method with which anthropologists are grappling in creative and innovative ways as media—ever more broadly conceived—moves increasingly to the center of anthropological inquiry.

Challenge #1: What's New About Digital Media?

One of the common tropes in contemporary media studies involves emphasizing the newness of digital media and the speed with which they have penetrated into everyday human life around the world. But what is meant by "new"? And what is meant by "digital"?

In the mid-1970s newspapers began to transition from typewriters to computer terminals wired to massive, refrigerator-sized mainframe computers and a system of code-based online typesetting. Twenty years later personal computers enabled news editors to receive stories on floppy disks and lay out pages of the newspaper on large screens using Adobe software. Similar transformations of technology took place in radio, cinema and television. Media has been "digital" for almost 50 years but this digitalization went largely unremarked when it was simply a tool for doing better what radial media had already been doing. In practice, media anthropologists (like other media scholars) tend to use the term "digital" primarily to refer to a broad range of convergent technologies, genres, practices, message forms and styles of interaction that have arisen since the establishment of the Internet in early 1990s.

Media anthropologists are increasingly paying attention to people's appropriations of media into such quotidian practices as shopping, cooking, finding a job, driving a car and raising children. New media technologies have enabled practices that empower and make visible marginalized, disenfranchised and oppressed groups. Yet these same technologies empower state surveillance, hate speech and new interventions into electoral processes.

In our focus on the new, it's important to recollect that "newness" is itself a discursive construct and needs to be scrutinized as part of public discourse rather than valorized as a descriptive or analytical term (Gershon 2017). "New media" is a shifting term, a moving target. New media become established, and eventually become the "old media" that subsequent technologies confront as "new media" (Armbrust 2012). These are processes that anthropologists need to be describing, particularly since social media genres, technologies and practices change so rapidly. As always, anthropologists must focus on similarities as well as differences, continuities as well and disjunctions in developing diachronic studies of human entanglements with media.

Challenge #2: Digital Divisions

In popular discourse, the term "digital divide" refers to a gap between those with, and those without access to the Internet and other information and communication technologies—or, more broadly, between those able to benefit from digital technologies and those who are not. The term is utopian in its assumptions about the value of online capacities, and simplistic in its assumption that the only significant hierarchical distinction in social media is access or lack of access. But it draws attention to two key points: first, media has penetrated into so many domains of human life that its lack becomes an issue of social concern, like malnutrition, and, second, this media penetration plays significant roles in creating and maintaining social distinctions.

Recent ethnographic work has certainly recognized media's influence in an ever wider range of social domains, such as cultural and political activism (Juris 2012, Postill 2013), development (Skuse, Gillespie and Power 2011) and revolution (Peterson 2017, Armbrust 2019), but also more intimately media's use in romantic entanglements (Gershon 2010), marketing oneself as a desirable employee on social media (Gershon 2014), and hospice patients use various media to engage with their social universe at the final stage of their lives (Miller 2017). Theoretically, the ubiquity of media has led to increasing attention to theories of "mediatization" (*Medialisierung*) and "mediation." Mediatization refers to both the long-term historical processes through which a "media logic" is said to have diffused across the modern world and, more proximately, into everyday human interactions (Couldry and Hepp 2013, Hepp, Hjarvard and Lundby 2015). Mediation theories seek to move media anthropology beyond the study of communications media to the ways in which meaning moves through people, practices and objects in transaction (Mazzarella 2004, Boyer 2012).

Anthropologists have also been keenly aware that there are many digital divides. Like all human artifacts, media play crucial roles in the creation of social hierarchies. Class, caste, race and gender identities (among others) can be inflected not only by whether one possesses a technology like a smartphone, but by which brand one owns, to which service one subscribes, which apps one uses to text and so forth. Shifts from one medium, site or service to another can both mark and create significant social distinctions. And media affordances are never only enabling and empowering; they are also always constraining, and these constraints can have marked social consequences for people with sensory impairments, physical disabilities and cognitive challenges.

As a term defining categories of "haves" and "have-nots," digital divide draws attention to issues of power and materiality that are only beginning to be explored. Platforms are not neutral spaces for content, algorithms literally "encode" the contexts of social relations within which they were produced (Seaver 2018), the "cloud" exists in the full materiality of digital storage centers (see Taylor's chapter in this volume). Ideas are owned, authored and authorized, and controlled through webs of irregularly enforced international intellectual property laws and regulations. All of our intimate, personal engagements with and through virtual media rest on very real and material infrastructures, and are incorporated within objects and supply chains, carbon emissions, waste management systems and the anthropocene environment, and these too contribute to digital divisions.

Challenge #3: Post-Radial Semiotics

Another fundamental challenge to media anthropology is moving beyond a semiotics of communication rooted in a model of speakers and hearers, or senders and receivers, which is embedded not only in much of media theory generally but also in the ethnography of communication (Hymes 1977, Jakobson 1960). The collapse of the radial model of media exchange as the primary paradigm for communication opens the need for new language to talk about exchange of media messages (including the concept of "message" itself). The metaphor of the "virus" dominates popular discourse, but there is much to recommend the concept of "spreadability" (Jenkins, Ford and Green 2013) as a way to understand the dissemination and circulation of media in many forms across multiple platforms.

The most significant value of "spreadability" for anthropologists is the issue of agency. In the metaphor of the virus, social actors are mere hosts for messages that, in essence, spread themselves through their hosts. Some hosts are non-receptive to the message, some receptive and, of the latter, some spread the message further. Spreadability, by contrast, emphasizes the agency of spreaders, and attends to the ways in which media may be edited, dubbed, re-imaged, reframed and otherwise transformed before being passed on to others. Engaging in the spreading of messages makes one part of "participatory culture," networks of people who are "shaping, sharing, reframing, and remixing media content" (Jenkins, Ford and Green

2013: 3). Participatory cultures are created through practices of exchange, communal acts of giving and receiving that link people together into networks.

In an environment of media convergence, mediation and polymedia, the ecology of communicative opportunities within which people carry out their social relations (Madianou and Miller 2012), spreadability and participatory culture appear as useful corollary concepts. One danger of the participatory culture concept has been a tendency for it to be celebrated rather than described and analyzed. Many accounts of participatory culture frame it as a construction of horizontal social relations rather than contextualizing these social relations within the broader political economies within which they operate. Platforms may not be culture industries in the way publishing and broadcasting companies are, but neither are they neutral.

Challenge #4: Imagining Communities

What are the processes of community formation by and through social media, Internet technology and gaming? The question of what constitutes a social unit of analysis in anthropology—the *ethnos* for our ethnography—is a longstanding question in the history of the discipline. Mass media created the possibility of "communities" of atomized individuals connected only by their common consumption of media. New media open up the possibility of people forming communities through exchanges of memes, clicking the "like" button or leaving a comment. Anderson's concept of "imagined communities"—communities of people who will likely never meet yet who imagine themselves as participating in a horizontal comradeship—has never been more salient. But what are the tools through which such communities are imagined?

The semiotics of identity in participatory cultures and cultures of connectedness is indexicality, which explores the meanings of connections in particular contexts. An index is any relation between signifier and signified based on relations of contiguity—that is, on connectedness. Through participation in online discourses, people link themselves to one another in complex webs of significance. While actual clicks and shares are important moments of identity construction (Hervik 2019), of even greater significance are the ways in which people imagine the community into which they have just clicked themselves. Models of people constructing identities by linking themselves to broader communities of taste, such as Silverstein's study of oenophilia (Silverstein 2003), offer interesting models for understanding the ways in which mediated communities as QAnon emerge and thrive.

Challenge #5: Play, Game and Design

Yet another challenge involves describing and analyzing the convergence of play and gaming into human engagements with media. Games have rarely been seen as communications media and have historically been excluded from the anthropology of media. This exclusion is no longer tenable. The rise of digital and online gaming has led to a distinctive convergence between games and media. Games can be played online with others both asynchronous and in real time, people can enter into online multiplayer games and interact with, and exchange resources with, other characters whose real bodies are displaced from one another in time and space (Nardi 2010), and people can share games, and invite others to play in participatory online gaming cultures. Role-playing games may have cinematic narrative plots that draw on, yet differ from traditional film, print, radio or television narratives in that player choices affect outcomes creating co-narrative activities. Issues of media representations of race, gender, class and other salient social distinctions are now as relevant to gaming as they are to radial media, yet may be experienced differently because of these co-narrative elements. Gamers and gamemakers create social worlds around these experiences with their own languages, social norms and systems of solidarity and conflict, and these live and online gaming communities engage in public discourses about play, with other players, in interactive media spaces of many different kinds, sometimes embedded in the game platforms themselves. These game communities often build group identities and alterities around representational politics in game production. These interactions can include trolling, hate speech and other genres.

Attention to games draws our attention to another historically ignored domain, that of play. Play is significant in media contexts because it is the wellspring of possibility, virtuality, liminality and contingency—the mysterious realms of "what if …?" that lie just beyond our everyday social worlds accessed by gaming (Stromberg 2009), but also by the many other elements of virtuality in contemporary mediation (Malaby 2007). An understanding of play as a social and cultural practice may be crucial to understanding much of participatory culture, as well as the activities of fan communities organized around media and the indexical webs creators and consumers weave out of interconnections between games, television and film, music, toys, costumes and myriad other media. Most of these interconnections do not emerge spontaneously but are professionally produced through acts of *design*, the social process of managing creativity and contingency in order to turn possibilities into tangible experiences that can transform social life. Designers inhabit professional worlds that seek to name, organize and systematize the creative process, generating competing and overlapping theories, ethics and practices through which contemporary media are created (Clarke 2011).

Conclusion

Over the past 25 years, the study of media can be seen as having moved from the periphery to the center of anthropological interest, as every domain of human life from ritual to kinship to political activity to flows of economic capital have become mediatized. It is difficult to imagine ethnographic studies of any human activity that will not at some point describe their hosts' entanglements with media, so there is a sense in which the anthropological study of media can be said to have gone mainstream. At the same time, there will continue to be a distinct subfield of media anthropology, focused more specifically on media practices and on what they can teach us about the human condition. Media anthropology in this more restricted sense will serve as a source of solutions to these ethnographic accounts of broader human activities in which media play a part.

References

Abu-Lughod, L. (1989) "Bedouins, Cassettes and Technologies of Public Culture," *Middle East Report*, 159: 7–11, 47.
Appadurai, A. (1996) *Modernity at Large: Cultural Dimensions of Globalization*, Minneapolis: University of Minnesota Press.
Armbrust, W. (2012) "A History of New Media in the Arab Middle East," *Journal for Cultural Research*, 16(2–3): 155–174.
Armbrust, W. (2019) *Martyrs and Tricksters: An Ethnography of the Egyptian Revolution*, Princeton: Princeton University Press.
Askew, K. and Wilk, R.R. (eds.) (2002) *The Anthropology of Media: A Reader*, Malden: Blackwell Publishers.
Auge, M. (1986) "Telecultural Heroes, or A Night at the Embassy," *Cultural Anthropology*, 27(2): 184–188.
Bateson, G. (1980) "An Analysis of the Nazi Film 'Hitlerjunge Quex'," *Studies in Visual Communication*, 6(3): 20–55.
Bean, S. (1981) "Soap Operas: Sagas of American Kinship," in W. Arens and S. Montague (eds.), *The American Dimension*, Van Nuys, CA: Alfred Publishing, 80–98.

Beeman, W. O. (1982) *Culture, Performance and Communication in Iran*, Tokyo: Institute for the Study of Languages and Cultures of Asia & Africa.

Beeman, W. O. (2000) "Margaret Mead and Cultural Studies: Introduction to The Study of Culture at a Distance," in M. Mead, R. Metraux and W. O. Beeman, (eds.), *The Study of Culture at a Distance*, Berghahn Books, xi–xxx.

Beeman, W. O. and Peterson, M. A. (2001) "Situations and Interpretations: Explorations in Interpretive Practice," *Anthropological Quarterly*, 74(4): 159–162.

Benedict, R. (1946) *The Chrysanthemum and the Sword*, Boston: Houghton Mifflin.

Bird, E. (1992) *For Enquiring Minds: A Cultural Study Supermarket Tabloids*, Austin: University of Texas Press.

Bird, E. (ed.) (2003) *The Anthropology of News and Journalism: Global Perspectives*, Bloomington: Indiana University Press.

Bishara, A. A. (2013) *Back Stories: US News Production and Palestinian Politics*, Stanford: Stanford University Press.

Boellstorff, T. (2008) *Coming of Age in Second Life: An Anthropologist Explores the Virtually Human*, Princeton: Princeton University Press.

Boyer, D. (2012) "From Media Anthropology to the Anthropology of Mediation," in R. Fardon and J. Gledhill (eds.), *The SAGE Handbook of Social Anthropology*, London: Sage, 383–392.

Boyer, D. (2013) *The Life Informatic: Newsmaking in the Digital Era*, Ithaca, NY: Cornell University Press.

Briggs, C. L. and R. Bauman (1992) "Genre, Intertextuality, and Social Power," *Journal of Linguistic Anthropology*, 2(2): 131–172.

Buszard-Welcher, L. (2018) New Media for Endangered Languages, in K. L. Rehg and L. Campbell (eds.), *The Oxford Handbook of Endangered Languages*, Oxford: Oxford University Press.

Carael, M., and Stanbury, J. B. (1984) "A Film Program in Health and Family Planning in Rural Zaire," *Human Organization*, 43(4): 134–142.

Caton, S. (1999) *Lawrence of Arabia: A Film's Anthropology*, Berkeley: University of California Press.

Caughey, J. L. (1984) *Imaginary Social Worlds: A Cultural Approach*, Lincoln: University of Nebraska Press.

Clarke, A. J. (2011) *Design Anthropology: Object Culture in the 21st Century*, New York: Springer.

Claus, P. J. (1982) "A Structuralist Appreciation of Star Trek," in J. B. Cole (ed.), *Anthropology for the Eighties*, New York: Free Press, 417–429.

Cleaver, H. M. (1998) "The Zapatista Effect: The Internet and the Rise of an Alternative Political Fabric," *Journal of International Affairs*, 51(2): 621–640.

Coleman, E. G. (2013) *Coding Freedom: The Ethics and Aesthetics of Hacking*, Princeton: Princeton University Press.

Coleman, P. (1986) "Music Carries a Message to Youths," *Development Communication Report*, 53: 1–3.

Cotter, C. (1999). "Raidió na Life: Innovations in the Use of Media for Language Revitalization," *International Journal of the Sociology of Language*, 140: 135–147.

Couldry, N. and Hepp, A. (2013) "Conceptualizing Mediatization: Contexts, Traditions, Arguments," *Communication Theory*, 23(3): 191–202.

Das, V. (1973) "The Structure of Marriage Preferences: An Account from Pakistani Fiction," *Man*, 8(1): 30–45.

Doostdar, A. (2004) "'The Vulgar Spirit of Blogging': On Language, Culture, and Power in Persian Weblogistan," *American Anthropologist*, 106(4): 651–662.

Dornfeld, B. E. (1998) *Producing Public Television, Producing Public Culture*, Princeton: Princeton University Press.

Enzenberger, H. M. (1970) "Constituents of a Theory of the Media," *New Left Review*, 64: 13–36.

Gershon, I. (2010) *The Breakup 2.0: Disconnecting Over New Media*, Ithaca, NY: Cornell University Press.

Gershon, I. (2014) "Selling Your Self in the United States," *POLAR: Political and Legal Anthropology Review*, 37(2): 281–295.

Gershon, I. (2017) "Language and the Newness of Media," *Annual Review of Anthropology*, 46: 15–31.

Ginsburg, F. (1991) "Indigenous Media: Faustian Contract or Global Village?" *Cultural Anthropology*, 6(1): 92–112.

Ginsburg, F. D., Abu-Lughod, L., and Larkin, B. (2002) *Media Worlds: Anthropology on New Terrain*, Berkeley: University of California Press.

Granzberg, G. (1982) "Television as Storyteller: The Algonkian Indians of Central Canada," *Journal of Communication*, 32(1): 43–52.

Hannerz, U. (2005) *Foreign News: Exploring the World of Foreign Correspondents*, Chicago: University of Chicago Press.

Hjorth, L., Horst, H., Galloway, A., and Bell, G. (2019) *The Routledge Companion to Digital Ethnography*, London: Routledge.

Hepp, A., Hjarvard, S., and Lundby, K. (2015), "Mediatization: Theorizing the Interplay Between Media, Culture and Society," *Media, Culture & Society*, 37(2): 314–327.

Hervik, P. (2019) "Ritualized Opposition in Danish Online Practices of Extremist Language and Thought," *International Journal of Communication*, 13: 3104–3121.

Himpele, J. (2008) *Circuits of Culture: Media, Politics and Indigenous Identity in the Andes*, Minneapolis: University of Minnesota Press.

Hymes, D. (1977) *Foundations of Sociolinguistics*, Philadelphia: University of Pennsylvania Press.

Jakobson, R. (1960) "Concluding Statement: Linguistics and Poetics," in T. Sebeok (ed.), *Style in Language*, New York: Wiley, 350–377.

Jenkins, H., Ford, S. and Green, J. (2013) *Spreadable Media: Creating Value and Meaning in a Networked Culture*, New York: New York University Press.

Jhappan, C. R. (1990) "Indian Symbolic Politics: The Double-Edged Sword of Publicity," *Canadian Ethnic Studies*, 22(3): 19–39.

Juris, J. S. (2012) "Reflections on# Occupy Everywhere: Social Media, Public Space, and Emerging Logics of Aggregation," *American Ethnologist*, 39(2): 259–279.

Karp, I. (1981) "Good Marx for the Anthropologist: Structure and Antistructure in 'Duck Soup'," in W. Arens and S. Montague (eds.), *The American Dimension*, Sherman Oaks, CA: Greenwood, 53–68.

Kottak, C. (1990) *Prime Time Society*, Belmont, CA: Wadsworth.

Lynd, R. and Lynd, H. M. (1929) *Middletown*, New York: Harcourt Brace.

Lynd, R. (1937) *Middletown Revisited*, New York: Harcourt Brace.

Madan, T. N. (1987) *Non-Renunciation: Themes and Interpretations of Hindu Culture*, Delhi: Oxford University Press.

Madianou, M. and Miller, D. (2012) "Polymedia: Towards a New Theory of Digital Media in Interpersonal Communication," *International Journal of Cultural Studies*, 16(2): 169–187.

Malaby, T. M. (2007) "Beyond Play: A New Approach to Games," *Games & Culture*, 2(2): 95–113.

Malaby, T. M. (2009) *Making Virtual Worlds: Linden Lab and Second Life*, Ithaca, NY: Cornell University Press.

Mankekar, P. (1999) *Screening Culture, Viewing Politics: An Ethnography of Television, Womanhood, and Nation in Postcolonial India*, Durham, NC: Duke University Press.

Manuel, P. (1993) *Cassette Culture: Popular Music and Technology in North India*, Chicago: University of Chicago Press.

Mazzarella, W. (2003) *Shoveling Smoke: Advertising and Globalization in Contemporary India*, Durham, NC: Duke University Press.

Mazzarella, W. (2004), "Culture, Globalization, Mediation," *Annual Review of Anthropology*, 33(1): 345–367.

McLagen, M. (1996) "Computing for Tibet: Virtual Politics in the Post-Cold War Era," in G. Marcus (ed.), *Connected: Engagements with Media at the Century's End*, Chicago: University of Chicago Press, 159–194.

Mead, M. and Metraux, R. (eds.) (1954) *The Study of Culture at a Distance*, Chicago: University of Chicago Press.

Michaels, E. (1994) *Bad Aboriginal Art: Tradition, Media and Technological Horizons*, Minneapolis: University of Minnesota Press.

Miller, D. (2017) *The Comfort of People*, Cambridge, Polity.

Miller, D. and Sinanan, J. (2013) *Webcam*, New York: Wiley.

Miller, D., Costa, E., Haynes, N., McDonald, T., Nicolescu, R., Sinanan, J., and Wang, X. (2016) *How the World Changed Social Media*, London: UCL Press.

Nardi, B. (2010) *My Life as a Night Elf Priest: An Anthropological Account of World of Warcraft*, Ann Arbor: University of Michigan Press.

Nyiri, P. (2017) *Reporting for China: How Chinese Correspondents Work with the World*, Seattle: University of Washington Press.

Pedelty, M. (1993), "Making Use of the (Alternative) Media," *Practicing Anthropologist*, 15(3): 29–30.

Peterson, L. C. (2014) "Made Impossible by Viewers Like You: The Politics and Poetics of Native American Voices in US Public Television," in D. A. Macey and K. Ryan (eds.), *How Television Shapes Our Worldview: Media Representations of Social Trends and Change*, New York: Lexington Books: 247–266.

Peterson, M. A. (2003) *Anthropology & Mass Communication: Media and Myth in the New Millennium*, Oxford, NY: Berghahn Publishing.

Peterson, M. A. (2017) "Mediated Experience in the Egyptian Revolution," in M. Zayani (ed.), *Digital Middle East: State and Society in the Information Age*, New York: Oxford University Press, 85–108.

Pink, S., Horst, H., Postill, J., Hjorth, L., Lewis, T. and Tacchi, J. (2016) *Digital Ethnography: Principles and Practice*, Thousand Oaks, CA: Sage.

Portes, A. (1976) "On the Sociology of National Development: Theories and Issues," *American Journal of Sociology*, 82(1): 55–85.

Postill, J. (2013) "Democracy in an Age of Viral Reality: A Media Epidemiography of Spain's Indignados Movement," *Ethnography*, 15(1): 51–69.

Powdermaker, H. (1950) *Hollywood: The Dream Factory: An Anthropologist Looks at the Movie-Makers*, New York: Little, Brown & Co.

Powdermaker, H. (1962) *Coppertown: Changing Africa*, New York: Harper & Row.

Redfield, R. and Singer, M. (1954) "The Cultural Role of Cities," *Economic Development and Cultural Change*, 3(1): 53–73.

Rodríguez, C., Kidd, D. and Stein, L. (eds.) (2010) *Making Our Media: Global Initiatives Toward a Democratic Public Sphere, Volume One: Creating New Communication Spaces*, Creskill, NJ: Hampton Press.

Rodgers, S. (1986) "Batak Tape Cassette Kinship: Constructing Kinship through the Indonesian National Mass Media," *American Ethnologist*, 13(1): 23–42.

Rothenbuhler, E. and Coman, M. (2005) *Media Anthropology*, Thousand Oaks: SAGE Publications.

Roudakova, N. (2017) *Losing Pravda: Ethics and The Press in Post-Truth Russia*, Cambridge, UK: Cambridge University Press.

Sapir, E. (1985) [1932] "Cultural Anthropology and Psychology," in D. Mandelbaum (ed.), *Selected Writings in Language, Culture and Personality*, Berkeley: University of California Press: 509–521.

Seaver, N. (2018) "What Should an Anthropology of Algorithms Do?" *Cultural Anthropology*, 33(3): 375–385.

Silverstein, M. (2003) "Indexical Order and the Dialectics of Sociolinguistic Life," *Language & Communication*, 23(3–4): 193–229.

Singer, M. (1960) "The Great Tradition of Hinduism in the City of Madras," in C. Leslie (ed.), *Anthropology of Folk Religion*, New York: Vintage Books, 105–166.

Singer, M. (1966) "Modernizing Religious Beliefs," in M. Weiner (ed.), *Modernization: The Dynamics of Growth*, New York: Bass Books.

Singer, M. (1972) *When a Great Tradition Modernizes: An Anthropological Approach to Indian Civilization*, New York: Praeger.

Singhal, A. and Rogers, E. (1989) *India's Information Revolution*. New Delhi: Sage.

Skuse, A., Gillespie, M. and Power, G. (eds.) (2011). *Drama for Development: Cultural Translation and Social Change*, New Delhi: Sage Publications India.

Sreberny-Mohammadi, A. and Mohammadi, A. (1994) *Small Media, Big Revolution: Communication, Change and the Iranian Revolution*, Minneapolis: University of Minnesota Press.

Stein, L., Kidd, D., and Rodríguez, C. (eds.) (2009) *Making Our Media: Global Initiatives Toward a Democratic Public Sphere, Volume Two: National and Global Movements for Democratic Communication*, Creskill, NJ: Hampton Press.

Stephen, L. (2012) "Community and Indigenous Radio in Oaxaca: Testimony and Participatory Democracy," in L. Bessire and D. Fischer (eds.), *Radio Fields: Anthropology and Wireless Sound in the 21st Century*, New York: New York University Press: 124–141.

Stromberg, P. G. (2009) *Caught in Play: How Entertainment Works on You*, Stanford: Stanford University Press.

Tenhunen, S. (2018) *A Village Goes Mobile: Telephony, Mediation, and Social Change in Rural India*, Oxford: Oxford University Press.

Toffler, A. (1980) *The Third Wave*, Toronto: Bantam Books.

Traube, E. G. (1992) *Dreaming Identities Class, Gender, and Generation in 1980s Hollywood Movies*, Boulder: Westview.

Turner, T. (2002) "Representation, Politics, and Cultural Imagination in Indigenous Video: General Points and Kayapo Examples," in F. Ginsburg, L. Abu-Lughod, and B. Larkin (eds.), *Media Worlds: Anthropology on New Terrain*, Berkeley: University of California Press, 75–89.

Udupa, S. and Pohjonen, M. (2019) "Extreme Speech and Global Digital Cultures," *International Journal of Communication*, 13: 3049–3067.

Warner, W. L. (1959) *The Living and the Dead: A Study in the Symbolic Life of Americans*, New Haven: Yale University Press.
Warner, W. L. and Lunt, P. S. (1941) *The Social Life of a Modern Community*, New Haven: Yale University Press.
Wilson, P. and M. Stewart (eds.) (2008) *Global Indigenous Media: Cultures, Poetics, and Politics*, Durham, NC: Duke University Press.

2
INDIGENOUS MEDIA
Anthropological Perspectives and Historical Notes

Philipp Budka

Introduction

Indigenous media matters because indigenous people do.

Wortham, 2013: 218

Anthropological research into Indigenous media has contributed to the formulation and construction of the field (or the sub-discipline) of media anthropology at the beginning of the 1990s (Askew, 2002; Ginsburg, Abu-Lughod and Larkin, 2002). However, the relationship between Indigenous people and media has been conceptualized and analysed in different ways and with different intentions. These research patterns are, of course, connected to historical developments, theoretical turns, and methodological changes in the discipline of anthropology and its growing interest in media and related phenomena. Around the middle of the 20th century, anthropologists were particularly interested in the sociocultural, linguistic, and cognitive consequences of new types and forms of media communication. They investigated how Indigenous people used and consumed "modern" media technologies and how these new media practices impacted their lives, their "original" and culturally distinct ways of perceiving the world (e.g., Worth and Adair, 1970). Some studies at that time even had a nostalgic and rather exoticizing tone; lamenting the loss of "traditional," "innocent" – or even "primitive" – culture because of "modern," "Western" media technologies (e.g., Carpenter, 1972). Towards the end of the 20th century, anthropologists became increasingly interested in how Indigenous people (re)appropriate and (re)interpret media technologies for their own needs and how they started to create their own media, media products, and media representations (Ginsburg, 1991). Such processes and practices have been integrated into anthropological research on media under the term "Indigenous media."

Indigenous media have been broadly defined as media and forms of media expression conceived and produced by Indigenous people (Ginsburg, 1991; Wilson and Stewart, 2008), as well as media practices involving members of Indigenous societies (Hafsteinsson, 2013; Hinkson, 2021). But who is Indigenous? What are defining characteristics of Indigenous people and societies? There is no inclusive definition of "Indigenous people(s)" that could be applied globally. The *United Nations Declaration on the Rights of Indigenous Peoples* was adopted in 2007 without any formal definition of Indigenous people(s) because "the identification of an indigenous people is the right of the people itself" (United Nations Department of Economic and Social Affairs, 2019: 4). Despite these identification difficulties, international organizations estimate that the overall number of the world's Indigenous population varies between 370 million (United Nations Department of Economic and Social Affairs, 2009) and 477 million (International Labour Organization, 2019), who live in more than 90 countries and speak more than 4,000 of the world's estimated 7,000 languages (United Nations Department of Economic and Social Affairs, 2009).

So, attempts to define Indigenous people – and consequently Indigenous media – are difficult, conflict-laden, sometimes contradicting, and always context-related. By drawing on different definitions and categorizations, Wilson and Stewart (2008: 14), however, suggest four points of reference to understand the term "Indigenous people": (1) priority in time of occupying and utilizing a particular territory; (2) cultural distinctiveness, including language, religion and social organization; (3) self-identification as "Indigenous" and recognition by other groups and entities as a distinct collectivity; (4) experience of marginalization, dispossession, and exclusion. The aspect of self-identification is particularly important in conceptualizing "the Indigenous" because it refers to self-determination or sovereignty "as the necessary response to the legacy of colonization and the only means to ensure the survival of Indigenous peoples" (Wilson and Stewart, 2008: 8).

The conception of "Indigenous people" has a strong sociopolitical connotation and is always shaped by different historical and sociocultural contexts that reflect the diversity of the world's Indigenous population. This is also true for Indigenous media projects that often aim to contribute to self-determined identity-making and forms of representation, albeit on different scales. Big Indigenous media schemes, such as national broadcasting initiatives (Hafsteinsson, 2013) or regional Internet projects (Budka, 2015), involve larger Indigenous collectives and networks, whereas smaller media projects, such as artistic articulations and expressions (Pitman, 2019), tend to represent smaller collectives and individuals.

The chapter traces developments in the anthropological study of Indigenous media, particularly since the 1990s when research in this field co-contributed to the widening area of media anthropology. For example, Indigenous media have been prominently conceptualized as a type of cultural activism that intends to spark, create, and support social and political change (Ginsburg, 2000; Landzelius, 2006). By (re)considering essential anthropological concepts, such as agency, change, and the cultural, it highlights the importance of activism and social change within Indigenous media engagements. However, this chapter is also critical of the cultural activist approach that tends to underestimate the sociocultural consequences of appropriating media technologies or to neglect Indigenous people's own articulations of media-related practices and experiences.

Moreover, this chapter foregrounds the technological and infrastructural dimensions of Indigenous media projects and initiatives, in particular by drawing on my own ethnographic research with the Keewaytinook Okimakanak Kuh-ke-nah Network (KO-KNET) in Northwestern Ontario, Canada, one of the world's leading Indigenous-owned and controlled Internet organizations (Budka, 2015, 2019). This relationship between media, mediation, technologies, and infrastructures has become more evident in explorations of digital media technologies, such as the Internet and social media platforms. By emphasizing the cultural dimension in processes of (digital) technology appropriation, Salazar (2007: 16) suggests that we might understand Indigenous media "as a socio-technical system of relations where technology becomes a cultural construction appropriated according to relevant cultural codes and social relations."

The chapter's next section discusses Indigenous media in the historical context of an anthropology of media by focusing and critically reviewing in particular the idea of understanding Indigenous media as cultural activism. The following section analyses aspects in the Indigenization of media. In doing so, it considers locally specific practices of media technology appropriation, global processes of identity-making, and the technological and infrastructural dimension of media projects. Especially important to these discussions are the concepts and the conceptualizations of (collective) action or agency and (sociopolitical) change. Ethnographic examples from the anthropological literature and from my own fieldwork in Canada complement these theoretical considerations. The chapter closes with a summary of key findings.

Indigenous Media in an Anthropology of Media

In 1984, when there was the famine in Ethiopia, the remote First Nation community of Sandy Lake in Northwestern Ontario, Canada, was raising money to support aid agencies that went to Africa to help the starving people. Since word-of-mouth fundraising was rather slow and not very successful, the people utilized locally available media technologies. A group of women went to the local communication centre where they switched off the TV transmitter of the Canadian Broadcasting Cooperation (CBC). They did this just before Saturday night ice hockey was going to be on, which was and still is one of the most popular TV shows, particularly among the community's male residents. After shutting down the transmitter, the women went on community radio, which is not only used to play music, but to communicate with community members and to organize social events such as bingo. They announced that they would not turn the transmitter back on until the men had given a certain amount of money. The following Monday, a group of Sandy Lake men went to the community centre and turned off the TV transmitter, just before another popular CBC programme was on: the soap opera *All my Children*, which was watched in particular by the community's women. The men then declared via radio that they wouldn't put the show back on until the women had donated money as well.

This story was told to me by one of my research partners just before my first visit to Sandy Lake in 2007 to exemplify the importance of local control and ownership in respect to the Indigenous utilization of media technologies. Even though the technical equipment was not owned by the community – it was the property of the CBC and therefore should not be manipulated – people of this remote Indigenous community used and manipulated available media technologies for their specific local aims. These practices can be characterized as being part of processes of media appropriation. To understand these processes, they must be contextualized by considering sociocultural and techno-historical specifics, such as the importance of media communication for remote settlements and the preference for oral communication in First Nation communities (Budka, 2009). Such contextualization adds to a deeper understanding of communicative environments or ecologies (Horst and Miller, 2006; Kummels, 2020). These environments include people, a variety of communication media and technologies, as well as changing relationships between media and people – for instance when Indigenous people in a remote area engage with new media technologies in creative and unexpected ways.

In the introduction to the seminal collection *Media Worlds: Anthropology on New Terrain*, Ginsburg, Abu-Lughod and Larkin (2002: 7) placed anthropological and ethnographic research on media at different positions in a sociocultural and sociopolitical continuum. At one end of this spectrum, anthropological research was dealing with mass media that were produced and distributed by commercial organizations and governmental institutions as well as with the consumption of media products. In the middle, processes and contexts related to the media production and consumption of diasporic and minority groups were the focal points of research. At the other end of the spectrum, they outlined anthropological research on media practices that aimed to empower marginalized and disfranchised people. This latter category included, in particular, Indigenous people and how they were utilizing media technologies to talk back to structures of power by producing their own media and by inserting their voices into mainstream media discourses. Related processes and practices have been investigated in different times by anthropologists in a variety of regions and sociocultural settings around the globe (e.g. Deger, 2006; Ginsburg, 1991; Hafsteinsson, 2013; Salazar, 2015; Turner, 1992).

As Ginsburg and colleagues (2002: 3) argued, anthropology situates media as a social practice within "shifting political and cultural frames" looking for "how media enable or challenge the workings of power and the potential of activism; the enforcement of inequality and the sources of imagination; and the impact of technologies on the production of individual and collective identities." Thus, media constitute different social fields for anthropological research. And media anthropology's models "must allow for the simultaneity of hegemonic and anti-hegemonic effects as we [anthropologists] examine how 'technologies of power' are created and contested within intimate institutional cultures, shaped by ideologies ranging from public services to audience appeal, to aesthetics, to political empowerment" (Ginsburg, Abu-Lughod and Larkin, 2002: 23).

This close connection between media, power, and activism becomes obvious when looking into Indigenous people's motives to create media. Ginsburg (2000: 29–30) identified four dimensions here: (1) the recognition of Indigenous people(s) and their cultural practices on a world stage; (2) the sustaining and transformation of contemporary Indigenous culture; (3) the enhancement of the struggle for Indigenous rights; (4) the critique of non-Indigenous representations of Indigenous people and culture(s). By (strategically) inserting their own narratives in the dominant media landscape – through films, TV, and radio programmes, and more currently, through websites and social media – Indigenous people also utilize media technologies as means for social change and political transformation. Such media-making practices include "the sense of both political agency and cultural intervention that people bring to these efforts" (Ginsburg, Abu-Lughod and Larkin, 2002: 8) and have become part of the "ongoing struggles for Indigenous recognition and self-determination" (Ginsburg, 2000: 30).

Media as Cultural Activism?

Considering the above aspects, Indigenous media-making practices can sometimes be understood as (a form of) cultural activism (Ginsburg, 1997; Turner, 1992). This view acknowledges Indigenous people's agency and their ability to respond to structures of power. Such an activist approach considers media technologies as tools to make the voices of marginalized and disfranchised people heard. This conception of media practices as activist practices relates to two basic ideas. First, the foundation of mediated activism is (the notion of) collective action or agency. This is a rather broad concept that can be further specified by relating it to (ideas of) conflict, solidarity, competition, cooperation, resistance, mobility, or ritual (Bräuchler and Budka, 2020; Melucci, 1996). Second, mediated activism usually intends to spark, create, and support social and political change. It is important here to distinguish between slow sustained social changes that are continuously happening, and "actual social change," as Postill (2017: 35–36) puts it. He describes this as concrete and abrupt moments of change that transform the way people communicate and interact, such as the introduction of broadband Internet networks and connectivity in remote First Nation communities in Northwestern Ontario in the early 2000s (Budka, 2015).

Contemporary phenomena of mediated activism can be traced back to historical moments and processes such as the increasing distribution and availability of Internet-based digital media technologies (Kidd and Rodriguez, 2009). These developments have also been characterized by changing terminologies, such as terms like "cyberactivism," "hacktivims," or "social media activism" indicate. The activist use of digital media and technologies has become characteristic of almost all sociopolitical movements, from anti-globalization and Occupy movements, to the Podemos movement in Spain and various movements related to what has been termed the "Arab Spring" (Gerbaudo, 2017; Postill, 2018). The basic ideas of collective action and change indicate the relatedness between Indigenous media projects and the use of media by social movements in their critiques of neo-liberal capitalism. Media-related activism – Indigenous or non-Indigenous – can be understood as mediated collective action that aims for sociopolitical change. Media activism, and of course Indigenous media activism, is furthermore related to a whole set of phenomena, such as different sociopolitical and economic power relationships, several forms and structures of conflict as well as processes of globalization and transnationalism.

However, critics of this activist approach in the 1980s and 1990s contended that the Indigenous appropriation of "Western" media technologies inevitably resulted in the loss of "traditional" culture, language, and knowledge. Weiner (1997) stated that in utilizing "Western" media, Indigenous people are also absorbing the dominant, "modern" world view. He therefore questioned the usefulness of (audio-visual) media technologies for Indigenous people at large. Carpenter (1972: 191) even went so far as to state that ("modern" mass) media "are so powerful they swallow [Indigenous] cultures." Weiner was correct in pointing out that media technologies are always developed, (re)produced, and distributed with specific sociopolitical and economic intentions and under locally distinct conditions. Structures of power are continuously inscribed into media. It is also true that media and related practices have effects on people and their sociocultural realities (see Postill this volume). There is hardly any doubt that "Western" media technologies lead to linguistic adaptation and acculturation. However, this does not necessarily mean the loss of distinct cultural features. Much of Weiner's account simply rested on an essentializing and static understanding of culture, including the underestimation or even the complete denial of Indigenous people's agency.

Ginsburg (1991), Turner (1992) and other anthropologists of media have shown that the Indigenous use of "modern" media technologies includes regaining the control over the mediation and representation of Indigenous culture and identity. This also means that to abstain from media appropriation – to "preserve" traditional culture, as Weiner (1997) suggested – would eventually result in losing control over Indigenous futures. For Turner (1992), Indigenous media are an important opportunity to insert Indigenous voices into the mainstream media. And Wood (2008) adds that Indigenous media production, in particular Indigenous film making, contributes to the correction of misrepresentation of Indigenous people by the dominant non-Indigenous media industry. According to Wood (2008: 81–83), Indigenous media makers – and I would add a majority of media anthropologists – therefore largely reject assumptions that "Western" media are so powerful that they "swallow cultures," and the resonating media determinism. While colonial narratives underlie the overall domination of "Western" media technologies, thus denying Indigenous agency, activist narratives, as responses to the inadequacy of coloniality highlight Indigenous media's potential for structural change, cultural representation, and political inclusion.

However, another strand of critique argues that the activism narrative tends to neglect Indigenous people's own articulations of media practices (Hafsteinsson, 2013). As an alternative to the colonial and the activism narrative, Hafsteinsson (2013: 51) suggests a democratic narrative about Indigenous media which not only considers structural changes, but also individual and local changes and related social transformations and consequences invoked by media. By analysing the relational aspects and characteristics of media through the case of communicative and journalistic practices of the Canadian Aboriginal Peoples Television Network (APTN), Hafsteinsson explores the sociocultural agency of Indigeneity and its (media) politics. Following Michaels (1985), who worked with Indigenous media producers in Australia in the 1980s, he pays particular attention to media's cultural, societal, and linguistic particularities and limitations. Thus, he focuses on the communicative constraints, norms, and regulations of knowledge and information production and circulation in a Canadian Indigenous context. Hafsteinsson (2013: 12) argues that APTN's media practices are basically democratic practices "which include respect, protection, promotion of diversity, and universal human rights." By conceptualizing democracy as an "emerging narrative field," which builds on the inclusion and participation of Canada's diverse Indigenous people as well as on the bridging between Indigenous and non-Indigenous people alike, Hafsteinsson (2013: 68) develops his account of Indigenous media as practices of "deep democracy," a term he borrows from Appadurai.

Hafsteinsson is right in reminding us to be careful when deploying "Western" concepts, such as activism, in interpreting and analysing Indigenous (media) practices. He is also correct in drawing our attention to individual and local changes which are related to processes of mediation. However, these "small" changes are not to be separated from structural changes, sociopolitical developments, and historical contexts. I therefore propose that to gain insights into the relationship between Indigenous individuals, collectives, and media technologies, it is necessary to consider the relational aspects of Indigenous media as tools for cultural activism as well as media's (technical) constraints and the distinct cultural norms and values of an Indigenous knowledge economy.

Media Anthropologists as Activists

It is important to recognize that the Indigenous media, information, and knowledge economy may also include anthropologists. Working together with Indigenous people to produce videos (Turner, 2002), websites (Forte, 2006), or films (Ginsburg, 2002a, 2002b), some anthropologists have actually become media activists, and hence cultural or political activists, themselves. Weiner (1997) was critical of the activist role anthropologists like Ginsburg or Turner played in Indigenous media projects. While actively being involved in such projects, anthropologists leave the describing outsider position that is, according to Weiner, necessary for conducting anthropological research. Considering the difficult and sometimes even desperate situations in which many Indigenous people have to live, I find it understandable that researchers turn into activists by moving beyond academic studies and descriptions to actively engage in media projects.

Anthropologists become deeply involved and incorporated into processes, procedures, and practices, which they may initially intend to examine from the "outside." This may be a response to the fact that an increasing number of Indigenous people, communities, and organizations strongly reject the objectification of their lives and cultures through anthropological and ethnographic research by cooperating only in work that contributes directly to Indigenous controlled projects or initiatives (Smith, 2005). Many methodological, ethical, and moral questions are emerging here, which not only have been discussed within the fields of applied and action anthropology, but also within anthropology at large, in attempts to decolonize the discipline (Harrison, 2010).

Turner, who worked with Kayapo communities in Brazil, understood the anthropology of media primarily as a form of action anthropology (Boyer, 2006). In such an anthropology, the sociopolitical and cultural self-realization of people through the (technological) mediation of human agency is put into the centre of research. In this respect, research in Indigenous media has become an important lesson for anthropology and media studies alike. In his collaborative work with a community-based Maya Q`eqchi' video project in Guatemala, Flores (2004: 35) suggests an applied visual media anthropology approach that has its roots in Rouch's "shared anthropology." This applied or shared anthropological endeavour is characterized by a shift from a seemingly objective observer-centred approach to an (inter)subjective positioning of the researcher. This may include the conscious creation of collaborative relationships between researcher and research participants – so that the latter actually become research partners – as well as the production of meaningful research outcomes for the respective communities, such as videos or films that support legal claims.

In this line, Pratt (2010: 163), being an Indigenous researcher herself, proposes "participatory research models" to answer questions about the future of Indigenous "communication needs and priorities." Indigenous researchers, she states, are particularly well equipped to examine new communication media and practices in Indigenous communities by offering a unique perspective (Pratt, 2010: 170). Such an applied, action-oriented approach to (Indigenous) media research holds the potential not only to empower research partners and the community by co-creating and sharing knowledge and research results, it is also the researcher herself who is empowered through close partnerships and bonds of trust.

Indigeneity and the Indigenizing of Media Technologies

Media technologies, and the control over their production and distribution, obviously play an important role in the representation and articulation of Indigenous people. Some Indigenous media initiatives have been jointly brought forward by Indigenous and non-Indigenous activists to mutually represent subaltern interests. These joint projects point to the idea of Indigeneity that connects to fields of sameness and otherness as well as to different processes in time and space. "Indigeneity, in other words, is at once historically contingent and encompassing of the nonindigenous – and thus never about untouched reality" (de la Cadena and Starn, 2007: 4). It is a relational field that needs to be understood in a historical context by considering processes of sociopolitical change and continuity as well as a larger structural framework of identification and ethnicity.

The past decades saw a worldwide increase of Indigenous activism which has been centring around land claims, language, and human rights, education and "the rights of indigenous peoples to speak for and represent themselves as opposed to being 'spoken for' by nonindigenous experts, bureaucrats, and policymakers" (de la Cadena and Starn, 2007: 10). The latter refers in particular to Indigenous media projects and initiatives that have become increasingly globalized. Wilson and Stewart (2008: 2) state that Indigenous media "have emerged from geographically scattered, locally based production centres to become part of globally linked media networks with increased effectiveness and reach." Media technologies have become central to Indigenous people(s)' movements and their organization. Indigenous issues, such as control over land, (de)colonization, cultural, and linguistic diversity, traditional and local knowledge, as well as questions of self-identification and the negotiation of identities, are put to the discursive foreground through Indigenous media on local, national, and global levels. This has also resulted in the explicit mentioning of Indigenous peoples' right to media (representation) in the *United Nations Declaration on the Rights of Indigenous Peoples* (United Nations, 2007: 6).

The active involvement of Indigenous people in global debates about Indigenous identity and definitions as well as about the rights of Indigenous people is key in the development and negotiation of a global Indigenous identity. While media technologies allow for the recognition and celebration of local cultural distinctiveness, they also enable the world's Indigenous people to connect, network, and collaborate across nation state borders. Pietikäinen (2008: 198) shows that Indigenous media in the case of the Sámi, who reside in a territory stretching across northern Norway, Sweden, Finland, and Russia, resonate on a local level and, at the same time, serve for transnational "pan-Sámi" political and sociocultural needs.

However, as Smith, Burke and Ward (2000) state, globalization has a dual effect on Indigenous people in terms of media; global media offer new possibilities of connecting and networking, while simultaneously creating new threats to property and knowledge rights (see also Ginsburg, 1991). On one hand, globalization threatens to accelerate the centuries-old process of colonization by facilitating new waves of "invasion" through mass tourism, globally distributed media technologies, and the domination of "Western" popular culture and its products. These processes, on the other hand, also enable Indigenous people to present themselves and their cultures to a wider audience and to connect and network with other Indigenous people on a global scale. The increasing public awareness of Indigenous distinctiveness and diversity as well as the networking between Indigenous people, who share the common experience of colonization, are fundamental for Indigenous empowerment. The creation of Indigenous networks with their implicit empowering character contributes to the process of decolonization which again transforms sociopolitical orders.

Sociopolitical Change

"Indigenized" media technologies are providing Indigenous people with possibilities to make their voices heard, to network and connect, to distribute information, to revitalize culture and language, and to become politically engaged and active (Budka, 2019; Ginsburg, 2002a). As Wortham (2004: 367) notes in her discussion of Indigenous video practices in relation to projects of self-determination in Mexico, "as the state builds its patrimony of pluralism, Indigenous activists are constructing forms of autonomy that redefine their communities through the use of audio-visual technology." And Brooten (2008: 111–12) demonstrates that Indigenous media in Myanmar contribute to in-group communication and outside representation by "identifying the patterns of resistance and survival that begin to alter stereotypes of Indigenous peoples as helpless, hopeless victims." Media technologies have thus become tools for sociopolitical change (see also Pietikäinen, 2008; Smith, 2010; Wortham, 2013).

In the early 1980s, Michaels (1985, 1994) started to investigate the role and implications of electronic communication in remote Indigenous communities in Australia. In doing so, he became particularly interested in the (changing) situation of Warlpiri media producers in an oral culture context. He examined the interaction and relations between "modern" electronic media, such as television and video, and "traditional" life worlds and practices by focusing on cultural phenomena such as "speech restriction" – that is, the prohibition of referring to specific names or terms in case of death or in relation to local modes of sacred knowledge production. Michaels (1985: 506) emphasized that Aboriginal orality depends on the control and ownership of communication and knowledge processes and that "constraints of knowledge" must be considered when producing, distributing, and utilizing media technologies in an economy of oral information. By understanding culture as the communication of traditions, the introduction of new means of communication is of crucial concern for Indigenous people (Michaels, 1994). He therefore proposes that without Indigenous-owned and controlled media, Indigenous people simply produce local content that only becomes "Indigenous" outside of its local context (Michaels, 1994: 43–44).

As Turner (1992, 2002) showed with the case of the Kayapo and their video making projects in Brazil, (Indigenous) media appropriation is just another cultural performance that is not necessarily replacing other performances or cultural practices. These new performative practices rather extend the cultural repertoire of Indigenous communities. By appropriating video technologies, the Kayapo continue, according to Turner (1992), their tradition of objectifying modes of representation. Video technologies in the Kayapo case have led to the objectification of Indigenous people's own culture for political struggle – what Ginsburg, Abu-Lughod and Larkin (2002: 10) have called "strategic objectification" – and, at the same time, to the hybridization of culture through the Indigenous incorporation of techniques and technologies of the dominating culture.

Moreover, video making has been used by the Kayapo to establish (political) facts and (social) reality. Kayapo video teams recorded meetings with Brazilian and international politicians as well as with other Indigenous representatives to later show and discuss these videos in their remote communities. Indigenous media have become key in mediating sociopolitical activities, for sociopolitical empowerment, and ultimately for sociopolitical change. According to Turner (1992), the Kayapo are transforming their culture and the conceptions of themselves through media technologies and related practices. He furthermore emphasizes the particularity of Indigenous media making as a process that also mediates sociocultural and political relationships in an Indigenous community and which differs considerably from an "outsider" mode of mediation, as initiated through anthropological projects (Turner, 2002). For him Indigenous media production is not about preserving culture, but about the empowerment of social actors by producing "their own cultural mediations" (Turner, 2002: 80). Through media technologies, Indigenous people with no writing tradition construct their own objectively determined social reality, thus "heightening their sense of control over the process of objectification itself" (Turner, 2002: 88).

Internet for Remote First Nation Communities in Canada

A key driver of increasing global interconnectedness, of self-controlled mediation and therefore of sociopolitical change has been digitally networked media technologies. Indigenous people have been utilizing digital media technologies since the early 1990s to communicate, represent, connect, network, and cooperate (e.g. Budka, 2019; Landzelius, 2006). Particularly in regions where Indigenous people had access to the necessary infrastructure, they became "early adopters" of digital technologies. Precisely because of their collective experience with marginalization and dispossession, they were among the first to make strategic use of these alternative, globally networked technologies; for instance, in the global movement of Indigenous peoples and for the construction of a global Indigenous identity (Forte, 2006; Niezen, 2005). Thus, the Indigenization of digital media technologies had and still has a strong sociopolitical meaning. Landzelius (2006: 4–6) therefore refers to Indigenous people's "self-authored engagements" with digital media technologies as "indigenous cyberactivism."

One of the first examples of Indigenous digital media activism is the Zapatista movement in Mexico (Cleaver, 1998). With the support of non-governmental organizations and solidarity networks and their utilization of early forms of online communication, the Zapatistas created a transnational counter-public to circulate their call for Indigenous rights. Digital media technologies contributed to the global popularization of the Zapatistas, the insertion of the

Indigenous cause into the national civil society, and eventually the survival of a regional sociopolitical movement. Globally distributed digital media and technologies also support the political endeavours of Indigenous groups for the recognition of their collective identity. Carib and Taino communities in the Caribbean and the diaspora have been utilizing the Internet to create forums of self-representation and networks of support to strengthen their struggle for cultural revival and Indigenous identity (re-)construction (Forte, 2006). Internet connectivity and the use of Internet technologies and services rely on digital infrastructures. The creation and maintenance of these infrastructures have been challenging for small, often remote, Indigenous communities (González, 2020; Sandvig, 2012).

By drawing on my own fieldwork with the Keewaytinook Okimakanak Kuh-ke-nah Network (KO-KNET) in Canada, I will show that Indigenous communities have been very successful in creating and maintaining their own Internet infrastructures and services (Budka, 2015, 2019, 2021). In 1994, the Oji-Cree tribal council Keewaytinook Okimakanak (KO) established KO-KNET to connect Indigenous people in the remote region of Northwestern Ontario to and through the Internet (Fiser and Clement, 2012). Remote communities in Northwestern Ontario have no year-round road access and are distant from other settlements and town service centres. At that time, a local telecommunication infrastructure in these communities was almost non-existent. KO-KNET started with a simple online bulletin board system that allowed community residents to communicate with family members who had to leave home to attend school or to find a job. The overall aim of this community-driven, sociotechnical development was to give people a choice and the possibility to stay in their home communities. By successfully competing for project funds, KO-KNET built the communities' digital infrastructure. Today, this infrastructure includes landline and satellite broadband Internet as well as Internet-based mobile phone communication, all under the control of the local communities (Beaton et al., 2016). Together with local, regional, and national partners, KO-KNET developed different services: from e-health and an Internet high school to different remote training programmes. The most mundane of those services was MyKnet.org, which enabled First Nations people to create personal homepages within a cost- and commercial-free space on the web.

MyKnet.org was set up in 1998 exclusively for the First Nations people of Northwestern Ontario. By the early 2000s, a wide set of actors across Northwestern Ontario, a region with an overall Indigenous population of about 45,000, had found a new home in this digital environment. During its heyday between 2004 and 2008, MyKnet.org had more than 30,000 registered user accounts and about 25,000 active homepages. With the advent and rise of commercial social media platforms, such as Facebook, user numbers began to drop. To reduce administrative and technical costs, KO-KNET decided to switch to Wordpress as hosting platform in 2014. Since this required users to set up new websites, numbers continued to fall. In early 2019, there were only 2,900 homepages left and MyKnet.org was shut down a couple of months later.

MyKnet.org used to be extremely popular among First Nations people for two reasons. First, people utilized MyKnet.org to establish and maintain social relationships across spatial distance in an infrastructurally disadvantaged region. They regularly visited the homepages of friends and family members, which could easily be found because of MyKnet.org's real name policy, to see what they were up to; they communicated via message boxes, and they linked their homepages to the pages of family members and friends. In doing so, MyKnet.org users created a "digital directory" of Indigenous people in Northwestern Ontario. Second, MyKnet.org contributed to different forms of cultural representation as well as individual and collective identity construction. Homepage producers used the platform to represent themselves, their families, and their communities by displaying and sharing pictures, music, texts, website layouts, and artwork. Such digital practices contributed to the creation of a great diversity of digital selves or digital biographies that also reflected the everyday life of Indigenous people in a remote region (Budka, 2021).

MyKnet.org can be conceptualized as a field of practices that included and interconnected several digital practices and activities that were co-constitutive of this environment (Budka 2015, 2019). The production, displaying, and sharing of images, website layouts, videos, or artwork can be connected to "social rewards" that again are related to social status as well as symbolic and cultural capital in this social field. In MyKnet.org, people were "extrinsically rewarded" for providing and sharing digital and visual material by an increase of website traffic and hits and thus an increase of social status, as indicated in an official list of the most popular websites. By connecting the practice of sharing visual material with the practice of measuring and displaying hits, website producers were also co-creating a digital "economy of recognition" (Stern 2008: 109). On the other hand, people were rewarded "intrinsically" for creating digital and visual content for their websites by utilizing this content for self-reflection, catharsis, and self-documentation. Creating digital artwork, for instance, also allowed for documenting personal growth and self-evolution, in respect to software skills as well as in respect to personal development. Thus, MyKnet.org and related digital practices are a good example of the entanglement of the collective and the individual, of media, technology, and infrastructure in an Indigenous media initiative.

Conclusion

As part of a wider set of sociopolitical practices, Indigenous media and related practices are closely connected to the mediation of culture and the construction of (collective) identities. Indigenous people have been appropriating media technologies for decades to communicate within and outside their communities, to resist outside domination, and for self-determination. Indigenous media thus contribute to the reflection and the transformation of the conditions of Indigenous lives. The mediation and (re-)construction of culture and identity through "modern" media technologies include cultural elements and characteristics of the dominant, non-Indigenous or settler societies which are recombined with Indigenous, "traditional" elements. Thus, Indigenous media practices contribute to the creation of a future in which "traditional" narratives and practices and "modern" technologies are combined.

As examples in this chapter show, Indigenous people are sometimes ambivalent and sometimes enthusiastic about media technologies. This very much depends on individual experiences and expectations as well as on sociocultural, political, and economic contexts and developments. Considering Indigenous people's colonial history and coloniality's effects on Indigenous communities, it is not surprising that many Indigenous representatives are particularly concerned about issues of power, control, and ownership related to media technologies and new digital ways of knowledge production, circulation, and representation (Fiser and Clement, 2012; Ginsburg, 2008). As the case of KO-KNET indicates, Indigenous people, communities, and organizations have been successfully appropriating digital media technologies to use them in self-determined and self-controlled ways. This case also shows that it is important to consider the technological and infrastructural dimensions of (Indigenous) media, because it is through technologies and infrastructures that communication, culture, and identity are mediated.

There is a strong sense of sociopolitical activism and agency in Indigenous people's collective engagements with media technologies which are closely connected to the (re-)construction and mediation of identity, cultural articulation, social intervention, and self-determination.

At the same time, Indigenous people's media practices are related to mundane necessities of everyday communication, social networking, family bonding, or self-expression. Digital and social media platforms have therefore become widely popular in Indigenous communities (Budka, 2015; Carlson, 2013; Fish, 2011). Media have become an important part of Indigeneity, as a global idea and as a practice of collective identity formation, which coexists with the sense of belonging to a distinct local Indigenous community. This is particularly because media allow for establishing social relations among Indigenous and to non-Indigenous people alike.

References

Askew, K. (2002) "Introduction" in K. Askew and R. Wilk (eds), *The Anthropology of Media: A Reader*, Malden, MA: Blackwell, 1–13.

Beaton, B., Burnard, T., Linden, A. and O'Donnell, S. (2016) "Keewaytinook Mobile: An Indigenous Community-Owned Mobile Phone Service in Northern Canada" in L. Dyson, S. Grant and M. Hendriks (eds), *Indigenous People and Mobile Technologies*, New York: Routledge, 109–125.

Boyer, D. (2006) "Turner's Anthropology of Media and its Legacies," *Critique of Anthropology*, 26(1): 47–60. https://doi.org/10.1177/0308275X06061483

Bräuchler, B. and Budka, P. (2020) "Introduction: Anthropological Perspectives on Theorising Media and Conflict" in P. Budka and B. Bräuchler (eds), *Theorising Media and Conflict*, New York: Berghahn Books, 3–31.

Brooten, L. (2008). "Media as Our Mirror: Indigenous Media of Burma (Myanmar)" in P. Wilson and M. Stewart (eds), *Global Indigenous Media: Culture, Poetics, and Politics*, Durham, NC: Duke University Press, 111–127.

Budka, P. (2009) "Indigenous Media Technology Production in Northern Ontario, Canada" in K.-D. Ertler and H. Lutz (eds), *Canada in Grainau/Le Canada à Grainau: A Multidisciplinary Survey of Canadian Studies After 30 Years*, Frankfurt am Main: Peter Lang, 63–74.

Budka, P. (2015) "From Marginalization to Self-Determined Participation: Indigenous Digital Infrastructures and Technology Appropriation in Northwestern Ontario's Remote Communities," *Journal des Anthropologues*, 142–143(3): 127–153. https://doi.org/10.4000/jda.6243

Budka, P. (2019) "Indigenous Media Technologies in 'The Digital Age': Cultural Articulation, Digital Practices, and Sociopolitical Concepts" in S. S. Yu and M. D. Matsaganis (eds), *Ethnic Media in The Digital Age*, New York: Routledge, 162–172.

Budka, P. (2021) "Kultur- und Sozialanthropologische Perspektiven auf Digital-Visuelle Praktiken. Das Fallbeispiel einer Indigenen Online-Umgebung im Nordwestlichen Ontario, Kanada" in R. Breckner, K. Liebhart and M. Pohn-Lauggas (eds), *Sozialwissenschaftliche Analysen von Bild- und Medienwelten*, Berlin: De Gruyter Oldenbourg, 109–132.

Carlson, B. (2013) "The 'New Frontier': Emergent Indigenous Identities and Social Media" in M. Harris, M. Nakata and B. Carlson (eds), *The Politics of Identity: Emerging Indigeneity*, Sydney: University of Technology Sydney E-Press, 147–168.

Carpenter, E. (1972) *Oh, What a Blow That Phantom Gave Me!* New York: Holt, Rinehart and Winston.

Cleaver, H. (1998) "The Zapatista Effect: The Internet and the Rise of an Alternative Political Fabric," *Journal of International Affairs*, 51(2): 621–640.

Deger, J. (2006) *Shimmering Screens: Making Media in an Aboriginal Community*, Minneapolis, MN: University of Minnesota Press.

de la Cadena, M. and Starn, O. (2007) "Introduction" in M. de la Cadena and O. Starn (eds), *Indigenous Experience Today*, Oxford, UK: Berg, 1–30.

Fiser, A. and Clement, A. (2012) "A Historical Account of the Kuh-Ke-Nah Network" in A. Clement, M. Gurstein, G. Longford, M. Moll and L. R. Shade (eds), *Connecting Canadians: Investigations in Community Informatics*, Edmonton: Athabasca University Press, 255–282.

Fish, A. (2011) "Indigenous Digital Media and the History of the Internet on the Columbia Plateau," *Journal of Northwest Anthropology*, 45(1): 89–110.

Flores, C. Y. (2004) "Indigenous Video, Development and Shared Anthropology – A Collaborative Experience with Maya Q'eqchi' Filmmakers in Postwar Guatemala," *Visual Anthropology Review*, 20(1): 31–44. https://doi.org/10.1525/var.2004.20.1.31

Forte, M. C. (2006) "Amerindian@Caribbean: Internet Indigeneity in the Electronic Generation of Carib and Taino Identities" in K. Landzelius (ed.), *Native on the Net: Indigenous and Diasporic Peoples in the Virtual Age*, London: Routledge, 132–151.

Gerbaudo, P. (2017) "From Cyber-Autonomism to Cyber-Populism: An Ideological History of Digital Activism," *TripleC*, 15(2): 477–489. https://doi.org/10.31269/triplec.v15i2.773

Ginsburg, F. (1991) "Indigenous Media: Faustian Contract or Global Village?" *Cultural Anthropology*, 6(1): 92–112.

Ginsburg, F. (1997) "'From Little Things, Big Things Grow': Indigenous Media and Cultural Activism" in R. G. Fox and O. Starn (eds), *Between Resistance and Revolution: Cultural Politics and Social Protest*, London: Routledge, 118–144.

Ginsburg, F. (2000) "Resources of Hope: Learning from the Local in a Transnational Era" in C. Smith and G. K. Ward (eds), *Indigenous Cultures in an Interconnected World*, Vancouver: UBC Press, 27–47.

Ginsburg, F. (2002a) "Screen Memories: Resignifying the Traditional in Indigenous Media" in F. Ginsburg, L. Abu-Lughod and B. Larkin (eds), *Media Worlds: Anthropology on New Terrain*, Berkeley, CA: University of California Press, 39–57.

Ginsburg, F. (2002b) "Mediating Cultures: Indigenous Media, Ethnographic Film, and the Production of Identity" in K. Askew and R. Wilk (eds), *The Anthropology of Media: A Reader*, Malden, MA: Blackwell, 210–235.

Ginsburg, F. (2008) "Rethinking the Digital Age" in P. Wilson and M. Stewart (eds), *Global Indigenous Media: Cultures, Poetics, and Politics*, Durham, NC: Duke University Press, 287–305.

Ginsburg, F., Abu-Lughod, L. and Larkin, B. (2002) "Introduction" in F. Ginsburg, L. Abu-Lughod and B. Larkin (eds), *Media Worlds: Anthropology on New Terrain*, Berkeley, CA: University of California Press, 1–36.

González, R. J. (2020) *Connected: How a Mexican Village Built its Own Cell Phone Network*, Oakland, CA: University of California Press.

Hafsteinsson, S. B. (2013) *Unmasking Deep Democracy: An Anthropology of Indigenous Media in Canada*, Aarhus: Intervention Press.

Harrison, F. V. (ed.) (2010) *Decolonizing Anthropology: Moving Further Toward an Anthropology of Liberation*. 3rd Edition, Arlington, VA: American Anthropological Association.

Hinkson, M. (2021) "Indigenous Media" in H. Callan (ed.), *The International Encyclopedia of Anthropology*, Hoboken, NJ: Wiley. https://doi.org/10.1002/9781118924396.wbiea1944

Horst, H. and Miller, D. (2006) *The Cell Phone: An Anthropology of Communication*, Oxford, UK: Berg.

International Labour Organization (2019) *Implementing the ILO Indigenous and Tribal Peoples Convention No. 169: Towards an Inclusive, Sustainable and Just Future*, Geneva: ILO, available at www.ilo.org/global/publications/books/WCMS_735607/lang--en/index.htm (accessed 6 December 2021).

Kidd, D. and Rodriguez, C. (2009) "Introduction" in C. Rodriguez, D. Kidd and L. Stein (eds), *Making our Media: Global Initiatives Toward a Democratic Public Sphere, Volume 1: Creating New Communication Spaces*, New York: Hampton Press, 1–22.

Kummels, I. (2020) "An Ayuuik 'Media War' over Water and Land: Mediatised Senses of Belonging between Mexico and the United States" in P. Budka and B. Bräuchler (eds), *Theorising Media and Conflict*, New York: Berghahn Books, 196–214.

Landzelius, K. (2006) "Introduction: Native on the Net" in K. Landzelius (ed.), *Native on the Net: Indigenous and Diasporic Peoples in the Virtual Age*, London: Routledge, 1–42.

Melucci, A. (1996) *Challenging Codes: Collective Action in the Information Age*, Cambridge, UK: Cambridge University Press.

Michaels, E. (1985) "Constraints on Knowledge in an Economy of Oral Information," *Current Anthropology*, 26(4): 505–510.

Michaels, E. (1994) *Bad Aboriginal Art: Tradition, Media, and Technological Horizons*, Minneapolis, MN: University of Minnesota Press.

Niezen, R. (2005) "Digital Identity: The Construction of Virtual Selfhood in the Indigenous Peoples' Movement," *Comparative Studies in Society and History*, 47(3): 532–551. https://doi.org/10.1017/S0010417505000241

Pietikäinen, S. (2008) "'To Breathe Two Airs': Empowering Indigenous Sámi Media" in P. Wilson and M. Stewart (eds), *Global Indigenous Media: Culture, Poetics, and Politics*, Durham, NC: Duke University Press, 197–213.

Pitman, T. (2019) "Indigenous New Media Arts: Narrative Threads and Future Imaginaries," *Transmotion*, 5(1): 184–206. https://doi.org/10.22024/UniKent/03/tm.738

Postill, J. (2017) "The Diachronic Ethnography of Media: From Social Changing to Actual Social Change," *Moment Journal*, 4(1): 19–43.

Postill, J. (2018) *The Rise of Nerd Politics: Digital Activism and Political Change*, London: Pluto.

Pratt, Y. P. (2010) "Taking a Stance: Aboriginal Media Research as an Act of Empowerment" in S. B. Hafsteinsson and M. Bredin (eds), *Indigenous Screen Cultures in Canada*, Winnipeg: University of Manitoba Press, 163–182.

Rouch, J. (1995) "The Camera and Man." in P. Hockings (ed.), *Principles of Visual Anthropology* (2nd ed.), Berlin: Mouton de Gruyter, 79–98.

Salazar, J. F. (2007) "Indigenous Peoples and the Cultural Construction of Information and Communication Technology (ICT) in Latin America" in L. E. Dyson, M. Hendriks and S. Grant (eds), *Information Technology and Indigenous People*, Hershey, PA: Idea Group, 14–26.

Salazar, J. F. (2015) "Social Movements and Video Indígena in Latin America: Key Challenges for 'Anthropologies Otherwise'" in S. Pink and S. Abram (eds), *Media, Anthropology and Public Engagement*, New York: Berghahn Books, 122–143.

Salazar, J. F. and Córdova, A. (2008) "Imperfect Media and the Poetics of Indigenous Video in Latin America" in P. Wilson and M. Stewart (eds), *Global Indigenous Media: Culture, Poetics, and Politics*, Durham, NC: Duke University Press, 39–57.

Sandvig, C. (2012) "Connection at Ewiiaapaayp Mountain: Indigenous Internet Infrastructure" in L. Nakamura and P. A. Chow-White (eds), *Race After the Internet*, New York: Routledge, 168–200.

Smith, L. C. (2010) "Locating Post-Colonial Technoscience: Through the Lens of Indigenous Video," *History and Technology*, 26(3): 251–280. https://doi.org/10.1080/07341512.2010.498639

Smith, L. T. (2005) *Decolonizing Methodologies: Research and Indigenous Peoples*, London: Zed Books.

Smith, C., Burke, H. and Ward, G. K. (2000) "Globalisation and Indigenous Peoples: Threat or Empowerment?" in C. Smith and G. K. Ward (eds), *Indigenous Cultures in an Interconnected World*, Vancouver: University of British Columbia Press, 1–24.

Stern, S. (2008) "Producing Sites, Exploring Identities: Youth Online Authorship" in D. Buckingham (ed.), *Youth, Identity, and Digital Media*, Cambridge, MA: MIT Press, 95–117.

Turner, T. (1992) "Defiant Images: The Kayapo Appropriation of Video," *Anthropology Today*, 8(6): 5–16.

Turner, T. (2002) "Representation, Politics, and Cultural Imagination in Indigenous Video: General Points and Kayapo Examples" in F. Ginsburg, L. Abu-Lughod and B. Larkin (eds), *Media Worlds: Anthropology on New Terrain*, Berkeley, CA: University of California Press, 75–89.

Warde, A. (2005) 'Consumption and theories of practice', *Journal of Consumer Culture*, 5(2): 131–153

United Nations (2007) *United Nations Declaration on the Rights of Indigenous Peoples. Resolution Adopted by the General Assembly on 13 September 2007*, A/RES/61/295. New York: United Nations, available at https://documents-dds-ny.un.org/doc/UNDOC/GEN/N06/512/07/PDF/N0651207.pdf (accessed 6 December 2021).

United Nations Department of Economic and Social Affairs (2009) *State of the World's Indigenous Peoples*, Volume 1 New York: United Nations, available at www.un.org/development/desa/indigenouspeoples/publications/state-of-the-worlds-indigenous-peoples.html (accessed 6 December 2021).

United Nations Department of Economic and Social Affairs (2019) *State of the World's Indigenous Peoples: Implementing the United Nations Declaration on the Rights of Indigenous Peoples*, Volume 4. New York: United Nations, available at www.un.org/development/desa/indigenouspeoples/publications/state-of-the-worlds-indigenous-peoples.html (accessed 6 December 2021).

Weiner, J. F. (1997) "Televisualist Anthropology: Representation, Aesthetics, Politics," *Current Anthropology*, 38(2): 197–235.

Wilson, P. and Stewart, M. (2008) "Indigeneity and Indigenous Media on the Global Stage" in P. Wilson and M. Stewart (eds), *Global Indigenous Media: Cultures, Poetics, and Politics*, Durham, NC: Duke University Press, 1–35.

Wood, H. (2008) *Native Features: Indigenous Films from Around the World*, New York: Continuum.

Worth, S. and Adair, J. (1970) "Navajo Filmmakers," *American Anthropologist*, 72(1): 9–34.

Wortham, E. C. (2004) "Between the State and Indigenous Autonomy: Unpacking *Video Indígena* in Mexico," *American Anthropologist*, 106(2): 363–368. https://doi.org/10.1525/aa.2004.106.2.363

Wortham, E. C. (2013) *Indigenous Media in Mexico: Culture, Community, and the State*, Durham, NC: Duke University Press.

3
A LONGITUDINAL STUDY OF MEDIA IN BRAZIL

*Conrad Phillip Kottak
and Richard Pace*

When co-author Kottak began planning research on Brazilian television in the early 1980s, media anthropology did not exist as a recognized field of study. Indeed, it was common for anthropologists to express hostility toward mass media's perceived potential for cultural destruction through homogenization—particularly television's global spread and its assumed threat to cultural distinctiveness. Kottak, however, recognized media's spread as a new frontier to extend anthropology's traditional penchant for cross-cultural testing, gaining a broader perspective on aspects of human behavior through systematic study in other cultures.

Kottak's interest in Brazilian television grew out of his ethnographic fieldwork in Arembepe, Bahia, which, when he began in 1962, was a fairly isolated Atlantic fishing community. Throughout the 1960s and into the 1970s, its residents, like many other rural and often nonliterate Brazilians, had no regular access to national and international information. Yet, when Kottak returned to Arembepe in 1980 after a seven-year absence, electricity had arrived, and television soon thereafter. He was struck by the changes. People were much more knowledgeable about national and international events than previously. This was a change worth further research. At the same time, Kottak was teaching a course at the University of Michigan on American popular culture, which included a section on TV studies. The material was heavily biased by Western-bound understandings of the medium and, clearly to Kottak, did not mesh well with his observations from Arembepe.

By 1983 Kottak had designed and obtained funding for TV research in Brazil.[1] The project included analysis of Brazilian television on a national level, from institutional organization to program content. More critically, realizing the value of the "before-and-after" approach to media from his Arembepe research, Kottak decided to conduct multi-site research in three additional communities, all previously studied by anthropologists. With a team of graduate students pursuing their PhDs in anthropology, of which co-author Pace was a member, Kottak sent the team into the field for year-long studies. They gathered information and produced findings that culminated in Kottak's (1990) book *Prime-Time Society: An Anthropological Analysis of Television and Culture*. In this chapter, we examine this early work and follow the project's trajectory as it has continued to evolve over the ensuing 35 years. As a long-term project, involving multiple researchers, the information collected presents a rich and rarely paralleled foundation of ethnographic knowledge on media engagement. By incorporating both qualitative and quantitative methods, the data demonstrates details of sociocultural trends, both change and stability, that to-date are fairly rare among media studies. The on-going nature of our research also underscores the ever-provisionary character of any research project which facilitates, if not requires, repeated research reassessment (see Royce and Kemper 2002: xv–xxv).

Prime-Time Society (PTS)

Originally published in 1990, and updated in 2009, PTS is an early example of an ethnographically focused media study, conducted between 1983 and 1987. It considered, both qualitatively and quantitatively, the creation, distribution, reception, and impact of televised messages. PTS also offered a comparative and historical framework that encompassed both Brazil and the United States. In the initial phase of the study, Kottak reviewed the institutional history and organization of Brazilian television, followed by a content analysis of programs watched on the dominant network—Globo. One of his main foci was Brazilian *telenovelas*, popular nightly serial melodramas often compared to American soap operas.

With this baseline in hand, Kottak joined with the graduate students to conduct ethnographies in four rural communities—Gurupá in the Amazon, Arembepe in the Northeast, Cunha in the Southeast, and Ibirama in the South. The team also administered 847 household and 1,032 individual surveys (interview schedules) in the four sites, plus two additional urban settings—Americana in São Paulo state and Níteroi across the bay from Rio de Janeiro. These sites were added later to provide contrast and context to the rural studies. Many questions on the survey paralleled inquiries typically asked in US TV research, intentionally included in order to assess cultural differences, as well as weigh underlying cultural assumptions about media's influence.

The study prioritized television's role as an agent of socialization. It focused on the impact of long-term exposure to the medium and how this interaction successfully, or unsuccessfully, molded or cultivated viewers' opinions, values, and world view, as well as affected behavior (see Gerbner et al. 1986 and Kitzinger 2004). Within the realm of TV impact studies at the time, the original research design was unique, because it offered three different ways of measuring exposure to television. The first was variable length of site exposure. The initial wave of TV sets with good reception reached our six field sites in different years (from 1955 to 1983); the communities in our study thus represented a continuum of exposure to television. Second was length of individual exposure. Our respondents began watching television at different times in their lives: some as children and some as adults. Third was current viewing habits. Some participants were heavy viewers (six hours or more per day), some watched TV rarely, and others had never seen TV at all. In some homes the set remained on almost all day while in others sets were absent, broken, or rarely turned on.

The study resulted in an insightful array of correlations linking media engagement with beliefs and behaviors, as well as challenges to common assumptions made by Western media researchers studying Western audiences. Among the most salient of the findings, three things stand out: the realization that TV impact occurred in well-defined stages in Brazil, the ability to connect levels of television viewing and the generation of liberal attitudes toward gender roles, and the subtle, but measurable link between TV viewing and family planning behavior.

The Stage Model

As noted, the study sample included the community of Gurupá in the Amazon, where television had arrived the year before our study began and where many residents had never seen the medium. At the other extreme, the southern cities of Americana and Níteroi had television since 1955, meaning that people younger than 30 years probably never remembered a time without the medium. The other three study sites, Ibirama, Cunha, and Arembepe, fell in between these endpoints of our timeline. Based on these examples, we developed a five-stage model for television engagement.

Stage I is the initial contact, lasting from 5 to 15 years depending on the speed of diffusion. The stage is marked by the strangeness and novelty of the new technology. Paraphrasing Marshall McLuhan's aphorism, at this point the medium rather than the message is the mesmerizer. In the study, Gurupá was in stage I. Pace observed people raptly watching any set and image available; rigid postures, eyes frozen on the small screen, not making a sound as they absorbed all. Notable changes in local discourse soon followed as viewers participated in and commented about Brazilian culture for the first time in real-time, while simultaneously witnessing global events and receiving an endless feed of novel information.

Stage II follows as people become more familiar with and accustomed to TV. Over a period of 10 to 20 years, viewers begin a process of selective acceptance, rejection, interpretation, and reworking of TV messages. Access to sets and therefore in-home viewing is only partial at this stage. Two of our research sites—Arembepe and Cunha—had reached stage II by the mid-1980s. Pace, who continued researching Gurupá over the ensuing years, also witnessed the advent of stage II there. He documented the decline in the initial excitement of televiewing witnessed in stage I, replaced by more tempered attitudes, although negative opinions toward television continued to be rare. Stage II also marked the end of the strict rules of spectatorship (such as silent watching and rules on communal viewing through open windows; see Pace 1993; Pace and Hinote 2013).

We found the strongest correlations between measures of TV exposure and other variables in our stage II communities. For example, years of home TV exposure strongly predicted liberal views on gender roles, more household possessions, perceptions that the local community is dangerous, less trust of people in one's social network, greater appreciation of international holidays, and higher rates of gift-giving and receiving (e.g., birthdays and Christmas). TV also carried important significance as a communication modality and material possession, particularly when TV sets had a limited distribution. In these cases, owning a set enhances social status in two ways: as a material token of conspicuous consumption, and, more subtly, as a source of privileged information. In Ibirama, for example, which was transitioning from stage II to stage III in the mid-1980s, high-status individuals watched TV attentively and frequently because it endowed them with special information. By disseminating this, they gained prestige and authority.

Stage III is the saturation point in terms of access to TV. It occurs as nearly all homes in a locale have a set. It transpires some 20 to 30 years after the medium's arrival. At this point TV loses its novelty, distinction, and status-enhancing value. Dismissive comments about the medium increase. Statistical measures of its impact among the population also becomes less evident. This is because as a phenomenon pervades a community, its presence differentiates less and less among residents.

Stage IV involves lifelong exposure to televiewing for adults. The more profound and long-term sociocultural effects of television as a powerful national agent of mass enculturation, become discernible at this point. This was most evident in the United States during the 1970s and early 1980s, abundantly studied by US media studies specialists. In the Brazil research sample, Americana and Níteroi had entered this stage.

Kottak first published his four-stage model in 1990. Since then, the arrival of the Internet offers multiple avenues of on-line content. In many parts of Brazil, computer screens and cell phones compete with, but also complement, the engagement with television, especially with the rise of social media (Facebook, YouTube, WhatsApp, Twitter, and Instagram being favorites throughout Brazil—discussed below). We can today suggest a stage V dominated by interactive and on demand content, giving viewers/users greater control over timing of engagement, as well as greater access to a wide variety of entertainment and news outlets. This capability transforms television and associated media from agents of mass enculturation into technologies of segmental appeal.

Liberal Attitudes

Among the project's most significant findings was the strong correlation between TV exposure and liberal or progressive views on sex-gender issues. The heavier and longer-exposed viewers were strikingly more liberal—less traditional in their answers to questions on such matters as whether women "belong at home," should work when their husbands have good incomes, should work when pregnant, should go to bars, should leave a husband they no longer love, should pursue men they like; whether men should cook and wash clothes; and whether parents should talk to their children about sex. We found that such questions elicit TV-influenced answers, in that Brazilian television (particularly telenovelas) depicts an urban-modern society in which sex-gender roles are markedly less traditional than in rural communities (Vink 1988; Afonso 2005; see also Benavides 2008).

Our research design permitted us to avoid one huge pitfall of quantitatively oriented TV research in the United States at the time, which routinely used current viewing level as the best available measure of TV impact. The problem with this measure is that it cannot easily differentiate cause and effect relationships from mere correlations. Questions like the following always arise: Does watching a lot of television cause people to be, for example, fearful of the outside world (as some have claimed)—or is it that already fearful people are more likely to stay home and watch more TV? *Effects* are clearer when, as in our study, variable length of direct exposure to television in the home can be measured independently of age of respondent (it is almost impossible to separate those two variables for American viewers, most of whom have had television in their homes since birth).

In our Brazilian study we concluded that liberalization was both a correlation and an effect. We found a strong *correlation* between liberal social views and *current* viewing hours. Liberal-leaning small-town Brazilians turned to TV to validate personal views that their local setting suppressed. However, confirming that long-term TV exposure also has an *effect* on Brazilians' attitudes, we found an even stronger correlation between years of home viewing by individuals and their liberal social views. We concluded that our Brazilian heavy viewers probably were predisposed to liberal views. However, over time, TV content—especially that of the Globo network's hugely popular telenovelas—when invited into the home on a daily basis, reinforced and augmented those views. TV-biased and TV-reinforced attitudes spread as viewers take courage from the daily validation of their unorthodox (local) views in (national) programming. More and more townsfolk accept non-traditional views as normal.

TV's Contraceptive Effect

Another important effect of Brazilian TV—on family planning—became evident only after PTS was published. Kottak first got the idea that TV might be influencing family planning in Brazil from an article in the *New York Times* (Brooke 1989) which suggested that TV (along with other factors) was influencing Brazilians to have smaller families. The article quoted George Martine, a Canadian demographer working then in Brasília: "Television transmits images, attitudes, values and habits of a modern, urban, industrial and middle-class Brazil … They are images of the small, affluent, consumer-oriented family, of a divorce between sexuality and procreation." Kottak immediately realized that our research project had collected data that allowed us to test, and as it turns out, to confirm the hypothesis that television had a contraceptive effect. Put simply, the longer the length of TV exposure, the smaller the family.

In the three communities in our study exposed to TV the longest, women with a TV set in their homes for an average of 15 years had 2.3 pregnancies. By contrast, in the three towns where TV had arrived most recently, the women with home TV for an average of four years had five pregnancies. Although length of site exposure was a clear predictor of female reproductive histories, we recognized that the presence of TV in a community reflects that town's overall access to external systems and resources, including improved methods of contraception. Nevertheless, the impact of long-term home TV exposure on fertility showed up not only when we compared sites, but also within sites, within age cohorts, and among individual women in our total sample.

Particularly fascinating was that this effect on family planning was occurring without any concerted, or even conscious, use of television to get Brazilians to limit their progeny. Brazilian TV's contraceptive effect was totally unplanned. In fact, the possibility that TV portrayals might be influencing family size has been denied vigorously by Brazilian TV executives (see Partlow 2009). How then has television encouraged Brazilians to plan smaller families? The answer lay in the depiction of Brazilian TV families—routinely portrayed on Globo's nightly telenovelas—which have fewer children than traditional small-town Brazilians do. From their content analysis of 115 Globo telenovelas appearing in the two most-watched time slots between 1965 and 1999, Eliana La Ferrara and her associates (2008) found that 72 percent of the main female characters (aged 50 or below) had no children, and 21 percent had only one child. The relevant point is that the daily TV programming most watched in our field sites has consistently and for years presented as normal and desirable nuclear families smaller than the traditional rural family. Telenovelas may well convey the idea that viewers can enjoy lives like those of their characters if they emulate their apparent family planning.

La Ferrara and associates (2008) also confirmed the specific role of Globo's telenovelas in this Brazilian demographic transition. They first determined when the Globo network had entered various markets between 1970 and 1991, and then found that women in areas exposed to Globo had significantly lower fertility than those in areas without the Globo signal. By contrast, the presence of a TV network showing mainly imported shows had no significant effect on fertility, suggesting that Globo's telenovelas specifically—rather than TV in general—were influencing family planning choices.

The Research Continues: *Amazon Town TV* (ATTV)

Grounded in this initial research project, both theoretically and methodologically, co-author Pace continued to look at television engagement in Gurupá over the next three decades. In addition to long-term ethnographic observations, he and his assistants administered two more interview schedules, one in 1999 and the other in 2009. Analyses of these results, conducted with co-author Brian Hinote, are reported in *Amazon Town TV: An Audience Ethnography in Gurupá, Brazil* (Pace and Hinote 2013). Using PTS's original model as a base for ATTV, however, gave rise to a number of challenges. Since PTS's original publication, media anthropology had emerged as a specialty, strongly influenced by globalist perspectives, models emphasizing viewer agency, and a turn to ethnography developed best by British Cultural Studies. Media anthropologists working in the 1990s followed their lead in addressing media and modernity, while pointing out ethnocentric miscues and misplaced Western assumptions through their ethnographic details. Many others have since followed, forming an eclectic mix of media scholars concerned with television and other media technology, nearly all using interpretive and/or practice theory approaches in their analyses. Lost in their midst, however, are the quantitative approaches which strive to measure media influence through correlations, if not causation. These approaches, now collectively classified as "media effects" research, have been ostracized from discussions for underplaying viewer agency, ignoring polysemic and contested messages, and missing the greater ethnographic context. To be sure, media studies have benefited greatly from qualitative and interpretive approaches, and have corrected many of the flaws of earlier approaches. But at the same time, relying so heavily on poststructuralist, cultural studies, and practice theory approaches (predominant in this current volume), to the neglect of others, obscures much of what we found to be of interest in the PTS research.[2]

Entering the fray of media studies polemics, Pace reframed the theoretical base of the project with a middle-ground approach which gauges the relative strength of television influence vis-à-vis viewers' ability to mediate it. Media power, media effects, and active audience readings of texts are understood not as mutually exclusive processes, but instead elements in a complex, and likely uneven process of influence, negotiation, and subversion (see also Kitzinger 2004). Reviewing the works of Brazilian and Brazilianist media scholars, Pace and Hinote (2013: 39–49) identify four key preferred messages broadcast over the years on Brazilian TV: consumerist, national identity, developmentalist, and political texts. Through ethnography and survey, they examine whether viewers accept or identify with these broad messages embedded in programming—heeding interpellation of the program's message in Althusser's (1971) sense[3]—and whether this leads to changes in behavior. Of particular interest is heeding messages when program creators or producers and program viewers do not share similar backgrounds, as is the case for nearly all residents of Gurupá. At the same time, they note how often viewers miss, ignore, and resist messages. Key here is viewers' cultural capital, following Bourdieu (1984), which, when applied to televiewing, includes knowledge of narrative structures, strategies of programs, genre rules, and familiarity with different types of images and characters (see also La Pastina 2004: 306; Straubhaar 2007: 203).

The setting of Gurupá has proven fortuitous to address this polemic, given its long isolation from pan-national Brazilian culture. The first widespread exposure occurred only in the 1950s via radio, followed by TV in the 1980s, and finally print matter in the 2010s—due to high illiteracy rates (which have been overcome, in no small part by desires to read social media). Pace has been able to trace the arrival of television and later media technologies, and to observe and analyze people's engagements from a number of angles: such as difficulties in gaining access to technology, signification of the medium as a communication and material modality, media displacement of public activities, creation of new habits of spectatorship, as well as the reception of broadcast messages (see Peterson's 2003 rubric). Although the space provided here does not allow detailed description of multiple ways people engage television (as the principal media technology impacting the community until recently), a brief overview with a few highlights must suffice.

In terms of heeding television's interpellation, Pace and Hinote identify five categories: TV-Talk, with subcategories of Identity and Awareness Talk; Consumerism; Material Display; Social Identity (particularly nationalism and gender roles); and Worldview Shifts (perceptions of development, fear of crime, best place to live). As an example, TV-talk refers to viewers engaging in TV discourse, processing the layers of novel information to rethink all kinds of social identities, worldviews, and behaviors. In the case of identity-talk, discourse becomes a way to establish links to national or regional cultures in real-time—as in repeating a trendy phrase used on a telenovela. It may also establish social boundaries, as in the particular case where the newly introduced term "gringo" was localized/indigenized to refer to anyone not from the North (Amazon), including southern Brazilians.

Identity construction likewise occurs with the local display of items or traditions shown on television, such as displays for World Cup competitions, Christmas decorations, and hair styles, clothing, and other adornments used by actors on TV. None of these patterns predate televiewing and all agreed, when queried in Gurupá, the ideas come from TV.

Texts with international foci impact national identity formation—whether it is Brazil's opposition to the US war in Iraq or outrage over racial slurs directed toward the Brazilian national soccer team by Argentineans. In these cases, opinions vary little from the preferred nationalistic position expressed in the media, and the televisual messages create feelings of national unity—especially when contrasted with an objectified international "other" whose foreignness accentuates Brazilian "sameness."

As mentioned earlier, exposure to the possibilities of expanded gender roles through television programming, especially for women, encourages liberal or progressive attitudes. In Gurupá, these changes occur in tandem with women taking on new public roles (doctors, mayors, union officials), and indeed, many people we interviewed linked these changes in part to role models observed on TV. At the same time, limitations abound as many women in new roles are expected to continue their domestic tasks. In other words, a baseline of machismo persists, despite TV's liberal messages, resulting in frequent social stresses (see Pace and Hinote 2013: 128–135 for further discussion).

On the other hand, missing interpellation occurs in cases where viewers lack the necessary cultural capital to recognize and understand what writers and producers wish to communicate. Pace and Hinote identify three categories of messages typically missed. The first involves product placement. Although inexpensive items (e.g., shampoos and beer) gain attention and are consumed, product placements that target middle- and upper-class consumers (e.g., cars, computers, pet foods, tutoring services) are missed. In Gurupá, these items are understood as props in the program narrative signifying modernity, rather than as consumables (see also La Pastina 2001). Second is social merchandising, or the insertion of contemporary social and political issues into storylines (e.g., abortion, racism, homosexuality, child labor, the Internet). These messages are understood by some, although typically localized, distorting the intended meaning into familiar contexts, but on the whole are simply overlooked (see Pace and Hinote 2013: 154–156). Last, intertextuality/extratextuality, referring to the practice of using one text implicitly or explicitly to refer to another, as in a television program cross-referencing another show, a film, or the Internet, are ubiquitously missed. The cartoon *The Simpsons* therefore becomes little more than slap-stick humor and the animated movie *Shrek* a strange story about a talking frog surrounded by unintelligible creatures.

Ignoring interpellation occurs when the audience perceives the preferred messages, but deems them uninteresting, irrelevant, or plainly false, and then ignores them. Pace and Hinote observed these processes in terms of local customs and tastes, from greeting and parting salutations (hugs versus kisses) to preferences in food and music. The preferred patterns shown on television, typically representing the lifestyles and habits of the middle- and upper-classes from Southeastern Brazil, proved less appealing than regional patterns already in place, sometimes for centuries. In addition, preferences for locally important Catholic saints supersede interest in saints celebrated and televised nation-wide (such as Brazil's patron saint, *Nossa Senhora de Aparecida* or Our Lady Revealed). One of the most curious findings was the devaluation of Carnaval—the ubiquitous and quintessential expression of Brazilian identity prominently shown on television—in favor of the regional June Festivals that celebrate three saints, rural culture, and Northern/Northeast identity, which until very recently were far less likely to be televised.

Resisting interpellation, whereby viewers subvert the texts by articulating alternative viewpoints, is rarer. Pace and Hinote speculate that sufficient cultural capital, needed to understand and thereby challenge televisual messages, is lacking. One exception, however, is belief in the rainforest supernatural. These are enchanted creatures, often of Indigenous origins, such as *botos* (shape-shifting dolphins that seduce unsuspecting humans), *curupiras* (small beings with their feet turned backward who will punish overzealous hunters by leading them astray deep in the forest or stealing their soul), or *cobra grandes* (gigantic anacondas seen at night with glowing eyes and the penchant to capsize river boats). Despite television's representations of these entities as folkloric and imaginary, persistent belief in them (as measured in three waves of surveys) is an affirmation of regional identity and overt resistance to preferred televisual texts.

In all these cases in which television messages miss their mark, the degree of cultural capital possessed by viewers and the proximity of the text to local realities are the key elements that shape reception results. Straubhaar (2007: 198) explains that a viewer's cultural capital is typically rooted in the local or subnational region. Local culture, therefore, will often supersede national culture in terms of viewers' perceptions and world views. Particularly in situations, as in Gurupá, where education systems are weak, the ability to travel outside the region is limited, and family and personal networks are key sources of information, the local will be preferred over the national and international. Missing, ignoring, and resisting preferred messages becomes an expression, consciously or not, of regional identity.

Even though the four categories of audience response, shaped by cultural capital, set the stage for a wide range of viewer interpretations of television messages, viewers are still responding to heavy barrages of repeated messages. Responses, the study found, are not limitless, nor are readings of texts always polysemic or interpretations aberrant. On the contrary, engagement is often highly patterned, affecting real-life, often measurable, behavioral changes. Our findings challenge assertions frequently found in the media anthropology and media studies literature disavowing the potential for discovering causation. Rajagopal (2001: 24), for example, opines that "television's influence has, then, to be presumed rather than discovered, contra media effects research." Such a view unnecessarily rejects or ignores evidence that does confirm such influence—as research in Gurupá has documented using longitudinal, ethnographic, and quantitative approaches.

Mēbêngôkre-Kayapó TV

In 2013, Kottak and Pace embarked on a third phase of the Brazilian study, funded by a National Science Foundation grant,[4] to restudy four of the original communities (Ibirama, Cunha, Arembepe, and Gurupá). Also, through research contacts from new team member Glenn Shepard, the project added the Mēbêngôkre-Kayapó Indigenous village of Turedjam— located on the fringe of Mēbêngôkre-Kayapó Indigenous Territories about 45 minutes by car from the Brazilian town of Ourilândia, Pará. The village had 24 hours a day electricity (a rarity among Mēbêngôkre-Kayapó villages), and television was newly arrived, allowing the study to once again witnessed stage I, but now in a very different cultural context.

When compared to the non-Indigenous communities in the study, Turedjam rates as lightly impacted: 71 percent of adults 18 years and older report six years or less of television viewing, while most reported daily viewing hours at one hour or less. Even though most people watch sparingly, our media inventories indicate that television, both as a device for watching commercial broadcasts and a monitor for DVDs (and now USB devices and memory chips), is nonetheless the most significant media technology in the village (at the time, more important than radio and cell phones, although the Internet was not yet available). Television's signification as a communication modality is ambiguous. Only a few villagers express negative opinions, over a third have positive opinions, but a surprising 52 percent are neutral in their opinions. By contrast, respondents in non-Indigenous communities elsewhere in the study's 2013 Brazil-wide sampling finds an overwhelming 61percent positive perception of television, 22 percent neutral, and 17 percent negative. Even among those in Turedjam who judge television in a positive light, one-fourth do so because of the television's usefulness as a medium for watching Mẽbêngôkre-Kayapó DVD productions—particularly recordings of their elaborate naming ceremonies, rather than Brazilian programming (see also Shepard and Pace 2021).

A similar ambivalence governs ends and goals for viewing. The people of Turedjam express an interest in gaining knowledge of the outside world through televiewing, particularly by monitoring political events, learning Portuguese, and understanding Brazilian culture. Yet they also express a clear distrust toward the medium and its messages. Villagers monitor events on the television news with a skeptical eye, often criticizing and frequently rejecting TV information as false or distorted. Globo's evening news program is a particular target, with vocalized distrust the loudest over news stories involving Indigenous people.

The semi-attentive viewing pattern we observed clearly relates to cultural disjunctions and incomplete comprehension of the messages. Hindrances to comprehension include limited Portuguese-language fluency (older groups speak little Portuguese, younger generations speak more, but only a few are fluent), lack of cultural identification with actors and settings, and difficulties with cultural capital needed to interpret narrative devices, plot, class and cultural stereotypes, product placement, intertextual messages, and so on. These difficulties detract from the pleasures of televiewing as indicated by the high levels of indifference to the medium. One illuminating example of the cultural capital barrier observed was the responses to a popular commercial aired on the Globo television network during the 2014 World Cup soccer tournament referred to as "Neymar's Hair." As described in Pace et al. (2018), the Brazilian soccer superstar Neymar da Silva Santos Jr. takes his friends on a back-country trek in a Volkswagen vehicle to reveal the secret of his creative and highly variable hairstyle: a wild-looking Indigenous medicine man, living in an isolated village. The arduous trek through the rain forest, the arrival in a "primitive" Indigenous village, the exotic but generic dress of the medicine man, and the grunting noise he makes all draw on stereotypes that sensationalize and trivialize Brazil's rich and varied Indigenous heritage.

However, Turedjam viewers, far from taking offense, laughed heartily at the commercial. When we asked why, several responded that the implausibility of such an important Brazilian celebrity actually visiting an Indigenous village just to get a haircut made the short clip absurdly funny. When we pressed further as to why they did not find the depiction of Indigenous people offensive, they saw no connection between the generic Indian depicted briefly in the clip and their own culture and lifestyle. In other words, the demeaning representation of Indigeneity, which speaks so directly to Brazilian prejudice and stereotype, made no connection with Mẽbêngôkre-Kayapó self-identity (i.e. they completely missed the message), and therefore rendered it irrelevant and hence inoffensive, at least from their point of view.

Overall opinions on the impact of television programming in the village are mixed. Because of the newness of the technology and the relatively light viewing practices, most (66 percent of survey respondents) claim that television has had no impact. For those who do see an impact, the most cited changes are in the use of certain Portuguese-language terms in discourse among the young and changes in clothing and hair styles. In addition, a small number mentioned growing challenges to adult authority by youth.

The Next Round

The attention paid to culturally appropriate, Mēbêngôkre-Kayapó-produced media (filming of their own ceremonies), in juxtaposition, if not opposition to their viewing of commercial TV, highlights the importance of understanding a combination of media technologies to correctly grasp media engagement. As our study continues in the five communities, we have expanded our research focus to include the Internet (particularly social media), accessed primarily through cell phones in our sites, and how it is linked to watching television, and vice-versa.[5] For example, in our latest round of surveys in 2021, respondents report they get their news (international, national, and local) from a combination of sources, with television most cited (78 percent of the sample reported it as one source), followed by radio (42 percent), print newspapers (21 percent), and now cell phones (69 percent). The most used apps on cells phones for news, in the order of engagement, are Instagram, Facebook, Twitter, and email—all critical for alternative as well as false or fake news.

That these media are being used in an overlapping and intertwining fashion is demonstrated in our observations of Brazil's nation-wide street demonstrations erupting in 2013 that protested declining living standards and government corruption. In our five communities, we found that the baseline information came from TV broadcasts. These images and narratives were accompanied by commentary filling up chat rooms and postings on social media—including homemade videos of protests that were then shown on television. Facebook, accessed through cell phones, in particular, was the conduit nation-wide to organize hundreds of thousands of protesters flooding the streets over several months in forceful, if somewhat unfocused protests. The results of this "Facebook revolution" is credited with expediting the eventual impeachment and removal from office of President Dilma Rousseff and was interpreted by many as part of a bold new world of digitally facilitated sociocultural change (see Cardoso, Lapa, and Di Fátima 2016). The research team followed the protests in each community, noting the access to social media in relation to TV, radio, and print, and observing how people engaged media to understand the protests, as well as plan their own (see Pace, Shepard, and Kottak 2014).

For example, in Ibirama, the tight-knit community of German, Polish, and Russian migrants, overwhelmingly middle class and conservative, with access to high-speed Internet for at least a decade, all protests were planned on Facebook and all focused on government corruption and dissatisfaction with the left-wing government of Rousseff. The protest drew hundreds in the small town. Upon request, one of the project's members filmed the event on her cell phone, which the protest leaders posted on Facebook, from which the regional TV station obtained it for the evening news. Confirmed by the footage on TV, protesters in Ibirama considered the event a great success.

At the other extreme in Turedjam village, where Internet was not available, the villagers followed the protests entirely on television. They realized the federal government was weakened by the intensity of the popular discontent and perceived a political opportunity. The men covered their bodies in black war paint and prepared arrows and other weapons as they planned to blockade the Transamazon Highway to force a government response. They maintained constant contact with other villages via short-wave radio and cell phones. In the end, a select group traveled to Brasília to express their grievances to the government—which they carefully filmed for their home audiences to counteract misrepresentations broadcast by commercial television or disseminated through print media.

As our project continues with fieldwork in 2021–2022, our research team continues ethnographic observations and surveys, now capturing people's engagement with the rise of fake news in Brazilian social media and on TV, the explosion of political radicalization and upswing of right-wing politics (much of it via Brazilian YouTube), and controversies surrounding combating the C-19 pandemic—all of which will be published elsewhere. But as a closing anecdote, recorded in Arembepe just before writing this chapter, the team observed the following contrasting encounters pointing toward new forms of media engagement evolving in the small towns that we study. The first was a public scolding of the research group by a 20-year-old male parked-car attendant who, upon learning about the teams' interest in researching social media, reacted angrily by spouting a string of conspiracy theories and accusations of communism and pedophilia that he felt underlie the research project—types of accusations commonly viewed on Brazilian YouTube. The event shocked people witnessing this atypical public berating, and bystanders, shaking their heads, said just ignore the outburst. Later key consultants explained to Pace that this public expression of social media "hate" was unusual, but not completely unforeseen given the deluge of extreme right-wing propaganda circulating on-line.

In the second example, we interviewed a local environmental activist who made good use of Facebook, Instagram, and YouTube to denounce illegal housing development on fragile marshlands protected by Brazilian law. He emphasized he was only one insignificant individual, but with the power of the cell phone camera and social media, his message is heard and people pay attention to the "assault on their paradise" (paraphrasing Kottak's book title about his long-term study of Arembepe)—making it to national and international environmentalist websites, and most importantly in his view, the big city TV news. He noted that his latest protest video had received 4,200 views, which along with TV exposure garnered the attention of local politicians and, in this particular case, resulted in both political and financial support for local environmental projects.

Final Remarks

The Arembepe anecdotes suggest opposing endpoints in a continuum for researching new media technologies in our small towns and village. Situated within our longitudinal foundation, we can continue to analyze how social media engagements are intertwined with television, radio, filmmaking, music, and other outlets in a complex media ecology. All of these analyses are encased within decades of research observations that have recorded television's arrival and initial engagement, its ensuing changes, and now followed by complex interactions with new digital technologies. Utilizing ethnographic and quantitative methods, our research provides a unique body of empirical evidence to contribute to the evolving literature. Our findings directly address the discussions of media power, influence, and effects, as well as viewer/user agency in interpreting messages, and how interactions with media may or may not alter people's lives over the short and long terms.

Notes

1 A 1983–1984 Wenner-Gren Foundation Grant to study electronic mass media and social change and a 1984–1986 National Science Foundation Grant 8317856—PI Conrad Kottak, to study the social impact of television in rural Brazil.
2 As readers may note, our approach aligns with Postill's "effects challenge" outlined in Chapter 8 in this volume. Postill's essay rephrases longstanding (and often acrimonious) debates invoking positivistic-humanistic, science-antiscience, or materialism-mentalist oppositions found throughout the theoretical history of anthropology and communication studies.

3 Interpellation denotes the point at which an outside voice calls an individual, who by acknowledging or responding to the call becomes a subject, in a sense being defined by the call. With TV, viewing the media is the act that brings the audience into existence as a subject, and interpellation describes how ideological messages in programming catch the viewers' attention and how that process can influence the viewers' thoughts and behaviors.
4 A 2013–2014 National Science Foundation Grant 1226335—PI Richard Pace and Co-PI Conrad Kottak, to study the evolution of media influence in Brazil.
5 The approach is known as media ecology, which provides a useful framework to understand how different media devices and platforms form interconnected parts of an ecological or polymediated system (see Strate 2006).

References

Afonso, L. (2005) *Imagens de Mulher e Trabalho na Telenovela Brasileira (1999–2001)*. Goiânia, Brazil: Editoria da Universidade Católica de Goiás.
Althusser, L. (1971) *Lenin and Philosophy and Other Essays*. London: NLB.
Benavides, H. (2008) *Drugs, Thugs, and Divas: Telenovelas and Narco-Dramas in Latin America*. Austin: University of Texas Press.
Bourdieu, P. (1984) *Distinction: A Social Critique of the Judgment of Taste*. Cambridge, MA: Harvard University Press.
Brooke, J. (1989) "Births in Brazil Are on Decline, Easing Worries." *New York Times* August 8. www.nytimes.com/1989/08/08/world/births-in-brazil-are-on-decline-easing-worries.html.
Cardoso, G., T. Lapa, and B. Di Fátima (2016) "People are the Message? Social Mobilization and Social Media in Brazil." *International Journal of Communication* 10: 3909–3930.
Gerbner, G. and L. Gross, M. Morgan, and N. Signorielli (1986) "Living with Television: The Dynamics of the Cultivation Process." In Bryant, J. and D. Zillmann (eds), *Perspectives on Media Effects*. Hillsdae: Laurence Erlbaum, 17–40.
Kitzinger, J. (2004) *Framing Abuse: Media Influence and Public Understanding of Sexual Violence against Children*. London: Pluto.
Kottak, C. (2009 [1990]) *Prime-Time Society: An Anthropological Analysis of Television and Culture*. Walnut Creek, CA: Left Coast Press.
La Ferrara, E., A. Chong, and S. Duryea (2008) "Soap Operas and Fertility: Evidence from Brazil." Inter-American Development Bank. Research Department, Working Paper #633.
La Pastina. A. (2004) "Seeing Political Integrity: Telenovelas, Intertextuality, and Local Elections in rural Brazil." *Journal of Broadcasting & Electronic Media* 48(2): 302–326.
La Pastina. A. (2001) "Product Placement in Brazilian Prime Time Television: The Case of the Reception of a Telenovela." *Journal of Broadcasting & Electronic Media* 45(4): 541–557.
Pace, R. (2009) "Television's Interpellation: Heeding, Missing, Ignoring, and Resisting the Call for Pan-National Identity in the Brazilian Amazon." *American Anthropologist* 11(4): 407–419.
Pace, R. (1993) "First-Time Televiewing in Amazônia: Television Acculturation in Gurupá, Brazil." *Ethnology* 32(2): 187–205.
Pace, R. and B. Hinote (2013) *Amazon Town TV: An Audience Ethnography in Gurupá, Brazil*. Austin: University of Texas Press.
Pace, R, G. Shepard, E. Galvão, and C. Kottak (2018) "Kayapó TV: An Audience Ethnography in Turedjam, Brazil." In Pace, R. (ed.), *From Filmmaker Warriors to Flash Drive Shamans: Indigenous Media Production and Engagement in Latin America*. Nashville, TN: Vanderbilt University Press.
Pace, R., G. Shepard, and C. Kottak (2014) "Street Protests and Electronic Media in Brazil: Views from Small Towns and Villages." *American Anthropology Newsletter*, Online (June).
Partlow, J. (2009) "Brazil's Novela May Affect Viewers' Lifestyle Choices." *Washington Post*, June 8, P. A07.
Peterson, M. (2003) *Anthropology & Mass Communication: Media and Myth in the NewMillennium*. New York: Berghahn Books.
Rajagopal, A. (2001) *Politics after Television: Religious Nationalism and the Reshaping of the Indian Public*. Cambridge: Cambridge University Press.
Royce, A. and R. Kemper (2002) "Long Term Fieldwork Research: Metaphors, Paradigms, and Themes." In Kemper, Robert and Anya Royce (eds), *Chronicling Cultures: Long-Term Field Research in Anthropology*. New York: AltaMira Press, xiii–xxxviii.

Shepard, G. and R. Pace (2021) "Authenticity and Anthropophagy in Kayapó Video Production." *Current Anthropology* 62(3): 309–332.
Strate, L. (2006) *Echoes and Reflections: On Media Ecology as a Field of Study.* Cresskill, NJ: Hampton.
Straubhaar, J. (2007) *World Television: From Global to Local.* Los Angles: Sage Pub.
Vink, N. (1988) *The Telenovela and Emancipation: A Study of Television and Social Change in Brazil.* Amsterdam: Royal Tropical Institute.

PART II

Approaches

A

Media as Infrastructure

4
"HERE, LISTEN TO MY CD-R"
Music Transactions and Infrastructures in Underground Hip-Hop Touring

Anthony Kwame Harrison

In January 2001, while working at Amoeba Music's San Francisco store, I received a phone call from a record executive at Nu Gruv Alliance asking me to stop by their offices that week to discuss my potential participation in an upcoming national tour. Founded in 1995, Nu Gruv Alliance was a prominent manufacturing, marketing, and distribution outlet that partnered with small independent record labels specializing in House Music, Drum 'n' Bass, Indie, and Hip Hop. A good deal of the company's success had been in the last genre. Indeed, by 2001, Nu Gruv made the decision to drop all other genres and focus exclusively on promoting a handful of promising hip-hop artists. This included launching its own sub-label: Ground Control Records.

I had appeared on Nu Gruv's radar through a research interlocutor who had close connections with the company's then head of A&R.[1] People in their offices were aware of my ethnographic research on underground hip hop and, needing an assistant manager for the tour, figured that the flexibility of my music store employment made me an ideal candidate. For me, being on tour offered a rare, behind-the-scenes glimpse into an aspect of the music industry I had only known as a fan. I additionally hoped it would allow me to make comparisons between what I was seeing and documenting in the Bay Area and what was going on in other local music scenes. The following week, after a short meeting in Nu Gruv's South San Francisco offices, I was on-board. When February rolled around, I joined 14 other Ground Control Allstars who departed from the company headquarters to begin a five-week, 27-show tour of cities and college towns across America. My responsibilities, as assistant tour manager, included calling ahead to confirm reservations and sound checks, putting up promotional materials at venues, waking up the artists and bus driver, and, most importantly, selling merchandise at every show.

In this chapter, I discuss my experience as the Ground Control Allstar tour "merch guy," focusing on one distinct and now virtually extinct media form: the recordable compact disc or CD-R. Whereas my job was to sell pre-recorded CDs, vinyl records, and T-shirts to the hip-hop fans we encountered, I did not expect that several of these show-goers would bestow artefacts of their own musical creativity on me.[2] Between the late 1990s—when CD recorders first became affordable—and the rise of streaming services in the 2010s, the CD-R reigned as the media of choice among avid music fans. Yet its utilization as a new means for novice hip-hop artists to engage their more-established music industry idols signals an important shift in

DOI: 10.4324/9781003175605-8

the ideologies, organizational arrangements, and practices of hip-hop music-making at the start of the twenty-first century. In reflecting on this unforeseen element of my ethnographic travels and building on my prior work, in this chapter I spotlight the importance of infrastructures in setting the governing logics through which exchanges occur and collective identities coalesce in fields of popular music. More specifically, in this turn-of-the-century moment, my role selling merchandise positioned me to experience an emergent infrastructural scaffolding that guided underground hip-hop devotees' interactions with one another as well as their assertions of belonging. At the core of these dynamics, the CD-R served as a repository for articulating personal commitments and conveying aspirational hopes.

Following the ideas of media anthropologist Brian Larkin (2013), I root my conceptualization of infrastructures in the duality of their physical and cultural presence. As structures, we can think of infrastructures as fixed things. For example, the interstate highway system that enabled travel from Albuquerque, New Mexico, to Austin, Texas (approximately 700 miles), for shows on successive nights or the pathways of internet communications that spread word to fans in Phoenix that one of the headlining artists on our tour had lost his voice the previous night in Las Vegas. Similarly stable but less material, infrastructures can include the regulations and capabilities surrounding economic transactions—for instance, who is allowed into a venue and what music media is available for purchase at what costs—or the chain of authority in managing a tour. Yet, the patterns of expected behaviour surrounding systems of exchange and the social connections they enable also comprise a type of infrastructure. Such *soft infrastructures* (Stahl, 2004), in the context of a national music tour, are often encoded with the imagination and desires of both individuals and the collective whole (Larkin, 2013). In this regard, they might be oriented towards imagined futures (De Beukelaer, 2019) and/or sustained through the emotional investments of the actors within them (Danely, 2016). Accordingly, a preliminary understanding of infrastructures might recognize them as ordered material, relational, and affective conduits that facilitate "the unfettered circulation of goods, ideas, and people" (Larkin, 2004: 94).

Despite the presumption that infrastructures are highly organized, cohesive, and durable, as a conceptual tool they remain surprisingly amorphous. Indeed, Larkin (2013: 335) observes that infrastructures "operate at multiple levels concurrently"; therefore deciding what to highlight is always a selective process. To the extent that material and social infrastructures, respectively, supply the architecture and ideologies for articulating cultural logics (De Beukelaer, 2019), it is important to recognize the fluidity of these logics—how they evolve over time and space, at key moments coming to be displaced by new logics. Changes in music format often signal and/or engender compatible shifts in the underlying logic of music circulation within a given scene. With my focus largely on these social and ideological qualities, I conceptualize music scene infrastructures as recurring, though impermanent, "configurations of local(ised) connections, instrumental to shaping relationships and options" for artists, fans, and other key actors (Magaudda, 2020: 28).

Whereas in my prior work I have focused on the sales of underground hip-hop cassette tapes within local music scenes (Harrison, 2006, 2018), in this chapter I utilize notions of infrastructure to examine the ambiguous place of the CD-R in the trans-local spaces of a national hip-hop tour. For a fleeting moment in history, the medium of the CD-R facilitated a series of unprecedented transactions, somewhere between a commodity and a musical gift, within the context of underground hip-hop tours. In this work, I am particularly interested in spotlighting a nascent hip-hop infrastructure that arose as an alternative to the existing arrangements and social practices regulating interactions between music industry insiders (including artists) and fans. These exchanges, I argue, were more than simply musical. They encapsulated sentiments of communion with and propositions for belonging to a resurgent arena of hip-hop music-making as a folk tradition. As such, this work responds to Magaudda's (2020) call for greater attention to infrastructures within popular music scenes. Yet where much of the existing scholarship on music scenes has been "especially prompted" by the music industry's turn towards digitized, non-material music formats (Magaudda, 2020: 25; see for example Stern, 2012; Morris, 2015), my interests centre on one of the late-stage physical music artefacts that preceded this shift.

In the pages that follow, I first explain the network of logistical and financial arrangements underlying the Ground Control Allstar tour and the pivotal position of the merchandise salesperson within them. After a brief introduction to underground hip hop and the terms through which I researched it, I next highlight the different functions of the CD-R as both a momentary medium of music storage and an update on the conventional music industry logic surrounding the "demo tape." In the final section of this chapter, I discuss the CD-Rs I acquired on tour, reflecting on their uniquely underground hip-hop character and considering the transactional nature of these media offerings. In doing this, I theorize that the terms and expectations surrounding these social and musical exchanges align with, or more accurately toggle between, two differing music-oriented infrastructures: a traditional one marked by self-interested actors seeking career advancement and pursuing a "big break" within a power-laden, vertically organized industry; and an emerging one that observes alternate logics of peer inter-action, mutual belonging, and affective regard (Molm, Collett, and Schaefer, 2007). Whereas many media anthropologists focus on a single infrastructure, my approach takes into account multiple, shifting infrastructural layers and the frictions and insights resulting from their concurrence. Ultimately, the value of the chapter is in showing how media forms like the CD-R are not only materials that circulate within infrastructural arrangements, but how such media encode the cultural logics and ambitions underlying the transactions they inspire.

Infrastructures of Industry, Touring, and Merchandise Sales

A national tour involves a complex series of arrangements. The Ground Control Allstar tour featured four acts, each from a different city. The Masterminds were an up-and-coming trio based in New York City. Bay Area emcee Rasco had made a huge splash in the underground hip-hop world with his 1997 debut single "The Unassisted" and, in 2000, had recently collaborated with rising star Planet Asia to form the duo Cali Agents. Boston's Ed O.G. had released the classic song "I've Got to Have It" in 1991, during what is commonly regarded as hip hop's "Golden Era." Though at the time of the tour, "Edo" had not released an album in eight years, he had made a few critically heralded appearances on compilation albums and was due to release a new CD in a few weeks. Last, the tour's headliner was Aceyalone—a Los Angeles rapper and key figure in the legendary group Freestyle Fellowship. Acey's highly anticipated third solo album, *Accepted Eclectic*, was officially released two weeks into the tour but early tour show-goers could purchase pre-release copies. In addition to these six (three members of the Masterminds and three solo artists), the tour included various deejays and "hype-men" (companions on stage) as well as a tour manager and assistant manager.

Beyond negotiating with the four acts featured on the tour, Ground Control Records had to coordinate with local promoters regarding dates, venues, ticket prices, guaranteed and additional pay-outs (i.e. the money we were promised and could potentially make if a show sold out), lodging (sometimes meals), sound checks, in some cases limousine pick-ups, and the like. Looking over the tour itinerary and budget, for 27 show dates the total guaranteed money was just over $54,000. Speculating on what Ground Control paid the artists and tour bus driver, not to mention per diem costs, it seems clear that the company was counting on successful promotion—in order to reach additional pay-outs that considerably outpaced the guarantees—as well as the revenue from merchandise sales to make the tour a financial success. These nuts-and-bolts of necessary machinery, services, and contractually bound arrangements comprise a dimension of infrastructures that are more-or-less formal, fixed, and regulated in accordance with laws of nature, physics, and the laws of the land.

The role of merchandise salesperson offers a unique perspective through which to experience a tour. This is perhaps even truer today than it ever was as, with the decline of record stores and physical music sales, touring and merchandise has taken on a bigger part of music industry revenues (Cordero, 2016). Being the "merch guy," I was typically the first tour member at the venue. While my fellow Ground Control Allstars were enjoying pre-show meals or making memories in the "green room" (the space reserved for performers to relax when not on stage), I was the first person to interact with local audiences. Throughout the night, I was often the most accessible tour member and, at the end of the show, when all the performances were finished, the audience would usually turn "180 degrees from the stage" and beeline for the merchandise (Vilanova and Cassidy, 2019: 99). Over the course of five weeks, it became abundantly clear that, whether it was a Saturday night at the Metro in Chicago or a Wednesday night at a club called "the Warehouse" in Charleston, South Carolina, each night when we arrived in a new city, we were *the event*—at least for people inclined towards the kinds of music we offered. Early entrants would often eagerly ask me if Planet Asia was accompanying Rasco on the tour or would cheer when I informed them that DJ Drez was deejaying for Aceyalone.

Scholarship on the music industry has presented it as a form of structured organizational relationships (Ryan and Peterson, 1982). To the extent that these structures are not visible to the typical music fan, but rather undergird the music recordings and performances that most fans enjoy, they comprise an infrastructure in the most conventional treatment of the term (Star, 1999). John Ryan and Richard A. Peterson (1982) shed light on an elaborate decision chain through which country songs pass in transitioning from a spark of inspiration or carefully crafted composition, by one (or a few) song-writer(s), to a hit record. At various links along the decision chain, a collection of distinctly qualified professionals decide which songs are selected for moving forward, how a song might be tweaked or revised to conform to the guiding product image, and how the song is best commodified—including decisions about the artist to perform it, the recording process, its packaging, and its promotion.[3]

Although recognized artists provide distinct contributions to music recordings (Becker, 1982), depending on the organizational structure of the record label and how established or experienced they are as artists, they may have very little decision-making power or knowledge of how music industry decisions are made. This is possibly most apparent within hip-hop music, where new artists have historically been recruited from backgrounds where they have little experience with complex music industry machinations and are therefore susceptible to exploitative contracts and fantasies of having "made it" after receiving a five-figure advance check (Negus, 1999).[4]

Whereas a music tour is different from a record release, it is nevertheless part of the same overriding music industry infrastructure and, accordingly, governed by similar, if at times less contractually bound, organizational and hierarchical relationships. As significant a function as the "merch person" serves, the job is, nevertheless, regarded as an entry-level position and accorded little status among the community of touring artists (Vilanova and Cassidy, 2019). In addition to being the first to arrive and last to leave the venue, and having to pack all the merchandise into the cramped storage space below the bus, I was also expected to pack and sometimes even tote other tour members' personal belongings. Indeed, my closest relationship on the tour might have been with a fellow service worker, the bus driver—although he kept mentioning, with a smirk, how Ground Control Records was paying him too much. This certainly was not the case with me!

I surmise that to fans attending the shows, I was simultaneously a peer (an ordinary person rather than a celebrity) and a representative of the music industry, albeit at the lowest rung. Accessibility often serves as an important vector through which to assess status. As the most accessible tour member, I was distinct from the headlining artists that fans were paying to see perform. Yet my position behind the merchandise table, or more specifically on the tour bus, meant that I was an initial but significant step closer to the artists and industry channels that aspiring hip-hop musicians who attended our shows might hope to engage.

Ethnographies of Underground Hip Hop

I had initially travelled to San Francisco, as a fieldwork site, intending to do research on the then recent emergence of Do-It-Yourself (DIY) hip-hop artists who recorded music in bedroom studios, using recently domesticated (i.e. affordable) recording technologies, and sold music on the internet and through supportive local retailers. I was fortunate to land a job working at Amoeba Music, a store in which "an estimated 70 to 75 percent of all local music brought into the store by artists themselves (for retail sales) fell under the category of hip hop" (Harrison, 2009: 39). Indeed, this new movement in underground hip hop—that positioned itself in direct opposition to commercial polish—impacted desired music formats as well as aesthetic preferences surrounding packaging and sound (Harrison, 2006). I had been drawn to the Bay Area because of my awareness of an initial generation of DIY hip-hop artists residing there—artists who were actively releasing music between 1995 and 1999. By 2000, I found that, owing to their modest celebrity, many of these artists were less accessible than I had hoped. As a result, the community I wound up doing research among (spending time with nearly every day) were mostly artists releasing or working on their first commercially available album—what I would call a second generation that came of age through their fandom and emulation of the first. I regularly encountered such artists on the streets, open mics, and house parties of San Francisco, Oakland, and Berkeley—as well as at my merchandise table while on tour.

My research had an additional racial component to it. Around the turn of the century, the role of the hip-hop emcee transitioned from a station that, throughout the 1990s (since the fall of Vanilla Ice), was occupied primarily by Black identified persons to something that now included emcees of all races, at least at its underground hip-hop tiers (Harrison, 2009). The simple explanation for this is that by circumventing major record-label decision-makers' notions of what an emcee should look like (i.e. he^5 must be Black), and instead relying on access to home production technologies, emerging underground hip-hop scenes oriented towards more middle-class, multi-racial constituents. Of course, things are never quite this simple. As both the dissertation I completed based on this research—notably titled "Every Emcee's a Fan, Every Fan's an Emcee" (Harrison, 2003)—and my first book (Harrison, 2009) underscore, race did matter. During the tour, my appearance as a Black, dreadlocked "merch guy" certainly conveyed the message to many majority white audiences—about a third of which were in college towns—that hip hop had come to town.

Unpacking the CD-R

While my job on the tour was to sell music, which both generated revenue for Ground Control Records and distributed their music to local audiences around the country, at the completion of the tour I was surprised to have accumulated a box of approximately 20 compact discs that aspiring artists/fans had given to me. The vast majority of these were DIY-duplicated CD-Rs (as opposed to professionally manufactured CDs).[6] In considering what this signifies about hip-hop music and the infrastructures supporting it, I maintain that the CD-R was instrumental in carrying forth meaningful shifts in understandings of hip hop as both a subset of the music industry and a music community. Many commentators mark the appearance of digital music files, most notably mp3s (Stern, 2012), as the medium that sparked the decline in physical music sales and the eventual closing of countless brick-and-mortar record stores. I maintain that the recordable compact disc is an equal if often overlooked accomplice. Returning to Larkin's definition of infrastructures as "built networks that facilitate the flow of goods, people, or ideas and allow for their exchange over space" (2013: 328), I see the CD-R as both symbolizing and enabling a new cultural logic surrounding these exchanges.

At the start of the twenty-first century, as peer-to-peer (P2P) file sharing via websites like Napster and KaZaA dominated music industry headlines, sales of CD-Rs exploded. For a brief moment before mp3 players became more widespread and domesticated, CD-Rs reigned as the dominant media for storing and playing this newly accessible music. The CD-R boom first appeared on college campuses, where high speed internet access made vast music catalogues available to thousands of young people (Boehlert, 2000). Concerns over music duplication were not new. In the early 1980s, the British Phonographic Industry launched a "Home Taping is Killing Music" campaign against the practice of recording music off the radio on blank cassettes; similar concerns hovered around dual-cassette recorders. Yet the CD-R had distinct advantages over the cassette. First, you could record instantaneously rather than in real time, which made it possible to duplicate huge quantities of music in short amounts of time. Second, the quality of the recording did not decrease with successive duplications. Finally, with P2P file sharing, any member of a musical community—namely sites like Napster but even a collection of students networked digitally on a college campus—could have access to the libraries of dozens if not thousands of other music fans. Such duplication capabilities launched the first major blow to record store retailers. In the coming years, music fans' reliance on physical media would wane and eventually even digital files would largely give way to streaming services.

CD-Rs were also transformational in replacing demo tapes as the prime media for home recordings. This occurred in a context of newly available quality recording technologies, including Digital Audio Workstations like GarageBand, which was common on Apple computers, and Pro Tools and Ableton Live. My research interests focused on this rise in home recording technologies. With the ability to make quality hip-hop recordings in bedroom studios, as well as a symbiotic shift in what many devoted hip-hop listeners found sonically valuable, demo tapes/CD-Rs were no longer exclusively a stage in the music production process. As the sonic imperfections associated with DIY production increasingly came to be heard as markers of authenticity, within underground hip-hop circles, these one-time demo recordings transformed into viable music commodities (Harrison, 2006). This alone signalled an important aesthetic change. Through my position in the Ground Control Allstar tour, I experienced first-hand the extent to which it also fundamentally altered the transactional logics underlying hip hop's infrastructures of exchange.

The "demo tape" (short for demonstration) is a longstanding feature of the music industry production infrastructure. One of its primary uses has been to audition serviceable renditions of an aspiring artist's music, recorded on the best available equipment, to someone networked within the music industry. Throughout music industry folklore, the "demo tape" has been hailed as a golden ticket to stardom. If a quality demo tape makes it to the right person—or more accurately gets listened to by the right person—an unknown group can suddenly find themselves with a hit song, leading to further success. Thus, the demo tape is thoroughly embedded in the traditional soft infrastructures of fantasy and desire (Stahl, 2004; Larkin, 2013) that facilitate exchanges and interactions between novice music-makers and the music industry personnel they aspire to work with or emulate.

The demo tape has been particularly revered in hip-hop circles. In 1989, one of the great duos of hip hop's Golden Era, EPMD, famously released the song "Please Listen to My Demo" that recounts their experiences trying to get signed to a record deal. Indeed, many hip-hop songs that explicitly highlight "paying dues" and/or struggles with the music industry prominently feature demo tapes in their narratives. Even as late as 2005, in the Academy Award winning film *Hustle & Flow*, the plotline climaxes around the main character, DJay (played by Terrence Howard), getting a demo tape of his recordings into the hands of a successful local rapper. In the scenes leading up to the fateful exchange, DJay truly believes he is on the cusp of stardom and that everything in his life is about to change (Allain, Singleton, and Brewer, 2005).

At one level, CD-Rs existed as later versions of the demo tape, the difference being that the medium had switched. Yet within underground hip-hop scenes, where many devotees defined themselves in fierce opposition to the major record companies,[7] CD-Rs could be exclusive and prized music commodities in an emerging cottage industry. Beyond being merely commodities to be bought and sold, these music-storing objects served as one of the primary vehicles for constructing and sustaining an alternative relational infrastructure.

CD-R Exchanges in Underground Hip Hop

In researching and writing about underground hip hop for close to two decades, I have often outlined the qualities distinguishing it, as a musical field, from its more commercial counterpart. While there is no single, all-encompassing delineation of what comprises underground hip hop, in prior work I highlight its DIY, anti-major-record-label stance; its recognition of localities outside of hip hop's established metropolitan hubs; its observance of hip hop's four foundational elements—namely, deejaying, break(danc)ing, emceeing, and graffiti writing; and the fact that it emerged as a distinct subgenre at the close of hip hop's Golden Era—suggesting that something had started to go wrong (see Harrison, 2006, 2009, 2018). In examining the CD-Rs I acquired on the Ground Control Allstar tour, with particular focus on the infrastructural networks they enabled, an additional demarcation became apparent. Nearly all of the CD-Rs had prominently displayed contact information.

As I previously discussed, accessibility serves as a valuable means through which to assess status. When purchasing an album released through Sony Music Entertainment (or any major label), there is no address, phone number, or email that would allow the consumer to directly contact the artist or anyone meaningfully involved in the music production process. If attempting to contact someone through the company, one is likely to encounter a succession of barriers (both people and processes) before reaching anyone of creative consequence. The difference between such major-label music artefacts and the ones I acquired reflect a significant difference in the respective *soft infrastructures* through which information flows. Drawing from the work of Charles Landry, *soft infrastructures* exist through "social networks, connections, and human interactions" that stimulate the circulation "of ideas between individuals and institutions" (cited in Stahl, 2004: 55). Whereas conventional hip-hop music industry infrastructures are hierarchical and gated, the cultural logics underlying underground hip hop encourage more free-flowing communications between music-makers and their listeners, artists and fans, as well as artists and other artists.

On one of the CD-Rs given to me, there is a small note clarifying that the "0" in the listed email address is the number zero and not the letter "O." I recall another underground CD-R with a phone number that included a note for the caller to ask for "Josh"—keep in mind that this was a time when many young people would not have had their own phones. If nothing else, in distributing CD-Rs of their music, these artists/fans were signalling that they welcomed being contacted. Yet in making this gesture—particularly to a member of the Ground Control Allstar tour—what kinds of contacts, interactions, and informational exchanges were they soliciting or expecting?

I cannot be certain which of the various CD-Rs that I acquired were also being sold—as opposed to solely being given away. Several were merely blank CD-Rs with marker writing (no additional packaging); others had elaborate packaging and a few were professionally manufactured; two had barcodes indicating that the music had been registered to the professional standards of the Universal Code Council; and a handful were shrink-wrapped. Such markers of professionalism, though not particularly common, might be motivated by strategic and aspirational self-presentations. For instance, one evening our tour manager handed me a CD-R that had been given to him wrapped in *Saran*. There was thus a complex and contradictory valuation of crudeness and professionalism as symbolizing music legitimacy (Harrison, 2006). To some degree, such considerations might impact whether a particular CD-R was considered a music commodity—for sale to paying consumers—or simply an example of an artists' music to be handed out. The aesthetics of underground hip hop powerfully swung towards the former. Yet all the CD-Rs I accumulated on tour were willingly given to me (or a fellow tour member) free of charge.

I am quite sure that this was largely connected to my position on the tour bus and my association, however tenuous, with Ground Control Records and Nu Gruv Alliance—the latter being a well-respected underground hip-hop distribution house. Yet returning to the question of what was being proposed through the act of gifting me this music, different industry infrastructures offer divergent explanations. On the one hand, observers of conventional hip-hop music industry logics would view me as the most accessible person through which aspiring artists could get their music played on this bus—and perhaps heard by one of their musical idols—or in the offices of Nu Gruv Alliance. The more horizontal infrastructures of underground hip hop, on the other hand, prioritized creating and sustaining networks of mutual appreciation and, likely, support and solidarity.

John Ryan and Michael Hughes have written persuasively about how the introduction of relatively inexpensive, high quality, recording technologies created a "new industry" model (2006: 240). Whereas the traditional model was based on a complex, collaborative yet hierarchical process in which record companies had ultimate decision-making power, within the newer alternative model, innovative artists were free to pursue their own creativity. In reflecting on the CD-Rs that I acquired on tour, I recognize how, at a transitional moment when an alternate underground hip-hop infrastructure was still nascent, these transactions encompass the expectations and fantasies of both music industry models.

The conventional model conforms to the narrative of the classic EPMD song referenced above. By getting their music into the hands of someone connected to the music industry, or even played on the tour bus, an aspiring artist gives themselves a better chance of being discovered. The music industry is abound with such narratives. For example, there is an oft-recounted story that after hearing a copy of the then relatively unknown Detroit rapper Eminem's *Slim Shady* EP, hip-hop producer Dr. Dre said "have this kid out here by Monday" and the rest is history (Taysom, 2021). Another version of this sought-after moment-of-discovery, one that may resonate particularly within hip-hop circles, involves being offered a guest appearance on an established artist's song. Hip-hop albums at all levels feature regular guest appearances and "posse cuts" (a song featuring four or more rappers). Had Ed O.G., for instance, heard one of my CD-Rs playing on the bus and concluded that the emcee was a special talent, he might have invited them to collaborate with him on a future song—a meaningful, though often inconsequential, first step for an aspiring artist to get noticed. Such fantasies motivate many up-and-coming artists' creative endeavours and enthusiasms about tour buses coming to town. In this way, they comprise a powerful affective dimension of these infrastructures (Danely, 2016), fuelling the creation and distribution of countless demonstration tapes and CD-Rs. Although appearing on a posse cut is a long way from achieving sustained music success, such ambitions and the activities they inspire are standard conventions for how differently positioned people in and around the hip-hop music industry approach and understand artist-related interactions.

The emergent infrastructure of underground hip hop offers a different framework of desires and expectations. By circumventing traditional music industry bureaucracies and hierarchies, DIY underground hip-hop artists are engaging with music in ways that eschew its commercial commodity value and uphold priorities of interpersonal music circulation. Instead of looking at these gestures—of giving the merch guy your CD-R—as strategic bids for entry into a regulated system involving negotiated contracts and monetized success, these acts of sharing music can be looked at as exchanges in the more generalized anthropological sense.

Starting with Malinowski (1922) and continuing through theorists like Claude Lévi-Strauss (1969) and Marshall Sahlins (1972), anthropologists have long recognized how strong social connections are created and supported through systems of *generalized exchange*—that is, the practice of giving something of value to another person without any expectation of immediate or direct return. People engaged in such exchange expect to benefit at some point in the future (if they have not already in the past) from an offering made to them by typically a different person. Accordingly, a sense of trust (in the network of exchange) and social unity prevail. Recent studies have shown that actors engaged in such generalized and indirect reciprocity are "likely to perceive themselves as a collective entity," sharing a strong sense of social solidarity (Molm, Collett, and Schaefer, 2007: 237).

Thus, rather than a request to "please listen to my demo," which presumably comes with the desired expectation of doing something that might facilitate the giver's "breaking" into the industry, the offering gesture of "here, listen to my music" is more in line with how music circulates among an allied network of peers. In offering the object of their CD-R as a form of music exchange, these artists/fans were making bids for recognizing their mutual participation in an alternative musical sphere that valued collectivity in response to the greater resourced and more hierarchal existing hip-hop music industry. Through circulations of such musical goods, and the ideas and aesthetics that underlie them, these artists played an active part in constructing and maintaining an alternative infrastructure that prioritized artistry over commerce.

The fact that these exchanges occurred at the merchandise table—the centre of commercial transactions for each show—is beyond ironic. Indeed, for me it signifies the complexities of these infrastructural emplacements. Building on the work of Larkin, Christiaan De Beukelaer (2019: 151) discusses the process through which newer infrastructures get superimposed on top of earlier ones, "creating a historical layering over time." The conventional music industry infrastructure, then—with its dreams of soon-to-be celebrity that animate interactions—never entirely disappears. For some (I am certain) it remains most prominent. Yet the aesthetic and aspirational changes facilitated through the emergence of underground hip hop generated new motivations and fantasies surrounding a national hip-hop tour coming to town. The dynamic relationship between these differing reasons for giving the "merch guy" a CD-R reflects the "palimpsests of practices, initiatives, economies, and dreams" resulting from additional infrastructural overlays (De Beukelaer, 2019: 151).

Through the emergence of underground hip hop, the fanfare surrounding rap music stardom waned for many long-time hip-hop devotees. Within middle-class enclaves particularly—like the college towns that made up a third of our tour—as more artists/fans acknowledged the virtues of being local performers, they came around to embracing the idea of making music as a hobby rather than a career. In the absence of the fixed rigidity characterizing established music industry bureaucracies and hierarchies, underground hip-hop practitioners invested in creating and supporting a soft infrastructure through which to bolster their sense of collective belonging (Stahl, 2004).

CD-Rs would eventually give way to a different mode of musical transfer. Within a decade, as digital music files and then streaming came to dominate, the traditional reliance on space and time compressions—that is, being in the right place at the right time—would become outdated (Straw, 2009). While some celebrate the convenience of music's lost physicality, I want to posit that through its very object-ness, the CD-R demands recognition (Straw, 1999). Without a physical artefact to mediate these social exchanges, I wonder if the dynamics of this infrastructural overlay would have been visible to me. Infrastructural provisions tend to be most observable when they fail or become unreliable. In this case, the surprise acquisition of so many of these physical artefacts alerted me to the idea that something different was happening. Although the *infrastructural turn* in popular music studies has largely been prompted by hyper-connected, virtual media technologies (Magaudda, 2020), refocusing on physical media might reveal new insights into the way infrastructures sustain themselves and interrelate to one another.

Conclusion

In this chapter, I have emphasized how shifts in hip hop's music creation practices and relational understandings introduced a new alternative infrastructural logic that, rather than displacing hip hop's conventional cultural (industry) logic, superimposed itself on top of it. Instead of using demonstration recording CD-Rs solely as means to potentially enter a hierarchically organized, gated music industry, many novice hip-hop artists began viewing them as mediums through which to assert their mutual identification, collective belonging, and underground hip-hop solidarity. While my role as merchandise person on a national hip-hop tour positioned me on the frontlines to experience these complex interactions, it was through the surprise acquisition of these soon-to-be fleeting media artefacts that I came to recognize the underlying differences surrounding such musical exchanges. Accordingly, I encourage anthropologists working in popular cultural fields to pay greater attention to the activities and terms through which media circulate and what they might reveal about the differing infrastructures that various social actors observe and operate within.

Music industries and the scenes that surround them are saturated with infrastructural architectures, networks, and arrangements. Whereas scholars may tend to focus on the fixed, material aspects of infrastructures (see Ryan and Peterson, 1982; Negus, 1999), in the realm of music, where emotions, aesthetics, and imagined narratives figure so prominently, there is tremendous value in attending to the social and ideological elements that comprise soft infrastructures. Through examining these more fluid aspects of culture, we gain greater understandings of how infrastructures emerge and evolve as well as how they can come to be emplaced and eventually even displaced. The recognition that, at any given moment, multiple infrastructures might co-exist and/or come into conflict with one another enhances our understandings of how different cultural actors make sense of and operate within the range of options available to them. In considering fields of popular music, past, present, and future mediums of exchange provide keys for accessing the networks of actors and ideas through which social collectivities form.

Notes

1. A&R is a common music industry colloquialism referring to Artists and Repertoire. This is typically the division or persons in a record label responsible for scouting and developing new talent. Thus, the A&R person serves as the official contact for most new artists affiliating with a record label.
2. An earlier version of this chapter was presented at the 2015 International Association for the Study of Popular Music (IASPM)—US Branch conference in Louisville, KY. Music from the CD-Rs is featured as part of the IASPM-US Mixtape Series at http://iaspm-us.net/please-listen-to-my-cd-r-underground-hip-hop-music-from-the-fans-by-anthony-kwame-harrison/
3. Some of these processes have become more visible with the popularity of programs like VH1's *Behind the Music*, ABC/MTV's *Making the Band*, and a flood of music documentaries. Yet even these, which not all fans watch, tend to foreground narratives of music creativity and downplay the bureaucracy behind it.
4. Advances are sums of money given to artists to pay for their music's recording. This money eventually needs to be paid back to the record label and should therefore be considered a loan or investment in the future profitability of their release. It is not free money.
5. I purposely use the masculine pronoun to highlight the gendered dimension of evaluating who should emcee.
6. For the remainder of this chapter, I used the term "CD-R" to reference all the discs I acquired on tour, although technically a few of them were CDs.
7. In 2000, this would have been the "Big Five" (i.e. Universal Music Group, Sony Music Entertainment, EMI, Warner Music Group, BMG)—formerly the "Big Six" and soon-to-be the "Big Four"—and their subsidiaries.

References

Allain, S., Singleton, J. (Producers), and Brewer, C. (Director) (2005) *Hustle & Flow* [Motion Picture], United States: Paramount Pictures.
Becker, H. S. (1982) *Art Worlds*. Berkeley, CA: University of California Press.
Boehlert, E. (2000) "The Death of Music Retail as We Know It?" *Salon*, 30 May, available at www.salon.com/2000/05/30/cd_r/ (accessed 2 September 2021).
Cordero, R. (2016) "Concert 'Merch' Comes of Age," *Business of Fashion*, 18 April, available at www.businessoffashion.com/articles/news-analysis/concert-tour-merchandise-justin-bieber-rihanna-kanye-west (accessed 2 September 2021).
Danely, J. (2016) "Affect, Infrastructure, and Vulnerability: Making and Breaking Japanese Eldercare," *Medicine Anthropology Theory* 3 (2): 198–222.
De Beukelaer, C. (2019) "The Social and Built Infrastructure of Cultural Policy: Between Selective Popular Memory and Future Plans," *International Journal of Cultural Policy* 25 (2): 140–153.
Harrison, A. K. (2003) "Every Emcee's a Fan, Every Fan's an Emcee": Authenticity, Identity, and Power within Bay Area Underground Hip-Hop, Unpublished Ph.D. Dissertation, Syracuse University.
Harrison, A. K. (2006) "'Cheaper Than a CD, Plus We Really Mean It': Bay Area Underground Hip Hop Tapes as Subcultural Artefacts," *Popular Music* 25 (2): 283–301.
Harrison, A. K. (2009) *Hip Hop Underground: The Integrity and Ethics of Racial Identification*, Philadelphia, PA: Temple University Press.
Harrison, A. K. (2018) "Preserving Underground Hip-Hop Tapes in Ethnographic Context," in N. Guthrie and S. Carlson (eds.), *Music Preservation and Archiving Today*, Lanham, MD: Rowman & Littlefield, 103–120.
Larkin, B. (2004) "Bandiri Music, Globalization, and Urban Experience in Nigeria," *Social Text* 22 (4 [81]): 91–112.
Larkin, B. (2013) "The Politics and Poetics of Infrastructure," *Annual Review of Anthropology* 42: 327–343.

Lévi-Strauss, C. (1969) *The Elementary Structures of Kinship*, revised edition, Boston, MA: Beacon Press.

Magaudda, P. (2020) "Music Scenes as Infrastructures: From Live Venues to Algorithmic Data," in T. Tofalvy and E. Barna (eds.), *Popular Music, Technology and the Changing Media Infrastructure*, Cham, CH: Palgrave Macmillan, 23–41.

Malinowski, B. (1922) *Argonauts of the Western Pacific*, New York: E. P. Dutton.

Molm, L. D., Collett, J. L., and Schaefer, D. R. (2007) "Building Solidarity Through Generalized Exchange: A Theory of Reciprocity," *American Journal of Sociology* 113 (1): 205–242.

Morris, J. W. (2015) *Selling Digital Music, Formatting Culture*, San Francisco: University of California Press.

Negus, K. (1999) "The Music Business and Rap: Between the Street and the Executive Suite," *Cultural Studies* 13 (3): 488–508.

Ryan J. and Hughes, M. (2006) "Breaking the Decision Chain: The Fate of Creativity in the Age of Self-Production," in M.D. Ayers (ed.), *Cybersounds: Essays on Virtual Music Culture*, New York: Peter Lang, 239–253.

Ryan, J. and Peterson, R. A. (1982). "The Product Image: The Fate of Creativity in Country Music Songwriting," in J. Ettema and D. C. Whitney (eds.), *Individuals in Mass Media Organizations: Creativity and Constraint*, Thousand Oaks, CA: Sage, 11–32.

Sahlins, M. (1972) *Stone Age Economics*, New York: Aldine-Atherton.

Stahl, G. (2004) "'It's Like Canada Reduced': Setting the Scene in Montreal," in A. Bennett and K. Kahn-Harris (eds.), *After Subculture: Critical Studies in Contemporary Youth Culture*, New York: Palgrave Macmillan, 51–64.

Star, S. L. (1999) "The Ethnography of Infrastructure," *American Behavioral Scientist* 43 (3): 377–391.

Stern, J. (2012) *MP3: The Meaning of a Format*, Durham, NC: Duke University Press.

Straw, W. (1999) "The Thingishness of Things," *In[]Visible Culture: An Electronic Journal for Visual Studies* 2, available at http://rochester.edu/in_visible_culture/issue2/straw.htm (accessed 28 April 2016).

Straw, W. (2009) "The Music CD and its Ends," *Design and Culture* 1 (1): 79–91.

Taysom, J. (2021) "The Moment Dr. Dre Discovered Eminem," *Far Out*, available at https://faroutmagazine.co.uk/when-dr-dre-discovered-eminem/ (accessed 2 September 2021).

Vilanova, J. and Cassidy, K. (2019) "'I am Not the Drummer's Girlfriend': Merch Girls, Tour's Misogynist Mythos, and the Gendered Dynamics of Live Music's Backline Labor," *Journal of Popular Music Studies* 31 (2): 85–106.

5

"TECHNOLOGY IS WONDERFUL UNTIL IT ISN'T"

Community-Based Research and the Precarity of Digital Infrastructure

Jerome Crowder, Peggy Determeyer, and Sara Rogers

Computers, tablets, and cell phones have gone from being luxury items to being necessities in just the past 20 years. Consider all the mediated technical accoutrements that we carry regularly. During the past year, a global pandemic has exacerbated our dependence on media technologies. Professional and personal meetings that used to occur in person are now regularly managed over various virtual platforms.

Whereas we have published the results of prior sessions on improvements of health literacy elsewhere (Crowder and Determeyer, 2019; and Determeyer and Crowder, 2019, Determeyer et al, 2021), this chapter tackles new terrain by focusing specifically on the challenges, failures, and future advice in creating information, digital infrastructures for use in community dialogues and other Community-Based Participatory Research programs. In fall of 2020, the three authors of this chapter elected to offer a session of community dialogues in a virtual format to address medication literacy and management using pharmacogenomics, which refers to how the genetic make-up of individuals responds to medications. A group of eight diverse community members met for five weeks to discuss the importance of health literacy, medication management, pharmacogenomics, and data/privacy issues. Community dialogues are an interactive gathering of a group of people to discuss topics of interest over multiple weeks (usually four to six). Participants receive information in a variety of formats and then discuss the topic for the week, led by a facilitator.

Community-based research requires coordinated efforts across multiple platforms, as it depends upon lines of communication, routinely used and maintained, synchronization of calendars, regular meetings and approvals, consents from many persons and data hosting, and distribution and storage. This particular session was a pilot on a new topic related to genetics that built on prior sessions covering Patient-Centered Outcomes Research (PCOR), end-of-life planning, and Senior Mental Health, conducted by Crowder and Determeyer in Galveston, Texas during the years 2012–2016, supported by grant number R24HS022134 from the Agency for Healthcare Research and Quality with the intent of improving health literacy and understanding of these topics.

DOI: 10.4324/9781003175605-9

While the most recent session was conducted virtually on Zoom, all of the sessions that the chapter authors have led relied heavily on technology, with mixed results: while the participants were empowered by the format, neither the researchers nor the participants anticipated the challenges that would be presented by the idiosyncrasies of the technologies, and in some cases, issues with technology literacy that were being applied. In this chapter, we wish to use a case study of Community Dialogues to illustrate the practical realities that have been discussed in the media anthropology literature regarding lack of access for various constituencies. Ultimately, we seek to move beyond critique and provide important lessons for other researchers who wish to engage communities through digital communication infrastructures. We will examine key access issues, identifying the challenges that we encountered, changes we made with subsequent dialogues, and the lessons that we learned about the precarity of digital infrastructure.

Background

It is well known that patients with low health literacy levels experience great difficulties in accessing the health care system and have poorer health status than patients with higher health literacy levels (Berkman, Sheridan, and Donahue, 2011; Wolf, 2010). For example, patients with low health literacy levels are often unable to name or describe how to use their current medications, have a limited understanding of their medications and the associated side effects, and are often less likely to ask questions of their pharmacists (Youmans, 2003). These difficulties in comprehending medication information have been linked to medication errors, misinterpretation of instructions and/or symptoms, poor medication and treatment adherence, lesser self-care behavior, worse health outcomes, and more visits to the emergency department (Hernandez and Landi, 2011). With the continuing complexity of healthcare, including trends toward personalized medicine, an expansion of health literacy and comprehension of concepts related to health technology is an essential need. The authors have been using community dialogues as a means of improving health literacy with a variety of African American, Latino, and white communities of seniors (65 years and older) in the Gulf Coast area of Texas, including Galveston, Houston, and surrounding counties (Brody et al., 2015; Crowder and Determeyer, 2019; Determeyer and Crowder, 2019).

Community members' understanding of the various health and medication issues has been exacerbated by the absence of technological literacy. As an example, more physicians and hospitals are relying on patient portals to provide details on diagnoses and test results to patients and their families. In addition, telehealth has emerged as an essential component of health care delivery. The demand for telehealth services is rapidly rising, with the expected long-term growth and adoption of telehealth services being hastily compressed to meet the urgent, pandemic-driven needs of practitioners and patients. Consequently, achieving health literacy requires technological and media literacy as well, since much of our "health" is placed and accessible primarily online. This ability to use information and communication technologies to find, evaluate, create, and convey information requires both cognitive and technical skills and is becoming a prerequisite to attain health literacy.

Anthropologist Brian Larkin (2013: 328) notes that infrastructures "facilitate the flow of goods, people, or ideas and allow for their exchange over space." Researchers often define infrastructure as "technical structures such as roads, power lines or databases that support particular forms of work and social life" (Niewöhner, 2015: 119). But the concept has been extended to think about how software infrastructures have far-reaching impacts on social life (Hsu, 2014). In this chapter, we define infrastructure as following Larkin's definition. Such a definition is advantageous because it emphasizes the interrelatedness of required information with acquisition pathways. For us, the media provided at community dialogues formed an infrastructure of information that revealed asymmetries of inclusion which complicated participants' ability to understand health issues and frame them in ways where values could be clarified and communicated to other community members.

All of this literacy returns to basic forms of infrastructure and access. Anthropologist Bryce Peake (2020: 7) discusses the culture infrastructure that is necessary to make a technical infrastructure usable. Internet infrastructure is, of course, an essential element of the economic, educational, and social inequalities between those who have computers and online access and those who do not. However, infrastructure alone does not necessarily translate into adoption and beneficial use. Local and national institutions, affordability and access, and the digital proficiency of users, all play significant roles—and there are wide variations globally along each of these.

As noted in the introduction, community dialogue sessions led by the authors have included a variety of topics in areas that participants are unlikely to have reviewed and discussed, as they are complex and not in the normal stream of conversation. For the researchers, the community dialogue sessions provide the means for investigating the participants' views and values of a topic in a bi-directional way intended to be informational and educational for the participants while providing the researchers with critical information on participants' values (Brody et al., 2015). As noted by Crowder and Determeyer (2019), participants found these sessions beneficial in many areas, including learning new information and becoming empowered to advocate for themselves in managing their own health care.

Overall, even with the benefits realized from holding the community dialogues, there were three areas in which the research leaders were surprised at the lack of digital inclusion that appeared: access to using digital media; application of digital and technical media in the conduct of the dialogues; and in the most recent session, the challenges of using the virtual environment for the conduct of the dialogues. Notably, the last dialogue session, conducted in the fall of 2020, is the inaugural application of virtual seminars to community dialogues.

In the original dialogue sessions (2014), the preparatory materials included readings, audio recordings made by the researchers, and videos. While some of the readings were provided in paper format, the digital materials were provided on a compact disc (CD) for the participants to access at their leisure. In providing these materials in a digital format, researchers hoped to simplify distribution of the information and make it more accessible to participants. When the dialogues were beginning in 2014, disks provided an easy, cost-effective way to share materials which participants could access easily on their computer (most computers still had CD-ROM drives at that time). These could also be handed out at the beginning of the dialogue and contained all materials necessary for the entire session.

The materials were intended to ensure that everyone was on the same level during the discussions. In fact, using this format did the opposite—most participants did not have the means for accessing the digital materials or did not know how to use them, and rather than try to learn new methods for accessing the materials, would simply not use them. After the first series of dialogues, we reverted to articles that could be provided in a paper format for distribution to participants. Subsequent dialogues included several groups who participated multiple times. Finally, with the most recent session, with an inability to meet in person due to the pandemic, the community dialogue session was held via Zoom, the only virtual option to support people participating with different operating systems and platforms. Participants were recruited by a variety of community organizations identified by the researchers. While most of the participants had a passing familiarity with virtual meetings, some had trouble with the computers, phones, or tablets that they were using to "attend" the meetings. Trouble-shooting issues as they arose was problematic—one of the leaders encountered difficulties when using her phone and computer, not realizing that the approach would create an echo during the transmission.

These examples demonstrate the need for advanced planning in establishing a media infrastructure that could adequately support the dialogues. Often, academic researchers tend to take technologies and their infrastructures for granted and assume that everything will work according to plan. However, as we have noted in the title, technology is wonderful until it isn't, and we use this chapter to explore the challenges that we encountered in greater detail, with an eye toward addressing the precarious nature of technology, particularly when planning community engagement projects.

"Not Quite Plumb": Squaring Fundamental Infrastructures and Foundational Knowledge

The promise of technology is to make what we normally do easier or improved in some way. Historically, anthropologists have studied cultures and how they develop technology to improve their lives and better adapt to their environments (Steward, 1972; White 2016; Harris, 2001). Larkin (2013) believes that infrastructures inherently have an enlightenment notion of progress and improvement, but recent experiences indicate otherwise. As an example, within the past two decades, anthropological researchers have focused on the impact the internet and smart phones have had on societies worldwide. The term "digital divide" became a popular way of distinguishing those who had access to these technologies and those who did not, and is now commonly referred to as issues of "digital inclusion" (Correa Pavez, and Contreras, 2018; Horst and Miller, 2012). Initially, this issue reflected basic access to computers; once households achieved this goal, the term more accurately described those who had access to the internet and those who did not (Hassani, 2006; Selwyn, 2006). Even among populations with some access to technology, digital inclusion is challenged in the form of lower-performance computers, lower-speed wireless connections, lower-priced internet use connections such as dial-up, and limited access to subscription-based content. In many ways, cell phone technology helped underserved communities leapfrog the personal computer moment and provided the internet and a handheld computing device simultaneously (Yates, Gulati, and Weiss, 2011). We are not overstating the revolutionary impact of cell phone infrastructure to distribute computation and internet access around the globe and into corners of it that have rarely seen much more than an AM radio.

However, availability and access are distinguishable. Availability means that infrastructures have been developed in an area while access identifies those persons or groups who can engage with the infrastructure. As Jenkins notes (2009: 8), "a focus on expanding access to new technologies carries us only so far if we do not also foster the skills and cultural knowledge necessary to deploy those tools toward our own ends." As with any commodity or resource, limitations to access are imposed by those who control the resource. In underserved areas, internet services may be available in limited forms as well as access due to pricing parameters (Turow and Kavanaugh, 2003; Warschauer, 2004). The cell phone offers easier access to the internet through phone plans, but due to service prices, offers limited bandwidth or restrictions on how much service is usable per period or cycle (Greengard, 2008). Jenkins (2009) underscores this observation. He states, "simply passing out technology is not enough. Expanding access to computers will help bridge some of the gaps between the haves and the have nots, but only in a context in which ... youth and adults learn how to use those tools effectively" (2009: 13). Ours is not a new story, and it reflects other narratives we have all heard about or experienced personally, in how people without much can make do in order to access technologies that are available to others who can pay or live where services are available (Crowder, Wilson, and Vredenburg, 2009; Dourish and Bell, 2011; Horst and Miller, 2020; Matthews and Doherty, 2009).

In order to conduct social science research in underserved areas of Houston and Galveston, we had to consider the residents and their access to the internet and other digital infrastructures. As our project engaged primarily with persons 65 or older, we confronted the human impediment to technology access (user error and comfort with digital technology) (Freese, Rivas, and Hargittai, 2006). While nearly everyone we worked with had an email account, a cell phone, and internet access, the use of certain apps and knowledge about how to make the technology work played the largest role in our potential success. Thus, the technologies squared with the communities' needs, but the users were not quite "plumb" with the infrastructures. Technology is only as good as the skills individuals have to access it.

The technology access and user issues became immediately evident as we began to prepare our community participants for the impending dialogues (Crowder and Determeyer, 2019). We had selected, on average, three readings (professional journal articles) for each of the four weeks of discussion, all of which we provided to participants in portable document format (PDF), commonly used by academics for sharing and storing articles and papers. We had unwittingly assumed several things about our participants regarding their technology use and understanding. First, we expected that our community liaisons (who identified and recruited our participants) would be able to manage the digital files and distribute them to everyone in the research project. Second, we further assumed that that our participants would be able to open and use PDF files, since they had the technology in hand to deal with them. We quickly learned that this was not the case, since some of our older participants only "received" email through their children or smart phones and could not easily read a digital document on a monitor. Despite our interest in saving paper by going digital, we found that it was easier for the elderly participants to receive a three-ring binder with all the readings printed for them to review. Third, we assumed that professional journal articles published on our topics were appropriate for the residents; they were not, and we were not able to obtain or find and provide the dialogue participants with less sophisticated readings in such a short period of time.

Once the dialogues began, participants were asked to read the materials for each week. It became apparent that many of the participants were not able to digest the academic writing style and vocabulary, while also considering the font size to be too small. Since the PCOR articles maintained a style and content that required careful reading, many of the participants balked and limited their engagement. Given the careful consideration that had gone into selecting the reading content, the research team decided to record ourselves discussing the basic arguments of the papers, so participants could listen to the banter and prepare themselves for the session. As previously noted, files were distributed digitally and copied to a CD-ROM to be played at home (it was 2014, so this technology was already obsolete, albeit accessible). Our idea was based on assumptions about people's use of audio files, expecting them to know how to open and listen to a digital audio file, or at least play the disk on a player (residing in a desktop or laptop computer). Even though participants were interested in listening to the discussion, they could not play the files on their computers; some even sat in their cars as that was the only CD player they had access to! Upon review, in subsequent dialogues, we selected more appropriate readings, in line with participants' expectations, taken from newspapers and magazines that provided similar information at an accessible reading level.

Regular communication with our participants relied on email, but as we quickly learned, our participants only checked email when they knew they had a message. Consequently, we developed a call tree, in which we shared each other's phone numbers and had an agreement to relay messages to the entire group via cell phone (not even text messaging). We were experiencing a crisis in technological literacy, which is the level at which users understand how to adequately operate the technology shared within the group. We could only operate using the group's common denominator. Clearly, some people are better users or more technologically savvy than others, but the entire group suffers at the hands of those who know the least—and in some cases, are the least willing to learn or engage. Oftentimes, we would hear participants complain about their phones not operating correctly—"there's something wrong with this phone, it has been acting up lately"—while others would comment "I'm not sure what I'm supposed to do with this, how do I open it?" There was frustration with the technology itself, the knowledge required to operate it, and the fear of not being able to perform at a level expected by the group. We had not realized just how technologically illiterate some of our participants would be. For some, there was an unapologetic refusal to accede to the technological world by having a cell phone or email address, while others eagerly consumed the materials and participated with their tablets or laptops weekly.

Despite the digital infrastructures available to our participants, we could not use them effectively because of user knowledge. We were not in the position to teach everyone how to engage with their cell phones and computers, and instead had to adjust by retrofitting the project with older technologies that were familiar to the users. As researchers, we were "backwards compatible," allowing for interoperability with older systems, and responded to our participants' needs. In the end, participants were content to avoid the "information highway" by reading from their binders, talking on the phone, and meeting every week.

Imaging Discussion: Exploring Possibilities and the Promise of Technology

When preparing for the second round of dialogues (2014–2016), we asked the community groups what they felt would increase participation in the neighborhood and help develop conversations with other residents. As the next chosen topic was *Mental Health and Aging*, we assumed that the participants would have more ideas about how to better structure and organize the dialogues, provide suggestions that would help them more easily engage with the materials, or share what they learned with others. Conversations on this topic were not remarkable, and few major suggestions were made regarding technology, other than selecting more accessible readings. Everyone was content with using printed materials, working the phone chain, and using email as backup. Much of the organization fell to the community members themselves, especially the moderator, as they worked with the participants directly, taking attendance, providing materials, and coordinating with the research team.

One group of participants was particularly eager to share their dialogues with the larger community. Their leader suggested that he would contact the local high school to check if their communications program would be able to video capture the discussions. The implication was that the recordings could be made by tech-savvy teenagers, who could then edit the footage and place it all online or distribute via DVD for residents to review and share beyond the neighborhood. They were excited by the process and the material and felt this information would be important for their family and friends to know about (beyond the report generated at the end of the session).

However, before the new round of dialogues began, we heard nothing about the prospect of video recording during the impending meetings. Although this one group seemed excited by the potential application of video technology, other dialogue groups were opposed to being video recorded during these sessions, both because of being identified and due to the distraction that such production would impose on the sessions. Some members became "possessive" of this time together while others felt the conversations were personal and not all stories needed to be shared with the wider world.

As noted earlier (Crowder and Determeyer, 2019), videotaping the dialogues is not necessary in order to perform appropriate project analyses. At one point, we considered the use of video tape as a research strategy for data capture in case we thought an analysis of proxemics or non-verbal body language would be worthwhile. However, the suggestion for videotaping was made by community members. In this bottom-up example, it seemed worthwhile because it would be driven and executed by the community rather than by the researchers, providing additional ownership in the dialogue process.

The day the dialogues on *Mental Health and Aging* began, no one from the high school appeared with their video equipment. Although the group consented to filming the dialogue and participants expected it would happen, there was almost no discussion about it when no one showed up. However, participants were interested in filming for both posterity and to share the recordings across their wider community. This group believed strongly that video recording their discussion would be worthwhile as a teaching instrument—without considering how it would be distributed. Having no other alternative for having their sessions filmed, they asked the research team if we could help them videotape the following meeting. Once set up, the static camera did not affect the proceedings and held a wide-angled view of the room. However, the frame could not capture everyone around the table, and those furthest away from the camera appeared quite small and difficult to view. Furthermore, we realized the product would not live up to the expectations the participants imagined.

By the end of the dialogue sessions, we had captured more than nine hours of single camera video. Little, if any, of the footage was usable in terms of producing it for others to view for learning or teaching purposes. There was no time allocated to edit it down to much more than soundbites to share in research presentations. No participants inquired about watching the video or obtaining copies for themselves. In the end, the researchers used it for presentations to offer our audiences an idea of how the dialogues work and key statements participants made about mental health and aging.

The lesson from this example is that sometimes it is not the technology or infrastructures themselves that deter or inhibit a project, but the expectations of those involved with the project as to what technologies can or cannot accomplish. In this case, participants are so accustomed to seeing video, somewhat effortlessly made, that they assumed it would be easy to video capture their dialogue and share it with their community members, much like a TV show they would watch. Alternatively, such productions, especially those requiring multiple cameras and subjects, also require a great deal of resources to make happen and meet expectations. Sometimes, technologies are so integrated into our worldviews that we do not recognize the infrastructures that support them (Di Nunzio, 2018; Poirier et al., 2019: 229). It was probably like this when electricity or telephone lines were initially installed, much like it is when we think about internet access and being on Wi-Fi. These technologies are taken for granted and there is very little, if any, recognition as to the immense structures that uphold these everyday gadgets and devices, until they fail (Horst and Miller, 2012; Niewöhner, 2015: 123).

More importantly to the point here, the technology was available to include in the project. However, the resources, in this case human capital, were not available; there were not enough persons to adequately capture the video and audio of the dialogues. The expectations of the technology failed the participants; cultural infrastructure was incommensurate to the task (Peake, 2020).

Zoom Matters: Technology Literacy and Community Dialogues During a Pandemic

We have learned from our assumptions and mistakes over the course of the various projects. Most recently, due to COVID-19, we held a virtual dialogue to discuss personalized medicine and pharmacogenomics. Crowder and Determeyer, two of the authors of this chapter, were introduced to Rogers, a pharmacist dedicated to decreasing risks caused by drug interactions. We began mapping out a dialogue to focus on genetics and personalized medicine. Since the theme was complex, the project became a pilot to test materials and presentations to understand how well persons already familiar with the dialogue process could engage with this science-heavy material.

The first wave of the COVID pandemic had passed when we were ready to begin recruiting participants. We contacted former dialogue participants who demonstrated leadership throughout the experience by taking their new knowledge back to their communities and remained in touch with us in the interim. Moving the dialogues to a virtual platform required persons who were not intimidated by technology and could make the most out of the technical/science grounded dialogue. Coordinating a dialogue that addressed real-life issues was difficult enough; would the promise of technology make the administration of this research project easier? We were uncertain but wanted to test the veracity of the community dialogue method.

We immediately superimposed our experiences with teaching and meeting online with the potential issues we had encountered holding dialogues via Zoom. Connectivity, literacy, etiquette, and availability were the challenges we foresaw with these sessions, and we began addressing them in our dialogue planning. One variable we could not control would be individuals' level of internet access that would allow them to maintain a sufficient presence during the dialogue. We were not sure who would have limited internet connectivity or older technology, so when reaching out to potential participants we asked about their virtual meeting literacy and access to adequate technology. We were pleased to learn that several former participants were interested in the topic and felt technologically confident enough to navigate a series of virtual meetings.

Another variable we recognized would be affected by the virtual platform is the duration of the online meeting: dialogues last three hours, offering a ten-minute natural break half-way through for refueling. By this time in the pandemic (fall 2020), it was clear that long online meetings were detrimental to individuals' focus and engagement, so we considered how to cut the sessions back while providing adequate time to learn from and discuss the materials. As these personalized medicine materials were significantly advanced, we anticipated hesitation from potential participants, so we developed entry-level materials that would help explain the nature of the theme and how it may apply to them.

Leading up to the opening dialogue, we initiated "practice" sessions with those who had committed to participate. As precursors to any group meeting, we also planned virtual meetings with individuals to talk with them about the theme, answer questions, and check how well they could navigate the technology. We found that nearly everyone was sufficiently literate with the virtual technology, although they demonstrated a wide range of proficiency and interest.

As dementia, diabetes, heart disease, and anxiety/depression are common conditions in the population we work with (65 and older), we assumed that participants would recognize how learning more about personalized medicine could affect their health care options and potential outcomes. In discussing the topic with potential participants, we realized that family members and caregivers should also be included in the group, so we expanded our age range to include younger persons who would appreciate the information provided by personalized medicine and how it could help the patient or their family member. We assumed that younger participants would increase the number of persons comfortable with the technology, making for a more pleasant experience overall.

The orientation meeting held the week before offered a sense as to how the participants would engage with the technology and how the virtual conversation would unfold in the following weeks. Like most Zoom meetings, people had problems with their cameras and virtual backgrounds, suffered low bandwidth, and most commonly were unintentionally muted. At first not everyone turned on their video, and then it became apparent that participants had logged in with multiple devices, as there were more screens visible than participants. Someone's laptop camera would not work, so they used their cell phone but left the computer mic on, broadcasting ambient background noise despite muting their phone when not speaking. The insistent, muffled noise continued throughout the session, making it difficult to hear and interrupting the flow of the dialogue. One of the researchers suffered from a poor quality built-in laptop mic, so we switched to a cell phone for audio, leaving the computer channel on, therefore appearing in two different places on everyone's screens.

Unlike the in-person dialogues, the virtual ones were significantly more difficult to focus on because of the many distractions, especially those caused by audio and video signals dropping out, people talking over each other, and random noises. One man had to go to work during the meeting and transferred from his home computer to his cell phone, staying with the meeting even while driving!

The story of the virtual dialogue is a testament to the robustness of the internet and Wi-Fi infrastructures throughout the country. A decade ago, these stories would have seemed implausible because the technology to carry out a virtual, multi-person, multi-device meeting was unthinkable due to low bandwidth and slower computer processing speeds. Now our commentaries rely upon the ineffable resilience of the infrastructure despite user error and the characteristics of the technologies themselves. While these technologies enable the research to be more inclusive and democratic, the mediated engagement serves to distance everyone involved. The technical infrastructures mediating interaction cannot replace, or be a substitute for, the in-person engagement (see Boyer, 2012 for further discussion). In our last case, we confess that despite all of the problems with using Zoom technology to carry out our dialogues, the common denominator remained the human element, and it is here that infrastructures break down because we are not conditioned to engage with each other the same as we would if we were in person. Despite our failures at this most basic level, we still learned about pharmacogenomics and personalized medicine, data security, and polypharmacy. But it has yet to be determined how much more productive, engaged, or revealing the dialogues would have been if we had met in person, around a table, without our phones and laptops mediating our conversations, instead physically interacting with each other across a table and over a beverage and notebook. However, with this pilot, we are engaging with the technological potential of conducting at least some future dialogues virtually, potentially expanding the participants.

As documented elsewhere (Crowder and Determeyer, 2019; Determeyer and Crowder, 2019), the major stumbling block for the community dialogues method is encouraging the participants to take what they have learned and to engage with officials and health care professionals with the purpose of directly responding to their reported comments and concerns. This chapter has further revealed that with the initial dialogues, the burden lay with the participants to engage with community leaders; however, given the reluctance and difficulty participants had when engaging with technology and other issues with regards to leadership, this was not likely to take place without an advocate. This represents an issue for integration in future dialogues.

Lessons Learned

Our experiences with community dialogues have illuminated a series of lessons regarding digital engagement among different groups, most of whom tend to be older. While we know that activities can be undertaken that were previously not possible, we have encountered challenges that demonstrate some of the limitations of technology. We share these lessons learned not only as a reminder of our finitude, but also with the hope that we can become better researchers and planners as we go forward.

Value of Technology. Digital media has opened a range of opportunities, not the least of which includes the ability to promote socialization (Chesley and Johnson, 2014), which has been particularly important during the COVID pandemic. Community dialogues provide an important opportunity for groups to engage in a range of educational programs while enabling researchers to investigate various topics. Moreover, families can utilize technology to engage with each other in health literacy education (Portz et al., 2019), which can be enabled with community dialogues, where participants not only expand their understanding of a wide range of topics, but also learn that they can disagree without being disagreeable, a skill that cannot be underestimated in times of deep division. Older adults comprise the fastest-growing population group and should be included in projects applying digital media.

Importance of Community Partnerships and Promotion of Digital Inclusiveness. Unertl et al. (2016: 66) note that

> applying Community Based Participatory Research in practice required strong academic community partnerships, and developing these relationships required time, energy, trust, and resources on all sides. Building rapport and trust between researchers, community members, and Community-Based Organizations demanded skills and knowledge that are not commonly taught or developed in academic research settings.

Part of this trust-building must include the mutual understanding of digital media and how it will be applied in the project. Consequently, the researchers need to include plans for maximizing digital inclusiveness. For the community dialogues, we are addressing this by including more training in the planning and budgeting process, with the hope that better technological literacy will be achieved. This includes the necessity of establishing sufficient boundaries around plans to use technology, being careful to avoid over-promising the media to be used. Glowacki, Zhu, and Bernhardt (2021) caution that availability of technology does not equal literacy in its use, and that lesson is clear from our experiences with the community dialogues.

Limit Assumptions. When we embarked on the dialogues, our intentions with regard to providing technical support were well-meaning, but occasionally misguided. We assumed that participants who had computers and smartphones would be able to access all of the technologies that we were offering. Likewise, in fall 2020, with our practice sessions, we assumed that the transition to the virtual world would be seamless. We learned that the idiosyncrasies of various equipment types caused challenges that needed to be addressed—as previously noted, problems are not limited to participants, with one of the researchers encountering equipment issues. With careful planning, audio and visual checks. and easy to follow trouble-shooting instructions, everyone can be on the same page.

Community dialogues provide reliable educational opportunities where participants can learn and disagree without being disagreeable, while allowing researchers a glimpse into values on the chosen topic. Our work thus far (as well as those we are planning) would be far more difficult without technological resources and methods. The most difficult lesson has been recognizing the limits of technological infrastructure with our demographic of (mostly) senior adults. It is incumbent upon us to recognize the opportunities that lie ahead for both participants and researchers while planning to assure that problems are minimized in executing the programs so that the experiences for both parties are beneficial.

References

Brody, H., Croisant, S., Crowder, J., and Banda, J. (2015) "Ethical Issues in Patient-Centered Outcomes Research and Comparative Effectiveness Research: A Pilot Study of Community Dialogue," *Journal of Empirical Research on Human Research Ethics*, 10(10): 22–30.

Berkman, N. D., Sheridan, S. L., and Donahue, K. E. (2011) "Low Health Literacy and Health Outcomes: An Updated Systematic Review," *Annals of Internal Medicine*, 155(2): 97–107.

Boyer, D. (2012) "From Media Anthropology to the Anthropology of Mediation." In J. Mitchell, R. Fardon, O. Harris, T. H. J. Marchland, M. Nuttall, C. Shore, V. Strang, and R. Wilson (eds), *The SAGE Handbook of Social Anthropology*. London: Sage, 411–422.

Chesley, N., and Johnson, B. E. (2014) "Information and Communication Technology Use and Social Connectedness over the Life Course," *Sociology Compass*, 8(6): 589–602.

Correa, T., Pavez, I., and Contreras, J. (2020) "Digital Inclusion Through Mobile Phones? A Comparison Between Mobile-only and Computer Users in Internet Access, Skills and Use," *Information, Communication & Society*, 23(7): 1074–1091.

Crowder, J. W., Wilson, J., and Vredenburg, E. (2009) "Wireless Networking in an Underserved Neighborhood: Ethnographic Methods for Understanding Technology and Culture," *Practicing Anthropology*, 31(1): 11–15.

Crowder, J. W., and Determeyer, P. L. (2019) "Optimizing Community Bioethics Dialogues: Reflections on Enhancing Bi-Directional Engagement on Health Care Concerns," *Narrative Inquiry in Bioethics*, 9(3): 259–273.

Determeyer, P. L., and Crowder, J. (2019) "Community Dialogues." In C. Klugman and E. G. Lamb (eds), *Research Methods in Health Humanities*. Oxford: Oxford University Press, 235–248.

Determeyer, P. L., Crowder, J., O'Mahany, E., Esquivel, B., Atwal, H., Atwal, P. S. and Rogers, S. L. (2021) "Application of the Community Dialogues Method to Identify Ethical Values and Priorities Related to Pharmacogenomics," *Pharmacogenomics*, (11): 693–701.

Di Nunzio, M. (2018) "Anthropology of Infrastructure," *LSE Cities, Governing Infrastructure Interfaces-Research Note* 01: 1–4.

Dourish, P., and Bell, G. (2011) *Divining a Digital Future Mess and Mythology in Ubiquitous Computing*. Cambridge, MA: MIT Press.

Freese, J., Rivas, S., and Hargittai, E. (2006) "Cognitive Ability and Internet Use Among Older Adults," *Poetics*, 34(4–5): 236–249.

Glowacki, E. M., Zhu, Y., and Bernhardt, J. M. (2021) "Technological Capital Within Aging United States-Based Populations: Challenges and Recommendations for Online Intervention Uptake," *Journal of Applied Communication Research*, 49(3): 347–367.

Greengard, S. (2008) "Upwardly Mobile," *Communication*, 51(12): 17–19.

Harris, M. (2001) *Cultural Materialism: The Struggle for a Science of Culture*. New York: AltaMira Press.

Hassani, S. N. (2006) "Locating Digital Divides at Home, Work, and Everywhere Else," *Poetics*, 34(4–5): 250–272.

Hernandez, L. M., and Landi, S. (2011) *Promoting Health Literacy to Encourage Prevention and Wellness Workshop Summary*. Washington, DC: National Academies Press, 2011.

Horst, H., and Miller, D. (2012) "Normativity and Materiality: A View from Digital Anthropology," *Media International Australia*, 145(1): 103–111.

Horst, H., and Miller, D. (2020) *The Cell Phone: An Anthropology of Communication*. New York: Routledge.

Hsu, W. F. (2014) "Digital Ethnography Toward Augmented Empiricism: A New Methodological Framework," *Journal of Digital Humanities*, 3(1): 43–61.

Jenkins, H. (2009) "Confronting the Challenges of Participatory Culture: Media Education for the 21st Century. An Occasional Paper on Digital Media and Learning," *John D. and Catherine T. MacArthur Foundation*. Boston: MIT Press.

Larkin, B. (2013) "The Politics and Poetics of Infrastructure," *Annual Review of Anthropology*, 42: 327–343.

Matthews, M., and Doherty, G. (2009) "The Invisible User," *Interactions*, 16(6): 13–19.

Niewöhner, J. (2015) "Infrastructures of Society, Anthropology of Humboldt-Universität zu Berlin," In J. Wright (ed.), *International Encyclopedia of the Social and Behavioral Sciences, 2nd ed.* Amsterdam: Elsevier, 119–125.

Peake, B. (2020) "Media Anthropology: Meaning, Embodiment, Infrastructure and Activism." In N. Brown, T. McIlwraith, and L. T. de González (eds), *Perspectives: An Open Introduction to Cultural Anthropology*, pp. 1–17, https://perspectives.americananthro.org/Chapters/Media.pdf

Portz, J. D., Fruhauf, C., Bull, S., Boxer, R. S., and Bekelman, D. B. (2019) "'Call a Teenager … That's What I Do!' – Grandchildren Help Older Adults Use New Technologies: Qualitative Study," *JMIR Aging*, 2(1): e13713–e13713.

Poirier, L., Fortun, K., Costelloe-Kuehn, B., and Fortun, M. (2019) "Metadata, Digital Infrastructure, and the Data Ideologies of Cultural Anthropology." In J. W. Crowder, M. Fortun, R. Besara, and L. Poirier (eds.), *Anthropological Data in the Digital Age: New Possibilities–New Challenges*. Washington, DC: Springer Nature, 209–237.

Selwyn, N. (2006) "Digital Division or Digital Decision? A Study of Non-users and Low-users of Computers," *Poetics*, 34(4–5): 273–292.

Steward, J. H. (1972) *Theory of Culture Change: The Methodology of Multilinear Evolution*. Urbana, IL: University of Illinois Press.

Turow, J., and Kavanaugh, A. L. (2003) *The Wired Homestead: An MIT Press Sourcebook on the Internet and the Family*. Cambridge, MA: MIT Press.

Unertl, K. M., and Schaefbauer, C. L. (2016) "Integrating Community-based Participatory Research and Informatics Approaches to Improve the Engagement and Health of Underserved Populations," *Journal of the American Medical Informatics Association*, 23(1): 60–73.

Warschauer, M. (2004) *Technology and Social Inclusion: Rethinking the Digital Divide*. Cambridge, MA: MIT Press.

White, L. A. (2016) *The Evolution of Culture: The Development of Civilization to the Fall of Rome*. New York: Routledge.

Wolf, M. S., Feinglass, J., Thompson, J., and Baker, D. W. (2010) "In Search of 'Low Health Literacy': Threshold Vs. Gradient Effect of Literacy on Health Status and Mortality," *Social Science & Medicine*, 70(9): 1335–1341.

Yates, D. J., Gulati, G. J., and Weiss, J. W. (2011) "Different Paths to Broadband Access: The Impact of Governance and Policy on Broadband Diffusion in the Developed and Developing Worlds," *System Sciences* (HICSS), 44th Hawaii International Conference on, 1–10.

Youmans, S. L., and Schillinger, D. (2003) "Functional Health Literacy and Medication Use: The Pharmacist's Role," *The Annals of Pharmacotherapy*, 37(11): 1726–1729.

6
MEDIA MIGRATION

Patricia G. Lange

In the world of mediation, why do some social media sites become hot while others cool? What causes people to migrate away from old sites to new ones? How do social media platforms as communicative infrastructures impact self-expression, sociality, and personal empowerment? Media anthropology scholars should explore how online sites are structured and how their features and general aura impact interaction. Of particular interest is studying media migration, in which people stop using media or leave an online site that was previously important to their sociality or self-actualization. A discernable break in usage occurs, and participants go elsewhere to escape inhospitable environments or to support their goals. Given that everyday interaction often requires using social media, media migration studies should analyze why people stop using a site or service to understand users' mediated desires and sites' participatory limits.

Social media sites, which enable public, vernacular posting of media and interaction, serve as forms of infrastructure that support and influence how media may be posted and exchanged. According to the Merriam-Webster Dictionary (n.d.), the prefix "infra" means below, and "infrastructure" refers to structures or systems containing features and capabilities that support required functionality, such as facilitating flows or exchanges of things (Larkin, 2013). Transportation infrastructures include roads and traffic laws, while media infrastructures refer in this ethnographic context to characteristics such as technical features, terms of service rules, and the site's participatory aura, all of which influence what may be posted and whether desired forms of sociality may be accomplished through video exchange. Anthropologists are interested in studying infrastructures in part to see how they might reveal "insights into other domains" (Larkin, 2103), which here refers to understanding how corporate changes to social media infrastructures both impact and reveal participants' creative and social opportunities and desires.

This chapter contributes to media anthropology scholarship by focusing on migration away from a media platform due to perceived infrastructural problems. Using a case study of early socially oriented YouTubers who migrated to Twitter, the chapter engages with digital media anthropology and traditional anthropological migration literature to understand how infrastructure impacts sociality. A key goal is exploring whether commercialized internet "architectures" (Wahl-Jorgensen, 2018) support sociality, to work toward achieving social justice. Reasons for leaving a site should be analyzed, and site administrators should be held accountable for how they support or complicate interaction, given that social media platforms are central to accomplishing sociality on public forums, yet are controlled by profit-oriented, private companies (Zuboff, 2019).

Two key factors undergird media migration studies. The first is the centrality of media in sociality in everyday life (Postill, 2017). Media anthropologists have explored how interaction and self-actualization require access to mediated spaces, taking on even greater importance than co-located community when access to community acceptance in physical locations is not available to marginalized groups (Boellstorff, 2008; Ito et al., 2010; McDonald, 2016; Miller et al., 2016). The second factor involves conceptions of place as moving beyond main associations with physical location. Pink (2015) argues that physical place is more productively theorized as a social "event" that includes interrelated constellations of people and things—including media.

Given media's central role in supporting sociality and changing conceptions of physical place, it is advantageous to explore similarities and differences between media migration and traditional physical migration concepts. Are the reasons for leaving physical places versus media sites too dissimilar for comparison? Or can traditional migration theories shed light on movement between media? Does media anthropology require new frameworks for analyzing why people leave one media infrastructure for another? Or are there meaningful similarities that invite comparison and use of both rubrics to broaden understanding of movement to support sociality and personal empowerment? Media migration sometimes exhibits motivations similar to those in transnational migration, which seek to expand and maintain human connection and social support systems (Baldassar, 2015; McKay, 2018)—although key differences also exist. Nevertheless, media anthropologists and migration theorists analyze why people change their loci of sociality, a fundamental aspect of humanity.

Anthropologists have investigated social reasons for leaving one's homeland, and for switching technologies. In addition to political concerns and economic opportunities, social motivations such as joining extended family networks also influence physical movement. Such motivations may even contradict economic logic or personal well-being (Baldassar, 2015). Notably, media migration is different from swapping back and forth between media to communicate. It is distinct from "polymedia" practices in which people choose from myriad communicative options to fulfill social or emotional needs (Madianou and Miller, 2012). Media migration centrally involves a visible and meaningful break from one platform or media to use another.

This chapter draws on a multi-year, multi-method ethnographic study of sociality-motivated YouTubers to analyze their migration away from the site due to its intensifying commercialized atmosphere. The chapter first outlines the ethnographic context and discusses past instances of media migration in response to infrastructural changes. It then compares media migration to anthropological conceptualizations of geographical migration, noting similarities and differences. The chapter next explores media migration categories, and shows how numerous scholarly terms might productively be theorized under the broader media migration category. My goal is to encourage a collective conversation by proposing and analyzing dynamics in the anthropology of media migration, particularly with regard to how specific media supports human sociality.

Ethnographic Context

The chapter draws on an ethnography of self-expression and sociality on the video-sharing site of YouTube. The study focused on a group of video bloggers (vloggers) who created video blogs (vlogs) to connect with people socially (Lange 2019, 2020a). Interviewees watched each other's videos, posted supportive comments, exchanged tips for improvement, sent private messages, and met offline in grassroots gatherings to hang out and have fun. Many wished to support each other's amateur video-making skills or help each other through personal tragedy. YouTube interviewees often worked in professions such as office support, web design, temporary agencies, social work, and retail. Most had access to numerous media—and thus migration opportunities—although some struggled financially with securing new equipment or stable internet access.

Data was examined from 152 interviews, video-sharing patterns, hundreds of video artifacts, and participant-observation online and in grassroots meet-ups across the United States, and one in Canada. Most YouTube interviewees were early adopters, having joined within the first year of YouTube's launch in 2005. The study originated in 2006–2009, with supplementary data collected in 2016–2020. I also maintained a YouTube vlog (*AnthroVlog*) and completed an ethnographic film entitled, *Hey Watch This! Sharing the Self Through Media* (Lange 2020a).

YouTube originally offered features common on "social media," which connotes "the collection of software that enables individuals and communities to gather, communicate, share, and in some cases collaborate or play" (boyd, 2009). Social network sites (SNS), one form of social media, offers features such as a "profile page" containing a self-description and hard-coded friendship links depicting one's site-organized social network. Initially mimicking the social network "profile page" feature was the YouTube "channel page" which is a participant's main YouTube page. It lists videos that the user has uploaded and self-entered personal information. In 2007, YouTube introduced monetization. Qualifying individuals could join YouTube's "partner" program, and receive a share of revenue earned through video-based ads. Official figures are not available but content creators report that YouTube's share of ad revenue is about 45 percent (Kaufman, 2014). YouTube's current hybrid structure privileges commercialized video streaming but retains a few social media features, such as an ability to post videos and comments. Although some interviewees became YouTube partners who earned ad revenue, most of the socially motivated YouTubers whom I studied bonded by exchanging videos and comments rather than using social network or monetization features.

Interviewees often used Stickam, a different live video chat service that ran from 2005 to 2013 ("Stickam," n.d.). YouTubers appreciated experiencing synchronous video chat versus asynchronously making and commenting on videos. One interviewee characterized waiting for comments as less "interactive" than Stickam's live, synchronous atmosphere. Yet synchronous interaction was insufficient to lure participants away from YouTube's platform. Instead, Stickam effectively functioned as a "satellite" (Lange, 2019) or "supplement" or "plug in" to YouTube (Burgess and Green, 2018: 101). YouTubers swapped between these modalities to post both videos and enjoy "live" interaction with YouTube friends, but they did not cease using YouTube to migrate to Stickam.

The longitudinal aspect of the study revealed important mediation patterns that were not apparent during initial YouTube participation. Key infrastructure characteristics include participatory rules and technical features. As monetization goals intensified, YouTube's rules tightened about integrating copyrighted material into videos—a common social and creative practice. In addition, algorithms were used to identify popular videos and promote them on recommendation lists. The way that infrastructures are organized not only facilitates flows of things but also provides a kind of "mentality or way of living in the world" (Larkin, 2013: 331). Through its rules and incentives, infrastructures aim to produce certain types of participants who can orient more efficiently to standardized behaviors (Larkin, 2013; Von Schnitzler, 2008). As a result of the site's infrastructural characteristics, YouTubers often posted content oriented less around friendship and more toward gaining views and achieving broad algorithmic success, all of which created a commercialized aura that prompted many interviewees to become disillusioned and leave, often after three to five years on the site.

Studying sites longitudinally reveals insight for analyzing responses to infrastructural changes, rhythms of usage, and response to changes in media. For instance, Kottak and Pace (this volume) observed recognizable stages in Brazilian television adoption, moving from novelty to saturation. YouTube interviewees exhibited a participatory rhythm moving from enthusiasm to social intensification to disillusionment. This chapter picks up where the ethnographic story of *Thanks for Watching* (2019) concluded, by delving more deeply into migration theory, rethinking terms such as "digital migration," and proposing a more general rubric of media migration. As YouTubers left, some joined Twitter or Facebook. Yet, YouTube as an orienting community framework did not disappear. Rather, it took new form in new social media sites—a phenomena that became visible by studying the site over time.

Media Migration Histories

Media migrations—including infrastructural disruptions to sociality—have occurred since the earliest online communities. One instance of media migration—albeit without use of the term—appeared in a study of the WELL (Whole Earth 'Lectronic Link), a computer-based community that Howard Rheingold (2000) studied between 1985–1993. Due to financial difficulties, it was sold to an entrepreneur whom many members disliked. Conflict drove some members to establish their own online community, which remained small and eventually experienced its own discord. Migration occurred because members became disenchanted with the community's infrastructure, including its operations and parameters.

Media anthropologists have observed that social media may exhibit a generational aura, such that young people collectively use a site to be with friends on a particular platform (Ito et al., 2010). Participants may leave amid changing age-based demographics. When older adults predominate, or as parents join sites to monitor their children (Miller, 2016), young people may migrate away to seek their own mediated social spaces. Youths in the United States have reportedly migrated away from Facebook and toward Instagram and Snapchat (Ross, 2019). Media migration may also exhibit apparent race and class dimensions as when media scholar danah boyd (2012) observed that many white, affluent, young people began migrating away from MySpace to Facebook, citing concerns about MySpace being overrun with spam and having a perceived broader user demographic in comparison to college-oriented Facebook users in its early years.

Numerous scholarly terms describing such dynamics may be subsumed under the rubric of media migration. Technologists and computer specialists speak of "user migration" when transferring people, data, or hardware from one system to another (Bourreau, Cambini, and Dogan, 2011). Additional terms include "cyber migration" (Zengyan, Yinping, and Lim, 2009), "digital migration" (Lange, 2019, 2020b), and "virtual diaspora" (Boellstorff, 2008). In their study of SNS, Zengyan, Yinping, and Lim (2009) argue that when users switch away from an SNS more permanently, their behavior constitutes "cyber migration."

Previously I used the term "digital migration" to characterize YouTubers' movements between digital sites (Lange, 2020b). This chapter proposes the broader term "media migration" as a productive general rubric, given that not all migration between media is digitally based, nor are digital properties always the most salient experiential characteristics of media migration. The theoretical category of media migration gathers disparate but related concepts to understand mediated movement. The idea is to compare various media migration experiences, and through comparison, identify important characteristics and patterns in media migration.

Media Migration Dynamics and Migration Theory

Migration scholars explore why people leave one experiential context, and how they create meaning when moving elsewhere (Baldassar, 2015; Brettell and Hollifield, 2015; Horst, 2007; Lanz, 2013; McKay, 2018). In media migration, people cease using or centrally orienting around one infrastructural medium and use other sites or services. Yet, what aspects of geographical migration apply when analyzing media migration? Classical migration theory previously emphasized escaping "poverty, conflict, or environmental degradation," yet the migratory landscape is complex, and poverty and violence are no longer the overwhelming factors driving physical migration (Castles, De Haas, and Miller, 2014: 5). Geographical migration often increases with development, "because improved access to education and information, social capital and financial resources increases people's *aspirations* and *capabilities* to migrate, while improved transport and communication also facilitate movement" (emphasis original; Castles, De Haas, and Miller, 2014: 25).

Media migration and geographical migration share similar characteristics. They both often exhibit socially oriented motivations for leaving, aspirations for self-advancement, and sometimes a longing to return. Yet, key differences exist in terms of the practical demands and types of relocation, the degree of emotional intensity of leaving, and whether a return to a participatory environment is feasible. Transnational migration scholarship shows that dispersed families often use social media to engage in intimate communications and maintain relationships (Baldassar, 2015; McKay, 2018, Sinanan, 2017). The present data suggest that these patterns differ from the contact that YouTubers exhibited when migrating to another platform, sometimes only casually maintaining friendships. Nevertheless, general similarities between media migration and geographical migration invite analytical comparisons to identify useful frameworks for analyzing media migration.

Motivations for Leaving

Geographical migration scholarship explores why people leave a social nexus. Such explorations are observable and worthy of investigation on social media, particularly with respect to infrastructural changes. In response to decreased video postings, "farewell videos" announcing participants' departures, and reports of increased Twitter use, I explored whether interviewees viewed their Twitter participation as a "migration" away from YouTube. Similar to geographical migration, interviewees described leaving an inhospitable environment to seek new opportunities.

At a meet-up in Santa Monica, California I interviewed a documentary filmmaker who requested that I refer to her by her YouTube channel name of K80Blog. A white woman in her 20s, she often vlogged about humorous life observations. As depicted in the documentary *Hey Watch This!* (Lange 2020a), she described patterns resembling a media migration away from YouTube.

PATRICIA: Do you think that YouTube is kind of over now, um, or is it still going strong?
K80BLOG: Uhh, I think it's on its way out. I mean, you know, MySpace had its time. Uh, Facebook might be on its way out as well. Twitter will be. You know, I mean that's what's interesting like websites, they don't last very long. [I] think YouTube is on its way out. [I] think it's because it became so corporate and so much about advertising that I think a lot of people are turned off. And then maybe just the novelty of it is kind of worn away.

PATRICIA: Are you still participating on YouTube?
K80BLOG: [Not] like I used to, no.
PATRICIA: Do you stay in touch with friends you met on YouTube?
K80BLOG: Yes, I do. I do. [And] that's what Twitter is good for ... [I'm on Twitter] because I'm keeping connected with the YouTube community.

Similar to other YouTubers, K80Blog faults infrastructural issues, specifically monetization and its effects, for complicating sociality. For her, YouTube was "on its way out," suggesting a decline in enthusiasm and intensity of use.

Many interviewees reported decreasing YouTube usage and instead using Twitter, a micro-blogging and social network site launched in 2006 that updates friends on thoughts and activities (Burgess and Baym, 2020). Twitter users post brief messages or "tweets," which were originally limited to 140 characters but expanded in 2017 to allow 280 characters ("Twitter," n.d.). I joined Twitter in April 2007 (eventually migrating to my current account in 2009 with a better online user name!) and followed publicly posting interviewees. Artifactual analysis supports K80Blog's contention. Her YouTube channel shows three videos posted in May 2020. Prior to that, her latest video was posted in 2015. In contrast, she tweeted 58 times between February and May 2020.

Geographical migration studies suggest that people leave when their current situation presents difficulties or when a new location facilitates achieving aspirations. YouTubers complained that excessive advertising supporting the site's monetization negatively impacted their social environment. Video makers began ending their videos with obnoxious exhortations to "Rate! Comment! Subscribe!" to their YouTube channel. To subscribe to a video maker at that time only required pressing a yellow "Subscribe" button, and an account holder would be alerted at no cost when the video maker uploaded a new video. The site has considerably expanded its technical features to include paid subscription options and monetization metrics that track aggregate video watch time and require minimum subscription thresholds to achieve monetization (Levin, 2018). Interestingly, even amid today's commercialized infrastructure, successful video makers still characterize their persona as oriented to creative self-expression rather than just making money (Stokel-Walker, 2019).

Interview narratives referenced not only individual choices, but also patterns of collective movement. An interviewee named Ryan (thetalesend on YouTube) similarly blamed YouTube's excessive commercial atmosphere for compromising sociality. Ryan was a 29-year-old man of Filipino descent and iReporter for the CNN.com website, who sadly, has since passed away. He posted about social issues, and made humorous vlogs. As recorded in *Hey Watch This!* (Lange, 2020a), he takes a broad perspective of YouTube's future in his interview in Santa Monica. Ryan opined that YouTube would continue offering interesting content, but had ceased to be an effective site for supporting vernacular social media.

RYAN: YouTube is still gonna go strong. But it's not gonna be mainly from user-generated content. It's [gotten] more commercial, you've seen all the ads pop up a lot more. As a community-based, kind of social media thing, YouTube is pretty much done. But as a place for people to find interesting videos, and videos that may be promoted by YouTube, it's not gone yet, but, uh, it may be. Someone [is] bound to make a service that is more user-friendly. And [whenever] someone finds or adopts that area, people will move on. It's like the rest of the internet. We had MySpace, now we have Facebook. No one's on MySpace anymore, now we have Twitter. So, it's just whoever gives the next best step, that's what's gonna go on. That's just the way the internet is.

K80Blog and Ryan reference intensive commercialization as prompting deep concerns about the site's *participatory* future. As in traditional migration theory, deprivation or inability to tolerate one's circumstances prompts change, particularly to fulfill goals of sociality and self-expression.

Notably, several participants used their YouTube name on Twitter, reflecting an internet pattern in which people retain their online names across sites. One study estimated that 45 percent of social network participants on Facebook, Twitter, and Foursquare use the same online name across sites (Li et al., 2018). Transporting a name from a prior social media site also potentially indexes how the original site may organize participants who travel to new interactive contexts. Conceptually, participants maintained an idea of YouTube sociality on a new infrastructural platform, suggesting that infrastructures may continue to retain influence beyond use in their original instantiation.

Migrating to Self-Actualize

Interviewees referenced being influenced by a new site's "novelty," a concept linked to self-actualization opportunities and aspirational aspects of geographical migration. In their study of massively multiplayer online role-playing games, Hou et al. (2011) observed that the novelty of an alternative served as an impetus for migrating to a new site. Closely associated with novelty is the "cool" factor, which by definition continually changes. Gladwell (1997) argues that "the act of discovering what's cool is what causes cool to move on." In interviews, participants described patterned movement to new sites, as seen in prior media adoption studies. A new medium initially feels "novel and strange" and accords prestige to early adopters, but upon saturation in a community, it loses its "novelty and distinction" (Kottak, 2016).

Research suggests that the "cool" factor constitutes much more than superficial fads. Rather, it connotes how infrastructural factors support achieving one's goals. Infrastructures have long been associated with "fantasy and desire," and a dream of "realizing the future" to achieve personal and societal progress and freedom (Larkin, 2013). In a study of public access to information and communication technologies (ICTs), Gomez and Gould (20010: 257) found that "cool" could be defined as a "set of subjective perceptions that make public access to ICT attractive: a combination of unrestricted internet access, friendly operators, and a comfortable space for social interaction." Venues such as libraries that offered instrumental uses of ICTs were perceived as less cool than cyber cafés that supported sociality. In a study of Facebook applications, Neale and Russell-Bennett (2009) quote researchers who argue that cool products are "inspiring and attractive" thus "providing *empowerment* to the user," eliciting the "best of their capacities and abilities" (emphasis added; Parvaz, 2003). Once a platform no longer inspires or empowers, it is no longer "cool." Participants move on to the "next best thing," as Ryan stated.

Floods of obnoxiously presented advertisements, competition between video makers, extreme videos with unsupported claims, and increasingly strict rules about producing content to attain monetization are all examples of infrastructural factors that socially motivated YouTubers cited as participatory complications (Lange, 2017). YouTubers complained that tight copyright prohibitions were enacted to facilitate lucrative partnerships with corporate advertisers. They believed these factors unfairly complicated self-expression and creativity. To the extent that what is "novel" and "cool" feeds creative empowerment, people may migrate away when they can no longer creatively express the self, in contrast to new sites where they hope to attain creative control and social support. Such patterns resemble a common motivation in traditional migration in which people move in the "hopes for a better life," one that enables self-actualization (Jackson, 2013), suggesting that understanding aspiration, infrastructural opportunities, and the "cool" factor are all important for studying both geographical and media migration.

Relation to Diaspora

Scholars call for analyzing the relationship between migration and diaspora (Butler, 2001; Clifford, 1994; Tölölyan, 1996), which typically refers to people who have been dispersed from their homeland. Common characteristics include violent separation, impossibility of return, trauma, and how people negotiate past identities in new locations. Two opposing analytical concerns have emerged. The first protests an overly restricted definition of diaspora to an "ideal type," thus ignoring new socially salient forms of diaspora (Clifford, 1994). An opposite concern opposes overly broad use to the point of disrespectfully losing analytical force, as in the so-called "egg cream diaspora," referring to that beverage's geographically dispersed consumers (Tölölyan, 1996: 10). To what extent, then, does the diaspora rubric apply to media migration?

Media migration is distinct from patterns of "digital diaspora" (Everett, 2009; Laguerre, 2010), at least where that term describes consistently used media that supports already-dispersed groups in an ongoing way to achieve economic, political, and social goals. The term digital diaspora has been used to characterize how a diaspora might "express and perform its *digital* identity" (emphasis original; Laguerre, 2010). However, media migration would become salient if a diaspora moved from one platform or media to another as its central participatory locus.

Research in media anthropology reveals that, infrastructurally, when a platform that is important to a social group is shut down, participants may feel intense sadness and loss. They may form a "virtual diaspora" (Boellstorff, 2008; Pearce, 2009) that seeks to bond on a different media platform. The term "virtual diaspora" (Boellstorff, 2008) describes forced and often traumatic mediated movement between online, virtual worlds, and is an important sub-category of media migration.

Participants may experience intense feelings over the loss of central interactive loci, particularly in marginalized communities in which online connections are vital to sociality, such as in disabled groups. In his study of *Second Life*, a site in which people play and interact in player-created graphical environments, anthropologist Tom Boellstorff (2008: 197) observed that "virtual diasporas" form "when a virtual world goes out of existence and some of its residents flee to other virtual worlds." Similarly, players of a massively multiplayer online game called Uru formed a virtual diaspora that Pearce (2009) called the "Uru Diaspora." When Uru developers discontinued the game, players migrated to platforms such as *Second Life*. Participants were "shocked" and exhibited "symptoms of posttraumatic stress" upon losing their social "homeland" (Pearce, 2009: 89). The players reportedly experienced "shared trauma" due to the "deep emotional connection" they formed with Uru community members—some of whom were disabled and relied on internet enclaves to obtain resources and facilitate social interaction (Pearce, 2009: 89). Hou et al. (2011: 1893) use the term "migration" to describe players' feelings of isolation when a game is shut down or no longer meets their needs, thus losing connection to their ludic "place of origin." Boellstorff (2008: 197–198) also observed "lesser forms of virtual diaspora" in which sites simply become "less popular" and participants migrate elsewhere, often bringing friends with them.

The data suggest that the present YouTubers did not form a tight-knit diaspora in traditional or updated media senses. The break that YouTubers experienced was voluntary rather than due to forced circumstances such as a site closure. Interviewees often said they left because the environment no longer met their needs, yet many retained connections to YouTube and its participants via other social media. Whether or not an instance of media migration constitutes a "diaspora," or group that suffers a violent break from a social nexus, must be evaluated in each case. However, given that some mediated groups have experienced infrastructural disruptions to central forms of interaction in ways that resemble diasporas, further ethnographic research should explore the relationship between new types of diaspora and media migration.

Migratory Return

In both geographical and media migration, participants may return to a prior social context. In her anthropological study of geographical migration, Brettell (2003: 47) quotes Gmelch (1980) who defines return migration as "the movement of emigrants back to their homeland to resettle." In the early 20th century, despite the costs, an estimated 25 percent of the 16 million Europeans who emigrated to the United States eventually returned to Europe, suggesting that return is a crucial area of migration studies (Brettell, 2003). Media participants at times similarly expressed a wish to return.

Yet, return is not always possible physically or online. A place of origin may no longer exist, such as when political boundaries change or a site permanently closes. YouTube still exists and people may post videos, yet personal and social factors may complicate a robust return. Many participants have not yet returned to YouTube to post videos to their original account with the same intensity, in part because their "media cohort," or group who arrived at the same time on the site also left (Lange, 2019). Still, interviewees sometimes conceptualized future participation in terms of a possible return. An interviewee who asked to be referred to by her YouTube channel name of lemonette illustrated a common theme. She is a white woman now in her 60s who helped organize YouTube meet-ups in the southern U.S. and was very social on the site. Often vlogging from her car, her videos are heartfelt and comedic.

In a birthday video posted in 2011 that she calls a "comeback video," or what I call a "return video" (Lange, 2019), she says she no longer makes videos but keeps up with YouTube friends by reading their Facebook posts. This disclosure suggests at least a partial migration to a different social media site—one that does not orient around the time-consuming activity of making videos. In her video *Check in with Lemonette* posted in 2013, she admits having lost interest in YouTube when the environment shifted to boasting "how many views you got," rendering the site no longer "fun" for her. She notes that receiving kind comments still gives her a warm feeling—and a twinge of guilt for not posting videos. She does not promise to make new videos, but hedges saying, "I'm not going to say I'm *not* going to make any either. We'll just wait and see what happens." Like many social YouTubers, she leaves the door open to return.

Issues complicating a full return for YouTubers included health challenges, family responsibilities, departure of friends from the site, and most especially, decreased interest given the site's commercialized infrastructure. Notably, participants were often reluctant to declare that they would never again post videos. Most YouTubers in the study retained the possibility that they might return, although not exhibiting the full force of prolific video-making that they exhibited when they first joined. Videos posted a decade later reveal a desire to communicate one day through video and to keep connected with members of an envisioned YouTube community—whether on YouTube or on other sites.

A Collective Conversation About Media Migration

Media migration scholarship should explore specific types of media migration as they emerge in socio-technical contexts. Scholars should examine arrivals and departures, and explore nuanced uses of the concept that pertain to mediated dynamics. For example, in traditional migration, ethnographic research shows that returnees may encounter difficulties in re-adjusting socially back home (Horst, 2007). Researchers might explore whether these and other dynamics are present when participants attempt to "return" back to a favorite media platform. Comparisons bring enhanced understanding of media usage patterns over time.

Types of Media Migration

The YouTube case study revealed that media migration exhibits several forms: *radical migration*, *in-migration*, and *conceptual migration* (Lange, 2019). In radical migration, a participant stops using a medium altogether. A YouTube participant may leave their channel nominally open, but post no videos, or post so infrequently as to effectively keep open a dead channel. In-migration refers to abandoning a prior channel and creating a new one *on the same site* that expresses a participant's current interests, goals, or persona. For example, an interviewee who wished to be referred to by her YouTube channel name of jenluv37 posted a video in 2012 in which she announced opening a new make-up review channel. Her prior channel exhibited no new videos after her announcement. Conversely, her new channel consistently showed many new videos from 2012 to 2020, often including several per week.

In conceptual migration, a participant may stop using a site or vastly reduce their usage, yet the idea of the site continues to provide an *orienting social context* for interaction on new sites. Conceptual migration is a useful umbrella term that folds in the "lesser virtual diaspora" that Boellstorff (2008) referenced—without overgeneralizing the term "diaspora." Conceptual migration does not presume the traumatic effects of diaspora, yet recognizes the desire for social continuity across sites. "YouTubers" may still wish to interact after they leave YouTube for Twitter. For example, K80Blog contextualized her decreased usage on YouTube by explaining that Twitter helps her keep "connected with the YouTube community." YouTube continues to provide a framework for organizing sociality on Twitter, but it is conceptual rather than practically infrastructural once participants no longer use the YouTube platform.

Departures and Arrivals

This chapter analyzed motivations for *leaving* YouTube. However, arrival stories are also crucial to the media migration saga. Anthropologists have analyzed the impact of arriving on immigrants, ramifications for the host populations, and tensions between them (Brettell, 2003; Horst, 2007; Rytter, 2019; Salem-Murdock, 1989). Colson (2003) argues that more research is needed in studying the impacts of new arrivals on existing communities. Similar categorical impacts are observable on social media. On YouTube, tensions emerged when popular users of the video-based Vine service migrated to YouTube after Vine was closed (Alexander, 2018). Vine was a video-hosting service founded in 2012, in which people shared 6-second long, looped video clips.

Viners with large audiences migrated to YouTube and Instagram after Vine uploads were disabled in 2016 ("Vine," n.d.). Referred to in YouTube videos as "Vine refugees," controversy erupted when certain popular Viners achieved rapid success on YouTube (Alexander, 2018). By transitioning their aesthetics to longer-form videos, successful Viners brought many of their followers to YouTube. YouTubers faulted Viners such as Jake Paul and Logan Paul for their abrasive personalities and negative impact on YouTube.

Using migration terminology, one pundit opined that the Viners' immigration to YouTube "may have started out as an invasion, but it's become a permanent settlement" (Alexander,

2018). Researchers on Vine lamented the death of that infrastructure's technical 6-second video requirement, which provided challenging and unique creative opportunities that spawned distinct aesthetics (Browne, 2017). The Vine tale may be just the beginning. Reports suggest that governmental bans on the short-form, video-sharing site of TikTok may prompt new waves of media migration to YouTube (Doval and Sarkar, 2020). Studying media migration arrivals—both voluntary and forced due to site closures—are very important to understand media migration's impacts, including the interactive dynamics on the receiving media service and its participants.

Studies of media participants' arrivals or returns to a former site might draw inspiration from return migration rubrics. Important analytical categories may emerge, such as examining closely how current participants on a social media site treat new arrivals, and whether returnees' behaviors exhibit similar or different patterns depending upon which media sites they are originating from. Horst (2007) for example, found that current residents felt that returnees to Jamaica exhibited different behavior depending on whether they were returning from England versus the United States. Research on migration and transnational movement may offer meaningful analytical categories for exploring new forms of media migration.

Conclusion

Media migration away from a particular medium is often prompted by dissatisfaction with the infrastructure of a prior site as well as opportunities and technical affordances of new sites. Media migration is an important chapter in the human mediation saga, particularly in terms of understanding the infrastructural reasons that complicate a site's perception as socially inviting and personally empowering. For socially oriented vloggers in the study, a prime migration motivation involved their disenchantment with YouTube's monetization requirements, changes in technical features, and heavily competitive, commercialized atmosphere. Infrastructures are never just about physical parameters but also include the economic, political, legal, and social systems with which they are intertwined (Larkin, 2013). Understanding the forces that prompt changes in media sites and services is important to design equitable interactive spaces that support participants' goals. Achieving self-expression online amid services that are owned by a few corporations presents challenges and may require activism to envision equitable participatory opportunities (Lange, 2017).

An important goal for this chapter has been to propose an umbrella term that gathers disparate phenomena to facilitate a collective anthropological conversation about media migration dynamics. It has presented a rubric that at times drew on traditional migration theory to explore how and why people break with prior media. It also provided analytical categories particular to media migration. Future research should investigate which type of media migration is present ethnographically. Not all online migration stories, for example, yield an emotionally driven "virtual diaspora" but may still exhibit a "conceptual migration" in which the sociality of a prior site retains socio-emotional force. Nor are all migrations online oriented around "digital migration" as the key salient aspect of their movement.

Future media migration studies might address: 1) motivations for leaving a site, service, or medium; 2) motivations for choosing a new site; 3) the impact of leaving a prior site or social group; and 4) the impact of the arrival of a new group. Knowing why people migrate away from media reveals important clues about what different cultural groups expect from media to fulfill their goals and desires for achieving self-expression and sociality. The term *media migration* broadly addresses media usage at points of origin and arrival, thus encouraging researchers to explore nuanced dimensions and sub-types that are salient for particular social groups. Media migration serves as a general rubric for understanding a wide range of phenomena that support human mediation, and offers rich terrain for understanding human interaction and creativity.

References

Alexander, J. (2018) "Vine's Closure Led to YouTube's Most Debated Trend," *Polygon*, January 17, available at www.polygon.com/2018/1/17/16901392/vine-youtube-jake-logan-paul-pewdiepie (accessed May 13, 2020).

Baldassar, L. (2015) "Guilty Feelings and the Guilt Trip: Emotions and Motivation in Migration and Transnational Caregiving Emotion," *Space and Society* 16: 81–89.

Boellstorff, T. (2008) *Coming of Age in Second Life: An Anthropologist Explores the Virtually Human*, Princeton, NJ: Princeton University Press.

Bourreau, M., Cambini, C., and Dogan, P. (2011) "Access Pricing, Competition, and Incentives to Migrate From 'Old' to 'New' Technology," *HKS Faculty Research Working Paper Series RWP11-029*, John F. Kennedy School of Government, Harvard University.

boyd, d. (2009) "Social Media is Here to Stay ... Now What?" Microsoft Research Tech Fest, Redmond, Washington, February 26, available at www.danah.org/papers/talks/MSRTechFest2009.html (accessed March 27, 2020).

boyd, d. (2012) "White Flight in Networked Publics? How Race and Class Shaped American Teen Engagement with Myspace and Facebook," in L. Nakamura and P. A. Chow-White (eds), *Race after the Internet*, New York: Routledge: 203–222.

Brettell, C. B. (2003) *Anthropology and Migration: Essays on Transnationalism, Ethnicity, and Identity*, Walnut Creek, CA: Altamira Press.

Brettell, C. B., and Hollifield, J. F. (2015) "Introduction," in C. B. Brettel and J. F. Hollifield (eds), *Migration Theory: Talking Across Disciplines*, 3rd ed., New York: Routledge: 1–36.

Browne, R. (2017) "The Death of Vine, and the Volatile Nature of New Media," *Researching Sociology @ LSE*, June 26, available at http://eprints.lse.ac.uk/82199/ (accessed May 13, 2020).

Burgess, J. and Baym, N. K. (2020) *Twitter: A Biography*, New York: New York University Press.

Burgess, J. and Green, J. (2018 [2009]) *YouTube: Online Video and Participatory Culture*, Cambridge, UK: Polity Press.

Butler, K. D. (2001) "Defining Diaspora, Refining a Discourse," *Diaspora: A Journal of Transnational Studies*, 10 (2): 189–219.

Castles, S., de Haas, H., and Miller, M. J. (2014) *The Age of Migration: International Population Movements in the Modern World*, 5th ed., New York: Guilford.

Clifford, J. (1994) "Diasporas," *Cultural Anthropology*, 9 (3): 302–338.

Colson, E. (2003) "Forced Migration and the Anthropological Response," *Journal of Refugee Studies*, 16 (1): 1–18.

Doval, P. and Sarkar, J. (2020) "TikTok Stars Migrate to other Platforms," *The Times of India*, July 1, available at: https://timesofindia.indiatimes.com/business/india-business/tiktok-stars-migrate-to-other-platforms/articleshow/76720891.cms (accessed July 20, 2021).

Everett, A. (2009) *Digital Diaspora: A Race for Cyberspace*, Albany: State University of New York Press.

Gladwell, M. (1997) "The Coolhunt," *The New Yorker*, March 17, available at www.newyorker.com/magazine/1997/03/17/the-coolhunt (accessed May 12, 2020).

Gomez, R. and Gould, E. (2010) "The 'Cool Factor' of Public Access to ICT," *Information Technology & People*, 23 (3): 247–264.

Horst, H. A. (2007) "'You Can't Be in Two Places at Once': Rethinking Transnationalism Through Jamaican Return Migration," *Identities: Global Studies in Culture and Power*, 14: 63–83.

Hou, A. C. Y., Chern, C-C., Chen, H-G., and Chen, Y-C. (2011) "'Migrating to a New Virtual World': Exploring MMORPG Switching through Human Migration Theory," *Computers in Human Behavior*, 27: 1892–1903.

Ito, M., S. Baumer, M. Bittani, d. boyd, R. Cody, B. Herr-Stephenson, H.A. Horst, P. G. Lange, D. Mahendran, K. Z. Martínez, C.J. Pascoe, D. Perkel, L. Robinson, C. Sims, and L. Tripp (2010) *Hanging Out, Messing Around and Geeking Out: Kids Living and Learning with New Media*, Boston, MA: The MIT Press.

Jackson, M. (2013) *The Wherewithal of Life: Ethics, Migration and the Question of Well-Being*, Berkeley, CA: University of California Press.

Kaufman, L. (2014) "Chasing their Star, on YouTube," *New York Times*, February 1, available at www.nytimes.com/2014/02/02/business/chasing-their-star-on-youtube.html (accessed December 12, 2020).

Kottak, C. P. (2016 [1990]) *Prime-Time Society: An Anthropological Analysis of Television and Culture*, New York: Routledge.

Kottak, C. P. and Pace, Richard. (2022) "A Longitudinal Study of Media in Brazil," in E. Costa et al. (eds), *The Routledge Companion to Media Anthropology*, New York: Routledge.

Laguerre, M. S. (2010) "Digital Diaspora: Definition and Models," in A. Alonso, and P. J. Oiarzabal (eds), *Diasporas in the New Media Age: Identity, Politics, and Community*, Reno: University of Nevada Press: 49–64.

Lange, P. G. (2017) "Participatory Complications in Interactive, Video-Sharing Environments," in L. Hjorth, H. Horst, A. Galloway, and G. Bell (eds), *The Routledge Companion to Digital Ethnography*, New York: Routledge: 147–157.

Lange, P. G. (2019) *Thanks for Watching: An Anthropological Study of Video Sharing on YouTube*, Louisville, CO: University Press of Colorado.

Lange, P. G. (2020a) Director, *Hey Watch This! Sharing the Self Through Media*, Ethnographic film, 54 minutes.

Lange, P. G. (2020b) "Digital Migration," *anthro{dendum}*, April 11, available at https://anthrodendum.org/2020/04/11/digital-migration/ (accessed May 6, 2020).

Lanz, T. (2013) "Migration," *Oxford Bibliographies*, July 24, available at www.oxfordbibliographies.com/view/document/obo-9780199766567/obo-9780199766567-0098.xml (accessed May 7, 2020).

Larkin, B. (2013) "The Politics and Poetics of Infrastructure," *Annual Review of Anthropology*, 42: 327–343.

Levin, S. (2018) "YouTube's Small Creators Pay Price of Policy Changes after Logan Paul Scandal," *The Guardian*, January 18, available at www.theguardian.com/technology/2018/jan/18/youtube-creators-vloggers-ads-logan-paul (accessed May 20, 2020).

Li, Y., Peng, Y., Zhang, Z., Wu, M., Xu, Q., and Yin, H. (2018) "A Deep Dive into User Display Names Across Social Networks," *Information Sciences*, 447: 186–204.

Madianou, M. and Miller, D. (2012) *Migration and New Media: Transnational Families and Polymedia*, Abingdon, UK: Routledge.

Merriam-Webster Dictionary (n.d.) "Infrastructure," available at www.merriam-webster.com/dictionary/infrastructure (accessed July 14, 2021).

Miller, D., E. Costa, N. Haynes, T. McDonald, R. Nicolescu, J. Sinanan, J. Spyer, S. Venkatraman, and X. Wang. (2016). *How the World Changed Social Media*, London: UCL Press.

McDonald, T. (2016). *Social Media in Rural China*, London: UCL Press.

McKay, D. (2018) "Sent Home: Mapping the Absent Child into Migration through Polymedia," *Global Networks*, 18 (1): 133–150.

Neale, L. and Russell-Bennett, R. (2009) "What Value do Users Derive from Social Networking Applications?" *First Monday*, 14 (9), available at https://journals.uic.edu/ojs/index.php/fm/article/download/2506/2278 (accessed May 11, 2020).

Parvaz, D. (2003) "They're on a Quest for What's Cool—Here and Everywhere," *Seattle Post–Intelligencer*, November 20, available at http://seattlepi.nwsource.com/lifestyle/149002_coolhunt.html (accessed May 12, 2020).

Pearce, C. (2009) *Communities of Play: Emergent Cultures in Multiplayer Games and Virtual Worlds*, Cambridge, MA: The MIT Press.

Pink, S. (2015) *Doing Sensory Ethnography*, 2nd ed., Los Angeles: Sage.

Postill, J. (2017) "Remote Ethnography: Studying Culture from Afar," in L. Hjorth, H. Horst, A. Galloway, and G. Bell (eds), *The Routledge Companion to Digital Ethnography*, New York: Routledge: 61–69.

Rheingold, H. (2000 [1993]) *The Virtual Community: Homesteading on the Electronic Frontier*, Cambridge, MA: MIT Press.

Ross, S. (2019). "Being Real on Fake Instagram: Likes, Images, and Media Ideologies of Value," *Journal of Linguistic Anthropology*, 29 (3): 359–374.

Rytter, M. (2019) "Writing Against Integration: Danish Imaginaries of Culture, Race and Belonging," *Ethnos*, 84 (4): 678–697.

Salem-Murdock, M. (1989) *Arabs and Nubians in New Halfa: A Study of Settlement and Irrigation*, Salt Lake City: University of Utah Press.

Sinanan, J. (2017) *Social Media in Trinidad*, London, UK: UCL Press.

"Stickam" (n.d.) *Wikipedia*. https://en.wikipedia.org/wiki/Stickam (accessed May 2, 2022.

Stokel-Walker, C. (2019) *YouTubers: How YouTube Shook Up TV and Created a New Generation of Stars*, Kingston Upon Thames: Canbury Press.

Tölölyan, K. (1996) "Rethinking Diaspora(s): Stateless Power in the Transnational Moment," *Diaspora: A Journal of Transnational Studies*, 5 (1): 3–36.

"Twitter" (n.d.) *Wikipedia*. https://en.wikipedia.org/wiki/Twitter (accessed May 2, 2022).

"Vine" (n.d.) Wikipedia. https://en.wikipedia.org/wiki/Vine_(service) (accessed May 2, 2022).

Von Schnitzler, A. (2008) "Citizenship Prepaid: Water, Calculability, and Techno-politics in South Africa," *Journal of South African Studies*, 34(4): 899–917.

Wahl-Jorgensen, K. (2018) "The Emotional Architecture of Social Media." In Z. Papacharissi (ed.), *A Networked Self and Platforms, Stories, Connections*, New York: Routledge, 77–93.

Zengyan, C., Yinping, Y., and Lim, J. (2009) "Cyber Migration: An Empirical Investigation on Factors that Affect Users' Switch Intentions in Social Networking Sites," *Proceedings of the 42nd Hawaii International Conference on System Sciences*, available at https://citeseerx.ist.psu.edu/viewdoc/download?doi=10.1.1.402.4797&rep=rep1&type=pdf (accessed January 18, 2021).

Zuboff, S. (2019) *Surveillance Capitalism*, New York: Public Affairs.

7

THE DIGITALLY NATURAL

Hypomediacy and the "Really Real" in Game Design

Thomas M. Malaby

'Dumb Money' Is on GameStop, and It's Beating Wall Street at Its Own Game

GameStop shares have soared 1,700 percent as millions of small investors, egged on by social media, employ a classic Wall Street tactic to put the squeeze – on Wall Street.
Matt Phillips and Taylor Lorenz, New York Times, *January 27, 2021*

Wall Street clearly underestimated a generation raised on highly coordinated Friday night World of Warcraft raids.
James F. Puerini (@J_Puerini), Twitter, 8:49 pm, Jan 27, 2021

The "fuzzy logic" (Bourdieu, 1977: 163) by which human beings improvise in new situations with old materials has long been known to anthropology, and anthropologists often find themselves pointing to practical innovation when making the case for how practice (alongside materiality and representation) can be consequential in social life. In the early 2021 stock market event referenced above, with its remarkable lifting of GameStop's (and other companies') stock market value by a loosely coordinated "raid" (springing from the subreddit r/wallstreetbets), Puerini invites us to consider the ways in which digitally networked games may be particularly potent sites for the generation of such improvisatory dispositions, and this may be because games are an increasingly prevalent aspect of the infrastructures that "generate the ambient environment of everyday life" (Larkin, 2013: 328). If we are to acknowledge that games today – primarily digitally networked ones – are making their presence felt in such ways, is there something about the combination of digital technologies and games that has made this kind and scale of impact possible? Is it possible to ask questions about how digital technologies have influenced games without indulging in one or another kind of digital exceptionalism?

To answer these questions means taking seriously the possibility that the infrastructures of digitally mediated environments can become naturalized for their users, just as more familiar infrastructures, such as road systems, do. By "digital infrastructure" here I mean the relatively durable structures that enable and constrain social action through the design and implementation of a combination of material technologies and coded protocols. While I have generally employed the word "architecture" in similar ways, media anthropology has rightly suggested that "infrastructure" signals more effectively both the broader scale, in time and space, as well as the ambient or implicit quality of infrastructure (Larkin, 2013). But I recommend here some further consideration of how this taken-for-granted quality is achieved, specifically the extent to which it may depend on the remediation of game elements in digital media. It is easy to recognize that computer games make use of remediation, "the formal logic by which new media refashion prior media forms" (Bolter and Grusin, 1999: 273) – the remediations of elements from cinema, print fiction, and other media are quite plain – and in this chapter I suggest that we recognize and consider how this process also includes the remediation of elements from analogue game design.

The empirical work presented below is primarily illustrative, and relies on work conducted through the Digital Cultures Collaboratory at the University of Wisconsin-Milwaukee. Rather than undertake solely more traditional ethnographic work (such as participant observation with the players of games, or with their designers), this group has supplemented this by approaching the playing and close reading of both analogue and digital games as an opportunity to examine them as infrastructural propositions; that is, we see any game as a complex presentation of constraints and possibilities that can command player attention and generate interpretable outcomes. Games, therefore, are contrived projects of the social institution that makes them (usually a specific, historically and culturally located game company or designer). Our approach shares qualities with material culture studies in its focus on the artifact, and is meant to challenge the tendency to treat digital infrastructures as the ambient background for social action and offer theoretical insights applicable to extended, ethnographically informed work.

Whereas previously my focus has been on developing an approach to games that helps us account for their capacity to command attention and contribute to institutional projects, here I wish to focus on how digital infrastructures so easily become taken as natural, and ask two questions: First, what can we learn about how this happens by examining the remediation of analogue game design elements in computer games? Second, how do these gaming-generated infrastructures become ambient and persuasive in setting reality for a potentially wide range of digital activity and sociality? After discussing and illustrating game remediation, I turn briefly to the topic of ritual, one that I have found to be repeatedly productive for checking our thinking about the cultural form of game. In this context, our approach to ritual can help us think more deeply about how digital games find new ways to produce what Clifford Geertz called the "really real," the "aura of utter actuality" that characterizes everything that goes without saying; the bedrock understandings of how the world works that inform our action (1973: 112). My aim is to suggest that when we give the cultural form of game its due (as we have for ritual and bureaucracy) – that is, when we incorporate a robust consideration of game features into our analyses – we will be in a better position to undertake the ethnographic work necessary for understanding the increasing social impact of computer games and how they contribute to the digital structuring of reality.

What is at stake here is nothing less than the often-silent dispositions toward how the world *is* that inform how we act within and beyond digitally mediated contexts. As shown by the GameStop phenomenon, social action is always already proceeding from practical understandings of what constraints and possibilities exist, not only within one context, but across contexts. There is an improvisatory attitude implicit in our engagement with the infrastructures, digital and otherwise, that we encounter, and we furthermore extend the action we find to be reliable into other domains. For media anthropology this is vital, because it is about the relationship between, on one hand, the cultural forms long available for institutional use (bureaucracy, ritual, game) and, on the other, the various media, and now digital media, through which such forms can be deployed to engage subjectivities and contribute to the construction of the real. This chapter is thus deeply indebted to several longstanding conversations in media anthropology, and especially to sections II and V of the landmark *Media Worlds: Anthropology in New Terrain* (Ginsburg, Abu-Lughod, and Larkin, 2002). Section II focuses on attempts to produce national subjects through media, while Section V pushes anthropology to look to the forms of media in all their materiality, most pointedly in Larkin's treatment of Nigerian cinema theatres (Larkin, 2002). In the collection, Richard Wilk, in his study of television and the national imaginary in Belize, articulated the common theme of several of these authors when he wrote of "the opportunity to think beyond programming and content to the form of the medium itself, to the way television constitutes a new form of cosmology and creates new social worlds" (Wilk, 2002: 171). Relatedly, Nick Couldry, a sociologist of media, asked directly of broadcast media how it contributed to the construction of reality, and looked to anthropology and its handling of cultural forms, specifically ritual, for insight into these processes (2003). I am inspired by that move, but wish to stay "closer to the ground" of mediated social action. The anthropological handling of both media and ritual have their best insights to offer when they provide the tools to delve closely into the practice and materiality as they unfold for participants.

Games and Remediation

For scholars interested in games, there has been a vexed fault line that has appeared to separate treatments of so-called "analogue" or "offline" games from "digital games." Digital exceptionalism in game studies is most visibly, and for scholarship consequentially, realized in perhaps the most active current scholarly association for studying games: DiGRA, or the Digital Games Research Association. There are nonetheless scholars who have sought to trouble this boundary (e.g., LaLone, 2019), and this group includes David Graeber, who meditates on how *Dungeons & Dragons* (D&D) resides in between the bureaucratically ordered structures of their rule systems and printed statistical resources, on one hand, and the contingency of their imaginative social play on the other. He goes on to raise questions about the digital remediation of game elements in the games that followed in D&D's wake. After noting D&D's peculiar mix of (anarchistic) free imagination and bureaucratic order (through its reliance on numbers to resolve events), he continues (2015: 189):

> Still, the introduction of numbers, the standardization of types of character, ability, monster, treasure, spell, the concept of ability scores and hit-points, had profound effects when one moved from the world of 6-, 8-, 12- and 20-sided dice to one of digital interfaces. Computer games could turn fantasy into an almost entirely bureaucratic procedure: accumulation of points, the raising of levels, and so on … This in turn set off a move in the other direction, by introducing role-playing back into the computer games (Elfquest, World of Warcraft …), in a constant weaving back and forth of the imperatives of poetic and bureaucratic technology.

Graeber seizes upon a transformation of media that demands our attention, a transformation of previously explicit elements into the veiled computation of code. His treatment tends toward a dichotomy, however, with Weberian rational bureaucracy on one side and the anarchy of free imagination on the other. What he does not take up is how analogue game elements such as the dice actually lie somewhere between these extremes. Neither bureaucratically determinative nor unbounded in their possibility, they are the tools for generating (stochastic) contingencies, the kinds of indeterminacy that, it should be noted, are anathema to bureaucracy (and digital computation, strictly understood).[1] In D&D, these stochastic contingencies circulate with other sources of the indeterminate (e.g., player and Dungeon Master's [DM] performances, and their guesswork about each other), as well as the various kinds of constraints that we find in games. But even these constraints, we must remember, are not simply rules (the bureaucratic) in other forms. The material or architectural (battle maps, dice trays, miniatures, DM screens) are their own kind of constraint, as are the social conventions (however partial) that shape participants' behaviours.

With this in mind, Graeber's meditation on the shift from the analogue to the digital for D&D takes on new dimensions. Rather than a ping-ponging back and forth between bureaucracy and imagination, we begin to notice that analogue games often (have had to) present their contrivance in explicit ways, especially when it comes to elements that allow for the generation of stochastic contingencies. Well-shuffled decks of cards, spinners, and dice are just the most familiar examples of game design elements vital for the production of indeterminacy beyond that introduced by players' actions and guesses (as well as alongside external sources of stochastic contingency, such as weather – for outdoor games, or even "lag" for networked computer games). What happens when these elements, as well as constraints such as rule systems, are remediated in the context of digital and digitally networked technologies so as to be less explicit, and more a part of the game's infrastructure? To put it bluntly: Does the experience of playing games that have increasingly implicit constraints and contingencies transform the impact it can have on dispositions cultivated through playing and related claims about the real?

One of the digital games that raised these questions some time ago was *Take Back Illinois*, Ian Bogost's single-player, flash-based game produced for the Illinois House Republican campaign of 2004. Players encountered the game on the campaign's website, and four versions (sub-games) of the game were released, three highlighting a different policy position of its sponsor, while the fourth focused on demonstrating the potential impact of the player-voter's participation in the campaign. In the policy sub-games, the player was presented with a few city blocks (or the state, depending upon the version) in 2.5D, slider-like controls, several blocks of information, and a calendar representing time marching on. (There is also a striking be-suited figure, every inch an expression of white, male, establishment power, looming over the frame from the lower right. This is Tom Cross, the Republican Illinois House Minority Leader at the time.) In the sub-game built in relation to the party's policies on capping medical malpractice awards, several hospitals were prominent on the landscape, and avatars of residents could be seen moving about, each with an emoji over their heads indicating happiness, dissatisfaction, or illness. The ill residents could infect others as they walked about the city and hospitals, if doctors were available and incented to work in them. The sliders represented simple metrics for "Medical Research Support" and "Maximum Non-Economic Damages" (see Figure 7.1).

Bogost's own discussion of his game focuses on the potential games have for modelling complex systems and reflecting ideologies, which they certainly do have (Bogost, 2006), but for the purposes of this chapter this game illustrates the remediation of game design elements in a helpful way. While its maker, Bogost, has framed its political action as a kind of persuasion – that is, as a rhetorical move taking place in a different guise – I would like to suggest that this and other games that make use of implicit game elements are not best understood in rhetorical terms. Instead, I suggest that they operate much more like ritual in how they enact and verify a particular reality. But first let us consider remediation further, as its application for games calls for some special handling.

In *Remediation*, Bolter and Grusin devote one chapter to computer games and focus their discussion primarily on the ways in which computer games remediate elements from tv, film, and computers themselves (1999: 88–103). This is an understandable emphasis and is consistent

The Digitally Natural

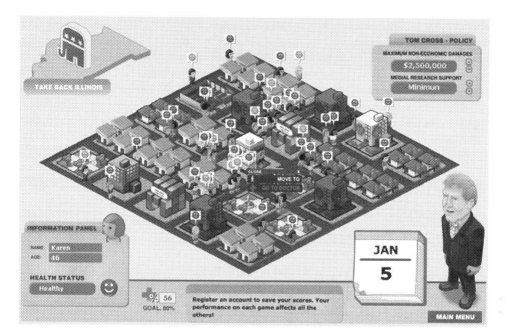

Figure 7.1 A screenshot of Persuasive Games' *Take Back Illinois* (medical malpractice version)
Source: http://persuasivegames.com/game/takebackillinois

with treatments of remediation elsewhere in the book. One of its effects, however, is that the discussion of player experience tends to hinge upon questions of visual fidelity and verisimilitude; in fact, the "player" is regularly replaced with the "viewer." At several points the authors do make note of the player's intimate involvement with the computer game through their input, but the overall discussion is framed with reference to television and film and the associations of these technologies with surveillance and monitoring (1999: 94). In this visual approach, two phenomena are central: hypermediacy, "a style of visual representation whose goal is to remind the viewer of the medium"; and (transparent) immediacy, "a style of visual representation whose goal is to make the viewer forget the presence of the medium" (1999: 272).

Grusin and Bolter join anthropologists in recognizing that, as I discuss below, at stake in the enactment of cultural forms like ritual and game is the construction of the real, but here this seems to be accomplished primarily through the transformations of visual experience: "Such games seek the real, sometimes through transparency and sometimes through hypermediacy – sometimes by encouraging the player to look through the surface of the screen and sometimes by dwelling on the surface with its multiplicity of mediated objects" (1999: 94). Notably, however, they do begin their chapter with an acknowledgement of how computer games remediate elements, and not necessarily visual ones, from games themselves (1999: 89), and in a later work Grusin extends this discussion with a consideration of mimesis and embodiment that leaves much of the bias toward the visual behind (Grusin, 2010).

It is this aspect of remediation that I suggest could be especially fruitful for anthropological considerations of digital games. What is at stake in the implicit incorporation (rather than explicit showcasing) of game design elements as they are remediated in digital games is, I suggest, something more than "(transparent) immediacy" (for a viewer). This phrase both accentuates the visual at the expense of these other considerations, and also misleadingly suggests that mediation could ever be wholly absent (immediate). If "hypermediacy" is "a style of remediation whose goal is to remind the [user] of the medium" (1999: 272), then here I would offer the term "hypomediacy" to pair with it, meaning the style of remediation whose goal is to conceal the medium from the user. Successful hypomediation in computer games and other digital contexts may be part and parcel of how their infrastructures become naturalized for their users. The advent of speech-driven interfaces (Alexa, Siri, and others) is perhaps the most common example of hypomediation as of this writing, and have for many users become naturalized infrastructures, ones that open up a vast array of opportunities for new institutional projects in even more intimate spaces. We can also note how the first-person perspective used in many computer games, but especially "first person shooters" (and, notably, also Pokémon Go), has served as a hypomediation that can be found in now-ubiquitous mapping software (such as GoogleMaps or AppleMaps). But can we say more about how such infrastructure, with the constraints and possibilities it offers for social action, involves the players of computer games in the production of the real?

Ritual and the Real

In attempting to answer such questions about how infrastructures help to produce the real, I have often found myself drawn back in time in our disciplinary conversations, if you will, than forward, and most often that has been to anthropological treatments of ritual and performance. Our discipline's long-fruitful approach to ritual can serve as a paradigm for how we may best approach a different cultural form, that of the game, provided we are ready to acknowledge ritual and game as peers, in a sense – ontologically on a par with each other (and perhaps with a third, bureaucracy).[2] While ritual and game differ in key respects, one of the great virtues of anthropology's approach to ritual has been how we long ago de-coupled our handling of particular ritual events from any determinate effects on participants; in short, anthropology treats rituals as fraught and provisional projects, any instance of which may succeed or fail. Games, of course, share this quality, but with a distinct and explicit commitment to producing such contingencies – without them, the "fix is in" (the game has been rigged) and the game becomes invalid (Malaby, 2007).

What is more, Clifford Geertz, and later Edward Schieffelin, drew anthropological attention to how ritual, as a cultural form, can verify – through its performance of cosmic orderings in the practice of the messy everyday – institutionally sponsored claims about the "really real." This performative construction of reality was, as Schieffelin stressed, not simply a matter of powerfully imparting symbolic information. It was accomplished through the concrete realization of an account of the world, as an active process of creation by its participants not reducible to one dimension of representation, practice, or materiality. And while certainly subject to various contingencies, rituals – as Lévi-Strauss recognized (1966: 31) – on the whole aim for something other than the surprise inherent in games. (In this discussion, I follow Schieffelin in taking a performative approach to ritual. For a full definition and discussion, see Tambiah, 1985: 128.)[3]

As Schieffelin makes clear, the constitution of the "really real" (almost always a project of a sponsoring institution) occurs along several dimensions, but the one to highlight here is the "dialogic" dimension – the back and forth between the audience and the enactors. As has been mentioned, the line between ritual and game is not absolute, and one way in which it is blurred concerns the ways in which ritual can, like games, make performative demands on its audience. This is common in rituals with the element of spirit possession, as when a medium becomes possessed by a powerful spirit, one that can perform cures of ill community members or provide information to participants. One such dialogic exchange that Schieffelin explores concerns the whereabouts of lost pigs, using his own ethnographic data from the Kaluli of Papua New Guinea (Schieffelin, 1985). After providing an overview of the limitations of viewing ritual's impact in purely representational terms, and giving a brief description of a Kaluli séance, he concludes (1985: 712):

> Understanding what is happening here, however, is more than a matter of showing that the séance provides a logically and symbolically plausible resolution for a problematic situation. It is also necessary to show why the Kaluli accept what they see in the séance as a convincing, even compelling, reality. That is, the question addressed here does not concern the content of Kaluli spirit belief, but how these beliefs are brought to life and galvanize social reality.

What follows is an extended discussion of the elements and practices that, as an unfolding process, contribute to the ritual's construction of the real. Because it relates directly to how computer games pose performative challenges for their players (and for the sake of space), I focus here on just one of Schieffelin's points of analysis. In the Kaluli séance, the information provided by the medium to help find the lost pigs is "markedly ambiguous." As Schieffelin describes (1985: 718):

> During one séance I observed, the medium's spirit child was sent to locate a missing pig described as a female with cropped ears and a white patch on the chest. Returning to the séance, the spirit later declared: "I saw the pig but I do not know the name of the ground." He went on to describe a place where a small brook ran into a larger creek with a particular kind of sago palm nearby …
>
> On the following day when the pig owner visited the place designated by the spirit he did in fact find a female pig with cropped ears and a white patch on its chest. But it was the wrong pig. The pig he was looking for was much larger and he returned disgruntled to the longhouse.

Following this disappointment, the audience takes up the question again, disputing the river previously suggested and substituting a different one they feel is more appropriate. After this change, "the various details suggested by the spirit were sufficient for the audience to piece together a picture and reach a consensus about where the pig was located," and "the séance participants doubtless felt that they had received it on spiritual authority, whereas to a Western observer, it appeared that they had constructed most of it themselves" (718). Schieffelin concludes:

> This event epitomizes the process of the social construction of reality in the séance. The spirit imparts information at once clear and ambiguous and the audience is induced to determine exact locations … That is, as the people search for clarification of the spirit's message they create the meaning they discover.
>
> 718–719

This co-construction of reality, achieved through the contingent (game-like) performative action of the audience, mirrors the discovery of the "truth" put forth implicitly by Bogost's *Take Back Illinois*. If we take a moment and consider, as an ideal type, no longer a ritual performer and audience, as was Schieffelin's reference point, but instead this encounter between a single digital game player and that game, we can wonder to what extent these roles have been distilled and reversed. The player is both audience and medium, through practice becoming familiar with, and able to affect, aspects of the world such as how caps on medical lawsuit damages influence the availability of doctors.

In contrast to ritual, games place contingency and the challenge of performative action centre stage. They constantly generate, as a matter of course, the performative challenges that Schieffelin saw as constituting part of some ritual events. Is it the case that, just as *TBI* implicitly constructs a reality claim about Illinois itself through its architecture's encounter with the player, similarly hypomediated games propose a set of claims about reality that are potentially enacted through their play? The game designer, perhaps initially imaginable as the "performer," has in these cases mobilized game remediation to diminish the signalling of contrivance, and thereby to bring the game's infrastructure of constraints and contingencies into potential alignment with the unbounded open-endedness of our experiences in more "naturalized" contexts. One widely experienced example of this was the advent of motion-sensitive controllers, such as the Nintendo Wii, which, with varying degrees of success, sought to align analogue bodily movement (such as swinging a bat, or sitting still in meditation) with their digital hypomediation. With these insights from the study of ritual in mind, we can return to the question of how analogue elements of games are remediated in computer games and draw deeper conclusions that can inform future research.

From Explicit to Implicit Participation

Explicit mechanisms – for example, written ("official" or "according to Hoyle") rules, concretely bounded fields of play, and stochastic tools (such as markers, dice, and spinners) – have played a central role in the history of games. They have been central to the ways in which games, rather than representing a starkly cordoned-off arena wherein things unfold in unique ways, instead configure and contrive, within arenas that are at most semi-bounded, the *same* types of constraints and contingencies that we encounter in our (unbounded) experience elsewhere. Games that command our attention are games that calibrate pattern and the unexpected just so, as Natasha Dow Schüll has demonstrated in her work on the production of video poker and slot machines (2012). But in most analogue games, throughout most of human history, these contrivances have been obvious, participatory, and vulgar in the original sense: rules are learned, applied, and enforced; game spaces are constructed and maintained; and mechanisms that generate contingency beyond the players' own contingent performance are manipulated and deployed directly.

In *TBI*, as in virtually all computer games, we may notice several things about the hypomediation of these game design elements. I will discuss each of these briefly, but first I note that the discussion here is of ideal types; that is to say, I am sure that many readers will be able to imagine examples of computer games (or analogue games) that trouble these observations (as well as that very distinction), but the aim here is precisely to get us thinking about what these ideal types of games owe to each other. After all, today's analogue games are themselves already remediating digital game elements (Matt Leacock's popular board game *Pandemic* is filled with the imagery of a digital game interface), although consideration of this is beyond the scope here.

Disappearing Rules. First, in *TBI* gameplay does not proceed through a process dependent on the "rules"; that is, there are no written rules to be learned and consulted, to be applied and enforced, to stand ready to be mistaken as "the game" (in the same way in which a score for Brahms' 2nd symphony could be mistaken for the symphony itself). Written game rules, in the Western tradition, have come to occupy an outsized place both in lay understanding of what games are and in scholarly research about them, leading to the strange situation (much like with the Brahms symphony) where one must actively remind researchers that games (like symphonies) only exist in their playing (see Malaby, 2007, 2009 for discussions of these issues and several examples).

This "misplaced concreteness" (Lambek & Boddy, 1997: 5) about games has not only worked very much against developing robust accounts of games and their significance, but it has also worked to obscure the role of written technical knowledge in institutional projects that seek to establish legitimacy and power. What kind of authority, when one thinks about it, do rulebooks for games have, and where does it come from? More to the point for this chapter, by learning and applying (and possibly modifying and rejecting) rules, players participate in a form of governance, enacting that government through their negotiated, social practice. Rules give them an opportunity to regulate, but also to "situationally adjust" (Moore, 1978). When, by contrast, the rules that dictate proper versus improper play are remediated, through digital code, into the much harder, infrastructural constraints of computer games (although never perfect; see Consalvo, 2007), the "givenness" of those rules becomes implicit in participating in the game at all; it is no longer produced through the social action of its players explicitly. Players of *TBI*, through playing *TBI*, enact implicitly the reality and legitimacy of what had been its rules.

Absence of Setup. Second, and relatedly, participants do not need to enact the material constraints of the game (such as through setting up a "field of play" or other distinct physical arena and its arrangements). As with the rules, to design a computer game is to construct the infrastructure, the durable conditions (including constraints and contingencies) under which player action can take place. What may have required governance by rules in a game like, say, *Monopoly*, is now taken care of materially. But even a computer game's materiality is not created in the same way as *Monopoly*'s material elements: the board, the tokens, the property cards, and so on. The handling and set up of these materials in the original game is also an occasion for the social production of the game, an event which itself highlights its contrivance and how much it depends upon human attention, negotiation, and effort – it is "hypermediated." In many computer games, such as *TBI*, there is no call for the pre-production that can contribute to the framing of the game as socially contrived and intersubjectively constituted. Instead, participation in these games has more of a quality of "thrownness" (in the Heideggerian sense; see Jackson, 1989); that is, players are in a sense thrown into a world not of their own making.

Attenuated Negotiation. Third, in most computer games there is no ongoing negotiation of expectations between players, as (in a game like *TBI*) the player has no contact with other players, or limited ability to raise questions of governance and adjustment when they can make such contact. Nor, should we note, is this unique to computer games; any solo ("solitaire") game has this quality. But in computer games the comparative absence of participatory pre-production and regulation, noted above, means also that the player is presented with a given landscape with which the player must contend. The infrastructure of the game is itself inscribed with the implicit value commitments of its creators, but that implicitness means that the ethical encounter between the player and the game producers occurs in a form similar to that which fascinated Michel de Certeau (1984): between the tactical, creative actor and the strategic, proper space-making institution.

Implicit Contingency. Fourth, in computer games like *TBI*, no turn to activating and consulting stochastic mechanisms (such as a spinner) is necessary; random events are handled by the code.[4] In *TBI*'s case, we can see this contingency's effects in how the simulated residents may infect each other as they move about the city blocks. When contingencies such as this become part of the background conditions against which social action takes place, a significant step, I suggest, has taken place: something like the "background of indeterminacy" that characterizes all human experience (Moore, 1978) has here an additional layer produced by the hypomediated handling of contingencies by the computer game's code.

I propose that in all the ways listed above, but perhaps especially in this folding of stochastic mechanisms into the background of an arena for performative action, the hypomediacy of many computer games makes them more potent sites for claims about the "reality" the player's performance helps to produce. Analogue games, then (again, speaking broadly) correspondingly tend to exhibit a kind of "hypermediacy"; that is, analogue games draw attention to their status as contrivances by making use of artifacts with only an arbitrary relationship to the interpretations of game outcomes. Interestingly, there are many examples of computer games and game-related environments which have remediated game design elements such as stochastic mechanisms *explicitly*. An example of this would be graphically animated (with apparent "desktop" physics and sound effects) dice-rolling within a browser window (such as on the D&D site dndbeyond.com). This kind of hypermediacy represents a turn away from the unbounded naturalization potential of hypomediacy in favour of engagement in a style that evokes the manipulation of physical objects. Such examples demonstrate the level of investment by designers (and significance for users) of these aspects of computer games and cry out for more analysis.

To summarize, I suggest that we need to push our exploration of remediation in games in three directions. First, we must be ready to think more broadly about what is (re)mediated. Games demand attention to their specific design elements, which are both ancient and ontologically distinct from what we find in other media (visual or otherwise). Second, we must be ready to look at the micro-level and become historical as we trace which elements are remediated in which ways, and as against what institutional projects. Third, we must avoid drawing *a priori* conclusions about the consequences of these remediations for their players. I have done so above to a certain extent, and thereby risked overdrawing these contrasts and interpretations, but I have done so for the sake of illustrating the specific kinds of remediation that attend digitally networked games; there is no doubt that ethnographic analysis would be required to ferret out the extent to which we can find illumination in these terms. But to attach these ideas more firmly to the anthropological tradition, I will close by identifying some of the ways in which our study of ritual can serve as a paradigm for thinking about how remediation in general, and hypomediacy in particular, in games may drive their potential for use in the infrastructures of today.

Conclusion

I am interested in the work that games are doing, in close relation to the verb-sense, particularly the work they are doing for institutions, after a great deal of time in which they have been largely unruly. They constituted a largely threatening presence, as in the underground national lottery of Brazil as described by Amy Chazkel (2011), and of course the Olympics of 1936 and other years are also classic examples. Today, however, games are coming to heel, as it were, becoming more and more tractable for institutions, and the material affordances of our digital circumstances have played a core role in making this possible. While power and institutional interest are not foregrounded in the preceding, they are at the heart of the approach to games and remediation that I recommend. As Geertz and Schieffelin understood, cultural forms are available for sponsorship and use as part of institutional projects, and my suggestion is that digital games fit more readily to that institutional hand than the hypermediated games in the past.

The recent history of remediation of games may illuminate this story. While I have focused, in a "micro" sense, on game design elements, these remediations involve those recognized by

Grusin and Bolter as well as others concerning networked communication, often with roots in technical practice around early computing. Soon after the rise of professionalized game design in the twentieth century came networked and digital communications infrastructures, and game designers in computing soon grappled with two significant remediations. In one, they drew from how tabletop roleplaying games like *Dungeons & Dragons* transcended the idea of games as bundles of rules in order to architect systems that were vastly more complex and open-ended. These systems became the basis for so-called "sandbox"-style computer games – whether for one player, a few, or many thousands – and beyond this continue to shape the design of complex social environments throughout the internet.

In the second, and relatedly, they developed infrastructures for inter-player and player-system communication that drew from a range of existing media conventions, often combining them in new ways. Elements that can be found in Twitch streams (for example) today that remediate these other forms include: synchronous, text-based chat (including emoticons/ emojis); textboxes for the streaming of game events (and related code); livestreaming of audio and visual media; and game interface design (such as maps, character portraits, resource bars, and the like). What is more, this bundle of remediations is now to be found in a vast array of contexts beyond Twitch and other game-related domains, including education management software (Canvas), team communication software (Slack), and large-scale social media (such as Facebook), to name a few.

Such broader permutations of remediations are beyond the scope of this chapter, but if we can begin to handle digitally mediated games with a fuller sense of how they make use of hypo- and hypermediacy, we will be in a better position to inquire deeply into how digitally mediated infrastructures accomplish the quality of ambience that underwrites the vast scope of their influence on human affairs.

Acknowledgments

The author wishes to thank the editors for the invitation to contribute to this volume, and also Stuart Moulthrop and Richard Grusin for their feedback on this piece. I am also in debt to the graduate student (and alumni) members of the Digital Cultures Collaboratory at the University of Wisconsin-Milwaukee (a.k.a. Serious Play), especially Matthew Keracher and Ryan House, who pointed me to key work I may not have otherwise found. The Digital Cultures Collaboratory is supported by UWM's Center for 21st Century Studies. The "Communities of Play Symposium" (April 2021) provided an opportunity for Ryan House and I to collaborate on a presentation of these ideas in connection with his work on *Death Stranding*, a video of which can be found here: https://youtu.be/uIKI4kDAtEM. My thanks also to all who participated in the question and answer discussion that followed.

Notes

1 The dramatic, long, and vexed encounter between modernity's project of rational control and contingency lies at the heart of many fascinating scholarly moments, such as Charles Darwin and James Clerk Maxwell's challenges to positivist science, the foundations of American pragmatism and legal realism, and the landmark shift of Wittgenstein's thought which led him to see language as a game. Among many other works, one could begin with Ian Hacking's *The Emergence of Unpredictability* (1975) and *The Taming of Chance* (1990; see also Hacking, 1983), or Louis Menand's *The Metaphysical Club* (2001).

2 Regarding the treatment of ritual and game as ontologically on a par with one another, see Lévi-Strauss's four-page discussion of the two forms, full of insights still relevant today, in *The Savage Mind* (1966: 30–33). Regarding cultural form, see Bourdieu's comment in *Outline of a Theory of Practice* on "form," specifically in the musical sense, as an appropriate metaphor for social action (1977: 198, note 8).

3 I wish to stress very strongly here that, while I may present these differences between "ideal types" of game and ritual, in reality many events that we may fruitfully treat under one or the other label nonetheless have elements of both (and of bureaucracy as well). The Olympics, of course, are the most prominent example of all three cultural forms running simultaneously and together.

4 Note that, in truth, these computer-generated contingencies are pseudo-random, as no digital computer can produce actual randomness. Interestingly, this pseudo-randomness is often achieved via a complex algorithm that makes use of, for example, the string of numbers (often in milliseconds) generated by the player's input. This is immaterial for the experience of the player, however, for whom it is *practically random*.

References

Bogost, Ian. (2006) "Playing Politics: Videogames for Politics, Activism, and Advocacy," *First Monday*, available at https://doi.org/10.5210/fm.v0i0.1617 (accessed November 1, 2021).

Bolter, Jay David and Richard Grusin. (1999) *Remediation*, Cambridge, MA: MIT Press.

Bourdieu, Pierre. (1977) *Outline of a Theory of Practice*, translated by Richard Nice, Cambridge: Cambridge University Press.

Chazkel, Amy. (2011) *Laws of Chance: Brazil's Clandestine Lottery and the Marking of Urban Public Life*, Durham, NC: Duke University Press.

Consalvo, Mia. (2007) *Cheating: Gaining Advantage in Videogames*, Cambridge, MA: MIT Press.

Couldry, Nick. (2003) *Media Rituals: A Critical Approach*, Abingdon: Routledge.

De Certeau, Michel. (1984) *The Practice of Everyday Life*, translated by Steven Rendall, Berkeley, CA: University of California Press.

Geertz, Clifford. (1973) "Religion as a Cultural System," in *The Interpretation of Cultures: Selected Essays*, New York: Basic Books: 87–125.

Ginsburg, Faye, Lila Abu-Lughod, and Brian Larkin. (2002) *Media Worlds: Anthropology on New Terrain*, Berkeley, CA: University of California Press.

Graeber, David. (2015) *The Utopia of Rules: On Technology, Stupidity, and the Secret Joys of Bureaucracy*, Brooklyn, NY: Melville House.

Grusin, Richard. (2010) *Premediation: Affect & Mediality after 9/11*, London: Palgrave MacMillan.

Hacking, Ian. (1975) *The Emergence of Probability*, Cambridge: Cambridge University Press.

Hacking, Ian. (1983) "Nineteenth Century Cracks in the Concept of Determinism," *Journal of the History of Ideas*, 44 (3): 455–75.

Hacking, Ian. (1990) *The Taming of Chance*, Cambridge: Cambridge University Press.

Jackson, Michael. (1989) *Paths toward a Clearing: Radical Empiricism and Ethnographic Inquiry*, Bloomington, IN: Indiana University Press.

La Lone, Nicholas. (2019) "A Tale of Dungeons & Dragons and the Origin of the Game Platform," *Analog Game Studies*, available at https://analoggamestudies.org/2019/09/a-tale-of-dungeons-dragons-and-the-origins-of-the-game-platform/ (accessed November 1, 2021).

Lambek, Michael and Janice Boddy. (1997) "Introduction: Culture in Question," *Social Analysis*, 41 (3): 3–23.

Larkin, Brian. (2002) "The Materiality of Cinema Theaters in Northern Nigeria," in *Media Worlds: Anthropology on New Terrain*, Berkeley, CA: University of California Press: 319–336.

Larkin, Brian. (2013) "The Politics and Poetics of Infrastructure," *Annual Review of Anthropology*, 42: 327–43.

Lévi-Strauss, Claude. (1966) *The Savage Mind*, Chicago: University of Chicago Press.

Malaby, Thomas. (2007) "Beyond Play: A New Approach to Games," *Games & Culture*, 2 (2): 95–113.

Malaby, Thomas (2009) "Anthropology and Play: The Contours of Playful Experience," *New Literary History*, 40: 205–218.

Menand, Louis. (2001) *The Metaphysical Club: A Story of Ideas in America*, New York: Farrar, Strauss, and Giroux.

Moore, Sally Falk (1978) *Law as Process: An Anthropological Approach*, Boston, MA: Routledge & Kegan Paul.

Phillips, Matt and Taylor Lorenz. (2021) "'Dumb Money' Is on GameStop, and It's Beating Wall Street at Its Own Game," *New York Times*, January 27, available at www.nytimes.com/2021/01/27/business/gamestop-wall-street-bets.html (accessed November 1, 2021).

Puerini, James [@J_Puerini]. "Wall Street Clearly Underestimated a Generation Raised on Highly Coordinated Friday Night World of Warcraft raids," *Twitter*, 8:49 pm, January 27, 2021, available at https://twitter.com/J_Puerini/status/1354622608000614402 (accessed November 1, 2021).

Schieffelin, Edward. (1985) "Performance and the Cultural Construction of Reality," *American Ethnologist*, 12 (4): 707–724.

Schüll, Natasha Dow. (2012) *Addiction by Design: Machine Gambling in Las Vegas*, Princeton, NJ: Princeton University Press.

Tambiah, Stanley. (1985) *Culture, Thought, and Social Action*, Cambridge, MA: Harvard University Press.

Wilk, Richard. (2002) "Television, Time, and the National Imaginary in Belize," in *Media Worlds: Anthropology on New Terrain*, Berkeley, CA: University of California Press: 171–187.

B

Media as Practice

8
MEDIA PRACTICES AND THEIR SOCIAL EFFECTS

John Postill

Not long ago I told a colleague I was writing a paper on the effects of media practices. She looked at me as if she'd just seen the ghost of Vlad the Impaler.

'Don't go there', she urged me. 'Do your digital activism thing instead'.

'Why?' I asked.

Shaking her head sadly, she explained that the notion of effects is crude and causally linear and cannot capture people's life experience (or words to that effect).

I gave this idea of jumping ship some thought but having calmed my nerves with a decent belt of Corona rum I decided to stay the course. After all, the question of media effects has dogged me for years. To quote King Gizzard & the Lizard Wizard: 'If not now, then when?'

But where to begin? It is not as if we media anthropologists had paid much attention to the effects of media practices – or so it seemed to me – precisely for the reasons noted by my spooked colleague. Most of us wouldn't want to be caught dead uttering the e-word, let alone in the title of a book chapter. We have metrics to massage, promotions to secure, mortgages to pay.

As it turns out, Nick Couldry's (2004) often cited essay 'Theorising media as practice' is a good starting point. Couldry proposes practice theory as the new paradigm for media studies, a paradigm focused on 'media-oriented practices'. 'What, quite simply', he asks, 'are people doing in relation to media across a whole range of situations and contexts?' (2004: 119). Although the new paradigm, adds Couldry, is meant to take media scholarship beyond its traditional focus on media institutions and media texts, we shouldn't abandon the fundamental question posed in the late 1940s by two pioneers of US mass communication research, Lazarsfeld and Merton (1969 [1948]), namely: 'What are the effects of the existence of media in our society?' (quoted in Couldry 2004: 130). In fact, writes Couldry, this is the question we must return to 'with all our theoretical energies'. This all suggests that the problem of media effects never really went away, not even among scholars with impeccable anti-positivist credentials.

In this chapter, I broach a slightly modified version of this question. First, and in keeping with a practice approach, instead of 'media' in general I will examine *media-related practices* ('media practices' for short). Second, in the place of 'our society', with its tacit reference to American society, I will refer to *people's social worlds* wherever these may be; that is, to the

DOI: 10.4324/9781003175605-13

hugely diverse social formations that media ethnographers study around the globe. My tweaked question, then, is:

> What are the effects of the existence of media practices in people's social worlds?

To this end, below I draw from the recent (media) practice theory literature and from a range of empirical studies, including my own anthropological research in Sarawak, Malaysia, to explore the effects of media practices in people's social worlds. I argue that these social effects are often complex, messy, and non-teleological and that they include two main varieties: mediatising effects and worlding effects. I also suggest that this area is ripe for further media anthropological work, so long as we overcome our customary aversion to the notion of effects.

Practices, Worlds, Effects

Let us start by clearing the ground around the three key terms in my question: media practices, social worlds, and effects. The notion of media practices can be retraced to a heterogeneous school of thought that emerged in the late 1970s known as 'practice theory' (Ortner 1984). Most scholars working within this tradition posit that social practices – rather than individuals, interactions, structures or systems – are central to human life (Hui, Schatzki and Shove 2017; Postill 2010a). Practices are the 'embodied sets of activities' that we perform 'with varying degrees of regularity, competence and flair' (Postill 2010a: 1). As such, practice theory can be aptly described as 'a body of work about the work of the body' (2010a: 11).

In media anthropology, the analytical centrality of practices – especially media practices – was a given for decades (see, e.g. Askew and Wilk 2002; Ginsburg, Abu-Lughod, and Larkin 2002). It is only in recent years that media anthropologists have explicitly addressed practice theory, especially since the publication of the edited volume *Theorising Media and Practice* (Bräuchler and Postill 2010). As Kubitschko (2018: 630) has noted, contributors to this volume replace 'rather detached investigations of media contents or media effects' with 'practice-oriented approaches that move human acting into the foreground'. This practice turn in media anthropology has since influenced interdisciplinary scholars working on a range of media-related topics, including information science (Cox 2012), social movements (Stephansen and Treré 2019), hacker politics (Kubitschko 2018), mobile phones (Tenhunen 2018), development (Slater 2014), and conflict (Budka and Bräuchler 2020).

The volume features a core conceptual debate. Thus, in his chapter's response to Couldry's (2004) call for a practice paradigm, Mark Hobart argues that the notion of media-related practices is more open-ended than Couldry's 'media-oriented practices' in that it doesn't limit itself to the study of 'institutionalised' dimensions of production and distribution (Hobart 2010: 67). For Hobart, media-related practices can refer to anything from negotiating the purchase of a home computer to preparing dinner in time for the family's favourite soap opera to making a video on one's phone (2010: 63).

In fact, there is no need to choose between the two concepts. In an ever more mediated world we need more, not less, conceptual vocabulary to map a changing social terrain. Accordingly, we can employ 'media-related' as the umbrella qualifier while retaining 'media-oriented', 'media-based', 'media-dependent' and cognate terms as more specific qualifiers. For instance, watching television is a media-related practice, yet it is also a media-oriented practice. To state the obvious, without a TV-enabled device we cannot watch television. In the remainder of this chapter, then, I use media practices as a shorthand for media-related practices.

Next on our list is the concept of *social worlds*. By this term I mean the kinds of social formations long theorised by the Chicago School of Sociology, most notably by Strauss (1978) and Becker (1982). For Strauss, who follows Shibutani (1955), social worlds are typically held together not by formal membership or territorial demarcations but by 'the limits of effective communication' (Strauss 1978: 119). Social worlds are enormously diverse in their character and scale. Some are large, others small. Some are new, others old; some local, others translocal. In the United States alone, argues Strauss (1978: 121), they range from 'opera, baseball, surfing, stamp collecting [and] country music' to 'homosexuality, politics, medicine, law, mathematics, science, Catholicism' and innumerable others.

The notion of social world, suggests Strauss, can help researchers with the perennial problem of how to gauge change by tracking concrete changes within bounded, yet porous, domains of social life. For instance, a scholar researching the world of professional tennis would have no choice but to consider its 'explosive' growth in the 1970s (Strauss 1978: 126). To do so, she would have to combine synchronic methods such as interviews and participant observation with diachronic ones like archival research. Studies of social worlds, says Strauss, make us attentive to their history – to their past, present and future. Is the world we are investigating 'evolving, disintegrating, splintering, collaborating, coalescing?' (Strauss, 1978: 127).

In my multi-sited study of 'nerd politics' (Postill 2018), I married Strauss' social worlds with Sewell's (2005) conceptual trinity of events, trends, and routines (or 'practices', in my renaming). This allowed me to write a history of nerd politics from its modest West Berlin birth in the early 1980s to its global diffusion and splintering into four 'subworlds' (Strauss 1978: 121) – data activism, digital rights, social protest, and formal politics (Postill 2018: 170). Also building on Strauss, Andreas Hepp (2013: 621) contends that most social worlds depend today on 'an articulation through media communication' and are bound together by '[an] intersubjective knowledge inventory, specific social practices and cultural thickenings'. Hepp (2013: 621) calls such domains 'mediatized worlds' (see below) and believes that they make the study of mediatisation more concrete and empirically viable.

Finally, to the controversial notion of *effects* – more specifically, to the social effects of media practices. In most existing overviews, the study of media effects is associated exclusively with US mass communication research. In fact, scholars from *all* media research traditions, not least media anthropology, have always written about media effects. Very few scholars of media practices, however, have discussed their social effects explicitly. One rare exception is McGovney-Ingram (2013) who examines the effects of media practices such as selecting sources and defining newsworthiness on how the mainstream media frame race and gender.

Far more common in the literature is to discuss the effects of media practices obliquely or euphemistically, or through cognates such as 'impacts', 'influences' or 'consequences'. Take, for instance, the media anthropology reader *Media Worlds* (Ginsburg, Abu-Lughod and Larkin 2002). In her chapter, Faye Ginsburg (2002: 44) explores how Inuit media practitioners responded to 'the impact of [Western] representational practices on Inuit society and culture'. She argues that:

> The activity of media-making has helped to revive relations between generations and skills that had nearly been abandoned. The fact of their appearance on television on Inuit terms inverts the usual hierarchy of values attached to the dominant culture's technology, conferring new prestige to Inuit 'culture-making'.
>
> *Ginsburg, 2002: 44*

Notice Ginsburg's use of the noun 'impact' to refer to Western representational practices, of the phrase 'helped to revive' to describe the effect such practices had on Inuit intergenerational relations, and of the term 'conferring' in relation to indigenous 'culture-making'. All three are effects formulations that posit a causal relationship between new media practices and concrete sociocultural changes among the Inuit. Another *Media Worlds* contributor, Mayfair Yang (2002), similarly writes about the 'deep impact' that singing karaoke songs from Hong Kong and Taiwan had on Mainland China audiences. Stressing the embodied nature of this media practice, she argues that it entailed 'the active performance and oral and bodily enactment of a different way to be Chinese' (2002: 198–199). Far from isolating this mediated effect from its sociohistorical contexts, Yang (2002: 198) links it to four simultaneous processes of mediated change unfolding in China at the time.

In his contribution to the volume, Mark Hobart (2002) likewise uses the term 'impact' to explore the social effects of media practices, in his case those of watching theatrical plays on television in Bali, Indonesia. Implicitly equating correlation with causation, Hobart writes: 'The impact of television on theatre can be judged by the fact that, according to the best estimate, over 80 percent of theatre troupes in Bali disappeared during the 1980s, when audiences became bent on watching only "the best" [Balinese theatre on television]' (2002: 372). For his part, Richard Wilk (2002) examines the 'important effect[s]' of television discourse in postcolonial Belize, including changing the 'terms of the debate' about local versus foreign culture. Since the arrival of television, writes Wilk (2002: 175), Belizeans 'talk about "culture" constantly, in ways that were not possible before'. He describes local people as 'voyeurs watching North America through an electronic peephole' united by 'their shared experience of voyeurism' (Wilk, 2002: 175) – or, to put it in practice-theoretical terms, by the shared *practices* of watching and talking about American TV shows.

Considered together, these media anthropological texts invite a number of propositions. First, *all media practices have social effects*. To repurpose Sheehy and Feaver's (2015: 395) general remark about social practices, a media practice is 'a human action that is repeated over time and that has social effects'. This shouldn't be a controversial point to make. The reason it still is in media anthropology and related fields is the negative connotations carried by the word 'effects'.

Second, *the social effects of media practices come in vastly different forms, scales, and durations*. While some effects will be small and fleeting, others will be large and long-lasting. Some will be direct, others indirect, and so on. To be able to study them, we must abandon the stereotype of 'effects' as necessarily referring to a crude, causally linear process (to recall my opening anecdote). Instead, we should assume that social effects are likely to be diverse, complex, and non-linear.

Third, because practice is always embodied, *media practices will have effects on practitioners' minds and bodies. This will, in turn, result in various social effects*. Here the practice-theoretical work of Cecily Maller (2017) is pertinent. Maller explores the potential epigenetic effects of eating practices resulting in cardiovascular disease and other health issues, which in turn can have major social and economic consequences. A similar approach could be applied to investigating, for instance, the social effects of social media burnout (Han 2018), or indeed of singing certain genres of karaoke in Mainland China (see Yang 2002 and above).

Fourth, as both the social media and karaoke examples show, media practices are always part of 'flows of people, ideas, and objects … mediated by communication technologies' (Ginsburg, Abu-Lughod, and Larkin 2002: 5). *These mediated flows will have multiscalar and multitemporal social effects beyond the immediate performative context of the media practice in question*. As Ginsburg, Abu-Lughod, and Larkin (2002: 5) note, both Benedict Anderson (1991) and Jürgen Habermas

(1989) are key figures in theorising such effects in connection to nationalism and public discourse, respectively.

In sum, the social effects of media practices are embodied, ubiquitous, heterogeneous, multiscalar, and multitemporal – a far cry from our received idea of media effects. Media anthropologists are well equipped to study such social effects through both synchronic and diachronic methods. But how can we begin to grapple with this vast question? How do we take stock of what we already know? To address these questions I wish to propose a working heuristic that links them to the notion of social worlds, a heuristic consisting of two main types of social effects: *mediatising effects* and *worlding effects*. These concepts, I suggest, can help us mine the rich media ethnographic literature and open new lines of investigation.

Mediatising Effects

Let us consider first the mediatising effects of media practices. The concept of 'mediatisation' has gained much traction over the past two decades. Originally it referred to the long-term historical process whereby a 'media logic' was said to have diffused across modern societies, colonising virtually every social world (Hjarvard 2008). In recent years it has been put to shorter-term uses, including ethnographic ones (see Couldry and Hepp 2013; Hepp, Hjarvard, and Lundby 2015). Here I am adjectivising ('mediatising') this noun to capture the process whereby a new media practice increases, enhances or deepens the technological mediation of an existing social world. We can distinguish two broad types of social world. First, worlds that began their life courses untouched, or barely touched, by modern media such as radio, television, mobile phones or the internet. Examples include villages in remote areas of the Global South, fields of practice rooted in the pre-modern age or centuries-old institutions like the Catholic Church or the university. Second, worlds that were already mediated by modern communication technologies when the particular media practice we are investigating took hold, for example, the addition of smartphone photography to the repertoire of photographers in Barcelona (San Cornelio and Gómez-Cruz 2014) or the spread of datafication practices across professional football in Germany (Schmidt 2017).

But how does my proposed notion of mediatising effects differ from the existing concept of mediatisation? It does so in three main respects. First, it foregrounds and makes explicit the underexplored question of the social effects of media practices. Additionally, by shifting the focus from the macro-historical process implied by the idea of mediatisation to the social effects of specific media practices it makes the inquiry more concrete and manageable. Finally, this is a notion aligned with social practice theory, not mediatisation theory. As such it is agnostic about the various mediatisation debates, for example institutionalism vs. constructivism (Hepp 2013).

In media anthropology, the mediatising effects of media practices have been commonly discussed in relation to the advent of television in a developing country. Mark Hobart, for example, has written about the mediatising effects (my term, not his) of watching television in Bali.

> Television viewing changed [Balinese] domestic and public activities in several ways. Some are familiar from studies of family viewing (e.g., Morley 1986; Lull 1990), like the impact of television watching on domestic routines including new kinds of power relations around choices of viewing. Village food stalls mostly went out of business except for the few that installed television, while public sets in village halls became the site for raucous humour and searing commentary on broadcast politics. Women's

arduous daily routines were enlivened by listening, if not always watching, television, and new kinds of working relationships emerged. The number of witchcraft accusations plummeted, as people developed other concerns. The impact upon agricultural and industrial labour patterns was complex. Television viewing has come to affect many aspects of rural and urban social life.

Hobart, 2010: 67–68

Observe this media anthropologist's unapologetic use of direct effect terms like 'changed', 'impact', and 'to affect' as well as indirect effects formulations such as 'went out of business', 'became the site for', 'were enlivened by', 'emerged', and 'plummeted'. This excerpt shows the great potential of rereading the media ethnographic record from a mediatising effects angle, not least in areas that were yet to be 'media-saturated' at the time of fieldwork (Couldry 2004: 121).

But can we really attribute mediatising effects to a single media practice like watching television, taking smartphone photos or working remotely? Given how fuzzy and entangled media practices are in real life (Hepp 2013), isn't the very idea of separate media practices an academic fantasy (see Christensen and Røpke 2010; Hobart 2010)? Shouldn't we be concerned solely with 'media ecologies', 'mediascapes', 'media figurations', and other holistic understandings of media? Indeed, the latest thinking in social practice theory places the locus of sociocultural change not in individual practices but rather in 'interconnected systems of practice' – what Hui, Schatzki, and Shove (2017) call 'the nexus of practices'. Analogously, a number of contributors to *Theorising Media and Practice* advocate a holistic, cultural version of media practice theory (Postill 2010a: 19).

Once again, as with most things in social science, there is no need to make an either-or decision. Here, it makes no sense to establish by fiat a single locus of change. As the Manchester School of Anthropology taught us long ago (e.g. Epstein 1958), sociocultural changes will typically have multiple loci. It follows that both individual (media) practices as well as 'constellations' (Hui, Schatzki, and Shove 2017) of (media) practices can have mediatising effects. In other words, we should not be hasty to disregard individual media practices, for one never knows when they may prove handy in research.

An example from my own fieldwork among the Iban, an indigenous group of Sarawak, East Malaysia, will demonstrate this point. When television began to percolate into the Sarawak countryside in the 1980s, an American acquaintance of mine could not believe that an old Iban friend would ignore his attempts at chatting while a Bollywood film was being shown on the screen. He found this to be 'a glaring breach of traditional norms of longhouse hospitality' (Postill 2006: 158) (A longhouse is a manner of 'village under one roof'.) This incident illustrates how local people invent new rules of etiquette around a new media practice, a phenomenon that ethnographers have documented for a range of media forms, most recently for social media (see Miller et al. 2016). By the time I carried out fieldwork in Sarawak – from 1996 to 1998 – both radio listening and television viewing were integral to the daily rounds of practices among rural Iban. Both had combined mediatising effects that, along with other sets of practices (schooling, waged labour, migration, etc.), helped to 'modernise' and nationalise Iban longhouses as Malaysia's successive governments pursued ambitious nation-building policies (Postill 2006). In this regard, it makes perfect sense to speak of Hui, Schatzki, and Shove's (2017) 'nexus of practices', but only as *one* significant locus of change.

On the other hand, it is still reasonable to argue that the individual, albeit fuzzy, media practice of watching television had mediatising effects in rural Sarawak longhouses that were distinctive from those of, say, listening to the radio, reading school textbooks or speaking through the PA system during a local event (Postill 2006: 102–105). For instance, in the mid-1990s, well before the advent of smartphones, radio listening helped to structure the everyday activities of women – who did most of the farming and housework – much more than those of men, whose time was already pre-structured by the demands of the waged workplace. In the evenings, though, it was watching television, not listening to the radio, that brought together all segments of the longhouse population (women, men, the elderly, and schoolchildren). It was primarily through the practice of watching television that family members jointly 'domesticated' the state's vision of a fully developed Malaysia by 2020. It was this media-related practice that had a profound effect on longhouse sociality, which in pre-television days had revolved around chatting (*berandau*) in the communal gallery (*ruai*). By the time I arrived in Sarawak in 1996, the more 'modernised' longhouses had little time for this form of evening conviviality (Postill 2006).

In sum, when it comes to the social effects of media practices – including their mediatising effects – we do not have to choose between being a practice 'lumper' or a practice 'splitter', to adapt Charles Darwin's phrase (Burkhardt and Smith 1990). We can be either, or both, depending on the questions at hand. Single media practices can have distinctive, albeit hard to ascertain, social effects; and so can 'congeries' (Hobart 2010) or 'constellations' (Hui et al. 2017) of such practices.

Worlding Effects

As we have just seen, new media practices – and clusters of them – can have the effect of changing an existing social world in significant ways. Some media practices can also have the compound effect of (co-)creating *new* social worlds. I will call this complex phenomenon *the worlding effects of media practices*. Here, too, we find that media anthropologists have already addressed this problem through an effects language, yet without explicit reference to either the media effects tradition or to social practice theory. For instance, Richard Wilk writes:

> By studying the advent of television in the developing world, anthropologists gain something that has largely been lost in the parts of the world where television is now a taken-for-granted social fact. That is the opportunity to think beyond programming and content to the form of the medium itself, to the way television constitutes a new form of cosmology *and creates new social worlds* ... Of course, the medium has also changed as it has expanded, and we can now *see some effects on and consequences for television* that earlier scholars did not predict.
>
> Wilk 2002: 171, *my emphasis*

This is an insightful remark, but it refers to media as form rather than media *as practice* (Couldry 2004). To add a single but crucial word to Wilk's passage, in this section we are interested in how *watching* television and other media practices make new social worlds. Let us consider, by way of ethnographic illustration, three very different types of social world: an online virtual world, an activist space, and a recursive public. Despite their notable contrasts, these are all worlds that owe their existence, evolution, and survival to the combined effects of media practices over time.

From June 2004 to January 2007, anthropologist Tom Boellstorff 'lived' in the 3D virtual world Second Life as the avatar Tom Bukowski. His book *Coming of Age in Second Life* (2008) describes in minute detail the daily practices and social relations of the local 'residents'. Boellstorff aimed to account for inworld practices on their own terms, not as pale imitations of 'real life' practices. Contrary to tabloid reports of Second Life as a cesspit of consumerism and bizarre cybersex, he found that most residents were perfectly happy carrying out mundane practices such as building, weaving, chatting, dancing, flying or trading. Unlike ordinary communication media, argues Boellstorff, platforms like Second Life allow residents to craft 'complete new worlds that are in themselves places for human sociality' (Fontana 2009: 28). 'I cannot meet a lover inside a novel and invite friends for a wedding ceremony there', he writes, 'nor can I and a group of like-minded persons buy joint property inside a television program' (Boellstorff 2008: 237). In other words, Second Life was not born fully formed in the minds of professional programmers at Linden Lab (Malaby 2011). Rather it was the resident avatars, both professional and amateur, who created this new world by developing virtual practices, the composite effect being the emergence and stabilisation of a subcultural web of norms, relationships and artefacts.

While some social worlds are coterminous with a specialist field of practice like journalism, sociology, rock-climbing or possum removal, others exist at the intersection of two or more fields. Take the fraught world of short-video-based (SVB) consumer activism in contemporary China (Yu 2021). Zizheng Yu sought to examine the working mechanisms behind the actions of Chinese SVB activists through an 'activist media practices' lens derived from Mattoni and Trere (2014). He soon discovered that this form of political agency is located at the intersection of four distinct fields, or subworlds (Strauss 1978), namely activism, journalism, business, and government – each with its own set of key media practices. Thus, businesses wanting to minimise the effect of negative videos will hire 'ghost writers' to post glowing comments about the firm (Yu 2021: 10). Yu's work is a timely corrective to both popular accounts about the supposedly runaway virality of today's media landscapes (e.g. Wasik 2009) and to overly simple portrayals of an all-powerful Chinese surveillance state where citizens have no outlets for their grievances (see Postill, Lasa, and Zhang 2020). It also suggests that we need to pay closer attention to the dynamic feedback loops of effects and counter-effects (in this case, the effects on consumer activists of the business practice of ghost commenting) that characterise media-based worlds, yet without falling into the crude cybernetic functionalism of earlier communication models (see Couldry 2004: 123; Craig 1999).

My final example of the worldmaking effects of media practices comes from the realm of free software production (Kelty 2008, 2010). Earlier I mentioned Strauss' (1978) point about the study of social worlds requiring a combination of diachronic and synchronic methods. In his long-term study of free software geeks, anthropologist Chris Kelty likewise combined archival (mostly listservs) and ethnographic research. The result is the monograph *Two Bits* (2008) which tracks the trajectories of five geeky practices: sharing source code, conceptualising openness, applying copyright licenses, coordinating/collaborating, and 'the movement' (the mostly online meta-practice of discussing the other four practices) (see Postill 2010a: 25). This dynamic nexus of practices drove the emergence and stabilisation of the free software world, which Kelty (2008) calls a 'recursive public'. The free software public, contends Kelty (2008), is held together not by a shared ideology but by the practices themselves. This echoes Couldry's point about Giddens' (1984) structuration theory positing that 'principles of order [can] both produce and be reproduced at the level of the practice itself (social order, in other words, is "recursively" present in practice and in the organisation of practice)' (Couldry 2004: 124).

These diverse worldmaking examples suggest that we have an arduous, but exciting, practice-theoretical task ahead of us as media ethnographers: to trace the emergence of new social worlds driven by media practices that are crafted by the denizens themselves, not by some external agency, ghostly structure or social system hovering above them (see Helle-Valle 2019; Hobart 2010).

Who Needs Effects?

At this juncture, some readers might still harbour doubts about the need for studying effects when researching media practices, especially given this notion's chequered history. Responding to an earlier version of this chapter, one reader noted that my examples focus on what digital technologies enable people to do, or how they appropriate new media into existing practices. Readers asked, what is gained by bringing back the language of effects?[1]

My response to this objection is that inquiring about the social effects of media practices is a logical, pragmatic corollary to the hard ethnographic work of studying such practices in the field. Indeed, it would be a wasted opportunity *not* to consider their social effects (or consequences). My principal point is that some sets of media and other practices will have the overall or compound effect of co-constituting new social worlds. These effects will often be complex, messy, indirect, and hard to document empirically but that is no reason to ignore them. Studying them does not commit us to a new paradigm of media anthropology. It merely expands our epistemological range should we wish to pursue this question. In fact, studying what new digital practices enable people to accomplish is an issue that an effects approach is well equipped to address.

Let me expand on this last point through the earlier example of Second Life. Boellstorff (2008: 245) argues that 'the cultures of virtual worlds are the product of techne'. By techne he means 'art or craft', that is, 'human action that engages with the world and thereby results in a different world' (2008: 64). In other words, virtual worlds come into being partly as the combined *effect* of inworld practices (alongside inworld objects, relationships, norms). The operative word here is 'partly', as it would make little sense to pass over the trajectories of objects, relationships, and norms in our worldmaking accounts (regardless of whether we are dealing with a virtual or an 'actual' world).

To be sure, this poses a major methodological challenge, namely how to reconstruct ethnographically the role of media practices in the making of an existing world. Strauss' (1978) aforesaid call for both synchronic and diachronic methods in the study of social worlds is again crucial – in our case, with a focus on reconstructing the evolution of a world's 'nexus' (Hui, Schatzki, and Shove 2017) of media practices. Here Boellstorff's (2008) ethnography offers some tantalising clues. In the early days of Second Life, he writes, Linden Lab conceived of the platform's economy as being object-based. However, over time, and partly through the actions of its virtual residents, it became a property-based economy. Put simply, through engaging with a range of building and other place-making practices, many residents reported a sense of accomplishment, agency, belonging and wellbeing. In terms of Warde's (2005) practice theory of consumption, residents found such practices to be intrinsically rewarding. As Boellstorff (2008: 182) notes, what really mattered to most residents was creating 'social places' where they could interact with other residents. At the same time, the building practices came with rewards 'extrinsic' to the practices themselves (Warde 2005: 147), in that property owners attained a higher standing in the virtual world than homeless residents – just like they do in physical neighbourhoods around the globe (see Postill 2011: 121 for a Malaysian example). To recast this in a causation idiom, the social effects of building practices in Second Life came in two main forms: intrinsic to the practices, and extrinsic to them. Taken together, such effects resulted in a specific type of sociocultural change: the remaking of inworld cultural values, norms, and relationships around virtual buildings rather than virtual objects.

This brings us to the agentive (or enabling) effects of media practices. Different media practices will enable – and sometimes disable, see below – practitioners to carry out different forms of action upon the world, that is, to exercise agency. The notion of effects does not, in other words, turn people into passive recipients of an external 'impact', thereby depriving them of agency. On the contrary, effects and agency are fully compatible ideas, not least via the sibling concepts of 'enabling effects' (Bartenberger and Grubmüller 2014; Collin et al. 2011; Hayes, Johnston, and King 2009) and 'agentive effects' (Iliopoulos 2020; Medina 2018). One clear illustration of this compatibility is my earlier example from Faye Ginsburg's (2002) Inuit research. Ginsburg argues that Inuit media-making practices helped to, among other things, 'revive relations between generations' (2002: 44). That is to say, such practices were a key enabling factor in the revival of intergenerational relations; this was one of their more significant *social effects*.

Barely explored in the media and communication literature, but crucially important from an 'applied' perspective, is the question of the disabling and/or disruptive effects of media practices. Isika, Mendoza and Bosua (2020), for instance, explore the 'enabling and disruptive effects' of social media (practices) on the self-management of chronic illness. Along similar lines, but lacking a media dimension, the Norwich Access Group in the UK have campaigned for legislative changes that will address 'the disabling effects of social practices and built environments' upon the lives of people with disabilities.[2]

Conclusion

The present chapter is a first attempt at creating a heuristic around the social effects of media practices that might raise interesting questions for future empirical and theoretical work. I hope to have demonstrated that there is no reason to fear the study of such effects. These are within our grasp as media ethnographers, as long as we are prepared to think diachronically (see Postill 2017) and 'follow the effects' wherever they may take us. In fact, one surprising discovery from my (re)reading of the media anthropology literature is that we know far more about this question than we think, although we have yet to write about it explicitly and synthesise our collective findings.

To further this line of enquiry, more epistemological and empirical groundwork is needed. I propose that, first, we develop a robust conceptual vocabulary that critically interrogates and builds on the working concepts I have just listed or that draws from different sources. Second, we should reach a basic consensus on what counts as evidence that a given media practice (or set of practices) had an effect on one or more social worlds, while rejecting the default position that media effects pose an insoluble problem. Third, we should not limit ourselves to the 'ordering' effects of media practices (see Couldry 2004; Hobart 2010), like I have done in this chapter for reasons of space and cohesion. There is much to be learned, too, from the *dis*ordering – and/or disabling – effects of certain media practices. Fifth, we could connect this line of research with relevant literatures on practice theory and media and communication, such as the effects of media framing (Druckman 2001; Scheufele 1999). Finally, there already exists a vast effects vocabulary across fields as diverse as economics, physics, genetics, biology, law or medicine to draw from when required. This lexicon consists of both familiar notions (e.g. butterfly effect, domino effect, chilling effect) and unfamiliar ones (e.g. cluster effect, catch-up effect, Diderot effect).[3]

To return to my tale of entry, it is time to retire the old caricature of media effects being crudely 'linear'. Instead, we should reclaim the notion of effects from the mass communication tradition and craft sophisticated accounts of the social effects of media practices. What we need, I suggest, is a version of causation that media anthropologists – and indeed other media and communication scholars – can put to good use; we need a more complex, nuanced causation that accommodates human agency and media appropriation, yet does not overlook the social effects of media practices.

Notes

1 See the European Association of Social Anthropologists' (EASA) Media Anthropology Network's 66th e-seminar on an earlier version of this paper, held in February 2021, https://easaonline.org/networks/media/eseminars
2 http://norwichaccessgroup.org.uk/page19.shtml
3 Wikipedia (2021), List of effects, https://en.wikipedia.org/wiki/List_of_effects

References

Anderson, B. (1991 [1983]) *Imagined Communities: Reflections on the Origins and Spread of Nationalism*, London: Verso.
Askew, K. M. and R. R. Wilk (eds) (2002) *The Anthropology of Media: A Reader*, London: Blackwell.
Bartenberger, M. and V. Grubmüller (2014) 'The Enabling Effects of Open Government Data on Collaborative Governance in Smart City Contexts', *JeDEM – eJournal of eDemocracy and Open Government*, 6 (1): 36–48.
Becker, H. S. (1982) *Art Worlds*, Berkeley: University of California Press.
Boellstorff, T. (2008) *Coming of Age in Second Life: An Anthropologist Explores the Virtually Human*, Princeton, NJ: Princeton University Press.
Bräuchler, B. and J. Postill (eds) (2010) *Theorising Media and Practice*, Oxford: Berghahn.
Budka, P. and B. Bräuchler (eds) (2020) *Theorising Media and Conflict*, Oxford: Berghahn.
Burkhardt, F. and S. Smith (eds) (1990) *The Correspondence of Charles Darwin (Volume 6: 1856–1857)*, Cambridge: Cambridge University Press.
Christensen, T.H. and I. Røpke (2010) 'Can Practice Theory Inspire Studies of ICTs in Everyday Life?' in B. Bräuchler and J. Postill (eds), *Theorising Media and Practice*, Oxford: Berghahn, 233–258.
Collin, P., K. Rahilly, I. Richardson and A. Third (2011) 'The Benefits of Social Networking Services', *Cooperative Research Centre for Young People, Technology and Wellbeing*. Retrieved from www.fya.org.au/wp-content/uploads/2010/07/The-Benefits-of-Social-NetworkingServices.pdf
Couldry, N. (2004) 'Theorising Media as Practice', *Social Semiotics*, 14 (2): 115–132.
Couldry, N. and A. Hepp (2013) 'Conceptualizing Mediatization: Contexts, Traditions, Arguments', *Communication Theory*, 23 (3): 191–202.
Cox, A. M. (2012) 'An Exploration of the Practice Approach and its Place in Information Science', *Journal of Information Science*, 38 (2): 176–188.
Craig, R. T. (1999) 'Communication Theory as a Field', *Communication Theory*, 9 (2): 119–161.
Druckman, J. N. (2001) 'On the Limits of Framing Effects: Who can Frame?' *The Journal of Politics*, 63 (4): 1041–1066.
Epstein, A. L. (1958) *Politics in an Urban African Community*, Manchester: Manchester University Press.
Fontana, E. L. (2009) *Virtual Worlds, Real Subjectivities: Media Anthropology at the Personal/Public Interface*, Unpublished Master's Thesis, University of California, San Diego.
Giddens, A. (1984) *The Constitution of Society: Outline of the Theory of Structuration*, Cambridge: Polity Press.
Ginsburg, F. D., L. Abu-Lughod and B. Larkin (eds) (2002) *Media Worlds: Anthropology on New Terrain*, Berkeley: University of California Press.
Habermas, J. (1989) *The Structural Transformation of the Public Sphere*, Cambridge, MA: MIT Press.
Han, B. (2018) 'Social Media Burnout: Definition, Measurement Instrument, and Why We Care', *Journal of Computer Information Systems*, 58 (2): 122–130.
Hayes, D., K. Johnston and A. King (2009) 'Creating Enabling Classroom Practices in High Poverty Contexts', *Pedagogy, Culture & Society*, 17 (3): 251–264.
Helle-Valle, J. (2019) 'Advocating Causal Analyses of Media and Social Change by Way of Social Mechanisms', *Journal of African Media Studies*, 11 (2): 143–161.
Hepp, A. (2013) 'The Communicative Figurations of Mediatized Worlds', *European Journal of Communication*, 28 (6): 615–629.
Hepp, A., S. Hjarvard, S. and K. Lundby (2015) 'Mediatization: Theorizing the Interplay between Media, Culture and Society', *Media, Culture & Society*, 37 (2): 314–324.

Hjarvard, S. (2008) 'The Mediatization of Society: A Theory of the Media as Agents of Social and Cultural change', *Nordicom Review*, 29 (2): 105–134.

Hobart, M. (2002) 'Live or Dead? Televising Theater in Bali', in F.D. Ginsburg, L. Abu-Lughod and B. Larkin (eds), *Media Worlds: Anthropology on New Terrain*, Berkeley, CA: University of California Press, 370–382.

Hobart, M. (2010) 'What do we Mean by "Media Practices"?' in B. Bräuchler and J. Postill (eds), *Theorising Media and Practice*, Oxford: Berghahn.

Hui, A., T. Schatzki, T. and E. Shove (eds) (2017), *The Nexus of Practices: Connections, Constellations, Practitioners*, Abingdon: Taylor & Francis.

Iliopoulos, A. (2020) 'Early Body Ornamentation as Ego-Culture: Tracing the Co-Evolution of Aesthetic Ideals and Cultural Identity', *Semiotica*, 232: 187–233.

Isika, N., A. Mendoza and R. Bosua (2020) 'An Affordance Perspective on the Enabling and Disruptive Effects of Social Media Tools on Self-Management of Chronic Illness', in K. Sandhu (ed), *Opportunities and Challenges in Digital Healthcare Innovation*, Hershey, PA: IGI Global, 36–56.

Kelty, C. M. (2008) *Two Bits: The Cultural Significance of Free Software*, Durham, NC: Duke University Press.

Kelty, C.M. (2010) 'Theorising the Practices of Free Software: The Movement', in B. Bräuchler and J. Postill (eds), *Theorising Media and Practice*, Oxford: Berghahn.

Kubitschko, S. (2018) 'Acting on Media Technologies and Infrastructures: Expanding the Media as Practice Approach', *Media, Culture & Society*, 40 (4): 629–635.

Lazarsfeld, P. and R. Merton (1969) 'Mass Communication, Popular Taste and Organised Social Action', in W. Schramm (ed), *Mass Communications*, Urbana: University of Illinois Press.

Lull, J. (1990) *Inside Family Viewing: Ethnographic Research on Television's Audiences*, London: Routledge.

Malaby, T (2011) *Making Virtual Worlds*, Ithaca, NY: Cornell University Press.

Maller, C. (2017) 'Epigenetics, Theories of Social Practice and Lifestyle Disease', in A. Hui, T. Schatzki, T. and E. Shove (eds), *The Nexus of Practices: Connections, Constellations, Practitioners*, Abingdon: Taylor & Francis, 80–92.

Mattoni, A. and E. Treré (2014) 'Media Practices, Mediation Processes, and Mediatization in the Study of Social Movements', *Communication Theory*, 24 (3): 252–271.

McGovney-Ingram, R. L. (2013) *Race, Gender, and Media Practices: A Critical Framing Analysis of the Media's Coverage of USDA Worker Shirley Sherrod*, Unpublished PhD Dissertation, Texas A&M University.

Medina, C. (2018) 'Digital Latin@ Storytelling: Testimonio as Multi-modal Resistance', in C. Medina and O. Pimentel (eds), *Racial Shorthand: Coded Discrimination Contested in Social Media*, Logan, UT: Computers and Composition Digital Press.

Miller, D., J. Sinanan, X. Wang, T. McDonald, N. Haynes, E. Costa, J. Spyer, S. Venkatraman and R. Nicolescu (2016) *How the World Changed Social Media*, London: UCL Press.

Morley, D. (1986) *Family Television*, London: Routledge.

Ortner, S. B. (1984) 'Theory in Anthropology since the Sixties', *Comparative Studies in Society and History*, 26 (1): 126–166.

Postill, J. (2006) *Media and Nation Building: How the Iban became Malaysian*, Oxford: Berghahn.

Postill, J. (2008) 'Localizing the Internet Beyond Communities and Networks', *New Media & Society*, 10 (3): 413–431.

Postill, J. (2010a) 'Introduction: Theorising Media and Practice', in B. Bräuchler and J. Postill (eds), *Theorising Media and Practice*, Oxford: Berghahn.

Postill, J. (2010b) 'Researching the Internet', *Journal of the Royal Anthropological Institute*, 16 (3): 646–650.

Postill, J. (2011) *Localizing the Internet*, Oxford: Berghahn.

Postill, J. (2017) 'The Diachronic Ethnography of Media: from Social Changing to Actual Social Changes', *Moment, Journal of Cultural Studies*, 4 (1): 19–43.

Postill, J. (2018) *The Rise of Nerd Politics: Digital Activism and Political Change*, London: Pluto.

Postill, J., V. Lasa and G. Zhang (2020) 'Monitory Politics, Digital Surveillance and New Protest Movements: An Analysis of Hong Kong's Umbrella Movement', in S. Maasen and J. H. Passoth (eds), *Soziologie des Digitalen-Digitale Soziologie?*, Baden-Baden: Nomos Verlagsgesellschaft, 453–466.

San Cornelio, G. and E. Gómez-Cruz (2014) 'Co-creation and Participation as a Means of Innovation in New Media: An Analysis of Creativity in the Photographic Field', *International Journal of Communication*, 8: 1–20.

Schatzki, T. (1996) *Social Practices: A Wittgensteinian Approach to Human Activity and the Social*, Cambridge: Cambridge University Press.

Scheufele, D. A. (1999) 'Framing as a Theory of Media Effects', *Journal of Communication*, 49 (1): 103–122.

Schmidt, R. (2017) 'Reflexive Knowledge in Practices', in A. Hui, T. Schatzki and E. Shove (eds), *The Nexus of Practices: Connections, Constellations, Practitioners*, London: Routledge, 141–154.

Sewell, W. H. (2005) *Logics of History: Social Theory and Social Transformation*, Chicago: University of Chicago Press.

Sheehy, B. and Feaver, D. (2015) 'Designing Effective Regulation: A Normative Theory', *University of New South Wales Law Journal*, 38: 392–425.

Shibutani, T. (1955) 'Reference Groups as Perspectives', *American Journal of Sociology*, 60: 522–529.

Slater, D. (2014) *New Media, Development and Globalization: Making Connections in the Global South*. New York: John Wiley & Sons.

Strauss, A. L. (1978) 'A Social World Perspective', in N. K. Denzin (ed), *Symbolic Interaction* 1, Greenwich, CT: JAI Press, 119–128.

Takhteyev, Y. (2012) *Coding Places: Software Practice in a South American City*. Cambridge, MA: MIT Press.

Tenhunen, S. (2018) *A Village Goes Mobile: Telephony, Mediation, and Social Change in Rural India*, Oxford: Oxford University Press.

Warde, A. (2005) 'Consumption and theories of practice', Journal of Consumer Culture, 5(2): 131–153

Wasik, B. (2009) *And Then There's This: How Stories Live and Die in Viral Culture*, London: Penguin.

Wilk, R. (2002) 'Television, Time, and the National Imaginary in Belize', in F. D. Ginsburg, L. Abu-Lughod and B. Larkin (eds), *Media Worlds: Anthropology on New Terrain*, Berkeley: University of California Press, 171–186.

Yang, M. M. H. (2002) 'Mass Media and Transnational Subjectivity in Shanghai', in F.D. Ginsburg, L. Abu-Lughod and B. Larkin (eds), *Media Worlds: Anthropology on New Terrain*, Berkeley: University of California Press, 189–210.

Yu, Z. (2021) 'An Empirical Study of Consumer Video Activism in China: Protesting against Businesses with Short Videos', *Chinese Journal of Communication*, 14 (3): 297–312.

9
TELEVISION IS NOT A DEMOCRACY

The Limits of Interactive Broadcast in Japan

Elizabeth A. Rodwell

On the third floor of Fuji Television's labyrinthian headquarters, staff circulate around a dimly lit, grey-carpeted television control room—typical, apart from the Apple laptops scattered on ledges around the switchboards. Two glass-walled rooms off to the side hold the technology and people responsible for this program's internet livestream, which runs longer than its parallel television broadcast (8–11 pm, versus 9–10:25 pm for the TV portion). Therefore, it has already been almost an hour since two of the hosts entered the leftmost room to start an internet discussion of North Korea's threat to Japan, while in the main studio below another male-female pair are having their hair combed and makeup touched up in final preparation for television broadcast. As an assistant director counts down, chatter in the big studio slows while the internet broadcast in the room above continues unaffected. "*Ippun!*" (one minute) calls the assistant.

"BS[1] *Fuji LIVE: Social TV The Compass*" (*BS Fuji Raivu: Sōsharu TV Za Konpasu*) (hereafter called *The Compass*)[2] was a hybrid online/tv news variety show and the project of an ambitious and idealistic cohort within Tokyo's television community. It would also soon be canceled by its parent network, which assigned it neither the resources nor time-slot necessary to succeed. The show's two broadcasts converge at regular intervals, as the internet hosts descend from their glass box to the main studio to join the conversation downstairs. By any standard, *The Compass* has a lot going on: while guest experts discuss current events, audiences weigh in via Twitter (#compassTV), Facebook, or Japanese streaming broadcast platform Nico Nico Douga (NND). And the NND viewing experience is especially unique: what began as a YouTube aggregator evolved into a forum for users to comment on streaming content in real-time, their words passing directly over internet broadcast screens (see Figure 9.1). Juggling television, NND, and social media is no small feat for the production staff. Behind the TV hosts' table, a ticker displays aggregated Twitter comments, while assistant directors periodically run polls of NND users' opinions and feature the results on both feeds. Hosts repeat users' Twitter comments and questions to its panel of commentators. If there is such a thing as too much user input, this could be it. Or it is the future.

It is the relationship between these components and professional practice that I will discuss in this chapter: the ways that television producers tried to push the limits of technology to create a current-events forum intended to be more democratic than the usual TV news fare. *The Compass* as a case study is significant for two reasons. First, the program illustrates how the

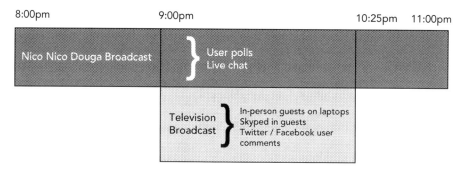

Figure 9.1 The Nico Nico Douga broadcast runs longer than the TV broadcast, and though they overlap at times, each involves different kinds of interaction
Source: Image by the author.

characteristics of a television broadcast are constituted by the composite practices of the production process, and how this broadcast changes when the TV cameras turn off, and webcams turn on. Second, the program was considered exemplary by the social television community, that is, a group of TV industry insiders seeking to evolve Japanese broadcast from a technological standpoint and circumvent a notoriously censorious and restrictive climate for news production through audience participation (Borowiec, 2016; Kingston, 2018; Snow, 2019). This group's attention to *The Compass'* structure and dissection of its successes made it one of the most prominent of the early social TV experiments in 2012.

Through this example, I will argue that the ways this program used technology—specifically its secondary and less formal internet livestream—introduced a rarely seen intimacy to television. However, despite any democratic overtures made by the inclusion of Twitter voices and NND comments, television remains transparently anti-democratic. While the collaboration represented by *The Compass* and more high-tech interactive TV programs complicated the relationship between audiences and expert producers of media content by relinquishing partial control over programmatic narrative to an unpredictable and unknown body, these programs remain subject to the traditional gatekeeping practices of mass media (Ihlebæk & Krumsvik, 2015, p. 472). I have previously written about "social TV" in conjunction with entertainment/games (Rodwell, 2021a), and about alternative news production in conjunction with strategies to bypass traditional gatekeeping (Rodwell, 2021b). By contrast, in this chapter, I wish to focus on the tension between the nature of *The Compass* as an interactive experiment, and the insular structure of the Japanese television industry. *The Compass* offers an opportunity to explore how social TV and experimental production strategies were combined to (attempt to) introduce diversity into the Japanese news landscape.

This account is based on my fieldwork in and around the television industry in Tokyo, including in-studio observation of many programs' production, and interviews with more than 30 producers, directors, bureau chiefs, writers, and camera operators. Anthropology as a field has historically approached the study of television from three overlapping perspectives: as an agent of cultural dissemination/tool of national hegemony or identity (e.g. Abu-Lughod, 2002; Barkin, 2013; Giusto, 2020; Howe, 2008; Kottak, 2016; Kottak & Pace, 2022; Mankekar, 2002); reception studies (e.g. Abu-Lughod, 2008; Kazi, 2018; Mankekar, 1999; Vidali, 2010); and a smaller body of literature on agents of television production (e.g. Dornfeld, 1998; Grindstaff, 2002; Lukács, 2010; Moll, 2018). This chapter belongs to the last category and is uniquely positioned by the length of time spent in television production spaces (18 months), access to the producers themselves, and the status of these field sites as major hubs of national television production.

On-site fieldwork has made it possible for me to examine the social practices surrounding experimental television production and the relationship between media authors and audiences as articulated by these authors and complicated by the structure of interactive TV. In this chapter I use Postill's (2010) explication of practice to interpret the routines, habits, and bodily discipline characteristic of television producers. Similarly, I draw on Bourdieu's notion of habitus, classified in his work as a product of history, a type of "negative freedom" (1995, p. 33), and the routine conditions associated with a class of existence. One's habitus, in Bourdieu's words, "produces individual and collective practices" (ibid., p. 34). Thus, practice and habitus intersect as conceptual categories, and are taken up in this chapter to interpret *The Compass* staff's diligent maintenance of the boundaries between their subjectivity and that of audiences.

Although this chapter focuses on the case study of an individual program, *The Compass* was closely linked to the broader landscape of Japanese experimental television and journalism and was the subject of many industry workshops and informal social events. As has been typical in fieldwork among media producers (Hannerz, 1998; Ortner, 2009), there was little participation involved in my "participant observation" of this show's broadcast. That is, until I was dragged onto the show's internet livestream and interviewed by its hosts as a form of reciprocal scrutiny. Most of the time, however, I shadowed producers and directors while they worked, my status closer to that of the audience members discussed here than the staff of these shows.

The Twenty-First Century Audience

Viewers of *The Compass*' NND internet stream were privy to an informal construction of the relationship between audience and presenter. The highly controlled comportment typical of a Japanese television newsreader was relaxed somewhat to allow for this reframing. Not just webcast, not quite formal broadcast, the internet-streaming portion of *The Compass* broke ground for its willingness to genuinely ad-lib, and for the feeling one gets in watching that its producers were experimenting with and through viewers. Having never done this before, television was willing to play within a context (news programming) that had historically preferred to use bodies as mere conduits for information.

The question of audience positionality and its relationship to professional practice is central to media anthropology (e.g. Englehart, 2003; Ganti, 2014; Kazi, 2018; Matza, 2009). In her canonical account, Ien Ang (1991) described audiences as an unknowable category, a discourse object useful for indicating something that cannot fully be measured or seen. And indeed, in conversations with television producers, the slipperiness of audiences, and the inadequacy of the antiquated means by which we still categorize and account for them is raised as a primary object of their concern. For one, audience capacity for self-assessment is lacking; when asked to locate themselves within survey boxes and account for time spent, audiences are suspected of aspirational thinking.

But participants in *The Compass* differ based on how much data they provide—voluntarily and involuntarily. More than an aggregate body whose engagement and interest are governed by ambiguity, these are individuals engaged in active self-representation and commentary on TV content. And although NND and Twitter bestow certain anonymity, both services classify users as they create accounts and track them afterwards. Simple data such as age, gender, and location are more than adequate to determine ratings and sell sponsorship, particularly when allied with commenting as a sign of active engagement. While the industry still tolerates the ratings derived from in-home aggregation hardware, websites like NND helpfully supplement older methods of data collection and complicate stereotypes of audiences as passive observers.

Anthropology has historically used sited fieldwork to complicate reductive assessments of audience reception by consuming mass media content with people in their homes or public spaces (Abu-Lughod, 2008; Englehart, 2003; Mankekar, 1999). But Nico Nico Douga also granted me the capacity to experience live television simultaneously with both audiences and broadcast professionals—to observe the convergence of their reactions and the effects of immediate feedback on the in-studio climate. Indeed, the users with whom I shared virtual space on Twitter and *The Compass*'s NND livestream were a lively and opinionated bunch whose commentary overlapped with that of the show's invited guests (but was expressed in less restrained language). Although some of these guests attended the TV broadcast from the studio, others joined remotely via Skype, and nearly everyone on both the NND livestream and TV broadcast sat behind a laptop computer regardless. Therefore, differences in overall comportment between guest and audience participants was usually attributable to established practice and habitus for each role. Credentialing and a mandate to represent an academic or journalistic habitus restricted guests' capacity to speak freely while also contradictorily granting them passage through television's gatekeepers. Typically for television, barriers to open audience participation remained intact despite the programs' promotion as interactive experiences.

Television is Not a Democracy

I attended *The Compass*'s final broadcast, and its multiple spaces of production felt charged. Many more people than usual milled about in the shadows of the cavernous studio space, some of whom were Fuji TV staff generally interested in social media and television, and who wished to bear witness to the end of this experiment. Tonight's internet audience was also larger than usual; before the television broadcast even began, 11,707 Nico Nico Douga users had already tuned in online. They banter about the prime minister, the underfunding of interesting television programs (such as *The Compass*), as well as tonight's theme: the political advantages to being media/tech savvy. On this last night of the program, the informality governing the internet livestream especially breaks with that of the main television broadcast, and while a lack of commercial break has always encouraged internet-streaming hosts to engage in corporeal gestures before the cameras such as putting in eyedrops, *The Compass*'s finale grants a certain permissiveness in which even the relaxed rules of internet streaming may be broken. For example, high ranking production staff who would typically remain off-screen wander in and out of the NND transmission room, briefly sharing space and bantering with the program's internet hosts in front of the camera.

While television writ large guides viewers towards acceptance of a pre-set narrative, it leaves room for subjective decoding and has been well-established as unfolding within a broader web of social practices (Abu-Lughod, 2008; Pace, 2009; Postill, 2009; Roald, 2016). And for Japanese TV producers, one of these practices is to direct audience responses by deploying the faces of celebrities in small boxes on screen to view content and react synchronously with home audiences. This phenomenon of replacing implicit narrative direction with overt assignation of meaning is not unique to Japanese TV, though many countries rely on less proscriptive strategies (Cushion & Thomas, 2013). Television-sanctioned interpretations such as this do not always resonate with audiences: one TV industry employee, Ujiie Natsuhiko (2013a) writes that a major problem with Japanese television is that its variety programming represents a highly one-sided (*ippōteki*) sense of fun, while information and news programs speak to their audiences as though removed, from above ("*ue kara mesen de tsutaerarete iru*") (ibid., para. 3).

That television should conservatively repeat successful formulae is only part of the story and the reason that media anthropology advocates for fieldwork to enrich our understanding of producers' practices and ground our theory in what they *do* as well as what they say (Hobart, 2007, p. 7). As Bourdieu theorizes, habitus can result in an unpredictable, but also homogenous range of practices, and television formulas reflect that (1995, p. 35). However, much can be learned by examining how programs are the products of conversations between their authors, and assembled by means of professional dialog that combines assumptions about the characteristics of audiences with self-referential discourse about the essential components of good television (Hill, 2016; te Walvaart, Dhoest, & Van den Bulck, 2017, p. 1141). In other words, something of the autopoietic nature of the medium is located in the repetitive nature of the production process itself, and the repetitive nature of professional enculturation. Time spent with producers therefore allows us to disentangle the contested meanings of production's cyclical flow (Postill, 2010).

Further, television endures what anthropologists Dominic Boyer and Cymene Howe have referred to, using Alexi Yurchak's term, as "hypernormalization" (2015, p. 32), defined as the relentless reproduction of standards already deemed acceptable by a conservative status quo and accounted for in their professional habitus. In their example, the speeches of local Russian communist leaders engage in political hedging and demonstrations of respect by creating speeches comprised of text directly appropriated from their political predecessors. Television producers (in Japan, and elsewhere) also deploy a normalized authorial voice, consistently reappropriating parts of TV's semiotic ecosystems within a production echo chamber and churning out new programming that closely resembles the old. This tendency of television reflects the condition (and plight) of expert practice in a conservative corporate setting, as a successful TV career demands an expression of expertise characterized by integration of the status quo. In the case of Japanese television, performance of habitus means shepherding original programs that neither deviate from standard formulae, nor attract negative attention from politicians.

Compared to the internet livestream, live television operates with as much control as possible and merging *The Compass*'s components into a coherent whole requires careful choreography: 1. An assistant holds up signs indicating whose turn it is to speak. 2. The TV broadcast hosts are responsible for posing discussion questions out loud to the embodied/remote panel. 3. Another assistant repeats the question on the NND internet stream as a user poll. 4. The poll results are conveyed on TV as part of the broadcast. 5. The discussion moves on to comments from the *nama koe* (literally, "raw voices") of Twitter. Meanwhile, 25,812 people are now in the NND chatroom.

That the comments of these individuals participating on Twitter, Facebook, and NND are incorporated into this program should not be inferred overly optimistically as part of a democratization effort (Karlsson et al., 2015). Indeed, the filtering practices of TV are on display as the commentary of online users is managed by assistant directors whose actions hinder the capacity of this program to function as democratic. The sheer volume of this kind of commentary is invoked to defend aggregation such as Beatrice Blaagaard's (2013, p. 1086) assessment that the increasing amount of news commentary has made the role of journalists all the more essential, as they are needed to "filter, to select, to think about information" in a way that simply is no longer feasible if it is not one's job to do so. A decade earlier, media scholar John Hartley (2000) made a similar observation, branding technologically advanced nations "redactional societ[ies]" within which there is simply too much information being generated at any one time for any single individual to apprehend the whole. He argued that under such conditions, organizations (composites of individuals) rather than individuals (by name) become trusted sources of truth as they engage in the work of redaction, revising information into new forms, and curating salient points on behalf of the public.

Mass media producers have internalized this perspective and use it to defend their role against the individualizing nature of social media. As global journalism has come to emphasize a stationary gathering of information over a mobile and embodied "pursuit of the truth"—journalistic practice has become about "gathering, filtering, structuring and disseminating" (Blaagaard, 2013, p. 1086; Boyer, 2013). That the comments scrolling by on my NND iPad application are generally "quick take" opinions without attribution is one of the ways that they depart from conventional journalism, especially in Japan. Social media input is processed (redacted) by *Compass* staff with a learned sense of appropriate tone and performance (habitus), who choose comments to broadcast on television largely based on what they exclude: overt racism, conspiracy theories, and derogatory comments about individuals.

Internet content proliferates because of the comparatively low barrier to entry required, but this means inconsistency in the quality of commentary, which television professionals attempt to eliminate as much as possible under the banner of "appropriateness." While the freedom granted online viewers in Japan can be attributed to a lack of accountability to institutional power sources, media executives circulate in proximity to politicians and are largely responsible for enforcing an institutional "trickle down" effect (Rodwell, 2021b). The system grants politicians a wide berth to manipulate TV broadcasters through mechanisms such as party boycotts and public censure, as each station depends on government approval for the renewal of their broadcast licenses (Mulgan, 2017; Nakano, 2017).

Research continues to suggest that differences in online and TV participation are attributable to both a smaller default audience and degree of anonymity anticipated by participants in online platforms (Løvlie, Ihlebæk, & Larsson, 2018). A lack of identification with key aspects of a journalistic habitus such as deference to credentialed facts, as well as an absence of training in journalistic neutrality provide secondary explanations (Eldridge II, 2019). In many countries, television is also often limited by legal and social considerations that impact its messaging, and TV commentators in Japan have faced substantial pushback for criticizing the government (Sekiguchi, 2013).

Further, required broadcast licenses keep the total number of Japanese television channels low and maximizes their audience share, while demanding the medium strike a balance between the fragmentation of targeted marketing, and forms of address suited to national bodies (Lukács, 2010). Simply put, with only six television stations, the task of representation is distributed among relatively few entities. Thus, online video streaming (like NND) has represented a form of competition for audiences that TV stations were not accustomed to. In Ujiie Natsuhiko's (2013b) interpretation, the privileged space of television infantilized it, allowed it to ignore the development of other media until: "the wall that has protected the television industry for more than half a century [began] to collapse" (para. 12).

Is Nico Nico Douga the Enemy?

Of the more than a third of Japan's population who had a NND account during *The Compass*, many are the *"datsu terebi"* (removed from TV) generation about whose experience it has been written: "in the era of bidirectional media, television feels 'pushy' somehow" (AsahiShimbun, 2013). Despite a tendency to taxonomically relegate them to the category of the nerdy/anti-social *otaku*, and/or the politically right wing and mostly male *netto uyoku*, NND's user base (comprised during the final broadcast of 80 percent individuals ages 10–30), is extremely desirable to marketers, and represents a body that is crucial to both understand and appropriate for marketing purposes (AERA, 2013). Nico Nico Douga's strength and its appeal to audiences lies partially in its capacity to allow viewers to interact with hosts, and with one another simultaneously.

But the newspaper *Asahi Shimbun*, who as the owner of one of Japan's television networks (TV Asahi), has a stake in defending television, reminded its readers that Japanese citizens turned to television immediately after the 2011 earthquake and Fukushima nuclear plant disasters, and can still reliably be counted on to prefer television for watching sporting events. Asahi also argues without substantiation that television remains a major source of accurate (*seikaku*) transmission about world affairs, and a major source of documentary-style content (AERA, 2013). Nonetheless, one of the advantages of platforms like NND is their capacity to circumvent a historical tendency for audiences to identify with individual reporters or newscasters only as legitimized by entrenched institutions. While NND grants users anonymity to push back against TV broadcast norms, the platform also functions like YouTube (and other video platforms) in allowing individual content creators to become trusted redactors.

The Compass, then, tries to appropriate the benefits of both social and conventional media: At 9:55 pm during a routine commercial break, staff scramble to touch-up makeup and hastily curate comments from Twitter and NND. Two assistant directors (ADs) peer into laptops, while those whose jobs are not more immediately pressing snap cellphone photographs of the stage set's final use. Ignoring the bustle around them, and even the finessing of their appearance, the TV broadcast hosts page through scripts to get a sense of the lines they will need to deliver. As another commercial pops up on the in-studio monitors, the two ADs select several comments from Twitter user @ray_luno, and a third calls out panelists' speaking order upon resumption of the television broadcast. Of the 35,967 individuals now in the NND chatroom, most are typing emphatic missives about the state of mass media, or about how the program ought to continue:

> "It's said that mass media came to an end fifteen years ago." (*Masu ga owari o tsugeta to iwarete, mō 15-nen darō.*)
> "It's the era of making mass media online." (*Netto de masukomi o kaku jidai.*)
> "There's still a wall between the net and TV." (*Kono jiten de terebi to netto ni kabe o tsukutteru kan aru na.*)
> "Television has no future. (Laugh)" (*Terebi no mirai wa naitte koto ja ne? w.*)
> "TV already doesn't have a bright future." (*Iya, mō terebi ni akarui mirai wa nai desu yo.*)
> "[It had] good contents." (*Ii kontentsu datta no ni.*)[3]
> (In response to a user question about why *The Compass* was cancelled):
> "Pressure from the top?" (*Ue kara no atsuryoku?*)
> "More people watched online than on TV?" (*Terebi de miru yori netto de miru hito ga ōkattan ja ne?*)
> "Money." (*Okane da ne.*)
> "So, what's next week? Just uncut NND broadcast?" (*De raishū wa? Niko-nama dake demo iin da ze?*)

And as the TV broadcast resumes, the scholars and staff on-stage engage in a meta-conversation about the necessity and importance of programs such as *The Compass*, and a collective instinct that such bidirectionality (*sōhōkō-sei*), at the very least, is the future of television. While the program approaches its finale, several of Fuji TV's most prominent innovators join the hosts on stage to close with a discussion of the network's intention to pursue this kind of programming as part of an overall modernization project. Then, as the TV program moves to commercial, the hosts turn off their webcams and the NND screen goes black. Meanwhile, the user comments continue their march from right to left over this black box, glowing green like input on an old computer terminal.

One producer at Japan's public broadcast station, NHK, revealed that shows like this answered the hopes of early interactive television, including a 1993 program he worked on that introduced the possibility of partial collaboration with audiences: "SIM TV" (*Kinmirai Terebi SIM*, or as Nishida[4] translated the name: "Simulating the Future with Technology"). In an early example of television that allowed audiences to act directly upon the appearance of a mass broadcast's visual presentation, viewers could call in with analog phones and change the graphics displayed on-set.

Nishida additionally sought to allow viewers selection of camera angles, anticipating work from media scholars like Jostein Gripsrud, who argued that television would eventually allow users to recover control over a critical aspect of their agency—the decision about where to look (2004). Nishida similarly imagined audiences taking on the work of control room broadcast technicians, whose job is usually to signal and execute camera changes. However, the limits of early 1990s technology challenged his vision, as it was impossible for a viewer to change the camera more than once every 20 seconds by phone. Based on the audience size anticipated by even a low-rated program, the process seemed guaranteed to generate a frustrated queue of audience members who never made it past a busy signal to take their turn with the camera, and the experiment was short-lived. In this case, producers excited by the concept of democratizing the viewing process were stymied by technological limitations, and while the barriers to digital participation have decreased, the conservatism of television (and its allocation of interactive TV to undesirable time slots or secondary channels) remains an impediment for the genre.

The Future of Television, the Status of Images

After a break, those who worked on the show sit down in the main broadcast studio and, although the final TV broadcast has ended, they turn the cameras on for the NND livestream to take questions from its chatroom. While the show's hosts join the discussion, as television "personalities" they receive another round of makeup and hair touch-ups before returning to the stage. This impromptu panel breaks with typical TV formality to discuss the difference between kinds of audiences (*shichōsha*) and "TV people" (*terebi no katagata*, rather than *geinōjin*–entertainers). The difference, according to one producer, is that internet comments are "straight" (*sutorēto*), while those of TV people are often "slanted." Speaking to the more than 30,000 people in the chat room by this time, another producer boldly claims that TV culture is contrary to freedom of the press, and to introduce any substance they must connect to spaces like the Nico Nico Douga chat room. His interpretation is consistent with my own, that the comportment and freedom allowed TV presenters exists in a sliding scale, with the TV hosts on one end and anonymous internet users on the other. "Straight" here means uninhibited, while "slanted" reflects the institutional and social influences mentioned above (the desire to keep one's job and to avoid censure, for example).

The wrap-up eventually progresses from the virtual space of NND to a nearby American Western themed restaurant for drinks, food, and a "straight" post-mortem on the program. Between toasts by the assembled staff of *The Compass*, a producer laments that he wants to make more programs of this sort, but that they are not valued by the networks. He invokes Marshall McLuhan by name, emphasizing loudly to be heard over the din: "*media wa messēji de aru!*" (the *media* is the message). This translation of the phrase, the use of the word *media* over the word *medium* initially startles me. I ask about it, and he paradoxically insists that it is always translated into Japanese in this way to remain consistent with McLuhan's intentionality. It is the *media* who become the message, as a group of people driving societal conversations and (in this case) seeking to connect with internet commentators as a means of engaging both the institutionally and individually enculturated parts of themselves. Recalling the staff's on-stage discussion, I ask if he's thinking about the comparative "straightness" of internet commenting when arguing that the media/medium constitutes the message. And would television always be considered "slanted," even if its objective in news contexts is to perform neutrality? He corrects me on this, too, and in so doing devises the perspective of this chapter: isn't forced neutrality a kind of slanting? Indeed, the medium's self-conscious refusal to take a position is notable, and commentators on *The Compass* habitually avoid personal identification with a viewpoint by acknowledging political positions in the passive voice and with practiced indirectness. This is characteristic of the professional practices of "TV people"— those whose job it is to host programs, in addition to those who make appearances on TV.

Another producer, Eki, is listening silently next to us. He changes the subject to the economic conditions of television labor, pointing out to me that the individuals drinking together are mostly employees of various production companies and not Fuji TV—and will be scattered to different programs soon. He later writes in an email:

> The Compass and BS Fuji Live (another program he worked on) were experimental, interesting programs that allowed professionals and the general public to discuss the news and social phenomenon, to exchange opinions. The style of the program was not fully realized, even immature—the program was cancelled before it could mature. But I think programming like this will become ubiquitous in the future.

Eki identified sports as the genre most likely to facilitate interactivity, as audiences were already inclined towards live participation and a desire to talk about it with others. "People already want to share the 'now' of sports viewing," he noted. But he was clear that he did not necessarily see "social TV" as the future of the medium and predicted:

> the devices on which television can be watched in the future will increase, and the content consumed on viewing platforms will include TV without being limited to it. The likelihood that social TV will spread in the future is high, but the future of television has no relation to social TV, and social TV has no relation to the future of television.

Conclusion

The hindsight provided by nearly two more decades of television development informs my challenge to this notion of television as ever being a slippery medium. If anything, TV has proven as exasperatingly wed to conventional practices as the corporations within which it is produced. Though affected by the same neoliberal economic forces that have pushed so many large companies to outsource jobs, rely on contingent labor, and pressure employees to cover jobs previously assigned to multiple individuals, television has adapted and is still producing hits. If anything, the logic of television as a medium remains intact, as it has spent the past two decades manipulating puzzle pieces in attempt to fit interactivity to television without significantly changing its practices or challenging the habitus of its staff. With television producers sharing many of the same ideals as academics about the potential sociopolitical ramifications of bidirectional mass media (and much the same skepticism/cynicism), it can be tempting to interpret the ways that viewer contributions have been integrated into programming with excessive optimism. But is the integration of Twitter comments into news broadcasts fundamentally different from practices begun in the past of reading audience letters onscreen, or taking calls from viewers? Television has remained remarkably stable even as technology in general has changed rapidly around it and the tools with which we engage it become smaller, more portable, and tailored to on-demand viewing. While Japan has developed the means by which to alter television technology through participatory TV show/games (Rodwell, 2021a), these tools have been appropriated by shows like *The Compass*, which was hindered by resource limitations that clashed with the ambitions of its creators and reflected a lack of institutional interest in expanding news discussion to include audiences. With its webcams attached to bulky laptops, and a visual interface resembling a Skype call, the program seemed almost retro at times. However, absent network willingness to pay for more expensive technologies, it also represented the work of visionaries trying to exploit all the interactive technology possible on a limited budget.

One of the major themes revealed by fieldwork in the Japanese television industry is the discrepancy between its conservatism as a product of institutions versus the experimentally minded ethos of individual producers working for the major broadcasters. These individuals, active within local interactive TV interest groups and impressive in their command of emergent technologies, identify participation as a means of making television content more compelling for audiences. Consequently, they fabricate programs around what audiences can *do* in relation to programming. As though informed by John Hartley's (2004) assessment that TV will never be considered alongside other "literate" forms of art until audiences can both read and write in response to it, production staff seek to elevate programs like *The Compass* by encouraging participation in current-events debates.

But access to the television screen is still tightly regulated, even as comments are unmoderated online. More so even than Twitter, Nico Nico Douga's enforced anonymity encourages open expression of even the most fringe perspectives, so its chatroom/window can never be shown on television. Indeed, user comments do not even pass over the same images that are shown on TV: as the NND hosts join the TV hosts in the main studio at designated intervals, *The Compass*'s internet livestream remains a separate feed that transmits only from its hosts' laptop cameras. Therefore, despite making gestures towards integrating viewer perspectives into the broadcast, this show is not a public forum. For television in general, gatekeeping practices remain integral to the production process and bidirectionality limited, with assistants sending questions and polls to the online chat and showing results of these polls alongside curated tweets as part of the program's cautious inscription of "raw voices."

While even countries with a liberal mass media perform gatekeeping and are influenced by public (and advertiser) pressure, TV will remain an especially regulated space in Japan so long as political disfavor can easily destabilize networks' capacity to keep individual programs or broadcasters on the air. Pressure on management in the networks was, during my fieldwork, frequently discussed by media professionals, and some topics (like the role of Tokyo Electric in the Fukushima nuclear disaster) were known to be risky or forbidden on air. Nonetheless, experimentally minded staff sought to reconnect disillusioned or distracted audiences to the medium by inviting them to contribute within designated spaces. Despite live television's capacity to engender *communitas*, the medium remains, as Rancière defined it, "an aesthetic community structured by disconnection" (2014, p. 59). This disconnection is enforced by the practices and habitus of its creators as a protective mechanism used to define their role, defend their status as professionals, and protect their employer.

Notes

1 BS stands for "broadcast satellite."
2 As of September 2021, you could still see a YouTube user uploaded video of how the show worked: https://youtu.be/y9eY_5OAwcg
3 A user poll featured at the end showed that 78.9 percent of NND users thought *The Compass* was "very good" (*totemo yokatta*) and 17.6 percent that it was "pretty good" (*ma ma yokatta*). (*Fieldnotes* March 26, 2013).
4 All names of television personnel used in this chapter are pseudonyms.

References

Abu-Lughod, L. (2002). Egyptian Melodrama: Technology of the Modern Subject? In F. Ginsburg, L. Abu-Lughod, & B. Larkin (Eds.), *Media Worlds: Anthropology on New Terrain* (pp. 115–133). University of California Press.
Abu-Lughod, L. (2008). *Dramas of Nationhood: The Politics of Television in Egypt*. University of Chicago Press.
AERA. (2013, Feb. 11). Hitto no Shigoto Jūtsu (The Art of Making a Hit). *Asahi Shimbun Weekly: AERA*, 10–15.
Ang, I. (1991). *Desperately Seeking the Audience*. Routledge.
Asahi Shimbun. (2013, Feb. 15). Netto ni Makenai 'Daradara Chikara' mo Ikasu Terebi no Dai Fukkatsu (a Revival of TV That Makes the Most of Its 'Dull Power' to Compete with the Internet). *Asahi Shimbun*. http://astand.asahi.com/webshinsho/asahipub/aera/product/2013021200006.html
Barkin, G. (2013). Reterritorialization in the Micromediascape: Indonesian Regional Television Amid the Rise of Normative Media-Islam. *Visual Anthropology Review*, *29*(1), 42–56.
Blaagaard, B. B. (2013). Shifting Boundaries: Objectivity, Citizen Journalism and Tomorrow's Journalists. *Journalism*, *14*(8), 1076–1090.
Borowiec, S. (2016). Writers of Wrongs. *Index on Censorship*, *45*(2), 48–50.
Bourdieu, P. (1995). Structures, Habitus, Practices. In J. D. Faubion (Ed.), *Rethinking the Subject: An Anthology of Contemporary European Social Thought* (pp. 31–45). Westview Press.
Boyer, D. (2013). *The Life Informatic: Newsmaking in the Digital Era*. Cornell University Press.
Boyer, D., & Howe, C. (2015). Portable Analytics and Lateral Theory. In D. Boyer, J. D. Faubion, & G. E. Marcus (Eds.), *Theory Can Be More Than It Used to Be: Learning Anthropology's Method in a Time of Transition*. Cornell University Press.
Cushion, S., & Thomas, R. (2013). The Mediatization of Politics. *The International Journal of Press/Politics*, *18*(3), 360–380.
Dornfeld, B. (1998). *Producing Public Television, Producing Public Culture*. Princeton University Press.
Eldridge II, S. A. (2019). Where Do We Draw the Line? Interlopers, (Ant)Agonists, and an Unbounded Journalistic Field. *Media and Communication*, *7*(4), 8–18.
Englehart, L. (2003). Media Activism in the Screening Room: The Significance of Viewing Locations, Facilitation and Audience Dynamics in the Reception of HIV/Aids Films in South Africa. *Visual Anthropology Review*, *19*(1–2), 73–85.
Ganti, T. (2014). The Value of Ethnography. *Media Industries*, *1*(1), 16–20.
Giusto, S. (2020). Through the Looking Glass: Televised Politics in Contemporary Populist Italy. *PoLAR: Political and Legal Anthropology Review*, *43*(1), 87–102.
Grindstaff, L. (2002). *The Money Shot: Trash, Class, and the Making of TV Talk Shows*. University of Chicago Press.
Gripsrud, J. (2004). Broadcast Television: The Chances of Its Survival in a Digital Age. In L. Spigel & J. Olsson (Eds.), *Television after TV: Essays on a Medium in Transition* (pp. 210–223). Duke University Press.
Hannerz, U. (1998). Other Transnationals: Perspectives Gained from Studying Sideways. *Paideuma: Mitteilungen zur Kulturkunde*, *44*, 109–123.

Hartley, J. (2000). Communicative Democracy in a Redactional Society: The Future of Journalism Studies. *Journalism*, *1*(1), 39–48.

Hartley, J. (2004). From Republic of Letters to Television Republic? Citizen Readers in the Era of Broadcast Television. In L. Spigel & J. Olsson (Eds.), *Television after TV: Essays on a Medium in Transition* (pp. 386–417). Duke University Press.

Hill, A. (2016). Push–Pull Dynamics: Producer and Audience Practices for Television Drama Format the Bridge. *Television & New Media*, *17*(8), 754–768.

Hobart, M. (2007). What Do We Mean by Media Practices? In B. Bräuchler & J. Postill (Eds.), *Theorising Media and Practice* (pp. 55–75). Berghahn.

Howe, C. (2008, June 10). Spectacles of Sexuality: Televisionary Activism in Nicaragua. *Cultural Anthropology*, *23*(1): 48–84.

Ihlebæk, K. A., & Krumsvik, A. H. (2015). Editorial Power and Public Participation in Online Newspapers. *Journalism: Theory, Practice & Criticism*, *16*(4), 470–487.

Karlsson, M., Bergström, A., Clerwall, C., & Fast, K. (2015). Participatory Journalism—The (R)Evolution That Wasn't. Content and User Behavior in Sweden 2007–2013. *Journal of Computer-Mediated Communication*, *20*(3), 295–311.

Kazi, T. (2018). Religious Television and Contesting Piety in Karachi, Pakistan. *American Anthropologist*, *120*(3), 523–534.

Kingston, J. (2018). Watchdog Journalism in Japan Rebounds but Still Compromised. *The Journal of Asian Studies*, *77*(4), 881–893.

Kottak, C. (2016). *Prime-Time Society: An Anthropological Analysis of Television and Culture* (Updated edn). Routledge.

Kottak, C. and Pace, R. (2022). A Longitudinal Study of Media in Brazil. In E. Costa, P. G. Lange, N. Haynes, & J. Sinanan (Eds.), *Routledge Companion to Media Anthropology*. Routledge.

Løvlie, A. S., Ihlebæk, K. A., & Larsson, A. O. (2018). User Experiences with Editorial Control in Online Newspaper Comment Fields. *Journalism Practice*, *12*(3), 362–381.

Lukács, G. (2010). *Scripted Affects, Branded Selves: Television, Subjectivity, and Capitalism in 1990s Japan*. Duke University Press.

Mankekar, P. (1999). *Screening Culture, Viewing Politics: An Ethnography of Television, Womanhood, and Nation in Postcolonial India*. Duke University Press.

Mankekar, P. (2002). Epic Contests: Television and Religious Identity in India. In F. Ginsburg, L. Abu-Lughod, & B. Larkin (Eds.), *Media Worlds: Anthropology on New Terrain* (pp. 134–151). University of California Press.

Matza, T. (2009). Moscow's Echo: Technologies of the Self, Publics, and Politics on the Russian Talk Show. *Cultural Anthropology*, *24*(3), 489–522.

Moll, Y. (2018). Television Is Not Radio: Theologies of Mediation in the Egyptian Islamic Revival. *Cultural Anthropology*, *33*(2), 233–265.

Mulgan, A. G. (2017). Media Muzzling under the Abe Administration. In J. Kingston (Ed.), *Press Freedom in Contemporary Japan* (pp. 17–29). Routledge.

Nakano, K. (2017). The Right-Wing Media and the Rise of Illiberal Politics in Japan. In J. Kingston (Ed.), *Press Freedom in Contemporary Japan* (pp. 30–39). Routledge.

Ortner, S. B. (2009). Studying Sideways: Ethnographic Access in Hollywood. In V. B. Mayer, Miranda J. Caldwell, J. T. (Eds.), *Production Studies: Cultural Studies of Media Industries* (pp. 183–197). Routledge.

Pace, R. (2009). Television's Interpellation: Heeding, Missing, Ignoring, and Resisting the Call for Pan-National Identity in the Brazilian Amazon. *American Anthropologist*, *111*(4), 407–419.

Postill, J. (2009). What Is the Point of Media Anthropology? *Social Anthropology*, *17*(3), 334–337.

Postill, J. (2010). Introduction: Theorising Media and Practice. In B. Bräuchler, & J. Postill (Eds.), *Theorising Media and Practice*. Berghahn.

Rancière, J. (2014). *The Emancipated Spectator*. Verso Books.

Roald, A. S. (2016). Satellitization of Arab Media: Perceptions of Changes in Gender Relations. *CyberOrient*, *10*(1), 87–114.

Rodwell, E. A. (2021a). The Machine without the Ghost: Early Interactive Television in Japan. *Convergence: The International Journal of Research into New Media Technologies*, *27*(5), 1376–1392.

Rodwell, E. A. (2021b). Open Access, Closed Systems: Independent Online Journalism in Japan. *Information, Communication & Society*, 1–18. Available at: www.tandfonline.com/doi/full/10.1080/1369118X.2021.1994627 (Accessed June 8, 2022).

Sekiguchi, T. (2013, July 15). *Japanese Politicians Bite Back against Media.* http://blogs.wsj.com/japanrealtime/2013/07/05/japanese-politicians-bite-back-against-me

Snow, N. (2019). NHK, Abe and the World. *Asian Journal of Journalism and Media Studies, 2,* 1–13.

te Walvaart, M., Dhoest, A., & Van den Bulck, H. (2017). Production Perspectives on Audience Participation in Television: On, Beyond and Behind the Screen. *Convergence: The International Journal of Research into New Media Technologies, 25*(5–6), 1140–1154.

Ujiie, N. (2013a). *Terebi No Mirai 6: Terebi Kyoku wa Media Sābisu Kigyō E Shinka Suru• Zenpin (The Future of Television Part 6: Television Channels Evolving into Media Services Companies).* Ayablog (blog). September 3. http://ayablog.com/?p=483

Ujiie, N. (2013b). *Terebi No Mirai: Terebi wa Fuben de Jidai Okure no Sābisu Da. (the Future of Television: Television Is an Inconvenient, Old-Fashioned Service).* Ayablog (blog). August 28. http://ayablog.com/?p=471

Vidali, D. S. (2010). Millennial Encounters with Mainstream Television News: Excess, Void, and Points of Engagement. *Journal of Linguistic Anthropology, 20*(2), 372–388.

10
PRODUCING PLACE THROUGH PLAY
An Ethnography of Location-based Gaming

Kyle Moore

In July of 2016, a former subsidiary of Google Inc., Niantic Labs, released the hugely popular location-based game *Pokémon Go*. The game was reportedly the fastest mobile game to reach $1 billion USD in revenue (Russell, 2017). Early discussions about the game usually focused on the rapid player uptake (Laincz, 2017) and the dangers of playing in public spaces (Leung and Blanco Munoz, 2016). Academic work focused on the role of audience (Goggin, 2017), the game as a form of nostalgia (Keogh, 2017), and as a method of surveillance (de Souza e Silva, 2017). Scholars also placed *Pokémon Go* historically in relation to other locative, augmented, and urban play (Licoppe, 2017; McCrea, 2017; Sicart, 2017). More recently, scholarly work has focused on the games' ability to form affective intergenerational relationships, challenging assumptions around who plays these types of games (Richardson, Hjorth, and Piera-Jimenez, 2020; Saker and Evans, 2021).

What many accounts of *Pokémon Go* fail to consider is how the game shapes place-making and urban mobility. *Pokémon Go* builds on Niantic's earlier games creating contested urban representations – a tension between user-generated maps and emerging practices of urban mobility and sociality. Through an ethnography of Sydney's *Ingress* community, this chapter argues that the platformisation of location-based games creates contested urban representation and differential mobilities – highlighted in tensions of playing in public and digital place-making. By focusing on play as a practice of place-making, players' everyday mobilities become unequally distributed. These differential mobilities – or unequal access to movement – become embedded within location-based games and produce contested access to and representations of public space. Through a case study of *Ingress* communities, this chapter investigates how place-making practices within *Ingress* were transferred to subsequent location-based games. A battle ensues over public space, as unequal access to space and mobility becomes encoded in ongoing representations of public space.

As of late 2021, *Pokémon Go* is still one of the most popular location-based games. It broke earning records in 2019, earning $900 million through in-application purchases (Statt, 2020). Players can contribute to developing the maps that *Pokémon Go* uses to power their locative infrastructure (Takahashi, 2020). Similarly, in Niantic's prior location-based game, *Ingress*, early adopters engaged in practices such as confirming locations, uploading photos, and contributing to co-creating the game's map (Ingress Help Center, 2017). Location-based gaming maps provide a point of reference, interaction, and navigation within urban environments. Niantic's recent announcement of creating a worldwide, real-time map (The Niantic AR team, 2020), yields serious implications for the ethics of augmented reality and map-based infrastructures (Carter and Egliston, 2020).

Understanding how maps are made in location-based games is important, as it helps us understand how individual and communal urban mobilities form part of a collective representation of urban space. These games are produced through communities and their remapping and reproducing of place via playful cartographic practices. How might gamers' practices, mobilities, and socialities result in tensions over space and representations of place? The goal of 'mapping the world' also raises concerns about community participants' labour in contributing to encoding deferential mobilities. This labour of mapping through play forms the backdrop of my ethnographic practices, which revealed ongoing territorialisation of place and tensions over public space.

This chapter draws from fieldwork of Sydney-based players of Niantic's earlier location-based game, *Ingress* (2012), and beta-testing of *Pokémon Go* in Sydney Australia, from February to July 2016. It explores the role of 'practice' in media anthropology, suggesting we think of play as a specific sociocultural practice performed around games and playable objects. Studying how these practices are formalised within communities and within tangible geo-locative maps, this chapter analyzes the differential mobilities that become encoded in representations of public space. Practices of place-making are examined in detail through *Ingress*'s map-making process and the clash of practices and place-making that occur when co-created in-game maps are reused for new, different games. This platformisation further embeds differential mobilities in representations of public space – creating ongoing contestations about how space can or should be used.

Play as a Media Practice

Media anthropologists often incorporate 'practice' as an object of study. As routines and rhythms embedded within everyday activity, I argue that play is a form of practice. Practices such as play become formalised through sociocultural norms – behaviours and patterns deemed acceptable or ideal within the game world, overlapping with expectations of moving within urban environments. Postill (2010, p. 1) defines practices as 'the embodied sets of activities that humans perform with varying degrees of regularity, competence and flair'. Drawing from a range of practice theorists, Postill (2010, p. 11) summarises practice theory as 'a body of work about the work of the body'. We can view practice as a structuring of the social world, or as Schatzki defines them, an ' array of activity' (in Postil, 2010, p. 10). Couldry (2010, p. 41) extends the notion of routine actions, defining them as unconscious or automatic. He suggests a 'practice turn' within sociology and media, suggesting we analyse media as sets of open practices relating to or orientated around media (2010, p. 36) What does this mean for how we view acts of play, locative media, or more specifically, location-based gaming?

I argue that play is best thought of as an embodied practice performed around 'gaming'. The concept of situated gaming (Apperley, 2010; Yate and Littleton, 1999) orientates play as an embodied action performed around 'gaming' as a 'cultural niche' (Yates and Littleton, 1999), understood at the intersection of individuals (gamers), technology (gaming), and culture (gaming cultures). Apperley (2010) incorporates the body and bodily rhythms as part of this niche. Grüter and Oks (2007) link the term 'situated play' to Dourish's (2001) 'embodied interaction' explicitly to define play as an activity that brings to life gaming technology. This is a problematic definition, as it limits definitions of play to 'gaming' technology. As Sicart

(2014) argues, play is 'portable'; it should be detached from the idea of games as objects. Conceptualising 'play' as a distinct phenomenon is not new. Sutton-Smith (2001) discusses the difficulty in defining play, as working towards understanding the ambiguity of play beyond games and playthings. Instead, viewing play as a practice – as something done around, or pertaining to, gaming (as a culture, technology, and identifier) – provides a more holistic conceptual framework for approaching the range of activities location-based games do across digital and material gameworlds.

The intersections of play, practice, and anthropology can be framed as a 'playful turn' within digital ethnography (Hjorth et al., 2017). This turn reflects a 'ludification' (Mäyrä, 2017) of culture, where play becomes a core component of the intersections of the digital and the human. Tensions between the human and the digital are central to digital anthropology (Horst and Miller, 2012), and reflect larger issues within digital gaming and ethnography (Boellstorff, 2008; Nardi, 2010; Taylor, 2006) where emergent in-game practices in digital spaces contribute to larger cultural practices in everyday life. With location-based gaming, this emergent co-creation of game space directly intersects with larger cultural issues that influence access to public space. Examining 'play' as a central practice in locative gaming has larger implications for how place is produced through locative media. Notably, play is not a practice fixed to any singular object. It is executed around and relates to gaming technology. With location-based games that build on dominant locative media infrastructures like Google Maps and Niantic's playable infrastructures, play as a practice must take into consideration these technologies. To take an infrastructure such as maps and representations of space that are produced by one community, and create new ones leads to serious issues of how gaming frameworks transcend any specific game, shaping access to playable public spaces and the representation of place through digital technologies.

Playable Locative Media

Location-based games are mobile games that utilise mobile devices' GPS coordinates as a key element of their game design and play. Leorke (2018) details how location-based technology was incorporated into pervasive and digital games before the mass adoption of smartphone technology. Within these games, the city is the primary site of play, with various forms of mobile and pervasive technology creating a playful mediation of these places. Some have argued that such forms of urban play owe themselves to histories of subverting the functional elements of 'the urban' through free movement, mobility, and playful tactics such as the *dérive* or parkour, in which people physically train by running, jumping, climbing, and other activity in the existing urban envrionment (de Souza e Silva and Hjorth, 2009; Stevens, 2007). With the mass adoption of smartphone technology, Google Maps became the dominant form of location-based infrastructure for contemporary location-based gaming. Wilken (2012) notes that the rise of a standardised mapping Application Programming Interface (API) lead to Google Maps setting itself as the paramount visual representation and navigational practice in locative media. From this connection between Google Maps as a dominant locative media infrastructure, Niantic Labs emerged as a development node within Google Incorporated (Mac, 2016), layering new forms of interaction on top of Google Maps. Niantic developed the site-seeing application *Field Trip* (Niantic, *Fieldtrip*, 2012) and released an invitation-only location-based game *Ingress* (Niantic, *Ingress*, 2012), which would later be downloadable for all Android devices, with iOS devices gaining access in 2014 (Ingress, 2014). As a subsidiary of Google Incorporated, Niantic was one of few companies with direct access to such an extensive and widely used representation of material space and geo-locative data.

Contestations over access to and representation of public space reveal problems. Location-based technology involves the creation of a hybrid space (de Souza and Silva, 2006) – a mediation of the material through a layering of geo-locative data. To play a location-based game is to do more than engage with these layers. It involves sufficient mobility to move through multiple spaces freely. This may mean access to public/private transport, proximity to urban centres, and access to reliable mobile technology. Such mobility is unequally distributed across members of the public. As Frith notes (2012; 2015), physical spaces have differential mobility or uneven access to movement within and across space. Examples include access to public or private transport, socioeconomic stratification of urban space, and broader issues of urban inequality. Uneven distribution of access to spaces form the sociocultural backdrop to location-based games. Examining differences in interactive locations in a small town versus a major city is illuminating. For instance, Niantic's Portal Criteria gives preference to heritage items found more in cities. As you move to suburbs or rural areas, there are fewer playable objects – meaning urban centres are overly represented within location-based games. As 'place' increasingly shifts towards 'location' (codified geo-coordinates), such differential mobilities are embedded in a centralised infrastructure. Unequal access contributes to these types of gaming infrastructures resulting in what Frith terms a 'splintered space' (2012; 2015). The need for places and urban objects to be 'playable' creates an overly urban-centric representation of space – reflecting the mobility of urban elites rather than a global player base. This creates contentious representations of public space within these games.

As locative media becomes more pervasive, the dominant way of viewing this technology shifts from place to 'location'. Goggin (2012) terms this a 'locational turn'. This turn emphasises location – the technical and material geo-coordinates that underpin location-based technology – thus directly influencing the production of place and space. Further investigating the notion of the material beyond boundaries of virtual/real, location-based scholars explore the underlying infrastructure of locative media. Zeffiro (2012) discusses the technical and social patterns of control that remain in location-based technology – a hangover from the technology's military origins. Similarly, Farman (2015) discusses visible and invisible power dynamics in location-based infrastructures. As Halegoua and Polson (2021) suggest, digital place-making involves using digital media to create a sense of place for oneself and others. Yet, digital place-making may fundamentally 'expose or amplify pre-existing inequities, exclusions, or erasures in the ways that certain populations experience digital media in place and placemaking' (Halegoua and Polson, 2021 p. 574). Understanding play as a form of practice, as a routine or rhythm that produces something beyond the act itself, reveals that location-based gaming is built around infrastructures of control and differential mobilities. As play becomes codified as a series of locations, the free movement of specific communities and individuals shapes how public space is formally encoded.

Through an anthropological approach to location-based technology, this chapter uncovers the human elements within location-based games like *Ingress* and *Pokémon Go*. Early adopters of these technologies not only set social and cultural standards for playing these games. They are key producers of user-generated maps, which create a conceptual hierarchy of places, encoding their value systems to inform future practices of play. These are points I have made elsewhere (Moore, 2020), examining how forms of playful engagement with place may risk the forming of homogenised playable objects. In contrast, in this chapter, I wish to focus on the role of practice. Practice, including routines performed with or around media technology, helps us understand the role of humans in building playable infrastructures. Moreover, it highlights tensions around the labour of creating representations of public space. Representation of public space is not fixed – it is constantly being re-written under new parameters; it represents moments in place-making. To say that *Ingress* and *Pokémon Go* represent public space the same way is to ignore the complexities of play as a form of practice.

In sum, dominant forms of mobility (who moves and maps the most) become formally encoded playable objects, ensuring that future players must also perform similar movements. As such, play does not just mean engaging with a dynamic locative media; it also involves examining the connection between human and non-human elements vital to the field of digital anthropology. Examining how place is made in specific games involves examining the practice of place-making in *Ingress* and how values and hierarchies of places and movements are reinforced within social gameplay. It also requires analysing the issues that arise from transferring these maps to *Pokémon Go*, thus illustrating the contested battle over public space and location-based gaming's importance.

Play as a Practice of Place-making

As of late 2021, Niantic Labs had released *Ingress* (Niantic, *Ingress*, 2012), now *Ingress Prime* (Niantic, 2018), the hugely successful *Pokémon Go* (2016), *Harry Potter: Wizards Unite* (Niantic, 2019), the soon to be defunct *Catan: World Explorers* (Niantic, 2020) (Campbell, 2021), and another Nintendo collaboration *Pikmin Bloom* (Niantic, 2021) (Peters, 2021). All of these games draw from maps made early on in *Ingress* – a stylised version of Google Maps with user-generated points of interest. While there have been tweaks to the underlying infrastructure (Frank, 2017), these playable infrastructures are the result of labour provided by *Ingress* communities across the globe. In *Ingress*, locations are known as 'Portals'. Each new game re-names and re-purposes these 'Portals', but these games draw heavily from the work of early adopters in the *Ingress* community. To play *Ingress* is to participate in a practice of place-making. Whether they are early adopters who submitted locations to the game, community leaders who organise events around specific locations, or casual players moving through urban spaces, each *Ingress* player re-enforced the codification of place. They are participating in digital place-making. It is not necessarily their intention to further differential mobilities. Yet, the practice of play (to engage with locations and other players) embeds these differences within a technological infrastructure. This embedding is abstracted in the underlying maps and locations that are re-purposed in new location-based games.

Portals are submitted by players through the game's interface and subjected to Niantic's Portal review criteria. As of September 2015, Portal submissions were closed (Ingress Help Center, 2017), with only the ability to edit images and details of existing locations within the dataset remaining. The ability to submit Portals and edit them was eventually reopened and given to a specific set of high-level players in particular locations (Ingress, 2017; Kumparak, 2016). Portal criteria dictate that locations must be 'a location with a cool story, a place in history or educational value, a cool piece of art or unique architecture, a hidden gem or hyper-local spot' (Ingress Help Center, 2017). Niantic also privileged places of worship and public libraries – considering both to be places that contribute to connecting people. During *Ingress*'s formative years, players needed to engage in several required practices such as visiting these locations, using the game's interface to access the Portal submission page, uploading a photograph and description, and confirming their geo-coordinates. The Portals were then submitted to Niantic for a submission process before being rejected or accepted. As of 2021, more than 5.39 million Portals have been created across 200 countries (Hanke, 2016).

Portals became key points of interaction within the game. Similarly, they are situated within a discourse of 'play as heritage', which befits *Ingress*'s Portal Criteria (Ingress Help Center, 2017) of engaging with and viewing sites of cultural and historical value while at play. While

Ingress nominally emphasises locations' historical significance (Ingress Help Center, 2017), the shifting focus towards formalised, hierarchy-based, and highly strategised play means that much historical significance of some elements are lost or eclipsed by their significance as in-game locations. It is also sometimes inappropriate to play games at sacred memorial sites, as I discuss below. When considering locative play in urban spaces, it is important to trace how it becomes situated within particular practices of being within the urban.

The incorporation of locations as playable objects is an important part of how locative media and location-based games produce a sense of place. The game's cartography is built on the routines of early adopters of *Ingress* and their desire to play as part of their daily practices, but also to push the boundaries of their everyday mobility. Reflecting on one instance, I and two players were on a lunch break discussing the nature of dense urban clusters around centres of work and major transportation hubs. One Resistance Agent player, Andrew (a pseudonym), was an early adopter of *Ingress* and reflected on not his own, but the broader communities' patterns of Portal submissions. Andrew's early Portal submissions revolved around the suburb in which he lived and his daily routine and movements. Like other early adopters, after photographing and submitting numerous Portals near his home, work, and commute, he to ventured to new locations. Travelling to new locations to submit Portals is rewarded with the in-game achievement 'Seer'. Andrew notes how this affected *Ingress's* map system, with anything that addressed the Portal criteria rapidly photographed and submitted. This speedily uploaded information – yet slow process of Portal approval by Niantic – resulted in a staggering of large clusters of Portals built on major points of mobility such as main transport routes, train stations, major bus stops, and open spaces encoded as 'accessible' to the public. The result is that within the game, urban hubs become over-represented in terms of overall types of space, portraying a splintered space of playable and non-playable places.

As a location-based game, *Ingress* is both a platform and a practice. It is a map, built by a community, that was then reused, re-skinned, and re-packaged to form *Pokémon Go*, *Harry Potter: Wizards Unite*, and *Ingress Prime*. But there is more to the game than just a digital representation of place and points of interest. As I suggest elsewhere (Moore, 2020) a playful form of mobility underlies the playable infrastructures of location-based games like *Ingress* and *Pokémon Go*, working with and against the prescribed use patterns – 'playing' with Portal criteria to create strategic locations, 'gaming' daily commutes, and creating friendly or not-so-friendly rivalries to undermine individual and team strategies. In doing so, *Ingress* creates unique playful engagements with place, and the cultural practices of 'place-making' (Moore, 2015; 2017; Stark, 2016). Engaging with these platforms are 'traces' of other players – signals of their actions broadcast in game, visible on the map. Such traces are viewable by other players, as forms of pervasive and haptic ambience (Apperley and Moore, 2019), or as a form of surveillance from the game developers themselves (Hulsey and Reeves, 2014). The visibility of other players' in-game actions contributes to a territorialisation of place – creating visible hierarchies and valuing of place. Suburbs and locations become 'known' as either Enlightened or Resistance, the game's two main teams. Locations and places become better for catching Pokémon. The more urban clusters are mapped and re-mapped as ideal sites to play, the more other places become excluded.

Social Place-making with Locative Media

Location-based games involve the intersections of play and place. With games like *Ingress*, which focus heavily on community, what constitutes play is often unclear. From micro-coordinating events, to meeting strangers in public places, to gathering and extracting resources, acts of play and labour often overlap. This section explores 'farming' as a primary example of playful activities that intersect with place, place-making, and the labour of gameplay. A farm is a social event – meeting at a predetermined location to collectively gather resources to play the game (weapons, items for claiming locations, and so on). Farms facilitate knowing how the social world of *Ingress* operates. First, there is a level of micro-coordination. Specific members of the community, usually those with a well-established presence, organise these events. Second, farms illustrate the organisation of communities, revealing key members of teams, and key strategic locations within specific places. Lastly, farms demonstrate a connection to place. They repurpose social spaces of bars, parks, or open public spaces as a meeting point for effective gameplay. They show the intersections of game space (maps), community (digital social media platforms), and public spaces (material place).

To organise a farm is to be a key member of a community, have a clear understanding of place both in and out of the game, to have accumulated enough 'gaming capital' (Consalvo, 2009), and/or to be seen as a leader within the gaming community. As Chess (2014) notes, *Ingress* communities are both global and local. While regional local distinctions are made in-game through points systems, there are distinct patterns and cultures of play unique to how cities are structured. Where people gather, how they move across or within cities, and how they incorporate play into their daily lives has much to do with the structure and rhythms of urban life. Global and local players are also present in community organisation – with global leadership coming from Niantic themselves, and local communities organising their own informal events. Farms are semi-formal events organised by local communities. Farming can exhibit consistent practices – occurring weekly on lunch breaks at work, to coincide with meal deals at the local pub or every weekend in a specific suburb. Each team is generally aware of the other team's routine, which yields both important information and also ethical issues around the collection of data, and how that data is shared. Patterns of play reveal structures and routines in players' days. This became apparent early on in fieldwork when another player told me they could estimate where I lived and worked based on the pattern of my in-game engagement on my walk from my apartment to collaborative research spaces.

Farms are just one example of how the material and social intersect in location-based games. They fit within the practices and rhythms of mobilities of localised communities. Furthermore, the embedded social elements of the game – catching up with the community, eating, and playing, cannot be overstated. 'Play' as tied to specific gaming objects becomes more difficult to apply to these fluid gaming situations. Drawing from Sicart's (2014) idea of detaching play from distinct objects and extending the work of Dourish (2004) allows us to examine play as a form of practice that is embedded in various social contexts. Games and play may be understood through these situated contexts while recognising that technologies are sociocultural and may be constantly redefined. The concept of situated play is a messy process situated across multiple localised and global contexts and practices.

While farms are social, semi-informal events, they add to a further territorialisation of place. Locations are strategically submitted to Niantic by early adopters to create 'clusters' in specific locations. This may be a set of multiple locations in a park, a bar, or any other place that allows a group of people to meet, sit, and play for a sustained period of time. Clusters create a unique problem when transferred to other games – they create an in-game location that yields substantial in-game items. In the case of *Pokémon Go*, the unexpected popularity of the game sent waves of players to the clusters to try and capture elusive Pokémon. What worked well for small, niche communities, to set up semi-formal social gatherings, created a splintered space, causing issues of access, mobility, and authority over how public space is represented and utilised.

Kyle Moore

Towards Locative Gaming Platforms: *Pokémon Go*

While *Pokémon Go* was officially launched in July 2016, Niantic offered an invite-only beta test to specific countries earlier in the year. Australia and New Zealand gained access in April (Frank, 2016). The beta involved playing an early version of the game and reporting bugs to Niantic via the platform. This beta test formed part of my fieldwork, with a direct overlap with Sydney's *Ingress* community. The beta test closed in late June, in time for the game's official launch in July 2016. *Pokémon Go* was a huge success (Turk, 2017). This matters, because the relatively niche and closed community of *Ingress*, and their unique locative gaming practices were suddenly overshadowed by the media-worthy, seemingly out of nowhere success of *Pokémon Go*. *Pokémon Go*'s maps were similar to those in *Ingress*. Many *Ingress* 'Portals' were reused as new in-game locations – Pokéstops and Gyms – both with different interactive modes. Locations that were frequented by *Ingress* players saw new waves of people gathering in those locations. Some research participants noted tensions between 'new' *Pokémon Go* locative game players and the 'old' *Ingress* players – a casual/hardcore dichotomy that forms a recurring theme within gaming culture (Juul, 2009). Players exhibited feelings of ownership to these locations, to a community that spent time and effort producing these locations, only to be co-opted by new waves of players.

Tensions arose as the place-making and maps of *Ingress* were reused. Maps produced by a community, for a specific community-centric purpose were re-purposed for a game that became more popular than the developers had expected. Examining two examples – inappropriate sites of play, and a location unique to Sydney's location-based community, a park in the suburbs of Rhodes – reveals a clash of practices that emerge from a platformisation approach to location-based gaming. Both examples reveal tensions over play in public and the practice of place-making. They reveal the issues with how digital information becomes layered over our everyday urban spaces, and the power dynamics embedded within locative media developers who, by all rights, own these representations of space. Such representations have a direct impact on urban mobility. The platformisation of location-based gaming creates tension over the use and representation of public space.

The labour practices within *Ingress* are best conceptualised as what John Banks (2013) terms 'co-creation'. Emerging from a new participatory culture – the breakdown between consumers and producers – co-creativity is 'rooted in the uncertainties and controversies about how these emerging cultural and economic relations are made' (Banks, 2013, p. 24). Players feel ownership when uploading a Portal, including a photograph, and naming the Portal. One participant, Andrew, explained to me his pride in taking excellent photographs and was embarrassed about one he took in haste. Each Portal creator's username was originally visible on *Ingress* but has since been removed in subsequent Niantic games. Such practices subtly erase the *Ingress* communities' labour in co-creating these digital places. Individual and community ownership and connection to place becomes obscured in platformisation processes. Knowing who submitted a location to the game may seem trivial, but a sense of community was built around this knowledge. It contributes to a sense of 'known users' – or key community members who organise farming events, or who frequent these locations. Known players were key figures in my fieldwork. They exhibited distinct patterns of movement, frequenting locations organised around their work, home, and third places. Locations were created for their own individual practice, and, in turn, embedded into the community. Once these 'known' cartographic and community practices become obscured or removed, serious issues around the appropriate or inappropriate nature of play arise.

The inappropriate nature of playing in public was a key theme of *Pokémon Go*'s news cycle. Most notably, sites of historical significance received media attention – due to a high volume of visitors, all wandering with phones in their hands. One of the most problematic locations of play was the US Holocaust Memorial Museum and Arlington National Cemetery (Guardian staff and agencies, 2016). The museum director went to considerable effort to have the site removed from the game. It is not the purpose of this chapter to provide a value judgement on these matters. There are places where play may be inappropriate and disrespectful. Rather, I wish to point out that the maps underlying *Pokémon Go* were produced under the *Ingress* Portal Criteria of 'sites of historical significance' (Ingress Portal Criteria, 2017). Herein lies the problem – there is a disconnect between the cartographic practice of incorporating sites of historical significance and the act of play. Play, as a practice, is socio-culturally encoded as 'not serious'. Once it moves into locations of serious concern, problems arise. Adding to these tensions is the realisation that these are not open and public spaces. They are closed off and may even be sacred sites. They are not 'open' to the public as sites of leisure such as parks may be. They do not allow for free and open movement, thus impacting different mobilities amid conflicting practices of memorialisation and play. Players perform the 'labour' of creating maps and place-making – but do not have a say over ongoing representation of the locations used within Niantic's games.

Despite these technological interventions in representations of space, *Pokémon Go* is still owned by Niantic. Within Sydney, no other example illustrates this better than Peg Paterson Park in the Sydney suburb of Rhodes. As Butler (2016) summarises, 'Rhodes, in the west of Sydney, became an early favourite spot for hardcore fans due to its high concentration of Pokéstop points – or item pickup locations – and the tendency for rare and powerful Pokémon to appear there'. Residents led a campaign to remove the locations from the game alongside interventions from the local Canada Bay government. The incident points towards appropriate behaviour in public space and was the centre of numerous local moral panics about quiet locations being overrun by unruly players. Yet it also points to issues of control. For local government, it means having to heavily regulate spaces; for residents it means a call to arms to protect their home from inappropriate uses of the spaces, and for both parties to petition and actively engage with Niantic's location removal system. Eventually, the Pokéstops were removed, and the location returned to a state of relative normalcy (Cellan-Jones, 2016). These tensions highlight a level of control and labour present in these platforms that yield differential mobilities, or asymmetrical access to places. Tensions over public space and the use and misuse of place reveal important issues with location-based gaming and play as practice. Play does not constitute homogenised forms of interaction. They are socially and culturally embedded. For *Pokémon Go* players, the issues raised at Peg Paterson Park in Rhodes reflect a desire for transparency in platforms regarding ownership and representation of public space.

Conclusion: Play as a Place-making Practice

This chapter explores the practice of digital place-making through playable locative media. It analyses the issues of media practices and digital place-making and the tensions between community co-production and corporate control over public space. As much as 'practice' is difficult to define, so is 'play'. An ambiguous set of routines and rhythms loosely related to gaming technology or playable objects – play transfers a specific meaning on to routines and objects. Rather than perform an ethnography of a game world, we must understand the intersections of playful practices – across digital and material technologies and objects.

Location-based media provides a unique example to examine the intersections of the digital and material, to understand place-making, and how specific meaning around mappable and material objects is produced. As we shift our understanding of locative media from 'place' to 'location', we can start to see tensions around how 'practices' become embedded in geo-locative locations – fixed in position and retaining specific meaning of those who produced such locative technologies. Place-making is a social practice, but also a technical practice – it is co-creating an interactive object. Looking at the practice of place-making, this chapter examined three major ethnographic encounters – the making of maps, the repurposing of maps for social structures, and the platformisation of maps for future location-based games. Each of these reveals a 'clash' of practices or, rather, the differential mobilities that are embedded within urban inequality. As we play in public, the contested nature of place, space, and location begin to create tensions over public and private representations and uses of place and space.

References

Apperley, T. & Moore, K. (2019). 'Haptic Ambience: Ambient Play, the Haptic Effect and Co-presence in Pokémon GO'. *Convergence*, 25(1), 6–17. https://doi.org/10.1177/1354856518811017

Apperley, T. (2010). *Gaming Rhythms: Play and Counterplay from the Situated to the Global*. Institute of Network Cultures.

Banks, J. (2013). *Co-creating Videogames*. Bloomsbury Academic.

Boellstorff, T. (2008). *Coming of Age in Second Life: An Anthropologist Explores the Virtually Human*. Princeton University Press.

Butler, J. (2016, August 2). 'Sydney "Zombie" Pokémon Hotspot Shut Down After Residents' Campaign'. *Huffington Post*. www.huffingtonpost.com.au/2016/08/01/sydney-zombie-pokemon-hotspot-shut-down-after-residents-campa_a_21443133/

Campbell, I. C. (2021, September 17), 'Niantic is Shutting Down its AR Catan Game after a Year of Early Access'. *The Verge*. www.theverge.com/2021/9/17/22680166/niantic-catan-world-explorers-shutdown-early-access

Carter, M. & Egliston, B. (2020). 'Ethical Implications of Emerging Mixed Reality Technologies'. https://doi.org/10.25910/5EE2F9608EC4D

Cellan-Jones, D. L. (2016, August 2). 'Troublesome Sydney Pokestop Shut Down'. *BBC News*. www.bbc.com/news/technology-36948331

Chess, S. (2014). 'Augmented Regionalism: Ingress as Geomediated Gaming Narrative'. *Information, Communication and Society*, 17(9), 1105–1117. https://doi.org/10.1080/1369118X.2014.881903.

Couldry, N. (2010). 'Theorising Media as Practice' in B. Bräuchler & J. Postill (Eds.), *Theorising Media and Practice* (1st edition). Berghahn Books.

Consalvo, M. (2009). *Cheating: Gaining Advantage in Videogames*. MIT Press.

de Souza e Silva, A. (2017). 'Pokémon Go as an HRG: Mobility, Sociability, and Surveillance in Hybrid Spaces'. *Mobile Media & Communication*, 5(1), 20–23. https://doi.org/10.1177/2050157916676232

de Souza e Silva, A. (2006). 'From Cyber to Hybrid: Mobile Technologies as Interfaces of Hybrid Spaces'. *Space and Culture*, 9(3), 261–278. https://doi.org/10.1177/1206331206289022

de Souza e Silva, A., & Hjorth, L. (2009). 'Playful Urban Spaces: A Historical Approach to Mobile Games'. *Simulation & Gaming*, 40(5), 602–625. https://doi.org/10.1177/1046878109333723

Dourish, P. (2001). *Where the Action Is: The Foundations of Embodied Interaction*. MIT Press.

Dourish, P. (2004). 'What We Talk About When We Talk About Context'. *Personal Ubiquitous Computing*, 8(1), 19–30. https://doi.org/10.1007/s00779-003-0253-8

Farman, J. (2015). 'Infrastructures of Mobile Social Media'. *Social Media + Society*, 1(1), 205630511558034. https://doi.org/10.1177/2056305115580343

Frank, A. (2016, March 4). 'Pokémon Go Heading Out to the Field in Japanese-only Beta Test'. *Polygon*. www.polygon.com/2016/3/4/11161010/pokemon-go-field-test-beta-japan

Frank, A. (2017, December 4). 'Pokémon Go's Maps Now Look a Lot Different'. *Polygon*. www.polygon.com/2017/12/4/16725748/pokemon-go-map-changes-openstreetmap

Frith, J. (2012). 'Splintered Space: Hybrid Spaces and Differential Mobility'. *Mobilities*, 7(1), 131–149. https://doi.org/10.1080/17450101.2012.631815

Frith, J. (2015). *Smartphones as Locative Media*. John Wiley & Sons.

Goggin, G. (2012). 'Encoding Place: The Politics of Mobile Location Technologies' in R. Wilken and G. Goggin (Eds.), *Mobile Technology and Place*. Routledge.

Goggin, G. (2017). 'Locating Mobile Media Audiences: In Plain View with Pokémon Go' in C. Hight & R. Harindranath (Eds.), *Studying Digital Media Audiences: Perspectives from Australasia*. Routledge.

Grüter, B. & Oks, M. (2007). 'Situated Play and Mobile Gaming'. www.digra.org/wp-content/uploads/digital-library/07312.21501.pdf

Guardian staff and agencies. (2016, July 13). 'Pokémon Go: US Holocaust Museum Asks Players to Stay Away'. *The Guardian*. www.theguardian.com/technology/2016/jul/13/pokemon-go-us-holocaust-museum-asks-players-to-stay-away

Halegoua, G. & Polson, E. (2021). 'Exploring "Digital Placemaking"'. *Convergence*, 27(3), 573–578. https://doi.org/10.1177/13548565211014828

Hanke, J. (2016, January 28). 'Three Years of Ingress and the Road for Niantic'. https://medium.com/@johnhanke/three-years-of-ingress-and-the-road-for-niantic-a991a2d6587#.gtyrsdmcf

Hjorth, L., Balmford, W., Greenfield, S., Gaspard, L., Naseem, A., & Penney, T. (2017). 'The Art of Play' in L. Hjorth, H. Horst, A. Galloway, & G. Bell (Eds.), *The Routledge Companion to Digital Ethnography*. Routledge.

Horst, H. & Miller, D. (Eds.). (2012). *Digital Anthropology*. Bloomsbury Academic.

Hulsey, N. & Reeves, J. (2014). 'The Gift that Keeps on Giving: Google, Ingress, and the Gift of Surveillance'. *Surveillance & Society*, 12(3), 389–400.

Ingress. (2014, July 14). 'Welcome to #Ingress iOS users. #Apple #iPhone #iOS [Google+ Post]'. https://plus.google.com/+FevenisSilverwind/posts/TmY7QfK6rwB

Ingress Help Center. (2017). 'Candidate Portal Criteria'. Ingress Help Center. http://support.ingress.com/hc/en-us/articles/207343987-Candidate-Portal-criteria

Juul, J. (2009). *A Casual Revolution: Reinventing Video Games and Their Players*. MIT Press.

Kumparak, G. (2016, November 17). 'Niantic's New Invite-only "Portal Recon" Tool Lets Players Vote Real-world Locations into Ingress'. *TechCrunch*. http://social.techcrunch.com/2016/11/17/niantics-invite-only-portal-recon-tool-lets-players-vote-new-real-world-locations-into-ingress/

Keogh, B. (2017). 'Pokémon Go, the Novelty of Nostalgia, and the Ubiquity of the Smartphone'. *Mobile Media & Communication*, 5(1), 38–41. https://doi.org/10.1177/2050157916678025

Laincz, J. (2017, July 6). 'Pokémon Go: The first year'. *The Verge*. http://apps.voxmedia.com/at/theverge-pokemon-go-the-first-year

Leorke, D. (2018). *Location-based Gaming: Play in Public Space*. Palgrave Macmillan.

Leung, C. & Blanco Munoz, B. (2016, August 11). 'The Dangers of "Pokemon Go"'. *CNN*. www.cnn.com/2016/08/11/asia/pokemon-go-dangers-bans/index.html

Licoppe, C. (2017). 'From Mogi to Pokémon GO: Continuities and Change in Location-aware Collection Games'. *Mobile Media & Communication*, 5(1), 24–29. https://doi.org/10.1177/2050157916677862

Mac, R. (2016, July 26). 'The Inside Story of "Pokémon GO's" Evolution from Google Castoff to Global Phenomenon'. *Forbes*. www.forbes.com/sites/ryanmac/2016/07/26/monster-game/

Mäyrä, F. (2017). 'Pokémon GO: Entering the Ludic Society'. *Mobile Media & Communication*, 5(1), 47–50. https://doi.org/10.1177/2050157916678270

McCrea, C. (2017). 'Pokémon's Progressive Revelation: Notes on 20 Years of Game Design'. *Mobile Media & Communication*, 5(1), 42–46. https://doi.org/10.1177/2050157916678271

Moore, K. (2015). 'Painting the Town Blue and Green: Curating Street Art through Urban Mobile Gaming'. *M/C Journal*, 18(4). http://journal.media-culture.org.au/index.php/mcjournal/article/view/1010

Moore, K. (2017). 'Playing with Portals: Rethinking Urban Play with Ingress' in A. Trammell, E. Torner, & E. L. Waldron (Eds.), *Analog Game Studies: Volume II*. ETC Press.

Moore, K. (2020). 'Playful Mobility and Playable Infrastructures in Smart Cities' in D. Leorke & M. Owens (Eds.), *Games and Play in the Creative, Smart and Ecological City* (1st edition). Routledge.

Nardi, B. (2010). *My Life as a Night Elf Priest: An Anthropological Account of World of Warcraft*. University of Michigan Press.

Peters, J. (2021, March 22). 'Pikmin is the Next AR Game from the Makers of Pokémon Go'. *The Verge*. www.theverge.com/2021/3/22/22345472/niantic-nintendo-pikmin-partnership-collaboration-ar-mobile-game

Postill, J. (2010). 'Introduction: Theorising Media and Practice' in B. Bräuchler & J. Postill (Eds.), *Theorising Media and Practice* (1st edition). Berghahn Books.

Richardson, I., Hjorth, L., & Piera-Jimenez, J. (2020). 'The Emergent Potential of Mundane Media: Playing Pokémon GO in Badalona, Spain'. *New Media & Society*, 24(3), 667–683. https://doi.org/10.1177/1461444820965879

Russell, J. (2017, February 1). 'Report: Pokémon Go Has Now Crossed $1 Billion in Revenue'. *TechCrunch*. http://social.techcrunch.com/2017/02/01/report-pokemon-go-has-now-crossed-1-billion-in-revenue/

Saker, M. & Evans, L. (2021). *Intergenerational Locative Play: Augmenting Family*. Emerald Publishing Limited.

Sicart, M. (2014). *Play Matters*. The MIT Press.

Sicart, M. (2017). 'Reality Has Always Been Augmented: Play and the Promises of Pokémon Go'. *Mobile Media & Communication*, 5(1), 30–33. https://doi.org/10.1177/2050157916677863

Stark, E. (2016). 'Playful Places: Uncovering Hidden Heritage with Ingress' in M. Willson & T. Leaver (Eds.), *Social, Casual and Mobile Games: The Changing Gaming Landscape*. Bloomsbury Publishing USA.

Statt, N. (2020, January 10). 'Pokémon Go Never Went Away – 2019 Was Its Most Lucrative Year Ever'. *The Verge*. www.theverge.com/2020/1/10/21060877/pokemon-go-record-revenue-2019-niantic-labs-ar-growth

Stevens, Q. (2007). *The Ludic City: Exploring the Potential of Public Spaces (1st edition)*. Routledge. https://doi.org/10.4324/9780203961803

Sutton-Smith, B. (2009). *The Ambiguity of Play*. Harvard University Press.

Takahashi, D. (2020, May 26). 'Niantic's Latest AR Features Add Realism to Pokémon Go'. *VentureBeat*. https://venturebeat.com/2020/05/26/niantics-latest-ar-features-add-realism-to-pokemon-go/

Taylor, T. L. (2006). *Play Between Worlds: Exploring Online Game Culture*. MIT Press.

The Niantic AR team. (2020, November 10). 'Mapping Reality: Building the Future of AR'. Niantic. https://nianticlabs.com/en/blog/building-future-ar-maps/

Turk, V. (2017, July 6). 'One Year On, Who Still Plays Pokémon Go?' *WIRED UK*. www.wired.co.uk/article/pokemon-go-first-anniversary-who-still-plays

Wilken, R. (2012). 'Locative Media: From Specialized Preoccupation to Mainstream Fascination'. *Convergence*, 18(3), 243–247. https://doi.org/10.1177/1354856512444375

Yates, S. J. & Littleton, K. (1999). 'Understanding Computer Game Cultures: A Situated Approach'. *Information, Communication & Society*, 2(4), 566–583. https://doi.org/10.1080/136911899359556

Zeffiro, A. (2012). 'A Location of One's Own: A Genealogy of Locative Media'. *Convergence*, 18(3), 249–266. https://doi.org/10.1177/1354856512441148

11
PHOTOMEDIA AS ANTHROPOLOGY
Towards a Speculative Research Method

Edgar Gómez Cruz

Introduction

One of the distinctive objects that became pervasive during the Covid pandemic that, while writing this in July 2021 was still far from over, were the facemasks. Australia, where I used to live, has been very privileged compared to the rest of the world and the number of infected people has been relatively low. Nevertheless, in July 2021, a growing number of cases, combined with a poor rollout of the vaccine, also saw increased use of facemasks in public places, shopping centres, public transport, and even in the common areas of residential buildings. I photographed all the facemasks I found on the street in Sydney, Australia, beginning around May 2020 (Figure 11.1).

These images (more than 1000 so far) inform an ongoing project of mine that seeks to position photography as a way of thinking, not as a way of representing, at the centre of a speculative method. I suggest that photography has great potential not only to represent the world but also to imagine it and, hopefully, to intervene within it. Building on my previous work, in this chapter I advance ideas about this particular use of photography, opening up new lines of thinking as inspired by the recent phenomena of global facemasks.

Visual Anthropology as a Practice

My approach considers photography as a set of everyday actions and habits that are improvised in situated contexts. I suggest we need a wider dialogue between media and anthropology that takes seriously media affordances as tools to develop anthropological thinking, particularly "in practice" (Costa, 2018), that is, situated in everyday processes. The particular types of practices I am interested in include both everyday vernacular habits and improvised usages of photography, such as using one's cellphone for taking visual notes, but also, evolving research-based practices such as walking methods of observing while taking photos. My goal is to present a different path to visual anthropology beyond the images focusing instead on the practice of producing them.

In terms of practice, from its early inception, photography was compared, contrasted, and defined in relation to paintings. By reproducing the same structure (an image within a frame), photography disrupted paintings as a visual medium, "liberating" it from its representational function. As Bazin states: "photography freed western painting, once and for all, from its

DOI: 10.4324/9781003175605-16

obsession with realism and allowed it to recover its aesthetic autonomy" (Bazin, 2060, p. 9). This understanding of photography as the "pencil of nature" (Talbot, 2020) permeated its development and uses. Since its beginnings, the practice of doing photography was reduced to the resulting images that were perceived as a *direct* representation of reality. While this idea of photography as representation has been contested and debated multiple times (Scruton, 1981; Brook, 1983) from very early on, photography was most of the time reduced to its documentarian function. That is, photography offered a way to "frame" reality. This relationship between framing and reality was also developed as a theoretical device in the analysis of particular phenomena based on cultural determinations (i.e. Goffman's "frame analysis", 1974), or as a way to acknowledge how media presents (frames) a given topic (Kitzinger, 2007).

All these elaborations contributed to a limited use of the camera in anthropology. Anthropologists adopted the idea of the camera capturing reality almost uncritically, and it quickly became the primary use of photography in anthropological inquiry (for an interesting discussion see Mead & Bateson, 2003). While I do not have space here to recount the history of photography in anthropological fieldwork nor to expand this discussion on the use of visual methods in social research (see Pink, 2020; Banks & Zeitlyn, 2015; Rose, 2016), I will note that, as with anything in the digital age, the use of visual elements in social research is increasing exponentially and there are a number of new journals, apps, and platforms that publish visual academic outputs. My point here is that, while there is a long tradition in the use of photographic images in anthropological research, these have been mostly understood as pieces of data to be captured, as representations of reality rather than a method of research in its own

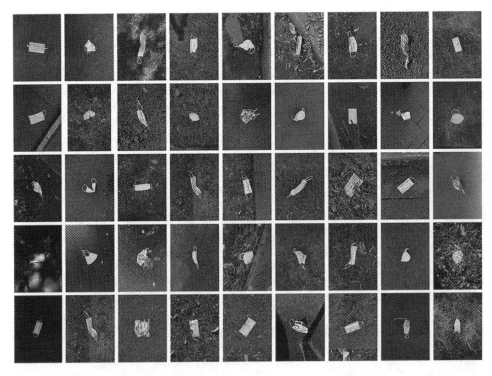

Figure 11.1 Discarded facemasks in Sydney, Australia
Source: Photo by author.

terms. MacDougall states that "Anthropology was inspired by zoology, botany, and geology to describe the world visually, and there was a corresponding emphasis upon those aspects of culture that could be drawn or photographed" (2005, p. 215). Therefore, the anthropological use of visual media was mostly reduced to "show and tell" aspects of fieldwork. Even in the multiple volumes that tackle the particular historical relationship between anthropology and photography (Edwards, 2015; 1992; Pinney, 2011), the focus is primordially on the use of images as ethnographic representations.

With the arrival of the digital, more people started doing photography. The use of photography increased in academic research but, also, people started photographing *differently*. Not only in terms of what was "picture-worthy" (Ito & Okabe, 2003), but using photography in a way that did not necessarily respond to a documentarian, representational, or memory function. These different uses seem to be finally "expanding" photography from its previous representational constraints (similarly to what happened to painting with the arrival of photography). While a number of vernacular practices contributed to this detachment, it was the art world that pushed for a more conceptual use of photography that was not inhibited and defined by the frame (or what the frame depicted). This transformation has allowed photography to become less fixed in "reality" and used more as a kind of magic:

> The connection of close-up magic to contemporary photography is in the idea that magic is something that happens in the viewer's imaginations ... photographic magic opens us to multiple possible meanings of our visual world, and calls upon our collective ways of looking at it; it also offers ideas of what the visual world might imply about our contemporary condition.
>
> *Cotton, 2015, p. 3*

Simultaneously, and I hope to make the connection of both tendencies in this text, one of the most interesting and revelatory approaches happening in anthropology is its detachment from ethnography as *the* method to do anthropology. Ingold presents the distinction by saying that "Ethnography aims to describe life as it is lived and experienced, by a people, somewhere, sometime. Anthropology, by contrast, is an inquiry into the conditions and possibilities of human life in the world" (2017, p. 22). Ingold emphasises that the detachment of anthropology from ethnography is intended not as a critique of the latter but as a way of expanding the reach of anthropology since, "an ethnographer can reasonably feel constrained in what he or she can write [or photograph] by the requirements of descriptive fidelity" (2017, p. 22) while, on the other hand, suggesting that "anthropology is nothing if not speculative, and I want to cherish and protect the intellectual freedom I have, as an anthropologist, to speculate on the conditions and possibilities of human life in this world" (2017, p. 22). Rees, in a project similar to Ingold's, suggests that, detached from ethnography, "anthropology has the potential to venture into the terrain it formerly left, unwittingly or not, to philosophy: a study of the conceptual grounds constitutive of the human and the real" (2018, p. 34).

Inspired mostly by contemporary art, I want to expand this debate to account for what a visual anthropology could be beyond a visual ethnography, moving to a more speculative terrain and away from its representational use. In a different text, Ingold states that "contemporary art and anthropology have in common that they *both* observe *and* speculate" (Ingold, 2019, p. 660 emphasis in the original). Critiquing the "ethnographic turn" in art (see Foster, 1996), Ingold suggests that "an art that is speculative and experimental, that explores the possibilities of being through open-ended conversation and comparison, cannot meet the standards of accuracy, of empirical depth and detail, expected of ethnography" (2019, p. 662). The traditional use of photography as a reliable tool for ethnography (see Collier & Collier, 1986) was based on the idea that, what was depicted on the frame was a clear representation of reality. Therefore, the frame provided security and reassurance. If, as Ingold suggests, there must be an anthropology that goes beyond ethnographic accounts, could it be an anthropological use of photography that responds to this invitation?

Acknowledging and building upon all these important ideas, I suggest that it is time to *think* outside the box and to *see* outside the frame. Inspired by the use of photography in contemporary art, I have started exploring moving away from the ethnographic use of the image (that frames reality), exploring instead what an anthropological use of the image that imagines and speculates *on the conditions and possibilities of human life* could be. Mirzoeff says: "at the heart of imagination is the image. Visual culture has to respond day to day in its effort to understand change in a world too enormous to see but vital to imagine" (2016, p. 281). It is this triple movement of observation, imagination, and speculation, that can create a fertile ground for two important shifts: situating photography as a media practice (that does not have to be documentary) and practicing a non-ethnographic anthropology. This double shift lies at the base for the *PhotoMedia as Anthropology* method presented here.

My concept of a *PhotoMedia as Anthropology* method as proposed in this chapter is centred in the combination of images and imagination as a form of anthropological inquiry, and it builds upon previous uses and reflections on photography as a medium. Therefore, I will discuss the three phases in my relationship with digital photography: as a research object, as a method, and as an intervention. I see each phase as a step towards the method I am presenting here. The ultimate goal of the chapter is to contribute to the development of a media anthropology that is not an anthropology *of* media (or media practices), or an anthropology that *uses* media, but a speculative and interventionist use of media that is anthropological in its aim: a *media anthropology*.

My work draws from the large and important literature on visual anthropology (Collier & Collier, 1986; Ruby, 2005), particularly its interest in the use of visual technologies for anthropological inquiry; design anthropology (Gunn, Otto, & Smith, 2013), especially its approach to "inquiring into the possible" (Halse, 2013, p. 194); and emerging developments in anthropological thinking (Ingold, 2013, 2017; Rees, 2018) that project an anthropological thinking not limited to ethnographic inquiries. I follow and recognise these important bodies of work in order to present how I have approached, studied, and evolved in my use of digital photography in the last decade. In this chapter I argue that photography, or any kind of media, can become a tool for anthropological thinking, expanding its current use as ethnographic representation. My goal is to expand the discussion of media anthropology to think about the practice of media production *as* anthropology.

Photography as an Object: Observing

Digital photography is better understood as a practice and not only reduced to the resulting image of this practice. This entails both particular photographic practices (such as selfies or urban representations), as well as more general discussions about the role of material visual practices in broader themes such as politics, social media, memory, and socialisation. To account for both, I focus on "networked images" (Gómez Cruz, 2012), aligning digital photography not only with the history of the photographic medium but with a broader assemblage of technologies, uses, and discourses that are set in motion to produce and distribute images. To conceptualise digital photography, we must consider the materiality of these networked images as well as the practices of their creation, processing, and distribution (Lehmuskallio & Gómez Cruz, 2016).

While the classic canon on photographic studies focuses on the ontology of the image, its representational, aesthetic, or semiotic characteristics, I suggest studying it as a process that considers a broader assemblage of technologies, from the camera to the internet connection, from platforms to hashtags and apps. This approach focuses more on how images are produced and used rather than the particular content of the photographs. In that sense, with the wide availability of digital cameras, observing and photographing have become increasingly entangled. My prior ethnographic findings in this area (Gómez Cruz, 2012) had led me to think about photography as a practice that starts before the images are taken and extends beyond their sharing. I was interested in understanding how people use, adopt, and adapt photography in their everyday lives and how, increasingly, digital practices are becoming visual, from platforms to communication; from photos to video; and from emojis to stickers (Gómez Cruz & Siles, 2021). One of the main findings of this research was that, increasingly, we are *observing* the world while *photographing* the world. That is, we are observing the world more *precisely* because we are looking for opportunities to photograph it.

This chapter contributes to the expanding conceptions of material visual practices, in order to understand the ways in which people use digital photography in their everyday lives. These uses are perhaps mundane and quotidian but nevertheless signal a number of important changes in how we use visual elements. For example, when doing fieldwork about digital photography practices with amateur photographers in Barcelona (Gómez Cruz, 2012), I witnessed the emergence of a visual practice that it is now absolutely normalised: taking and sharing images as *visual notes*. The participants in my research took many photographs that were intended as a shared-observation experience, sometimes with themselves, sometimes with others. They took visual notes that ranged in uses from presenting different options when they wanted someone else to choose one (as in a takeaway menu), to books they photographed in bookstores to later search for them in public libraries. Notes were used in various ways, from collecting particular signs, objects, and situations they were interested in, to photographing products they wanted their partners to purchase in the grocery store.

While many of the early accounts on mobile photography documented similar uses and they were one of the most important findings of these early studies of mobile photography (Villi, 2007; Van House et al., 2005), the normalisation of the practice has turned our attention away from them. The important point here is that, in many of these cases, the use of photography was not only to *remember* but increasingly as a way to *observe*. I mention this ethnographic finding because the way participants in my study used images to exchange and share information was *different* than how photography was understood and studied traditionally and, on many occasions, the meaning of the photograph was conveyed not with the content of the image per se but with the context, a shared history, the hashtag used, and other elements that informed the practice of visual notetaking. That is, creating a conceptual scaffold for the image to make sense. The photograph then was part of a larger assemblage of meaning.

While this was an ethnographic finding, it became an inspiration to launch an exploration that was not ethnographic but anthropological in the sense of being more speculative of the human condition rather than representational of a particular group. Many of the uses I saw in Barcelona were systematic and consistent; people used photography almost as a "method" in the sense of its constant use to reach certain goals (communicate, manage, organise), a practice that increased exponentially with the proliferation of mobile phones. People incorporated these *vernacular methods* in their daily life, that is, routines and techniques that people use systematically without necessarily constructing and following them with the rigour that, for example, academic methods usually need.

I find it useful to think about these practices as methods because they are bottom-up processes that become integrated into everyday practices. Since many of these "methods" were visual and had the aim of communicating and not only documenting, I also realised these vernacular methods could indeed become an inspiring resource for *academic* methods. On the one hand, they are systematic enough but, perhaps more importantly, they are integrated into wider practices of thinking and doing. Taking images as notes seems to have become a widespread practice in work settings (Thakur, Gormish, & Erol, 2011).

The next iteration of using images to think with was their use not as memory devices or as representational tools, but as a way to imagine things that were not necessarily present in the image. And this became the first building block of the method.

Photograph(ing) as a Method: Thinking

After years of studying material visual practices ethnographically, I revisited these "vernacular methods", and I found the practice of taking notes visually particularly interesting. Cartier-Bresson already claimed that the camera "is a sketchbook, an instrument of intuition and spontaneity" (1999, p. 15). Taking this idea as a starting point, we can consider the materiality of photography (the cameras, the lenses, the connectivity) and explore how different camera technologies could be used to develop research methodologies that respond to their affordances.

Figure 11.2 Discarded facemask in Sydney, Australia
Source: Photo by author.

This informed my current project on facemasks. The social meaning of these facemasks is not reduced to the image of the masks or even the masks themselves. It is, as we have seen around the world, highly contested and praised. I started taking these images of facemasks as a "survey", in the sense of photographing them every time I found one on the street. (see Figure 11.2)

At the same time, images became increasingly used as a data interface (Gómez Cruz, 2016b), that is, a practice of making connections with images. This use of images as data became pervasive with the use of Quick Response (QR) codes during the pandemic. Quick Response codes are two-dimensional barcodes that can be read and interpreted by a camera device with an online connection. In Sydney, where I lived during the pandemic, QR codes were required to check-in into all public places. The "reading" of the QR code with the mobile phone takes the user to a "checking-in" website that helps the health ministry trace the movements of people and stop the spread of the virus. This use of the mobile camera—not to create photographs, but as an interface—initiated my quest to develop new methods based on camera affordances, thus creating conversations, collaborations, and experimentations with colleagues who were studying and using emerging vision technologies such as drones, eye-tracking systems, and GoPros, among other devices.

While anthropologists have been "largely ignoring the decisive role that particular camera technologies have played in steering the trajectory of anthropological work" (Luvaas, 2019, p. 77), it has become clear that the use of certain visual, digital emerging technologies has the potential for expanding the methods developed in anthropological inquiry: for example, using different technologies influences analysis in terms of scale (using cameras in drones to show large scenes from above), presence (using automated cameras that detect movement), and temporalities (using time-lapse functions to see changes that are slow to be appreciated in real time).

While this exploration led me to engage with cutting-edge visual technologies, I realised two important things. On the one hand, the most important technology for visual research was the one we all carry with us at all times: the mobile phone. And, second, it was precisely this constant availability that could become the key to methodological uses of photography beyond the engagement with a particular group, that is, beyond ethnographic inquiry. The constant availability, increased image quality, and permanent connectivity turned the camera-phone into the most important (audio)visual technology, exponentially increasing the scope and reach of photographic practices but also expanding the times, types, and reach of the practice of photography for anthropological thinking. This expansion in how we do photography opened the door to a more speculative approach to image-creation in which the connection and conceptual use of images becomes more relevant than the representational use. The camera became not only a way to see the world, but also to imagine it. I started taking lots of photos, particularly when going for long walks in the city. These strolls can be connected with another emerging exploration in ethnography: walking methods (Bates & Rhys-Taylor, 2017) as a "way of engaging with the social world and allowing it to ask questions of us" (p. 4). The combination between seeing photographically and walking was interesting because, ultimately, it became a sensory experience that allowed me "to think of images as being produced and consumed in movement and of 'the visual sense' being part of (multisensory) perception in movement" (Pink, 2011, p. 7).

Sometimes the resulting images of these strolls are mere fragments of things I observe that catch my attention: architectural details, objects, people, or streets. At other times they are a specific exploration about a particular embodied phenomenon, for example the ways people exercise in public parks, or how cars may have protective covers on them, or people sleeping in public places. This use is similar to how Mead and Bateson used photography in *Balinese*

Character (1942) in which images were not illustrations of points, but the images were the points themselves. Walking and shooting have become almost a combined meditative practice that mixes the dynamic of thinking while walking and the reflexive action of looking while photographing. As Brent Luvaas has written: "The camera (is) engaged in the project of seeing ethnographically *along with me*" (2019, p. 78). The more I practice this walking-visual-thinking, the more I realised that the activity itself is becoming more important than the resulting images.

It was because I went for long walks, with my camera in hand, that I was able to encounter and photograph these facemasks. While my gaze focused on them, my reflections were about the pandemic at large. Facemasks were reminders of the close presence of people and the distance the pandemic had forced between us. In a way, it was a co-presence (we are all in this together) and a reminder that we need to be separated to be able to be together once again. But they were also political, cultural, and material objects themselves that were central to many discussions about community responsibility, environmental protection, and health practices.

Photography as an Intervention: Imagining

Thanks to the photographic walks I took using photography as a method of seeing/thinking, I started noticing things that I did not notice before (see Forrest, 2016). I started making connections that I had not perceived until that very moment. In my exploration, photography as a method evolved from a way of seeing to a way of thinking and to a way of imagining. It was this imagining that turned later into an intervention in the sense that my intention was not to describe something but to interrogate it.

All this noticing, observing, and connecting led me to imagine a number of things that were not necessarily reduced to what I had in front of the lens when I took the photos. These images were not necessarily representations of a particular group of people, or a given situation, or an observable phenomenon, and were more than the sum of its parts. Many of the things that I was photographing ignited my imagination in different directions. For example, photographing cars with protective covers made me think about mobility, the abuse of fossil fuels, and human priorities (people were protecting their cars from nature!). Or, photographing people doing exercise allowed me to think about the body, the role of culture shaping them, and the connection between class, physical activity, and subjectivities.

As with the facemasks, one important example that I have theorised and photographed has to do with adhesive bandages. I started photographing adhesive bandages out of curiosity, thinking about them as traces of the presence of wounded people. I started looking for these *traces* whenever I walked. While I used the concept of *trajectories* to reflect on my relationship with the space while in movement and photographing (Gómez Cruz, 2016a), I used the concept of traces, inspired by the work of Napolitano (2015) that defines traces as an index that "embeds affective circulations" (p. 52). I use the concept of trace as a way to acknowledge the affective connection between an object (such as adhesive bandages or facemasks) and my encounter with them. Adhesive bandages indexed an unseen presence (that of the humans who discarded/wore/lost them) which prompted broader questions about human fragility, the environment, and social life. I wrote a small piece along with a "visual essay" that focused on these very quotidian and insignificant but visually pervasive objects. The goal of the visual essay was not to present some findings using the images as data, nor to elaborate a theoretical discussion based on empirical elements. The visual essay simply wanted to make a point: humans are playing a central role in the climate catastrophe in spite of our own fragility as a species. The images of the discarded adhesive bandages were more metaphorical than representational, and they called for the reader's imagination to *see* the connection that could not be *seen* in the photos. Therefore, the most important element with the images, and the key point in the piece, was not what was *in the frame* but what was out of it, something so big that it cannot be *framed*. Inspired by conceptual art, it was the accompanying text that provided the suggested meaning.

The second iteration of this particular project is still unfolding, this time focusing on discarded facemasks. I have taken more than a thousand images of discarded facemasks in the streets. Facemasks that are wet, thorned, ragged, dirty, spotless. Some are old, some are new, sometimes they are covered (in dirt, plants or leaves) (Figure 11.2), or under objects (plants, cars, trees) (Figure 11.3).

As with the discarded adhesive bandages, these facemasks are a clear reminder of the Covid-19 pandemic. Encountering them triggers my imagination about distribution networks, materials, policies, the sense of community and solidarity, health, the rollout of the vaccine, and so on. Facemasks are used by humans to prevent the virus from spreading but they are also a reminder that we are fragile beings in a pandemic originated in the disruption of natural environments. These images are evocative of how we have broken the fragile balance in the planet and are experiencing the consequences of it. By showing the images of facemasks together, the aim is to turn them into an intervention, as a form of visual activism because "once we have learned how to see the world, we have taken only one of the required steps. The point is to change it" (Mirzoeff, 2016, p. 293).

Figure 11.3 Discarded facemask covered in leaves
Source: Photo by author.

Towards a Future-oriented *Media Anthropology*

While I have traced my relationship to photography, from research object to method to intervention, explaining how we can use images to imagine and not only to represent, it is time for me to come back to the original point I wanted to make, paraphrasing the famous speech made by John F. Kennedy, it is time to think not what anthropology can do for media but what media can do for anthropology. I suggest three avenues to develop this media anthropology: going beyond ethnography; imagination and speculation; and techno-reflexivity. While I am only able to outline them here, my goal is to invite an ongoing dialogue.

MacDougall, talking about visual anthropology, stated that it "may offer different ways of understanding but also different things to understand" (2005, p. 220). While the examples I presented in this chapter are related to photography, and they could be framed within discussions of visual anthropology, I suggest that they can also become a fertile ground when discussing media anthropology. Similar experimentations and innovations could use other media forms such as audio, video, installations (Hartblay, 2018), theatre, or performance to make similar points (see Schneider & Wright, 2020 for some examples, and Ingold, 2013 for a theorisation). The argument that I want to highlight is that the affordances of media can go beyond its use to create representational illustrations and become key tools in our methodological innovations, but, more importantly, they can be a game changer element as an academic intervention into how we think, see, and act in the world.

Inspired by an anthropology detached from ethnography, I make a call for the use of media to study the human *beyond* its connection to specific cultures and peoples. That is, to explore the non-ethnographic uses of media *as* anthropological thinking. This requires imagination and new ways of acknowledging and engaging in photographic practices. While the examples presented here could be seen as ethnographic in their base, they do not reflect a particular group and are not connected (nor reduced) to specific people, culture or collective (facemasks, while highly contested, became normalised and sometimes mandatory in many parts of the world). The use of these images, when combined with a more speculative approach, become anthropological by speaking to potentially all forms of humanity.

Imaginative Speculation

Inspired by techniques and approaches developed and used in contemporary art, the idea of a speculative use of media as anthropology can potentially revitalise our methods but also our theoretical tools. In this chapter I have mentioned three concepts that I developed for three visual essays: trajectories (Gómez Cruz, 2016a), traces (Gómez Cruz, 2021), and *imagenation* (a wordplay between image and imagination) (Gómez Cruz, 2020). These theoretical devices were used to account for movement, encounters, paths, reflexivity, ways of seeing, and ways of thinking. In this chapter, I bring them together to propose them as a speculative method. These theoretical devices became useful in explaining methodological processes that were created in response to less directive, more organic, and improvisational ways of inquiry that involve everyday practices of photography. We need, therefore. a methodological theory that is connected to our technological empiricism and experimentation. I propose the new term *PhotoMedia*[1] as a first step in that direction. *PhotoMedia* is a methodological approach that can be simultaneously empirical, theoretical, and technical. Moreover, working in this way, the distinction between what is theoretical, what is empirical, and what is imaginative becomes blurred. While in the past this might have been an outrageous idea, the significant challenges that lie ahead require us to be innovative, bold, and creative. Anthropology is well situated to respond to these challenges, particularly with a future-orientation (Kazubowski-Houston & Auslander, 2021; Salazar et al., 2017; Bryant & Knight, 2019). As Pandian (2019, p. 4) poetically suggests: "anthropology is the endeavour to conceive a humanity still yet to come". Now, more than ever, we need this approach.

Key to this endeavour is pushing the boundaries of media beyond its current use as representations and illustrations and towards its imbrication in practices of meditation, thinking, and speculation, approaches which have been proposed for years without being fully embraced by the anthropological community. If we accept two premises, that photographic images can be more than representations and that ethnography is not the only method for anthropology, these could allow us to discuss the idea of a media anthropology moving forward. This would require not only to rethink our use of media but perhaps more importantly to rethink anthropology itself. A way to do that would be to take seriously what media can afford.

Techno-reflexivity

The idea that technologies hold the potential to become tools to think with is not new. McLuhan famously stated that "We shape our tools, and thereafter our tools shape us". Nevertheless, media technologies are still undertheorised in this way. While there has been an "ethnographic turn" in art and media studies, at the same time there seems to be an "artistic turn" in anthropology, particularly in ethnography (Schneider & Wright, 2020; Wright & Schneider, 2010; Marcus & Myers, 1995; Willim, 2017). While media production is an essential component of this convergence, on many occasions their uses are either in collaborations, using creative ways to engage with ethnographic fieldwork, or with the presentation of ethnographic data. We need to develop methodological strategies that respond to our use of particular media, constructing them as theoretical devices.

The third element of this method is intended to push the technical boundaries and the traditional uses of media, turning them into tools for thinking by applying what I call techno-reflexivity. While the concept has been used in the past to acknowledge the subjectivity of people building technological systems, I am repurposing it to account for the constant dialogue and reflection about how we use media technologies, how we could use them differently, and what kind of questions we imagine can be responded by them.

In this sense, the mobility and constant access to a quality camera, afforded by smartphones, has become a central element in this techno-reflexivity. It is the constant availability of an image-making device when in movement that has shaped most of the projects that I have discussed here.

Conclusion

I still photograph facemasks every day. I constantly find new ones, on the pavement, in the park, many outside hospitals, on the beach, and in the bush. The facemask has become the image of a pandemic that is still killing people all over the world. It is a barrier, a protection but also an isolator, a thin hope of survival that has been used in protests to counteract global surveillance systems, and by people to stop the virus that was born out of destruction of natural habitats.

This chapter reflected on a body of work that is currently being developed, photographic explorations of what does it mean to be human in these times. While this is not a topic traditionally associated with anthropological approaches to media, I contend that media can become a powerful tool for anthropological inquiry. Combining practice-based approaches such as walking methodologies, visual anthropology, speculative approaches, techniques of contemporary art, and current debates in anthropology, I suggest that media anthropology could expand its reach with a combination of a more imaginative use of media as a way of thinking, imagining, and acting.

Moving toward a more future-oriented speculative reflection can become a fruitful way to think beyond the constraints of both disciplinary and theoretical boundaries. I suggest that we can expand the toolkit of media anthropology by adopting and adapting approaches that incorporate movement and embodiment but mostly by thinking not only anthropologically *about* media but producing anthropological knowledge *with* media. This *media anthropology* is particularly suitable for inquiries about the future and we need it now more than ever.

Note

1 The methodological use of the concept is mine but the concept itself is not. There is a very important conference in Finland with that title.

References

Banks, M. & Zeitlyn, D. (2015). *Visual methods in social research*. Sage.
Bates, C. & Rhys-Taylor, A. (Eds). (2017). *Walking through social research*. Taylor & Francis.
Bateson, G. & Mead, M. (1942). Balinese character: A photographic analysis. *New York Academy of Sciences*, 17–92.
Bazin, A. (1960). The ontology of the photographic image. *Film Quarterly*, *13*(4), 4–9.
Brook, D. (1983). Painting, photography and representation. *The Journal of Aesthetics and Art Criticism*, *42*(2), 171–180.
Bryant, R. & Knight, D. M. (2019). *The anthropology of the future*. Cambridge University Press.
Buckingham, D. (2009). Creative visual methods in media research: Possibilities, problems and proposals. *Media, Culture & Society*, *31*(4), 633–652.
Cartier-Bresson, H. (1999). *The mind's eye: Writings on photography and photographers*. Aperture.
Collier, J. & Collier, M. (1986). *Visual anthropology: Photography as a research method*. UNM Press.
Costa, E. (2018). Affordances-in-practice: An ethnographic critique of social media logic and context collapse. *New Media & Society*, *20*(10), 3641–3656.
Cotton, C. (2015). *Photography is magic*. Aperture.
Edwards, E. (2015). Anthropology and photography: A long history of knowledge and affect. *Photographies*, *8*(3), 235–252.
Edwards, E. (1992). *Anthropology and photography, 1860–1920*. Royal Anthropological Institute of Great Britain and Ireland.
Foster, H. 1996. The artist as ethnographer? in H. Foster (Ed.), *The return of the real: The avant-garde at the end of the century*. MIT Press, 171–203.
Forrest, E. (2016). Exploring everyday photographic routines through the habit of noticing, in E. Gómez Cruz & A. Lehmuskallio (Eds.), *Digital photography and everyday life: Empirical studies on material visual practices*. Routledge.
Frosh, P. (2018). *The poetics of digital media*. John Wiley & Sons.
Garrett, B., & Anderson, K. (2018). Drone methodologies: Taking flight in human and physical geography. *Transactions of the Institute of British Geographers*, *43*(3), 341–359.
Goffman, E. (1974). *Frame analysis: An essay on the organization of experience*. Harvard University Press.
Gómez Cruz, E. (2021). Everyday anthropo-scenes: A visual inventory of human traces. *Cultural Geographies*, *28*(1), 193–201.
Gómez Cruz, E. (2020). Black screens: A visual essay on mobile screens in the city. *Visual Communication*, *19*(1), 143–156.
Gómez Cruz, E. (2017). Immersive reflexivity: Using 360 degree cameras in ethnographic fieldwork. In E. Gómez Cruz, S. Sumartojom, & S. Pink (Eds.), *Refiguring techniques in visual digital research*. Palgrave Pivot.
Gómez Cruz, E. (2016a). Trajectories: Digital/visual data on the move. *Visual Studies*, *31*(4), 335–343.
Gómez Cruz, E. (2016b). Photo-genic assemblages: Photography as a connective interface. In E. Gómez Cruz & A. Lehmuskallio (Eds.), *Digital photography in everyday life: Empirical studies on material visual practices*. Routledge, 228–242.

Gómez Cruz, E. (2012). *De la Cultura Kodak a la imagen en red. Una etnografía sobre fotografía digital.* Editorial UOC.
Gómez Cruz, E. & Siles, I. (2021). Visual communication in practice: A texto-material approach to Whatsapp in Mexico City. *International Journal of Communication, 15*, 21.
Gunn, W., Otto, T., & Smith, R. C. (Eds.). (2013). *Design anthropology: Theory and practice.* Taylor & Francis.
Halse, J. (2013). Ethnographies of the possible. In W. Gunn, T. Otto, & R. C. Smith (Eds.) *Design Anthropology.* Routledge, 180–196.
Hartblay, C. (2018). This is not thick description: Conceptual art installation as ethnographic process. *Ethnography, 19*(2), 153–182.
Ingold, T. (2019). Art and anthropology for a sustainable world. *Journal of the Royal Anthropological Institute, 25*(4), 659–675.
Ingold, T. (2017). Anthropology contra ethnography. *HAU: Journal of Ethnographic Theory, 7*(1), 21–26.
Ingold, T. (2013). *Making: Anthropology, archaeology, art and architecture.* Routledge.
Ito, M. & Okabe, D. (2003). Camera phones changing the definition of picture-worthy. *Japan Media Review, 29*, 205–215.
Jacknis, I. (1988). Margaret Mead and Gregory Bateson in Bali: Their use of photography and film. *Cultural Anthropology, 3*(2), 160–177.
Kazubowski-Houston, M. & Auslander, M. (2021). *In search of lost futures: Anthropological explorations in multimodality, deep interdisciplinarity, and autoethnography.* Springer Nature.
Kitzinger, J. (2007). Framing and frame analysis, in E. Devereux (Ed.), *Media studies: Key issues and debates.* Sage, 134–161.
Lehmuskallio, A. & Gómez Cruz, E. (2016). Why material visual practices. In E. Gómez Cruz and A. Lehmuskallio (Eds.), *Digital photography and everyday life: Empirical studies on material visual practices.* Routledge, 1–16.
Luvaas, B. (2019). The camera and the anthropologist: Reflections on photographic agency. *Visual Anthropology, 32*(1), 76–96.
MacDougall, D. (2005). *The corporeal image: Film, ethnography, and the senses.* Princeton University Press.
Marcus, G. E. & Myers, F. R. (Eds.). (1995). *The traffic in culture: Refiguring art and anthropology.* University of California Press.
Mead, M. & Bateson, G. (2003). On the use of the camera in anthropology, in Y. S. Lincoln & N. K. Denzin (Eds.), *Turning Points in Qualitative Research, Tying Knots in a Handkerchief.* Altamira Press, 265–272.
Mirzoeff, N. (2016). *How to see the world: An introduction to images, from self-portraits to selfies, maps to movies, and more.* Basic Books.
Nadolny, P. (2011). A walk in Melbourne: A street documentary. *India International Centre Quarterly, 38*(1), 90–111.
Napolitano, V. (2015). Anthropology and traces. *Anthropological Theory, 15*(1), 47–67.
Pandian, A. (2019). *A possible anthropology: Methods for uneasy times.* Duke University Press.
Pink, S. (2020). *Doing visual ethnography.* Sage.
Pink, S. (2011). Sensory digital photography: Re-thinking "moving" and the image. *Visual Studies, 26*(1), 4–13.
Pinney, C. (2011). *Photography and anthropology.* Reaktion Books.
Rees, T. (2018). *After ethnos.* Duke University Press.
Rose, G. (2016). *Visual methodologies: An introduction to researching with visual materials.* Sage.
Ruby, J. (2005). The last 20 years of visual anthropology—A critical review. *Visual Studies, 20*(2), 159–170.
Salazar, J. F., Pink, S., Irving, A., & Sjöberg, J. (Eds.). (2017). *Anthropologies and futures: Researching emerging and uncertain worlds.* Bloomsbury Publishing.
Scruton, R. (1981). Photography and representation. *Critical Inquiry, 7*(3), 577–603.
Schneider, A. & Wright, C. (Eds.). (2020). *Contemporary art and anthropology.* Routledge.
Talbot, W. H. F. (2020). *The pencil of nature.* Good Press.
Thakur, A., Gormish, M., & Erol, B. (2011). Mobile phones and information capture in the workplace, in *CHI'11 extended abstracts on human factors in computing systems.* Association for Computing Machinery, 1513–1518.
Van House, N., Davis, M., Ames, M., Finn, M., & Viswanathan, V. (2005, April). The uses of personal networked digital imaging: An empirical study of cameraphone photos and sharing. In *CHI'05 extended abstracts on human factors in computing systems.* Association for Computing Machinery, 1853–1856.
Vannini, P. & Scott, N. (2020). Mobile ethnographies of the city, in B. Jensen, C. Lassen, V. Kaufmann, M. Freudendal-Pedersen, & I. S. Gøtzsche Lange (Eds.), *Handbook of Urban Mobilities.* Routledge, 59-67.

Vannini, P. & Vannini, A. (2008). Of walking shoes, boats, golf carts, bicycles, and a slow technoculture: A technography of movement and embodied media on Protection Island. *Qualitative Inquiry, 14*(7), 1272–1301.

Villi, M. (2007). Mobile visual communication: Photo messages and camera phone photography. *Nordicom Review, 28*(1), 49–62.

Willim, R. (2017). Evoking imaginaries: Art probing, ethnography and more-than-academic practice. *Sociological Research Online 22*(4), 208–231. doi:10.1177/1360780417726733.

Wolf, S. (Ed.) (2019). *PhotoWork: Forty photographers on process and practice*. Aperture.

Wright, C. & Schneider, A. (2010). *Between art and anthropology: Contemporary ethnographic practice*. Berg.

Yi'En, C. (2014). Telling stories of the city: Walking ethnography, affective materialities, and mobile encounters. *Space and Culture, 17*(3), 211–223. doi:10.1177/1206331213499468

12
CONTENT-AS-PRACTICE

Studying Digital Content with a Media Practice Approach

Christoph Bareither

Introduction

Studying media through media-related practices has long been a leading approach in media anthropology (Bräuchler and Postill, 2010). Given the interdisciplinary nature of the field, media practice is a valuable concept for developing shared key interests across disciplinary lines. The conceptual foundations of practice theory – building on the works of Pierre Bourdieu, Michel de Certeau, Anthony Giddens, Sherry Ortner, Andreas Reckwitz, Theodor Schatzki, and many others (for an overview, see Postill, 2010) – have given rise to different strands of media practice thinking. Together, they constitute what I call the "media practice approach," which includes any analytical perspective employing practice theory to understand the relationships between media technologies, human actors, and everyday life.

My first aim is to identify a conceptual and methodological desideratum of the media practice approach. Nick Couldry, in his foundational text for the study of media practices, describes the key aim of this "new paradigm": "to decentre media research from the study of media texts or production structures (important though these are) and to redirect it onto the study of the open-ended range of practices focused directly or indirectly on media" (2010: 16–17). In following the media practice approach, then, media anthropologists do not only turn towards practices; they *decentre* media texts. As Couldry explains, the decentring of media texts allows media researchers to go beyond content analysis (and beyond questions of production and direct reception) so as to "get a better grip on the distinctive types of social process enacted through media-related practices" (Couldry, 2012: 55).

It is not my intention to interrogate the plausibility and analytical usefulness of practice-oriented media research. On the contrary, my intention is to contribute to the media practice approach by pointing out the lack of conceptual and methodological clarity about how to fit media content into research designs inspired by practice theories, *despite* their decentring of media texts. This is important because, for scholars working on media practices, "media cannot be studied without an acknowledgement of their content," as Sarah Pink puts it (2015: 12).

In their seminal work "How the World Changed Social Media," a comprehensive summary of a multi-researcher anthropological study on social media practices around the globe, Daniel Miller et al. (2016) go one step further. They argue that anthropologists of social media need to pay close attention to user content because it constitutes the relevance of social media in the first place: "It is the *content* rather than the platform that is most significant when it comes to why social media matters" (ibid.: 1).

But how do we best approach content when following a media practice approach? This question has special relevance for "old" and "new" media, but it is especially important for media anthropologists working on and in digital environments, which is why I focus on *digital content* below. By digital content, I mean any kind of digital image, video, text, or audio recording presented on or circulated via digital media technologies such as social networking sites (e.g. Facebook, Instagram), dating and messenger apps (e.g. WhatsApp, Tinder), and other online repositories (e.g. YouTube). I deliberately avoid the term "user-generated content" because it implies a dichotomy between professional producers on the one hand and users or consumers on the other, which does not capture the complexity of social media entanglements (Ardèvol et al., 2010: 264–265). Digital content has become an essential part of many media anthropological studies, but its hybrid, fluid, and manifold nature makes it all the more challenging to conceptualise within complex sets of media practices. How can we conceptualise digital content with the media practice approach? What can we gain analytically from its conceptualisation? And what methodological consequences does it have for media anthropology in general?

In fleshing out conceptual and methodological responses to those questions, I will draw on my work in the multi-researcher project Curating Digital Images (Bareither et al., 2021), which examines the transformations caused by digital image technologies in heritage and museum contexts. I focus in particular on my ethnographic study of Berlin's Memorial to the Murdered Jews of Europe (Bareither, 2019, 2021a, 2021b), colloquially referred to as the Holocaust memorial. Widely known for its uncommon aesthetics, the memorial consists of 2,711 concrete blocks covering 19,000 square metres. It is located next to the Brandenburg Gate at the very centre of the German capital, and is one of the city's most popular tourist destinations and one of the most frequently visited sites of Holocaust remembrance in the world. In my study, I describe the digital media practices of Holocaust remembrance at the Berlin site as practices of "past presencing," which anthropologist Sharon Macdonald regards as "the ways in which people variously draw on, experience, negotiate, reconstruct, and perform the past in their ongoing lives" (Macdonald, 2012: 234). My research also relies on approaches to the study of digital memory practices (e.g. Hoskins, 2018), theories of emotional and affective practices (Scheer, 2012; Wetherell, Smith, and Campbell, 2018), the ethnographic study of digital photography (e.g. Gómez Cruz and Lehmuskallio, 2016), and social media practices more generally (e.g. Costa, 2018).

My previously published articles have focused on the empirical results of my study (Bareither 2021b) and on discussions of digital media's "emotional affordances" at sites of Holocaust remembrance (Bareither 2019, 2021a). By contrast, this chapter raises general theoretical, conceptual, and methodological questions regarding the role of digital content from my ethnographic work. I am particularly interested in revisiting my ethnographic data to explore new theoretical terrain in developing an anthropological understanding of digital content that builds upon the media practice approach.

My study comprised participant observation at the memorial and online, 17 face-to-face interviews with 41 visitors at the site, and 24 chat interviews with Instagram and Facebook users. The interviewees had an equal gender balance, ranging from 12 to 77 years of age (most between 20 and 40), and representing 29 nations. The interviews and participant observation were accompanied by a computer-assisted ethnographic analysis of 800 social media posts taken from Instagram and Facebook. The posts typically include one or more digital images (and occasional videos), text captions (often in combination with emojis, hashtags, and geo-tags), and comments from other users. In the following, I use these posts as well as the material I gathered from my fieldwork and interviews in outlining my approach to digital content.

In order to illustrate some of the arguments, I provide links in the endnotes to examples of Instagram posts, which can be viewed without creating a user account. All links were active as of June 2021. Alternatively, readers may visit the Instagram subpage that brings together all posts tagged with the Holocaust memorial location.[1] The subpage's source code indicates that it contains more than 314,000 posts related to the memorial, although the exact number is unclear. All examples that I mention can be easily identified by browsing the page.

Understanding Digital Content-as-Practice

Digital content is an elusive analytical object. It consists of binary code that appears to us as an image, video, text, symbol, and, as in the case of social media posts, a combination of all three. The term "content" usually does not refer to the medium itself – for example the image as a medium, the video as a medium, the text as a medium, and so on. Rather, it directs our attention to what the media *contain* – for example the image of a particular person at a particular place, a video showing a particular activity, a text containing particular words, and so on. But digital media technologies do not contain content in the way that a photo album does. Instead, they store and/or access digital data and process it in such a way that it can be displayed on electronic interfaces such as smartphones, cameras, and computers. This makes the question of what digital content *is* difficult to answer.

My aim is not to resolve the ontological status of digital content or to offer a static definition in its place. My concern is epistemological: how can we understand digital content through the lens of the media practice approach? To answer that question, one could turn to Theodor Schatzki's ideas about the relationships between practices, sayings, texts, and discursive formations (2017), to Andreas Reckwitz's notion of discursive practices (2008), or to Guido Ipsen's semiotic reading of the media practice approach (2010). Though I find these approaches helpful, I propose a practice-theory approach to digital content that does not rely on categories of text, discourse or representation.

To that end, I suggest a simple analytical shift: instead of making a clear-cut distinction between digital content and its associated practices, we can understand digital content itself *as* practice. Whereas a media text approach focuses on the meanings or semiotic implications of digital content, a media practice approach allows us to ask: What does digital content *do*? This is not to suggest that digital content is itself an actor in the sense of actor-network theory (e.g. Latour, 2005: 71–72). My position is much simpler: I argue that the practices of content creators *live on* through digital content while being shaped by the affordances of digital technologies. I call this constellation *content-as-practice*.

This may first seem counterintuitive. Can an image, a text, or an emoji be understood in a meaningful way as a practice? I believe it can. Consider the example of selfies taken at the Holocaust memorial showing a person or persons with sad facial expressions, which I term the "sad selfie."[2] When we think of the bodily routine of making a sad facial expression (independently from any technological device), we can certainly conceptualise this as a practice in the sense of practice theory, and the same goes for taking photos in front of memorials and posting them on social media. So why should the practices lose their status once they are transformed by digital technologies and appear as digital images on social media? A social media post showing a sad selfie taken at the Holocaust memorial is a digital continuation of the bodily gesture captured by a camera. It sustains the original practice in digital form.

The conceptual challenge here is the temporal delay. It might seem that a sad selfie simply encapsulates something that happened in the past, that it *results* from a practice. But from a practice-oriented perspective, it is impossible to determine where practice ends and the digital object is all that remains. Think of a person who shows a friend a picture of herself making a sad facial expression at the Holocaust memorial. We certainly would consider it to be a practice. So why shouldn't we think of this as a practice when the same process is enacted and multiplied (sometimes thousands of times) at a later time on digital interfaces, albeit without the presence of the original creator?

The same goes for other types of content such as textual captions. Writing captions can surely be regarded as a media practice. Why would we think the practice constituted by writing stops once the writing stops? For example, visitors to the Holocaust memorial frequently articulate their emotional relationship to the past through captions and through the hashtags and emojis embedded in them. The captions themselves continue to articulate the visitors' emotional experiences, even after the visitors who posted the content log off.

The content-as-practice approach draws from the theoretical work of Kevin Pauliks and Jens Ruchatz, who regard digital images such as those circulating on social media as materialised practice. While my own approach attends to texts, emojis, hashtags, and the like as well as to images, their key argument is nevertheless helpful for my purposes: "A picture materializes a practice insofar as it is the result of a practice that gains a perceivable, definable, and at least to some extent stabilized (because reproducible) form in the aesthetic object" (Pauliks and Ruchatz, 2021: 124). The notion of a materialised practice allows us to think of digital content as both object *and* practice. In contrast to Pauliks and Ruchatz, however, I argue that digital content is not only the "result" or the "trace of practices" (ibid.); instead, it allows practices to live on in digital form. In other words, digital content-as-practice is both materialised *and* lived practice.

Like other practices, digital content-as-practice does not exist in a vacuum (Pink et al., 2016: 57). It is closely entangled with other media-related practices. For instance, a digital image taken at the Holocaust memorial and then posted on social media is connected to the practices of visiting the memorial, finding a good place to take a picture, and positioning one's own body or the bodies of others, before finally taking the picture, editing it, and posting it online. A digital caption is shaped by practices of reading, writing, and online communication (e.g. using emojis). Images and captions related to the Holocaust memorial are also bound to broader social and cultural practices such as visits to other heritage sites and emotional performances of Holocaust remembrance. For example, a sad selfie is connected to the bodily routines of displaying sad facial expressions when being present at sites of atrocities such as the Holocaust, which many visitors have internalised in accordance with their particular social and cultural backgrounds. The content-as-practice approach always understands digital content to be imbricated in a whole range of social, cultural, and emotional practices and assigns it an active role within them.

Human Actors, Practical Sense, and Technological Affordances

To recapitulate, the content-as-practice approach considers how the practices of content creators live on through digital content. But who or what is the "actor" behind content-as-practice? Practice theories assume that actors are not subjects preceding practices but "body/minds who 'carry' and 'carry out' social practices" and who "'consist in' the performance of practices" (Reckwitz, 2002: 256). The bodies linking practices and actors have incorporated a "practical sense" (Bourdieu, 1990) – a "shared practical understanding" (Schatzki, 2001: 11), or a "practical knowledge" (Hörning, 2001) – that guides everyday actions.

The consideration of human bodies and their practical sense is crucial for understanding the agent who enacts digital content and who performs media-related practices more generally. But this is only the first step. For media technologies are not passive objects; they bring specific potentials of their own. Analytical tools are needed to comprehend how media technologies actively participate in media practices. One approach that meets this need is actor-network theory (ANT), which understands technical devices as *actors* (Latour, 2005: 71). Media anthropology has a somewhat ambivalent relationship with the ANT approach, however. While it has certainly influenced work in the research area, ANT implies (or is at least understood to imply) a strong decentring of human actors, which is not suited for every kind of ethnographic description, and has thus been rejected by many practice theorists (Schatzki, 2001: 20).

Another approach, which relies more strongly on practice theories, understands media practices to result from the interplay between human bodies and the practice potentials within media technologies. In the mid-1990s, Stefan Beck developed an approach for the study of technology and media that became very influential in German-speaking cultural anthropology (1997). Building on the practice theories of Bourdieu and others, Beck pointed to the role of the body as repository for incorporated knowledge that guides everyday practices, including the use of technologies and media (ibid.: 272). As Beck puts it, the body enacts "the social and cultural formation of comparatively 'soft' cultural orientations, dispositives and habitualisations" that shape our everyday relationships to technology (ibid.: 169, my translation). In other words, our bodies are infused with a practical sense shaped by cultural and social conventions for handling technological devices in our everyday lives.

Beck maintains that technological devices themselves are not passive objects; rather, they unfold what he calls "object potentials" (ibid.: 169; my translation) that offer or prompt a range of practices while restricting others. Crucially for Beck, the potentials go beyond the physical properties of a given technology. Instead, they are highly relational: what kind of practices a technological device allows, prompts, or restricts, depends on an actor's practical sense. By calling our attention to the interdependency of technology practices with human bodies, social conventions, and technological potentials, Beck offers a practice-theory approach to the study of technology and media that remains valuable today.

The book in which Beck lays out his approach was never translated into English, so its impact on the international field of media anthropology has been limited. Similar approaches have evolved through the rise and popularity of affordance theories, however. Growing out of the work of James W. Gibson (1986), the idea of affordance has become a key concept for describing the relationship between media technologies and everyday practices. "Affordances," Ian Hutchby writes, "are functional and relational aspects which frame, while not determining, the possibilities for agentic action in relation to an object" (2001: 444). In contrast to Beck's approach, affordance theories have not been explicitly developed to extend practice-theory thinking. They are nevertheless highly compatible with practice theories, especially when we consider the many similarities between Beck's approach and the practice-oriented language used by Hutchby and others.

Elisabetta Costa has argued that affordances always exist in relation to the practices through which they are enacted. Her concept of "affordances-in-practice" means that "affordances are not intrinsic properties that can be defined outside their situated context of usage, but ongoing enactments by specific users that may vary across space and time" (2018: 13). Costa's concept, which inspired my idea of "content-as-practice," contains an implicit criticism of approaches that reduce the affordances of technologies to their functions (ibid.:10). Costa and other authors such as Julian Hopkins (2016) advance a decidedly relational notion of affordance, which emphasises the role of social and cultural context. Combine their approach with Beck's emphasis on the body's practical sense, and we have a framework that acknowledges complexity of the interplay of human bodies, their practical sense, the cultural and social conventions in which both are embedded, and the affordances of media technologies.

From Social Media Algorithms to Routinised Practices

How does this contribute to my understanding of digital content? First, it helps us to treat digital content not simply as a practice enacted by human actors in isolation, but as an integral part of the complex entanglements of bodily knowledge, social and cultural conventions, and media technologies. At the same time, it allows us to see what sets digital content-as-practice apart from other types of media practices. We can say that typical media practices (taking photos, writing, editing, posting, etc.) depend on both human bodies and media affordances, but human actors are the primary agents. Once these practices become digital content, however, the agency shifts towards the media technologies. Through their affordances, media technologies allow human practices to live on through digital content, even when said creators are not actively involved in the process anymore. But this also means that the affordances control, shape, and restrict how these practices unfold over time.

As the platforms' affordances take over control, they employ a complex system of algorithms. Recall that digital content does not exist per se. It consists of binary code that is processed in such a way to appear as specific images, texts, and symbols. Algorithms are important to consider because they shape that process. For example, social media algorithms can determine which posts are displayed to whom and when. A complex example for this is Instagram's use of artificial intelligence, which determines what is shown to individual users through the platform's personalised "explore" feature (Medvedev, Wu, and Gordon, 2019). Two more well-known and comparatively simple examples for social media algorithms are location feeds and hashtag feeds. These are continuously growing lists – or "unruly archives" (Geismar, 2017) – that can be easily accessed by Instagram users. A location feed brings together all public posts with a particular geo-location tag. A hashtag feed does the same for particular hashtags such as "#holocaust" (Lundrigan, 2020).

From the content-as-practice perspective, the algorithms social media sites use carve out *routines* from a vast amount of seemingly random posts. Practice is never a random, one-off activity, but a form of repetition. Indeed, "for practice theory," Andreas Reckwitz observes, "the nature of social structure consists in routinization ... [and] the idea of routines necessarily implies the idea of a temporality of structure: routinized social practices occur in the sequence of time, in repetition" (2002: 255).

The notions of routine and repetition can easily be applied to media practices that are repeated by the same person every day. Someone who reads the news on her smartphone every morning enacts a routinised media practice. Ditto for those who routinely publish the same type of digital content. But now consider digital content dispersed across platforms, media formats, and hundreds or thousands of online user accounts. Many sad selfies taken at the Holocaust memorial and other sites of Holocaust remembrance appear on social media platforms. From the perspective of their creators, each post is a unique, individual act. Can we then still understand sad selfies as *routinised* practice?

This is where the algorithmic affordances of social media platforms come into play. For an individual user, a sad selfie might be an individual act. But scroll through the several hundred thousand posts on the location feed for the "Memorial to the Murdered Jews of Europe," and it becomes apparent that the sad selfie is one routinised practice among many. The social media algorithm that assembles all sad selfies under a geo-location tag renders individual acts into collective routines. In the following, I discuss these routines co-constituted by human actors and the affordances of digital technologies and living on through digital content-as-practice.

Content-as-Practice and the Holocaust Memorial

I employed computer-assisted ethnographic coding (Emerson Fretz, and Shaw, 2011: 171–200) to analyse 800 social media posts on Instagram and Facebook taken from location feeds linked to the Holocaust memorial. The sample was based on an inductive selection process. I collected smaller samples first and used the coding to identify the most relevant practices within them. The sad selfie is one example. In the process, I sought to deepen my insights into specific practices and identify new ones that previous samples did not include. In this way, I was able to pinpoint the most common and most dominant types of content-as-practice related to the Holocaust memorial. I was not looking for the meaning ascribed to the content. Instead, I focused on what a particular type of content is *doing*, how it functions as a routinised practice.

It's worth noting that the analytical distinction between different types of content-as-practice is relative. The routines I outline here do not describe objective characteristics. Rather, they emerge inductively from the particular interests of my work and the specifics of the ethnographic data. Accordingly, they represent a broad selection of different types of content-as-practice related to the site.[3]

As a first example, let us return to the sad selfie. First and foremost, I submit, it presences the past by articulating and mobilising emotions: the visitor in the photo looks directly at the camera while expressing sadness; the memorial in the background connects the emotion to the commemoration of the Holocaust. The sad selfie's past presencing engages in a thoughtful remembrance of past atrocities that honours victims and, through its emotional power, raises awareness for Holocaust remembrance, and may even help prevent future atrocities.

Another type of social media image shows visitors as they look into the distance as if lost in thought.[4] Typically, visitors sit on one of the concrete blocks or stand between them. These images, too, are practices of past presencing that work through the display of emotions. In contrast to sad selfies, however, they achieve this goal by documenting how visitors interact with the memorial (instead of interacting directly with the camera). Notably, these photos are often taken by friends or family members, but it is the persons portrayed who post them on social media. For them, the social media posts allow their emotional practices to live on and to participate in shared routines of Holocaust remembrance.

Other digital images posted on social media refrain from depicting human bodies at the memorial, and instead foreground its materiality and spatial structure. The photos articulate relationships to the past by visually capturing the memorial space. For example, one type of content-as-practice consists of shots with seemingly endless rows of grey stone.[5] An interviewee who took such a photo explained that "when I was really inside, I really felt like, you know, that you are … like a depressing feeling, because it's so tight, so that's what I kind of tried to fit in the picture, that you are [so] small in this huge, massive structure." Images that capture the spatial structure of the monument can articulate the photographer's emotional experiences at the site and share them with others. While they do not show the visitors' bodies, they are still a practice of presenting emotional relationships to the past.

These image-based practices are usually accompanied by text-based practices. The writing styles and text types used for social media captions come in many forms. Text-based practices that articulate one's own emotional experiences at the monument are particularly dominant. An analysis of more than 300 such captions revealed many variants. For example, captions articulate how visitors were emotionally moved by the memorial,[6] how they felt small, isolated or lost when walking through the blocks,[7] and how some felt hopeful and positive.[8] The overwhelming number explicitly or implicitly articulate sadness, melancholia, compassion, and remembrance[9] – in this way, they sustain the practices of past presencing enacted by their creators.

An integral part of many captions is emojis. They display hearts, praying hands, falling leaves, or sad faces that supplement or replace textual captions.[10] A visitor who posted a sad emoji (followed by 30 hashtags) under a photograph of the memorial explained to me: "I didn't really know what to write. So the emoji was only to express how I was feeling at that moment. I really think that it says more than everything."

Again, we see here how digital content functions as a practice. All types of images, texts, and emojis mentioned here are practices of past presencing in relation to the Holocaust. In addition, we see how digital content-as-practice is entangled not only with other media-related practices such as taking pictures, writing texts, and so on, but also with each other. Images, texts, and emojis are not singular and isolated routines; they often work together. The notion of content-as-practice always denotes an entanglement of practices that move and flow into one another.

Methodological Consequences

The content-as-practice approach also raises methodological questions, and one issue is central here: Is it sufficient to analyse *only* content-as-practice in order to provide thick ethnographic descriptions of digital media practices? I believe that the answer is no. The content-as-practice approach is truly productive only as part of more comprehensive ethnographic research. While the approach enables the study of visitors' media practices via the interfaces of social media platforms and uncovers specific routines and relationships in digital networks, it also needs participant observation, qualitative interviews, and other ethnographic approaches that provide contextualisation.

To clarify, whether it is necessary to combine the content-as-practice approach with other methods depends on one's disciplinary perspective. Pauliks and Ruchatz convincingly argue that their "materialised practices" allows the analysis of media practices from the perspective of a "praxeological media philosophy" (Pauliks and Ruchatz, 2021: 124) *without* resorting to interviews and fieldwork. For studies in the field of media anthropology, however, I believe that any analysis of digital content needs as much ethnographic context as possible under the circumstances provided by the given empirical field (see also Hobart, 2010: 64–65).

To understand why, consider photos of visitors to the Holocaust memorial looking into the distance. If we examine these posts only through what we see on a social media platform, we would conclude that they capture and display the creators' bodily practices in digital form. But participant observation at the site and conversations with visitors show this practice from a different perspective: most of the time, visitors adopt such reflective poses for a mere matter of seconds. They have family or friends take the photo, check the picture, perhaps repeat the process once or twice and then immediately share the image on social media.

This is not to say that digital content-as-practice reveals only the "surface" of the actual practice; on the contrary. My research shows that, from the perspective of the posts' creators, the act of commemoration is not constituted in the bodily practice on site but through the social media post itself. That is to say, the post *is* the act of commemoration. And thanks to the algorithms of the social media platform, each act of commemoration is connected to similar acts of commemoration, forming a clearly visible and routinised practice. My methodological point is that it is precisely these links that remain hidden if we study digital content-as-practice in isolation. This means that ethnographic research cannot be replaced by an analysis of digital content alone. It requires triangulating the analysis of content-as-practice with participant observation, interviews, and other methods.

Conclusion

My aim in proposing the content-as-practice approach is not to introduce a new theory. Instead, I want to provide an analytical tool enabling the analysis of digital content as media practice. What can we gain from this perspective? The answer to this question depends on the analytic purpose we assign to practice-theory thinking. As an ethnographer of digital cultures, I want to better understand the role of particular media-related routines in everyday life. And understanding content not only in terms of text and meaning but also as an entanglement of active routines that sustain the practices of their creators serves that purpose.

In the case of digital content related to the Holocaust memorial, this has clear analytical consequences. While text-centric methods focus on the meaning of the content and how it reflects contemporary memory cultures, the content-as-practice approach makes plain that digital content is not simply a reflection or representation of practices of remembrance. Digital content is a way for memory practices to *live on* through social media and, in this way, co-constitutes contemporary cultures of Holocaust remembrance on a massive scale.

The practice-theory perspective also points us to the role of practical sense and how it connects human bodies to media affordances. A content-as-practice such as the "sad selfie" shows how distinct everyday routines – taking of selfies and expressing sadness at a site of Holocaust remembrance – flow into one another to create a new practice. Integrating smartphones, digital cameras, and social media in everyday life gives rise to a practical sense for new routines that forge personal relationships to the past in different ways. In terms of affordance theories, this means that the analysis of content-as-practice shows how digital media do indeed afford new kinds of past presencing in contemporary Holocaust remembrance. Speaking on a more general level, digital content is one more area besides fieldwork and interviews in which to examine how the affordances of media technologies enable and shape different kinds of lived practice.

Several core questions have emerged from my concept of content-as-practice: How do the practices of content creators live on through digital content? How is content-as-practice shaped by the interplay of human bodies, their practical sense, the social and cultural conventions surrounding them, and the affordances of media technologies? How does digital content-as-practice constitute routines? What role do the algorithmic affordances of social media platforms play here? How are these routines entangled with other practices? And why do they matter in everyday life?

By proposing the content-as-practice approach, I do not wish to claim that digital content should be analysed *only* as practice. "Practice," Mark Hobart observes, "is not a natural object but a frame of reference that we use to interrogate a complex reality" (2010: 62). In the field of media anthropology, the content-as-practice approach can help us to better combine the study of digital content with the study of everyday life. In doing so, it provides a new form of ethnographic content analysis and a new tool in the expanding toolbox of media anthropological research.

Notes

1 www.instagram.com/explore/locations/213676284/memorial-to-the-murdered-jews-of-europe/
2 www.instagram.com/p/BdF_ZaWD5zd/, www.instagram.com/p/BebPrjIF7M4BE5Q4AIGWC8ld CqUgoFcolkLfjg0/

3 For example, I deliberately ignore the many "happy" social media posts related to the memorial: photos with visitors smiling brightly in front of the Holocaust memorial, climbing on the blocks, making funny faces or gesturing towards the camera. While these images are certainly salient and highly controversial for the digital cultures of Holocaust remembrance, they require a much deeper empirical analysis that would distract me from the conceptual questions at the heart of this chapter (but see Bareither, 2021b).
4 www.instagram.com/p/BcFSqbOHqiL/, www.instagram.com/p/BdADaXIDH4F/
5 www.instagram.com/p/BcFapmhhvdD/?taken-at=213676284, www.instagram.com/p/BcF4-lml4-j/
6 www.instagram.com/p/BcHv6i4AxFD/, www.instagram.com/p/BcJGAXJBxt3/
7 www.instagram.com/p/BjcpyfuHv43/, www.instagram.com/p/BjKmR39FJWG/
8 www.instagram.com/p/BcBAhSGDOsb/, www.instagram.com/p/BjarVqzHum9/
9 www.instagram.com/p/BbpEfqvDSrT/, www.instagram.com/p/BbxFzwego7j/
10 www.instagram.com/p/BZL12TnFvPE/, www.instagram.com/p/BkLQCUoFzQo/

References

Ardèvol, E., Roig, A., San Cornelio, G., Pagès, R., and Alsina, P. (2010) "Playful Practices: Theorising 'New Media' Cultural Production" in B. Bräuchler and J. Postill (eds), *Theorising Media and Practice*, New York: Berghahn, 259–279.

Bareither, C. (2019) "Doing Emotion Through Digital Media: An Ethnographic Perspective on Media Practices and Emotional Affordances," *Ethnologia Europaea*, 49 (1): 7–23.

Bareither, C. (2021a) "Capture the Feeling: Memory Practices in between the Emotional Affordances of Heritage Sites and Digital Media," *Memory Studies*, 14 (3): Special Issue: "Locating 'Placeless' Memories: The Role of Place in Digital Constructions of Memory and Identity," edited by Huw Halstead: 578–591.

Bareither, C. (2021b) "Difficult Heritage and Digital Media: 'Selfie Culture' and Emotional Practices at the Memorial to the Murdered Jews of Europe," *International Journal of Heritage Studies*, 27 (1): 1–16.

Bareither, C., Macdonald, S., Greifeneder, E., Geis, K., Ullrich, S., and Hillebrand, V. (2021) "Curating Digital Images: Ethnographic Perspectives on the Affordances of Digital Images in Heritage and Museum Contexts," *International Journal for Digital Art History*, 8 (1), "The Digital Image – A Transdisciplinary Research Cluster," edited by Hubertus Kohle and Hubert Locher: 87–102.

Beck, S. (1997) *Umgang mit Technik: Kulturelle Praxen und kulturwissenschaftliche Forschungskonzepte*, Berlin: Akademie Verlag.

Bourdieu, P. (1990) *The Logic of Practice*, Cambridge: Polity Press.

Bräuchler, B. and Postill, J. (eds) (2010) *Theorising Media and Practice*, New York: Berghahn.

Costa, E. (2018) "Affordances-in-practice: An Ethnographic Critique of Social Media Logic and Context Collapse," *New Media & Society*, 22 (1): 1–16.

Couldry, N. (2010) "Theorising Media as Practice" in B. Bräuchler and J. Postill (eds), *Theorising Media and Practice*, New York: Berghahn: 35–54.

Couldry, N. (2012) *Media, Society, World: Social Theory and Digital Media Practice*, Cambridge: Polity.

Emerson, R. M., Fretz, R. I., and Shaw, L. L. (2011) *Writing Ethnographic Fieldnotes*. Second edition, Chicago: University of Chicago Press.

Geismar, H. (2017) "Instant Archives?" in L. Hjorth, H. A. Horst, A. Galloway, and G. Bell (eds), *The Routledge Companion to Digital Ethnography*, New York: Routledge, 331–343.

Gibson, J. J. (1986) *The Ecological Approach to Visual Perception*, Hillsdale, New Jersey: Lawrence Erlbaum Associates.

Gómez Cruz, E. and Lehmuskallio, A. (eds) (2016) *Digital Photography and Everyday Life: Empirical Studies on Material Visual Practices*, London: Routledge.

Hobart, M. (2010) "What Do We Mean by 'Media Practices'?" in B. Bräuchler and J. Postill (eds), *Theorising Media and Practice*, New York: Berghahn, 55–75.

Hopkins, J. (2016) "The Concept of Affordances in Digital Media" in H. Friese et al. (eds), *Handbuch Soziale Praktiken und digitale Alltagswelten*, Wiesbaden: Springer Fachmedien, 1–8.

Hörning, K. H. (2001) Experten des Alltags: Die Wiederentdeckung des praktischen Wissens [*Experts of Everyday Life. The Rediscovery of Practical Knowledge*], Weilerswist: Velbrück Wissenschaft.

Hoskins, A. (ed.) (2018) *Digital Memory Studies: Media Pasts in Transition*, New York: Routledge.

Hutchby, I. (2001) "Technologies, Texts and Affordances," *Sociology*, 35: 441–456.

Ipsen, G. (2010) "Communication, Cognition and Usage: Epistemological Considerations of Media Practices and Processes" in B. Bräuchler and J. Postill (eds), *Theorising Media and Practice*, New York: Berghahn, 171–189.

Latour, B. (2005) *Reassembling the Social: An Introduction to Actor-Network-Theory*, Oxford: Oxford University Press.

Lundrigan, M. (2020) "#Holocaust #Auschwitz: Performing Holocaust Memory on Social Media" in S. Gigliotti and H. Earl (eds), *A Companion to the Holocaust*, Hoboken, NJ: Wiley, 639–655.

Macdonald, S. (2012) "Presencing Europe's Pasts" in U. Kockel, M. Nic Craith, and J. Frykman (eds), *A Companion to the Anthropology of Europe*, Chichester, UK: John Wiley & Sons, Ltd, 231–252.

Medvedev, I., Wu, H., and Gordon, T. (2019) "Powered by AI: Instagram's Explore Recommender System." https://ai.facebook.com/blog/powered-by-ai-instagrams-explore-recommender-system/

Miller, D., Costa, E., Haynes, N., McDonald, T., Nicolescu, R., Sinanan, J., Spyer, J., Venkatraman, S., and Wang, X. (2016) *How the World Changed Social Media*, London: UCL Press.

Pauliks, K. and Ruchatz, J. (2021) "Towards a Praxeological Media Philosophy of the Digital Image. Theorizing Pictorial Picture Critique in Social Media," in H. Kohle and H. Locher (eds), *International Journal for Digital Art History*. E1 "The Digital Image – A Transdisciplinary Research Cluster," 121–136.

Pink, S. (2015) "Approaching Media through the Senses: Between Experience and Representation," *Media International Australia*, 154 (1): 5–14.

Pink, S., Horst, H. A., Postill, J., Hjorth, L., Lewis, T., Tacchi, J. (2016) *Digital Ethnography: Principles and Practice*, Los Angeles: Sage.

Postill, J. (2010) "Introduction: Theorising Media and Practice" in B. Bräuchler and J. Postill (eds), *Theorising Media and Practice*, New York: Berghahn, 1–31.

Reckwitz, A. (2002) "Toward a Theory of Social Practices: A Development in Culturalist Theorizing," *European Journal of Social Theory*, 5 (2): 243–263.

Reckwitz, A. (2008) "Praktiken und Diskurse: Eine sozialtheoretische und methodologische Relation" [Practices and Discourses: A Sociotheoretical and Methodological Relation], in H. Kalthoff, S. Hirschauer, and G. Lindemann (eds), *Theoretische Empirie: Zur Relevanz qualitativer Forschung*, Frankfurt am Main: Suhrkamp, 188–209.

Schatzki, T. R. (2001) "Introduction: Practice Theory" in E. von Savigny, K. Knorr-Cetina and T. R. Schatzki (eds), *The Practice Turn in Contemporary Theory*. London: Routledge, 10–23.

Schatzki, T. R. (2017) "Sayings, Texts and Discursive Formations" in A. Hui, E, Shove and T. R. Schatzki (eds), *The Nexus of Practices: Connections, Constellations, Practitioners*. London: Routledge, 126–140.

Scheer, M. (2012) "Are Emotions a Kind of Practice (And Is That What Makes Them Have a History)? A Bourdiesian Approach to Understanding Emotion," *History and Theory*, 51: 193–220.

Wetherell, M., Smith, L., and Campbell, G. (2018) "Introduction: Affective Heritage Practices" in L. Smith, M. Wetherell and G. Campbell (eds), *Emotion, Affective Practices, and the Past in the Present*, Milton: Routledge, 1–21.

Funding

The ethnographic research underlying this paper was carried out in the context of Christoph Bareither's membership at the Centre for Anthropological research on Museums and Heritage (CARMAH) in Berlin, funded by the Alexander von Humboldt Foundation as part of the research award for Sharon Macdonald's Alexander von Humboldt Professorship. At the same time, the research is part of the ongoing project "Curating Digital Images: Ethnographic Perspectives on the Affordances of Digital Images in Heritage and Museum Contexts" funded by the Deutsche Forschungsgemeinschaft (DFG, German Research Foundation) – GZ: BA 6440/2-1 AOBJ: 660775.

C

Media as Materiality

13
THE MATERIALITY OF THE VIRTUAL IN URBAN SPACE

Jordan Kraemer

Digital media technologies are central to constructing social worlds and spaces in material, embodied ways. In the context of new social and spatial mobilities, media technologies contribute to distinct and diverging ways of inhabiting the same spaces. From knowledge workers in postunification Berlin to neighborhood organizers in pandemic Brooklyn, these technologies constituted key sites where the transition to an information economy was lived out. As I contend in this chapter, digital platforms comprise and shape the material environments and infrastructures of urban life, restructuring encounters with friends and neighbors. Drawing on ethnographic research in two "creative" urban cities, Berlin between 2007–2015 and Brooklyn during the COVID pandemic in 2020, I analyze how material engagements with networked media fostered mutuality, intimacy, and publicness. Turning to accounts of media's materiality, I show how technology practices rework social and spatial mobilities, public experiences of mutuality and care, and contestations over social inequalities, in places transformed by precarity and displacement.

Media anthropologists have analyzed extensively the role of mass and new media in constructing shared identities, in relation to globalizing processes (e.g., Appadurai 1996), national selfhood and the nation online (Abu-Lughod 2005; Bernal 2014; Mazzarella 2004), transnational flows, such as among migrant families (Alinejad 2019; Madianou and Miller 2012), and new formations of class and youth (Geertman and Boudreau 2018; Liechty 2003; Luvaas 2010; Smith-Hefner 2007). Technologies like social and mobile media require retheorizing media in anthropology, in terms of what media are and how they rework spatial relations. Where mass media enabled national identities and forms of selfhood in the 19th and early 20th centuries (Anderson 1989; Gellner 1983; Spitulnik 1996), many scholars linked digital media in the late 20th and early 21st to emerging global and transnational formations. Marshall McLuhan, for example, envisioned media would link people across time and space in a shared "global village" (McLuhan 1968), while David Harvey located new global flows in time-space compression (Harvey 1989; see also Castells 1996). But social and mobile media call into question these scalar formations, weaving together relationships at multiple geographic levels (Kraemer forthcoming; 2014) that highlight the construction of spatial scales (cf. Brenner 2001, 1998 and Tsing 2000 on scalemaking). Along with transforming social formations and selfhood at multiple scales, emerging media rework, in material ways, multiple and divergent experiences of urban space.

DOI: 10.4324/9781003175605-19

In this chapter, I discuss what it means for analyses of urban space to approach digital media as material, linking digital materiality and media infrastructures to questions of gentrification and the information economy. Across sites of urban change, a multiplicity of media technologies—social network sites, text messaging, visual media, video conferencing—structured experiences of development and gentrification, from an emerging middle class in Berlin to mutual aid networks and anti-gentrification organizers in Brooklyn. Toward the end of the first decade of the 21st century in Berlin, many young Germans and Europeans were incorporating digital practices in daily life in ways that allowed for fleeting but deeply embodied connections in shared and communal spaces (Kraemer forthcoming). Mobile media, such as laptops and mobile phones, were linked to articulations of class and transnational mobility, operating as a new site of contestation over public space. At other times, shared media, from an illicit film screening to electronic dance parties to makeshift World Cup viewings (sometimes in the literal public street), generated new forms of mutuality and reshaped urban encounters.

These media practices in postunification "New Berlin" were entwined with, and constitutive of, economic transformations associated with the influx of capital and transition to flexible (and precarious) "knowledge" or "creative" work, following the *Wende*, the fall of the Wall and re-unification in 1990 (Bauer and Hosek 2019; Boym 2001; Huyssen 1997). In New York City in 2020, social, economic, and technological changes were similarly remaking the city's boroughs and neighborhoods, from mobile broadband, smartphones, and social media to the gig work and platform labor of the "sharing economy" (Cardullo 2017; Rosenblat 2018; Sadowski 2020). In Brooklyn neighborhoods undergoing gentrification, these changes fomented new pressures and inequalities for poor and working-class residents as work became more precarious and housing prohibitively expensive (Lees 2016; Trinch and Snajdr 2016; Safransky 2019). The arrival of the COVID-19 pandemic in March 2020 intensified inequalities that neighborhood associations and anti-gentrification activists had been contending with for decades, sparking the formation of new mutual aid groups and business relief efforts, alongside renewed racial justice protests. Digital media were central to neighborhood organizing during the pandemic, as existing groups organized over apps like Zoom, while new groups formed across platforms like Slack, WhatsApp, and Facebook. Organizing online lowered barriers to participation for some but excluded others. The mutual aid groups were formed in many cases by younger residents, many new to organizing, as were the racial justice protests. The lockdown and economic devastation, especially for the already precarious, opened new spaces for organizing while intensifying neighborhood fractures of race and class. For both new and existing groups, media practices reproduced and reworked divided ways of living in the same neighborhoods, through bodily and material enactments.

Media Materiality and Urban Placemaking

Tension between the local and global or particular and universal have long animated anthropological inquiry, what Geertz described as "a continuous dialectical tacking between the most local of local detail and the most global of global structure in such a way as to bring both into view simultaneously" (Geertz 1974: 43; see also Lambek 2011). Anthropological interest in urban space and place is more recent (Low 1996, 2000, 2009, 2016; Weszkalnys 2010, 2008), with a growing literature examining media technologies in urban placemaking. This research considers ways media technologies shape class formations (Weidman 2010), media networks and community organizing (Berger Funke, and Wolfson 2011; Chesluk 2004), news media in the production of the local (Udupa 2012), and computer-generated visualization in urban imaginaries (Melhuish, Degen, and Rose 2016). Urban studies and information scholars have also considered the role of digital media in urban divides (Graham 2002; Graham and Marvin 2001), particularly shifting ways of moving through urban space (Humphreys 2010; Hjorth and Pink 2014; Licoppe 2016.) and digital placemaking (Halegoua 2020). Such scholarship is increasingly attentive to technocratic neoliberal urbanism through datafication, automated systems, and machine learning, including algorithmic reinstantiations of "redlining" (Safransky 2019), the use of corporate digital platforms in "platform urbanism" (Sadowski 2020), and "smart city" discourses in austerity politics (Pollio 2016). These accounts detail ways that deregulation and tech solutionism shape urban life and development in deeply unequal ways, increasing surveillance, regulation, and precarity for poor, minoritized, and working-class inhabitants.

One tendency in studies of digital media, however, is to view media practices as semiotic and informational, sometimes framed as cognitive or immaterial labor (e.g., Jarrett 2016; cf. Graham 2013). This approach risks limiting digital practices to online spaces rather than situating them in material, embodied experiences, such as how racialization works in cognitive economies (Amrute 2015). As sociologist Mona Sloane argues, urban inequalities are structured by spatial design that manifests through material qualities, such as housing materials (Sloane 2019). Viewing media as material brings into view how media practices are equally located in built environments with consequences for how those environments are constructed and experienced. In Joshua Bell and Joel Kuiper's collection on cell phone materialities, the authors call attention to mobile media "as material objects that affect the social world" to bring into "analytical focus how these devices are discrete things in the world that are assemblages of materials" (Bell and Kuipers 2018: 12). Although materiality can be read as concrete, inert durability which limits or constrains, such as the speed of wires or deteriorating storage (Blanchette 2011), other studies emphasize the lively, dynamic qualities of digital worlds and technologies (Pink, Ardévol, and Lanzeni 2016; see also Dourish and Mazmanian 2013; Ingold 2007; Hayles 2004). Media materialities are often analyzed separately from the production of urban space, but as Paolo Cardullo argues in his study of wireless mesh networks and gentrification, urban space shapes the development of media and communication technologies: "the production of urban space is crucial to the development of such technologies—wireless networks are, after all, very local and territorial" (Cardullo 2017: 406). Cardullo compares cyberspace with urban space, arguing that both "can be described by the way in which bodies move through them" (*ibid.*). With the rise of mobile media, these movements have become more tightly interwoven, entwining co-present and digital encounters in urban living.

Along with studies of digital materiality, anthropological attention to infrastructure highlights the built, material, and regulatory systems—often provisional or incomplete—that shape digital worlds and urban environments (Larkin 2004, 2013; see also Sandvig 2013; Dourish and Bell 2007). As these approaches show, urban space shapes technology, but technologies also produce urban space. Digital media technologies equally foster new inequalities and urban divides, often exacerbating infrastructural unevenness (Graham 2002; Graham and Marvin 2001). Mobile media have played a role in processes of gentrification and displacement, increasing connectedness and economic opportunities for elites while further disenfranchising the poor, elderly, disabled, and other marginalized people (Jansson 2019; Cardullo 2017; Berger, Funke, and Wolfson 2011). Digital technologies are often imagined as creating new possibilities for urban life, from enabling the mobile "knowledge" work of the new creative classes to optimized smart cities where sensors and algorithms regulate and allocate resources (Pollio 2016). But such technologies have become central to casualizing labor, through the rise of gig work such as ridehailing apps, food delivery services, and other examples of platform labor (Rosenblat 2018; Sadowski 2019; Schor et al. 2020). Work under these conditions is becoming more precarious for knowledge and service workers alike, even as these technologies hold new possibilities for generating mutuality, organizing, and re-appropriations of space.

Mobile Media in Café Culture

Among an emerging middle class of young Germans and Europeans in Berlin in the mid-to-late aughts, online practices had become key to maintaining connections among small translocal "friend circles" (*Freundeskreise*) and wider transnational networks (Kraemer forthcoming; 2014). From 2007–2015, primarily over ten months in 2009–2010, I conducted sustained fieldwork with two friend circles (as they termed them) in Berlin. This fieldwork included participant observation, online and co-present, approximately 21 semi-structured interviews with 19 participants, numerous informal conversations, and content analysis of digital platforms. While mobile phones were central to everyday check-ins, text chats, and get-togethers, laptop computers occupied a contested niche in public space, associated with newcomers, "tourists," and hipsters, particularly mobile, "self-employed" people and *Ausländer* (foreigners). Most people in my research owned a laptop, often older machines they found heavy and less portable. As Sabine, a music journalist explained, her laptop was "too old, heavy, and big" ("ganz alt, schwer und gross") to lug around, although she sometimes brought it on the train to visit family. A record shop owner, David, explained that he mainly brought his laptop when traveling: "yes, I take my laptop to work and for travel, but less often to cafés—that's rare." Cafés were seen instead as a space for meeting with friends, drinking coffee or tea, or reading a magazine. In U.S. cities, cafés and coffeeshops are often harbingers of gentrification, but in much of Europe they have long histories as public gathering places (see Oldenburg 1999 on "third places" necessary for creating community; Kleinman 2006; cf. Habermas 1989). The material (and semiotic) qualities of mobile computing reworked how many experienced these intermediate spaces.

As Berlin became popular in the early 2000s with *Ausländer* (typically a term for Turkish Germans but among my interlocutors, non-Germans from the E.U. or anglophone countries), cafés became a new site of contestation over digital networking in public life. Cafés dot Berlin, but in gentrifying central districts, there was often a division between "laptop cafés" and unmarked ones. One weekend, I met my friends and interlocutors Katrine and Milo at a cozy café with mismatched furniture, not exclusively a "laptop café" (Figure 13.1). I was working on my laptop, but when they arrived, I stopped to chat over tea. Katrine pulled a fashion magazine from one of the ubiquitous racks and perused it. I often observed groups of two or three friends come through this café and others, order drinks, spend an hour together, then leave. After about 45 minutes, Katrine and Milo seemed wordlessly to agree it was time to go. While for some, the café was a space for solitary work, for them, it was a "third space" for shared sociality.

Despite the social connotations of laptops, these devices were often necessary for students. Bettina, a graduate student, stated her concern with violating the norms of cafés and being marked as part of the burgeoning knowledge class. She maintained she would take her laptop to her university's library but never to a restaurant:

> [I take it] to school, a lot, to the library, and sometimes to cafes and occasionally to [a friend's place]. And, when I travel, I take it a lot ... I think subconsciously I do choose [cafés] according to appropriateness, just because, you know, you don't really take it to a restaurant. Anywhere where you can sit and hang out, I might take it along.

She described making fun of hipsters and the self-employed ("Ich-AGs," short for Ich-Arbeitgeber, self-employer), explaining:

The Materiality of the Virtual in Urban Space

Figure 13.1 Cozy café in Kreuzberg, 2015
Source: Photo by author.

> It's frowned upon because … it's perceived as arrogant. This is the stereotype, people who go with their laptops, you would see it in Prenzlauer Berg where, you know, hipster-looking people, really nicely dressed, they'd sit in there … They're creative. And they're just they're perceived as a bit upper class—I guess bourgeois would be the word. And so I think that's why it's frowned upon.

Bettina's anxieties about laptops in public reflect broader concerns about gentrification and forms of sociality new technologies risked foreclosing, and perhaps, how new forms of work were reshaping her own life.

Those who did bring their laptops often felt conspicuous, such as Erik, a public relations manager in Hannover who regularly visited friends in Berlin. He considered his laptop his "communication device" and brought it with him "everywhere I go, basically." But doing so provoked critical commentary from a prior circle of friends:

> For *Gotts* sake, a lot of my friends are nerdy like me, but all my friends that I know from, like, seven years ago are like, why are you carrying your laptop with you, and what are you doing? I get some comments quite a few times.

Using laptops in public also depended on infrastructure such as wireless networks. Pascal, a design student, preferred the computers at his university's computer lab for their faster Internet connection, while Alex, a DJ and promoter, favored his smartphone for checking email because wireless (WLAN) access on campus was uneven:

> In one of the buildings where there is Internet, then I can work a bit, but during Bachelor's studies, I took my computer all of the time, because, for example, my university had a really good Internet connection, so I could, like, upload stuff within seconds. I took it daily and now I only take it if I have a presentation or I have to go through some through some work with my classmates.

Wireless infrastructure shaped these spaces by determining when and where it was possible to make use of mobile computing.

Among one Berlin friend circle that had formed growing up together in a nearby rural region, Nathan, an Ausländer from the UK, described bringing his laptop to cafés in Berlin. As a student in the UK, he had worked in cafés without reservation, as he explained: "I did bring it around to cafés—I often worked in cafés, because the library did me in, so I really brought my computer with me a lot, and whenever I was traveling." But in Berlin, he felt self-conscious and feared he was breaking norms of "café culture": "I do go out with it, and if café owners didn't look at me so weird, and if I didn't feel weird for killing café culture by bringing out my laptop, I definitely would bring it out even more." For Nathan, anxieties about laptop use in public correlated with his position as the type of cosmopolitan, mobile Ausländer transforming Berlin.

Laptops in these contexts were perceived as conspicuous, associated with the itinerant work of E.U.-Ausländer, tourists, "hipsters," and the mobile self-employed. In contrast, mobile phones were not associated with creative capital in the same way. Smartphones, which few owned at the time, could garner public opprobrium, signifying access to capital and elite mobility. Few of my interlocutors articulated this norm verbally, but I rarely observed them scrolling through social media feeds or attending to mobile screens during public events. Instead, it was material engagements with laptops and smartphones that reworked—or threatened—the social norms of these third spaces.

Diverging practices between phones and laptops organized ways of using digital media in urban space, marking those perceived as "tourists" or "hipsters." Such distinctions did not map to German identity or citizenship—both friend circles included Ausländer and people some might consider "hipsters." Instead, these distinctions demarcated spaces in Berlin—cafés, but also nightclubs or popular shopping thoroughfares—along lines of class, nationality, and imagined authenticity. Some places, such as workshops, studios, small offices, or even trains, were figured as the appropriate spaces for creative work, associated with music or art. But laptops in cafés enacted the wrong kind of knowledge work: the appropriation of public spaces by global capital, catalyzing Berlin's transition from a countercultural site of openness, possibility, and experimentation to a gentrified capital of development and consumption (Bauer and Hosek 2019).

Public Media Mutuality

In other circumstances, media practices in Berlin fostered mutuality and affective connection, through improvised setups and ad-hoc arrangements of shared space. Although some people criticized tourists for consuming Berlin's alternative and countercultural legacy, most participated in the semi-licit parties and events for which Berlin was known. West Berlin in the postwar era had been a destination for musicians and artists, a refuge for gays and lesbians, and home to alternative social movements. After the Wall came down in 1989, many Berliners left for work in the West, which, compounded with neglect and ambiguous building ownership, left East Berlin with low occupancy and inexpensive rents (Boym 2001; Huyssen 1997). The following decade, from the early 1990s to the early aughts was famed for illicit and underground techno parties (Borneman and Senders 2000; Denk and von Thülen 2014; Nye 2013; Partridge 2008) in abandoned and unrenovated spaces. By the mid- to late aughts, East Berlin had transformed rapidly, especially central districts like Mitte (the old city center) and Prenzlauer Berg. One famed event space, the Kunsthaus Tacheles, was an anarchist art collective in a repurposed 20th-century department store. The massive prewar building became an increasingly isolated, graffiti-covered relic as upscale stores and boutique hotels sprouted around it (Boym 2001; Stewart 2002). Mitte in particular was seen as having gentrified or "yuppified" in the early aughts (Sark 2019; Ward 2019; see also Weszkalnys 2008, 2010), followed by Prenzlauer Berg.

The legacy of postunification Berlin informed public media practices among mobile young people, practices that often coalesced around ad-hoc or semi-licit events. Informal or illicit media activities created spaces for unspoken mutuality, what Garcia 2013 describes as "liquidarity." Liquidarity, in counterpoint to Durkheimian solidarity, constitutes affective, embodied experiences of connectedness that cohere temporarily. In Garcia's account of Berlin nightlife, shared moments dancing to techno fostered fleeting sentiments of commonality and belonging, a form of stranger sociability where tacit norms materialized through gestures of care. Liquidarity is a transient and contingent mutuality, in Garcia's words: "the sense of fluid solidarity arises from the embodied improvisation of an intimate public" (Garcia 2013: 247).

Media practices similarly contributed to experiences of mutual affect and connection in in public. Three scenes illustrate examples of public media mutuality in Berlin: an unofficial film screening in a warehouse in Prenzlauer Berg; granting friends free entry into events through *guestlisting*, and makeshift setups for watching World Cup matches. I was invited by friends to the film screening through a Facebook event page with directions to meet at a nearby underground (U-Bahn) station. There, the organizers led a gathered crowd through a courtyard and across a parking lot to an empty warehouse. The warehouse had been converted to an impromptu theater, with folding chairs and overturned buckets for seats and a projector connected to a laptop. The film, a semi-fictional biopic of an Appalachian dancer, was an independent release that had been featured at a Berlin film festival. An uneven sound system with frequently shifting volume accompanied a cacophonous soundtrack and difficult to follow speech. The directions and setup were more reminiscent of illicit warehouse parties than a film screening. Like other illicit media practices in Berlin, such as pirating and filesharing (see Kraemer forthcoming), the screening offered a workaround to patchwork international distribution agreements, rather than to avoid paying. The shared viewing comprised a tactic of managing this infrastructural unevenness, a way of getting by with a long history in Berlin. This tactic also fostered a shared experience of mutual, if fleeting, connection.

In other instances, practices such as guestlisting generated linkages across overlapping music scenes. The nightclub Berghain, one of Berlin's most notorious, situated in a cavernous former power station, was infamous for its strict door policy and formidable bouncers. One evening, in line with Alex, a DJ and promoter, we overheard two young Irish men loudly arguing after being rejected: "What? Is it because we don't speak German?" before leaving angrily. As Alex and I reached the head of the line, he quickly said "I'm on the guest list, and they're with me." The door staff waved us in without comment. On another evening, I met Alex at Tacheles, a venue he typically associated with "tourists," but a close friend of his was DJing. "I think we're on the guestlist," he told the door staff, who ushered us in once they found his name. Like the warehouse screening, the club setup seemed ad-hoc—a sparsely furnished, dimly lit space with a folding table for a bar. Though not a media practice, guestlisting generated diffuse cohesion across a constellation of music scenes, as a form of subcultural capital (Thornton 1996) that fostered unspoken mutuality. More than (or alongside) not paying, guestlisting crystalized networks of mutual recognition and affective ties. After his friend Viktor's set, Alex said, "Let's go say hello to Viktor," so we could support him with our presence—but not with actual money.

These makeshift, illicit, and improvisational practices spilled into the literal public street during the World Cup football championship, highlighting how media materiality could transform urban space. During the World Cup, public spaces in Berlin metamorphosized in ways I hadn't seen before. Bars and cafés suspended capacious flatscreen TVs over sidewalk tables or projected the games on floor-to-ceiling screens. Over two months, public viewings remade the spaces of cafés, parks, clubs, and city streets. One notoriously licentious outdoor club and radical commune, Bar 25, dedicated its open-air theater to screening the matches. Like the film showing, the screening fused elements of Berlin's underground dance parties with communal media viewing. The improvised materiality of these arrangements structured shared media practices, fostered unspoken affective ties, and reworked the urban streetscape in ad-hoc ways.

For the semi-finals between Germany and Spain, a group of architecture students set up a projector and folding chairs on a quiet sidewalk in Kreuzberg. Someone connected a laptop to a projector, both stacked precariously on crates and a folding table, with a tangle of wires snaking into their building (Figure 13.2). Folding chairs were arranged in semi-circular rows

Figure 13.2 Laptop and projector streaming the World Cup 2010 final match on the sidewalk in Kreuzberg
Source: Photo by author.

out into the street, where a few cars passed slowly by. As at the warehouse screening, material, ad-hoc arrangements allowed for public viewing, transforming the quiet streetscape into a space of mutual connection. A friend who arrived late admitted: "I like watching the big games, but I don't actually care who wins, you know?" A growing crowd clustered behind the seats, until, eventually, Spain scored a winning goal and a cheer went up from Spanish speakers in attendance. Though the German team's fans were disappointed, the feelings of mutuality and camaraderie extended to Spain's fans, as part of a cosmopolitan class linked by shared media viewing that remade European nationalism as hip, urban, and acceptable (Kraemer 2018).

Digital Materiality and Organizing in Pandemic Brooklyn

In Berlin, media devices and infrastructures contributed to placemaking, as sites of conflict over class and gentrification. During the COVID-19 pandemic in Brooklyn in 2020–2021, digital materiality structured experiences of urban space in new ways as public practices moved online and into homes. I conducted fieldwork with neighborhood groups and organizers from 2020–2021, as part of a grant-funded study on urban inequalities and digital platforms. The fieldwork, spanning about a year, involved remote and digital participant-observation with neighborhood groups in gentrified parts of Brooklyn that were historically West Indian and Puerto Rican. I attended weekly Zoom calls, followed channels on Slack, NextDoor, and WhatsApp, and (remotely) interviewed 11 participants in-depth. Large development projects, along with demographic shifts and rising housing costs, had spurred waves of anti-gentrification activism and tenant organizing in the preceding decades. The pandemic, however, forced residents and city agencies alike to host meetings and canvassing efforts on digital platforms, including Zoom, Webex, Facebook Groups, and WhatsApp. Meeting online allowed for new means to challenge racial and economic inequalities, such as mutual aid groups on Slack and Zoom or racial justice protests coordinated on Instagram (Figure 13.3). But digital platforms produced new exclusions as well, especially for older, poorer residents without broadband Internet or smartphones. Members of one neighborhood association described publicizing community board meetings and land-use hearings with printed flyers, but found that many who had attended in person were absent online.

In these contexts, embodied engagements with digital tools and interfaces reworked public space, making visible social distinctions. Remote meetings, for example, brought organizing activities into members' homes, remaking boundaries of public and private. This context brought arrangements of devices and home spaces into new juxtapositions, with some people creating dedicated setups for videoconferencing while others positioned smartphones on coffee tables or in kitchens. One mutual aid group had formed in response to the pandemic and instituted weekly community calls around themes such as alternatives to policing or tenant organizing.

Initially, the group publicized its efforts on Facebook and distributed print flyers to reach residents not on social media. Group Zoom calls effectively became public spaces, in the sense of being open to all residents, even as they took place within private homes. Most participants situated themselves in semi-public spaces of the home—at a sofa or desk, or sometimes dining or kitchen table. Because only a small portion of the space was visible, some differences could be flattened—some members lived in rental apartments in 19th-century townhouses, while others lived in newer buildings, some with high-end amenities. But on Zoom, most displayed comparable backgrounds, typically showing white walls. Visual elements provided cues about tech setups, such as camera angles (upwards often meant a laptop or tablet), the rotation of

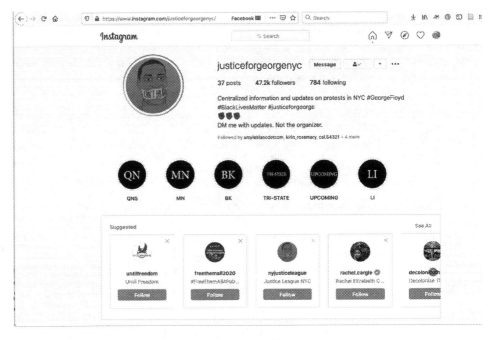

Figure 13.3 JusticeforGeorgeNYC Instagram page, June 2020

the frame (vertical was typical of smartphones), or lighting (such as well-lit faces versus backlit ones). A few participants called in over their phone or opted to turn their video off.

The group's channels on Slack (a chat and productivity platform) and WhatsApp (a mobile group chat app) each counted hundreds of members. The Zoom calls, however, typically attracted 15 to 25 participants, eventually decreasing to twice-monthly when attendance declined. On one call about a year into the pandemic, in the spring of 2021, eight members met to discuss programs such as grocery support and a community refrigerator. The meeting consisted mainly the group's core organizers, mostly younger white people. Each appeared seated, with video on, in front of a white wall, some with framed photos or art behind them. Most sat upright and focused their attention on their screen, embodied practices which contributed to a sense of formality—less like being in each other's homes and more like a shared public space.

The sense of formality was heightened by interactional norms, such as little cross talk (which can garble speech on video calls) and few side conversations (which are difficult except in the chat, see Figure 13.4). Yet most members had been working together for over a year. When one member accidentally spoke over another, she quickly apologized. Although these practices owe in part to the affordances of Zoom, in prior research, I observed closeness and informality through emoticons and other affective signifiers over chat (Sloane and Kraemer 2021). Most used the chat window instead to share occasional links, for example, to shared meeting notes, except one participant who responded to scheduling a fundraising call, typing: "I could do it Saturday morning." These embodied and material practices, from posture and conversational norms to minimalist backgrounds, produced a shared space that was neither fully public nor fully private.

Many organizers described these meetings as more public than closed or internal meetings, but less public than platforms like Facebook or NextDoor or "really open public space" like parks, as one participant put it. Public and private distinctions were not fixed, but varied

The Materiality of the Virtual in Urban Space

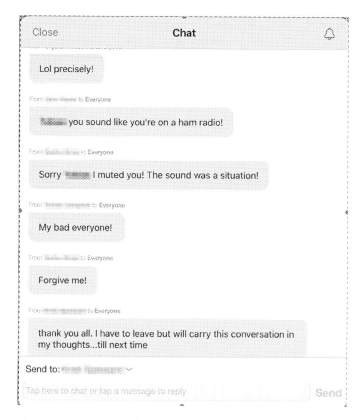

Figure 13.4 Screenshot of the chat window from a mutual aid group Zoom call, August 2020. One member's poor sound quality garnered more discussion in the chat than was typical

across contexts. Bodily interactions with digital artifacts and interfaces structured these spaces and contributed to the kinds of publics they produced. The following week, I attended the monthly meeting of a neighborhood association that had formed in response to large-scale development projects. These meetings previously took place in spaces like a condo building's meeting room, but switched to Zoom during the pandemic. Participants were generally older than the mutual aid organizers, predominantly white, and had in many cases lived in the area for 20 years or more. The materiality of the shared virtual space differed from the carefully curated semi-formality of the mutual aid group call. Each person's background varied, some with bookshelves, others showing kitchens or living spaces, often dimly lit or backlit. A few called in from mobile phones, their video vertical in the frame.

Along with visual and material differences, conversational norms were relaxed and informal. Members seemed familiar with each other, frequently using first names and speaking rapidly back and forth, including crosstalk. Some used the chat, what one person called "the chat room," to comment on negative experiences with police the previous summer (during the George Floyd protests). When one person mentioned it was his birthday, others typed in in "Happy Birthday!" Despite this easy familiarity, tensions often surfaced. Some members were upset about developers' upzoning proposals, fearing higher property values and further displacement. One man insisted the project wouldn't worsen the lack of affordable housing. In response, a Latina woman countered that previous rezoning had pushed her family members out of the neighborhood, who were now "scattered" across the city's boroughs. She was afraid she would be forced out as well. These material and interactional norms constructed a shared space that was more informal but not necessarily less "public" than the mutual aid group's meeting. Publicness here was enacted through different means and dimensions in terms of tech competence, social class, age, race, and other aspects of social location.

Media materiality, from digital interfaces to the arrangement of devices, intersected with interactional norms such as using first names or turn-taking, to generate multiple experiences of publicness. Videoconferencing technologies constituted lively material tools whose features were co-constructed by shared practice, what Elisabetta Costa calls "affordances-in-practice" (Costa 2018), ways of engaging with digital platforms that are never fixed. The curated backgrounds, direct lighting, and dedicated webcam setups in the mutual aid call reflected the class status (and generational divides) of young, tech savvy knowledge workers comfortable with remote work, in contrast to less formal arrangements and bodily positionings among neighborhood association members. The same technological features conveyed and materialized social distinctions, which reflected the diverging goals of each group. Where the mutual aid group (mostly younger renters in their 20s and 30s, often new to the area) emphasized direct, non-hierarchical aid and support, the neighborhood association (mostly longer-term residents, often homeowners in their 50s and 60s) focused on resisting largescale development and rezoning. These disparate foci were themselves sites of contestation that played out across neighborhood channels on Slack, WhatsApp, and NextDoor, where group membership often overlapped. Attending to the materiality of media technologies highlights how these platforms produced multiple and often conflicting experiences of the same public spaces.

The Virtual Matter of Urban Space

Media's materiality across these sites generated new forms of urban mobility and community organizing. In the early 2000's Berlin, emerging technologies served as new sites of contestation over class, capital, and transnational mobility when public use of laptop computers came to signify the mobility of Ausländer, viewed as inauthentic "tourists" or "hipsters." Cafés were recast either as "laptop" cafés for mobile, self-employed workers or as gathering spaces for genuine public sociality, reworking these shared spaces. In other instances, public media produced new experiences of provisional mutuality and embodied connection, from semi-licit events and parties to ad-hoc viewings of the World Cup. Repurposed warehouses, nightclubs, and the literal public street were reconfigured by shared media as temporary spaces of felt connection.

In Brooklyn during the COVID-19 pandemic, the materiality of media intermingled with social norms and interpretive practices to create shared public spaces over video calls. Publicness was reworked through these encounters, produced through arrangements bodies and technologies in ways specific to (and constitutive of) social location. Curated videocall setups with flattering lighting and whitewashed backgrounds reflected and connoted class status for young, mobile professionals working remotely, in contrast to the more varied setups and arrangements of older, sometimes less tech savvy residents and homeowners. Material engagements with the same technologies such as Zoom produced disparate, sometimes conflicting experience of public space and understandings of publicness.

In these sites, digital media took shape as generative material interfaces through shared practice. Technological artifacts and arrangements, from laptops to video interfaces, intersected with bodily activities to situate these practices in contestations over gentrification and publicness. This dynamic materiality, rather than restrain or limit spatial experiences, engendered manifold instances of the same places and technologies. Laptops, for example, structured Berlin cafés as sites of elite, transnational mobility and capital, yet equally supported media practices that fostered sentiments of acceptable European nationalism. In Brooklyn, video calls produced conflicting experiences of shared spaces. As in Berlin, contestations over class and gentrification often played out as debates about imagined Others—whether foreign tourists and hipsters or vulnerable residents. In both sites, what counted as public depended on often temporary and ad-hoc arrangements of technologies and practices. Media materiality draws attention to how media technologies are not only a resource for fashioning identity, but the enacted means of living out tensions over social and class position during times of intensive social, economic, and technological change.

References

Abu-Lughod, L. (2005) *Dramas of Nationhood: The Politics of Television in Egypt*, Chicago: University of Chicago Press.
Alinejad, D. (2019) "Careful Co-Presence: the Transnational Mediation of Emotional Intimacy," *Social Media + Society*, 5 (2): 1–11.
Amrute, S. (2016) *Encoding Race, Encoding Class: Indian IT Workers in Berlin*, North Carolina: Duke University Press.
Anderson, B. and Harrison, P. (2010) *Taking-Place: Non-Representational Theories and Geography*, Farnham: Ashgate.
Appadurai, A. 1996. *Modernity at Large: Cultural Dimensions of Globalization*. Minneapolis: University of Minnesota.
Bauer, K. and Hosek, J. (2019) *Cultural Topographies of the New Berlin*. New York: Berghahn Books.
Bell, J. and Kuipers, J. (2018) *Linguistic and Material Intimacies of Cell Phones*. New York: Routledge.
Berger, D., Funke, P., and Wolfson, T. (2011) "Communications Networks, Movements and the Neoliberal City: The Media Mobilizing Project in Philadelphia," *Transforming Anthropology*, 19 (2): 187–201.
Bernal, V. (2014) *Nation as Network: Diaspora, Cyberspace, and Citizenship*, Chicago: University of Chicago Press.
Blanchette, J. F. (2011) "A Material History of Bits," *Journal of the American Society for Information Science and Technology*, 62 (6): 1042–57.
Borneman, J. and Senders, S. 2000. "Politics Without a Head: Is the 'Love Parade' a New Form of Political Identification?" *Cultural Anthropology*, 15 (2): 294–317.
Boym, S. (2008) *The Future of Nostalgia*, New York: Basic Books.
Brenner, N. (1998) "Between Fixity and Motion: Accumulation, Territorial Organization and the Historical Geography of Spatial Scales," *Environment and Planning, D*, 16: 459–81.
Brenner, N. (2001) "The Limits to Scale? Methodological Reflections on Scalar Structuration," *Progress in Human Geography*, 25 (4): 591–614.
Castells, M. (1996) *The Rise of the Network Society*, Malden, MA: Blackwell Publishers.
Cardullo, P. (2017) "Gentrification in the Mesh?" *City*, 21 (3–4): 405–19.
Chesluk, B. (2004) "'Visible Signs of a City Out of Control': Community Policing in New York City," *Cultural Anthropology*, 19 (2): 250–75.
Costa, E. (2018) "Affordances-in-practice: An ethnographic critique of social media logic and context collapse." New Media & Society, 20 (10): 3641–56.
Denk, F. and von Thülen, S. (2014) *Der Klang der Familie: Berlin, Techno und die Wende* [*The Sound of the Family: Berlin, Techno, and Reunification*], Norderstedt: Books On Demand.
Dourish, P. and Bell, G. (2007) "The Infrastructure of Experience and the Experience of Infrastructure: Meaning and Structure in Everyday Encounters with Space," *Environment and Planning B: Planning and Design*, 34 (3): 414–30.
Dourish, P. and Mazmanian, M. (2013) "Media as Material: Information Representations as Material Foundations for Organizational Practice," in P. R Carlile, D. Nicolini, and A. Langley (eds.), *How Matter Matters: Objects, Artifacts, and Materiality in Organization Studies*, Oxford: Oxford University Press: 92–118.
Garcia, L-M. (2013.) "Crowd Solidarity on the Dancefloor in Paris and Berlin," in F. Holt and C. Wergin (eds.), *Music Performance and the Changing City: Post-Industrial Contexts in Europe and the United States*, New York: Routledge, 227–55.

Geertman, S, and Boudreau, J. A. "'Life as Art': Emerging Youth Networks in Hanoi and the Tree Hug Movement," *City & Society*, 30 (2): 210–36.
Geertz, C. (1974) "'From the Native's Point of View': on the Nature of Anthropological Understanding," *Bulletin of the American Academy of Arts and Sciences*, 28 (1): 26–45.
Gellner, E. (1983) *Nations and Nationalism*, Ithaca: Cornell University Press.
Graham, M. (2013) "Geography/Internet: Ethereal Alternate Dimensions of Cyberspace or Grounded Augmented Realities?" *The Geographical Journal*, 179 (2): 177–82.
Graham, S. (2002) "Bridging Urban Digital Divides? Urban Polarisation and Information and Communications Technologies (ICTs)," *Urban Studies*, 39 (1): 33–56.
Graham, S, and Marvin, S. (2001) *Splintering Urbanism: Networked Infrastructures, Technological Mobilities and the Urban Condition*, New York: Routledge.
Habermas, J. (1991) *The Structural Transformation of the Public Sphere: an Inquiry Into a Category of Bourgeois Society*, Thomas Burger and Frederick Lawrence (trans.), Cambridge, MA: MIT Press.
Halegoua, G. R. (2020) *The Digital City: Media and the Social Production of Place*, New York: New York University Press.
Hayles, N. K. (2004) "Print Is Flat, Code Is Deep: The Importance of Media-Specific Analysis," *Poetics Today*, 25 (1): 67–90.
Harvey, D. (1992) *The Condition of Postmodernity*, Malden: Wiley-Blackwell.
Hjorth, L. and Pink, S. (2013) "New Visualities and the Digital Wayfarer: Reconceptualizing Camera Phone Photography and Locative Media," *Mobile Media & Communication*, 2 (1): 40–57.
Humphreys, L. (2010) "Mobile Social Networks and Urban Public Space," *New Media and Society*, 12 (5): 763–78.
Huyssen, A. (1997) "The Voids of Berlin," *Critical Inquiry*, 24 (1): 57–81.
Ingold, T. (2007) "Materials Against Materiality," *Archaeological Dialogues*, 14 (01): 1–16.
Jansson, A. (2019) "The Mutual Shaping of Geomedia and Gentrification: the Case of Alternative Tourism Apps," *Communication and the Public*, 4 (2): 166–81.
Jarrett, K. (2016) *Feminism, Labour and Digital Media: the Digital Housewife*, New York: Routledge.
Kleinman, S. (2006) "Cafe Culture in France and the United States: A Comparative Ethnographic Study of the Use of Mobile Information and Communication Technologies," *Atlantic Journal of Communication*, 14(4): 191–210.
Kraemer, J. (2014) "Friend or Freund: Social Media and Transnational Connections in Berlin," *Human-Computer Interaction*, 29 (1): 53–77.
Kraemer, J. (2018) "Of Spargel and Spiegel: Networked National Feelings in Berlin," *Anthropological Quarterly*, 91 (4): 1385–416.
Kraemer, J. (forthcoming) *Mobile City: Emerging Media, Space, and Sociality in Contemporary Berlin*, Ithaca: Cornell University Press.
Lambek, M. (2011) "Catching the Local," *Anthropological Theory*, 11 (2): 197–221.
Larkin, B. (2013) "The Politics and Poetics of Infrastructure," *Annual Review of Anthropology*, 42: 327–43.
Larkin, B. (2008) *Signal and Noise: Media, Infrastructure, and Urban Culture in Nigeria*, Durham: Duke University Press.
Leès, L. (2016) "Super-Gentrification: The Case of Brooklyn Heights, New York City," *Urban Studies*, 40 (12): 2487–509.
Licoppe, C. (2016) "Mobilities and Urban Encounters in Public Places in the Age of Locative Media. Seams, Folds, and Encounters with 'Pseudonymous Strangers'," *Mobilities*, 11 (1): 99–116.
Liechty, M. (2003) *Suitably Modern: Making Middle-Class Culture in a New Consumer Society*, Princeton, NJ: Princeton University Press.
Low, S. M. (2016) *Spatializing Culture: The Ethnography of Space and Place*, London: Taylor and Francis.
Low, S. M. (1996) "The Anthropology of Cities: Imagining and Theorizing the City," *Annual Review of Anthropology*, 25: 383–409.
Low, S. M. (2000) *On the Plaza: The Politics of Public Space and Culture*, Austin: University of Texas Press.
Low, S. M. (2009) "Towards an Anthropological Theory of Space and Place," *Semiotica*, 2009 (175): 21–37.
Luvaas, B. (2010) "Designer Vandalism: Indonesian Indie Fashion and the Cultural Practice of Cut'N'Paste." *Journal of Linguistic Anthropology*, 1–16.
Madianou, M. and Miller, D. (2012) *Migration and New Media*, London: Routledge.
Mazzarella, W. (2004) *Shoveling Smoke: Advertising and Globalization in Contemporary India*, Durham: Duke University Press.
McLuhan, M. (2003). *Understanding Media: The Extensions of Man*, Corte Madera, CA: Gingko Press.

Melhuish, C, Degen, M., and Rose, G. (2016) "'The Real Modernity That Is Here': Understanding the Role of Digital Visualisations in the Production of a New Urban Imaginary at Msheireb Downtown, Doha," *City & Society*, 28 (2): 222–45.

Nye, S. (2013) "Minimal Understandings: The Berlin Decade, the Minimal Continuum, and Debates on the Legacy of German Techno," *Journal of Popular Music Studies*, 25 (2): 154–84.

Oldenburg, R. (1989) *The Great Good Place: Cafés, Coffee Shops, Community Centers, Beauty Parlors, General Stores, Bars, Hangouts and How They Get You Through the Day*, New York: Paragon House.

Partridge, D. 2008. "We Were Dancing in the Club, Not on the Berlin Wall: Black Bodies, Street Bureaucrats, and Exclusionary Incorporation Into the New Europe," *Cultural Anthropology*, 23 (4): 660–87.

Pink, S., Ardévol, E., and Lanzeni, E. (2016) *Digital Materialities Design and Anthropology*. London: Bloomsbury Academic.

Pollio, A. (2016) "Technologies of Austerity Urbanism: the 'Smart City' Agenda in Italy (2011–2013)," *Urban Geography*, 37 (4): 514–34.

Rosenblat, A. (2018) *Uberland: How Algorithms Are Rewriting the Rules of Work*. Oakland: University of California Press.

Sadowski, J. (2020) "The Internet of Landlords: Digital Platforms and New Mechanisms of Rentier Capitalism," *Antipode*, 92 (1): 10–19.

Sandvig, C. (2013) "The Internet as Infrastructure," in W. H. Dutton (ed.), *The Oxford Handbook of Internet Studies*, Oxford: Oxford University Press Oxford, 86–106.

Safransky, S. (2019) "Geographies of Algorithmic Violence: Redlining the Smart City," *International Journal of Urban and Regional Research*, 123 (5): 1118–19.

Schor, J., Attwood-Charles, W., Cansoy, M., Ladegaard, I., and Wengronowitz, R. (2020) "Dependence and Precarity in the Platform Economy," *Theory and Society*, 49: 833–61.

Sloane, M. and Kraemer, J. (2021) *Terra Incognita NYC: Mapping New York City's New Digital Public Spaces during the COVID-19 Outbreak*, New_ Public, March. https://newpublic.org/terra-incognita

Smith-Hefner, N. J. (2007) "Youth Language, Gaul Sociability, and the New Indonesian Middle Class," *Journal of Linguistic Anthropology*, 17 (2): 184–203.

Spitulnik, D. (1998) "Mediated Modernities: Encounters with the Electronic in Zambia," *Visual Anthropology Review*, 14 (2): 63–84.

Stewart, J. (2002) "Das Kunsthaus Tacheles: the Berlin Architecture Debate of the 1990s in Micro-Historical Context," in S. Taberner and F. Finlay (eds.), *Recasting German Identity: Culture, Politics, and Literature in the Berlin Republic*, Rochester, NY: Camden House, 51–66.

Thornton, S. (1996) *Club Cultures: Music, Media and Subcultural Capital*, Middletown, CT: Wesleyan University Press.

Trinch, S. and Snajdr, E. (2016) "What the Signs Say: Gentrification and the Disappearance of Capitalism without Distinction in Brooklyn," *Journal of Sociolinguistics*, 21 (1): 64–89.

Tsing, A. (2005) *Friction: An Ethnography of Global Connection*, Princeton, NJ: Princeton University Press.

Udupa, S. (2012) "News Media and Contention Over 'the Local' in Urban India," *American Ethnologist*, 39 (4): 819–34.

Ward, S. (2019) "Reconfiguring the Spaces of the "Creative Class" in Contemporary Berlin," in K. Bauer and J. R. Hosek (eds.), *Cultural Topographies of the New Berlin*, New York: Berghahn Books.

Weszkalnys, G. (2010) *Berlin, Alexanderplatz*, New York: Berghahn Books.

Weszkalnys, G. (2008) "A Robust Square: Planning, Youth Work, and the Making of Public Space in Post-Unification Berlin," *City & Society*, 20 (2): 251–74.

Weidman, A. (2010) "Sound and the City: Mimicry and Media in South India," *Journal of Linguistic Anthropology*, 20 (2): 294–313.

14
ANTHROPOLOGY AND DIGITAL MEDIA
Multivocal Materialities of Video Meetings and Deafness

Rebekah Cupitt

During these pandemic-driven video meetings, some of us may have even noticed that a key event of the video meeting is that moment right before the meeting starts. This is the moment where the technology and the human meet in awkward and visible ways. Configuring the software, the hardware and even the physical space around us, as well as placing ourselves in view of the camera and establishing a social rapport with colleagues are all core components of preparing for a video meeting. As we have become more familiar with video meetings, most of us will have refined our routines but even so, these vary depending on the kind of meeting we are having, with whom we are meeting, and where we are. Because of the looming meeting, we do not often reflect on what we do or why. This chapter offers some pre-pandemic reflections on the kinds of meanings our actions during video meetings can convey within the context of meetings in Swedish Sign Language (SSL). I argue that during these meetings, the socio-material processes of becoming d/Deaf become more visible in the routines, contexts and multiple participants that meet via video.[1]

Evoking the pandemic-tinged forms of video meetings is a prompt to the reader to take some of the shared, embodied experiences of video meetings with them in the reading of this chapter. In this way, the kinds of video meetings that were happening at Swedish television (SVT) will be interpreted as different in some ways, but as sharing commonalities. I focus on the first moments of a video meeting and highlight the often invisible, human labour that draws video meeting technology into ontologically multiple socio-material complexes (see Mol, 2002 in Hine, 2017: 23). Video meetings can thus be understood as human-technology-human intra-actions (Barad, 2007) that speak to ways of being Deaf, deaf, interpreter, hearing, and other ways of being.

Digital Media Anthropology

The media anthropology of today is inherently digital; be it mass media anthropology (Spitulnik, 1993), the anthropology of broadcasting media, audiences, and audience participation (Pertierra & Turner, 2013; Costa, 2017), social media (Haynes, 2016; Miller et al., 2016), mobile media (Horst and Miller, 2006), or media and arts production (Ginsburg, Abu-Lughod, & Larkin, 2002, Uimonen, 2009). Therefore the overlap between important insights from digital anthropologists and media anthropologists such as Hine (2017), Costa (2017), Ginsburg et al. (2002), Pertierra (2018), and Abrams and Pink (2015) are relevant. Design anthropology (Pink, 2014; Murphy, 2016; Ventura & Bichard, 2017) is also of relevance, especially as we acknowledge the insights of MacKenzie and Wajcman, who write that technologies are not just products of innovation but are "thoroughly social in their development and use" (1985, cited in Hine, 2017: 23). Taking this confluence of design, media, and the digital and noting that the anthropologist focuses not only on the impact of technologies but the conditions under which technologies "come to be" (Hine, 2017: 23), this chapter highlights the agency of the employees at SVT Teckenspråk and how their daily workplace practices constitute a technology (as in Hine, 2017: 23). By extension, I address how people use technology to *become* (with) – deaf, Deaf, hearing, and allies.

Anthropological studies on media technologies and their use in the context of television production in SSL, offer a new avenue for media anthropology beyond content production/consumption paradigms (Pertierra, 2018: 155). It is an avenue not without its methodological and epistemological challenges. One challenge is how these materialities of deafness change depending on the contexts of communication, the media in use, but even differ when understandings of deafness are, in fact, not shared by hearing colleagues, deaf colleagues, and even technologies. To illustrate these potential changes, I present an example of how deafness materialises differently during two separate video meetings and qualify these as individual embodiments of deaf identities that shift, like the brittlestar (Barad, 2007: 375), depending on the viewpoint, the contexts, the people, the technologies, and their agendas. These different ways of being deaf (Monaghan, Nakamura, Schmaling & Turner 2003), relate to the media technologies used for video-mediated communication (video meetings) and to human-technology relations or intra-actions. I also emphasise that the context for each video meeting and the individual's agenda are central to how deafness and Deaf culture manifest creating subjective materialities (Cupitt, 2017).

In this chapter I take Spitulnik's seminal piece on mass media anthropology as a starting point and use it to demonstrate that media technologies like video meeting technologies make up a central matter for concern within media anthropology. Speaking specifically about mass media, Spitulnik writes, these media are "artifacts, experiences, practices and processes ... economically and politically driven, linked to developments in science and technology and ... bound up with the use of language" (1993: 293). Applied to a specific media (video media technologies), this statement holds true. Video meeting technologies are simultaneously artefacts embedded within the experiences of meeting participants' past, present and preferable futures (referring here to Candy as cited in Dunne & Raby, 2013: 27; Cupitt 2017). The video meeting examples presented here point to what d/Deaf SVT Teckenspråk employees see as important markers of their d/Deaf identity and how this identity is tied to practices of video-mediated communication in SSL and Swedish. From this standpoint, an individual's or collective's labour makes visible these markers and articulates them through video meeting communication practices (Cupitt, Forstorp & Lantz, 2019).

A Video Meeting at SVT Teckenspråk

I am in the large, newly designed meeting room called *Stora stöten* at Swedish television's regional offices in Falun (central Sweden). The room is bright. I position myself at the back of the room on one of the hard, corrugated, grey felt chairs that epitomise Swedish design with their bright yellow metal legs and minimalist, modern design that inserts a playfulness into the sometimes drab feel of an office meeting room. The chair is placed a bit away from the hard white surface of the large oval table that seats at least 20 people around it. There are two televisions at standing head-height (approximately 170 cm), and an assortment of video meeting "black boxes" that house the system hardware. Cables trail down the backs of these stands and two video cameras are set atop the stack of media technology. It appears as if these cameras are ready to capture all that goes on in the room and relay it, faithfully, to colleagues seated in a much smaller, cluttered video meeting room in Stockholm.

At this meeting, the large table in Falun has been dismantled. A small, round table has been formed and two chairs placed on one curved side with one of the television stands pulled up close to it. The Head of SVT's Division for Television Programming in Swedish Sign Language (*SVT Teckenspråk*), and the programme directors for two of SVT Teckenspråk's content and production teams, Children's television (*Barn- och ungdomsredaktionen*) and Culture and Society (*Kultur och samhälle*) were holding their regular meeting. Anna and René were in Falun, a town located about three hours north of Stockholm by train. Louisa, the director of the Culture and Society division, had yet to dial in from Stockholm and Anna was fiddling with the remote, trying to get the best camera angle for a meeting in SSL.

After tipping the camera up and down, then zooming in and out using the buttons on the remote, Anna seemed satisfied and sat down on one side of the round table. Sitting down, she quickly realised that only the top of her head was now visible and began to tilt the camera a little more to readjust the image that Louisa would see in Stockholm. As she began to laboriously (and unsuccessfully) do this, René came in and Anna turned and asked him to take over. René adjusted the camera so that the image that he could see on the monitor to the left of the room showed Anna's torso and head. He then sat down himself and, as if on cue, Louisa sat down at her table in Stockholm. An image of her head and torso was framed nicely by the monitor on the right in Falun which was opposite the table at which René and Anna sat. All signed a greeting. Louisa is Deaf and has worked for SVT Teckenspråk for many years producing television shows that both speak to the Swedish d/Deaf community and also educate hearing Swedes about Deaf culture. Anna has also worked for SVT Teckenspråk for many years. Her work with children's programming in SSL predates the Division's incorporation with Swedish television and started when it was a part of *Dövas TV* (TV for the Deaf). Dövas TV was a community-initiated television station and closely linked with the Swedish d/Deaf community in the Leksand region of Sweden and had strong ties with *Sveriges dövas riksförbund* (the Swedish Association of the Deaf). René was newest to SVT Teckenspråk but had been with the team for at least five years at the time of the meeting in 2012. Both Anna and René could communicate in SSL (*teckenspråk* in Swedish). René usually had an interpreter with him at meetings as, although he could understand it, he was not a fluent signer. At this meeting, there were no interpreters available, and all had decided that they could go ahead without. Louisa was extremely careful with her signing and used to bridging any gaps that hearing colleagues might have when communicating in SSL. Anna was capable of relaying what was signed if needed. In fact, at this meeting I was the one who was least proficient and although I could follow the general gist of what was being discussed, Anna's intermittent translations of what Louisa signed (mostly for my benefit) helped facilitate the meeting and my participant observation.

In the vignette above, I have focussed on the work Anna and René, two hearing SVT Teckenspråk employees, put into creating a meeting space that catered to both their needs, as well as to their perception of their d/Deaf colleague, Louisa's needs. This short retelling highlighted how Anna and René interacted with the media technology of the video meeting system: its interfaces (the remote, the television monitors, and the cameras). These interactions are part of the labour needed to configure a meeting space for SSL communication and occurred within the conceptual space of a video meeting, the physical space of two distant meeting rooms in Stockholm and Falun, and a part of SVT Teckenspråk employees' work-related duties as television producers. The human-technology interactions are *intra*-actions in the way Barad has defined them where meanings matter (2007, see also Cupitt, 2017). In the second example, I will discuss how these (re)configurations of video meetings, to draw on Suchman's work on human-non-human intra-action (2007), are in fact materialities of mediated communication (as in Barad (2007) in Cupitt, 2017: 278f). Through interpreting the intra-actions of d/Deaf and hearing employees at SVT Teckenspråk with video meeting technologies as performances of hearing *and* deaf ways of being, the material subjectivities of d/Deaf and hearing become visible (Cupitt, 2017). Using analyses of video meetings to show the ways in which d/Deaf employees, in particular, use video meeting technologies, I show media technologies are not only tools for communication but also for articulating what it means to be d/Deaf. [Digital] media technologies, such as video meetings, are thus understood as "dynamic sites of struggle over representation, and complex spaces in which subjectivities are constructed and identities are contested" (Spitulnik, 1993:296).

Being d/Deaf at SVT Teckenspråk

This chapter contains a necessarily fragmented but central account of the institutional histories in which media technologies at Swedish television (SVT) are embedded (see Postill, 2009). The key characteristics of the organisation are the principles on which Swedish public service broadcasting are anchored (see Syvertsen, Enil, Mjøs & Moe, 2014; cf. Thorbjørnsrud, 2013), the fundamental values of Swedish democracy (Kautto, Fritzell, Kvist & Uusitalo, 2001; Nissen, 2013; Ferrell Lowe & Martin, 2014; Djerf-Pierre & Ekström, 2013) and the organisation's goal to bring media content to the whole of Sweden as "*hela Sveriges television*."[2] While the extent to which these characteristics are enacted in the workplace is a matter for further discussion, it is these core principles and values that underlie the enactments of employees' material subjectivities in video meetings at SVT Teckenspråk.

The SVT Teckenspråk team at the time of this study (between 2010–2013), consisted of deaf and hearing employees who have as their goal to increase Swedish citizens' awareness of Sign Language, as well as providing a cornerstone of cultural exchange for the Swedish d/Deaf community. This community is (unsurprisingly) far from homogeneous and is characterised by numerous understandings and ways of being d/Deaf (see Monaghan et al., 2003). This chapter presents a moment in the institutional history of SVT Teckenspråk, when employees understand deafness as more than clinical definitions of deafness, and where focus is instead turned on SSL as an embodied expression of Deaf culture. SSL from this perspective becomes a shared canon of meanings conveyed through the primarily visual media of film, television, and video meeting technologies. Taking my cue from the SVT Teckenspråk employees, who understand deafness as a visually rich culture, I examine the performance of d/Deaf identities through SSL, television production, and video-mediated communication.

In part because of the centrality of SSL within the organisation and public service's democratic ideals, meetings at SVT Teckenspråk were held in two languages, Swedish and SSL. They usually involved an interpreter (one of the in-house interpreters or an external interpreter, depending on the type of meeting and the in-house interpreters' workloads). Video meetings were a part of the daily workflow as SVT Teckenspråk had offices in both Stockholm and Falun. The division also prided itself on being a *tvåspråkig redaktion* (a dual-language division). Perhaps because of the politically charged nature of being Deaf among hearing and also due to the SVT Teckenspråk team's goal to spread knowledge and awareness of d/Deaf lived experiences, holding meetings in two languages became instances of asserting d/Deaf ways of communicating and opportunities to forefront the different needs that visual communication in SSL placed on both hearing colleagues and the media technologies used to mediate the meetings. It was this politically charged use of video media technologies that had initially drawn me to SVT Teckenspråk as it offered a unique example of how video meetings could function, despite their challenges – challenges which are often used as excuses for not meeting via video (Cupitt, 2013). The configuration needed in order to set up a video meeting like those at SVT Teckenspråk was a mundane occurrence for the d/Deaf and hearing employees. Video meetings were scheduled daily and a certain amount of fiddling with the remote was factored into to the meeting preparations. At times, staff like Anna turned up a few minutes early to set up the room, establish a video link, and place the camera in the best position. When interpreters were involved in the video meetings, these configurations became more complex than for this meeting.

The two examples of video meetings with members of SVT Teckenspråk discussed in this chapter illustrate how people, media technologies, and their politically and morally charged contexts all intersect with deafness. These examples are used to identify key elements of SSL communication, deaf visual culture, and how subjective ways of being d/Deaf materialise. What emerges is a sense that SSL and media technologies are inherently bound to reconfigurable, embodied, and performative enactments of material subjectivities (as suggested by Spitulnik, 1993; and further detailed in Cupitt, 2017). I approach video meetings as convergences of social practices and digital media to examine them not only as communicative practices within institutions, but as constitutive of moralities, and as playing a part in "the construction of community" and identity (Spitulnik, 1993: 293).

"Artifacts"

Video meetings are an example of media technology in action. Inserting this technology into the realm of media anthropology is a conscious broadening of the field through a redefinition of media. This move builds on the work of Ginsburg, Abu-Lughod, and Larkin to include all forms of technology that produce content (however fleeting) and provide connections between people and technologies and people (2002: 4). Compared to the television content they produced, the video meetings of the SVT Teckenspråk team were in fact temporary instances and configurations of the SVT employees and reflect the situatedness of people and technology at one particular point in place and time (Suchman, 2007).

Following on from Spitulnik's (1993) framing, I consider what might be the "artifacts" of video meetings and this particular media anthropology. The video meeting technologies used at SVT were slightly different from the video meeting platforms most of us have used daily during the pandemic and which are the kinds of video meeting applications that work on existing multi-purpose devices such as mobile phones or personal computers. The video meeting technologies were purpose-built and configured for their singular function – to host video meetings. At SVT Teckenspråk, the offices in Falun and Stockholm contained a dedicated, albeit mismatched, assemblage of proprietary software and hardware located in a "meeting room." For SVT employees, a video meeting meant using three remotes, two monitors, two cameras, one video meeting hardware box, and connecting all these to the SVT networks. The video meeting technology being used was admittedly less than optimal with older components combined with newer, and work-arounds implemented by the information technology staff to prolong the life of the most outdated of parts (which dated back to the early 2000s). This contrasts starkly with the intended use of well-known, high-end video meeting systems designed by large telecommunication companies and which require significant outlay

Anthropology and Digital Media

and space in order to deliver the high quality, "as good as face-to-face" meeting experiences (see Cupitt, 2013).

Experiences

In the example of the video meeting with which I started this discussion, the meeting had not yet begun and when Louisa sat down and greeted her Falun colleagues, she immediately saw

(a)

(b)

(c)

Figure 14.1 (a) Louisa signing to René and Anna that she only sees half of René; (b) A view similar to the one that Louisa would see of René and Anna was shown on a secondary monitor in the Falun meeting room; (c) Louisa's image as seen by those in Falun and taken from the view of the anthropologist

that René was not entirely visible on her screen in Stockholm. She signed to him that his face was cut in half by drawing her open hand, long-ways down her face (see Figure 14.1a). René made a small grunt and signed, speaking at the same time saying, "*Jag är delad; jag är kluven*" ("I'm split; I'm divided" or more figuratively, "I am torn"). The trio shared a chuckle at this word play, and then René reached for the remote, fiddling once more with the arrow buttons that controlled the camera and angled it so that he was fully visible. This was not enough, however, due to the limitations of the camera's range of focus. René and Anna moved closer to each other but this meant they would not always be able to see what the other signed (see Figure 14.1b). Had René and Anna been d/Deaf, this solution would have been suboptimal. They were hearing however, and once Louisa gave a thumbs-up the meeting officially commenced.

This need to make adjustments before the meeting could start – both with the technology and also with the positioning of human bodies and furniture – was necessary for meetings in SSL to succeed. Through observing over 74 video meetings over a three-year period, I learnt that for video meetings in SSL and Swedish to be possible, the images of people's torsos, hands, and faces should be clear and large enough so that facial expressions are visible on screen. A classic head and torso with a tight focus works well and Louisa, knowing this, had set up her camera this way (see Figure 14.1c). Anna and René had worked to set up their image properly, but were not sitting near enough to each other to be able to zoom in that close and instead of two tightly framed torsos, Louisa saw a smaller version with some of the white table in frame. This framing might have meant that Anna and René were thrown into relief as their skin tone would have been darkened as the camera adjusted to the bright white of the table in the foreground. This technological limitation had caused issues in video meetings. On this occasion, soft morning light ameliorated the camera's limitations and Louisa was also prepared to accept less-than-optimal video meeting conditions; adapting to these without demanding further changes.

Practices

Historically, this view that it is the d/Deaf who need to accept and adapt to hearing worlds has been the approach educators, governments and other social bodies have taken to deafness (with oralism in Swedish schools (Göransson & Westholm, 1995) being the prime example). Globally researchers have highlighted how this need to adapt to a hearing way of life is still a fact of life for employed d/Deaf people (Punch, Hyde, & Power, 2007; O'Brien, 2020; Stokar & Orwat, 2018). By the same token, the expectation that hearing will make accommodations for d/Deaf colleagues is frequently absent (Mattson, Nylund, & Rassmussen Öberg, 2012: 33). This last reality was not the case at SVT. At SVT Teckenspråk, a dual-language workplace, hearing colleagues were asked to take lessons in SSL and in-house interpreters were on hand to facilitate communication, even chats in the lunch room, as well as staff meetings and events. D/deaf employees in Falun could therefore expect hearing colleagues to accommodate communication in SSL. It was this expectation and the institutionalised right to ask that these accommodations be made while at SVT Teckenspråk that was articulated so expertly by Deaf journalist, Axel in the second example.

We are once again in a video meeting. This time, I am seated in Stockholm in the tiny room Louisa occupied in the first example. I am joining Axel, a video and web journalist for the SVT Teckenspråk news team, *Nyhetstecken*. The group are having a meeting to discuss upcoming content, delegation of work, and the week that was. The connection has already been established with Falun and most of the team are seated in the stark white room around the large, reassembled white table. From Stockholm, Axel and I can see four of his colleagues: Rickard (head of the Nyhetstecken team), Tova (a journalist and the newest team member), Tracy (the interpreter), and Jenny (an SSL news presenter). Of these, Rickard is hearing and fluent in SSL, Tova is hearing and does not understand SSL, while Jenny is *teckenspråkig döv* (d/Deaf and an SSL user). Axel, in Stockholm is also *teckenspråkig döv* but unlike his d/Deaf colleagues, he sometimes speaks Swedish as he had partial hearing as a child.

The meeting has not yet officially started as there is at least one team member missing. Axel, who is in Stockholm, takes the opportunity to optimise the image he sees by asking his colleagues to adjust the camera and rearrange themselves. His goal is to be able to see everyone who will be signing. He is also considering his d/Deaf colleagues in Falun when he makes these re-arrangements. He begins by asking the group in Falun to zoom out so that he can see everyone there. Rickard obliges using the remote – one of three lying on the table. Once he has made the adjustments, Rickard puts down the remote and starts signing to Axel. The interpreter, Tracy, begins to translate what Rickard was signing to Axel for hearing team member, Tova's, benefit as she was not familiar with SSL.

RICKARD: Peter's coming too. (Tracy: *Peter kommer också.*)
AXEL: Aha. Ok. He's there then? (Tracy: *Jajaja ok. Han är där alltså?*)

RICKARD SIGNS TO AXEL: What? Don't you know who works here? (Tracy: *Va? Du vet vilka det är som jobbar hos oss alltså?*)

Rickard is joking and he and the interpreter in Falun chuckle. Axel sees Tracy's facial expression but missed Rickard's joke and replies with a question.

AXEL: What did you say? (Tracy: *Vad sa du?*)

Rickard who has not noticed the miscommunication, continues joking around.

RICKARD: But you know, that guy … (Tracy: *Men du vet den där killen …*)
AXEL (stops him mid-joke): Rickard, I can't see you! You're only half there. Riiiiiickard???? (Tracy: *Du syns inte! Jag ser dig bara till hälften. Riiiickard??*)

Axel and Rickard are both signing and communicating directly with each other without the mediation of the interpreter but it is clear that they are not quite understanding each other. I am relying on the interpreter's spoken dialogue, so follow the jovial exchange and chuckle in the background. Unable to hear the interpreter however, Axel needs to see Rickard signing. Unfortunately, Rickard is sitting half in, half out of frame, as Axel finally points out with mild exasperation (see Figure 14.2a, and the section transcribed above). Rickard's signs are therefore half lost and cannot be seen from Stockholm. Tracy, the interpreter, sees them clearly from her position in Falun and interprets them to spoken Swedish which I hear and understand. But for Axel who does not benefit from Tracy's spoken Swedish interpretation of Rickard's SSL, the joke is only partially conveyed.

Once Rickard realises this mistake (with help from Axel), he leans forward to put himself back into frame for us in Stockholm. Saying nothing, he picks up the remote and, looking at the second monitor in Falun to guide his adjustments, he shifts the camera angle slightly (see Figure 14.2b). Presumably happy with the camera angle, Rickard puts down the remote and moves his chair forward but is still only *just* visible to us in Stockholm. It is only when he hunches over the table that he is fully seen; not when he leans back in the chair. He moves a little more, waves and Axel responds.

AXEL: Ah now – Ah. I wonder if Tracy and Tova should swap places. (Tracy: *Ah nu – Ah. Jo, jag funderar lite grann om Tracy and Tova ska byta plats.*)

Resigned to only seeing a part of Rickard in much the same way Louisa also made do with an imperfect image in the first example, Axel is now focusing on making sure that the interpreter is sitting in the optimum position for him and his d/Deaf colleague in Falun, Jenny. Tracy and Tova stand up and swap seats so that Tracy is now sitting between Rickard and Tova and can more easily see Jenny, as well as still being able to see Axel on the monitor. Jenny has not said anything so far and seems a bit disinterested in the proceedings. Axel signs:

AXEL: There. Now Tracy can see better. (Tracy: *Då ser Tracy bättre.*)

Axel is referring to Tracy and how she needs to be able to see what Jenny signs. In reply, Jenny signs a short and nonchalant "Yep." Which is not translated by Tracy who is looking at the monitor to see what Axel is going to sign next while making herself comfortable in her chair. Rickard is still only partially visible for us in Stockholm. Tracy and Tova are sitting in the centre of the image and the set-up is, from Axel's perspective, now optimised for SSL communication.

Processes

In this video meeting, it is the machinations of Axel, his steering of the camera, the organising of his colleagues, and his positioning of himself so that the video meeting could successfully take place that are unmistakable, intentional acts. The discussion here is much more directed than in the first meeting where Louisa's comment on how René was only half visible led to minor (and probably imperfect) adjustments on the Falun team's part. In this meeting, Axel was not only letting his colleagues know that he needed to be able to see those who signed as well as

Figure 14.2 (a) The image Axel sees from his Stockholm meeting room. Note how Rickard is only half visible on the right-hand side of the screen; (b) Rickard leaning forward and waving to make sure he is visible before he picks up the remote and starts moving the camera angle

the team leader, Rickard; he was also making sure they experienced the needs of technologically mediated SSL communication. This experience was embodied as each team member had to physically move to different places in the room. This is what I have previously referred to as the materialisation of D/deaf subjectivity (Cupitt, 2017; Cupitt et al., 2019). If we also consider this request in light of the view that d/Deaf people are often those who are expected to adapt to hearing worlds, then Axel's actions can be understood not only as everyday articulations of deafness, but as holding a political significance.

Video meetings at SVT Teckenspråk show the ways in which both d/Deaf and hearing colleagues worked hard to establish and maintain the dual-language work environment (den teckenspråkiga miljön). The example with Axel demonstrates not only that hearing colleagues adapted to SSL communication and d/Deaf colleagues' needs, but also that media is used in "mundane ... practices to create and contest representations of the self and the other" (Nair & Sharma, 2015). Through his manipulations of the camera, the video meeting system, and his colleagues, Axel configures himself as Deaf (strongly identifying with the right to communicate in SSL), but also as deaf. He needs to see and be seen and zooms in on himself so that Falun can easily follow his signs. He asks Tracy and Tova to move places so that he can follow what Tracy signs more easily, but also so that she can see his signing. He transfers his understanding of deafness onto Jenny and places Tracy so that she can be seen easily even for his d/Deaf colleagues in Falun. This is part of the deaf experience – understanding and positioning themselves in relation to d/Deaf colleagues and also the interpreters. Axel also tries to position Rickard so that he is visible and can communicate in SSL but is thwarted by the limitations of the camera and video meeting technology. Rickard, with his knowledge of SSL communication, tries to oblige but is also limited by the technology – the layout of the room, the furniture, and the camera angle.

I have approached this meeting in terms of Axel's practices. Axel instructs people to move, requests the camera angle be changed, and that colleagues swap seats in an articulation of his needs and identity as a Deaf Sign Language user (teckenspråkig döv). Yet it is through the *process* of negotiating these changes with colleagues that his Deaf identity and status as a Deaf materialises. It is through following his instructions that hearing colleagues show their allyship and share his understanding of what it means to be Deaf. Axel's d/Deaf colleague, Jenny, possibly has a different way of being d/Deaf, but in this moment and through becoming a part of the process of setting up a video meeting with an interpreter and in SSL, Jenny, too, takes on a version that aligns with Axel's. These processes of setting up a video meeting take place not only in relation to colleagues, but in relation to the video meeting's media technologies. Therefore it is fair to say that a variety of ways of being "become with" (as in Haraway, 2007), and are embodied through, the digital materiality of video media technologies. We can see what it means to become with these technologies in Falun and Stockholm; what it means to become d/Deaf in its many forms; to become allies; and to become interpreters. In this short fragment, being d/Deaf, hearing, ally, and interpreter materialise in the orchestrations that preceded the actual meeting discussion but they are ongoing processes that are reconfigured throughout the meeting and the intra-actions of people and media technologies (see Suchman, 2007).

Conclusion

The material-discursive nature of these reconfigurations illustrated quite literally by Axel's instructions and their material consequences, speak to the ways in which media technologies are embedded within cultural processes of meaning-making and identity work. In the first example with Louisa, René, and Anna, we find another version of how these reconfigurations might play out. Less explicit in her instructions and relying more on her SSL-fluent, hearing colleagues and their pre-existing understandings of SSL communication, Louisa's agenda could be understood as less about identity and more about collaborating with hearing colleagues. Axel's practices, on the other hand, were more overt and had an obvious agenda of reminding old (and teaching new) colleagues (and observing anthropologists) about SSL communication via video-mediated means. Looking closer, Axel's orchestrations go beyond this and can be interpreted through the analytical lens of critical design studies, to serve as the perfect example for what Costa calls "strategies of resistance to the structuring forces of technological design" (2017: 8). Here we have a video meeting technology that is design by hearing for hearing. It is a technology whose design is predicated on the fact that video meeting participants will be able to hear as well as see. Designers of these kinds of hardware and software often unintentionally exclude those of us who do not conform to a preset notion of an intended user (Cupitt, 2017: 294ff). Video media technologies thus amplify inequality and further push the marginalised into situations of surveillance and precarity, but not just in situations of crisis (see Madianou, 2020: 9). For d/Deaf employees to take part in these meetings, they and their hearing colleagues need to adapt to and accommodate the technological limitations of the "artifacts" that are a part of their communicative practices during video meetings. In the case of Louisa and her two SSL-fluent colleagues, this was relatively straightforward. For the Nyhetstecken team and the much larger group meeting that also involved non-SSL-fluent colleagues, multiple d/Deaf SSL users, a hearing, SSL-fluent colleague, and an interpreter, the accommodations were more complex.

That there are many ways of being deaf is a perspective already established in deaf studies (see Nakamura, 2013; Monaghan et al., 2003). These differences refer to identity and what it means to be a part of d/Deaf cultures yet such variation is also manifest in everyday practices, like Axel's, Jenny's, and Louisa's ways of being deaf in video meetings. Deafness comes into being with technologies through intentional intra-actions with people and media technologies, as Axel's orchestrations show. These materialities almost defy generalisation and it was as if there was a new way in which SVT Teckenspråk employees enacted deafness for every meeting I observed. The circumstances were seldom the same even though the video meeting technology and the people involved might be. For the digital media anthropologist, the reasons behind these different materialisations of deafness are overshadowed by the practices and processes through which they came about, two of which I have reviewed here.

Media anthropologists have seen technology as a means for subversion (Abrams & Pink, 2015: 12), as empowering (Michaels (1986) in Pertierra, 2018: 66; Larkin, 2008; cf. Wallis, 2011), as a catalyst for community building (Kraemer, 2017; Boellstorff, 2008; Stephen, 2012), and as a tool for political ends and nation building (Abu Lughod, 2008; among many others). For this *digital* media anthropologist, the most interesting social phenomenon is how people draw on, manipulate, and interact with the media technology present in video meetings. In the two cases presented in this chapter, not only the people but the video technologies are active agents in co-creating what it means to be d/Deaf, hearing, and ally at SVT Teckenspråk. Those competent or confident in interacting with video meeting technologies use them to effect; punctuating the differences between material subjectivities to reinforce their own (political) agendas. The multiple and subjective experiences of human interactions with video media technologies and the ways these interface with articulations of being coalesce to form the many co-existing, material subjectivities of human-technology intra-actions in video meetings. It is this "multivocality of media" and human intra-actions with media technologies that presents a challenge for digital media anthropology. Meeting this challenge head on, this chapter has given two brief examples that demonstrate how video meetings in SSL embody complex socio-technical materialities that make visible the many different ways of being in video meetings and notes the central task of paying attention to these differences in order to better demonstrate that digital media materialities are socio-technical processes, constantly in flux.

Notes

1 I use "deaf" to describe the medical diagnosis associated with a loss of hearing or hearing impairment *and* in the case where the person has not explicitly identified as belonging to the Swedish deaf community, as being a part of the Deaf culture (Padden & Humphries, 2005), or communicated that they belong to the SSL community (or as *teckenspråkiga döva*) (Fredäng, 2003). Where someone is making a political statement through identifying with the Deaf culture movement, I have used "Deaf" to signify this. In scenarios where it is not made explicit, I have used, "d/Deaf" which acknowledges both positionalities (Napier, 2002).
2 "*Hela Sveriges television*" can be translated as "television for all of Sweden." See https://omoss.svt.se/ (last accessed: 29.10.2021).

References

Abu-Lughod, L. (2008) *Dramas of Nationhood: The Politics of Television in Egypt*. Chicago: University of Chicago Press.

Barad, K. (2007) *Meeting the Universe Halfway: Quantum Physics and the Entanglement of Matter and Meaning*. Durham, NC: Duke University Press.

Boellstorff, T. (2008) *Coming of Age in Second Life: An Anthropologist Explores the Virtually Human*. Princeton: Princeton University Press.

Costa, E. (2017) "Social media as practices: An ethnographic critique of 'affordances' and 'context collapse'." *Working papers for the EASA Media Anthropology Network's 60th e- Seminar*. https://easaonline.org/downloads/networks/media/60p.pdf (last accessed: 15.8.2021).

Cupitt, R. (2013) "Phantasms collide: Navigating video-mediated communication in the Swedish workplace." In *GMJ AU, Global Media Journal, Australian Edition Special Issue: Communication Technology and Social Life: Collaboration, Innovation, Conflict and Disorder* 1(1). www.hca.westernsydney.edu.au/gmjau/?p=247 (last accessed: 14.11.2021).

Cupitt, R. (2017) *Make Difference: Deafness and Video Technology at Work*. Doctoral Thesis No. 3, KTH, Royal Institute of Technology.

Cupitt, R., Forstorp, P.-A., & Lantz, A. (2019) "Visuality without form: Video-mediated communication and research practice across disciplinary contexts." *Qualitative Inquiry* 25(4): 417–431.

Djerf-Pierre, M. & Ekström, M. (eds) (2013) *A History of Swedish Broadcasting: Communicative Ethos, Genres and Institutional Change*. Göteborg: Nordicom.

Dunne, A. & Raby, F. (2013) *Speculative Everything: Design Fiction, and Social Dreaming*. Cambridge, MA: MIT Press.

Ferrell Lowe, G. & Martin, F. (eds) (2014) *The Value of Public Service Media*. Göteborg: Nordicom.

Fredäng, P. 2003 *Teckenspråkiga döva: Identitetsförändringar i det svenska dövsamhället*. Doctoral Thesis, Uppsala Universitet.

Ginsburg, F., Abu-Lughod, L., & Larkin, B. (2002) "Introduction." In F. Ginsburg, L. Abu-Lughod & B. Larkin (eds) *Media Worlds: Anthropology on New Terrain*. Berkeley: University of California Press, pp. 1–36.

Göransson, S. & Westholm, G. (1995) *Nästan allt om döva*. Stockholm: Tolk- och översättarinstitutet, Univ. TÖI.

Haraway, D. J. (2007) *When Species Meet*. Minnesota: Minnesota University Press.

Haynes, N. (2016) *Social Media in Northern China*. London: UCL Press.

Hine, C. (2017) "From virtual ethnography to the embedded, embodied, everyday internet." In L. Hjorth, L., Horst, H., Galloway, A., & Bell, G. (eds), *The Routledge Companion to Digital Ethnography*. New York: Routledge, pp. 21–28.

Horst, H. A. & Miller, D. (2006) *The Cell Phone: An Anthropology of Communication*. Oxford: Berg.

Kautto, J., Fritzell, B.H., Kvist, J., & Uusitalo, H. (2001) "Introduction: How distinct are the Nordic welfare states?" In J. Kautto, B. H. Fritzell, J. Kvist, & H. Uusitalo (eds), *Nordic Welfare States in the European Context*. London: Routledge, pp. 1–17.

Kraemer, J. (2017) "Locating emerging media: Ethnographic reflections on culture, selfhood, and place." In L. Hjorth, H. Horst, A. Galloway, and G. Bell (eds), *The Routledge Companion to Digital Ethnography*. New York: Routledge, pp. 179–190.

Larkin, B. (2008) *Signal and Noise: Media, Infrastructure, and Urban Culture in Nigeria*. Durham, NC: Duke University Press.

MacKenzie, D. A. & Wajcman, J. (1985) *The Social Shaping of Technology: How the Refrigerator Got Its Hum*. Milton Keynes: Open University Press.

Madianou, M. (2020) "A second-order disaster? Digital technologies during the COVID-19 pandemic." *Social Media and Society* 2020: 1–5.

Mattson, K., Nylund, E., & Rassmussen Öberg, C. (2012) *Dövas plats i arbetslivet*. Samordningsförbundet Centrala Östergötland. Rapport nr: 2012:1. Gryt: Mediahavet AB.

Michaels, E. (1986) *The Aboriginal Invention of Television: Central Australia 1982–6*. Canberra Institute of Aboriginal Studies.

Miller, D., Costa, E., Haynes, N., McDonald, T., Nicolescu, R., Sinanan, J., Spyer, J., Venkatraman, S., & Wang, X. (2016) *How the World Changed Social Media*. London: UCL Press.

Moll, A. (2002) *The Body Multiple: Ontology in Medical Practice*. Durham, NC: Duke University Press.

Monaghan, L., Nakamura, K. Schmaling, C., & Turner, G. (2003) *Many Ways to be Deaf: International Variation in Deaf Communities*. Washington, DC: Gallaudet University Press.

Murphy, K. (2016) "Design and anthropology." *Annual Review of Anthropology* 45(1): 433–449.

Nair, P. & Sharma, N. (2015) "Media anthropology: An Emerging discipline in India." *Loyola Journal of Social Sciences* XXIX(1): 7–25.

Nakamura, K. (2006) *Deaf in Japan: Signing and the Politics of Identity*. Ithaca: Cornell University Press.

Napier, J. (2002) "The D/deaf – H/hearing debate." *Sign Language Studies* 2(2): 141–149.

Nissen, C. S. (2013) "Organisational culture and structures in public media management: In search of a model for the digital era?" In M. Glowacki & L. Jackson (eds), *Public Media Management for the Twenty-First Century: Creativity, Innovation and Interaction*. Routledge Research in Cultural and Media Studies. New York: Routledge, pp. 81–102.

O'Brien, D. (2020) "Mapping Deaf academic spaces." *Higher Education* 80: 739–755.

Padden, C. & Humphries, T. (2005) *Inside Deaf Culture*, Cambridge, MA: First Harvard University Press.

Pertierra, A. C. (2018) *Media Anthropology for the Digital Age*. Cambridge: Polity Press.

Pertierra, A. C. & Turner, G. (2013) *Locating Television: Zones of Consumption*. New York: Routledge.

Pink, S. (2014) "Digital–visual–sensory-design anthropology: Ethnography, imagination and intervention, Arts and Humanities." *Higher Education* 13(4): 412–427.

Pink, S., & Abram, S. (2015) "Introduction: Mediating publics and anthropology" In S. Pink & S. Abram (eds), *Media, Anthropology and Public Engagement*. Oxford: Berghahn Books, pp. 1–22.

Postill, J. (2009) "What's the point of media anthropology?" *Social Anthropology/Anthropologie Sociale* 17(3): 334–344.

Punch, R., Hyde, M., & Power, D. (2007) "Career and workplace experiences of Australian university graduates who are Deaf or hard of hearing." *The Journal of Deaf Studies and Deaf Education* 12(4): 504–517.

Spitulnik, D. (1993) "Anthropology and mass media." *Annual Review of Anthropology* 22: 293–315.

Stephen, L. (2012) "Community and Indigenous radio in Oaxaca: Testimony and participatory democracy." In L. Bessire (ed.), *Radio Fields: Anthropology and Wireless Sound in the Twenty-First Century*. New York: New York University Press, pp. 124–141.

Stokar, H. & Orwat, J. (2018) "Hearing managers of deaf workers: A Phenomenological investigation in the restaurant industry." *American Annals of the Deaf* 163 (1): 13–34.

Suchman, L. (2007) *Human-Machine Reconfigurations. Plans and Situated Actions*. Cambridge: Cambridge University Press.

Syvertsen, T., Enli, G., Mjøs, O. J., & Moe, H. (2014) *The Media Welfare State: Nordic Media in the Digital Eram*. Series: New Media World, Ann Arbor: University of Michigan Press.

Thorbjørnsrud, K. (2013) "The autonomy of Scandinavian public service broadcasters during election campaign periods: Principles and practices." *Nordicom Review* 34: 63–76.

Uimonen, P. (2009) "Internet, arts and translocality in Tanzania." *Social Anthropology* 17: 276–290.

Ventura, J. & Bichard, J-A (2017) "Design anthropology or anthropological design? Towards 'Social Design'." *International Journal of Design Creativity and Innovation* 5(3–4): 222–234.

Wallis, C. (2011) "Mobile phones without guarantees: The promises of technology and the contingencies of culture." *New Media & Society* 13(3): 471–485.

15
CLOUDWORK

Data Centre Labour and the Maintenance of Media Infrastructure

A.R.E. Taylor

I am standing in one of the server rooms of a 100,000-square foot data centre. The facility is owned and operated by GigaTech, a UK-based cloud provider who currently manage three data centres in the London metropolitan area and multiple facilities across geographic regions in Asia (Thailand, India, Singapore and China). I am being given a personal tour of their newest "hyperscale" facility, located on an industrial estate in the outskirts of East London.[1] The server room is blindingly white (Figure 15.1). At one end sit a number of server cabinets, arranged in neat symmetrical aisles. Aside from those cabinets, the room is largely empty, anticipating future growth. Heating, ventilation and air conditioning (HVAC) units, embedded within the walls and ceiling panels, funnel cold air down the aisles, preventing the servers from overheating. If the servers got too hot, their performance decreases, making them more likely to lose data. The noise made by the HVAC system is incredibly loud. I adjust my ear plugs, taken from one of the many dispensers mounted to the walls throughout the data centre. Ear plugs are provided to help engineers avoid hearing damage during long working hours in the noisy server rooms.

I am being guided through the facility by Mike Antin, GigaTech's East London Operations Manager. I had met Antin at a data centre security expo in London. When he heard that I was conducting fieldwork on cloud storage he invited me to GigaTech's newly built data centre. Antin has worked for GigaTech for ten years. He has spent the last few months overseeing the installation of equipment in the new data centre. As we walk down one of the aisles we meet Paul Bradford, one of the data centre's network operations centre (NOC) engineers, who is busy re-bolting a server that he noticed was slightly loose in its rack. He is wearing a large pair of earmuffs, as well as gloves and steel toe-capped boots. "Server racks are made from really sharp metal which can cut your hands up pretty badly", he shouts to me over the ambient noise, "they're also heavy, so you don't want them falling on your feet!". The floor around Bradford is littered with bags of cage nuts and cable off-cuts. He explains that he is now "cabling up" the server, the final stage of the maintenance job. This involves cutting and crimping the cables plugged into the server, in order to keep them neat and tidy. "If your cables aren't in order", Bradford explains, "they can get easily damaged and you run the risk of potentially taking your clients offline". Picking up on Bradford's point, Antin explains that "the whole point of a data centre is to stop downtime at any cost". Downtime refers to the time that a data centre's services are unavailable or offline. "So many services now depend on the cloud", Antin tells me, "that

DOI: 10.4324/9781003175605-21 213
This Chapter has been made available under a CC-BY-NC-ND License

Figure 15.1 One of the server rooms in GigaTech's East London facility
Source: https://jamesbridle.com/works/the-cloud-is-a-lie. Photo by author.

if a data centre should momentarily go offline it can cause widespread societal and economic disruption, as well as lasting financial and reputational damage for the data centre provider and their clients".

Data centres provide the cloud computing resources that form the operational backbone of digital societies. Commerce, consumption, distribution and production systems are now mediated on many levels by data centres, which strive to ensure their smooth, reliable and continuous operation. Financial services (banking and insurance), transportation systems (air traffic controls, road and rail signals, driverless cars), global logistics, communications (telephone networks, satellites, messaging apps, videoconferencing platforms), government and emergency services, utility providers (gas, water, electricity), online data storage (iCloud, Dropbox, OneDrive, Google Drive) and internet media services (music and video streaming, online gaming, advertising, social media) now all rely on data centres. With cloud services now connecting and enabling such a large number of sectors across government, business and society, Jean-François Blanchette (2015: 3) has suggested that we think of the cloud as a "meta-infrastructure". Indeed, the apps, software and communications systems provided by data centres are now perceived to connect such an incredible range of services and utilities that, we are told, "modern life wouldn't function without them" (TechUK 2014).

GigaTech was founded in 2011 and serve a large number of national and international customers, ranging from UK-based financial firms and government bodies to global media companies and retail chains. While some data centres house a single company's data and IT equipment, such as Facebook's or Google's facilities, the vast majority of data centre providers operate in public cloud or colocation markets, providing clients with access to computing resources – from storage capacity to processing power – that they pay for in a pay-as-you-go fashion. This means that clients do not need the large capital outlays required to build and service their own data centres. Many online media corporations, such as Twitter and Netflix, do not operate their own data centres but opt to lease public cloud infrastructure, like Amazon Web Services (AWS).

The GigaTech facility where I conducted my fieldwork forms part of what they call their London data centre "ecosystem". The location on the outskirts of London enables for a variety of connectivity options with different telecommunications carriers while operating at a safe distance from the high-risk city centre (a potential terrorist target), to satisfy disaster recovery requirements. As we continue our walk through the East London facility, Antin turns the conversation towards the growing pressures of the job. "Everyone is moving their data into the 'cloud'", he tells me, placing the word "cloud" in air quotes. "This is great for business", he says, "but they all expect their online services to be constantly available". His words echo out into the whitescape surrounding us. "The problem is", he continues, "end-users tend to forget that their cloud services rely on physical computing machines that are prone to failure, [and] maintaining all of this is exhausting, high-pressure work". Despite the image of immateriality that the "cloud" metaphor conjures, during my tour of GigaTech's facility I learned that, for those who work in the data centre industry that underpins the cloud, this infrastructure is experienced as material, fragile and precarious, and that it takes considerable labour to ensure that cloud services remain constantly online and available.

This chapter follows the high stakes work of those tasked with operating and maintaining cloud infrastructure. I draw from my tour at GigaTech and from subsequent visits and interviews with staff to explore the lived experiences of data centre labour that form the conditions of possibility for cloud media cultures and digital societies. In doing so, I centre "maintenance" as a key, but overlooked, form of media labour. A rich body of ethnographic work has explored the labour of media makers, producers, consumers and distributors. From Powdermaker's (1950) ethnography of the Hollywood studio system, to newsroom ethnographies (Schlesinger 1978; Gans 1979; Tuchman 1991; Born 2005; Boyer 2013), to online content creation (Boellstorff 2008), labour has been widely discussed in empirical studies of media production. Such work has directed attention to the social context of media production, shedding light on the material conditions, professional standards, institutional structures, social relations and values, that shape media workplaces and that ultimately affect the content and meaning of media texts. Beyond media production labour, anthropologists have also explored the work of media consumption, with ethnographic observations of household media habits making valuable contributions to audience reception studies (Moores 1993; Horst 2012). Ethnographies of media labour have also drawn attention to the work involved in media distribution, from the exchange of photographic images (Edwards 2012) to the circulation of hard drives (Cearns 2021).

If production, consumption and distribution have been understood as key media processes, much less attention has been paid to maintenance, and to those who operate and fix media infrastructure. Data centres are essential to the storage, distribution and maintenance of internet media and require continuous upkeep to facilitate the "on-demand", "real-time" and "instant" access that characterises online consumption. A focus on data centres thus invites us to expand the scope of media labour to include the work of those who maintain media infrastructures. If end-users experience online consumption as a relatively smooth process, with content and services available at the click of a button, it is because a vast array of human workers, material infrastructure and extracted energy and resources support that process. A growing body of scholarly literature and investigative journalism is now exploring the invisible forms of labour that take place "behind the screens" of digital media economies, challenging popular perceptions that online services are driven primarily by automated and algorithmic labour.[2] The "human cloud" is a phrase that has been used to refer to the invisible human labourers that conduct work for cloud platforms (O'Connor 2018), such as the remote "click work" of crowdsourced (or "cloud-sourced") microwork platforms like Amazon Mechanical Turk, and the gig economy jobs generated by on-demand work platforms like Uber, Deliveroo, TaskRabbit, PeoplePerHour, Upwork, Freelancer and Fiverr. Scholarship on digital labour has drawn attention to the unseen workers whose labour produces the smooth-running experience of online services. Yet, while data centres underpin and enable these myriad forms of digital labour, the work that takes place in these buildings has largely remained absent from this literature. One of the key promises of a media-anthropological approach to cloud infrastructure lies in the attention an anthropological focus can direct towards the people and human labour of the data centre industry. This chapter thus aims to develop a more expansive understanding of the "human cloud" by bringing the work of those tasked with operating and maintaining data centres into discussions of digital labour.

The Transcendental Media Imaginary

Popular imaginaries of media technologies often turn around their immaterial and transcendental properties. Historians of communication have illustrated how imaginaries of transcendence over the material constraints of space, time and the human body have been central to understandings of modern media and communications technologies, from the electric telegraph, to the wireless radio, to the telephone (Carey 1989). The transcendental imaginary is certainly not limited to pre-digital communications. Digitisation is often presented as a process of dematerialisation. This was perhaps best characterised by MIT technologist Nicholas Negroponte (1995: 4), who famously described digitisation as a shift "from atoms to bits". As a system of interconnected digital computer networks, the internet, in particular, has been persistently dematerialised in popular discourses and imaginaries, often presented as an "electronic world", "cyberspace" or an "information superhighway" (Mosco 2004). Today the "cloud" metaphor continues this conceptual history of imagining the internet as an immaterial, weightless and ethereal nonplace.

Cultural commentators have noted that the metaphorical conceit of the cloud problematically presents online data storage as a transcendental and placeless operation (Carruth 2014; Taylor 2021a). This imaginary erases any sense of the physicality of the infrastructure and labour that underpin online services and, by extension, renders the geopolitical, social and environmental costs of cloud infrastructure largely invisible. As Arjun Appadurai and Neta Alexander (2020: 16) have observed of cloud computing companies: "the language of immateriality [is] often used to disguise their energy-consuming and environmentally destructive infrastructures". Often understood as sites where the cloud "touches the ground", data centres have surfaced as key buildings through which the materiality of the internet has been unpacked (Holt and Vonderau 2015; Amoore 2018). Data centres are resource-intensive enterprises. They require enormous amounts of electricity and water to power and cool the servers on which they store digital data (Hogan 2015). Their construction often greatly impacts the landscapes, ecologies and communities in which they are sited (Vonderau 2018; Johnson 2019; Brodie 2020). "Grounding the cloud" has become both a mantra and a method for problematising popular metaphors that present digital communications as immaterial and ethereal, often by directing attention to the politics of data centres and their impact on the geographies and communities amidst which they are built (Fard 2020).

This growing interest in the materiality of internet infrastructure has arisen against the backdrop of the "material turn" in media research. This has seen scholarly attention expand from the study of screened content towards the materialities of digital media technologies and their supporting infrastructures (Parks and Starosielski 2015). As Ramón Reichert and Annika Richterich (2015: 7–8) observe "Rather than looking at what happens on the screen and hence concentrating on the representative, accessible side of digital media, the focus shifts to what happens 'behind the screen'". Infrastructure, in particular, has emerged as a valuable ethnographic object and analytic through which scholars have grappled with the materialities of networked cultures. Rather than dismiss transcendental digital imaginaries, scholars of media infrastructure have paid attention to the work that such imaginaries enact in social worlds, approaching infrastructures as simultaneously material, discursive and imaginary.

Human labour has been recognised as a key component of the materiality of media infrastructure (Parks and Starosielski 2015; Roberts 2019). In the early 2000s, communications theorist Greg Downey (2001: 225) observed that studies of internet infrastructure often "fail to include most workers in the mix at all". Downey was writing against popular tendencies to dematerialise internet infrastructure. Today, internet labour issues are generating a tremendous amount of interest from scholars and journalists alike, drawing much-needed attention to the invisible workers of digital economies (Dyer-Witheford 2010; Fuchs and Sevignani 2013). Media exposés have highlighted the poor working conditions of those on the bottom rung of global tech, from those who work in Apple's assembly plants and Amazon's fulfilment centres, to the underpaid labourers (often in Asian countries) who spend their days "farming" resources in virtual worlds on behalf of wealthy gamers in the Global North (Chatfield 2010). Critical data studies scholars have problematised the claims of big data rhetoricians that position data as a "raw" resource that "can speak for itself" (Gitelman 2013), by foregrounding the scientific and technical human labour that goes into cleaning datasets prior to their insertion in the databases of big data science (Ribes and Jackson 2013; Irani 2015; Walford 2017; Plantin 2019). Others have investigated the ways in which online leisure activities, such as live-streaming and content creation, convert the play of users into a form of unremunerated labour ("playbour") by generating value for big tech organisations (Terranova, 2000; Ritzer and Jurgenson, 2010; Goggin 2011). The labour of social media content moderation has also been investigated, tracing the often-traumatic work involved in screening and removing offensive material posted online (Gillespie 2018; Roberts 2019). Studies of "digital labour" now cover a diverse array of work practices in the digital economy.[3] As Jarrett (2020) observes, the concept of "digital labour" now spans an array of phenomena, ranging from "digital transformations of paid work, to creative labor in digital media industries, to the exploitation of user data, to mineral extraction, manufacturing, and electronic waste disposal" (see also Jarrett 2022). Together, scholarship on digital labour has shown that, despite hype surrounding automation, robotics and algorithmic processing, human labour remains a key component of digital capitalism.

The People in the Cloud

Without data centres many of these forms of digital labour would not be possible. The connectivity, apps and access to large data sets that these buildings facilitate, enable the data-driven labour landscapes of the digital economy. Yet little attention has been directed to the work that goes into operating, maintaining and servicing the data centre infrastructure that supports the datafication and digitisation of labour. In much the same way that digital work, such as social media content moderation, may appear automated at the user-end, data centres themselves are often represented as automated data spaces rather than workplaces. In popular media and industry marketing materials, data centres are typically depicted as machinic worlds full of futuristic computing equipment and flashing server lights, with few, if any, humans in sight (Taylor 2019). These corporate visual communications generate a vision of the data centre as a technological "world without us". Relatedly, the term "infrastructure", which is often used to conceptualise data centres (and which I also use in this chapter), tends to conjure an image of technical systems or nodes, rather than buildings in which people work. But infrastructures are also worksites. While data centres, as buildings, may not immediately be associated with media industries labour (unlike, say, the newspaper publishing houses, film and broadcasting studios, or other monumental buildings of media organisations [Ericson and Riegert 2010; Wallace 2012; Evans 2022]), they are now vital sites of media distribution and maintenance work, with data centre professionals responsible for ensuring that online content reaches its audiences.

To be sure, these buildings are primarily designed for machines, rather than humans. This was highlighted during a data centre management training programme I attended. The course instructor explained that

> the data centre is not a people space. This needs to be made clear up front as it can lead to serious consequences and costs if it is overlooked. The primary aim must always be to support the IT assets which, in turn, support the business need.
>
> Taylor and Velkova 2021: 295

For this reason, Kate Jacobson and Mél Hogan (2019) have described the working environment of the data centre as "hostile" to human labour. The structural accommodations needed for the human labour force – the kitchens and toilets, the server aisles wide enough for maintenance staff to access – are often perceived by industry professionals as an inconvenient barrier to data centre optimisation because they reduce the space available for data compute and storage.

The question of human labour has not been neglected in critical studies of the data centre industry. Ethnographic work in regions where these buildings are being constructed has explored how negotiations and agreements to develop data centres are persistently tied to local hopes of regional rejuvenation, particularly in relation to promises of job creation for local working-class labour markets (Vonderau 2018; Johnson 2019; Burrell 2020; Mayer 2019). Asta Vonderau (2018) has explored how the construction of a Facebook data centre in Luleå, Sweden, was tightly entangled with municipal leaders' hopes for job creation. Ultimately, however, Vonderau (2018: 18) observes that the data centre resulted in a "lack of new jobs for locals". Rather than draw from the local labour pool, large tech firms often rely on contractual workers, or import staff from their Silicon Valley offices (Gray and Suri 2019). This is not always the case, as Julia Velkova (2020) has shown in her ethnography of a Yandex data centre in Finland, where she observes that most of the data centre's operators are "locals who live close by the facility" (Velkova 2020: 48).

In another ethnographic context, Alix Johnson (2019: 78) has traced how the development of the data centre industry in Iceland was similarly linked with anticipations for "new high-paying, high-prestige jobs for Icelanders" that never materialised. Elsewhere, Jenna Burrell (2020) has shown how, after the initial building work of a Facebook data centre in Prineville, Oregon, which temporarily provided some job opportunities for local construction workers, it was unclear exactly whether the local labour pool would benefit from the data centre in the

Figure 15.2 "The Cloud is a Lie", James Bridle (2011). Courtesy of the artist
Available online: https://jamesbridle.com/works/the-cloud-is-a-lie

long term. As Burrell (2020: 301) notes: "In Prineville, if one tries to project forward into the future, there are no certainties or stabilities around the question of data center jobs".

Accounts of the data centre industry in the popular press frequently describe these buildings as "cloud factories" (Glanz 2012; see also Cook 2011). However, the factory metaphor is typically invoked to highlight the environmental impact of the data centre industry, drawing a connection between the smoke-cloud-emitting chimney stacks of industrial capitalism and the polluting "cloud" arising from the data centres of digital capitalism, which often rely on fossil fuels to power their equipment (Figure 15.2).

While the factory metaphor does important work in drawing attention to the carbon relations in which the cloud is entangled, there are, as architectural historian Kazys Varnelis (2014) reminds us, "crucial differences between data centers and factories". In comparison to the factories of industrial capitalism, which were key drivers of economic growth through job creation, data centres typically employ a relatively small workforce in proportion to their size. Many data centres have in fact been retrofitted inside former factory buildings (Pickren 2018). However, in repurposing the ruins of industrial capitalism to service the needs of post-industrial digital capitalism, the labour relations of these sites have dramatically shifted (Jacobson and Hogan 2019). This is something that Graham Pickren (2018) has observed in his exploration of the data centre sector that has taken root in former printing and bread-making factories in Chicago's South Loop. Pickren (2018: 26) notes that, while the industrial factory buildings once brought many jobs to the area, in their repurposed form as data centres these buildings "do not employ many people". Commenting on the absence of workers in these buildings Pickren (2018: 26) asks: "If the data centre is the 'factory of the 21st century,' whither the working class?" Scholarship on data centre labour has thus often focused on the promises of job creation that accompany data centre development, and the lack of jobs that data centres provide, rather than the everyday work that takes place in these buildings after their construction. As such, the experiences and perspectives of data centre professionals who work in these spaces has been less often considered.

Cloud Pressure

GigaTech employ 26 people in their East London data centre. These people work across a range of technical, managerial and administrative positions. The team is headed by the Chief Technology Officer (CTO), to whom Antin, the facility Operations Manager, reports. There are seven service desk operators who work in an open-plan office on site and who are responsible for answering support tickets and telephone calls from clients, as well as conducting basic network administration functions. The sales and marketing team, which consists of three people, are also based in the office. There are three receptionists, the only females on site (aside from cleaners), who work in alternating ten-hour shifts, from 8 am to 6 pm. The East London facility is also staffed by a five-man team of security guards who rotate between night and day shifts. They monitor the perimeter of the facility, man guard posts and conduct clearance checks on visitors. There are six technicians who are responsible for installing, repairing and upgrading hardware and software, as well as conducting other basic operational necessities (Figure 15.3). They deal with reported faults and problems that are issued to them via the service desk team. In addition to the core workforce, there are a range of contractors (plumbers, electricians, janitors) who carry out routine cleaning and maintenance work, such as servicing fire alarms and HVAC systems. Aside from the receptionists and cleaners, the staff at GigaTech's East London data centre are all white males. The lack of diversity is not unique to GigaTech but is reflective of larger diversity issues that the industry faces (Judge 2018).

In an economic context that demands "always-on" access to cloud services, there is significant pressure on data centre operators to ensure their systems remain constantly available. For the managers, technicians and security teams who work in the cloud, the day-to-day job is characterised

Figure 15.3 A technician running diagnostic tests to ensure equipment is correctly functioning
Source: Photo by author.

by a state of anticipation for IT failure that could occur at any moment (Taylor 2021a). Their task is to avoid data loss and downtime. As tech journalist Rich Miller (2019a) reminds us, the data centre industry "was created to ensure that mission-critical applications never go offline". During my visit to GigaTech East, Antin explained to me that data centre professionals "always need to be prepared", highlighting that his work rarely stops because he must remain perpetually "on call" in case a failure event should occur. Antin, along with the technicians at GigaTech, uses mobile apps to remotely check the current service levels of the facility when not at the workplace. Data centre work does thus not only take place within the data centre but unfolds across multiple spatial and temporal scales. As Ned Rossiter (2016: 142) observes: "The 24/7 maintenance of servers, for instance, may combine onsite technicians with remote network operators residing in different time zones".

The daily pressure to ensure uninterruptible uptime is especially felt by the technicians who are responsible for installing, testing and servicing the IT equipment. During an interview with GigaTech technician Paul Bradford, who we met at the beginning of this chapter, he described his job as "stressful [because] so much depends on us [technicians] making sure nothing goes wrong". The technicians are one of the few groups of people in the data centre that have access to the server rooms. They spend a large portion of their day moving in and out of the server rooms, maintaining the computing equipment. Bradford explained that he enjoys the mobility of his role. "Most people assume IT guys spend their lives sitting at a computer desk", he said, "but if you work in a data centre, it's hard graft … lots of physical labour, lifting and moving equipment most days … it can be pretty back-breaking work". He explained that the worst part of the job was the night shifts. Like the security guards, the technicians work in shifts, ensuring that the site is manned 24-hours-a-day, all year round. Once or twice a week, depending on the rota, the technicians are required to work a night shift, which generally lasts from 7 pm to 7 am. The majority of a night shift is spent in the network operations centre, a large control room with a range of screens mounted to the walls, displaying power, cooling and network activity, as well as CCTV feeds. Every 90 minutes the technician must inspect the facility. They check the Uninterruptible Power Supply (UPS) rooms and the server rooms, as well as the generators outside the building to make sure they are set to "auto mode". This enables the generators to automatically detect and fix problems without requiring manual intervention (though, somewhat ironically, a member of staff must still be on site to regularly check auto mode is enabled).

During exceptional periods of anticipated service demand, the injunction to ensure uninterruptible service continuity has even led some data centres to invest in sleeping equipment for data centre staff who may have to work around the clock. During the 2012 Olympic Games the London-based data centre, Interxion, installed "sleeping pods" so its staff could remain on site (Miller 2012). More recently, during the Covid-19 pandemic, data centre staff were classed as "key workers" by a number of authorities (Judge 2020a). With schools and workplaces closed, data centre services enabled for a valuable degree of business and societal continuity as many organisations shifted to online remote working. The pressure to ensure uptime during an extended period of increased demand for digital services led some data centre providers to organise on-site sleeping and food supplies for staff. As one data centre provider highlighted, staff had to be prepared "to stay at the data center for a long period of time if need be" (Moss 2020). The requirement for data centre staff to continue working on site during the multiple lockdowns was a reminder that, when "uptime is mandatory" (Miller 2012) there can be no time off.

Antin highlighted that there is also little room for "time off" due to major staffing shortages that the industry is facing. Some industry insiders have suggested that job vacancies in the data centre industry now number 300,000 (Judge 2021). A 2021 report on data centre staff requirements, titled "The People Challenge" (Uptime Institute 2021), highlights the need to recruit and train a new generation of data centre workers, predicting that growing demand for cloud services "will exacerbate staffing shortages" (Uptime Institute 2021: 1), pushing data centre staff workloads to increasingly unsustainable levels. Indeed, a 2019 forecast highlighted that the work entailed in meeting consumer expectations for uninterruptible service delivery is testing "the endurance of key specialists" (Miller 2019b). Highlighting the exhausting levels of work involved, the forecast states that "There is a real risk that the level of activity causes burnout on your network team" (Miller 2019b). In a 2021 survey collecting feedback about the future of the data centre workforce, the pressure of ensuring uninterrupted uptime was identified as one feature that may deter young people from entering the industry, with the survey asking participants whether they agree that "The always-on urgency associated with data centers is off-putting to most graduates" (Data Center Dynamics 2021).

Caring for Data

When we centre the people that run cloud infrastructure, questions of maintenance inevitably rise. As Kate Jacobson and Mél Hogan (2019: 89) have observed, "the vast majority of work currently done in data centres is what would best be termed 'maintenance' labour". As a sphere of work, maintenance has been historically undervalued in cultures obsessed with technological novelty and "innovation" (Russell and Vinsel 2020). Media studies scholars and anthropologists have now begun to seriously engage with practices of maintenance and repair (Jackson 2014; Starosielski 2015; Mattern 2018). The work of data centre professionals plays an important but neglected role in the maintenance of online media cultures.

Data centre technicians loosely divide data centre maintenance into two temporal categories: "anticipatory" and "reactive". Reactive maintenance is work that takes place after an incident has occurred. This could be the work of a plumber repairing a broken air conditioner or efforts to diagnose a software bug that has disrupted service delivery. Despite efforts to anticipate downtime, disconnection and failure events invariably occur. Server maintenance, hacker-led server overloads due to DDoS attacks (see Parikka 2015) or surges in active users (e.g. when a new app launches or when content goes viral) can all result in service disruptions. These moments of connective disruption often materialise at the user-end in the form of loading screens, buffering icons or error messages. While data centres tend to exist at a remove from end-users, sometimes these error screens attempt to visualise data centre maintenance, providing non-technical end-users with a vague sense of their relationship to data centre staff (Figure 15.4).

In the data centre industry, significant time, money and energy is invested in efforts to anticipate breakdowns and thus avoid reactive maintenance labour. Anticipatory maintenance seeks to pre-empt downtime through a range of preparedness measures, such as regularly servicing generators, updating ventilation ductwork, ensuring that all redundant electrical components are frequently tested and in working order, and stress-testing equipment to make sure that it can operate under heavy or unexpected demand. The importance of stress-testing was highlighted by Bradford: "Before any new kit goes into our core we load it onto a test [server] rack to make sure that it doesn't crap out under duress, … this helps to avoid phone calls from concerned clients at 2 am in the morning". Another key practice of anticipatory maintenance is the retiring of servers before their mechanical parts begin to deteriorate. Despite marketing metaphors that present online data storage as a transcendental and immaterial operation, for data centre technicians like Bradford, digital storage media, like servers, are fragile material

Figure 15.4 LinkedIn's service disruption error screen visualises data centre server maintenance, providing users with a momentary hint of the labour and infrastructure that otherwise remains distant and unseen behind the screen

Source: Screenshot by author.

things that must be handled with care to ensure the data stored on them is not damaged or lost. Servers are upgraded roughly every twelve months in the data centre industry. A considerable part of data centre work thus involves regularly migrating data to new servers in an effort to ensure the terabytes of data stored on them remain accessible not only in the present but into the future (Taylor 2021b).

Through these anticipatory and reactive maintenance practices, data centre technicians enact a specific form of "care for the data" (Fortun and Fortun 2005: 47). This is a phrase that Kim Fortun and Mike Fortun have used in their fieldwork with toxicologists who work with large volumes of toxicogenomic data. Through the lens of "care" they describe the various ways that toxicologists strive to practice "good science" by ensuring the accuracy of their insights through careful analysis of the data made available to them. In the data centre industry, relations of care are enacted through the routine maintenance practices that aim to avoid data loss and ensure the uninterrupted delivery of cloud services – from handling hardware with care to carefully arranging cables in server cabinets.

While "care" is essential to data centre maintenance, human "carelessness" is considered a key vulnerability. Indeed, human error, rather than machine error, is often positioned in industry discourse as a leading cause of data centre downtime (Taylor 2019). Automation is widely seen to offer a means to reduce the vulnerabilities associated with human workers. In contrast to human operators that must be trained, paid, placed on call, and who may make mistakes, the automated data centre, decoupled from human labour, promises to "predict its own maintenance, diagnose its own errors, and implement its own recovery plan" (Munn 2020: 172). Faced with the growing pressures arising from understaffed data centres coupled with an increasing demand for always-on digital services, attempts to automate the monitoring and maintenance of data centres are now accelerating. A growing number of data centres are investing heavily in artificial intelligence (AI) and robotics, with the hope that intelligent nonhuman systems will eventually carry out technical tasks, such as removing and replacing faulty servers, that are currently conducted by human technicians (Burrell 2020: 299; Munn 2020: 172). In 2020, the data centre provider Switch announced that they were developing self-driving sentry robots to patrol their facilities (Judge 2020b). It is unclear whether this project ever materailised. Hyperlinks to the Switch sentry webpage no longer work, possibly suggesting that this attempt to automate the work of security guards failed.

While the development of fully automated, self-healing data centres may eventually reduce or eliminate jobs for human maintainers, for understaffed and overwhelmed technical departments in the present, these developments promise relief. As Antin told me: "Automation isn't being driven by the need to improve data centre efficiency but by staff shortages ... There's simply too much work to do and not enough people to do it".

Conclusion

Visions of AI-driven maintenance and "lights-out" or "dark" data centres (facilities in which no lights are needed because there are no human operators) are proliferating in the sector. At the moment, however, data centres remain, for the most part, largely reliant on human labour to function. Cleaners, contractors, receptionists, facility managers, disaster recovery officers, security guards, service desk operators, technicians and sales and marketing teams are just some of the people that run and maintain GigaTech's East London data centre. Data centres are enabling developments in algo-robotic automation, which threatens to render many high- and low-skilled jobs obsolete – perhaps including the work of data centre professionals themselves – but the human has yet to be completely removed from the loop.[4] The industry's continued reliance on human labour was made glaringly obvious throughout the sector during the Covid-19 pandemic. In a news article on the industry's response to the pandemic, one data centre provider highlighted the importance of on-site staff when it comes to delivering uninterruptible services, explaining that "essential operations staff" will remain "on-site to continue guaranteeing 100 percent uptime" (Moss 2020). The data centre provider emphasised that "We will always have someone [at the data centre], so if an immediate quarantine was called where no one can leave, there will be someone present ... There never is and never will be a moment when it goes completely unoccupied".

Anthropology's attunement to the human offers an understanding of data centres not as automated data spaces but as workplaces that are reliant on myriad forms of upkeep and maintenance. A media-anthropological focus on the labour of data centre workers draws attention to the importance of infrastructure maintenance as a critical form of media labour for online cultures, highlighting practices of maintenance as vital to the storage, circulation, preservation and distribution of internet media and communications services. While the circulation and consumption of online media is often described using the language of "flows" and "streams", it takes considerable work to make media flow smoothly. The work of data centre staff, along with the work of other media infrastructure maintainers, such as Wi-Fi engineers and fibre-optic cable engineers, facilitates the smooth flow of online media, cultivating the fiction of digital automation in the process. As Antin put it, "without us [data centre workers] the digital world stops". Through the often-exhausting work of regularly servicing, updating and upgrading servers and other IT equipment, data centre technicians aim to ensure that cloud services remain instantly and constantly available, ready to be accessed, streamed or downloaded at the click of a button, at any time. The goal is to render these services "uninterruptible", that is, to eliminate the possibility of a single moment when online services are not available. By extension, of course, this work serves to maintain the constant connectivity, voracious online consumption (the "binge-watching" and "infinite scrolling"), and continuous data extraction that characterises cloud capitalism.

Notes

1. All names have been changed to protect the privacy of the data centre professionals with whom I worked during the period of field research presented in this chapter.
2. This literature builds on a longstanding body of scholarship exploring the invisible labour of IT workers and service technicians (Orr 1996; Nardi and Engeström 1999; Star 1999; Downey 2001).
3. Given the sheer breadth of work activity that is now being brought together under the category of digital labour, some have questioned the meaningfulness of this umbrella term (Gandini 2021).
4. As Gavin Mueller (2021: 115) has stated, "automation never completely erases human labour".

References

Amoore, L. (2018) "Cloud Geographies: Computing, Data, Sovereignty", *Progress in Human Geography*, 42: 4–24.
Appadurai, A. and N. Alexander (2020) *Failure*, Cambridge: Polity Press.
Blanchette, J. (2015) "Introduction: Computing's Infrastructural Moment", in C.S. Yoo and J. Blanchette (eds), *Regulating the Cloud: Policy for Computing Infrastructure*, Cambridge, MA: MIT Press: 1–20.
Boellstorff, T. (2008) *Coming of Age in Second Life: An Anthropologist Explores the Virtually Human*, Princeton: Princeton University Press.
Born, G. (2005) *Uncertain Vision: Birt, Dyke and the Reinvention of the BBC*, London: Secker and Warburg.
Boyer, D. (2013) *The Life Informatic: Newsmaking in the Digital Era*, Ithaca, NY: Cornell University Press.
Brodie, P. (2020) "'Stuck in Mud in the Fields of Athenry': Apple, Territory, and Popular Politics", *Culture Machine*, 19: 1–34.
Burrell, J. (2020) "On Half-Built Assemblages: Waiting for a Data Center in Prineville, Oregon", *Engaging Science, Technology, and Society*, 6: 283–305.
Carruth, A. (2014) "The Digital Cloud and the Micropolitics of Energy", *Public Culture*, 26: 339–364.
Carey, J.W. (1989) *Communication as Culture: Essays on Media and Society*, Boston: Unwin Hyman.
Cearns, J. (2012) "Connecting (to) Cuba: Transnational Digital Flows between Havana and the Cuban Diaspora", *Cuban Studies*, 50: 161–185.
Chatfield, T. (2010) *Fun, Inc. Why Games are the 21st Century's Most Serious Business*, London: Virgin Books.
Cook, G. (2011) "How Dirty is Your Data?" available at www.greenpeace.org/international/Global/international/publications/climate/2011/Cool%20IT/dirty-data-report-greenpeace.pdf (accessed 23 October 2021).
Data Center Dynamics. (2021) "What is the Impact of the Skills Gap on the Data Center Industry?" available at: www.datacenterdynamics.com/en/whitepapers/the-impact-of-the-skills-gap-on-the-european-data-center-industry/ (accessed 21 October 2021).
Downey, G. (2001) "Virtual Webs, Physical Technologies, and Hidden Workers: The Spaces of Labor in Information Internetworks", *Technology and Culture*, 42(2): 209–235.
Dyer-Witheford, N. (2010) "Digital Labour, Species-becoming and the Global Worker", *Ephemera*, 10(3): 484–503.
Edwards, E. (2012) "Objects of Affect: Photography Beyond the Image", *Annual Review of Anthropology*, 41: 221–234.
Ericson, S. and Riegert, K. (2010) *Media Houses: Architecture, Media and the Production of Centrality*. New York: Peter Lang.
Evans, E. (2022) "Bricks, Mortar, and Media: Understanding the Media Industries through their Buildings", in P. McDonald (ed.), *The Routledge Companion to Media Industries*. London: Routledge: 212–222.
Fard, A. (2020) "Cloudy Landscapes: On the Extended Geography of Smart Urbanism", *Telematics and Informatics*, 55: 1–11.
Fortun, K. and Fortun, M. (2005) "Scientific Imaginaries and Ethical Plateaus in Contemporary U.S. Toxicology", *American Anthropologist*, 107(1): 43–54.
Fuchs, C. and Sevignani, S. (2013) "What Is Digital Labour? What Is Digital Work? What's Their Difference? And Why Do These Questions Matter for Understanding Social Media?" *tripleC: Communication, Capitalism & Critique*, 11(2): 237–293.

Gandini, A. (2021) "Digital Labour: An Empty Signifier?" *Media, Culture & Society*, 43(2): 369–380.
Gans, H.J. (1979) *Deciding What's News. A Study of CBS Evening News, NBC Nightly News, Newsweek and Time*, New York: Pantheon Books.
Gillespie, T. (2018) *Custodians of the Internet: Platforms, Content Moderation, and the Hidden Decisions that Shape Social Media*, New Haven, CT: Yale University Press.
Gitelman, L. (2013) *Raw Data is an Oxymoron*, Cambridge, MA: MIT Press.
Glanz, J. (2012) "The Cloud Factories: Power, Pollution and the Internet", *The New York Times*, 22 September, available at www.nytimes.com/2012/09/23/technology/data-centers-waste-vast-amounts-of-energy-belying-industry-image.html (accessed 16 October 2021).
Goggin, J. (2011) "Playbour, Farming and Leisure", *Ephemera*, 11(4): 357–368.
Golding, P. and Elliot, P. (1979) *Making the News*. London: Longman.
Graham, S and Thrift, N. (2007) "Out of Order: Understanding Repair and Maintenance", *Theory, Culture & Society*, 24(3): 1–25.
Gray, M.L. and Suri, S. (2019) *Ghost Work: How to Stop Silicon Valley from Building a New Global Underclass*, Boston, MA: Houghton Mifflin Harcourt.
Hogan, M. (2015) "Data Flows and Water Woes: The Utah Data Center", *Big Data & Society*, 2(2): 1–12.
Holt, J. and Vonderau, P. (2015) "'Where the Internet Lives': Data Centers as Cloud Infrastructure", in L. Parks and N. Starosielski (eds), *Signal Traffic: Critical Studies of Media Infrastructures*, Urbana, IL: University of Illinois Press: 71–93.
Horst, H.A. (2012) "New Media Technologies in Everyday Life", in H.A. Horst and D. Miller (eds) *Digital Anthropology*, London: Berg: 39–60.
Irani, L. (2015) "Justice for 'Data Janitors'", available at www.publicbooks.org/justice-for-data-janitors/ (accessed 6 October 2021).
Jarrett, K. (2022) *Digital Labor*, Cambridge: Polity.
Jarrett, K. (2020) "Digital Labor", in K. Ross, I. Bachmann, V. Cardo, S. Moorti and C.M. Scarcelli (eds), *The International Encyclopedia of Gender, Media, and Communication*, available at https://onlinelibrary.wiley.com/doi/full/10.1002/9781119429128.iegmc008 (accessed 3 October 2021).
Jackson, S.J. (2014) "Rethinking Repair", in T. Gillespie, P.J. Boczkowski and K.A. Foot (eds), *Media Technologies: Essays on Communication, Materiality, and Society*, Cambridge, MA: MIT Press: 221–240.
Jacobson, K and Hogan, M. (2019) "Retrofitted Data Centres: A New World in the Shell of the Old", *Work Organisation, Labour and Globalisation*, 13(2): 78–94.
Johnson, A. (2019) "Data Centers as Infrastructural Inbetweens", *American Ethnologist*, 46: 75–88.
Judge, P. (2018) "Diversity Won't Solve Itself", available at www.datacenterdynamics.com/en/opinions/diversity-wont-solve-itself/ (accessed 23 September 2021).
Judge, P. (2020a) "Data Center Staff Classed As 'Essential' During Pandemic", available at www.datacenterdynamics.com/en/news/data-center-staff-classed-essential-during-pandemic/ (accessed 12 October 2021).
Judge, P. (2020b) "Switch plans to launch security robots for data centers", available at www.datacenterdynamics.com/en/news/switch-plans-launch-security-robots-data-centers/ (accessed 20 September 2021).
Judge, P. (2021) "Data Centers Need to Find 300,000 More Staff by 2025", available at www.datacenterdynamics.com/en/news/data-centers-need-find-300000-more-staff-2025/ (accessed 15 September 2021).
Mattern, S (2018) "Maintenance and Care", available at https://placesjournal.org/article/maintenance-and-care/ (accessed 6 October 2021).
Mayer, V. (2019) "The Second Coming: Google and Internet Infrastructure", *Culture Machine*, 18: 1–10.
Miller, R. (2012) "Interxion Readies Staff 'Sleeping Pods' for Olympics", available at www.datacenterknowledge.com/archives/2012/04/12/interxion-readies-staff-sleeping-pods-for-olympics (accessed 4 October 2021).
Miller, R. (2019a) "Rethinking Redundancy: Is Culture Part of the Problem?" available at https://datacenterfrontier.com/rethinking-redundancy-is-culture-part-of-the-problem/ (accessed 4 September 2021).
Miller, R. (2019b) "The Eight Trends That Will Shape the Data Center Industry in 2019", available at https://datacenterfrontier.com/the-eight-trends-that-will-shape-the-data-center-industry-in-2019/ (accessed 3 September 2021).
Moores, S. (1993) *Interpreting Audiences: The Ethnography of Media Consumption*, London: Sage.
Mosco, V. (2004) *The Digital Sublime: Myth, Power, and Cyberspace*. Cambridge, MA: MIT Press.

Moss, S. (2020) "Italy's Coronavirus Lockdown: The View from SuperNAP", available at www.datacenterdynamics.com/en/analysis/italys-coronavirus-lockdown-the-view-from-supernap/ (accessed 3 October 2021).

Mueller, G (2021) *Breaking Things at Work: Why the Luddites Were Right About Why You Hate Your Job*. London: Verso.

Munn, L. (2020) "Injecting Failure: Data Center Infrastructures and the Imaginaries of Resilience", *The Information Society*, 36(3): 167–176.

Nardi, B. and Engeström, Y. (1999) "A Web on the Wind: The Structure of Invisible Work", *Computer Supported Cooperative Work* (CSCW), 8: 1–8.

Negroponte, N. (1995) *Being Digital*, New York: Knopf.

O'Connor, S (2018) "The Human Cloud", *Financial Times*, 30 October, available at www.ft.com/content/5fe8991e-dc2a-11e8-8f50-cbae5495d92b (accessed 12 September 2021).

Orr, J.E. (1996) *Talking About Machines: An Ethnography of a Modern Job*. Ithaca and London: Cornell University Press.

Parikka, J. (2015) "Denials of Service", in I. Kaldrack and M. Leeker (eds), *There is No Software, There are Just Services*. Lüneburg: Meson Press: 103–111.

Parks, L. and Starosielski, N. (2015) *Signal Traffic: Critical Studies of Media Infrastructures*. Urbana, IL: University of Illinois Press.

Pickren, G. (2018) "The Factories of the Past are Turning into the Data Centers of the Future", *Imaginations: Journal of Cross-Cultural Image Studies*, 8(2): 22–29.

Powdermaker, H. (1950) *Hollywood, the Dream Factory*, Boston: Grosset and Dunlap.

Plantin, J. (2019) "Data Cleaners for Pristine Datasets: Visibility and Invisibility of Data Processors in Social Science", *Science, Technology, & Human Values*, 44(1): 52–73.

Reichert, R. and Richterich, A. (2015) "Introduction. Digital Materialism", *Digital Culture & Society*, 1(1): 5–17.

Ribes, D. and Jackson, S.J. (2013) "Data Bite Man: The Work of Sustaining a Long-Term Study", in L. Gitelman (ed.), *"Raw Data" is an Oxymoron*. Cambridge, MA: MIT Press: 146–166.

Ritzer, G. and Jurgenson, N. (2010) "Production, Consumption, Prosumption: The Nature of Capitalism in the Age of the Digital 'Prosumer'", *Journal of Consumer Culture*, 10(1): 13–36.

Roberts, S.T. (2019) *Behind the Screen: Content Moderation in the Shadows of Social Media*. New Haven: Yale University Press.

Rossiter, N. (2016) *Software, Infrastructure, Labour: A Media Theory of Logistical Nightmares*. London: Routledge.

Russell, A.L. and Vinsel, L. (2020) *The Innovation Delusion: How Our Obsession with the New Has Disrupted the Work that Matters Most*. New York: Random House.

Schlesinger, P. (1978) *Putting "Reality" Together: BBC News*. London: Constable.

Star, S.L. (1999) "The Ethnography of Infrastructure", American Behavioral Scientist, 43(3): 377–391.

Starosielski, N (2015) *The Undersea Network*. Durham, NC: Duke University Press.

Taylor, A.R.E. (2019) "The Data Centre as Technological Wilderness", *Culture Machine*, 18: 1–30.

Taylor, A.R.E. (2021a) "Standing by for Data Loss: Failure, Preparedness and the Cloud", *Ephemera*, 21(1): 59–93.

Taylor, A.R.E. (2021b) "Future-proof: Bunkered Data Centres and the Selling of Ultra-secure Cloud Storage", *Journal of the Royal Anthropological Institute*, 26(S1): 76–94.

Taylor, A.R.E. and Velkova, J. (2021) "Sensing Data Centres", in N. Klimburg-Witjes, N. Poechhacker and G.C. Bowker (eds), *Sensing In/Securities: Sensors as Transnational Security Infrastructures*. Manchester: Mattering Press: 287–298.

TechUK. (2014) "Data Centre Publications", available at www.techuk.org/insights/reports/item/1858-data-centre-publications (accessed 6 September 2021).

Terranova, T. (2000) "Free Labor: Producing Culture for the Digital Economy", *Social Text*, 18(2): 33–58.

Tuchman, G. (1991) "Qualitative Methods in the Study of News", in K.B. Jensen and N. Jankowski (eds), *A Handbook of Qualitative Methodologies for Mass Communication Research*. London: Routledge: 93–106.

Uptime Institute. (2021) "The People Challenge: Global Data Center Staffing Forecast 2021-2025", available at https://uptimeinstitute.com/global-data-center-staffing-forecast-2021-2025 (accessed 3 September 2021).

Varnelis, K. (2014) "Eyes That Do Not See: Tracking the Self in the Age of the Data Center", *Harvard Design Magazine*, 38, available online www.harvarddesignmagazine.org/issues/ 38/eyes-that-do-not-see-tracking-the-self-in-the-age-of-the-data-center (accessed 12 October 2021).

Velkova, J. (2020) "The Art of Guarding the Russian Cloud: Infrastructural Labour in a Yandex Data Centre in Finland", *Digital Icons: Studies in Russian, Eurasian and Central European New Media*, 20: 47–63.

Vonderau, A. (2018) "Technologies of Imagination: Locating the Cloud in Sweden's Global North", *Imaginations: Journal of Cross-Cultural Image Studies*, 8(20): 8–21.

Walford, A. (2017) "Raw Data: Making Relations Matter", *Social Analysis*, 61(2): 65–80.

Wallace, A. (2012) *Media Capital: Architecture and Communications in New York City*. Urbana: University of Illinois Press.

16
MEDIA ANTHROPOLOGY AND EMERGING TECHNOLOGIES

Re-working Media Presence

Sarah Pink, Yolande Strengers, Melisa Duque, Larissa Nichols, and Rex Martin

Emerging technologies have implications for all domains of life, including our homes, mobilities, and health. They are part of how our future lives are imagined in media, industry, and policy narratives in the form of, for instance, smart homes, self-driving cars or digital health devices. Increasingly automated and connected technologies and systems form part of the sensorial and material media ecologies of both the present and imagined futures. Emerging technologies, the digital data they produce and use, and the automated systems they participate in involve new modes of materiality, mediated communication, content, and connection with third parties. These evolve and shift our relationships with existing media and communications technologies in the present and anticipated futures. For example, in the present, there are existing opportunities to dialogue with and make purchases suggested by Google Home voice assistants, such as subscriptions to paid online music channels. In imagined futures, self-driving car pods or other future mobilities devices may involve algorithms which will decide on and make available personalised news or advertising content based on passengers' digital profiles.

Given these shifts, empirical research in media anthropology needs to accommodate a world where everyday life with media includes how we live with new automated and connected technologies, the material devices through which they are manifested, the predictive data analytics they involve, and the anticipatory modes through which people engage with them. This chapter demonstrates an approach to media anthropology through which these questions might be investigated. Theoretically rooted in phenomenological anthropology, the chapter shows how attention to the experiential dimensions of the presence of media leads us to new insights concerning how people live with emerging technologies. It argues for an applied media anthropology through which the insights of such work might inform smart technology design, and thus participate in the processes through which new technologies emerge in everyday life.

To develop this, we build on Sarah Pink and Kerstin Leder Mackley's (2013) argument that by the second decade of the twentieth century everyday life with media in home environments was shifting. At this time, much existing work had accounted for how people experienced media in homes (Morley 1986, 2000, Couldry and Markham 2008) constituting what was referred to as "media life" (Deuze 2012), which was saturated by media content. Pink and

Leder Mackley showed how in addition to the proliferation of media content in everyday life, a new experiential layer of "media presence" had come about in the form of the diversified statuses and standby modes that complicated on/off binaries. This meant that it was not only media content that mattered in the home but that, additionally, the material and sensory presence of media and technologies being "on" had become part of everyday domestic environments and routines. In this chapter we update this concept of media presence in such a way that accounts for emerging intelligent and smart home technologies. In 2013, Pink and Leder Mackley showed how people engaged and improvised with media presence to create home environments that would "feel right" to them (2013: 689). Here we show how, in 2020, people engaged with the new modes of media presence associated with smart home technologies.

We draw on the ethnographic example of older people's experiences of living with smart home technologies in regional Australia. Our ethnography revealed how new modes of media communication with voice assistants, use of media content from Google, and the continuous presence, and possibility of activation of these technologies were experienced and anticipated in everyday life. We examine how relationships between media content, communication and presence, are reconfigured through the modes of sensory and affective presence and anticipation associated with smart tech, data, and automation and how they participate in the constitution of the feeling of home. This has two layers of implications: first, it demands a theoretical and methodological framework which engages media anthropology more closely with emerging technologies; second, it develops an applied or interventional research agenda.

We use the term emerging technologies to refer to devices that are technologically possible, but might not have entered markets, or reached their full intended or desired market. The example of smart home technologies discussed here refers to the latter, since the technologies trialled by our participants are commercially available, but not established as everyday technologies amongst older people. The applied objective of our research was to identify where smart home technologies could benefit older people, by supporting their wellbeing and independence.

In what follows we: outline the shifting theoretical, methodological, and technological context that frames our research; explain our ethnographic research process; discuss the experiences of two participants to demonstrate these new modes of smart home technology and media presence; and reflect on the implications of our findings for an applied media anthropology.

Shifting Modes of Media and Technological Presence

In the first decades of the twenty-first century non-media-centric media studies (Moores 2012, Couldry 2012) revealed how media content was used in homes (Couldry and Markham 2008) and how the smartphone became embedded in routines of communication invoking shared human presence (Wilken and Goggin 2012: 16). Media anthropology scholarship added a material culture focus (Miller and Horst 2012). It also generated insights into how digital media and technologies were becoming entangled with everyday routines through which the home was ongoingly reconstituted and maintained, entailing new modes of non-binary and often continuous media presence (Pink and Leder Mackley 2013). For instance, media content was attached to particular feelings of home, such as the atmosphere needed for people to fall sleep – ranging from classical music to TV shows involving car chases. However, media presence, and the anticipation that technologies would be activated, played a further role, for instance, in the constitution of the night time home, which might involve: charging mobile or smartphones; the waiting alarm clock; the WiFi that was never off; leaving technologies on standby; needing to switch off devices "at the wall" so they would feel "right" (as in electrically safe) at bed time; or keeping a landing light on at night. Pink and Leder Mackley developed a three-stranded approach to media in everyday life in the home, through distinct analytical prisms, each of which drew on recent "turns" in social theory: "environment/place; movement/practice; perception/sensory embodied experience" (Pink and Leder Mackley 2013: 683). An ethnographic focus on the routines of everyday life – the familiar and repeated but never absolutely identical activities that people perform and sense as they move through their domestic environments – created insights across these three strands. Theoretically the strands were interrelated through the assumption based in phenomenological anthropology that people, media and technologies are all moving co-constituents of shared everyday environments, with which we engage through sensory, affective, performative dimensions of everyday digital media experience.

Subsequent research has analysed participants' sensory and affective relations with technologies through a futures anthropological focus by engaging the anticipatory concepts of trust and anxiety (Pink, Lanzeni, and Horst 2018), far future concepts of hope and aspiration to explore how mundane futures with digital technologies are imagined (Pink and Postill 2019), and social practice imaginaries (Strengers, Pink, and Nicholls 2019). This body of work highlights how different modes of anticipation are experienced and articulated in everyday life encounters with digital media, technologies, and data. It reinforces the significance of routine and everyday improvisation in securing a sense of "ontological security". That is, by obscuring or alleviating anxieties in the context of everyday futures that are ultimately uncertain, but can be made to feel familiar – such as through data saving routines (Pink, Lanzeni, and Horst 2018).

The implication of this work is that new technologies, media, and data are incorporated into everyday life in homes, in ways that follow similar patterns to earlier technologies. Anthropologists have explained such phenomena through theories of appropriation (Miller 1988), or exaptation (concerning the refinement of things in use) (Ingold 1997). Digital futures anthropology (Pink 2021) advances this in two ways. First, by focusing on the processual and unfinished nature of digital materiality (Pink, Ardevol, and Lanzeni 2016), where the digital and material are inseparable, and part of the same artefact, environment or experience. Second, through its commitment to concepts of emergence (Smith and Otto 2016), contingency (Bessire and Bond 2014, Irving 2017), and improvisation in uncertainty (Akama, Pink, and Sumartojo 2018). These concepts belong to a processual theoretical rendering of the world, echoed in recent media phenomenology, through emphasis on "the experience of everyday digital life" (Markham 2020: 1). This approach understands contingency as a background to the improvisatory actions through which people feel at home (Markham 2020).

This emphasis on contingency and improvisation in anthropology and subsequently in media studies represents a processual and phenomenological disposition in media anthropology itself and its disciplinary constituents. It invites us to consider how emerging technologies, the contingency they introduce, the improvisatory stances through which people engage with them, and how anticipatory feelings (e.g. trust, anxiety, hope and aspiration) are entangled in emerging home-based media ecologies. These considerations therefore underpin our discussion of how the *content*, *communication*, and *presence* associated with emerging technologies and media, are implicated in the contingent circumstances of everyday life.

Interventional Ethnography

Our project was undertaken in partnership with McLean Care, a not-for-profit health care provider, and Deakin University's CADET Virtual Reality Training and Simulation Research Lab. The project aimed to gain new understanding of the wellbeing and independent living benefits these households gained from their participation in a six-month trial of new technologies, including the Google Home voice assistant, smart kettles, smart lighting, and automated (robotic) vacuum cleaners. The project involved teamwork on two levels; both as an interdisciplinary collaboration with the technical team, and within our social science and design team. Because our ethnographic work was developed within the particular interventional circumstances of an applied and trial-based project, this created possibilities for us to directly focus on the anticipatory modes through which participants experienced the technology.

In 2020 we undertook intensive fieldwork with 33 older Australians aged between 73 and 93, and living across 22 separate households in towns in rural and regional New South Wales. We took a team ethnography approach to this project, with five of us undertaking varying amounts of fieldwork, sharing our materials and all being involved in the analysis and writing up. Our analysis was undertaken jointly with two Deakin University technical colleagues to, where possible, match their quantitative data regarding the use and commands given to the technologies with our qualitative materials. In this chapter we concentrate on the ethnographic findings.

Our ethnographic methods built on video tour and re-enactment methods developed for research into everyday digital media and smart home technologies (e.g. Pink et al., 2017, Strengers and Nicholls, 2018). These were adjusted to focus on participants' experiences of the smart home technology trial intervention. They were designed to enable researchers access to participants' everyday lives and worlds and to reveal otherwise invisible aspects of their spoken and performative experiences of using the devices.

Our research was undertaken in three stages. The first stage involved video and audio recorded face-to-face encounters with participants in their homes (Figure 16.1). We began

Figure 16.1 Edna participating in the video tour of her home during the first stage of our research with Sarah and Melisa

Source: Video still from *Smart Homes for Seniors* (Pink dir. 2021) by Sarah Pink. Copyright: Emerging Technologies Research Lab.

Figure 16.2 Bob, Edna's husband participating in the online ethnography during the final stage of our research with Sarah and Melisa

Source: Video still from *Smart Homes for Seniors* (Pink dir. 2021) by Sarah Pink. Copyright Emerging Technologies Research Lab.

with interviews in a comfortable part of the home chosen by the participant – such as the kitchen table or living room – to cover a checklist of questions around participants' experiences and definitions of wellbeing and independence, and their experiences and future hopes for the smart home devices. They then took us on a tour of their homes to show us where the devices were situated, when appropriate demonstrating how they accessed content, communicated with and through the devices, and their experiences of each device's presence. We next spent time with the technical team member, as participants discussed challenges they had experienced and learned to use the technologies in ways that supported their needs. On leaving we invited participants to keep diaries of their experiences for our follow-up meetings. The second stage was a short keeping-in-touch phone call. This stage was undertaken in the context of the 2020 COVID-19 pandemic, which was also to frame the following stage of our research. The third fieldwork stage (Figure 16.2) was originally planned as a face-to-face home video ethnography visit. However, due to the COVID-19 restrictions was undertaken remotely using digital tools including mobile phones and tablets for voice and video calls. We reflected with participants both on their own experiences and how they imagined the technologies might participate in their own and other people's futures.

Content, Communication, and Presence

We now outline the modes of content, communication, and presence associated with the smart home technologies our participants experienced and our insights regarding how they engaged with them, in relation to existing research. In the following section we bring this to life by situating these experiences through the ethnographic stories of two households.

Our participants already accessed media content from material and sensory sources including television, radio and newspapers, and social media accessed through their iPads or computers, similar to earlier studies of digital media use in homes in the UK and Australia (Pink et al. 2017, Pink et al. 2018). The introduction of the Google Home voice assistant offered new ways of accessing and experiencing media content such as news, music, and weather information through the material devices and voice commands. For instance, single automated commands, such as "Good Morning Google", could activate a sequence of content delivery such as local weather and news, the date and time, and scheduled diary activities. Such content delivery became part of participants' routines, as they learned when and how to use the Google Home device. However, the use of these services did not completely replace other media content. Rather they augmented and supplemented existing news, weather, and music provision from existing sources and technologies, contributing to the multiplication of complementary devices in the home which earlier studies have found (Røpke, Christensen, and Jensen 2010) and provided additional "small conveniences" (Strengers and Nicholls 2017, Nicholls and Strengers 2019) in accessing new forms of content. The services were also limited in some ways. Sometimes Google Home's search identified paid content which could only be accessed if the participants subscribed to the sites and services that provided it. As Groot and Costera (2019) note, existing research already suggests that smart technologies introduce different modes of agency to "request, demand, allow, encourage, discourage, and refuse" actions (David and Chouinard 2016). Participants thus also came into contact with a mediated world of not only new content, but of blockages and inequalities.

The smart home technologies also introduced new possibilities for learning and engaging in new modes of communication. Living with the Google voice assistant, which participants gendered as "her" in line with the device's default feminine voice, involved learning to use new command-based communications. Most participants appreciated the voice command options. However, communication issues were frequently reported. For instance, when participants told us that Google Home did not appear to understand or seemed to misinterpret their commands, (as is common for voice assistants – see Schönherr et al. 2020), or would respond when not required. Some participants found Google "herself" difficult to follow and struggled to understand if her speech was too fast or the volume too low. However, over time, by interacting with Google, participants learned new modes of communication that complied with the "command-based speech" common to voice assistants (e.g. "find x", "play x") who need to be clearly directed to perform specific tasks following statement of their "wake words" or words that activate a device, such as "hey Google" (Schiller and McMahon, 2019). This directed and redirected what they could ask Google to do, and how they could ask. As participants learned to live with the new presence of the voice assistant, additionally new modes of personal communication also emerged. In media and communication studies the concept of "digital intimacy" is used to denote intimacy experienced through digital social media apps and platforms. This includes, for instance, the private intimacy of texting as well as public shows of intimacy by YouTubers (Andreassen, Nebeling Petersen, and Harrison 2017; Dobson, Carah, and Robards 2018).

Our ethnography revealed how new kinds of digital intimacy can come about through communication with smart technologies. Participants already used a range of communications technologies which were implicated in their intimate relationships with others, including smartphones, simpler mobile phones, landlines, email, social media messaging, and the VitalCall necklace for emergencies. Additionally, during the COVID-19 pandemic lockdown period the "Google Nest Hub Max" tablet was introduced to the households and set up for participants to make video calls. This opened up new opportunities for digital intimacy through audio and visual communication with loved ones during isolation. The Google Home assistant added the possibility of joking dialogues with Google herself. The device was also sometimes embroiled in domestic disputes and discussions, where she was enlisted as a "third party" to provide authoritative or definitive advice on a particular matter or issue under question, similar to a third person being called in to settle a family debate. This inspired participants to reflect on the social etiquette or "manners", as they put it, which they felt were appropriate when communicating with her. Many participants struggled with command-based speech without polite additions, such as "please" and "thank you", seeking to avoid being rude to Google Home. Command-based speech was therefore complicated by participants' anthropomorphising of the Google Home device as she/her and the robotic vacuum cleaner which was identified as both he/him and she/her and given a variety of names.

Human and gendered characterisations of the devices led participants to engage with them in gendered ways, and to attempt to treat them politely and respectfully, in line with the social mores and gestures common to older Australians. Indeed, such findings reflect the anthropomorphising of social robots, voice assistants, and other AI that take on the physical embodiment of human or other identifiable forms, have autonomous mobility, and/or an ability to perform social behaviours (Darling 2016). Existing research shows that such attributes make people more likely to treat these technologies as "friends", or other familiar human roles, such as those of wives, housekeepers, servants or butlers (Sorrell 2017, Strengers and Kennedy 2020). Thus, as present, and as participants, in these intimate spheres of life, voice assistants can be seen as helping to constitute new modes of digital intimacy, which are embedded in the specificities of everyday life as lived through particular relationships and circumstances.

In research undertaken a decade earlier, we saw how standby and other modes which challenged the binaries of on/off (Pink and Leder Mackley 2013) were generating a new media presence in everyday life in the home. Smart home technologies, which are "always on" have a markedly different way of being present. The technological, material and sensory, and media presence of the smart devices did not overly worry participants or lead them to withdraw from the trial. Instead they experienced, sensed, and represented concerns relating to: the materiality of the large black "box" that accompanied the devices (the black box ensured their connectivity and links to the tech team but disrupted participants' homes spatially and aesthetically); whether their private conversations were listened to by the technologies; impact on their electricity use and bills; and about being unable to re-start the system if it went off and being unable to switch power sources off at night or when going on a trip. These concerns broadly reflect privacy, security, and cost concerns identified in other ethnographic and qualitative studies of smart home technologies (e.g. Hargreaves and Wilson, 2017, Jensen et al. 2018, Strengers et al. 2019). However, additionally for our older participants, the technological presence during the trial period was inseparable from the technology support and research team. Thus, the technological and media presence was entangled with human presence in multiple ways, ranging from: the support humans who are co-engaged with the technology; the human design of algorithms for automated technologies; and the digital intimacy of communications with close others through technologies.

Bringing the Experience of Smart Home Technologies to Life

Above we have outlined how new modes of content, communication, and presence came about as smart technologies and media were embedded in the social material and sensory environments of participants' homes. We now draw on the experiences of two households to show how this was experienced within the contingent circumstances of everyday life and the digital intimacies this entailed. Here, content, communication, and presence are much more entangled than in the wider analysis reported on in the last section. We emphasise that we do not intend these two examples as representative of all participants but note that participants' experiences, such as of joking or playing music with Google, concerns about privacy and questions around switching technologies off, resonated across our sample (see for example Duque et al. 2021, Pink 2021). In this section we both introduce the specificities of the participants' homes and experiences and structure our discussion according to the key questions of content, communication, and presence.

When we visited them, Edna and Bob were in their eighties and living independently in their own spacious one-floor family home with Cheeky, their cockatoo. Their home was filled with the things of a lifetime, and photos of their children and grandchildren. Edna was active at home and in her community, cooking, cleaning, and caring for her home with the help of a fortnightly service, knitting and checking Facebook about once a day for family and her musical and religious interests. Edna agreed to be part of the trail because "Why not?", thinking it was a survey. She was surprised and daunted when so much equipment was installed, but even though her daughter-in-law had suggested that she should give it back because she didn't need it, she decided to continue.

The ongoing technological presence of Google Home and the content it made available introduced positive new spatial and sensory encounters. Edna showed us her joy in asking Google to play her favourite music, while she made her bed. Like other participants, she and Bob also had fun joking with Google, in gendered ways, as they told us together:

BOB: I said to her one day, "Are you married? … Are you married?"
EDNA: and she said, "I'm in a relationship" [laughing].

However, sometimes communicating with Google Home created challenges since the technology was rule-bound and difficult to use when the voice commands were not correctly given. Edna and Bob did not always remember the exact form of the "Hey" command, and Edna found the commands themselves to be ill mannered, as she put it:

> I think that's rude to say, "Hey Google". I'd rather say, "Excuse me, Google. Could you do this?", but because that's how it's set, that's how it has to be. … . I'd never say, "Hey" … It's not comfortable … I mean that's foreign. I don't ever even say to Bob, "Hey, come in here", unless I'm very cross.

There were several ways that the presence of the technology created uncertainty: the cables went down the back of Edna's oven, which she now didn't use in case it was unsafe; her kitchen surface was cluttered with the voice assistant and buttons; she wanted to switch the technology off during a planned trip away from home, but feared it would not work again when she switched it back on; and worried about "What's this going to do to our power bill?"

The presence of the technology ensured immediate access to content, but shifted the auditory environment of the home. Edna told us

> We just act normal because there's nothing we say or do or anything, it doesn't matter to anybody because we're not coming out and saying this shouldn't be happening and that shouldn't be happening or whatever. If I yell at him and Madam here listening, well, so be it. [laughter].

Edna and Bob were in fact careful about what they said. The idea that "she" might be listening to them was a concern in case they accidentally gave a command to Google. Simultaneously, the sound of Google and their commands became integrated into the domestic soundscape.

As such, Edna's home became a socio-technically active space in a number of ways. Her and Bob's relationships with the technologies, including Google Home, shifted the feel of home and required them to learn to live in relation to contingencies shaped by the smart home technologies. As our research unfolded so did the complexities that surrounded the use of different technologies. For instance, Edna explained how the automated vacuum cleaner might start on its own, necessitating action where other things and species – Cheeky the cockatoo and Edna's doll collection – must be protected. Cheeky was hidden behind the larger oven, and Edna imagined that a broomstick could be placed in front of the dolls to prevent the vacuum cleaner getting too close. Another example involved the smart kettle, which was activated by voice command but only used when visitors came (including our visit), as it was too large for only two cups of tea and too heavy for Edna to lift when full.

Such contingencies played out in the lives of all of our participants. Some brief insights from the experiences of Ernest, who lived with his wife in their one-storey home, offer further examples. For Ernest a highlight of the ongoing presence of the smart technologies was the medication light, which was connected to his kitchen cupboard and reminded him to take his medication. He explained how:

> It's set up in this cupboard. It's got a sensor up there and as soon as you open it, the light comes on. So I've got it set for six, twelve and six [o'clock] so it'll come on and tell you to open and shut the door. It stays on. See the sensor up there, up to there? So when I shut the door it should go off. You see that? Terrific, isn't it?

When we asked how it helped him he told us that:

> It reminds me [laughing]. Because I have forgotten, especially the lunchtime one. Every now and again I've missed out on the night one and it's fairly important for my heart. I can be lying there awake with heart trouble and I don't put two and two together. Sometimes I do.

Ernest was more experienced with technology and software than Edna and Bob, but found the technical support team's troubleshooting – such as their modifications to the "sensitivity" of Google Home – essential. Like Edna and Bob, he had also made the technologies present in his routines selectively, improvising to bring them together with existing technologies. For example, the smart kettle had become part of his morning routine, where first thing he would "Get [his wife] a cup of coffee. So we generally ask the kettle to come on now which is good. I can do it from the bed [laughing] as I'm getting up". He combined this with putting country music on the radio – rather than accessing it through the smart home technology. As well as using voice commands to activate his devices, Ernest also enjoyed accessing content such as jokes through Google Home. However, while this ongoing technological presence was welcome, Ernest had always switched off his devices at night, and the electricity when going away. Now, like other participants, he felt unsure; he told us: "I'm scared if I turn them off they won't come on again. We're just talking about when we go away what are we going to do about all this? Do we turn it all off?"

For both households, smart home technologies were implicated in a complex and sometimes contradictory set of feelings and functions. The functionality of some of the devices was easily incorporated into some everyday routines and into intimate relations, while the presence and possible breakdown of the technology became a mundane but noted disruption, in relation to which participants generated particular anticipatory stances and strategies.

Towards an Applied Media Anthropology

Unsurprisingly, our participants improvised to make smart technologies part of their everyday lives in generationally and culturally specific ways. However, as outlined above, our research produced new insights into how smart home technologies participate in the shifting ecologies of media presence, content and communication. In the previous section we showed, by example, how older people learned and lived with the devices, in their intimate spaces of home and their intimate relationships both with the technologies themselves and with other people. In doing so they engaged with the continuous presence of smart home technologies as part of their everyday life materialities, sensory environments, and relationships. Three dimensions of this are particularly pertinent to our interest in this chapter in extending earlier discussion of the content, communication, and presence of media and technology in homes to the emerging smart home technology context.

First, the routines of everyday life are partly anticipatory actions that mark time, prepare for what is to come later, and when accomplished engender feelings of security and familiarity. Pink and Leder Mackley's (2013) research showed that people used media content to create atmospheres at home in anticipation of what would happen next: for instance, by using content not for its informational or entertainment possibilities but as background to help them get to sleep in anticipation of the day ahead. In the 2020 study we discuss here how our participants embedded the smart home devices' functionality and the content they provided into existing everyday routines, which likewise mark time, such as Ernest's morning routine and Edna's bed-making routine. In doing so, they improvised by shaping the use of the devices to their own needs and their anticipation of what they would be doing next, with the support of the technical team.

Second, voice assistants became embedded in the digital intimacies of everyday life. While earlier research has suggested that digital intimacies are generated through the use of a range of smart devices and platforms, the introduction of voice assistants signified new modes of everyday digital intimacy. Participants were careful with the language they used to communicate with Google Home, and each other. Working with the technical support team, they learned to use the right commands in order to accomplish the actions they wished for. The continued presence of Google Home and the devices associated with it meant that even where they did not find the commands to be polite, expectations of what would happen next were bound up in issuing successful commands and avoiding the issuing of accidental ones.

Third, participants responded to the contingencies of their new technological environments in ways that changed their routines and disrupted those very actions that made the home "feel right", for instance in their abandoning life-long routines of switching devices off at night. Pink and Leder Mackley's (2013) earlier research showed that technologies available a decade ago had shifted the binary on/off possibilities towards a context where devices could be activated from standby mode. In 2020, we found that with smart home devices being always on, participants began to plan their medium future actions in relation to the presence of the technology. They considered if they could switch it off completely when they went away, contemplated if it would smoothly switch on again, and asked what technical support might be needed to ensure that this went smoothly.

Generally, the devices were welcomed by participants and many of them decided to continue the trial. Yet, each of these three dimensions reveals elements of the presence of the devices which have future design implications. Attention to how they experienced and used the content and functionality of devices shows how they were *selectively* engaged to support everyday life routines and the sense of wellbeing that is derived from their accomplishment. These findings imply that if research into everyday routines informs the design of future smart devices for older people, it is likely to lead to uptake of more devices and further wellbeing outcomes. Attention to the communications element of technological presence reveals how participants' experience of the devices shifted their affective and social ways of being in and experiencing the home in ways that were helpful but *not ideal*. Future design therefore might attend to the "manners" and communicational preferences of older people, and the possibility of creating tailored or flexible communication design for this (and other groups). Attention to how the presence of the devices disrupted established everyday routines suggested some *anxieties* which were resolved through anticipated support needs. The design implication of this finding is that for older people it is likely that, at least in present iterations, smart home devices should not be understood as a standalone service or solution that can be applied separately from a human support service.

The applied agenda of our research project was to discover how smart home technologies might support the independence and wellbeing of older people. Exploring this question through a media anthropological focus on content, communication, and presence offers a specific set of insights which are coherent with the interdisciplinary project's wider findings and recommendations (Strengers et al 2021). It also demonstrates the potential of applied research in generating and consolidating conceptual work in media anthropology.

Conclusion

In this chapter, we have shown how the introduction of smart home technologies participates in how the experience of media content, communication, and presence is configured. Our work has two implications regarding: the advancement of a phenomenologically inspired media anthropology; and the possibilities of an applied media anthropology.

Our ethnographic research has shown how the older participants in our research experienced shifts in the anticipatory modes through which everyday routines, materialities, socialities, and communications are played out, and in how it "feels" to be at home, through their engagement with the smart home technology trial. The implication is that the object of study of media phenomenology of home has again shifted, that researchers in this field should attend to how new modes of presence have become part of the contingency of home and human improvisation associated with it. The concept of media presence was originally developed in an applied research context, to explain how standby mode entailed the "use" of a device rather than a waste of energy. In the research discussed here it has a second applied purpose, to explain the experience of smart home devices as a shift that comes about in relation to different dimensions of the experience of the continuous digital-material presence of smart home technology, and to reveal the design implications of this.

Acknowledgements

The Intelligent Home Solutions for Independent Living project was undertaken through a collaborative partnership between McLean Care, Deakin University, and Monash University and received funding from the Australian Government through a Department of Health CHSP Innovation Grant.

References

Akama, Y., S. Pink, and S. Sumartojo (2018) *Uncertainty and Possibility*. London: Bloomsbury.
Andreassen, R., M. Nebeling Petersen, K. Harrison, et al. (eds) (2017) *Mediated Intimacies: Connectivities, Relationalities and Proximities*. London: Taylor & Francis.
Bessire, L. and D. Bond (2014) "Ontological Anthropology and the Deferral of Critique". *American Ethnologist 41* (3): 440–56.
Cho, M., S. Lee, and K. Lee (2019) "Once a Kind Friend Is Now a Thing: Understanding How Conversational Agents at Home are Forgotten" in *Proceedings of the 2019 Designing Interactive Systems Conference*. New York: ACM, 1565.
Couldry, N. and T. Markham (2008) "Troubled Closeness or Satisfied Distance? Researching Media Consumption and Public Orientation". *Media, Culture & Society 30* (1): 5–21. https://doi.org/10.1177/0163443707084347
Couldry, N. (2012) *Media, Society, World: Social Theory and Digital Media Practice*. Cambridge: Polity Press.
Darling, K. (2016) "Extending Legal Protection to Social Robots: The Effects of Anthropomorphism, Empathy, and Violent Behavior Towards Robotic Objects" in R. Calo, A.M. Froomkin, and I. Kerr (eds.), *Robot Law*. Cheltenham, UK: Edward Elgar Publishing, 213–231.
Davis J.L. and J.B. Chouinard (2016) "Theorizing Affordances: From Request to Refuse". *Bulletin of Science, Technology & Society 36* (4): 241–248. doi:10.1177/0270467617714944
Deuze, M. (2012) *Media Life*. Cambridge: Polity.
Dobson A.S., N. Carah, and B. Robards (2018) "Digital Intimate Publics and Social Media: Towards Theorising Public Lives on Private Platforms" in A.S. Dobson, B. Robards, N. Carah (eds), *Digital Intimate Publics and Social Media*. Cham: Palgrave Macmillan, 3–27.
Duque M., S. Pink, Y. Strengers, R. Martin, and L. Nicholls (2021) "Automation, Wellbeing and Digital Voice Assistants: Older people and Google Devices". *Convergence 27* (5):1189–1206. doi:10.1177/13548565211038537.
Groot Kormelink, T. and I. Costera Meijer, (2019) "Material and Sensory Dimensions of Everyday News Use". *Media, Culture & Society 41* (5), 637–653. https://doi.org/10.1177/0163443
Hargreaves, T. and C. Wilson (2017) *Smart Homes and Their Users*. Cham, Switzerland: Springer.
Ingold, T. (1997) "Eight Themes in the Anthropology of Technology". *Social Analysis 41* (1): 106–138.
Irving, A. (2017) "The Art of Turning Left and Right" in J. F. Salazar, S. Pink, A. Irving, and J. Sjoberg (eds), *Anthropologies and Futures*. London: Bloomsbury, 23–42.
Jensen, R.H., Y. Strengers, J. Kjeldskov, L. Nicholls, and M.B. Skov (2018) "Designing the Desirable Smart Home: A Study of Household Experiences and Energy Consumption Impacts". *CHI '18 Proceedings of the 2018 CHI Conference on Human Factors in Computing Systems*.
Markham, T. (2020) *Digital Life*. Oxford: Polity Books.
Miller, D. (1988) "Appropriating the State in the Council Estate". *Man 23*: 353–372.
Miller, D. and H. Horst (2012) "The Digital and Human: A Prospectus for Digital Anthropology" in H. Horst and D. Miller (eds), *Digital Anthropology*. London: Bloomsbury, 3–35.
Moores, S. (2012) *Media, Place and Mobility*. Basingstoke: Palgrave Macmillan.
Morley, D. (1986) *Family Television: Cultural Power and Domestic Leisure*. London: Comedia.
Morley, D. (2000) *Home Territories: Media, Mobility and Identity*. London: Routledge.
Nicholls, L. and Y. Strengers, 2019) "Robotic Vacuum Cleaners Save Energy? Raising Cleanliness Conventions and Energy Demand in Australian Households with Smart Home Technologies". *Energy Research & Social Science 50*: 73–81.
Pink, S. (2021) "Digital Futures Anthropology" in H. Geismer and H. Knox (eds), *Digital Anthropology*. London: Bloomsbury, 307–324.
Pink, S. and K. Leder Mackley (2013) "Saturated and Situated: Rethinking Media in Everyday Life". *Media, Culture and Society 35* (6): 677–691. doi 10.1177/0163443713491298.
Pink, S., K. Leder Mackley, R. Morosanu, V. Mitchell, and T. Bhamra (2017) *Making Homes: Ethnographies and Designs*. Oxford: Bloomsbury.
Pink, S. E. Ardevol and D. Lanzeni (2016) "Digital Materiality: Configuring a Field of Anthropology/Design?" in S. Pink, E. Ardevol, and D. Lanzeni (eds), *Digital Materialities: Anthropology and Design*. Oxford: Bloomsbury, 1–25.
Pink, S., L. Hjorth, H. Horst, J. Nettheim, and G. Bell, (2018) "Digital Work and Play: Mobile Technologies and New Ways of Feeling at Home". *European Journal of Cultural Studies 21* (1): 26–38.

Pink, S. and J. Postill (2019) "Imagining Mundane Fuures". *Anthropology in Action* 26 (2): 31–41. doi:10.3167/aia.2019.260204.

Røpke, I., T. Haunstrup Christensen, and J. Ole Jensen, (2010) "Information and Communication Technologies: A New Round of Household Electrification". *Energy Policy 38* (4): 1764–1773.

Schiller, A. and J. McMahon (2019) "Alexa, Alert Me When the Revolution Comes: Gender, Affect, and Labor in the Age of Home-Based Artificial Intelligence". *New Political Science 41* (2): 173–191.

Schönherr, L., M. Golla, T. Eisenhofer, J. Wiele, D. Kolossa, and T. Holz (2020) "Unacceptable, Where Is My Privacy? Exploring Accidental Triggers of Smart Speakers. arXiv preprint arXiv:2008.00508

Sorrell, S. (2017) *Consumer Robotics: From Housekeeper to Friend*. Basingstoke: Juniper Research. www.juniperresearch.com.

Smith, R. C. and T. Otto (2016) "Cultures of the Future: Emergence and Intervention in Design Anthropology" in R. C. Smith, K. T. Vangkilde, M. G. Kjærsgaard, T. Otto, J. Halse, T. Binder (eds), *Design Anthropological Futures*. London: Bloomsbury, 19–36.

Strengers, Y., M. Duque, M. Mortimer, S. Pink, A. Eugene, R. Martin, L. Nicholls, B. Horan, and S. Thomson (2021) *Smart Homes for Seniors: Intelligent Home Solutions for Independent Living*, Final research evaluation report, McLean Care, Monash University and Deakin University, Melbourne, Australia.

Strengers, Y., S. Pink, and L. Nicholls, (2019) "Smart Energy Futures and Social Practice Imaginaries: Forecasting Scenarios for Pet Care in Australian Homes". *Energy Research & Social Science 48*: 108–115.

Strengers, Y., K. Kennedy, P. Arcari, L. Nicholls, and M. Gregg, (2019) "Protection, Productivity and Pleasure in the Smart Home" in *Proceedings of the SIGCHI Conference on Human Factors in Computing Systems: Weaving the Threads of CHI*. New York: ACM.

Strengers, Y. and J. Kennedy (2020) *The Smart Wife: Why Siri, Alexa and Other Smart Home Devices Need a Feminist Reboot*. Cambridge, MA: MIT Press.

Strengers, Y. and L. Nicholls (2017) "Convenience and Energy Consumption in the Smart Home of the Future: Industry Visions from Australia and Beyond". *Energy Research & Social Science 32*: 86–93.

Wilken, R. and G. Goggin, (2012) "Mobilising Place: Conceptual Currents and Controversies" in R. Wilken and G. Goggin (eds), *Mobile Technology and Place*. New York: Routledge, 3–25.

D

Media as Representation

17

#EVEREST

Visual Economies of Leisure and Labour in the Tourist Encounter

Jolynna Sinanan

Manish was 27 years old when we spoke in a small café in the back streets of Kathmandu's outer suburbs in 2019. His friend Dawa had introduced us: Manish had previously worked for Dawa, first as a porter and then as an assistant guide at an international trekking company where Manish stayed on when Dawa left to join a local company. Manish and Dawa had continued to remain friends, Manish considered Dawa a mentor, especially at that time as he was starting his own small business in trekking tourism. That afternoon, we chatted over tea in the back room of the café, which was owned by a family friend of Dawa's. Most of its customers were young porters and assistant guides for local and international companies, many of which lived in the area. Around us, other young men sat with tea, mostly scrolling on their phones. We had met there as it was the neighbourhood hub for young porters and assistant guides – mobile workers in the trekking industry who left their families in Kathmandu for weeks at a time to work in popular Himalayan trekking and mountaineering regions to the country's north. Manish scrolled through images he had taken on his phone; picturesque landscapes of 'the giants' of the Khumbu region: Nuptse, Lhotse and Everest, trekking clients crossing suspension bridges and groups together at Everest Base Camp. He recalled that many of these photos had been taken at the request of clients and some of these photos have been posted to his Facebook profile, some were sent to clients via Messenger and WhatsApp and a handful would go on the website for his small trekking business. He explained that taking photos of landscapes, of and with clients, was a common expectation of his job as an assistant guide.

Manish grew up in Kathmandu and he became a porter when he was 17. Although the legal age to work as a porter was 18, many boys who joined international and local trekking companies in the mid-2000s were as young as 15, as at the time, Nepal's tourism industry was making a rapid recovery after years of a decline in tourism due to civil unrest in the early 2000s. Manish was typical of that generation of young men who were introduced to working in tourism by fathers and uncles; relatives who themselves had been working with mostly international companies as cooks for treks and mountaineering expeditions. As the industry expanded and the number of trekking agencies grew, so did the demand for young men, which they saw as an opportunity for work by extending their skills and networks. Around a decade later, many of these young men were in their late 20s and early 30s, some had young families of their own and they were in different stages of starting or had expressed wanting to start their own small business in trekking tourism. This was much of the cohort Dawa introduced me to in Kathmandu.

Like Manish, many spoke in the vernacular of entrepreneurship, expressing they wanted to draw on their years of experience working as porters, assistant guides and guides. Unsurprisingly, a major part of their business strategy integrates websites and social media platforms Instagram and Facebook. The affordances of social and mobile media facilitate a marketing strategy that includes spectacular panoramic images of the Himalayan mountain scapes, detailed, intimate snapshots of life during a trek and portraits of exhilarated tourists on their bucket list adventures – visual tropes that all seem quite obvious after 15 years of the integration of mobile media into tourist experiences. However, the role of images in the work of Everest tourism goes beyond aesthetics, they are part of themes that have long held the interest of anthropologists; images as digital visual communication form a significant part of social exchange: images function as part of a strategy to create longer-term relationships, as well as patron–client relations between workers and tourists that may be mutually drawn upon into the future. These relationships may secure further, more lucrative work, resources through the sending of consumer goods and personal relationships of support through friendships.

In this chapter, I examine the intersection of visual cultures and the 'work' of Mount Everest tourism. Anthropologists have described Nepal as a country of contradictory global imaginaries (Leichty 2017; Norum 2013). Early visitors were drawn to Nepal for the images it evoked of solitude, spiritualism and heroic mountain exploration. Since the mid-1990s, the global mediatisation of Mount Everest has played a key role in attracting visitors to the region. Arguably, Everest has always been mediatised: historically, its appeal as an idea has existed in part through technologies of visual cultures (Mu and Nepal 2016; Mazzolini 2015). Everest may be especially mediatised now; recently improved mobile infrastructure in the northern Himalayas has coincided with an increase in the number of tourists arriving between 2016 and 2018 (Ministry of Culture, Tourism and Civil Aviation 2017). Using Deborah Poole's visual economy (1997) as a starting point, I examine how the production and circulation of images through digital technologies shape how tourists imagine and experience Everest in Nepal. Drawing on fieldwork conducted in the Solukhumbu region with tourists, guides and porters, I argue that mobile and visual communication are part of tourist experiences, but they are also part of the strategies for meeting aspirations of life projects for workers whose livelihoods depend on the tourist industry and digital practices reveal shifting expectations and cultural understandings of Everest. Visual economies of Everest capture a double bind: on the one hand, images produced within the tourist encounter reinforce the narratives of solitude, spiritualism and mountain exploration. And on the other, enduring themes contributing to the appeal of Everest result in more tourists embarking on visiting the region and shapes their expectations for particular experiences. Such expectations may increase pressure on a workforce whose livelihoods depend on a region already fraught with increasing environmental challenges.

This chapter focuses on the tourist encounter to contribute to the intersection of media anthropology and an anthropology of mobilities by considering the aesthetic value of Everest within locally bound and across global networks. The chapter contributes to furthering studies in media anthropology by considering the relationship between images produced and circulated through mobile and social media and social exchange (Edwards 2012; Pertierra 2018; Pinney 2002). Through instrumentalising the potency of the imagination of Mount Everest, images as representation can become part of networks of obligation and reciprocity through digital practices that facilitate further material exchange.

Between 2017 and 2019, I conducted three visits to Kathmandu and the tourist hub of Namche along the Everest Base Camp trek, which lasted between three and four weeks each.

Visual Economies of Leisure and Labour

My visits in 2017 and 2018 provided the ground work for fieldwork conducted in 2019. Further fieldwork was scheduled during the April–May summit season during Nepal's 'Visit Nepal year of Tourism 2020', but was cancelled due to the global COVID-19 pandemic. The pandemic is the second major disruption to Nepal and the Everest tourism industry in five years, after the earthquake and subsequent avalanches in 2015. With Nepal's peak tourism season cancelled and workers remaining in Kathmandu or in villages in surrounding regions, the future of the tourism workforce in upcoming months remains uncertain.

The material presented in this chapter draws on insights gained from time spent in Namche with 26 tourists (seven women and 11 men, aged between 22 and 64), six guides (all men, aged between 24 and 42), six porters (all men, aged between 19 and 25), two managers of a guest house (one couple, a man aged 37 and a woman aged 35, who were parents to an 11-year-old daughter) and three managers of a porters' accommodation house (two sisters aged 22 and 19 and another woman). Contrary to the visibility of Khumbu Sherpa, who have been traditionally associated with Everest mountaineering, significant numbers of guides and porters are from the Tamang and Rai ethnic groups – populations from other parts of Nepal who have historically been at the economic margins of Nepali society (Nepal 2005). Most of the workers involved in this study were Tamang and Rai who worked seasonally in the Khumbu region.

The wider project combines ethnographic methods of participant observation and interviews with digital ethnography. This approach investigates mobile media's role for workers and tourists in the Everest tourist industry, and the implications for the interconnectedness of work, tourism and mobilities. Digital ethnography has been drawn on in media studies and cultural studies and there is now a significant number of volumes that instruct how researchers might "do" digital ethnography (see Hjorth et al. 2017; Pink et al. 2016). Taken as an assemblage (of visual content, digital practices, interviews and researcher and participant reflection), digital ethnographic inquiry can allow for a deeper understanding of a distant geographical or social site, and the meanings they generate. More often than not, addressing complex questions about how populations engage with digital devices and spaces cannot be answered by simply looking at what is posted to websites and platforms without reference to the context which produced them. Unlike other approaches to digital visual communication such as content analysis, digital ethnography retains an anthropological sensibility by locating digital media practices within regional media ecologies and how they are reflective of wider social and cultural factors such as such as class, ethnicity, gender, inequality, economic decision making and political engagement. The key methodological approach in this study draws from a previous monograph *Visualising Facebook* (2017), where Daniel Miller and I examined images posted to Facebook in the same period we were conducting ethnographic fieldwork (in England and Trinidad respectively), where we had already gained insights to observable and generalisable cultural norms. The research presented in this chapter builds on this approach for understanding the experiences of mobile populations such as workers and tourists in the tourist encounter.

Visibility and Everest in Global Visual Cultures

In *Vision, Race and Modernity: A visual economy of the Andean image world* (1997), Deborah Poole coins the term visual economy to draw attention to the circulation of objects and images in local political economies. Poole relates these locally produced objects and images to their movement across global networks to investigate the commercial and private individual stakeholders in image production. Economy connotes an organised, systematised mode that constructs gradients in fields of vision along the lines of visibility and invisibility that has "as much to do with social relationships, inequality, and power as with shared meanings and community" (Poole 1997: 8). In her ethnography of African diasporic aesthetic practices, Krista Thompson draws on visual economies to emphasise how certain aesthetic qualities or ephemeral visual effects give value to objects which are then circulated in wider social life (2015: 24). Thompson's analysis of significance of light, lightness and 'bling' in African diasporic aesthetics and in Jamaican aesthetic cultures in particular emphasises how eye-catching objects relate to the visibility of an individual in society. In a similar way, my earlier ethnography *Social Media in Trinidad: Values and Visibility* (2017) argued that visibility and visuality (being eye-catching according to the norms of socially constructed categories) are reflective of personhood: the crafting of appearance becomes a moral reflection of who a person is. It is no coincidence that ethnographies of Caribbean and Caribbean diasporic populations highlight the centrality of visibility to personhood where crafting external appearances through consumer goods, aesthetics or performance refutes how one is structurally positioned in society due to the legacies of colonial histories based on slavery and indentureship (Miller 1994). In the book I further argue that while visuality is appropriated to convey aspects of personhood, the crafting of appearances is also highly intertwined with displaying aspirations (even though they might not yet be attained). This is not simply for the purpose of 'showing off' but to show that one subscribes to culturally appropriate social aspirations (in Trinidad: a middle-class lifestyle, a respectable profession and retaining the importance of family and household and, for many, idioms of freedom signified through Carnival culture).

Social media more than represents who a person is; it is an extension of visibility and appearance that determines who a person is in social terms, which in turn can secure cultural capital (Sinanan 2017). For those who are unable to attain social capital through economic or educational means, social media also facilitates gaining a following, social kudos or notoriety through posting eye-catching, shocking and spectacular images of oneself or sharing similar posts of others to platforms such as Facebook. Experiences of travel have become a form of cultural capital for middle-class populations, globally, seen through the popularity of travel influencers for example (Polson 2016). Mount Everest has become symbolic for embodied, material values of aspiration and achievement and climbing it has become the highest form of attainable cultural capital by commercial means for tourists. At the time of writing during the COVID-19 pandemic, the number of climbing permits issued by the Nepali government in 2021 so far (377), is expected to exceed the record number of permits (381) issued in 2019 (*The Guardian*, 27 April 2021).

In *The Everest Effect*, Elizabeth Mazzolini argues that Mount Everest 'provides a narrative that has strongly influenced Western people's sense of what it means to be a human in the twentieth century' (2015: 13). She takes a cultural rhetorical approach to science studies to examine how 'material assemblages have produced seemingly immaterial values related to Mount Everest, and how those immaterial values have had intensely material consequences' (ibid). Everest became intensified in the 20th-century imagination as within hours of Sir Edmund Hillary's and Tenzing Norgay reaching the summit, they become national and international celebrities. Journalist James (later known as Jan) Morris was under pressure to deliver news of the successful summit attempt to the *The Times* of London from deep in the Himalayas using encrypted messages carried by couriers while preventing the story from being leaked to other press outlets. Hillary and Norgay reached the summit on the same day as the queen's coronation in 1953, however, Mazzolini argues that their infamous ascent in many ways marked the end of an era of nationalistic achievement and the beginning of the age of individual achievement (2015: 29). As a distinctly late modern phenomenon, Mazzolini further argues that mountain climbing and climbing Everest in particular is so appealing because it symbolises a distinctly modern contradiction. That is, Everest represents purity and permanence but also human ability to conquer the extremity of nature through team work as well as exceptional individual achievement (Mazzolini 2015: 9, 13).

Hillary and Norgay became instant celebrities through iconic images in global media while squabbles over their nationality continued – Hillary was a New Zealander on a British expedition and Norgay was claimed as a Tibetan Sherpa, a Nepali and an Indian. Norgay became symbolic of the appropriation of colonised territories leading up to independence movements in the 1960s (Liechty, 2017). In their study of Everest tourism, Mu and Nepal argue that the increase in the number of mountaineers and trekkers in high mountain destinations like Mt. Everest in subsequent years is symptomatic of contemporary society's fixation with personal glory and ambition (2016: 509). The first commercial trek to the Everest region was organised in 1966, and, since, the Khumbu valley has seen growth in tourism from around 20 visitors in the 1960s to 18,200 during the 1997–1998 seasons (Mu and Nepal 2016: 501–503). The most recently available statistics from 2017 reports that 45,000 trekkers visited the Khumbu valley (Ministry of Culture, Tourism and Civil Aviation 2017).

Scholars on Nepal and Everest tourism agree that the mediatisation of Everest plays a significant role in drawing visitors to the region (Liechty 2017; Ortner 1999). The contemporary imagination of Everest is shaped by constructions of Everest as 'the commercialisation of risk', 'selling adventure' and 'made for Hollywood disaster' (Palmer 2002), exemplified by the popularity of recounts of the 1996 disaster in Jon Krakauer's novel *Into Thin Air* and the 1998 IMAX film *Everest*. More recently, since the avalanches of 2014 and again in 2015 due to the Nepal earthquake, the government of Nepal has made a committed effort to increase telephone connectivity in the region. Alongside the government's efforts, private telecommunications corporations have invested in under-resourced and under-serviced areas in the Himalayas by providing digital connectivity through WiFi accessible on mobile phones. Two mobile providers (NCell and Everest Link) now service a region where, until 2000, the only form of communication was through letter writing. Residents of the Khumbu region can recharge through pay-as-you-go cards and tourists can purchase a data sim card valid for a month as soon as they land in Tribhuvan Airport in Kathmandu (Figure 17.1). Although lucrative tourism accelerated the demand for telecommunications alongside earthquake recovery efforts, tourism has also ushered a new phase of communicating the imagination of the Everest region, predominantly through images facilitated by newly established mobile media infrastructures.

The growth of mobile phone infrastructure provides some of the background for a genre of image that has become familiar on news and social media: queues of people along the narrow corridor of the Hillary Step waiting in turn to reach the summit. *Washington Post*'s coverage of the deaths from the summit attempts on 24 May 2019 quoted Eric Simonson, director at International Mountain Guides, who commented that since commercial expeditions become more popular and Mount Everest appeared more in the media from recounts of the 1996 disaster to travel blogging, 'it crossed over from just climbers being interested to everybody being interested'. Today, images and videos from Everest summit expeditions and treks to Everest Base Camp can be posted to social media platforms from an altitude of 5,000 metres (16,400 feet) in very close to real time. The hundreds of thousands of images posted to Instagram with #everest or #everestbasecamp indicates the extent to which mobile phones broadcasting experiences of treks or summit expeditions have become a normal part of Everest tourism and, in turn, they play a key role in shaping the value and perception of Mount Everest in the contemporary global imagination. Visual themes that appear in these images capture contradictory values that have remained pervasive throughout the history of the commodification of Everest. These include local burdens of tourism and the servitude of regional populations through

Figure 17.1 A screen advertising NCell data SIM cards featuring Mount Everest in the baggage claim area of Tribhuvan Airport, Kathmandu
Source: author.

work, changing perceptions of identity in Nepal and the valorisation of nationalism of Sherpa populations while rendering other regional ethnic groups less visible and the continuation of colonial legacies through narratives of individual achievement and the legitimation of colonial ownership of space.

In his study of visual motifs of tourism on Instagram, Smith argues that narratives of the most common visual tropes reinforce unequal power relations which prefigure tourists as the rightful users of local spaces (2018: 173). His concerns with aspects of the tourist gaze and the tourist imagination that reinforce colonial imaginaries of Other lands (see Edensor 2001; Kothari 2015; Urry and Larsen 2011) play out through mobile media platforms such as Instagram. Smith further argues that images taken and posted in situ are a form of travel writing; images narrate an actual experience and they are autobiographically rendered as users take the images themselves (2018: 175). Mountainscapes in particular represent elite experiences, where mountaineering emerged as an 19th-century leisure activity for the European wealthier class, which influenced the growth in the popularity of mountain panoramas adorning the walls of middle-class homes (Wood 2001).

More generally, artistic and photographic depiction of landscapes is deeply associated with narratives of power; however, scholarship on the production of images in tourism tends to focus on the role of tourists only (Smith 2018). Chio argues that tourism research has the tendency to perceive tourism as a host or guest endeavour that does not take into account contemporary mobile realities of the role of workers and the tourist encounter as a total phenomenon (2011: 209). In her study of the production of rural Chinese villages as sites for

Chinese tourists, Chio examines the visual economy of such villages to highlight the dual mobility of workers in tourism as well as the emerging middle-class Chinese who visit, a population for whom local tourism is a recent phenomenon (2014). By drawing on the visual economy to emphasise not only the circulation of images, the meanings, values and mobilities they enable, Chio provides a more in-depth account of how within the tourist encounter, individual experiences and communication about them can now be treated as commercial objects to be owned and exchanged.

Further, for cultural minorities living in remote areas, the affordances of internet technologies can be appropriated for self-representation in relation to local, regional and national boundaries, while remaining cognisant of global audiences. In *Inuit in Cyberspace* for example, Neil Blair Christensen's portrayal of Inuit from Arctic Canada, Alaska and Greenland emphasises a 'practicality' through which Inuit engage globally; that is, even though Inuit surf the net, order consumer goods online and consume 'global' media, they do so while asserting cultural identities that are anchored regionally (2003).

These insights resonate strongly with the ethnographic vignettes of the Everest tourist encounter that follows. Throughout its history, Everest has always existed in the minds of ordinary people as an idea through technologies of visual culture (Mazzolini 2015). The last 20 years have seen a dramatic shift from trips made mostly by mountaineers and 'serious' trekkers to mostly the same ordinary people who cite 'achieving a dream' and ticking Everest off 'the bucket list' as a main motivation. In this next section, I present three ethnographic vignettes that illustrate the ways in which the visual economies of Everest impact upon the tourist counter.

Digital Communication as Building and Disrupting Relationships in the Everest Tourism Industry

These stories represent particularities of individual circumstances as well as typical themes that emerged in narratives of the tourism encounter from fieldwork. In the first example, Pasang was fairly representative of young tour operators in Kathmandu trying to navigate technological and social change within the tourism industry. Pasang's insights to the role that digital technologisation in tourism plays in transforming the relationships between operators and tourists speaks to the shift in Nepal's tourism history.

In 2019, Pasang was 36 years old and had been running his small business in organising treks for eight years. Originally from the north of the Dhaulagiri region in the midwestern Himalayas, Pasang and his mother moved to Kathmandu when he was in high school. He worked as an assistant guide and then a guide before opening his office in the tourist hub Thamel, a suburb that went from being a backwater to a centre for local businesses and entrepreneurs, high and mid-end accommodation, and entertainment (Liechty 2017; Linder 2017). As the first arrival point from the airport for most tourists embarking on treks or mountaineering expeditions, Thamel is an 'Everestland' of sorts, from bars and restaurants with Himalayan themed names such as 'Fat Monk's Bar', 'Everest Irish Pub' and 'Yeti Tap Room' side by side with mountain gear shops. However, as much as Thamel is denigrated by tourists and locals alike for its consumerist inauthenticity, it is also a site of Nepali cosmopolitanism (Linder 2017). Nepalis like Pasang have been influential in the regeneration of businesses following the economic downturn related to the military coup in the early 2000s and again in the reconstruction following Nepal's earthquakes. Today, relatively young Nepalis frequent many of Thamel's nightclubs and bars, because as Pasang described, 'there is always somewhere to go out with your friends, any night of the week'. The rapid changes of Thamel as a tourist hub and a Nepali cosmopolitan centre coupled with the emergence of WiFi data sim cards have had varying impacts on his and trekking businesses owned by Nepalis. Pasang explained:

> When I opened the business, it was much easier to get clients. Young people spend a lot of time in Nepal, months, they come here after going to India or Thailand and they have more ideas of what they want to do ... they stay in Thamel and they walk around to the different companies. They talk to you and you can talk about a trek that is good for them, how much time and how much money they want to spend there and where they want to go. If they go to Pokhara, they want a trek and rafting, we can do that for them. But now it's more difficult. People will look up websites in their home country and they book everything online. They come to Thamel, meet their group, stay in the hotel or go to a restaurant with their group and they don't see much themselves. Or they stay in Thamel for a few days after the trek and they go to some restaurants, bars, shop for souvenirs but that's it.

Pasang further explained the impacts mobile phones were having on trekking businesses as well as for disrupting the potential to build relationships between guides and clients.

> It's the first thing trekkers want when they arrive in Kathmandu. I organise my tour leaders to take clients to mobile phone shops, where they can copy their passport and buy a sim card. Some people do this at the airport, but many ask me on email or Messenger if we can arrange it when they arrive. Bigger companies also rely on this for their advertising. They ask clients to leave reviews and their photos on TripAdvisor or to send to them so they can use on their website. And the better the photos, the happier the clients, any person who wants to do the trek, this is what they also expect.

The significance of Pasang's experience as emplaced in Thamel, which has a formidable history for its emergence as a tourist hub, is beyond the scope of the chapter. However, his narration of tourists spending more time in the area previously is anchored in Nepal's long history of hippie tourism and being a destination for counter-cultural seekers (Liechty 2017). Similar to many destinations in South and South East Asia, Nepal attracted tourists who would spend longer amounts of time, weeks to years in the country, and would embark on individual travel. More recently, tourists embark on shorter trips due to time constraints of holiday leave from work. Trekkers such as Ciaran provide another viewpoint as to how shifts to increased technologisation in tourism play out.

Ciaran was 32 and lived in Dubai with his girlfriend, where they were both teachers in international schools. Ciaran explained that Everest Base Camp had always been on his bucket list and he had been planning for the trip for six months, as he only had a limited amount of time to travel during his school holidays. In his day pack, he carried a GoPro and monopod, his iPhone which he kept charged on a portable solar panel attached to his bag, and his copy of *Into Thin Air*, which he pulled out in the afternoon after his group had reached their destination for the day. On his phone, he had several photos that he had taken but also of himself on significant points on the trek: crossing a suspension bridge and at the Everest View Point Hotel in Namche, which offered the first panoramic view with Everest. Ciaran explained that his fellow trekkers had taken some of the photos of him, but also their guide and a couple of porters (Figure 17.2). He noted the skill with which their guide in particular took photos,

Visual Economies of Leisure and Labour

Figure 17.2 A trekking guide taking a photo of a group of trekkers
Source: author.

Taraj knows where all the good spots are to take photos. Like you're walking on a ridge and you want to go exploring by yourself, you take some pics of each other but he's hanging back and when you meet him again he points in another direction and says 'the view is better over there'. He's taken some great photos of us, you can see mountains properly in the background, he takes a few at a time so you can choose the best ones, he's a pretty good photographer!

After leaving Namche, Ciaran's group continued the trek which included the Thukla Pass, two days' itinerary from Everest Base Camp. The route follows a steep hill paved with stones and the top of the ridge meets a plateau that has been converted to a memorial ground for mountaineers and Sherpa who have lost their lives on Everest summit expeditions. Memorials are constructed with stone and some are adorned with bronze plaques and Tibetan prayer flags. Cloud at 4,800 metres (15,748 feet) causes poor visibility and trekkers can spend up to an hour exploring the plateau for figures they have seen portrayed in films or have read about. Ciaran saw other trekkers asking their guides where the memorials to Scott Fischer and Rob Hall were located, where guides responded that they didn't know.

The '96 disaster is a pretty well-known bit of Everest history, so I'm surprised guides didn't know about those memorials. You come this far, you're on your way to Base Camp, so of course you want to see them if you can. Taraj knew where they were, he asked if any of us wanted to see them and a few of us went along. I took some video on the GoPro and a couple of photos but I'm not sure I'll post them anywhere; it doesn't feel right. But I'm glad we saw them.

A couple of the bars and restaurants in Namche show Everest movies and documentaries nightly. As it is an acclimatisation point, trekkers will spend two to three nights in Namche before continuing their ascent, and main leisure activities are to sit in one's lodge, drink in one of the local bars or watch movies in these local improvised cinemas. Recognising the various media cultures that Everest has been a part of and building it in to key points of the trek, including taking photos, enhances the experience for trekkers such as Ciaran and likely influences their desire to join the same companies treks on return visits to Nepal. In my final example, 53-year-old Matt from Australia somewhat represented two generations of Nepali tourists, having spent significant time in the country in the late 1990s and again in the 2010s.

In 2018, Matt used his two months of accrued annual leave from his job in the Queensland mining industry to holiday in Nepal. In the first month, he joined a group to summit a small Himalayan peak in the Khumbu region but had to forego the midnight summit attempt due to gastro. Two friends had travelled with him from Brisbane and were embarking on the Everest Base Camp trek, where they all met in the village of Dingboche on the way down. Now independent of their respective group itineraries, the three friends were being accompanied by a solo guide who Matt had met on his previous trip in 2016. Matt had independently employed the guide to lead him on the Annapurna circuit and they had stayed in touch via Messenger. He had planned the next leg of the trip through his contact, who met them in Dingboche and was accompanying them off the main trekking route back to Lukla and Kathmandu, where he had then organised hired motorbikes for their second month to ride from Chitwan to Pokhara and back again. Matt explained they had to cut the trip short as one of his friends then fell ill with gastro so they turned around and completed a more comfortable, shorter trip in the region surrounding the south of Kathmandu. Despite these setbacks, Matt described the trip as a success and reminisced how much had changed since he first motorbiked in Nepal in the 1990s. He did not have the opportunity to employ someone locally active in the tourism industry and was grateful to have someone 'on the ground' to organise his trip as he has less time than he did when he was younger.

Six months later, I caught up with Matt in Brisbane. He showed me photos of the remainder of the 2018 trip including several photos of him and his friends taken by their guide, or sent to them by their guide when they returned to Kathmandu. He talked about his plans to visit again, but when asked if he would work with the same guide again, Matt sighed.

> He was a really nice guy, really professional, organised and good company. It was like he was one of us lads on the trip. He was the same on the last trip too. But this time, after I got home, he kept messaging, which is fine, how are you et cetera, but then after a couple of months, he started sounding a bit desperate. He told me about some family problems and his finances and then he started asking for money. I was bit uncomfortable, and I said sorry I couldn't help, but he kept asking. Then he started saying that we're friends so you should help your friends, I live in a richer country so it shouldn't be a problem and I just started ignoring his messages. I felt bad about it but I think he crossed a line.

'Keeping in touch' after a trek was fairly common between trekkers in the same group as well as porters, guides and trekkers. Several interactions turned into positive longer-term relationships of exchange, which included bringing gifts of branded goods or bringing goods for reimbursement on return visits. However, as Matt's story highlights, these relationships that were initially based on mutual interest surrounding tourism as a leisure activity and as a livelihood strategy can start to resemble themes that appear in anthropological research in migration. These include networks that can be drawn on for support or resources, but also need navigating in relation to obligation (Baldassar and Merla 2016). Digital communication as practices of taking photos but also circulating them, draws on the mediatisation of Everest to enhance tourist experiences. These can become an entry point for ongoing conversational exchange with varied implications.

These brief examples have illustrated different kinds of relationships that emerge in the tourist encounter and the ways they are navigated through digital technologies. In particular, I have highlighted the role of digital visual communication and genres of images from the global imaginaries of Everest and how they are integrated into different aspects of tourist experiences. Manish, who appeared at the opening of the chapter, has integrated images taken while working on treks into his marketing strategy, where his experience working with international trekking agencies revealed the value of being a good photographer as part of working as a guide. Pasang's description of working in Thamel captures the many and often contradictory iconographic motifs of tourism and Nepal that greet tourists as soon as they arrive. Yet, these motifs have been encountered in advance through trip planning stages via the internet and shape their expectations for the trip ahead. Ciaran emphasised attributes of guides as extending to knowledge of Everest in global cultures and skills with photography, reinforcing Manish's experiences. Finally, Matt's story reveals the ambiguities that can emerge with establishing friendships from multiple trips that resemble patron-client relations. Digital communication may facilitate informal, dyadic relationships and shift relationships from being transactional to reciprocal; these forms of reciprocity remain anchored in unequal power relations of exchange – a long-standing theme in tourism scholarship.

Conclusion: the Aesthetics of Everest for Mediating Aspirations

Through digital technologies such as smartphones, the place-based relationships that emerge from the tourist encounter between tourists and mobile workers can influence how people may imagine their futures and work towards meeting their individual or collective family aspirations. The relationship between those whose aspirations include 'bucket list' destinations and the livelihoods that benefit from them call for deeper analysis beyond being a host or guest endeavour (Chio, 2011). Fischer (2014: 5) argues that aspirations are a navigational capability, mapping the steps from here to there based on cultural imaginations of the future. Anthropologists have developed a distinct approach to studying the imagination by paying attention to the role of materiality and to 'the conditions, relations and situations external to the imagining individual' (Harris and Rapport 2015: 7). Media in particular, as technologies of the imagination in a colloquial sense, provide unique insights to social and material processes that enable particular relationships between people, objects and places, including their potential narratives.

This chapter has provided a brief portrait of how collective imaginings of Everest have impacted upon individual aspirations, played out through digital technologies and navigating relationships in the tourist encounter. The intricacies of the history of tourism in Nepal, Nepal in the global imagination, Nepali inflections of hospitality and the economic development of Nepal is far beyond what can be achieved in a chapter and will be developed elsewhere. Here, I have emphasised the multiple impacts that mobile and visual communication have had on the Everest tourist encounter in the initial years since digital infrastructures have emerged in the remote Himalayan region. The chapter has drawn together approaches in media anthropology and visual cultures to examine the ways in which media practices and images produced in situ move across local and global networks. Mobile livelihoods as a form of intrastate migration may be especially significant as an example of a population who appropriate the imaginings of place to secure future opportunities. For such populations, digital technologies, social and mobile media enable a wider repertoire of cultural and social imaginings and expand the means through which they may be attained.

References

Baldassar, L. and Merla, L. (eds) (2014) *Transnational Families, Migration and the Circulation of Care: Understanding mobility and absence in family life*, New York: Routledge.

Chio, J. (2014) *A Landscape of Travel: The work of tourism in rural ethnic China*, Seattle: University of Washington Press.

Chio, J. (2011) Know yourself: Making the visual work in tourism research. In C. Michael Hall (ed.), *Fieldwork in Tourism: Methods, issues and reflections*, London: Routledge, pp. 209–219.

Christensen, N.B. (2003) *Inuit in Cyberspace: Embedding offline identities online*, Copenhagen: Museum and Tusculanum Press and University of Copenhagen.

Edensor, T. (2001) Performing tourism, staging tourism: (Re)producing tourist space and practice. *Tourist Studies*, 1(1): 59–81.

Edwards, E. (2012). Objects of affect: Photography beyond the image. *Annual Review of Anthropology*, 41: 221–234.

Fischer, E. F. (2014) *The Good Life: Aspiration, dignity, and the anthropology of wellbeing*, Berkeley: Stanford University Press.

Glick Schiller, N. and Salazar, N. B. (2013) Regimes of mobility across the globe. *Journal of Ethnic and Migration Studies*, 39 (2): 183–200.

Harris, M. and Rapport, N. (eds) (2015) *Reflections on Imagination: Human capacity and ethnographic method*, London: Routledge.

Hjorth, L., Horst, H., Galloway, A. and Bell, G. (eds.) (2017). *The Routledge Companion to Digital Ethnography*, London: Routledge.

Kothari, U. (2015). Reworking colonial imaginaries in post-colonial tourist enclaves. *Tourist Studies*, 15 (3): 248–266.

Liechty, M. (2017) *Far Out: Countercultural seekers and the tourist encounter in Nepal*, Chicago: University of Chicago Press.

Linder, B. (2017). Of 'tourist' places: The cultural politics of narrating space in Thamel. *HIMALAYA, the Journal of the Association for Nepal and Himalayan Studies*, 37 (1): 10.

Madianou, M. (2019) Migration, transnational families, and new communication technologies. In J. Retis and R. Tsagaousianou (eds), *The Handbook of Diasporas, Media and Culture*, London: John Wiley & Sons, pp. 577–590.

Mazzolini, E. (2015). *The Everest Effect: Nature, culture, ideology*. Alabama: University of Alabama Press.

Miller, D. 1994. *Modernity: An ethnographic approach*. Oxford: Berg.

Miller, D. and Sinanan, J. (2017) *Visualising Facebook*. London: UCL Press.

Ministry of Culture, Tourism, and Civil Aviation (MOTCA) (2017) *Nepal Tourism Statistics 2016*, Kathmandu, Nepal: MOTCA.

Mu, Y. and Nepal, S. (2016) High mountain adventure tourism: Trekkers' perceptions of risk and death in Mt. Everest Region, Nepal. *Asia Pacific Journal of Tourism Research*, 21 (5): 500–511.

Nepal, S. (2005) Tourism and remote mountain settlements: Spatial and temporal development of tourist infrastructure in the Mt Everest region, Nepal. *Tourism Geographies*, 7 (2): 205–227.

Norum, R. (2013). *The Hypersocial: transience, privilege and the neo-colonial imaginary in expatria, Kathmandu* (unpublished Doctoral dissertation, University of Oxford).

Ortner, S. B. (2001) *Life and Death on Mt. Everest: Sherpas and Himalayan mountaineering*, Princeton: Princeton University Press.

Palmer, C. (2002) 'Shit happens': The selling of risk in extreme sport. *The Australian Journal of Anthropology*, 13 (3): 323–336.

Pertierra, A. C. (2018) *Media Anthropology for the Digital Age*, Cambridge: Polity.

Pink, S., Horst, H., Postill, J., Hjorth, L., Lewis, T. and Tacchi, J. (2016) *Digital Ethnography: Principles and practices*. London: Sage.

Pinney, C. (2002) The Indian work of art in the age of mechanical reproduction: Or, what happens when peasants 'get hold' of images. In F. Ginsburg, L. Abu-Lughod and B. Larkin, (eds), *Media Worlds: Anthropology on new terrain*. Berkeley: University of California Press, pp. 355–369.

Polson, E. (2016) *Privileged Mobilities: Professional migration, geo-social media, and a new global middle class*. New York: Peter Lang.

Poole, D. (1997) *Vision, Race, and Modernity: A visual economy of the Andean image world*, Princeton: Princeton University Press.

Sinanan, J. (2017). *Social Media in Trinidad: Values and visibility*, London: UCL Press.

Smith, S. P. (2018) Instagram abroad: Performance, consumption and colonial narrative in tourism. *Postcolonial Studies*, 21 (2): 172–191.

Sørensen, N. and Olwig, K. (eds), (2002) *Work and Migration: Life and livelihoods in a globalizing world*. London: Routledge.

The Guardian. *Everest Covid Cases Shine Harsh Light on Nepalese Decision to Open Mountain*. 27 April 2021 www.theguardian.com/world/2021/apr/23/everest-covid-cases-shine-harsh-light-on-nepalese-decision-to-open-mountain Accessed 27 April 2021.

Thompson, K. A. (2015) *Shine: The visual economy of light in African diasporic aesthetic practice*, Durham: Duke University Press.

Urry, J. and Larsen, J. (2011). *The Tourist Gaze 3.0*, London: Sage.

Washington Post. How Mount Everest became a tourist destination. 31 May 2019 www.washingtonpost.com/sports/2019/05/31/how-mount-everest-became-tourist-destination/ Accessed 1 June 2019.

Wood, M. (2001). The mountain panorama and its significance in the Scottish context. *Cartographica: The International Journal for Geographic Information and Geovisualization*, 38 (1–2): 103–118.

18
POSTCOLONIAL DIGITAL COLLECTIONS

Instruments, Mirrors, Agents

Haidy Geismar and Katja Müller

This chapter explores the relationship between digital media in collections and postcolonial and decolonial critique focusing on the politics of representation on the politics of representation. By working at two scales, a top-down exploration of postcolonial theories of representation and how they may be applied to digital collections, and a bottom-up case study of how these issues are engaged with on the ground in museums and archives (with a particular focus on India), we aim to open up questions about the importance of digital media in challenging the global power relations, and ideas about normativity, that are often implicitly encoded within museum projects. Here we link to what Udupa, Costa, and Budka (2018) call the "digital turn" in media anthropology: a turn towards unravelling the conceptual, material, and infrastructural qualities of digital media as a social process and cultural practice (see also Larkin, 2013). Our discussion brings to media anthropology a connection to the growing literature focused on critical histories of digital technologies in museums and their relationship to past practices of collection and display (Geismar, 2018; Turner, 2016), in the broader context of aspirations for what Risam terms a "postcolonial digital humanities" (2019).

We follow Tariq Jazeel by utilizing an understanding of postcolonialism drawn not from the anticolonial political movements of the twentieth century, such as Negritude or Black Marxism, but rather from 1970s literary studies to focus particularly on the forms, structures, and institutional aesthetics and representational practices that both embody and resist colonialism (Jazeel, 2019: 8). Despite a lengthy excavation of the colonial legacies of collecting and ordering within museums and archives, it remains the case that the promises of postcolonial theories of both power and representation are not always realized within the everyday practices of museums and archives. Some of this is *because of* the close historical, and ongoing, relationship between museums, collections and archives, and colonial orderings. In recent years there has been a shift in critical discourse away from the term "postcolonial" towards the concept of the "decolonial," in order to recognize the ongoing presence and instantiation of colonial knowledge systems and political authorities, and to signify commitment to the ongoing work of unravelling and refusing the colonial project (see Lonetree, 2012).[1] In the absence of a truly *post*colonial commitment in many places, particularly in the Global North, decolonizing projects now abound within museums and archives around the world (see Jilani, 2018).

The present turn to decolonization in museums and the convergences of these movements with other social justice movements are worth a study in their own right. Here, we draw on some key postcolonial and decolonial theories of representation, to explore how they may be productively linked to digital museum practices and media (see Fernandez, 1999). Media, and visual, anthropology has long been a space in which practices of cultural difference, and unequal global power structures have been explored (e.g. Pinney, 2002; Pinney and Peterson, 2003). We continue this perspective turning towards the digital infrastructures that are increasingly the idiom through which knowledge of collections is both contained and produced. We acknowledge our own positions as European scholars and curators, who have been privileged both to access European collections and to work collaboratively with stakeholders around the world (in India, Vanuatu, and New Zealand).

Throughout the chapter we move between two entwined registers: the first explores the key questions provoked by the convergence of postcolonial theories of representation and the structuring of cultural collections by digital media. We start by introducing some of the tensions between theory and practice that have emerged within cultural institutions since the putative end of European Imperialism, and explore the ways in which the digital may be less "new" than is first imagined, perpetuating colonial legacies as well as constituting new global discourses of access and citizenship. We then explore a range of digital museum projects, and link them to some of the key tropes of postcolonial theory, focusing on how we can understand digital practices as an instrument, a mirror, and an agent.[2]

Framed by a politics of resistance, decolonial theory draws attention to the continued structures of domination that inflect contemporary experience (Mignolo and Walsh, 2018; Anderson and Christen, 2019). Colonial power relations in India have been subject to intense critique (e.g. Cohn, 1996; Dirks, 1993; see also Stoler, 2009). This has led many to challenge the temporal linearity that initially seems self-evident in the very category of the *postcolonial*, which as a term is suggestive of a before and an after. Indeed, many commentators have challenged this linear thinking and highlight the ongoing systems of domination within which these debates are taking place (e.g. Hall, 1995). The case of India demonstrates the temporal complexities and geopolitical entanglements that underscore contemporary practices in museums and archives. Our focus here on India highlights the importance of recognizing historical, cultural, and geographical specificity within these broader set of global questions and debates, but also emphasizes the partiality that underscores a challenge to the perceived (or perhaps desired) holism of digital representation. Two big questions have underpinned our thinking: *When is the postcolonial? What is the digital?* These questions help us to explore how political and social theory might be transformed into code and enacted within digital platforms, which may then be understood to presence (and perhaps perpetuate, but hopefully decolonize) the ongoing legacies of colonial systems. Drawing on notions of the digital as an instrument, a mirror, and an agent, we end by positing we might in fact reverse our big questions to ask *When is the digital? What is the postcolonial?*

Situating the Postcolonial in Museums

The robust body of historical, sociological, aesthetic, and literary engagement with colonialism has for a long time interrogated how museums and archives have been, and continue to be, implicated in colonial projects and in some instances extend the legacy of colonial history into the present day (see e.g. Anderson and Christen, 2019; Basu and de Jong, 2016; Gosden and Knowles, 2001; Hicks, 2020; Thomas, 1994; Zeitlyn, 2012). Museums and archives have been prominent sites of knowledge production, where national collecting practices have historically emerged hand in hand with imperial expansion. Museums and archives have long been understood as integral to the fashioning of colonial knowledge systems and epistemologies, as sites where the ideologies of colonialism, imperialism, and nationalism are mediated and re-presented to the world (see e.g. Barringer and Flynn, 1998; Bennett et al., 2016; Henare, 2005; Jasanoff, 2006; Mathur, 2007).[3]

In India, after independence national leaders envisioned the museum after colonialism as one central aspect in building the newly partitioned nation-state. The opening of the National Museum of India in Delhi in 1960 explicitly aimed to demarcate the transition from colonial rule to independent nationhood (Singh, 2015; Shivadas, 2015). However, inside the museum, many of the museological conventions established in colonial times persisted. To this day, many of the galleries reflect the layout and ideas of an exhibition of Indian art and artefacts displayed at the Royal Academy in London in the winter of 1947–48 (see Singh, 2015). While the 1980s was a decade when the National Museum – as many other Indian museums – grappled to find its place between spectacle, entertainment, education, and state power (Appadurai and Beckenridge, 2015), and the 2000s and 2010s saw some galleries at the National Museum and other institutions undergoing renovation, they show little deviation from exhibition patterns laid out pre-Independence. These museum galleries display globally recognized "great masterworks," predominantly sculpture arranged according to time periods or religion.

Elliott's ethnography of the Indian Museum in Kolkata, another government museum founded in 1814, describes how "staff are very conscious of their institutions' historic legacy" (Elliott, 2006). When searching for the "postcolonial" in these institutions, we are not tracking a stringent evolution from colonial instruments of power in the peripheries of empire to postcolonial centres that reshape the relationship between the country and its Indigenous population. Rather, we encounter a (sometimes uncritical) continuation of work within institutional structures established during the colonial period during which museums were established as tools of political authority and governance (see e.g. Anderson, 1991). Similar patterns emerge in contemporary archiving culture in India, in which the National Archives, for instance, are still organized today in similar lines to their predecessor the "Imperial Record Department" that the British established in 1891. Today, 125 years into its existence and more than 70 years after independence, the National Archives continue to perform the legacy of the "paper Raj" (see Hull, 2012; Mattur, 2015; Rajpal, 2012). Access is frequently denied on the grounds of political sensitivity, interests of the nation, inappropriate content for females, or not explained at all (Balachandran and Pinto, 2011: 24).

These examples of colonial establishments, demarcations, and continuities within museum and archival practices highlight that the postcolonial period continues to raise tensions about archival and curatorial authority, the materialization of national identity through collections, and to perpetuate exclusion and hierarchy in national cultural institutions. The postcolony, as Mbembe (2001) has pointed out, can continue, rather than supersede, "the banality of power," and we may see archives and museums as instances of the banal authority of representational media within the contemporary nation-state.

Into the Digital

In 2012, the Indian Ministry of Culture started an initiative to digitize all museum collections (Figure 18.1), starting with ten major governmental museums, who created a national database called Jatan (see Müller, 2021). The Ministry sees Jatan as part of a broader national digitization programme, converging with "Digital India": a national "vision to transform India into

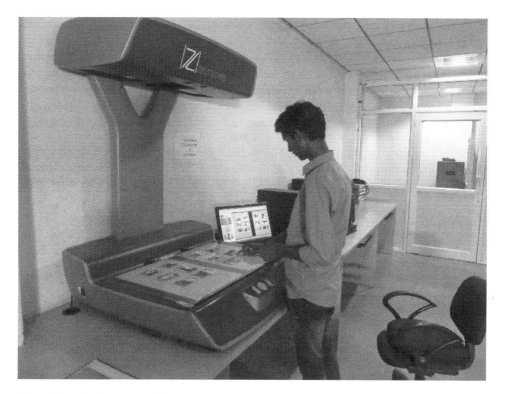

Figure 18.1 Digitizing in an Indian museum
Source: Photograph by K. Müller.

a digitally empowered society and knowledge economy."[4] Digital India aims to integrate all government departments and develop digital literacy to "empower" citizens of India, focusing on an expansion of digital infrastructure, including the connection of rural areas to high-speed internet, and the availability of government services in online format. "Digital India" aims at penetrating all parts of society (see Sen, 2016). The basis for this digitization agenda of the national government is the success story of India's ICT industry in the 1990s and 2000s. It provided a highly valued export commodity and made India a key player within the global information economy; arguably being the first relevant good that the country has contributed to the world market since independence (Sen, 2016).

This success and the current push for digitizing society have been praised for its ambitions and scale, but signals also signal some of the dominant narratives uncritically praising contemporary digital media (Sneha, 2016: 4). The compressions of both time and space, form and content within digital technologies has in many ways created an interpretive palimpsest with the category of the digital, or new media, often erasing histories of mediation across different forms (see Gitelman, 2006). Conceptual erasures of the past surrounding the discourse of "new media" have also entered into museums and archives, sometimes obliterating the past in ways that have significant consequences. Rather than overlaying the past with an ever-new present, neglecting these histories can result in the tacit import of norms and conventions from old media into new (see Geismar, 2018). Part of a decolonial agenda is to insist that the historical legacy of colonialism be fully addressed in order to transcend its own constraints (see for example Kassim, 2019 writing back to Hunt, 2019).

India's digitization campaign has rendered invisible the colonial legacy that in fact underpins it. Nair (2018) argues that the techniques and technologies underpinning the digital identification programme, *Aadhar*, emerge directly from colonial genealogies (where India was the colonial laboratory for the development of imperial technologies such as fingerprinting and anthropometry) and work to create neocolonial forms of citizenship with ongoing tensions between the extension of governance into digital form, and the exclusions, imbalances, and global politics that these projects inevitably encode.

This sense of the digital ushering in the new, and in a sense wiping the slate clean, is also felt in regards to the Jatan database. The discourse of Jatan being a postcolonial and democratizing venture, making collections accessible online, celebrates the digital as open and free. One director summarized Jatan as "an invaluable tool for scholars working from anywhere in the world who can come up within minutes with what exactly is where and then send requests."[5] But others are less enthusiastic. Another director stresses the continuity of structural inequalities, and views the digital as an important site of national autonomy and ownership:

> I don't mind others all over the world doing research on these topics, but when we as representatives of the Indian state are in charge of the collection, I also think that we should be the ones to have the right to first research and publish.[6]

What can be read as a gatekeeper's reluctance to make heritage accessible at the same time discloses how the digital tends to overwrite lessons learned in the past. The director worries that the Indian state is establishing itself internationally as a digital front-runner at the cost of protecting India's digital resources (Figure 18.2). He sees Jatan as a continuation of India's colonial history: a country where resources are extracted from, rather than nationally consumed, to benefit others, usually in the Global North. He refers to the context of structural inequalities, resulting and persisting from colonial domination, within which Jatan is situated, in particular the worldwide hegemony of museum research and academia in the Global North.

Three Postcolonial Theories of (Digital) Representation

We argue that it is productive to switch registers of questioning between the postcolonial and the digital: to explore the temporal and historical registers of the digital and to try to understand the material foundations and practices of postcolonial theories of representation. In this section we develop a framework for understanding the ways in which digital media might be mobilized for decolonial practices in the museum or archive. In so doing, we propose three tropes from broader and well-established postcolonial theories of representation that might help us to understand many contradictions we have seen emerge in digital museum projects.

The Digital as Instrument

In *Orientalism*, Said influentially argued for the instrumentality of aesthetic form in colonial political projects (2003). Literature and visual arts rendered cultural images as objective or evidential facts that then served to justify or legitimate cultural stereotypes of the colonized others in the minds of Europeans. This emphasis on instrumentalism brought in by Said's representational critique of colonialism helps us to understand how digital systems are used to act out intentions that are always entangled in pre-existing architectures of knowledge and power. We may see digital collection management systems, for example, as tools that constitute the

Postcolonial Digital Collections

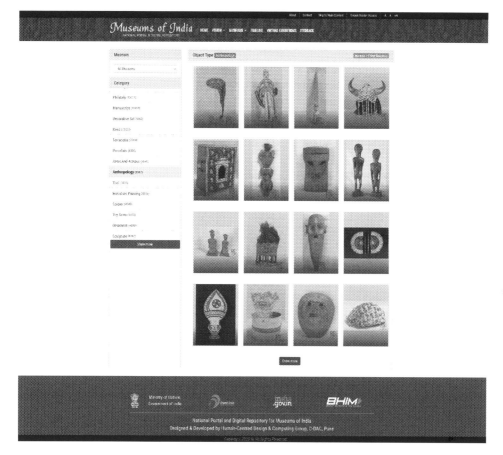

Figure 18.2 Screenshot of Jatan's frontend

knowledge necessary to organize, classify, and manage people as objects, reinforcing colonial values and world-views.

The Digital as Mirror or Mimesis[7]

We can extend this understanding of the instrumentality of the digital to think about the capacity of the digital to refract and mirror, changing the way we understand the world, and our place in it. Mimesis has been explored by theorists such as Homi Bhabha and Michael Taussig to highlight the ways in which representational technologies were complicit in producing a reverse or relational gaze in which the subjectivity of the viewer is produced as much as that of the viewed. This form of mimesis – "the nature that culture uses to create second nature, the faculty to copy, imitate, make models, explore difference, yield into and become Other" (Taussig, 1993: xiii) – supports Bhabha's notion of hybridity (1994) in which the facts of identity continually refract within one another. Moving beyond the realism implicit in instrumental theories of technology's capacity to act in the world, a focus on the mimetic pushes us to think about a more magical realism that might creatively inflect shared representational projects in colonial contexts (see Eaton, 2013). Bhabha uses this as a tactic to read resistance into the representational record. The notion of mimesis explores the digital not just as an instrumental domain of power, but also as a space that co-produces aesthetics, and knowledge, in which categories and classificatory judgments emerge from many different sites which work collectively to produce an understanding of the digital as much as an understanding of the knowledge or culture contained within it.

The Digital as Agent

Concepts of instrumentality and mimesis help us to understand the recursive ways in which digital media are entangled within existing structures of knowledge and power, but we also need to pay attention to the power of technology itself. Within postcolonial theories of representation, the notion of agency is intimately bound up with understandings of resistance, as a way of reading both along and against the grain of colonial history and the archive. Anne Stoler (2009) and others have been tracing voices that have conventionally been muted or obliterated. The digital can (re-)engage with and enhance these readings and the re-discovery of alterity within the colonial archive, which contains an implicit theory of agency, as an assertion of presence, activating the subject as a wilful player with capacities to alter the world.

Postcolonial Digital Projects in Theory and Practice

Risam (2019) argues that the promise of a postcolonial digital humanities is in the ways in which it can link theory, praxis, and pedagogy, linking critical thinking to the craft of building new projects in the world. For Risam,

> postcolonial digital humanities examines the possibility of recovering technologies being used for humanities scholarship beyond their complicity with colonialism… where examples of how computational technologies have been used against power – such as hacking, open access, and open source development – offer hope.
>
> *2019: 37*

The next section outlines some museum projects in India that we see as working towards this aim, and we use on the representational tropes from within postcolonial theory as a scaffold.

New Forms of Digital Collecting

A few years prior to the founding of Jatan in 2004, new heritage actors from outside of established institutions started to use digital forms to critique and remake the historical record. Indian Memory Project (www.indianmemoryproject.com) is one example of a newly created non-state archive aiming at engaging people in memory making and reflections on the nation's past. Anusha Yadav, a Bombay-based graphic designer, photographer, and curator, founded the project in 2010. She crowdsources and scans pre-1990 photographs, which she publishes online along with a written testimony focussing on the image. The 200+ entries stimulate online exchanges between people near and far, commenting and exchanging thoughts and memories on the website and beyond (see Müller, 2017a). Similarly, but with a larger audience of more than 900,000 followers on Facebook, the 1947 Partition Archive (www.1947partitionarchive.org) publishes written summaries of the entries of its newly created collection: an archive of 9,000+ digital video recordings of partition survivors telling their life stories. Guneeta Bhalla, the founder of the archive, leads a team of a dozen members and volunteers – with offices in Delhi and the USA – who set out to video-interview people who lived through partition, and subsequently upload the video content – recorded mostly in India and Pakistan – to this online archive.[8] Setting up an archive is, here, a consequence of missing reconciliation and memorial sites, and a way of recognizing the discrepancy between the continuing importance of the Indian partition in 1947 for people's everyday lives and the wide neglect of the issue in national cultural institutions. The partition not only created the states of India and Pakistan, but a huge refugee crisis with up to 20 million displaced and up to two million dead people. The violence during partition affects the relationship of the two countries until today (see e.g. Talbot and Singh, 2009). The voices from below, from amidst the subcontinent's society, are to fill perceived gaps in memory making and reconciliation, and enter the political arena of making the past.

Instrumentalizing the Database

A large amount of postcolonial digital critique has focused on altering and intervening in the knowledge systems and epistemologies constructed by collecting, archiving, and categorizing in museums and archives (see Risam, 2019). Following Verran and Christie, we might term this "postcolonial databasing" (2014). Postcolonial databasing is not only a theoretical concept but a practical means to bring Indigenous or alternative knowledge systems into the knowledge architectures of collections, intervening into the classificatory systems that organize collections. If, as Verran and Christie note, databasing "is a contemporary way of 'doing knowledge' with information and communications technologies" (2014: 57), postcolonial databasing aims to open up these technical structures to alternative knowledge systems, and in doing so undoes the overwriting of these systems by colonial epistemologies. This movement began within the very particular context of Anglophone settler-colonialism, emerging prominently in projects in Canada, New Zealand, and Australia. Postcolonial databasing acknowledges the classificatory power (or instrumentalism) of the database and inserts Indigenous agency into the very structures of classification. Verran's own work in Australia, working to explore how Aboriginal knowledge can be used to structure digital projects, has emerged alongside projects such as *Ara Iritija* and *Mukurtu*, which have been developed explicitly as archives in which Indigenous knowledge and protocols structure accessibility, aesthetics, and intellectual property of the archive as well as forming the content of new archival initiatives (Verran and Christie, 2013; Christen, 2005; Thorner, 2010; Povinelli, 2011, 2016).

Within the Indian subcontinent, there exists to our knowledge no comparable cultural databasing initiative in the cultural sector, although interesting work has commenced in the area of the digitization of traditional knowledge across a range of other contexts (medical, scientific, and environmental) in initiatives such as the Traditional Knowledge Digital Library.[9] In the cultural sector, projects include archiving and book publishing projects like *adivaani*[10] and *Sahapedia*,[11] founded in the aftermath of a government digitization project, or the archive *Tasveer Ghar*.[12] All of these are web-based projects that gather and tag or order articles, contemporary and historical images, projects, and videos on India's (visual) heritage, which are accessible for everyone through ubiquitous search platforms. Here, the move away from centralized government owned databases towards civil society projects that run on the engines of social media and web-based applications poses a number of challenges to the capacities of national museums and archives to fully open their collections and also challenges our formulation of the instrumental mapping of the museum/archive and the nation onto one another.

Digital Objects and Mimetic Returns

A third space of postcolonial digital practice and intervention into existing collections is to use the promise of new media to allow what especially in trans- or international contexts is sometimes called digital repatriation[13] or digital return. One Indian example of this was the *Purvajo-ni Aankh* exhibition event in Gujarat in 2012. Narayan and Vikesh Rathwa, curators at the Museum of Voice, Adivasi Academy, in collaboration with the local Indigenous Rathwa community simultaneously exhibited and worshipped photographic images that had returned to the Rathwa after being stored in Europe for several decades. The photographs, produced by Europeans between the 1920s and 1950s, depict various Indigenous communities in India. The photographs have been housed at the Museum for Archaeology and Anthropology in Cambridge and the Dresden Museum für Völkerkunde, who in response to demands also from the Adivasi Academy digitized and "returned" the digital copies to India. It was left to the Adivasi Academy to decide if and how to use the digital reproductions. Narayan and Vikesh Rathwa chose to exhibit them and selected, enlarged, printed and framed, and installed photographs in an open-air gallery at Koraj Hill, a sacred site. The exhibition comprised the procession with many of the local Rathwa singing and dancing, and the local priest consecrating some of the images. Curators, priest, and local village men later explained the photographs' worship at Koraj Hill (and subsequently in private houses, where they were arranged as adjunct to shrines and religious paintings) as the praise and worship of ancestors.

The return of these photographs in digital form was originally framed in terms of digital accessibility and circulation (see Rycroft and Müller, 2013). However, during the exhibition the Rathwa appropriated them as returning ancestors, who require respectful treatment and periodic worship. They gave new meaning to digitized and re-materialized photographs in accordance with local visual systems and religious reference points (Müller, 2017b, www.vimeo.com/66922942). Moving beyond notions of accessibility, and drawing on notions of mimesis, this form of exhibition can be seen to continue a long-standing trajectory of public engagement with Indian museums in which collections are co-opted into alternative aesthetic and experiential orders, running parallel but often completely counter to the rational order of colonial display, reading against the grain of typical readings of Indian museums that we started this article with (see Mathur and Singh, 2017). What is more, this act of mimetic reproduction facilitated a form of cultural appropriation that completely transformed the viewing structures of the collection within the European museums. The focus for the Rathwa was on returned ancestor images to be integrated into local visual and religious systems. Asked if they were interested in the story of the original photographs and their itineraries, the Rathwa answered in the negative. This was not to repudiate the collections' importance as a reference to the past, but rather shows that holding institutions still practice, and arguably fetishize, a distinction between original and copy. By elevating the (rematerialized) digital reproductions through exhibition and consecration, the Rathwa incorporate an appraisal of historic records and (new) originals while at the same time annulling it. Conversely, the European museums can draw on this "story of impact" (Marsh et al., 2016) and turn the neglect of interest in their "original" collections into an asset once more.

Digital returns and digital objects often provoke such negotiations of and further conversations about authenticity, ownership, and the circulation of collections. Digital technologies are being used to image and reimagine the form of collections, using not only reprints of digital/digitized photographs, but also techniques such as 3D and 2D scanning, sound and moving image, as well as the sharing of databases and files (see Al Badri and Nelles, 2017). Such projects provoke complex articulations and understandings, often culturally located, of digital materiality as well as drawing our attention to the colonial politics of digital circulation (e.g. Ngata, Ngata-Gibson, and Salmond, 2012; Hogsden and Poulter, 2012). Digital resources are not only currently creating new and complex materialities but also permit new kinds of access to collections.[14] They allow for objects to return not only to so-called source communities, but simultaneously to several different communities, or evoke novel forms of engagement, surrounding the authenticity of collections, and contesting the status of digital files as museum or community property (Isaac, 2015; see also Hollinger et al., 2013). Mimetic performances emerging around the digital return of cultural materials constitute new forms of symbolic ownership and appropriation, and can thereby undo the hegemony of national and international museum values and representations.

Conclusion

We have shown the promises, and limitations, of digital media, in the context of both postcolonial theory, and postcolonial practices in contemporary India. Whilst the Indian projects we have discussed may be informed by and linked to the representational critiques of postcolonial theory, particularly around ideas about instrumentalism, mimesis, and agency, they also make explicit some of the tensions that remain within museums and archives as fundamentally colonial institutions that have become sites for both the perpetuation of colonial power relations and epistemologies *as well as* for their unravelling. The constitution of new digital cultural sites in India, the introduction of digital technology to museums, and digital returns from Europe to India facilitate new forms of engagement, and extend postcolonial critiques of the nation. But as postcolonial projects they are also fraught with tension and ambiguity. Within this engaged set of material practices, postcolonial theory may be understood as a form of critique that is leveraged both for and against the state, as well as an imaginary from which to reimagine these cultural collections and institutions. We are arguing here that rather than defining the postcolonial in relation to periods of history, postcolonial theories of representation may be seen as an extended set of practices, tools, or objects in the so-called digital age. In turn, rather than focusing on the materiality of the digital, we may also understand the digital in temporal terms, as a moment within longer histories of museums and collections. This historicizing perspective on the digital allows us understand the complex ways in which digital technologies are entangled with existing institutional conventions, knowledge structures, memory politics, and forms of accessibility.

Digital media, rather than simply being understood as a set of practices, tools, or objects, is itself a powerful imaginary, incorporating dreams of modernity and constituting an imagined global community. This imaginary is often placed out of history, where the digital is imagined simply as a vessel for collections rather than a formative substance from which collections and archives are generated. It is important to pay attention to the complex ways in which digital technologies are entangled with existing knowledge structures, hierarchies, forms of accessibility, expertise, circulation, and property relations. Understanding the digital as a temporal as well as material register allows us to be mindful that the digital is just as complicit within nation-making, and globalizing projects as it is within projects that resist them.

Acknowledgments

We would like to acknowledge the participants in the *Postcolonial Digital Collections* symposium generously funded by the Fritz Thyssen Siftung (2017-01467): Wayne Modest, Ciraj Rassool, Sarah Kenderdine, Andrea Scholz, Nora Al-Badri, Anuba Singh, Laura Gibson, Kate Hennessy,

Hannah Turner, Jane Anderson, Tunde Opeibi, Angelica Serna, and Puthiya Purayil Sneha. Thanks also to Antonia Walford, Kostis Arvanitis, and Jolynna Sinanan for valuable critical feedback on previous drafts of this essay.

Notes

1. As Bhambra notes, the term postcolonial has emerged more prominently in relation to culture than that of decolonial that "was strongly linked to world systems theory from the outset as well as to scholarly work in development and underdevelopment theory and the Frankfurt School critical social theory tradition" (Bhambra, 2014: 118). In turn, there is a regional slant to these discussions: talk of postcolonialism emerged the Middle East and South Asia, Decolonialism in Latin America. Both terms write largely back to European colonialism and recognize the entanglement of colonialism and modernity. In this paper we continue to explore the legacy of the theorists we cite who cluster their thinking around the term postcolonial but advocate for a broader decolonial stance to enact such theory in practice.
2. This chapter emerges from a workshop we organized together at the University of Halle in 2017, entitled *Postcolonial Digital Collections*, which brought together scholars and practitioners to discuss the intersections of postcolonial theory and practices within museums and archives in a global and comparative context. The workshop was held on 16/17 May 2018 at the Center for Interdisciplinary Area Studies (ZIRS) at Halle University and was organized by Katja Müller and Haidy Geismar with support from the Fritz Thyssen Siftung. Thanks to the participants: Ciraj Rassool, Wayne Modest, Sarah Kenderdine, Hannah Turner, Tunde Obeibi, Anubha Sinha, Andrea Scholz, Nora Al-Badri, Laura Gibson, Puthia Purayil Sneha, and Angelica Serna for feedback during the workshop which contributed to this chapter. Many of the presentations have been archived at https://web.archive.org (last accessed 22 August, 2021).
3. The emergence of local cultural centres, ecomuseums, and other institutional structures aimed to undo the inequality between centre and periphery established by imperial expansion (see e.g. Isaac, 2007). This institutional rethinking has underscored an important strand of contemporary decolonial museology, especially in the settler-colonies of the USA, Canada, Australia and New Zealand where Indigenous peoples continue to struggle for sovereignty over collections that remain under a colonial jurisdiction. In this context, a broader critique of colonialism has not only created new institutions and centres for collections, but has reformed national museums (see Henare, 2004; Lonetree and Cobb, 2008; Williams, 2005; Schorch and McCarthy, 2019).
4. See http://museumsofindia.gov.in/repository/page/digitization_initiative, last accessed 30 December 2019, and www.museumsofindia.gov.in/repository/page/msg_hcm, last accessed 6 June 2019. http://digitalindia.gov.in/content/about-programme
5. Quote from field interview with K. Müller, March 2019.
6. Quote from field interviews with K. Müller, March 2019.
7. "The menace of mimicry is its double vision which in disclosing the ambivalence of colonial discourse also disrupts its authority. And it is a double vision that is a result of what I've described as the partial representation/recognition of the colonial object" (Bhabha, 1994: 126).
8. So far, only a small number of the full video interviews is available for view through several university servers. Almost all interviews are online in the form of short written summaries along with one to three photographs of the interviewee.
9. See www.tkdl.res.in/tkdl/langdefault/common/Home.asp?GL=Eng, last accessed 7 February 2020.
10. https://adivaani.org/
11. www.sahapedia.org
12. www.tasveergharindia.net
13. The notion of digital repatriation has been heavily critiqued by some people and communities, who rightly note that receiving digital files or hard disks usually does not free collections from their institutional home in museums, and rather reinforces the existing status quo of ownership and authority for colonial collections. Robin Boast's and Jim Enote's critique of Clifford's notion of the Contact Zone as neo-colonial underpins their argument that virtual repatriation is often "neither virtual or repatriation," rather suggesting that ideas of digital simulation are used to perpetuate existing relational dynamics within collections (Boast and Enote, 2013).

14 A collection of essays, generated by a series of workshops at the Smithsonian National Museum of Natural History, entitled "After the Return" summarizes many of these initiatives (Bell, Christen, and Turin, 2013).

References

Appadurai, A. and Breckenridge, C. (2015) "Museums are Good to Think: Heritage on View in India" in S. Mathur and K. Singh (eds), *No Touching, No Spitting, No Praying: The Museum in South Asia*, London: Routledge, 173–183.

Anderson, J. and Christen, K. (2019) "Decolonizing Attribution: Traditions of Exclusion," *Journal of Radical Librarianship*, 5, available at www.journal.radicallibrarianship.org/index.php/journal/article/view/38 (accessed 17 January 2021).

Al-Badri, N. and Nelles, J. N. (2017) *Not a Single Bone*, Berlin: NOME Gallery.

Balachandran, A. and Pinto, R. (2011) "Archives and Access," New Delhi/Bangalore: The Centre for Internet and Society, Researchers at Work online publication, available. https://cis-india.org/raw/h (accessed 17 January 2021).

Basu, P. and De Jong, F. (2016) "Utopian Archives, Decolonial Affordances. Introduction to Special Issue: Utopian Archives, Decolonial Affordances," *Social Anthropology*, 24 (1): 5–19.

Barringer, T. and Flynn, T., eds. (1998) *Colonialism and the Object: Empire, Material Culture and the Museum*, London: Routledge.

Bell, J. A., Christen, A. and Turin, M. (2013) "Introduction: After the Return," *Museum Anthropology Review*, 7 (1–2): 1–21.

Bennett, T., Cameron, F., Das, N., Dibley, B., Harrison, R., Jacknis, I., and McCarthy, C. (2016) *Collecting, Ordering, Governing: Anthropology, Museums, and Liberal Government*, Durham: Duke University Press.

Bhabha, H. K. (1994) "Of Mimicry and Man: The Ambivalence of Colonial Discourse" in *The Location of Culture*, London: Routledge, 121–131.

Bhambra, G. K. (2014) "Postcolonial and Decolonial Reconstructions" in *Connected Sociologies*, London: Bloomsbury Academic, 117–140.

Boast, R. and Enote, J. (2013) "Virtual Repatriation: It Is Neither Virtual nor Repatriation" in P. F. Biehl and C. Prescott (eds), *Heritage in the Context of Globalization: Europe and the Americas*, New York: Springer New York, 103–113.

Christen, K. (2005) "Gone Digital: Aboriginal Remix and the Cultural Commons," *International Journal of Cultural Property*, 12 (3): 315.

Christie, M. and Verran, H. (2013) "Digital Lives in Postcolonial Aboriginal Australia," *Journal of Material Culture*, 18 (3): 299–317.

Cohn, B. S. (1996) *Colonialism and its Forms of Knowledge: The British in India*, Princeton: Princeton University Press.

Dirks, N. B. (1993) "Colonial Histories and Native Informants: Biography of an Archive" in C. Breckenridge and P. van der Veer (eds), *Orientalism and the Postcolonial Predicament: Perspectives on South Asia*, Philadelphia: University of Pennsylvania Press, 279–313.

Eaton, N. (2013) *Mimesis across Empires: Artworks and Networks in India, 1765–1860*, Durham: Duke University Press.

Elliott, M. (2006) "Side Effects: Looking, Touching, and Interacting in the Indian Museum, Kolkata," *Journal of Museum Ethnography*, 18: 63–75.

Fernandez, Maria. 1999. "Postcolonial Media Theory," *Art Journal* 58 (3): 58. https://doi.org/10.2307/777861.

Geismar, H. (2018) *Museum Object Lessons for the Digital Age*, London: UCL Press.

Gitelman, L. (2006) *Always Already New: Media, History, and the Data of Culture*, Cambridge: MIT Press.

Gosden, C. and Knowles, C. (2001) *Collecting Colonialism: Material Culture and Colonial Change*, Oxford: Berg.

Hall, S. (1995) "When Was the 'Post-Colonial'? Thinking at the Limit" in I. Chambers and L. Curti (eds), *Post-Colonial Question: Common Skies, Divided Horizons*, London: Routledge: 242–260.

Henare, A. (2004) "Rewriting the Script: Te Papa Tongarewa the Museum of New Zealand," *Social Analysis*, 48 (1): 55–63.

Henare, A. (2005) *Museums, Anthropology and Imperial Exchange*, Cambridge: Cambridge University Press.

Hicks, D. 2020. *The Brutish Museums: The Benin Bronzes, Colonial Violence and Cultural Restitution*. London: Pluto Press.

Hogsden, C. and Poulter, E. K. (2012) "The Real Other? Museum Objects in Digital Contact Networks," *Journal of Material Culture*, 17 (3): 265–286.

Hollinger, R. E., Edwell, J., Jacobs, L., Moran-Collins, L., Thome, C., Zastrow, J., Metallo, A., Waibel, G., and Rossi, V. (2013). "Tlingit-Smithsonian Collaborations with 3D Digitization of Cultural Objects," *Museum Anthropology Review*, 7 (1–2): 201–253.

Hull, M. S. (2012) "Documents and Bureaucracy," *Annual Review of Anthropology*, 41: 251–267.

Hunt, T. (2019) "Should Museums Return their Colonial Artefacts?" *The Guardian*, 29 June, available at www.theguardian.com/culture/2019/jun/29/should-m (accessed 17 January 2021).

Isaac, G. (2007) *Mediating Knowledges: Origins of a Zuni Tribal Museum*, Tucson: University of Arizona Press.

Isaac, G. (2015) "Perclusive Alliances," *Current Anthropology*, 56 (12): 286–296.

Jasanoff, M. (2006) *Edge of Empire: Conquest and Collecting in the East 1750–1850*, London: Harper Perennial.

Jazeel, Tariq. 2019. *Postcolonialism*. 1st ed. New York: Routledge, https://doi.org/10.4324/9781315559483.

Jilani, S. (2018) "How to Decolonize a Museum," *Times Literary Supplement Online*, 7 June, available at www.the-tls.co.uk (accessed 17 January 2021).

Kassim, S. (2019) "The Museum is the Master's House: An Open Letter to Tristram Hunt," *Medium*, July 26, https://medium.com/@sumayakassim/the-museum-is-the-masters-house-an-open-letter-to-tristram-hunt-e72d75a891c8 (accessed 17 January 2021).

Larkin, B. 2013. "The Politics and Poetics of Infrastructure," *Annual Review of Anthropology* 42 (1): 130828114652000. https://doi.org/10.1146/annurev-anthro-092412-155522.

Lonetree, A. and Cobb, A. J. (2008) *The National Museum of the American Indian: Critical Conversations*, Lincoln: University of Nebraska Press.

Lonetree, Amy. 2012. *Decolonizing Museums: Representing Native America in National and Tribal Museums*, Chapel Hill: UNC Press Books.

Marsh, D. E., Punzalan, R. L., Leopold, R., Butler, B., and Petrozzi, M. (2016) "Stories of Impact: The Role of Narrative in Understanding the Value and Impact of Digital Collections," *Archival Science*, 16: 327–372.

Mathur, S. (2007) *India by Design: Colonial History and Cultural Display*, Berkeley: University of California Press.

Mathur, S. and Singh, K. (2017) *No Touching, No Spitting, No Praying: The Museum in South Asia*, London: Routledge.

Mattur, N. (2015) *Paper Tiger: Law, Bureaucracy and the Developmental State in Himalayan India*, Cambridge: Cambridge University Press.

Mbembe, A. (2001) *On the Postcolony*, Berkeley: University of California Press.

Müller, K. (2021) *Digital Archives and Collections: Creating Online Access to Cultural Heritage*, London: Berghahn Books.

Müller, K. (2017a) "Online Documents of India's Past: Digital Archives and Memory Production," *Museum Worlds: Advances in Research*, 5: 149–161.

Müller, K. (2017b) "Reframing the Aura: Digital Photography in Ancestral Worship," *Museum Anthropology*, 40 (1): 65–78.

Nair, V. (2018) "An Eye for an I: Recording Biometrics and Reconsidering Identity in Postcolonial India," *Contemporary South Asia*, 26 (2): 143–156.

Ngata, W., Ngata-Gibson, H., and Salmond, A. (2012) "Te Ataakura: Digital Taonga and Cultural Innovation," *Journal of Material Culture*, 17 (3): 229–244.

Pinney, C. (2002) "Creole Europe: The Reflection of a Reflection," *The New Zealand Journal of Literature* 20 (Settlement Studies: Special Issue): 125–161.

Pinney, C. and Peterson, N. (2003) *Photography's Other Histories*, Durham: Duke University Press.

Povinelli, E. (2011) "Routes/Worlds," *E-Flux* 27, available at www.e-flux.com/journal/routesworlds/ (accessed 17 January 2021).

Povinelli, E. (2016) *Geontologies: A Requiem to Late Liberalism*, Durham: Duke University Press.

Rajpal, S. (2012) "Experiencing the Indian Archives," *Economic & Political Weekly* XLVII (16): 19–21.

Risam, R. (2019) *New Digital Worlds: Postcolonial Digital Humanities in Theory, Praxis, and Pedagogy*, Evanston: Northwestern University Press.

Rycroft, D. and Müller, K. (2013) "The Future of Anthropology's Archival Knowledge: An International Reassessment (FAAKIR)," *Jahrbuch der Staatlichen Ethnographischen Sammlungen Sachsen* 46: 221–226.

Said, E. W. (2003) *Orientalism*, London: Penguin Books.

Schorch, P. and McCarthy, C., eds. (2019) *Curatopia: Museums and the Future of Curatorship*, Manchester: Manchester University Press.

Sen, B. (2016) *Digital Politics and Culture in Contemporary India: The Making of an Info-nation*, New York: Routledge.

Shivadas, V. (2015) "Museumising Modern Art: National Gallery of Modern Art, the Indian Case Study" in S. Mathur and K. Singh (eds), *No Touching, No Spitting, No Praying: The Museum in South Asia*, London: Routledge, 148–169.

Singh, K. (2015) "The Museum is National" in S. Mathur and K. Singh (eds), *No Touching, No Spitting, No Praying: The Museum in South Asia*, London: Routledge, 107–131.

Smith, P. C. (2009) *Everything You Know about Indians Is Wrong*, Minneapolis, London: University of Minnesota Press.

Sneha, P. P. (2016) "Mapping Digital Humanities in India," available at http://cis-india.org/papers/mapping-digital-humanities-in-india (accessed 17 January 2021).

Stoler, A. L. (2009) *Along the Archival Grain: Epistemic Anxieties and Colonial Common Sense*, Princeton, NJ: Princeton University Press.

Talbot, I. and Singh, G. (2009) *The Partition of India*, Cambridge: Cambridge University Press.

Taussig, M. T. (1993) *Mimesis and Alterity: A Particular History of the Senses*, New York: Routledge.

Thorner, S. (2010) "Imagining an Indigital Interface: Ara Iritija Indigenizes the Technologies of Knowledge Management," *Collections: A Journal for Museums and Archives Professionals*, 6 (3): 125–147.

Udupa, S. (2016) "Middle Class on Steroids: Digital Media Politics in Urban India," available online at https://casi.sas.upenn.edu/iit/sudupa (accessed 17 January 2021).

Udupa, S., E. Costa, and P. Budka (2018) "The Digital Turn: New Directions in Media Anthropology" in *E-Seminar on the EASA Media Anthropology Network Panel "The Digital Turn."* Stockholm, Sweden. https://easaonline.org/downloads/networks/media/63p.pdf.

Vartanian, H. (2018) "Growing Coalition Calls Brooklyn Museum 'Out of Touch' and Demands Decolonization Commission," *Hyperallergic*, 12 April, available at https://hyperallergic.com/437542/growing-coalition-calls-brooklyn-museum-out-of-touch-and-demands-decolonization-commission/ (accessed 17 January 2021).

Venkatraman, S. (2017) *Social Media in South India*, London: UCL Press.

Verran, H. and Christie, M. (2014) "Postcolonial Databasing? Subverting Old Appropriations, Developing New Associations" in J. Leach and L. Wilson (eds), *Subversion, Conversion, Development: Cross-Cultural Knowledge Encounter and the Politics of Design*, Cambridge: MIT Press, 57–78.

Webster, G. C. (1990) "The U'mista Cultural Centre," *The Massachusetts Review*, 31 (1-2): 132–143.

Williams, P. (2005) "A Breach on the Beach: Te Papa and the Fraying of Biculturalism," *Museum and Society*, 3 (2): 81–97.

Zeitlyn, D. (2012) "Anthropology in and of the Archives: Possible Futures and Contingent Pasts. Archives as Anthropological Surrogates," *Annual Review of Anthropology*, 41 (1): 461–80.

19
ETHNOGRAPHIES OF THE DIGITALLY DISPOSSESSED

Heather Ford

In 2011 the "Oral Citations Project" was created and funded by the Wikimedia Foundation, the non-profit organisation based in the United States that hosts Wikipedia. The project was first documented on "Meta", a site used for coordinating and planning Wikimedia projects. The project was introduced on the site as follows:

> Imagine a world in which every single person on the planet is given free access to the sum of all human knowledge. To many within the Wikimedia movement, this idea is the guiding ambition that drives us. The problem with the sum of human knowledge, however, is that it is far greater than the sum of printed knowledge.

The Oral Citations Project was a response to Wikipedia's dearth of published material about topics relevant to communities in places outside North America and Western Europe. To the project director, Wikimedia Foundation Advisory Board member, Achal Prabhala, the source of this problem was Wikipedia's policy that defines "reliable sources" as published texts.

According to Prabhala, Wikipedia policies suggest that only printed knowledge can be used as a basis of articles. But books and printed material are a luxury of only the "rich economies (of) Europe, North America, and a small section of Asia". In the introduction to the project, he noted that there was very little scholarly publishing in languages other than English in India and that most South African languages other than English and Afrikaans have had a "primarily oral existence".

Because of this disparity, the knowledge of some communities is privileged on Wikipedia, while for others, it remains hidden. The lack of written, printed and published material in countries and languages outside the Global North was not only problematic for Wikipedia editions written in languages other than English and other major European languages. It also resulted in a less rich Wikipedia, one that couldn't possibly fulfil its goal to represent "the sum of all human knowledge" (Wikimedia Foundation, n.d.).

> As a result of this disparity, everyday, common knowledge – things that are known, observed and performed by millions of people – cannot enter Wikipedia as units of fact because they haven't been written down in a reliably published source. This

means that not only do small-language Wikipedias in countries like India and South Africa lose out on opportunities for growth, so also does the Wikimedia movement as a whole lose out on the potential expansion of scope in every language.

Prabhala suggested that a new type of source, an "oral citation", be employed in cases where no published information about a topic exists on Wikipedia. The Oral Citations Project team visited communities where oral tradition had facilitated the transfer of knowledge about local customs and culture. Wikipedia editors involved in the project conducted in-person interviews with community members in the rural village of Ga-Sebotlane in Limpopo province, South Africa and over the phone with interviewees from Kannur, a city in North Kerala, India. They uploaded recordings and transcripts of those interviews onto Wikimedia Commons, a sister site to Wikipedia where multimedia files are stored. They then wrote Wikipedia articles using the oral citations as references.

In response to the project, many other Wikipedia editors attempted to discredit, delete and vandalise the articles, while debates about the validity of oral citations for the encyclopedia raged on mailing lists and working groups. One of the articles based on oral citations was about "surr", a game that was once popular among children living in the villages of northern India. Surr is a game played by two teams of four players each. A rectangular playing field is divided into four equal quadrants. One team gathers in the first quadrant, while the other team gathers along the lines of defence at the borders of the adjoining quadrant. The objective of the game is for a team to enter the other three quadrants without being touched by a player from the opposing team. If all members of a single team survive and reach the final quadrant, then they will win the game. Once all the surviving players gather in a new quadrant, they shout, "Bol Den Goivan Surr!"

Surr is no longer commonly played in India. Some say that it is because children prefer video games or that they now live in high-rise apartments and aren't allowed to run and play outside by their increasingly vigilant parents. Despite this, surr is a phenomenon etched in the memories of those who once played it. It animates the memories of their childhood. It reminds them of a culture unique to where they come from. A man born in the neighbourhood of Ayodhya in Uttar Pradesh, who played the game in his childhood, talked about how surr was played by *Bahujan* people. *Bahujan* is the Hindi word for Dalits and "Other Backward Classes" (OBC), a collective term used by the Government of India to classify castes which are educationally or socially disadvantaged.

> (G)ames like Surr have a strong connection with soil and agriculture. Surr used to be played at the barren or emptied fields. And in most cases, the people who used to inhabit near to these fields were those, who work in the fields, minimum waged workers. Their kids used to play Surr. In rare cases, when the kids from metropolitan cities, like Mumbai, visited the village and happened to see kids playing Surr, they might join them.
>
> *Interview, 17 June 2021*

On Wikipedia, the article explained where the game was played and its rules. Statements were referenced to transcribed audio interviews with two Indian public servants about their experience of the game. But not everyone agreed with the validity of the knowledge represented there. Many Wikipedians opposed the use of the interviews as sources in Wikimedia mailing lists and working groups dedicated to Wikipedia policy discussion. The hope that at least on

Wikipedia, a space would be offered to share the knowledge of those already suffering from significant hardship born by class and caste, was dashed.

One of those who weighed in on oral citations via the Wikimedia listserv was the long-time Wikimedia volunteer, Ziko van Dijk, who has been a Wikimedian since 2003, has a doctorate in history and has played a significant role in Wikimedia in the Netherlands and Germany. He argued that only academic experts ("historian, ethnologist etc") could legitimately record knowledge held by "illiterates".

> There are good reasons for this way. One is, that it is not very practical to cite from audiotapes/audiofiles. Another, that what this individual is describing may be true for his personal environment but cannot be generalized to others. For that, one needs the scholar. Remember: witnesses are the most unreliable source ever. People tell you plain nonsense – not because they want to (lie) or are stupid but because the human brain is simply not created to be a historian. It has the greatest difficulties to store information truthfully. So you need to record, and compare the different assertions from different people.
>
> It is a possibility to record oral and visual expressions from illiterates, and only later to do something with it scholarly. But all this has nothing to do with Wikipedia.
>
> *Ziko van Dijk, Wikimedia-l mailing list, 25 February 2012*

Former Wikimedia Foundation Board Chairperson, Ting Chen responded that van Dijk's was the traditional view of how encyclopaedia should be produced, but that Wikipedia could produce the encyclopaedia differently; Wikipedia, *was* in fact, already doing things differently:

> Yes, it is the way classic encyclopedia[s] worked. But Wikipedia is not a classic encyclopedia, and I don't see the sense to bound ourselves ... just to please some old traditional rules ... Scholars have limited capacities ... Scholars cannot pay attention to everything. [If we] give everyone the possibility to pay attention to what they think is interesting and important in their life, we can free a lot of potential.
>
> *Ting Chen, Wikimedia-l mailing list, 25 February 2012*

The story of surr is difficult to reconcile with the dominant paradigm of Wikipedia. By most accounts, Wikipedia is a platform that offers the only viable, virtuous alternative to Big Tech. Wikipedia is among the 15 most popular websites in the world, used daily by nearly 500 million people. Featuring more than 40 million articles, it works through what Yochai Benkler (2006) calls "commons based peer production", in which large numbers of people work cooperatively to produce collective, public goods.

Wikipedia is open to contributions by anyone who has an Internet connection and its content can be freely used, reused and modified for commercial and non-commercial purposes. It is operated by the Wikimedia Foundation, a non-profit organisation that is headquartered in San Francisco, with chapters in 39 countries. Early in its development, Wikipedia's co-founder, Jimmy Wales pronounced that the site's goal was to give freely "the sum of all human knowledge". The project's logo is a globe represented as a puzzle that is yet to be completed. This dream of global accord in a universal encyclopedia continues a tradition from ancient encyclopedic efforts to H.G. Wells' "World Brain" that would bring forth "a common understanding" (Reagle, 2010: 25).

Wikipedia's apparent pluralism was what attracted me to the project. When I co-founded Creative Commons in South Africa in 2005, I recognised that Wikipedia was important not only because it provided free *access* to knowledge but because it provided a platform for local *participation* on a global platform. When I was appointed as the Executive Director of iCommons, a non-profit organisation set up by Creative Commons to lead international efforts around Creative Commons, I recognised that Wikipedia was the world's greatest example of the power of free and open source software and open content.

I became a passionate activist for Wikipedia in Africa. On 10 November 2007, I co-organised the first Wikipedia Academy (as edit-a-thons used to be called) in Africa (Wikimedia Foundation, 2007). The event was hosted by CIDA City Campus, a university that served a majority of disadvantaged students at their campus in Johannesburg, offering students a full scholarship for tuition and living expenses. Jimmy Wales and Swahili Wikipedian, Ndesanjo Macha, came to the event to talk about the importance of Wikipedia for preserving local knowledges. Students from a local tertiary education institution enthusiastically started articles in their home languages. On South Africa's annual Heritage Day, the iCommons team set up a stall in our local mall to accept donations of old photographs and artefacts to Wikimedia Commons, the site where most of the photographs used on Wikipedia are housed. We enthusiastically accepted a dribble of donations and proselytised to the already converted about the value of "free knowledge". I believed, at that time, that Wikipedia was truly open to the knowledge of all, and that it only required our acceptance of the invitation to participate in building "the sum of all human knowledge".

But a few years on and I had become increasingly sceptical of the global promise of the movement from my vantage point in South Africa. Even Wikipedia was being unmasked as a project riddled with bias and ignorance about knowledge from outside the West. When the Oral Citations Project was launched in 2011, I was in graduate school, trying to understand how social norms and organisational rules could create barriers to information and knowledge sharing, despite the existence of open licenses. I started researching Wikipedia for a small project during my Master's degree at UCBerkeley and started my ethnographic study of Wikipedia in 2012, when I worked as an ethnographer for the Kenyan non-profit technology company, Ushahidi.

Media anthropology inspired me to discover Wikipedia from an alternative perspective to the one that dominated the field known as Wikipedia Studies at the time. In this chapter, I argue that, in addition to the ethnographic studies of platforms' pro-users, its dominant actors, its most popular or active groups, we need ethnographies of the digitally dispossessed: those who are routinely ignored, omitted, denigrated and denounced by platforms. In the case of Wikipedia, ethnographies of the digitally dispossessed enable us to understand how platforms shape the world, how we see one another, and how we might improve the ways in which they work for the benefit of underserved groups.[1]

Media Anthropology and the Sources of Power/Knowledge

Media anthropology's principles for understanding the *multiplicity* of peoples' experiences of global platforms is key to its value in studying global digital cultures. At the heart of media anthropology is the idea that media practices are not universal. Media anthropologists study the ways in which media are designed or adapted for use by specific communities or groups. Borrowing a phrase coined by postcolonial theorist, Dipesh Chakrabarty (2000), the media anthropologist, E. Gabriella Coleman (2010) writes that ethnography is a useful methodology to study digital media platforms that are supposedly global because of how they can "provincialize" digital media. This enables ethnographers to "push back against peculiarly narrow presumptions about the universality of digital experience" (Coleman, 2010: 489).

For some ethnographers, these details are used to reveal "the splendour of sociocultural life" (Coleman, 2010: 497). In this tradition, ethnographies of Wikipedia have generally answered the question: how can Wikipedia exist? Wikipedia seems like an impossibility. Why would people give their labour for free to build an encyclopedia? Answering this question, Wikipedia ethnographers have illustrated the importance of the principle of "good faith collaboration" for how Wikipedia operates (Reagle, 2010) and the unique organisational form that constitutes Wikipedia work (Jemelniak, 2014).

For Joseph Reagle (2010), participant observation meant "observing – and occasionally participating in – the Wikipedia online community by "follow[ing] them 'in real time' via a number of venues" including Wikipedia pages and edits to them, talk pages, mailing lists, newsletters and Wikipedia meetups (Reagle, 2010: 9). For Dariusz Jemelniak, it resulted in significant Wikipedia labour which saw him "moving through all the ranks of the Wikipedia parahierarchy" (Jemelniak, 2014: 197). Jemelniak eventually became a steward (the role with the widest access to technical privileges across all Wikimedia projects) and the Chair of the Funds Dissemination Committee, a global advisory body to the Wikimedia Foundation.

For other ethnographers, details are "ethically deployed to push against faulty and narrow presumptions about the universality and uniformity of human experience" (Coleman, 2010: 497). It is this orientation that aligns most strongly with my own ethnographic approach. Like other ethnographies, my own study of Wikipedia involved conversing with editors and participant observation of practice both in the work of the encyclopedia and in the context of the face-to-face events that Wikipedians gather at. But my choice of articles to follow, people to interview and practice to participate in is shaped by a commitment to the subaltern perspective. By subaltern, I mean those who are "removed from all lines of social mobility" (Spivak, 2005: 475). The subaltern, in this sense, is not just Other, minority, or disadvantaged. They are essentially unable to speak for themselves within existing power structures that constitute Wikipedia as a knowledge project.

Previous ethnographies of Wikipedia have tended to explore Wikipedia from the perspective of its most active contributors, that is, through the lens of those who already have significant power on Wikipedia. Other ethnographies have pointed to the multiple alternative ways of seeing and experiencing Wikipedia. My own ethnographic study of Wikipedia is situated from the perspective of those that exist in the shadow of the encyclopedia – those who edit Wikipedia far from its cultural centre in Silicon Valley, those who have been banned, whose articles have been deleted and who are opposed to what they believe is the hegemony of the mainly-Western, white, male Wikimedia community (Ford, 2011; Ford and Geiger, 2012; Ford, 2016, 2017). This orientation has influenced how I have situated myself within the field, who I have chosen to interview, which articles I have chosen to select as cases, what kinds of practice I have observed and participated in.

Indeed, when faced with the opportunity to study a platform ethnographically, there are a myriad of choices that need to be made. Wikipedia is made up of millions of articles, hundreds of working parties (or Wikiprojects) and article types, a myriad policy pages and "meta" discussions taking place on wiki and on mailing lists and other social media platforms. There are over 300 language versions of Wikipedia and Wikipedia is only one of a number of Wikimedia projects interconnected with one another. Wikimedia Commons stores media files, for example; Wikidata stores infobox data, interwiki links and other data. Projects are often distinguished by their own rules, norms and cultures. I found myself asking: How can one claim to capture Wikipedia's culture when one can only experience a tiny slice of it? More importantly: which slice to capture? Which projects to follow? Which practice to participate in?

In the sections that follow, I present three strategies that I used to explore Wikipedia from the perspective of the digital subaltern. First, I focus on how the surr article raised questions about how factual claims are obstructed, refused or demeaned by others. Second, I explore how different forms of authority were used to support (or oppose) these claims and what kinds of expertise are ignored or downplayed. Finally, I trace how claims about the authority of the surr article were (or were not) constituted and animated by data and what this means for how knowledge becomes authoritative (or not). I explain how I applied these strategies in the context of the article about surr on English Wikipedia, demonstrating the ways in which digital and increasingly datafied knowledge representations gain purchase or stop in their tracks via online platforms like Wikipedia.

Entering via Flagged Erasures

The ethnographer, Jenna Burrell suggests seeking entry points to networks rather than identifying sites in order to locate one's fieldwork. This requires first establishing "what position(s) to take within the network" (Burrell, 2009: 190). Wikipedia's articles that had been flagged for deletion were useful entry points in line with my focus on the subaltern perspective and enabled me to learn more about the practices by which some knowledges are excluded from Wikipedia. In order to facilitate the representation of phenomena in Wikipedia, a space needs to be created for the recording of facts surrounding the phenomenon. The ideal form of space creation in Wikipedia is the creation of an article. The new article contains no baggage of previous articles, with their embedded authors, narrative frames, and teeming desires.

Anyone can create a new Wikipedia article if a topic doesn't yet exist. But those articles can be just as quickly deleted by other editors. Wikipedia's editors are patrolling new articles with the assistance of automated tools that mark up the articles according to some of the traces of their construction. Those traces include the edit experience of the authoring editor, the existence of categories in the article, and links to other Wikipedia articles.

One of the key features of the software and the practice of page review is to be able to rapidly remove what Wikipedia calls "bad-faith contributions", such as "attack pages" or copyright violations. The feed enables editors to view metadata related to the article, such as who "patrolled" (reviewed) the article or whether it has been nominated for deletion, as well as data about the article itself (its size, a preview of the text, whether it has been categorised, and how many users have contributed to it). Page patrollers' first view of the article is through its data.

In the case of surr, I followed edits made to the Hindi and English version of the article (including attempts to delete and vandalise it), discussions about the article on the Reliable Sources Noticeboard on English Wikipedia and the global Wikimedia mailing list (Wikimedia-l). I interviewed editors involved in creating articles and sources, and one editor leading efforts to discredit them. The article flagged for deletion generated a wide map of people, discourses and practices and technologies while centring on the topic of exclusion.

Following Sources and Their Characterisation

Articles can be accepted or deleted on Wikipedia, but another significant way in which knowledge is included or excluded is via the sources that are cited in support of facts in articles. Wikipedia is built on the principle of verifiability, where all statements must be able to be verified by a "reliable source".

Reliability on Wikipedia has specifically been equated with "secondary" sources published according to institutional standards, rather than sources as people themselves (as in the tradition of journalism or social science). English Wikipedia policy forbids the publishing of "original research". This means that articles "may not contain any new analysis or synthesis of published material that serves to reach or imply a conclusion not clearly stated by the sources themselves" (Wikipedia: No Original Research, n.d.).

The ways in which Wikipedians decide which sources are reliable, as well as the ways in which they summarise those sources, all involve Wikipedians actively creating knowledge by deciding what is excluded. Wikipedia practice involves discourse and actions that serve to classify some sources as reliable and other sources as unreliable. Following the ways in which local sources of knowledge on Wikipedia are accepted, rejected, debated or not, is central to understanding the practices of exclusion on the platform.

In the case of surr, the article became a site of controversy because it challenged the idea that Wikipedians do not actively curate knowledge. The oral citations model enabled activist Wikipedians to record the knowledge of ordinary people who they recognised as authorities on local culture. But many Wikipedians fought back, re-asserting the expertise of institutional academics (in this case, historians and anthropologists) as the proper authority on knowledge and reinforcing the idea that they, the editors, were merely passive curators.

Following discussions about citations for the Wikipedia surr article makes visible multiple layers of sources for the facts stated in Wikipedia articles. These include the editors themselves, who make decisions about what facts to select, which sources are cited and how facts are summarised. It includes secondary sources, which may reflect a topic alternatively or in opposition. In the background are the knowledge holders, who are not always represented accurately (or at all) by sources. They include the witnesses to events, or those identified by information.

I followed discussions about the oral citations used in surr in at least two key sites outside the article to understand how decisions are made to exclude knowledge on Wikipedia. The Reliable Sources Noticeboard on English Wikipedia, for example, is a place where editors can go to query and discuss the appropriateness of particular sources being used in articles. In the case of surr, a number of editors weighed in on the reliability of oral citations on the surr article by pointing to the identities of those involved in producing the citations (interviewees, interviewers and Wikipedia editors). In one example, the local expert interviewed in the audio clip was described as "a layperson".

> (T)he person interviewed has no academic authority in the field. He is simply a layperson, who has played a game of unknown notability.
> *NativeForeigner, Reliable Sources Noticeboard discussion,*
> *13 February 2012*[2]

In another statement, the publisher of the source on Wikimedia Commons (Aprabhala) is labelled as a mere "commons content creator". Reliability, according to these editors, is determined not by the quality of the source but by the identity of its producers.

> I'm sorry, but commons user Aprabhala is not a professional or academic ethnographer; they're a commons content creator.
> *Fifelfoo, Reliable Sources Noticeboard discussion,*
> *13 February 2012*

A week after the debate on the Reliable Sources Noticeboard, the Oral Citations Project was discussed on the Wikimedia-l mailing list. Wikimedia-l is one of about 400 mailing lists administered by the Wikimedia Foundation but it occupies a special position in the Wikimedia network because of its role in providing a forum for issues relating to Wikimedia Foundation projects. The Wikimedia-l mailing list is used to discuss issues relating to new projects, new chapters, polling and fundraising and is where the majority of high-level, strategic and long-time discussions about movement-wide issues take place between the Wikimedia Foundation and non-Foundation members of the Wikimedia community.

The discussion about oral citations began when the project lead, Achal Prabhala, sought advice from the Wikimedia community about the Oral Citations Project.[3] Fourteen editors weighed in on the question, many were significant members of the Wikimedia movement. Disagreements centred around the role of Wikipedians in terms of the knowledge that they represent, and about the subjects of knowledge and the role of those subjects in the representation process.

The discussion about oral citations ended after less than a week of replies with no clear consensus on whether allowing oral citations as defined by Prabhala and his colleagues was conducive to Wikipedia's goals or identity. None of the editors participating in the thread on Wikimedia-l edited the surr article during or after this discussion, but work continued on the article by a variety of actors engaged in the daily practice of article maintenance and construction.

Opposing editors attempted to label the article as unreliable and incomplete. They added warning tags to the article in order to cast doubt on the content of the article, they deleted text, thereby discrediting claims within the article and they removed the links to the oral citations hosted on Wikimedia Commons. They also threatened to delete the citations themselves by adding a request for copyright permissions in the format specified by policy and denied the authority of the Oral Citations Project page on Meta (Wikimedia's coordination site) by arguing that Meta was irrelevant to the work of English Wikipedia.

Analysing the Networks That Traverse Articles

Wikipedia is increasingly a data project rather than a traditional encyclopedia project. Its facts are extracted to populate vast knowledge bases that present single answers to our questions about the world on search engines and digital assistants. Asking Google or Siri who won the Russian election, what happened in Egypt in 2011 or what is the capital city of Israel results in facts often gleaned from Wikipedia.

In order for facts to travel to more popular sites like Google, they must be structured as data on Wikipedia. This primarily happens in the infobox, the box on the right-hand side of an article that lists its key facts. Starting in 2013, Wikipedians began to develop infoboxes as structured data. Structured data differs from digital data in that it is tightly controlled by a data model that dictates its structure and order. It is well-defined in this way so that it can be easily accessed by computer programs.

The structuring of claims, it turns out, is determined by a particular kind of representational politics. The heterogeneity of these networks creates power dynamics because only certain users are able to control representation in multiple spaces, each of which requires familiarity and specialised literacy. Tracing how facts travel across networks and how they are structured as data, then, is a useful way of understanding how power is inscribed according to the ways in which claims are able to circulate.

Some knowledge doesn't seem to fit the data models provided, some claims haven't yet been structured because of a lack of interest or understanding by Wikipedians who care about them. Whereas the sport of cricket on Wikipedia has an infobox that is richly detailed, including facts about when and where the sport was first played, for example, surr has no infobox. It lists just one other "interwiki" link to the Hindi version of the article and it links to only two categories on Wikipedia. It is thinly described on Wikidata, the Wikimedia project where structured data from infoboxes is stored.

The arrival of Wikidata has shifted power relations among knowledge communities in Wikimedia. Even though Wikidata's entities are open for public scrutiny and editing, many Wikipedia editors lose their ability to make meaningful changes to the facts that they constructed once they move to Wikidata. Editing a semantic database turns out to require very different expertise and the ways in which editors think about the topics that they edit are different still. If there is conflict in the ways that items are edited, discussions about those items need to take place in English because Wikidata is a centralised database for Wikipedia's more than 300 language projects.

Analysing the networks that traverse articles, I uncovered a universe of new relations that were being discounted as "merely technical" but had real, material effects on the ways in which people and their knowledge was represented. The structured data projects in which Wikimedia is currently involved will have an impact on how minority language groups are able to control representations on Wikipedia and outwards to the wider Web. Understanding the metadata that drives those representations along silent transport routes are critical to engaging with knowledge platforms like Wikipedia. The question, as the Wikipedia ethnographer Stuart Geiger (2017) writes, is "for whom are algorithmic systems (and the organizations that rely on them) formal, rigid, and consistent, and for whom are they in flux, revisable, and negotiable?"

Structured data matters in the context of Wikipedia because it is a new means of making knowledge visible – not only on Wikipedia but on the Web, since structured data claims travel more readily to powerful platforms like Google, Siri and Alexa. In order to understand how knowledge is being excluded, we have to trace the circulation of data in addition to focusing on where it lands. It is not enough for knowledge claims to be represented on platforms like Wikipedia. If they aren't discoverable, then they will be buried and ignored, unmaintained and unrecognised. The ways in which communities are represented by factual claims on platforms like Wikipedia (and consequently, Google) matters to people who are so often unseen and whose knowledge and experience are unacknowledged in global systems. Data makes knowledge visible and it is in data's circulation that new centres of power/knowledge arise.

New Centres of Power/Knowledge

The arrival of the Internet was accompanied by a new idealism about global solidarity. The Internet enabled people to come together on a common platform to share knowledge and understanding. As John Perry Barlow (1996) famously stated about the Internet in his "Declaration of the Independence of Cyberspace", "We are creating a world that all may enter without privilege or prejudice accorded by race, economic power, military force, or station of birth". More than 15 years on and we now scoff at Barlow's idealism. As Science and Technology Studies scholar, Sheila Jasanoff (2004: 36) writes that power is continually reinscribing itself in institutions, practices, discourses, claims and products of science and technology. No platform exists outside of this constant process.

How can we best understand how power is reinscribing itself in the context of digital systems, beyond the simplistic claim that platforms or algorithms are the only subjugating force? How can we conduct research that will actually help to change the conditions in which so many have to endure when attempting to present their knowledge as legitimate? The dominant framing of research in the context of digital inequalities is in terms of platform "bias". The majority of studies exploring platform bias use statistical models to compare how certain subjects or sources are represented compared to others. In the context of Wikipedia, much work has been done to demonstrate how Wikipedia over-represents current history rather than events from the distant past (Graham, Hale and Stephens, 2011), men rather than women (Reagle and Rhue, 2011), places in the Global North rather than the Global South (Graham et al., 2014; Sen et al., 2015).

Although this work has been instrumental in determining what gaps exist, they don't get us any closer to understanding the sources of bias or what might be done to solve such problems. Furthermore, knowledge claims are increasingly made accessible to the world not via the platform itself but by its data doppelgangers, copied automatically across to digital assistants and smart search engines as answers to users' queries. The types of content, topics and language versions of content that are highlighted in these systems also demonstrates biases. Some content is more likely to be represented in more popular engines than others, but the source of that content is often obscured. What does platform bias mean in the context of a Web that is increasingly interconnected and fragmented at the same time?

Ethnographies that follow disputed claims, their incumbent authorities on both sides of the debates and the networks that traverse them are a useful alternative to the quantitative methodologies exploring bias. Starting from deleted or disputed knowledge claims as entry points to heterogeneous networks, ethnography can surface the conversations and actions that work to disable and destabilise certain types of knowledge. The example of surr demonstrates how the power to represent knowledge is lodged in discourses concerning the sources of reliable knowledge, representations that determine who the expert and subject are, and identities that authorise certain knowledge holders as legitimate and others as illegitimate.

Achal Prabhala completed the Oral Citations Project but it left him bitterly disappointed at Wikipedia's response. In my interviews with him, he talked about opportunities lost in favour of what he saw as the Western conservatism of Wikipedia. Although surr remains on English Wikipedia, ten years after it was first published, it is thinly described. The potential for including many more local sports and aspects of cultural life was abandoned as proponents of the Oral Citations Project were left dismayed at the attitudes of Wikipedia's dominant groups. Wikipedia rejected the Oral Citations Project because they thought it would move them out of the passive curator role they thought they inhabited. But Wikipedians are active curators of knowledge, as discussions like this confirms.

Advocates of the project chose players of surr, rather than historians or anthropologists to be interviewed for the surr article, effectively upending Wikipedia's notions of expertise as located within institutions, particularly academia. The project advocates were effectively suggesting that the source of knowledge is in the embodied experience of phenomena rather than through institutional certification. This idea represented a threat, not only to the series of articles using oral citations, but to Wikipedia's conceptions about its own role in the system of expertise more broadly. By choosing to interview individuals in the community who had first-hand knowledge of the game, the editors representing surr in the original Hindi had effectively transformed those community members into experts. Similarly, the editors who conducted the interviews also displayed expertise because of their knowledge of both the phenomenon and how to identify and contact the experts in the villages.

The response by some English Wikipedia editors was to reaffirm the expertise of academics and institutions, thereby denigrating the embodied experience of the villagers. When the article entered English Wikipedia's socio-technical system, the voices of those who experience the game were no longer available since the link to the audio file had been removed. Instead of the community members being recognised as experts, they were relegated to being the subjects of the newspaper article about surr that constitutes the only linked citation within the article when this study was conducted. Wikipedia editors' success lay in their ability to define the roles and identities of Wikipedians and the experts that they rely on.

It seems that the call from the "Critical Point of View: A Wikipedia Reader" is still as relevant as it was in 2011. "The task is to create new encounters and point to new modes of inquiry, to connect the new with the old, and to give voice to different, 'subjugated' histories" (Lovink and Tkacz, 2011: 10). What platforms include and exclude is not just a technical data point on a map about coverage. In the case of surr, for example, the acceptance or rejection of an article about cultural activity in rural India is symbolic of whether colonial attitudes towards former colonies have been abandoned or whether those attitudes have merely taken on a new form.

The results of platform ethnographies are constituted according to decisions made at every step in forming a fieldsite within these massive territories. I advocate for exploring how subaltern populations try to use supposedly global platforms in order to be heard, how those attempts often fail and what this says about how they can be more inclusively designed. In the context of an Internet that is increasingly subject to the logic of automation and AI, voice is enabled through one's mastering of practice within data centric representational forms.

My research on the surr Wikipedia article is intended to push back against the idea that Wikipedia can only be one thing to all people. This orientation aligns strongly with my desire to study systems not only to understand them, but in order to improve their workings for those who can most benefit from them. Ethnographies of the digitally dispossessed are one key component of this ongoing task. Connecting knowledge platforms to the stories of the subjugated, dispossessed and disenchanted is a valid goal as we remain under the influence of their representations.

Notes

1 I am indebted to Dr. Jasbeer Musthafa Mamalipurath who conducted and translated interviews for this project.
2 The RS/N discussion about oral citations is archived at https://en.wikipedia.org/wiki/Wikipedia:Reliable_sources/Noticeboard/Archive_115#Oral_Citations.
3 Archived discussion available at https://lists.wikimedia.org/pipermail/wikimedia-l/2012-February/thread.html.

References

Barlow, J.P. (1996). A Declaration of the Independence of Cyberspace. Retrieved 1 August from www.eff.org/cyberspace-independence.
Burrell, J. (2009). The fieldsite as a network: A strategy for locating ethnographic research. *Field Methods*, 21(2): 181–199. doi: 10.1177/1525822X08329699
Chakrabarty, D. (2000). *Provincializing Europe: Postcolonial Thought and Historical Difference*. Princeton, NJ: Princeton University Press
Coleman, E.G. (2010). Ethnographic approaches to digital media. *Annual Review of Anthropology*, 39: 487–505.
Ford, H. (2011). The missing Wikipedians. In G. Lovink and N. Tkacz (eds), *Critical Point of View: A Wikipedia Reader*. Amsterdam: Institute of Network Cultures.
Ford, H. and Geiger, S. (2012). Writing up rather than writing down: Becoming Wikipedia literate. *Proceedings of the Eighth Annual International Symposium on Wikis and Open Collaboration (WikiSym '12)*. Association for Computing Machinery, New York, Article 16: 1–4. https://doi-org.ezproxy.lib.uts.edu.au/10.1145/2462932.2462954
Ford, H. (2016). Wikipedia and the sum of all human information. *Nordisk Tidsskrift for Informationsvidenskab og Kulturformidling*, 5(1): 9–13.
Ford, H. (2017). The search for Wikipedia's edges. In L. Hjorth, H. Horst, A. Galloway, G. Bell (eds), *Routledge Companion to Digital Ethnography*. New York: Routledge.

Ford, H. and Wajcman, J. (2017). 'Anyone can edit'. Not everyone does. Wikipedia and the gender gap. *Social Studies of Science Journal* 47(4): 511–527.

Geiger, R.S. (2017). Beyond opening up the black box: Investigating the role of algorithmic systems in Wikipedian organizational culture. *Big Data & Society* 4(2). https://doi.org/10.1177/2053951717730735

Graham, M. (2009, 2 December). Wikipedia's known unknowns. *The Guardian*. www.theguardian.com/technology/2009/dec/02/wikipedia-known-unknowns-geotagging-knowledge

Graham, M., Hale, S. and Stephens, M. (2011). *Geographies of the World's Knowledge*. Technical report. London: Convoco.

Graham, M., Hogan, B., Straumann, R.K. and Medhat, A. (2014). Uneven geographies of user-generated information: Patterns of increasing informational poverty. *Annals of the Association of American Geographers*, 104(4): 746–764.

Jasanoff, S. (ed.) (2004). *States of Knowledge: The Co-production of Science and the Social Order*. London: Routledge.

Jemielniak, D. (2014). *Common Knowledge? An Ethnography of Wikipedia*. Stanford: Stanford University Press.

Lovink, G. and Tkacz, N. (eds) (2011). *Critical Point of View: A Wikipedia Reader*. Amsterdam: Institute of Network Cultures.

Raymond, E. (1999). The cathedral and the bazaar. *Knowledge, Technology & Policy*, 12(3): 23–49.

Reagle, J. (2010). *Good Faith Collaboration: The Culture of Wikipedia*. Cambridge, MA: MIT Press.

Reagle, J. and Rhue, L. (2011). Gender bias in Wikipedia and Britannica. *International Journal of Communication*, 5: 21.

Sen, S. W., Ford, H., Musicant, D. R., Graham, M., Keyes, O. S. and Hecht, B. (2015). Barriers to the localness of volunteered geographic information. In *Proceedings of the 33rd Annual ACM Conference on Human Factors in Computing Systems*, 197–206.

Spivak, G. (2005). Scattered Speculations on the subaltern and the popular. *Postcolonial Studies*, 8(4). https://doi.org/10.1080/13688790500375132

Wikimedia Foundation. (2007, 31 October). Wikipedia founder Jimmy Wales leads South African Wikipedia Academies in Johannesburg. Wikimedia Foundation Website. https://foundation.wikimedia.org/wiki/Press_releases/Wikipedia_Academies

Wikimedia Foundation. (n.d.) Our Work. Retrieved 1 August 2021, from https://wikimediafoundation.org/our-work/

Wikipedia: No original research policy. (n.d.) Retrieved 1 August 2021, from https://en.wikipedia.org/w/index.php?title=Wikipedia:No_original_research&oldid=1012596131

PART III

Thematic Considerations

A
Relationships

20
"FRIENDS FROM WECHAT GROUPS"

The Practice of Friendship via Social Media among Older People in China

Xinyuan Wang

Introduction

Based on ethnographic fieldwork on the use of the smartphone among older people in Shanghai, this chapter brings focus on a novel mediated friendship facilitated by WeChat, the dominating social media in China. In daily conversation, older people frequently mentioned 'my friends from WeChat groups' as a common resource of information and social network. Curiously, 'friends from WeChat groups' are different to 'WeChat friends', as the latter refers to WeChat contacts that one can have a one-to-one conversation with, whereas the former are contacts that exist in various WeChat groups and with whom one obtains a certain degree of connection within the groups. This specific social category, with its growing significance in social life, provides us with an opportunity to investigate evolving mediated friendship practices in the age of the smartphone.

The main ethnographic fieldwork that supports this chapter took place between 2018 and 2019 when I moved into an ordinary low-rise residential compound called *ForeverGood*, in the city centre of Shanghai. *ForeverGood* consists of 23 residential buildings, housing 941 households. The average age of the residents is around 60 (32 per cent were over 60). *ForeverGood* was my immediate neighbourhood during the 16-month stay in Shanghai, where I immersed myself in the daily rhythm of people's lives.

One of the benefits of the long-term fieldwork was that research participants gradually grew to trust me and felt comfortable not only sharing their personal stories, but also 'opening' their smartphones up to me to have a closer look at. I therefore gained first-hand material about what people do with their smartphones and how they navigate various social relations via WeChat. Specifically, interviews focusing on the use of WeChat groups were conducted among 52 key research participants (30 women, 22 men) between age 45 to 75 in 2019. In these interviews, research participants displayed all the WeChat groups they joined and revealed their experience in these groups.

The chapter starts with a discussion of friendship practices via social media. The ethnography then provides a close look at a variety of situations of interpersonal interaction. With a systematic review of different types of WeChat groups, the chapter showcases how a new kind of friendship is taking form in the age of social media.

Mediated Friendship in the Chinese Context

The very understanding of the 'mediated' nature of interpersonal relationship allows anthropologists to study friendship from a variety of aspects of social life, from religion to politics (e.g. Bell and Coleman, 2020; Killias, 2017). More specifically, with the proliferation of the digital communication technology, a growing body of scholarship is now assessing the ways that social media are being drawn on to sustain personal relationships and reconfigure ideas and practice of intimacy and friendship (e.g. Chambers, 2013). Prior research on the internet-mediated friendship focuses on discussing the sociality facilitated by the internet and the relationship between online and offline friendships (e.g. Boase and Wellman, 2006; Ellison, Steinfield, and Lampe, 2007; Parks and Floyd, 1996; Tang, 2010). Studies of social media also highlight the sophisticated self-management and negotiation in digital-mediated social relationships, through the lens of 'networked friendship', facilitated by the technical affordance of persistence, replicability, scalability and searchability (boyd, 2011; Chambers, 2017). The concept of 'scalable sociality', proposed by the 'Why We Post' project, an anthropological study on the global social media use,[1] provides a useful framework for understanding how 'social media has colonised the space of group sociality between the private the public. In so doing it has created scales, including the size of the group and the degree of privacy' (Miller et al., 2016: x). The subject of this chapter, 'friends from the WeChat group', provides an example of such 'scalable sociality' in Chinese context.

The discussion of mediated friendship in the Chinese context also needs a reflective discussion of the very concept of 'friendship' *per se* in the context of Chinese social relations. Kinship-orientated Chinese society traditionally sees non-kinship ties as less significant compared to the three closest relationships: the ties between father and son, emperor and official, and husband and wife (Li, Du and Van de Bunt, 2016). Non-kinship ties were sought as an extension of familial forms of support when kinship support was not sufficient (Bell, 2000). The term state (*guo jia*) in Chinese literally means 'state-family', with the implication that the state is modelled on the principles of kinship organisation and the hierarchical and obligatory bonds of mutual devotion between 'father-son' as well as 'ruler and ministers', which form the web of Confucian social relationships (Kutcher, 2000). In the article 'The fifth relationship: dangerous friendships in the Confucian Context', Kutcher (2000) further points out that traditionally, in Chinese society, friendship, with the potential to be non-hierarchical, is viewed by Confucian writers as subversive. Friendship was therefore constructed as the social bond whose function was the service of the other bonds: a good friend should make the person a better son, brother or official (ibid.). Meanwhile, anthropological research in China also points out that, even though 'friendship' occupies a rather marginal position according to Confucian moral orthodoxy, in practice, a specific strategy of fictive/ritual kinship, such as 'same-year siblingship', has been deployed to facilitate the development of friendship between same-sex persons of the same age/generation (Santos, 2008). That is to say, the friendship always plays an important role in people's social lives even though in many cases, it is 'disguised' as kinship.

Furthermore, the concept and practice of friendship among this older generation in China require specific consideration of this cohort's life experience, which has been charged with significant social transformations, including the redefinition of a variety of social relations during the communist revolutions in modern China. Chinese people in their 50s and 60s, who were the main focus of this study, were born in communist China (from 1949 onwards) and often deeply involved in the Cultural Revolution (1967–1977), a decade-long period characterised by major political turmoil in their youth. They also witnessed a series of major social shifts during their adulthood, such as the post-Mao economic reform and the one-child policy. 'For China, the Cultural Revolution functions as this sort of watershed event, as it influenced not only the life course of Chinese people, including those born after it, but also the very construction of the Chinese life course' (Gold, 1991).

Since 1949, the party-state had effectively replaced the norms of 'friendship' with communist 'comradeship' in people's interpersonal interaction outside of their kinship ties (Vogel, 1965). As Vogel argues, the new morality of 'comradeship' requires people not to distinguish between people on the basis of personal preference, but to 'help' each other to fall in line and do what is expected of them in the communist regime. The underlying logic of comradeship has also been that one should not have a special bond with a certain person as that would interfere with the obligations to other comrades, therefore a common sense of friendship (special relationship between two persons) could be considered suspect and even illegitimate during the revolutionary time.

In addition to the weakening of 'friendships' during the communist regime, kinship organisation was also significantly weakened. The once all-encompassing organisation of kinship became dysfunctional during the revolutionary time, when individuals were first mobilised by the party-state to break away from the extended family and then organised to join the newly established urban socialist 'work units' (*danwei*). As anthropologist Yan (2010) eloquently argues, it was exactly because of the pervasive control coming from the party-state that at a deeper level, Chinese individuals were 'dis-embedded', in many cases forcefully, from traditional networks of kinship (Yan, 2010).

Daily Use of WeChat and WeChat Groups among Older People in Shanghai

One-third of Shanghai residents are in their 60s and above, and the average life expectancy in the city has reached 81 years for men was and 86 years for women.[2] The social and technological transformations older people in China experienced in their lifetime are unprecedented. Almost every research participant in their 60s and 70s uses a smartphone and it is important to note that the use of these devices in mainland China did not develop from 'PC-centric' culture in a linear fashion as it did in Europe and the United States, where computers constituted the main device used by individuals before smartphones took off. This is even more so in the case of 'information have-less' segments of the population, such as older people and rural migrants (Cartier, Castells and Qiu, 2005) in China, as for them, the mobile internet facilitated by the smartphone is the first time they have gained personal access to the internet (also see Wallis, 2013). A more general statistic shows that around 98.6 per cent[3] of internet users in China use smartphones to access the internet, arguably making the smartphone the major 'internet device' when it comes to online access in China. In Shanghai, it has become increasingly unusual to see a person below 70 not using a smartphone.

One of the major reasons that older people have adapted to smartphones is the social expectation and perceived need for WeChat. WeChat dominates all of the research participants' phone use. By 2015, the penetration rate of WeChat in main Chinese cities had already reached 93 per cent.[4] The app is similar to WhatsApp in the sense that in China, it has become the dominant interpersonal messaging app, but its functionality goes beyond WhatsApp's in the sense that it is an all-in-one app: it provides text and audio messaging, audio and video calls, location sharing, multimedia sharing, contactless payment in shops, restaurants, and so on, a money transfer service which includes the sending of 'red envelopes', as well as a wide range of functions (WeChat mini programmes) from taxi-hailing, paying for metro rides to making hospital appointments and more. Unlike WhatsApp, in WeChat, two persons who have not mutually confirmed each other's connection cannot have a 'one-to-one' conversation. In addition, WeChat is also different to WhatsApp in that it also functions as the major social media profile of an individual, which can be likened to a profile that combines data that one would only find on Facebook plus Instagram. That is to say, being a WeChat contact not only gives one access to private communication but also to private content that people would post on social media profiles.

It is worth noting that the use of email, a digital application normally associated with the PC era, is rather limited among the Chinese. Usually, WeChat is the first choice of communication channel, including for formal communication in the workplace. The most frequent use of email is for practical reasons such as registering for an online service, rather than interpersonal communication. The use of email is even more scarce among older people, as the majority first engaged with digital media when the popularity of email had long given way to the proliferation of smartphone-based applications in mainland China. The fieldwork revealed that only about 15 per cent of research participants[5] (ranging from people in their 50s to people in their 70s) owned an email account and only less than 5 per cent had checked their email in the past month. Considering the use of WeChat groups in the context of email, including mailing lists, being almost absent from daily communication and information circulation, it is not difficult to recognise the indispensable role WeChat groups occupy in older people's interpersonal communication and wider social engagement. In the next section, the story of research participant Dihua provides a typical portrait of the daily use of WeChat groups among older people in Shanghai.

Dihua is a 65-year-old retired factory manager. The brand-new Vivo smartphone she uses is her third. Following a recommendation from her friends in a photography-themed WeChat group, Dihua chose a Vivo for its superior camera. It is a normal day in May 2019. In the morning, Dihua wakes up to a series of morning greeting emojis being exchanged in eight different WeChat groups. 'Before, I used to say good morning to my neighbours and colleagues on my way to work, now I send Good Morning stickers to much more people via WeChat when I am still in bed', she remarks. The WeChat groups' traffic reaches its peak time around 9 am when most of her peers, Dihua included, have dropped off their grandchildren at school and done some morning housekeeping. On Dihua's WeChat, there are 23 WeChat groups, ranging from three to 315 participants. Dihua actively participates in eight of them, messaging on a daily basis. Throughout the day, within one particular WeChat group made up of her former 'classmates' from a folk musical instrument course at the local 'senior citizen university' that she set up one year ago, she receives more than 50 messages, including short videos and WeChat stickers, related to the upcoming rehearsal of their performance at the community art festival. Dihua also constantly praises (by sending various WeChat stickers) the photos posted in a WeChat group consisting of 229 amateur photographers.

From time to time, Dihua checks new messages in another WeChat group about stock market investments and saves some of the articles as 'WeChat favourites' for later reading and sharing. In the afternoon, her attention is drawn to a rather urgent 'family meeting' in a WeChat group with her four siblings. The meeting is about hiring a live-in care worker for her 90-year-old mother and how much money each household should contribute. Audio messages and multiple screengrabs of WeChat conversation about various care workers are exchanged back and forth in the group. Simultaneously, Dihua's younger sister is sending her one-to-one WeChat messages, complaining about their elder sister being stingy in taking care of the care bill.

At dinner time, Dihua takes a few photos of herself cooking and her grandson having dinner, then sends them to the smaller family WeChat group, which only contains her husband and their daughter's nuclear family. Dihua explains: 'His (grandson) mother is keen on a balanced diet, I can't feed him too much meat ... sending photos to them to check is like my daily reporting duty'. After dinner, Dihua takes 10 minutes to produce a short video via a WeChat mini-programme called 'animation affection album' and sends it to the WeChat photography group. The short video she made is a one-minute animation with background music and consists of 15 photos selected from the images people had posted on the WeChat group during the day. According to Dihua, making a short video out of others' posts is her way of acknowledging others' contribution to the group, and by doing so, she 'gives face' (*gei mianzi*) to active group members. At night, Dihua talks to her good friends in another WeChat group about having problems getting a carer for her mother. Meanwhile, she also forwards the useful stock market report she had saved as 'WeChat favourite' from her investment WeChat group and shares the news of the opening of a new park that her 'friends from WeChat groups' told her about.

After that, Dihua has a final round of group 'patrolling', especially in the two groups where she is the group founder, so-called *qunzhu*. Slowly scrolling up and down her smartphone screen, Dihua carefully reads through hundreds of messages exchanged during the day within the groups to see if there are any interesting or important messages that escaped her attention or whether there is any problem that would require her immediate intervention or mediation. Talking about her 'friends from WeChat groups', Dihua says: 'I may not know some of them in person, but we are somehow connected ... They definitely provide me with a lot of 'positive energy' (zheng nengliang)'.

In 2014, when WeChat started to gain popularity among all age groups in urban China, the average size of WeChat groups used by people in Shanghai[6] was rather small, mainly covering the family, close friends and essential work-related ties. This observation was also in line with the general observation about WhatsApp groups being relatively small in other societies, as studied by the 'Why We Post' project (Miller et al., 2016) which took place in 2013–2014. However, just a few years later, during the fieldwork for this project, the average size of WeChat groups that research participants participate regularly in is much more varied. Larger WeChat groups, such as those with more than 50 group members, have become much more common in people's daily lives.

As found in the specific interview focusing on the use of WeChat groups among 52 key research participants as mentioned above, the average number of WeChat groups individuals joined was about 11 with the total amount of WeChat groups ranging from four to 69. In practice, the overlap between 'friends from WeChat groups' and 'WeChat friends' which are the direct contacts on WeChat, is even smaller than what was estimated by some research participants themselves. For example, one retired schoolteacher, Mr Jiang, in his 60s, claimed that he knew most of the people he interacted with on WeChat, however when he showed me his WeChat groups, it turned out that he had been active in six WeChat groups with about 450 different online contacts (each group has about 60 to 200 group members) and could only recognise less than 10 per cent of them. During interviews on WeChat groups, older people often felt surprised to realise that the number of contacts they were connected with via WeChat groups was larger than they had expected.

Different Types of WeChat Groups

As shown in the case of Mr Jiang, even though small-scale WeChat groups (group members less than 30, typically less than 10) occupy an essential role in people's social lives, medium-scale

(30–50 members) and large-scale (more than 50, typically more than 100 members) WeChat groups have become more and more common among older people. Also, within larger WeChat groups, members typically only know a small proportion of the contacts within the group.

The different types of interpersonal ties proposed by Hwang in his influential article 'Face and favor: The Chinese power game' (1987) are useful in analysing the different types of WeChat groups according to different types of social bonds existing within the groups. According to Hwang (ibid.), there are essentially three kinds of interpersonal ties in China: expressive, instrumental and mixed ties. The 'expressive tie' refers to a relatively permanent and stable social relationship (such as family and close friends), which fosters feelings of affection and a sense of belonging. People can certainly use expressive ties to attain material resources, however, the expressive component of the tie usually far outweighs the instrumental component. The 'instrumental tie' stands in opposition to the expressive tie in the sense that the latter is usually regarded as the means rather than the end – people establish such ties in order to attain other goals and the affective component is minimal. Between 'expressive ties' and 'instrumental ties', lie the 'mixed ties', which cover all the social connections that usually have relatively 'balanced' affective and instrumental components. This type of tie is frequently found among relatives, neighbours, classmates, colleagues, and so on.

Different types of interpersonal ties are generally guided by three different sociality rules (Hwang, 1987). The 'need rule' guides the expressive ties in the sense that members do their best to meet each other's needs to promote the harmony and integrity of the relationship. Social exchanges and resource distribution among expressive tie are governed by the 'need rule' as individuals' interests are so closely associated with one another and the affective attachment is considerable, to the degree that it makes no sense to make a distinction between 'you' and 'me'. However, within the 'instrumental tie', the ideal principle is equity – take the shopkeeper who is supposed to treat all customers equally. The equity rule also indicates social exchanges at equal values with a minimal affective component. Finally, a mixed tie is guided by the *guanxi* rule, where individuals seek to influence others through *guanxi* management and *guanxi* building.

Guanxi, the 'special Chinese form of social capital' (Qi, 2013), can be roughly described as a personalised connection between two individuals (Bian, 2019). 'Personalised' is the key to *guanxi*, as social interactions do not automatically generate *guanxi* between people unless such a connection results in active and intimate interactions in the personal worlds (Kipnis, 1997). In *guanxi* practice, concerns related to the 'face' (*mianzi*) are essential. As a typical 'front-stage' behaviour (Goffman, 1990), *Mianzi*, known as 'Chinese face', is a sophisticated felling with regards to one's own sense of dignity and reputation in a community (Hu, 1944).

During the fieldwork, I observed that WeChat groups have covered the full range of social relations people can possibly engage within their daily life, from families to strangers. Therefore, Hwang's model provides a useful frame to map out different interpersonal communication strategies applied to different types of mediated relationships on WeChat. There are three general types: instrumental groups, mixed groups and expressive groups (Figure 20.1). It is important to note that Hwang's model of interpersonal ties in China has its limitations in the sense that the clear division runs the risk of oversimplifying the complicated interpersonal relations in people's daily life, as observed in the fieldwork. Therefore, the practice of the curation of different WeChat groups based on Hwang's model aims to present a brief sketch of the basic outline of different WeChat groups, which then provides the base for a further nuancing of the interpersonal interactions within these WeChat groups.

In the chart (Figure 20.1), the coloured part of the rectangles stands for the affective component and the white part the instrumental component. The dashed lines dividing the three categories indicate that the different types of boundaries are slippery in practice and depend

The Practice of Friendship via Social Media

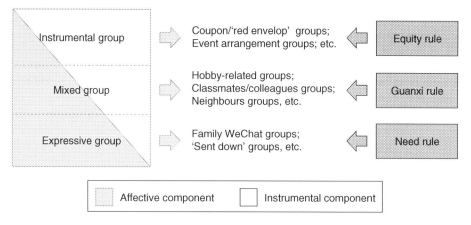

Figure 20.1 WeChat groups can be broken down into three types, based on three interpersonal ties. This chart is adapted from the original chart called 'a theoretical model of face and favor in Chinese society'
Source: Hwang, 1987: 949, reworked by the author.

on specific situations. For example, expressive groups can, though rarely, develop from mixed groups, mixed groups can also develop from, or become instrumental groups. With regards to the 'instrumental' compound in interpersonal ties, it is important to note that utility is always a part of friendship and kinship in China, and it is utility that made for the highest forms of friendship which ultimately bolstered the family and the society (Kutcher, 2000: 11).

In terms of 'expressive groups', all of the research participants[7] have at least one family WeChat group, and many of them have three family WeChat groups – two groups for the extended family from both sides of the couple and one for the nuclear family. Sometimes, siblings and family members belong to the same generation, or closer siblings would have their own specific groups. Also, it is common to see separate groups set up for specific reasons among family members, such as taking care of the elderly parents. Besides family groups, groups for former classmates and former colleagues are also present on the smartphones of the majority of the research participants.

Another specific expressive group among this older generation is the 'sent-down' group. The 'sent-down' WeChat group is a unique group category which only exists among the cohort of people who were born in 1950s. During the decade-long Cultural Revolution (1966–1976), schools were shut down and massive amounts of urban youths who were supposed to receive secondary school education were instead 'sent down' to rural areas to undertake heavy labour in the fields and to be re-educated by the farmers. Having been 'sent down' is the trademark of many older people who participated in the research, and friends people made during that specific time are widely and profoundly valued as people they share deep bonds with. In a way, the revolutionary time is when young people cultivated strong interpersonal relations outside of their family.

More than two-thirds of the research participants were part of a WeChat group consisting of formerly 'sent-down youth'. The specific life experience shared by the previously 'sent-down' urban youth is frequently mentioned by this older generation nowadays as an unforgettable collective memory and individual experience. As one person remarks: 'The affection formed during the tough 'sent down' period is so special and probably the deepest bond in my life'. Another one comments: 'They (the sent-down youth who used to work in the same 'production team' in the countryside) are my good comrades during the tough time … like family without blood ties and actually they are closer to me even more than my family'. This acknowledgement and appreciation of these special bonds, as evidenced in the popularity of the 'sent-down' WeChat groups among older people today, reflects the profound influence of the party-state on Chinese people's friendship, at the time better known under the name of 'comradeship'.

Even so, not all of the 'sent-down' groups can be qualified as 'expressive groups'. Like former classmates' groups, larger 'sent-down' groups, formed on the basis of the original admin unit rather than personal preference, were usually mixed groups where members are keen to present themselves in group interaction following the rule of *guanxi*.

'Expressive groups' such as family groups, 'sent-down' groups or other small WeChat groups of close friends represent people's essential social life based on closest ties, and typically, group members know each other very well. In 'instrumental groups', however, the chance that people know other group members in person is meagre. As observed during fieldwork, 'instrumental groups' are not uncommon, and about a third of research participants[8] had such a group on their WeChat. Normally, people were added to instrumental WeChat groups by their online contacts. It is common to hear people explain them as follows: 'One of my previous colleagues "dragged" (*la*) me along into this group'. Or: 'I asked my friend to "drag" me into the group'. 'Drag' (*la*), a verb which indicates a certain degree of dependency and passivity, is the most colloquial way of describing how people joined a group. It also reflects that most instrumental WeChat groups grow gradually through each member 'dragging' their own personal online contacts along.

Typical instrumental groups include 'red envelope' group (*hong bao*), where people simply post links to coupons that contain rewards and discounts, so-called 'red envelopes'. In eCommerce, it is common for customers to be rewarded discount coupons for their next purchase and the red envelope group works like a collective 'coupon box' so that every member contributes a coupon, and, in turn, every member can always benefit from others' coupons.

Some visit the red envelope group on a weekly basis, but it is very rare to see any other interaction among group members except sharing coupon links. As one person says, 'Whenever I order take-aways, I will first check the red envelope group to see whether there is a coupon available there … we go there for coupons, no one would go there for making friends'. Another common type of 'instrumental group' is the joke group which works based on a similar logic as the red envelope group, except here, the shared subject is jokes and funny short videos. Interaction among group members is minimal as people visit these groups mainly for their content. Mr Jiang is a member of one joke group, and for him, it is a great resource of funny content, with daily updates which he can further forward to many other WeChat groups. Mr Jiang would also frequently share jokes that he received from different groups to this joke group, as, according to him, 'give and take should be equal to be fair' (see the 'equity rule').

Usually, there is no reaction at all from others to whatever he posts in the joke group, but Mr Jiang feels this is completely fine. He explains, 'most of them don't know me and why people need to give me a "face" if they don't know me? I don't react to them neither'. Curiously, once Mr Jiang posted a joke in the WeChat group of his previous classmates, which is a typical 'mixed group', and there was no reaction for a couple of hours. Mr Jiang immediately started to worry that this silence was indicative of some subtle collective discontentment against him, and he had to message one of his close friends, urging him to reply to his joke in the group to save his 'face' in front of the whole class. The discrepancy between Mr Jiang's attitudes towards being ignored in 'instrumental group' and being ignored in the 'mixed groups' he is part of exemplifies the way in which these two types of groups are guided by different sociality rules, with only the latter requiring the maintenance of *guanxi*, which sees people care about 'face'.

In many ways, the 'instrumental group' is like a busy shopping mall where many people gather for the goods that they want – most of them do not expect to have interpersonal communication with other customers. WeChat instrumental groups also provide an example of online 'strangership', as proposed by McDonald (2019) based on his ethnographic study of the use of social media in rural China. However, the difference here is that in McDonald's fieldsite, people in the village were aware of the negative social implications of strangers in an offline situation and social media provides a place that makes it possible to interact with strangers; whereas in the example of the WeChat groups in Shanghai, the personal desire for interacting with strangers online for social reasons is rather limited and strangers within 'instrumental groups' don't have a stigma attached to them, being commonly regarded as a potential information resource.

The third type of group described, the 'mixed group', is also the type that hosts the majority of 'friends from WeChat groups' as it includes groups of former classmates, colleagues and neighbours, and various hobby-related groups. It is also within mixed groups that people are more likely to make new friends outside of their previous social network.

Friend-making and *Guanxi* Practice in WeChat Groups

Tang, a 66-year-old retired teacher, regards WeChat as the place to make new friends after retirement. Talking of making friends, Tang remarks:

> Unlike young kids, for whom making friends is a common thing, our older people feel reluctant to make friends because we have been used to only a few old friends for long and making new friends is somehow strange at the later stage of life, plus, we don't have many opportunities to make new friends after retirement and we may have lost the capability for making new friends due to the lack of practice…WeChat is the only place where I get to know new people nowadays.

As Tang says, it is common to see older people find it challenging to make new friends, especially after retirement, when 'the centre of life is supposed to return to the home', as another research participant put it. In practice, WeChat is deployed in many ways to maintain as well as make friends. Here, we will focus mainly on making friends.

The 'scalable sociality' facilitated by the WeChat groups can foster potential friendships among group members who did not know one another before. It is common for WeChat groups to be set up for specific activities and events for the convenient circulation of information. Often, these groups are rather short-lived as all the group participants become silent once the group has served its original purpose. Short-lived as these groups were, they served another major function: providing a platform where people can gain access to other members' WeChat accounts because they are part of the same group. In some cases, the main reason for setting up WeChat groups is to avoid the possible embarrassment of asking to connect as WeChat friends in person. Occasionally, these groups would remain active for a long time. For example, one research participant once organised a trip to a water town with a couple of her former classmates and their friends. She set up a WeChat group called '16 May water town group' to share details of tickets, hotel bookings, real-time location and photos. During the trip, the group of six got along very well and decided to meet regularly back in Shanghai and have more trips together. The WeChat group name was then changed from '16 May water town group' to 'More journeys to go'.

As mentioned before, unlike WhatsApp, which is mainly used for messaging, WeChat includes Facebook-like personal profiles. In practice, given the extent of self-exposure on WeChat, becoming personal WeChat friends (contacts) is widely regarded as an endorsement of meaningful social connection. WeChat users can tailor their privacy settings to block selected WeChat friends from viewing their profile content. However, in practice, unless the contacts are clearly instrumental, it is regarded as rude to impose 'visiting limits' on WeChat friends among older people.[9] In this context, 'friends from WeChat group' is a group that lies between strangers and WeChat friends and has as a unique advantage its flexibility in dealing with new contacts. On the one hand, within a WeChat group, the opportunity to send friend requests is available in most cases;[10] on the other hand, in many cases, there is no explicit social expectation of adding one another as WeChat friends immediately. Therefore, people can take their time to observe group members' interaction and performance within the group and decide whether it is worthwhile to get to know the person as a new friend.

Tang has made new friends from various WeChat groups. For example, once, there was a discussion about one specific piece of Qing dynasty furniture in a group about Chinese history, and to Tang's surprise, a few group members shared some very interesting posts and made insightful comments. As Tang recalls, 'I immediately sent friend requests to two of them after reading their comments, and they both confirmed my requests very soon'. Later, Tang went through these two new friends' WeChat profiles only to find that one had even worked in the same 'production team' as him during the 'sent-down' period. Like Tang, a few research participants also report cases of making new friends 'naturally' outside of large WeChat groups.

WeChat groups also provide multiple social networks, which one may lack in their 'offline' immediate living situation. For example, 60-year-old Maling joined a WeChat group after taking part in a flower arranging workshop 'in real life' and found that she prefers the lifestyle encouraged by its members. Unlike many of her friends from childhood, Maling does not have any grandchildren so does not take part in daily grandparenting duties. Maling wants to look beautiful, but her surrounding friends and siblings think it is not necessary for older women to put on make-up and wear fashionable items. Maling constantly feels 'out of place'. However, in the flower arrangement WeChat group, sharing photos of new dresses is welcomed and would receive praise.

Conclusion

This chapter discusses the consequence of pervasive WeChat use, particularly the wide and mundane applications of WeChat groups and the practices of friendship among older people in contemporary Chinese society. 'Friends from WeChat groups' gains its very existence thanks to the pervasive use of WeChat groups among Chinese people in their daily communication. Furthermore, this chapter argues that 'friends from WeChat groups' should be treated as a new social category in contemporary China, given its unique function in social networking and its subtle position between friendship.

The goal of this chapter has been to present emerging social norms surrounding the new type of mediated friendship in the context of social media. As shown by the variety of scenarios discussed above, the social expectations and cultural preferences that form the normative usage of WeChat groups have become part and parcel of people's everyday lives. The different types of WeChat groups not only represent the full range of people's social lives, but also reflect sophisticated sociality rules applied in different interpersonal interaction scenarios.

Embedded in people's everyday interpersonal interaction, WeChat groups have become one of the major places where older people make new friends. This is due to three reasons – first, the online space plays an even more important role in people's social life given the offline space (e.g. workplace) where interpersonal interactions regularly take place starts to shrink after retirement. Second, in practice, the WeChat group serves as an 'incubator' which provides a relatively friendly field, allowing potential friendships to grow. Third, the WeChat group works as a friendship 'scalable threshold' where people have perceived control over how they develop friendships via the privacy setting.

The lived experience of older people in China is characterised by periods of time that were deeply embedded in socialist communities where regional relationships (such as those between 'sent-down youth') and work-related relationships (comrades, colleagues) occupied the gap left by the somewhat 'forced' absence of kinship during the socialist revolution. The 'friends from WeChat groups' category, which is mediated not only by social media, but also by the shared past and ideals of friendship among older people in China, finds its niche in people's social lives after retirement. The increasing significance of 'friends from WeChat groups' provides a particular perspective for understanding the evolving concept and practice of friendship in a society where Confucian and communist legacies intersect with the social possibilities facilitated by digital media.

Acknowledgement

This study was funded by the European Research Council under the European Union's Horizon 2020 research and innovation programme (No. 740472).

Notes

1. From 2012–2017, the author's ethnographic research about the use of social media in industrial China was part of the global comparative project Why We Post. www.ucl.ac.uk/why-we-post/
2. www.statista.com/statistics/1081645/china-life-expectancy-of-registered-population-in-shanghai/#:~:text=In%202019%2C%20the%20average%20life,male%20persons%20was%2081.27%20years
3. www.statista.com/statistics/255552/penetration-rate-of-mobile-internet-users-in-china/, data by December 2018.
4. '2015 WeChat Impact Report' https://www.sohu.com/a/66255816_293227
5. The inquiry of people's general use of various digital applications took place in different stages of the fieldwork in different forms (observations, interview and questionnaire). The valid data about the use of email is based on 170 research participants.
6. In addition to the 15-month fieldwork in a factory town in southeast China, the author also did one month's (July 2014) fieldwork in Shanghai about people's use of WeChat. See X. Wang, 2016. *Social Media in Industrial China*. UCL Press, 24.
7. Among 52 research participants (30 men and 22 women) aged between 45 and 75 who self-counted their WeChat groups and took part in in-depth interviews about their smartphone in 2019.
8. Among 52 research participants (30 women and 22 men) between age 45 to 75 who self-counted their WeChat groups and received in-depth smartphone interviews in 2019.
9. Among younger people who have a large professional network, sometimes blocking work-related contacts from viewing their profile is acceptable. Although people would still rather not post private things on WeChat at all, they can tailor each post's privacy setting rather than blocking WeChat contacts from viewing private content, as the latter is always associated with unwelcoming attitudes and causes them to lose face, therefore doing harm to work/business relationships, which are also guided by *guanxi* rules.
10. The privacy setting allows users to switch off the 'add a friend via WeChat groups' function, which means nobody can send a friend request through the WeChat group. However, among older research participants, it is very uncommon to see people apply this privacy setting.

References

Bell, D. (2000) 'Guanxi: A Nesting of Groups', *Current Anthropology*, 41(1): 132–138.
Bell, S., and Coleman, S. (eds.), (2020) *The Anthropology of Friendship*. London: Routledge.
Bian, Y. (2019) *Guanxi: How China Works*. Cambridge: Polity.
Boase, J. and Wellman, B. (2006) 'Personal Relationships: On and Off the Internet', in A. L. Vangelisti and D. Perlman (eds), *The Cambridge Handbook of Personal Relationships*, Cambridge: Cambridge University Press, 709–724.
boyd, d. (2011) 'Social Network Sites as Networked Publics: Affordances, Dynamics, and Implications', in Z. Papacharissi (ed.), *A Networked Self: Identity, Community, and Culture on Social Network Sites*. New York: Routledge, 39–58.
Cartier, C., Castells, M. and Qiu, J. L. (2005). 'The information have-less: Inequality, mobility, and translocal networks in Chinese cities', *Studies in Comparative International Development*, 40(2): 9–34.
Chambers, D. (2013) *Social Media and Personal Relationships: Online Intimacies and Networked Friendship*. New York: Palgrave Macmillan.
Chambers, D. (2017) 'Networked Intimacy: Algorithmic Friendship and Scalable Sociality', *European Journal of Communication*, 32(1): 26–36.
Ellison, N. B., Steinfield, C. and Lampe, C. (2007) 'The Benefits of Facebook "Friends": Social Capital and College Students' Use of Online Social Network Sites', *Journal of Computer-Mediated Communication*, 12(4): 1143–1168.
Goffman, E. (1990) *The Presentation of Self in Everyday Life*. London: Penguin.
Gold, T. B. (1991) 'Youth and the State', *The China Quarterly*, 127: 594–612.
Hu, H. (1944) 'The Chinese Concept of "Face"', *American Anthropologist*, 46 (1): 45–64.
Hwang, K. (1987) 'Face and Favor: The Chinese Power Game', *The American Journal of Sociology*, 92 (4): 944–974.
Killias, O. (2018) 'Distant Friends and Intimate Strangers: On the Perils of Friendship in a Malaysian Apartment Building', *Urban Studies*, 55(3): 554–569.
Kipnis, A. (1997) *Producing Guanxi: Sentiment, Self, and Subculture in a North China Village*. Durham, NC: Duke University Press.
Kutcher, N. (2000) 'The Fifth Relationship: Dangerous Friendships in the Confucian Context', *The American Historical Review*, 105(5): 1615–1629.
Li, Y., Du, J. and Van de Bunt, S. (2016) 'Social Capital Networking in China and the Traditional Values of Guanxi', in M. Ramady (ed.), *The Political Economy of Wasta: Use and Abuse of Social Capital Networking*. New York: Springer, 173–183.
Miller, D., Costa, E., Haynes, N., McDonald, T., Nicolescu, R., Sinanan, J., Spyer, J., Venkatraman, S. and Wang, X. (2016) *How the World Changed Social Media*. London: UCL Press.
McDonald, T. (2019) 'Strangership and Social Media: Moral Imaginaries of Gendered Strangers in Rural China', *American Anthropologist*, 121(1): 76–88.
Parks, M. R. and Floyd, K. (1996) 'Making Friends in Cyberspace', *Journal of Computer-Mediated Communication*, 1(JCMC144).
Qi, X. (2013) '*Guanxi*, Social Capital Theory and Beyond: Toward a Globalized Social Science', *British Journal of Sociology*, 64(2): 308–324.
Qian, W., Razzaque, M. and Keng, K. (2007) 'Chinese Cultural Values and Gift-giving Behaviour', *Journal of Consumer Marketing*, 24(4): 214–228.
Santos, G. D. (2008) 'On "Same-Year Siblings" in Rural South China', *Journal of the Royal Anthropological Institute*, 14(3): 535–553.
Tang, L. (2010) 'Development of Online Friendship in Different Social Spaces', *Information, Communication & Society*, 13(4): 615–633.
Vogel, E. F. (1965) 'From Friendship to Comradeship: The Change in Personal Relations in Communist China', *The China Quarterly*, (21): 46–60.
Wallis, C. (2013) *Technomobility in China*. New York: New York University Press.
Yan, Y. (2010) 'The Chinese Path to Individualization', *The British Journal of Sociology*, 61(3): 489–512.

21
MEDIATED MONEY AND SOCIAL RELATIONSHIPS AMONG HONG KONG CROSS-BOUNDARY STUDENTS

Tom McDonald, Holy Hoi Ki Shum and Kwok Cheung Wong

The field of media anthropology has made a significant contribution to the overall discipline, foregrounding how social relationships are shaped by ongoing transformations in media use taking place in different societies. Work in this area has led scholars to consider broader definitions of what constitutes "media", with technological advances and changing communications practices expanding the scope of mediated social actions. This is particularly apparent in the domain of money, which Swartz (2020) posits is itself increasingly becoming a form of social media. This chapter investigates the anthropological implications that emerge from treating money as a *kind* of social media, especially for charting the interconnections between contemporary forms of money, media and social relationships.

The chapter addresses this issue through examining how Hong Kong cross-boundary schoolchildren manage their personal monies within the context of their frequent passages between Hong Kong and Mainland China. We reveal how the increasingly mediated nature of money makes it an important site through which these individuals reflect upon and manage relationships with both their parents/guardians and also consumptive service providers. As cross-boundary students enact lives that span the two regions, they represent an ideal group through which to observe how the increasingly mediated nature of money may be reshaping how people perceive and experience their social relationships with individuals, organisations and places.

This chapter argues that money's propensity to act as a form of social media is not of a homogenous nature, but is instead inherently contextual and significantly determined by specific locational and relational factors. For our school-aged participants, money is typically felt to be comparatively more like social media when they are located on Mainland China than is the situation for when they are in Hong Kong. This apparent distinction in the perceived social mediation of money correspondingly shapes students' (and their parents') attempts to use different monies to enact kinship relations within and across geographical spaces.

The early sections of this chapter will review scholarship on money as a communicative media, outline the methods used in this study and describe the payment landscapes of the two regions. The chapter then turns to examine students' use of money pertaining to two key categories of social relations. First, parents intentionally adopt distinctive monetary technologies for disbursing differentiated allowances to their offspring for use in each region. This strategy allows parents to both care for and monitor their offspring in ways tailored to the expectations of activities to be engaged for each locale. Second, the subsequent effects this has on the kinds of consumptive relations enacted by students are examined, detailing how these shape their perceptions of the regions as sites of primarily study or leisure. The conclusion reflects on the potential contribution of treating money as social media for our anthropological understandings of how social relationships are enacted and maintained.

Money as Media

Scholars have long acknowledged the communicative dimensions of money. Simmel compared money to language. He argued that money's rendering of activities/possessions in terms of abstract monetary value was analogous to the way that thoughts must be expressed in a "universally understood language" in order to achieve practical ends (Simmel 2004: 210). Kant (1887) asserted that money's capacity for transmitting thought made it a technology akin to printed books, likening "the freedom to trade" with the "freedom of the pen" during German enlightenment. Parsons described money as a "generalised medium of communication" (Parsons 1963: 39), expressing how money as a medium enables the generation and communication of various symbolic expressions which carry a built-in preference structure.

Hart (2009) has outlined the need to move beyond the money-as-language metaphor, instead calling for greater attention to be paid to *how* people actually communicate through money. This approach, which asks "What does money *do*, and how?" (Hart 2009: 138), foregrounds the various social relationships, behaviours and meanings emerging from money's communicative dimensions. Maurer warns against reducing money to mere economic functions, instead pointing towards how "money is infused with meaning, morals, and material traces of our relationships with others" (Maurer 2015: 48). Swartz (2020) has sought to situate the act of payment within communication and media studies by arguing that money not only transmits value, but also encompasses aspects of ritual communication that produce shared social realities:

> Payment is a form of communication, a way of transmitting information that produces shared meaning. Communication through payment knits us together in a shared economic world: a *transactional community*, by which I mean the set of relations that are produced by transactional communication.
>
> Swartz 2020: 16, author's emphasis

This treatment of money as a form of communication is rendered all the more powerful given that the process by which money's communicative qualities work appears to be undergoing significant changes owing to novel monetary technologies (Moor 2017). Digital devices (smartphones in particular) are establishing themselves as the primary interfaces through which the storage, transferral, tracking and payment of money is achieved, in turn transforming the nature of what money *is* (Maurer, 2015). Swartz (2020) portrays this as a transition away from the "mass money media" of state-issued currencies, instead towards a world of "social money media" where diverse forms of payment are "increasingly being *produced*, *practiced* and *understood* as a form of 'social media'" (Swartz 2020: 18–19, author's emphasis). Swartz's description of a macro-level shift away from "transactional communities that are the size and scope of the nation" appears to elide with Dodd's (2014) observation of the increasing detachment of money from the geopolitical space. Treating social media as simultaneously an industry, a collection of technologies and a series of norms and practices that acts both *within* and *beyond* particular territorial boundaries, Swartz's approach thus provides a powerful theoretical lens for understanding the social impacts of the novel spatial flows of mediated money.

The everyday monetary practices of cross-boundary school children moving between Hong Kong and Mainland China constitute an ideal phenomenon through which to explore how the concept of money as a form of social media might work across multiple spaces. China resumed the exercise of sovereignty over the formerly British-administered territory of Hong Kong in 1997. Hong Kong's status as a Special Administrative Region of the People's Republic of China means that it maintains its own currency, customs and immigration controls. Many individuals frequently travel between Hong Kong and Mainland China for reasons related to work, study or leisure. In 2018, 236 million cross-boundary passenger trips occurred between the two regions (Legislative Council of HKSAR 2019).

Taylor and Horst's (2018) research on everyday experiences of financial inclusion and exclusion on the Haiti–Dominican Republic border provides a particularly useful framework for considering similar issues. Through examining the use of ordinary technologies such as mobile money, the authors deploy the concept of the "living fence" to examine how the contingencies of power relations become embedded within various economic and social relations formed across the regions. Likewise, Latonero and Kift's (2018) idea of "digital passages" provides a meaningful reminder that digital infrastructures both traverse and materialise boundaries, often carrying with them complex sets of normative ideals. Cross-boundary schoolchildren's own passages—both physical and digital—between Mainland China and Hong Kong thus afford a distinctive opportunity to think through the anthropological implications of mediated money.

Methods and Social Context

This study employed a methodology tailored to understanding the use of digital money and payments technologies by cross-boundary secondary school students. The category of "cross-boundary students" is a formal designation for young people who are Permanent Residents of Hong Kong, but who normally reside in the city of Shenzhen in the Chinese Mainland and who commute to Hong Kong to attend primary or secondary school. Such trips typically occur every weekday during term time, although some students may stay for longer periods if they also have family members or access to alternative accommodation in Hong Kong. One of the historic reasons for this arrangement was that, prior to 2017, these young people were generally not eligible to receive state-subsidised schooling in Mainland China, as they lacked a household registration (*hukou*). Waters and Leung (2020) note that after a policy change in 2017 which permitted certain students to enrol in Shenzhen designated schools, many parents nonetheless continued to send their offspring to study in Hong Kong for multiple reasons, including perceived greater educational mobility, lower costs associated with schooling and more widespread use of English.

In many cases, parents of cross-boundary school children are Mainland Chinese residents who may themselves possess limited rights to travel to Hong Kong. Their offspring typically gained Hong Kong permanent resident status by virtue of simply being born in the city. According to the HKSAR Education Bureau, the number of cross-boundary school pupils grew from 9,899 in 2010–2011 to 28,106 in 2015–2016 (HKSAR Government 2016). Revised immigration measures introduced by the HKSAR Government in 2013 have resulted in a significant reduction of births by Mainland mothers in Hong Kong (HKSAR Constitutional and Mainland Affairs Bureau 2019). However, many cross-boundary students born prior to these changes are currently still in the primary or secondary stages of their education at Hong Kong schools.

Authorities in both regions provide numerous support measures for cross-boundary students, including priority clearance lanes at immigration facilities and subsidised bus transport between the boundary control point and their school. Students' frequent cross-boundary passages and extended daily commutes nonetheless produce distinctive life experiences (Waters and Leung 2020). Their use of digital money therefore provides a unique lens for understanding how such passages—and the social relations pertaining to them—might be experienced and managed on an everyday level.

Recruitment involved approaching principals of various Hong Kong public secondary schools (by letter and telephone communication), who were asked to publicise the project amongst their cross-boundary students aged 16–18 years old. Upon gaining informed consent from both student participants and their parents/guardians, students completed a week-long financial diary documenting their everyday transactions (including details of expenditure/income/exchange, value and currency of transaction, platforms/payment methods used, parties involved). Shortly after completion of the financial diaries, follow-on interviews were conducted with selected participants. Fifteen financial diaries and 12 interviews were completed in total.

Interviews covered specific phenomena highlighted by the diary, while also eliciting students' general practices surrounding and attitudes toward digital money. Because of lengthy mandatory quarantine requirements for travellers that were in place on both sides of the boundary for much of the fieldwork period in response to Covid-19, students generally experienced difficulty travelling between the two regions as normal. Many schools instead opted to deliver classes through online means. Considering this, both the financial diary and interview were carried out online, with video interviews being conducted in either Standard Chinese (Mandarin) or Cantonese. This chapter primarily focuses on students' narratives of their monetary practices under "normal" (i.e., pre-pandemic) conditions, when travel was largely unconstrained. We have discussed the impacts of reduced travel between the regions on everyday monetary flows in a separate publication (McDonald, Shum, & Wong 2021).

While the methods used in this study generally would not be regarded as representing "traditional" ethnography, various ethnographic sensibilities were nonetheless encompassed in our approach. One unexpected benefit of our methodology were the glimpses into everyday family life that interviews conducted via videocall offered. Because student participants usually preferred to schedule such interviews when they were at home (this being one of the few places where they had access to reliable internet connections), videocalls were often received in living or dining rooms. Being able to view students' living surroundings provided a glimpse into their everyday life and the likely financial situation of their family, sometimes helping to contextualise interview question responses, leading to a more nuanced understanding of how digital money was affecting social relations.[1] We argue that deploying such an approach in this study helps demonstrate the value of anthropological perspectives even with the absence of long-term ethnographic methods, owing to the way that such perspectives effectively place social relationships at the fore of analysis.

Digital Money Differentials: Payment and Place

One of the earliest themes to emerge in conversations with cross-boundary students regarding how they managed their money was an awareness of asymmetries in the uptake of mobile payment methods amongst the general population in each of the two regions. Many participants remarked on how the use of mobile money and payment platforms on the Mainland was almost ubiquitous, while they had the impression that the uptake of such technologies in Hong Kong remained comparatively uneven. Most students recalled how they had long been accustomed to relying on mobile payment platforms when they were in Shenzhen, whereas such payment methods had only started to gain traction amongst the general public in Hong Kong from around 2018. Admittedly, one explanation for the comparatively slower adoption of mobile payments in Hong Kong might have been the already widespread use of other payment technologies (such as bank-issued credit cards and Octopus store cards) in the city, alongside the continued prevalence of cash-based payments. In keeping with this trend, most participants reported that they themselves were yet to register for, or make use of, Hong Kong-based mobile payment platforms.

Beyond the general distinctions between online versus offline payments, attitudes were also shaped by the asymmetrical prevalence of specific payment platforms. In Mainland China, the rapid ascendence and dominance of two predominantly smartphone-based payment platforms—Alipay and WeChat Wallet—had resulted in these becoming almost universally accepted means of payments in the region, largely replacing cash-based transactions. In Hong Kong, the closest thing to a *de facto* non-cash-based payment method was the Octopus card, a contactless stored value card first introduced in 1997 for use on the territory's mass-transit system, which is also widely accepted for small-value payments in shops and convenience stores. However, at the time of writing, a significant minority of Hong Kong retailers still only accepted cash.

The Hong Kong Monetary Authority (HKMA) has dedicated efforts to encouraging innovation and competition in digital payments, including by issuing 18 stored value facilities licences since 2016.[2] Hong Kong now boasts a comparatively variegated ecology of competing digital payment technologies such as EPS, Octopus Wallet, Apple Pay, Android Pay, Samsung Pay and PayMe (from HSBC), along with Hong Kong localisations of Alipay and WeChat Wallet. However, these varied payment methods tend to remain less frequently used in Hong Kong than either cash or traditional Octopus cards—especially amongst our school-aged participants. The plethora of payment options available in Hong Kong also forms a distinct contrast to Shenzhen, where participants described Alipay and WeChat Wallet as effectively the default choice for everyday payments.

Mediating Family Relations: Parental Nurturance and Control of Offspring

Disparities in students' attitudes towards mobile payments across the two regions were enmeshed in and generative of their own varied sets of social relationships. Central amongst these were students' relationships with their parents/guardians, whom they relied on as their primary source of money. Stafford (2000) has persuasively described the deeply held Chinese cultural principle whereby parental nurturance of offspring (*yang*) is regarded as involving the creation of parent–child debt, which offspring have an obligation to repay when their parents reach old age. Such acts of nurturance are particularly foregrounded during ritual festivals (such as the gifting of red envelopes during the Lunar New Year festival), but they also occur throughout everyday life in more mundane ways, for instance through the everyday provision of clothing and food. For our participants, the supply of money by parents to support their offspring's everyday spending may be regarded as a channel through which participants discerned parental care to be acting upon them. This raises questions regarding how the digitisation of such parental provisioning of money to offspring may affect such relations.

The affordances of specific monetary types (whether digital or non-digital)—along with their anchoring in specific regions—plays a key role in leading these monies to become "earmarked" (Zelizer 2017) in certain ways, a process through which money is assigned specific social uses and given social meaning. For instance, one student described cash as primarily being used when attending school in Hong Kong, whereas WeChat Pay was associated with leisure time in Shenzhen. Applying the notion of earmarking to the use of money by cross-boundary school children can provide an analytical perspective that moves beyond seeing money as a practical "tool" for settling transactions, instead demonstrating it as a meaning-laden media through which parents engage in ongoing negotiations with their offspring with the aim of shaping norms surrounding the kinds of activities that their cross-boundary lifestyles ought to be comprised of.

Participants often described how their parents managed the supply of different kinds of monies in an effort to encourage them to prioritise their academic studies. Many students detailed how although they received spending money in *both* Chinese Yuan and Hong Kong Dollars from their parents, they usually received a greater overall amount of the former than they did the latter. Parents typically gave Hong Kong dollars in cash to support everyday spending when in Hong Kong (either through cash-based transactions or by first depositing on an Octopus card for later spending). Chinese Yuan tended to instead be given in digitally mediated fashion, with parents sending it to their offspring using smartphones via the WeChat Wallet or Alipay apps. As one student recalled:

> Because, I guess you could say I'm in a one-parent family, I normally live with my Dad in Hong Kong, so during holidays or weekends I'll go and stay with my Mum [in Shenzhen]. So, for spending money, it's troublesome for my Dad to come to Shenzhen to give me it, so he will directly send it to my WeChat.
>
> Sze Wan, female secondary school student[3]

The above factors tended to result in students having comparatively less personal budget for spending in Hong Kong than when in Shenzhen. Furthermore, several students commented that the digital nature of Chinese Yuan transactions and their integration in the popular WeChat messaging platform made it easier to immediately request (and receive) further additional "top-ups" of money in Chinese Yuan from one's parents, when needed. In this sense, the specific affordances of mobile money platforms (ability to send money alongside messages, and to enact payments remotely) facilitated many more ad-hoc transactions, shaping the frequency and size of parent's Chinese Yuan money transfers with their offspring. For instance, male student Ming Fai commented that although he received more Chinese Yuan than Hong Kong dollars from his parents, each individual Chinese Yuan transfer tended to be comparatively small, as it was easier for parents to more flexibly and regularly send their offspring small amounts of Chinese Yuan via the app than was the case with cash.[4] By contrast, students' reliance on seemingly "off-line" money infrastructures of cash and Octopus cards for handling Hong Kong dollars often obliged them to collect Hong Kong dollar cash from their parents *in person* when they were at home in Shenzhen.

These variances in the degree to which students' personal monies have converged into smartphone technologies were further intensified by differentials in parental provision of internet access to their offspring across the two regions. Several participants described experiencing comparatively more limited access to the internet when they were in Hong Kong than when in Shenzhen. This seemed to have little to do with network coverage or smartphone access,[5] but rather appeared to be a situation that was, to a certain extent, intentionally engineered by their parents. Most parents had chosen to provide their offspring with types of Mainland Chinese mobile phone SIM cards that had been selected on the basis that they lacked support for data roaming while in Hong Kong.[6] Even amongst the few student participants who reported possessing an additional dedicated Hong Kong SIM card, these had been carefully selected for plans that provided only voice call and SMS functionality, not mobile data. Such a situation was well encapsulated by one female cross-boundary student, Kwai Wah, who commented: "I have two SIM cards in my phone: one Mainland, one Hong Kong. The Hong Kong one can only make calls, while with the Mainland one it's [also] possible to access the internet."

Students' comparative lack of access to mobile data in Hong Kong cannot be solely attributed to cost factors. Indeed, data packages on Hong Kong SIM cards were generally inexpensive. Rather, participants suggested that their parents believed that having internet access while in Hong Kong might distract their offspring from their studies. Notably, when asked about whether they were inconvenienced by not having ready access to mobile data while in Hong Kong, some students seemed to echo their parents' sentiment, commenting that they felt they had limited need for internet access during their busy school days in Hong Kong.

Returning to the central issue of monetary practices, this situation meant the comparatively limited internet access that participants experienced when they were located in Hong Kong tended to further amplify their reliance on "simple" offline forms of payment such as cash and Octopus card. This also resulted in there being relatively little impetus for them to experiment with the wide array of digital money platforms on offer in the region. Some students expressed concern that even if they were to sign up for Hong Kong-based mobile payment services, they doubted whether they would be able to fully rely on such technologies for making payments, given that they lacked a separate Hong Kong SIM card that could guarantee dependable internet access. While parents' efforts to shape their offspring's activities through asymmetrical provision of both money and internet access across the two regions may have the initial appearance of being somewhat overbearing, students' own cognisance and internalisation of many of the ideals embedded in such parental oversight are also testimony to the effectiveness of the dual role that smartphones often play as technologies of both surveillance and care within social relationships (Miller et al. 2021).

Students' preference for non-mobile payments while they were physically located in Hong Kong was further intensified by their willingness to appropriate such offline monetary forms to preserve a degree of privacy from their parents. While students acknowledged that their own reliance on cash and Octopus card when in Hong Kong largely restricted them to face-to-face transactions, they nonetheless viewed such monies as offering a greater control over the degree of oversight that their parents had on their everyday spending than when compared to the mobile payment platforms that they were accustomed to using when in Shenzhen. Students may have enthused about the multiple possibilities for spending their money on WeChat and Alipay, but they conversely expressed concern regarding the degree to which their parents were able to "observe" certain online traces of their transactions. These concerns related to transaction records stored within payment platforms, as well as debit card transactions of cards linked to the platforms (some parents would link their own bank accounts to their offspring's payment app in order to automatically settle transactions on their behalf). One student explained the concerns she had regarding having her parents' bank card linked to her account.

> Suppose I wanted to connect [Alipay] to my mum's bank card, the inconvenient thing is that when I buy something, my mum will know. There's no privacy, so I can't be bothered to connect it. Using money is more convenient, as she won't know.
> *Yuk Yee, female secondary school student*

These situations display certain resemblances to boyd's (2014) observation that American parents often engage in surveillance of their teenage offspring's social media activities as "acts out of love but fail to realise how surveillance is a form of oppression that limits teens' ability to make independent choices" (boyd 2014: 74). In contrast, the relatively undifferentiated nature of money in the form of cash or Octopus cards appeared to provide students with a greater sense of agency over their money, since transactions in Hong Kong occurred largely beyond the purview of their parents.

Beyond the issue of parental surveillance, another aspect of agency related to mobile money platforms arose from how participants tended to perceive these technologies as opening up possibilities for accessing income streams from non-parental sources, thus potentially reducing their financial dependency on parents. For instance, Yuk Yee described how she often engaged in the popular pastime of collecting virtual red envelopes in WeChat. Virtual red envelopes are a digital version of the paper red envelopes containing banknotes that are traditionally exchanged during ritual occasions such as Chinese New Year or weddings. The digitisation of this tradition introduced new gamified elements for use even in non-ritual occasions. Yuk Yee recalled how when friends sent virtual red envelopes into group chat messages on the platform, she would race to "grab" the envelope before others to be awarded a randomly allocated share of the total envelope value. Significantly, Yuk Yee would earmark digital red envelopes gathered on WeChat for uses distinct from the money that she received from her parents:

> I am always grabbing virtual red envelopes [on WeChat], then after grabbing them into my WeChat, I have 400-500 RMB! Wouldn't it be a shame if I just kept it there and didn't use it? Since I have this money, and I know that I have this money, so I won't need to go to my parents and ask for more cash. Then I'll just use the money that I have managed to grab myself to buy things … then I'll use my own money that I received [from parents] for the Lunar New Year [for other purposes]. My parents won't control how I spend it, or how I use it. So, when I purchase things, I will have a little bit of freedom
>
> Yuk Yee, female secondary school student

These contrasting examples therefore demonstrate how the different levels of integration between money and social media generate new possibilities for parents to both care for and monitor their offspring in ways tailored to the specific contexts of each region.

Consumptive Relations: "Simple" and "Complex" Payment Repertoires

Cross-boundary students tended to gravitate towards specific monetary technologies for use in particular regions based primarily on the perceived appropriateness of the level of convergence between money and social media, which in turn had an impact upon the social relations that students formed with providers of consumptive services. Many student participants consistently observed that their practices surrounding the use of money in Hong Kong were deemed to be "relatively simple" in contrast to the comparatively more complex monetary practices they described themselves as carrying out when in Shenzhen. This distinction was not because of a lack of payment options in Hong Kong, but instead seemed to stem from how social media money in Mainland China was already a central component of the comprehensive "platformatisation of everyday life" (de Kloet et al. 2019) in the region. Many students attributed this to an understanding that digital money seemed to offer especially diverse affordances in Shenzhen, allowing for the enactment of a broad array of consumptive relations.

Both Alipay and WeChat Wallet can be thought of as forms of social media because they act as "super sticky" apps (Chen, Mao, and Qiu 2018) offering an endlessly growing variety of functions that keep users glued to the platforms. These apps serve as gateways, making possible the convergence and co-ordination of multiple spheres of social and economic life. Participants recounted using these payment platforms for seemingly all manner of activities: online shopping, restaurant dining, food delivery, theme parks, pet grooming, mobile games and taxi rides (to name but a few). These apps were social not only in the sense of enacting monetary transactions with Mainland providers of consumptive services, but also because they frequently became the actual medium through which participants compared between the services and products of different companies, as well as subscribing to and receiving ongoing updates from them. This was especially the case for WeChat, which by virtue of its position as the region's most popular instant messaging platform, meant that even ostensibly "offline" activities—such as visiting a cinema to watch a film with a friend—were organised and paid for in advance through integrated online platforms. Indeed, this points to how the relations social media money made possible were not always purely dyadic but could also encompass participants' friends or family, with whom such consumptive experiences were shared.

Another example of how social media money made possible the construction of expansive, digitally mediated social relations came from Alipay's integration into the popular shopping platform Taobao. Taobao provided participants with access to an especially diverse array of affordable goods through a multitude of small online sellers. The incorporation of other friends into these relations also occurred here, with several cross-boundary students reporting having Hong Kong-based classmates requesting their assistance in making purchases (in Chinese Yuan) on their behalf using Alipay, which were delivered to cross-boundary students' family homes in Shenzhen. Participants would then hand-carry these purchases to school in Hong Kong to give to their classmates, who would reimburse them in Hong Kong dollars.

> Classmates will ask me to go onto Taobao to shop, and after I have purchased, I will bring the goods to Hong Kong and receive Hong Kong dollars from them according to the exchange rate. Because I'm often crossing the boundary, so I can offer the "real" exchange rate for purchase.
>
> *Yuk Yee, female secondary school student*

Aside from helping classmates to access affordable goods, this practice therefore also serves as an informal, improvised means by which cross-boundary students could occasionally exchange small amounts of Chinese Yuan for Hong Kong dollars to supplement the Hong Kong dollars they received from their parents. In so doing, cross-boundary students successfully use digital payment and shopping platforms to mediate (and conjoin) social relations with both online sellers and their classmates.

Cross-boundary students often contrasted what they regarded as the complex kinds of relations they enacted through WeChat and Alipay when in Shenzhen with their comparatively "simple" monetary practices when in Hong Kong. Participants saw this quality of simplicity as primarily emerging out of their reliance on "old-fashioned" payment methods of cash and Octopus cards when in Hong Kong. Most participants reported not holding Hong Kong bank accounts or debit cards.

> Previously, I had [a Hong Kong bank account] ... now I've got rid of it again ... because I didn't use it often, so it expired ... because [when I'm in Hong Kong] I just put cash in my wallet ... I wouldn't often go to the bank to pay in or take out money.
>
> *Siu Ming, female secondary school student*

In contrast to the above quote, one participant described feeling her Mainland Chinese bank account to be indispensable, owing to it being connected to her WeChat Pay account allowing her to automatically fund payments made using the platform. Noteworthy here is that while the nearly ubiquitous acceptance of mobile payments in Shenzhen led participants to view having a bank account there as necessary for funding their payment platforms, this sentiment did not appear to easily carry over to the Hong Kong context. This is relevant because it persuasively highlights how the consumptive relations mediated by money go beyond purely dyadic relations between retailer and consumer. They may also encompass social relationships that people held with various kinds of financial institutions.

Considering students' reliance on cash and Octopus cards when in Hong Kong foregrounds a distinctive constellation of consumptive relations. Their everyday spending patterns while in Hong Kong tended to be heavily centred on items such as public transport fares to and from school, along with the purchase of cheap food in or around their Hong Kong school campuses. Students seemed to regard the "no-frills", almost humdrum monetary technologies of cash or Octopus cards as being ideal for such mundane, low-value expenditures. Indeed, Octopus cards merit particular attention here, as participants regarded them as the ideal alternative to carrying cash. Although a maximum of up to HK$3,000 ($386 USD) could be stored on a single Octopus card, most participants reported only ever keeping minimal amounts of spending money on their card:

> At most [I'll keep] HK$200–300 ($26–39 USD) [on my Octopus], because it's not possible for me to use that much ... I wouldn't use Octopus that much. Instead, I'll use cash a little bit more for payment.
>
> *Mei Ying, female secondary school student*

> Normally speaking, on a Monday my Octopus card will have HK$500–600 ($64–77 USD) stored inside, by Friday there will be very little left. If I feel like I will want to go out shopping, then I'll remember to put an extra few hundred dollars in my wallet beforehand.
>
> *Man Yee, female secondary school student*

The above quotes reveal how participants primarily viewed Octopus cards as being a handy store of money that could be used to fulfil everyday incidental expenses when in Hong Kong. This was likely helped by the fact that Octopus cards had minimal barriers to entry, since they could be purchased from any metro station for a nominal fee, required no registration or passwords and could easily be recharged at metro stations and convenience stores across the city.[7] Indeed, it is possible to posit that students seemed more comfortable in forming a relationship with Octopus than they were with banks because the former was perceived to offer affordances of storage and convenient payment that surpassed cash, but without the kinds of bureaucratic attachments that they associated with traditional financial institutions.

Taken together, both cash and Octopus cards, with their seemingly "low tech" and accessible qualities, appeared to fulfil (at least in student's own perceptions) a relatively narrowly circumscribed set of practical uses: in-person, small-value transactions for day-to-day incidental expenses while in Hong Kong. These were almost always undertaken by participants during travels to or from school, or while on school campuses. The fleeting, consumptive relations that were being mediated by these monetary technologies (e.g., buying snacks at convenience stores, transportation fares, etc.) spoke to the primacy of face-to-face transactions tied to the actual physical locations that students visited over the course of each school day.

To summarise, this section demonstrates how students' preferences for particular monetary technologies were generative of distinctive constellations of consumptive relations between regions. The nature of these relations in turn reinforced perceptions amongst many cross-boundary students that Hong Kong was chiefly a place that they associated with study, while they viewed the time that they spent in Shenzhen as being more associated with leisure and enjoyment. While one might argue that this finding is perhaps unsurprising given that the primary reason our participants had for travelling to Hong Kong was to attend school, examining the kinds of social relationships that emerge from different monetary technologies nonetheless remains an anthropologically fruitful exercise as it allows us to better appreciate the role that different everyday monetary transactions play in the formation and reproduction of such sentiments.

Conclusion

Our interactions with cross-boundary students have highlighted distinctions between the monetary technologies they utilised when in Hong Kong and Shenzhen. These variations stemmed from and further influenced their relationships with parents, consumptive service providers and classmates. Participants' reliance on cash and Octopus cards[8] while they were located in Hong Kong appeared to conform more closely to Swartz's (2020) description of the "mass money media" of traditional state-issued currencies, while their comparatively greater dependency on Alipay and WeChat Pay when in Shenzhen reflects their active involvement in producing, practicing, and understanding money as a form of "social media". While Swartz suggested that payment was increasingly becoming social media as a result of the development of novel monetary technologies and corresponding shifts in behaviour, our case study adds an additional dimension to such claims, demonstrating how intertwining modalities of money can occur geospatially both within and across regions, becoming discerned by participants through the rhythms of their daily migratory passages.

Anthropological approaches can be of particular utility in helping to better appreciate the variegated convergences of money and media. The ethnographic sensibilities deployed in this chapter have been indispensable in eliciting participants' everyday economic behaviours and grounding them within the broader social context of their lives. By paying attention to the interweaving transactional communities that a formed through multiple configurations of money and media, fruitful glimpses of the varied possibilities of social relationships emerging from them have been offered.

Furthermore, the study of money has the potential make a valuable contribution to media anthropology precisely because it provides an outstanding opportunity to rethink what we understand media to be. Anthropological perspectives have already played an important role in challenging ideas of money as being a purely economic entity, by highlighting the way money is a central force in social relationships. Anthropologists have also made similar arguments for media, asserting that beyond simply being a mode of communication for imparting information, media—along with its attendant practices and behaviours—is itself constitutive of social relations. By combining the two together, we can clearly see how payment frequently fulfils the role of communication, while also making clear the role that media plays in facilitating exchange. Such an approach can deliver valuable nuance when it comes to considering how transactions and exchanges occur both within and across regions, and the unique kinds of human engagements that this produces.

Acknowledgements

This research project (Project Number: 2019.A8.089.19D) is funded by the Public Policy Research Funding Scheme from the Policy Innovation and Co-ordination Office of The Government of the Hong Kong Special Administrative Region.

Notes

1 By way of example, when one video interview with a participant touched on the theme of saving money, the respondent showed researchers the physical "piggy bank" that they kept at home for such purposes.
2 Including three licensed banks, which are regarded as SVF licensees by the HKMA.
3 All participant's names have been altered for the purpose of preserving confidentiality.
4 These mobile money platforms typically did not provide currency exchange or cross-boundary money transfer features.
5 All student participants in the study possessed their own smartphone.
6 While some Mainland Chinese SIM cards offered data roaming services when in Hong Kong, costly roaming charges meant that most students did not have such services enabled on their subscription plans.
7 Since 2016, Octopus offered a mobile money account named Octopus Wallet (formerly O!ePay). However, none of our student participants reported using this service.
8 The majority shareholder (57.4 per cent) of Octopus Cards Limited is MTR Corporation Limited, which operates the city's mass-transit service (Octopus Cards Ltd 2021). The Hong Kong SAR Government holds a 74.8 per cent stake in MTR Corporation Limited (MTR Corporation 2021).

References

boyd, d., 2014. *It's Complicated: The Social Lives of Networked Teens*. New Haven, CT: Yale University Press.
Chen, Y. J., Mao, Z. and Qiu, J., 2018. *Super-sticky WeChat and Chinese Society*. London: Emerald Publishing.
de Kloet, J., Poell, T., Zeng, G. and Chow, Y. F. 2019. The platformization of Chinese society: Infrastructure, governance, and practice. *Chinese Journal of Communication*, 12(3), 249–256.
Dodd, N., 2014. *The Social Life of Money*. Princeton, NJ: Pinceton University Press.
Hart, K., 2009. The persuasive power of money. In Gudeman, S. ed., *Economic Persuasions*. New York: Berghahn Books, 136–158.
HKSAR Constitutional and Mainland Affairs Bureau, 2019. *Number of Live Births Born in Hong Kong to Mainland Women*. Hong Kong.
HKSAR Government, 2016. *LCQ11: Cross-boundary Students (Annex)*. Hong Kong.
Kant, I., 1887. *The Philosophy of Law*. Clark, NJ: Lawbook Exchange.
Latonero, M. and Kift, P., 2018. On digital passages and borders: Refugees and the new infrastructure for movement and control. *Social Media + Society*, 4(1), 1–11.
Legislative Council of HKSAR, 2019. *Land-based Cross-boundary Passenger Trips*.
Maurer, B., 2015. *How Would You Like To Pay? How Technology is Changing the Future of Money*. Durham, NC: Duke University Press.
McDonald, T., Shum, H. K. H. and Wong, K. C., 2021. Payments in the pandemic: Orchestrating and imagining cross-boundary digital money infrastructures in China during COVID-19. *Media International Australia*, 181(1), 44–56.
Miller, D., Abed Rabho, L., Awondo, P., de Vries, M., Duque, M., Garvey, P., Haapio-Kirk, L., Hawkins, C., Otaegui, A., Walton, S. and Wang, X. 2021. *The Global Smartphone: Beyond a Youth Technology*. London: UCL Press.
Moor, L., 2017. Money: Communicative functions of payment and price. *Consumption Markets & Culture*, 21(6), 574–581.
MTR Corporation, 2021. Share Information [online]. Available from: www.mtr.com.hk/en/corporate/investor/shareservices.html [Accessed 1 August 2021].
Octopus Cards Ltd, 2021. Corporate Structure [online]. Available from: www.octopus.com.hk/en/corporate/about-octopus/profile/structure/index.html [Accessed 1 August 2021].

Parsons, T., 1963. On the concept of influence. *Public Opinion Quarterly*, 27(1), 37–62.
Simmel, G., 2004. *The Philosophy of Money: Third Enlarged Edition*. London: Routledge.
Stafford, C., 2000. Chinese patriliny and the cycles of yang and laiwang. In Carsten, J. ed., *Cultures of Relatedness: New Approaches to the Study of Kinship*. Cambridge: Cambridge University Press, 37–54.
Swartz, L., 2020. *New Money: How Payment Became Social Media*. New Haven, CT: Yale University Press.
Taylor, E. B. and Horst, H. A., 2018. A living fence: Mobility and financial inclusion on the Haitian–Dominican Republic border. In Maurer, B., Musaraj, S. and Small, I. eds., *Money at the Margins: Global Perspectives on Technology, Financial Inclusion and Design*. New York: Berghahn Books, 23–43.
Waters, J. L. and Leung, M. W. H., 2020. Rhythms, flows, and structures of cross-boundary schooling: State power and educational mobilities between Shenzhen and Hong Kong. *Population, Space and Place*, 26(3), e2298.
Zelizer, V. A., 2017. *The Social Meaning of Money*. Princeton, NJ: Princeton University Press.

22
NARRATIVES OF DIGITAL INTIMACY
Romanian Migration and Mediated Transnational Life

Donya Alinejad and Laura Candidatu

Introduction

With the European Union (EU) visa liberalization policies implemented in 2002, intra-EU migration from Romania intensified and multiplied in types. With the subsequent expansion of the EU in 2007, Romanian migration to OECD countries more than doubled in 2007 (compared to the previous year), and the period signaled a diversification of Romanian migration (Sandu, 2010: 91). This included an increase in temporary, circular migration to Western Europe,[1] and the rise of brain drain. This all took place in tandem with a mushrooming of digital media usage rates, meaning that over the past two decades, transnational intimate life for many Romanians has not only been intensified by higher migration rates but has also rapidly become a primarily digitally mediated experience.

Mass migration is by no means new to Romania, and the country has an extensive and dynamic migration history (Nica and Moraru, 2020). Romanian mass emigration was first sparked after the fall of the state socialist regime in 1989, as international mobility restrictions were loosened. This marked the country's symbolic "return to Europe" (Gal and Kligman, 2000). Acknowledging the social effects of these mass migration events helps understand how social media uses within transnational families emerge with relation to collective memories of migration, transnational imaginations, and formations of cultural diaspora. In this chapter, we focus on the implications of migration's traces for mediated experiences of intimacy by looking at how narratives about migration relate to accounts of social media uses that help families stay in touch, transnationally. We do this by focusing on two cases based on fieldwork carried out in 2018: one examines the perspectives of relatively recently migrated Romanian mothers in the Netherlands; the other investigates the experiences of those who remained in Romania (as minors or young adults) when their parents or other family members migrated to Western Europe between the 1990s and the early 2000s.

In each case, we focus on a different positioning within transnational Romanian families and a different migration phenomenon. Together, the two cases demonstrate how social media communications are given meaning through "social discourses" (Spitulnik, 1997) about migration experiences. Debra Spitulnik advanced this idea to discuss how mass media discourses circulate in popular culture to discursively produce communities. She takes Anderson's (1983) pivotal theory of imagined communities, which focuses on textual production and top-down processes of nation-formation, and builds on it by emphasizing how discourses circulate horizontally among people. While Spitulnik discussed the circulation of these discourses through mass media, our analysis draws on her ideas to analyze narratives about social media. Hence, we see transnational family intimacy as being shaped not only by everyday practices of long-distance communications, but also by the related process of "cultural mediation" that forms collective belonging (Ginsburg, 1991). As Faye Ginsburg elaborates with relation to national identities, it is important to understand that just as the media involved in (re)producing social collectives such as nations and provincial communities help to construct cultural difference within and across societies, these national and local social forms "mediate identities" in ways that shape experience (1994: 137). Dominic Boyer's similar use of "social mediation" (Boyer, 2012: 418) draws on Ginsburg and others to argue for the broad idea of an "anthropology of mediation," under which the study of a phenomenon like migration would be connected with the study of print and broadcast media because all are involved in the movement of images, discourse, persons, and things (Boyer, 2012: 384).

Tracing social discourses in our research participants' accounts of their social media uses helps us understand how meanings of communications technologies become discursively integrated within people's narratives about living intimate lives marked by transnational migration. The notion of mediation mobilized here also mirrors that of cultural studies approaches to culture; namely, culture as the process through which mere events take on significance and are made sense of through language, narrative, and representation (Hall, 1980). There is an important parallel here with the idea of mediation advanced by media anthropologists who saw culture as mediating all human conduct rather than being a separate domain (Rosaldo, 1994). As social discourses about migration (from/to a particular national context) circulate and shape people's experiences of belonging within transnational social spheres, they also discursively implicate social media. It therefore becomes important to examine the discourses people produce about the role that social media plays in their lives. Hence, the question we address in this chapter is: how do social discourses about social media become part of the way people experience living within transnational family relationships?

In what follows, we answer this question by primarily analyzing interview accounts. We show that as media becomes embedded within the everyday experience of distanced family relationships, the meanings it is given are shaped by wider discourses about migration. Cultural reproduction in the diaspora, shared cultural memories around mass migration phenomena, and imaginations about the lives of loved ones abroad, all shape the ways people make sense of their online communication practices. Hence, as first-generation migrant mothers facilitate online communication between their parents' and their children's generation, they not only fulfill their social role as mothers. Their accounts also reflect that they use these media in their role as the first generation of Romanian cultural diaspora producers. Likewise, as the loved ones of migrants who stayed behind in Romania reflect on their everyday emotional lives in digitally mediated families, they do so not only in terms of present-day family sociality, but also through the lens of cultural memories of various historical waves of migration that shaped their generation. As such, we use concepts from the study of migration to suggest that "diaspora culture" (Hall, 1990; Gilroy, 2008) and "cultures of migration" (see Bal and Willems, 2014) shape media users' experiences of their online, long-distance relationships.

"Culture of migration" is one of the ways anthropologists have understood how those who have not migrated are affected by the migration of others around them. Bal and Willems (2014: 252–23) build on the work of Kandel and Massey (2002) to emphasize how a more comprehensive view of migration processes needs to consider the unmaterialized and culturally mediated "migration aspirations" and collective imaginations of migration destinations (Bal and Willems, 2014: 254). "Diaspora culture" has been used by such scholars as Stuart Hall (1990) and Paul Gilroy ([1993] 2008) to discuss how diaspora culture is seen as a *sui generis* post-migration cultural formation process. This conceptualization accounts for lived social experiences marked by syncretism and diasporic belonging, foregrounding diaspora as a space of transcultural exchange and "imagined" community-making between the "host" and the "home" land. The ways in which these cultural formations shape and inform media use has been long argued for in scholarship conceptualizing digital diaspora (see for example Everett, 2009; Brinkerhoff, 2009; Gajjala, 2004; Georgiou, 2006; Madianou and Miller, 2013; McKay, 2012; Nedelcu, 2018; Candidatu, Leurs, and Ponzanesi, 2019). Our aim in this chapter is to demonstrate how narratives about migration experiences help to understand the meanings given to social media uses.

This focus on narrative representation not only helps us understand the ways in which migration experiences shape social media's significance. It also demonstrates the value of bringing early media anthropological ideas and cultural studies theories – developed in relation to mass media – to the fore of the contemporary anthropological study of social media. Our focus on narrative representation and the discursive significance given to social media within people's everyday lives offers a counterpoint to material culture perspectives on media practices in anthropology. In what follows, we further frame our argument with relation to how mediation and transnational digital intimacy have been discussed in the literature. We then introduce the case and the dual-sited methodological approach of the empirical investigation, highlighting how this helps us look at the traces of historical migratory patterns alongside newer transnational mobility phenomena. Each of the two empirical sections that follows is dedicated to discussing our respective findings from field sites in Romania and the Netherlands. We conclude by distilling the implications of the two case discussions for the research question about the relationship between social discourses about social media and narrated experiences of living in migrant families.

Digital Intimacies as Discursive Formations

Families are not only the location of the biological production of generations, they are also collections of inter-personal relationships. As such, they are the anchor of common-sense generational models for understanding cultural change and continuity over time. Social generations (Mannheim, 1972), understood in terms of cohorts (Pilcher, 1994: 483), are cultural productions that rely on media, memory, and collective narratives of change and continuity (Vittadini et al., 2013: 67). Hence, social generations stand in contingent but non-arbitrary relation to biological generations within families. For families affected by migration and long-term resettlement, this picture is further complicated by how transnational everyday social life is experienced differently across generations, as well as how international mobility affects cultural change.

Jennifer Scuro (2004), in her work on the interpretation of oral history in research on women's migration and history writing, examines the specific impact migration had on the life of her Italian grandmother before and after migrating to America in the 1920s and 1930s. She draws extensively on the ethnographic work of Goddard (1996) in the South of Italy and carefully traces the changes migration brought to the local cultural context, both in Italy and in America, in order to emphasize the strong impact migration has on culture. This reading challenges earlier works on Italo-American communities that read South-Italian culture as atomistic and failed to see South-Italian migrant women's "exaggerated individualism" as a "complex consequence of assimilated native social structures" in the context of migration (Scuro, 2004: 62). Along the same lines of re-centering the significant ways in which migration and culture are inextricably connected, our investigation of border-crossing digitally mediated relationships traces the development of changing and complex social roles that are formed in the overlapping processes of being part of a family while experiencing migration or having loved ones abroad.

Migration contexts have offered particularly relevant settings in which to investigate how extensive reliance on social media in intimate social spheres may give rise to emergent forms of long-distance intimate life. And research on transnational family intimacy has been the empirical focus of much of the investigation into long-distance relationships through private digital communications. In this body of work, theorizations of care and relationships have proven important in the study of transnational intimacy (Baldassar et al., 2016; Graham et al., 2012), and discussions of "co-presence" have helped grasp how transnational family sociality is oriented toward feelings of togetherness at a distance (Alinejad, 2019; Baldassar, 2016; Baldassar et al., 2016; Itō, Okabe and Matsuda, 2005; Madianou, 2016; Nedelcu and Wyss, 2016). Previous research has also suggested the importance of developing our understanding of the ways transnational intimacy is maintained, shifted, and adapted in the context of digital media's proliferation (Alinejad and Ponzanesi, 2020).

In building on this research, we expand our analytical focus from the family to include relevant insights from the mediation of diasporic belonging and transnational culture. This approach is broadly informed by how the anthropology of globalization has previously brought media into the fold of theorizing cultural processes affected by flows and circulations of meaning across contexts and geographical scales (see Appadurai, 1996; Mazzarella, 2004). In line with this scholarship, we do not understand intimate family relationships as having come to be mediated for the first time with the arrival of communications media. Rather, we approach facets of transnational social life such as collective memory, imaginations of migrant destinations, and diaspora formation as inherently involving processes of mediation. We also draw on the important work of Madianou and Miller (2012) on transnational families' communication practices, which argues that social conceptions of motherhood mediate the ways family members make choices about the media they communicate with. We suggest that situated discourses about migration and diaspora mediate people's experiences of using social media in their long-distance family relationships.

Case Background and Research Methodology: Studying Romanian Transnational Cultural Formations

Romanian postsocialist migration to Western Europe after the fall of state socialism was supported by ideological factors such as the circulation of European friendly sentiments (Trandafoiu, 2013: 31–32). The austerity measures introduced during the economic recession of this period further affected migration (Sandu, 2010: 59), and migration patterns suggest that these changes affected men and women's mobility differently (see Verdery, 1996, 35; True, 2000; Pascall and Kwak, 2005: 29; Miroiu, 2004: 222–3). While men migrated more during the first decade of the postsocialist period, the expansion of the freedom to circulate within the Schengen area freely after 2002 also saw women become more mobile (Sandu, 2006). In the period that followed, men tended to work in construction jobs, and women migrated to do care work and work in the domestic sector, with Spain and Italy becoming the two main preferred destinations (Sandu, 2010: 37–8). With the 2007 EU accession, temporary migration grew so intensively that, according to United Nation's 2015

International Migration Report, Romania occupied the second place after the Syrian Arab Republic in 2015 in the annual growth rate of the diaspora.[2] According to Eurostat, as of January 1, 2019, Romania had the highest number of citizens residing in any of the other 27 EU member states. More highly skilled migrants left Romania as well (Sandu, 2010: 38) complicating the dominant image of the construction worker and the domestic worker in migration scholarship.

In the context of these different migration patterns, little information is available on the (temporary and permanent) mobility of Romanians during the post-2007 stage, leading its heterogeneity to be under-addressed. Migration from Romania to the Netherlands became significant after the 2007 EU enlargement, when Romania and Bulgaria became member states (Gijsberts and Lubbers, 2015: 24). Most of the officially registered Romanian people in the Netherlands are highly educated and came to the Netherlands as labor, family, or study migrants—categories that may overlap in some cases (ibid.: 101, 105). By looking at the Netherlands, we highlight a less conventional focal point than the usual emphasis on the economic impacts of low-skilled migration to Southern European countries. And by looking at Romania, we highlight the current traces of historical migration flows, updating post-soviet memory in an age of digital ubiquity.

While Romania has among the lowest rates of daily internet use of all EU member states,[4] it has also undergone a striking recent surge in internet use on mobile devices, with this rate more than tripling between 2012 and 2017.[5] Contemporary Romania therefore complicates a static/simple notion of a geographic "digital divide" by exhibiting both a relative lack (in comparison to EU) and abundance (in comparison to its own recent past) of networked communications. Scholarship on Romanian digital media usage has so far tended to focus on (middle-class) migrants rather than those staying behind (see Ducu, 2018 for a multi-sited research exception). Yet, the communication practices of those "left behind" in the home country by their migrating loved ones are an understudied but equally important part of transnational families' communication and care dynamics (Cabanes and Acedera, 2012).

The fieldwork on which this chapter draws was conducted by the two authors, each in different research settings within the Netherlands and Romania. Candidatu carried out four-month long ethnographic field research (participant observation and interviews) within Amsterdam in April, and September to December, 2017, among women who had migrated from Romania in the period after 1989 and mostly after Romania's EU accession in 2007. Alinejad conducted interview-based research in and around Bucharest among those who had stayed behind in Romania while their parents and/or siblings had migrated to other European countries years prior, mostly in the early 2000s but a few in the early 1990s. This took place in the course of two months from July, 2018. Candidatu's selection of participants was focused on women who were mothers, while Alinejad's participants were mostly part of transnational family constellations as children or siblings of migrants. The interviews conducted in Romania were translated to English via live interpreter. The Amsterdam interviews were conducted in Romanian.[3] Both cases involved migration shaped by labor demand. Together, they offer two vantage points within the social processes around Romanian migration within Europe, which span across borders, locations, and time. We do not focus on the same families, and the specific kinds of labor migration the research in each location focuses on differ: while Candidatu focused on highly skilled migration from Romania to the Netherlands, Alinejad's focus was on economic migration to European western countries, in general. Yet, the collaborative exchange and analytical synthesis allows us to cover a wider variety of migration circumstances and positionings within experiences of Romanian transnational mobility rather than focusing on a single migration phenomenon.[4]

The fieldwork of both authors was conducted within a common research design inspired by the work of Pink et al. (2016) on the use of ethnography for research in a digitally mediated context. Inasmuch as ethnography represents a type of research that involves contact with human agents within the context of their daily lives (Pink et al., 2016), digital ethnography necessarily implies looking at the digital as it unfolds in those everyday lives. Both authors conducted a short-term ethnographic study, with Pink and Morgan's "Short-Term Ethnography: Intense Routes to Knowing" (2013) proving to be useful for how the research unfolded. Pink defines short-term ethnography as a theoretically informed approach to doing research that involves "intensive excursions" into people's lives, focused observation, and clear-cut selection of informants. While the research participants were approached within a wider project that involved short-term immersive fieldwork and observation, the analysis presented in this chapter is based on the interview material gathered in the respective research settings.

Mothers' Diasporic Efforts Toward Cultural Reproduction

In her fieldwork on the Romanian diaspora in the Netherlands in 2017, Candidatu identified mothering as an important experience that shaped women's participation in digital diaspora-making. Indeed, research on migrants' media use shows the strong relation between kin-work and the maintenance of transnational ties and digital media use (Baldassar, 2007; 2008; Nedelcu and Wyss, 2016). Furthermore, there is a strong gendered aspect to this relationship, with mothering practices being central to processes of diasporic cultural transmission and community maintenance (Tsolidis, 2001: 206–7; Collins, 2000: 178–83; see also Candidatu, 2021 for a discussion on diasporic mothering and gendered diasporas). This scholarship sees mothers' digital media use as part of a broader gendered process though which diaspora materializes, both locally and transnationally. We argue that the expectations and norms that give rise to diaspora culture formation blend into the mutual co-constitution of mothering and digital media. Specifically, Romanian mothers' preoccupations with language transmission become the main reasoning through which they make sense of their participation within the Romanian diaspora in the Netherlands (i.e. regular participation to classes and events organized by the Amsterdam Romanian weekend school for children). These mothers then explain their digital media uses with relation to the social expectations of mediating communication with family abroad. One of Candidatu's key participants, Elena, identified becoming a mother as an important trigger for her diasporic consciousness and related digital media practices. Elena is in her early forties, has lived in Amsterdam for almost 20 years, and has two children. She manages a website and a Facebook page where she shares news pieces about Romania. She describes her motivations to create these media spaces about Romania in the following way:

> [My daughter] was born and when my [daughter] was born that was the moment when … I went with her, I remember she was a baby, and I went with her to the park and I realized that I was not comforting her in Romanian. I was ashamed to talk in Romanian. And one day, I remember, I was breastfeeding in the park and I was talking to her, caressing her, and I thought: what is happening to me? Where is my self-esteem if I cannot stand up and talk in my own language with my child? And then something changed, and I thought, OK, now everything will change.

Mothering was thus the experience that triggered a conscious connection between Elena and her Romanian identity and made her take on the role of "culture bearer." Like Elena, many other participants later referred to the intricate relation between mothering, diaspora participation, and language transmission. These mothers realized that speaking Romanian with their children is directly connected with them consciously assuming a Romanian identity that is later to be transmitted, generationally. This is in line with previous studies on migration and heritage language that identify the desire to pass on the mother tongue as being closely related to the intent of transmitting parents' cultural legacies (Nesteruk, 2010: 273).

Many of the women interviewed by Candidatu participate in digital diaspora-making via their specific interest in supporting their children in learning and speaking their mother tongue. Many of them take their children to the Romanian school in Amsterdam, a weekend school that offers classes of Romanian culture and language to children. These Romanian mothers also use a variety of digital platforms to keep in touch with their parents and extended family; video calls and chats on WhatsApp, Facebook Messenger, or Skype are part of their diasporic polymedia environment. In terms of everyday practices of connecting with family members from the homeland, my informants have regular video calls in which their children also take part. They develop digitally mediated "keeping in touch" routines (Nedelcu, 2012) and mediated "ordinary co-presence" practices (Nedelcu and Wyss, 2016) as an integral part of maintaining inter-generational, transnational ties, not only between them (the daughters) and their parents but also between their children and their children's grandparents.

The two diasporic practices of language transmission and regular digitally mediated contact with family and friends from Romania collapse in the mothers' discourses about their everyday lives. The unique position of mothering while migrant, together with the gendered responsibilities that come with that (in terms of cultural transmission and community maintenance), merge both practices of language acquisition and Romanian school participation as well as the digital practices involved in regular communication with the grandparents and extended family members. For both Alexandra, a member of the coordination team of the Romanian school in Amsterdam, and Elena, diasporic identity negotiations and reflections are ultimately crystallized around the issue of language and language acquisition. Below, Alexandra reproduces a dialogue in which she tries to convince her daughter of the many benefits that speaking Romanian has:

> And don't forget, when you will grow up, you will be the only one from your environment who speaks Romanian. You never know what you will do with this language when you will be twenty. Maybe you will do something, it will help you in life. And besides, when we go to Romania, my love, you only speak Romanian, you cannot speak any other language. Do you think your family from Romania will ever learn Dutch? No, it is my duty to teach you Romanian so you can speak with your grandmother.

Many of the respondents relate their children's Romanian language acquisition to the ability to speak Romanian with family and friends from Romania. This engagement is sometimes considered so important that, in certain situations, it overcomes children's own unwillingness to do so or the mothers' own lack of interest for ethnic-based diasporic ties. Ada, a former teacher of the school, whose children also attend the classes, talks about her son's difficulties to relate to the language and his reluctance to learn it: "He says that 'I don't know, I find it hard … I do not need to speak it.'" In a similar way to Alexandra's insistence with her daughter, Ada reminds her son of the importance of being able to communicate with extended family members from Romania: "And how are you to talk with the grandparents, my brother, your uncle?" Indeed, for the mothers, language is also a vital tool to keep the connection with family from abroad alive. This also exemplifies previous scholarly claims about how language facilitates communication across generations within Eastern European migrant communities. Members of these migrant communities highly value extended family relationships and the grandparents' presence in their grandchildren's lives (Kuroczycka Schultes, 2016: 179), and media (and, more recently, digital media) is an important way to maintain these connections when there is a geographical distance (see Nesteruk and Marks, 2009; Nesteruk, 2010).

Normative expectations about the maintenance of kin ties and the preservation of transnational intimate relationships, especially those with grandparents, seem to play a particularly important role in why and how mothers use digital media. Both language transmission and digitally mediated practices of keeping in touch with family members from Romania are intentional processes (Nedelcu and Wyss, 2016: 205) strongly marked by gendered norms about the role of the mothers in processes of diasporic cultural reproduction. These practices attest to the role of diasporic belonging and diasporic cultural formations in how social media uses are given meaning. The two practices of language transmission and regular digital connectedness with family and friends from Romania are two sides of the same diasporic cultural reproduction coin. Romanian mothers' various digital media practices of connectedness with family from Romania are therefore part of a larger web of diasporic cultural reproductive work that includes the transmission and preservation of the maternal language so that their children can develop and maintain a sense of closeness and intimacy with members of the extended family.

How Cultures of Migration Shape Mediated Transnational Relationships

Dana was a 50-year-old psychologist working out of her private practice in Bucharest. Her husband, Cristi, worked as a sailor and an engineer for the Romanian fleet, and was gone for weeks at a time for his job. Now that the oldest of their two daughters had started her 20s and moved in with her boyfriend, Dana and Cristi lived together with their youngest daughter. Dana described the times spent away from her husband as having been very difficult during earlier periods in their marriage, when social media apps were unavailable to them while he was away on voyages for months at a time without access to the telephone. But having spent part of her youth and all her adult life with a brother who had moved abroad, permanently, Dana talked about this distance from loved ones as something familiar. Her brother had left in 1992, soon after the revolution. "Many people left then," she said. "The borders were opened and it was easy. So he got a scholarship and moved to Glasgow to get his PhD in chemistry." Dana went on to describe the material hardships she recalled her brother having endured during his graduate studies, having had to work in a factory and tutor students while studying. He then had to live on little while getting his doctorate while his wife joined him from Romania and started her PhD.

> In those years he couldn't afford to come here much. It was difficult times because my father had died young and he had been the main provider for us if we needed anything. So my brother knew he had no help—he knew he had to work very hard because there was no one he could ask for financial support.

The idea that "things were hard before the revolution too, but afterwards it was a different kind of hard" also penetrated Dana's account of her husband's mobility abroad for work in the period that followed. She explained how the fall of the communist regime had led to Cristi being away for longer periods—the fleet he worked for was eventually sold off after the change of leadership, leaving him working for the foreign companies to whom Romania's commercial shipping needs were outsourced.

> They knew we had good education for our engineers, like Cristi had. So Romanians were easily hired by these companies in those times ... We could only talk with each other on radiogram then. I had no idea how he was doing. Radiogram is a very specific kind of communication—one man on the ship was in charge of it and they had to pay big money so they could talk once a month with their spouses from the ship. Or if they had emergencies. So this is how I told him I was pregnant with our first child. I went to the lady in the post office and told her to write: I am well. Stop. We'll be three. Stop. I love you. Stop. It was standard six months that he would be away in those times, and we didn't have satellite communication like there is now in order to stay in contact from the ship. Now by international law there is a limit of between two and four months or so, and now I really can't imagine it differently—that we wouldn't have Facebook Messenger. Although I've been through that, I can't. How could I live without it? It's so much easier. It would be a tragedy for me. To go back there.

Dana's intimate family memories were embedded within memories of the overthrow of communism in Romania and the impacts on international mobility that rippled out from this event. The technological possibilities for communication also colored the emotional dimensions of memories of long-distance, mediated intimacies. Dana was astutely aware of how her familiarity with living at a distance from loved ones was both individually specific and collectively shared, and she reflected on how her stories of distance from loved ones related to experiences of many others with memories from post-communist Romania's emigration patterns. The collective meaning-making around the migration of loved ones in light of political histories complicates the significance of intra-family distance and separation and ways of remembering and narrating it.

Like Dana, many other respondents also acknowledged the personal psychological challenges of distance in the family as part of a collective coming to terms with the emotional consequences of the post-communist past and its lasting effects. Indeed, this past is far from being over because many of these young people now enter adulthood in Romania as their parents retire and remain abroad. During the fieldwork conducted by Alinejad in Romania, a number of young people in their 20s were interviewed who had grown up with both their parents working abroad in Western European countries. They now stayed in touch with their parents, especially their mothers, on a daily basis via social media apps; WhatsApp, in particular. Apart from sharing in common a sense that their parents' remittances had helped them access higher education and upward social mobility, a strong theme across the accounts of their respective upbringings (by next of kin—usually grandmothers or aunts) and current mediated relationships with their parents was an emotional ambivalence about their parents' migration. Each in their own ways, their reflections on their childhoods and young adulthoods of staying in touch with their parents from a distance involved acknowledging their feelings of loss and sadness about the absence, while also empathizing with their parents to various degrees, and situating their feelings with relation to circumstances outside the family. Their accounts of their relationships reflect a common awareness about how their parents' generation was situated both with relation to the family and to European labor markets of the time for other parents like their own. The social discourses they produced about their mediated relationships were themselves mediated by collective memories about mass migration phenomena.

For example, 25-year-old Eliza talked about both her parents being away for work in Italy—her mother as a care worker and her father as a truck driver. She described feeling special as one of the children in the class who had a parent abroad. They would get sent things like candy and clothes that were not yet available in Romania. She remembered thinking at the time that "it was very cool to have your parents in another country … and when you're a child you get used to it and you think it's normal." But she also explained how, among the children she knew who stayed behind, she felt like one of the "lucky" ones because her mother was able to come and visit often for weeks or sometimes months at a time when Eliza and her sister were younger. Her younger sister, Anka, who was also in her 20s, talked about a process by which she, too, "got used to" the situation of her parents being away, and came to understand their financial motives for leaving.

> Soon I realized that this is the better thing to do, you know? And I saw this as a positive thing, not as a negative thing. So I didn't quite feel the need to talk about this as a problem or as something like: oh my god, I'm so sad that my parents [left]. It was hard at first but little by little... it became a part of me. Maybe I wouldn't be this same person who knows how to take care of myself.

Others who stayed behind also had mixed/changing feelings, as Corina described intensely missing her parents—and especially her mother—when they left to go to Italy for work during her high school period. But she also came from an extended family where this distance had become a norm as stories of migration benefits circulated. "Imagine that my grandmother saw all her kids leave to go all over the world. Only my one aunt stayed here with her." The memories of these young people, now in their 20s, of when their parents had left in their pre-teen years, recalled not only a particular moment in Romania's migration history in the early 2000s when mobility was increasing amid hopes of prosperity through remittances. They also recalled this as period in their lives as being shaped by the communications technologies of the time, all recalling receiving landline calls from their parents abroad (who were the ones who could afford to make these calls, not the family members they were living with), and taking their turn speaking on the phone in the family living room. These were conditions of the past, as all these young people now had smartphones with mobile internet connections and could afford to stay in touch at any time of day. Alongside having grown older and gained greater understanding of the circumstances of their parents' distance, these technological developments had made living at a distance far more bearable for them. As Corina says, "if I would have had FaceTime or something back then, I think it would have been easier because you're able to see them." For Corina, as for Dana and others, social media apps are given meaning within a broader narrative about weighing the difficulties and benefits of loved ones being distant due to the well-known phenomenon of Romanian labor migration to Western Europe.

These memories of family intimacy from earlier years are shaped not only within family dynamics but also by a broader "culture of migration" (Bal and Willems, 2014). This idea refers to the imaginings and aspirations that circulate (within the migration *sending* context) about distant places and lives, the social implications of migration, and the structural impacts of mass migration phenomena on those who never migrate, themselves. Hence, cultural histories of migration shape the meanings of distance within the family. The contemporary everyday practices of intensively communicating with parents outside Romania through social media apps are experienced through the lens of the shared social discourses that circulate within a particular culture of migration in Romania. These discourses relate the migration of loved ones to events in Romanian national politics and transnational imaginations of Romania's marginal position in relation to Europe. Reproduction of social discourses about migration's legacies in family relationships shape the perspectives of those who are left/stayed behind, making up ambivalent and even optimistic narratives of simultaneous upward social mobility and technological advancement that has made living in a transnational family more manageable.

Conclusion

The rich scholarship around long-distance family relationships has established how intimacy is digitally mediated in a variety of ways. Yet, the experience of living in a long-distance relationship did not only start to be a mediated experience with the growing reliance on long-distance communications technologies. Rather, anthropologists and cultural studies scholars alike have advanced the idea that people's very experiences of their everyday lives have never been unmediated, as mediation already takes place when people produce narratives or discourses to represent—and, thus, make sense of—the events around them (Hall, 1980; Mazzarella, 2004). Such narratives take shape through mass media production, but also through the reproduction of social discourses that circulate horizontally through collectivities. We have sought to demonstrate how social media communications are given meaning by becoming discursively integrated within narratives about mass intra-EU migration events. People's discourses about how social media help them maintain their long-distance family relationships spill seamlessly into shared narratives about their situated experiences of migration. These narratives include cultural imaginations about the future of a growing Romanian diaspora and its connections with Romania, as well as cultural memories of how migration has affected and continues to affect Romanians in Romania. We understand these social discourses as the contours within which people's modes of staying in touch online take on significance, thus pushing our discussion beyond the dynamics of intra-family communications and toward the ways in which diaspora culture and cultures of migration mediate sense-making about social media and distance in the family.

Notes

1 Chapter 2: Recent Trends in Romanian Migration in OECD Report, Talent Abroad: A Review of Romanian Migrants www.oecd-ilibrary.org/sites/00fb26e2-en/index.html?itemId=/content/component/00fb26e2-en last accessed 15/07/2021
2 United Nations. 2016. International Migration Report 2015 Highlights www.un.org/en/development/desa/population/migration/publications/migrationreport/docs/MigrationReport2015_Highlights.pdf
3 While the positionality of the researchers with relation to the respondents bore differences in each case, the goal was not to ensure uniformity but to analyze the findings in terms of each research context. More than comparing interview findings, the analytical purpose was relating the two situated analyses to one another.
4 The research was conducted within the project, "Digital Crossings in Europe: Gender, Diaspora and Belonging," funded by ERC consolidator grant, 647737.

References

Alinejad, Donya. 2019. "Careful Co-presence: The Transnational Mediation of Emotional Intimacy." *Social Media+ Society* 5 (2): 1–11. https://doi.org/10.1177/2056305119854222
Alinejad, Donya, and Sandra Ponzanesi. 2020. "Migrancy and digital Mediations of Emotion." *International Journal of Cultural Studies* 23 (5): 621–38. https://doi.org/10.1177/1367877920933649
Anderson, Benedict. 1983. *Imagined Communities*. London: Verso.
Appadurai, Arjun. 1996. *Modernity at Large: Cultural Dimensions of Globalization*. Minneapolis: University of Minnesota Press.

Bal, Ellen, and Roos Willems. 2014. "Introduction: Aspiring migrants, Local Crises and the Imagination of Futures 'Away from Home'." *Identities* 21 (3): 249–58. https://doi.org/10.1080/1070289X.2014.858628

Baldassar, Loretta. 2007. "Transnational Families and the Provision of Moral and Emotional Support: The Relationship Between Truth and Distance." *Identities* 14 (4): 385–409.

Baldassar, Loretta. 2008. "Missing Kin and Longing to Be Together: Emotions and the Construction of Co-Presence in Transnational Relationships." *Journal of Intercultural Studies* 29 (3): 247–66.

Baldassar, Loretta. 2016. "De-demonizing Distance in Mobile Family Lives: Co-presence, Care Circulation and Polymedia as Vibrant Matter." *Global Networks* 16 (2): 145–63. https://doi.org/10.1111/glob.12109

Baldassar, Loretta, Nedelcu, Mihaela, Merla, Laura, & Wilding, Raelene. 2016. "ICT-based Co-presence in Transnational Families and Communities: Challenging the Premise of Face-to-face Proximity in Sustaining Relationships." *Global Networks* 16 (2): 133–44.

Boyer, Dominic. 2012. "From Media Anthropology to the Anthropology Of Mediation." In *The Sage Handbook of Social Anthropology*, edited by Richard Fardon, Olivia Harris, Trevor Marchant, Mark Nuttal, Chris Shore, Veronica Strang, and Richard Wilson. Thousand Oaks: Sage.

Brinkerhoff, Jennifer M. 2009. *Digital Diasporas: Identity and Transnational Engagement*. Cambridge: Cambridge University Press.

Cabanes, Jason Vincent A., and Kristel Anne F. Acedera. 2012. "Of Mobile Phones and Mother-Fathers: Calls, Text Messages, and Conjugal Power Relations in Mother-away Filipino Families." *New Media & Society* 14 (6): 916–30. https://doi.org/10.1177/1461444811435397

Candidatu, Laura. 2021. "Diasporic Mothering and Somali Diaspora Formation in the Netherlands." *Journal of Global Diaspora & Media* 2 (1): 39–55.

Candidatu, L., Leurs, K., and Ponzanesi, S. (2019). "Digital Diasporas: Beyond the Buzzword. Towards a Relational Understanding of Mobility and Connectivity." In *The Handbook of Diasporas, Media & Culture*, edited by Jessica Retis and Roza Tsagarousianou. Hoboken: John Wiley.

Collins, Patricia Hill. 2000. *Black Feminist Thought. Knowledge, Consciousness, and the Politics of Empowerment*. New York: Routledge.

Ducu, Viorela. 2018. *Romanian Transnational Families: Gender, Family Practices and Difference*. Gewerbestrasse: Springer.

Engbersen, Godfried, Arjen Leerkes, Maria Ilies, Erik Snel, and Robbert Meij. 2011. *Arbeidsmigratie in Vieren. Bulgaren En Roemenen Vergeleken Met Polen*. IMIC: Citizenship, Migration & the City.

Everett, Anna. 2009. *Digital Diaspora: A Race for Cyberspace*. Albany: State University of New York Press.

Gajjala, Radhika. 2004. *Cyber Selves: Feminist Ethnographies of South-Asian Women*. Lanham: Rowman & Littlefield.

Gal, Susan, and Gail Kligman. 2000. *The Politics of Gender After Socialism: A Comparative-Historical Essay*. Princeton: Princeton University Press.

Georgiou, Myria. 2006. Diaspora, *Identity and the Media*. Cresskill: Hampton Press.

Gijsberts, Mérove Isabelle Léontine, and Marcel Lubbers. 2015. *Roemeense Migranten. De Leefsituatie in Nederland Kort Na Migratie*. The Hague: SCP.

Ginsburg, Faye. 1991. "Indigenous Media: Faustian Contract or Global Village?" *Cultural Anthropology* 6 (1): 92–112.

Ginsburg, Faye. 1994. "Culture/Media: A Mild Polemic," *Anthropology Today* 10 (2): 5–15.

Graham, Elspeth, Lucy P. Jordan, Brenda S.A. Yeoh, Theodora Lam, Maruja Asis, and Su Kamdi. 2012. "Transnational Families and the Family Nexus: Perspectives of Indonesian and Filipino Children Left Behind by Migrant Parent (s)." *Environment and Planning A* 44 (4): 793–815. https://doi.org/10.1068/a4445

Goddard, Victoria A. 1996. *Gender, Family, and Work in Naples*. Washington: Berg.

Hall, Stuart. 1980. "Cultural Studies: Two Paradigms." *Media, Culture & Society* 2 (1): 57–72.

Hall, Stuart. 1990. "Cultural Identity and Diaspora." In *Identity: Community, Culture, Difference*, edited by Jonathan Rutherford. London: Lawrence and Wishart.

Heyma, Arjan, Ernest Berkhout, Siemen van der Werff, and Bert Hof. 2008. "De Economische Impact van Arbeidsmigratie Uit de MOE-Landen, Bulgarije En Roemenië. Een Studie Naar Omvang, Aard En Economische Effecten van Arbeidsmigratie." Ministerie van Sociale Zaken en Werkgelegenheid SEO-rapport nr. 2008-70.

Hoschild, Arlie. 2012. *The Managed Heart: Commercialization of Human Feeling*. Berkeley: University of California Press.

Ito, Mizuko Ed, Daisuke Ed Okabe, and Misa Ed Matsuda. 2005. *Personal, Portable, Pedestrian: Mobile Phones in Japanese Life*. Cambridge: MIT Press.

Kremer, Monique, and Erik Schrijvers. 2014. "Roemeense En Bulgaarse Arbeidsmigratie in Betere Banen." WRR Policy Brief nr. 1.

Kuroczycka Schultes, Anna. 2016. "Foreign Mothers, Native Children: The Impact of Language on Cultural Identity among Polish Americans in Chicago." In *The Migrant Maternal: 'Birthing' New Lives Abroad*, edited by Anna Kuroczycka Schultes and Helen Vallianatos. Bradford: Demeter Press.

Kandel, W., & Massey, D. S. (2002). "The culture of Mexican migration: A theoretical and empirical analysis." *Social Forces*, 80(3): 981–1004. https://doi.org/10.1353/sof.2002.0009

Madianou, Mirca. 2016. "Ambient Co-presence: Transnational Family Practices in Polymedia Environments." *Global Networks* 16 (2): 183–201.

Madianou, Mirca, and Daniel Miller. 2012. *Migration and New Media. Transnational Families and Polymedia*. Florence: Taylor and Francis.

Mannheim, Karl 1893–1947. 1972. *Essays on the Sociology of Knowledge*. International Library of Sociology and Social Reconstruction. London: Routledge & Paul.

Mazzarella, William. 2004. "Culture, Globalization, Mediation." *Annual Review of Anthropology*. 33: 345–67.

McKay, Deirdre. 2012. *Global Filipinos: Migrants' Lives in the Virtual Village*. Iniana: Indiana University Press.

Miroiu, Mihaela. 2004. *Drumul Catre Autonomie: Teorii Politice Feministe*. Iasi: Polirom.

Nedelcu, Mihaela. 2012. "Migrants' New Transnational Habitus: Rethinking Migration Through a Cosmopolitan Lens in the Digital Age." *Journal of Ethnic and Migration Studies* 38 (9): 1339–56.

Nedelcu, Mihaela. 2018. "Digital diasporas." In *Routledge Handbook of Diaspora Studies*, edited by Robin Cohen and Carolin Fischer. London: Routledge.

Nedelcu, Mihaela, and Malika Wyss. 2016. "'Doing Family' through ICT-mediated Ordinary Co-presence: Transnational Communication Practices of Romanian Migrants in Switzerland." *Global Networks* 16 (2): 202–18. https://doi.org/10.1111/glob.12110.

Nesteruk, Olena. 2010. "Heritage Language Maintenance and Loss among the Children of Eastern European Immigrants in the USA." *Journal of Multilingual and Multicultural Development* 31 (3): 271–86.

Nesteruk, Olena, and Loren Marks. 2009. "Grandparents Across the Ocean: Eastern European Immigrants' Struggle to Maintain Intergenerational Relationships." *Journal of Comparative Family Studies* 40 (1): 77–95.

Nica, Felicia, and Madalina Moraru. 2020. "Diaspora Policies, Consular Services and Social Protection for Romanian Citizens Abroad." In *Migration and Social Protection in Europe and Beyond*, edited by Jean Michel Lafleur and Daniela Vintila. Gewerbestrasse: Springer.

Pascall, Gillian, and Anna Kwak. 2005. *Gender Regimes in Transition in Central and Eastern Europe*. Bristol: Policy Press.

Pilcher, Jane. 1994. "Mannheim's Sociology of Generations: An Undervalued Legacy." *The British Journal of Sociology* 45 (3): 481–95.

Pink, Sarah, and Jennie Morgan. 2013. "Short-Term Ethnography: Intense Routes to Knowing." *Symbolic Interaction* 36 (3): 351–61. https://doi.org/10.1002/symb.66

Pink, Sarah, Heather Horst, John Postill, Larissa Hjorth, Tania Lewis, and Jo Tacchi. 2016. *Digital Ethnography: Principles and Practice*. New York: SAGE.

Pohrib, Codtruta Alina. 2019. "The Romanian Latchkey Generation Writes Back: Memory Genres of Post-Communist Facebook." *Memory Studies* 12 (2): 146–83.

Rosaldo, Renato. 1994. "Whose Cultural Studies?" *American Anthropologist* 96 (3): 524–9.

Sandu, Dumitru. 2006. *Locuirea Temporara În Strainatate: Migratia Economica a Românilor: 1990–2006*. Bucharest: Fundatia pentru o Societate Deschisa.

Sandu, Dumitru. 2010. *Lumile Sociale Ale Migratiei Romanesti in Strainatate*. Iasi: Polirom.

Scuro, Jennifer. 2004. "Exploring Personal History: A Case Study of an Italian Immigrant Woman." *The Oral History Review* 31 (1): 43–69.

Spitulnik, Debra. 1997. "The Social Circulation of Media Discourse and the Mediation of Communities." *Journal of Linguistic Anthropology* 6 (2): 161–87.

Trandafoiu, Ruxandra. 2013. *Diaspora Online: Identity Politics and Romanian Migrants*. New York: Berghahn Books.

True, Jaqui. 2000. "Gendering Post-Socialist Transitions." In *Gender and Global Restructuring: Sightings, Sites and Resistances*, edited by Marianne H Marchand and Anne Sisson Runyan. London: Routledge.

Tsolidis, Georgina. 2001. "The Role of the Maternal in Diasporic Cultural Reproduction−Australia, Canada and Greece." *Social Semiotics* 11 (2): 193–208. https://doi.org/10.1080/10350330120018319

Verdery, Katherine. 1996. *What Was Socialism, and What Comes Next?* Princeton: Princeton University Press.

Vittadini, Nicoletta, Andra Siibak, IRENA Reifová, and Helena Bilandzic. 2013. "Generations and Media: The Social Construction of Generational Identity and Differences." *Audience Transformations: Late Modernity's Shifting Audience Positions: Shifting Audience Positions in Late Modernity*, 65–81.

Williams, Raymond. 2001. *The Long Revolution*. Ontario: Broadview Press.

B

Social Inequality and Marginalisation

23
MEDIATING HOPES
Social Media and Crisis in Northern Italy

Elisabetta Costa

Introduction

In 2008, Italy entered a period of protracted economic crisis that brought profound transformations to the lives of millions of people. Most working adults in Milan, the main economic and productive centre of Italy, would describe their lives as characterised by a turning point: some lost their jobs, others saw their salary significantly reduced, others started experiencing poor working conditions, and many went back to live with their parents because they could not pay their bills anymore. More than ten years after the financial crisis, the lives of many adults in Northern Italy continue to be characterised by high levels of uncertainty, precarity, and unemployment. In 2019, the unemployment rates in Italy were 10 per cent, with youth unemployment in the region of Lombardy at 18.3% (statista.com). In January 2019, the main Italian newspapers reported that Italian industrial production had dropped by 22% since 2007 (D'Aloisio and Ghezzi 2020). This extended economic crisis has been worsened even further at the time of writing in winter and spring 2021, due to the Covid-19 pandemic.

This chapter examines the role of social media in shaping hope and visions for a better future among people affected by the global economic crisis that started with the Wall Street crash in 2008 and went on to hit Italy and the world. In Northern Italy, online self-branding has become increasingly common among unemployed and precarious workers and professionals, across a large variety of fields. Against a backdrop of general resignation and pessimism caused by the scarcity of job opportunities and alternative routes out of the crisis, people continue to search for ways to make positive changes to their life, and social media plays a significant role in imagining a better future and coping with present-day uncertainties.

Building on the large body of work in anthropology of hope (amongst others, see Appadurai 2013; Hage 2003; Han and Antrosio 2020; Jansen 2021; Keane 2015; Kleist and Jansen 2016) and anthropology of social media (Miller et al. 2016), this chapter describes how digital practices contribute to shaping hopes for a better future when people feel 'stuck'. It shows the way in which social media and hope are interconnected and co-construct each other. In this chapter, hope is viewed as practice that occurs within specific social contexts and is mediated by digital platforms rather than someone's quality or affect (Hauer, Østergaard Nielsen, and Niewöhner 2018). The practices of social media usage enable and shape hope. Building on these principles, this chapter shows that unemployed or precarious workers often do not fully believe that digital platforms can help them find a job or better succeed in their professions as self-employed workers. Many expressed their doubts about online promotion being the way to find a job. Nevertheless, they engage in online self-branding and persist against reason (Han and Antrosio 2020). They do this, first, because they have exhausted all the other available opportunities to find a way out of their situation, and nothing has worked. There are not many other remedies, but opening and updating an Instagram or LinkedIn account and implementing a self-branding strategy can generate the positive feeling of being active and 'going somewhere' when other opportunities have already been explored without results. Second, self-branding can help maintain social relationships. It can help people make new friends or strengthen ties with old acquaintances and friends. However, if not properly applied, personal branding can also damage pre-existing relations because it follows social norms that are different from those of friendship. Third, by using social media, people conform to new normative expectations of how innovative and creative workers should craft their careers and find jobs, something that makes them feel positive about themselves. In newspapers and at hiring agencies, discourses on the potential of social media for self-promotion position digital platforms as tools to overcome structural problems. Digital technologies create imaginaries of possibilities and shining futures, as exemplified in the stories of successful influencers that became famous and rich thanks to Instagram or YouTube.

In short, the hope mediated by social media is more about surviving the difficulties of the present rather than working towards a better future. In many instances, practices of social media use play an important role in people's wellbeing, but do not necessarily bring significant changes to career paths. As such, they can become a force for political and social conservatism more than a way to actively transform the present and the future (see also Jakimov 2016). This form of hope helps people better cope with the consequences of structural inequalities in the present, which eventually reproduces precarious workers' subordinations. Also, by bringing more users to social media sites, this form of hope benefits social media companies. Online branding thus tends to simultaneously reproduce social inequality at two different scales of the neoliberal economies: in the local labour market and in the global political economy of social media.

Based on the study of the lived realities of middle-age adults who share a vulnerable and precarious working path under a multiplicity of legal working statuses and professions, this chapter sheds light on the important role of social media in shaping people's hopes and aspirations for better lives in the context of protracted crisis in neoliberal Italy. It argues for a media anthropology that addresses wider anthropological debates, while at the same time making use of all the rich conceptual and analytical tools that come from almost three decades of research on media-related practices (amongst recent examples, see Ardevol and Gomez-Cruz 2013; Bird 2011; Bräuchler and Postill 2010; Costa 2018; Couldry 2004; Ginsburg, Abu-Lughod, Larkin 2002; Hobart 2010; Miller et al. 2016; Peterson 2004). Particularly with the rise of digital technologies in the last two decades, media have become central to and entangled with many more aspects of people's everyday life that were not part of the traditional foci of media anthropology. A closer dialogue between different subfields in anthropology has the potential to enrich current research on the ways in which media are intertwined with people's everyday experiences and social inequality.

Crisis in Northern Italy

After rapid industrialisation and economic growth in the second half of the 20th century (Molé 2012), in the mid-1990s, Northern Italy entered a period of economic transformations characterised by a significant increase in the number of temporary, precarious, and sub-employed workers (Molé 2012). In the new century, transformations of work and production under a variety of globalised production strategies have created what Victoria Goddard (2017) described as a 'complex landscape consisting of different forms of production and particular concentrations of economic activity'. D'Aloisio and Ghezzi (2020) show that the variety of precarious forms of labour in the industrial north of Italy can be associated with two main transformations: the crisis of the traditional manufacturing system and the emergence of highly skilled self-employees in the growing service industries. The individuals I describe in this chapter have been affected by the long-lasting crisis. As children and young adults in the years before that financial crisis of 2008, they did not face significant economic insecurities. However, at the time of my research in 2019, they had to cope with unemployment, a precarious working life, and the consequences of austerity that have generated lower standards of living and consumption (Knight and Stewart 2016). While a longing for protected labour in the new precarious economy has been reported to be part of Italian workers' aspirations in the first few years of the new millennium (Molé 2012; Muhelebach 2011), my research participants lived with a general acceptance of workforce casualisation and lack of job protections. They instead looked for possibilities to increase their income and wellbeing within the neoliberal framework of temporary jobs and scarcity of employment.

The ethnographic material for this chapter was primarily collected from April to July 2019. I conducted fieldwork in Milan, combining in-depth interviews and life-history narratives with observation of online platforms. I conducted ten interviews with job seekers/underemployed people in the age range of 30 to 55 and ten interviews with human resources professionals and trade unionists in Milan. Some of the ten job seekers/underemployed people were interviewed again during the course of 2020 and 2021. The research participants were selected through multiple channels: an announcement on a local Facebook group, personal contacts, and snowball techniques. I also observed two local Facebook groups, four WhatsApp groups, and the social media accounts of the people I interviewed. The chapter is also informed by my participation in social events, gatherings, parties, and informal conversations with adults living in Milan during my regular visits to the city over the decade 2011–2020. The effects of the crisis on people's working and private lives has been a never-ending topic of conversation and concern throughout these years, across multiple social circles. Unemployed and precarious workers' conditions were worsened by the lack of community centres, charities, or municipality projects providing support. This also means that my research was primarily situated in private spaces and online, rather than in a public physical environment.

Online branding and local forms of socialities

The idea that social media can help people find a job is a frequent theme among hiring agencies, career counsellors, and employment agencies. In 2019, Adecco organised several courses on how to find a job or change career with the help of LinkedIn and other platforms, and Adecco webpages provide guidelines on how to find jobs through social media. Job seekers attend these courses to learn how to better promote themselves, fashion their own brands, and connect with people. And many branded themselves on social media. While freelancers and employees in many highly skilled and creative professions often successfully engage in social media branding, this is not always the case. When there are no jobs, people tend to express scepticism about the efficacy of online branding.

This scepticism certainly comes from the failure of social media in helping them. As explained to me by human resources professionals and labour policy makers, most companies do not take LinkedIn, Instagram, or other social media profiles seriously into account. Yet distrust towards the role of social media in finding a job also reflects the disrupting role of online branding in local forms of sociality and public presentations of the self. In Northern Italy, professional networks tend to remain largely separated from the larger circles of friends, and, on platforms like Facebook and Instagram, acquaintances from work are often kept divided from friends. For example, Carlotta, a 37-year-old woman who worked as an executive secretary for large international companies for many years, has never added any of her colleagues on Facebook. She doesn't like it. She is afraid that her colleagues might make fun of her 'real' life because she comes from a middle-upper-class family and can afford restaurants and hotels that her colleagues cannot. Above all, she has only had negative experiences of distrust and antipathy with colleagues and thinks that time with them should be reduced. She uses Facebook and Instagram massively with friends and relatives but cannot imagine how these platforms can be used to maintain contacts with former colleagues, or even worse, become branding tools. Anna, who works as a researcher at the university, has two different Facebook accounts. One is used with her larger network of more than 600 friends and acquaintances. The other is her 'professional' account that she uses with around 200 people she knows from work. She does not actively engage in personal branding but maintains relationships with colleagues and promotes academic events via this second Facebook account. These two stories show the local tendency to keep professional and social spheres divided and to approach the former with a certain level of mistrust. Molé (2012) and Muehlebach (2011) described the shifts from an era of protected labour, which provided resources to construct identities, friendships, and sense of self, towards a distinctly Italian post-Fordist condition. In the context of Italian cultural traditions that value solidarity and collective social ties, and have high levels of distrust in institutions (Alessandro Cavalli 2001 in Molé 2011), the collapse of protected labour pushed people to different spheres of their lives to construct their significant relationships, recognition, and belonging. As a result, urban Italy shows high levels of social participation and lively social environments (see also Walton 2021) that are largely divided and independent from the sphere of work.

The division between these two spheres does not facilitate online branding. This can lead to the unpleasant situation of 'context collapse', the flattening of several social contexts and audiences onto one another (Boyd 2014). Self-promotion is not always welcome in the circles of friends, which are often characterised by registers of informality and collegiality. For example, one day Carla shared in a WhatsApp group a YouTube video made by Mirko, a friend who promoted himself as a pedagogical consultant on Facebook. Carla posted the video, followed by the comment: 'It cracks me up!' (*mi fa morire*) and four laughing emojis. This message was followed by many other comments by all the other members of the WhatsApp group. They were all amused by the video and teased their old friend for presenting himself as a serious and capable professional. One person wrote, 'He is very good at social media strategies!' and added several laughing emojis. The video contained nothing funny in itself, but the group thought that the view of their old friend branding himself on Facebook and YouTube was hilarious. Mirko was teased on Facebook too. He opened a new professional Facebook page, a new website, and uploaded several videos on YouTube. When he also changed his profile picture on his old Facebook account, within in a few hours the image received 20 messages from friends who joked about his new look: 'you are hot!', 'you look super professional!', and 'The new year is starting with a miracle!'

People tend to consider self-branding unsuitable for the Italian context, as also shown by the statement of a university student in Milan:

> In Italy you cannot brand yourself on social media. People will immediately label you as an egocentric, self-centred, and arrogant person. It is not something that you can easily do here.

Another element that contributes to people's increased reluctance to engage in practices of self-branding is that publicly disclosing to friends and acquaintances the condition of unemployment or under-employment is considered inappropriate. Three interviewees described their friends' negative reactions at seeing requests for help in Facebook or larger WhatsApp groups. Sara is a 45-year-old social researcher who has been freelancing for several institutes, research centres, and charities all her working life. One day, after a long period with no income or work, she was stressed and angry and posted a message on Facebook to promote herself and ask for jobs. She did not receive any comments on the public wall, but her post elicited several private messages from friends who rebuked her for an inappropriate public post that could have ruined her reputation. Maria, an electronic engineer from Colombia who has lived in Milan for a few years, had a similar experience. She was surprised to see how inappropriate it was to be seen as a job seeker/unemployed in Italy, whereas using personal contacts on social media to find a job was common practice in Colombia. A third research participant told me, 'It is all about shame! Being publicly seen jobless is shameful here in Northern Italy and you cannot make it public!'

While none of the people I interviewed fully believed in the efficacy of digital branding, for all the reasons described above, everyone did believe that social connections and networking were key to finding a job. This idea was so widespread and widely accepted that the then-Minister of Labour and Social Policy, Giuliano Poletti (Democracy Party of the Left), stated in a meeting with university students at the University of Bologna in 2017, 'You have more opportunities to find a job while playing football on Monday evening, rather than sending your CVs to companies.' This news was on the front page of the main Italian newspapers and elicited heated discussions. If recommending someone for a job is current practice in Northern Italy, why were my research participants sceptical of the efficacy of online branding? Unlike branding on social media, offline personal recommendation is private and is often surrounded by some degree of shame because it is supposedly not done on the basis of merit. And, unlike branding on social media, it builds on long-lasting relationships that are embedded in traditional forms of sociality like family, neighbourhood, or established circles of friends. In addition, personal recommendations imply exchange and reciprocity that maintain relationships over a long period of time, while online branding on social media is meant to meet the need of a flexible job market characterised by short-term relations and frequent career transitions and shifts (Gershon 2017).

To conclude, the scepticism towards online branding should be understood contextually and historically. It is not only structural conditions, such as the lack of job opportunities and low labour mobility, that generate the perception that online branding does not help. Distrust of online branding as a means to find or create jobs is also grounded in its disrupting role in local forms of socialities, presentation of the self, and divisions between different social spheres.

Giulia: Social Media and the Practice of Hoping

I don't know if self-promotion and personal branding only give people hope or really work. Come back in one year, and I will tell you if it is one or the other!
Giulia, 40-year-old creative director

Giulia, a 40-year-old creative director with many years of experience working in the television industry, became unemployed after her international corporation made her redundant. When I saw her in summer 2019, she had been looking for a new job for almost a year, without success, and was living on unemployment benefits that would end in a few months. She described how the job market had changed since the crisis hit the television sector in 2011:

> In Italy there are ten television channels, of which seven are based in Milan. I have already worked with all of them, and I know all the creative directors there. ... In the last ten years, the number of jobs available has decreased, but more people are on the job market. It is very simple. There are no jobs!

Overall, Giulia was optimistic and enthusiastic about the possibility of finding another job as a creative director and strongly believed that luck played an important role in making this happen. Contacts and networking from previous jobs in television were not helpful because the very few temporary positions available were taken by young freelancers who accepted low wages that Giulia did not want to accept anymore. Because she did not want to wait for something to happen, she designed a social media strategy. She had already had a LinkedIn and Vimeo account for around ten years and a website and Instagram account for one year. She had used Facebook for promotion purposes a lot in the past but did not want to do that anymore. Facebook was for her personal life, and she wanted to keep her professional and personal spheres divided. It was time to work harder on self-promotion on Instagram. Although she had little funding available, she planned to hire a professional social media expert who could implement the strategy, create content, and regularly update her Instagram page for a few thousand euros. Giulia had the knowledge and skills to do this herself, but she disliked self-promotion. She thought that it makes people narcissistic and self-centred. It was also stressful for her to draw lines between private and public life and decide what aspects of herself to promote in public. She thought that Instagram was the place to display those aspects of private life that would have contributed to build her public persona. She explained: 'Instagram is the place where you display what you want people to know about you, like hobbies and interests. But it is better if another person does it on my behalf, or I will become insane.' She decided to commit herself to online branding even though she did not fully believe it could help and she did not like doing it. Yet online branding was a very good way to *actively* hope for a better life. Self-branding served the important function of making her pro-active when very few actions seemed to be effective.

A year and a half after the interview, Giulia was still unemployed and her unemployment benefits had ended. The Covid-19 pandemic did not help in finding a job, nor had the social media strategy. She had stopped investing time and effort in her social media presence and online self-branding. Education afforded more hope. She enrolled herself in a BA program in business and administration at the University of Milan. Eventually, in summer 2021, after three years of unemployment, Giulia was offered a permanent position as senior manager of communication in a large Italian company. When I asked if social media helped her find this job, she replied, 'Not at all, I found it thanks to previous connections and a lot of luck!'

Social media did not help Giulia to find a job, expand her network, or increase her notoriety. They instead shaped what Kuehn and Corrigan (2013) called 'hope labour', 'the uncompensated work carried out in the present, often for experience or exposure, in the hope that future employment opportunities may follow'. At the same time, social media also served the important function of making her feel that she was actively doing something. By viewing hoping as a set of mediated practices – designing a strategy, hiring a social media expert, opening new social media accounts, creating content – Giulia's story shows that *doing* is an integral part of the hoping process and gives it a specific temporal dimension. Active hoping, namely active doing, contributes to surviving the present. Following Berlant (2011) and Jakimov (2016), I can also argue that practices of self-branding on social media tied Giulia to the mainstream lifestyle of the digital era, which helped her cope with present-day insecurities. Jakimov (2016), in his study of hope among marginalised people in India, showed that education is critical to one's sense of self, and people keep investing in it for this reason, even when it does not help them go anywhere in life. In a similar manner, engaging with online branding gave Giulia the 'sense of what it means to keep on living on and to look forward to being in the world' (Berlant 2007: 33). In the following section, I explore other rewards produced by social media in the present, which are the creation and maintenance of social relationships. As pointed out by Alacovska (2019) in relation to her study of creative workers from South-East Europe, social relationships are a form of compensation that help people cope with the difficulties of everyday life.

Laura and Luca: Self-Branding and the Crafting of Meaningful Relationships

Laura is a 54-year-old single woman who has been employed in the same company for more than 25 years. In 2011, her company started to struggle. She was put on furlough (*cassa integrazione*). She lived for a few months with unemployment benefits and the fear that the company could have fired her for good and she could not enter the job market anymore. At that time, her main hobby was the production of organic soaps and skin creams for herself and few close friends. She thought that she could turn this hobby into earnings and asked a local market if she could sell soaps and creams there. Since then, she has been selling her products at the market every other weekend, while her company went through a long period of crisis and decline that led them to cut a few hundred employees. Laura spent the last eight years alternating months of being laid off and reduced working hours with other periods of full-time employment. The production of soaps and creams thus became a second job. She viewed it as a form of safety net (*ammortizzatore sociale*) that gave her an extra salary of up to 400 euros a month and the possibility of a higher salary in the future if she lost her current job. Laura sold her products at the local market and not online, but she used social media to increase her visibility and maintain the possibility of turning her small-scale production into her main source of income if she lost her main profession in the future.

She opened dedicated pages on Facebook and Instagram to promote the production of organic soap and skin cream and created a WhatsApp group with around 30 members that she used to keep contact with her most affectionate customers. She explained,

> If I had a secure job until my retirement, I would sell these products only to my friends, and only for fun! And I would stop updating these social media accounts. But social media are a way to keep the possibility of an income open!

She viewed Instagram, Facebook, and WhatsApp as the main way to expand her small production. She also enjoyed scrolling through the Instagram accounts of those who became successful skin product influencers or entrepreneurs. Above all, the use of social media to promote her products was a way to meet new friends and maintain relationships with new 'customers/friends' (*clienti/amici*) who did not belong to her old circles. On WhatsApp, she publishes videos of new soaps being made and chats with her most loyal customers about the process of cream and soap production. On Facebook, she remains in touch with many more people, such as a woman who was undergoing chemotherapy who Laura first met at the market. Laura was pleased that this woman felt cared for and loved in a difficult moment of her life, and they kept in contact for months. This and other relationships started or were maintained via social media and made Laura happy. Creating new relationships and being part of new groups of friends was an important outcome of her online branding and social media presence.

Acquiring social belonging and recognition via online branding while unemployed also characterised Luca's experience. Luca is a 46-year-old man who was born in Milan and lived there all his life. We met to drink coffee in a nice bar with tables outside and chatted for more than two hours. It was a sunny day with a fresh pleasant breeze, and Luca looked happy. He felt relieved to no longer be working for the employer that had made his life miserable for the previous ten years. Up until six months before my interview, when he decided to quit the job, Luca had worked as a shop assistant in a supermarket for 26 years. In the years before the 2009 crisis, he did not have problems at work. He was able to carry out all his tasks in a peaceful environment and received a decent wage. His working conditions started deteriorating in 2009 and increasingly worsened in the following years. He was continuously re-allocated from one supermarket location to another and forced to work overtime. His workload and that of his colleagues doubled while the salary remained the same, and he did not have any opportunity for career development. Exhausted and frustrated, he started thinking of quitting his job. After a few more years, he woke up one morning and resigned. Following a couple of months of rest and holiday, he actively began working on the project he had been envisioning for a while: launching an e-commerce activity to sell second-hand CDs and vinyl records. Luca is a music lover with an extensive knowledge of indie-progressive rock and underground rock bands. He loved hanging out in second-hand markets and shops, buying and collecting second-hand albums. Years before my interview, he started selling CDs and vinyl on eBay, earning around 300 euros a month. He thought that with a bit more effort and time this could become his main income. He thought of opening a website with a VAT number, linking it to his page on eBay, and increasing the number of CDs that he bought in stores and resold on eBay. His goal was to reach the income of 1000 euros a month. He did not have to pay a mortgage and had no children, so these earnings would have allowed him to realise his idea of a 'good life': turning his passion for music into a source of income, while not spending 40 hours a week inside a supermarket.

Luca had never used social media before. A few years earlier, a friend had created a Facebook account for him that remained inactive. Luca did not like social media and did not feel the need to use them. But he heard from friends that Facebook could help him to promote his project. Without a professional strategy or massive investment of time, he decided to use Facebook to brand himself as a music expert and to promote his new e-commerce activity. He friended all his old friends and acquaintances from school and the neighbourhood and started posting covers of CDs and links to videos on YouTube. He explained:

> I don't exactly know how it can be useful for my e-commerce activity, but you never know. I want to open all the possible channels and contacts available, and then we will see! ... I have time now, and I love to share the music I like. I might post rare songs that people do not know. My friends always trust me when we talk music, and I am happy to suggest to them what they can listen to. I don't have a clear strategy, but I have time now, and I like using Facebook in this way. I am not sure it really helps, but I will wait and see!

Nine months after my chat with Luca, the Covid-19 pandemic hit the north of Italy. Throughout 2019 and 2020, Luca regularly shared music and music-related posts and images on his Facebook wall. Almost every day, and sometimes multiple times per day, he posted links to music videos on YouTube or images of covers of his favourite albums. For every post, he received likes or comments from Facebook friends. Unlike Laura, Luca did not use social media to reach out to new people. On Facebook, he branded himself as music lover and expert among his large established circle of friends and acquaintances. And, unlike the other social media users described in the previous section, he presented a self that did not contradict the identity he had among his friends. Both Laura and Luca stated that the main reason for using social media was to increase the chance of having higher income in the future, but on the other hand, social media facilitated the creation of new relationships or the strengthening of older ones. Social relationships were the immediate rewards that motivated them to be active online, and these also compensated for the lack or shortage of social connections brought by an unstable work path and unemployment.

Social Media and the Mediation of Hope

Social media practices are hope. They produce promises for a better future life that are not always fulfilled, while at the same time affording present-day rewards. The anthropological study of hope emerged during the first decade of the twentieth century and is now a rich and diverse field of inquiry. In his comprehensive review, Jansen (2021) identifies a large number of studies on the role of hope in upward social mobility and search for better lives, including among underemployed and precarious workers 'in Egypt (Schielke 2015), Ethiopia (Mains 2011), Georgia (Demant Frederikse 2013), Mongolia (Pedersen 2012), and Iran (Khosravi 2017)'. Ethnographies of hope have shown its relational character, which stresses that past, present, and future are entangled with each other and that hope is always embedded in specific temporal orientation. They also share the idea that hope is always to some extent grounded in people's present practices. For example, Elliot (2016) describes the 'labour of hope' of young women in Morocco and demonstrates that, despite their belief in predestination, women actively engage in activities to increase the possibility of marital success. Alacovska (2018) conceptualises hope among creative precarious workers as the practices oriented to the present that are necessary to coping with precarity. Even Crapanzano (2003), who conceptualises hope mostly as a passive activity – 'the passive counterpart' of desires – recognises its embodiment in specific practices. Kleist and Jansen (2016) think that hope always includes agency and can be conceptualised as the moving away from suppressions. Finally, Ahmed (2010) describes hope as something 'that teaches us about what we strive for in the present' (2010: 181–182).

This chapter complements and adds to this growing literature in the anthropology of hope by bringing to the fore the role of social media in enabling practices that are meaningful in the present. On the one hand, social media practices attach people to imaginaries for a better future, which are also influenced by public discourses on the importance of online branding to secure a job. Social media practices facilitate an imaginative response to insecurity. Building on the work of Berlant (2011), Ahmed (2010), and Jakimov (2016), I view this imaginary as providing a sense of inclusion into the 'mainstream' life that enables 'the continuity of the subject's sense of what it means to keep on living on and to look forward to being in the world' (Berlant 2011: 24). I suggest that precarious and unemployed workers in Northern Italy engage in online branding because they feel that they are doing the right thing. They adjust their behaviours to what is portrayed as being the latest innovative ways to improve life and working conditions. The influence of discourses portraying social media as the more efficient way to find a job emerged in all the three stories described in this chapter. On the other hand, social media enable practices that are rewarding in the present: updating a profile, embellishing the public self through the decoration of a Facebook wall, creating new friendships, expanding older social networks, reading about other people's stories. Laura, for example, enjoys being active on Instagram and Facebook. Although she describes her social media use as aimed at building up a new profession, her narrative revolves around the sense of fulfilment brought by her new relationships and the exploration of other DIY experiences in Europe and Asia. And Luca loved becoming a source of inspiration for the few hundred friends who followed him on Facebook. The dual temporal component of hope explains why precarious workers and unemployed people keep investing in online branding even though this rarely translates into better job opportunities and often clashes with local norms ruling sociality and friendships.

In this chapter, I built on a practice approach to hope (Hauer, Østergaard Nielsen, and Niewöhner 2018) and social media (Costa 2018) to describe the experiences of people at the margin of neoliberal societies in Europe. I also took as my starting point the main principle of media anthropology, which is the study of media practices as embedded in people's everyday life and relationships. These approaches allowed me, first, to shed light on the temporality of mediated hope. Second, they allowed me to show that online branding is not homogenous across places and cultures, but rather grounded in and interconnected with local forms of sociality in multiple and complex ways. Social relationships constitute, at the same time, the main obstacle and the main reward in the use of social media for online branding and explain why people do not lose hope and keep persisting even when the promises of better futures are not fulfilled.

A productive strand of research has described the interplay of material culture, infrastructure, and hope, counter-balancing the human-centric perspective of previous works (Cross 2015; Harvey, Jensen, and Morita 2017; Hauer, Østergaard Nielsen, and Niewöhner 2018; Knox 2017; Reed 2011; Reeves 2017). Yet little ethnographic research has investigated digital media as generators of future-oriented aspirations and desires. In this chapter, I foreground the role of social media in shaping people's hopes in situations of marginalisation and social inequality. I also advocate for the use of the conceptual tools from media and digital anthropology to investigate a large variety of human experiences. Dominic Boyer suggested that '

> media anthropology's most generative moments (like indigenous media research of the 1980s and 1990s) succeeded precisely because they addressed wider anthropological debates on aspects of social mediation such as representation, technology, exchange and knowledge.
>
> 2012: 389

Thirty years later, media anthropology continues to play a crucial role in addressing wider anthropological debates. As shown in this chapter, a media practice approach to online branding offered a fruitful perspective to investigate social inequality, hope, and personal relationships in a particular historical conjuncture of late neoliberalism in Europe.

References

Ahmed, S. (2010). *The Promise of Happiness*. Durham, NC: Duke University Press.
Alacovska, A. (2019). 'Keep Hoping, Keep Going: Towards a Hopeful Sociology of Creative Work.' *Sociological Review* 67 (5): 1118–1136.
Appadurai, A. (2013). *The Future as Cultural Fact: Essays on the Global Condition*. London: Verso.
Ardevol, E. and Gomez-Cruz, E. (2014). 'Digital Ethnography and Media Practices.' In Valdivia, A. N. (ed.), *The International Encyclopedia of Media Studies*. Malden, MA: John Wiley.
Berlant, L. (2007). 'Cruel Optimism: On Marx, Loss and the Senses.' *New Formations* 63: 33–51.
Berlant, L. (2011). *Cruel Optimism*. Durham, NC: Duke University Press.

Bird, E. (2011). 'Are We All Produsers Now? Convergence and Media Audience Practices.' *Cultural Studies* 25 (4–5): 502–516.

Boyd, D. (2014). *It's Complicated: The Social Lives of Networked Teens*. New Haven, CT: Yale University Press.

Boyer, D. (2012). 'From Media Anthropology to the Anthropology of Mediation.' In Fardon, R. et al. (eds), *The SAGE Handbook of Social Anthropology*. London: Sage.

Bräuchler, B. and Postill, J. (2010). *Theorising Media and Practice*. New York: Berghahn.

Cavalli, A. (2001). 'Reflections on Political Culture and the "Italian National Character".' *Daedalus* 130(3): 119–137.

Couldry, N. (2004). 'Theorising Media as Practice.' *Social semiotics* 14(2): 115–132.

Costa, E. (2018). 'Affordances-in-practice: An Ethnographic Critique of Social Media Logic and Context Collapse.' *New Media & Society* 20(10): 3641–3656. doi:10.1177/1461444818756290

Crapanzano, V. (2003). 'Reflections on Hope as a Category of Social and Psychological Analysis.' *Cultural Anthropology* 18(1): 3–32.

Cross, J. (2015). 'The Economy of Anticipation: Hope, Infrastructure, and Economic Zones in South India.' *Comparative Studies of South Asia, Africa and the Middle East* 35(3): 424–437.

D'Aloisio, F. and Ghezzi, S. (2020). *Facing the Crisis: Ethnographies of Work in Italian Industrial Capitalism*. New York: Berghahn Books.

Demant Frederiksen, M. (2014). 'To Russia with Love: Hope, Confinement, and Virtuality Among Youth on the Georgian Black Sea Coast.' *Focaal* 70: 26–36.

Elliot, A. (2016). 'The Makeup of Destiny: Predestination and the Labor of Hope in a Moroccan Emigrant Town.' *American Ethnologist* 43(3): 488–499.

Fischer, E. F. (2014). *The Good Life: Aspiration, Dignity, and the Anthropology of Wellbeing*. Stanford, CA: Stanford University Press.

Gershon, I. (2017). *Down and Out in the New Economy*. Chicago: University of Chicago Press.

Ginsburg, F. D., Abu-Lughod, L., and Larkin, B. (2002). *Media Worlds: Anthropology on New Terrain*. Berkeley: University of California Press.

Goddard, V. (2017). 'Work and Livelihoods: An Introduction.' In Goddard, V. and Narotzky, S. (eds), *Work and Livelihoods: Histories, Ethnographies and Livelihood at Times of Crisis*. London: Routledge.

Hage, G. (2003). *Against Paranoid Nationalism: Searching for Hope in a Shrinking Society*. Annandale, Australia: Pluto/Merlin.

Han, S. and Antrosio, J. (2020). 'The Editors' Note: Hope.' *Open Anthropology* 8 (2). www.americananthro.org/StayInformed/OAArticleDetail.aspx?ItemNumber=25812

Harvey P., Jensen C., and Morita A. (2017). *Infrastructures and Social Complexity: A Companion*. London: Routledge.

Hauer, J., Østergaard Nielsen, J., and Niewöhner, J. (2018). 'Landscapes of Hoping: Urban Expansion and Emerging Futures in Ouagadougou, Burkina Faso.' *Anthropological Theory* 18(1): 59–80.

Hobart, M. (2010). 'What Do We Mean by "Media Practices"?' In Bräuchler, B. and Postill, J. (eds), *Theorizing Media and Practice*. New York: Berghahn.

Jakimow, T. (2016). 'Clinging to Hope through Education: The Consequences of Hope for Rural Laborers in Telangana, India.' *Ethos: The Journal of the Society for Psychological Anthropology* 44(1): 11–31.

Jansen, S. (2021, January 22). *The Anthropology of Hope*. Oxford Research Encyclopedia of Anthropology. Retrieved 4 March 2021, from https://oxfordre.com/anthropology/view/10.1093/acrefore/9780190854584.001.0001/acrefore-9780190854584-e-182

Keane, W. (2002). 'Sincerity, "Modernity," and the Protestants.' *Cultural Anthropology* 17(1): 65–92.

Khosravi, S. (2017). *Precarious Lives: Waiting and Hope in Iran*. Philadelphia: Pennsylvania University Press.

Kleist, N. and Jansen, S. (2016). 'Introduction: Hope over Time – Crisis, Immobility and Future-Making.' *History and Anthropology* 27(4): 373–392, doi: 10.1080/02757206.2016.1207636

Knight, D. M. and Stewart, C. (2016). 'Ethnographies of Austerity: Temporality, Crisis and Affect in Southern Europe.' *History and Anthropology* 27(1): 1–18.

Know, H. C. (2017). 'Affective Infrastructure and the Political Imagination.' *Public Culture* 29(2): 363–384. doi:10.1215/08992363-3749105

Kuehn, K. and Corrigan, T. F. (2013). 'Hope Labour: The Role of Employment Prospects in Online Social Media Production.' *Political Economy of Communication* 1(1): 9–25.

Mains, D. (2011). *Hope is Cut: Youth, Unemployment, and the Future in Urban Ethiopia*. Philadelphia: Temple University Press.

Miller, D., Costa, E., Haynes, N., McDonald, T., Nicolescu, R., Sinanan, J., Spyer, J., Venkatraman, S., and Wang, X. (2016). *How the World Changed Social Media*. London: UCL Press.

Molé, N. (2011). *Labor Disorders in Neoliberal Italy: Mobbing, Well-being, and the Workplace.* Bloomington: Indiana University Press.
Molé, N. (2012). 'Hauntings of Solidarity of Post-fordist Italy.' *Anthropological Quarterly* 85(2): 371–396.
Muehlebach, A. (2011). 'On Affective Labour in Post-fordist Italy.' *Cultural Anthropology* 26(1): 58–82.
Pedersen, M. A. (2012). 'A Day in the Cadillac: The Work of Hope in Urban Mongolia.' *Social Analysis* 56(2): 136–151.
Peterson, M. A. (2004). *Anthropology and Mass Communication: Media and Myth in the New Millennium.* New York: Berghahn Books.
Reed, A. (2011). 'Hope On Remand.' *Journal of the Royal Anthropological Institute* 17(3): 527–544.
Reeves, M. (2017). 'Infrastructural Hope: Anticipating "Independent Roads" and Territorial Integrity in Southern Kyrgyzstan.' *Ethnos* 82(4): 711–737.
Schielke, S. (2015). *Egypt in the Future Tense: Hope, Frustration and Ambivalence Before and After 2011.* Bloomington: Indiana University Press.
Walton, S. (2021). *Ageing with Smartphones in Urban Italy.* London: UCL Press.

24
DIGITAL INEQUALITY AND RELATEDNESS IN INDIA AFTER ACCESS

Sirpa Tenhunen

The digital divide concept emerged in the 1990s to refer to the unequal access and usage of digital technologies. The idea is well summarized by Castells (2002: 269), who argued that being disconnected from the internet is tantamount to marginalization in the global, networked system. In this chapter, I will first discuss how the approaches to digital divides and inequality have evolved as access to digital media has increased. Drawing from my ethnographic fieldwork[1] on smartphone use in rural and urban India among low-income and little-educated people, I then propose a novel way to understand digital inequality through the concept of digital relatedness. I demonstrate that understanding digital inequality requires exploring how people's digital media use is embedded in social relationships and how media use serves to refashion relationships and hierarchies. To conclude, I discuss the implications of the relational understanding of new media use for digital inclusion.

Whereas the lion's share of the research on the appropriation of new media has tended to focus on the early adopters, the notion of the digital divide directed attention to the people excluded from digitalization. Hence, the notion helped build a critical stance towards the ideas about digital media as bringing about development and prosperity for all (Gunkel, 2003). Early debates on digital divides tended to assume that information and communication technologies (ICTs) are inherently good and progressive, that the non-use is solely caused by a lack of access, and that providing ICT resources for socially disempowered groups is a means to empower them (Green and Haddon, 2009). The critiques of the concept, which first emerged at the beginning of the 21st century, found the notion technologically deterministic and crude in emphasizing access to media and dividing people into information have and have-nots (Carpentier, 2003; Gunkel, 2003; van Dijk, 2006). Yet, much of the academic, policy, and popular discourse around ICTs has continued to centre on this notion, while policies worldwide seek to bridge the divide or enable a digital leap.

Inequalities after Access

Identifying the conceptual flaws of the digital divide notion has not been accompanied by the disappearance of digital inequality. Stark differences in people's abilities to access digital data persist not only between countries but also within countries. The global access rate to the internet has increased from nearly 17 per cent in 2005 to over 53 per cent in 2019; yet, only 19 per cent of individuals in the least developed countries had access to the internet in 2019, while 97 per cent of the population was able to go online in developed countries (International Telecommunication Union, 2019). Even high-quality and low-price access to the internet does not necessarily translate into an equal capacity to use it. In Europe, half of the less-educated and the elderly do not use the internet regularly, and about 58 million EU citizens (aged 16–74 years old) have never used it at all (Negreiro, 2015). The digitalization of governmental and private sector services worldwide has helped those tech-savvy enough to access these services, but it has increased digital inequality for others. The Covid-19 pandemic has exacerbated the situation further as an increasing number of activities, which used to take place face-to-face, have been transferred to the digital sphere (Lai and Widmar, 2020). Children without access to distant learning have borne the brunt of digital inequality—two-thirds of the world's school-age children have no internet access at home (United Nations Children's Fund and International Telecommunication Union, 2020).

Mobile broadband subscriptions exceeded the number of fixed connections in 2008, and much of this growth now occurs in developing countries (World Bank, 2012: 11–30). While the coverage gap—those living outside of areas covered by mobile broadband networks—has narrowed to 7 per cent of the world population, the usage gap—the difference between total potential use and actual usage—has grown faster than usage (Bahia and Delaporte, 2020). Like much of the developing world, India witnessed unprecedented growth in teledensity from less than one per 100 persons to 93.27 during 1991–2018 (Telecom Statistics of India, 2019). Mobile internet use increased in India particularly after the service provider company Jio launched an affordable smartphone along with a free internet trial offer in 2016. Other service providers responded by introducing rate cuts; as a result, India's data usage quadrupled in one year. By 2018, when I returned to India for fieldwork, India was one of the largest and fastest-growing markets for digital consumers, with 560 million internet subscribers, second only to China (BBC, 2019). Yet, the usage gap of mobile internet in South Asia was highest among the continents—61 per cent of the population who live in regions covered by mobile internet did not use it in 2020 (International Telecommunication Union, 2020). Affordability has remained a pivotal barrier to connectivity, especially in lower-income countries and among low-income people in countries worldwide; consequently, around half of the world population was offline in 2020 (International Telecommunication Union, 2020).

Those connected to the internet through smartphones do not get the same affordances as those using a broadband connection through a computer, as Donner's (2015) research in South Africa and India demonstrates. In addition to reading on a small screen, it is hard to use smartphones to author internet content, which is one of the vital internet affordances compared to printed text. Furthermore, the same properties responsible for mobile telephony's rapid growth in developing countries, such as usage-based pricing, present significant constraints to effective internet use. When every click on the internet costs money, users are likely to conserve airtime and their data bundle balance carefully—families have to decide how to allocate and balance bytes to different uses such as Facebook versus work. Hence, instead of unlimited surfing and browsing the internet, the hundreds of millions of new internet users are, likely to use it briefly and occasionally. In Donner's (2015:124,125) words, they "dip and sip," conserving airtime and the balance on their data bundles (2015: 135).

Similar to Donner, media anthropologists (for instance, Archambault, 2017; Burrel, 2012; Costa, 2016; Hobbis, 2020; Horst and Miller, 2006; Tenhunen, 2018; Ventkatraman, 2017) have challenged universalizing claims about the impact of digital technologies. They have revealed the diversity in people's new media use and demonstrated that many users have to use new media sparingly due to the high cost of connections. However, although media anthropologists have provided rich data on digital inequality as well as insights into the new media use as a social practice, they have seldom explicitly addressed the debate on digital divides and inequality. Drawing from media anthropology, I aim to develop a nuanced understanding of digital inequality by exploring technologies and social relatedness based on my ethnographic fieldwork in rural and urban India. I have carried out fieldwork in Janta, a multi-caste village in the eastern state of West Bengal with 2,441 inhabitants (Census of India, 2011) since 1999. In 2012–2013, I observed how people moved from simple handsets to smartphones (Tenhunen, 2018). In 2018, I carried out fieldwork among environmental refugees in Kolkata, a mega-city in Eastern India. I also visited a few of these Kolkata residents' villages in the coastal region of Sundarban, which they had left due to the extreme weather events.

Understanding Gradations of Use

As digital technology has become increasingly ubiquitous, the discussion on the divides has moved from access to contextualizing the usage of technology (Tsatsou, 2011: 319). For access to matter, people must find the use of ICTs socially and culturally meaningful; they must fulfil people's needs, desires, skills, and capacities to make a difference in how and whether they access technologies (Loader, 1998; Mansell and Steinmueller, 2000: 37). In addition to access to technological means, divides can exist in terms of the autonomy of use, use patterns, social support networks, and skills (DiMaggio and Hargittai, 2001). The "digital divide" is now commonly understood as consisting of three levels: the first one refers to the inequality in access, the second one to skills and use,[2] and the third one[3] to the unequal outcomes and benefits of digital media use (Van Dijk, 2020). Since even when the divides are understood as multiple, the term reinforces splitting people into haves and have-nots, the notion of the digital divide is more usefully described as digital inequality to reflect the gradations of use. The scholarly interest, in turn, has shifted from divides to approaches that consider the relationship between social and digital inequality (Helsper, 2012 and 2021).

The concept of intersectionality has offered a fruitful way to address the social complexity of the appropriation of new media. The term coined by legal scholar Kimberlé Crenshaw (1989: 139) refers to how mutually reinforcing vectors of race, gender, class, and sexuality constitute subjectivity. Crenshaw availed the concept to make the law more sensitive to different registers of identity—she developed her insights by drawing from legal cases involving African American women's arguments that they were facing compound discrimination. The concept has since been used in many contexts across disciplines to highlight how focusing on one aspect of identity, such as gender or class as apart, does not do justice to social complexity. Wallis (2015) applied the concept to media studies exploring how multiple axes of identity and modes of power among migrant women in China relate to mobile phone use. She argued that social constructions of gender, class, age, and place produce particular engagements with mobile technologies, which reproduce and restructure these identities. By demonstrating that migrants' social identity as migrants and not as Beijing people remained intact, despite the virtual mobility and inclusion in expanded and enriched social networks that phones offered, Wallis emphasized social barriers of media use. Yet, smartphone-mediated encounters can facilitate users' agency. For instance, McCaffrey and Taha (2019) challenged assumptions of refugee incompetence by demonstrating how Syrian migrants in the US harnessed such smartphone interfaces as Google Translate and YouTube videos to negotiate linguistic and cultural differences and lower the interpersonal language barriers.

In this chapter, I introduce the term digital relatedness to pay attention not only to the barriers of media use but also how the use of digital media is embedded in human and non-human relationships and networks, which are inherently open and emergent. Relatedness is a term coined by Carsten (2000) to refer to the processual nature of kinship relationships produced through social interaction and the exchange of substances. Kinship studies have focused mainly on how substances as bodily fluids are understood to constitute kinship relationships. Carsten's ethnographic research in Malaysia and Scotland broadened the understanding of substances from bodily fluids to small acts of everyday life, which could create kinship where it did not previously exist. By digital relatedness, I refer to how media use is not only embedded in pre-existing social relationships as revealed by the intersectionality approach but how it can serve to refashion the meanings of social relationships and hierarchies. Consequently, the term relatedness helps to highlight the potential emergence of new relationships, identities as well as concomitant novel media ideologies. I will start by describing how my interlocutors used their smartphones, including the barriers they faced in using the phones. I then demonstrate how people were able to develop novel digital practices. Next, I explore how people refashioned their relationships and local hierarchies through their smartphone use. I provide ethnographic vignettes from my fieldwork during 2012–2013 and 2018, in order to analyse how the new availability of inexpensive branded phones contributed to digital practices and inequality.

The Diversity of Digital Practices after Access

When I arrived in the village of Janta in 2012, one of the first things I was told was that the lowest caste group,[4] the Bagdis, had acquired fancy phones. The news surprised me since Bagdis had been among the last people in the village to purchase phones. The fancy phones turned out to be Chinese-made phones with smartphone facilities: a music player, camera, the internet, video camera and player, radio, double-sim facility, and a memory chip. These multiple-facility Chinese phones were offered at much lower prices—the cheapest cost Rs 700 (around 10 euros)—than even the simplest branded phones. Nevertheless, mere smartphone ownership did not mean that people accessed the internet or were even interested in doing so. Most phone owners used even the calling function of their phones sparingly. Wealthier people could make and receive tens of calls a day, whereas low-income families only receive and make a few brief calls weekly. The importance of education for phone use was highlighted when I observed a 12-year-old Bagdi girl effortlessly learning to browse English language information from the internet using a smartphone. At the same time, the older, less-educated generation in the same family needed help to type in a number. Yet, an inability to read English numbers and text does not exclude anyone from calling because phones are shared, and younger family members could help their elders use the phone's calling function. I witnessed both young men and women acting as phone use experts in their families.

The few people in the village who had used their phones to browse the internet all had a college education and therefore belonged to a minority. In 2013, I found 33 villagers (1.3 per cent of the village population) who either had a college degree or were studying at a college. The few who had tried the internet had found many uses for it: downloading music and movies, finding out about prices, products, jobs, and exam results, as well as sending e-mail and accessing study sources such as literature and dictionaries, and using Facebook. In 2013, browsing the internet directly on a mobile phone cost Rs 98 per month for a limited amount of gigabytes, which low-income people found too expensive. Service providers had also introduced inexpensive data plans (starting from Rs 12), allowing the internet to be browsed for a limited period and amount of data, which could mean just one night. Consequently, people tended to access the internet by means of their phones only sporadically. Moreover, browsing the internet on an inexpensive, low-end handset was not easy—these phones were not user-friendly. I, for instance, failed to teach a young woman who had studied up to class 10 (first year of high school) to access the internet and use e-mail on her mobile phone. I, too, found it difficult to operate the low-end phone model to access the internet. But it must have been more challenging for someone who had never browsed the internet with the help of a computer even to grasp the idea of the internet when accessed on a small phone screen.

Most people who possessed cheap smartphones, however, had accessed the internet but not directly with their phones. Instead, they bought music, videos, and pictures, which are downloaded on their phone's memory chips at a village shop. Although this practice differs crucially from the more autonomous use of smartphones to browse the internet, it offers easy and inexpensive access to internet content. The amount of downloaded material depended on the size of the memory chip, but the usually downloaded package contained hundreds of songs, dozens of pictures, and a few films. Each download cost Rs 10–30, and the cost of memory chips was around Rs 150–350. Villagers found these costs more affordable than buying a monthly or daily internet package.

In 2018, my interlocutors in a squatter settlement in Kolkata used their smartphones much the same way as the villagers I encountered in 2012–2013 despite the new availability of inexpensive branded phones and data plans. Some people had continued to use old simple handsets because they were not comfortable using the touchscreen phones, while others had bought branded smartphones. For most people, the phone's calling function continued to be more valuable than internet-based applications. The families were dispersed into several units in different locations, and phones helped them stay in touch. Moreover, phones' calling functions were crucial for their livelihoods. Most men's work was tied to construction projects—they were hired to carry out a specific part of the project, and once it was over, phones helped them to find a new job. Other urban opportunities for men included small-scale business or working as a ricksha or car driver for which phones' calling functions were also necessary. Women, who mainly found employment as domestic workers, said that without owning a phone one could not get a job, as employers want to stay in constant touch with their employees by calling them.

I met persons who possessed Jio phones and were aware of the three-month free internet offer; yet, they had not availed themselves of the offer. Like villagers in 2013, most people indirectly accessed the internet by purchasing music and films on their phone's memory chip from the nearby shops. The difference was that the urban shops charged more and offered their customers more possibilities to select the content[5] than the village shops in 2013. The two college-educated residents of the Kolkata neighbourhood possessed a good understanding of the various ways one can use the internet—both had learned how to use a smartphone's internet applications from their teachers and peers at the college. However, only one of these persons owned a smartphone and could practice what he had learned. He had used the smartphone for his studies by accessing information about exams. He also mentioned using WhatsApp, Facebook, and Google maps. He was the only person I met in this community who had used internet banking applications. The Indian state's Digital India campaign, which has among other things sought to develop digital financial services in 2017 (Ministry of Electronics & Information Technology, Government of India, 2019) had not reached this community. They preferred to send money to their families through a trusted person who could travel and deliver the cash in person. Some people mentioned having used other people's bank accounts to send money.

The rest of the internet users I met in this urban neighbourhood were either young or middle-aged people whose sons or daughters could help them use the smartphone. The smartphone users with little education could access the internet, but their range of use was much narrower than that of the above-mentioned college-educated man. Popular ways to use the internet over smartphones included watching films on YouTube and series on television channels, which were provided on their phones. Most people used the phone for recreation, but some people also mentioned watching educational videos on YouTube. For instance, a young woman had learned cooking and hairstyling from YouTube videos. Some people also made video calls or exchanged videos of their daily lives. Children played games and watched cartoons on smartphones.

The branded phones and cheaper data connections had made using the internet easier: consequently, the range of use had diversified. Nevertheless, accessing the internet still required social learning. My findings are similar to many ethnographic studies, which have revealed how people who lack skills and abilities are often helped to use digital media. Bakardjieva (2005), who studied computer use at homes in the United States, coined the term "warm expert" to refer to nonprofessional persons who help inexperienced users come to terms with digital devices. The crucial role that warm experts play in the appropriation of new media means that inclusion in the digital world takes place through social interaction. For instance, Oreglia (2014) discovered how older women in rural China had learned the basics of mobile phone and computer use. These women pursued their goals of maintaining relationships and accessing online entertainment after receiving training from their children, through collaboration and knowledge sharing with their peers, and through frequent reliance on other people to perform specific actions. In contrast, exclusion from digital services can result from the scarcity of social contacts or networks lacking people with digital skills. However, the social appropriation of new media is not only about passing technological know-how on how to use the device. People also have to learn to use different media in socially appropriate ways. Gershon (2010) argues that people devise the proper ways to use a specific medium together—she calls the process an idiom of practice. Gershon maintains that the medium shapes the message because people have media ideologies that shape how they think about and use different media, while media ideologies about one medium are always affected by the media ideologies people have about other media. The notions of media ideology and warm expert help us to understand how digital media use tends to be firmly embedded in pre-existing social relationships. As such, even when people use digital technologies seemingly autonomously, the use remains predominantly social in that people need to learn to use smartphones and application from other users. Hence, in addition to missing access, differential use of digital media emerges from patterns of social interaction.

Refashioning of Social Hierarchies

The social relationships in which the media use is embedded are not static but emergent, and media use can contribute to the changes in social hierarchies. Next, I turn to explore how my interlocutors refashioned and reconstructed hierarchies through their smartphone use—in both research locations, smartphones played a role in how people navigated within social hierarchies, even refashioning them. The low caste, Bagdi neighbourhood was the last one in the village to receive electricity; therefore, unlike the upper castes and classes in the village, they had not previously owned televisions. Consequently, smartphones had allowed the Bagdi neighbourhood to leapfrog a whole range of gadgets—cameras, music players, and televisions—which most of the world has acquired one after another as separate technologies over many decades. Although the Bagdis did not buy branded phones, their smartphones were identity statements, signifying their position's relative improvement in relation to the upper land-owning castes in the village. Smartphones represented the Bagdis' new inclusion in services and consumer products from which they had previously been excluded. This exclusion, in turn, had contributed to their social standing in neo-liberal India, where media images have delineated the urban middle classes as the consumers of not just the newly available commodities but also of the new India produced through the meanings of these commodities (Fernandes, 2000). The widespread ideology, according to which not being connected is a sign of exclusion from global currents and development, has also contributed to how owning digital technology has become a significant symbolic act through which people can seek to improve their position and challenge hierarchies. Throughout India and South Asia, it has become common for elites to demonstrate social and economic changes through anecdotes of how someone's driver, cook, or maid has suddenly acquired a mobile phone (Nisbett, 2007). Nisbett (ibid.), who repeatedly heard the story from the IT elites in Bangalore, notes that the comment entails a dual discourse—the pride that these working-class people could have acquired something so symbolic of hi-tech India, mixed with the uneasiness about how the lower classes have suddenly managed to catch up in a hi-tech sphere considered the preserve of the elite. When I told my upper-caste friends in the nearby town of Vishnupur about the popularity of smartphones among the Bagdis, they commented that common people's use of phones as entertainment centres entails the misuse of phones, which should be used for making calls. The low castes' and classes' use of mobile phones for entertainment stirred controversy because their new ability to possess such advanced technological gadgets was experienced as disruptive of local hierarchies—a Bagdi caste person owning a smartphone challenged the upper-caste views of lower castes as backward. By labelling low caste people's smartphone use as misuse, the upper-class people sought to downplay the potential rise in the hierarchy that the possession of smartphones could signify.

The Kolkata community, where I did fieldwork in 2018, was an informal squatter settlement characterized by more social fluidity and diversity than the village. Most of the residents of this community had left their villages in the coastal region of Sundarban (South 24 Parganas district) after the cyclone Aila, which caused large-scale destruction in the area in 2009. For some, displacement had meant social decline and poverty; yet, for others, the chance to move to the city and engage in paid labour had made it possible to save money and move upward. The neighbourhood looked shabby with its houses made of mud, bamboo sticks, and plastic sheets; yet, the interiors of the homes were usually neatly furnished and included such expensive items as flatscreen television and branded smartphones. Even the few wealthy people of this community did not have many incentives to improve their houses because they could be evicted any day. The city had zoned the area as a park, but it could not evict the people until it could rehouse them. Residents had built their houses and lived there without paying rent by bribing the local police and the party office.

As mentioned before, people of this community found phones useful for coordinating family relationships and work, but smartphones were also used to navigate the social fluidity in families whose members had drifted apart socially. For instance, a woman who worked as a maid had arranged her daughter's marriage to a well-to-do family. Her interaction with her daughter and the in-laws was now limited because visiting her informal neighbourhood would have disturbed the upper-class status of the daughter's in-laws. Mother and daughter were, therefore, able to see each other only seldomly, but they exchanged videos of each other and especially the daughter's children over their branded smartphones. Another couple kept in contact with their sons by calling them, despite the rift with their sons' families. The parents had converted from Hinduism to Pentecostal Christianity; thus, their sons' wives forced them to move out of their own house. They relocated to the informal settlement and did not visit their sons' families;

however, they could stay in touch with their sons over the phone despite the social rift. The possibility that phones offer staying in touch despite social ruptures contributes to the changes in how social hierarchies are experienced and understood.

Digital Recreation as Social Change

In both locations and research periods, the internet was used directly or indirectly for recreation. The digital divide debate has overlooked the use of digital media for pastime and amusement since these uses have not been considered as offering potential for users' agency. However, far from passive time-pass, recreational activities, too, involved social negotiations about family relationships and the line between the spheres of everyday life in terms of who watches which contents in which social contexts. The use of smartphones for entertainment challenges ideas about phone users as rational individuals in search of useful information with the help of ICTs, although entertainment is not entirely devoid of information. Television viewers in India, for instance, use soap operas to gain new knowledge on phenomena such as urban lifestyles and alternative family types (Johnson, 2001; Munshi, 2012). Rangaswamy and Cutrell (2012), who have observed that low-income youths in urban India used phones for recreation just as the villagers of Janta did, suggest that these entertainment practices have the potential to lead to new skills and abilities being discovered by offering a space to experiment with technology. They also argue that the use of smartphones to access entertainment can have a valuable social effect of binding people and creating an informal technology hub.

Both accessing and sharing music and films directly from the internet are fluid activities because one has great freedom to choose when to watch and listen and with whom to share the content. Even phone memory chips offered this kind of freedom. Most people find the way they can now reshape the line between work and leisure exciting and energizing. Whereas television and cinema hall audiences have to follow the program schedules, a person possessing a smartphone can select the time and the company they wish to share the content of their phone's memory chip. Hence, leisure activities can be constructed as more relational than before. A young woman, for instance, said that the smartphone allows her to watch serials while her husband watches films on the television. On the one hand, smartphones enabled household members to make their own choices on what to watch, and, on the other hand, parents found it easy to control how children used the shared family smartphone. For example, parents of a young girl preferred the smartphone to television because the daughter could only watch cartoons when her father was at home with his smartphone—had they owned a television, it would have been more difficult to keep her from watching television and neglecting her homework. However, for adult family members, smartphone ownership increased their opportunities to make individual choices over what to watch. Most families lived in one-room-houses and owned one television set, which meant that they had to agree to watch the same programs, whereas people could make individual choices about what they watched on smartphones. Women prefer to watch soap operas since they are designed for female audiences—they depict strong female characters and address topical issues from women's perspectives. The leisure practices enabled by smartphones, hence, can help transform gendered kinship relations by giving women access to a greater variety of programs than they could access by watching television. Watching films and serials on smartphones offers a new freedom of choice and social experiences both in rural and urban India, similarly to Hobbis's (2020) description of the role of movie watching on smartphones for kinship relations in Melanesia.

Conclusions

Attention to digital relatedness helps understand how media use is embedded in social hierarchies and their meanings, revealing how digital inequality emerges and how social hierarchies are transformed. The slashing of the prices of branded phones and internet access has diversified smartphone use among the people I observed in India in 2018. The branded phones have enabled such online activities as filming and sending video clips as well as watching television and films much better than the cheap semi smartphones used in 2013 did. Most young people who owned smartphones had acquired these skills, helping the older generation of their households master them. However, in 2018, it was still rare to find people using a greater variety of internet affordances—possibilities for action offered by internet—such as textual contents of the internet, payment, banking, and navigation applications, or even WhatsApp. Only those people who had a college education and a network extended to tech-savvy people could become skilled in using a variety of internet services. For them, smartphones opened up a wealth of useful information and data from which they could reap practical and even professional benefits through their access to educational contents. Hence, digital practices corresponded largely with social relatedness. The ability to use the many affordances offered by the internet was rare as it required higher education and interaction with people who already possessed these skills. Consequently, smartphone use has strengthened pre-existing rifts between the more and less-educated people. At the same time, the calling functions of the phones continued to be more significant for most low-income people's livelihoods and support networks compared to the textual information offered by the internet. The internet hardly offers useful contacts for people who seek work in the informal economy. Moreover, informal sector workers' social security was largely based on family and kinship; hence, the ability to call was more crucial in times of crisis than searching for useful information from the internet. However, as I have demonstrated, people who are seemingly digitally marginalized can develop unexpected ways to use digital technologies and refashion their relationships. Although these practices do not translate into drastic improvements or changes, for instance in economic power relationships, over time, these small changes can lead to epochal changes.

The workaround practices to tackle the high cost of internet access and lack of internet skills, such as buying content on memory chips, enable novel recreational practices. However, these novel practices by no means diminish the value of the ability to use the internet for a wide range of essential purposes, for instance economic transactions or remote learning. The pre-existing scholarship on digital inequality and divides has relied mainly on quantitative data and such general criteria for digital inequality as access, motivation, skills, and the autonomy of use to measure the empowering effects of internet access. However, even seemingly autonomous media use is embedded in social relationships in the sense that people learned how to use services from others. Moreover, the focus on autonomous use can leave unacknowledged a great variety of digital practices, which users can find valuable and even transformative. The third-level digital divide—for example unequal outcomes and benefits of digital media use—is often understood through tangible benefits such as economic and political empowerment, although users increasingly avail of digital media for recreation, which can play a part in social and cultural change in multiple ways.

The central policy goal in India and elsewhere has been to tackle digital inequality by providing affordable access. Despite the slashing of internet prices, low-income people still tend to find mobile internet too expensive, which largely explains the wide usage gap in South Asia. My study demonstrates that although the high cost is the main barrier for internet use among low-income people, even affordable access may not translate into a broad range of internet uses. Being able to avail multiple affordances of the internet tends to require a higher-than-average level of education. In turn, this hinders the successful use of the internet for increasing equal opportunities in learning, which is one of the goals of the Digital India program (Ministry of Electronics & Information Technology, Government of India, 2019). Moreover, learning to use the internet to access useful information and services requires developing social networks that extend across social boundaries to those who are already practising these internet skills. My research exemplifies how digital inequality is influenced by both rigid social hierarchies and insufficient attention to the role of social interaction for digital inclusion. Instead of access to digital services promoting learning and social mobility, higher educational level and social mobility tend to promote digital inclusion. Highlighting the importance of digital relatedness brings the complexity of digital use, relationships, and power into focus.

Notes

1 The research in 2018 for this article was funded by the Academy of Finland (project 318782) as part of the project "Sustainable Livelihoods and Politics at the Margins: Environmental Displacement in South Asia."
2 Attewell (2001) coined the widely used terms first level divide and second level divide.
3 Robles and Torres Albero (2012) first used the term third divide to address the outcomes and benefits of digital media use.
4 The dominant caste, both numerically and in terms of land ownership, is the Tilis (50 per cent). Other major caste groups are the Bagdis (15 per cent) and Casas (16 per cent). Most Tilis and Casas own land, while most Bagdis, who are classified as a scheduled caste, earn their livelihood by means of daily labor—agricultural work or work in the brick factories.
5 These shops charged Rs 20–25 per film and Rs 2–3 per song, whereas one could purchase a large selection of songs and films in the village with just Rs 25.

References

Archambault, J. (2017) *Mobile secrets: Youth, intimacy, and the politics of pretence in Mozambique*. Chicago: Chicago University Press.
Attewell, P. (2001) "Comment: The first and second digital divides," *Sociology of Education* 74 (3): 252–9.
Burrell, J. (2012) *Invisible users: Youth in the internet cafés of urban Ghana*. Cambridge: MIT Press.
Bahia, K. and Delaporte, A. (2020) *The State of Mobile Internet Connectivity 2020*. GSM Association. www.gsma.com/r/wp-content/uploads/2020/09/GSMA-State-of-Mobile-Internet-Connectivity-Report-2020.pdf. (Accessed 30 June 2021.)
Bakardjieva, M. (2005) *Internet society: The internet in everyday life*. London: Sage.
BBC "Mobile data: Why India has the world's cheapest," available at www.bbc.com/news/world-asia-india-47537201, (accessed February 16, 2021).
Carpentier, N. (2003) "Bridging cultural and digital divides: Signifying everyday life, cultural diversity, and participation in the online community Video Nation," *EMTEL Conference New Media and Everyday Life in Europe*, 1–37.
Carsten, J. (2000) *Cultures of relatedness: New approaches to the study of kinship*. Cambridge: Cambridge University Press.
Castells, M. (2002) *The internet galaxy: Reflections on the Internet, business, and society*. New York: Oxford University Press.
Census of India. (2011) *Primary census abstracts*. West Bengal. New Delhi: Office of the Registrar General and Census Commissioner.
Chakraborty, S. (2015) "Investigating the impact of severe cyclone Aila and the role of disaster management department—A study of Kultali block of Sundarban," *American Journal of Theoretical and Applied Business* 1 (1), 6–13.
Cho, S., Crenshaw K., and McCall L. (2013) "Toward a field of intersectionality studies: Theory, applications, and praxis," *Signs* 38 (4): 785–810.

Choo, H. and Ferree M. (2010) "Practicing intersectionality in sociological research: A critical analysis of inclusions, interactions, and institutions in the study of inequalities," *Sociological Theory* 28 (2): 129–149.
Costa, E. (2016) *Social Media in Southeast Turkey*. London: University College Press.
Crenshaw, K. (1989) "Demarginalizing the intersection of race and sex: A black feminist critique of antidiscrimination doctrine, feminist theory, and antiracist politics," *University of Chicago Legal Forum* 1 (8): 138–167.
DiMaggio P. and Hargittai E. (2001) From the "Digital Divide" to "Digital Inequality": Studying Internet Use as Penetration Increases. Working Paper Series, 15. Princeton University: Center for Arts and Cultural Policy Studies.
Donner, J. (2015) *After access: Inclusion, development, and a more mobile internet*. Cambridge, MA: MIT Press.
Fernandes, L. (2000) "'Nationalizing the global': media images, cultural politics and the middle class in India," *Media, Culture & Society* 22 (5): 611–628.
Gershon, I. (2010) *The breakup 2.0: Disconnecting over new media*. Ithaca, NY: Cornell University Press.
Green, N. and Haddon L. (2009) *Mobile communications: An introduction to new media*. Oxford: Berg.
Gunkel, D. (2003) "Second thoughts: Toward a critique of the digital divide," *New Media & Society* 5 (4): 499–522.
Helsper, E. J. (2012) "A corresponding fields model for the links between social and digital exclusion," *Communication Theory* 22 (4): 403–426.
Helsper, E. (2021) *The digital disconnect: The social causes and consequences of digital inequalities*. Thousand Oaks, CA: Sage.
Hobbis, G. (2020) *The digitizing family: An ethnography of melanesian smartphones*. London: Palgrave Macmillan.
International Telecommunication Union (2019) "Measuring digital development: Facts and figures 2019," Geneva: ITU Publications.
International Telecommunication Union (2020) "Measuring digital development: ICT price trends 2020," Geneva: ITU Publications.
Jodhka, S. S. (2016) "Revisiting the rural in 21st century India," *Economic and Political Weekly* LI (26 and 27): 5–7.
Johnson, K. (2001) "Media and social change: The modernizing influences of television in rural India," *Media, Culture & Society* 23 (2): 147–169.
Lai, J. and Widmar, N. (2020) "Revisiting the digital divide in the COVID-19 era," *Applied Economic Perspectives and Policy* 43 (1): 458–464.
Loader, B. (1998) "Cyberspace divide: Equality, agency, and policy in the information society." In B. D. Loader (ed.), *Cyberspace divide: Equality, agency, and policy in the information society*. London: Routledge.
Lowrie, I. (2018) "Algorithms and automation: An introduction," *Cultural Anthropology* 33 (3): 349–359.
Mansell, R. and Steinmueller, W. (2000) *Mobilizing the information society: Strategies for growth and opportunity*. Oxford: Oxford University Press.
McCaffrey, K. and Taha, M. (2019) "Rethinking the digital divide: Smartphones as translanguaging tools among middle eastern refugees in New Jersey," *Annals of Anthropological Practice*, 43 (2): 26–38.
Ministry of Electronics & Information Technology, Government of India (2019) India's Trillion Dollar Digital Opportunity. www.digitalindia.gov.in/ebook/MeitY_TrillionDollarDigitalEconomy.pdf. (Accessed 2 July 2021).
Munshi, S. (2012) *Remote control: Indian television in the new millennium*. Westminster: Penguin.
Negreiro, M. (2015) "Bridging the digital divide in the EU," *European Parliamentary Research Service*.
Nisbett, N. (2007) "Friendship, consumption, morality: practising identity, negotiating hierarchy in middle-class Bangalore," *Journal of the Royal Anthropological Institute* 13 (4): 935–950.
Oreglia, E. (2014) "ICT and (personal) development in rural China," *Information Technologies and International Development* 10 (3): 19–30.
Rangaswamy, N. and Cutrell E. (2012) "Anthropology, development, and ICTs: Slums, youth, and the mobile internet in urban India," *Proceedings of the Fifth International Conference on Information and Communication Technologies and Development*, 85–93.
Robinson, L., Cotton, S. Ono, H., Quan-Haase, A., Mesch, G., and Chen, W. (2015) "Digital inequalities and why they matter," *Information, Communication & Society* 18 (5): 569–582.
Robles, J. M. and Torres Albero, C. (2012) "Digital divide and the information and communication society in Spain," *Journal for Spatial and Socio-Cultural Development Studies* 50 (3): 291–307.
Telecom Statistics of India. (2019) Economics Research Unit: Department of Telecommunications Ministry of Communications. Government of India. New Delhi.

Tenhunen, S. (2018) *A village goes mobile: Telephony, mediation, and social change in rural India*. New York: Oxford University Press.

Tsatsou, P. (2011) "Digital divides revisited: What is new about divides and their research?" *Media, Culture and Society* 33(2): 317–331.

United Nations Children's Fund and International Telecommunication Union. (2020) How many children and young people have internet access at home? Estimating digital connectivity during the COVID-19 pandemic. New York: UNICEF.

Van Dijk, J. (2005) *The deepening divide: Inequality in the information society*. London: Sage.

Van Dijk, J. (2006) "Digital divide research, achievements, and shortcomings," *Poetics* 34 (4-5): 221–235.

Van Dijk, J. (2020) *The digital divide*. Oxford: Polity Press.

Wallis, C. (2015) *Technomobility in China: Young migrant women and mobile phones*. New York: New York University Press.

World Bank. 2012. *Information and communications for development 2012: Maximizing mobile*. Washington, DC: World Bank.

Ventkatraman, S. (2017) *Social media in South India*. London: University College Press.

25

IN THIS TOGETHER

Black Women, Collective Screening Experiences, and Space-Making as Meaning-Making

Marlaina Martin

Introduction

From September 2015 through November 2016, I studied the production and distribution strategies of Black women media-makers working across the New York City boroughs of Brooklyn, Manhattan, and Queens. Over time, I noticed that several preferred to share media they made with audiences in real-time, real-world milieus. I appreciated this push for collective bodily presence as it was conducive to ethnographic research. However, I have since revisited this penchant, now curious about what creators believed such a requirement could offer their media in terms of impact. Why was the preference for in-person screening so common, and for some a deal breaker as to whether they would let their work show in certain capacities (i.e., film festivals versus streaming platforms versus museum exhibits)? This chapter takes up this prompt through two driving questions. First, how do screening programs – agendas that assemble people in time and space for critical conversations – shape viewers' interpretations of media? Second, how might more attention to community exhibition (Ross 2013) by media anthropologists broaden our understanding of the kinds of cultural, narrative, spatial, and bodily reclamation that collective viewing experiences can promote differently than home or commercial theatre viewing?

Collective screening events thrive on what Black feminist icon bell hooks (1989) calls 'choosing the margins of a space of radical openness'. To trace lived examples of such 'radical openness', this chapter analyses a film/video program I attended in Fall 2016 to examine how atmospheres intentionally constructed for collective witness, feedback, and dialogue can transform film-watching into communal, interactive, and intimate experiences for those involved. Organized by a five-member Black women's film collective, this program screened social issues film and video content directed and/or produced by self-identified Black women in three blocks (clusters of two or three works, depending on each's length). The clusters were in turn broken up by Question-and-Answer (Q&A) sessions with representatives of the preceding block's film teams and gaps improvised by the organizers for individual and group reflection.

Additionally, the screening's location in the back space of a dimly lit bar that was otherwise still open for business amplified its already alternative – even rebellious – feel. We came to bare and share our gripes with systems that teach Black people to stay quiet about discriminatory infrastructures of hyper-surveillance and state violence. In that reserved bar area, our self-selected crowd of organizers, creators, and viewers worked to validate and brainstorm solutions with each other without having to tiptoe around unspoken terms of structural racism. Those familiar with the hosting collective and city's broader Black independent film circuit attended screenings like this precisely because they did not have to pander to or even consider acquiescing to whiteness, nor Black women to misogynoir. This chapter examines what 'value added' creators associate with in-person screenings – namely, their expansion of viewers' social, intellectual, physical, and emotional engagement with media, their creators, and fellow spectators with whom they share social interests if not cultural backgrounds.

This chapter earmarks two major reasons to increase anthropological attention to collective screening experiences. First, a focus on screening *events* widens our purview to see the physical, socio-cultural, and ideological terrains in and through which people make meaning(s) about and with media. At screenings, media are not incidental background noise to people's everyday lives – as could be the case for television or YouTube. Rather, they play primary roles in setting a tone for the event and prompting attendees not only to discern patterns and themes, but to also question, bend, bridge, reframe, and relate them to their own experiences. Everyone's historical knowledges, personal and community backgrounds, past experiences, and aspirations have the potential to layer, rework, or redirect how conversations unfold. In shifting from interpreting media as bounded objects to situating them as processes, hubs, and launch pads for social critique and dialogue, analysis of collective screenings stands to include more perspectives (e.g., event organizers, media production and distribution teams, audience members, etc.) and points of debate than an analytical approach that treats film as texts to be properly deciphered by scholars alone.

Second, studying screenings challenges conceptions of media as 'disembodied' by recognizing how attendees' corporeal and affective engagements shape their takeaways. Realistically, people come to these events for the film as well as other reasons, such as to (1) lay symbolic claims to public space as members of socially marginalized groups, (2) hold deliberative and intimate space between Black people and allies, and (3) build more conscious connections to their own physical and emotional selves. While some people presume that the meaning of an audio-visual work is fixed because its plot points are fixed, this chapter argues that screenings allow audiences to speak back to media and their creators as well as other attendees in directions guided by each's unique mix of participant personalities and surrounding current events. Excited by learned anticipation of what collaboration can spark, the film collective channelled into this event their deep understanding of film and video as creative works meant, not to draw conclusions, but to lay groundwork for braver reflections and discussions. Black women creatively and logistically spearheaded the event focused on the theme of 'threat'. Most of them were motivated by their broader social lives as observant, creative, and resourceful women determined to succeed despite the multiple forms of marginalization they experience.

Distance and Distancing in Black Women's U.S. Media Histories

Media allow creators to separate themselves from what – and in this case, who – they depict. Such distance – and the creative license it permits – has been weaponized historically to advance colonial and Empire-building projects. For instance, European explorers circulated dehumanizing images of non-white 'Others' to majority white target audiences as educational materials about mystically primitive, 'less civilized' worlds. European travelogues detailed heroic quelling of African 'savages' (Burton 2000); flyers advertised 'Jardin Zoologique d'Acclimation' (Amusement and Leisure zoos) that toured captured Africans such as Saartjie Baartman around

18th- and early 19th-century Europe as freak show-esque attractions (Gordon-Chipembere 2011); Louis Aggasiz created notorious daguerreotypes of enslaved persons on a plantation in the state of South Carolina, as evidence of their inferiority (Wallis 1995); and W.E.B. Griffith's 1915 feature-length Ku Klux Klan-revering film *The Birth of a Nation* was screened by then-United States President Woodrow Wilson in the White House's East Room, despite mass offense taken by Black communities (Green 2000:6). Ringing of violence, such distances devalued and disregarded Black life without space for Black objection.

Terms of distance grew even more complicated with the advent of 1920s race films in the United States. An alternative media ecosystem championed racial uplift but maintained gender conservatism. Despite a commendable rise of racial counter-images, most credit went to Black men. Studies of this era tend to celebrate creators such as Oscar Micheaux, director of *The Homesteader* (1919) and *Within Our Gates* (1920), and William D. Foster, *Foster Photoplay* production company founder and *The Railroad Porter* (1912) director. Yet there was little recognition of Black women. However, as film historians Claudia Springer (1984) and Jacqueline Bobo (1998) have documented, Alice B. Russell (actress/producer and Oscar Micheaux's wife) and Eloyce King Patrick Gist (co-director of 1933's *Verdict Not Guilty* and 1935's *Heaven-Bound Traveler*) were just a few Black women film creatives active in the U.S. film industry's early years.

Distancing also shaped U.S. Black film's second pronounced wave in the 1990s, which scholars heavily correlate with the rise of Spike Lee's directorial career (Ebert 1991). As Ed Guerrero suggests,

> By exploring in his films a number of socially charged issues that have expanded the nation's perceptions about what it means to be Black in America, Lee has been able to place elements of the African-American experience at the centre of America's popular culture agenda and social imagination.
>
> *1993: 171*

Lauded for works showing gritty and cultured realities of Black life, Lee has stirred both applause and rebuttal. While he has condemned Quentin Tarantino's 2012 U.S. slavery epic *Django Unchained* and the gentrification of New York City, his own depictions of Black women have garnered criticism. For instance, Black feminists have memorably critiqued *She's Gotta Have It* at the risk of being branded 'race traitors'. Michele Wallace (2007) argued that uncritically rallying behind the film because Lee directed it backhandedly worked to fortify stereotypes of Black women as innately and selfishly hypersexual. She attests that, for such defenders, it does not 'appear relevant to mention that *She's Gotta Have It*, the showpiece of the new Black aesthetic, was about a Black woman who couldn't get enough of the old phallus and who therefore had to be raped' (2007: 24). Extreme in its opinion, this comment speaks to issues that arise when people read the progress of Black men as representative of progress of the racial whole, as Black women enter the public zeitgeist in image but not voice.

Returning to the screening at hand, the hosts worked to control for and collapse these ideological, discursive, and physical distances. On top of enabling distortions, such distance can dishearten and convince those represented that they are alone in their struggles. Rather than divide-and-conquer, this screening sought to bring people together to confront 'taboo' topics of racial disparity and distress, and encourage collective critique of standardized racial dogmas. Building on Miriam Ross's assertion that 'films were given meaning through this dialogue and the co-authorship delivered by the audience' (2013: 450), this chapter centres community exhibition as means through which participants co-author and co-reimagine a society built on their labour yet to their disadvantage. However, unlike Ross's interest in community exhibition as interstice between home and commercial theatre viewing, I analyse the relational and embodied dynamics of community exhibition – or what I am calling 'collective screening events' – to observe how they motivate and sanction not only attendees' politics, but their psyches and heartstrings as well.

Furthermore, in studying collective screening events and the experiences they inspire, I stress that participants' diverse backgrounds, bodies, ambitions, and emotions are both integral to and indivisible from event outcomes. Against narratives that mythicize Black agency behind valiant tales of white male ascendance (Trouillot 1995), media anthropology can alternately spotlight the time-proven alienation of Black women from their images and labour by centring situations in which Black women's generative mobilization of bodily and social intimacies are not tangential but fundamental.

A Night Out: Alternatives of Black Media Screening and Engagement

I first met Tanya and the four other members of her Black women film collective at a screening of theirs in 2015. I listened intently during the Q&A as they reflected on what it meant for and required of them to work in (and sometimes around) media systems dominated by white men's finances and thus, their priorities. With varying degrees of boldness, they explained their politicized investments in film/video-making, offered advice to greener and aspiring creators, and denounced racial, gendered, and classed hierarchies that course through contemporary media systems. Touched by their passion, I tried my best to keep in touch with several collective members by phone and social media throughout my 14-month fieldwork period. My mixed-methods research design included participant observation, archival research, content analysis, and approximately 40 semi-structured interviews with Black women and allies I met through them. Occasionally, I would hear from a member notifying me of some project's development or upcoming event. This chapter recalls a 2016 program that I learned about through such an update. However, unlike the first screening I attended, this one did not feature only their works. Instead, it curated some works from their catalogues and others by Black women who were not part of the collective but aligned with its members' radical sensibilities.

Just after dusk on the scheduled date, I hustled down a Brooklyn sidewalk, repeating the building's street number to myself so as not to forget or mistakenly rush past it. Eventually, I came upon a tripod bulletin board with the event's title scrawled across it in neon pink, orange, and green chalk. Slightly confused by the location, I yanked open the front door of a faintly lit 'L'-shaped bar. The entryway led occupants down a relatively narrow walkway alongside the bar counter before opening up into a spacious rectangular atrium. I squeezed through the crowd and soon spotted Tanya leaning against the bar's far end donning her signature bright red lipstick and regally perched locks. She saw me as I made my way over and briefly glanced up from enthused conversation with early arrivals to wave in acknowledgement. As I caught a better view of the layout, I realized that the collective had reserved and flipped this bar's back section into a makeshift screening area. With limited seating, most attendees would remain standing throughout the program. Behind Tanya, a Black DJ hooked up her equipment to fill transitional silences and play atmospheric music throughout the evening. The other collective members multitasked like Tanya: double-checking agenda items and responsibilities, testing equipment, and greeting attendees.

Tanya assumed a main announcer role from the start, welcoming us and naming the program's intentions to critique and reimagine racist structures that delimit possibilities of Black people around the world. Next, she described the night's overarching theme: Black speculative meditations on 'threat' both as Black people are deemed threatening and as they navigate threats that are mundane and spectacular. Maya Stovall speaks to this climate of threat, stressing the self-sacrifice that Black people are expected to perform for others' comfort. She writes that society 'teaches us [Black people] to genuflect to a founding myth – a founding myth made possible with African American people's legislated sacrifice and destruction' (2020: 4). U.S. society makes courage necessary for Black people to do things as ostensibly mundane as walking through residential complexes or driving one's officially licensed car, for fear they will not make it home alive. Hence, gatherings such as this can help affirm the very real basis of social anxieties and expose injustices that Black people are socialized to either 'prove' or bottle up inside. The films and videos creatively dissected norms that push African-descended people to internalize both guilt for threats they allegedly 'present' to others (Shange 2019, Steele 2010), and environments of threat they are made to face because of such stereotyping (Ahmed 2004). Whether via revisitation, revision, or reimagination, the curated mix of media used innovative Black women-made amalgams of image, word, sound, and silence to catalyse our group confrontation with toxic tropes of Blackness as menacing, thuggish, and deserving of containment and harm.

The program proceeded in three rotations, each including a block of three to four short film and video screenings, Q&A sessions with affiliated cast and crew, and interceding periods for responsive contemplation and dialogue. Overall, the event urged viewers to critically confront difficult topics, but in a context salved with community support. The evening's pieces flouted various aesthetics; lighting, sound, and colour designs; genres (or blurring thereof); countries of origin; storytelling styles; and degrees of commitment to (or abandonment of) realism. The works not only spotlighted anti-Black structures and standards but foregrounded their human costs (i.e., feelings, fears, fatigues, and frustrations). In this purposefully conjured space, creatives and interested community members came together to watch media that recognized and reflected their ethno-racial identities and gave them opportunities to ask questions and be in conversation with creators and each other during Q&A talkback sessions.

The event assembled films and videos that diversely addressed intersections of Blackness, policing, surveillance, white supremacy, and threat. As marginalized social subjects, the Black women who helmed this event and created its constitutive projects had already done the immense, and at-times uncomfortable work of translating the ambivalence of threat – especially Blackness-concerned threat – into audio-visual forms. Among such threats are disparate mortality and incarceration rates, structural racism, housing, and employment precarity, and higher risk of suffering police brutality. Some of the night's creators goaded critical thought with utopian imaginings of equity and/or achievement. Others took a different approach, thinking up dysphoric scenarios to call attention to social ills via hyperbole. Some pieces mused on the abuse of Black bodies by way of gunfire, batons, drug epidemics, and governmental neglect. Others foregrounded surrealism, using jolty sensations of jump-cuts, phrase repetition, animated graphic overlays, documentary-narrative hybrids, unrealistic pacing, and audio-visual misalignment among other effects to punctuate the absurdity of racial hierarchy and herald Afro-inspired rhythms, values, and auras borne from loss but also resourcefulness and innovation (Yearwood 2000). No matter how conceptual or concrete these portrayals leaned, they all explored threats against Black embodiment and social mechanisms cultivated to reduce if not obviate them.

While the works ranged in aesthetic style, geographic locale, and levels of investment in (or divestment from) realism, they all mulled over the presence, actions, and capacities of Blackness via the explicit centring (or omission) of Black bodies. One film followed a dark-skinned Black Cuban woman as she danced joyously through the streets to claim (an ultimately precarious) mobility and freedom. Another condemned the endemic rates of slain Black people through an experimental piece on the murder and memorialization of Trayvon Martin. A third exposed structural absentia and amnesia by ruminating on the high percentages of Black men removed from everyday society by either death or incarceration. Thus, the promise of engaging Black imaginative media lay not only in its alternative histories, settings, characters, and takeaways, but also its aims to centre viewers in vantage points and reveries that general society has largely bastardized as a subhuman and inferior 'Other'. As a special benefit to shared screening contexts, the films' addressing of Blackness with, through, or tellingly absent of Black bodies (vis-à-vis incarceration or homicide) invited viewers to weave their own bodily and embodied knowledges into their modes of interpreting the evening's offerings. Here, media texts operated as reflections of creators' thoughts and what Black visual culture scholar Tina Campt calls *still-moving-images*, which

> require us to engage the *overlapping sensory realms of the visual, the sonic, the haptic, and the affective labour* that constellates in, around, and in response to such images. Still-moving-images demand our affective labour through their capacity to touch or move us and through the labour they require to manage, refuse, or deny their affects.
>
> *2019: 27, emphasis added*

The curated film/video pieces may be understood as *still-moving-images* because one of their primary goals is to emotionally provoke audiences into deep thought and engagement. To stir affective response, these pieces took advantage of technology's capacities for non-realism. They de- and re-centred, re-paced, and in some cases completely rewrote histories and powerholders into media forms able to address race, gender, and other social discourses with greater expressive leniency and imprints of creators' own lessons learned. Nonetheless, these works were meant to be sincerely questioned, digested, and built upon by every viewing audience – a grand co-production of meaning, indeed.

Co-Production of Meaning: Why Screening Events are Important Sites of Inquiry

As media anthropologists have long argued, media's meanings are not fixed at the moment of creation, but evolve. After all, media are cultural artefacts that people interpret through lenses coloured by their backgrounds, values, expectations, commitments, and questions. Media's significance comes from people's ability to relate to its interests, learn lessons, and engage in conversations with others who consume the same thing but come away with completely different interpretations.

Although early uses of media by anthropologists popularly assumed its greater 'objectivity', our discipline has grown to understand media as a human creation. Cameras entered ethnographic toolkits in the late 19th century as a way to visually document supposedly 'vanishing' societies' (Mead 2003). Therefore, a major reason to adopt video and audio recording into one's research methods was to invisibly – unseen by the camera – and supposedly 'objectively' capture visual 'data' (Weinberger 1992). Such 'evidence' was thought irrefutable by some because, as the idiom goes, 'seeing is believing'. However, with time and debates such as those around Robert J. Flaherty's controversial *Nanook of the North*, anthropologists have increasingly recognized that media's greatest potential lay not in representation of some absolute Truth, but in the situated dialogues and dissonances they help bring to light. After all, as Civil Rights activist James Baldwin (1962) asserts, 'Not everything that is faced can be changed. But nothing can be changed until it is faced.'

So, if we accept the futile and unhelpful impossibility of the age-old search for Truth (Rosaldo 1989), how might we study media otherwise? Perhaps we can look instead to social thought, practice, and action, and focus not on media *per se* but on conditions, spaces, interactions, and politics of media engagement that helped them get made. In such a situation, screenings serve as ideal research 'sites'. Mechanically, they are concentrated hubs of communication prepped and primed to nurture people's varied engagements with media forms and other attendees – and with relatively low stakes. Such media curation and usage operate on the presumption that media are not finite nor unchangeable. Conversely, they can be mobilized as creators' modes of expression as well as tone-setters for collective screening sessions. These sessions, unlike the everyday 'colorblind racisms' (Bonilla-Silva 2003) of U.S. neoliberalism, take sexism, racism, misogyny, classism, and other systemic disparities as givens rather than exceptions to some discursively upheld advertisement of structural equity. Undeterred by distractions lobbed by white supremacist culture (Bonilla-Silva 2003, Morrison 1975), these experiences also raise baselines of engagement. They push viewers to actively digest pieces, sounds, storylines, and dialogues that take structural racism and misogynoir as given. In doing so, they seek higher-level analysis of Black struggle – and also Black joy – amid racist global systems and their local iterations.

Beyond instincts to treat media as factual objects, anthropologists have increasingly understood them to be constructed interpretations of moments, situations, and interactions passed – that is, if they ever happened at all (Baudrillard 1994). Nick Couldry challenges media studies scholars' tendency to privilege content analysis, theorising 'media as practice' as means to 'decentre media research from the study of media texts or production structures (important though these are) and to redirect it onto the study of the open-ended range of practices focused directly or indirectly on media' (2004: 117). Along similar lines, Dominic Boyer posits 'social mediation' to broaden media anthropology's interests beyond the material text. He writes,

> it is very difficult to separate the operation of communicational media cleanly from broader social-political processes of *circulation, exchange, imagination and knowing* … what we might gloss as processes of social mediation: i.e. social transaction in its broadest sense of the movement of images, discourse, persons and things.
>
> *2012: 383*

Also interested in what such reframing could yield, I too ask what interpersonal relations, commitments, and conflicts might get clearer when studied not through media texts but people's behaviours, tensions, talks, and testimonies as enabled by and through them.

A much-cited paradigm shift, Black cultural studies mainstay Stuart Hall penned 'Encoding and Decoding in the Television Discourse' to trace pathways through which people create, interpret, attribute, adapt, and splinter media's meaning(s). Hall complicates misinterpretations of media consumption as bounded, passive, and unidirectional by – via words and charts – describing co-constitutive ebbs and flows of meaning that happen across producers' and consumers' respective 'frameworks of knowledge', 'structures of production', and 'technical infrastructure'. This intervention is significant because it reiterates that media's meanings are not copied-and-pasted onto mindless receivers. Rather, meanings morph and blossom as they circulate through local and global contexts. Hall also acknowledges that power inequities and overarching social relations inevitably shape how differently positioned social subjects interpret and experience media, and in what situations and company. He explains,

> The degrees of symmetry – that is, the degrees of 'understanding' and 'misunderstanding' in the communicative exchange depend both on the degrees of symmetry/a-symmetry

> between the position of encoder-producer and that of the decoder-receiver: and also on the degrees of identity/non-identity between the codes which perfectly or imperfectly transmit, interrupt or systematically distort what has been transmitted.
>
> Hall 1973: 4

Here, Hall frames interpretation as a process that can monopolize power but can also radically reroute and reclaim it. Catered to attract people from relevant social and cultural interest groups, these non-mainstream screening events produce outcomes much different than those organized for more general audiences. In support of this narrower focus, Clyde Taylor insists that Black cinema must be located in socio-political conditions that precede, succeed, and surround it: 'The screen and theatrical space of the new Black cinema is one the spectator can enter and exit without carrying away the glazed eyes and the afterglow of erotic-egotistic enchantment that identifies the colonized moviegoer' (1983: 46). Insistent that Black cinema has a 'responsibility to social reality' that makes cinematic escape for escape's sake more of the exception than the rule, Taylor ardently blurs lines typically drawn between character and person, and between producer and consumer. In his words,

> Both filmmakers and spectators can move easily and interchangeably before and behind the camera without drastic alterations of character…It is a space open *to wide-ranging possibilities, yet free of the illusionism whose effects make mainstream commercial films so superficially enchanting.*
>
> 1983: 46, emphasis added

Ethnographic study of collective screening experiences asks questions that media anthropologists have studied more in casual, recurring, and longitudinal contexts such as families' living room chatter over broadcast television serials (Schulthies 2013, Abu-Lughod 2005) or radio show hosts' on-air chats with listeners (Squires 2000, Spitulnik 1997). Some such questions include: How do people's real-time engagements with media enable new meanings to be made of the themes, provocations, and takeaways? What benefits and oversights come from viewing media – especially socially-oriented media – with others? However, on top of studying media consumption as social practice, a 'collective screening' approach adds elements of creator intentions and public space. In screening situations, media are not happenstance or background to more conscious everyday life (i.e., family conversations, driving to work). Instead, they are critical to proceeding interactions. Event organizers commit money, labour, and time to design one-time events that put attendees in direct and potentially unnerving relation with and around these media's driving themes. The media docket and encompassing event are meant to inspire attendees to collaboratively name injustice, negotiate stake, and imagine alternatives. Ultimately, the screened media endorse curiosity and encourage participants to grab hold of the cathartic comforts of collective social critique.

At this juncture of media anthropology and Black radical imagination, a 'collective screening experience' framework leans into the uncertainty, irresolution, and complexities that characterize *Blackness* not as systems try to contain it, but as people actually *live* it. Especially considering its central subjects and themes, this analysis intuits a Black feminist politic convinced that one must account for the many registers, cultural capitals, embodied knowledges, and communal investments at work in efforts to elevate the talents and takes of people that U.S. structures have exploited and diminished for centuries. This chapter then extends Couldry's and Boyer's attention to media as practice and process, Hall's to the dynamism of media's semantic flows, and Taylor's to social and cultural pragmatics. Combining the work of these scholars with Black feminist thought is intended to redirect inquiry from media texts to media events, as they are planned and facilitated to prod oft-shunned conversations in close, intentional quarters – here, in the back of an unassuming bar. Such condensed but extremely rich conditions allow us to follow detailed interactions as they happen. They also allow us to discover what other questions and realizations might arise when dialectics of meaning and power become possible through people encountering media not in distanced succession between geographic sites, but in interactive and intimate proximity with media content, creators, and other viewers.

Visceral Validation: Reclaiming Space, Body, and Affect

Societal leaders have long used notions of the public – and variations such as 'public sphere' and 'public space' – to imprint rules of inclusion and exclusion on perceived community members and, consequently, non-members. This event space fostered radically different terms of belonging. Thus, in addition to being more cost-effective than renting out a commercial theatre, the bar was a public space to claim. We shimmied around that bar's still very much public space, aware – however subconsciously – of the potential dangers of 'being in public' and the socio-political statement of 'taking up space' while Black in the United States. As a unit, we watched Black people dance and make music in the streets, or fashion home lives 'safe' from the ominous unpredictability of public space, or probe GPS images of streets existing far beyond the Black lives stolen on them.

All participants had ventured to that bar in search of solace and solidarity, effectively reversing perceptions of danger Black people come to expect outside – and in cases, also inside – their homes. Thus, beyond symbolism, space has meaning in the literal sense of being located in the world. As a group, we not only dared to occupy public space, but to reserve and revamp it to meet our needs. With the collective's leadership, we flipped the arrangement and usage – and in so doing, the utility and purpose – of the space to assist us in critiquing Black subservience and assimilation, and uplifting Black cooperation, expression, and social support. We, an intergenerational group committed to social justice, lingered, and lavished in the space on both embodied and symbolic levels. The rest of this chapter dives into these bodily and affective possibilities as a particularly salient gain that collective screening experiences open up.

Squeezing into what was a tight fit for the 20 or so people present, attendees had little choice but to stand in clusters, some of us even grazing shoulders. While the bar space generally felt more welcoming than the individuating setup of commercial theatre seats faced forward and literally separated with arm rests, it did not offer much in terms of seating. I only saw some odd stools absconded from elsewhere in the bar and a few small booths – most rightly reserved for elderly and physically disabled attendees and the rest filled by V.I.P.s (e.g., mentors, colleagues) and a few lucky early arrivals. Curious about this non-normative setup, I let myself think both outward and inward, noting how attendees' bodily dispositions and orientations here differed from both conventional screening environments and bar patrons using the front of the establishment. Remarkably, the patrons' levity and drink-induced disconnect from reality clashed with our dive into some of reality's most pressing mortal threats. From several directions, the night's agenda enlisted our bodies in a jarring union of a non-normative screening atmosphere and media depicting the maddening normality of structural anti-Blackness.

As we braced ourselves to watch films about Black life in settings threatened with Black death, our corporeal forms were not to be ignored. Over time, I noticed more and more people swaying or shifting weight between their legs, whether to find chance sightlines between the heads of people in front of them or relieve aches and numbing tingles that gradually crept up through their ankles, calves, thighs, and lower backs. While I cannot know how everyone felt inside about each film/video piece, I can attest that our hours'-long communion prompted us to hone not just intellectual but also 'somatic modes of attention'. As Thomas Csordas explains, 'to attend to a bodily sensation is not to attend to the body as an isolated object, but to attend to the body's situation in the world ... a mode of attending to the intersubjective milieu that give rise to that sensation' (1993: 138). Tasked with simultaneously attending 'with' and 'to' our bodies, we commingled (and commiserated) in a dull soreness that conversely attuned and forced us to reckon with our embodied present. While some people cycled out and late arrivals did appear, most stuck around from start to finish to rotate through screening periods to conversations and back again. Rather than zoning out and mentally fleeing into some alternate universe, the screening experience in that bar was designed to return us to bodies that society had repeatedly taught us to overlook.

In its setup and the asks it makes of attendees, the space ushered forth a co-negotiation that compelled me to contemplate not only the social assumptions and signifiers imposed on my and others' bodies, but also how my physical body filled and felt in this shared space. This also cued me to consciously consider fatigue, cosiness, and emotional pulls on my body, and wonder where, how, and why I – as a rotund, mocha-skinned Black cis-woman in the United States – had learned to ignore my body's aches and needs. Our bodies-in-attendance were not just conceptually, but actively enrolled as pivotal parts of the screening experience itself. This visceral bringing-back of one's body to mind and one's mind to body proved cathartic, especially against a society that teaches non-white non-men to discount, disguise, or disappear their bodies whenever and however possible (Fordham 1993, Fanon 1952).

Beyond physical considerations, this screening experience compelled us to feel and feed off one another's energies differently. We benefitted from an affective charge resonant with Judith Butler's analysis of crowds and public protest. She rejects romantic abstractions of 'protest' to acknowledge real bodies partaking in them. She suggests that studies of protestors' performative claims on public space must go beyond stated demands to consider 'the bodily dimensions of action, what the body requires, and what the body can do, especially when we must think about bodies together, what holds them there, their conditions of persistence and of power' (Butler 2011: 1–2). With this, Butler traces the potential power of social actions not to individuals nor protest sites, but to the unscripted exuberance that comes of people who convene in public space to air grievances and press for social change. Stressing the importance of bodily presence in meaningful protest demonstrations and politics more broadly, she attests:

> For politics to take place, the body must appear. I appear to others, and they appear to me, which means that some space between us allows each to appear.... No one body establishes the space of appearance, but this action, this performative exercise happens only 'between' bodies, in a space that constitutes the gap between my own body and another's. In this way, my body does not act alone, when it acts politically. Indeed, the action emerged from the 'between.'
>
> 2011: 2

While most do not happen on public streets, collective screening experiences also carve out explicit domains for people to gather to confront, digest, interpret, and discern lessons from potentially sensitive media, each person reminding the next they are not alone. Hence, screening events work not only through media content they show and conversations they promote, but also conditions they create for social, interpersonal, spatial, and physical engagement. The organizers leveraged closeness and capacity for real-time dialogue to encourage discussions about topics that might be deemed 'radical' and 'improper' in more general industry screening and networking contexts. Introspections that the films and videos provoked in viewers were cradled and magnified by other audience members' reactions and commentaries. Gathering made signals such as gestures, sighs, head nods, and shoulder pats more noticeable – leaving marks that would probably be dampened over a video chat and lost on a phone call. Assemblies such as these – helmed by marginalized people in public space – expand what media can signify and accomplish for participants, particularly on registers of spatial, bodily, and affective reclamation. The intimate, immediate, and in-person nature of screenings goes beyond supporting resistance to help people embody, enact, and connect with it, recalibrating the conversation's very baseline of racial knowledge and sensitivity.

Emotions are also part of both protest and collective screening events. While protest organizers utilize social media invites and chants to regulate participants' expectations, screenings orient attendees to the event's inquiring tone and intent via an introductory script (by Tanya at the top of the night) and its curation of emotionally provoking – some heartening, some heart-wrenching – and fittingly progressive media. Rather than swallowing or hiding signs of these, whatever anger, sadness, and joy that overcome them behind dense intellectual terminology, viewers rested on group dynamics of understanding, care, and solidarity whenever the feelings got to be too much. This is particularly comforting for Black people used to the silencing tactics of whiteness and patriarchy. Aware that people's emotions are indivisible from projects of socio-political advancement, the screening's hosts positioned attendees' bodies and embodied experiences as legitimate sources of knowledge and attached the most value, not to the event site nor the films, but to people's active engagement with both of these and one another. The program utilized the bar and film blocks as scaffolding on which to have rich conversations to help participants attain sharper awareness of their fragility and vulnerability as well as their strength, determination, and support networks both pre-existing and possible. Across ages, countries of origin, and race, gender, and class identities, participants cared less about media's degrees of facticity than about the sensorial and bodily revelations they could elicit and channel into conscious modes of reflection and dialogue.

Conclusion: Black Un/Imagining in Collective Screening Spaces

Breaching templates that jump to study media as object makes space to recognize both hurdles that creators navigate throughout production and distribution, and – as this chapter's focus – people who voluntarily attend and participate in exhibition programming. Such approaches, when totalizing, are not only misguided but they restrict our ability to do due diligence to the web of forces at play in collective screening events. Some of these include the creator's project intentions and behind-the-scenes accounts; event organizers' choices in film curation, film/video screening order, and other program components; and audience members' various ways of interpreting, relating to, and drawing conclusions about the media and ensuant conversations. Combined, these elements guide attendees on journeys of collective awareness- and narrative-building that are ultimately unique to the mix of people, films, recent world events, and interventions that shape screenings individually.

Overall, this collective screening event assembled films, creators, and viewers to challenge white supremacist norms and ask participants to engage on such terms. Counter to a society that expects them to act 'strong' or 'flawless' to earn respect, these screenings give people permission to release reductive facades and express life's doubts and uncertainties with people likely to have similar questions. Dispelling industry norms that have gilded in-theatre screenings and white men directors as standards, these events presume that media can present, travel, and even *feel* different depending on how, where, and among whom people produce and consume them.

Concentrated on the latter, this chapter highlighted decentralized, non-mainstream exhibition events as ethnographic sites with which to better understand what intentional collective witness and engagement can add to intellectual and emotional experiences of media-watching. During a program beholden to Black women's visions, attendees were not just cognizant but made active use of this climate to re-conceptualize and articulate issues frequently left unquestioned if not shallowly entertained for optics' sake in dominant media contexts.

Restricting outsiders' wanton access to Blackness, the hosts and involved media-makers organized this event to challenge framings of Black people as inherently accessible, transparent, subordinate, and 'threatening', especially in groups. Alternatively, these media and conversations called out ideological lineages that have enduringly marked Blackness as distinctly dangerous in order to get away with structural exploitation and abuse of Blackness. Putting action behind their belief in Black excellence, the hosting collective provided space and activities that questioned the hollow and opportunistic terms on which society has labelled them and their gatherings 'dangerous'. After all, they met *en masse* to talk about racism without masking codes, euphemisms, or witty turns-of-phrase – and without any hint of the violence and destruction that political discourse has attributed to Blackness-centric gatherings. Quite the opposite, our group sought to be in intimate relationship with each other and, it turned out, our own bodies. We aimed to 'be in' and 'take up' space to rejuvenate our spirits and recoup hope from the everyday drain of white supremacy, and to claim as principle our legal and moral right to public space. This collective screening experience succeeded because its hosts, featured creators, and participants united in 'the margin as a space of radical openness'. Rather than seeing the bar as a budget-friendly but inferior compromise, we treated it as means to drive home the radically different criteria they would use to assess value of media content as well as its social lives and implications – among them, emotional honesty, historical revisionism, culture-minded aesthetics.

In conclusion, collective screening events and the experiences they enable deserve much more attention in media anthropology and the wider discipline. This purview can examine terms, tones, tensions, and triumphs of public interface to shine light on wider-reaching themes. Media do not have fixed meanings. Rather, meanings accrue, fracture, and change as people contemplate, debate, and apply them. The organizing collective – and I, via this chapter – contend that media programming such as this not only curates but encourages commitment to the continued cultivation and elevation of radical Black visions unafraid to repurpose public space, and to go beyond mere presence in shared space to create re/generative community with one another.

References

Abu-Lughod, Lila. 2005. *Dramas of Nationhood: The Politics of Television in Egypt*. Chicago: University of Chicago Press.
Ahmed, Sara. 2004. 'Affective Economies.' *Social Text* 79, 22(2): 117–139.
Baldwin, James. 1962. 'As Much Truth as One Can Bear.' *New York Times*.
Baudrillard, Jean. 1994. *Simulacra and Simulation*. Translated by Sheila Glaser. Ann Arbor: University of Michigan Press.
Bobo, Jacqueline. 1998. *Black Women Film & Video Artists*. New York: Routledge.
Bonilla-Silva, Eduardo. 2003. *Racism without Racists: Color-blind Racism and the Persistence of Racial Inequality in the United States*. 2nd Edition. New York: Rowman & Littlefield.
Boyer, Dominic. 2012. 'From Media Anthropology to Anthropology of Mediation.' In *The SAGE Handbook of Anthropology*. Thousand Oaks: Sage.
Burton, John. 2000. 'Disappearing Savages? Thoughts on the Construction of an Anthropological Conundrum.' *Journal of Asian & African Studies* 35(4): 453.

Butler, Judith. 2011. 'Bodies in Alliance and the Politics of the Street.' #*Occupy Los Angeles Reader* 1–3: 1–11.
Campt, Tina. 2019. 'The Visual Frequency of Black Life: Love, Labor and the Practice of Refusal.' *Social Text* 37(3): 25–46.
Couldry, Nick. 2004. 'Theorising Media as Practice.' *Social Semotics* 14(2): 115–132.
Csordas, Thomas. 1993. 'Somatic Modes of Attention.' *Cultural Anthropology* 8(2): 135–156.
Ebert, Roger. 1991. 'A High Tide for Black New Wave.' Rogerebert.com. Accessed 12 January 2022. Electronic Resource. www.rogerebert.com/roger-ebert/its-high-tide-for-black-new-wave.
Fanon, Frantz. 1952. *Black Skin, White Masks*. New York: Grove Press.
Fordham, Signithia. 1993. '"Those Loud Black Girls": (Black) Women, Silence, and Gender "Passing" in the Academy.' *Anthropology & Education* 24(1): 3–32.
Foster, William D. 1912. *The Railroad Porter*. The Foster Photoplay Company.
Gordon-Chipembere, Natasha (ed.). 2011. *Representation and Black Womanhood: The Legacy of Sarah Baartman*. New York: Palgrave MacMillan.
Green, Ronald. 2000. *Straight Lick: The Cinema of Oscar Micheaux*. Bloomington: Indiana University Press.
Griffith, D.W. and Thomas Dixon. 1915. *Birth of a Nation*. Los Angeles, CA: Triangle Film Corp.
Guerrero, Ed. 1993. *Framing Blackness: The African American Image in Film*. Philadelphia: Temple University Press.
Hall, Stuart. 1973. Encoding and Decoding in the Television Discourse. Colloquium Paper. Centre for Contemporary Cultural Studies, University of Birmingham
hooks, bell. 1989. 'Choosing the Margin as a Space of Radical Openness.' *Framework: The Journal of Cinema and Media* 36: 15–23.
Mead, Margaret. 2000. 'Visual Anthropology in a Discipline of Words.' In *Principles of Visual Anthropology*, Paul Hockings (ed.). Berlin: De Gruyter Mouton, 1–10.
Micheaux, Oscar. 1919. *The Homesteader*. Micheaux Book & Film Company.
Micheaux, Oscar. 1920. *Within Our Gates*. Micheaux Film Corporation.
Morrison, Toni. 1975. *Keynote*. Portland: Portland State University.
Rosaldo, Renato. 1989. 'After Objectivism.' In *Culture & Truth: The Remaking of Social Analysis*. Boston: Beacon, 46–67.
Ross, Miriam. 2013. 'Interstitial Film Viewing: Community Exhibition in the Twenty-first Century.' *Continuum: Journal of Media & Cultural Studies* 27(3): 446–457.
Schulthies, Becky. 2013. 'Reasonable Affects: Moroccan Family Responses to Mediated Violence.' In *Discourses of War and Peace*, Adam Hodges (ed.). Oxford: Oxford University Press.
Shange, Savannah. 2019. *Progressive Dystopia: Abolition, Antiblackness and Schooling in San Francisco*. Durham: Duke University Press.
Spitulnik, Debra. 1997. 'The Social Circulation of Media Discourse and the Mediation of Communities.' *Journal of Linguistic Anthropology* 6(2): 161–187.
Springer, Claudia. 1984. 'Black Women Filmmakers.' *Jump Cut: A Review of Contemporary Media*. 29: 34–37.
Squires, Catherine. 2000. 'Black Talk Radio: Defining Community Needs and Identity.' *Press/Politics* 5(2): 73–95.
Steele, Claude. 2010. *Whistling Vivaldi: How Stereotypes Affect Us and What We Can Do*. New York: W.W. Norton & Company.
Stovall, Maya. 2020. *Liquor Store Theatre*. Durham: Duke University Press.
Tarantino, Quentino. 2012. *Django Unchained*. The Weinstein Company.
Taylor, Clyde. 1983. 'New U.S. Black Cinema.' *Jump Cut* 28: 46–48.
Trouillot, Michel-Rolph. 1995. *Silencing the Past: Power and the Production of History*. Boston: Beacon Press.
Wallace, Michele. 2007. 'Spike Lee and Black Women.' In *The Spike Lee Reader*, Paula Massood (ed.). Philadelphia, PA: Temple University Press.
Wallis, Brian. 1995. 'Black Bodies, White Science: Louis Agassiz's Slave Daguerrotypes.' *American Art* 9(2): 38–61.
Weinberger, Eliot. 1992. 'The Camera People.' *Transition* 55: 24–54.
Yearwood, Gladstone Lloyd. 2000. *Black Film as a Signifying Practice: Cinema, Narration and the African American Aesthetic Tradition*. Trenton: Africa World Press.

26
BLACK GAMER'S REFUGE
Finding Community within the Magic Circle of Whiteness

Akil Fletcher

Introduction

So, why do you play video games when it can be harmful to play?
Because I grew up playing video games! And I refuse to let people run me out of a space that I grew up loving.

Sapphire—Black Girl Gamers

In 1938, Johann Huizinga in his work *Homo-Ludens* theorized games as unique social spaces in which the specific rules of the game supplant the rules of society and create a realm of play. This allows for the existence of a game and its unique behaviours (Phillips 2020), or the "magic circle." Those who break the rules of this space, however, shatter this game realm and become what Huizinga calls a "spoil sport." While these definitions have been useful in understanding how game zones are unique from other spaces in society, both game scholars and anthropologists alike have critiqued the short comings of viewing a game as a vacuum or closed-off space (Taylor 2018). Indeed, with the rise in popularity of online gaming it has become harder to view gaming spaces as the closed magic circles Huizinga put forth in his work. Online games through their connection to the internet exist in a state of intermediality, where they are connected to multiple forms of social media, streaming websites, and communication apps. However, this does not mean that games as a form of polymedia (Miller and Madianou 2013), do not exist without boundaries. After all, digital anthropologists such as Boellstorff (2008) and Nardi (2010) have written extensively on the fact that games exist and create their own unique cultures. Rather, it is that the boundaries of what many consider a game have expanded and become porous. They are similar to a cell filtering content in and out while remaining its own unique entity.

Yet, as these boundaries expand to include multiple forms of media and digital communities, there has been a need to reframe what is thought of as a game or gaming space itself. This is because online video games today are sites for more than just gameplay. Most notably, games and gaming spaces have become powerful sites for anti-Black discrimination, in part through numerous attacks on marginalized gamers and streamers. In 2021, musician Faheem Rasheed Najm, better known by his stage name, "T-Pain," was attacked while streaming on Twitch by an opposing team calling him the N-word. Events like these display that online video games are more than just the game itself, but an interweaving of gameplay and anti-Black social dynamics. We must understand this instance not simply as T-Pain being called the N-word as an insult, but as an integral part of the gameplay for his white attackers.

For this reason, when considering race and gaming, typical definitions of a game or gaming space simply do not fit. But how then does one make sense of an evolving gaming space that is not only deeply affected by race, but sees race become a tool of gameplay? Here, while Huizinga's definition of a game/gaming space is not without its shortcomings, I believe it can be useful in understanding the role race plays within multiplayer online games and the media which connects to them. This is because despite its limitations, Huizinga provides a definition which sees the world of a game constructed through a set of rules—for example if you are playing chess the world demands that you move your pieces correctly to maintain the game. But what if instead of a set of game rules, the boundaries of the magic circle or "game" were instead formed by a set of cultural rules or logics? Specifically, what if the "magic circle" of online games weren't just formed by the guidelines of the game, but reconceptualized to be formed by the cultural logics of a hetero white male gaming culture? This conceptualization could be used to understand the ways in which race has come to influence online gaming—a conceptualization that I coin "the magic circle of whiteness" (MCW).

I define the magic circle of whiteness as a conceptual tool which builds upon Huizinga's definition of the magic circle by viewing online games and connected medias not just as isolated spaces maintained by a set of rules or guidelines, but as spaces dictated and maintained by a set of white cultural logics. This is because, historically, video games in the U.S (both online and off) have been typically viewed as the domain of white men seeking to affirm their identity in technological know-how, constructing a form of what Kocurek (2015) calls "technomasculinity." Indeed, with about 70 per cent of game developers in the U.S being white men (Browne 2020), and most human-appearing main video game characters being of the same demographics, video games in the U.S have centred whiteness in their creation and proliferation. This, along with the popular trope within media of the downtrodden white gamer, has resulted in many games and gaming spaces being viewed as predominantly white, with many white male gamers coming to internalize and act upon this belief. This can be seen in examples such as #Gamergate[1] which was a hate campaign against women and people of colour by white men who largely felt that their games were being threatened by diversity (Gray 2016). However, the MCW is not formed or maintained simply by individual attacks, but rather is the coalescence of a white hegemony within gaming, that sees its industries, products, and players act upon and maintain a white status quo.

Here, I build upon other scholars, such as Everett and Watkins' (2008), who have discussed how games can work as sites of harmful racial learning in what they call "racialized pedagogical zones." Further, anthropologists such as Malaby (2007), have stressed the importance of realizing that games are influenced directly by those who play them, writing that they are "processes" which "always contain the potential for generating new practices and new meanings." (Malaby 2007: 102). However, it is through my own research that the premise for the MCW comes to form, as throughout my time researching Black gamers and Black gaming spaces, I have come to see the ways in which white forces have come to terrorize and deject Black gaming spaces.

Specifically, throughout 2019 I had the opportunity to play with, talk to, and interview several Black gamers as a part of my ongoing research on Black gaming spaces and communities. Many of them commented on the reality of "games not being made for them," and expressed feelings that the industry only catered to white individuals. Additionally, within my research I also spent time with multiple Black groups on popular gaming communication apps like

Discord where many of the Black members (including myself) experienced harassment from white actors spewing insults and invading the space. One group I participated in was Black People Discord (BPD), a public Black online group on Discord, which unfortunately dissolved due to a deluge of similar white discrimination and harassment during my time of research. However, BPD was unique in that members were not simply scared into leaving the app, but instead the group was slowly transformed from Black space to generalized space by a combination of white attackers and white individuals who joined the space to find their own pleasure. It was from their fate that I developed the concept of the MCW to help better understand how Black space was deconstructed and overwhelmed by whiteness, not just in the form of racist attacks but by the consumption of Black space for white play or pleasure.

It should be said that not everything I experienced in my research was negative. In fact, through engaging with my participant and friend Sapphire I was shown the possibilities for Black joy in larger anti-Black online settings. She was a member of the group Black Girl Gamers (BGG), an organization of Black women gamers spread through multiple websites and spaces. While she and others in BGG have been attacked for being Black women in gaming spaces, they have found ways to not only exist, but thrive in a larger anti-Black gaming industry. Utilizing private online spaces such as Facebook groups and Discord channels, this UK- and US-based group have found ways to build community despite being bombarded by non-Black attackers. In fact, they are so successful that it is here where I found the second half of my theoretical framework. Just as Huizinga's spoil sport denied the rules of the game, shattering the magic circle, Sapphire and her comrades portrayed this same outcome. By finding joy and community in a white space structured to prevent this, they denied the logics of the MCW. Instead, they exemplified what I term the "Black Spoil Sport," an identity which I base within the acts of refusal and fugitive expressions performed by these gamers in the MCW.

It is this dichotomy between the MCW and the Black Spoil Sport, which serves as the core of this chapter. I seek to provide anthropology a better way to understand the reality of Blackness and gaming, and display how online video games, connected media, and participants in the U.S are shaped by race. Specifically, I explore how a hegemonic whiteness marks Blackness and Black players as a "gaming other" working to remove Blackness to maintain itself. Thus, in this chapter, I will engage with the ethnographic data I have collected from my time with BPD and my interviews with Sapphire about BGG and her own experiences to explore how a white hegemony or "whiteness as default" within gaming influences the experiences and navigational practices of Black gamers and online users.

Ironically, I will not be discussing any specific game in this chapter but instead placing the focus of my analysis on Black media spaces connected to the larger gaming ecosystem, to understand the challenges Black individuals face when trying to use these spaces to circumvent or cope with the racism they experience when gaming. The body of this chapter is broken into two parts. The first will recount the collapse of the online/gaming community BPD, to explore how Black communities are at risk within the MCW. Specifically, I discuss the ways in which whiteness in both deleterious and well-meaning forms can work to eject Black online community from gaming spaces and reaffirm the MCW.

The second section will elaborate on the concept of the Black Spoil Sport by exploring the tactics of BGG to maintain a Black presence within the circle. I illustrate the possibilities for Black existence within the circle and demonstrate how through their success in navigating and finding space within it, they come to resist the logics of the MCW and encapsulate the identity of the Black Spoil Sport. By applying these two concepts, I contribute to both the anthropology of media and digital spaces, with a way to interpret racial trends among interconnected forms of polymedia. Providing this framework aids in the study of multi-sited digital projects, but more broadly provides a useful tool in understanding spaces that are dictated by hegemonic white forces within a period of rapidly growing digital media.

The Dissolution of Black People Discord

When setting out to study how Black people experienced, navigated, and made sense of online gaming spaces, Discord was immediately one of the first places I went to. This is because since its launch in 2015, Discord has become a staple among a wide variety of gaming communities. Created by Jason Citron and his partner Stanislav Vishnevsky, Discord is a form of video, speech/audio, and text chat communication program similar to predecessors like Skype, but unique in that it was targeted towards gamers. It was created to allow them to join persistent servers (both private and public) which served as hubs for interaction. These servers allow anyone moderators approve into a space where users can send messages and communicate with the other members of the server. They function like a giant group text, where individuals could leverage the functionality of their computers/phones, to do things like hop into conference calls, stream videos with friends, or simply share images. By homing in on the idea of providing a fast and reliable connection for gamers looking to communicate while they played, Discord exploded in popularity and use. However, because Discord offers a multitude of features ranging from advanced tools like bots (automated programs which conduct tasks), which could perform features like automatically filtering incoming people or moderate chat rooms—Discord also gained the attention of audiences beyond gaming, making it unique for understanding Black community in gaming spaces.

Having used Discord myself, I knew it would be a suitable place to begin looking for Black gaming communities as many gamers would use it as a communication hub to speak with friends over a broad range of games. By utilizing a feature on Discord's website that lets you search through public servers, I began looking for anything that might lead me to Black space. To my surprise, at least three pages of Discord servers with titles or references to Black culture popped up in response to my inquiry. Servers like *Black Gamers*, *The Black Experience*, and *Blerd Stasis* (a combination of Black and nerd) came up on my screen, filling me with both hope and surprise. These search results seemed to indicate that not only were there Black gaming/nerd communities online, but that efforts to create such were consistent and plentiful. However, my hope would not last long, as upon closer inspection I saw that mixed into the servers that sought to celebrate Blackness, there were many servers that directly mocked and played with Black imagery and text.

Like minstrel posters, many of these servers were listed with overtly racist server names like "Niqqers be Wildin" and "Niqqer Server"[2] with Qs instead of Gs (likely to avoid alerting Discord's sensors). Others utilized derogatory Black imagery such as Black cartoon characters or celebrities which were edited to wear things like du-rags or eat watermelon. This would mark some of the earliest signs of anti-Blackness which inspired my initial conceptualization for the MCW, because not only were these images disconcerting, but they also served as digital markers of space. They reminded individuals of the anti-Blackness which existed in online spaces and reminded users of the possibility and fear that they might unknowingly join an anti-Black space. But, when I did finally join servers, ten out of the 15 initial servers I joined remained eerily inactive. Like digital ghost towns, these servers had little to no activity for over a year.

While this is common, as Discord is host to countless abandoned servers, the sheer amount of "dead Black space" stuck out like a thorn. As Taylor (2002) has noted, it is the people and players that give a digital space "life," so seeing this left me asking why. It would not be until I joined the group BPD that I would begin to find answers. BPD, a group created to celebrate Blackness, would come to end during the time of my research. In 2019, I witnessed BPD slowly collapse under a deluge of white harassment, infiltration, and non-Black folk seeking their own play and joy within the space. As within BPD, I would come to witness first-hand the reality of an openly Black community in a space rife with anti-Black behaviours.

Created in March 2019 by a Black man I will refer to as "Gold," *BPD* was a creation of chance. Gold had only created the space after he was removed from another Black server for defending a potential racist who had joined the group. Gold advocated that the individual not be removed without sufficient evidence of racism, to which the leaders of the group promptly kicked them both out. Disgruntled and left without a community, Gold created BPD, a public server dedicated to what he believed Black community should be. He hoped for a community that was open and welcoming to all participants provided they were respectful and understood that the community was primarily a Black space. By creating multiple channels (contained spaces within the server, like subreddits but with audio capabilities), Gold deftly created sites for discussion about topics such as food, politics, and memes, organizing the server in hopes that all kinds of Black folks would find space there. Additionally, remembering the situation he had come from, he went on to set up a gamified governing system to ensure no one would be removed the way he was from his previous group. He provided a levelling system for people in the community, where the more time they spent engaging and helping, the higher the level they would achieve, and subsequently the higher their position in the community. To Gold's credit, this system succeeded in attracting many Black members to join the community. The group had reached around 50 members when I joined in June 2019 with around half being Black. Many used the space to find friends, play video games, or simply vent about the day with one another. Through his group, Gold displayed how "Blackness could expertly utilize the internetwork's capacity for discourse to build out a social, cultural, and racial identity" (Brock 2020: 5).

Unfortunately, it did not take long for Gold to run into issues. In opening his community to all participants, he also opened it to attacks which had a drastic impact on the space. For example, on multiple occasions the space was invaded by random attackers spamming the N-word and saying things like "fuck Black people." While this was infrequent and the individuals would be removed, it remained a significant detriment to the community as many became too annoyed or bothered and would simply leave the space. Additionally, the group faced another issue in the form of individuals joining and pretending to be Black, performing what Leonard (2004) calls high-tech Blackface. Many individuals in fact made it a game, and would find fun in pretending to be Black, using a Black profile picture or simply claim to be Black, only to one day go on a racist rant resulting in their removal. However, while they had their fun, their actions would often leave the rest of the group questioning whether they could trust the remaining members. As part of an ongoing issue specific to online gaming spaces, online anonymity provided cover to attackers that they would not have in a physical setting. These issues became so common that Gold assigned key positions to other members to help moderate the channel and ensure the safety of the community. But even this became complicated.

Gold's levelling system came back to bite him, as many of the individuals ranking up in the space weren't Black but were instead white members who came to enjoy the company of Black users. When the time came to select moderators for the group, Gold had little choice but to rely on the white members who were most active in the community to help safeguard it. One example was a white Australian man who called himself "Babatunde," a name based on an African character played by Black British Youtuber KSI. This character was stereotypically poor and could not afford shoes. The Discord user Babatunde would make no effort to hide the fact that he was white and would consistently remind everyone of this in an attempt to remain "racially sincere" (Jackson 2005) since his profile picture was of KSI (a Black man) and not himself. Surprisingly, this honesty gained him a key position in the group as he become both a moderator and a staple of the space, spending almost every day engaging in conversation in a wide array of topics. In fact, because of their time zone differences, when Gold went to bed, Babatunde would often become the de facto leader of the channel, kicking out racist assailants and holding down the fort for Gold until he logged in again. Babatunde was quite earnest about carrying out the job; when I asked him why a white man would seek out a Black group he answered:

> To be honest, I just joined this group chat because living in my country I feel like there isn't a lot of black people. Growing up in school my two best friends were black until high school came, they had to go to other schools, and I lost touch. I sorta just felt like I could be friends with anyone and seeing all the negativity towards people for the colour of their skin I figured I should just join the group and spread some more positivity if you will, ha-ha.

It is unclear if Babatunde was aware of the irony in his words. Between a white administrator gaining power and the continued verbal attacks on the community, more and more Black people started to leave, while more non-Black individuals started to join. This continued steadily with one Black woman telling me before leaving: "I want to join a group that's for only Black people, I don't trust all this." She and many others raised important concerns about the boundaries of their Black space, specifically asking if they could even still call what they had a Black community. While Black users rarely made these concerns public, they expressed fear that too many non-Black members joining would result in the space no longer being made safe for Black individuals. This is not to say members objected to or had any dislike of non-Black members, but rather expressed a concern about how one could be truly vulnerable and free in their expression of Blackness if they still had to encounter aspects of the white world they hoped to escape.

After all, Blackness often resides as both a foil and peripheral force to whiteness, as Blackness is often made to be the bar in which whiteness is measured against, and the tool in which whiteness comes to realize itself as what Benjamin (2019) calls "the invisible centre." The normalization of whiteness as raceless comes to reinforce Blackness as the raced other (Harrison 1995), "for not only must the black man be black; he must be black in relation to the white man" (Fanon 1952). This combined with a global history of seeing Black spaces demonized and terrorized by white forces (Hartman 2019). Rendered the questions these Black members were asking not only fair, but pivotal to the group's survival.

This all came to a head when Gold finally met his breaking point and left the group after a specific case of high-tech Black face. A member, calling himself "Dashiki Brown," spent a little over a month pretending to be a Black person. Surprisingly, Dashiki did not partake in the usual racist behaviour. In fact, he was a cordial member of the group. However, one day when another person was accused of committing digital Black face, Dashiki became adamant, demanding that the person be removed, telling the group: "digital Black face is a thing, and he's got to go." Ironically, many members had suspected that Dashiki himself was not Black (Dashiki was a little on the nose), but since no one had proof, everyone decided to let it go, arguing that if he remained civil it would not matter. But with his newfound fervour for removing people,

Gold found him threat enough and performed his own investigation by joining other Black groups and asking if anyone had heard of him.

Through his Discord hopping, Gold discovered that not only was Dashiki a white Greek man, but also that he had been removed from another group for having meltdowns and verbally attacking Black women. When this news came to light, Gold, Babatunde, and two other moderators confronted Dashiki with the information. They held a synchronous ad hoc trial through text chat for his behaviour, posting screen shots Gold had collected from another group. Faced with this, Dashiki admitted his wrongdoings. He claimed that he joined Black groups because he didn't feel at home in his Greek community offline, saying he was often mocked for being too pale compared to other individuals in Greece. Thus, he figured Black people would understand what it felt like to be ostracized so he joined BPD. He bargained that he would change his picture and name as penitence, and surprisingly the admins let him stay. Flabbergasted by the decision, I spoke to Gold privately about it, where he admitted to me that he did not trust him at all, remarking: "Oh, he's crazy for sure."

But it was in this conversation that Gold told me that he planned to leave the group. He remarked that running a group was a lot more work than he imagined, and he planned to pass it down to the most active member, Babatunde. By the end of that day, Gold announced his departure and said his goodbyes. With that, BPD went from being a Black space to one that had a white owner overnight. I never spoke to Gold after he left the group as he did not log back in, but I did stay to witness the aftermath of the transition of power. First, Babatunde realized that it was inappropriate for a white person to own a server named Black People Discord, so he changed the name along with his own username. This catalysed the remaining Black-identifying members to leave the group. Slowly the transformation was complete—BPD was no longer a Black space but instead became a hangout for white and other non-Black users with a completely different name. While it did not share the same fate as the servers I had found at the start of my search, it joined the "dead Black space" in a different way, one that despite its continuing existence, left no trace of the Black community it once was.

While this was as solemn moment, it was one which displayed the ways the MCW worked to remove Blackness. Its tactics were not found just in the aggressive and consistent berating of Black online users. They also worked through the co-opting of space, the acts of deceit which made Black members question their space, and the inundation of behaviours which simply exhaust Black communities. Simply put, the MCW is not a space simply maintained by random acts of white racism, but is instead the culmination of racists behaviours, anti-Black histories, and an adherence to whiteness as default. It is a space which like many other social formations centred in whiteness, has come to be informed through an interlinking of multiple cultural spheres which make up and empower it (Delany and Yanagisako 1995). Most frightening of all is how within the MCW, BPD became a source for white pleasure, a game within a gaming space, both for those who attacked, and those who came to claim their joy within Black space.

Black Girl Gamers, the Black Spoil Sport, and Possibilities within the Magic Circle of Whiteness

With a history of gaming as a white player space (Newman 2017) and an industry which struggles with diversity and inclusion (Brock 2011, Russworm and Blackmon 2020), I came to worry if anything could properly disrupt the MCW. After all, BPD was not unique in its problems as many Black gamers have echoed the issues of anti-Black discrimination in their gaming (Gray 2020). This was made worse by the realization that these attacks were happening unprovoked, as this harassment was not targeting a specific behaviour, but rather the identity and idea of Blackness itself. However, it was from this reality that I developed the concept of the Black Spoil Sport, to help explain why Black individuals were being targeted just for existing. As Huizinga writes:

> The player who trespasses against the rules or ignores them is a "spoilsport". The spoilsport is not the same as the false player, the cheat; for the latter pretends to be playing the game and, on the face of it, still acknowledges the magic circle. It is curious to note how much more lenient society is to the cheat than to the spoilsport. This is because the spoilsport shatters the play-world itself. By withdrawing from the game, he [sic] reveals the relativity and fragility of the play-world in which he had temporarily shut himself with others. He robs play of its illusion. ... Therefore, they must be cast out, for they threaten the existence of the play-community.
>
> *Huizinga 1938: 11*

In this way, Blackness and Black individuals become the spoil sport within the MCW, just as the spoil sport shatters the illusion of the magic circle, so too does the Black Spoil Sport shatter or disrupt the idea that gaming is an inherently white space. Simply put, the Black Spoil Sport through their mere existence becomes a type of "gaming other" and a wrench in the idea that gaming spaces are fundamentally white, thereby unsettling the status quo. This can be seen clearly in the outrage towards the addition of Black characters in video games where many claim that they "break the immersion of the game" or that they make games "too political." By this logic, in a medium with talking dragons and blue hedgehogs, Black people become the most unbelievable factor. This underlines the reason Blackness comes under attack in white gaming spaces, as Blackness shatters the "immersion" of white space, and thus must be attacked, cast out, or absorbed in ways similar to those causing the demise of BPD.

However, this is not all that the Black Spoil Sport is, as Black gamers aren't just passive participants in gaming spaces, but are actors who develop their own space, communities, and joy. This is something I would fully realize in the conversations I had with my participant Sapphire, as she and her group BGG accomplished what BPD could not—they managed to create a sustained Black gaming group and existence online. But this did not happen overnight, and in fact took years to grow into the popular space it is today. Created in 2015 by a Black woman named Jay-Ann Lopez, BGG is a multi-platform community and organization that seeks to enact change within the larger gaming community and industry (Blue 2021). It began as a safe space for Black women to find friends, hang out, and game, and was created in response to the immense amount of anti-Black/misogynoir harassment Black women faced in gaming (Gray 2018). Harassment which caused many, including Sapphire, to change the way they played, often choosing to mute their mics and limit interaction with others, lest they be attacked if anyone discovered that they were women or Black. For this reason, BGG operates on sites such as Facebook, Twitter, Instagram, and Discord. Where the group utilizes the connective nature of the internet to expertly create both public and private spaces to first find members, and then provide them with safe spaces. By managing features in Facebook or Discord, members build boundaries to ensure that only Black women are allowed into the space. These boundaries were even extended toward me as a Black man, as Sapphire made clear that I would not be able to enter their private Facebook or Discord group. Sapphire did welcome me to follow their public work posts on Twitter and Twitch; a request I was happy to oblige, after witnessing what had happened to BPD.

It was because of these boundaries that BGG was able to maintain their space. As with BPD, many would try to invade the BGG spaces. Sapphire noted that as BGG grew, they started to get a lot of requests from men and white women who wanted to join their space. This reflected the need for their boundaries, as anytime Black individuals wanted to keep something to themselves there was consistently a force trying to take it away. This resulted in strict moderation of their private spaces including checking every profile that requested access, surveying current member activity, and assigning and rotating jobs to avoid moderator fatigue, all in order to maintain a space where their members felt safe and welcomed. This was one of the benefits of creating Black community online: By establishing boundaries and checking systems, they were able to keep out anyone that might harm the space, allowing BGG to flourish into the prominent organization it is today. After all, since 2015 BGG has evolved into a multi-faceted coalition. On one hand, they run a deep private network of Black knowledge, where their members teach each other technical skills like how to improve in video games, build stream setup, and how to navigate their respective industries. While, at the same time, they manage a public-facing brand that has been featured on billboards in New York's Time Square and partnered with large companies like Marvel for their "Women of Marvel" event and celebration. This was in part only possible because BGG members prioritized protecting their space.

While there are many ways to create online Black gaming communities, it is worth noting how effective BGG is at leveraging the intermediality of games and media. After all, anthropologists such as Marcus (1997), Ginsburg (2005), and Coleman (2010) have pointed to the fact that the internet and burgeoning media have expanded what we consider community or the "field." BGG is a prime example of this. By interacting with so many individuals, games, websites, and digital spaces, BGG has formed an international community. In doing so they undermine the white gaming hegemony and create spaces which allow for the existence of Blackness. However, it is this unique management of borders, a deft understanding of media space, and the ability to navigate and protect one's community by reorganizing it along those media lines which fully encapsulates the Black Spoil Sport.

It is this ability to carve out space which disrupts the hegemony of the MCW, which encapsulates the Black Spoil Sport not just as a passive existence but as what Campt (2007) and Sojoyner (2017) call "fugitivity." As Sojoyner writes: "the concept of fugitivity highlights the tension between the acts or flights of escape and creative practices of refusal, nimble and strategic practices that undermine the category of the dominant" (Sojoyner 2017: 516). The Black Spoil Sport can be interpreted as a fugitive identity which through tactics displayed by BGG (such as turning off their mics, creating spaces which deny whiteness, and utilizing a vast network of digital spaces to create sites which celebrate Black womanhood both publicly and privately) shapes itself in ways which resist the practices that hold the MCW together. In this way, the Black Spoil Sport is not merely a recolouring of Huizinga's terms, but instead builds on concepts such as Sara Ahmed's "feminist kill joy" (2010) and Bonnie Ruberg's "too-close player" (2019), to exist as an identity which passively and actively challenges the makeup of the MCW. After all, Black resistance has taken on multiple forms throughout history, and while there were times which we have actively resisted deleterious powers, there were also others where just surviving was a form of resistance. Thus, the conceptualization of Black Spoil Sport seeks to consider both these realities to display how Blackness and, in this case, Black women like those in BGG resist the MCW, in which Blackness is often incongruent in white gaming spaces. After all, "[B]lack women have always embodied, if only in their physical manifestation, an adversary stance to white male rule and have actively resisted its inroads upon them and their communities in both dramatic and subtle ways" (The Combahee River collection citing Angela Davis 1971).

Conclusion

While there is much more to be said about these groups and Black community online, overall, this chapter has provided one way to look at gaming spaces. By introducing the concept of the "Magic Circle of Whiteness" and the "Black Spoil Sport," I have offered anthropology a conceptual framework which seeks to better understand how whiteness as default shapes interconnected online gaming spaces. Specifically, through my discussion of BPD I recount the challenges faced by this group and Black gamers at large. This chapter displays how Black individuals face a bevy of dangers in online gaming spaces, such as verbal assault, racist imagery, and individuals pretending to be Black, both as a game and a form of harassment. This, in conjunction with the poor portrayal of Black characters in games and an industry which has been and continues to be predominantly white, coalesces to form the MCW. Through this concept I seek to expand our understanding of online gaming spaces—not just as games, but as interconnected with larger internet media spaces dictated by white logics.

This, however, is just one half of the framework, as Black individuals are not without agency within the MCW, as no hegemonic force completely dictates the lives of those found within. While Black gamers may face steady peril within the MCW, many Black individuals have developed methods to cope and undermine the white logics of the space. It is this ability to resist and find space within the MCW which I frame as the Black Spoil Sport, exemplified by BGG. This group has cleverly utilized digital boundaries and multiple media sites to find and build community within sites of anti-Blackness. At the core of these concepts is the need to understand how gaming operates as white space and how Black folks come to resist it. As games continue to rise in prevalence, anthropology at large will need to adapt new ways of looking at how these gaming communities influence and intersect with media at large. This will require a transformation in how we look at how we examine at gaming spaces, as video games have never, and will never exist within a vacuum.

Notes

1 #Gamergate was an online harassment campaign which took place predominantly in the U.S, UK, and Canada after which it first targeted game developer Zoë Quinn but saw many individuals being attacked and having their personal information released in a trend called doxing.
2 Servers like these were much more common at the time of this research. Since then, Discord has been more active at shutting down these servers and many of these have been removed from their system.

References

Ahmed, Sara. The Promise of Happiness. Durham, NC: Duke University Press, 2010.
Benjamin, Ruha. "Race After Technology: Abolitionist Tools for the New Jim Code." Social Forces, 2019. https://doi.org/10.1093/sf/soz162
Blue, Rosario. "How Black Girl Gamers Is Changing the Gaming Landscape for the Better." TechRadar. 6 September 2020. Accessed 25 February 2021.
Brock, André. "'When Keeping it Real Goes Wrong': Resident Evil 5, Racial Representation, and Gamers." Games and Culture 6(5) (2011): 429–452.
Brock, André and Jr André Brock. Distributed Blackness. New York: University Press, 2020.
Browne, R. (2020, August 14). The $150 billion video game industry grapples with a murky track record on diversity. CNBC. Retrieved 13 May 2022, from www.cnbc.com/2020/08/14/video-game-industry-grapples-with-murky-track-record-on-diversity.html
Boellstorff, Tom. Coming of Age in Second Life: An Anthropologist Explores the Virtually Human. Princeton: Princeton University Press, 2008.
Campt, Tina M. Listening to Images. Duke University Press, 2017.

Coleman, E. Gabriella. "Ethnographic Approaches to Digital Media." Annual Review of Anthropology 39 (2010): 487–505.

Du Bois, W.E.B. 2015 "The souls of black folk." In The Souls of Black Folk. New Haven: Yale University Press.

Everett, Anna, and S. Craig Watkins. "The Power of Play: The Portrayal and Performance of Race in Video Games." MacArthur Foundation Digital Media and Learning Initiative, 2008.

Fanon, Frantz. 2008. Black Skin, White Masks. New York: Grove Press.

Goodwin, Marjorie Harness. "The Serious Side of Jump Rope: Conversational Practices and Social Organization in the Frame of Play." The Journal of American Folklore 98(389) (1985): 315. https://doi.org/10.2307/539938.

Gray, Kishonna L. "Solidarity Is for White Women in Gaming." Diversifying Barbie and Mortal Kombat: Intersectional Perspectives and Inclusive Designs in Gaming (2016): 59–70.

Gray, Kishonna L. 2018. "Gaming Out Online: Black Lesbian Identity Development and Community Building in Xbox Live." Journal of Lesbian Studies 22 (3): 282–96.

Gray, Kishonna L. Intersectional Tech: Black Users in Digital Gaming. Baton Rouge: Louisiana State University Press, 2020.

Hartman, Saidiya. Wayward Lives. New York: W. W. Norton & Company, 2019.

Huizinga, Johan. Homo Ludens: A Study of the Play Element in Culture. Boston: Beacon, 1938.

Jackson, John L. Real Black: Adventures in Racial Sincerity. Chicago: University of Chicago Press, 2005.

Kocurek, Carly A. Coin-operated Americans: Rebooting Boyhood at the Video Game Arcade. Minneapolis: University of Minnesota Press, 2015.

Leonard, David. "'Live in Your World, Play in Ours': Race, Video Games, and Consuming the Other." SIMILE: Studies in Media & Information Literacy Education 3(4) (January 2003): 1–9. https://doi.org/10.3138/sim.3.4.002.

Madianou, Mirca, and Daniel Miller. "Polymedia: Towards a New Theory of Digital Media in Interpersonal Communication." International Journal of Cultural Studies 16(2) (2013): 169–187.

Malaby, Thomas M. "Beyond Play: A New Approach to Games." Games and Culture 2(2) (2007): 95–113.

Marcus, George E. "Ethnography in/of the World System: The Emergence of Multi-sited Ethnography." Annual Review of Anthropology 249(1) (1995): 95–117.

Nardi, Bonnie. My Life as a Night Elf Priest: An Anthropological Account of World of Warcraft. Ann Arbor: University of Michigan Press, 2010.

Newman, Michael Z. Atari Age: The Emergence of Video Games in America. Cambridge, MA: MIT Press, 2017.

Noble, Safiya Umoja. Algorithms of Oppression: How Search Engines Reinforce Racism. New York: New York University Press, 2018.

Phillips, Amanda. Gamer Trouble. New York: New York University Press, 2020.

Rothenbuhler, Eric W. and Mihai Coman, eds. Ginsburge, Faye "An Introduction" Media anthropology. Thousand Oaks: Sage Publications, 2005.

Ruberg, Bonnie. Video Games Have Always Been Queer. New York: NYU Press, 2019.

Russworm, TreaAndrea M. and Samantha Blackmon. "Replaying Video Game History as a Mixtape of Black Feminist Thought." Feminist Media Histories 6(1) (2020): 93–118.

Russworm, TreaAndrea M. "A Call to Action for Video Game Studies in an Age of Reanimated White Supremacy." Velvet Light Trap 81(2018): 73–77.

Sojoyner, Damien M. "Another Life Is Possible: Black Fugitivity and Enclosed Places." Cultural Anthropology 32(4) (2017): 514–536.

Taylor, T. L. 2018. Watch Me Play: Twitch and the Rise of Game Live Streaming. Princeton: Princeton University Press.

Taylor, Tina L. "Living Digitally: Embodiment in Virtual Worlds." In The Social Life of Avatars. London: Springer, 2002, pp. 40–62.

The Combahee River Collective. "A Black Feminist Statement." Women's Studies Quarterly 42(¾) (2014): 271–80. Accessed 18 July 2021. www.jstor.org/stable/24365010.

Yanagisako, Sylvia and Carol Delaney. "Naturalizing Power." Naturalizing Power: Essays in Feminist Cultural Analysis, London: Routledge, 1995.

C
Identities and Social Change

27
INKING IDENTITY
Indigenous Nationalism in Bolivian Tattoo Art

Nell Haynes

Introduction

In June 2016, I traveled with my friend Gus from La Paz, Bolivia to Sucre where he had been invited to work as a guest tattoo artist for a week. I met Gus in 2011 when he was still an apprentice, but by 2016 he had opened his own studio in La Paz, and occasionally traveled to other cities in South America to work as a guest artist. Though Gus identified primarily as mestizo (mixed Indigenous and Spanish ancestry), he was particularly interested in going to Sucre because the city was the site of the country's Museum of Indigenous Art.

Gus's primary style falls within "American Traditional" tattooing, featuring black outlining, bold colors, and familiar designs such as skulls, roses, daggers, and "pin up girls." But he also often catered to clients' desires for tattoos that had a particular "Bolivian" or "Andean" element. This might include pre-Incan or Incan symbols, elements of Bolivian folklore, and common fauna and flora of the region. Gus had recently taken a particular liking to designing swallows based on traditional sailor tattoos, but in his variations, he would fill the bird's outline with designs from traditional Bolivian textiles. At the museum, he took copious notes and photographs of textile collections to incorporate in his tattoo designs. A year later at a tattoo convention, one of his swallow designs was a finalist in the category for "Best Bolivian Tattoo."

When I first encountered this category of "Bolivian" or "Andean" tattooing in 2012, I asked Dylan, another tattoo artist from La Paz, what exactly it meant. He responded that "it's representative of history and culture … it's not about the technique or style, but the message that you transmit with your design. It has to show something distinctive about Bolivia." Designs deemed by tattoo artists and clients as "Bolivian" usually have symbolism related to Aymara and Quechua culture or broader notions of indigeneity. As a result of shifting definitions and social status of indigeneity in Bolivia since the early 1990s, "being Indigenous" is anything but straightforward. Most tattoo artists and clients identify as primarily mestizo/a, but often note that they have some Indigenous ancestry. Thus, these "Bolivian-style" tattoos demonstrate a particular orientation toward Indigenous symbolism as a more generalized identity claim available to anyone living in the Andes.

From 2009–2017 I spent over 24 months in La Paz while working on different ethnographic research projects. In 2011, I coincidentally became friends with Gus, Dylan, and several other tattoo artists in the city. Most were men (with the exception of two women) and represented a range of class and ethnic identifications. Most had been tattooing between 5 and 20 years when we first met. Over the years, I have spent many hours in their studios talking, eating, drinking, and trying to stay warm during cold altiplano winters. I rented rooms in their homes, spent Christmas and New Year's Eve with them, attended family weddings, and traveled with them to conventions. I connected with them on Facebook, Instagram, and WhatsApp, where I would see images of their tattoos and advertisements for their shops, in some cases, almost daily. When I began to think of tattooing through an academic lens in 2019, I already had a wealth of experience with these men and women, knowing their histories, challenges, and triumphs, based on both shared time offline and our interactions online. When I proposed to each of them that tattooing would make an interesting research topic, all were enthusiastic, and many ended up participating and connecting me to their clients with tattoo designs relevant to this project.

In this chapter, I discuss tattooing in La Paz, Bolivia, as an important medium in which identity is enacted—both for tattoo artists as well as their clients. Tattoos are at times a performance to the self, and at other times are an outwardly directed self-representation performed for those one encounters in daily life. But tattoos are not simply individual. They also reflect prevailing ideologies related to such realms as ethnicity, regionalism, and nationalism (not to mention gender, social class, and a host of other social categories).

I concentrate here on the ways tattoos are enmeshed in conceptions of nationalism that center indigeneity. Drawing from Néstor García Canclini's (1989) concept of hybridity, I explore tattooing as an identity-making project that draws from multiple referents—on local, national, and global levels. I argue that indigeneity in 21st-century Bolivia may be understood through the concept of suffusion,[1] in which representations of indigeneity have so thoroughly penetrated wider urban altiplano culture that separating what is "Indigenous" and what is "Bolivian" is no longer possible. I use suffusion here drawing upon its traditional meaning of the spreading of a fluid into surrounding tissues, resulting in inundation. Just as fluid may irreversibly spread, forever changing that which it penetrates, so too has indigeneity suffused urban altiplano culture. In part, this is due to the ways complex cultural knowledge can be flattened into recognizable iconic symbols of indigeneity divorced from historical meaning. While some suffusion of indigeneity into understandings of Bolivianness has happened as a slow seepage over time, there have been important state projects in which it has been a conscious process. This flattening of symbolism is obvious in tattooing and other forms of pop culture but is also central to political discourse of "indigenismo" in the 1950s, and discourses of "Indigenous nationalism" in the first decades of the 2000s.

As society has shifted, so too have the content and meanings of tattoos. Rather than considering tattoos as simply visual art, I understand them through the concept of ideology, which has been central to studies of media in Latin America (see Pertierra et al., 2019). By understanding ideology as embedded in various kinds of media, including visual art rendered in skin, I point to the ways hegemonic notions of the nation can become embedded in even the most "rebellious" of identity representations. As such, this exploration is not focused on whether these tattoos are "authentic" or not, but instead takes up questions related to the ways different forms of power may be advanced or diminished through self-representation and Indigenous symbolism in tattooing.

Tattoo, Identity, and Place

Most scholarly explorations of modern tattooing describe it as a mode of performing identity and belonging. In doing so, writers acknowledge that identity is not a static inherent aspect of a person, but is a dynamic social relation that is actively produced and performed (Brubaker and Cooper, 2000; Bucholtz and Hall, 2004). As part of broader symbolic culture, tattooing is a medium through which individuals and groups constitute and represent themselves, both privately and publicly. Like other forms of art and adornment, tattooing has been described by anthropologists as a mode of claiming or being assigned subjectivity related to gender, ancestral lineage, social stratification, occupation, religion, personal experiences, and national patriotism (Caplan, 2000; Faris, 1988; Strathern and Strathern, 1971; Turner, 2012). Beverly Yuen Thompson also points out that some tattoo enthusiasts may be considered "collectors" as well, traveling far and wide to pay for tattoos from well-known artists. She writes,

> This leisure pursuit reflects the collector's identity, through the actual images represented on their body, which provide insight to their tastes and passions. It also makes them into a new type of "heavily tattooed" person, which they now share with a select group of Others.
>
> *2019, p. 286; see also Kierstein and Kjelskau, 2015*

In this explanation, Yuen Thompson points out the ways that in the 21st century, tattoo-associated identity works on multiple levels—first, being "a tattooed person"; second, through meaning attached to the style(s) of tattoos; and third, in relation to specific imagery depicted in the tattoos. Each of these reflect choices the individual makes in creating a visible form of identification[2] and modes through which others evaluate the individual.

There is often a cleavage between studies related to tattooing and identity in contexts of global circulation, and those focusing on traditional practices that concentrate more heavily on indigeneity and the importance of place to tattooing. I attempt here to bridge this cleavage, again with reference to García Canclini's notion of hybridity, and make clear the ways that the local converges with the global in tattoo, rather than being subsumed by it.

As Kuwahara points out, in focusing on tattooing as an Indigenous practice, tattoos are often seen as deeply rooted in place. "They are invented in the place, belong to the place and consolidated in the place. Thus, styles of tattooing are often distinguished by adjectives describing the places they originated, such as 'Tahitian' or 'Japanese'" (2005, p. 19). In Bolivia, however, most tattoo artists describe the styles they tattoo as traditional/old school American [*tradicional, tradi, old school*], neo-traditional [*neo-tradicional, neo-tradi*], new school [*new school*], realism [*realismo*] black-and-grey [*negro y gris*], biomechanical [*biomecánica*], or watercolor [*acuarela*]. Rather than developing from an Indigenous tradition of tattooing, the practice in Bolivia has always been part of global circulations.

Though some of the oldest tattoos in the world have been found in the Andes among the Chinchorro civilization (Pabst et al., 2009; Allison, 1996), tattooing fell out of practice when the Spanish colonized the Inca. It did not resurface with any consistency in the Andes until the late-1800s, when tattooed sailors began docking in Chilean ports. The custom eventually made its way from the coastline up the mountains, but in Bolivia was primarily confined to career military men until the end of the 20th century.

In the 1990s, amongst the increasing circulation of media related to punk music, rock n' roll, and other "rebellious" artforms and lifestyles, young Bolivians' desires for tattoos began to surface. Many Bolivian tattoo artists who have now spent years tattooing note that their first exposures to tattooing were MTV music videos and tattoo magazines imported from the United States and Europe. Thus, the present-day style of tattooing in La Paz is more closely connected to global music that arrived via television and print media, than an ancestral practice of tattooing. For several years, these tattoos primarily featured global tattoo symbols such as skulls, roses, Pacific Island "tribal" styles, ships, and classic lettering. Yet as tattooing in the city has developed, the use of Incan, other pre-colonization, and Indigenous symbolism in those tattoos has proliferated. This shift has coincided with the emergence of important Indigenous movements in Bolivia, beginning in the 1990s, and increasing in the early 2000s with the political rise of Evo Morales, Bolivia's first Indigenous-identified president.

In placing tattoos within contexts of global media circulation and Bolivian social changes, I argue this art form is best approached using media anthropology. Tattoos may be understood as media in that they are a form of visual communication (see Worth, 1980)—a social practice resulting in cultural documents which circulate, mediate social relations, and can be "read" for indications of shifts in both individual identity, and larger social formations. Most anthropological explorations of tattooing, whether looking at contemporary practices (Kuwahara, 2005) or archaeological examples (Deter-Wolf and Diaz-Granados, 2013; Krutak and Deter-Wolf, 2017) focus on small-scale, "traditional," and "tribal" practices, echoing a focus on "primitive art" that can be traced back to Boas (1927). But as anthropological approaches to art have increasingly considered consumption, commodification, interpretation, circulation, and positioning in local, national, and global spheres, they now overlap with anthropologists' considerations of media. Indeed, both art and media may be understood as "space in which difference, identity, and cultural value are being produced and contested" (Marcus and Meyers, 1995, p. 11).

Considering connections between art and media acknowledges the ways media and art in the 21st century draw on the same symbolism and cultural understandings for meaning-making, creating inextricable intertextual linkages between them. Artworks and other forms of media may converge in some ways, conflict in others, but are always mutually influential, and significant to wide swaths of the population. In considering art (whether found in the museum, the Indigenous village, or the tattoos of La Paz) as media, we attend to a number of important considerations: the ways in which ideology is embedded within, contested through, or reinforced in representation and communication; the importance of circulation to meaning and interpretation; and the ways in which meaning and interpretation mediate relationships and notions of selfhood. Thus, these themes of ideology, circulation, and mediation of identity are central to my explorations of tattoo art using Indigenous symbolism in Bolivia.

The Politics of Indigeneity

Contemporary understandings of what it means to "be Indigenous" (*ser indígena*) constantly shift in the Andes. A vast majority of Paceños (residents of La Paz) characterize themselves as Indigenous to some extent, but do not necessarily engage in traditional or religious practices, speak a native language, or trace their lineage directly to Indigenous ancestors. There are people who may identify as Indigenous in particular situations and not others, leading Canessa to caution against falling into an essentialist trap in describing Indigenous peoples. He suggests that "who is and who isn't Indigenous and what it means to be Indigenous in Latin America is highly variable, context-specific and changes over time" (2012, pp. 9–10; see also de la Cadena, 2000; Goodale, 2006).

As a result, when I asked tattoo artists and clients about their ethnic or racial identification[3] most hesitated to give a definitive answer. Their responses included: Mestizo; Indigenous; from an Indigenous region; "It's complicated"; and "I can't define it." Many explained how histories of colonization had shaped Bolivia ethnically. Others contemplated the color of their skin, and how it related to that of their parents and siblings. Some chose to identify simply as "Bolivian," given that their parents were from different parts of the country, with different histories of colonization and even understandings of racial categories.

Vlad, a 40-year-old client with 10 tattoos, explained that he hadn't ever learned Indigenous languages and customs at home. He then continued: "I can't tell you 'No I don't have any Indigenous lineage in me,' because that would be lying, you know." Vivi, a Paceña in her mid-30s who is currently studying for a doctorate in psychology offered a more academic perspective:

> Well it's complicated because I think ethnicity is something we're always constructing, right? The theme of race is difficult, because I'm a person with … confusion. I can call myself mestiza, but that doesn't quite capture it. I'm also Indigenous, I have Indigenous roots. I have Indigenous [phenotypic] characteristics, but I don't speak any Indigenous language. It's difficult to define.

In many ways, these answers reflect the range of ways tattoos relate to indigeneity. Some tattoos present Indigenous imagery quite explicitly and in a more traditional looking manner. Others mix imagery into a "complicated" meshing of different regional, or local/global symbolism. There is no direct correspondence between the type of tattoo and the artist's or client's ethnic or racial identity. For example, Beto was the only person I interviewed to give a definitive answer of "Indigenous"—which was then followed by "We're a mix here because of Spanish colonization, in reality. So we're mestizos from Indigenous people, let's say." Beto tattoos almost exclusively in a black and gray style, highlighting horror and skull imagery. On the other hand, Nacho, a client in his early 40s who had five tattoos with explicitly Indigenous imagery, responded to the question with the longest answer of all my interviews. He began by saying "I consider myself Bolivian, but without any ethnicity," and continued clarifying for more than four minutes.

Though a majority of Bolivians have similarly complicated relations to Indigenous ancestry, there is certainly still much discrimination levied against those who appear as unmistakably Indigenous in Bolivia.[4] While somewhere between 40 and 60 percent of Bolivians identify as Indigenous in national censuses (INE 2003, 2012), there is enormous diversity among those who do. Differences between urban and rural Indigenous-identified people, as well as among different highland and lowland groups are notable. Those who are more visibly Indigenous—usually through their style of dress and language use—are easily distinguished from a more "Westernized" majority and, as a result, face social exclusion. Their educational and literacy levels lag, and poverty levels far surpass those of non-Indigenous Bolivians.

However, the first two decades of the 2000s have marked important changes. Beginning with his first term in 2006, Evo Morales appointed many Indigenous people to head government ministries, and championed a new 2009 constitution which guarantees Indigenous representation in congress, community control over justice, and other forms of sovereignty for Indigenous communities. The World Bank has reported significant increases in Indigenous communities' access to electricity, potable water, and sanitation. Morales also made great strides in combating lack of education and poverty (decreasing rates from 59.5 percent in 2006 to 36.4 percent in 2018) which both affect Indigenous peoples at a much higher rate. But Morales, and those in his political party MAS (Movimiental a Socialismo) who continue to govern, have not been able to entirely reverse 500 years of colonial legacy. "Evo," as he is often called in Bolivia, has been a figurehead for MAS and progressive politics in the country more broadly. However, it's important to see his accomplishments as embedded in historical, social, and political processes that pre-empted his rise to power (see Farthing and Kohl, 2014, pp. 5–7; Postero,

2017, p. 26), represented a movement made up by diverse social actors, and have already proven to outlive his position in office, after his ousting in 2019 amid accusations of election fraud and then civil unrest (Farthing, 2020).

As part of this broader movement, Evo Morales was instrumental in promoting discourse that framed Bolivia as an Indigenous nation. Previously, Bolivian governments had promoted mestizaje as an ideal of cultural sameness which erased Indigenous culture (Martinez-Echazabal, 1998). This national project of mestizaje was particularly prominent in the 1950s, when Indigenous folklore began to be valorized as national culture, even as real Indigenous peoples remained divorced from political power—a phenomenon referred to as "indigenismo." As Himpele points out, since the 1950s, "conspicuous scenes of native Andean peoples have been attached to the national project in photography, film, dance, and music, originated and disseminated from the rising non-Indigenous mestizo middle class of politicians, artists, intellectuals, and writers" (2008, p. xiv).

Hempele suggests indigenismo of the 1950s is an important context for understanding the current politics of indigeneity in Bolivia. He sees a relationship between "the popularization of indigenismo and the indigenization of the popular." Imagery of Indigenous folklore was previously depoliticized and framed as quaint tradition, important to Bolivia's heritage, but no longer a living reality for the modern, mestizo nation. This visual and performance-based discourse has recently been reconfigured to frame the nation as deeply rooted in and re-politicized through these traditions. Albro has described Morales as replacing the ideal of mestizaje with a new framework focused on Indigenous plurality as the articulatory focus for a new national project (2005). Yet, this re-envisioning of Bolivia as an Indigenous nation has not been positive for many Indigenous peoples (Hempele, 2008, p. 9). These discourses have served to highlight the political stakes of more populous and politically connected Indigenous groups over others (see Fabricant & Postero, 2015), and have been critiqued as yet another homogenizing rhetoric which takes emphasis away from the most vulnerable by framing all Bolivians as similarly positioned.

Postero draws attention to the importance of representation within this shift, suggesting MAS has united its diverse constituencies within an ideal of "Indigenous nationalism" with a focus on a politics of recognition (2017, p. 26). This is exemplified by Evo's attention to the symbolism of indigeneity in state ceremonies and his general self-presentation. This institutional use of symbolism amplified a rising appreciation of the aesthetics of indigeneity and a more general cultural valuation of indigeneity which has resulted in Indigenous identification across a much wider swath of the population. A variety of cultural forms now incorporate Indigenous symbolism in the ways that would have previously been seen as "backward." Youth listen to rap music in Aymara, Quechua, and Spanish with lyrics that speak to Indigenous or otherwise marginalized identities (see Goodale, 2006, p. 634). Graffiti art combines Indigenous imagery with more widely recognizable tagging style. Fashion designers incorporate Aymara textiles in their garments. And it is not unusual to find an upper-middle-class home decorated with Andean art that two decades ago would have been considered vulgar. This has led to a cultural conundrum in which the bounds of indigeneity appear to be ever-elastic, resulting in debates about who and what might be considered "authentically" Indigenous, with not even Evo Morales escaping critique (Albro, 2006, p. 417). These cultural forms also contribute to nationalism by framing Bolivia as an Indigenous nation whose streets, entertainment, and styles of self-expression reflect this heritage, without questioning "who owns Native culture" (see Brown, 2004).

The resulting brand of Indigenous nationalism conflates and claims indigeneity as part of globally marginalized identity. These discourses rightly point to the histories of colonization that have positioned Bolivia as one of the "least developed" countries in the hemisphere and despite recent advances, a country that still has low GDP and high poverty rates. At the same time, they collapse diversity within the country, at times subsuming the interest of the nation's most vulnerable Indigenous peoples within a majoritarian claim to indigeneity. From some perspectives, this reinstantiates earlier forms of indigenismo, once again divorcing real Indigenous peoples from Indigenous aesthetics taken up by the majority. This is not to say that most Bolivians have un-critically taken up the notion of an Indigenous nation. Rather this ideology has set a backdrop for more subtle ways in which many Bolivians reinforce this discourse implicitly, even while they may recognize it as regressive or opposing the politicians who are the architects of this positioning.[5]

These discourses were partially founded as a conscious effort to promote Indigenous nationalism by MAS and sympathetic media producers (who may have had quite good intentions of acting against anti-Indigenous discrimination). But these messages have worked iteratively, making their way into films, television shows, music, fashion, and art that young Bolivians encounter every day. Media has become one of the primary vehicles for ideological dissemination in modern society (Althusser, 1968), and as a result has contributed to shaping national imaginaries (see Anderson, 1983; Ginsburg, Abu-Lughod, and Larkin, 2002, p. 11). As these discourses are naturalized, they are less likely to be critiqued and are reproduced unconsciously, and in increasingly mundane and independent ways—including individuals seeking out "Bolivian tattoos" which incorporate Indigenous symbolism.

Tattoos with Indigenous Symbolism

In a discussion of tattoos with Indigenous symbolism, it would be inattentive to omit discussion of the particularities of race, identity, and tattoo directly in relation to skin. Though anthropologists recognize race as a social construction—a way in which people delimit categories and attach meaning to otherwise neutral biological variation—in the collective consciousness of most of the world, race is most often conceptualized and recognized through skin color. Tattooing places imagery not *over* the skin, covering it, as we might describe for clothing, but creates images *in* the skin in such a way that not only is the skin color (and other attributes) visible through the tattoo, but affects the ways tattoos are planned and executed. Darker skin tones require additional attention to creating contrast, selection of colors, ink types, and other considerations in the actual tattooing process.

Of course, many Indigenous scholars from across the globe note that lighter-skinned Indigenous individuals are often erased through representations of Indigenous peoples as exclusively dark with quintessential features, which in the Americas usually include dark straight hair, large noses, and hairless bodies. While certainly there are Bolivians who are lighter skinned while having every claim to indigeneity, the colonial history of the country has resulted in understandings of Indigenous peoples as darker. As a result, lighter-skinned Indigenous Bolivians have not been subjected to the kinds of discrimination darker-skinned Indigenous peoples face. Given the contextual nature of "being Indigenous" in the Andes discussed above, skin color remains a central organizing referent in understandings of indigeneity. Thus, the skin color on which Indigenous-related visuals are tattooed, immediately serves as a layer of meaning which melds with the inked image such that it is *part of* the tattoo, rather than simply a neutral canvas on which the tattoo is applied. Indigenous symbolism on lighter skin then may be interpreted differently than the exact same symbolism would be on darker skin—each inflected by the interpretant's own understandings of the relationship between indigeneity and skin tone.

With this in mind, many "Bolivian" tattoos combine locally recognizable cultural icons with globally circulated tattoo aesthetics. These hybrid forms reflect García Canclini's (1989) understanding of the ways global media and consumer goods combine with Latin American cultural formations. He argues that globally hegemonic products never entirely override national, regional, or local popular culture. Further, Latin Americans do not simply modify these forms to fit the new context, but *remix* (Rivera-Rideau, 2015) such forms in ways that de-hierarchize the assumed prominence of media and goods from Western industrialized countries. Yet, these concepts of hybridity and remixing may not fully capture the ways in which the Indigenous, the local, the historical, and the global meld together. I use the term suffusion to describe the ways these different sources of symbolism become inextricable from one another as they are flattened into an icon placed in the skin. The following examples illustrate how meanings become not only remixed in the tattooing process, but more profoundly reflect a longer cultural process of suffusion in which Indigenous imagery comes to symbolize the local and national.

(1) Tattooing Text—Jallalla

Mateo was one of the youngest tattoo artists among my group of friends, and while apprenticing had received tattoos from almost all the other artists I knew in the city. One of his favorites was the word "Jallalla" [pronounced huh-YIE-yuh] which had been tattooed on his forearm by one of his mentors, Raúl.

Jallalla is an Aymara and Quechua term that unites concepts of hope, festivity, and blessings. But even those Paceños that don't speak any Indigenous language would recognize this word. It is commonly used by Bolivians in celebratory contexts, such as a toast or a shout in a crowd after one's favorite football team wins a match ("Jallalla Tigre!"). It might also be used on a national holiday ("Jallalla Bolivia") or on July 16th celebrations of the founding of La Paz ("Jallalla Chuquiago Marka"). The word is so prolific in La Paz that it often appears in municipality funded banners or painted walls such as "Jallalla La Paz, con fuerza y con ñeque" [with strength, first in Spanish, then Aymara].

In many ways, during the presidency of Evo, the word jallalla, likely the most recognizable of any Indigenous word in Bolivia, was used as a way of promoting a particular orientation to decolonization. Evo was well-known for performative gestures aimed at ridding the country of foreign influence—expelling the United Nations, US ambassador, and Peace Corps from the country, threatening to oust Coca Cola, and even replacing the clock mounted atop the façade of the congressional building with one that turns counter-clockwise, urging Bolivians to "question established colonial norms in order to think creatively." The increasing use of widely-known Indigenous words during his term coincided with this same line of thinking. The municipal government of La Paz often incorporated these kinds of terms, thereby establishing them as referents not only of Quecha and Aymara language, but of the city and regional identity. When I asked Mateo about the tattoo, he brushed it off, saying "I just like the sentiment behind it. It's pride, it's happiness." But given the ways the term circulates in the context of 21st-century Bolivia, it has become closely connected with the kinds of discourses of Indigenous nationalism espoused by the MAS party. Thus, this one word simultaneously references mundane Bolivianness as well as a politics of indigeneity.

(2) Tattooing Cultural Symbols—The Ñatita with Chullo and Coca Leaves

In 2015 I helped Gus and his friend Miguel at their table at a local tattoo convention. As attendees passed the table, they perused the binders both artists had set out with photos of their

Inking Identity

recent designs. One young woman approached the table saying she was looking for an "Andean design" and Miguel showed her a page with designs of Inti the sun deity most often associated with the pre-Incan Tiwanaku culture, as well as the chakana, or Andean cross which represents the cardinal directions and three levels of existence. Instead of these straightforward designs that come from pre-Colombian culture of the Andes, she chose a design that combines three elements related to "Bolivianness."

The design (similar to Figure 27.1) centered on a ñatita, a skull (usually *not* of a family member), which acts as a vessel housing the soul of the former living person. Ñatitas are kept in the home and thought to bestow blessings on its caretaker. The practice is Aymara in origin, though widely practiced by Paceños hoping to benefit from the ñatita's association with fertility, luck, and protection. Atop the head of the ñatita sat a chullo, the iconic Andean hat with earflaps, which is based on an Inca style of headwear. While a generation ago these hats would have been associated with a "backward," Indigenous style of dress, their recent popularity among tourists has increased their popularity among urban Paceño youth. Below the skull were two coca leaves, representing the plant that is often used in Indigenous rituals. Because of its association with indigeneity, the coca leaf has lent a particular sense of credibility to those involved in Indigenous social movements (see Grisaffi 2010, 427). At the same time, the practice of chewing coca for its mild stimulant properties (similar to coffee) have made their use in Bolivia quite widespread, and are just as often associated with working-class people who must

Figure 27.1 Tattoo of ñatita with chullo and coca leaves
Source: Tattoo and photo by Rodrigo Jimenez Ross.

labour for long hours, as associated with Indigenous identity. The coca leaf has also become a political symbol in recent decades, associated with MAS, and more specifically Evo Morales, who began his political career as president of the coca-growers union.

Unlike an Inti or chakana design, this young woman's choice reflects the ways material goods with Indigenous origins have become embedded in local practices that are now more superficially connected to indigeneity. While ñatitas, chullos, and coca leaves all have origins in Indigenous practice, they have now become so widely possessed and used among Paceños that they, much like Mateo's jallalla tattoo, more closely reflect local context than reference Indigenous cosmovision, ritual, or practice. This underscores the way indigeneity itself has become available for identity claims to the wider Paceño public.

(3) Tattoo as Hybridity—Textile Swallows

While the ñatita tattoo appears as Indigenous symbolism but actually reflects local material goods, the swallow tattoos designed by Gus (see Figure 27.2) reflect Indigenous symbolism converging with global tattoo symbolism. The swallow tattoo dates to sailors in the 1800s, and has a number of different meanings attributed to it—sailing 5000 nautical miles, going around Cape Horn or the Cape of Good Hope, or possibly getting one swallow before a first voyage and a second swallow upon return. In any event, the swallow is one of the most longstanding and well-recognized tattoos today, across the world. At the same time, the textiles Gus studied at the museum, as well as in books and online resources, seem to reflect the hybridity García Canclini discusses, but bring the local into the global. The textiles reflect designs from the Yampara and Jalq'a cultures, and Gus paid specific attention to which were created by women and which by men, which were used in quotidian life, and which reflected ritual imagery.

Figure 27.2 Tattoo of swallow with aguayo textile design
Source: Tattoo and photo by Gustavo Palacios Gutierrez.

But to an undiscerning Bolivian eye these designs might appear quite mundane, reminiscent of the aguayo textiles ubiquitous in La Paz. Aguayos serve as tablecloths in corner restaurants and most homes have a few lying around for various purposes. The textiles are also visible on city streets as they're used by market women to carry their wares on their backs. These women are known as "cholas," a formerly derogatory term for rural to urban migrant women who make a living selling wares in outdoor markets. Mary Weismantel (2001) explains that historically these women, as urban dwellers, were "not quite" considered Indigenous, yet, were not wholly mestiza either. Today however, the chola is considered to be more of an icon of indigeneity, represented in festival dances, advertisements for dessert brands, and lending an air of "being from this place" to local political candidates (see Albro, 2000). The chola is indeed a national icon. Thus, this symbol uses a very specific form of representing local place but can easily be interpreted in nationalist terms through indexing the chola, and is literally enveloped by the global symbol of the swallow.

From Abstraction to Appropriation?

These examples of tattoo imagery present a range of symbolic associations, from Indigenous-related politics, Indigenous ancestry, Incan iconography, fauna indigenous to the region, quintessential gendered social types, festival characters, and favorite sights of the city. These categories of symbolism though, often overlap, particularly as exemplified by coca, which simultaneously indexes Indigenous ritual, and working-class practice. In each of these, then, we see a string of linkages which eventually brings us back to indexing indigeneity.

Each of these symbols has already accumulated various meanings related to pre-colonization cultures, colonial traditions, and current politics. In the process, they have become culturally recognized and associated with certain social categories, reified over time and transferred into symbols and signs of identity or belonging (Butler, 1999). As Clare Sammells points out, abstraction of indigeneity into symbols is part of what has made Indigenous culture "real and powerful" for Bolivians (2012). While each of these symbols retains indexicality oriented toward indigeneity, they also have come to stand in for "Bolivianness" more generally. The idea of Bolivia as an Indigenous nation has taken hold among many social sectors, particularly with younger urban Bolivians who do not retain the biases and stigmas their parents and grandparents may have had toward Indigenous peoples. Yet, the distillation of these complex histories into a flattened symbol means that these links are not easily pried open. In essence, notions of Andean indigeneity have become completely suffused in notions of Bolivianness in the altiplano.

Not all tattoo artists see this as a positive development. Like the general population, some question whether the Indigenous nationalism of both political speeches and pop culture might verge on appropriation. When I interviewed Gus in 2020, he reflected, almost five years later, on the type of tattoo he had been pursuing back when we visited Sucre's Museum of Indigenous Art.

> I was trying to use folkloric elements in order to create valorisation of our Andean culture. But I've realized that it's a cultural exploitation that I don't like and I don't feel comfortable with it, because it [feels like] I'm selling a culture that doesn't belong to me, to people that it doesn't belong to.

He then explained that tattooing folkloric designs is simultaneously good and bad. It valorizes an important part of Bolivian culture, but only by transforming it into a product that is bought and sold. On one hand, tattooing tradition has long been steeped in replication of iconic symbols (such as sailor tattoos or famous artists like Bert Grimm),[6] but in thinking about the specific context of Indigenous nation ideology, we can see a tension between positive and negative cultural effects.

Critiques similar to that of Gus are levied at times in Bolivia but are counter to the prevailing way of understanding indigeneity as part of national identity. However astute Gus's stance may be, my point is not to shame individuals by suggesting that they are appropriating Indigenous culture as outsiders. Michael Brown's claim that "the hybrid nature of Indigenous cultural life today argues against rigorous separation of Indigenous knowledge from the public domain of global society" (2004, p. 248) seems quite relevant to the Bolivian context. Rather, I reflect on the change of perspective Gus details to emphasize that representations of "Bolivia" or "Bolivian identity" have become thoroughly steeped in notions of being an "Indigenous nation."

Conclusion

The tattoos I describe which incorporate Indigenous-related symbolism may simultaneously be read in conflicting ways. Many individuals do see them as reflecting an increasing valuation of indigeneity, of connecting the artist and client to an Indigenous ancestry, and even indexing affinity with Indigenous-associated social movements and politics. But others might equally read these same tattoos as appropriations of Indigenous culture by urban, middle-class, mestizo-appearing bodies who (should) have no claim to Indigenous symbolism. Through such a reading, these tattoos may be considered a microcosm within Bolivian society of the global tendency to appropriate Indigenous "tribal" tattooing. Seeing these tattoos not as simply appropriation, but a reworking of identity within a context of the nationalization of indigeneity then opens up greater possibilities for understanding identity formation in late capitalist Bolivia.

What is perhaps most surprising about these tattoos is the ways in which tattooing itself is still seen as quite "rebellious" in Bolivia, by the general public as well as those who make and have them. But in analyzing the tattoos themselves, we see how they still quite strongly draw from and reinforce the ideological discourses that are hegemonic among politicians in the first two decades of the 2000s. While not as exploitative as the indigenismo of the 1950s, today's discourses may equally marginalize the most vulnerable in the country in favor of majoritarian political projects. Tattooing Indigenous symbolism may be understood as a reflection of these ideological discourses, but they also serve to reinforce them through their quotidian presence. Understanding the ways once vibrant cultural symbols become flattened in tattoo imagery demonstrates how media, even when produced from the margins, may both reflect and strengthen hegemonic discourses related to identity and nationalism.

Notes

1 I draw in part from Albro's (1998) astute evaluation of transactions with yatiris at Quillacollo's festival of the Virgin of Urkupiña as going beyond a syncretic "combination of Andean and Christian cosmological systems in the colonial context" (p 134; see also Himpele, 2008, p xiv). In the case of tattooing in La Paz, indigenous symbolism is flattened into iconic representation without the complexity of ritual (or other forms of cultural) knowledge.
2 Identification here might also include counteridentifying with hegemonic social norms through the use of tattoo or reworking such norms in a form of disidentification (see Pecheux, 1982; Muñoz, 1999).
3 I asked, "Que consideras tu etnia o raza?"
4 See Haynes, 2015, p. 273 for explanation as to what characteristics make a person "visibly Indigenous" in Bolivia.

5 In fact, during the 2019–2020 political crisis in Bolivia, I found through personal conversations, small WhatsApp group discussions, and public social media posts that almost all tattoo artists discussed here, and many clients, openly opposed Evo Morales, and the MAS party.
6 Charlie Connell, Editor in Chief at *Inked Magazine* notes that reproduction and replication have always been central to tattoo art, and in the context of Indigenous symbolism poses new questions as to what constitutes commodification (personal communication, June 28, 2021).

References

Albro, R. (2000). The Populist Chola: Cultural Mediation and the Political Imagination in Quillacollo, Bolivia. *Journal of Latin American Anthropology*, 5(2), 30–88. https://doi.org/10.1525/jlca.2000.5.2.30

Albro, R. (2005). The Indigenous in the Plural in Bolivian Oppositional Politics. *Bulletin of Latin American Research*, 24(4), 433–453.

Albro, R. (2006). Actualidades Bolivia's "Evo Phenomenon": From Identity to What? *Journal of Latin American Anthropology*, 11(2), 408–428. https://doi.org/10.1525/jlca.2006.11.2.408

Allison, M. J. (1996). Early Mummies from Coastal Peru and Chile. In K. Spindler, H. Wilfring, E. Rastbichler-Zissernig, D. zur Nedden, & H. Nothdurfter (Eds.), *The Man in the Ice: Human Mummies, a Global Study of their Status and the Techniques of Conservation* (Vol. 3, pp. 125–130). Springer-Verlag.

Althusser, L. (1968). *Lenin and Philosophy, and Other Essays*. Monthly Review Press.

Anderson, B. (1983). *Imagined Communities: Reflections on the Origin and Spread of Nationalism*. Verso.

Boas, F. (1927). *Primitive Art*. Harvard University Press.

Brown, M. F. (2004). *Who Owns Native Culture?* Harvard University Press.

Brubaker, R., & Cooper, F. (2000). Beyond "Identity." Theory and Society Theory and Society: *Renewal and Critique in Social Theory*, 29(1), 1–47.

Bucholtz, M., & Hall, K. (2004). Theorizing Identity in Language and Sexuality Research. *Language in Society*, 33(4), 469–515. https://doi.org/10.1017/S0047404504334020

Butler, J. (1999). *Gender Trouble: Feminism and the Subversion of Identity*. Routledge.

Canessa, A. (2006). Todos somos indígenas: Towards a New Language of National Political Identity. *Bulletin of Latin American Research*, 25(2), 241–263. https://doi.org/10.1111/j.0261-3050.2006.00162.x

Canessa, A. (2012). *Intimate Indigeneities: Race, Sex, and History in the Small Spaces of Andean life*. Duke University Press.

Caplan, J. (2000). *Written on the Body: The Tattoo in European and American History*. Reaktion.

de la Cadena, M. (2000). *Indigenous Mestizos: The Politics of Race and Culture in Cuzco, Peru, 1919–1991*. Duke University Press. http://search.ebscohost.com/login.aspx?direct=true&scope=site&db=nlebk&db=nlabk&AN=1362471

Deter-Wolf, A., & Diaz-Granados, C. (Eds.). (2013). *Drawing with Great Needles: Ancient Tattoo Traditions of North America*. University of Texas Press.

Fabricant, N., & Postero, N. (2015). Sacrificing Indigenous Bodies and Lands: The Political–Economic History of Lowland Bolivia in Light of the Recent TIPNIS Debate. *The Journal of Latin American and Caribbean Anthropology*, 20(3), 452–474. https://doi.org/10.1111/jlca.12173

Faris, J. C. (1988). *Nuba Personal Art*. University of Toronto Press.

Farthing, L. (2020). In Bolivia, the Right Returns with a Vengeance. *NACLA Report on the Americas*, 52(1), 5–12. https://doi.org/10.1080/10714839.2020.1733217

Farthing, L. C., & Kohl, B. H. (2014). *Evo's Bolivia: Continuity and Change*. University of Texas Press.

García Canclini, N. (1989). *Hybrid Cultures: Strategies for Entering and Leaving Modernity*. University of Minnesota Press. https://archive.org/details/hybridculturesst0000garc

Ginsburg, F., Abu-Lughod, L., & Larkin, B. (Eds.). (2002). *Media Worlds: Anthropology on New Terrain*. University of California Press.

Goodale, M. (2006). Reclaiming Modernity: Indigenous Cosmopolitanism and the Coming of the Second Revolution in Bolivia. *American Ethnologist*, 33(4), 634–649. https://doi.org/10.1525/ae.2006.33.4.634

Grisaffi, T. (2010). We Are Originarios ... "We Just Aren't from Here": Coca leaf and Identity Politics in the Chapare, Bolivia. *Bulletin of Latin American Research*, 29(4), 425–439.

Haynes, N. (2015). UnBoliviable Bouts: Gender and Essentialisation of Bolivia's Cholitas Luchadoras. In C. R. Matthews & A. Channon (Eds.), *Global Perspectives on Women in Combat Sports—Women Warriors around the World* (pp. 267–283). Palgrave-McMillan. www.palgrave.com/us/book/9781137439352

Hempele, J. (2008). *Circuits of Culture: Media, Politics and Indigenous Identity in the Andes*. University of Minnesota Press.

Himpele, J. D. (2008). *Circuits of Culture: Media, Politics, and Indigenous Identity in the Andes*. University of Minnesota Press.

Institute Nacional de Estadistica (INE), Bolivia. (2012). *Censo Nacional*. www.ine.gob.bo/index.php/censos-y-banco-de-datos/censos/

Kierstein, L., & Kjelskau, K. (2015). Fascination and the Decision to Become Tattooed. *Current Problems in Dermatology, 48*, 37–40.

Krutak, L., & Deter-Wolf, A. (Eds.). (2017). *Ancient Ink: The Archeology of Tattooing*. University of Washington Press.

Kuwahara, M. (2005). *Tattoo: An Anthropology*. Berg.

Marcus, G. E., & Meyers, F. (1995). *The Traffic in Culture: Refiguring Art and Anthropology*. University of California Press.

Martinez-Echazabal, L. (1998). Mestizaje and the Discourse of National/Cultural Identity in Latin America, 1845–1959. *Latin American Perspectives, 25*(3), 21–42.

Muñoz, J. E. (1999). *Disidentifications: Queers of Color and the Performance of Politics*. University of Minnesota Press.

Pabst, M. A., Letofsky-Papst, I., Bock, E., Moser, M., Dorfer, L., Egarter-Vigl, E., & Hofer, F. (2009). The Tattoos of the Tyrolean Iceman: A Light Microscopical, Ultrastructural and Element Analytical Study. *Journal of Archaeological Science, 36*, 2335–2341. https://doi.org/10.1016/j.jas.2009.06.016

Pecheux, M. (1982). *Language, Semantics, and Ideology*. Palgrave.

Pertierra, A.C., Salazar, J.F., Valdéz, S.M., 2019. Media Cultures in Latin America: An Introduction, in: Media Cultures in Latin America: Key Concepts and Debates. Routledge, New York, pp. 1–21.

Postero, N. (2017). *The Indigenous State*. University of California Press. www.ucpress.edu/book/9780520294035/the-indigenous-state

Rivera-Rideau, P. R. (2015). *Remixing Reggaetón: The Cultural Politics of Race in Puerto Rico*. Duke University Press.

Sammells, C. A. (2012). The City of the Present in the City of the Past: Solstice Celebrations at Tiwanaku, Bolivia. In D. F. Ruggles (Ed.), *On Location: Heritage Cities and Sites* (pp. 115–130). Springer New York. https://doi.org/10.1007/978-1-4614-1108-6_6

Strathern, A., & Strathern, M. (1971). *Self-decoration in Mount Hagen*. University of Toronto Press.

Turner, T. S. (2012). The social skin. *HAU: Journal of Ethnographic Theory, 2*(2), 486–504. https://doi.org/10.14318/hau2.2.026

Weismantel, M. J. (2001). *Cholas and Pishtacos: Tales of Race and Sex in the Andes*. University of Chicago Press.

Worth, S., 1980. Margaret Mead and the Shift from "Visual Anthropology" to "The Anthropology of Visual Communication." Studies in Visual Communication 6, 15–22.

Yuen Thompson, B. (2019). Women Covered in Ink: Tattoo Collecting as Serious Leisure. *International Journal of the Sociology of Leisure, 2*, 285–299.

28
BEING KNOWN AND BECOMING FAMOUS IN KAMPALA, UGANDA

Brooke Schwartz Bocast

Introduction

In contemporary Kampala, there are two dominant media streams that engage female university students: one tells them to abstain from sexual activity while the other tells them to take their clothes off. Consider the following two anecdotes, in which Makerere University students, Agnes[1] and Winnie, encounter these media streams:

> One weekend afternoon, Agnes, Winnie, and I were hanging out in their university hostel (a privately-run dormitory) when conversation turned to the tabloid press. As is common for stylish university women, Agnes and Winnie occasionally find their photos in Uganda's leading tabloid newspaper, the *Red Pepper* (see Figure 28.1). The paper once ran a full-page story on these young women complete with photographs and fabricated descriptions. One image – captioned "Fine Kampala city babes in Ntinda[2] partying" – pictured the women walking down the street wearing tight, trendy clothing. Agnes and Winnie shouted over each other as they described the images to me. They were eager to elaborate on the "publicity" they gained from this experience.

> On another occasion, we rounded the corner of the Makerere's law faculty to confront a mural covering the side of a campus building. Produced by Kampala-based NGO, Artivists 4 Life (A4L), the mural illustrates two middle-aged men attempting to entice female students into their cars (see Figure 28.2). The woman in the background complies while the woman in the foreground resists. The men display fancy cell phones and big bellies – two distinct signifiers of "sugar daddies," or wealthy businessmen who date younger women. The mural offers a directive to female students to discourage their participation in what public health officials call cross-generational sex: "Have self-worth. Care about tomorrow." When I asked Agnes and Winnie to describe their reactions to the mural, Winnie dismissed it with a tisk of her tongue: "I'm like, 'eh.' I don't want to know."

Figure 28.1 An example of the *Red Pepper*'s coverage of female university students

These instances demonstrate the relative presence of two forms of media – tabloid press and public health awareness campaigns – in the lives of female university students in Kampala, Uganda. Public health NGOs target female students in behavior change campaigns meant to reduce the spread of HIV while tabloid papers profit from the circulation of sexually explicit images of female students. The differences between the above images are obvious. The mural preaches sexual restraint based on notions of respectable womanhood and future-orientation, while the *Red Pepper* encourages young women's promiscuity and "hedonism." In popular conversation, these media entities are frequently positioned as "opposite" in that public health campaigns are presumed to help young women while the *Red Pepper* is thought to exploit them.

These apparent oppositions mask the fundamental *similarities* between these media productions. Within Uganda, women's bodies have emerged as a central site for contestations over modernity and national development. Cross-generational sex is a key motif for development and tabloid media, due to its epidemiological centrality to intergenerational disease transmission, and to the symbolic potency of the sexually liberated female student, respectively. The hegemonic portrayal of university women within Uganda's public sphere obscures students' self-fashioning as modern, moral women. This disjuncture has profound consequences for Uganda's population health because media misrecognition of female students contributes to gender dynamics that drive Uganda's rising HIV rate.

From 2010 to 2012, I conducted doctoral fieldwork with Agnes, Winnie, and their friends at Makerere University. I was curious about their experiences at East Africa's top university in the wake of Uganda's decades-long overhaul of its education system. Like many sub-Saharan

Figure 28.2 A4L mural on Makerere University Campus

African countries in the 1990s and early 2000s, Uganda adopted a World Bank-dictated structural adjustment program that privatized state-run industries like higher education and public media. These reforms also redressed long-standing gender disparities in education. Makerere University instituted an affirmative action policy that dramatically increased admissions numbers for female students. These dual outcomes – skyrocketing enrollments and girls' novel presence at schools throughout the country – profoundly altered Uganda's education landscape. The public began to contend with a new archetype born from neoliberal education and media restructuring: the "campus girl."

This chapter considers media representations of the campus girl as a lens onto the interplay of media messaging and audience reception as they relate to performative constructions of personhood (Barber 2007). I first demonstrate that despite apparent opposition between public health and tabloid media organizations, both entities construe themselves as knowledge producers engaged in pro-woman "sensitization" projects. "Sensitization" is an oft-deployed (though ill-defined) term in the field of international development. Within Uganda, it loosely refers to activities meant to raise awareness or otherwise enlighten ignorant populations.[3] While NGO directors hope to "sensitize" female students so that they behave more responsibly, Kampala's most notorious tabloid editor insists that his paper "emancipates" young women by sensitizing them to their right to flaunt their bodies in public.

Second, I show that NGOs and tabloid newspapers draw upon overlapping claims to modernity in their discursive constructions of female students, and that *both* of these constructions present female students as promiscuous and immoral. NGOs produce media that promote a vision of modernity in which young women engage in monogamous, romantic, same-age, heterosexual relationships that lead to marriage and a nuclear family; on the other hand, tabloid newspapers traffic in tropes of licentious, sexually liberated female subjects. I argue that both discourses do violence to young women's claims to personhood by constructing them as promiscuous (either because they are too ignorant to practice what NGOs define as "safe" sex, or because they are "modernized") and hence, immoral.

Students engage with these media messages in surprising and sometimes contradictory ways, rooted in self-making practices that locate value in the extension of one's personhood through publicity and reputation. I combine insights from media and performance studies with analyses of African personhoods to reveal how female students manipulate NGO and tabloid images in order to cultivate their ideal state of "being known" (*okumanyika*). While students couch this state in contemporary celebrity discourse, it also resonates with "fame" in the Munnian sense. Writing about exchange relations in Melanesian society, Munn describes how fame as a "virtual form of influence" is key to the positive expansion of the self in intersubjective space-time (1986: 117). For the purposes of our discussion, it is enough to note that female students create value though activities designed to build personal renown. While linked to long-standing models of African personhood, students' innovations reveal profound shifts in techniques of gendered selfhood in post-liberalization, post-HIV success Uganda.

From Taboo to Tabloid: Sex and Development in Uganda's Public Sphere

In the late 1980s, Uganda's newly appointed President Museveni sought to revitalize Uganda's economic and political institutions following decades of civil conflict. In concert with the IMF and World Bank, he instituted a platform of political and media liberalization with far-reaching effects for Uganda's public sphere. The country's media outlets had previously been few and government-owned. The 1990s and 2000s spawned multitudes of independent radio and print outlets operating in English[4] and dozens of local languages. Concurrently, Uganda witnessed a proliferation of international development agencies and NGOs.

The above developments aligned most dramatically in the form of Uganda's national HIV awareness campaign in the early 1990s. Funded by major international donors, the "ABC" (Abstain, Be faithful, use Condoms) initiative was the first large-scale AIDS awareness campaign in sub-Saharan Africa. In the wake of Uganda's lowered rates of HIV during the 1990s, the ABC campaign was hailed as a success, though its effectiveness has since been re-evaluated by public health experts and social scientists. Regardless of the ABC campaign's success or failure, its architecture and machinery ushered Ugandans into the ongoing era of sensitization.

Today, Ugandans are regularly "sensitized" on issues ranging from hygiene to girlchild education to voting rights. Sensitization campaigns often draw upon international human rights discourse. For example, in 2013 a roadside billboard informed commuters that internet access is an UN-sanctioned "human right." Sensitization campaigns hinge upon the figure of the autonomous, rights-bearing, decision-making individual.[5] It is this individual who is meant to adopt specific behaviors regarding sexual expression.

Prior to the ABC campaign, matters of sexuality were absent from mainstream Ugandan media. The proliferation of HIV awareness messaging normalized public discussion of sex.[6] A combination of this new-found openness and media liberalization policies wrought an efflorescence of tabloid newspapers. Uganda's tabloid sector is now the most robust on the continent. Along with the tabloids, mass media began to feature images of modern romance tied to the fidelity espoused by public health campaigns and to multinational consumer marketing.

Music videos, magazine advice columns, radio shows, and soap operas contribute to emergent discourses of romantic love, commodity consumption, and modern courtship.

It is important to emphasize that media does not represent a pre-existing reality. Media is implicated in the *production* of persons and social life. Media productions provide shared public possibilities for ways of thinking about the world and one's place within it. In recent considerations of ethical personhood, Michael Lambek writes that "Personhood draws on public – that is, social or cultural – criteria, concepts, models, and vehicles for its realization" (Lambek 2013: 837). These public vehicles include a Ugandan soap opera called *The Hostel* that chronicles the lives and loves of university students. *The Hostel* introduces characters who operate within ethical frameworks made explicit through the medium of scripted television. As characters – and audience members – discuss and evaluate each other's actions, *The Hostel* enters into a "dialogic relationship" with viewers that generates potential ways of being at university (Howe 2008: 50).

Young women integrate popular media into person-making practices that accrue value through renown and reputation. Anthropologist Karin Barber demonstrates how the circulation of Yoruba praise poetry – one form of textual media – facilitates this type of value production. She writes, "In the act of recognizing and publicizing reputation, it consolidates forms of social being achieved and precipitated through networks of social relations" (Barber 2007: 109). As praise poems are passed through social networks, the subjects of the poems expand their "reach" across space and time. Similarly, as tabloid papers circulate photos of Agnes and Winnie, they gain recognition among a young urban readership. Uganda's explosion of private media is therefore inseparable from the production of new forms of selfhood.

The Producers

Population Services International's (PSI) office is located in one of Kampala's poshest suburbs, Kololo. European residents jog and walk their dogs throughout this neighborhood of paved roads and manicured shrubbery. PSI, headquartered in Washington DC, is one of three major global health NGOs that operate in Kampala. PSI's health promotion initiatives are funded by multi-million-dollar grants from USAID, European governments, and UN agencies. Their Kampala office is cluttered with artifacts of social marketing campaigns, such as branded condoms and glossy brochures. PSI's staff primarily comprises Ugandan and European development professionals.

Artivists 4 Life does not have a permanent office. The young artivists (a neologism that combines "artists" and "activists") meet in the studio of a larger global health project affiliated with Makerere University. Their Canadian board of directors oversees the organization's local staff in the design and production of A4L's public awareness materials.

A4L and PSI differ in scale and overall mission but their philosophies, strategies, and products are remarkably similar. Both organizations rely on Western donor funding to operate, both are staffed by American, European, and Ugandan development professionals, and both are imbricated in mainstream international development flows of ideologies, materials, and human resources.

In contrast to the earnestly professional workspaces of PSI and A4L, the *Red Pepper*'s newsroom – located far outside of town due to security concerns[7] – has but one piece of A5 paper affixed to the wall. It bears an image of a bikini-clad woman with a handwritten message declaring, "If you play pussy, you get fucked." At least one male staffer displays pornographic images as his computer wallpaper. When a BBC reporter asked a female *Red Pepper* staffer whether the décor made her feel uncomfortable, the staffer replied that it did, but that she felt powerless to address it. The *Red Pepper*'s internal gender dynamics mirror the politics of its print matter. One of the *Red Pepper*'s most popular features is a comic strip called *Hyena*. In this comic, the Hyena character graphically recounts his sexual escapades – many, if not all, of which fit legal definitions of rape in various countries. Western readers and socially conservative Ugandans often find the *Red Pepper* to be offensive and in poor taste.

The *Red Pepper*'s editor, Rugendo, aims to provoke, and his strategy is paying off. Rugendo founded the *Red Pepper* in 2001while he was a student at Makerere University. He modeled the paper after his favorite British tabloid, *The Sun*. Currently, the *Red Pepper* has one of the widest readerships in Uganda. The paper draws international attention for its investigative political journalism and no-holds-barred approach to nudity and violent imagery. In 2012, the African Leadership Institute awarded Rugendo an Archbishop Tutu Leadership Fellowship to recognize his contributions to press freedom in Uganda.

The Sensitization Model

Despite the idiosyncrasies of the above three media producers, they exemplify their respective sectors regarding working assumptions about "sensitization." Like all buzzwords, the meaning of sensitization is ambiguous and polysemous.[8] However, it is possible to identify key features of what I term the "sensitization model" as it is commonly deployed in Uganda. PSI, A4L, and the *Red Pepper* instrumentalize assumptions about knowledge, personhood, and modernity in their sensitization projects. This model can be extrapolated from PSI and A4L's statements of purpose:

> Encouraging healthy behaviors and empowering the vulnerable in the countries we serve to make smart decisions regarding their health is at the center of PSI's work
>
> *PSI n.d.*

> Artivists 4 Life seeks to "inform, sensitize and empower our communities on issues that effect [sic] them."
>
> *A4L n.d.*

These statements make several assumptions about the workings of knowledge in the lives of their target populations; these assumptions underpin the sensitization model. The statements suggest that vulnerable people make poor decisions because they are unaware of the consequences of their actions and/or the existence of alternative choices. This lack of awareness mires them in a state of disempowerment. It is therefore the task of NGOs to intervene in individuals' and communities' ways of being by introducing actionable knowledge. These interventions are predicated on the assumption that once a target group is "sensitized," or informed, about their problematic behavior, group members will terminate said actions and adopt new, NGO-sanctioned forms of behavior. This "behavior change" is often glossed as "empowerment."

Taken together, public health organizations and tabloid media producers espouse an understanding of development (and hence, modernity)[9] that manifests in individual rights and agency, especially with regards to decision-making. Producers from both sectors see themselves as knowledge distributors such that the given knowledge will prompt recipients to make choices in line with national development objectives, whether that be reduced HIV transmission rates or the realization of new rights for women. However, these understandings become muddled when deployed in outreach efforts and media productions.

Modernity claims, morality claims

In this section, I look more closely at how NGO and tabloid media outfits deploy the sensitization model in their engagements with, and depictions of, university women. Despite their differing and, at times, ambivalent stances toward female students' sexuality, public health and tabloid discourse produce surprisingly uniform constructions of female students as promiscuous and, hence, immoral.

From 2007 to 2009, PSI ran a USAID-funded multi-media campaign entitled "Cross-generational sex stops with you!" The cornerstones of this campaign were billboards around university campuses and major traffic intersections, radio spots, and a university peer outreach program called "Go-Getters." I interviewed PSI and A4L staff, analyzed their internal documents and public awareness materials, and observed their staff meetings and art-making workshops. These data reveal a framework similar to sociologist Anthony Giddens' vision of modernity. Giddens suggests that the modern subject orients his actions to "the future" by virtue of calculated, information-based choices taken with particular goals in mind (Giddens 1991).

Although neither campaign explicitly instructs female students as to what sort of relationships they *should* be pursuing, when placed in the context of PSI's overall platform, it is clear that students should prepare themselves for monogamous marriages with same-age partners in which they will utilize family planning methods and produce small nuclear families. Presumably, this is "the future" to which students (and the nation at large) should orient themselves.

According to a PSI program brief, the campaign's "key message" to female students is "plan for long-term goals and consider the consequences of short-term gains" (PSI n.d.). In a popular PSI radio spot, a female narrator elaborates this message and reprimands young women for their consumerist desires and supposed ignorance about HIV transmission.

> Girls! The gifts, the nights out, the cash, can never be worth your life and future. Older men are taking advantage of you and putting you at risk of HIV infection in exchange for these bu [small] things. This practice is called cross generational sex. Respect yourselves, do what I do. Say "no" to sugar daddies. Cross generational sex stops with you.
>
> *PSI n.d.*

PSI implicitly underlines its role in creating the marked category of "cross-generational sex." Although intergenerational relationships have long been the norm in Uganda, public health organizations – in accordance with UNAIDS and other major donors – seek to "rebrand" these relationships as aberrant.

Finally, PSI billboards picture young, attractive university students surrounded by expensive consumer goods. The text encourages girls to distinguish between their "wants" and "needs," and reject relationships with "sugar daddies":

> You might *want* these material things … but do you *need* HIV? Say no to Sugar Daddies.
>
> You might want the phone, meals out and fancy clothes … but do you need HIV?

These PSI productions, in concert with the A4L murals, present a hegemonic framing of cross-generational relationships as something that older men tempt young women into with promises of material goods. PSI and A4L presume that female students participate in these

Figure 28.3 Juxtaposition of tabloid and public health representations of female university students

relationships because they lack self-worth, "life skills," and biomedical knowledge, and prioritize "wants" over "needs." They further presume that young women's desires for material goods and older male companionship are ignorant, short-sighted, and self-defeating. PSI and A4L attempt to sensitize young women to the ignorance of their choices by introducing knowledge about the value of romantic love and the importance of "the future." In this formulation, young women demonstrate empowerment by resisting men's advances, as illustrated in the A4L mural that introduced this chapter.

The vision of modernity promoted by PSI and A4L is devoid of desire, both sexual and consumer-based. Morality is demonstrated through physical and financial restraint. The heavy-handed nature of these campaigns enforces the image of the female university student as weak-willed, irrational, ignorant, and improperly desirous of sex and material commodities.

While public health campaigns promote modern forms of personhood, the execution of these campaigns undermine the very qualities that constitute this personhood. PSI's Go-Getters program claims to empower young women to be assertive, but the program's effectiveness is measured in terms of how well young women comply with external directives (for example, PSI's internal literature classifies students into "behavers" and "non-behavers" based on the type of romantic relationships they engage in). The word "empower" literally means "to give power or authority to" which is hardly the sense portrayed in the radio presenter's invective to "do what I do." Further, the billboards showcase coveted consumer goods and attractive college students who access them while simultaneously chastising young women who pursue these goods. NGOs appeal to girls to reject tangible symbols of modernity (phones, fancy clothes, cars) in favor of intangible constructs of modernity such as "true love" and "the future." These contradictions are not lost on female students.[10]

Much like PSI and A4L, the *Red Pepper* defines female university students according to the things they consume or wish to consume. However, unlike public health NGOs, the *Red Pepper* celebrates the physical trappings of modernity. A recent article lauds a female student for her ability to extract capital from her older male partner. The title reads "Rewards! MUBS[11] glamour girl Karungi eats big. Top lawyer buys her ride" (see Figure 28.3). The photo accompanying the article pictures Karungi smiling next to a new car, presumably the one that she has just been gifted. The article continues, "The pair have been spotted countless times having fun at exclusive places. In fact, we are further told, Karungi and her loaded counsel recently visited Malaysia for just shopping and fun." The image of modernity portrayed here is one of hedonism and conspicuous consumption on a global scale, with the university woman as its primary driver. While departing from public health discourse in terms of proper modes of consumption, this image capitalizes on the figure of the autonomous individual involved in a pure romantic relationship.

The image ties into Rugendo's philosophy about development and personal freedoms.

> For us, the way I understand women emancipation, it is also about the physical emancipation, the appreciation of your dress. The appreciation of your appearance is also part of the women, feminist cause ... For us, we are saying this is perfect and women are free to come out and even pose for our cameras. There's nothing wrong with it. That's what I was calling physical emancipation.

Despite Rugendo's feminist rhetoric, the *Red Pepper*'s coverage of young women seems designed to titillate, rather than extol. A recent *Red Pepper* article titled "Campusers looking for rich men exposed" features a full-page spread of female students in provocative poses wearing very little clothing. The article states that these photos were downloaded from the women's Facebook pages. Much like Karungi, the women appear smiling and confident, and they apparently authored and disseminated the images of their own volition via Facebook. While Rugendo undoubtedly considers this an example of women's "physical emancipation," the headline introduces an element of public shaming. By claiming to "expose" these women, the *Red Pepper* suggests that their dress and actions are worthy of public censure. The *Red Pepper*'s dual axis of shame and celebration undermines the modern womanhood it claims to promote by implicitly conjuring – and valorizing – the specter of traditional modesty that female students circumvent.

The contexts in which public health and tabloid representations of female students are embedded differ pointedly. But when removed from these contexts, the representations are almost interchangeable. In each image, an attractive young woman is surrounded by coveted modern commodities. It is only the immediate relationship between the woman and the commodities that differs. In the public health image, the woman desires the commodities; in the tabloid image, she already possesses them. This distinction is reflected in the women's facial expressions. The former appears distraught while the latter appears content. Both representations define university women in terms of their consumerist accoutrements. Likewise, both images present the women in a relationship with an older man or considering the benefits of such a relationship. These images reflect and reinforce each other and produce a powerful, almost hegemonic, media construction of the female university student.

Agnes and Winnie suggest that by advertising the relationship between sugar daddies, desirable commodities, and "educated" women, these billboards inadvertently promote cross-generational sex:

AGNES: Actually, it can even attract [girls] more.
WINNIE: Yeah, for real.
AGNES: Because, like, these things they do if, like, a sugar daddy's going to give you this, this, and that. Now that person is, like, getting an idea of that. So me, I think it's even worsening things.
WINNIE: Like, ok, if I got a sugar daddy I might …
AGNES: Get that.

By calling for university women to refrain from engaging in sugar daddy relationships, PSI and A4L establish that university women (at least, those who have not yet been taught how to "behave") are immoral and promiscuous. By "exposing" university women who participate in these relationships, the *Red Pepper* draws the same conclusion. But why do students find the first discourse riveting and the second one, passé? Agnes and Winnie provide clues to this discrepancy.

Cross-Generational Sex Starts with You!

Winnie and Agnes never mentioned public health campaigns of their own volition except for a joking post on Agnes' Facebook wall that read, "cross-generational sex *starts* with you!" This presented a marked contrast to students' frequent and enthusiastic talk about tabloid papers. While this discrepancy is not an absolute measure of students' levels of engagement, it does point to certain social facts about their modes of engagement with the above media productions. These modes of engagement, in turn, reveal features of female students' self-making strategies, or what the Comaroffs refer to as the "praxis of self-construction" (2001: 271).

Agnes and Winnie are presumably the intended targets of public health and tabloid media. They engage in sexual relationships with older men and flaunt the spoils of these relationships, such as iPhones and fancy watches. They frequent Kampala's most expensive clubs and bars (never paying for their own drinks) and sport the latest urban fashions, such as four-inch heels and miniskirts in bright, or "shouting," colors. Both come from middle-class urban families and are academically adept. Agnes serves as something of a leader among her peers, and doles out advice on sex, love, and relationships. Agnes and Winnie have given birth to one child each; these children are cared for by their extended families. When asked about their reactions to public health interventions on campus, they dismissed the relevance of such campaigns to their own goals and concerns:

BROOKE: When you saw [the A4L mural] on campus what was your thought when you saw it?
WINNIE: No, I just looked. I'm like "eh." I don't want to know.
AGNES: Usually it doesn't create an impact.
WINNIE: Nothing at all. We do what we want to do. No one is going to put up posters and tell me not to see a sugar daddy when I have my issues. I want … as in, that is what makes me happy. …
WINNIE: Yea. Then [NGOs] would say AIDS and all that, yet the little ones also have AIDS. They are actually worse than the sugar daddies … seriously. Me, I used to fear

big men and now I'm like, "this guy's so sweet!" And afterwards I'm like, "ok." The little boys are actually worse. They stray too much. The big guy is thinking about money, his family. He's looking for money. He's not going to cheat on you like a little boy.

AGNES: I don't even know why they call them sugar daddies.

WINNIE: White people, they don't look at age as anything.

Agnes and Winnie express resistance to public health interventions on several grounds. First, when Winnie insists that "little ones" (male college students) are more likely to be infected with HIV than sugar daddies, she prioritizes campus, or local, knowledge over expert knowledge generated by international public health actors. Second, in an implicit recognition of NGOs' claims to modernity, Winnie stakes a counterclaim by referencing "white people's" acceptance of cross-generational relationships. Winnie insinuates that because "white people" are the originators of modernity, their habits and predilections trump local billboards' directives. Finally, Winnie and Agnes are simply not inclined "to know" what NGOs want to teach them.

Agnes and Winnie explain that college students are too assured of their own expertise to pay such programs any heed:

Agnes: At times it is like sensitization ...

Winnie: At campus usually people don't have time for those.

Agnes: The people usually don't have time. If it was in high school you would listen.

Winnie: Yeah, high school they would teach us about using always condoms. They do that in high school.

Agnes: Yeah, it really, really helped me in high school. But in campus I never attended any of them, never. Not even a rally, not even what. I'm too busy. And again, you're like "I know everything". By now you know, you think you know. Even if you don't, you just think you know. But in high school, you know you're green. In high school, yeah, it really helped. Campus, I think very few people went. Have you ever?

Winnie: Uh uh. Me, I didn't have time. I would just go for my lectures.

Agnes explains that she valued HIV awareness programs in high school because she was "green" and aware of her ignorance regarding sexual and reproductive health. She insists that university students are confident in their understandings about sex and relationships and foreclose the possibility of assimilating new knowledge.

The above conversations reveal fundamental discord between public health NGOs' assumptions of female students' ignorance and receptivity to technical knowledge, and students' self-conceptions as well-informed and secure in their understanding of "issues that effect [sic] them." In an ironic twist, the key behaviors that PSI and A4L seek to induce in female students are acts of refusal and self-assertion. These are the very acts that Winnie performs when she rejects public health messaging and proclaims, "We do what we want to do."

Anthropologist Kristen Cheney (2007) has noted the "paternalism" of sensitization programs in Uganda, which partially accounts for Agnes and Winnie's resistance to these campaigns. I suggest that students take umbrage not just at the paternalistic tone of sensitization messaging, but at the negation of forward progress these messages embody. Winnie and Agnes perceive a disjuncture between their secondary school selves and their university selves that indicates a life cycle progression. Despite PSI's insistence that "the future" will be ushered in through sexual abstention and consumer restraint, students experience PSI's campaigns as a call to stagnation. Agnes and Winnie are engaged in processes of building and expanding the self through knowledge production and dissemination in order to progress through the life course. PSI would have them reverse this process and revert to younger (both in terms of chronological and social age) versions of themselves.

While one might argue that Agnes, Winnie, and their friends represent only a fraction of MAK's student body, Agnes' impressions of the futility of public health campus outreach campaigns are born out in PSI's internal monitoring and evaluation reports (PSI n.d.). PSI's Uganda Country Director informed me that she declined to renew their anti- cross-generational sex campaign after reports revealed that, while students correctly identified the "risks" of cross-generational relationships as portrayed in PSI's campaign, their relationship behavior did not change over the course of the campaign. In other words, while students' "knowledge" of the risks of cross-generational relationships was high, they did not incorporate this knowledge into their decision-making processes. This failure was read by PSI staff as a failure of students' reflexivity and further proof that students had not yet appropriated modern ways of being, despite the NGO's best efforts.

On the other hand, students actively engage with the *Red Pepper*. Many times throughout my fieldwork, I found students huddled around issues of the *Red Pepper*, giggling and gossiping over the images within. Students co-opt the language of celebrity in their discussions. They strategize how to avoid *Red Pepper* photographers, whom they term "paparazzi," but delight in their "fame" when pictured. *Red Pepper* images at times revealed students' romantic partners in compromising positions with other women, thereby troubling these relationships. At the same time, being pictured in the *Red Pepper* with one's current beau reifies that relationship. Students would occasionally submit unflattering photos of *each other* to the *Red Pepper* in the context of peer disputes. This example of media ambivalence underlines the efficacy of tabloid papers as a tool for expanding the self and building a reputation in Kampala.

Here we recall Barber's characterization of texts, or media, as central to the production of personhood. People engage with texts strategically "to shape social knowledge about themselves and others" (2008: 112). Media amplifies personal renown through what Barber describes as "texts' creation of inhabitable spaces through the expansion of a name" (Barber 2007: 112). Young women capitalize on tabloid papers' affordances – mass production, circulation, and consumption among a young, urban, educated readership – to expand their own names and tarnish others'.

Students incorporate tabloid newspapers into their self-making projects based on an understanding of "the self" as relational and performative. One endeavors to continuously expand the "reach" of oneself (glossed by Agnes and Winnie as "being known") by cultivating channels through which select information can flow. It is important to remember that "Far from being understood in terms of individual autonomy or self-sufficiency, [this form of personhood's] signature was control over the social production of reality itself" (Comaroff and Comaroff 2001: 274). And what better way to control the social production of reality than by manipulating representations of yourself and your peers in Uganda's "most loved"[12] newspaper?

Agnes and Winnie tack back and forth between discussion of the *Red Pepper*, Facebook, and real-time interactions with peers, all in reference to their larger project of "being known."

AGNES: And the other time [the *Red Pepper*] got my picture from Facebook, they put me there as Kampala's what? Kampala's hot campus chick, something like that. They put my full names, the company I work for ... Like how I'm sassy and sexy and what, oh God! It was so annoying.

WINNIE: Did you feel good? That was a good comment.

AGNES: I didn't feel good cause they're making money on me, yet they're not paying me, and they don't have my permission. I don't feel good ... *Red Pepper* had downloaded all our photos on Facebook, all ... Yeah, I've realized that I'm so famous, so known. I have 5,000 friends [on Facebook], 5,000 subscribers. Everywhere I go they're like "I know you from Facebook!" and I'm like "Ok, now what's your name?"

WINNIE: Like celebrity.

BROOKE: Did you say it's also part of your job, "being known" and meeting people?

AGNES: Yeah, yeah. It's part of my job, being known, cause when [*Red Pepper* readers] know me they know who I work for. They always get to know my company. It's part of my job description, PR.

This conversation reveals students' ambivalence about having their photos published in the *Red Pepper*. While Agnes initially expresses annoyance for having her photos published without her consent or financial compensation, Winnie prompts her to recognize the positive nature of the coverage. As the conversation continues, Agnes reveals connections between *RP* coverage and her cultivation of the positive state of "being known," both in terms of her job in the public relations department of a building supply company, and in her personal life wherein she revels in being recognized by strangers. Barnes' analysis of pre-colonial equatorial African personhood is strikingly prescient of contemporary social media. According to Barnes, "a following was the sine qua non of power" and "The measure of one's power and prestige was taken in numbers" (Barnes 1990: 254). Agnes' accumulation of 5,000 Facebook followers indicates her skill at the value production inherent to wealth-in-people.

Barber notes that audiences are not "ready-made congregations," but that "[performances] convene those congregations and by their mode of address assign them a certain position from which to receive the address" (Barber 1997: 353–354). In the sense that public health and tabloid media productions are "performances," we can take a closer look at how they delineate and shape who is and is not among their addressees. Because public health organizations position themselves as arbiters of modernity, the students they address are necessarily positioned as premodern. The *Red Pepper* similarly positions itself as a bastion of modernity but considers the female students within its pages as simultaneously modern subjects-in-the-making and already-modern collaborators. When I asked Agnes to describe students who do *not* appear in the *Red Pepper*, she answered as below:

If, you do not hang out, you do not ... you're not on Facebook, actually. And you're not hot (laughs). And you're not hot, definitely not hot, cause it's hard for *Red Pepper* to put in someone who's not hot. They always look for the hotties in town.

Thus, according to Agnes, those students who do not appear in the *Red Pepper* are those who don't participate fully in modern lifeways. Broadly speaking, the *Red Pepper* crystallizes who is important and worthy of "being known" in Kampala. PSI and A4L, on the other hand, attempt to convene an audience with so many internal contradictions – empowered/not empowered, modern/premodern, assertive/obedient – it ceases to exist.

Not only does *Red Pepper* convene an audience that Agnes and Winnie identify with and aspire to belong to, but the publication acts as a resource for entering the world of the "known."

Agnes and Winnie capitalize on *Red Pepper* coverage to convene *their own audiences* of admirers. Agnes values the reputation she gains through Facebook and the *Red Pepper*, and she speaks derisively of peers who do not command the same renown. Agnes' valuation of this "publicity" is not narcissism or self-aggrandizement – it is evidence of successful "being through becoming" in which oneself "ranged over the sociophysical space-time occupied by the sum total of its relations, presences, enterprises" (Comaroffs 2001: 275).

In this chapter, I have argued that young Ugandan women participate in self-making projects in which personhood is a "mode of becoming" dependent on the continuous cultivation of relationships and reputation. Media is key to this process. NGO and tabloid media producers circulate images of young women in sensitization campaigns meant to influence audience behavior. I have focused on one segment of this audience – university students – to illustrate how people integrate media into their ongoing praxis of self-construction. In contemporary Kampala, it is more valuable and life-affirming to produce and disseminate highly curated knowledge about oneself than to receive pre-packaged knowledge from external actors. To refrain from sugar daddy relationships as the NGOs instruct, or to be absent from the pages of local tabloids, would be to court "social death." To Agnes and Winnie, this is a much more immediately troubling prospect than the risk of biological death from HIV/AIDS.

Notes

1 All names are pseudonyms except for the author and public figures.
2 Ntinda is a neighborhood of Kampala with popular bars and clubs.
3 Like much development jargon, "sensitization" does not translate directly into Uganda's dominant local language, Luganda. The most common translation is *okuyigiliza*, which gives a sense of acquiring new information. But speakers usually code-switch to English when referencing "sensitization."
4 English is one of Uganda's national languages.
5 Cheney (2007) and Christiansen (2011) identify this feature of BCC campaigns in Uganda.
6 See Parikh (2004); Sadgrove (2007).
7 The *Red Pepper* antagonizes the federal government with its political coverage and is periodically subject to police raids and vandalism attempts.
8 See Cornwall (2007) on the role of buzzwords in international development.
9 As Karp (2002) explains, development discourse always comprises ideologies of modernity.
10 According to Agnes, "modern" is rendered in Luganda as *okyilongosemu*, which includes the meanings of "newer" and "better," and is often linked to technology. Thus, PSI's calls to reject consumer electronics in the name of modernity are particularly ironic.
11 Makerere University Business School.
12 This accolade was reported by *Kampala Dispatch* (2011).

References

Artivists 4 Life. 2012. Idealist.org Non-profit organization listing "About Us" section.
Barber, Karin. 1997. Preliminary notes on audiences in Africa. *Africa* 67(3).
Barber, Karin. 2007. *The Anthropology of Texts, Persons, and Publics*. New York: Cambridge University Press.
Barnes, Sandra. 1990. Ritual, power, and outside knowledge. *Journal of Religion in Africa* 20(3): 248.
Cheney, Kristen. 2007. *Pillars of the Nation: Child Citizens and Ugandan National Development*. Chicago: University of Chicago Press.
Christiansen, Catrine. 2011. Youth religiosity and moral critique: God, government and generations in a time of AIDS in Uganda. *Africa Development* XXXVI(3 & 4): 127–145.
Comaroff, Jean and John Comaroff. 2001. Millennial capitalism: First thoughts on a second coming. In *Millennial capitalism and the culture of neoliberalism*. J. Comaroff and J. Comaroff, eds. Durham: Duke University Press, 1–56.
Cornwall, Andrea. 2007. Buzzwords and fuzzwords: Deconstructing development discourse. *Development in Practice* 17(4–5): 471–484.

Giddens, Anthony. 1991. *Modernity and self-identity: Self and society in the late modern age.* Stanford: Stanford University Press.

Howe, Cymene. 2008. Spectacles of sexuality: Televisionary activism in Nicaragua. *Cultural Anthropology* 23(1): 48–84.

Karp, Ivan. 2002. Development and personhood: tracing the contours of a moral discourse. In Critically modern: alternatives, alterities, *anthropologies*. B. Knauft, ed. Bloomington: Indiana University Press, 83.

Lambek, Michael. 2013. The value of performative acts. *Hau: Journal of Ethnographic Theory* 3(2): 141–160.

Munn, Nancy. 1986. *The fame of Gawa: A symbolic study of value transformation in a Massim (Papua New Guinea) society.* Durham: Duke University Press.

Parikh, Shanti. 2004. Sugar daddies and sexual citizenship in Uganda: Rethinking third wave feminism. *Black Renaissance* 6(1): 82–107.

Population Services International. n.d. Uganda anti-cross-generational sex campaign description. Internal Document.

Sadgrove, Jo. 2007. "Keeping up appearances": Sex and religion amongst university students in Uganda. *Journal of Religion in Africa* 37: 116–144.

29
THE HALL OF MIRRORS
Negotiating Gender on Chilean Social Media

Baird Campbell

> Either a day before or the same day that Kaitlyn Jenner was on the cover of Vanity Fair, that was the same day that I said publicly that my name was going to be Alexa. And it was my first public post as Alexa, and it was really long, and it had my whole life story, and how I had come to feel like a trans girl, and I asked that people call me Alexa … The next day I woke up and my social media was exploding. It was shared more than 300 times, and it had more than 1000 likes.[1]
>
> *Alexa Soto*

I first interviewed Alexa Soto in June 2016 at a sushi bar a few blocks from Santiago, Chile's central Plaza Baquedano, since (unofficially) renamed Plaza de la Dignidad (Dignity Plaza) in the context of the ongoing *estallido social* (social explosion) (Ashley 2021.) We first met in 2015 at OTD Chile (*Organizando Trans Diversidades* or Organizing Trans Diversities), one of Chile's major trans rights organizations, where I was beginning preliminary fieldwork, and where Alexa had first arrived while still questioning and exploring her gender identity. Though I witnessed some of this identity negotiation in person during our time together at OTD, a parallel and inextricably linked process was playing out publicly on her social media accounts, to which I had not yet become privy.

During my fieldwork with trans and gender diverse/dissident[2] activists in Santiago over a period spanning 2013–2018, I heard countless stories of coming out on social media. In addition to 18 months of participant observation with both organizations and individual activists, I also conducted semi-structured interviews that increasingly pointed to the importance of social media technologies as a key part of the negotiation of gendered subjectivities for trans Chileans, as well as a source of intracommunity pedagogy in the context of scant reliable information available to most Chilean trans people. While Chile is home to a thriving and growing trans community and trans rights movement, many sectors of society—for example, the medical, educational, and criminal justice systems—have been reticent to create and implement explicitly pro-trans policies. For example, until the 2018 passage of the country's Gender Identity Law—guaranteeing Chilean trans adults the right to change their legal name and sex markers on all official documents—informal networks were crucial in spreading information about spaces and institutions that would respect trans identities without a legal obligation. As such, trans Chileans must often learn to navigate society and their identities through trial and error, as well as explicit and implicit instruction from others in the community.

Through these informal channels, some were able to help each other access higher education, medical care, and employment. This kind of "whisper network" has been especially important for trans people seeking help with biomedical transition (access to hormones, surgical interventions, etc.). The vast majority of Chilean hospitals do not explicitly offer these services, meaning that trans Chileans often learn from the experiences of peers about which hospitals, doctors, and insurance plans provide the services they need. As such, many make use of a relatively small number of hospitals and doctors, proven over time to be at least marginally trans affirming. In the absence of institutional guidance, trans Chileans develop and create trans-specific expertise through their lived experiences of success and failure navigating both institutional and public spaces.

Though gender and sexual minorities have long built and developed their own strategies for identity formation and strategic visibility through available media infrastructure (McKinney 2020; Brouwer and Licona 2016), and while the process of coming out has quickly become socially obligatory in much of the world, the advent and rapid spread of social media in countries like Chile[3] has rendered this experience more visible than ever before. In this piece, I argue that social media functions simultaneously as a queer and normative force in the lives of some trans Chilean activists, existing in a reciprocal relationship with the embodied self. That is, social media is neither simply a space of gender freedom nor gender policing. Rather, social media—and the people who use it—exist in a constant state of feedback and flux, leading to moments of both radical possibility and the solidification of normative gender expressions. Additionally, drawing on Daniel Miller's theorization of material mirrors through which subjectivity is negotiated, I account for the polyvocal nature of social media by suggesting that the relationship between the subject and social media might be more akin to a hall of mirrors, to which I will return in a moment.

Identity Construction on Social Media

Much of social media's current structure corresponds to a historical demand that we render ourselves intelligible (Cover 2014) through discursive acts (Foucault 1988), which are shaped by the very technologies, platforms, and algorithms that incite us to enunciation in the first place. This emphasis on the role of mediation in self-construction aligns with Judith Butler's (1993) theorization of gender performativity, which asserts that gender is the result of iterative acts of performance, mediated by discourse and culture (see also: King 2016.) This genealogy of thought is key to understanding selfhood in the social media age, in which subjectivity is quite literally constructed through the creation, curation, and sharing of texts—broadly understood to include words, images, videos, ephemera, and the body itself (Kennedy 2006; Lejeune 2014).

Nonetheless, even this capacious and non-prescriptive framing of the process of online self-making does not exist in a vacuum. Rather, as anthropologist of media Daniel Miller asserts, "We cannot know who we are, or become what we are, except by looking in a material mirror, which is the historical world created by those who lived before us" (2006, 8). That is, the subject positions available to us are always informed, limited, and shaped by the sociocultural and historical contexts reflected in the media in which they coalesce. Though this idea is by no means limited to self-construction online, the inherently relational, public, and rapid-paced nature of social media brings these processes into stark relief, leaving traces of processes that—offline—are largely internal and more difficult to access. However, I propose that social media might be more productively understood as a hall of mirrors, in which seemingly infinite reflections, refractions, and distortions force the subject to navigate (in this case) their gender identity and expression, guided by perpetually shifting signposts toward a static but as-yet-unknown outcome. In this way, the inextricability of online and offline processes of subject formation is brought into relief.

Put another way, while identity construction writ large is always a relational and mediated process, this piece will demonstrate that social media presents a seemingly infinite amount of publicly visible input from an ever-broadening range of interlocutors, all of whom play a role in shaping and reshaping each other's subjectivities through continual acts of identity performance and construction both on- and offline, in both direct and indirect ways.

Alexa

Alexa always looks impeccable: her hair expertly styled, makeup carefully applied to her *morena* skin, and her short, slender frame dressed to the nines. Though she is admittedly striking, embodying a "transnormative" (Spade 2015) or "hegemonically feminine" (Schippers 2007) gender expression, Alexa is more than a pretty face. In addition to her carefully curated image, Alexa's sharp wit, sense of humour, and kindness give her an ability to navigate multiple, seemingly opposed social worlds in a way I have seen few others do. A professional cosmetologist and co-owner of her own salon, she is equally at home rubbing elbows with TV stars as she is at a protest, at Congress, or a photoshoot. Simply put, she has a certain intangible quality that puts people at ease. At least partially for these reasons, she is a well-known figure in Santiago's diverse/dissident community, friendly with all but beholden to none. Offline, she can often be found at speaking engagements, parties, and organizing meetings. Online, she blends social media influencer aesthetics with activism, making use of the platform she has built to spread information about her experiences as a trans woman in Chile to both other trans people and to the general public.

Nonetheless, when I first met Alexa, she was not the public figure she is today, but a young Chilean from the working-class neighbourhood of Estación Central, coming to terms with an identity she had little vocabulary for. When I asked her why she had chosen to come out on social media—as opposed to gradually, in person—she pointed to a fundamental lack of accessible (e.g., free, Spanish-language, approachably written) information on the realities of living as a trans person. That is, because she had initially bumbled through her transition with little guidance, she felt that her personal experiences might help to fill the information vacuum for others like her. As a millennial, social media was the obvious choice for circulating her experiences to a wider audience.

> I just didn't really know anything about what [being trans] was all about, just because I didn't have any information. I think that lack of information is what made me spend such a long time not realizing that I was transgender.

Alexa's comments echo those of many of my interlocutors who came of age as the at the turn of the millennium, who almost unanimously signalled the importance of social media in the coalescence and articulation of their gender identities. This dearth of information Alexa describes is at least partly due to the place of gender in the Chilean imaginary. Rigid, binary gender roles have historically been framed as fundamental to the formation and preservation of the Chilean nation-state (Castillo 2005; Valdés and Olavarría 1998), becoming a particular (though often unspoken) component of the military dictatorship of Augusto Pinochet (Carvajal 2018), which lasted from 1973–1990. Even after the return to democracy in 1990, state refusal to address the already rampant HIV/AIDS epidemic (Donoso et al. 2015)—particularly devastating for trans

The Hall of Mirrors

women, *travestis*,[4] and gay men—reinforced in the minds of many Chileans that deviance from gender norms was a dangerous and deadly proposition.

As a result, widely available information about trans realities in Chile was generally limited to occasional, salacious reports on news magazine shows, and transphobic jokes and sketches on late-night talk shows. While this kind of programming was targeted at a cisgender[5] audience with a certain level of morbid curiosity, it reinforced to Alexa—and many others like her—the message that non-cisnormative expressions of gender were inherently laughable, shameful, and grotesque. Ultimately, Alexa highlights this context as the reason she chose to come and out and transition so publicly, "so that people could see in a very close-up and empathetic way what it's like this live this process." She continued,

> I think my story was really sincere, like I was telling a story that was really personal and really about my feelings. How I felt, how I wanted to feel, and how I had felt this whole time. And that when I decided that I was going to share my hormone treatment, too.

Alexa, like many trans people in the Internet age, made a conscious decision to document and share the steps of her biomedical transition (Raun 2015). Beginning with her initial "coming out" post, Alexa began to document her experience through both images and text. For example, images of pill container (for hormone pills), a doctor's office, or even of herself recovering in bed after her vaginoplasty, were also accompanied by sometimes lengthy texts that put the photos in context, shared her physical and emotional state, and invited questions from others looking to access these services. Even today, though the images she posts are now less focused on the transition itself, she still often posts side-by-side photos of herself now and as a child (see Figure 29.1), sharing reflections on her experience growing up trans in Chile.

Figure 29.1 This photo, posted to Alexa's Instagram in December 2016, appears with the (translated) caption: "We can all be what we want to be. In the first photo I was 7 and dreamed of being a girl. Now, at 24, I can say that I am definitely a woman"

These images are at once radical and quotidian, highlighting both a stark contrast between the two images, while also demonstrating a continuity of subjectivity that transcends the physical body. That is, the juxtaposition of the images invites the viewer to witness both the radical and normative potential of biomedical transition, a process that is always already inscribed within particular understandings of normative gender. The two photos putatively depict the same subject, and at the same time do not. The hall of mirrors of social media paradoxically allows for the presentation and policing of multiple versions of the self, while still ultimately leading the subject toward a specific yet arguably un-predetermined outcome, in this case, normative femininity.

A popular genre in trans social media (Vipond 2015; Horak 2014), these transition narratives are both archival and pedagogical in nature, what I have termed elsewhere the "archive of the self" (Campbell 2021). On one hand, they serve as an archive of physical and emotional changes, a genre of self-expression and identity negotiation that predates social media. On the other, because of the inherent relationality of social media and the dearth of trans-specific guidance in Chile, they often serve as a guide for other trans people who encounter them online. To some extent, as explored above, this is simply a part of subject formation within a particular sociohistorical framework. As Maurice Merleau-Ponty (2007) argues, changes in our self-representational strategies—in the case of trans people, including their names, clothing, tone of voice, and physicality—are necessarily also indicative of a change in our understandings of our own subjectivities and "the self" writ large.

While I do not disagree, this does not fully capture the complex nature of trans temporalities, which simultaneously highlight, question, and reify the cisheteronormative nature of linear time. Jay Prosser (1998) theorizes the importance of autobiography for many trans people, arguing that "post"-transition autobiographic practices "[allow] trans people to retroactively bring order to what is often experienced as a confusing and chaotic time;" in short, the benefit of time allows trans people to retroactively make sense of—and narrativize—their transitions into often neat, linear stories.

However, as Kadji Amin points out, "if the retrospective construction of a coherent transsexual plot narrative proves healing to some, it is at the expense of episodes, or even fleeting moments, that would fracture or exceed it" (2014, 220). That is, while Alexa and other trans social media personalities undoubtedly provide a crucial perspective for Chileans considering transitioning, the very act of narration often obscures the messiness of day-to-day identity negotiation. Given the lack of information and the relatively few examples of trans Chileans in the public sphere, it is easy to see how people like Alexa become emblematic not of one personal, possible outcome, but of a set of instructions to follow in the absence of other visible options (Siebler 2018). The polyvocality of social media presents seemingly endless possibilities for gendered selfhood emanating from and reflecting back at each user. Thus, while other authors have pointed to social media as a space for challenging transnormativity (J. F. Miller 2019; Eckstein 2018), it is perhaps more accurate that online spaces hold the potential to both trouble *and* reify gendered subjectivities that adhere to normative binary gender identity and expression. That is, despite its radical potential, social media is at once both a space of gender experimentation and one of gender policing. Much like in a real hall of mirrors, trans Chileans like Alexa cannot count on universal or coherent guidance, but must learn by trial and error, bumping into mirrors reflecting variously gendered subjectivities along the way.

Due to a combination of her content, her openness, and the algorithmic infrastructure of social media that rewards views with more views, Alexa became not only an abstract point of reference, but a reliable source of concrete support and advice to thousands of followers/young trans users. Through the process of negotiating her own subjectivity in public, she has become "the mirror" for her followers, who now see a possible version of themselves reflected in her, even as her own identity continues to shift. As might be expected, her audience skews younger due to the demographics of Instagram. However, her clever use of provocative images also elicits a notable amount of engagement from ostensibly cisheterosexual men, who may be attracted by the image but learn something about trans experience from the caption. Additionally, Alexa, like many highly visible trans people on social media, also regularly receives direct requests for help and guidance. In her own words, "And little by little, I started getting more likes and comments, and then I started to get people directly asking me for help."

Nonetheless, as I explore in the remainder of this piece, this increase in visibility and recognizability gives rise to new pressures, in some ways unique to the trans—and especially transfeminine—experience of social media, in which the performance of normative femininity is both rewarded and punished, but which also often presents the possibility for creative and subversive uses of normatively gendered imagery for the proliferation of resolutely nonnormative ideas about gender.

Normative Gender, Radical Potential

Alexa is under no illusion about the role that her gender expression has played in her acceptance both within the diverse/dissident community and more generally. While she is always quick to critique this influence, she recognizes that at least some of her ability to navigate society with relative safety is due to her performance of hegemonic femininity.

> Probably the time when I have felt most accepted in my life has been now, like, less discriminated against. Even though I obviously experience moments of discrimination or aggression, despite all that I think—and it's sad to say—but I think upon becoming more heteronormative I made myself more acceptable. Like people started to tolerate me more, because obviously they're going to prefer a woman to a *maricón*[6] in heels.

Alexa's use of the word "obviously" in the above remarks signals the power and ubiquity of binary gender norms in contemporary Chilean society, such that for her it is a foregone conclusion that people will "prefer"—react more positively to—trans expressions of gender that map neatly onto binary gender norms. This in turn presents trans people like a Alexa with a sort of Catch-22, in which visibility, security, and the ability to create change in her national and cultural context are predicated on a gender expression that is ultimately rooted in the oppressive sexualization of femininity, especially in and on bodies read as male (Serano 2009).

Nonetheless, Alexa's negotiation of when and how to acquiesce to and resist normative gender expression is calculated, based on safety as well as the idea that the public she hopes to reach with important information about trans issues will be more receptive to the message if the messenger embodies a certain aesthetic. It is for this reason that Alexa's Instagram account is a mixture of photos with friends, records of attending protests and marches, and overtly sexual photos that reify a particular aesthetic model of femininity the privileges puckered lips, lingerie, and a thin yet curvy frame. Accordingly, it is often these more sexualized images that are accompanied by the most overtly political messages. For example, in this post from October 2020 (see Figure 29.2), the image itself falls into a familiar influencer format, that of the effortlessly beautiful woman, fully made up, lounging in bed as if she has just awoken.

Figure 29.2   A post from Alexa from October 2020

Nonetheless, the caption accompanying the photos is a forceful rebuke of misogyny, clearly rooted in her own experiences. Translated, it reads:

> If I find myself in the company of a *machista*, whoever it may be, I will always tell him he's a pathetic *machista*. I will never make an effort to understand people who refuse to understand, simply because they don't want to. Because they live comfortable as little *machitos* in a world where their lives are easy and free from fear. We women are not responsible for dealing with their violence, the *machitos* are the ones who need to cut the shit and respect us. To allow people to think this way because they're "old" or because they grew up in that reality is to endorse *machismo* and patriarchal violence against us.

Thus, what appears to be a simple, somewhat sexy Instagram post by a popular influencer is revealed as a sort of feminist bait and switch, taking advantage of the sexualization of trans women on the Internet to transmit a resolutely feminist message, decrying the prevalence of *machismo* in Chilean society. Nonetheless, this fact exists in tension with the inescapable fact that the aesthetic of this photo conforms to ideas of femininity many in the trans and diverse/dissident communities feel are harmful. Further still, Alexa's photo and the accompanying caption will inevitably be seen by both trans and cis audiences, reinforcing for members of both groups the putative importance and attainability of transnormative gender expressions, in reality available to only a small percentage of trans Chileans.

Here Alexa's chosen occupation also plays a role, highlighting the intersections of gender, race, and class in the performance of acceptable gendered subjectivity. As mentioned above, Alexa is the co-owner of her own salon, as well as a somewhat well-known figure in the worlds of fashion and *farándula*, Chilean celebrity culture. She participates in these worlds both behind the scenes—doing the makeup and hair of many of Chile's cultural elite—and in front of the camera, promoting herself, her business, and her activism in both traditional and social media spaces.

In early July of 2016, Alexa hosted what she called a *Chochatón* (roughly, a vagina-thon) to raise money for her upcoming vaginoplasty. In Chile, where gender affirming healthcare is generally not covered by the national healthcare system nor by private insurers, it was and is common for trans people to hold one-off fundraising events to offset the high costs of surgery and aftercare. Held at *Nómade* (Nomad), a nightclub in a converted colonial house in Santiago's Bellavista neighbourhood, the event was massively attended by Alexa's friends, social media followers, and—notably—enough celebrities to draw the attention of several media outlets, including the national network TVN. Throughout the evening, stars from the worlds of Chilean television, music, and fashion appeared, not as paid performers, but as guests. The casual nature with which they interacted with Alexa and at the event emphasized that these were not paid celebrity appearances, but rather a glimpse into one of the social worlds Alexa felt comfortable navigating. Though I am unaware of the behind-the-scenes machinations that made this possible, the event clearly communicated Alexa's comfort and belonging within this community of famous, "beautiful people." In this context, it seemed that the version of Alexa reflected in the social media hall of mirrors was, in fact, just as glamorous as it appeared.

It is no small feat for a trans woman to be granted this level of access to this echelon of society, especially in Chile, a country marked by stark racialized and gendered class differences (Barandiarán 2012; Correa Téllez 2016). By bringing together her cosmetology skills, her social media following, and the social world of celebrities and media personalities she works with and for, Alexa is afforded a certain class position that shores up her gender identity, and vice-versa. That is, though Alexa herself does not come from an upper-class family and is racialized as *morena*, her gender expression, social world, and occupation coalesce to afford her entrée into the worlds of the rich and famous, worlds that are all but closed, off-limits to a brown-skinned "*maricón* in heels." And by her admission, a significant part of what allows Alexa to navigate and feel at home in these spaces is her normative gender presentation. Nonetheless, despite her significant cultural cachet, Alexa is still a trans woman on social media, a space known for its hostility toward femininity, and one that was in many ways constructed to actively exclude gender expressions outside the cisnormative gender binary (Bivens 2017).

Damned if you do …

In early 2018, Alexa made headlines not for her work, image, or activism, but because of targeted sexual harassment she experienced on Instagram (Cooperativa.cl 2018). As her image and clout have grown, Alexa has joined many influencers in doing paid promotion for certain products and events. This arrangement has many perks—free makeup, clothes, and lingerie to name a few—that are especially appealing to a trans woman like Alexa, who had begun building her feminine wardrobe in earnest only a few years prior. Consequently, this also means that she is regularly in contact with the official accounts of brands looking to forge a mutually beneficial relationship. Thus, she was not initially surprised to see a message in her Instagram inbox from DC Shoes Chile, the Chilean branch of a US company. However, when she opened the message, she was surprised to see not a job offer, but an attack. The message, in translation, read: "Haven't you ever thought about making porn videos? I'd love to see you."

Alexa, conscious of the power of social media to apply pressure, posted the message to her own Instagram, with the following caption (my translation).

> A few days ago, I received from @dc_shoes_chile an unpleasant and unnecessary message, that offended me not because I have anything against pornography, but because I think it shows a lack of respect that we *minas* (girls) have to put up with this, without even being able to identify a specific person, in this case from the official account of a brand. It's even more disappointing (*da más lata aún*) because they assume there won't be any consequences.

A few months later, when I interviewed Alexa again, I asked her almost offhandedly "What ever happened with the DC Shoes thing?"

"*Nada*," she replied, deadpan. "*Obvio*." Nothing. Obviously.

Again, Alexa's awareness that consequences for transphobia and misogyny are exceedingly rare is telegraphed by her seeming resignation to this fact, through another use of the word *obvio*. That transphobic violence can occur online with no negative consequences for the abuser—even from the official account of a multinational apparel company—is so obvious to Alexa that it almost doesn't bear mentioning.

However, this example also demonstrates the limitations of Alexa's normative gender presentation and its trappings as a mechanism for fostering acceptance and, ultimately, security. The 26,000 Instagram followers, famous friends, and glamorous public life it has provided her are ultimately no match for the misogyny and transphobia her very presence online provokes. With no official response from DC Shoes, and the rejection of her lawyer's request for an order of protection, Alexa felt there was nothing more she could do.

Ultimately though, she was much more bothered by the collateral abuse she received as a result of her initial accusation, much of which blamed the events on her own social media presence and gender presentation.

> I got a lot of abuse from followers of DC, especially girls who told me that if I like to walk around naked then I just had to deal with it. In fact, it was girls who said those things to me the most. That if I was going to show my body on social media like that, then I just had to accept that people were going to treat to me like that.

In this way, we see the influence of multiple forms of online feedback in Alexa's life. Despite presenting normative femininity, her gender expression and sexuality are ultimately still stigmatized. The same posts that regularly receive thousands of likes and follows are also revealed as a pretence for the continued abuse and policing of her gendered body. This incident demonstrates the seeming impossibility of navigating social media free from abuse as a trans person, and especially as a trans woman. Almost universally, interlocutors who identified as trans women and *travestis* related stories of having to significantly adjust or limit their social media presence—and in some cases leave social media altogether—because of the constant onslaught of abuse and sexual harassment they received from strangers. This is exacerbated by the *de facto* sexualization of transfeminine and *travesti* bodies regardless of context. That is, though much of Alexa's social media content is purposefully and overtly provocative, the nature of the content in question ultimately has little impact on the often violent reactions trans women and *travestis* receive as a consequence of simply existing on social media.

Damned if you don't …

Despite similarities in their age and social class, Catalina (or Cata) is in many ways the polar opposite of Alexa. Though she lives as openly trans in all areas of her life, when I first met her in 2017, she was working as a risk prevention engineer in construction—a decidedly male-dominated field—under her assigned name and gender. She would often arrive at weekly OTD meetings dressed like a male construction worker, emerging from the organization's tiny bathroom minutes later with clothes and makeup that reflected her feminine gender identity. Faced with the high costs of biomedical transition in Chile, keeping her job by any means necessary was key to eventually being able to live the life she wanted.

For these reasons Cata, like many of her trans peers, is acutely aware of the risks and benefits of being publicly visible as trans online. While, as discussed above, Alexa's choice of profession, social connections, and gender presentation all coalesced into some level of qualified acceptance, Cata's circumstances instead highlighted the importance of being judicious about when to share her gender identity and with whom. Her social media presence, especially at the time, was heavily filtered and curated, and existed alongside the content and accounts she had created under her assigned name and gender.

Though this effort to organize and navigate the online hall of mirrors was helpful in the short term—allowing her a greater degree of control of her visibility as trans—it also had offline ramifications for Cata that significantly impacted her quality of life, dictating where she could go, when, with whom, and under what identity, as she tried to navigate the shifting and mutually exclusive expectations of her dual gender presentation on social media. This was a common coping strategy for many of my interlocutors, who often find themselves torn between their desire to live and present their gender as they see fit, and the reality that living openly as a trans person in Chile often results in in the loss of the same material conditions that might make this possible. Contrary to "coming out" narratives that frame the moment of announcing one's gender identity as a momentary, all-encompassing act, Cata's social media strategy was in fact much more in line with the lived experiences of many of my interlocutors, who described this process as contextual and ongoing.

In 2017, I interviewed Cata about this and a variety of topics. The interviews I had already done, most notably with trans YouTubers, had revealed a disproportionate number of trans men vloggers in relation to trans women. Though Cata is not herself a vlogger, I asked her for her thoughts about the reasons behind this underrepresentation of transfemininity online. She responded,

> Why are there never any trans women on social media? Because of discrimination and censorship. … If they're going to show their bodies, it has to be at the beginning of the video and in a bikini, on the beach. Because otherwise everyone will say, "What's she doing in a bikini?" And they report you.

The emphatic tone of Cata's response is indicative of someone who has experienced this type of marginalization firsthand, and who is conscious of how it has affected her subsequent online behaviour. As she mentions, her previous experiences of targeted transmisogyny have made her much more reticent to show her body, which conversely is often an important part of transmasculine transition narratives on social media. However, it is also illustrative of an important if often unacknowledged facet of social media; though much content moderation is now done by algorithms, this moderation often depends on which posts individual users report (Crawford and Gillespie 2016), a reality that has disproportionately negative consequences for non-normative subjects online. That is, moderation is often triggered by a "report" by a specific individual, whose own biases and prejudices necessarily dictate which content they deem "inappropriate." It is this reality that is ultimately partially responsible for the seeming inescapability of misogynistic abuse for trans women online. Even a successful performance of normative femininity results in both acceptance and abuse, precisely because transfemininity—and femininity more generally—is at once exoticized and reviled, both the object of sexual desire and a pretext for further abuse.

I should clarify here that I establish this juxtaposition between Alexa and Cata not because I seek to rank or pass judgement on their individual choices, but precisely because—despite a continued pattern of victim-blaming—these choices ultimately have had little effect on their experiences of transmisogyny online. That is, though Alexa's social media identity is significantly more tied to sexualized notions of cisnormative of womanhood than Cata's, their experiences of online abuse have not been notably different, except perhaps in scale.

Though many of my transmasculine interlocutors expressed an increased sense of bodily autonomy as their transitions progressed, especially in terms of displaying their changing bodies without fear of censorship, trans women like Cata and Alexa experienced the contrary. As Cata's remarks above demonstrate, as her gender expression became more feminine, her body also became subject to increased policing and surveillance. However, unlike Alexa, Cata has a markedly "private" social media presence. While Alexa has a verified "public figure" account on Instagram, Cata's accounts are not explicitly public facing. That is, while all social media accounts are somewhat public, Cata's are largely available to people with whom she has a direct connection. Nonetheless, the similarities between their negative experiences of being trans women online illustrate that while the performance of hegemonic femininity is often rewarded with acceptance and increased social capital, it can still ultimately be weaponized against trans women. In the social media hall of mirrors, what seems like the "right" path can quickly reveal itself as a trap, dead end, or detour.

Conclusion

Though the performance of hegemonic femininity is often framed as key for the increased safety and acceptance of trans women, the experiences of many trans women on social media belie the limitations of this approach. That is, despite the efforts of Alexa's Instagram attackers to blame her online abuse on her own behaviour, similar experiences of abuse toward trans women like Cata demonstrate that efforts to keep one's experiences of transition and transness somewhat private do not ultimately result in freedom from misogyny online. Importantly for this piece, these often-unpredictable experiences of validation and abuse contribute both to a silencing of diverse transfeminine experiences online and to a reduction in the range of available models of transfemininity that are ultimately allowed to circulate on- *and* offline. This is made clear in the case of Alexa's resigned acceptance of the fact that her abuse at the hands of DC Shoes would provoke no substantive changes to safeguard against future incidents. We also see this tense relationship between online feedback and offline gender performance in the case of Cata, who was only briefly able to maintain a separation between her two different online identities and her offline gender presentation. Here we see that in the hall of mirrors, the illusion of choice is just that: an illusion. Ultimately, Cata found it untenable to juggle multiple gendered subjectivities and seemingly mutually exclusive demands and was ultimately led along the path of normative femininity. Since my original interviews with Cata, she has legally changed her name and gender markers, moved in with a partner, and had a baby, a testament to both her drive and ability and to the power of performing normative femininity.

In this piece, I have endeavoured to expand upon Daniel Miller's theorization of media as mirrors through which subjectivity is shaped and solidified. Given the seismic shift in the media landscape provoked by the polyvocality of social media, I have then proposed that a more productive analytic for social media might be that of a hall of mirrors, a space of both reflection and distortion, and one that is ultimately always teleological. Though subjects are presented with a seemingly limitless array of options, just like a real house of mirrors, in contexts such as Santiago, there is only one "correct" path: in this case, that of normative gender. However, I have further argued that the "successful" navigation of the hall of mirrors—the embodiment and performance of normative femininity—is ultimately still revealed as a trap; normative gender presentation does not prevent abuse, it simply gives it a different shape. In this way, social media demonstrates the underlying bind of transfemininity and femininity online; for Chilean trans women online, there may be no exit from the hall of mirrors, but simply a new set of mirrors. This reframes the ongoing debate concerning social media as either a space of homogenization or transgression of existing gender norms, making clear that these technologies—like offline spaces—present opportunities for both.

Notes

1 All interviews were conducted in Spanish, and all English translations are mine.
2 While the global movement often exists under the banner of the "LGBTQ" or "LGBTI" rights, these acronyms overlook a great variety of non-Anglo-centric dissident subjectivities and political orientations, often glossed as "Queer." Scholars in and of the Global South (Rivas San Martín 2011; Concilio 2016) have increasingly questioned the imperialist nature of adopting terms like Queer from the Global North uncritically. As such, throughout this piece I combine two local terms—diverse and dissident—to gesture toward the two poles of a movement united by gender and sexually diverse people fighting for security, recognition, and protection, though often through very different strategies.
3 As of January 2021, roughly 82 percent of Chileans had regular access to internet (DataReportal 2021).
4 A feminine non-binary category, in Chile often associated with sex work and societal marginalization.
5 A person who identifies with the gender assigned to them at birth; and heterosexual, a person who is sexually attracted primarily or exclusively to members of the "opposite" gender within a binary gender system.
6 A common slur for male homosexuals throughout Latin America. It should be clarified that Alexa uses the word here in the way many in Chile's diverse/dissident community do, as a way of reclaiming it and emphasizing the discrimination it entails.

References

Amin, Kadji. 2014. "Keywords: Temporality." *Transgender Studies Quarterly* 1 (1–2): 219–21.
Ashley, Jennifer. 2021. "A Radical Recentering of Dignity." *Sapiens*, February 9, 2021. http://web.archive.org/web/20210210124533/https://www.sapiens.org/culture/chile-democracy-dignity/.
Barandiarán, Javiera. 2012. "Researching Race in Chile." *Latin American Research Review* 47: 161–76.
Bivens, Rena. 2017. "The Gender Binary Will Not Be Deprogrammed: Ten Years of Coding Gender on Facebook." *New Media & Society* 19 (6): 880–98.
Brouwer, Daniel C., and Adela C. Licona. 2016. "Trans(Affective)Mediation: Feeling Our Way from Paper to Digitized Zines and Back Again." *Critical Studies in Media Communication* 33 (1): 70–83. https://doi.org/10.1080/15295036.2015.1129062.
Butler, Judith. 1993. *Bodies That Matter: On the Discursive Limits of "Sex."* New York: Routledge.
Campbell, Baird. 2021. "The Archive of the Self: Trans Self-Making and Social Media in Santiago de Chile." Dissertation, Rice University. https://scholarship.rice.edu/handle/1911/110457.

Carvajal, Fernanda. 2018. "Image Politics and Disturbing Temporalities: On 'Sex Change' Operations in the Early Chilean Dictatorship." *TSQ: Transgender Studies Quarterly* 5 (4): 621–37.
Castillo, Alejandra. 2005. *La república masculina y la promesa igualitaria*. Santiago de Chile: Palinodia.
Concilio, Arielle A. 2016. "Pedro Lemebel and the Translatxrsation." *TSQ: Transgender Studies Quarterly* 3 (3–4): 462–84. https://doi.org/10.1215/23289252-3545167.
Cooperativa.cl. 2018. "Joven Expuso 'Desagradable' Mensaje Machista Enviado Por Marca de Zapatillas – Cooperativa.Cl." *Cooperative.Cl*, January 19, 2018. http://web.archive.org/web/20210215184242/https://www.cooperativa.cl/noticias/sociedad/minorias-sexuales/joven-expuso-desagradable-mensaje-machista-enviado-por-marca-de/2018-01-19/175652.html.
Correa Téllez, Josefina. 2016. "La Inmigración Como 'Problema' o El Resurgir de La Raza. Racismo General, Racismo Cotidiano y Su Papel En La Conformación de La Nación." In *Racismo En Chile: La Piel Como Marca de La Inmigración*, edited by María Emilia Tijoux, 35–47. Santiago de Chile: Editorial Universitaria.
Cover, Rob. 2014. "Becoming and Belonging: Performativity, Subjectivity, and the Cultural Purposes of Social Networking." In *Identity Technologies: Constructing the Self Online*, edited by Anna Poletti and Julie Rak, 55–69. Madison, WI: The University of Wisconsin Press.
Crawford, Kate, and Tarleton Gillespie. 2016. "What Is a Flag for? Social Media Reporting Tools and the Vocabulary of Complaint." *New Media and Society* 18 (3): 410–28. https://doi.org/10.1177/1461444814543163.
DataReportal. 2021. "Digital in Chile: All the Statistics You Need in 2021—DataReportal—Global Digital Insights." DataReportal. 2021. https://datareportal.com/reports/digital-2021-chile.
Donoso, Amelia, Víctor Hugo Robles, Luz María Yaconi, Malucha Pinto, Cecilia Sepúlveda Carvajal, Karen Lee Anderson, Sonia Covarrubias Kindermann, et al. 2015. *SIDA en Chile: historias fragmentadas*. Santiago de Chile: Siempreviva Ediciones.
Eckstein, Ace J. 2018. "Out of Sync: Complex Temporality in Transgender Men's YouTube Transition Channels." *QED: A Journal in GLBTQ Worldmaking* 5 (1): 24–47. www.jstor.org/stable/10.14321/qed.5.1.0024.
Foucault, Michel. 1988. *Technologies of the Self: Seminar: Selected Papers*. Amherst, MA: University of Massachusetts Press.
Horak, Laura. 2014. "Trans on YouTube: Intimacy, Visibility, Temporality." *TSQ: Transgender Studies Quarterly* 1 (4): 572–85. http://tsq.dukejournals.org/cgi/doi/10.1215/23289252-2815255.
Kennedy, Helen. 2006. "Beyond Anonymity, or Future Directions for Internet Identity Research." *New Media & Society* 8 (8): 59–76.
King, Brian W. 2016. "Becoming the Intelligible Other: Speaking Intersex Bodies against the Grain." *Critical Discourse Studies* 13 (4): 359–78.
Lejeune, Philippe. 2014. "Autobiography and New Communication Tools." In *Identity Technologies: Constructing the Self Online*, edited by Anna Poletti and Julie Rak, 249–58. Madison, WI: The University of Wisconsin Press.
McKinney, Cait. 2020. *Information Activism: A Queer History of Lesbian Media Technologies*. Durham, NC: Duke University Press.
Merleau-Ponty, Maurice, Ted Toadvine, and Leonard Lawlor. 2007. *The Merleau-Ponty Reader*. Evanston, IL: Northwestern University Press.
Miller, Daniel. 2006. "Materiality: An Introduction." In *Materiality*, edited by Daniel Miller. Durham: Duke Univ. Press.
Miller, Jordan F. 2019. "YouTube as a Site of Counternarratives to Transnormativity." *Journal of Homosexuality* 66 (6): 815–37. https://doi.org/10.1080/00918369.2018.1484629.
Prosser, Jay. 1998. *Second Skins: The Body Narratives of Transsexuality*. New York: Columbia University Press.
Raun, Tobias. 2015. "Archiving the Wonders of Testosterone via YouTube." *TSQ: Transgender Studies Quarterly* 2 (4): 701–9.
Rivas San Martín, Felipe. 2011. "Diga 'Queer' Con La Lengua Afuera: Sobre Las Confusiones Del Debate Latinoamericano." In *Por Un Feminismo Sin Mujeres*, edited by Territorios Sexuales Ediciones, CUDS, 59–75. Santiago de Chile.
Schippers, Mimi. 2007. "Recovering the Feminine Other: Masculinity, Femininity, and Gender Hegemony." *Theory and Society* 36 (1): 85–102. https://doi.org/10.1007/s11186-007-9022-4.
Serano, Julia. 2009. "Psychology, Sexualization and Trans-Invalidations." Philadelphia: Keynote lecture presented at the 8th Annual Philadelphia Trans-Health Conference. www.juliaserano.com/av/Serano-TransInvalidations.pdf.

Siebler, Kay. 2018. *Learning Queer Identity in the Digital Age*. London: Palgrave Macmillan UK.

Spade, Dean. 2015. *Normal Life: Administrative Violence, Critical Trans Politics, and the Limits of Law*. Brooklyn, NY: South End Press.

Valdés, Teresa, and José Olavarría. 1998. *Masculinidades y equidad de género en América Latina*. Santiago: FLACSO-Chile: UNFPA.

Vipond, Evan. 2015. "Resisting Transnormativity: Challenging the Medicalization and Regulation of Trans Bodies." *Theory in Action* 8 (2): 21–44. https://doi.org/10.3798/tia.1937-0237.15008.

D

Political Conservatism

30
MEDIA ANTHROPOLOGY AND THE CRISIS OF FACTS

Peter Hervik

Introduction

In the current age of economic crisis, moral outrage, and digitalization of everyday life, issues of strategic ignorance and racialized inequality are two particularly troubling and intellectually challenging areas. According to surveys conducted by the World Economic Forum, massive cyberattacks and breakdown of critical information infrastructure and networks are regarded as the second highest risks to society in 2019, hence the crisis of fact. The increasing influence of the attention economy, political communication, the shift to omnipresent personal searching, user generated sites, and global Internet access have accelerated the practice of pseudo-science, vitriol, disinformation, popular memes, slogans, and symbols. User activists have contributed to a global crisis of facts that takes a strong toll on the functioning of democratic society and seems irreversible. This is a challenge media anthropology need to address.

At the turn of the millennium, I realized that my approach in two research projects in Denmark echoed key questions in the anthropology of media as formulated mostly clearly by Kelly Askew (2002), including: "What meanings do people construct out of mass-mediated images and sounds?" "How do they negotiate embedded ideologies, politics, and economics?" The projects coincided with "history-in-progress" as the far-right Danish People's Party, established in October 1995, grew dramatically in a symbiotic relationship with the news media. The second research project on the media coverage of religion in Danish news media began in early 2001 and ended in 2002. Core research questions were inspired by Askew and others included: "How do people know about migrants, descendants and refugees?" "What were the sources of their knowledge?" "How did basic perceptions about these populations form?" Since few Danes personally know minorities, yet still hold strong opinions about them, the media was a primary source of (dis)information but not reducible to any single, identifiable outlet. Our analysis yielded substantive documentation of a dominant conservative media with a neonationalist, anti-migration, and anti-elitist platform (Hervik 2011). With the global rise of neonationalism came discourses of racialization and racist political programs, policies and administrative routines. These projects I identified as falling within an anthropology of media and political anthropology, which by the time of publishing the book *The Annoying Difference: The Emergence of Danish Neonationalism, Neoracism, and Populism in the Post-1989*

World in 2011 could be identified as "Media Anthropology" – the new contact field as pioneers of the discipline framed it (Postill 2009).

In a recently concluded team research project entitled "A Study of Experiences and Reactions to Racialization in Denmark" (SERR), as well as in a subproject on "Danish exclusionary reasoning in social media and web news commentaries" (DER), the public space, and the media in particular, was not what it used to be (Hervik 2018: 98ff). This space was degenerated through processes of hyper commercialization, monopolization, and competitions among private interests over state-directed resource allocation (ibid., see also Cody 2011). We found that the use of media sources to gain information had to a large extent remolded into clashes between radically different and often extreme opinions. Opinions and attitudes stripped of context in service of creating click bait, moral panic and moral outrage allowed little space for increased understanding. The corporate national news media increasingly used racialized and bifurcated terminology: one for "white" Danes and one for new "non-Danes." In particular, Islam and Muslims became targets of a nationalist project promoting "Danish values" understood and organized as a defense of a nation in danger (Hervik 2018, 2019a).

The research findings resonated with what Robert N. Proctor coined agnotology (the study of ignorance), and argued that strategic ignorance is a sign of the times we live in (2008). Ignorance, say of practices of racism and nationalism, should not be seen as merely lack of knowledge, but is a construction that can be reproduced both actively and passively. Strategic ignorance is the active use of ignorance, where certain people don't want you to know certain things, or will actively work to organized doubt or uncertainty by any means available (Hervik, 2021b, Proctor 2008). Proctor's own key examples are the Tobacco Industry and the military, while more current examples could be climate crisis denialism as well as the denials of nationalism and racism (Proctor 2008; Hervik 2021b). In addition, strategic ignorance is the heart of political communications, well captured in two book titles. When Bill Press published his book on spinning the news in 2001, he adequately gave it the subtitle *All the Ways We Don't Tell the Truth*, and Danish author Christian Kock, called his book *They Don't Answer (De svarer ikke)* (2011). Again, the political communication industry is powerful contributor to the crisis of fact.

Such a process of strategic ignorance is not unique to racialization but is a suggested a part of a broader phenomenon that is of a global dimension as Proctor suggested. In addition, racialization in Denmark is in an inseparable partnership with nationalism and neoliberalism (Hervik 2011). As such, these isms form the pillars of decolonial relations (Udupa 2020; Udupa, Galiardone and Hervik 2021). This will become clear in the illustrations. Racialization is interwoven with gender and class-based discrimination and a dominant, ubiquitous theme and home turf for vitriol and exclusionary reasoning. In fact, the "us-them" division in nationalism and racism dovetails with the structure and priorities of the news media and to the extent that media culture and the web of culture are inseparable from each other (Bird 2003: 2–3).

In this article, the aim is to show how strategic ignorance in the field of racialization, racism, and nationalism works by using illustrations from Denmark. The original epistemology on how people know what they know, now need to include ignorance. Charles Mills has suggested that the epistemology of ignorance as a way to conceptualize the intellectual efforts to produce ignorance and being indifference to fact (2007). For the authors of the edited volume *Agnotology: The Making and Unmaking of Ignorance* the ignorance that underpins racism is not a simple accidental gap of knowledge of racial ideology and actual practice; ignorance is often actively produced for purposes of domination and exploitation (Stockly 2011). Race, racialization and racism are produced at particular moments to serve particular ends, which is also known as racial formation or simply racialization (Kumar 2021).

The basis for the research is the social practice theory premise well known in anthropology, which is to start with the specific problem in front of you and not a detached view from nowhere in particular. Such a start could be asking how come when our interlocutor, Lissy, uses toilet habits in her talk about concerns about the presence of non-white Danes in the country? My intention is to draw from the pool of many small social practice theory studies that is added together through analysis, which have revealed important issues about ignorance and inequality relevant for media anthropology to deal with (Hervik 2019b). One of the elements of social practice theory that moves further than Bourdieu's practice theory as well as the cultural studies circuit of cultural production is the insistence on including a person-centric approach that can improve our understanding of the complexities of the use of general media as a primary source of knowledge, or indirectly through social interaction where other persons draw on their recollection of the media event. To include a person-centric dimension can also be seen as a response to the use of the individual as an anonymous monad. Instead, we insist that persons are unique, psychologically complex, the product of a development process, and often, but not always, acting in an intentional, conscious manner. In this manner, persons are not reduced to simple effects of discourse – or cannot reduce the individual to an unthinking mélange of virtual identities proposed (Linger 2005). Accordingly, it becomes more obvious that from a specific person's perspective that the offline-online media outlets are complementary. After going through the illustrations, I argue that strategic ignorance is a huge new challenge to be addressed collectively by media anthropology.

Drawing on a pool of specific minor media events identified in the SERR and DER projects, I intend to include the forces and circumstances these events are situated in. An example of an event is radical right-wing party activists putting up road signs up "Syria 4426" (km) and "Baghdad 5317" outside a winter camp of tents housing asylum seekers. The signs were covered by a mainstream newspaper, which shifted the frame from the horrific winter conditions by the moral appeal: "How do you like the signs?" (Hervik 2019c). These minor media events are set within and in response to mainstream media coverage, and revealed ten nationalist responses for each one more accommodating and pragmatic (ibid.). Therefore, and as the *first* task, I will argue that professional political communication and right-wing dominance shape the daily news media stories today, while insisting that the ideology and investment in the news media *existed prior to* social media. This dominance is sometimes phrased as a "1 to 8" relationship reflecting the size and impact of the political conservative media. The number is obviously a figurative way to capture this relationship of power in the political orientation of the news media in the USA and Denmark. In the material gathered in these projects, we identified the consistent twin axes of true and false, civil and uncivil, whether in the minor media events themselves or in commentaries on them. I deal with this axis in the second section. Following a conceptual treatment of these ideas, I use cases from the Danish scene regarding indifference to research-based knowledge and the use of civility to control public discourse about racism to present and discuss how ignorance plays out. In the final concluding section, I discuss the implications of the long-term political conservative, nationalist, and populist media dominance across "old" and "new" media technologies in Denmark that shows how facts are no match for strategic ignorance.

Overall, the DER project includes the study of 35 minor media events, commentaries and ethnographic interviews with commentators mostly conducted in their homes. Of the 21 interviews, eight were commentators others would categorize as far or extreme right. All of them talk about FB friends, groups, and sites where people whom they shared views with, who are arming themselves to defend themselves, their families and their countries. None of the interviews distanced themselves from this aspect of violence, although they understood why this could be found necessary. The project took place mostly in Denmark, while the SERR project included the Nordic countries and France but with an eye to the decolonial relations in general (Hervik 2019b).

"One to Eight": The Dominance of Media-Driven Political Right

Right before the turn of the millennium, the subscribership of newspapers declined dramatically across the world in a structural shift towards the new free dailies and to the Internet. Advertising giants made enormous profits from the Internet, which left national newspapers in financial distress. Media conglomerates continued to expand news coverage and become more commercially oriented toward drama, images, opinions, entertainment, and domestic news, with less emphasis on substance, analysis and responsibility.

Since the 1920s the saying "In war, truth is the first casualty" has been emphasized again and again. Fewer people have noted how the politics of fear and crisis can create a sense of emergency in which truth and legal principles are set aside. Despite the grave historical truth of the Nazi Party declaring Germany in a state of emergency on February 28, 1933, discourses of national identity- and security-crisis as well as news media-driven moral panics bring the same assault on truth that allows for legal changes otherwise not obtainable (Buzan, Wæver, and de Wilde 1998). Neonationalist characterizations of Denmark as a nation in danger have increasingly invoked a rhetoric of war, occupation, intrusion, self-defense, and skepticism of international binding conventions.

According to Susan Carruthers, the "Vietnam syndrome" refers to the popular notion that it was the media that lost the Vietnam War. Particularly since the Falkland War (1982), the invasion of Grenada (1983), the invasion of Panama (1989), the Gulf War (1991), and the Iraq war (2003) (Carruthers 2000), the media has played a strong role in determining the success of new conflicts. The last five of these armed conflicts have been influenced by radical right, neo-conservative media policies under the leadership of American mavericks Dick Cheney and Donald Rumsfeld.

The Vietnam War also generated another concern about the media coverage. Because the war had dominated the media, it was difficult to attract new, younger conservative thinkers to academia and politics. This is precisely what Lewis Powell, a Supreme Court nominee, wrote in a memo to the Chamber of Commerce and the conservative business sector four years before the Vietnam War ended. Leaders in the American business sector subsequently outlined a long-term plan for maximizing influence. This entailed establishing institutes within universities, thinktanks, magazines, scientific journals, and publishers; all of which, Powell argued, should be well-funded. Then-Secretary of the Treasury, William Simon, took up this plan and made it a reality (Lakoff 2012).

Today, enormous sums of money have been donated to conservative and neo-conservative thinktanks, including the Heritage Foundation, Manhattan Institute, American Enterprise Institute, Hoover Institute, John M. Olin Center for Law, and the Cato Institute, to name but a few of the existing 60–80 thinktanks. In addition, conservatives own a large part of the news industry, controlling all phases of production through vertical integration (Lakoff 2012).

Thinktanks offer research and advice within conservative and neo-conservative paradigms, including profound analysis of political opponents. Any issue in public debates is given a conservative frame. In Lakoff's assessment, Republican politicians know what voters are thinking, whereas their Democratic counterparts hold onto the Enlightenment belief that everyone thinks in the same way and that is what makes them human. With intense dialogue and reasoning, higher understandings can be reached precisely as Einstein claimed (Lakoff 2012).

Given this dominance of media ownership and control which is not confined to within national borders, Lakoff argues that power discrepancies in the media world at all levels can be simplified as a relationship of 1:8. The mainstream right is roughly eight times more powerful than the mainstream left, for instance, in the number of talk show hosts, air time, frequency of sources used and financial support. The ratio is roughly similar in many European countries.

Interlinked with this development is a significant transnational shift in political communication that best can be described as a process of strengthening strategic ignorance at the expense of research-based facts in the traditional sense of the term. A proper starting point is Newt Gingrich's project "Contract with America," but in this context, I will only refer to the short text "Language: A Key Mechanism of Control" (Gingrich, 1994).

In 1994, Gingrich sent out a list of words to Republican leaders and representatives, instructing them to keep it by the phone or learn it by heart. Use these (negative) words for Democrats, and the (positive) words for Republicans.

Republican	Democrat
Peace	Crisis
Liberty	Greed, self-serving
Hard work	Corruption
Family	Family
Prosperity	Decay, collapse
Success	Failure
Pioneers, passionate	Traitors
Truth	Lie

This is a minor example of the new process of political control of media and voters. Consistent use will stick with voters after a few years.

One other political communication relevant to mention is the use of "talking points," in which leading spokespersons, communications staff, and talk show radio hosts receive the same short description of an argument and metaphor to be repeated during the day as often as possible.

Today, the communication industry offers lists of positive words and negative words to be used in advertisement and media dialogue. In Denmark, "draconian foreigner policy" and "Danish values" are positive phrases, while words associated with negativity such as "nationalism" and "racism" are carefully avoided. The professionalization of political communication emerged with the new Danish People's Party in 1995, which was headed by one of the most effective spin doctors in Danish media history, Søren Espersen. With prime minister, Anders Fogh Rasmussen, in charge of government in 2001, a Tony Blair style news media management took effect and included spin doctors for all cabinet minister (for analysis of the political spin of the Muhammad Cartoon story of 2005/2006, see Hervik 2011, 2012). Bill Press defined spin as an "angle of truth" and presenting yourself or your case in the most favorably light (despite facts) (2001), today this is better conceptualized as the production of strategic ignorance.

A Concern with Civility and Incivility

The notions of civility and incivility turned out to be key features of the evolving public debate and its private appropriations in Denmark. Civility involves a way of talking or writing about how people relate to one another despite apparent differences (Thiranagama, Kelly and Forment 2018:153), irrespective of ritual opposition or content in true dialogue. "Civility is part of a complex of associated terms, such as citizen, civilization, civic, civil society, which are, even more forcefully, concepts which both describe and order reality around them." (ibid.: 156). As such, the notion of civilization carries within it the concepts of barbarism and savagery (ibid.: 164), finding expression in oppositions of the civil, civilized, and cultivated against the uneducated, crude, and the brute. These latter expressions range historically from silencing dissent; excluding people from public discourse; and recasting disagreement in terms of etiquette, manners, proper tone, and civilized behavior (ibid.: 154). Accordingly, the concept of civility is tied up with class, gender, and race privilege, effectively producing and reproducing inequality and legitimizing violence (ibid.: 155). In a study of online incivility, authors describe "A manner of offensive interaction that can range from aggressive commenting in threads, incensed discussion and rude critiques, to outrageous claims, hate speech and harassment" (Antoci et al. 2016: 1).

Talk About Racism As Lack of Civility

These features of (appeals to) civility becomes particularly clear in the following mediatized event consisting of an exchange in the Danish Parliament (Folketinget) between the Chair of the Parliament, Pia Kjærsgaard, (one of the highest positions in the country), and a podium speaker, Pelle Dragsted, of the Red-Green Alliance (RGA) (a left-wing party) on February 21, 2019. Kjærsgaard is a member of the Danish People's Party (DPP) and was its Chair since its formation in October 1995 until 2012. Before that, Kjærsgaard was Chair of the former Progress Party (Fremskridtspartiet).

The following response to talk of racism in the Parliament illustrates broader a discursive response to racism and coloniality.

> KENNETH KRISTENSEN BERTH, DPP, POSED A QUESTION TO PELLE DRAGSTED (RGA): Isn't the truth just this that integration of people from predominantly Muslim countries is not possible?
>
> PELLE DRAGSTED: I am still shocked by such racist statements, where a whole section of the population is made into object of hatred.
>
> PIA KJÆRSGAARD, CHAIR OF PARLIAMENT: That there (*det der*) I won't have any of that. We do not accuse each other of that. We have a decent tone.
>
> PELLE DRAGSTED: If he says that a whole section of the population cannot be integrated, I reserve myself the right to call it a racist statement.
>
> PIA KJÆRSGAARD: One does not discuss with the Chair at all. I ask that this is complied with.
>
> *Kristiansen, Jacobsen, and Holm 2019*

The exchange is known to most people in Denmark and sparked huge debates in the news media, blogs, Facebook, tweets, and elsewhere.

By using the term "racist," Dragsted steps into Kjærsgaard's moral universe of Danish neonationalism. Kjærsgaard reprimands Dragsted for being uncivil, which is a use of the label as a symbol of bad and not a statement that represent a message about race. Then, she further reprimands him for breaking with etiquette and demands respect for her institutional position of power.

In the media coverage, the form becomes the content when Kjærsgaard argued that the left wing is playing the racist card.

> It is typical, that the left wing unfortunately has this inclination to use the word racist, when all other arguments have been attempted.
> The racism-card is pulled out when you are a little cornered in the debate.
> https://nyheder.tv2.dk/politik/2019-02-27-pia-kjaersgaard-venstrefloejen-siger-racist-naar-argumenterne-slipper-op

Further in the exchange, Kjærsgaard evokes moral authority from referring to, or mastering, the layman's understanding of what race and racism are. Such an understanding is assigned the status of the "real truth" or "new realism" (Prins and Saharso 2010). In the Parliament racism becomes literally "that there" (*det der*). She ignores what racism is and at no points in the media coverage does she ask for research-based knowledge.

Twenty years ago, and a few weeks after 9/11, Kjærsgaard aligned herself with the side of the "civil," the West, the U.S. and the powerful in a speech in the Parliament.

> It has been argued that 11 September is the start of a war between civilisations. In that I disagree since there is only one civilization, and it is ours. Our enemies cannot claim that they belong to a civilization, as a civilized world would never accomplish such an attack, which encompasses so much hate, savagery and devilishness … They want to implement savagery, the primitive, the barbary and Middle Age conditions.
> http://webarkiv.ft.dk/Samling/20011/salen/R1_BEH1_3_4_223.htm
> Folketinget, 4 oktober, 2001, 1. Samling, Tale 223, Pia Kjærsgaard

Kjærsgaard aggressively critiques domestic political opponents on the left as well as global adversaries for this talk about a war between civilizations. Our opponents are uncivil, as are Muslims and the Muslim countries that support terrorists. This is a logic that I will describe later as operating as a mechanism of fractal scalarity and spatiality: when the same reasoning is applied across space, back in time, and at the micro as well as macro level (Hervik 2018; 2019a; 2021b) and edits out information that does not fit the logic. In other words, it is producing a strategic truth.

Ali Does Know How to Use the Toilet

From earlier research comes the media story of Ali (Jørgensen and Bülow 1999), where civility and ideas of modernization are evoked in a depiction of African migrants living in Denmark. A tabloid newspaper, *Ekstra Bladet*, spearheads its anti-migrant campaign in 1997 with a story about a Somali man who had been given a residence permit in Denmark, along with his wife, ex-wife and 11 children. The story became the key media event of the newspaper's, three-month-long campaign in 1997. A campaign that had closely tied to the birth of the far-right party, The Danish People's Party, headed by Pia Kjærsgaard.

> At Wichmannsvej 19 Ali keeps his circumcised, illiterate wives in strict isolation according to Somali custom … The school age children must come home straight away and only play indoors … [Ali knows] nothing about modern European electrical installations … The Danish Refuge Council has, for instance, not told him how a toilet is used … The house in Nysted will be left so neglected that renovation will cost the taxpayers approximately 100.000 kr [13.500 Euro]. It has happened before, the Somalis are nomads, and Ali has lived seven different places.
> *Ekstra Bladet* May 23, 1997, *Hervik 1999; Jørgensen and Bülow 1999*

The archaic reality underlying modernity (Wilmsen 1996) surfaces with Ali, who does not know how to use a toilet because he wasn't taught how, conveying an image of incivility. The journalist authoring the story, Ulla Dahlerup, later authored most of the Danish People's Party's book-long manifesto *Danmarks Fremtid. Dit land – Dit valg* (*Denmark's Future, your country, your choice*).

Incivility of Toilet Habits

Keeping the theme of toilet knowledge in talks about non-Danes, the next illustrations come from a long home visit and ethnographic interview with Lissy, who is a very active radical right-wing commentator on Facebook. Lissy, a well-educated, wealthy, older woman supports the radical right. Like the activists in the Tea Party Movement and other radical movements, Lissy does not see herself as racist. She is outraged when the term comes up.

> We are neither racists, fascists, or Nazis because we like to have the good, old order in our mother country and we like to have a homogeneous population.
>
> Hervik 2021a

Lissy describes an episode in a local public swimming facility:

> They don't even respect waste bins. They just throw their rubbish where they please.
> They pee in the water. And I am sorry to say, they defecate in the water. The indoor public swimming pool. I don't go there. I read in our local newspaper … that they relieve themselves in the water. That is obvious harassment. Peeing in the changing rooms. That makes you furious.
> Slowly, a minority [could begin to] to transform our culture. We [would have] to put up with politicians turning our food into halal food. We [would have] to put up with … more and more scarves. I dare to say that we are more civilized.

Lissy's depictions of Muslims do not come from scientific analysis or research-based literature. While she is correct that a story in a local paper reported that people were urinating and defecating in the public pool (Warming 2014), this original story does not mention Arab boys or Muslims. In fact, it does not speculate about the identities of the perpetrators. The only sources that venture such claims are extreme right ideological websites, "Den Korte Avis" and "Uriasposten," who traffic in speculation and rumors. This incident illustrates a common trend of social media news exchanges, wherein accuracy of information goes unchecked and stories are not criticized, and reposted endlessly. Lissy's reference to a local newspaper and the two sites becomes a pseudoscientific search to verify an already established "fact."

When we asked interviewees about the source of their stories, these were never public service stations or leading mainstream newspapers, in spite of their right-wing ownership and values and therefore potentially "useful" as sources. Instead, interviewees listed the extreme right websites mentioned above as well as the "Avpixlat" (Later "Samsnytt"), and "Gates of Vienna"; the latter two are among terrorist Anders Breivik's favorite sites.

The use of sources is a prime example of choosing frames and values already available that matches one's own core beliefs. Other news sites are characterized as trafficking in rhetoric of falsehoods and conspiracies and so avoided. The use of these extreme sites is truly perplexing given the ordinary lives of users in suburban residences that signal the safe caves (oxytocin) as used by psychologists. Facts are not able to counter such ingrained beliefs and practices.

Freedom to Eroticize Torture

I now turn to an example of the pre-social media convergence of racialized thinking with entertainment. For more than ten years, the Danish daily, *Politiken*, has published a cartoon series called The Stripe (*Striben*) on the reverse side of the paper's second section. The Stripe is authored and drawn by Wulffmorgenthaler, which is a contraction of two names, Mikael Wulff and Anders Morgenthaler, who run a small company with five to ten employees. The August 4, 2011 edition of The Stripe illustrates how racialization emerges uncritically and furthermore suggests a sense of desensitization and denial of responsibility just a few weeks after the Anders Breivik massacre in Norway on July 22, 2011. The cartoon appears as copied from the infamous photograph of a pile of naked bodies of prisoners in the Abu Ghraib prison. The key difference is that the foreign prisoner guard is absent from the cartoon, suggesting the cartoon may have been drawn from recall. The cartoon caption goes: "Am I the only one who is a little aroused?" "Bizarre moment in Abu Ghraib" (*Politiken*, August 4, 2011).[1]

On August 10, 2011, a well-known Danish writer Niels Barfoed wrote a commentary also in *Politiken* criticizing Wulffmorgenthaler's cartoon for misanthropy (2011).

> The platitude has shown a clear new face, namely the clean face of misanthropy. Or, phrased in newspeak: All utterances are permitted. Only criminal code sets limits. … The point of this Stripe was that misanthropy in the Abu Ghraib prison in Iraq must have given the victims some sexual opportunities while the torture was done.

Barfoed goes on to argue that the communication that the cartoon represents is the outcome of a new fundamentalist free speech ideology and increasing hysteria around censorship and self-censorship, which blunts critical thinking (Barfoed 2011).

In the following week, the cartoon publication of August 4th is discussed in several threads with more than 200 commentaries. However, it is not so much the cartoon as it is Barfoed's commentary that sparks a critical discussion of the eroticization of torture at Abu Ghraib. Some commentators agree with Barfoed that there is an "anything goes" norm in Danish society and a "fundamentalist free speech ideology." This is also illustrated by the fact that no one argues against the cartoonists' entitlement to publish the cartoons. A second group downplays the discussion, stating, "it's just a picture"; "the funniest in a long time"; and that some people do not get the irony, sarcasm, or humour. A third group argues that there is no humour, no satire, only a "platitude"; "finger pointing"; "moralizing"; and that the artists went "under the mark" and "too far."

The day after Barfoed's criticism, Wulffmorgenthaler decided to remove the cartoon from their homepage. The cartoonists stated they didn't want to hurt anyone, yet they showed no remorse and did not apologize. They felt sorry that some readers were sad about the cartoon, and conceded that it might have appeared too close to the tragic events at Utøya in Norway on August 11, 2011.

One commentator asks whether the cartoon would be similarly funny if it had depicted Danish prisoners, captioned with the same text, in the Shell building (a building in Copenhagen bombed on March 21, 1945, where Danish prisoners were detained by Gestapo as human shields). I think few people would have found it funny if perverse torture had taken place there. An expert source similarly proposes the counterfactual of siting the joke at Utøya. The answer is a clear no, thus demonstrating the embedded racialization of non-Westerners in Iraq, who are excluded from the category of "Us."

But who is the target of the satire, if not the "politically" or "ethically" correct who want to limit publication? The desire to publish and not apologize seems – on first glance – to gain strength from its relationship to perceived critics – those who can be provoked. Yet the provocation is linked to Abu Ghraib prisoners, to whom are attributed masochistic desires, rendering the torture harmless (Brink 2011). The target is not the prisoners, who were brutally tortured and sexually humiliated in the process, but rather the domestic adversaries who would oppose the publication of the eroticized cartoon.

One commentator is outraged with the way the cartoon references the original intention of the photograph, since it ridicules a specific historical episode. This comment is the only one that cites the scandal at the Abu Ghraib prison. Let's turn to the original Abu Ghraib photographs.

Photographs of the brutal torture of Iraqi prisoners at the infamous prison, Abu Ghraib, appeared in October 2003. The prison was first used by Saddam Hussain's regime for torture and execution, and later used by American forces as a prison and for torture and public humiliation.

Susan Sontag argues that instead of exclusively focusing on the accuracy of an image to the object represented, the significance of images may lie simply in our relationship to them; that is, the way we consume them, for example forward them to friends or family, and edit and recontextualize them often with footage captured via mobile phones (Facebook did not exist until 2004 and only became widely popular a few years later). In line with studies of language and communication (Hanks 1996), the meanings of photographs and texts are now seen more and more as relational and should be understood in terms of their reception, that is, pre-understandings in the cognitive apparatus. "We begin to understand a photograph already before we see it" is a notion in linguistics that focuses on sites of meaning and sense-making (Sontag 2003). The soldiers circulated the pictures like souvenirs or trophies. Perhaps torture is more "attractive," as something to record when it has a sexual component, with the exception of The Hooded Man with sprouting wires who was reportedly told he would be electrocuted if he fell off. Soldiers were having great fun (Sontag 2003).

Sontag asks the difficult question: were the Abu Ghraib photos shocking because of the torture being represented, or for the apparent normality of the photographers, who looked as if they were enjoying themselves while taking holiday souvenir photos? In grotesque fashion, both sides of the question are in play in the Danish cartoon.

It appears as if Wulff and Morgenthaler have little historical knowledge about what happened when Abu Ghraib photographs of torture and humiliation struck horror throughout the world. If they did, they would not have depicted the cartoon as they did. Laughing and having fun with the soldiers is reproduced with the laughing of Danish consumers.

But who is the target of the satire? Who is supposed to laugh and who is supposed to be provoked? If the first observation is correct, that the lack of historical knowledge and the reproduction of the soldier's enjoyment were both factors, then the satire is directed at "the politically or ethically correct" who would censure the publication of such dehumanizing and vulgar cartoons along racialized lines. The desire to publish and not apologize seems – on a closer look – to gather its strength from its relationship to those who can be provoked.

In her work on "entitlement racism," Essed noted that it is a sign of the times we live in that people believe that one should be able to express oneself publicly without limits (Essed 2013). Essed first conceptualized freedom of expression as a form of racism that easily evolves into the notion that one has the right to offend and to humiliate, and even the duty to do so. With disregard for history, lack of self-reflexive scrutiny of racializing relations, and a celebration of free speech ideology without limits, we approach nihilism and perhaps the "badass" era's valorization of a lack of social responsibility.

The indifference to historical accuracy and the absence of social responsibility enables the Abu Ghraib cartoon to become an object of entertainment and celebration of eroticism as a means to provoke and a consolidating an image of unrestricted daring. As such, it becomes a nihilistic manoeuvre unable to grasp the meaningful, while adding a pseudo-civil contribution that celebrates the fun-loving soldiers, and reproducing the soldiers' dehumanization of the tortured.

In the next case, multiple dimensions converge in this cartoon and its commentaries: civility, incivility, ignorance, strategic ignorance, free speech, eroticization. Again and again, Danish illustrators are the ones caught up in claims of civility and the right to portray others in uncivil terms, and in the process, reveal no sense of responsibility or interest in the surrounding facts of the original story and the human suffering in the historical events.

The "Nation in Danger" and the Indifference to Facts

Exclusionary reasoning in Danish politics and in the popular consciousness has evolved over the last 25 years. The media has played a crucial role in tandem with political conservatism and the professionalization of political communication in producing a foundational neonationalist system of belief, the logic of which I identified as a "nation in danger" (Hervik 2018; 2019a). A large majority of the population has internalized this view. Today, it has become hegemonic for how most Danes view minorities, particularly Muslims, in the country. The confrontational and relentless anti-migrant approach was documented 25 years ago, but today it has proliferated by way of new media technologies with endless outlets of (mis)information to be played out against each other in a battle to win support and at the expense of common understandings and research-based insights. The news media, like the large daily *Jyllands-Posten*, has shifted its extreme speech from editorials and articles in the paper version and its web edition to associated bloggers, who are paid by the news institutions.

In addition to the shift of vitriol to social media, the difference between the popular consciousness of the 1990s and 2021 is the cultural assemblage of negative emotions. This accumulation stems from media repetition of the same stories, where moral and social evaluations of what is right, wrong, and natural guide stories, rather than journalistic analysis and expert-guided contextualization. We concluded through a figure of speech that 90 percent of all media stories could be done away with and the world would be a better place for it.

Entrenched cognitive understandings have led to rejection of the most obvious evidence. Since people find it crucial to maintain core beliefs, they will rationalize, ignore, and even deny anything that doesn't fit with these beliefs, as Frantz Fanon argues (2008). Facts that are inconsistent with totalizing ideologized visions either go unnoticed or are explained away. Creating an axis of differentiation requires selecting some qualities and ignoring or downplaying others. Erasure simply implies an explanation or explaining away the phenomenon that does not fit, leaving the observer's vision of the world intact (Gal and Irvine 2019).

Understanding the recurrence of extreme speech, digital hatred, neonationalist exclusionary reasoning posed a challenge to the SERR research project. Again and again new stories came up in new areas in which migrant presence and identities were contested and Danish national values celebrated in a classic us/them division. In the course of the project, we concluded that fractal analysis is the most constructive way to understand our data, even though the concept was little used in social sciences and humanities, let alone media anthropology.

Through a close reading of the original theory of fractals and literature in other fields, we used three concepts to analyze our wide-ranging material: fractal boundaries, fractal scalarity, and fractal spatiality (Hervik 2021b). Once these fractal dimensions are in play, something else is erased and, thus, becomes a contributor of strategic ignorance. Like the practice of "angles" in news stories. The reporter sticks to the angle decided beforehand like a scavenger who searches only for food. Anything else is irrelevant. Fractal reasoning captures the key characteristic of fractals in that they reiterate the same irregular shapes indefinitely regardless of whether you move up or down in what is ordinarily talked about as levels or extending to new spaces. This principle is present in nature from snowflakes to broccoli, ferns, clouds, in the human body including the brain and its neurons and multitubinals. Fractal boundaries are boundaries that from afar look sharp and clear; for instance, the public-private division; the coastline (between land and sea); racial binary categories (us/them); national categories (us/them). We found that such binaries were in fact separated between blurred areas or grey zones significant for the understanding of polarization, recruitment, demonization, and civil rights. Fractal scalarity and spatiality helps to explain how a foundational thought or primary spin can be scaled up or down and repeated endlessly across scales and social space. Primary concepts are repeated indefinitely regardless of time and space. For example, the "nation in danger"; "I am my body"; and the Danish news spin, "If you are criticized by non-Westerners, it is due to their lack of understanding free speech and democratic values," your opponents' speech is "an expression of their uncivil manners and thinking," or "If you criticize Israel, it is an expression of anti-Semitism." The concept of a nation in danger is used when legislating forced handshakes but also spoken of as guarding Denmark against radical Islam from the Middle East.

Conclusion

This chapter has argued for the strong need to situate studies of strategic ignorance about visible minorities within a longer historical process and as a decolonial critique. The latter is not dealt with in the chapter that instead aims to show how strategic ignorance works. The specific media event illustrations were media had to be related to the 1:8 division of power and access to news and popular media, which refers figuratively to the ratio of commercial, private, right-wing, news institutions vs. independent, public or liberal media institutions in the larger media landscape. This division is similar in the USA and Denmark. Although Danish news outlets receive some government support, they are run as commercial enterprises and widespread paywalls. When it comes to news about migrants, refugees, and minorities, most people in most societies say they get most of their information and opinions from a multitude of outlets on social media. And the younger half of the population more than the elder. But again, these often unfiltered sites and technologies similarly seem to reflect the 1:8 division in terms of what they offer to the consumer. However, as unfiltered, the extremism in form, content, and style is widespread and seemingly irreversible since they are in the hands of the largest advertisement companies on the planet that in and of themselves earn their profits from communication and identity over factual information (Curran, Fenton and Freedman 2012).

Media anthropology have edged towards taking up this huge challenge in society, which is the media-related crisis of fact. In this article, facts refer to systematic inquiries and insights about racialization, racism, nationalism, and other forms of inequality. Talk about racism in the Parliament became in itself a site for a brute manifestation of institutional power used to establish that such talk is uncivil, while at the same time strategically ignoring and being indifferent to fact-based knowledge of racial inequality in Danish society.

This chapter has shown how strategical ignorance works through specific illustrations. Media anthropology needs to take up the challenge of the strategic ignorance and the larger crisis of fact; for instance, by using its collective energy to explore, develop, and establish an epistemology that is not only about the source of knowledge but also the source of ignorance and how it is produced (Mills 2007). This task should be informed by material based on Kelly Askew's frequently quoted shorthand for media anthropological work: "ethnographically informed, historically grounded, and context-sensitive analysis of the ways in which people use and make sense of media technologies" (2002: 3), which must include a person-centric and experience-near approach that defies easy binaries and more adequately documents how knowledge is embodied and how it becomes embodied. An epistemology of ignorance needs less emphasis on documenting what is false, which again often comes years after the event or statement was made, and instead on reaching and understanding how strategic ignorance and cognitive processes work.

Note

1 The two cartoonists known publicly for their support for freedom of speech declined giving permission to republish the cartoons in this article. In previous analysis and presentations in non-commercial settings, I show slides of the cartoon and original photograph and discuss them as part of an anthropological analysis of contemporary expressions of strategic ignorance and racial dehumanization. The cartoon is accessible in various editions on the internet as well as on my website (peterhervik.dk).

References

Antoci, Angelo, Alexia Delfino, Fabio Paglieri, Fabrizio Panebianco, and Fabio Sabatini. (2016) "Civility vs. Incivility in Online Social Interactions: An Evolutionary Approach." *PLoS ONE* 11(11): e0164286.
Askew, Kelly. (2002) "Introduction." In Kelly Askew and Richard R. Wilk (eds), *The Anthropology of Media: A Reader*. Oxford: Blackwell Publishers, 1–13.
Barfoed, Niels. (2011) "Commentary." *Politiken*, August 10.
Bird, Elisabeth. (2003) *The Audience in Everyday Life: Living in a Media World*. New York: Routledge.
Brink, Dennis Meyhoff. (2011) Commentary. *Politiken*, August 11.
Buzan, Barry, Ole Wæver, and Jaap de Wilde. (1998) Security: A New Framework for Analysis. Boulder: Lynne Reiner.
Carruthers, Susan L. (2000) *The Media at War*. New York: Palgrave MacMillan.
Cody, Francis. (2011) "Publics and Politics." *Annual Review of Anthropology* 40: 37–52.
Curran, James N., Natalie Fenton, and Des Freedman (2012) *Misunderstanding the Internet*. New York: Routledge.
Ekstra Bladet. (1997) 2 sektion, s. 2 23 May.
Essed, Philomena. (2013) "Entitlement Racism: License to Humiliate." In *Recycling Hatred: Racism(s) in Europe Today: A Dialogue between Academics, Equality Experts and Civit Society Activists*. Brussels: European Network Against Racism (ENAR), 62–76.
Fanon, Frantz (2008)[1952]. *Black Skin, White Masks*. New York: Grove Press.
Gal, Susan and Judith T. Irvine. (2019) *Signs of Difference. Language and Ideology in Social Life*. Cambridge: Cambridge University Press.
Hanks, William F. (1996) *Language and Communicative Practices*. Boulder, CO: Westview Press.
Hervik, Peter. (1999) Den generende forskellighed. Danske svar på den stigende multikulturalisme. Copenhagen: Hans Reitzels Forlag.
Hervik, Peter. (2021a) "Racialization, Racism and Anti-Racism in Danish Social Media Platforms." In Sahana Udupa, Iginio Gagliardone, and Peter Hervik (eds.), *Digital Hate: Global Perspectives on Online Extreme Culture*. Bloomington: Indiana University Press, 131–145.
Hervik, Peter. (2021b) *Sådan er det bare! Antropologiske perspektiver på oplevelser og reaktioner på racialisering i Danmark* [*That's just the way it is! Anthropological perspectives on experiences and reactions to racialization in Denmark*]. Aarhus: Klims Forlag.
Hervik, Peter (2019a) "Denmark's Blond Vision and the Fractal Logic of the Nation in Danger." *Identities: Global Studies in Culture and Power* 26(5): 529–545.

Hervik, Peter (ed.). (2019b) *Racialization, Racism and anti-Racism in the Nordic Countries*. Series: Approaches to Social Inequality and Difference. New York: Palgrave Macmillan.

Hervik, Peter. (2019c) "Ritualized Opposition in Danish Practices of Extremist Language and Thought." *International Journal of Communication* 13: 3104–3121. Special journal issue: "Global digital media cultures and 'extreme speech'. Guest editor, Pohjonen, Matti and Udupa Sahana.

Hervik, Peter. (2018) "Refiguring the Public, Political and Personal in Current Danish Exclusionary Reasoning." In Claudia Strauss and Jack Friedman (eds.), *Political Sentiments and Social Movements: The Person in Politics and Culture*. New York: Palgrave Macmillan, 91–117.

Hervik, Peter. (2012) *The Danish Muhammad Cartoon Conflict*. Current Themes in IMER Research 13, Malmö Institute for Studies of Migration, Diversity and Welfare (MIM), Malmö: Malmö University.

Hervik, Peter. (2011) *The Annoying Difference: The Emergence of Danish Neonationalism, Neoracism, and Populism in the Post-1989 World*. New York: Berghahn Books.

Jørgensen, Rikke Egaa and Vibeke Søderhamn Bülow. (1999) "Ali og de fyrretyve k)r)oner. En analyse af Ekstra Bladets kampagne 'De Fremmede'." In Peter Hervik (ed.), *Den Generende Forskellighed*, 81–107.

Kock, Christian. (2011) *De Svarer Ikke*. Copenhagen: Gyldendal.

Kristiansen, Toke G.C., Sebastian R. Jacobsen, and Jeppe M. Holm. (2019) "Se klippet: Pia Kjærsgaard skælder EL-ordfører ud for racisme-anklager i Folketingssalen." www.altinget.dk/artikel/el-ordfoerer-irettesat-for-at-sige-racisme-af-pia-kjaersgaard (May 23, 2002).

Kumar, Deepa. (2021) *Islamophobia*. 2. Revised and expanded version. Chicago, IL: Haymarket Books.

Lakoff, George. (2012) "George Lakoff: Don't Think of an Elephant." Talk at the Commonwealth Club of California, July 12.

Linger, Daniel. T. (2005) *Anthropology Through a Double Lens: Public and Personal Worlds in Human Theory*. Philadelphia: University of Pennsylvania Press.

Mills, Charles W. (2007) "White Ignorance." In Shannon Sullivan and Nancy Tuana (eds.), *Race and Epistemologies of Ignorance*. Albany: State University of New York Press, 13–38.

Politiken. (2011) August 4. Second Section.

Postill, John. (2009) "What Is the Point of Media Anthropology?" *Social Anthropology*, 17(3): 334–345 (with response by Mark Allen Peterson).

Press, Bill. (2001) *Spin This" All the Ways We Don't Tell the Truth*. New York: Pocket Books.

Prins, Baukje and Sawitri Saharso. (2010) "From toleration to repression: The Dutch backlash against multiculturalism." In Steven Vertovec and Susanne Wessendorf (eds), The Multiculturalism Backlash. London: Routledge, 72-91.

Proctor, Robert N. (2008) "Agnotology: A Missing Term to Describe the Cultural Production of Ignorance (and its Study)." In Robert N. Proctor and Londa Schiebinger (eds.), *Agnotology: The Making and Unmaking of Ignorance*. Stanford: Stanford University Press, 1–33.

Sontag, Susan. (2003) *Regarding the Pain of Others*. New York: Picador/Farrar, Straus & Giroux. http://archive.truthout.org/article/susan-sontag-regarding-torture-others

Stockly, Olaf Dana Thomas. (2011) "The Epistemology of Ignorance." *Anthós* 3(1): 1–8.

Thirangama, Sharika, Tobias Kelly, and Carlos Forment. (2018) "Introduction: Whose Civility?" *Anthropological Theory* 18(2–3): 153–74.

Udupa, Sahana, Iginio Gagliardone, and Peter Hervik. (2021) *Digital Hate: The Global conjuncture of Extreme Speech*. Bloomington: Indiana University Press.

Udupa, Sahana. (2020) "Decoloniality and Extreme Speech." Paper presented at the 65th e-seminar, Media Anthropology Network, European Association of Social Anthropologists, June 2020, 17–30.

Warming, Martin. (2014) "Svømmehal plages af bæ-terror: Hvem gør det i vandet?" http://Lokalavisen.dk, http://www.lokalavisen.dk/112/2014-02-08/Svømmehal-plages-af-bæ-terror-Hvem-gør-det-i-vandet-1337674.html (February 22, 2021).

Wilmsen, Edwin N. (1996) "Introduction: Premises of Power in Ethnic Politics." In Edwin N. Wilmsen and Patrick McAllister (eds.), *The Politics of Difference: Ethnic Premises in a World of Power*. Chicago: University of Chicago Press, 1–23.

31
CONSPIRACY MEDIA ECOLOGIES AND THE CASE FOR GUERILLA ANTHROPOLOGY

Leighton C. Peterson and Jeb J. Card

Mark Allen Peterson (this volume) suggests that anthropological study of media emerged in a particular time before social media and more democratized tools of production and distribution. He argues this should give us pause to reconsider foundational assumptions and theories about media, including what is "new" about digital media and how emergent media processes have fundamentally shifted the semiotics of communication and belonging. He suggests that we engage the concepts of participatory culture and spreadability (Jenkins, Ford, and Green, 2013), as well as "indexical communities" such as Qanon, that is, communities that are negotiated through the adoption, sharing, and emblematization of rarefied symbols and discourses that mark participation (see Silverstein, 2006). To address this call, we weave a contemporary media narrative of U.S.-focused, politically conservative communities that originated in the creation, mixing, and spreading of conspiratorial, paranormal, and pseudoscientific media. This particular participatory culture has resulted in an emergent phenomenon known as "Qanon." Qanon refers to both an initially narrow community once completely emergent in online spaces and a broader conspiracy theory and "conspirituality" worldview that links New Age religiosity and celebrity culture with political disenchantment and conspiracy media ecologies (Ward and Voas, 2011). Qanon has an increasing memetic presence offline linked to U.S. conservative politics, and it has absorbed older conspiracy culture tropes and symbols. We explore the production and circulation of these discourses and the resulting ostensions through the lens of conspirituality and stigmatized knowledge, the spreadability of conspiracy genres, and paranormal and pseudoscientific mediascapes. This case provides us with the foundation for understanding complex media practices and intersections of old and "new" media, mediated interactions, and the offline world. It also provides a useful tale for "media anthropologists" who wish to engage these dangerous discourses in the public sphere (Allen, 2005; Pink and Abrahm, 2015).

Conspiracy communities, fake news, and popular documentary media based on pseudoscience are all part of a "conspiracy media ecology" whose intertextual links and recurring tropes include ancient aliens, nephilim, and other paranormal phenomena, as well as liberal satanist pedophile politicians. We argue that part of this ecology is the "myth and conspiracy genre" of seemingly mainstream media products. These alternative discourses, simultaneously conspiratorial and unscientific, are built upon an epistemology of *stigmatized knowledge* or those "claims to truth that the claimants regard as verified" despite their marginalization by scientific, scholarly, or cultural experts (Barkun, 2013: 26). Beliefs in conspiracies linked to paranormal phenomena are long-standing in American culture, with direct links between beliefs in the paranormal and beliefs in conspiracy (Bader, Baker, and Mencken, 2017; Wood, 2017). The underpinnings of conspiracy genres lie in alternative archaeology, also known as pseudoarchaeology, a framework rooted in racist concepts that reconfigures archaeological "evidence" to support dubious claims. Cinema, television, and YouTube have had a direct impact on the perpetuation of alternative archeological myths such as "ancient astronauts" theories that attribute past indigenous accomplishments to extraterrestrials (Hiscock, 2012). North American media stars such as Graham Hancock and podcaster Joe Rogan (*The Joe Rogan Experience*) recontextualize and spread outlandish theories that emerged from Erich von Däniken's *Chariots of the Gods?* (1968) through documentary films, streaming simulcasts, and prolific series such as History Channel's *Ancient Aliens* that provide the mythic charter for political extremism like Qanon and white supremacy (Card and Peterson, 2022; Hoopes, 2019).

What makes this concerning and what links politically conservative communities together are social networks that spread and amplify these narratives. Like UFO abductee communities and the growth and spread of UFO abduction stories, it is less about the story itself than it is the "intertextual, poetic process of recognizing the resemblances and patterns of other, and using that chime to cast a new story" based on apophenia (Lepselter, 2016:18). This results in a kind of intertextual parallelism where mimetic and recurring words, tropes, and symbols reappear in a variety of conspiratorial discourses. This is also what links pseudoscience and paranormal media content to fake news, user-generated content, and political activism. For this project, we used a process of digital and hashtag ethnography (Bonilla and Rosa, 2015) to follow evidence through a feedback loop of media myths, offline events, and social media conspirituality. We interviewed guerrilla media creators engaged in activist media interventions and have produced guerrilla interventions of our own. We begin our story with American conservative politics: In 2019 and 2020 numerous mainstream U.S. media outlets produced "What is Qanon?" pieces as the movement's symbols and adherents became prominent at rallies and events in support of former President Donald Trump, and at protests on issues against which Trump stood, particularly COVID anti-mask protests. The presence of Qanon symbols and slogans in the January 6, 2021 insurrection attack on the United States Capitol brought widespread media attention and concerns that the movement – and conspiracy politics generally – might have real-world dangers. One particular phrase core to Qanon seemed particularly relevant on that day: WWG1WGA, or "Where We Go One, We Go All," a call to violent revolution shared in memes, on T-shirts, and in social media as a life-style emblematization used to identify community members within this complex social network.

America's Stonehenge Vandalized

In October 2019, the *New Hampshire Union Leader* published a story of archaeological mystery and crime: "Sacrificial stone at America's Stonehenge vandalized with power tools." The paper reported that a supposed 4,000-year-old "sacrificial stone tablet" in Salem, New Hampshire was damaged by vandals using a grinding tool and a sledgehammer (Lessard, 2019). Curiously, they left behind "a wooden cross with images attached hanging between two trees." The *Union Leader* story echoed claims that the stone features, which are part of a private attraction, were thought to be one of the oldest man-made constructions in the United States, built by ancient people thousands of years ago who were well-versed in astronomy. According to the site's website and companion video, the stones remain a mystery: Some have theorized a Native American origin, while alleged evidence of Ogham (Irish line inscriptions), Phoenician, and Iberian Punic script have been found at the site. These interpretations suggest an incredibly early European presence in the Americas (America's Stonehenge, n.d.).

By the following day, the vandalism story was disseminated by the Associated Press, who added two unrelated theories: the "skeptics'" idea that the stone features were the work of a 19th-century shoemaker, and a law enforcement theory that the perpetrators were "trying to reenact a scene in a [unnamed] fictional book" – the latter an idea potentially influenced by the site-owners' associations with the world of alternative archaeology. Neither report described the vandal's etchings or the imagery on the cross, although the stories did include clear, photographic evidence of the aftermath. Both stories circulated on Twitter and other online spaces garnering a range of reactions. While not "accurate," as we will explain, neither story was an example of "fake news." Rather, the stories resulted from journalistic practices where "getting the story" means getting "both sides" and providing background information from legitimate sources (Peterson, 2001), in this case the owner's website (designed to attract tourists) or law enforcement officials (who had yet to crack the case). However, neither angle could begin to scratch the surface of the underlying reality in the way the grinding tool had scratched the stones. What did the vandals inscribe into the stone, and why did they leave the cross?

The vandalism story from 2019 was not the first media appearance for "America's Stonehenge," which was known as Pattee's Cave in its early years, and then dubbed Mystery Hill in the 1930s by owner William Goodwin. Goodwin promoted the site as a tourist attraction, claiming it as a religious space built by pre-Columbian Irish monks, linking the site with alternative archaeology (Card, 2018: 272). Such interpretations are ripe for media spread. In 1977, Mystery Hill was featured in the episode "Strange Visitors" in the TV series *In Search Of*, hosted by Leonard Nimoy. The episode suggested it was the product of Bronze-Age Minoans, precursors to the Classical Greeks. In 2001, the *History's Mysteries* show on the History Channel alluded to subsequent ancient Old World migration and conquest by Phoenicians. The History Channel returned to the topic in 2013 in an episode of *America Unearthed* focusing on alleged astronomical alignments to make claims involving those Phonecian (or Minoan, or Druid) creators, and linking it to an alignment with the UK's Stonehenge and astral projections related to the summer solstice. Flashy graphics and earnest university professor-experts (a geologist from Mount Holyoke College) with science-sounding explanations support the findings. The host's visit to the UK Stonehenge site then provided the semiotics of indisputable evidence.

Television portrayals of the site moved into the paranormal in 2019 when the History Channel's *Ancient Aliens* series featured America's Stonehenge in "The Druid Connection" (Season 14 Episode 7). Here, the host as well as famous alien abductee Whitley Strieber explain how sites like this focused "vortex" energy and facilitated communication with paranormal or "space" entities (Colavito, 2019). Actual archaeology at the site found 19th-century materials and older materials related only to indigenous North Americans (Vescelius, 1956). The "sacrificial stone" is clearly similar to historical lye or cider presses in the region, and does not resemble the fictitious sacrificial altars of Druids nor any Bronze Age or Celtic nor Phoenician objects. The site has no documentable exotic or paranormal elements but the truth of the 2019 vandalization of the stone cider press was far stranger. The cross placed at the site hinted at spiritual warfare. The inscription carved into the rock in 2019, the only *actual* inscription at the site, included "WWG1WGA." This is the initialism of the phrase "Where We Go One, We Go All," one of the main emblems of, and indexicals to, the Qanon political conspiracy movement (Peterson and Card, 2019).

Qanon is a portmanteau including the word "anon" that also originally referred to an online community, the Anonymous hacker movement. Beginning in 2003, people claiming to act in the name of Anonymous carried out cyber actions against a variety of groups in and out of government that they saw as mixing real-world damage and a lack of information transparency. Corporations and government institutions were significant targets, though early in the group's history there was a focus on the Church of Scientology. The group's prominence grew significantly not just with its actions, but the adoption of the stylized Guy Fawkes mask featured in the 2005 film *V for Vendetta*. The masks provided effective online counter-cultural branding and allowed for easier offline demonstrations and actions, where *anyone* could be part of Anonymous (mirroring the final scene in the film in which the people of London don these masks and rise up against a fascist government). The anon word grew not just for the movement, but also for the users of spaces in which the movement was hosted, anonymous message boards, most infamously, 4chan. Ostensibly set up as an image board for potentially offensive content, 4chan and similar places became virtual organizing spaces outside of institutional interference. Anon was adopted as a cultural moniker for those at home in a place where the old Internet promises of anonymity and that "information wants to be free" persisted when a majority of global users joined more regulated social media.

This setting proved ideal for the spreadability of large-scale conspiracy movements. The 2016 Presidential election in the United States was surrounded by conspiracies such as "Pizzagate" (deriving from spurious interpretations of leaked emails from the Hillary Clinton campaign, and sharing much of the ideology of Qanon as well as earlier conspiracy theories). But Qanon was more directly rooted in the nature of the anons and the chans, and was able to exploit their role in remixing semiotic forms and shared indexicals disseminated as code phrases and memes in social media. In November 2017 messages began to appear on 4chan from an anon with alleged "Q clearance," suggesting that they were deep inside the government and predicting "The Storm," imminent arrests of vile global conspirators. These usually focused on Hillary Clinton, echoing the Trump campaign and then administration's attacks on their opponent, threatening to "Lock Her Up." Clinton and others were engaged, they claimed, in clandestine demonic warfare against the good people of the world, often with explicit references to Christian End Times rhetoric. These prophecies, known as "drops" (much of the terminology of Qanon comes from military and espionage stereotypes) were coded in cryptic language using code words and concepts from conspiracy culture. The initial prophecies did not pan out but the drops continued as did growing interest in the ideology and in participating in a community through social media. Initial observation of Qanon focused on the core of anons at the chans, but by 2020 the movement had become a standard part of conservative, right-wing online political rhetoric, with symbols, memes, catchphrases, and other elements routinely being shared on all major platforms.

Mediated conspirituality

The America's Stonehenge vandalism and the Qanon movement are related to a segment of the American mediascape that mirrors conspiracy theories and claims of "fake news" that have become central to U.S. politics and media since 2016. The conspiracy media ecology relies on alternative readings of facts and evidence and on the idea that reality is being withheld from the public (Bader, Baker, and Mencken, 2017; Barkun, 2013). The core conceit is that institutions and experts hide the truth, but outsiders can reveal it. "Conspirituality" describes the blend of conspiracy theory, political disillusionment, and alternative spirituality fueled by celebrities and high-profile media exposure (Ward and Voas, 2011). It describes how seemingly contradictory social movements such as culturally liberal New Agers and far-right anti-globalist/antisemitic conspiracy theorists share common ideological topography in their quest for a "new paradigm worldview" to replace the current world order of materialism and modernity. Social networks linked through conspirituality and stigmatized knowledge seek new epistemologies or social orders akin to bricolage; Lévi-Strauss' (1966) concept of myth-making by self-sustaining feedback loop.

By 2017, when Qanon emerged, the paranormal mediascape from which it sprang had significantly changed. Beginning in the 1980s, paranormal topics became increasingly successful on U.S. network television, especially on emerging basic cable television. By the 1990s "learning" channels made UFOs a small but prominent staple of their programming. The rise of reality television post-1999, as well as the success of cheap paranormal-themed found footage films in the wake of the monumentally profitable *The Blair Witch Project* led to an explosion of cheap-to-produce reality ghost hunting shows in the 2000s. These shows, such as *Most Haunted* (2002–2010) in the UK and *Ghost Hunters* (2004–2016) and *Ghost Adventures* (2008–present) in the U.S. created numerous imitators. This genre inspired thousands of groups of ghost hunters to follow the practices seen on television, producing an industry of paranormal tourism and fan events (Hill, 2010). *Ancient Aliens*, indexically linked to Qanon and UFO communities, is one of the most egregious mainstream media products (Card and Peterson, 2022). We argue it is a part of the "myth & conspiracy" media genre that exists to destabilize knowledge and make the world "unknowable." It appropriates, rather than "mocks," documentary genre conventions; it omits or trades scholarly "facts" as "evidence" for "relative facts" as evidentiary markers. The "obfuscated knowledge" plot line outlines the errors and omissions of the elite materialist world, finds wonders in reclaiming knowledge, and allows the audience to participate in uncovering that knowledge through anomalies. Out of context, and with compelling talking heads, conspiracy media objects appear like any other historical, documentary, or journalistic offering. Low-cost editing and filming technology has led to independent paranormal and conspiracy content made for streaming consumption, ranging from seemingly legitimate documentaries to ranting activists, the descendants of public-access television, that illicitly edit into their content clips and CGI from more professional media products (Card and Peterson, 2022). Many people consuming myth and conspiracy media today likely do so through illicit copies of these shows on crowdsourced streaming media. Media activist Stephan Milo, whose work seeks to counter alternative archaeology, notes that

> Graham Hancock's books sell very well, but way more people are introduced to his ideas through Joe Rogan's podcasts and YouTube channels talking about his ideas. It's really through this social media that people are coming into contact with these things.
>
> *Milosavljevich, 2021*

Spreadability, or engaging in the recontextualization and spreading of media narratives, is foundational to indexical communities such as Qanon. Spreadability is related to what folklorists call "amplification," which allows "fake news" narratives to spread and morph beyond the contexts of an original (non)event. Amplification accounts for the agency and participation of users as well as algorithms of social media platforms (Peck, 2020). Algorithms are not solely to blame for the spread of conspiracy content, as many scholars and media commentators hope (e.g. Lange, 2019). Clicks are acts of agency by users (Hervik, 2019) who themselves "teach" the algorithms in a feedback loop; both are, nonetheless, creations of social actors. The same processes are involved in the spreadability of stigmatized knowledge. Qanon spreads through streaming video, particularly YouTube and Facebook. Videos that "redpill" new believers increasingly incorporated conspirituality elements of UFOs, ancient aliens, lost civilizations, and other topics of the conspiracy media ecology.

Peterson and Lindberg (n.d.) illustrate how paranormal reality show hosts legitimize pseudoscience through discursive practices such as "science talk," co-narrating apophenia, and marking intertextual bricolage. By looking at how ghost hunters entextualize evidence and ghost narratives, and how subsequent producers recontextualize these discourses, we mapped the spreadability and amplification of "scientifically legitimized" indexicals. These patterns allow stories and experiences to "grow powerful through the sense of truth that accumulates out of a cultivated apophenia and its build up, intertextual parallelism" (Lepselter, 2016: 18). Once Pattee's Cave/America's Stonehenge was embedded in alternative archaeology it became a spreadable concept for the rest of paranormal culture, including the "Third Wave spiritual warfare" movement (McCloud, 2013). Self-proclaimed spiritual warriors hunt for demonic sites but with ties to paranormal culture, the demonic spreads to include Pleidian and Reptilian aliens, the Deep State, the Anunaki alien overlords of the Middle East, the fallen angels and their Nephilim giant offspring being covered up by the Smithsonian, and the Illuminati projecting signals into pop culture. In the case of "America's Stonehenge," the indicted perpetrator was identified not only by the spiritual warfare components, but because he had carved his Twitter handle into the "altar" and posted on social media about damaging the site as an action against the Satanists confronted by Qanon (Peiser, 2021).

This movement is centered in the United States, but is not unique to it. Spiritual warriors spread oil on Olmec archaeological monuments in Mexico to sanctify them (notably, in both well-known cases, many of the vandals were foreigners, attacking remains related to what is considered a "mother culture" in Mexico). Olmec colossal heads are a staple of alternative archaeology due to unfounded suggestions they are evidence of African colonization of the Americas. In October 2020 widescale vandalism occurred in several museums in Berlin, Germany. This case appears similar in the motive of "sanctifying" artworks interpreted as "satanic altars." COVID anti-lockdown protests in 2020 in Trafalgar Square, London, England, replete with Qanon and other conspiracy imagery (claiming the virus is caused by 5G wireless networks), have found one of their leaders in David Icke, the most prominent theorist that the world is run by shapeshifting Reptilian aliens. Icke is a staple of conspiracy culture and has been criticized for echoing antisemitic blood libel including reprinting the Tsarist hoax *The Protocols of the Elders of Zion*. Influential UFO conspiracy theorist William Milton Cooper also reprinted *The Protocols* in *Behold a Pale Horse*, a major source of UFO and other conspiracy lore and a prototype for Qanon conspiracy maps.

The Case for Guerrilla Archaeology

As an antidote, we call for building upon an emerging "guerilla archaeology" that requires understanding the media ecologies in which Qanon, spiritual warriors, and other bricoleur circulate, spread, and amplify. One confounding element is that much of alternative archaeology draws upon earlier antiquarianism and archaeology cast out in the process of professionalism. In British archaeology, the new professionals of Oxbridge and other seats of professional power established themselves in part through clashes with ley line hunters (Stout, 2008). The "Gogmagog Affair" of the 1950s, in which a new generation of professionally trained archaeologists squared off against claims of a mythically informed hill figure being found south of Cambridge marks one of these clashes. Folklore and pagan-friendly older archaeologists supported claims of older dubious methods finding a fertility symbol on the landscape while university-based archaeologists saw an opportunity to draw a boundary of what real archaeology is. In the aftermath, the old-school mythics found a new place in the mystical realm of dowsing, ancient aliens, and witches (Lethbridge, 1957; Welbourn, 2011). Similarly, Americanist archaeology found a professional footing by rightfully critiquing hyperdiffusionist models of culture change by transoceanic migration rather than better evidence of social processes and ecological adaptation (Rowe, 1966; Wauchope, 1962). These and other moves toward the processual and "scientific" defined professional archaeology as a study of material remnants of largely mundane past human activities.

This development spawned two reactions to the rejection of "alternative" archaeologies by the profession. The first, with deep roots within the practice of studying the past to explain the present, was a search for the mythic, and in most cases, a rejection of materialist scientific paradigms. Within and without the profession, the lure of antiquity as a pathway to mythic origins and re-enchantment has been strong, resulting in dowsing, psychic archaeology, and related approaches that are not satisfied by analyzing old stones and bones (Bond, 1921; Cameron, 1976; Goodman, 1977; Hopkinson-Ball, 2007). While in some cases the mystical is meant to serve archaeology, in most cases the archaeology is meant to serve as a proof of non-material consciousness and psychical phenomena. This impulse fits within a broader rejection of the materialist scientific paradigm in favor of models of science being a subset of a broader knowledge seated in consciousness, the imaginal realm, magic, religion, and the "super natural" (Radin, 2018; Strieber and Kripal, 2016).

The second reaction to archaeological professionalization, more common among a small but persistent minority of academics, has been a critique of the profession through protest of the exclusion of alternative archaeology. This approach notes the "sharp elbows" of kicking dowsers, ley walkers, Atlantis-seekers, and hyperdiffusionists out of the field as a form of zealous gatekeeping or "crusading" (Cremo, 2012; Cusack, 2012; Derricourt, 2012; Fagan and Feder, 2005; Holtorf, 2005). Real-world events, such as the alternative archaeology symbols and themes in Qanon and the January 2021 insurrection at the U.S. Capitol such as the "Q-Shaman" wearing garb reminiscent of the Bad Dürrenberg Mesolithic burial (Porr and Alt, 2006), or the use of megalithic sites by supporters of Brexit (Brophy, 2019) suggests that these arguments, meant as a critique of a small profession, ignore much bigger and more damaging uses and abuses of the mythic past in alternative archaeology.

A more fruitful and scholarly approach is perhaps the most common since 2000: that of historical examination of alternative archaeologies and their entanglements with the history of the field. These fit within a broader social and cultural examination of paranormal and alternative worldviews as important cultural phenomena rather than anomalies to be dismissed as irrelevant (Bader et al., 2017; Barkun, 2013; Hanks, 2015; Laycock, 2012). Regarding archaeology, these studies have taken three paths. The first emphasizes the esoterically tangled seeking of mythic origins of the archaeologist's assumed ancestors on topics such as faery races, haunted houses, screaming skulls (Clarke and Roberts, 1996; Silver, 1999), or more broadly incorporating the mystical as method or motive (Kurlander, 2015; Link and Hare, 2015; Lowe, 2007; Michlovic, 1990; Moshenska, 2006; Vinson and Gunn, 2015). The second is the historical study of alternative archaeological ideas such as lost continents and transcendent knowledge from a global spiritual legacy (Desmond, 2009; Desmond and Messenger, 1988; Gere, 2009; Herva and Norden, 2015; Hornung, 2001; Iversen, 1993; Picknett and Prince, 2003; Sitler, 2012; Whitesides, 2019). A subset of this approach is the examination of colonialist constructions of a "cursed" indigenous archaeology such as the "native burial ground" or "the mummy's curse" (Bergland, 2000; Caterine, 2014; Day, 2006; Luckhurst, 2012; Lupton, 2003). These concepts, popular and born of colonialism, have either been transformed into new forms outside of traditional academia (Drieskens and Lucarelli, 2002) or have become part of an indigenous colonial reclamation of the past (Boyd, 2011).

The above sociohistorical approach to alternative archaeology garners less attention, as it is aimed at a predominantly humanities academic audience than the debunking perspective decried by some of the relativist advocates of alternative archaeology discussed above. While many debunking works are published in academic journals and volumes, a significant proportion of these works also aim at a broader public, and may be accompanied by public-facing efforts inviting conflict with alternative archaeology proponents. The earliest major debunking work was Wauchope's (1962) criticism of hyperdiffusionists, but with the popularity of paranormal media in the 1970s debunking was more common in the 1980s (Card and Anderson, 2016; Cole, 1980; Daniel, 1979; Feder, 1984, 2018; Williamson and Bellamy, 1983). These works take two forms: debunkings of specific claims (Burgess, 2009; Di Peso, 1953; Godfrey, 1951; Lepper and Gill, 2000, Mainfort and Kwas, 2004; Neudorfer, 1980; Sax et al., 2008), and broader examination of alternative archaeology as a phenomenon at odds with archaeological method and theory (Trigger, 1984; Williams, 1991). Debunkings were more common in the middle to later 20th century in academic literature, but with professionalization, such efforts moved into the public sphere in blog posts, non-peer-reviewed magazines, podcasts, and similar efforts. Academic approaches either became more historical (see above) or more critical of the broader notion of pseudoarchaeology.

The public-facing approach has reached more eyes and ears than academic works on alternative archaeology, but has fallen into traps that degrade the effectiveness of these efforts. Tracing the origins of anti-pseudoarchaeology websites is difficult given the temporary, and oft uncached, nature of Internet resources. An early effort in the 2000s was the *Hall of Ma'at*,[1] aimed at the alternative Egyptology that emerged in the 1990s (Picknett and Prince, 2003). A major site emerged in the 2000s in the writings of Jason Colavito, who has chronicled virtually all of alternative archaeology cable television and related efforts.[2] The main creators of these and other websites are rarely professional or academic archaeologists. Sites run by academics or professionals quickly face a common issue: sparring with fans of alternative authors, who are often hostile or litigious.

Many of the non-professional authors of anti-pseudoarchaeology websites, blogs, and social media groups aligned with the "skeptic" movement that challenged paranormal, alternative science and medicine, and conspiracy theory. This approach dates back to at least magician Harry Houdini's debunking of spiritualist mediums in the 1920s, with deeper roots in schisms within psychical research in the late 19th and early 20th centuries. The "skeptic" movement expanded with responses to claims of extraterrestrial visitation (UFOs) and catastrophism (the Velikovsky affair) in the 1950s, the popularity of psychic and New Age practices in the 1970s, and widespread paranormal media in the 1990s and on. In the 2000s this movement became linked with "New Atheism" led by figures such as Richard Dawkins and Christopher Hitchins in the wake of rising political religiosity or religious politics, including high-profile legal cases regarding Creationism and public education. The nature of the New Atheists was inherently combative and eminently adaptable to sound and fury in the emerging world of social media, signifying little of long-term impact.

Aftermath

In April 2021, Legendary Pictures, a major film production company contributing to many of the blockbuster films of the 21st century, announced that it was adapting the *Ancient Aliens* television show to a feature film (Kit, 2021). As Hiscock (2012: 174) notes, by employing myth and fantasy, "fictional images of the human past offered by Hollywood films are immediately persuasive and accessible to people without archaeological training." It is difficult to think of a more obvious sign that efforts by public archaeologists to control past media depictions have failed. Professional archaeologists and other scholars are not in charge of the narrative, and we must all realize that. We have argued elsewhere (Card and Peterson, 2022) that advocates of UFO legitimacy in the U.S. created a social media ecology exposing only superficial aspects of their worldview that appeal to mainstream media without being too "weird." Social media communities ignored the historical evidence of a more complex and dubious situation of psychical research and mysticism around the UFO topic, quietly embraced by these same advocates. By contrast, the defacement of America's Stonehenge is the direct result of an emergent bricolage and ever-expanding worldview.

The never-ending recycling of "mysterious" and paranormal topics in the conspiracy media ecology and the participatory cultures that remix and recontextualize these narratives provide fuel for the creation of universal conspiratorial worldviews like Qanon. We have illustrated how Qanon and Q-aligned communities mark their participation with tropes and symbols that indexically entail notions of, for example, spiritual warfare and ideological counterculture. In other words, the alternatives-seeking social media actor becomes the politically conservative conspiritual community member by mixing and spreading rarefied alternative discourses and symbols, thereby adopting a similar level of conspiratorial belief. In a "post truth world" where even academics are complicit (if not active) in this kind of bricolage (Sidky, 2020), it is especially urgent that media anthropologists begin to take the world of pseudoscience mediascapes and conspiracy media ecologies seriously. While our case study examines archaeology, it most certainly applies to anthropology more broadly, and indeed, to all concerned scholars and disciplines. In order to engage and counter these dangerous discourses, we must understand and examine how – and why – these narratives and communities continue to proliferate. And, most importantly, we should heed the warning of conspirituality: Not all "political conservatism" emerges from whence we think, and it is not about alternative candidates, social policies, or "right-wing vs. left-wing." It is ultimately about a new paradigm, alternative worldview.

Notes

1 www.hallofmaat.com/
2 www.jasoncolavito.com/

References

Allen, S. L. (2005) "Activist Media Anthropology: Antidote to Extremist Worldviews," in E. W. Rothenbuhler and M. Coman (eds), *Media Anthropology*, Thousand Oaks, CA: Sage, 285–294.
America's Stonehenge (n.d.) available at www.stonehengeusa.com/ (accessed October 8, 2019).
Bader, C. D. and Baker J. O., and Mencken, F. C. (2017) *Paranormal America: Ghost Encounters, UFO Sightings, Bigfoot Hunts, and other Curiosities in Religion and Culture*. Second Edition. New York: NYU Press.
Barkun, M. (2013) *A Culture of Conspiracy: Apocalyptic Visions in Contemporary America*. Berkeley: University of California Press.
Bergland, R. (2000) *The National Uncanny: Indian Ghosts and American Subjects*. Reencounters with Colonialism: New Perspectives on the Americas. Dartmouth College, Hanover, NH: University Press of New England.
Bond, F. B. (1921) *The Gate of Remembrance: The Story of the Psychological Experiment which Resulted in the Discovery of the Edgar Chapel at Glastonbury*, Fourth Edition, New York: E. P. Dutton.
Bonilla, Y. and Rosa, J. (2015) "#Ferguson: Digital Protest, Hashtag Ethnography, and the Racial Politics of Social Media in the United States," *American Ethnologist*, 42 (4): 4–17.

Boyd, C. E. (2011) "'We Are Standing in My Ancestor's Longhouse': Learning the Language of Spirits and Ghosts," in C. E. Boyd and C. Thrush (eds), *Phantom Past, Indigenous Presence: Native Ghosts in North American Culture and History*, Lincoln: University of Nebraska Press, 181–208.

Brophy, K. (2019) "The Moggalithic Antiquarian: Party Political Broadcasts from Stone Circles," Blogpost, *AlmostArch*, available at https://almostarchaeology.com/post/189644783963/moggalithic (accessed December 13, 2019).

Burgess, D. (2009) "Romans in Tucson? The Story of an Archaeological Hoax," *Journal of the Southwest*, 51 (1): 3–135.

Cameron, C. (1976) *Archaeology and Parapsychology*. Master of Arts Thesis, Department of Anthropology, California State University, Fullerton. Proquest/UMI, Ann Arbor, MI.

Card, J. J. (2018) *Spooky Archaeology: Myth and the Science of the Past*. Albuquerque: University of New Mexico Press.

Card, J. J. and Anderson, D. S. (2016) "Alternatives and Pseudosciences: A History of Archaeological Engagement with Extraordinary Claims," in J. J. Card and D. S. Anderson (eds), *Lost City, Found Pyramid: Understanding Alternative Archaeologies and Pseudoscientific Practices*, Tuscaloosa: University of Alabama Press: 1–18.

Card, J. J. and Peterson, L. C. (2022) "Guerrilla Archaeology and Ancient Aliens: Countering the Mediascapes of Stigmatized Knowledge," in K. Ryan and D. Staton (eds), *Interactive Documentary: Decolonizing Practice-Based Research*, Abington: Routledge: 187–203.

Caterine, D. V. (2014) "Heirs through Fear: Indian Curses, Accursed Indian Lands, and White Christian Sovereignty in America," *Nova Religio: The Journal of Alternative and Emergent Religions*, 18 (1): 37–57.

Clarke, D. and Roberts, A. (1996) *Twilight of the Celtic Gods: An Exploration of Britain's Hidden Pagan Traditions*. Foreword by A. Ross. London: Blandford.

Colavito, J. (2019) "Ancient Aliens Reviewed," available at www.jasoncolavito.com/blog/review-of-ancient-aliens-s14e07-the-druid-connection (accessed July 19, 2019).

Cole, J. R. (1980) "Cult Archaeology and Unscientific Method and Theory," *Advances in Archaeological Method and Theory*, 3: 1–33.

Cremo, M. A. (2012) "An Insider's View of an Alternative Archaeology," in A. Simandiraki-Grimshaw, and E. Stefanou (eds), *From Archaeology to Archaeologies: The "Other" Past*, Oxford: BAR International Series 2409, 14–19.

Cusack, C. M. (2012) "Charmed Circle: Stonehenge, Contemporary Paganism, and Alternative Archaeology," *Numen*, 59: 138–155.

Daniel, G. (1979) "The Forgotten Mile Stones and Blind Alleys of the Past," *Royal Anthropological Institute News*, 33: 3–6.

Day, J. (2006) *The Mummy's Curse: Mummymania in the English-speaking World*, New York: Routledge.

Di Peso, C. C. (1953) "The Clay Figurines of Acambaro, Guanajuato, Mexico," *American Antiquity*, 18 (4): 388–389.

Derricourt, R. (2012) "Pseudoarchaeology: The Concept and its Limitations," *Antiquity*, 86: 524–531.

Desmond, L. G. (2009) *Yucatán Through Her Eyes: Alice Dixon Le Plongeon, Writer and Expeditionary Photographer*, Albuquerque: University of New Mexico Press.

Desmond, L. G. and Messenger, P. (1988) *A Dream of Maya: Augustus and Alice Le Plongeon in Nineteenth-Century Yucatan*, Albuquerque: University of New Mexico Press.

Drieskins, B., and Lucarelli, R. (2002) "Untying the Magic of the Pharaoh," in R. Pirelli (ed.), *Egyptological Essays on State and Society*, Napoli: Dipartimento di Studi e Ricerche su Africa e Paesi Arabi: Serie Egittologica 2. Università degli Studi di Napoli "L'Orientale," 79–93.

Fagan, G. G. and Feder, K. L. (2005) "Crusading against Straw Men: An Alternative View of Alternative Archaeologies," *World Archaeology*, 38 (4): 718–729.

Feder, K. L. (1984) "Irrationality and Popular Archaeology," *American Antiquity*, 49 (3): 525–541.

Feder, K. L. (2018) *Frauds, Myths, and Mysteries: Science and Pseudoscience in Archaeology*. 10th ed., Cambridge: Oxford University Press.

Gere, C. (2009) *Knossos and the Prophets of Modernism*. Chicago: University of Chicago Press.

Godfrey, W. S., Jr. (1951) "The Archaeology of the Old Stone Mill in Newport, Rhode Island," *American Antiquity*, 17 (2): 120–129.

Goodman, J. (1977) *Psychic Archaeology: Time Machine to the Past*, New York: Berkley.

Hanks, M. (2015) *Haunted Heritage: The Cultural Politics of Ghost Tourism, Populism, and the Past*, Walnut Creek, CA: Left Coast Press.

Herva, V. and Nordin, J. M. (2015) "Unearthing Atlantis and Performing the Past: Ancient Things, Alternative Histories and the Present Past in the Baroque World," *Journal of Social Archaeology*, 15 (1): 116–135.

Hervik, P. (2019) "Ritualized Opposition in Danish Online Practices of Extremist Language and Thought," *International Journal of Communication* (19328036) 13.

Hiscock, P. (2012) "Cinema, Supernatural Archaeology, and the Hidden Human Past," *Numen*, 59: 156–177.

Hill, A. (2010) *Paranormal Media: Audiences, Spirits and Magic in Popular Culture*. Abingdon: Routledge.

Holtorf, C. (2005) "Beyond Crusades: How (Not) to Engage with Alternative Archaeologies," *World Archaeology*, 37 (4): 544–551.

Hoopes, J. W. "Introduction," SAA Archaeological Record 19, 5(2019): 8–9.

Hopkinson-Ball, T. (2007). *The Rediscovery of Glastonbury: Frederick Bligh Bond, Architect of the New Age*. Foreword by R. A. Gilbert. Stroud: Sutton Publishing.

Hornung, E. (2001) *The Secret Lore of Egypt: Its Impact on the West*. Translated by D. Lorton. Ithaca, NY: Cornell University Press.

Iversen, E. (1993) *The Myth of Egypt and its Hieroglyphs in European Tradition*. Princeton, NJ: Princeton University Press.

Jenkins, H., Ford, S. A. M., and Green, J. (2013) *Spreadable Media Creating Value and Meaning in a Networked Culture*. New York: NYU Press.

Kit, B. (2021) "'Cobra Kai' Creators Tackling 'Ancient Aliens' Movie for Legendary," *Hollywood Reporter*, www.hollywoodreporter.com/heat-vision/cobra-kai-creators-tackling-ancient-aliens-movie-for-legendary (accessed 14 October, 2021).

Kurlander, E. (2015) "Hitler's Supernatural Sciences: Astrology, Anthroposophy, and World Ice Theory in the Third Reich," in M. Blak and E. Kurlander (eds), *Revisiting the "Nazi Occult": Histories, Realities, Legacies*, German History in Context: Rochester, NY: Camden House, 132–156.

Lange, P. G. (2019) *Thanks for Watching: An Anthropological Study of Video Sharing on YouTube*. Louisville: University Press of Colorado.

Laycock, J. P. (2012) "Approaching the Paranormal," *Nova Religio: The Journal of Alternative and Emergent Religions*, 18 (1): 5–15.

Lepper, B. T., and Gill, J. (2000) "The Newark Holy Stones" *Timeline*, 17 (3): 16–25.

Lepselter, S. C. (2016) *The Resonance of Unseen Things: Poetics, Power, Captivity, and UFOs in The American Uncanny*. Ann Arbor: University of Michigan Press.

Lessard, R. (2019) "Sacrificial Stone at America's Stonehenge Vandalized with Power Tool, Cross Left Behind," *New Hampshire Union Leader*, www.unionleader.com/news/crime/sacrificial-stone-at-america-s-stonehenge-vandalized-with-power-tool-cross-left-behind/article_f12416d6-5e7f-5796-bd18-3cbfeb32221f.html (accessed October 3, 2019).

Lethbridge, T. C. (1957) *Gogmagog: The Buried Gods*. London: Routledge and Kegan Paul.

Lévi-Strauss, C. (1966) *The Savage Mind*. London: Weidenfeld & Nicolson.

Link, F., and Hare, J. L. (2015) "Pseudoscience Reconsidered: SS Research and the Archaeology of Haithabu," in M. Blak and E. Kurlander (eds), *Revisiting the "Nazi Occult": Histories, Realities, Legacies*, German History in Context: Rochester, NY: Camden House, 105–131.

Lowe, N. J. (2007) "Gilbert Murray and Psychic Research," in C. Stray (ed.), *Gilbert Murray Reassessed: Hellenism, Theatre and International Politics*, Oxford: Oxford University Press, 349–370.

Luckhurst, R. (2012) *The Mummy's Curse: The True History of a Dark Fantasy*. Oxford: Oxford University Press.

Lupton, C. (2003) "'Mummymania' for the Masses – Is Egyptology Cursed by the Mummy's Curse?" in S. MacDonald and M. Rice (eds.), *Consuming Ancient Egypt*, Encounters with Ancient Egypt, London: Institute of Archaeology, UCL Press, 23–46.

Mainfort, R. C., and Kwas M. L. (2004) "The Bat Creek Stone Revisited: A Fraud Exposed," *American Antiquity*, 69 (4): 761–769.

McCloud, S. (2013) *American Possessions: Fighting Demons in the Contemporary United States*. Oxford: Oxford University Press.

Michlovic, M. G. (1990) "Folk Archaeology in Anthropological Perspective," *Current Anthropology*, 31 (1): 103–107.

Milosavljevich, S. (2021) Interview with the authors.

Moshenska, G. (2006) "The Archaeological Uncanny," *Public Archaeology*, 5: 91–99.

Neudorfer, G. (1980) *Vermont's Stone Chambers: An Inquiry into their Past*, Barre, Vermont: Vermont Historical Society, available at www.google.com/url?q=https://accd.vermont.gov/sites/accdnew/files/documents/HP/Vermonts%2520Stone%2520Chambers.pdf (accessed October 15, 2021).
Nichols, B. (2016) *Speaking Truths with Film: Evidence, Ethics, & Politics in Documentary*. Oakland: University of California Press.
Peck, A. (2020) "A Problem of Amplification: Folklore and Fake News in the Age of Social Media," *The Journal of American Folklore*, 133 (529): 329–351.
Peiser, J. (2021) "N.J. Man Allegedly Carved a QAnon Hashtag into a Centuries-old Stone at 'America's Stonehenge'," *The Washington Post*, March 4, accessed on October 15, 2021.
Peterson, L. C. and Lindberg E. E. (n.d.) "Legitimizing Pseudoscience in Paranormal Reality Ghost Hunting Shows: A Discourse-Centered Approach."
Peterson, M. A. (2001) "Getting to the Story: Unwriteable Discourse and Interpretive Practice in American Journalism," *Anthropological Quarterly*, 74(4): 201–211.
Peterson, L. C. and Card J. J. (2019) "Documentary Film & Guerrilla Archaeology." BEA On Location Conference, October 9, 2019, Boulder, CO.
Peterson, M. A. (2005) "Performing Media: Toward an Ethnography of Intertextuality," in E. W. Rothenbuhler and M. Coman (eds), *Media Anthropology*, Thousand Oaks, CA: Sage Publications, 129–138.
Picknett, L., and Prince C. (2003) "Alternative Egypts," in S. MacDonald and M. Rice (eds), *Consuming Ancient Egypt*, Encounters with Ancient Egypt, London: Institute of Archaeology, UCL Press, 175–193.
Pink, S. and Abram, S. (2015) *Media, Anthropology and Public Engagement*, New York: Berghahn Books.
Porr, M. and Alt, K. W. (2006) "The Burial of Bad Dürrenberg, Central Germany: Osteopathology and Osteoarchaeology of a Late Mesolithic Shaman's Grave," *International Journal of Osteoarchaeology*, 16 (5): 395–406.
Radin, D. (2018) *Real Magic: Ancient Wisdom, Modern Science, and a Guide to the Secret Power of the Universe*, New York: Harmony.
Rowe, J. H. (1966) "Diffusionism and Archaeology," *American Antiquity*, 31 (3): 334–337.
Sax, M., Walsh, J. M., Freestone, I. C., Rankin, A. H., and Meeks, N. D. (2008) "The Origins of Two Purportedly Pre-Columbian Mexican Crystal Skulls," *Journal of Archaeological Science*, 35: 2751–2760.
Sidky, H. (2020) *Science and Anthropology in a Post-Truth World: A Critique of Unreason and Academic Nonsense*. Lanham: Lexington Books.
Silver, C. (1999) *Strange and Secret Peoples: Fairies and Victorian Consciousness*, Oxford: Oxford University Press.
Silverstein, M. (2006) "Old Wine, New Ethnographic Lexicography," *Annual Review of Anthropology*, 35: 481–496.
Sitler, R. K. (2012) "The 2012 Phenomenon Comes of Age," *Nova Religio: The Journal of Alternative and Emergent Religions*, 16 (1): 61–87.
Stout, A. (2008) *Creating Prehistory: Druids, Ley Hunters and Archaeologists in Pre-war Britain*. Oxford: Blackwell.
Strieber, W., and Kripal, J. J. (2016) *The Super Natural: A New Vision of the Unexplained*. New York: Tarcher Perigee.
Trigger, B. G. (1984) "Alternative Archaeologies: Nationalist, Colonialist, Imperialist," *Man*, 19: 355–370.
Vescelius, G. S. (1956) "Excavations at Pattee's Caves," *Bulletin of the Eastern States Archaeological Federation*, 15: 13–14.
Vinson, S. and Gunn, J. (2015) "Studies in Esoteric Syntax: The Enigmatic Friendship of Aleister Crowley and Batticombe Gunn," in W. Carruthers (ed.), *Histories of Egyptology: Interdisciplinary Measures*, New York: Routledge, Routledge Studies in Egyptology, 97–112.
Ward, C. and Voas, D. (2011) "The Emergence of Conspirituality," *Journal of Contemporary Religion*, 26 (1): 103–121.
Wauchope, R. (1962) *Lost Tribes and Sunken Continents: Myth and Method in the Study of American Indians*. Chicago: University of Chicago Press.
Welbourn, T. (2011) *T. C. Lethbridge: The Man Who Saw the Future*. Winchester: O-Books.
Whitesides, K. A. (2019) "The Highest Common Factor: Heterodox Archaeology and the Perennialist Milieu," *Nova Religio: The Journal of Alternative and Emergent Religions*, 22 (4): 22–43.

Whitesides, K. A., and Hoopes, J. W. (2012) "Seventies Dreams and 21st Century Realities: The Emergence of 2012 Mythology," *Zeitschrift für Anomalistik*, 12: 50–74.

Williams, S. (1991) *Fantastic Archaeology: The Wild Side of North American Prehistory*, Philadelphia: University of Pennsylvania Press.

Williamson, T. and Bellamy, L. (1983) *Ley Lines in Question*. Kingswood: World's Work.

Wood, M. J. (2017) "Conspiracy Suspicions as a Proxy for Beliefs in Conspiracy Theories: Implications for Theory and Measurement," *British Journal of Psychology*, 108 (3): 507–527.

32
RESEARCHING POLITICAL TROLLS AS INSTRUMENTS OF POLITICAL CONSERVATISM IN TURKEY

A Historical Framework and Methodological Reflections on a Discourse Community

Erkan Saka

Introduction

In the early 2000s, especially after September 11, Turkey would be seen by the western world as a model Muslim country (Tugal, 2016). But in the following years, a growing body of literature started portraying Turkey as a country that made an authoritarian turn in the early 2010s. The same party, AKP, led by the current President Erdoğan, has ruled Turkey since 2003. Yeşil (2016) labels the existing regime as authoritarian neoliberalism, what Poulantzas and Hall define as a mixing of the strong state with free-market politics (Jones, 2020). In Turkey, there was never a coherent reform plan for a more democratic state (Erensü and Alemdaroğlu, 2018). Internet freedoms continuously declined throughout the AKP rule (Saka, 2019). Islamist-inspired political conservatism would gradually shape the public sphere, and political trolls would be one of the critical instruments in creating political and cultural discourses while suppressing opponents. This chapter studies politically motivated pro-government internet trolls, named Aktrolls after the initials of AKP, as actors that served the production of political conservatism in Turkey. They were allegedly organised and paid within the party structure. However, my ethnographic work on Aktrolls revealed that they were mostly volunteering with no regular payment structure (Saka, 2018). In this chapter, I present how political trolls were viewed as a discursive community that became the mediative instrument of the ruling party when Turkey took an authoritarian turn. Political trolls have an evasive media appearance and their tactics frequently change in relation to ongoing political events. Through ethnography, I drew connections between different types of troll content and I came to define political trolls as a discourse community. The linguist John Swales defines discourse communities as groups with their own goals and purposes, that use communication to achieve these goals (Borg, 2003). The term discourse community is criticised for being imprecise and inaccurate and emphasising uniformity (Bazerman, 2009). Yet, this is precisely the reason why I use this term. Political trolls operate as a community that serves the authoritarian regime, and represents a uniform discourse for outsiders, while at the same time including complexities, ambiguities, loopholes and shifting alliances.

Why Study Political Trolls?

The term political trolling derives from the better-known concept of internet trolling. The latter describes arguing for the sake of provoking users into "expressing easily challenged positions, then exhausting them through mockery" (Aspray, 2019). In Flores-Saviaga, Keegan and Savage's (2018) words, political trolling is arguing and provoking for a political purpose, such as calling like-minded people to action over a political matter. Political trolling has emerged as an important political actor in Turkey in the immediate aftermath of the Gezi Park Protests in 2013. The Erdoğan-led AKP government encountered an unprecedented civilian uprising fuelled and coordinated through social media.

The protests started against a government plan to replace Gezi Park, a park next to the famous Taksim Square in Istanbul, with urban development plans. A small environmentalist protest was crushed by police brutality, which triggered nationwide protests. An environmental cause became a pretext to protest increasingly authoritarian government policies (Amnesty International, 2013). Protesters used social media effectively in mobilising citizens nationwide and in circulating protest news (Jenzen et al., 2021), which helped elevate the protests to international headlines.[1] This use of social media caused a reaction among Turkish government leaders. Some explicitly stated that they would have their own social media activists as counter-insurgents on the online platforms. Critics of the government labelled these trolls as "Aktrolls", which became a commonly used label that even some trolls themselves liked to use. However, little was known about Aktrolls, and nearly all media representation about them relied on speculation or media reports of political trolls in other countries such as Russia. My long-lasting and ongoing ethnographic study of these so-called Aktrolls started in 2014 and aimed to bring insights from the field and thus to verify or challenge existing media representations. My earlier work demonstrated that Aktrolls are not a close and stable network but an online alliance of volunteers whose boundaries changed continuously (Saka, 2018). My later work then showed that this discursive community acted following the authoritarian regime's policy changes. Initially, Aktrolls functioned as a surveillance tool to target anti-government agents. As the Gezi Park Protests stopped, political trolls became agents to promote the government cultural policies (Saka, 2019). When the ruling government lost many significant municipalities in the 2019 local elections, their new role was to monitor the failings of opposition municipalities (Saka, 2021). Aktrolls knew that they were part of a broader network of AKP party establishment, from municipalities to media outlets and bureaucrats, that served political conservatism. The ethnographic study of the role of Aktrolls within this network helped me understand the making of a new political system. Designing this research, in turn, allowed me to think about the methodological implications of this type of research.

Turkey's media ecology promotes affect-driven, post-truth media consumption, whether pro-government or not. The Turkish media structure is polarised and most outlets are keen on maintaining their political positions and have no interest to negotiate (Hoyng and Es, 2017). In such an environment, expert hierarchies dissolve rapidly, and lay individuals who use social media can have as much impact as established columnists. Objective standards become hard to sustain, and troll discourses have as much power as more rational actors and experts. Media is subject to rivalries between ever-increasing numbers of troll collectives. Within this context, political trolls found a fertile social media environment, and aligned themselves to pro-government traditional media and the existing authoritarian regime.

My long-term study of trolls demonstrated how trolls had both continuous and switching roles. The discontinuity in their different functions and practices made the boundaries of the troll community hard to pinpoint. Aktrolls frequently changed as intra-party alliances shifted. For this reason, understanding trolls was difficult, and ordinary observers or media reports misidentified this situation as a covert operation. While it was true that political trolling had secretive aspects, my ethnographic study debunked this.

In the Field: Different Historical Moments, Multiple Methods

In my study of political trolls, I adopted a multi-platform and a multi-method approach. There is not a single formula that can be applied, and ethnographers have to redesign and re-adjust their methods to the contingencies of the research. For example, Coleman (2014) started as an observer of IRC (Internet Relay Chat) rooms and web forums, and she then employed different and multiple ethnographic practices. Zimmermann (2016) relied on Tweetdeck and NodeXL software to capture and analyse social media data, and used screen captures to portray troll discourse and practices. Bradshaw and Howard (2017) collected data from news media articles and think tank reports and interviewed cybersecurity experts and other relevant persons. Pohjonen and Udupa (2017) employed multi-sited Internet-related ethnography (Wittel, 2000) and ethnographic interviews that aimed at gathering data across different media forms (Madianou and Miller, 2013). Last but not least, Gehl's (2016) work on the Dark Web includes discourse analysis of online interactions. My research builds on these previous studies and their methods, to shed light on the multiple discursive practices of Aktrolls.

In conducting research from 2013 to 2021, I observed changes over time as the current AKP regime formation took several turns. I identified three significant turns in this period. In every turn, trolling had a different primary role and function: (1) In the immediate aftermath of Gezi Park Protests in 2013, when the government announced counter-moves against protesters on social media, Aktrolls surveilled and intimidated the activists. (2) After the 2016 coup attempt, when Erdoğan's Islamist ally, the Gulen movement, allegedly led a coup attempt against the government, political trolls acted as agents of culture wars. AKP used the state of emergency after the coup attempt to suppress the followers of the Gulen Movement and other vocal opposition groups. In the lack of visible opposition, political trolls served the government-led Islamisation efforts. (3) After the local elections in 2019, when the ruling party lost in most of the major cities in Turkey, political trolls switched to a defensive mode and invested their energies to defend government development projects and criticise opposition municipalities. In what follows, I describe these three main stages of Aktrolling and the different methods that I used to study them.

The first stage began in the middle of the summer 2013. This stage of research aimed at defining trolling networks and their role against the protesters. Protesters were evacuated from the Gezi Park by security forces in the early days of June 2013, but the street protests all over the major cities continued at least until the end of the year. The first statements about a pro-government "social media army" appeared in the summer after the evacuation of Gezi Park. The claim of pro-government troll armies in support of the authoritarian regimes was concretised in a *Guardian* piece (Soldatov et al., 2015). When a few Turkish government representatives talked about establishing social media armies to counter government critics, both the opposition and the pro-government circles accepted the existence of a centralised troll army with virtually no suspicion. The news of Russian troll farms organised by the Russian government contributed to the acceptance of this explanation of Turkish opposition. People in Turkey thought that a similar centralised structure would occur in Turkey too. However, concrete evidence of such an army was surprisingly lacking. At this stage, I went beyond social media platform data analysis. I conducted fieldwork that combined offline and online observation. It is difficult for ordinary citizens, journalists and researchers to identify troll networks because they rely on semi-anonymity or secretive tactics. Since trolling content is on social media, most research had previously relied on publicly available data. However, I gained access to troll circles and this provided valuable ethnographic insights that could complement, challenge and also confirm existing knowledge on Aktrolls. One of my major access points was a group of cafes in the neighbourhood of At Pazarı Meydanı in Istanbul's conservative district, Fatih. The most famous cafe was called *Eski Kafa*, whose manager happened to be my close friend. Many Islamists from different factions frequented these cafes. For example, one day I witnessed a fistfight between an Islamist from one faction and an IHH member. IHH was the Turkish NGO that organised the Mavi Marmara flotilla to send aid to Palestine. Israeli security forces stopped the flotilla, and in the ensuing clash, nine activists were killed. This event became a propaganda tool for AKP (Migladovitz, 2010). My acquaintances in this cafe and others in the same district helped me contact political trolls. Some of them were already frequenting these cafes. When the Gezi Park Protests began, some of the people I met there saw their presence in the café' as an opportunity to get closer to government circles by offering their expertise on social media to counter the Gezi Park protesters. After the first interviews with the café goers, I was given new contacts, and my research then progressed beyond this specific site. As the research continued, I used some other ties, such as former high school classmates, to reach other networks I could not access before. This led me to interview a few bureaucrats who were involved in the ruling party's social media campaigns and functioned as liaisons with trolls. I was also able to interview two self-identified Aktrolls. One was a digital media producer with close ties to AKP circles, whose documentaries have been broadcast on state TV channels. Another troll was, according to AK party circles, a "Gülenist organiser" on Twitter. I also interviewed a relatively high-level bureaucrat specialising in Turkey's communication sector (more on this can be found in Saka, 2018).This primary method of data gathering was coupled with archival research in which. I analysed media representations of political trolling in mainstream newspapers and social media.

The second stage in the field began with the coup attempt of 2016, which led to a new political system in 2017. The Erdoğan-led government declared a state of emergency after the coup attempt. It was not only Gülenists who were allegedly behind the coup attempt who were massively purged in the bureaucracy and academia during this state of emergency (Göztepe, 2018), but also leftist and pro-Kurdish critics. Under these conditions, Turkey adopted a new political system: a presidential system with extraordinary executive powers ((Lowen, 2017). It was a break from the parliamentary system that had been in effect since 1950. Erdoğan became the first President in this system (Paul and Seyrek, 2017). Until the local elections in 2019, the ruling party's hegemony over the state apparatus went unchallenged. This meant that political trolls were needed less for surveillance and instead they began to assist the government efforts for political conservatism.

During the state of the emergency period, when political opponents were under pressure, I moved to digital spaces because I felt more secure: I stopped visiting the abovementioned district as I expected more heated arguments and hostility towards me. I created a master private list on Twitter (which I named "Akgossip") to monitor accounts I listed and mapped in the previous period (Saka, 2018). The list itself generated new additions as the interactions with the monitored accounts evolved, and I could note shifting alliances and changing political positions. Thus, methodological variety and offline ethnography were replaced by digital media monitoring. This period coincided with a consolidation of troll power. During the first stage, there were more independent and voluntary troll circles and a group named Pelikan, mostly financed by Erdoğan's son-in-law's family, began to control most of the Aktrolls. As the opposition was undergoing various waves of persecution, there were fewer critical voices on social media. Aktrolls now invested their labour not on the surveillance over their opponents but to actively promote a conservative agenda. For example, the campaign against gender equality that started at this time ended up with Turkey's withdrawal from the Istanbul Convention.[2] Nonconformist Islamist groups or thinkers would be targeted. Media content that did not conform to the regime's cultural rhetorics were chastised (as Netflix became a usual target) (more on themes can be found in Saka, 2021).

The third stage in my research on political trolls started with the local elections of March 2019. The ruling party, AKP, lost in most major cities, including İstanbul and Ankara. This was the first significant electoral defeat for the party leader and President, Erdoğan (Esen and Gumuscu, 2019). At this moment, Aktrolls retreated to more defensive lines. Nearly every day, trolls would criticise newly won municipalities. Istanbul and Ankara mayors were important targets. Acting as if the traffic jams were a new issue, political trolls continuously complained about municipality-governed public transportation. The opposition felt encouraged with the local election victories, and political trolls invested in targeting party defectors and opposition policy proposals. Trolls were now in an entirely defensive mood: Erdoğan's alliance with nationalists (Kucukgocmen, 2018) to preserve his presidency forced pro-Erdoğanist political trolls to take new positions or create defensive arguments. There are at least two vital issues in which trolls found difficulties crafting a smooth discursive line: the first is the Syrian refugees in Turkey. Due to Erdoğan's policy towards the Syrian civil war, Turkey adopted a pro-refugee position for various reasons (Polat, 2018), and Aktrolls rarely acted in a hostile way to increasing numbers of refugees. However, even the AKP constituencies became critical of the government's refugee policy (Yayan, 2019). Aktrolls had to innovate to conform with Erdoğan's policies. This led to some ruptures. More nationalist Aktrolls switched sides and became explicitly anti-refugee. The other vital issue was the vaccination process in the Covid-19 pandemic. AKP leadership had a relatively pro-vaccination position during the pandemic, but some trolls imported discourses from the American anti-vaccination circles on social media. This constituted strong ambiguities in pro-AKP social media discourses. Some became anti-vaxxers (i.e. Abdurrahman Dilipak[3]) without leaving the party line altogether. As the early post-coup attempt days had passed, I could again extend my inquiries beyond the Twitter list. However, pandemic conditions forced all citizens to spend more time on digital screens. Twitter usage increased again, but there happened to be a diversification of digital outlets (DHA, 2020). More digitally literate trolls started *Telegram* groups and channels. Trolls used it to organise and create content, while using WhatsApp to disseminate content to broader audiences. I had access to several groups at this point and remained there as a passive observer. I observed the emergence of new troll initiatives that could challenge the Pelikan group, the one financed by Erdoğan's son-in-law's family. For instance, the *Telegram* group "Ebabil" had its own agenda that did not always correspond with the troll agendas I was monitoring on my Twitter list. This stage signified a diversification of content modality too. The number of videos and GIFS, among other media content, increased. As a new wave of multi-platformed diversification occurred, I extended my inquiries beyond the Twitter list I followed during the second stage, sometimes to offline forays. Some deserters from AKP provided clues about the transformations of the troll scene in their social media appearances or speeches at independent media outlets. I was able to revisit some of the interviewees for further questions, and some hometown connections led me to be accepted into a private WhatsApp group. As newcomer, pro-Erdoğan groups joined the game, and they would publicly invite like-minded users to *Telegram* groups for social media coordination such as Twitter hashtag campaigns or doxxing (releasing private data about anti-government activists). These heterogeneous and emergent forms and practices shaped the way I conducted my investigation.

Throughout all these three stages, it was not easy to access troll circles. I followed digital traces, constructed rhetorical wholes and identified semi-anonymous figures while constructing the research site itself. Researching pro-government trolls implied the study of people that wield more power and status than the researcher. This type of research may be related to big tech companies. Here, Bonini and Gandini's (2020) fieldwork in music platforms such as Spotify and Deezer are helpful examples. The impermeability of these platforms led the researchers to find tactics to circumvent access problems. I had to find tactics, not because of the platform structure but because of the power and secrecy of political actors that functioned semi-clandestinely. Like Bonini and Gandini (2020), I turned to Seaver (2017), who reminded us that "challenges to access—hidden meetings, reluctant interlocutors, non-disclosure agreements—are part of the field, not simply barriers around it" (p. 7). These challenges are already data, and I believe that scientific research plays a political role in reducing this opacity or at least making it public. While Crosset, Tanner and Campana (2019) focused on a particular platform to track traces, Seaver extended the focus beyond a platform: scavenging information in disparate places, treating interviews as fieldwork, parsing corporate heteroglossia, detecting ambivalences and contradictions in the speech of respondents (Seaver, 2017). My data scavenging field was not the corporations but still demanded a similar effort. Trolls operated semi-secretly through mostly ephemeral media content. It may be easy to capture content in a particular moment, but it becomes harder to get data for an extended period on a specific medium. Some accounts in my long-lasting Twitter list were closed voluntarily by their users or by Twitter. Other new ones opened up. Sometimes, trolls switched to private settings, other times they preferred to operate in a different medium such as Telegram. More interestingly, they sometimes switched political sides.

Postill and Pink's (2012) discussion of social media as a research site informed my methodological choices. They explained the nature of their research object, and questions required them to go beyond two main research methods traditionally used in digital communications: web content analysis of large data sets and social network analysis. In a similar way, I designed my research beyond these two methods. I moved between online and offline contexts and followed the digital traces in between them. I was tasked with building relations between different venues as the discourses emerged and flowed in a cross-platform manner (Jenkins, 2010). It is important to note that social media produces phatic talk and discussions that are not necessarily coherent. Analysing large data sets can only bring more incoherency. This incoherency can easily be found in trolls' content. The researcher is responsible for connecting the dots in intra- and inter-media conditions. It is not even necessarily contained in media venues alone. Postill and Pink (2012) noted that the idea of a bounded social unit is not suitable for the study of trolls. While online community strongly implies the presence of a bounded social unit, troll practices and relationships can better be viewed as a discursive community that shares a set of discourses, but does not necessarily constitute a homogenous and bounded social unit.

Trolling as a Discourse Community in the Service of Political Conservatism

In this section, I view Aktrolling as a discourse community, and I show how this analytical approach accounts for trolls' multiple, diverse and incoherent media practices. This approach also shifts the focus from an exhaustive search on who political trolls are to what and how they perform. Udupa and Pohjonen's (2017) use of "extreme speech" instead of "hate speech" serves to reframe trolls' evasive manoeuvres. While hate speech is relatively well defined, and its boundaries are relatively well established, extreme speech includes explicitly described hate speech and speech acts that escape hate speech regulations. Trolls' tactical moves allowed them to evade hate speech regulations and create a discursive terrain that could not be immediately regulated. Many non-anonymous political trolls benefited from these evasions and escaped social network moderation rules. Among Aktrolls, anonymity was never a target to achieve. Aktrolls relied on the authorities' power, and in most cases showed who their real identities were. Yet, like in the study by Udupa and Pohjonen (2017), Aktrolls also constituted a heterogeneous discursive terrain. And many bureaucrats and columnists contributed to define these discourses as extreme speech with impunity.

Aktrolls made use of discursivity. They relied on "troll science" to enter into cultural battles with the opposition users. A similar use of discursivity is seen in Eslen-Ziya's argument about a "troll science" in her study of anti-gender movements in Europe: "(distorted) scientific arguments moulded into populist discourse, creating an alternative narrative on the conceptions of gender equality" (2020, p. 1). With Aktrolls it was not only gender issues but also historiography and other relevant fields that were at stake. Discursivity also brings in rhetorical loopholes. There were moments when pro-AKP women groups, such as KADEM, clashed with others who contributed to pro-government troll discourses that carried a more anti-feminist and anti-woman rights tone (T24, 2020). Although KADEM had a significant role in circulating pseudoscientific arguments to counter feminist equality arguments, this did not stop them from clashing with other trolls. This "troll science" case is a case for a broader understanding of trolls as a discursive community. As noted in the introduction, a discourse community reaches uniformity in terms of a common cause, but this uniformity is gained through many different discursive practices by many actors. Communicative tools are at the centre of uniformisation. "Troll science" contributes to this process by providing rhetorical devices on gender justice issues.

In delineating Aktrolls as a discursive community, Crosset, Tanner and Campana's (2019) methodological piece on researching far-right groups on Twitter becomes an invaluable guide. They describe their method as recontextualisation in which the researcher puts into context the digital traces trolls produce and construct trolls' rhetorical boundaries. In the case of Aktrolls, cues from the politicians or other opinion leaders are brought into social media, explained, meme-fied and diversified and these outcomes are used by the AKP leaders again. Thus, the statements by two former ministers – "Turkish women are the decoration of their home" and "Mothers should not center a career other than motherhood" – would be elaborated on Twitter as "Children have never been more unhappy because of the mother role rejected by the 'free woman' model" and "Mothers have never been alone like in these times as their children grew up and left their mothers in nursing homes".[4] Lieback (2019, p. 16) adds anger and hostility in the forming rhetoric when trolls become political: "a rhetoric grounded in provocation and aiming to undermine opposing arguments by casting them as emotional, biased, totalitarian, and unrealistic" (Lieback (2019, p. 16). Aktrolls, in their discursive formation, used their anger towards the individual political opponents first. Still, gradually their energy was directed towards cultural themes like women's rights as part of the government's regime building. Their anger and political agenda towards supposed enemies seemed to have made some citizens united in Aktrolls circles, who were not directly linked to the party headquarters.

I define Aktrolling as a discourse community, also because Aktrolls do not share a common ideology. Apart from loyalty to Erdoğan and a general tendency for authoritarianism, it is hard to imagine trolls as a closed social unit with a definable set of ideological themes. Erdoğan himself is known to change his political positions frequently as long his regime is maintained (Gontijo and Barbosa, 2020).

Finally, Aktrolls vary from platform to platform, from online to offline settings and, of course, contextually. Crosset, Tanner and Campana (2019) define digital traces as data generated by individuals with digital tools. Marres and Weltevred (2013, p. 943) describe two types of digital traces: detection and recording of action online and the tools used to produce and detect these actions. In many troll studies, memes occupy a significant role. But among Aktrolls, humour and related memes are never substantial. At best, Erdoğan-related imagery predominates as a source of possible image analysis. In the quest for traces, a significant difference in the Aktrolls case is that many are not too keen on protecting their anonymity. They do not need to overly hide because they cooperate with the authorities, and strong anonymity will prevent them from benefiting the material and political riches. I could not find a systemic and centralised payment system, but Aktroll benefited from the regime in myriad ways (I extensively list these ways in Saka, 2018).

Conclusion

There has been much speculation about the organisation and economic structure of political trolling collectives. My troll research started to explain the nature of political trolling and explore its allegedly centralised and paid structure. While Ong and Cabanes (2018) present the best case of how trolling becomes an industry in the Philippines, my own research did not find a similar industry fed by creative industries and digital advertisers. From the outset, pro-government media had accused creative industry personnel of supporting Gezi Park Protests by providing social media content (Yeni Şafak, 2013). For various reasons, advertising and PR people did not become pro-government. This led the ruling government to ask its sympathisers to form new agencies. However, the new agencies and their personnel did not have the same digital skillset despite gaining big government contracts. Sourcing budget information is limited worldwide, but Bradshaw and Howard (2017) found some figures from Syria, Ecuador and Russia. Sindelar (2014) could even show Russia's increasing military expenditure for social media manipulation. Some news items from Turkey also claimed some budgetary information, but these mostly remained unproven or partial. Aktrolls were also not in a militarised hierarchy; they could not be named "cyber troops", as portrayed by Bradshaw and Howard (2017) when researching political troll organisations in other parts of the world. My ethnographic findings pointed out the voluntary nature of trolling circles.

In various ways, trolls need attention. Motivations may vary, from recruitment to message amplification or just personal benefits. They may not use their real names, but most trolls like to create a well-known digital persona. When their content trends on Twitter, it is seen as a success (Pohjonen and Udupa, 2017). Their desire for media exposure may give clues for their identities and workings. This desire means there will never be a smooth discursive front as trolls want to emphasise their individual contribution to the discourse. As a case in point, when AKP leadership may have aimed for totalitarian surveillance over citizens by using political trolls, this did not lead to domination on social media. Trolls with various motivations, on the one hand, and new opponents, rivalries and defectors, on the other hand, made it hard to maintain a united singular front in the service of the AKP leadership.

Troll activities in Turkey constitute a discourse community at the service of a neoliberal authoritarian regime. On the one hand, trolls remain a heterogeneous field that forced me to act as an investigator following various traces. They are non-stable mazes. On the other, troll collectives do have a structure and pattern that evolve throughout the formation of the political regime. Although the term discourse community may trigger a series of critics, I hope this concept leads to a productive debate within anthropological circles. Trolls' complicated existence and inconsistencies and their decentralised formation, on the one hand, and their uniform discursive front against the government's enemies, on the other hand, signify the conservative regime's vulnerability: not systematic and permanently anxious about losing power.

Notes

1 An online archive for the Gezi Park Protests: www.geziarchive.net/
2 The Council of Europe Convention on preventing and combating violence against women and domestic violence was signed in 2011 in İstanbul so it is better known as the Istanbul Convention.
3 https://twitter.com/aDilipak
4 https://twitter.com/SireneOznur/status/1371820976716050433

References

Amnesty International. (2013). *Gezi Park protests: Brutal denial of the right to peaceful assembly in Turkey*. London: Amnesty International.
Aspray, B. (2019). On trolling as comedic method. *JCMS: Journal of Cinema and Media Studies, 58*(3), 154–160.
Bazerman, C. (2009). *Issue brief: Discourse communities*. Champaign, IL: National Council of Teachers of English.
Bonini, T. and Gandini, A. (2020). The field as a black box: Ethnographic research in the age of platforms. *Social Media+ Society, 6*(4), 1–10.
Borg, E. (2003). Discourse community. *ELT Journal, 57*(4), 398–400.
Bradshaw, S., and Howard, P. (2017). *Troops, trolls and troublemakers: A global inventory of organised social media manipulation*. Oxford, UK: Oxford Internet Institute.
Coleman, G. (2014). *Hacker, hoaxer, whistleblower, spy: The many faces of Anonymous*. New York: Verso books.
Crosset, V., Tanner, S. and Campana, A. (2019). Researching far right groups on Twitter: Methodological challenges 2.0. *New Media & Society, 21*(4), 939–961.
DHA. (2 May 2020). *Koronavirüs etkisiyle televizyon izleme oranı yüzde 23 arttı*. CNN Türk. www.cnnturk.com/turkiye/koronavirus-etkisiyle-televizyon-izleme-orani-yuzde-23-artti
Erensü, S. and Alemdaroğlu, A. (2018). Dialectics of reform and repression: Unpacking Turkey's authoritarian "turn". *Review of Middle East Studies, 52*(1), 16–28.
Esen, B. and Gumuscu, S. (2019). Killing competitive authoritarianism softly: The 2019 local elections in Turkey. *South European Society and Politics, 24*(3), 317–342.
Eslen-Ziya, H. (2020). Right-wing populism in New Turkey: Leading to all new grounds for troll science in gender theory. *HTS Theological Studies, 76*(3), 1–9.
Flores-Saviaga, C., Keegan, B. and Savage, S. (2018). Mobilising the trump train: Understanding collective action in a political trolling community. *Proceedings of the International AAAI Conference on Web and Social Media, 12*(1).
Gehl, R. W. (2016). Power/freedom on the dark web: A digital ethnography of the Dark Web Social Network. *New Media & Society, 18*(7), 1219–1235.
Gontijo, L. C. and Barbosa, R. S. (2020). Erdoğan's pragmatism and the ascension of AKP in Turkey: Islam and neo-Ottomanism. *Digest of Middle East Studies, 29*(1), 76–91.
Göztepe, E. (2018). The permanency of the state of emergency in Turkey. *Zeitschrift Für Politikwissenschaft, 28*(4), 521–534.
Hoyng, R. and Es, M. (2017). Conspiratorial webs: Media ecology and parallel realities in Turkey. *International Journal of Communication, 11*, 20.

Jenkins, H. (2010). Transmedia storytelling and entertainment: An annotated syllabus. *Continuum*, 24(6), 943–958.

Jenzen, O., Erhart, I., Eslen-Ziya, H., Korkut, U. and McGarry, A. (2021). The symbol of social media in contemporary protest: Twitter and the Gezi Park movement. *Convergence*, 27(2), 414–437.

Jones, P. K. (2020). *Critical theory and demagogic populism*. Manchester: Manchester University Press.

Kucukgocmen, A. (21 February 2018). Erdogan's AKP says to ally with nationalists for 2019 elections. *Reuters*. www.reuters.com/article/us-turkey-election-regulation-idUSKCN1G52DP

Lieback, H. (2019). Truth-telling and trolls: Trolling, political rhetoric in the twenty-first century, and the objectivity norm. *Aspeers*, 12.

Lowen, M. (16 April 2017). *Why Did Turkey Hold a Referendum?* www.bbc.com/news/world-europe-38883556

Madianou, M. and Miller, D. (2013). Polymedia: Towards a new theory of digital media in interpersonal communication. *International Journal of Cultural Studies*, 16(2), 169–187.

Marres, N. and Weltevrede, E. (2013). Scraping the social? Issues in live social research. *Journal of Cultural Economy*, 6(3), 313–335.

Migdalovitz, C. (2010). *Israel's blockade of Gaza, the Mavi Marmara Incident, and its aftermath*. Fort Belvoir, VA: Defense Technical Information Center.

Ong, J. C. and Cabañes, J. V. A. (2018). *Architects of networked disinformation: Behind the scenes of troll accounts and fake news production in the Philippines*. Leeds: University of Leeds.

Paul, A. and Seyrek, M. (2017). Constitutional changes in Turkey: A presidential system or the President's system. European Policy Center, www.epc.eu/en/Publications/Constitutional-changes-in-Turkey-A-presidential-system-or-the-preside~1d617c

Pohjonen, M. and Udupa, S. (2017). Extreme speech online: An anthropological critique of hate speech debates. *International Journal of Communication*, 11, 19.

Polat, R. K. (2018). Religious solidarity, historical mission and moral superiority: Construction of external and internal "others" in AKP's discourses on Syrian refugees in Turkey. *Critical Discourse Studies*, 15(5), 500–516.

Postill, J. and Pink, S. (2012). Social media ethnography: The digital researcher in a messy web. *Media International Australia*, 145(1), 123–134.

Saka, E. (2018). Social media in Turkey as a space for political battles: AKTrolls and other politically motivated trolling. *Middle East Critique*, 27(2), 161–177.

Saka, E. (2019). *Social Media and Politics in Turkey. A Journey through Citizen Journalism, Political Trolling, and Fake News*. Washington, DC: Lexington Books. https://books.google.com.tr/books?id=W8C9DwAAQBAJ&dq=Social+Media+and+Politics+in+Turkey:+A+Journey+through+Citizen+Journalism,+Political+Trolling,+and+Fake+News+&lr=&source=gbs_navlinks_s

Saka, E. (2021). Networks of political trolling in Turkey after the consolidation of power under the presidency. In S. Udupa, I. Gagliardone and P. Hervik (eds), *Digital hate: The global conjuncture of extreme speech*. Bloomington: Indiana University Press. https://iupress.org/9780253059253/digital-hate/

Seaver, N. (2017). Algorithms as culture: Some tactics for the ethnography of algorithmic systems. *Big Data & Society*, 4(2), 1–12.

Sindelar, D. (2014). The kremlin's troll army. *The Atlantic*, 12.

Soldatov, A., Borogan, I., Shearlaw, M., Walker, S., Burrows, M., Harding, L. and Shearlaw, M. (8 September 2015). What spawned Russia's "troll army"? Experts on the red web share their views. *The Guardian*. www.theguardian.com/world/live/2015/sep/08/russia-troll-army-red-web-any-questions

T24. (9 October 2020). *Yeni Akit yazarı Dilipak: AK Parti ve KADEM'in suç duyurularında son ifademi de verdim, hatırlatırım bir de bu işin öbür dünyası var*. T24. https://t24.com.tr/haber/yeni-akit-yazari-dilipak-ak-parti-ve-kadem-in-suc-duyurularinda-son-ifademi-de-verdim-hatirlatirim-bir-de-bu-isin-obur-dunyasi-var,908234

Tugal, C. (2016). *The fall of the Turkish model: How the Arab uprisings brought down Islamic liberalism*. New York: Verso Books.

Wittel, A. (2000). Ethnography on the move: From field to net to internet. *Forum Qualitative Sozialforschung/ Forum: Qualitative Social Research*, 1(1).

Yayan, İ. (11 September 2019). Metropoll araştırdı: Her dört kişiden üçü iktidarın Suriyeli politikasını onaylamıyor, üç kişiden biri "Savaş sürse bile geri gönderilsinler" diyor. *Medyascope*. https://medyascope.tv/2019/09/11/metropoll-arastirdi-her-dort-kisiden-ucu-iktidarin-suriyeli-politikasini-onaylamiyor-uc-kisiden-biri-savas-surse-bile-geri-gonderilsinler-diyor/

Yeni Şafak. (8 June 2013). *Reklam ajanslarında "organize işler"*. Yeni Şafak. www.yenisafak.com/gundem/reklam-ajanslarinda-organize-isler-530424

Yesil, B. (2016). *Media in New Turkey: The Origins of an Authoritarian Neoliberal State*. Champaign: University of Illinois Press.

Zimmermann, Ç. (13 October 2016). Feature: Turkey trolls' use of insults stifling reporting. *International Press Institute*. https://ipi.media/feature-turkey-trolls-use-of-insults-stifling-reporting/

33
PERFORMING CONSERVATISM

A Study of Emerging Political Mobilisations in Latin America using "Social Media Drama" Analysis

Raúl Castro-Pérez

Introduction

Media scholars such as P. David Marshall argue that the 21st century is the time in which we think and experience through the plurality of our publics rather than through a single public sphere or a public life (Marshall, 2016; also, Drucker and Gumpert, 2015; Gutsche and Hess, 2018). He suggests that, regardless of whether we define the public in reference to public opinion and self-serving interests (Lippmann, 1954) or to influencing political action through the public sphere (Habermas, 1989), "most (if not all) iterations of 'public' have contained this overriding communicative relationship of the individual to unity" (Marshall, 2016: 2). The emergence of strong citizen activism consisting of multiple discourses and signs facilitated mainly by the cultures of connectivity and their current participatory practices (Bennett and Segerberg, 2013; Van Dijck, 2013) is putting that plurality on display. The activity of the "digital publics" (Roberts, 2014), the "micro publics" (Marshall, 2015), or what danah boyd defines as the "networking publics" (2010) then makes necessary an analytical turn towards understanding contemporary politics as a "plurality of publics" that has been dominated by parallel, overlapping and usually competing "social worlds" (Pink et al., 2016).

Current politics in European democracies—for example Spain, France, Germany, the Netherlands, and the United Kingdom—or in those of the Americas—such as the United States, Peru, Brazil, Mexico, and Argentina—is increasingly yielding useful case studies of competing publics, all of them characterised by high levels of fragmentation (Bergsen, 2019; also, Boulianne, Koc-Michalska, and Bimber, 2020; Brinks, Levitsky, and Murillo, 2020) and confronted with underlying moral division. Feinberg and Willer refer to this division as a "moral empathy gap" that functions as a "technique for effective and persuasive communication across political divides" (Feinberg and Willer, 2019). Clearly recognisable is a rhetorical game defined by opposed political positions—liberal and conservative—that are founded upon the moral beliefs of each speech community. The empathy gap arises in the form of opposed sets of features that morally reframe the distinct discourses (Feinberg and Willer, 2019). These features—such as care/harm, fairness/cheating, loyalty/betrayal, authority/subversion, sanctity/degradation, liberty/oppression—are dichotomous categories that align along a wide ideological spectrum and reorder social discussion of topics such as schooling, the administration of justice, the politics of reproduction (e.g., abortion), and even those related to identity politics about sexuality and gender.

In this article, I apply an anthropological approach to the "moral empathy gap" among emerging, mobilised political groups in Latin America who, since 2016, have been adopting increasingly inflexible postures. I analyse conservative mobilisations that I consider representative of the trend of competing groups using moral rhetoric to confront one another. Inspired by Ginsburg's research on the abortion debate in an American community reported in *Contested Lives* (1998 [1989]), I discuss the political discourses and practices of analogous competing pro-life factions in Lima and Bogota. I also show that these conservative groups share platforms for communicative action with peers elsewhere in Latin America and organise sets of fluid and highly collaborative public assemblies and ceremonies in a participatory manner. I study these discourses and practices as a "social system" or "field" rather than as "loosely integrated processes" (Turner, 1986), following a method of research that Turner (1986) called "social drama analysis", where "social drama" denotes "a device for describing and analysing episodes that manifest social conflict" (Turner, 1974: 78). A "social drama", then, is a concept referring to dramatic, performative acts that are indicative of what a given community believes to be factual reality in crisis and which must be displayed—in a performed-for-an-audience manner—as an irreparable schism between competing parties in the search for social recognition and legitimation of the crisis (Turner, 1986).

The "social drama" concept will inform my approach to the pro-life public assemblies and ceremonies in Peru and Colombia in the same way it served Turner's analysis of power handover in the African Ndembu society (Turner, 1986) and Myerhoff in her analysis of "invisibility" among very old Jewish immigrants from Eastern Europe in California (Myerhoff, 1986). But, in addition, I will present a modification to the social drama concept that I call the "social media drama", in reference to the kind of mediatisation (the term is defined by Couldry and Hepp, 2013) that participants and wider audiences experience when attending public assemblies and ceremonies through the social media. In that regard, a "social drama" is explicitly designed and produced to livestream on Facebook, Twitter, or other social media sites and be subsequently re-experienced through uploaded and released videos. To validate this conceptual adjustment, using interviews and direct observation I analyse both the comments that participants share during an event—written on walls and in threads—and the subsequent discourse they engage in about the experience. The purpose of this adjustment is to understand more comprehensively the sense of participation experienced by the contributors to these movements as they at once constitute the congregation at public gatherings and use social media to share the principal messages.

To the extent that my approach is ethnographic and that we need to understand the public acts of conservative mobilisation in their social, historical, and political context, I, like Turner (1986), bring to bear Singer's concept of "cultural performance" (1972). This idea denotes concrete and observable units of analysis, such as "plays, concerts and lectures … but also prayers, ritual readings and recitations, rites and ceremonies, festivals, and all those things we usually classify under religion and ritual …" (Singer, 1972: 71). Turner conceives of "cultural performances" as spectacles that emerge from processual "social dramas" and become recognised narrative genres for participants and audiences alike. Turner differentiates "social drama" as the "raw" material for the "cultural performances", claiming that "what began as an empirical social drama may continue both as an entertainment and a metasocial commentary on the lives and times of the given community" (Turner, 1986: 39). In this chapter I show how conservative cultural performances function both as a play or a story for participants and, simultaneously, as a pedagogical medium for large-scale moral and political statements.

Media production of the protest and its recording and delivery in the form of self-broadcast videos shared on social media networks represents systematic use of media to publicise the activity and accentuate its instructional purpose for wider audiences. This systematisation is present in the experience of live streaming and the subsequent repeated viewing of videos on sites like Facebook and Twitter, a form of ritualised viewing and reviewing of the cultural performance enacted by the collective.

The final element for this study I borrow from Rabikowska (2015). My proposal is that watching social videos as re-experienced acts constitutes for the mobilised conservative activists what she calls the "everyday of memories". This term refers to how individuals in former communist countries of Eastern Europe performed everyday personal memorial practices enjoyed through the era's art and literature as acts with the power to resist the new capitalist social order. I will equate the concept with the re-experiencing through shared videos.

My research strategy relied on four qualitative methods. First, I interviewed activists who produced, shared, and re-watched the cultural performances on social media. During these interviews I played a selection of videos to elicit responses. Second, I observed research participants re-watching the online videos during remote interviews and then analysed their responses. Third, for the Lima mobilisation I attended and undertook participant observation. Finally, for the Bogota mobilisations, I undertook digital ethnography by analysing the Facebook account of one of the activists and then applying a qualitative research software package (QDA Miner Lite) that allowed me to analyse comments as systematic data and identify keywords.

Morally Centred Social Movements: The State of Affairs

At the start of the 21st century, social scientists generally considered conservative political mobilisations to be diverse in character and motivation (Blee and Creasap, 2010; Westermeyer, 2019). Blee and Creasap use the word *conservative* to denote "movements that support patriotism, free enterprise capitalism, and/or traditional moral order" and, in respect of the latter, report that "some scholars underscore how they mirror religious fundamentalism in their speeches: dualisms of good and evil, millennialism, and sharp boundaries between believers and others" (Blee and Creasap, op.cit.: 270). For example, conservative traditionalism is found in movements that consider sex education or teaching evolution in schools antithetical to the Biblical narrative and seek to ban them. In the US and Europe, some traditionalist movements also seek to limit access to abortion, pornography, gambling, or prostitution as "violations of morality" (Blee and Creasap, op. cit: 272).

Morals usually condition these movements and shape their interactions with the State (Karapin, 2007; McIvor, 2018). Moreover, their rhetoric in favour of individual citizen rights aims to establish a "balance of obligations" between citizens and the State (McIvor, 2018: 8) and demands respect from the State for the recognition of people's right to live according to their own moral traditional values. For example, conservative movements defend parental authority and fight for choice in the schooling their children receive or promote deregulation of their productive activities and private business (Blee and Creasap, op.cit.: 272). Such traditional cultural values, along with opposition to State intervention in the economy and emphasis on law and order, define their agenda, as they do for formal right-wing formal parties in the US,

Europe, and Oceania (Gidron and Ziblatt, 2019). Zealous activism by these actors competes persistently with progressive global policies, with conservative movements and parties acting and lobbying at world summits and international forums (Bob, 2012).

In Latin America, where they are driven by popular participation rather than the political establishment, morality-centred social movements and parties should be analysed in terms of meaning creation rather than resources and organisation. Just as Westermeyer (2019) found in his account of the Tea Party Movement in the US, in Latin America we find a massive mobilisation of grassroots conservative social groups from diverse backgrounds acting in alliance with political elites and with a sector of the media that makes their movement visible. In this sense, conservative groups in both the US and Latin America are gaining followers by providing the "space for collective political identities to be developed [and] lived ... [resulting in] vibrant local spaces of cultural production and political activism" (Westermeyer, 2019: 11). This process has led to conservative positions gaining considerable influence over public debate in recent years. For Bolcatto and Souroujon (2020), it explains why the continent is facing a *sorpasso* (takeover of political power) through which different right-wing traditions increasingly embody power.

Although their influence over the political landscape in the Americas is increasing, morality-centred mobilisations and parties face tension over how they are perceived in the public arena (Ginsburg, 1998; Blee and Creasap, 2010). They have been battling, on the one hand, against the authoritarian labelling they attract because of occasional sympathies with dictatorial regimes (Loxton, 2016), and on the other, against the resonance of acts of violence coming from the Far-Right, the Alt-Right, and other extreme positions (Ginsburg, 1998). Accordingly, conservative movements have become very active in managing their image. To distance themselves from violent positions, they use elaborate strategies, including conferences, recitals, activities in parks, and family-oriented cultural events. Moreover, they also run a very active self-promotion agenda drawing on their own set of hybrid media: information and opinion for the press, radio, and television, and social media that pursues "a particular ideological bent ... able to circumscribe media exposure easily and effectively to one consistent perspective" (Jamieson and Cappella cited in Westermeyer, 2019: 8). They represent a network that controls its message and seek to attract non-political groups into politics (Blee and Creasap, 2010).

It is the proficiency for self-management of their own media exposure by conservative social movements that has led some to identify their condition of "autonomy", particularly because of the ways they strategically use the multimedia resources of the platforms. As Shroeder (2018:7) explains: "the internet extends the mediation of politics, from above, such that political elites can target and respond more directly to their publics, and from below, such that people or citizens can engage in more diverse ways with politics". Shroeder's comparative analysis of mobilisations in countries such as Sweden, the US, India, and China also underscores how these new conservative forces can circumvent traditional gatekeepers and how their expert handling of digital media sustains their autonomous practices (Shroeder, 2018).

A "Social Media Drama" Analysis for Conservative Mobilisation

I have compiled a set of observations about what I regard as a new and emerging political contest: a morality-centred mobilisation and public debate. It is distinguished by a robust constellation of traditionalist social movements with a cross-cutting agenda centred on issues of gender, education, social identity, public health, and the politics of reproduction. While this process unfolds, an increase in cultural performances by the conservative mobilisations can be seen, many of which are significantly influencing the terms of contemporary public debate;

examples of which are the two Latin American cases I will approach in this study, both as cultural performances assembled collaboratively on public spaces and shared as mediatised ceremonies on social media sites like Facebook and Twitter.

In addition to the work of Turner (1974, 1986), my concept of morality-centred cultural performances as "social media dramas" draws on other developments that refer to the crossroads where art and political processes in highly mediatised social environments meet, such as Postill's concept of "Internet drama" (Postill, 2011). Postill applied the "social drama" device to analyse citizen conflict in Subang Jaya, Malaysia. Here, mediatised cultural performance in the form of a residential group's photo-protest published in Chinese-language media caused friction not only between the residents and the municipal council, but also between the residents themselves. Postill (2011: 89) used the term "Internet drama" to stress the increasing Internet mediatisation of the performance. In common with Postill's work, my study of Latin American conservative mobilisations regards their performances as the confluence of distinct collectives participating in networked online spaces for political expression. However, my study notes something additional: the groups in Latin America are aware of both the broad reach they achieve through social media and the pedagogical power that entails. For this reason, when they conceive and produce a performance for a given event, they do so with its long-term systematic use as an instructional resource in mind. By using the "social media drama" concept as an analytical device to explore and explain conservative cultural performances, my approach to the case studies in Peru and Colombia will primarily interrogate the participants' capacities to collaboratively construct a particular cultural identity and political discourse expressed through the display of a set of symbolic resources produced for mediatised public gatherings. The participants themselves recognise that structuring these gatherings in that context is a process of participatory design and interlocutory co-creation. They simultaneously self-perceive as users and *producers* (Ingold, 2014). My approach will borrow from Shroeder (2018) by focussing on the proficiency that participants must self-manage their social media resources and exposure, and on the transformative consequences the mediatisation of performances have, particularly when participants experience those performances as forms suitable for social media interactions (Couldry, 2008).

Regarding the latter, the research explores the forms of "ritualisation" that the social media interactions under analysis acquire (Bell, 2009). Evidence comes, on the one hand, from the way participants experience and share "direct events" through streaming on social media, and, on one other, from the way the participants practice their "everyday of memories" in personal routine acts in which they re-experience events online. Hence, I draw on Catherine Bell's "ritualisation" concept to interpret participants' "strategic way of acting", seeking to differentiate their mobilisation from others that lack a systematic rationality (Bell, 2009). Also consistent with Bell's approach, I explore how the ritualised way of acting evident in Latin America's conservative performances represents a disruptive political position and stresses a "moral empathy gap" with other positions aiming to warn about an alleged long-term moral crisis in society.

My principal aim is to lend support to Bell's insights about how ritualised, everyday, personal social media interactions lead to social cohesion and control of the participant's sense of reality—and at the same time, to a 'social pedagogy' (Bell, 2009: 176)—through extensive use of symbolic forms in public exposure. That is why an approach to conservative mobilisations from a "social media drama" analytical perspective must recognise the instructional power of a cultural performance: as a "public display of symbols" (Peterson, 2003: 18), or "sets of assumptions about the way things are and should be" (Bell, 2009: 176). My proposal, therefore, is to grasp the educative ability of the conservative symbolic forms to "model ideal relations and structure of values" (Bell, 2009: 175), in their helping "to define as authoritative certain ways of seeing society" (ibid.) A processual, analytic scheme like the "social media drama" also allows to us understand these sets of ritualised actions as a comprehensive social system.

Performing Conservatism in Latin America

I present in this section my two cases studies of ceremony ritualisation experienced in the form of social media interactions: a pro-life performance in Lima, Peru; a similar event in Bogota, Colombia. I consider each to be a cultural performance apt for analysis using the concept of "social media drama".

Performing Conservatism and Co-Creation in Lima

The first social media drama was a ritualised action that closed the Marcha por la vida (Pro-Life march [my translation]) in 2018, a massive rally that replicates similar events in major capitals around the world. Since the first such annual gathering in Lima, in 2008, participation levels have steadily grown, and the most recent event attracted a crowd measured in the hundreds of thousands. It mobilised various conservative groups claiming a moral and political case for the "right-to-life" of the "unborn". These activists conceive the right-to-life to include the life of a foetus; they do not address the mother's right-to-life in the event of pregnancy complications and nor do they consider health factors related to poverty. They are driven by an implacable opposition to the legalisation of abortion and assisted death (euthanasia), to the *ideologia de genero* (gender ideology) at school and to any practices that threaten what their publicity refers to as *diseño original de la familia* (the original design of the family [my translation]).

My particular focus is the ritualised action known as *un minuto de silencio* (the minute of silence [my translation]) in memory of the unborn, a performance previously documented in similar contemporary demonstrations like one observed in the United Kingdom (Lowe, 2016). Customised to be suitable for the local context, the performance included a particular sequence filled with meaningful elements and represented the climax of an hours'-long event that began with a caravan moving east to west across the entire city and ended with a massive Christian concert on the city's oceanfront. At the end of the musical performance, the then Archbishop of Lima and a dozen conservative parliamentarians, activists and other religious leaders took to the stage to call for an act of contemplation—the minute of silence—while the scene of a little boy in a hospital bed played on a giant screen. The child, Alfie Evans, suffered a terminal illness and had been at the centre of a dispute between his parents, who had fought to take him from the United Kingdom to Italy for further treatment, and the British government, which had obtained a court order to turn off his life support. A lone trumpet performance of "Il Silenzio" (the melody of "Taps", traditionally played at military funerals) resounded across the area. Cameras on mobile telephones filmed the ritualised performance, and some participants on social media shared the sorrowful moment in real-time with a wider audience.

"Alfie is a symbol", according to Fernando, one of the hundreds of volunteers who worked in the organising group and an important source for my research. He is also the founder of the Viva Vida Perú collective (Long Live Life Peru: [my translation]), an enthusiastic group mobilised in support of the family as "the fundamental unit of society and the State" (my translation of the objective stated on its Facebook account). Since its creation in 2016 the group has grown to 13,000 members. It provides a space for debate about current affairs considered to affect pro-life causes. Fernando explained to me that Alfie's drama had become an impasse reported in global media, the embodiment of an irreducible moral dispute that became political

Performing Conservatism

Figure 33.1 Portrait of the event "A Minute of Silence": religious leaders and parliamentarians at the closing ceremony of the Pro-Life march, held in Lima on 5 May 2018
Source: © Carolina Paullo.

due to its broad public exposure. On 28 April 2018, following the court order that withdrew his life support, Alfie passed away (BBC, 2018).

The centrality of Alfie's images to the minute of silence ceremony came as a surprise for those in attendance and had significant impact. "How touching, how great, how timely", tweeted Úrsula, a research participant and freelance journalist consultant, when commenting on the video of the event she shared on her Twitter account. The social media drama was experienced by all participants—those physically present and those remotely viewing a streamed performance—all of whom were able to view captions (such as "Alfie Evans' fight for life") on the giant screen and the branding of the original source of the video: the Pro-Life Weekly program (from the Catholic Church's TV channel EWTN, aired worldwide via cable). All participants also noted a banner from a pro-life British activist support network—popularly dubbed "Alfie's Army"—which was credited on the images and had mobilised on the streets and social media in support of Alfie's parents. The purpose of Alfie's Army transcends the case that inspired it; on its official Facebook account the group defines its purpose as "to protect the rights of parents to care for their own children".

According to Úrsula, "There it is an action plan ... to trample over the rights of the parent ... There are parents who will say: 'let's not have him suffer' ... But there are others who say no ... who have religious faith". For her, the problem is "that the State can say no ... That is a very dangerous precedent". According to Fernando, the drama of Alfie represented an extreme example of the State displaying its power and its authority over "public policy", even where such policy extends to an issue as sensitive as euthanasia. He explained, "we have to respect life until right up to natural death and give [the person] all treatment necessary to reduce the physical and emotional suffering".

It is notable the way in which the participants make sense of their experience of the minute of silence through the empowerment that each feels upon joining the Pro-Life march and becoming part of the political statement its performance embodies and represents. The performance communicates to different publics a latent social conflict and a deep moral schism that a militant conservative collective feels compelled to bring to the attention of the institutional establishment. When we view the act through the prism of "social media drama" analysis, we can observe in it the four processual stages that Turner identifies for a social system's complete action set: an initial breach precipitated by a norm-governed social ordinance; an evident crisis widely discussed in public; redressive actions ranging from personal mediations to formal judicial proceeding; and a social recognition of a deep, moral empathy gap between contesting parties (Turner, 1986). In the words of research participant, Fernando:

> All the parishes and organizations were like a massive boombox … There we were defending a right, raising awareness about the political use of euthanasia by the State, and about the suffering of people victimised by that use. That is what the case of little Alfie is about.

Schieffelin states that performances are compelling because "they somehow formulate or 'make sense' of particular, often problematic, cultural situations and then reframe, transform, or intensify this 'sense', leading to a new orientation of the participants to the situation" (Schieffelin, 1985: 707). This process becomes clear in the minute of silence through the participative construction of its dramatic action set by an engaged community. Voluntary activists, authorities, media networks, social media followers, and a supporters' 'army'—from inside the country and beyond—are all acting together and feeding meaningful resources into the action set. The contributions are often organised into themes. Research participant Fernando, for example, organised groups of disabled children, who participated through dance and theatre. "They are a demonstration that life must go on under any circumstances", he commented. Others, like Úrsula, fed the social media experience of the performance by live retweeting and sharing of video excerpts. Still more contributed by adding comments (for example, "it is not enough to be believers, you have to be credible", "This is a tribute to Alfie from Peru"); tagging media broadcasters, such as the BBC; and using hashtags such as (my translations in parentheses) #marchaporlavida (#pro-life march), #unidosporlavida (# unitedforlife) or #graciasmama (#thanksmum). Prior to the event, Alfie had become a major talking point across various publics, including in the press and on blogs, social media threads, and walls. Father Mario Arroyo, for example, states that the fight over the fate of Alfie's was based on the broader struggle by some members of civil society, including well-known members, to ensure the right of parents to decide their children's future (Arroyo, 2018).

In a symbolic game, the performance of the minute of silence restores that sense of authority—particularly parental—for the participants and at the same time pays homage to someone considered a hero offered in sacrifice. As the subjects of this research testify, the performance establishes for the network community a ritualised commemoration ceremony of someone who "lost a battle" in a moral fight with the State. The act "collectively bonds" its participants to a connected community in the same social world each time its participants again watch the video, creating a sense of reestablishment of the moral order between them.

Performing Conservatism in Bogota's Autonomous Media

The second cultural performance under analysis took place in Bogota on 5 September 2020 in the form of a live event called the Plantón por la vida (Pro-Life Sit-In [my translation]).

Figure 33.2 Young people participating at the concert of Lima's Pro-Life march on 5 May 2018
Source: © Carolina Paullo.

Bringing together various pro-life groups from around Colombia, the objective was to oppose demands for the decriminalisation of abortion put forth by the feminist organisation Causa Justa (Just Cause [my translation]). By staging it in front of the Constitutional Court of Colombia in the heart of the capital's historic centre, the event attracted considerable attention and gained significant news media coverage. Local channel City TV transmitted live from the site and a reporter interviewed a spokesperson for the collective, who claimed that the attendees were tired "of the discourses of death and violence" and "tired of others [presuming to] speak on our behalf", in reference to the way in which feminist collectives claim to represent all women in Colombia. "Empowered women have no need to murder their children", she declared bluntly to the camera (City TV, 2020).

According to the television reports and the organiser's own Facebook broadcast, more than 200 activists participated in teams that had been organised through their own networks. One volunteer, an anonymous informant for my research, explained to me via Messenger that the mobilisation involved "different groups or pro-life communities, from different parts and cities, united for the same cause, fighting for the same purpose and interest", with volunteers providing details of "the specific day, time and place" using all available means, including "on the radio, through newspapers, and handing out flyers". The resulting web of networks led to broad participation, with a notable preponderance of young people evident in the principal video recording of the event that the organisers uploaded to Facebook for subsequent viewing and reviewing. The video record also provides information about who led the event, its organisers, the volunteers, and those responsible for its communication, mainly journalists managing the Facebook live performance. The latter are social media teams acting in what Gerbaudo (2017) refers to as the movement's digital vanguard: mediums who convey an autonomous position to the public and question mediation by the mainstream press.

The event streaming was assembled on the Facebook account of one of the principal organisers: the Unidos por la Vida (United for Life [my translation]) collective. The video of the event streaming is still available on this social network, a cultural performance planned and developed from the start as a social media video that participants could later re-experience. The 14 minutes of footage also portray an interactive play with a life of its own, designed and assembled as part of the groups' overall strategy to widely disseminate their position by its viral delivery. The carefully prepared script is one in which, through a "social media drama" analysis, we can identify the classic four stage action set: a breach born out of the abortion decriminalisation proposal; a crisis regarding its possible social and legal acceptance; several redressive actions by mobilised pro-life collectives; and finally, a public statement of a social schism at which activists promise don't rest until you have overcome it. It begins with a young female volunteer who initiates the performance by reciting a sort of normative framing: "the protection of the rights of the child and of the unborn [in accordance with] binding international agreements signed by Colombia". An adult male then calls for resistance to the decriminalisation of abortion. The audience erupts by chanting *déjalo latir* (let it [the heart] beat [my translation]) as a collective response. Next, a young mother offers her testimony on abortion and her process of awakening: "My child is the living proof that a pregnant woman in crisis does needs support not an abortion." She is followed by a male participant-researcher who intervenes by complaining about the absence of reliable government data: "We have no information, no one is responsible for abortion in this country." Finally, a young female reporter appears to sum up and provide unity to the story, ending the sequence with the words: "this struggle is just beginning".

To explain the rationale for the use of an interactive device like that, my anonymous informant claimed that participants to the mobilisation were motivated by scorn for the way the mainstream media reports on the issue. She commented: "There is perhaps censorship by the media, the news programs, etc., because when there are protests in favour of abortion, they report it extensively ... but when there are pro-life demonstrations it does not happen like that." As evidence for her claim, she pointed to an earlier sit-in that had filled Bogota's Plaza Bolívar but had only been reported at its conclusion when most people had left: "They did not show the reality ... Luckily there were many people belonging to the movement and participants to the sit-in who took photos and videos of the moment and what really happened."

Production and materialisation of devices like the Plantón por la vida video, are mediatised cultural performances designed to be repeatedly viewed by users through social media. Their production and materialisation are important for the Colombian conservative movement because they are resources to employ in what Bell refers to as "social pedagogy" (2009). The ritualised practices I discovered, in which conservative mobilisation participants re-experienced public ceremonies by re-watching videos on social media, are filled with instructional meaning for individuals themselves and educational guidance for other audiences. By eliciting responses to the Plantón por la vida video and through my QDA Miner Lite analysis of the video comments, I identified several words in habitual use by the engaged online community as of 31 December 2020. They fell into three morally charged categories: [my translation: the Spanish words bracketed] (i) The right-to-life [derecho a la vida], (ii) nation [nación], and (iii) religion [religión]. Habitual words like these determine morally centred political commitments that instruct the participants: in a core motto—the right-to-life; in a vision of the intended scope and target for its efforts—the nation; and in a powerful ideological glue that binds the assembly—religiosity.

The testimonies of my informants speak to the way in which revisiting the events on social media normalise their sense of duty. Through an interview by teleconference, I spoke to Francisco, a middle-aged businessman and politician, about the Plantón por la vida experience. "It was a reminder", he pondered, in reference to abortion:

Let me explain. When I see something that I consider correct, I file it away in my mind. When the Plantón por la vida video again appeared, I clicked on it because I recognised in it a political campaign struggling against people who want to make acceptable something that is immoral and currently illegal", he said, in reference to abortion.

For Francisco, when people who hold different points of view but share the same values and principles re-experience instructional events, it becomes possible to align different publics behind a common cause. "You cannot go against the law of gravity", he says. He considers that the mobilised have a role to play in warning society about the perils upsetting its moral equilibrium.

Concluding Remarks

I have argued that the emergence of a robust morality-centred mobilisation and public debate in Latin America, particularly in Peru and Colombia, responds to the call by a constellation of conservative social movements in that region to resist public policies that affect their pro-life principles and values. These conservative movements react against legal abortion under any circumstances, against medically assisted death, and against actions by the State that affect and eventually remove parents' rights over schooling and the formation of their children's personal identity. Their rhetoric in defence of traditional values, parental control, and citizen rights able to counterbalance state power activates a cross-cutting agenda that inspires each member of the movement to engage with the construction of an autonomous body of political demands.

These aspects are evident in the mobilisation and practices of pro-life activists in Peru and Colombia. The "social media drama" is a useful conceptual device to analyse the cultural performances played out by these individuals. The Plantón por la vida and Un minute de silencio deliver categorical evidence for the emergence of renewed and defiant narratives over disputed moral issues and represent personal acts of cultural resistance against progressive social reforms.

Performing conservativism in Latin America is, on balance, both a project of social pedagogy in progress and a transformative experience for its participants, thanks to the recurrence with which they re-experience their social media dramas as everyday vivid memories. The participants insist on the educational commitment they have in the fight for the mainstream morals they feel called to defend. "It is not much, but it is good as a beginning", reflected my informant, Fernando. This claim expresses the potential that many of them feel exists to transform not only people's stories but also the main social narratives of their societies.

References

Arroyo, M. (2018) "Alfie Evans o ¿Cuánto vale una vida humana?" *Universidad de Piura, Blog Campus Lima*, 27 April, available at www.udep.edu.pe/hoy/2018/04/alfie-evans-o-cuanto-vale-una-vida-humana/ (accessed 15 February 2021).
BBC News (2018) "Alfie Evans: Legal Battle Toddler Dies," *BBC News*, 28 April, available at www.bbc.com/news/uk-43933056 (accessed 15 February 2021).
Bell, C. (2009) *Ritual Theory, Ritual Practice*, Oxford: Oxford University Press.
Bennett, W. and Segerberg, A. (2012) "The Logic of Connective Action: The Personalization of Contentious Politics," *Information, Communication & Society*, 15 (5): 739–768.
Bergsen, P. (2019) "Don't Be Afraid of Political Fragmentation," *Chatam House*, 16 December, available at www.chathamhouse.org/2019/12/dont-be-afraid-political-fragmentation (accessed 15 February 2021).

Blee, K. and Creasap, K. (2010) "Conservative and Right-Wing Movements," *Annual Review of Sociology*, 36: 269–286.

Bob, C. (2012) *The Global Right Wing and the Clash of World Politics*, New York: Cambridge University Press.

Bolcatto, A. and Souroujon, G. (2020) "Il sorpasso de las derechas latinoamericanas" in Bolcatto A. and Souroujon, G. (eds), *Los nuevos rostros de la derecha en América*, Santa Fe: Ediciones UNL, 14–15.

Bouliane, S., Koc-Michalska, K., and Bimber, B. (2020) "Right-wing Populism, Social Media and Echo Chambers in Western Democracies," *New Media & Society*, 22 (4): 683–699.

boyd, d. (2011) "Social Networking Sites as Networked Publics" in Papacharissi, Z. (ed.), *A Networked Self: Identity, Community and Culture on Social Network Sites*, New York: Routledge, 38–59.

Brinks, D., Levitsky, S. y Murillo, M. (eds) (2020) *The Politics of Institutional Weakness in Latin America*, Cambridge: Cambridge University Press.

City TV (2020) "Plantón por la vida: en rechazo por la práctica del aborto en Colombia," *City TV*, 25 September, available at www.youtube.com/watch?v=EqVCB_v2NoA (accessed 15 February 2021).

Couldry, N. (2008) "Mediation or Mediatization? Alternative Understandings of the Emergence Space of Digital Storytelling," *New Media & Society*, 10 (3): 373–391.

Couldry, N. and Hepp, A. (2013) "Conceptualizing Mediatization: Contents, Tradition, Arguments," *Communication Theory*, 23 (3): 191–202.

Drucker, S. and Gumpert, G. (2015) "The Unsquared Square or Protest and Contemporary Publics," *First Amendment Studies*, 49 (2): 138–149.

Feinberg, M. and Willer, R. (2019) "Moral Reframing: A Technique for Effective and Persuasive Communication Across Political Divides," *Social and Personality Psychology Compass*, 13 (12): 1–12.

Gerbaudo, P. (2017) "Social Media Teams as Digital Vanguards: The Question of Leadership in the Management of Key Facebook and Twitter Accounts of Occupy Wall Street, Indignados and UK Uncut," *Information, Communication & Society*, 20 (2): 185–202.

Gidron, N. and Ziblatt, D. (2019) "Center-Right Political Parties in Advance Democracies," *Annual Review of Political Sciences* 22: 17–35.

Ginsburg, F. (1998) *Contested Lives. The Abortion Debate in an American Community*. Berkeley: University of California Press.

Graham, J., Haidt, J., Koleva. S., Motyl, M., Iyer, R., Wojcik, S., and Ditto, P. (2013) "Moral Foundations Theory: The Pragmatic Validity of Moral Pluralism," *Advances in Experimental Social Psychology*, 47: 55–130.

Groskopf, C. (2016) "European Countries Are More Polarized Than Ever, and These Numbers Prove It," *Quartz*, March 30, available at https://qz.com/645649/european-politics-is-more-polarized-than-ever-and-these-numbers-prove-it/ (accessed 15 February 2021).

Gutsche Jr., R. and Hess, K. (2018) "Contesting Communities," *Journalism Practice*, 12 (2): 136–145.

Habermas, J. (1989) *The Structural Transformation of the Public Sphere. An Inquiry into a Category of Bourgeois Society, Studies in Contemporary German Social Thought*, Cambridge, MA: MIT University Press.

Ingold, T. (2016) "Introduction: the Perception of the User-Producer" in Gunn, W. y J. Donovan, J. (eds), *Design and Anthropology*, London: Routledge.

Jamieson, K. and Cappella, J. (2008) *Echo Chamber: Rush Limbaugh and Conservative Media Establishment*, Oxford: Oxford University Press.

Karapin, R. (2007) *Protest Politics in Germany: Movements on the Left and Right since the 1960s*, University Park, PA: Penn State University Press.

Lippmann, W. (1954 [1922]) *Public Opinion*, New York: Macmillan.

Loxton, J. (2016) "Authoritarian Successor Parties and the New Right in Latin America" in Levitsky, S. Loxton, J. Van Dyck, B and Domínguez, J. (eds), *Challenges of Party-Building in Latin America*, Cambridge: Cambridge University Press.

Lowe, J. (2016) "Growing Pro-Life Movement Presents a Challenge to Defenders of Abortion Rights," *The Conversation*, 16 May, available at https://theconversation.com/growing-pro-life-movement-presents-a-challenge-to-defenders-of-abortion-rights-59478 (accessed 15 February 2021).

Marshall, P.D. (2015) "Intercommunication and Persona: Intercommunicative Public Self," *International Journal of Interdisciplinary Studies in Communication*, 10 (1): 23–31.

Marshall, P.D. (2016) "The Plurality of Publics" in Marshall, P.D., D'Cruz, G., McDonald, Sh., and Lee, K. (eds), *Contemporary Publics. Shifting Boundaries in New Media, Technology and Culture*, London: Palgrave McMillan UK.

McIvor, M. (2019) "Human Rights and Broken Cisterns: Counterpublic Christianity and Rights-Based Discourse in Contemporary England," *Ethnos*, 84 (2): 323–343.

Myerhoff, B. (1987) "Life, Not Death in Venice: Its Second Life" in Goldberg, H. (ed.), *Judaism Viewing from Within and from Without*, Albany: State University of New York Press.

Peterson, M. (2003) *Anthropology and Mass Media. Media and Myth in the New Millenium*. New York: Berghahn.

Pink, S., Horst, H., Hjorth, L., Lewis, T., and Tacchi, J. (2016) *Digital Ethnography. Principles and Practice*. Los Angeles, CA: Sage.

Postill, J. (2011) *Localising the Internet: An Anthropological Account*, New York: Berghahn Books.

Rabikowska. M. (2013) *The Everyday of Memory. Between Communism and Postcommunism*, Berna: Peter Lang.

Roberts, J. (2014) *Digital Publics: Cultural Political Economy, Financialization and Creative Organizational Politics*, New York: Routledge.

Schroeder, R. (2018) *Social Theory after Internet: Media, Technology and Globalization*, London: UCL Press.

Schieffelin, E. (1985) "Performance and The Cultural Construction of Reality," *American Ethnologist*, 12: 707–724.

Singer, M. (1972) *When a Great Tradition Modernizes: An Anthropological Approach to Modern Civilization*, New York: Praeger Publishers.

Turner, V. (1974) *Dramas, Fields, and Metaphors: Symbolic Action in Human Society*, Ithaca, NY: Cornell University Press.

Turner, V. (1986) *The Anthropology of Performances*, New York: PAJ Publications.

Van Dijck, J. (2013) *Culture of Connectivity: A Social History of Social* Media, Oxford: Oxford University Press.

Westermeyer, W. (2019) *Back to America: Identity, Political Culture and the Tea Party Movement*, Lincoln, OR: University of Nebraska Press.

E

Surveillance

34
ALGORITHMIC VIOLENCE IN EVERYDAY LIFE AND THE ROLE OF MEDIA ANTHROPOLOGY

Veronica Barassi

Introduction

On a warm evening in 2018, I sat down in a crowded restaurant in the heart of West Los Angeles. I had arranged to meet Cara, one of the parents involved in my project on the datafication of children. That evening we started talking about her experience of surveillance in everyday life, from her use of social media to home technologies like Amazon Echo, and Cara rather than focusing on the issue of surveillance, immediately shifted the discussion to tell me how angry and irritated she felt about the fact that she was being sent targeted ads because she was being profiled as a single 50+ woman. She told me that she felt stereotyped and belittled by those practices of digital profiling. Although it was true that she was single and in her fifties, she said that this aspect did not define her because 'There is so much more to me as a person.'

I met Cara for the first time in 2016, when I launched the Child | Data | Citizen project. It was just one year after I had my first daughter, and I suddenly realized that most of the families that I met in my daily life shared multiple, almost unimaginable data traces of children. I launched the project because I was curious to understand how families negotiated and interacted with the systematic, relentless, and worrying practices of data tracking of their children. At that time, I was living in London and found myself immersed in the ethnographic reality of datafied families. But shortly after, my husband was relocated for work to Los Angeles. Hence I started studying the datafication of family life in both cities dealing with two homes, two health and education systems, and of course two very different data environments.

For three years (2016–2019) I documented how it felt to live in a world where not only me, my family, and children were being datafied. I became a participant observer in my own intercontinental life and started writing fieldnotes about how it felt to have to sign Terms and Conditions, even if I knew that my consent was somehow coerced and certainly not informed. I started to observe what other parents were doing in parks, school meetings, children's parties, and playdates. This auto-ethnographic research enabled me to start tackling the lived experience of the datafication of children from a parent's perspective. In both cities I worked with families with children between 0 and 13 years of age, whose personal information online – in both countries – is ruled by the Children's Online Privacy Protection Act (1998). I carried out 50 semi-structured interviews and eight months of digital ethnography of eight families' 'sharenting' practices, which involved a weekly analysis of the pictures, news, and updates they posted on their social media profiles (most parents posted regularly on Facebook and Instagram, and some on YouTube) and observed how people interacted with the information posted.

Over the last several years the field of media anthropology – which I define as the field built by those scholars and research communities who rely on anthropological knowledge and ethnographic practice in anthropology to study media and technological processes – has been preoccupied with the rapid rise of algorithmic logics and data technologies in everyday life. Some have focused on the rise of big data as a new form of knowledge and meaning construction (Boellstorff, 2013; Boellstorff and Maurer, 2015), others have analysed the powerful discourses associated with algorithmic logics in culture (Dourish, 2016; Seaver, 2017) or the multiple ways in which people were negotiating with data technologies in everyday life and their data narratives (Pink, Lanzeni, and Horst, 2018; Dourish and Cruz, 2018). These works are extremely insightful because they draw on classical anthropological theory to shed light on the cultural complexities that have defined the techno-historical transformation of our times.

In this chapter I want to add to these debates by focusing more specifically on algorithmic profiling and its impacts on parents. I will draw on some of the ethnographic data that I gathered during the Child | Data | Citizen project to offer a new intervention for this chapter. It will demonstrate that we can no longer talk about 'tech-surveillance' in everyday family life without dealing with the question about 'algorithmic profiling', and explore how algorithmic profiling in everyday life makes people feel belittled and objectified, and is often experienced as a form of violence. I also want to demonstrate that the experience and understanding of algorithmic profiling varies immensely if the participant comes from a privileged position or one of inequality, this is because algorithmic profiling impacts groups differently.

Over the last decades we have seen many scholars – outside of the field of media and digital anthropology – who have explored and analysed the relationship between surveillance, algorithmic profiling, and social inequality (Barocas and Selbts, 2016; Madden et al., 2017; Eubanks, 2018). In the last few years we have also seen scholars referring to concepts such as data violence (Hoffmann, 2018, 2020) or algorithmic violence (Onuhoa, 2018; Safransky, 2020; Bellanova et al., 2021) to explain how algorithms and data feed into specific forms of violence. Although insightful, these works seem to ignore anthropological theory and its key understanding that bureaucratic processes play a role in yielding symbolic and structural violence. In this chapter I would like to draw on this theory of bureaucracy and symbolic violence (Appadurai, 1993; Herzfeld, 1993; Gupta, 2012; Graeber, 2015) to shed light on the relationship between algorithmic profiling and bureaucratic processes and to reflect on the impact of algorithmic violence in everyday life.

Tech-Surveillance and the Question about Profiling

One evening in 2018, I drove to Mabel's house. Mabel worked as a manager in the entertainment industry. She was a single mom and lived in a beautiful house in Pasadena, Los Angeles with her son – who at the time of the interview was six years old – two dogs and a cat. As she opened her front door, I noticed the camera right above my head. She picked up her phone, laughed, and told me: 'Look the app just informed me you are here.' Mabel's security camera was connected to her phone and would inform her if there was movement at the front door or at the back door of her house. When we sat down in her beautiful living room overlooking the garden, I asked her if she was ok with me recording her. Influenced by years of ethical research practice, I told her that if – at any point in the interview – she wanted me to turn off my device she just needed to let me know. During the interview, I asked Mabel to talk about all the ways in which she thought that her son's data and her own data were being surveilled. She started talking about all the data that was being tracked on her social media accounts, her security system, her fitness apps, and of course Alexa, the voice-operated virtual assistant of Amazon that is included in the home hub Amazon Echo. As she mentioned the 'wake word' Alexa, the Amazon Echo turned on and started recording our interview. I immediately thought how paradoxical that simple fact was for ethnographers who are committed to preserving the anonymity of their participants in the interviews. Also Mabel noticed, she laughed and added:

M: You see we have Alexa, we are surveilled all the time and she records everything. I read that she also records without the wake word.
V: Does that bother you?
M: No I am not concerned, my life is very boring, but also I am not stupid enough to buy into the promise of it. So for instance if Alexa surveilles me to decide that I like blue, I won't go out and buy blue items.

When Mabel said that she was not stupid enough to buy into the 'promise of it', she was referring to algorithmic profiling. That is the business logic behind the technologies – that inhabit the homes of many families in the UK and US – for which the analysis of users' data traces could be used to predict their desires and future behaviors and sell them new products.

During the Child | Data | Citizen project, which took place as mentioned in the introduction between 2016 and 2019 in London and Los Angeles, I walked into many different living rooms, which varied in style, wealth, and location. Some were in wealthy neighborhoods, others were in very poor ones. Those living rooms reflected what anthropologist Arturo Escobar (2018) calls the 'pluriverse', which is defined as 'a place where many worlds fit'. I too observed a pluriverse of experiences in London and Los Angeles. In my multi-sited ethnography, I worked with parents who came from a variety of cultural, ethnic, and national backgrounds. The parents were extraordinarily diverse not only in terms of ethnicity (e.g. Asian, Latinos, Indian, Black, Indigenous, Multiracial, White), but also in terms of cultural and national heritage (e.g. Afghani, Mexican, Brazilian, Indian, German, Italian, Hungarian, Icelandic, Zimbabwean, and Scottish, among others). I also made a genuine attempt to seek parents from different classes, by interviewing parents working in low-income jobs (such as nannies, cleaners, buskers or in administration) as well as parents working in high-income jobs (such as lawyers, film-producers, journalists, and marketing, for example). I also came across a plurality of family situations that challenged the heteronormativity or the structure of the 'nuclear family', so I interviewed gay parents, divorced parents who had to juggle with a complex living arrangement, and single mothers who chose to adopt a child. Some of the living rooms I only visited once, but others became familiar spaces in the unfolding of my project, and I would return to them over and over again.

Despite the extraordinary variety of settings, locations, and backgrounds, many of the parents that I worked with shared Mabel's experience and described a wide range of surveilling technologies in their homes: from social media to apps and virtual assistants. They also talked about how their children were being surveilled and tracked not only at home, but by a multiplicity of other technologies and data collection practices that they encountered in their everyday life such as their online school platforms or the data gathered through their doctor's office. Some parents, unlike Mabel, were really concerned and tried to limit the number of technologies they used in their homes, as they did not want to expose themselves and their children to daily surveillance.

In 2017 for instance I found myself sipping coffee in a small and cosy living room in South London with Alina, the mother of two children aged one and four, and she described the change in everyday life, as well as the feeling of a lack of alternatives. Alina had moved to London from Germany five years before our interview. She had been pregnant or a full-time mom since she had arrived in the UK and lived in a low-income neighborhood in South-East London. Alina was particularly worried about the issue of surveillance; she had been brought up in East Germany. Even though she was very young in 1989, she knew of the surveillance tactics of the former German Democratic Republic (DDR). As we sipped our coffee, she started to tell me how uncomfortable she felt with the increased surveillance in everyday life:

> It feels that you have to give up a lot of information to actually get a service; you don't really have an alternative. Think about the car insurance you cannot really not buy. The lack of alternative is concerning, but also the lack of security. It's everywhere, they are starting with health care, they are starting with the chips in things, which it could be a good thing but they can be misused. There are cameras everywhere; you can't really escape this transformation.

During my research I met different parents who like Alina when talking about surveillance would often relate a lack of alternative and a feeling of powerlessness. Like Mabel had done, Alina related her worry about the ways in which 'data was being used to make assumptions and build profiles about her or her children' and added:

> It's scary. It's a new fear of our lives. In the 1980s during the Cold War you would always be worried about an atomic bomb, now you have to be worried about these things together with other things. It's too much. You should really stop thinking about it.

Although Mabel and Alina saw the issue of surveillance in different ways and with different degrees of worry, both of them could not discuss the issue without thinking about how data traces were being used to profile them and their children.

A few months after interviewing Alina, I interviewed Dan. His living room was in Central London, in a large modern flat conversion of an old school. The modernist and minimalist furniture contrasted with the children's toys, books, and items of clothing that were scattered around the room on chairs, sideboards, and an old trunk. Dan was a stay-at-home dad. He used to work in IT for a digital marketing company, but when he was made redundant, he decided to support his wife's career and take care of the house and kids. During the interview Dan told me – like Mabel and Alina had done – that he was very well aware of the fact that his family was being surveilled through a variety of technologies. He also told me that he worried that data that was being collected from his children today would be used by artificial intelligence (AI) systems in the future to determine key aspects of their lives including whether they would get access to a job, a rental accommodation, or a university degree, and then added:

> I'd like to think that we can change how it is done, but the world is a big marketing and profiling machine. I'd like to think that I can protect my children from that, but I don't think I can do it.

My research thus led me to the conclusion that it was impossible for me to explore the issue of tech-surveillance in family life without shedding light on the ways in which families were being affected and negotiated with algorithmic profiling. In particular, this chapter moves beyond prior scholarly emphases on 'big data' to understand the violence that occurs in everyday lived experiences. It concludes by calling for deeper exploration of the connection between anthropological theory on bureaucracy and the structural violence of algorithmic profiling.

'There is so much more to me as a person': Everyday Negotiations with Algorithmic Profiling, Human Reductionism, and Inequality

The evening that I interviewed Cara and she told how she was being profiled as '50+ and single', she said that this annoyed her because 'there was so much more to her as a person'. Then she added she felt that the data trackers on the internet were like 'gossipers' and then added:

> When others talk about you, when people seem to infer something about you on the basis of a certain information or rumor, then that is wrong, it feels like gossiping. When I get targeted for a search I have done on Google it feels exactly like that; like someone has been gossiping about me.

If Cara talked about data trackers as gossipers, Amy, another friend I met through the project, talked about the meanness of algorithmic profiling and the fact that data companies seemed to judge and define people on the basis of their weaknesses. She told me, for instance, that she was trying to lose weight and found it demeaning and unforgiving that every time she went on Facebook she was offered a new diet or plus-size clothing. She explained that she knew she was overweight and was trying to lose weight, but the fact that online data trackers kept reminding her of this hurt her feelings. She told me, as Cara had done, 'that there is more to her as a person' than her weight.

The fact that Cara and Amy used the same sentence ('there is more to me as a person') reveals a fundamental aspect of the experience of algorithmic profiling: the problem of human reductionism.

Media anthropologists have long been arguing that one of the problems behind the rapid rise in use of big data and algorithms to profile individuals is the belief that 'data is raw' and objective and that the large amounts of personal data ensure a good understanding of people's practices, beliefs, and desires. In fact, this is very far from being true. There is no such thing as raw data because data collection itself requires processing of narration and framing (Gitelman, 2013; Boellstorff and Maurer, 2015; Dourish and Cruz, 2018). Boellstorff (2013) has demonstrated that, in anthropology, the debates about data not being raw have been influenced by Levi-Strauss' distinction between raw, cooked, and rotted data (Levi-Strauss in Boellstorff, 2013: para 52) and Geertz's reference to the *ethnographic algorithm* to discuss the work of interpretation that comes from processes of data collection (Geertz in Boellstorff, 2013: para 56). In addition to the fact that data is neither raw nor objective, most of the data collected from people today is systematically taken out of context and thus the gathering of large amounts of personal data is not necessarily an indicator of quality especially when we are trying to understand humans (Boellstorff, 2013). Although not a media-anthropologist, Costanza-Chock (2018) has discussed this problem at length and has argued that human identity and experience are violated and belittled by binary data systems and computer reductionism as they do not take into account the variety and complexity of human existence.

Our technologies are not designed to take into account human variety and complexity. A key example, which is close to the heart at the time of writing, can be found in COVID-19 contact-tracing apps. In her fascinating work, Milan (2020) has shown that most of these apps are based on a 'standard' experimental subject that hardly allows for exploring the role of variables such as gender, ethnicity, race or low income. Both Costanza-Chock (2018) and Milan (2020) show how the roots of this reductionism stem from design practice itself. It is for this reason that the anthropologist Escobar (2018) has advanced a new vision for design theory, one that takes into account the complex and intersectional pluriverse we live in.

It is by understanding the human reductionism implicit to processes of algorithmic profiling that we can shed light on why – in everyday life – these processes are perceived as belittling, with people like Cara and Amy arguing that 'there is so much more to them as a person'. One aspect that surprised me, however, during my research was to notice that there were multiple ways in which people were negotiating and resisting algorithmic reductionism. Cara told me, for instance, that she would 'play the algorithm' and that many times she would consciously choose not to like someone's post on Facebook, even if she liked it, because she realized that if she did not like things, her news feed became much more 'democratic' and open to chance rather than likes. She also told me that she often tried to create a 'happy day on Facebook' for herself. She had different tricks to do this: either she would start liking the photos of animals posted by her friends, and she would get bombarded with cute animal feeds on Facebook, or if she was having a bad day, she would do a web search for a '2-bedroom house in Fiji' over and over again 'just to be targeted with beautiful advertising of amazing places'.

What emerged clearly from my research was that, as I mentioned also elsewhere (Barassi, 2020), there was a fundamental difference in the ways in which the families that were in a position of inequality or a position of privilege thought about algorithmic profiling and surveillance. Mabel for instance talked about algorithmic profiling only with reference to targeted ads, whilst Mariana, a Mexican immigrant who worked as a cleaner and lived in Los Angeles with her four children, told me during the interview that:

> You have to be aware of the technologies, because, you are also checked by the government, when you pass the border, they check it and they can push you back. We are being checked by everyone, insurances, doctors, police, everyone knows what we do as a family, where we go, what we eat.

Mariana was particularly worried about how immigration enforcers used that information to make entry decisions and related the story of her sister who had been refused a visa, because the border control had seen from her profile that she had too many family members in the US and were doubting the fact that she was just visiting.

Lina who migrated from Latin America to the UK over ten years ago shared the same worry. She lived in a small apartment at the top floor of a housing estate in one of the most deprived areas of South London. She shared the apartment with her two daughters, an eight-year-old and a teenager, and her husband. Both she and her husband were highly educated and aware of the transformations that were taking place when it came to data surveillance. In the interview, Lina told me:

> When I think about all this surveillance I feel as if I were an object, like I was being constantly objectified. We do not have a choice, you don't have privacy, you don't have anything. I feel as if I am being belittled, minimized, and invaded. I feel little

– how else can I explain it? I feel that it is too big for me, I can't fight it. I can't defend myself. I am completely powerless. I feel as if I am being used, because they could do whatever they want with your data and turn it against you.

These findings are not new or surprising. In fact, over the last five years different researchers, outside the field of media anthropology, have shown that marginal communities are more exposed to the injustices of tech-surveillance and algorithmic profiling (O'Neil, 2016 Barocas and Selbst, 2016; Eubanks, 2018). What is becoming clear is that data technologies and automated systems are not equal or fair, and the experience of data harms depends on one's position in society. This emerges clearly in the work of the legal scholar Gilman (2012) who shows that the poor are more exposed to privacy intrusions by government surveillance and other agents, and that current privacy law does not address the disparity of experience. Marginal communities are more exposed to privacy intrusion and data harms, because in their everyday life they are subjected to systemic surveillance and discrimination. In addition to this, as Madden et al. (2017) have rightly argued, poor and marginal communities are exposed to 'networked privacy harms', because they are held liable for the actions of those in their networks and neighborhoods.

Yet in the data something more emerged: algorithmic profiling, because of its reductionism and intrusiveness, was often perceived as a form of *violence* especially by people like Lina and Mariana who came from a disadvantaged position in life. Over the last few years some scholars, outside of anthropology, have focused on the notion of violence when reflecting on the impact of data technologies and algorithmic logics. Hoffmann (2018) argues that when we think about the inequality of algorithmic profiling and automated systems we need to talk about 'data violence' to understand the many ways in which these systems reinforce existing forms of structural violence against marginal communities and the poor. In contrast to Hoffmann (2018, 2020), during my research I often referred in my notes to the analytical and methodological idea of *algorithmic violence* instead of data violence to describe why people like Lina and Mariana felt violated and harmed by algorithmic profiling. I understood algorithmic violence, defined by Onuoha (2018), as the violence that an algorithm or automated system inflicts on people which – like other forms of violence – encompasses everything from micro-occurrences to life-threatening realities. It can materialize itself in political economic structures, as Safransky (2020) shows with research on smart cities or as Bellanova et al. (2021) portray in numerous examples such as drone attacks planned by tracking mobile phones, anti-riot police using face recognition, AI systems used for warfare and international politics, immigration agents using Twitter, and algorithmic profiling used for security intervention. Although in the understanding of algorithmic violence I believe it is pivotal to focus on structures of power, I also believe that it is essential to explore how algorithmic violence has become, for people like Lina and Mariana, but also for Mabel and Amy, an everyday sensory reality. In my theoretical and analytical use of the term algorithmic violence, therefore, I am more concerned with the way in which this violence was experienced and negotiated on a daily basis.

There is something more that sets my approach away from current positions on algorithmic violence. In fact, I was surprised to notice that – although Onuhoa (2018) briefly mentions the work of Graeber on bureaucracy – all the articles I read do not mention anthropological theory when they suggest that it is important to refer to the social sciences in understanding the violence of our algorithmic cultures. The lack of engagement with anthropological theory implied that they overlooked the fact that algorithmic logics are tightly linked with bureaucratic processes and hence with symbolic and structural violence as understood in anthropology. As we shall see below, the anthropological literature on bureaucracy and symbolic violence

(Appadurai, 1993; Herzfeld, 1993; Gupta, 2012; Graeber, 2015) is pivotal if we really want to understand the violence of data and algorithmic logics in everyday family life.

Algorithmic Violence, Bureaucracy, and the Role of Anthropology

We cannot understand the rise of big data and the cultural logics of algorithms without considering a key economic transformation that happened over the last few decades, which has transformed our cultures and institutions globally. In her work, Zuboff (2015, 2019), for instance, talks about the rise of a new economy of *surveillance capitalism*. She argues that it was Google that played a fundamental role in the emergence of surveillance capitalism, when in 2002 the company discovered behavioral surplus. The company, according to Zuboff (2019), played a very similar role to those that the Ford Motor and General Motors companies played in the establishment of industrial capitalism. This is because, according to Zuboff (2019), Google has not only introduced a new economic logic which revolved around data extraction, accumulation, and analysis, but the discovery of behavioral surplus has affected human practices and behaviors, restructured institutions, and transformed everyday life.

In anthropology the change has been theorized by David Graeber (2015). David Graeber never discussed the 'turn to data' as the rise of a new economic model, or as the emergence of the new age of surveillance capitalism like Zuboff does. His analytical eye did not focus on disruption and novelty, rather on the dialectical relationship between continuity and change. In his collection of essays, *The Utopia of Rules: On Technology, Stupidity and the Secret Joy of Bureaucracy* (2015), he shows that what has paved the way for today's environment is a structural transformation of corporate bureaucracy away from the workers, and towards shareholders and eventually towards the financial structure as a whole. This led to a double movement of a sort. On the one hand, corporate management became more financialized; on the other hand, the financial sector became more corporatized, and as a result the investor and executive class became indistinguishable, and hence numbers, measures, and bureaucratization became associated with value production.

One of the most fascinating aspects of David Graeber's theory of transformation in corporate bureaucracy is that he shows how this led to a broader cultural transformation whereby bureaucratic techniques (e.g. performance reviews, focus groups, and time allocation surveys) that were developed in the financial and corporate sector invaded different dimensions of society – education, science, government – and eventually pervaded every aspect of everyday life (Graeber, 2015: 19–21).

Graeber believed that we had seen the establishment of a 'culture of evaluation'. He argues that much of what bureaucrats do is to 'evaluate things' as 'they are continually assessing, auditing, measuring, weighting the relative merits of different plans, proposals, applications etc.' and of course constantly evaluating human beings (Graeber, 2015: 41). This culture of evaluation, he believes, is not only the product of financialization but the continuation of it since 'what is the world of securitized derivatives, collateralized debt obligations, and other such exotic financial instruments but the apotheosis of the principle that value is ultimately a product of paperwork' (Graeber, 2015: 42).

These processes of evaluation and documentation function as modern rituals. Anthropologists have long studied human rituals and focused precisely on those symbolic acts or phrases that defined social reality, for example a phrase such as 'I pronounce you husband and wife'. According to Graeber (2015: 49–50), in our societies, documents and the bureaucratic process function as rituals because they make things socially true. For example, we are not citizens of a nation if we don't have a passport, we are not experts on a subject without a diploma, among many other examples.

Around the 2000s, this bureaucratic process that is so fundamental to our societies was quickly digitized and given over to computers. In addition, at the turn of the 2000s something else happened. On the one hand, thanks to the advent of new technologies like social media or apps, the amount of personal information that could be collected, correlated, and used to profile people increased dramatically. For example, on a single day in 2019, according to one study, 350 million photos were posted on Facebook and 500 million tweets sent (Crawford, 2021: 106). On the other hand, developments in big data and artificial intelligence have led to an expansion of profiling technologies used by governments to all dimensions of everyday life (Elmer, 2004; Kitchin, 2014).

In the last decade, profiling technologies such as predictive analytics have started to be used to gather as much data about an individual as possible from different sources (e.g., family history, shopping habits, social media comments) and aggregate this data to make decisions about individuals' lives. These technologies are used everywhere. Banks use them to decide on loans, insurance companies use them to decide on premiums, and recruiters and employers use them to decide whether or not a person is a good fit for a job. Even the police and courts use them, to determine if an individual is a potential criminal or if there is a risk that an offender will repeat a crime.

Algorithmic profiling, like any form of bureaucracy, is defined by forms of symbolic violence, because it pigeon-holes, stereotypes, and detaches people from their sense of humanity. As Hertzfeld (1993) would argue, bureaucracy is based on the 'social production of indifference' by which bureaucrats insulate themselves from social suffering. Yet there is something more at stake. Bureaucratic systems emphasize numbers and rationality over individual lives and the unpredictability of human experience. They have often been used as tools of social oppression and control. Appadurai (1993), for example, demonstrated that in the British colonial imagination the numbers and classifications of population censuses were used as a form of control and imposition of a colonial and racist ideology.

In his work on bureaucracy, Graeber (2015) was particularly concerned with the relation between bureaucracy and violence. In the *Utopia of Rules* he refers to the feminist anthropological literature and a rereading of the concept of structural violence, and argues that the bureaucratization of everyday life is always built not only on symbolic violence, but also on some 'threat' of physical violence. The threat of physical violence he believes can be seen everywhere, but we have become so used to it that we actually do not see it. It is embodied in the many security guards, cameras, technologies, and enforcers entering different areas of social lives from schools to parks and public spaces, who are there to remind us that we have to stick to the rules or have the right papers. The violence of bureaucratization cannot only be perceived as the threat of physical violence but also as 'a near-total inequality of power between the bureaucratic structure and individuals' (Graeber, 2015: 59–60).

According to Graeber (2015), historically the everyday experience of bureaucratic violence is different for the poor or marginal communities, because they have constantly been exposed to continued surveillance, monitoring, auditing, and to the lack of interpretative work of the bureaucratic machine. As Gupta (2012) shows, the violence of the bureaucratic machine is not arbitrary in the sense that it does not affect everyone in the same way. This is because through classifications, rules, and systems the bureaucratic machine reinforces the structural inequality of a given society. Gupta's ethnographic work focused on India and the postcolonial state and one example that he uses is the fact that any application submitted by a woman in a bureaucratic office needs to indicate the name of the father or husband, and this simple fact not only reinforces and institutionalizes the patriarchal order but also normalizes heterosexual relations (2012: 26).

As media anthropologists, when we think about the rise of algorithmic violence we cannot fail to engage with the anthropology of bureaucracy because it clearly shows us that structural violence and human suffering are a fundamental aspect of our data-driven societies.

Conclusion

Over the last several years the field of media anthropology has explored the impact of algorithmic logics and data technologies in everyday life. Whilst much needed attention has been placed on the powerful discourses associated with algorithmic logics and data in society (Dourish, 2016; Seaver, 2017; Boellstorff, 2013; Boellstorff and Maurer, 2015), media anthropological research on how data technologies, flows, and narratives are experienced and negotiated in everyday lives is still limited (Pink, Lanzeni, and Horst, 2018). In this chapter I decided to focus on these processes of negotiation to demonstrate that we can no longer talk about 'tech-surveillance' in everyday family life without dealing with the question about 'algorithmic profiling', and explore how algorithmic profiling in everyday life makes people feel belittled and objectified, and is often experienced as a form of violence. In the last few years we have also seen scholars referring to concepts such as data violence (Hoffmann, 2018, 2020) or algorithmic violence (Bellanova et al., 2021) to explain how algorithms and data feed into specific forms of violence. Although insightful, as this chapter has shown, these approaches fail to engage with anthropological theory and hence with the understanding that there is a clear interconnection between algorithmic profiling, bureaucratic processes, and symbolic and structural violence. The aim of this chapter was to shed light on this relationship and how this is experienced in everyday life.

Yet there is much more work to do. At present the research on algorithmic violence, including mine, is based on US and western-centric understandings of data inequality. The anthropology of bureaucracy and structural violence teaches us that, although bureaucratic processes may be similar in different cultural contexts, they sustain and amplify culturally specific inequalities and injustices. Media anthropologists have much work to do when it comes to understanding algorithmic violence in everyday life. They can shed light on the multiple and complex ways in which algorithmic logics intersect with local understandings of violence and on context-specific processes of meaning construction and negotiations.

References

Appadurai, A. (1993) 'Number in the Colonial Imagination.' In Orientalism and the Postcolonial Predicament: Perspectives on South Asia (pp. 314–339). Philadelphia: University of Pennsylvania Press.

Barassi, V. (2020) *Child Data Citizen: How Tech Companies Are Profiling Us from Before Birth*. Cambridge, MA: MIT Press.

Barocas, S. and Selbst, A. D. (2016) *Big Data's Disparate Impact* (SSRN Scholarly Paper ID 2477899). Social Science Research Network.

Bellanova, R., Irion, K., Lindskov Jacobsen, K., Ragazzi, F., Saugmann, R., and Suchman, L. (2021) 'Toward a Critique of Algorithmic Violence.' International Political Sociology, 15(1), 121–150. https://doi.org/10.1093/ips/olab003.

Boellstorff, T. (2013) 'Making Big Data, in Theory.' *First Monday* 18(10). http://firstmonday.org/ojs/index.php/fm/article/view/4869.

Boellstorff, T. and Maurer, B. (Eds.) (2015) *Data: Now Bigger and Better!* Chicago, IL: Prickly Paradigm Press.

Costanza-Chock, S. (2018) 'Design Justice, A.I., and Escape from the Matrix of Domination.' *Journal of Design and Science, MIT*. https://jods.mitpress.mit.edu/pub/costanza-chock/release/4.

Crawford, K. (2021) *Atlas of AI: Power, Politics, and the Planetary Costs of Artificial Intelligence*. New Haven: Yale University Press.
Dourish, P. (2016) 'Algorithms and Their Others: Algorithmic Culture in Context.' *Big Data & Society*, 3(2): 1–11. https://doi.org/10.1177/2053951716665128.
Dourish, P. and Gómez Cruz, E. (2018) 'Datafication and Data Fiction: Narrating Data and Narrating with Data.' *Big Data & Society*, 5(2): 1–10. https://doi.org/10.1177/2053951718784083.
Elmer, G. (2004) *Profiling Machines: Mapping the Personal Information Economy*. Cambridge, MA: MIT Press.
Escobar, A. (2018) *Designs for the Pluriverse: Radical Interdependence, Autonomy, and the Making of Worlds*. Durham: Duke University Press.
Eubanks, V. (2018) *Automating Inequality: How High-Tech Tools Profile, Police, and Punish the Poor*. New York: St. Martin's Press.
Gilman, M. E. (2012) *The Class Differential in Privacy Law* (SSRN Scholarly Paper ID 2182773). Social Science Research Network.
Gitelman, L. (2013) *'Raw Data' Is an Oxymoron*. Cambridge, MA: MIT Press.
Graeber, D. (2015) *The Utopia of Rules: On Technology, Stupidity, and the Secret Joys of Bureaucracy*. Brooklyn: Melville House.
Gupta, A. (2012) *Red Tape: Bureaucracy, Structural Violence, and Poverty in India*. Durham: Duke University Press.
Herzfeld, M. (1993) *The Social Production of Indifference*. Chicago: University of Chicago Press.
Hoffmann, A. (2018) 'Data Violence and How Bad Engineering Choices Can Damage Society.' *Medium*. https://medium.com/s/story/data-violence-and-how-bad-engineering-choices-can-damage-society-39e44150e1d4.
Hoffmann, A. L. (2020) 'Terms of Inclusion: Data, Discourse, Violence.' *New Media & Society*, 23(12): 3539–3556. https://doi.org/10.1177/1461444820958725.
Kitchin, R. (2014) *The Data Revolution: Big Data, Open Data, Data Infrastructures and Their Consequences*. 1st edition. Los Angeles, CA: Sage.
Madden, M., Gilman, M., Levy, K. and Marwick, A. (2017) 'Privacy, Poverty, and Big Data: A Matrix of Vulnerabilities for Poor Americans.' *Washington University Law Review*, 95(1): 53–125.
Milan, S. (2020) 'Techno-solutionism and the Standard Human in the Making of the COVID-19 Pandemic.' *Big Data & Society*, 7(2): 1-7. https://doi.org/10.1177/2053951720966781.
O'Neil, C. (2016) *Weapons of Math Destruction: How Big Data Increases Inequality and Threatens Democracy*. New Bremen, OH: Crown Archetype.
Onuhoa, M. (2018) *Notes on Algorithmic Violence*. https://github.com/MimiOnuoha/On-Algorithmic-Violence.
Pink, S., Lanzeni, D. and Horst, H. (2018) 'Data Anxieties: Finding Trust in Everyday Digital Mess.' *Big Data & Society*, 5(1): 1–14. https://doi.org/10.1177/2053951718756685.
Safransky, S. (2020) 'Geographies of Algorithmic Violence: Redlining the Smart City.' *International Journal of Urban and Regional Research*, 44(2): 200–218.
Seaver, N. (2017) 'Algorithms as Culture: Some Tactics for the Ethnography of Algorithmic Systems.' *Big Data & Society*, 4(2): 1–12. https://doi.org/10.1177/2053951717738104.
Zuboff, S. (2015) 'Big Other: Surveillance Capitalism and the Prospects of an Information Civilization.' *Journal of Information Technology*, 30 (1): 75–89.
Zuboff, S. (2019) *The Age of Surveillance Capitalism: The Fight for a Human Future at the New Frontier of Power* (1st edition). New York: Public Affairs.

35

QUEER AND MUSLIM?

Social Surveillance and Islamic Sexual Ethics on Twitter

Benjamin Ale-Ebrahim

Let there be among you a community (*ummah*) calling to the good, enjoining right (*ya'murūna bi-l-ma'rūf*) and forbidding wrong (*yanhawna 'ani-l-munkar*). It is they who shall prosper.

Qur'an 3:104

Enjoining the right and forbidding the wrong (*al-amr bi-l-ma'rūf wa-n-nahy 'ani-l-munkar*) is a foundational concept in Islamic social ethics, rooted in Qur'anic injunctions to promote proper behavior and denounce sinful acts within the universal community of Muslims (*ummat al-islām*). Throughout the past 15 centuries of Islamic history, Muslim exegetes (*mufassirūn*) and philosophers have debated the specific implications of a Muslim's duty to be accountable for the actions of their fellow Muslims (Cook, 2001). Regardless of their interpretive stance, as a collective duty (*farḍ al-kifāyah*) or an individual obligation (*farḍ al-'ayn*), many prominent Muslim thinkers agree that enjoining the right and forbidding the wrong empowers Muslims to monitor the actions of other Muslims, encouraging them to speak out against any unethical behavior they observe. This is, of course, easier said than done. What happens when, as is often the case, Muslims cannot agree on what is ethically right (*ma'rūf*) or wrong (*munkar*)? How do Muslims use social media platforms to carry out this ethic of interpersonal surveillance, circulating information about the behavior of other Muslims to expose and critique their moral failings?

In this chapter, I argue that *al-amr bi-l-ma'rūf* can be understood as a form of social surveillance (Marwick, 2012) that has a long history within Muslim communities. I discuss the example of recent debates on Twitter regarding the ethical standing of lesbian, gay, bisexual, transgender, and queer (LGBTQ) Muslims as legitimate members of the universal Muslim community (*ummat al-islām*). As an ethnographer of social media and LGBTQ Muslim communities, I have been actively following debates about gender and sexuality on Muslim Twitter since 2018. Whereas in my previous research I have concentrated primarily on LGBTQ communities based in Morocco and their experiences navigating life on social media, in this chapter, I study LGBTQ Muslims living in the U.S. and U.K. In this way, I contribute to a growing body of research on the experiences of contemporary Muslim minorities by analyzing how English-speaking Muslim Twitter users engage each other on the question of LGBTQ belonging through acts of technologically mediated social surveillance.

I focus here on a series of roughly 20 viral tweets published between November 2020 and February 2021, each of which addresses the moral standing of LGBTQ Muslims from within an Islamic ethical framework. In these posts, queer Muslim Twitter users defend themselves against accusations from fellow Muslims claiming that they are sinful apostates (*kuffār*) who, by sole virtue of their sexual orientation or gender identity, exist outside the boundaries of Islamic morality. By sharing humorous Twitter posts and memes, queer Muslims expose the hypocrisy of their homophobic critics to argue that their sexuality and gender identity have little to do with their moral standing as Muslims. Based on the information shared on their public Twitter profiles, the authors of these tweets all live in Anglophone countries with large Muslim populations, especially the United States and the United Kingdom. They represent themselves as LGBTQ young adults who are familiar with Islamic source materials and norms of ethical behavior, either because they were raised in a Muslim family or currently practice Islam. Retweets, likes, and comments come from accounts around the world, though most are from other English-speaking Twitter users who also represent themselves as practicing Muslims. All names referenced in this chapter are pseudonyms unless otherwise specified. This is to protect the confidentiality and safety of individuals involved in this research.

I analyze this series of interactions as an example of how contemporary Muslims are using popular social media platforms like Twitter to enjoin the right and forbid the wrong (*al-amr bi-l-maʿrūf*), calling each other to account for their status as moral Muslim subjects through reciprocal social surveillance. In these digital exchanges, Muslim Twitter users enact contrasting visions of appropriate Islamic ethical behavior and promote divergent understandings of the qualities that determine a Muslim's moral standing within the *ummah*. I conclude by considering how this ethnographic example can advance contemporary debates on surveillance and privacy in media anthropology.

Enjoining the Right and Forbidding the Wrong as Social Surveillance

One of the central goals of this chapter is to consider how the Islamic concept of enjoining the right and forbidding the wrong (*al-amr bi-l-maʿrūf*) can complicate ongoing debates in surveillance studies and media anthropology. Within the past 20 years, in the aftermath of 9/11 and the expansion of the Global War on Terror, social scientists have developed an extensive vocabulary to analyze the complex ways in which new technologically mediated regimes of surveillance are reshaping privacy, individual freedom, and the exercise of power. Muslims are often the explicit target of contemporary regimes of surveillance, from countering violent extremism (CVE) programs in the United Kingdom (Qurashi, 2018; Brown, 2019) to the Uyghur Muslim genocide in China (Byler, 2019; Leibold, 2019) and the practice of U.S. intelligence agencies using personal user data taken from popular Muslim prayer apps in an attempt to identify potential "terrorist threats" (Cox, 2020; Khan, 2020). Many researchers have written about how digital technologies facilitate the surveillance of Muslims by the state and its intelligence agencies (Kamali, 2017; Renton, 2018). These regimes of state surveillance conflate markers of Muslim religiosity with the threat of terrorism, turning otherwise innocuous expressions of Islamic piety such as mosque attendance, listening to Qur'anic recitations, or a refusal to eat pork products into actionable indicators of a violent ideological stance that must be suppressed. What remains understudied, however, are the ways that Muslims use digital technologies to resist surveillance or engage in surveillance amongst themselves (Shams, 2017; Selod, 2018).

When media anthropologists have studied surveillance, they have tended to focus on the methods through which states and institutions exercise surveillance of their citizens or the means through which activists resist institutional scrutiny (Coleman, 2010; Nardi, 2015). For example, in analyzing the role of digital media in the 2009 Iranian Green Movement, anthropologists Annabelle Sreberny and Gholam Khiabani (2010) describe how Iranian citizens used anti-censorship software distributed via CDs to ensure news about the protests reached mainstream media outlets. Other anthropologists of media and visuality have described how police use CCTV to enact racial profiling in Canada (Walby, 2005) and how Google Maps facilitates Israeli surveillance of the occupied Palestinian territories (Goodfriend, 2021). Few studies in media anthropology have conceptualized surveillance as an aspect of interpersonal relations rather than as a means of enacting or resisting institutional power (see Shakhsari [2020] for an exception, in which she analyzes how Persian-language bloggers use personal critique to promote normative visions of Iranian national consciousness). By attending to the power relations enacted and critiqued through digital practices of sharing posts and memes, I argue that media anthropologists can begin to understand how surveillance operates within the realm of interpersonal relationships rather than just as an aspect of institutional governance.

Canadian engineer and social theorist Steve Mann offers a useful framework for understanding surveillance that is rooted in an analysis of power relations. Mann proposes that the concept of "surveillance" as a process of "watching from above" (from the French *sur* for "above" and *veiller* "to watch") cannot adequately describe the multiple ways in which power flows between those who watch and those who are being watched. Mann argues that institutions of authority, like the police or state security agencies, no longer possess a monopoly on the capacity to observe others in detail. Due to widespread easy access to handheld cameras and smartphones in much of the world today, individuals can now turn the power of surveillance against institutions and "observe those in authority" from below (Mann, Nolan, and Wellman, 2003: 332).

Mann calls this process "sousveillance," from the French *sous* for "below," in which individuals use technology to "observe the organizational observer," as exemplified by video recordings of police brutality (Mann, Nolan, and Wellman, 2003: 333). Through the exercise of sousveillance, individuals have the capacity to "access and collect data about their surveillance and to neutralize surveillance" (Mann et al., 2003: 333) through the deliberate observation of social actors occupying positions of authority. He argues that a more comprehensive theory of surveillance requires analysts to recognize that "we now live in a society in which we have both 'the few watching the many' (surveillance), AND 'the many watching the few' (sousveillance)" (Mann, 2013: 1). Mann complicates Foucault's (1995[1977]) discussion of the panopticon by proposing that the disciplinary power of observation shapes not only the behavior of individuals (through surveillance or "oversight" in the panopticon) but also the actions of organizations and authoritative institutions like the police (through sousveillance or "undersight" in the "inverse panopticon") (Mann, Nolan, and Wellman, 2003). A growing body of research in surveillance studies extends Mann's theorization of the multifaceted relationships of power and observation that are now facilitated by the proliferation of digital media technologies and the expansion of big data (e.g. Browne, 2015; Cho, 2018; Lee, 2018; Benjamin, 2019).

Internet researcher Alice Marwick (2012) draws upon Mann's discussion of power relations to consider how social media technologies resituate surveillance and observational discipline in the realm of interpersonal relations. She argues that popular social media platforms like Facebook, Twitter, and Instagram present their users with a particular set of technical affordances that facilitate not just surveillance (institutions watching individuals) or sousveillance (individuals watching institutions) but also interpersonal forms of observational discipline (individuals watching other individuals). Marwick (2012: 378–79) writes that social media platforms compel their users to "continually investigate digital traces left by the people they are connected to," a process which has the effect of "domesticating surveillance practices [in] day-to-day life and interpersonal relationships." She identifies social media platforms as spaces that are "characterized by both watching and a high awareness of being watched," where a person carefully "[monitors] their digital actions with an audience in mind, often tailoring social media content to particular individuals" (Marwick, 2012: 379).

In this environment, the disciplinary power of surveillance is exercised "between individuals, rather than organizational entities and individuals (e.g. governments surveilling citizens or corporations surveilling consumers)" (Marwick, 2012: 379). Surveillance on social media is also reciprocal, since "each participant is both broadcasting information that is looked at by others and looking at information broadcast by others" (Marwick, 2012: 379). The interpersonal and reciprocal nature of surveillance on social media is what Marwick defines as "social surveillance," the "increasingly common situations in which people of relatively equal power are watching each other and acting on the information they find" (Marwick, 2012: 380).

By observing the digital actions of others, sharing likes and comments, and internalizing the feedback they receive on their posts, social media users exercise the disciplinary power of surveillance from a relatively equal footing in relation to each other as fellow members of a larger social network. While Marwick recognizes that surveillance and sousveillance take place on social media, she argues that what sets these platforms apart from other media technologies is their capacity to enable more intensive forms of lateral social surveillance between individuals in everyday life. It is from this understanding of social surveillance as an interpersonal and reciprocal method of exercising behavioral discipline that I now turn to a discussion of the Islamic concept of enjoining the right and forbidding the wrong (*al-amr bi-l-maʿrūf*). The phenomenon of social surveillance that Marwick identifies as a characteristic feature of social media platforms has many important parallels with the concept of enjoining right and forbidding wrong in Islamic ethics, shaping how contemporary Muslims use social media to engage with each other and enact contested visions of Islamic morality.

In his detailed survey of *al-amr bi-l-maʿrūf* throughout the history of Islamic thought, Michael Cook (2001) explains that the majority of classical Islamic scholars:

> understand the duty [to enjoin right and forbid wrong] primarily as one to be performed by individual believers to each other, and not, say, by the community as a whole towards the world at large; [they] see its scope as in the first instance response to specific misdeeds, rather than vague and general ethical affirmation.

31

While enjoining right and forbidding wrong can take the form of an authority figure rebuking a subordinate (such as Caliph al-Maʾmūn reprimanding one of his overly zealous subjects [Cook, 2001: 10]) or a peasant challenging the authority of a king (as in Abū Ḥanīfa's account of a goldsmith who spoke out against the unjust actions of the ruler of Marw [Cook, 2001: 9]), it is generally promoted as a duty to be exercised between individual Muslims to uphold the collective moral standing of the universal Muslim community (*ummah*). In other words, though the concept of enjoining right and forbidding wrong encompasses surveillance and sousveillance, it is most often invoked as a way to promote social surveillance (Marwick, 2012), the collective and reciprocal effort of individual Muslims to keep each other in check, to be accountable for each other's actions, and to encourage one another to behave according to communal expectations of Islamic morality.

Cook's research demonstrates that centuries of Muslim exegetes (*mufassirūn*) and jurists (*fuqahā*) have ascribed great ethical value to the duty to enjoin right and forbid wrong, framing this as an essential quality of a proper Muslim ethical disposition. In an authoritative prophetic tradition (*hadith*) recorded in the corpus compiled by Abū Dawūd (d. 889 CE), the Prophet Muhammad reportedly said:

> Whoever sees a wrong (*munkar*) and is able to put it right with his hand (*an yughayyirahu biyadihi*), let him do so; if he can't, then with his tongue (*bi-lisānihi*); if he can't, then with [or in] his heart (*bi-qalbihi*), which is the bare minimum of faith.
>
> *Cook, 2001: 33*

This *hadith* indicates that the duty to enjoin right and forbid wrong can encompass a range of appropriate responses, from physical action and verbal reproach to (at the very least) internal disapproval. All of these acts signify one's status as a pious and moral Muslim. What is not acceptable, however, is to observe another Muslim commit a sinful act and simply stand by without taking some kind of action, whether externalized (in deed or in word) or internalized (as silent disapproval).

Muslim scholars and jurists from many different traditions consistently describe:

> the most pious (*atqā al-nās*) [as those who are] most zealous in performing the duty (*amaruhūm bi-l-maʿrūf*) and most loyal to their kinsfolk; he who commands right and forbids wrong is God's deputy on earth (*khalīfat allāh fī-l-arḍ*), and the deputy of His book and of His Prophet. Conversely, "a dead man among the living" is explained as one who fails to perform the duty; one who abandons it is no believer.
>
> *Cook, 2001: 38*

Muslim scholars thus frame enjoining right and forbidding wrong as the quintessential act which signals one's moral standing as a Muslim, since it is the very act which ensures the implementation of Islamic ethical ideals in the field of actual human relations. To be a good Muslim, according to these scholars, requires the detailed observation of other Muslims and their behavior as well as the internalization of an awareness that one's own actions are always subject to observation and critique from other Muslims. In other words, collective and reciprocal social surveillance is at the heart of authoritative scholarly discourse on Islamic social ethics.

In recent years, with the emergence of popular *da'wa* (lit. "invitation" or "proselytization") movements in many Muslim communities, the duty to enjoin right and forbid wrong has taken on a new political urgency as a method of challenging the perceived moral corruption of modern secular society. In her ethnography of a women's piety movement in Cairo, anthropologist Saba Mahmood (2005) analyzes *da'wa* as a central organizing paradigm for understanding the exercise of Islamist political agency. She writes that:

> while *da'wa* may also be directed toward non-Muslims, the contemporary piety movement in Egypt primarily understands it to be a religious duty that requires all adult members of the Islamic community to urge fellow Muslims to greater piety, and to teach one another correct Islamic conduct.
>
> *Mahmood, 2005: 57*

Actions encompassed by the category of contemporary *da'wa* include verbal admonishment of wrongdoing, establishing mosques, forming social welfare organizations, and preaching.

Enjoining right and forbidding wrong is thus an essential aspect of popular *da'wa* movements like the one Mahmood analyzes; it is the implementation of the duty to "invite" (*yad'ū*) other Muslims to greater piety through verbal admonishment and collective accountability. Mahmood demonstrates how *da'wa* movements serve as an important conduit for the exercise of Islamist political agency in contemporary Egypt, particularly among women (Mahmood, 2005: 3–5). These movements challenge the perceived secularization and attendant corruption of modern Egyptian society, seeking a "return" to an idealized past when Islam served as the moral foundation uniting all Egyptians (Coptic Christians notwithstanding). Within the past 20 years, as similar piety movements have gained adherents across the Muslim world (e.g. Deeb, 2006 on Shi'i movements in Lebanon; Bayat, 2007 on Iran, Palestine, and Egypt), social media sites like Twitter have become important platforms for the exercise of *da'wa* as a call to embrace Islam against the moral corruption of Western secularism (Mellor, 2018; Solahudin and Fakhruroji, 2020).

With this context in mind, I now turn to analyze a series of recent English-language tweets involving LGBTQ Muslims and those who criticize them. I am interested in what emerges from these digital interactions when they are understood not just as examples of homophobic trolling or internet humor but rather as instances of social surveillance enacted through the Islamic ethic of enjoining right and forbidding wrong. By facilitating the intensive reciprocal observation of others from a position of relatively equal social footing, social media sites like Twitter are discursive environments where the logics of digital social networking and Islamic social ethics intersect to reveal tensions within the Muslim community around how to define what is ethically right (*ma'rūf*) and wrong (*munkar*) in the context of contemporary debates about gender and sexuality.

"LGBT is Disgusting"/"You Are Married to Your Cousin": Islamic Sexual Ethics on Twitter

In November 2020, Aliyah Ali (@thetranshijabi on Twitter) posted a response to recent hateful messages she had been receiving from other Muslims online targeting her for her identity as a transgender Muslim woman. Aliyah is a prominent member of a growing network of queer Muslim social media influencers based in the United States who asked me to use her real name and username in this chapter. As a young activist and prolific social media user, Aliyah has developed a Twitter following of over 25,000 people by sharing intimate moments from her life and her gender transition alongside political commentary on queer liberation. In this tweet, Aliyah argues that homophobic and transphobic Muslims misunderstand the story of the Prophet Lūt when they critique her transgender identity, a common reference point for Muslims who deny the legitimacy of LGBTQ identities by labeling queer Muslims as contemporary "people of Lūt" (*qawm lūt*) who are condemned in the Qur'an, supposedly for acts of "sodomy" (Ali, 2006: 81–82). Aliyah explains to her thousands of followers that the real sin committed by the people of Lūt was "doxxing god's angels to a bunch of rapists," not "supporting lgbtq+ rights," as anti-LGBTQ Muslims claim. In a later tweet, she critiques Muslims who claim that "believing homosexuality isn't a sin is mental gymnastics." She quips that:

> if refusing to believe that our creator would make someone an unchangeable way and then forbid their existence is mental gymnastics then smack my ass and call me simone biles [a famous U.S. Olympic gymnast].

Aliyah thus asserts the legitimacy of her transgender identity by appealing to Islamic tradition and offering an interpretation of the story of the Prophet Lūt, defusing the critiques made by other Muslims against her as illegitimate attempts to forbid something that God has created (namely, her inherent disposition [*fiṭrah*] as a transgender woman). She uses humor to expose the hypocrisy of anti-LGBTQ Muslims who, she implies, criticize her out of hate and ignorance rather than in accordance with foundational Islamic values of mercy, respect, and decency.

Rather than interpret this exchange as an example of facetious internet debate, I argue that Aliyah's tweets represent an attempt to enjoin the right and forbid the wrong from within a network of Muslim Twitter users. Aliyah responds to surveillance and online critique from other Muslims in this interaction; she turns the critical gaze imposed upon her back against transphobic Muslims to expose the illogical nature of their rhetoric. This is not sousveillance (an individual observing an institutional authority), since the transphobic Muslims here are not scholars or other authority figures but simply other Muslim Twitter users who message her claiming that she is committing a sin by being openly transgender. Aliyah positions herself with just as much claim to Islamic authority as her critics here, since she frames everyone involved in this interaction as a believing Muslim (*mu'min*) debating with other believing Muslims. By speaking out against the hateful online messages she receives, Aliyah enacts a vision of Islamic ethics rooted in respect for human difference as fellow creations of God. She calls out transphobic Muslims for disobeying God's commands to act in a kind and decent manner, saying that, in fact, they are the ones who are committing sin by condemning her when she is doing nothing more than living her life as God created her. Through her witty and humorous tweets, she enjoins other Muslims to respect queer identities and forbids homophobic and transphobic rhetoric as an example of un-Islamic behavior. Aliyah is therefore acting like both a social media user (engaging in social surveillance within a networked public; Marwick, 2012) and a believing Muslim (exposing moral corruption within the Muslim community by speaking out against unethical behavior; Cook, 2001: 31).

Aliyah is not the only queer Muslim who uses Twitter to turn the gaze of Islamic ethical critique back against anti-LGBTQ Muslims. Shortly after Aliyah posted her tweets, in late December 2020, other queer Muslim Twitter users began circulating variations of the "Doomer Girl" meme to expose the hypocrisy they observed in the behavior of anti-LGBTQ Muslims (KnowYourMeme, 2021). In this genre of meme, popular on Twitter and Facebook since early 2020, two characters, usually one male smoking a cigarette and one female with curly black hair, face one another and ask each other a question. This meme is normally used to criticize interlocutors or express disbelief. In the queer Muslim iterations of this meme that I analyze, however, the characters comment on each others' actions or appearance rather than ask a question and both are visibly Muslim or Arab and South Asian.

In one example, a presumably-Muslim young male character smoking a cigarette criticizes a dark-skinned *hijabi*, saying "you're queer? that's so haram [sinful] you're not even muslim." For her part, the young woman stares back at the man, looking confused (with question marks "???" above her head) as she attempts to make sense of his criticism of her behavior while he smokes a cigarette next to his two girlfriends ("girlfriend #1" and "girlfriend #2"). It is clear that she does not take him seriously, questioning his moral standing to critique others while he openly flaunts normative Muslim expectations of proper sexual behavior (dating two women at once, and thus presumably engaging in premarital sex) and the consumption of intoxicants (many Muslims consider tobacco consumption to be prohibited alongside alcohol and other addictive substances).

This meme depicts a familiar social scenario for many queer Muslims in which a straight cisgender man attempts to exercise social surveillance against them by invoking a normative Islamic ethical framework. Here, queer Muslims speak back against those who label their sexuality and gender identity *ḥarām* ("forbidden" or "sinful") by exposing the hypocrisy of homophobic *takfiris* (Muslims who accuse other Muslims of "disbelief" or *kufr*, a serious sin in Islam). By circulating Muslim-centered parodic adaptations of the Doomer Girl meme, queer Muslims on Twitter call out the hypocrisy of homophobic and transphobic Muslims who focus an inordinate amount of attention on the actions of queer Muslims while ignoring how their own actions could be considered sinful from within an Islamic ethical framework.

Other queer Muslims soon began sharing their own versions of this meme to speak out against anti-LGBTQ rhetoric in Muslim communities. In one example posted by a young gay Muslim Twitter user, a bearded young Muslim man attempts to flirt with a *hijabi* by asking her, "I hate gay people so much, do you?" She responds simply by saying, "u smoke, drink and have sex," dismissing his homophobia by redirecting criticism back at him and his own "sinful" behavior. This post earned over 12,000 "likes" and over 1,600 "retweets," indicating that a large number of Muslim Twitter users resonated with the message of this meme.

In another example, Aliyah (from above) shares an image of a bearded young Muslim saying "lgbt is disgusting" while a *hijabi* responds "you are married to your cousin." Again, this meme defuses anti-LGBTQ rhetoric by exposing it as an illegitimate and hypocritical attempt by heterosexual and cisgender Muslims to claim moral superiority over their queer Muslim counterparts. This post earned over 179,000 "likes" and 15,000 "retweets." After generating so much attention with this tweet, Aliyah clarified in a later post that:

> the point of this was to show how stupid queerphobic muslims look spreading hate. y'all are no one to talk down on ppl ESPECIALLY when you could be seen by others as supporting/doing something immoral yourself. don't expect respect if you cannot give it.

By drawing a connection between LGBTQ identities and the relatively common practice of cousin marriage in some Muslim communities, Aliyah implies that anti-LGBTQ Muslims unfairly critique homosexual and transgender Muslims while ignoring other potentially "queer" sexual practices when they are performed by cisgender heterosexual Muslims.

It is important to note here that I am not claiming that the queer Muslim Twitters users who circulate these memes are arguing that other Muslims should have no right to criticize them at all. In fact, they agree that there are a set of ethical behaviors and dispositions that all Muslims should adhere to, including kindness, respect, tolerance, and honesty. Where queer Muslims on Twitter disagree with their homophobic critics is in their insistence that queer and trans subjectivities can align with Islamic ethical norms. They echo the arguments of contemporary feminist and queer Muslim scholars like Kecia Ali (2006), amina wadud (2009), and Scott Kugle (2003) in their claim that patriarchy, oppression, and social injustice are the real sins representing a threat to Muslims today, not the acceptance of same-sex sexuality and transgender identities. In this sense, their actions on Twitter do not represent a departure from Islamic ethical frameworks in favor of Western secular liberalism and its motto of "mind your own business" (Cook, 2001: 594), as many of their *takfiri* critics claim. Instead, they promote the idea of a universal Muslim community that actually lives up to what they understand as the foundational Islamic values of social justice and respect for human diversity, including acceptance of the full range of human sexual orientations and gender identities. This is why they turn the gaze of social surveillance back against their critics rather than claim that Muslims have no right to criticize the private lives of other Muslims. It is perfectly valid and necessary to observe and critique each other's behavior as fellow Muslims; conflict arises because the two sides disagree about what constitutes appropriate Islamic ethical behavior.

In a tweet posted two months later in February 2021, a young queer Muslim woman whom I call Nadia summarizes this social justice-oriented approach to Islamic ethics and social surveillance. Speaking out against misogynistic rhetoric commonly circulated within conservative Muslim networks on Twitter, she writes that "islam is literally like 'hey be kind to people pray and fast [smiley emoji]' and you mfs come on this app like 'WHY WOMEN SHOULDN'T ATTEND CO-ED GROCERY STORES' like are you guys ok???" With this humorous and slightly exaggerated representation of common misogynistic rhetoric on Muslim Twitter, Nadia critiques those who, she claims, misunderstand the fundamentals of Islamic ethics by focusing so much of their attention on enforcing a rigid heteronormative gender binary. She encourages her fellow Muslims to focus on what she argues are the fundamental aspects of Islamic piety ("be kind," "pray," "fast") rather than engage in what she frames as superficial boundary policing around gender norms. Speaking as a Muslim woman to other Muslims, Nadia admonishes those who commit wrongdoing (misogynists, homophobes) in the name of Islam, critiquing their behavior and encouraging them to act in a kinder and more ethical manner.

Through these tweets, LGBTQ Muslims engage in the process of enjoining right and forbidding wrong (*al-amr bi-l-maʿrūf*) within networks of their fellow Muslims on Twitter. As Marwick (2012) identifies, social media platforms like Twitter allow people to observe each other's everyday lives in intimate detail. However, surveillance encompasses more than just direct observation of behavior. Through their humorous posts and relatable memes depicting social scenarios familiar to many queer Muslims in their daily lives, these Twitter users draw from both their online and offline experiences in navigating widespread anti-LGBTQ rhetoric to express moral judgment on the general beliefs and practices of their fellow Muslims. Although queer Muslims resist attempts by homophobic and transphobic Muslims to exercise observational discipline against them, they do not do so by appealing to a universal right to individual privacy and limitless personal freedom. Instead, they expose anti-LGBTQ rhetoric as illegitimate moral critique based on a misreading of Islamic sources. By calling out the hypocritical behavior of those Muslims who single out LGBTQ Muslims for the harshest moral critique, queer Muslims challenge the broader Muslim community to live up to its highest ethical potential by enacting core Islamic values of kindness, decency, and respect for human diversity through acceptance of LGBTQ identities within an Islamic ethical framework.

What queer Muslim Twitter users are objecting to in their posts is not necessarily that homophobic Muslims have somehow infringed upon their right to exercise individual agency in claiming a non-heteronormative sexuality or gender identity. Instead, they situate affirmation of LGBTQ subjectivities as an expression of fundamental Islamic values, including respect for the diversity inherent within God's creation and the importance of treating others with kindness and humility. It is therefore less of a problem that homophobic Muslims are constantly observing them through social media; this is to be expected (another Twitter user, whom I refer to here as Sana, muses that "I know that no matter how lonely I get, there will be at least one homophobic Muslim thinking about me"). What matters instead is how they choose to live within the universal community of Muslims (*ummah*), an environment with a long tradition of social surveillance that is currently being intensified by the constant interpersonal contact enabled by increasing social media use (Marwick, 2012: 378–79). Queer Muslims on Twitter therefore do not seek an escape from social surveillance, since they argue that there are fundamental Islamic values that all Muslims should abide by. By contrast, they embrace the power to enact social surveillance themselves by turning the gaze of observational discipline against those who promote anti-LGBTQ rhetoric. They engage in what they understand as their duty to act as "God's deputy on earth (*khalīfat allāh fī-l-ard*)" (Cook, 2001: 38) by exposing the unethical nature of homophobia, transphobia, and patriarchy from within an Islamic ethical framework.

Conclusions: Toward a Theory of Contingent Privacy Online

In his discussion of the concept of privacy in classical Islamic thought, Michael Cook (2001: 593–94) argues that "while Islam has definite notions of privacy and gives them strong articulation," information about ethical wrongdoing "may be only contingently private" and can be the source of valid social critique if it is ever made known to other Muslims. In other words, within the thinking of authoritative Islamic scholars, it is not legitimate for a Muslim to defend themselves against accusations of sin by responding, "it's nobody's business but my own, and I have a right to do what I want." Instead, these scholars contend that Muslims have a duty to act ethically and avoid wrongdoing in all aspects of life, including in their personal lives. They interpret the Qur'anic duty to enjoin right and forbid wrong (*al-amr bi-l-maʿrūf*) as an obligation to expose corruption, hypocrisy, and unethical behavior anywhere it becomes evident, even if this means critiquing the behavior of others in their own bedroom. The only legitimate defense against an accusation of sin from a fellow Muslim is to claim "it's between me and God, and I disagree with your interpretation of God's commandments." Debates about privacy in Islamic ethics are thus rooted in debates about fundamental Islamic values; what is at stake is not necessarily the limits of one's personal freedom but the extent to which one enacts a comprehensive vision of Islamic ethics in all aspects of life.

While this logic might seem at odds with expectations about privacy and personal freedom promoted within secular liberal ideologies, it is actually not so different from how many people engage in debates about ethics in mainstream U.S. society, for instance. Consider the perennial fascination with politicians embroiled in sex scandals, or recent social media campaigns intended to expose the unethical or morally questionable behavior of celebrities, athletes, and business leaders in their personal lives. Many Americans would agree that acts of racism and sexism are indefensible in any situation, public or private, no matter who performs them. Instead, the debate is about what specifically constitutes racism or sexism. Observing other people who occupy a similar social position and making moral judgments about their behavior – what Marwick identifies as social surveillance – has long been at the heart of American politics and social justice movements.

While most debates about privacy and its limits in the U.S. have historically focused on instances of surveillance (e.g. the state observing citizens) and sousveillance (e.g. citizens observing institutional authorities, like the police, politicians, or influential celebrities), growing access to social media platforms precipitates a need to consider social (or lateral, interpersonal) surveillance in more detail. As ever more data about our personal lives, preferences, and everyday activities are being archived and circulated within social networks like Twitter, it is now easier than ever for individuals to observe and comment on the behavior of other individuals whom they may have never met in person. What we are used to thinking of as private or ephemeral information, such as our religious beliefs and sexual preferences or our conversations with family and friends, are being made increasingly durable and visible on social media, leaving us more susceptible to surveillance from institutional authorities as well as from other individuals within our social networks. Through the reciprocal broadcasting and observation of everyday life (Marwick, 2012), social media users enact a logic of lateral interpersonal surveillance, empowered by these technologies to circulate and comment on the behavior of others and to internalize the feedback they receive from other users as an assessment of their moral and social standing. Media anthropologists must learn from recent developments in internet and surveillance studies in order to fully explore how observation and control operate in the field of interpersonal relations.

Queer Muslims on Twitter offer a set of strategies for living in such a situation of contingent privacy and intensive social surveillance. Rather than attempt to resist observational discipline from anti-LGBTQ Muslims by claiming a universal right not to be surveilled or judged by others, they assert their right to express their sexualities and gender identities by invoking a communal ethical framework. They respond to social surveillance by engaging in the process of social surveillance themselves, exposing hypocrisy by enjoining right and forbidding wrong they observe in the actions of others. Like Mann's description of those who use the tools of observation to "watch the watchers" from a position of institutional subordination (Mann, Nolan, and Wellman, 2003; Mann, 2013), queer Muslims engage in the process of social surveillance by using the same tools of interpersonal observation as their critics – namely, the capacity to share their interpretations of authoritative Islamic sources in public Twitter posts, critiquing the behavior of other Muslims as misaligned with their vision of proper Islamic ethics.

However, power flows in this interaction in a more equalizing manner than Mann's hierarchical framework allows. Rather than a subordinate attempting to evade the observational discipline of an institutional authority through the exercise of "undersight," as in sousveillance, queer Muslims on Twitter refuse to accept a subordinate position in relation to their straight cisgender critics. While anti-LGBTQ Muslims attempt to frame themselves as the authoritative custodians of Islamic moral tradition and queer Muslims as their illegitimate and immoral subordinates (i.e. establishing a vertical relationship of observational discipline), Aliyah, Nadia, Sana, and other queer Muslim Twitter users assert that they are no different from any other Muslims and that they should not be singled out for moral critique (i.e. establishing a horizontal relationship of observational discipline). They embrace the contingent nature of privacy online, arguing that all Muslims should be held to the same ethical standards and demonstrating that they are not afraid to exercise the power of observational discipline to expose the hypocritical behavior of other Muslims when they encounter it.

Social surveillance therefore offers the potential to further entrench the marginalization of certain subjects (i.e. LGBTQ Muslims) at the same time as it offers the promise of furthering social justice by holding the members of a social network accountable for their actions (i.e. through exposing hypocrisy, homophobia, and transphobia). I suggest that this ethnographic example can offer a degree of optimism for those who seek to understand social media as a means of resisting injustice through social surveillance. Rather than fixate exclusively on the very real and worrying reality that these technologies work to sustain regimes of authoritative control and surveillance, social media platforms must also be studied as a means for marginalized people to call out their oppression and expose injustice.

References

Ali, K. (2006) *Sexual Ethics and Islam: Feminist Reflections on Qur'an, Hadith, and Jurisprudence*, London: Oneworld Publications.
Bayat, A. (2007) *Making Islam Democratic: Social Movements and the Post-Islamist Turn*, Stanford: Stanford University Press.
Benjamin, R. (2019) *Captivating Technology: Race, Carceral Technoscience, and Liberatory Imagination in Everyday Life*, Durham, NC: Duke University Press.
Brown, K. (2019) "Gender, governance, and countering violent extremism (CVE) in the UK," *International Journal of Law, Crime and Justice*. www.sciencedirect.com/science/article/abs/pii/S1756061619304537.

Browne, S. (2015) *Dark Matters: On the Surveillance of Blackness*, Durham, NC: Duke University Press.
Byler, D. (2019) "Ghost world," *Logic Magazine*, https://logicmag.io/china/ghost-world/.
Cho, A. (2018) "Default publicness: Queer youth of color, social media, and being outed by the machine," *New Media & Society* 20(9): 3183–3200.
Coleman, E. G. (2010) "Ethnographic approaches to digital media," *Annual Review of Anthropology* 39: 487–505.
Cook, M. (2001) *Commanding Right and Forbidding Wrong in Islamic Thought*, New York: Cambridge University Press.
Cox, J. (2020) "How the U.S. military buys location data from ordinary apps," *Vice News*, www.vice.com/en/article/jgqm5x/us-mi.
Deeb, L. (2006) *An Enchanted Modern: Gender and Public Piety in Shi'i Lebanon*, Princeton: Princeton University Press.
Foucault, M. (1995 [1977]) *Discipline and Punish: The Birth of the Prison*, Sheridan, A., trans., New York: Vintage Books.
Goodfriend, S. (2021) "A street view of occupation: Getting around Hebron on Google Maps," *Visual Anthropology Review* 37(2): 225–245.
Kamali, S. (2017) "Informants, provocateurs, and entrapment: Examining the histories of the FBI's PATCON and the NYPD's Muslim surveillance program," *Surveillance & Society* 15(1): 68–78.
Khan, A. (2020) "Muslim Pro, a popular prayer app, stops providing user data to firm selling to US military," *Religion News Service*, https://religionnews.com/2020/11/18/muslim-prayer-times-app-stops-providing-user-data-to-firm-selling-to-us-military/.
KnowYourMeme. (2021) "Doomer Girl," https://knowyourmeme.com/memes/doomer-girl.
Kugle, S. (2003) "Sexuality, diversity, and ethics in the agenda of progressive Muslims," in *Progressive Muslims: On Justice, Gender, and Pluralism*, Safi, O., ed., New York: Oneworld Publications.
Lee, C. S. (2019) "Datafication, dataveillance, and the social credit system as China's new normal," *Online Information Review* 43(6): 952–970.
Leibold, J. (2019) "Surveillance in China's Xinjiang Region: Ethnic sorting, coercion, and inducement," *Journal of Contemporary China* 29(121): 46–60.
Mahmood, S. (2005) *Politics of Piety: The Islamic Revival and the Feminist Subject*, Princeton: Princeton University Press.
Mann, S., Nolan J., and Wellman B. (2003) "Sousveillance: Inventing and using wearable computing devices for data collection in surveillance environments," *Surveillance & Society* 1(3): 331–355.
Mann, S. (2013) "Veillance and reciprocal transparency: Surveillance versus sousveillance, AR glass, lifeglogging, and wearable computing," in *IEEE International Symposium on Technology and Society (ISTAS): Social Implications of Wearable Computing and Augmediated Reality in Everyday Life*, Toronto, ON: 1–12.
Marwick, A. (2012) "The public domain: Surveillance in everyday life," *Surveillance & Society* 9(4): 378–393.
Mellor, N. (2018) *Voice of the Muslim Brotherhood: Da'wa, Discourse, and Political Communication*, New York: Routledge.
Nardi, B. (2015) "Virtuality," *Annual Review of Anthropology* 44: 15–31.
Nasr, S. H. (2013) *The Study Quran: A New Translation and Commentary*. Sūrah Āl 'Imrān, verse (āyah), 104.
Qiang, X. (2019) "The road to digital unfreedom: President Xi's surveillance state," *Journal of Democracy* 30(1): 53–67.
Qurashi, F. (2018) "The Prevent strategy and the UK 'war on terror': embedding infrastructures of surveillance in Muslim communities," *Palgrave Communications* 4(17).
Renton, J. (2018) "The global order of Muslim surveillance and its thought architecture," *Ethnic and Racial Studies* 41(12): 2125–2143.
Selod, S. (2018) *Forever Suspect: Racialized Surveillance of Muslim Americans in the War on Terror*, New Brunswick, NJ: Rutgers University Press.
Shakhsari, S. (2020) *Politics of Rightful Killing: Civil Society, Gender, and Sexuality in Weblogistan*, Durham, NC: Duke University Press.
Shams, T. (2017) "Visibility as resistance by Muslim Americans in a surveillance and security atmosphere," *Sociological Forum* 33(1): 73–94.
Solahudin, D. and Fakhruroji, M. (2020) "Internet and Islamic learning practices in Indonesia: Social media, religious populism, and religious authority," *Religions* 11(1): 1–12.

Sreberny, A. and Khiabani, G. (2010) *Blogistan: The Internet and Politics in Iran*, New York: I.B. Tauris.
wadud, a. (2009) "Islam beyond patriarchy through gender inclusive Qur'anic analysis," in *Wanted: Equality and Justice in the Muslim Family*, Anwar, Z., ed., Selangor, Malaysia: Musawah.
Walby, K. (2005) "How closed circuit television surveillance organizes the social: An institutional ethnography," *The Canadian Journal of Sociology/Cahiers canadiens de sociologie* 30(2): 189–214.

36
QUEER SOUSVEILLANCE
Publics, Politics, and Social Media in South Korea

Alex Wolff

In 2015 the Seoul-based Presbyterian college Chongshin University caught wind of Facebook and Twitter pages that had been recently registered by *Hop-Hop* (*Kkangchong-Kkangchong*), a school club for LGBTQ+ students and alumni. The administration issued public statements that claimed there were no "homosexuals" within the university and threatened a defamation lawsuit against the group. In response, *Hop-Hop*'s members circulated anonymized photos of a student bearing their flag at Seoul's annual Queer Cultural Festival, and statements denouncing the school's "repression, contradiction, and violence" using social media. Group members also posted redacted versions of their student registration certificates, proving that there were queers organizing at one of the most conservative Christian universities in South Korea. The school then called the bluff of largely unenforced anti-discrimination ordinances by trying to reveal and expel "homosexuals and those who support homosexuality" through surveillance measures (SOGI, 2016). Students were encouraged to report each other, and the administration undertook an investigation of all those who had "liked" *Hop-Hop*'s social media pages and posts on Twitter and Facebook (Yang, 2016). Despite these events, *Hop-Hop* has continued to hold face-to-face meetings and anonymously promote anti-discrimination through news interviews and social media. As one group member put it in an interview during fieldwork, "The most we can do is hide and be more active online. More than we've expected, there are many people online who cheer us on, and support us in solidarity."

While a severe case, this situation highlights the fraught relationships among surveillance and new media framing the prospects of politics for LGBTQ+ young adults in South Korea. Despite unprecedented levels of public awareness, diverging from normative models of gender and sexuality can still entail severe legal, economic, and social discrimination for LGBTQ+ folks. As a result, many LGBTQ+ Koreans are not "out" to certain family and friends, and are also not out in the workplace. While there is no anti-homosexuality or anti-sodomy clause in civil law, there is an anti-sodomy law in the Military Penal Code, with most men serving under mandatory military conscription (Jeong and Lee, 2018). Furthermore, people living with HIV/AIDS often encounter difficulty and stigmatization when receiving routine care at medical centers and hospitals, at times turned away for procedures like dental scaling or dialysis for fear of viral contamination (KNP+, 2017). Trans people additionally face profound discrimination in legally changing their gender, as they require documentation from doctors and even their parents (Na, 2014). The financial insecurity that South Korean young adults contemporarily face as a result of economic liberalization and high rates of under- and unemployment (Song, 2009; Jung 2017) exacerbates the economic risk that LGBTQ+ people already endure. With no national anti-discrimination laws to protect them in the workplace and more young adults requiring economic and housing support from immediate and extended kin to stay afloat, "passing" as heterosexual or cisgender is often necessary for survival (Shin, 2020).

When combined with a heteronormative gaze, the predominance of surveillance in South Korea poses additional challenges to LGBTQ+ sociality and politics. At one level, infrastructures of surveillance are pervasive, and technologies of self-and-other monitoring are a facet of everyday life. For instance, there are almost 90,000 CCTV cameras installed in public and private institutions, most drivers use car dash-board cameras (called *black boxes*) for the purpose of recording car accidents, and people's daily routes are logged by their banking institutions; especially due to the dominant practice of using credit and debit cards for public transportation fare (Yoo, 2018). As recent state-led COVID-19 prevention efforts involving contact-tracing have emphasized, personal information and geolocation data from cellphones, banking transactions, and CCTV footage can be readily combined and utilized by government officials to monitor and track civilians (Yang 2021).

At another level, there is interpersonal or "social surveillance" (see Marwick, 2012), which describes how individuals reciprocally publicize and observe information about one another, especially through social media. In South Korea, a vast majority of citizens own smart phones and utilize applications like Instagram, Twitter, the messaging service Kakaotalk, and blogs (*cafés*) hosted by the popular search engine Naver. As such, many phrases have emerged around online social surveillance. Much like the English term "lurking," the phrase *nunting*, which is a portmanteau of the Korean word for eye (*nun*) and "chatting," refers to the practice of observing people's personal information or conversations online without any form of interaction. While it is uncommon for people to maintain multiple public-oriented social media profiles, because South Korean government censors online pornography many anonymously use platforms such as Tumblr and Twitter to share adult content and DIY pornography (Yi Jones, 2020).

The relationships among public homophobia, surveillance infrastructure, and social surveillance, for example, came to a head in May 2020 when state-led COVID prevention efforts increased the risk of "outing" (*auting*) for many patrons of Seoul's queer-friendly Itaewon neighborhood. After a 29-year-old man who had visited several clubs and bars tested positive for COVID, officials tracked who had been in the area using social media analysis, CCTV footage, banking transactions, and cellphone location data. They then publicized this information online for the purposes of contact-tracing. As certain news outlets began to emphasize the clubs and bars as *gay*, and even publish information about patrons' ages and workplaces, it led to a significant uptick of homophobia online, making many LGBTQ+ individuals anxious about being outed and possibly losing their jobs or social networks (Kim, 2020).

While rife with the danger of exposure, social media platforms are important domains for LGBTQ+ subject formation, social collectives, and political work. Over the past two decades, LGBTQ+ South Koreans have formed activist groups and college organizations at over 70 universities, organizing projects that advocate for social acceptance, legal reform, and anti-discrimination. Within these communities, markers such as lesbian, gay, bisexual, trans, and asexual are commonly used for self-identification, along with the loan-word queer (*kwieo*) and the more formal phrase "sexual minorities" (*seongsosuja*) for collective identification. Their work includes protests, public speaking, and social media campaigns for repeal of the military's anti-sodomy clause, the formation of an anti-discrimination law, and the passage of a marriage equality law. More generally it also involves work towards making themselves and the struggles they face in everyday life socially legible to a broader public. Like those actions undertaken by *Hop-Hop* such as uploading deidentified enrollment documents and photos to politicize their existence, much queer activism in South Korea is anonymized due to the risk of outing. As a result, this situation is bringing about interconnected online and in-person political strategies that are predicated on survivability, endurance, and possibility.

In this chapter, I seek to create dialogues between anthropological literature on new media, gender, and sexuality in order to examine and theorize these emergent relationships among social media, surveillance, and queer politics. This analysis is based upon my ethnographic research on gender, sexuality, and politics in South Korea over the past decade, with preliminary research carried out from 2015–2019 and a year of fieldwork between 2020–2021. This chapter builds upon data gathered through participant observation and interviews, primarily with lesbian, gay, trans, pansexual, non-binary, and bisexual interlocutors in their 20s and 30s who hail from cities like Seoul, and numerous other locales in South Korea. This research additionally draws upon my research experiences with queer college political groups and LGBTQ+ activist organizations, which often involved participating or volunteering in group meetings, protests, conferences, and festivals. While my current research project focuses on relationships among economic insecurity, social conceptions of the life-course, and queer politics in Korea, this chapter marks a deeper engagement with media anthropology and the politics of surveillance—specifically as they connect to sexuality and social media.

I understand the mass-mediated politics of discretion carried out by LGBTQ+ young adults in South Korea to be acts of *queer sousveillance*. If "sur" in the word *surveillance* suggests forms of oversight and social hierarchy then the term *sousveillance* indexes acts that reverse these dynamics of power (Fuchs, 2011; Browne, 2015; Mann, Nolan, and Wellmann, 2003). Sousveillance may also entail countersurveillance or anti-surveillance practices, which attempt to prevent or obscure the act of being monitored or being made visible by another party (Brunton and Nissenbaum, 2016). Elaborating this framework further, Simone Browne (2015: 21) conceptualizes "dark sousveillance" as oppositional tactics that have historically "appropriated, co-opted, repurposed and challenged" forms of racializing surveillance in order to escape and endure—for instance, the historic forging of freedom papers that allowed enslaved individuals from the South to travel to the North in the United States. Browne identifies dark sousveillance as a site of imagination and possibility from which participants are able to articulate critiques of anti-black surveillance and racism.

If anthropological studies of surveillance often examine mass-monitoring carried out by the state (Feldman, 2015), police (Al-Bulushi, 2021), and corporations (Huberman, 2021), this chapter calls for greater attention to how practices of surveillance can be politically repurposed, as well as given new signification. Research in media anthropology dealing with social media and activism often examines how online platforms like Instagram, Tumblr, and Twitter facilitate political discourse in grass-roots movements (Juris, 2012; Postil, 2014), trans and asexual counterpublics (Renninger, 2015; Jackson, Bailey, and Welles, 2017), and in protests of racialized police brutality (Bonilla and Rosa, 2015; Mcnair, 2019). Within this literature the negative potential for these platforms to enable state or corporate-directed data collection and governance has been well established. However, I argue for a broader focus on how these very same techniques of social media surveillance, whether it be the quantification of users or the publicization of identifiers, can be repurposed as political strategies by those who they normally oppress.

Practices of queer sousveillance do more than just afford a sense of anonymity, or protection from being "outed." The activism of LGBTQ+ young adults in South Korea undertakes anti-surveillance measures, such as adopting unique activist nicknames, or anonymizing member recruitment through private chat rooms and online survey tools. However, groups also actively engage in depersonalized political organizing which builds upon the archival and circulatory affordances of social media. Linking their on-the-ground and online efforts to cultivate public recognition and anti-discrimination, group members participate in meetings, protests, and conferences which are then documented, de-identified, and circulated through their social media pages. Though acts like publishing censored identity documents or group photos where members' faces are pixelized may seem mundane, they are redirecting the power encoded in everyday forms of homophobic surveillance. These are political tactics that critically respond to larger cultural discourses on privacy and long-standing forms of anti-LGBTQ+ backlash in South Korea.

For example, a common tactic used by conservative protestors at Korea's annual queer culture festivals involves photographing and recording queer bodies, then circulating this media on social media in the hope that someone will "out" them. This surveillance is animated by a politics of *erasure via exposure*. They intend to intensify discrimination against aberrant queer bodies, to the point where they are forced to retreat from public life and politics. In contrast, young adults' practices of queer sousveillance assert a form of ontological politics. By archiving and circulating depersonalized representations of LGBTQ+ young adults around campuses, on the streets, and at pride festivals through social media and other online outlets, it enables durable political claims to existence and enumeration. These abstracted sets of data assert that they do in fact "exist," in large numbers, but also trouble attempts to schematize individuals into discrete identity categories for processes of administration. As a population desirous of greater legal protections and social recognition, they become bodies to be counted, but not identified.

These strategies defy commonly assumed connections between visibility and the impulse to make oneself "known." In the act of de-identifying photos and circulating them online, it becomes difficult, and even impossible, for viewers to "read" participants by placing them into assumed categories of identity or make judgements about the "demographic" composition of their organizations. Furthermore, when LGBTQ+ young adults organizing pride festivals or participating in these groups post statements on social media, they primarily refer to themselves through collective categories such as "queer" or "gender and sexual minorities." In obscuring the face, but representing and quantifying queer bodies, they defy what anthropologist Tom Boellstorff has critiqued as "the assumption that political … efficacy can only exist through naming each category of selfhood or experience" (2007: 19). Their strategies, made even more radical through an annual queer festival that consistently reports tens of thousands of participants, uses documentation to instantiate a population in need of recognition, and the social and legal protections that can come with it. At stake is the very knowledge production regarding those who are "sexual minorities" (*seongsosuja*) as a population. As such, LGBTQ+ folks are attempting to regulate what knowledge is generated about them by creating it themselves. This is what makes queer sousveillance analytically rich: it intervenes in the relations of power and knowledge production that underlie enumeration and surveillance as modes of discrimination and governance. While anonymizing online photos protects LGBTQ+ individuals from public outing, it also emerges from a political strategy to produce quantifiable knowledge of a queer population and community.

Surveillance Studies and Social Media

The proliferation of social media in everyday life has brought scholars to focus not only on the ways it mediates communication and sociality, but also how others become privy to the information users post online through surveillance. Through readings of Foucault (1995), surveillance has historically been conceptualized as asymmetrical forms of social control organized by state, corporate, educational, and medical institutions (Gandy, 1989; Lyon, 2001; Andrejevic, 2006). Scholars of surveillance studies and new media focused on the U.S. and Europe have theorized how technologies of surveillance have become larger aspects of securitization regimes (e.g., Dubrofsky and Magnet, 2015), the carceral state and policing (Beutin, 2017; Kerrison et al., 2018), employment (Hedenus and Bachman, 2017), and the mass-collection of personal data for marketing purposes (Pridmore and Zwick, 2011). Furthermore, scholars have come to account for how politics of race, gender, and sexuality become intertwined with surveillance systems and apparatuses (Phillips and Cunningham, 2007; Nakamura and Chow-White, 2011).

Important ethnographic and anthropological work dealing with social media and surveillance outside the U.S. and U.K. has focused on issues like social media and activism in Azerbaijan (Pearce and Kendzior, 2012) and how intimacy and politics are mediated by social media in Southeast Turkey (Costa, 2016). Additional work has focused on how social media relates to class and marginalization in South America (Speyer, 2017; Haynes, 2016), social norms in Trinidad (Sinanan, 2017), issues of stratification in South India (Venkatraman, 2017), and urban transformation in China (McDonald, 2016; Wang, 2016). In South Korea scholars from disciplines outside anthropology have researched the ways social media usage shapes gendered ideologies about the body and beauty (Jeon, Sung, and Yang, 2018) as well as how perceptions of anonymity online are related to peoples' comfort with public disclosure (Yoon, 2017; Oh and Lim, 2018).

But surveillance is not always connected to sprawling security apparatuses and institutions. At a more fundamental level, it can be understood as any set of relations involving monitoring and power. The expanding presence of social networking services in everyday life has brought about a renewed focus on the relational aspects of surveillance which operate in multi-dimensional and capillary ways (Foucault, 1995; Marwick, 2012; Christensen and Jansson, 2015). As it has become increasingly difficult to know who is viewing one's digital footprint, as well as to what ends, scholars have begun theorizing how actors navigate online discretion, as well as the larger ideologies that emerge around social media and surveillance.

For example, social media can have a flattening effect on domains of social interaction commonly held to be discreet, if not mutually exclusive (Marwick and boyd, 2014). The convergence of audiences such as friends, family, peers, and employers upon a single platform has led many to undertake practices of discretion, as well as the usage of different platforms for different kinds of self-presentation (van Dijck, 2013), or the expert manipulation of privacy settings and the use of multiple public accounts to navigate self-performance (Costa, 2018). Awareness of this situation has also brought about what Duffy and Chan (2019: 121) refer to as "imagined surveillance," a concept that describes how "individuals conceive of the scrutiny that could take place across the social media ecology and, consequently, may engender future risks or opportunities." As they argue in the case of young adults in the U.S., the anticipatory threat of scrutiny by college admission boards, employers and other prying eyes brings them to alter, or conceal their online self-presentation (ibid: 134). Building upon discussions of self-surveillance (Vaz and Bruno, 2003), or the ways surveillance shapes processes of subject formation and self-care, they hold that curating ones' online representation with regard to employability or using secondary profiles to avoid scrutiny may normalize pervasive online surveillance and economic logics of self-branding (Duffy and Chan, 2019: 134).

Consideration of gender and sexuality invites additional layers of complexity. If "imagined surveillance" has been argued to structure acts of self-governance in line with normative standards of employability, the threat of surveillance shapes the boundaries of how queerness can be enacted and "known" in South Korea. A commonly cited annoyance within the workplace and family is others' insistence to know more about one's personal life, which is often described through the term *ojirap*. This kind of social "nosiness" takes on a different significance for queer folks, as extended kin, co-workers, and superiors often lobby questions about the absence or presence of romantic partners and plans for marriage. When faced with these questions, interlocutors have reported having to come up with excuses such as not having enough time for relationships due to school or work, changing the gender of their current partner to a more socially acceptable one, or even making up a romantic partner out of whole cloth.

Because the *ojirap* encountered in everyday life dovetails with the ways people observe one another on social media, LGBTQ+ South Koreans often utilize the affordances of social media to avoid surveillance by family members, employers, and "straight" peers.

While many in South Korea do not necessarily recognize "queer-coded" style as such, interlocutors have explained that things like non-gender normative hairstyles, an excessive interest in same-sex celebrities, or using rainbow stickers can sometimes garner suspicion (*uisim*) from others. Additionally, posting LGBTQ+ flag emoticons, queer memes, or statuses about romantic encounters and celebrity crushes can increase the risk of being outed. While in the workplace interlocutors have reported having to sometimes change their hairstyles and self-presentation, or avoid using decorations involving LGBTQ+ affiliated symbols, social media offers multiple different strategies. Though a relatively uncommon practice for others, LGBTQ+ South Koreans often maintain multiple social media accounts (such as on Facebook, where alternative queer-friendly accounts are sometimes referred to as "Gay-book"), adopt pseudonyms or nicknames specifically for the purposes of activism (*hwaldong-myeong*), utilize privacy settings to make sure family members or unfamiliar users do not follow them, and upload non-representative or blank profile pictures to their accounts.

These are sousveillance practices oriented at the level of self-care. They allow for survival; the ability to maintain queer lives and sociality. At the same time, queer sousveillance practices can also project outwards, towards critique and political possibility. When viewed politically, imagined surveillance on social media is not only about how the increased scrutiny of LGBTQ+ embodiment may produce future risks. It is also about how this heightened attention can create new opportunities for activists to shape knowledge about LGBTQ+ publics. New media and countersurveillance practices afford different ways for LGBTQ+ Koreans to enumerate themselves, to create deliberate portrayals of the size and power of their political organizations. For LGBTQ+ Koreans, this queer sousveillance takes multiple forms. As I explore in the following section, it can include acts of counting, and refusing to individually identify, the attendees at queer festivals in ways that contradict the head-counts given by authorities. It also takes visual forms, such as de-identifying and circulating photographs of themselves, often in large groups, at meetings, protests, and pride festivals through social media and other webpages. As I argue, these are political processes of knowledge production. In working towards making their populations "count," they inhabit an unstable, yet productive, zone between biopolitical categorization and the possibilities of recognition that could lead to broader legal and social protections (Currah and Stryker, 2015: 4).

Enumeration and Practices of Queer Sousveillance

When the Seoul Queer Culture Festival was first held at Seoul City Hall Plaza in 2015—a sprawling green field at the heart of the city—much attention was paid to the record number of participants. Festival organizers estimated that the event garnered roughly 30,000 participants (Im, 2015; Bang, 2016), while police estimated only about 6,000 (Im, 2015). In a similar comparison, organizers estimated that 50,000 participants attended the 2017 Festival, also held at

Seoul City Hall Plaza, while police estimated only 9,000 (Im, 2015). Each year the number of participants has increased, but they also correspond with other reported statistics. In 2015, the police mobilized 4,000 officers from 60 companies and estimated that more than 9,400 Christians attended opposition events near the Festival (Im, 2018). In 2017, the Festival had 105 organizations in attendance, including 13 official government embassies, and the partnered film festival featured 72 works from 24 countries (Im, 2018). That the first Festival, held in 2000, had only 50 participants is a common reference point used to draw attention to its exponential growth (see Im, 2018). These numbers then pair with pictures that LGBTQ+ activists and organizations circulate online of members attending the Festival, including group photos with organizations' banners, where participants' faces are covered by pixel mosaics to hide their individual identities. The point is to demonstrate an enumerative existence, not individual identities.

The politics of enumeration and quantification have been well-discussed by anthropologists and science and technology studies scholars alike. For instance, anthropologist Vincanne Adams (2016: 8–9) notes that "quantification strategies and the metrics we rely on to *avoid* politics often do not avoid politics at all; they become a form of politics in their own right." For Adams (2016: 9), quantification is a form of "storytelling" given how numbers are produced and circulated, and so the stories global health projects tell of, say, causes of death or cost effectiveness are stitched within the statistics and move beyond the "truth-telling" of numbers. The seeming apolitical nature of numbers, quantitative data, and quantification itself "renders quantification so seductive," anthropologist Sally Engle Merry (2016: 1) writes, due to "the capacity of numbers to provide knowledge of a complex and murky world." Quantification embodies a "promise to provide accurate information that allows policy makers, investors, government officials, and the general public to make informed decisions … [it] appears to be objective, scientific, and transparent" (ibid: 3). Yet as both suggest, quantification, indicators, and metrics decontextualize local circumstances and situations, providing partial knowledge that is in fact political in its claims to objectivity. Merry's (2016: 4) intervention lies in the types of knowledge produced and the forms of "governance effects" that emerge from mobilizing quantitative data as a method of knowing an "unknowable world." Taken together, enumeration and the practices of surveillance and sousveillance that enable enumeration craft stories of the people and populations these numbers represent. By staking claims to forms of knowledge production, the politics of enumeration draw attention to the way power permeates this process.

As with the visual documentation numbering the members of LGBTQ+ college groups discussed in the previous sections, the data produced in and through the Seoul Queer Culture Festival—including the various statistics and visual documentation of unidentifiable LGBTQ+ organization members circulating online—sidestep identification and individualizing mechanisms in favor of "massifying" (see Prasse-Freeman and Ong, 2021). Enumeration and its visualization are tools that Festival organizers wield to draw attention to their massified existence, the growing numbers of *both* LGBTQ+ and LGBTQ+ supportive people. On the one hand, enumeration acts as a form of representation, showcasing not only the fact that LGBTQ+ Koreans exist, but that the numbers of LGBTQ+ Koreans and allies are steadily growing each year. The intended effect would thus be, for instance, creating greater recognition and awareness of LGBTQ+ peoples and the issues facing them, such as stigmatization, marginalization, and financial insecurity, which could lead to anti-discriminatory legal protections. On the other hand, the focus on and visual representation of such large numbers of people may also lend itself to outside interpretations of diversity and tolerance, that such large quantities of participants represent the growing tolerance of LGBTQ+ folks in Korea, whereby an over-played narrative of "progress" is used to read the data and conclude that Korea is "getting better." The pitfall here is that such enumeration-backed tolerance hides the need for actual conversations about LGBTQ+ discrimination in Korea. What, then, do these numbers do? What do they account for?

Taken together, the enumeration of the Seoul Queer Culture Festival participants tells a story of not just the Festival, but the state of LGBTQ+ folks in South Korea. Given the lack of any substantial social, economic, and legal protections, enumeration seeks to challenge a well-circulated assumption that "there are no queer Koreans" while simultaneously indexing this population's precarious existence. LGBTQ+ folks exist, but contentiously so. When festival organizers estimate tens of thousands of more participants than the police, it signals not only comparative politics of enumeration, but also the contestation of dominant forms of counting and surveillance. Foucault (2001: 216–211) suggests that government acts either directly or indirectly on populations as categories in themselves, and is concerned with the "welfare of the population, the improvement of its condition." Making use of the "mechanism of security," government acts at the level of the population, whereby the "essential function of security … is to respond to a reality in such a way that this response cancels out the reality to which it responds—nullifies it, or limits, checks, or regulates it" (Foucault, 2007: 69). The radically different estimations of Festival participants are not entirely surprising, for in underestimating the reported number of participants, the police—and, by extension, government—is able to "respond to a reality … [that] cancels out the reality to which it responds" (ibid). The police's markedly lower estimation instantiates erasure.

In this framework, such a small number represents such a miniscule fraction of the population, that it need not even be addressed as a "target" of government. For the police, enumeration is a tool, a mechanism of power, to delimit government involvement, as the "welfare of the population" is not in jeopardy. Interesting then is that the enumeration, quantification, and visual documentation of participants also indexes the population quality of government. If the police underestimate to sidestep broader intervention into the "welfare" of gender and sexual minorities, then Festival organizer's higher estimations, paired with the depersonalized images circulated online, stake a claim to government involvement. They may very well be a "minority" of the population, but this enumeration argues that they are significant enough to span LGBTQ+ individuals and allies in ways that warrant greater protections.

Acts of surveilling, documenting, and enumeration act as the outwardly political function of *queer sousveillance*. Sousveillance may at once be an act of anti-surveillance or countersurveillance, acts that aim to hide, circumvent, or resist the often state-led surveillance assemblage. If Browne's (2015) intervention with dark sousveillance is the reversal or manipulation of visibility to hide in order to escape and endure, then my intervention with queer sousveillance is attention to a radical form of visibility that makes use of the same security mechanism of population to shine an even brighter light on those already surveilled and documented—thus surveilling more, and counting higher. If enumeration enables political action, including social policy, then acts of queer sousveillance respond to acts of surveillance with even *more* visibility at the level of the population. Recall that these are unidentifiable sets of quantitative data. In many pictures of participants circulating online, the only quality documented is their presence at the festival, and in the case of the LGBTQ+ college organizations, their faces are anonymized while their bodies are countable. What makes these acts of sousveillance queer is not just a shared sexuality or gender identity, but a shared attention to a possibility of actions. Queer sousveillance is thus a set of techniques that counteract surveillance practices attempting to delimit existence and enumeration, thereby insisting upon action aimed at a specific population.

Conclusion

While technologies of surveillance may enact disciplinary forms of social control or the demarcation of populations for governance, they can also be methods towards self-preservation and political representation. In using broader practices of monitoring and classification queer sousveillance practices intervene in relationships among numbers, knowledge, and power. Writ large, this can position LGBTQ+ populations and the publics they create in relation to practices of governance. Recent scholarship on sexuality and surveillance examines the double-edged nature of biopolitical projects based on enumeration (Kafer and Grinberg, 2019; Currah and Stryker, 2015; Ball et al., 2009). They may universalize and flatten differences among LGBTQ+ folks through categorization, subjecting some populations to greater state administration while at the same time violently excluding others. On the other hand, they may also provide access to critical resources, social services, and protections for certain populations. The queer sousveillance practices of LGBTQ+ publics in South Korea operate within these tensions. Their work towards quantification through festival head-counts and circulating images of LGBTQ+ and LGBTQ+ friendly groups on social media create the prospect of greater recognition, the kind of attention that could invite greater legal rights and social protections.

The enumeration of the individualized body into numbers and the subsequent circulation of this information online calls attention to multiple issues underlying the relationships among politics, publics, and social media. As the COVID-19 pandemic has created new strains on LGBTQ+ folks' mobility, housing, and economic situations, it has created new pressures upon their sociality and political organizing. For example, due to social distancing measures and the risk of large in-person gatherings, 2020's Queer Cultural Festival and Queer Film Festival were adapted into an online form—in ways that garnered many participants but did not allow for the same representational strategies and impact as years previous. Furthermore, as members of many LGBTQ+ college organizations have reported, a lack of in-person sociality paired with the mounting pressures of everyday life have significantly impacted their ability to recruit new members and carry out political activities, activities that are often used to index LGBTQ+ presence online. As a number of scholars have argued, publics operate through mass media, utilizing self-abstraction and the discursive circulation of texts to instantiate themselves (Warner, 2002; Cody, 2011). However, as this chapter has demonstrated, there is a complex, and oftentimes delicate, relationship between LGBTQ+ political actors' in-person and online tactics which highlights the relationship between digital selves and offline versions of individuals (Boellstorff, 2012). LGBTQ+ Koreans are mobilizing and molding social media in ways that call attention to their existence and contributing to queer community building, transforming the tools of their own surveillance into the means of their resistance, recognition, and rights.

References

Adams, V. (2016) "Introduction," in *Metrics: What Counts in Global Health*, edited by Vincanne Adams, Durham: Duke University Press: 1–17.

Al-Bulushi, S. (2021) "Citizen-Suspect: Navigating Surveillance and Policing in Urban Kenya," *American Anthropologist*, 123 (4): 819–832.

Andrejevic, M. (2006) "The Discipline of Watching: Detection, Risk, and Lateral Surveillance," *Critical Studies in Media Communication*, 23: 391–407.

Ball, K. N. Green, H. Koskela, and D. Phillips. (2009) "Surveillance Studies Needs Gender and Sexuality," *Surveillance & Society*, 6 (4): 352–355.

Bang, H. (2016) "Queer Culture Festival Held as Scheduled ... Dismissal of Application to 'Block'," *Yonhap News*, (accessed February 1, 2021).

Beauchamp, T. (2019) *Going Stealth: Book Transgender Politics and U.S. Surveillance Practices*, Durham: Duke University Press.
Beutin, L. P. (2017) "Racialization as a Way of Seeing: The Limits of Counter-Surveillance and Police Reform," *Surveillance & Society*, 15 (1): 5–20.
Boellstorff, T. (2007) "Queer Studies in the House of Anthropology," *Annual Review of Anthropology*, 36: 17–35.
Boellstorff, T. (2012) "Rethinking Digital Anthropology," in *Digital Anthropology*, edited by Heather A. Horst and Daniel Miller, New York: Routledge: 39–60.
Bonilla, Y., and J. Rosa. (2015) "#Ferguson: Digital Protest, Hashtag Ethnography, and the Racial Politics of Social Media in the United States," *American Ethnologist*, 42 (1): 4–17.
Browne, S. (2015) *Dark Matters: On the Surveillance of Blackness*, Durham: Duke University Press.
Brunton, F., and H. Nissenbaum. (2016) *Obfuscation: A User's Guide for Privacy and Protest*, Cambridge: MIT Press.
Christensen, M., and A. Jansson. (2015) "Complicit Surveillance, Interveillance, and the Question of Cosmopolitanism: Toward a Phenomenological Understanding of Mediatization," *New Media & Society*, 17 (9): 1473–1491.
Cody, F. (2011) "Publics and Politics," *Annual Review of Anthropology*, 40: 37–52.
Costa, E. (2016) *Social Media in Southeast Turkey: Love, Kinship, and Politics*, London: UCL Press.
Costa, E. (2018) "Affordances-in-practice: An Ethnographic Critique of Social Media Logic and Context Collapse" *New Media & Society*, 20 (10), 3641–3656.
Currah, P., and S. Stryker. (2015) "Introduction," *TSQ: Transgender Studies Quarterly*, 2 (1): 1–12.
Dave, N. (2011) "Indian and Lesbian and What Came Next: Affect, Commensuration, and Queer Emergences," *American Ethnologist*, 28 (4): 650–665.
Dijck, J. van (2013) "'You Have One Identity': Performing the Self on Facebook and LinkedIn," *Media, Culture & Society*, 35 (2): 199–215.
Dubrofsky, R. E., and S. A. Magnet. (2015) *Feminist Surveillance Studies*, Durham: Duke University Press.
Duffy, B. E., and Chan, N.K. (2019) "'You Never Really Know Who's Looking': Imagined Surveillance across Social Media Platforms," New Media & Society, 21 (1): 119–138.
Feldman, I. (2015) *Police Encounters: Security and Surveillance in Gaza under Egyptian Rule*, Stanford: Stanford University Press.
Foucault, M. (1995) *Discipline and Punish: The Birth of the Prison*, New York: Vintage Books.
Foucault, M. (2001) *Power*, edited by James D. Faubion. New York City: New Press.
Foucault, M. (2007) *Security, Territory, Population: Lectures at the College De France 1977–1978*, New York: Picador.
Fuchs, C. (2011) "How Can Surveillance Be Defined?" *MATRIZes*, 5 (1): 109–33.
Gandy, O. H. (1989) "The Surveillance Society: Information Technology and Bureaucratic Social Control," *Journal of Communication*, 39 (3): 61–76.
Haynes, N. (2016) *Social Media in Northern Chile: Posting the Extraordinarily Ordinary*, London: UCL Press.
Hedenus, A., and C. Backman. (2017) "Explaining the Data Double: Confessions and Self-Examinations in Job Recruitments," *Surveillance & Society*, 15 (5): 640–654.
Huberman, J. (2021) "Amazon Go, Surveillance Capitalism, and the Ideology of Convenience," *Economic Anthropology*, 8: 337–349.
Im, K. (2015) "LGBTQ Festival Participants 'Rainbow March' in Downtown Seoul." *Yonhap News* (accessed May 24, 2022).
Im, R. (2018) "Queer Festival in Downtown Seoul on Weekend … Will There Be Another Spark of Conflict Following the Demonstration at Hyehwa Station?" *Korea Economic Daily* (accessed February 1, 2021).
Jackson, S. J., M. Bailey, and B. F. Welles. (2018) "#GirlsLikeUs: Trans Advocacy and Community Building Online," *New Media & Society*, 20 (5): 1868–1888.
Jeon S., Y. Sung, and E. Yang (2018) "Social Media and College Women's Body Image Concerns: Investigating the Role of Online Social Grooming on Facebook," *Korean Journal of Women's Psychology*, 23 (1): 69–81.
Jeong, S., and N. Lee. (2018) "Invisible Others: Institutional Homophobia and Identities of Sexual Minority in the Korean Military," *Culture & Society*, 26 (3): 83–145.
Jung, M. (2017) "Precarious Seoul: Urban Inequality and Belonging of Young Adults in South Korea," *Positions*, 25 (4): 745–67.

Juris, J. (2012) "Reflections on #Occupy Everywhere: Social Media, Public Space, and Emerging Logics of Aggregation," *American Ethnologist*, 39 (2): 259–279.

Kafer, G., and D. Grinberg. (2019) "Editorial: Queer Surveillance," *Surveillance and Society*, 17 (5): 592–601.

Kerrison, E. M., J. Cobbina, and K. Bender. (2018) "'Your Pants Won't Save You': Why Black Youth Challenge Race-Based Police Surveillance and the Demands of Black Respectability Politics," *Race and Justice*, 8 (1): 7–26.

Kim, N. (2016) *The Gendered Politics of the Korean Protestant Right: Hegemonic Masculinity*, London: Palgrave Macmillan.

Kim, N. (2020) "South Korea Struggles to Contain New Outbreak Amid Anti-Gay Backlash," *The Guardian* (accessed June 29, 2021).

Korean Network for People Living with HIV/AIDS (KNP+) (2017) "Unknown Lives: Initial Findings from *The People Living with HIV Stigma Index in South Korea 2016-17*," (accessed May 24, 2022).

Lee, A. (2018) "Invisible Networked Publics and Hidden Contention: Youth Activism and Social Media Tactics under Repression," *New Media & Society*, 20 (11): 4095–4115.

Lyon, D. (2001) *Surveillance Society: Monitoring Everyday Life*, Buckingham: Open University Press.

Magnet, S. A. (2011) *When Biometrics Fail: Gender, Race, and the Technology of Identity*, Durham: Duke University Press.

Mann, S., J. Nolan, and B. Wellman. (2003) "Sousveillance: Inventing and Using Wearable Computing Devices for Data Collection in Surveillance Environments," *Surveillance & Society*, 1 (3): 331–355.

Marwick, A. (2012) "The Public Domain: Social Surveillance in Everyday Life," *Surveillance & Society*, 9 (4): 378–393.

Marwick, A., and d. boyd. (2014) "Networked Privacy: How Teenagers Negotiate Context in Social Media," *New Media & Society*, 16 (7): 1051–1067.

McDonald, T. (2016) *Social Media in Rural China: Social Networks and Moral Frameworks*, London: UCL Press.

Mcnair, K. (2019) "Beyond Hashtags: Black Twitter and Building Solidarity across Borders," in *#identity: Hashtagging Race, Gender, Sexuality, and Nation*, edited by Abigail De Kosnik and Keith Feldman, Ann Arbor: University of Michigan Press: 283–300.

Merry, S. E. (2016) *The Seductions of Quantification: Measuring Human Rights, Gender Violence, and Sex Trafficking*, Chicago: University of Chicago Press.

Moon, S. (2005) *Militarized Modernity and Gendered Citizenship in South Korea*, Durham: Duke.

Muñoz, J. E. (2009) *Cruising Utopia: The Then and There of Queer Futurity*, New York: New York University Press.

Na, T. Y. (2014) "The South Korean Gender System: LGBTI in the Contexts of Family, Legal Identity, and the Military," translated by J. Han and S. Koo. *Journal of Korean Studies*, 19 (2): 357–377.

Nakamura, L., and P. Chow-White. (2011) *Race After the Internet*, New York: Routledge.

Oh J. and S. Lim. (2018) "The Effect of Personality Traits and Motivation on Anonymity of SNS Profile: How Instagram Users' Narcissism and Self-Monitoring Alter Visual and Discursive Anonymity," *Korean Journal of Broadcasting and Telecommunication Studies*, 32(4): 33–64.

Paz, P., and B. Fernanda. (2003) "Types of Self-Surveillance: From Abnormality to Individuals 'at Risk'," 1 (3): 272–291.

Pearce, K., and S. Kendzior. (2012) "Networked Authoritarianism and Social Media in Azerbaijan," *Journal of Communication*, 62, 283–298.

Phillips, D. J., and C. Cunningham. (2007) "Queering Surveillance Research," in *Queer Online: Media, Technology & Sexuality*, edited by Kate O'Riordan and David J. Phillips, New York: Peter Lang.

Postill, J. (2014) "Democracy in an Age of Viral Reality: A Media Epidemiography of Spain's Indignados Movement," *Ethnography*, 15 (1): 51–69.

Postill, J., and S. Pink. (2012) "Social Media Ethnography: The Digital Researcher in a Messy Web," *Media International Australia*, 145: 123–134.

Prasse-Freeman, E., and A. Ong (2021) "Expulsion/Incorporation: Valences of Mass Violence in Myanmar," in *Political Violence in Southeast Asia since 1945: Case Studies from Six Countries*, edited by Eve Monique Zucker and Ben Kiernan, New York: Routledge: 41–55.

Pridmore, J., and D. Zwick. (2011) "Marketing and the Rise of Commercial Consumer Surveillance," *Surveillance & Society*, 8 (3): 269–277.

Renninger, B. J. (2015) "'Where I Can Be Myself … Where I Can Speak My Mind': Networked Counterpublics in a Polymedia Environment," *New Media & Society*, 17 (9): 1513–1529.

Shin, L. (2020) "Avoiding T'ibu (Obvious Butchness): Invisibility as a Survival Strategy among Young Queer Women in South Korea," in *Queer Korea*, edited by Todd Henry, Durham: Duke University Press.
Sinanan, J. (2017) *Social Media in Trinidad: Values and Visibility*, London: UCL Press.
Society of Law and Policy on Sexual Orientation and Gender Identity Korea (SOGI) (2016) "Human Rights Situation of LGBTI in South Korea 2016," (accessed May 24, 2022).
Song, J. (2009) *South Koreans in the Debt Crisis: The Creation of a Neoliberal Welfare Society*, Durham: Duke University Press.
Spyer, J. (2017) *Social Media in Emergent Brazil: How the Internet Affects Social Mobility*, London: UCL Press: 295–322.
Sung, M. (2019) "The Triad of Colonialism, Anti-Communism, and Neo-Liberalism: Decolonizing Surveillance Studies in South Korea," *Surveillance & Society*, 17 (5): 730–33.
Uldam, J. (2018) "Social Media Visibility: Challenges to Activism," *Media, Culture & Society*, 40 (1): 41–58.
Vaz, P., and F. Bruno. (2003) *Surveillance & Society* 1 (3): 272–291.
Venkatraman, S. (2017) *Social Media in South India*, London: UCL Press.
Warner, M. (2002) *Publics and Counterpublics*, New York: Zone Books.
Wang, X. (2016) *Social Media in Industrial China*, London: UCL Press.
Yang, H. (2016) "Stop Persecution Against LGBT People's Rights Group Kang Chong Kang Chong," *Nodongja Yeondae (Worker's Solidarity)* (accessed February 1, 2021).
Yang, H. (2021) "Behind South Korea's Success in Containing Covid-19: Surveillance Technology Infrastructures," *Social Science Research Council* (accessed June 28, 2021).
Yi Jones, S. S. (2020) "Jemok Eopseum: The Repurposing of Tumblr for Gay South Korean DIY Pornography." *Porn Studies*.
Yoo, J. (2018) "Concerns Over Privacy Invasion, 'Significant Improvement in Night Road Security, Etc." *Dong-A Ilbo* (accessed February 1, 2021).
Yoon, M. (2017) "Is the Privacy in the Digital-Mediated Society Disappearing? – Networked Privacy and Selective Self-Exhibition," *Culture & Society*, (8) 183–217.

F

Emerging Technologies and Contemporary Challenges

Data, AI and VR

37
THE ALGORITHMIC SILHOUETTE
New Technologies and the Fashionable Body

Heather A. Horst and Sheba Mohammid

The introduction of new media technologies and the ways people around the world express, communicate, create and imagine connection and community with them has always been a key focus of media anthropology. As digital anthropologists demonstrate (Horst and Miller, 2006, 2013; Geismar & Knox, 2021), the growth of digital technologies has shifted our attention from media objects to some of the less visible, yet still material platforms, software and related infrastructures where data such as audio and video files, photographs, word documents, email and other information are stored (Horst, Sinanan and Hjorth, 2021). These are also structured by the companies, consumers, states and state agents that govern and regulate these digital infrastructures across local, national and transnational spaces (Foster and Horst, 2018, Horst, 2013; Pink, Lanzeni and Horst, 2018). Systems that form part of the digital infrastructure such as algorithms and other forms of automation influence the digital worlds that we have access to on social media and other platforms through mechanisms that largely remain invisible to people who use them. Smartphones, PlayStations and other systems also rely upon workers who lay the submarine cables, collect coltan and other minerals, or work to sort and classify the information that form digital infrastructures (Horst, 2021). The ghost workers, as Mary Gray and Siddarth Suri (2019) characterize the invisible labourers who support large multinational corporations, interpret guidelines provided by companies that are shaped by American legal frameworks and determinations of what online content, information and practices should entail. These forms of classification are then encoded into the systems such as Facebook, Amazon and Google, determining in part what information may or may not be censored or whether such information should be made available to a particular 'market segment'.

Alongside the invisible labour that contributes to determining how digital infrastructures and technologies mediate what we do and do not see, anthropologist Nick Seaver (2019) interrogates how we should approach the study of infrastructures such as algorithms. Like corporate anthropologists Thomas, Nafus and Sherman (2018), Seaver contends that the algorithm should not be understood as a monolith or an object that is fixed in space and time. Rather, he argues that algorithms are always 'enacted' and only become meaningful when we understand how differently positioned people engage with them. Seaver further suggests that algorithms are made meaningful through practice and that a range of different individuals are involved in shaping what algorithms mean – from those who we may recognize as having 'expertise' in algorithms such as engineers and computer scientists to governments, state-like entities such as humanitarian development organizations, marketers and others in a particular company or context who share a discursive understanding of what an algorithm does in the world. Importantly, and as we suggest elsewhere (Horst and Mohammid, forthcoming), this also includes the people who use devices and themselves imagine and engage with algorithmic recommendation systems. Despite this increasing attention to algorithms and other forms of automation (Besteman and Gusterson 2019, Horst, Baylosis and Mohammid, 2021; Knox and Nafus 2018; Mehta and Nafus 2016; Nafus and Sherman 2014; Seaver 2017), we are only at the beginning of understanding how technologies that rely upon algorithms, machine learning and Artificial Intelligence may be shaping our practices and worlds. Through attention to the study of algorithmic technologies and AI in contexts like the Caribbean that are rarely at the centre of new technologies, we challenge the homogeneity of assumptions and norms that emerge in algorithmic recommendation systems. At the same time, by centring decision-making processes rather than the technology, we highlight how people respond to and resist the inevitability of these systems to predict, or more aptly, recommend how people in different places and contexts make their worlds.

This chapter explores this new space of algorithms and associated automated decision-making technologies through the examination of a new fashion consumer product, the Amazon Echo Look (henceforth Echo Look). It focuses upon how women in Trinidad engaged with the Echo Look and the algorithmic recommendations the device provided. Through a closet ethnography, an innovative approach to researching everyday decision-making practices that involved a mediated diary study approach and traditional approaches in material culture studies (Horst, et al., 2021; Woodward, 2007), we situate our participants within the broader context of dress, clothing, and identity in Trinidad and the Caribbean. We then hone in on two issues that emerged in participants' interactions with the app and its associated device: algorithmic bias and misrecognition. Algorithmic bias occurred through the kinds of patterns, styles and silhouettes that were given primacy in the app and the associated recommendations that often failed to consider local contexts and aesthetics. More challenging, however, were the forms of misrecognition of brown and black bodies in the vision recognition software which, in some cases, rendered bodies invisible. We conclude by reflecting upon the necessity of media anthropology as a discipline to interrogate the norms and values that are reproduced in algorithmic and automated systems, particularly given the fact that they rely upon the further extraction of data from 'users' to sustain them.

Closet Ethnography: Dress, Clothing, and Identity in the Caribbean

Clothing and dress represent one the most important ways to understand cultural norms and values across different societies (Weiner and Schneider, 1989). From textiles, patterns and style to the examination of the global processes underpinning production, marketing, consumption and circulation (Hansen, 2000; Norris, 2010), anthropologists have focused upon the meanings and significance of clothing, style and dress across a range of contexts (Hansen, 2004). In a seminal article on the sociology of fashion, sociologist Joanna Entwistle (2000) conceptualizes the act of dressing as situated practice arguing that dress is not only an external shell but intimately intertwined with both the experience and presentation of the self. In many Western contexts presenting the self is a way of making what is often characterized as the true and internal self-visible on the body. However, in the Caribbean the self is made in and through the external body, what Daniel Miller (2013) characterizes as 'surface ontology'. The focus upon the surface of the body and associated notions of selfhood are closely linked to the historical realities that constituted modernity in the Caribbean and other parts of the African diaspora (Pearce, 2014). Transatlantic slavery worked to destroy connections and continuity between families and cultures and, in turn, set the conditions for the constitution of new forms of connection and new forms of institution building among Caribbean peoples.

Within this context, women's bodies and dress are key sites of control and commentary about moral values and the nation (Horst, 2011). In the Caribbean two concepts have often been used to describe gendered norms: 'respectability' and its counterpoint 'reputation' (Abrahams, 1983). Whereas the moral values associated with reputation have been linked to economic skill, men and the world outside the home, respectability is associated with proper manners, education, church membership and the institution of marriage. These values emerged in the transition from the plantation system to emancipation as the church sought to create a group of individuals and families who could carry out law and order and maintain a system of colonial-inspired morality. The new Creole class attended church, lived quiet, non-public lives, sent their children to private schools, trained children in the arts and restricted their access to the potential influence of lower status Jamaican children. While there is evidence of exceptions to and resistance of these norms (Besson, 2002), women were perceived to be responsible for maintaining order and cleanliness, a key marker of respectability (Sobo 1993; Smith 1988; Wilson, 1969, 1973). As such, the cleanliness of clothes, shoes and the skin of anyone leaving the home and yard reflected the moral order of the family and household.

The sense of morality around dress and the body also extended to women whose working lives took them outside of the home. Women working in civil service and 'professional' occupations were expected to differentiate themselves from women working in markets, bars, music venues or other settings (Cooper, 2004). A quintessential image is the country higgler who travelled in the early mornings on public transport to sell their wares in the market and were known for wearing long skirts which were perceived as cooler and made it easy to sit on the ground. T-shirts and other clothes could hide dirt and higglers often wore fabrics that could breathe in the hot sun of the day. At the other extreme is the display of women's bodies and sexuality associated with dancehall music which Cooper (2004) and others argue reflect Jamaican and other Caribbean women's resistance to Eurocentric notions of sexuality (Bakare-Yusuf, 2006). As we see in Carla Freeman's (2000) research with 'pink collar' workers in Barbados, it was not uncommon for women who worked in banks and other professional settings to be issued with dress codes which dictated the length of clothing like skirts or dresses, the need to polish shoes and iron clothes, or wear 'appropriate' jewellery and makeup.

Cabatingan's (2018) ethnographic work among professional women in the Trinidad-based Caribbean Court of Justice echoes Freeman's account of regulation of professional identity, although in their case appropriate clothes involved wearing suits and high heels and detailed attention to grooming. In the absence of any written policy, informal practices of enforcement were practised and managers faulted employees for wearing skirts or tops that were too tight, showing their arms or failing to wear a jacket even when outside of the office in the heat of the sun. Consistent with Cooper's (2004: 75) observations, this 'extraordinary attention on their extraordinary dressing' in Trinidad among professional women often resulted in spending a great deal of money to curate a professional look that ultimately functioned 'to distinguish its workers from those employed in more rote occupations, from those with no occupation at all, and from everyday life in general' (Cooper, 2004: 75). Nevertheless, curating a professional look had significant consequences for the possibilities of maintaining status or achieving social mobility.

Fashioning Silhouettes

The Echo Look was launched into the consumer market for limited release in 2017 and made fully available in the USA in 2018. It was marketed as a personal stylist tool and included a voice-activated camera and associated app that provided recommendations and outfit comparisons to give the user fashion advice based upon algorithmic material and fashion experts and was designed to help users make decisions about what to wear. Marketing scholar Zahy Ramadan (2019) suggests that the Echo Look represents a process of democratizing intangible luxury since the average user who can purchase the Echo Look (US$199) would never have access to customized advice and expertise daily. While the broader aspirations of the Echo Look were global, the first release was targeted at US clients who were familiar with the Amazon family of smart and home automation technologies. As designer Nassim Parvin (2019) highlights, the promotional ad of the Echo Look distinctly portrayed and targeted the device to successful upper-middle-class women who desired an on-demand personal stylist and would seamlessly add the device to their morning dressing routine. Like many US multicultural advertising campaigns (Davila, 2008; Shankar, 2012), the promotional material featured racially diverse women of different skin tones using the device in their everyday lives.

The Echo Look encouraged users to take photos as well as 360-degree videos of themselves to see their outfits from all angles. It also included a speaker and microphone whereby users could interact with the voice assistant Alexa and they could then gain feedback on the outfit as the device compared them using the Style Check feature on the app. To use Style Check, the user selected and put on two outfits for the device to compare and the device recommended an outfit by ranking it with a percentage preference. In addition, it provided a narrative outlining the reasons for the ranking on parameters such as outfit fit, shape or colour. To understand the ways in which our participants interpreted the use and meaning of the device, we began with an initial interview where participants described their dressing habits, their relationship with fashion and how this evolved throughout different phases of their lives. After reviewing materials provided about the device, participants often wanted to take some time to experiment with the best place to position the Echo Look to get the best quality photos in terms of lighting and the height where the device rested. Amazon had largely marketed the device as a solution for daily dressing dilemmas and decisions on what to wear, suggesting that users would get dressed with the device as part of their morning routine. We designed a diary study to capture these daily decisions and their use of the device. However, it became clear that our participants preferred to create an overview of their wardrobe where they could compare outfits, often on the weekends when they had more time. Rather than exploring the patterns and logic of their existing wardrobe as Woodward (2007) prioritized, participants were most interested in ascertaining trends in what the device thought looked best on them or what it rated as the best combinations of pieces in their wardrobe. Participants recounted their experiences and opinions to us through semi-structured in-person and online Zoom interviews. They also sent us pictures of the outfits and Style Check preferences on WhatsApp and their corresponding views on the Echo Look feedback, including the discussions they had with their peers or trusted friends regarding its feedback.

The women in our study noted the Echo Look was useful in providing recommendations and affirming the professionalism of their clothing choices. For example, Kim, a 46-year-old event planner of Chinese and Portuguese descent, considered fashion and the projection of a particular image to be essential in her professional life, part and parcel of the performance of confidence. Yet, unlike the values associated with the new Creole class, confidence meant owning rather than hiding or covering up one's own sexuality. This was not always straightforward, and she noted the tension between wanting to attract the right type of attention in the right context. One of the ways that Kim managed her performance of professionalism and confidence was through the cultivation of a desired silhouette. Kim believed there was a very clear idea of what a woman should look like and what would be perceived as 'sexy':

> In Trinidad they always used to be like the ideal figure was a 'thick girl'. You always say they always like to see meat on the woman … Growing up I was skinny. I felt inferior because I felt as if I need to put on weight … get a bigger butt [and] get more muscles in my legs. I needed to strive for this so then I would eat more protein and workout in the gym and try to build muscle, … up to today … I will always choose styles that would emphasize the hip or the butt part.

The curation of the body from having a skinny or 'magga' (in Caribbean parlance) figure to one that fits the more ideal image of a woman in Trinidad was a theme Kim discussed throughout her life. She recalled when tent dresses were in fashion, feeling that she was 'too skinny and looked like a tree, straight up and down'. To counter this look, she procured a thick piece of elastic to carve out a waist which would give herself more of a shape. She noted creating an hourglass shape had become a global trend in Western Culture with the popularity of Latin icons such as Jennifer Lopez and Shakira. Indeed, when she visited Miami or Los Angeles, the idealized curvy figure was more popular and she did not feel that it was about being fat or skinny per se but about proportions in the silhouette. For those who could not achieve this look, Kim believed that 'you have to make it up in some other way so your fashion … you had the best jewellery, and you had your best clothing and handbags and shoes'.

The Echo Look and the Style Check feature created the proportions she desired: to be nipped in and flared at the bottom to create an illusion of more curves. Kim had curated her wardrobe to include a variety of short dresses that fit that silhouette. She used Echo Look as an opportunity to choose what she looked best in and might give her 'an edge'. She imagined that she could use these recommendations to get noticed by social media at Carnival fetes. In many ways, Kim noted that the Echo Look review often confirmed what she had originally thought. She appreciated this and started to develop trust in the device. In fact, when the Echo Look rated a pair of shorts poorly, she decided to stop wearing them to the gym. She also realized that her husband had been telling her that those shorts were not the best fit for her for years, but she had only taken that advice seriously when Echo Look provided the feedback. Kim was pleased that the Echo Look's recommendations were aligned with her own. She relished its capacity to help her refine her wardrobe and to perform the kind of confidence and sexuality to which she aspired.

Whereas Kim's professionalism and confidence involved the curation of a silhouette that reflected her sexuality, other workplaces require different performances and dress codes. Jamilla, for example, was a 28-year-old Trinidadian woman of African descent who lived in Port of Spain and worked as a quantity surveyor in a local construction firm. Jamilla enjoyed getting dressed up and wearing dresses in her active social life in the capital, but her wardrobe at work was constrained. As she worked in a male-dominated industry and was younger than many of her male colleagues, she felt that it was necessary to downplay her sexuality to avoid unwanted attention. As she described,

> Most times you will be the only female on site, so you don't want to draw any attention unnecessarily because you know how things go … so you try to be as low key as possible, not to draw any attention because you just want to go, you want to get your job done. You want to be professional.

At work she deliberately wore long-sleeved shirts and never wore dresses or skirts. In the past she felt uncomfortable because of comments from construction workers at the sites she had to visit for work. In effect, Jamilla adapted her wardrobe into a binary of conservative, simple jeans and shirts for work and more form-fitting dresses for her life outside of work.

Importantly, Jamilla's job required her to downplay her sexuality, but outside of work she was still expected to display the fact that she was a professional. She felt that looking good in Trinidad was extremely important to many of her peers. In her life outside of work she wore form-fitting clothes that created 'that sexy vibe'. But overall, Jamilla felt that her fashion journey outside of work had evolved from youthful into her dressing more maturely. This was not about looking older but, rather, to demand respect and be treated as a 'big woman'. She felt that being a 'big woman' in Trinidad conferred autonomy, authority and the opportunity to assert oneself. Achieving this status involved finding the right combination of fashion and makeup while still looking professional and natural. It meant that someone did not seem like they were trying too hard but rather dressed, acted and performed with effortless confidence. Projecting confidence was key to being treated with respect. Being a 'big woman' meant that a woman was able to convey a sense of fashion while finding her own style and not seeming too contrived. Jamilla found that the Echo Look was useful in recommending clothing that would assist her in dressing like 'big woman' and, in turn, achieve the confidence and professionalism necessary to move forward in life.

Visibility and Misrecognition

A growing body of literature on algorithms within and beyond media anthropology draws attention to the implications of using existing data sets and algorithms to inform and, in the cases of more complex systems, influence how recommendations and information appear. From the emergence of filter bubbles in our communication practices to decisions about if and how healthcare should be provided (Obermeyer, 2019; Noor, 2020) to shaping the ways in which people are recommended in job searches or criminal justice decisions (Silberg and Manyika, 2019), the data sets that inform algorithms introduce and reinforce bias by using information that predicts an outcome for a particular population that is uncritically applied to another population or context (Osoba and Welser, 2017; van Nuenen et al, 2020). Sociologist Eszter Hargittai (2020), for example, argues that big data often draws from social media sites used by more privileged populations and/or those with better media skills; these have implications for the kinds of conclusions that can be drawn from particular social media sites to inform public opinion or public policy. Indeed, one of the fundamental biases that we see being reproduced and amplified in AI systems is data discrimination (Noble, 2019; Crawford, 2021). Building upon the long history of bias in visual technologies such as cameras which used white women as the metric to determine colour balance (Roth, 2009) and other forms of structural racism that inform the coding of data sets, the digital media industry continues to perpetuate forms of misrecognition, low recognition and classification inaccuracy for non-white populations who use or are subjected to or using facial recognition technology (Furl et al., 2002; Lohr, 2018), such as the Echo Look (Garvie and Frankle, 2016).

The Echo Look used photography and other visual recognition technology. While we can see in the previous cases that these 360-degree views of the body are valued by people who use the device, some participants reported that their experiences left them feeling misunderstood, misrepresented or even unseen. Our first example of misrecognition returns to Jamilla. Jamilla enjoyed the Style Check feedback and saw it as skill-building enabling her to acquire knowledge on how to dress her body in more optimal ways to flatter her build, shape and skin tone. While this aspect of the device led to a fruitful interaction, there were some aspects of the Echo Look that she did not like. She was frustrated that the device restricted particular items of clothing. Jamilla tried on bikinis and wanted to take advantage of the 360-degree view to see all the sides of her body. Rather than taking the picture and evaluating the two swimsuits, the Echo Look did not allow her to compare a bikini and threatened to ban her from adding further images if she did not follow community guidelines. As she described,

> One of the instances was with … the black bikini. One of them was with the coverup and one was without the coverup. But I noticed that it compared the picture with the coverup with another picture, so I think that that one was fine because I was not exposed. But in trying to compare the bikini with the one-piece or the bikini with anything else or the one-piece with anything else, it didn't take that comparison … It said 'we could not complete your Style Check. Make sure your photos follow our community guidelines. If this problem continues, we will not allow you to submit images to Style Check.'

Jamilla was perturbed that the Echo Look would not allow her to use Style Check and found it difficult to even discern what the 'community guidelines' were especially because she had not joined a community or shared her account with anyone else. As she summarized,

> The fact that they would ban us, so something like that from the Style Check for submitting something that's just natural to our sense of style in Trinidad is kind of disappointing and a little unnecessary. And they didn't even say why it's not appropriate. It just said, you know, don't compare that again or don't come back on the app, basically. It should be something limitless and something so much broader than restricting something so simple as a bathing suit. As a bikini … it is your style they're trying to collect data on. So, you can't really collect data on somebody's style if you're restricting what they could wear on the app.

She thought that the device was extremely useful in the feedback for professional and mature looks, but it did not allow her to compare all the types of clothes she wanted to wear. Jamilla felt it was a shame because the device played a role in enhancing how she built her outfits and finding new proportions and dressing styles. While her overall experience with the Echo Look was positive and she wanted to use it again, issues of censorship and the lack of recognition that other participants experienced led her to question the overarching values embedded in the device. As she stridently argued, the Echo Look practised censorship and she wondered whether there was a gendered dimension to this issue. She questioned whether a man posing in a swimsuit like a Speedo would be treated the same way.

Our next participant, Tamar, was a 25-year-old teacher of African descent who lived in Port of Spain. Having finished university, she was focused upon building her career and establishing a wardrobe that complemented an image as a young professional (Miller and Sinanan, 2017; Miller, 2003). As a Christian, a key aim of her dressing was to find outfits that were both modest, flattering and accentuated her curves, but she avoided clothing that showed her cleavage, was too high or too exposed. In her discussions of attitudes to clothing she recalled a particular instance of an uncle sending her home to change because of the short, fitted pants she was wearing to go on a holiday in Tobago. She was upset but felt that, in retrospect, the pants were probably too form-fitting. As Tamar synthesized her aesthetic, she wanted clothes that would be 'flattering' but not ones that would 'make me look straight or look like I'm in a box ... Yes, I want to be modest, but then I'm ... also a woman.'

Tamar was not fond of the camera. She thought that it distorted her shape in an unflattering way, describing 'how it blurs out the background and puts you in the foreground ... None of those look good. Like, it doesn't look like my actual shape, like the shape of my body that I would like to see in the mirror.' In response, Tamar adjusted the device to find a position that would take pictures that she felt better represented what she would see in the mirror and were a more positive reflection of what she looked like. Tamar's enthusiasm was dampened when she noticed that the Echo Look did not identify that she was present in one of her early attempts to take a picture of herself. She questioned whether its failure to distinguish her silhouette from the background was attributed to her race and darker skin colour.

With her enthusiasm for the device dwindling, Tamar also confessed that she was ambivalent about the choices that the Style Check app recommended. In ranking dresses that were cinched at the waist and more form-fitting higher than other options, she observed that it was gravitating to a slimmer silhouette. In effect, the device assumed that the aim was to look slimmer, which she felt was a flawed assumption. As she summarized,

> It's assuming that you want a slimmer silhouette, less curves, less flare, ...clothes that are not straighter in terms of just boxy, but clothes that generally tend to be more fitting. I believe that's what it's looking for. So, like with my flared dress, it didn't really choose that. If I chose something that was more flattering to my figure ... it doesn't take into consideration me, like my personal preferences. It's comparing me basically using its algorithm and how do I know that your algorithm is as inclusive as it should be, you know?

When she realized the device was primarily marketed to US consumers, Tamar was even more convinced that this was a flaw as US women also had different body types, ethnicities and a diversity of ways in which women wanted to present their bodies. Indeed, there has been a call for greater workplace diversity in high tech industries to recognize and reduce bias in algorithmic design and execution to tackle what sociologist Nichol Turner Lee (2018) argues is an embedded bias that both implicitly and explicitly causes harm to historically disadvantaged populations. We turn to the implications of bias and recognition in the next section.

Algorithmic Silhouettes in Context

In her article on fashion and the body in the Caribbean, Cultural Studies scholar Marsha Pearce (2014) applies Entwistle's framing to argue that clothing in Trinidad is used by people to refashion themselves. Pearce questions how personhood in Trinidad is constructed through fashion and cultural assumptions that 'Clothing became a strategy of subversion in the colonial era – a tactic of making sub-people look like people' (Pearce, 2014: 859) As she underscores:

> The idea of nothing becoming something signals a key point of engagement ... that of 'a no*body*' becoming 'some*body*.' I give deliberate emphasis to 'body' here as a means of maintaining a linkage between the somatic dimension, clothing and acts of dressing.
>
> *Pearce, 2014: 863*

The use of the Echo Look in Trinidad demonstrated how women managed their dressing as situated practice in complex negotiations of their presence and presentation of selves. This included contextual (de)codifications and fashioning their silhouettes through cultural sensitivity of what would be considered conservative, vulgar, professional, socially confident (Mohammid, 2017; Sinanan, 2017) and ultimately enabled them to achieve their aspirations. The silhouette was then constructed and experienced as intertwined with a range of intimate personal and cultural meanings. The Echo Look demonstrated the challenge of creating an aspirational silhouette through construction of normative body images. Some participants were able to successfully negotiate this while others felt unseen or challenged when they were trying to achieve a particular silhouette. Participants regularly noted that they would prefer greater dialogue with the device (Horst and Mohammid, forthcoming). Through listening and learning, the Echo Look may tailor the recommendations to an individual's preferences rather than assuming what they would like.

Taking a device like the Echo Look out of the US context and into the closets of women in Trinidad highlights the complexities of moving algorithmic- (and machine learning-) based technologies to different populations and cultural contexts. As feminist design scholar Nassim Parvin (2019) explains this tension,

> The normative judgment of Alexa substantiates the pitfalls of a code that is simultaneously absolutist and relativistic. It is absolutist in the sense of assuming that a universal set of principles could provide the basis for fashion choices, therefore undermining individual and cultural diversities in fashion expression … It is relativistic in the sense that it looks to majority opinion to identify and fix this universal code, elevating already powerful voices.

A key issue highlighted throughout the chapter is how the idea, ideology and reification of an idealized silhouette is embroiled in complex negotiations about norms and values around sexuality, confidence and professionalism, and the ways in which these might change across contexts. Journalist Khari Johnson (2018) has critiqued the inescapability of the human gaze in the Echo Look's recommendations and the inherent bias that this confers. He argues that, despite Amazon's efforts to train specialists to broaden the definitions of fashion, there has still been the challenge of a recognizable level of homogeneity in styling preferences. Johnson further contends that the fashion specialists assigned to direct the Echo Look's decision-making came from similar backgrounds that mainly included young women living in the Seattle area with employment history at companies like J. Crew, Nordstrom and Zulily. Other scholars have drawn attention to the perceived aesthetics of whiteness in AI (Phan, 2019) and the need to decolonize the field through the integration of different perspectives and voices into the design teams (Adams, 2021; Cave and Dihal, 2020). MIT's Algorithmic Justice lab is also systematically developing processes to hold commercial companies accountable for bias (Raji and Buolamwini, 2019). Such initiatives examine the gendered, racial and other forms of bias that underpin particular data sets (Buolamwini and Gebru, 2018), and their application in different socio-cultural contexts. While it is clear that algorithms and automation reproduce structural inequality, we need analysis that can give feedback to designers and others at particular points in the life of algorithms and automation processes.

Conclusion

In his article in *Big Data & Society*, Seaver (2019) distinguishes between two key orientations to researching algorithms. The first approach, what he refers to as *algorithms in culture*, 'hinges on the idea that algorithms are discrete objects that may be located within cultural contexts or brought into conversation with cultural concerns' (Seaver, 2019: 4). By contrast, Seaver suggests an alternative conception when he argues for an approach to understanding *algorithms as culture* because they 'are composed of collective human practices' and, as such, recognize the ways in which people from different perspectives and contexts work to make and unmake algorithms in their everyday lives. From an *algorithms in culture* perspective, one could argue that the Echo Look and the associated recommendations failed to take into account specific contexts and aesthetics. Instead, the recommendations were positioned as set principles and norms for codes of dress and, as such, failed to deliver upon Amazon's marketing promise of personalized recommendations as the device was used in and among Trinidadians. By contrast, an *algorithms as culture* approach might account for the ways in which forms of misrecognition that were both cultural and technological in nature appeared; not being able to detect black and brown bodies and censoring particular styles normalizes particular values, as our participants very clearly articulated.

From our vantagepoint, media anthropologists interested in algorithms should aspire to what we might conceptualize as a *social life of algorithms* approach. Following Dourish (2016) and others (e.g. Dourish and Cruz, 2018), a *social life of algorithms* approach acknowledges the dynamic and relational dimensions of a particular device, app or service employing algorithms at a particular point in time. It attends to the ways in which a particular algorithm is embedded within social and cultural processes, be these in settings such as companies or other contexts where particular values become normative. Through processes such as circulation, it draws attention to the different forms that algorithms may take, whether this is mediated through data, coders and designers or the feedback that is received from people who use or engage with a particular algorithm over time, such as interpreting data and algorithmic recommendations. It also leaves space for reuse, recycling or end of life processes as we experienced with the Amazon Echo Look itself which was discontinued in mid-2020 and integrated into the Amazon Echo Show app. But most importantly, a *social life of algorithms* approach enables us to analyse and understand the relationships between algorithms and power. Whether this involves the power to design and 'decide' what people can see through an algorithmic process, the ghost work that contributes to these systems or the increasing use of algorithms to influence and even make when employed by institutions, governments and state agencies, companies and others. What remains important about this framework is making the entire social life – or phases in its life – visible in order to challenge the sense of inevitability that often comes with new and future technologies. Only through media anthropologists' continued commitment to de-centring the North American and European canon by integrating the diverse experiences of differently positioned individuals and communities can we continue the tradition of Faye Ginsburg and others who employ media anthropology to make alternative media worlds.

References

Abrahams, R. (1983) *The Man-of-words in the West Indies: Performance and the Emergence of Creole Culture*, Baltimore: Johns Hopkins University Press.

Adams, R. (2021) 'Can Artificial Intelligence Be Decolonized?' *Interdisciplinary Science Reviews*, 46(1–2): 176–197.

Bakare-Yusuf, B. (2006) 'Fabricating Identities: Survival and the Imagination in Jamaican Dancehall Culture. Fashion Theory,' *The Journal of Dress, Body & Culture*, 10(4): 461–483.

Besson, J. (2002) *Martha Brae's Two Histories: European Expansion and Caribbean Culture-building in Jamaica*, Chapel Hill: University of North Carolina Press.

Besteman, C. and Gusterson, H. (Eds.). (2019) *Life by Algorithms: How Roboprocesses Are Remaking Our World*, Chicago: University of Chicago Press.

Buolamwini, J. and Gebru, T. (2018) "Gender Shades: Intersectional Accuracy Disparities in Commercial Gender Classification," *Proceedings of Machine Learning Research*, 81:1–15, Conference on Fairness, Accountability, and Transparency.

Cabatingan, L. (2018) 'Fashioning the Legal Subject: Popular Justice and Courtroom Attire in the Caribbean,' *PoLAR: Political and Legal Anthropology Review*, 41(S1): 69–84.

Cave, S. and Dihal, K. (2020) 'The Whiteness of AI,' *Philosophy and Technology*, 33: 685–703.

Clarke, A. and Miller, D. (2002) 'Fashion and Anxiety,' *Fashion Theory*, 6(2): 191–213. doi:10.2752/136270402778869091

Cooper, C. (2004) *Lady Saw Cuts Loose, In: Sound Clash*, New York: Palgrave Macmillan.

Crawford, K. (2021) *The Atlas of AI*, New Haven: Yale University Press.

Davila, A. (2008) *Latino Spin: Public Image and the Whitewashing of Race*, New York: NYU Press.

Dourish, P. (2016) 'Algorithms and their Others: Algorithmic Culture in Context,' *Big Data and Society*, 3(2): 1–11.

Dourish, P. and Gómez Cruz, E. (2018) 'Datafication and Data Fiction: Narrating Data and Narrating with Data,' *Big Data & Society*, 5(2): doi:10.1177/2053951718784083

Entwistle, J. (2000) 'Fashion and the Fleshy Body: Dress as Embodied Practice,' *Fashion Theory*, 4(3): 323–347.

Entwistle, J. (2009) *The Aesthetic Economy of Fashion: Markets and Value in Clothing and Modelling*, Oxford: Berg.

Foster, R. and Horst, H., Eds. (2018) *The Moral Economy of Mobile Phones: Pacific Perspectives*, Canberra: ANU Press.

Furl, N., Phillips, P. J. and O'Toole, A. J. (2002) 'Face Recognition Algorithms and the Other-race Effect: Computational Mechanisms for a Developmental Contact Hypothesis,' *Cognitive Science*, 26(6): 797–815.

Freeman, C. (2000) *High Tech and High Heels in the Global Economy: Women, Work, and Pink-collar Identities in the Caribbean*, Durham: Duke University Press.

Garvie, C. and Frankle, J. (2016) 'Facial-recognition Software Might Have a Racial Bias Problem,' *The Atlantic*, 7. www.theatlantic.com/technology/archive/2016/04/the-underlying-bias-of-facial-recognition-systems/476991/

Geismar, H. and Knox, H., Eds (2021) *Digital Anthropology*, 2nd Edition, Oxford: Routledge.

Gray, M. L. and Suri, S. (2019) *Ghost Work: How to Stop Silicon Valley from Building a New Global Underclass*, New York: Eamon Dolan Books.

Hansen, K. (2004) 'The World in Dress: Anthropological Perspectives on Clothing, Fashion, and Culture,' *Annual Review of Anthropology*, 34: 369–392.

Hansen, K. (2000) *Salaula: The World of Secondhand Clothing and Zambia*, Chicago: University of Chicago Press.

Hargittai, E. (2020) 'Potential Biases in Big Data: Omitted Voices on Social Media,' *Social Science Computer Review*, 38(1): 10–24.

Horst, H. (2011) 'Reclaiming Place: The Architecture of Home, Family and Migration,' *Anthropologica: Journal of the Canadian Anthropological Society*, 53(1): 29–39.

Horst, H. (2013) 'The Infrastructures of Mobile Media: Towards a Future Research Agenda,' *Mobile Media and Communication*, 1: 147–152.

Horst, H. and Miller, D. (2006) *The Cell Phone: An Anthropology of Communication*, New York: Berg Publications.

Horst, H. and Miller, D., Eds. (2013) *Digital Anthropology*, 1st Edition. London: Bloomsbury.

Horst, H. and Mohammid, S. (Forthcoming) 'Automated Decision-Making in Everyday Life: Learning with the Amazon Echo Look,' in S. Pink et al. (Eds.) *Everyday Automation*, London: Routledge.

Horst, H. and Sinanan, J. (2021) 'Digital Housekeeping: Living with Data,' *New Media & Society*, 23(4): 834–852.

Horst, H., Sinanan, J. and Hjorth, L. (2021) 'Storing and Sharing: Everyday Relationships with Digital Material,' *New Media & Society*, 23(4): 657–671.

Horst, H. A., Baylosis, C. and Mohammid, S. (2021) 'Looking Professional: How Women Decide What to Wear with and Through Automated Technologies,' *Convergence*, 27(5): 1250–1263.

Johnson, K. (2018) 'Amazon's Echo Look Fashion Assistant Lacks Critical Context,' *Venture Beat*, available at https://venturebeat.com/2018/08/03/amazons-echo-look-fashion-assistant-lacks-critical-context/ (accessed September 12, 2021).

Knox, H. and Dawn, N. (2018) *Ethnography for a Data-Saturated World*, Manchester: Manchester University Press.

Lee, N. T. (2018) 'Detecting Racial Bias in Algorithms and Machine Learning,' *Journal of Information, Communication and Ethics in Society*, 16(3): 252–260.

Lohr, S. (2018) 'Facial Recognition Is Accurate, if You're a White Guy,' *New York Times*, 9(8): 283.

Mehta, R. and Nafus, D. (2016) 'Atlas of Caregiving Pilot Study Report,' *San Francisco: Family Caregiver Alliance*. Retrieved November 10, 2021.

Miller, D. and Sinanan, J. (2017) *Visualising Facebook: A Comparative Perspective*, London: UCL Press.

Miller, D. (2003) 'Fashion and ontology in Trinidad,' in *Design and Aesthetics*, Oxford: Routledge, 143–169.

Mohammid, S. (2017) *Digital Media, Learning and Social Confidence: An Ethnography of a Small Island, Knowledge Society* (Doctoral dissertation, RMIT University).

Noble, S. (2019) *Algorithms of Oppression: How Search Engines Reinforce Racism*, New York: NYU Press.

Norris, L. (2010) *Recycling Indian Clothing: Global Contexts of Reuse and Value*, Bloomington, Indiana University Press.

Noor, P. (2020) 'Can We Trust AI Not to Further Embed Racial Bias and Prejudice?' *BMJ*, 368.

Obermeyer, Z., Powers, B., Vogeli, C. and Mullainathan, S. (2019) 'Dissecting Racial Bias in an Algorithm Used to Manage the Health of Populations,' *Science*, 366(6464): 447–453.

Osoba, O. A. and Welser IV, W. (2017) *An Intelligence in Our Image: The Risks of Bias and Errors in Artificial Intelligence*, Santa Monica, CA: Rand Corporation.

Parvin, N. (2019) 'Look Up and Smile! Seeing through Alexa's Algorithmic Gaze,' *Catalyst: Feminism, Theory, Technoscience*, 5(1): 1–11.

Pearce, M. (2014) 'Looking Like People; Feeling Like People: The Black Body, Dress and Aesthetic Therapy in the Caribbean,' *Culture Unbound*, 6(4): 857–872.

Phan, T. (2019) 'Amazon Echo and the Aesthetics of Whiteness,' *Catalyst: Feminism, Theory, Technoscience*, 5(1): 1–38.

Pink, S., Lanzeni, D. and Horst, H. (2018) 'Data Anxieties: Finding Trust in Everyday Digital Mess,' *Big Data & Society*, 5(1): doi:10.1177/2053951718756685

Raji, I. and Buolamwini, J. (2019) Actionable Auditing: Investigating the Impact of Publicly Naming Biased Performance Results of Commercial AI Products. *Proceedings of the 2019 AAAI/ACM Conference on AI, Ethics, and Society*, 429–435.

Ramadan, Z. (2019) 'The Democratization of Intangible Luxury,' *Marketing Intelligence & Planning*, 37(6): 660–673.

Roth, L. (2009) 'Looking at Shirley, the Ultimate Norm: Colour Balance, Image Technologies, and Cognitive Equity,' *Canadian Journal of Communication* 34(1): 111–136.

Silberg, J. and Manyika, J. (2019) 'Notes from the AI frontier: Tackling bias in AI (and in humans),' *McKinsey Global Institute (June 2019)*. www.mckinsey.com/~/media/mckinsey/featured%20insights/artificial%20intelligence/tackling%20bias%20in%20artificial%20intelligence%20and%20in%20humans/mgi-tackling-bias-in-ai-june-2019.ashx

Seaver, N. (2017) 'Algorithms as Culture: Some Tactics for the Ethnography of Algorithmic Systems,' *Big Data & Society*, 4(2): doi:10.1177/2053951717738104

Seaver, N. (2019) 'Captivating Algorithms: Recommender Systems as Traps,' *Journal of Material Culture*, 24(4): 421–436.

Shankar, S. (2012) 'Creating Model Consumers: Producing Ethnicity, Race, and Class in Asian American Advertising,' *American Ethnologist*, 39: 578–591.

Sinanan, J. (2017) *Social Media in Trinidad*, London: UCL Press, 250.

Smith, R.T. (1988) *Kinship and Class in the West Indies: Modern Marriage and other Arrangements*, London: Cambridge University Press.

Sobo, E. J. (1993) *One Blood: The Jamaican Body*, New York: SUNY Press.

Thomas, L., Nafus D. and Sherman J. (2018) 'Algorithms as Fetish: Faith and Possibility in Algorithmic Work,' *Big Data & Society*. January 2018.

van Nuenen, T., Ferrer, X., Such, J. M. and Coté, M. (2020) 'Transparency for Whom? Assessing Discriminatory Artificial Intelligence,' *Computer*, 53(11): 36–44.

Weiner, A. and Schneider, J. (1989) *Cloth and the Human Experience*, Washington DC: Smithsonian Institution Press.
Wilson, P. J. (1969) 'Reputation and Respectability: A Suggestion for Caribbean ethnology,' *Man*, 4(1): 70–84.
Wilson, P. J. (1973) *Crab Antics: The Social Anthropology of English-Speaking. Negro Societies of the Caribbean*, London: Yale University Press.
Woodward, S. (2007) *Why Women Wear What They Wear*, Oxford: Berg.

38
UNLOCKING HERITAGE *IN SITU*

Tourist Places and Augmented Reality in Estonia

Christian S. Ritter

Augmented reality technologies have intermittently caught the attention of anthropologists over the last decade (e.g. Boellstorff, 2011; 2014). Since the infrastructures of their production are opaque and widely unknown, the situated interfaces of augmented reality apps installed on smartphones serve as entry points for much ethnographic research. Recent anthropological investigations into these emerging technologies have mainly evaluated the educational potential of augmented reality apps (e.g. Simeone and Iaconesi, 2011; Fuentes, 2017) or place-making practices facilitated by the mobile phone game *Pokémon GO* (e.g. Denyer-Simmons, 2016; Hjorth and Richardson, 2017). In contrast to ethnographic studies of fully developed augmented reality apps, the research on which I report in this chapter casts light on design practices shaping augmented reality apps and the transformative role of these emerging technologies in the construction of tourism imaginaries. The theoretical approach of this investigation draws on the anthropology of smartphones, providing a holistic assessment of the development of smartphone apps and their implementation in the media ecology of tourist places. Such a socio-technical ecology entails production sites, code repositories, heritage objects, data infrastructures, places of usage, tourists, heritage workers, and app makers. As I explore in the chapter, the locative interfaces of the researched augmented reality apps facilitate touristic flânerie while setting in motion personal re-imaginings about people and places among tourists. In contemporary tourism, augmented reality technologies predominately occur as apps nested in the versatile smartphone. This global technology has been intensively assessed in recent years, and anthropological studies have approached the smartphone, inter alia, as a technology for maintaining close relationships (e.g. Horst, 2021), a multisensory device for photo-sharing (Fors, 2015), a means of facilitating smart aging (e.g. Garvey and Miller, 2021), or a place-making device (Waltorp, 2017). Exploring the mobile media ecology of Estonian tourist places in depth. this investigation demystifies how smartphones become technologies of emplacement.

There is already a considerable body of research that examines the manifold uses of augmented reality (e.g. Yu et al., 2009; Kim et al., 2018). Augmented reality technologies superimpose digital images onto a live view through a smartphone camera or smart glasses. Whereas augmented reality enhances the human vision against a shifting background of physical environments, virtual reality enables a completely simulated immersive experience. By the early 1990s, functioning prototypes of augmented reality solutions had been developed for work environments and theatre productions. Since the beginning of the 2010s, the utilisation of augmented reality technologies has burgeoned in a myriad of other contexts, including museums (e.g. Zeya, Wu, and Li, 2018), educational institutions (e.g. Bacca et al., 2014), hospitals (e.g. Zhu et al., 2014), family life (Saker and Evans, 2021) and tourist places (e.g. Wei, Ren, and O'Neill, 2014; Johnston et al., 2020). Although augmented reality features were implemented in head-mounted displays and laptops as early as the 1990s, it was the rise in the use of mobile devices that made these features accessible to mass audiences. Crucially, the ubiquity of the smartphone in everyday life opened up new possibilities for augmented reality technology to converge with mobile phone games (Keogh, 2017). However, the ways in which augmented reality apps transform the experiences of tourist places have not yet received sufficient scholarly attention. The augmented reality apps in this study reshaped how tourists make sense of heritage objects and embody imaginings about Estonia's maritime history. The constant presence of mundane software on smartphones paved the way for the appification of numerous realms of experience, including travel and tourism (Morris and Murray, 2018: 9). This exploratory chapter sets out to trace the transformations of tourism imaginaries through augmented reality apps in the Estonian context. Drawing on long-term fieldwork in Estonia, I address the following questions about the role of smartphone apps in tourist places: How do local app makers put into practice their design aspirations for creating augmented reality apps for Estonian tourist sites? In what ways do augmented reality apps represent cultural heritages? And, finally, how can answers to these empirical questions provide insights into the reordering of tourist imaginaries about Estonia through augmented reality technology?

The methodology of the investigation combined in-depth interviews with participant observation in tourist places, at professional events and on digital platforms. During the summer and winter holiday seasons of 2018 and 2019, I immersed myself in numerous Estonian tourist places where the researched apps were implemented. By taking part in guided tours, I investigated how tourists made use of smartphones during their travels. In total, I spent eight months in Etonian tourist sites. Since tourist places are in many ways fleeting phenomena, anthropological tourism researchers have often been required to carry out their fieldwork in multiple short spells (Graburn, 2002: 20). The observational roles that I took on resembled the daily experiences of local professionals as, for example, I regularly helped out at stalls during local festivals in Tallinn's Old Town. Furthermore, I studied the off-season routines of local tourism professionals and made contact with Estonian app developers while attending numerous start-up events and industry conferences. In addition to my boots-on-the-ground presence in local places, I studied the skilled practices of app makers through co-presence on digital platforms (Beaulieu, 2010; Pink et al., 2018). For instance, I participated in conversations on Slack channels, Unity forums, and the Twitter spaces #gamedev and #indiedev. Hiring a desk in co-working spaces in Tallinn and Tartu enabled me to shadow the daily practices of app makers. In doing so, I could gather priceless information about the versioning, production cycles and developer platforms for augmented reality apps. The participant observation in Estonian tourist sites was complemented by walkthroughs of app interfaces (Light, 2017; Light, Burgess, and Duguay, 2018; Ritter, 2021). In addition, I conducted interviews with six Estonian tourism professionals and four app makers. The first part of the chapter dives into the world of app makers and is followed by a detailed analysis of the representation of maritime heritage in augmented reality apps. Ultimately, the chapter argues that the researched app makers forged augmented reality technologies capable of emplacing experiences of Estonian heritage objects and instigating re-imaginings of cultural heritages among tourists.

Christian S. Ritter

Making Apps for Tourist Sites

At 5 pm on one particular Friday afternoon, the small square in the heart of Telliskivi Loomelinnak rapidly fills with young people eager to start their weekend. This area of Tallinn is home to numerous cultural establishments, including an alternative theatre and a photo gallery. Surrounding three-storey buildings are decorated with street art. Every Friday evening, clubs and bars open their doors, transforming the area into a nightlife district. Residing in Estonia's capital during the investigation enabled me to participate in the occasional get-togethers of local app developers. While attending these meetings, I could identify the online forums where they share their professional skills and visions. One of Estonia's largest co-working spaces is located in Telliskivi Loomelinnak, hosting numerous small start-up companies. Many of those sharing the two open-plan offices and four meeting rooms are programmers. On this occasion, I attend a panel discussion on the future of app design. Small crowds have already formed in several corners of the large lobby area. Free drinks and snacks are offered on a large wooden table. The expert panel is already seated on a stage. A CEO of a local start-up presents her experiences from a business trip to Japan, allowing her to meet with colleagues from Japanese companies developing games and transportation apps. All panel members passionately debate two contrasting design models emphasizing either user experiences (UX) or interface design (UI). After a 90-minute discussion, the attendees engage in informal chats over a drink while house music plays in the background. The panel discussion is part of a series of events bringing together different players from the local developer scene. The event has an intentionally casual atmosphere as the start-up scene seeks to remove bureaucratic hurdles that may hinder the smooth circulation of ideas and skills.

As apps are embedded in global infrastructures of production and distribution, ethnographic studies of smartphone cultures can oscillate between the global and local, but also between surface and deeper structures (Coman and Rothenbuhler, 2005: 9). Based on an immersion in the Estonian start-up scene, I examine how local app makers put into practice their design aspirations for creating augmented reality apps for Estonian tourist places. Anchored in specific local contexts of production (e.g. Suchman, 2011, Pink, 2014), the skilled practices of app makers are directed towards tools and materials. To forge app interfaces, they need to master a specific digital craft (DeNicola, 2016: 35). Apps are experienced as a series of interfaces, including dynamic maps, menus, and buttons. In the Estonian context, apps which involved dynamic maps and components of pathfinder games were widely considered precursors of augmented reality apps to be used in tourist sites. Tourists devote much of their time to laid-back flânerie while observing local sceneries. Such touristic flânerie can be significantly enhanced by locative media, which enables users to experience data, sounds, and images about specific geo-tagged locations, on the go. Locative app interfaces are nested in portable devices, which are equipped with a microprocessor and multiple sensors. These interfaces help users navigate unknown locations and frequently involve map-based games.

A walkthrough analysis of the app *Secret Path* illustrates how app making transitioned from apps enhancing touristic flânerie to those employing augmented reality in the Estonian context. Following a boot screen and a user registration, the first central interface was a dynamic map of Tallinn's Old Town. A pin indicated the actual location of the user on a medieval-style map. Ornaments on the app interfaces and music amplified the medieval ambience of the tourist places. The app guided its users to tourist attractions such as St. Catherine's Dominican Monastery. For each attraction, users could unlock textual information and a photographic puzzle, receiving gold coins for correct answers. Designers of augmented reality components mostly integrate a reward culture building on partially hidden information and additional pleasures while searching discovery points in the game play (McCrea, 2017: 44). QR codes embedded in the app interfaces could be activated to redeem the gold coins for discounts in local businesses, such as cafés, bars or souvenir shops. Another interface, which was developed as a minimal viable feature, was labelled "AR prototype test". While switching to camera mode, this interface displayed the overlaid object of a treasure chest against the background of the actual urban environment. By shaking the phone, gold coins fell out of the virtual chest, which could then be collected by the user.

Whereas traditional mass media were famously conceived as sensorial extensions of the human nervous system (McLuhan, 1964), the widespread use of handheld mobile devices has complicated the socio-technical dynamics of touristic flânerie. Smartphones and tablets incorporate their very own sensorial capacities, including location trackers, ambient light sensors, biometric sensors, magnetometers, accelerometers, gyroscopes, and camera lenses. Due to their numerous sensorial default features, handheld devices generate data about their whereabouts and orientation. Locations are primarily defined by fixed geographical coordinates, but can also take on complex, multi-faceted identities (de Souza e Silva and Frith, 2012: 78). Converging with location-aware apps, mobile phones and tablets act as locative media and make possible media practices that are functionally bound to a location (Wilken and Goggin, 2015: 3). Augmented reality apps amplify the capacities of smartphones by enabling emplaced experiences. Touristic flânerie is elevated by the exquisite experiences of animated content superimposed onto urban landscapes. While users direct their smartphone cameras over the surrounding environments, the augmented reality technology can recognise geo-tagged locations or shapes of markers to trigger the emergence of animated objects and characters. The experience of these animated features is emplaced by the interfaces of the smartphone app, since users are guided to such "discovery points" on embedded maps.

During my investigation into tourism media in Estonia, I quickly realised that local app makers regularly received support at incubator events. Furthermore, they received seed funds through a governmental initiative, encouraging them to commence the production of innovative apps. Digital design entails an affinity to reflection-in-action, and makers of digital artefacts mainly deploy a reflective production process, including iterative sequences of modifications to their various components (Salen, 2007: 302). Local app makers were predominately committed to a Kanban-based, data-driven design process. They mainly referred to Kanban, a Japanese term for signboard or billboard, as a form of workflow management. The Kanban method originally developed as a production system in car manufacturing in the late 1940s, but later established itself as an alternative to the waterfall model for agile software development. To track their work progress, developers order cards visualising tasks in the columns titled "requested", "in progress", and "done".

Smartphone apps such as *Secret Path* constantly generate large amounts of data. A Tallinn-based app designer expresses his stance on data-driven app design in the following statement:

> I use a service that provides an API [Application Programming Interface, C.R.]. And what I do in the code is … Next to the code for the button, I file an event. For instance, I send the data for the game button to the Internet, to the server, and I can find it in the analytics backend of the Google platform Firebase. They provide an interface, a web app. There, I can filter the data. I can find out, for example, how many users started and finished the tour or created an account. … When I create apps, I either ask for their age in the app or I try to get that data from Google or Facebook. I try to find out the age range for each tour.

The researched app makers were particularly interested in navigational data providing insights into the routes of users in tourist areas and the datafied "popularity" of tourist attractions. Furthermore, digital traces of on-screen actions can indirectly drive the development of apps. Programmers can build "funnels" and "event tracking" features into location-aware apps, enabling a tailor-made data collection on which further versions of the apps can be based. Although these technologies of quantification are embedded in infrastructures, the skilled practices of data analytics are enacted in the particularities of local worlds (Douglas-Jones, Walford, and Seaver, 2021: 10).

Ethics for data-driven app making can be directed towards the everyday practices and decision-making of developers. As apps can be designed to constantly collect data, ethical debates about the transparency and data ownership should go beyond the wrangle surrounding the Facebook Cambridge Analytica data scandal. Moral judgements about app making are shaped by the underlying attitudes and values of designers (Mittelstadt et al., 2016: 7), which are embodied in communities of knowing and educational institutions. Many of the researched app makers envisioned augmented reality features as a design challenge for improving location-aware apps and used the concept of a treasure hunt game as inspiration. *Secret Path* was a specific version of a location-aware collection game tailored for the navigational needs of tourists. Augmented reality components were mainly designed as additional features to be unlocked and experienced by the wandering tourist. Anchored in a data-driven production process, the app developers under investigation primarily materialised their aspirations for augmented reality apps as upgrades of location-aware apps that facilitate playful flânerie for tourists.

From touristic flânerie to augmented heritage

In the latter half of the 2010s, multiple locally funded design projects were dedicated to the creation of augmented reality apps for tourist sites in Estonia. Walkthrough analyses of two marker-based augmented reality apps demonstrate the ways in which Estonian heritages are portrayed on smartphones. While the app *Fat Margaret* was commissioned as a prototype by the Estonian Maritime Museum, the purpose of another app *(Re)start Reality* was to enhance the experience of street art. Named after a famous fortification tower built in Tallinn in the 16th century, *Fat Margaret* features historic sailing artefacts. *(Re)start Reality* guides its users to animated characters representing Estonians from the early 20th century, celebrating the era when the nation gained independence. Drawing on evidence from app interfaces and participant observation in the featured tourist places, I explore how augmented reality apps represent cultural heritages in the Estonian context. Tourist sites around the world increasingly adapt to the emergent mobile media ecology, providing visitors with geo-tagged information about local landmarks, heritages and numerous forms of entertainment on the go.

On the occasion of the centenary of Estonian independence, an anonymous, Banksy-inspired street artist began to create stencil and spray paintings at public sites in the Estonian cities of Tartu and Tallinn, but these wall paintings also became discovery points on the dynamic map in *(Re)start Reality*. Artists had been experimenting with location-aware technologies from the early 2000s (Gordon and de Souza e Silva, 2011: 44). To mark the centenary of the Estonian Republic, which was established in 1918, the characters displayed on the murals wore costumes from the early 20th century. The artist painted similar murals featuring Estonian historical figures in several cities, including Berlin, Brussels, Helsinki, London, Paris, Riga, and Rome. Information about the murals was shared on multiple web locations, including websites and digital platforms. Adjacent explanatory texts provided instructions on how to download the accompanying app. The Estonian tourist board regularly referred to the murals on its website and various digital platforms.

The mysterious stencil and spray paintings were a series of eight historical characters. For instance, the folk-tale character Lembit was painted on a wall next to the small deer garden in Tallinn's Old Town, proudly sporting a pipe and a top hat while sitting on a boulder. The painting depicted a scene in which he was about to light his pipe. The mural was embedded in the dynamic map of *(Re)start Reality*, guiding its users to the deer garden. By pointing the smartphone at the painting, users could see clouds of smoke emanating from his pipe against the background of the mural. The static subject of the mural metamorphosed into an animated character on the phone's screen. The unlocking of the discovery point also revealed textual information about the character available to users. A hidden meaning of the Estonian name Lembit was revealed on the various websites associated with the app. Lembit is also the name of a particular submarine built by the British Army and bought by the Estonian Republic prior to World War II. During the Soviet era, the vessel was incorporated into the Soviet fleet. When the Estonia regained independence in 1991, the submarine was returned to the nation, and following extensive preservation it remains on display as a shared heritage object at the Estonian Maritime Museum.

While *(Re)start Reality* symbolically commemorates Estonia's maritime heritage in a piece of polysemic artwork, *Fat Margaret* addresses Estonia's seafaring past in a more direct fashion. For many individuals, heritage simply refers to practices, places, objects, or ways of knowing which were sustained over generations. However, heritage can also be conceived as a hegemonic, highly institutionalised project of commemoration which reshapes collective identities and bolsters nation-building (De Cesari, 2010: 625). *Fat Margaret* illustrates the representation of heritage on smartphone screens. Following the boot screen and a menu for language options, the main interfaces of the app were part of its augmented reality component. The marker for triggering the augmented reality effects was a specific shape on a sticker, which was situated at Tallinn's airport and harbour, for instance. When a smartphone camera recognised the shape, two animated characters and a miniature version of the Estonian Maritime Museum appeared against the background of the surface on which the sticker was placed. Therein, the exhibition curators Priit and Feliks presented a series of exhibits through a text feed at the bottom of the screen. Subsequently, the user could swipe to the museum and select one of the six icons representing exhibited heritage objects, including a shipwreck, a figurehead of an ancient ship, an old barrel, a ship mast, a sea chest, and a half hull model ship.

Augmented reality components can primarily generate two modes of representation. Scenery and animated characters appearing on the interfaces of an augmented reality app can set in motion a mode of representation which is widely described as *indirect augmented reality*. This mode transforms the full screen to a 3D graphics environment, mixing the physical exterior of a device with augmented content displayed on its screen (Wither, Tsai, and Azuma, 2011; Liestøl, Ritter, and Ibrus, 2019). By pointing a mobile device at specific objects within a given location, users can unlock alternative visual narratives generating re-imaginings of these objects. The frame of the screen is the boundary between the scenes constructed by computer graphics and the physicality of the location where the device is held (Liestøl and Morrison, 2015: 209). When such sceneries are unlocked at a specific location, the entire display of the mobile device is filled with a simulation. The re-imaginings that users embody about artefacts or persons resemble the re-imaginings that movies or video games can initiate. In contrast, *(Re)start Reality* and *Fat Margaret* demonstrate a further mode of representation: *mixed reality*. This mode combines a video feed with layers of 3D graphics, which are superimposed onto the physical impression of a location. The superimposed content, such as objects or animated characters, are directly surrounded by the unique local environment which is visible through the camera of the mobile device. By seeing physical settings and augmented content simultaneously, users receive composite impressions, which instigate unique re-imaginings of objects or persons. Since physical places are filled with particular local atmospheres, strolling app users always make different experiences. Both modes of representation emplace experiences of objects, practices and persons as the appearance of the augmented content is triggered in geo-tagged locations. The mixed reality mode, however, reconfigures tourism imaginaries in new ways since it creates a seamless experience of augmented content and local ambience.

Given the manifold representations of heritages on digital media, they form a constantly evolving entity, which is crucially shaped by heritage workers (Samuels, 2015: 11). Heritage work refers to the conservation and management of material and immaterial heritages, including landscapes, languages, songs, traditions, historic buildings, and monuments. The preservation of heritages involves various professional groups, ranging from museum curators and heritage officers to history professors and archivists. By commissioning an augmented reality app, the heritage workers of the Estonian Maritime Museum introduced animated characters to the meaning-making process for heritage objects. Through the representation of maritime heritages on smartphone screens, *Fat Margaret* weaved the past into the present and assigned new meanings to Estonian heritage objects. The interfaces of this app and *(Re)start Reality* facilitated situated representations of cultural heritages, mixing overlaid artefacts and local ambience. App users could experience augmented reality features *in situ* while new personal imaginings about Estonia's maritime heritage were constructed.

Embodying Imaginings in Tourist Places

Although the implementation of augmented reality technologies in the media ecologies of popular travel destinations is still in its infancy, ethnographic evidence from Estonian tourist sites indicates that early forms of augmented reality content can emulate heritage objects and invite tourists to play serious mobile games in tourist sites. A huge variety of media, including newspapers, TV shows, travel literature, guide books, and messages on digital platforms, contribute to disseminating images about tourist sites in Estonia. Augmented reality apps are among the latest digital media technologies to reshape the construction of tourism imaginaries. Based on ethnographic evidence from tourist sites in Estonia, I assess how augmented reality technologies shift tourism imaginaries about Estonia.

Tourists and local tourism professionals are constantly entangled in cultural processes that shape imaginaries of places, people and practices (e.g. Jackson, 2005; Gravari-Barbas and Graburn, 2016; Mostafanezhad and Norum, 2019). Such imaginaries regularly serve as sociocultural frameworks for encounters with others. Tourism imaginaries can be conceived as socially transmitted representational assemblages which are used as meaning-making and worldshaping devices and interact with personal imaginings (e.g. Salazar and Graburn, 2014: 1). The main components of these representational assemblages include the imaginings of individual travellers, globally circulating images of local places, the collective identities of the people encountered, and, finally, the beliefs that tourists develop about locals and vice versa (Leite, 2014: 261). The study of tourism imaginaries can thus reveal worldviews, discourses, stereotypes, and fantasies. Although tourism imaginaries became a substantial subtheme of the contemporary anthropology of tourism, only a few in-depth studies address the ways in which personal imaginings are constructed. The ubiquitous uses of smartphones reconfigure the mobile media ecologies of tourist places, which disrupts the circulation of tourism imaginaries and the embodiment of imaginings about places, people, and practices. Augmented reality technologies thus contribute to the creation of new imaginings *in situ*.

A walkthrough analysis of further interfaces of *(Re)start Reality* demonstrates how augmented reality technologies actively participate in the circulation of imaginings about tourist attractions. The app's interfaces contained for instance textual information about the birth of the Estonian Republic in 1918, retelling episodes of her struggle for independence. Similar to newspaper articles or guide books, the app contributed to the circulation of historical connotations and shaped personal imaginings among tourists through textual information. One particular mural, which app users could find on the dynamic map, is another example showing how the app restructures tourism imaginaries. This wall painting depicted an Estonian street musician playing the bagpipes (*torupill*). Once the augmented reality content was activated in front of the mural, the musician began to rhythmically move and play the traditional Estonian instrument. Such augmented reality features also elicited personal imaginings about Estonia's history among tourists. The composite experience amalgamated overlaid artefacts unlocked during the virtual game play with their physical surroundings. Since such experiences were location-bound, they added a touch of uniqueness to the tourist's walk. *(Re)start Reality* blurred distinctions between the virtual world of play and the physical world of play.

The analysis of *Fat Margaret* also indicates how augmented reality features transform tourism imaginaries. Its interfaces primarily facilitated the construction of imaginings about historical maritime practices. App users could playfully discover various overlaid artefacts, such as an old barrel or a sea chest. The orientation sensor of the rotating mobile device was used to launch the episodes for the different overlaid artefacts and the text feed of the curators. The artefacts of the miniature museum could be experienced against an urban landscape backdrop. Augmented reality mobile games are played on the haptic interfaces of small screens and accompany multitudes of contemporary tourists in their everyday lives. While playing a game, they need to be attentive to and engage in both the virtual world and the physical world. Serious games for mobile phones, which are increasingly tailored to the needs of their users, create hybridised places (Keogh, 2015: 267). The corporeal existence of mobile gamers is increasingly incorporated into the virtual world and displayed on the mobile screen through location tracking technologies and camera technologies enabling new ways of seeing urban environments. Players are simultaneously present in, and aware of, a virtual and physical world. They are also embodied in both worlds through haptic interfaces in the virtual world and through their boots-on-the-ground presence in the physical world. The corporality of the app user is distributed across both worlds while the boundary between game play and physical settings collapses (Richardson, 2012; Hjorth et al., 2020). The appification of touristic experiences changed encounters between local residents and tourists. While augmented reality apps do not replace encounters with local tourism professionals, tourists can independently identify tourist attractions prior to and during their travels. Furthermore, the navigational features of tourism apps provide users with accurate routes in travel destinations, which may reduce their vulnerability to tourist scams.

In stark contrast to console-based video games, augmented reality technologies are embedded in the individualised materiality of smartphones and stimulate bodily movement throughout the game play. Locative media translated maps from public to private signs (Chesher, 2012: 324). Their locative interfaces encourage the strolling smartphone user to complete itineraries on dynamic maps, offering rewards, such as points and unlocked features, for reaching "check-in points". Other contemporary digital media technologies that participate in the construction of contemporary tourism imaginaries, such as travel vlogs shared on YouTube and travel photos posted on Instagram, carry signifiers of given tourist places, but their circulation is solely constrained by digital infrastructures. A photograph of a viewing platform in Tallinn's Old Town may reference local buildings, landscapes, and individuals, but the experience of looking at such an image is completely detached from its local context. However, the occurrence of the superimposed artefacts that augmented reality apps generate is place-bound. The locative sensors of smartphones guide tourists to particular locations where they can make unique experiences. Augmented reality apps retell stories from the past and make possible lived experiences of tangible, historical objects in a contemporary site.

Mass media, such as newspapers and television, tend to detach experiences from localities. They incorporate the capacity to make texts, photographs, and audiovisual materials accessible to large remote audiences. Live TV broadcasts have transformed how spectators can experience events, and users of hashtag-based platforms can engage in live reporting of events occurring in physical settings. Augmented reality technologies seem to reverse a centuries-old media trend. Smartphone users are freed from the physical constraints of traditional forms of media consumption, such as television, radio, theatre, and cinema. The ways in which augmented reality apps enable users to approach tourist attractions fundamentally differs from traditional techniques of representation, such as lithography, photography, or film making. Personalised gestures performed on haptic interfaces are central to the unlocking of augmented content. Designers of haptic interfaces aim to enhance effective interactivity using touch screens, whereby gesture and computer response are rendered almost instantaneous (Farman, 2012: 73). Augmented reality technologies make possible an emplacement of representation and touristic experience. The term emplacement generally relates to the rootedness of a person, practice, or object in their surrounding environment. However, emplacement cannot be reduced to physical localization as it also designates a state of being situated in a relational landscape (Englund, 2002: 263). In the context of location-aware apps, forms of emplacement can be theorized as the sensing subject's and sensing objects' ongoing process of engagement and entanglement with the lived environment (e.g. Pink, 2011: 348).

Augmented experiences are not solely grounded in the physical properties of material objects and their surrounding contexts, they add a new layer to the complex processes of developing and reinventing tourist places and the constantly ongoing negotiation of cultural representation (Bruner, 2005: 67; Skinner and Theodossopoulos, 2011: 4). Furthermore, the aura of heritage objects is not exclusively delineated by the experience of their material qualities, but requires their semiotic embeddedness in the fabric of tradition (Benjamin, 1969). The researched augmented reality apps rearranged how imaginings about Estonia as a travel destination were embodied. Symbolic meanings were re-ascribed to tourist attractions in hybridised places where tourists simultaneously experienced a virtual and a physical world. The augmented meaning-making of the researched apps enabled the emplacement of touristic experiences by mixing connotations from the mobile screen and physical surroundings.

Conclusion

In this chapter, I have drawn on ethnographic fieldwork to assess the role of augmented reality apps in tourist places. This emerging technology is increasingly being implemented in tourist sites around the world. Based on an immersion in the Estonian start-up scene, this investigation brought to light that local app makers predominately realised their aspirations for augmented reality apps as upgrades of location-aware apps that facilitate playful touristic flânerie. In the Estonian context, the production of augmented reality apps was largely envisioned as a data-driven design process. The researched augmented reality apps enabled situated representation of heritage objects and other tourist attractions, mixing impressions of superimposed artefacts and local ambience. Reconfiguring the mobile media ecology of Estonian tourist places, the researched app makers forged augmented reality technologies capable of emplacing experiences of Estonian heritage objects and instigating re-imaginings of cultural heritages among tourists. The research into augmented reality apps in Estonian tourist sites revealed how smartphones can be re-purposed as technologies of emplacement. Augmented content re-ascribes meaning to heritage objects while enabling tourists to engage in representational practices which unlock digital content *in situ*. For these reasons, augmented reality technologies reshuffle the construction of tourism imaginaries by adding new semiotic layers to the meaning-making surrounding the presentation of cultural heritages in tourist sites.

Engaging in a digital-physical continuum, users of augmented reality apps perform fine-grained gestures on the sequential texture of their interfaces and simultaneously stroll through urban landscapes. The analysis of the mobile media ecology of Estonian tourist places reveals the dynamics inherent in the socio-technical interplay between human perception and sensorial technologies. The senses of smartphones, such as location-tracking and camera lenses, play a constitutive role in augmented meaning-making. Although ethnographic research into augmented reality technologies is still scarce, ethnographic fieldwork is well suited for unravelling both socio-technical dynamics of augmented meaning-making and cultural processes shaping app making. Further ethnographic research into the skilled practices and moral convictions of app makers can provide crucial insights into the diversification of contemporary mobile media ecologies. The ethnographic assessment of early augmented reality technologies in Estonian tourist sites also raises ethical issues for the production of other location-aware smartphone apps. Operational transparency is necessary for the socio-technical processes of data-driven app development, and users should be comprehensively informed about the digital traces they leave in obscure databases embedded in digital infrastructures. The gamification of locative media carries great potential for mitigating at least some of the risks commonly associated with digital gaming, such as addiction and the glorification of violence. The collapse of the global tourism industry in the aftermath of the outbreak of the COVID-19 pandemic has considerably slowed down the implementation of further augmented reality apps in tourist sites. Despite ongoing concerns over the future of tourism, augmented reality technologies will continue to disrupt touristic experiences and populate tourist places with animated characters.

References

Beaulieu, A. (2010) "Research Note: From Co-Location to Co-Presence: Shifts in the Use of Ethnography for the Study of Knowledge," *Social Studies of Science*, 40(3): 453–470. doi.10.1177/0306312709359219.

Benjamin, W. (1969 [1935]) "The Work of Art in the Age of Mechanical Reproduction," in H. Arendt (ed.), *Illuminations* (trans. by H. Zohn), New York: Schocken Books: 214–218.

Boellstorff, T. (2011) "Virtuality: Placing the Virtual Body: Avatar, Chora, Cypherg," in F. Mascia-Lees (ed.), *A Companion to the Anthropology of the Body and Embodiment*, Oxford: Blackwell Publishing: 504–520.

Boellstorff, T. (2014) "An Afterword in Four Binarisms," in M. Grimshaw (ed.), *The Oxford Handbook of Virtuality*, Oxford: Oxford University Press: 739–746.

Bruner, E. (2005) *Culture on Tour: Ethnographies of Travel*, Chicago: University of Chicago Press.

Chesher, C. (2012) "Navigating Sociotechnical Spaces: Comparing Computer Games and Sat Navs as Digital Spatial Media," *Convergence: The International Journal of Research into New Media Technologies*, 18(3): 315–330. doi:abs/10.1177/1354856512442762.

Coman, M. and Rothenbuhler, E. (2005) "The Promise of Media Anthropology," in E. Rothenbuhler and M. Coman (eds), *Media Anthropology*, London: Sage: 1–11.

De Cesari, C. (2010). "Creative Heritage: Palestinian Heritage NGOs and Defiant Arts of Government," *American Anthropologist*, 112(4): 625–637. doi:10.1111/j.1548- 1433.2010.01280.x.

Douglas-Jones, R., Walford, A., and Seaver, N. (2021) "Introduction: Towards an Anthropology of Data," *Journal of the Royal Anthropological Institute*, 27: 9–25. doi:10.1111/1467-9655.13477.

DeNicola, L. (2016) "Forging Source: Considering the Craft of Computer Programming," in C. Wilkinson-Weber and A. DeNicola (eds), *Critical Craft: Technology, Globalization, and Capitalism*, London: Bloomsbury Academic: 35–56.

Denyer-Simmons, H. (2016) "Pokémon GO and Placemaking: Positive Side Effects of Using Augmented Reality Applications," *Journal of Visual and Media Anthropology*, 2(1): 55–63.

Englund, H. (2002) "Ethnography after Globalism: Migration and Emplacement in Malawi," *American Ethnologist*, 29(2): 261–286. doi:10.1525/ae.2002.29.2.261.

Farman, J. (2012) *Mobile Interface Theory: Embodied Space and Locative Media*, New York: Routledge.

Fors, V. (2015) "Sensory Experiences of Digital Photo-Sharing – 'Mundane Frictions' and Emerging Learning Strategies," *Journal of Aesthetics & Culture*, 7: 1–12. doi:10.3402/jac.v7.28237

Fuentes, J. (2017) "Augmented Reality and Pedagogical Anthropology: Reflections from the Philosophy of Education," in J. Ariso (ed.), *Augmented Reality*, Berlin: De Gruyter: 255–272.

Garvey, P. and Miller, D. (2021) *Ageing with Smartphones in Ireland: When Life Becomes Craft*, London: UCL Press.

Giddings, S. (2014) *Gameworlds*, London: Bloomsbury.

Gordon, E. and de Souza e Silva, A. (2011) *Net Locality: Why Location Matters in a Networked World*, Oxford: Wiley.

Graham, M., Zook, M. and Boulton, A. (2013) "Augmented Reality in the Urban Environment: Contested Content and the Duplicity of Code," *Transactions of the Institute of British Geographers*, 38(3): 464–479. Available at SSRN: https://ssrn.com/abstract=2427629.

Graburn, N. (2002) "The Ethnographic Tourist," in G. Dann (ed.), *The Tourist as a Metaphor of the Social World*, Wallingford: CAB International: 19–39.

Graburn, N. and Gravari-Barbas, M. (2016) "Introduction: Tourism Imaginaries at the Disciplinary Crossroads," in Gravari-Barbas, M. and Graburn, N. (eds), *Tourism Imaginaries at the Disciplinary Crossroads: Place, Practice, Media*, New York: Routledge: 1–32.

Hjorth, L., Ohashi, K., Sinanan, J., Horst, H., Pink, S., F. Kato, and Zhou, B. (2020) *Digital Media Practices in Households: Kinship through Data*, Amsterdam: Amsterdam University Press.

Hjorth, L. and Richardson, I. (2017) "Pokémon GO: Mobile Media Play, Place-making, and the Digital Wayfarer," *Mobile Media & Communication*, 5(1): 3–14. Doi:10.1177/2050157916680015.

Horst, H. (2021) "The Anthropology of Mobile Phones," in H. Geismar and H. Knox (eds), *Digital Anthropology*, London: Routledge: 65–84.

Jackson, R. (2005) "Converging Cultures; Converging Gazes; Contextualizing Perspectives," in D. Crouch, R. Jackson and F. Thompson (eds), *The Media and the Tourist Imagination: Converging Cultures*, New York: Routledge: 183–197.

Johnston, L., Galloway, R., Trench, J., Poyade, M., Tromp, J., and My, H. (2020) "Augmented Reality at Heritage Sites: Technological Advances and Embodied Spatially Minded Interactions," in J. Tromp, D. Le, and C. Le (eds), *Emerging Extended Reality Technologies for Industry 4.0*, Oxford: Blackwell Publishing: 101–116.

Keogh, B. (2015) "Paying Attention to Angry Birds," in G. Goggin and L. Hjorth (eds), *The Routledge Companion to Mobile Media*, New York: Routledge: 267–275.

Keogh, B. (2017) "Pokémon Go, the Novelty of Nostalgia, and the Ubiquity of the Smartphone," *Mobile Media & Communication*, 5(1): 38–41. Doi:10.1177/2050157916678025.

Leite, N. (2014) "Afterword: Locating Imaginaries," in N. Salazar and N. Graburn (eds), *Tourism Imaginaries: Anthropological Approaches*, London: Berg: 260–279.

Light, B. (2017) "Ashley Madison: Introduction to the Walkthrough Method," in J. Morris and S. Murray (eds), *Appified: Culture the Age of Apps*, Ann Arbor: University of Michigan Press: 31–41.

Light, B., Burgess, J., and Duguay, S. (2018) "The Walkthrough Method: An Approach to the Study of Apps," *New Media & Society*, 20(3): 881–900. doi:10.1177/1461444816675438.

Liestøl, G. and Morrison, A. (2015) "The Power of Place and Perspective: Sensory Media and Situated Simulations in Urban Design," in A. de Souza e Silva and M. Sheller (eds), *Mobility and Locative Media: Mobile Communication in Hybrid Spaces*, London: Routledge: 207–223.

Liestøl, G., Ritter, C., and Ibrus, I. (2019) "Audiovisual Industries and Tourism: Forms of Convergence," in I. Ibrus (ed.), *Emergence of Cross-innovation Systems: Audiovisual Industries Co-innovating with Education, Health Care and Tourism*, Bingley: Emerald: 165–172.

Morris, J. and Murray, S. (2018) "Introduction," in J. Morris and S. Murray (eds), *Appified: Culture the Age of Apps*, Ann Arbor: University of Michigan Press: 1–22.

Mostafanezhad, M. and Norum, R. (2019) "The Anthropocenic Imaginary: Political Ecologies of Tourism in a Geological Epoch," *Journal of Sustainable Tourism*, 27(4): 421–435. doi:10.1080/09669582.2018.1544252.

McCrea, C. (2017) "Pokémon's Progressive Revelation: Notes on 20 years of Game Design," *Mobile Media & Communication*, 5(1): 42–46. doi:10.1177/2050157916678271.

McLuhan, M. (1964) *Understanding Media: The Extensions of Man*. New York: McGraw-Hill.

Mittelstadt, B., Allo, P., Taddeo M., Wachter S., and Floridi L. (2016) "The Ethics of Algorithms: Mapping the Debate," *Big Data & Society*, 3(2): 1–21. doi:10.1177/2053951716679679.

Pink, S. (2011) "From Embodiment to Emplacement: Re-thinking Competing Bodies, Senses and Spatialities," *Sport, Education and Society*, 16(3): 343–355. doi:10.1080/13573322.2011.565965.

Pink, S. (2014) "Digital–Visual–Sensory-Design Anthropology: Ethnography, Imagination and Intervention," *Arts and Humanities in Higher Education*, 13(4): 412–427. doi:10.1177/1474022214542353.

Pink S., Hjorth, L., Horst, H., Nettheim, J., and Bell, G. (2018) "Digital Work and Play: Mobile Technologies and New Ways of Feeling at Home," *European Journal of Cultural Studies*, 21(1): 26–38. doi:10.1177/1367549417705602.

Richardson, I. (2012) "Touching the Screen: A Phenomenology of Mobile Gaming and the iPhone," in L. Hjorth, J. Burgess and I. Richardson (eds), *Studying Mobile Media: Cultural Technologies, Mobile Communication, and the iPhone*, New York: Routledge: 133–154.

Ritter, C. (2021) "Rethinking Digital Ethnography: A Qualitative Approach to Understanding Interfaces," *Qualitative Research*, 1–17. Doi:10.1177/14687941211000540.

Saker, M. and Evans, L. (2021) *Intergenerational Locative Play: Augmenting Family*, Bingley: Emerald.

Salazar, N. and Graburn, N. (2014) "Introduction: Toward an Anthropology of Tourism Imaginaries," in N. Salazar and N. Graburn (eds), *Tourism Imaginaries: Anthropological Approaches*, London: Berg: 1–30.

Salen, K. (2007) "Gaming Literacies: A Game Design Study in Action," *Journal of Educational Multimedia and Hypermedia*, 16 (3): 301–322.

Samuels, K. (2015) "Heritage as Persuasion," in K. Samuels and T. Rico (eds), *Heritage Keywords: Rhetoric and Redescription in Cultural Heritage*, Boulder: University Press of Colorado: 3–28.

Simeone, L. and Iaconesi, S. (2011) "Anthropological Conversations: Augmented Reality Enhanced Artifacts to Foster Education in Cultural Anthropology," *IEEE 11th International Conference on Advanced Learning Technologies*: 126–128. doi:10.1109/ICALT.2011.43.

Skinner, J. and Theodossopoulos, D. (2011) "Introduction: The Play of Expectation in Tourism," in J. Skinner and D. Theodossopoulos (eds), *Great Expectations: Imagination and Anticipation in Tourism*, Oxford: Berghahn: 1–26.

de Souza e Silva, A. and Frith, J. (2012) *Mobile Interfaces in Public Spaces: Locational Privacy, Control, and Urban Sociability*. New York: Routledge.

Suchman, L. (2011) "Anthropological Relocations and the Limits of Design," *Annual Review of Anthropology*, 40(1): 1–18. doi:10.1146/annurev.anthro.041608.105640.

Waltorp, K (2017) "Digital Technologies, Dreams and Disconcertment in Anthropological World-making," in J Salazar, S Pink, A Irving and J Sjöberg (eds), *Anthropologies and Futures: Researching Emerging and Uncertain Worlds*, New York: Bloomsbury Academic: 101–116.

Wilken, R. and Goggin, G. (2015) "Locative Media: Definitions, Histories, Theories," in R. Wilken and G. Goggin (eds), *Locative Media*, New York: Routledge: 1–19.

Wither, J., Tsai, J., and Azuma, R. (2011) "Mobile Augmented Reality: Indirect Augmented Reality," *Computer and Graphics*, 35(4): 810–822. doi:10.1016/j.cag.2011.04.010.

39
PRECARITY, DISCRIMINATION AND (IN)VISIBILITY
An Ethnography of "The Algorithm" in the YouTube Influencer Industry

Zoë Glatt

YouTube's algorithmic recommendation system—known colloquially as The Algorithm—is a powerful character in the lives of professional and aspiring social media content creators, exerting various pressures on them in their struggles for visibility and income in the influencer industry. Every creator has tales of woe and theories to share about The Algorithm, and every industry event has panels and discussions dedicated to it: how it works, what content it is currently preferencing, who it is discriminating against, and, most importantly, how to navigate it in order to achieve success.

Drawing on four years of ethnographic fieldwork in the London and LA influencer industries (2017–2021), I have argued (Glatt, 2022) that the introduction of algorithmic recommendation systems as a key mechanism marks an escalation of the conditions of precarity for platformised creative workers as compared to more traditional cultural industries. In addition to broader conditions of precarity, some creators are subject to *algorithmic discrimination*, which I define as a process whereby certain content, identities, and positionalities within the platform economy are deprioritised from recommendation, in an industry where visibility is key to success (ibid.). This chapter moves from the macro to the micro, digging deeper into these findings by exploring with an anthropological lens the multifaceted and situated ways that YouTube content creators understand and respond to The Algorithm in their working lives, through a close reading of their *discourses*, *practices* and *experiences*.

There is a particular urgency underlying this study; with an ever-increasing number of people seeking careers in the influencer industry, it is vital to interrogate the emerging and problematic technological structures that are core to this new form of creative labour. By attending to questions of power in the "messy web" (Postill and Pink, 2012) of online and offline fieldsites where the sociotechnical assemblage of The Algorithm emerges, the chapter contributes to this volume on media anthropology by drawing on critical algorithm studies, creative labour, and influencer cultures research, and builds on existing methods literature on the ethnographic research of algorithms (Bishop, 2019; Christin, 2020; Hine, 2015; 2017; Seaver, 2017).

Context: The Influencer Industry and Rise of Professional Content Creators

In her 2008 book *CamGirls*, Teresa Senft coined the term "microcelebrity". She defines this as "the commitment to deploying and maintaining one's online identity as if it were a branded good, with the expectation that others do the same" (2013: 346). Over the past decade, what began as the informal culture of microcelebrity has developed into a popular career path and a new creative industry, dubbed by Cunningham and Craig as "Social Media Entertainment" (2019), made up of a mature infrastructure of diverse and competing social media platforms, such as YouTube, TikTok, Instagram, and Twitch. Self-titled *content creators*, or *influencers*, amass online followings and monetise their content through a combination of ad revenue, brand deals, crowdfunding, merchandise sales, and public appearances. The average age of influencers has gone up as the original generation has aged, but this is a decidedly young industry; most successful content creators are under the age of 35, with two of the top earning YouTubers of 2020 under the age of 10 (Berg and Brown, 2020). There are nuances and disagreements around the distinction between what constitutes a "content creator" or an "influencer" in both academia and popular culture, but broadly speaking "content creator" is a catch-all term for an entrepreneurial social media creator working across any genre and with any level of followers or income, whereas "influencer" is a term utilised by the social media marketing industry, most often describing a particular subset of high-profile professional creators (Abidin, 2015) commonly associated with female-skewing lifestyle-related genres. In this chapter I use both designations, reflecting the self-titling practices of my participants.

Whilst influencers are regularly depicted in mainstream media and journalism as frivolous, lazy, and narcissistic—critiques, I found, that are often aimed at younger generations by those in power—this does them a grave disservice. During fieldwork it became clear to me that the majority of influencers are hardworking, multitalented creatives within a highly competitive industry. They possess a wide range of skills, simultaneously working as videographers, editors, photographers, on-screen talent, brand ambassadors, merchandise producers, marketers and PR reps, until they gain enough income to delegate some of the labour.

Elite influencers with multiple millions of fans can attract huge incomes; according to Forbes the top 10 highest-paid YouTube stars of 2020 earned a combined $211 million (Berg and Brown, 2020). However, these success stories fuel unrealistic expectations for the majority of hopeful content creators. According to a 2018 study by Mathias Bärtl, 97 percent of all aspiring YouTubers won't make it above the US poverty line of around $12,000 a year, with only 3 percent making a living wage (Stokel-Walker, 2018). Whilst some "microinfluencers" (those with 1000–100,000 followers) manage to defy the odds and earn a decent income—such as one tech reviewer creator I interviewed with only 10,000 YouTube subscribers who earnt £30k a year through a lucrative partnership with a gaming company—this is a metric-driven industry. A creator's number of views, likes, and subscribers is a major factor in determining income, and they are on a constant treadmill to maintain, or better to increase, these figures if they hope to earn a sustainable living.

In the anthropological tradition, Miller and Slater (2000), Postill and Pink (2012), and Hine (2017) have argued that the Internet is intimately and ubiquitously woven into the fabric of everyday (offline) life, and therefore needs to be studied within this context. The turn towards a geographical place-based approach to studying Internet cultures is more aligned with traditional forms of ethnographic engagement than the purely online ethnographies that emerged in the 2000s (for example, Baym, 2000; Boellstorff, 2008). This project was concerned with the lived experiences of creatives within an industry context, so I conducted and synthesised participant observation in both the multi-platform social media environment and in settings where the community-industry converges, including industry events such as VidCon UK & USA and Summer in the City. Drawing on immersive participant observation of anthropologists in digital spaces (Boellstorff, 2008; Hine, 2017; Lange, 2019; Nardi, 2009), I became a content creator myself in addition to watching, liking, and commenting on videos. Practises of becoming a YouTuber allowed me to reflect on the testimonies of my participants and gain a deeper level of understanding for their lived experiences. As Hine puts it, in "taking part for real … I experience how it feels in a visceral way that would be hard to access in an interview or observational setting" (2015: 99). The research also included formal semi-structured interviews with 30 London-based content creators. Interviewees represented a broad range of identity categories (in terms of gender, race, sexuality, class and ability), and worked across a wide variety of prominent and niche genres, including lifestyle, beauty, gaming, BookTube, education, video essays, animation, LGBTQ+ and feminism, political commentary, film and tech reviews, travel, trending vlog challenges and tags, comedy, and short films. In order to counteract the overemphasis on elite creators in the existing literature, whilst some of my participants were full-time professional influencers, others were aspiring to make the leap from hobbyist to full-time; interviewees ranged widely from 2.2 million subscribers to a single solitary subscriber (myself). Despite this range, all participants emphasised that they regularly struggled with The Algorithm in their work.

Critical/Ethnographic Approaches to Algorithms in Cultural Work

In recent years there has been a growing interest in the sociocultural dimensions of algorithms across the social sciences and humanities. Whilst taking an anthropological approach, this chapter draws on influential work from such disciplines as sociology, media and communications, critical race theory, and STS. Algorithms are an important aspect of the digital media landscape providing the foundational architecture for how social media platforms are structured, sorting and offering content to viewers according to the likelihood that they will watch it based on a variety of metrics, as well as determining which content should be (de)monetised. Rather than view algorithms simply as technological black boxes to be opened, critical qualitative approaches understand them as "complex sociotechnical assemblages involving long chains of actors, technologies, and meanings" (Christin, 2020: 898), as "heterogeneous and diffuse sociotechnical systems … [that are] part of broad patterns of meaning and practice" (Seaver, 2017: 1), and as "material-discursive" systems that generate particular formations of power and politics in social life (Bucher, 2018).

Research into the gig economy and crowdwork on platforms such as Uber, Deliveroo, and Amazon Mechanical Turk has provided vital insights regarding the relationship between algorithms and labour (Chen, 2019; Gray and Suri, 2019; Rosenblat, 2018). For example, in their ethnographic research Gray and Suri argue that for low-income earners with extremely limited bargaining power, the "algorithmic cruelty" of work dependent on the "thoughtless processes" of AI has severe economic and social consequences, in contexts where platforms have little to no accountability to workers (2019: 68). However, the cultural industries have distinct histories and social formations that require their own analysis in the context of platformisation, as Duffy, Nieborg, and Poell have argued (2019; 2021). Most notably, unlike the gig economy, labour in the cultural industries has long been marked by a "passionate attachment to the work and to the identity of creative laborer" (Gill and Pratt, 2008: 20), with cultural workers willing to endure precarious working conditions as a result (Bishop, 2018; Duffy, 2017; McRobbie, 2016). Whilst a multitude of structural factors combine to form an overall system of what Duffy et al. refer to as the "nested precarities" (2021) of social media work—such as a lack of regulation and fragmented and changeable multi-platform working environments—algorithms demand scrutiny as a central mechanism with wide-ranging sociocultural and economic implications for both hobbyist and professional content creators.

In her study of sociality on YouTube, Lange found that creators are subject to significant "algorithmic anxiety", drawing on an example of one creator who was unable to control his public image in the face of trolls producing highly searchable video with his name attached (2019: 197). From a cultural industries perspective, creators' income and career prospects are in large part determined by how widely their content is recommended by a platform's algorithms, but platforms rarely share information as to how their algorithms work or what factors they are preferencing. As Bishop observes, even highly successful creators "are not safe from algorithmically induced platform invisibility" (2018: 71), and consequently influencers with hundreds of thousands of subscribers will commonly still work other jobs in order to protect their financial stability. This chapter builds on and dialogues with Bishop's substantial body of critical feminist research into the role of algorithms in the influencer industry, which has addressed such topics as algorithmic gender inequalities and feminised labour (2018), practices of *algorithmic gossip* (2019), and the sub-industry of "growth hackers" (2020).

Researchers have highlighted that algorithms pose unique challenges for researchers due to their opacity as so-called "black boxed" technologies (Christin, 2020), a characterisation that has in turn been explored, challenged, and subverted by a number of qualitative researchers, who variously argue that rather than fetishise or obsess over the opacity of algorithms, understanding them as sociotechnical assemblages offers openings for creative methodological possibilities and more nuanced understandings of their impacts (Bishop, 2019; Seaver, 2017). Ethnography is particularly well suited as a methodology for examining how algorithms emerge through these sociotechnical assemblages in everyday life, able to encompass cultural practices, forms of sociality, and broader institutional factors, as well as discourses (Gray and Suri, 2019; Lange, 2019; Seaver, 2017). In his seminal piece on the ethnography of algorithmic systems, Seaver presents a vision of algorithms *as* rather than *in* culture, whereby they are "not singular technical objects that enter into many different cultural interactions, but are rather unstable objects, culturally enacted by the practices people use to engage with them" (ibid.: 5).

Building on these approaches, I investigate not what YouTube's algorithmic recommendation system does or how it works in some objective sense, but the diverse cultural meanings and values that content creators attach to it, and how platforms, the influencer industry, and the nature of platformised creative work are constituted through these processes. Thus, in the following sections I explore The Algorithm through three distinct but parallel lenses: what content creators *say* about it (their imaginaries and cultural discourses), their *actions* with regards to it (their cultural practices), and how they *feel* about it (their experiences). In triangulating these three dimensions, this chapter aims to provide both a well-rounded and systematic framework for the ethnographic study of algorithms in culture, as well as a detailed account of how YouTube content creators experience and respond to The Algorithm in their working lives.

Algorithmic Hearsay and Folk Theories

YouTube's algorithmic recommendation system plays a central role in the working lives of content creators, as one of the key mechanisms controlling their metrics in an industry built upon visibility. Ethnographers have highlighted that the opaque nature of algorithms makes them inherently difficult to centre in research, but the influencer industry provides a rare case study wherein algorithms are the object of such intense scrutiny and discussion that the challenge instead becomes sifting through and understanding the myriad, divergent, and strongly held beliefs and practices surrounding them. In this first of three empirical sections, I explore the prominent role of hearsay and folk theories in producing the various *algorithmic imaginaries* (Bucher, 2017) at work in constructing The Algorithm in the YouTube creator community. I investigate what types of narratives are shared about The Algorithm, and discuss two prominent themes that emerged from fieldwork and interviews: first, its framing as an omnipotent and unknowable God, and second, the community detective work—or *algorithmic gossip* (Bishop, 2019)—that occurs as creators try to decipher it in order to gain some control over their work.

Pleasing The Algorithm Gods

The Algorithm was often painted by participants as an anthropomorphised mythical creature or vengeful God with the power to determine the destinies of creators. Stories of wild victories were attributed to it, such as animation reviewer Steve who had jumped from 1000 subscribers to over 70k in two short months after a video he made went viral. Working full-time in IT, Steve was grappling with what to do with his new-found but fragile success. Equally, I heard about instances of catastrophic failures blamed on the pernicious Algorithm, such as a major children's content creator who told me that her channel had gone from receiving 500k views a day to almost zero overnight as a result of changes to the recommendation of kids' content in July 2019.

Discussing a recent video that hadn't performed as well as anticipated, science creator Dr Simon Clark explained:

> The viability of what I make is largely determined by an algorithm that nobody understands ... Talking about The Algorithm is like medieval Christians talking about God. Make a sacrifice by putting a clickbaity thumbnail on it and we'll pray to The Algorithm.
>
> *Simon Clark interview, October 2018*

Despite his humour, he described his work and income being at the mercy of an unknown algorithmic system as making him feel "powerless". This quote highlights the uncertainty of work for content creators, who are subject to unknown and ever-changing algorithmic and platform contexts. My participants commonly framed The Algorithm as an omnipotent, mysterious, and unknowable being, further obfuscating the human agency and commercial interests at work on YouTube.

Algorithmic Detectives and Conspiracy Theorists

In their attempts to understand and respond to the caprices of The Algorithm, my participants had become algorithmic detectives. I witnessed a prime example of this in January 2019 at my first London Small YouTubers (LSY) meeting, a community organisation for small creators (<20,000 subscribers), carrying out seemingly endless free *aspirational labour*, diligently approaching social media content creation as an investment in a future self that will hopefully be able to "do what they love" for a living (Duffy, 2017: x). The 40 attendees were a diverse group and covered a broad spectrum of content genres—from music composers and film reviewers, to petfluencers and beauty vloggers—but they were all there for the same reason: to learn how to grow and monetise their YouTube channels.

The majority of the meeting was dominated by a discussion about how small creators can gain visibility in the face of a hostile Algorithm; it is the received wisdom that until creators reach a minimum of 1000 subscribers (considered to be a nano-micro-atomic-*insert-synonym-for-small*-influencer), YouTube's algorithms refuse to push their content out to anyone at all. Confronted by this significant technological barrier to entry, the group were crowdsourcing all the information they could to sway it in their favour. For example, one creator said "I've heard a rumour that it's at 60% of watch time retention that The Algorithm starts to pay attention and promote your content", and another shared that they'd heard that video tags were no longer as important as watch time, clicks, titles, and thumbnails for driving traffic to content. These comments resulted in a lengthy discussion about the weighting of various metrics in determining algorithmic recommendation. Bishop (2019: 1) has described this as *algorithmic gossip*, defined as "communally and socially informed theories and strategies pertaining to recommender algorithms, shared and implemented to engender financial consistency and visibility on algorithmically structured social media platforms". She argues that taking this kind of community-industry gossip seriously provides a valuable resource for understanding the sociocultural, political, and economic dimensions of algorithms.

During an interview with Steve after the meeting, I asked if the intensity with which YouTube's algorithms had been discussed was the norm. He explained that the meeting was a typical example of the obsessive hearsay and folk theories shared between content creators, putting it:

> No one quite knows what The Algorithm is, but everyone likes to theorise and speculate and it's basically, like if you can picture this visually, everyone would be in a room with tin foil hats on with conspiracy theories about "I saw that YouTube did this and that means that The Algorithm is working in that way" and they will try and connect all the dots. It's like a detective film where they have post it notes all over the board and they are connecting it with string and they think they've figured it out but then something else happens like "uh-oh hats back on, now this is happening.".
>
> Steve Simpson interview, August 2019

Within this context of apprehensive peer-to-peer algorithmic detective work, an entire sub-industry of self-titled "algorithmic experts" or "growth hackers" has emerged in which individuals accrue social and economic capital by claiming privileged access to knowledge about how YouTube's algorithms work, as Bishop (2020) has explored in detail. Often successful and famous content creators in their own right, these are (overwhelmingly white and male) individuals who function as official and unofficial intermediaries between YouTube and content creators by selling theorisations of how to achieve algorithmic visibility on the platform (ibid.: 4). Responding to the uncertainties and anxieties that creators face, growth hackers present YouTube's algorithmic recommendation system as a black box to be opened, embracing the neoliberal logics of hard data over softer feminised forms of social media labour (Bishop, 2020; Duffy and Schwartz, 2018).

Influencer Practices: Gaming The Algorithm

Algorithmic discourses inform creator practices (Bishop, 2019; Bucher, 2017; 2018), but there is not a straightforward correlation between the two. In this section, I examine the common tactics that content creators employ in order to maximise visibility within unstable and unpredictable algorithmic contexts, and how such contexts can lead to broader shifts in the norms and genres of content creation. Whilst these tactics are commonplace, I argue that creators often find themselves in a double bind as they simultaneously try to avoid the appearance of being overly invested in metric popularity, with its connotations of inauthenticity.

Feeding the Hungry Algorithm

Aspiring and professional creators are on a relentless treadmill, employing sophisticated techniques to optimise their metrics within fluctuating and mysterious algorithmic contexts, or else risking the oblivion of invisibility. Common tactics include strategically timing posts to coincide with spikes in platform usage (Duffy, 2017: x), producing eye-catching thumbnails and "clickable" titles, participating in content trends and challenges, finding and sticking narrowly to a strong content niche for algorithmic visibility, scrutinising backend channel analytic data in attempts to reverse engineer YouTube's algorithms, and filming "collabs" with other content creators. Most importantly, it is common knowledge amongst content creators that YouTube's algorithms prefer channels with regular uploads; posting at least one video a week is seen as the bare minimum requirement to gain any traction, and daily uploads are understood as the ideal for maximum visibility. All of this has led to inevitable burnout, as creators frantically compete with one another in both quantity and quality of content output.

A simple shift in how YouTube recommends content can send shockwaves through the creator community, upending how they approach making videos and even what genre of videos they make. An example of such a shockwave was in 2012 when, in an attempt to combat clickbait (content with hyperbolic or misleading titles and thumbnails, designed explicitly with the aim of attracting clicks) on the platform, YouTube shifted the primary metric for algorithmic recommendation from the number of clicks a video had to the amount of watch time (Alexander, 2019a). Where previously all content creators had to do to make a "successful" video (i.e. one that would be recommended widely to viewers) was to attract initial clicks and it didn't matter how long viewers stayed on it, suddenly creators had to pivot to make videos that would keep viewers watching for as long as possible. Whilst this move was somewhat effective in reducing the prevalence of clickbait, it also profoundly shifted the entire YouTube ecology; where most videos used to sit well below the 10-minute mark, they have gradually become much longer across most major genres—including vlogs, tutorials, gaming livestreams, video essays, and documentaries—to the point where half hour or longer videos are now a cultural norm (Alexander, 2019b). YouTube further incentivised this transformation by allowing mid-roll ads on videos over 10 minutes, with creators receiving a cut of the revenue. On the other side of the coin, genres that were unable to adapt to become longer were all but decimated, most notably animation, which had previously been a thriving segment of YouTube culture. I heard animator panellists at VidCon UK 2019 talk about how animations are far more labour intensive to make per minute of content as compared to most other genres, and how they struggled to keep up with the video length and output that creators in other genres could achieve. Simi, a creator with 272k subscribers at the time of our interview, explained:

> I'd spend maybe a month working every day on a video and I'd be able to get, if I'm lucky, a 10-minute animation, but probably 6 minutes. But with let's say the video where I talked about why I stopped animating, I did that in a week, and it was 20 minutes long. So for me it was just like yeah, I should probably go in that direction then.
>
> *Simi Adeshina interview, October 2018*

The pressures to create longer videos, more quickly, had driven Simi away from animation and towards gaming commentary and livestreaming. As one interviewee noted, these days it is rare to see animation channels recommended in the "trending" tab, a good indicator of what is popular on YouTube. On social media platforms, all different types of content vie for viewers' attention within the same space, and the way that their recommendation algorithms are calibrated plays a key role in determining which genres will thrive and which will die. As prominent long-form video essayist Lindsay Ellis told The Verge in an interview, "I kind of lucked out that the algorithm eventually favored the type of content that I wanted to make" (Alexander, 2019b).

Stuck Between a Rock and a Hard Place: Algorithmic Optimisation Versus Authenticity

There is a pervasive sense of injustice amongst many creators that YouTube's algorithms reward channels that churn out mediocre, bloated, clickbaity daily content over painstakingly crafted weekly or monthly videos, a structure that benefits large content farms and production houses over independent creators. Within this context, creators must negotiate the extent to which they are willing to shape their content to fit with what the platform is preferencing, whilst simultaneously trying to avoid the negative cultural connotations surrounding practices of "gaming The Algorithm".

The ways in which creators understand and navigate this issue varies greatly, as I found during interviews when I asked creators to what extent they embraced tactics to optimise visibility. Some said that they never made content based solely on trends and metrics, whereas others were fairly matter of fact about it as a reality of the job. Whilst some who resisted algorithmic optimisation understood themselves as having more artistic integrity and authenticity—they were being *true to themselves* and didn't want to produce content only to gain views—others were clear that visibility was the main goal of their job, and they were willing to make any content that would lead to it. The majority of creators sat somewhere in the middle of these two extremes, trying to find an equilibrium between creating content they were proud of whilst maintaining financial stability.

Several creators had some kind of self-imposed rule for balancing their output of popular versus other types of content; they "allowed" themselves a certain quota of videos that they knew would not perform well in terms of metrics, but that they really wanted to make for artistic, educational, or other reasons. Simi told me that he made "whatever he wanted" most of the time, but that every third video or so on his channel had to be a trending/popular one in order to keep his numbers up. His rationale for this was that, according to hearsay, channels that have big lulls or are too erratic in their viewing figures stop being recommended by The Algorithm. The last thing he wanted was for his channel to crash, so committing to "playing the game" for every third video seemed to him to be a reasonable compromise and acted as a kind of buoy for the channel.

It is well established in the literature on influencers that being perceived as *authentic* by viewers—whatever authenticity looks like for a particular creator-audience community—is fundamental for success in social media entertainment (for example, Abidin, 2015; Duffy, 2017). Every creator I interviewed struggled with balancing the pressures of producing content of sufficient quality and quantity to please YouTube's algorithms, whilst simultaneously performing the *relational labour*—defined by Baym as the "ongoing, interactive, affective, material, and cognitive work of communicating with people over time to create structures that can support continued work" (2018: 19)—required to maintain the core proposition of authenticity and intimacy with their audience. Whilst it is common practise to modify content on the basis of algorithmic hearsay and folk theories, during fieldwork I found that creators who appear to only chase metric (and financial) success are often perceived as lacking the all-important authenticity required of influencers and can thus be met with disapproval by audiences. It is not simply a matter of knowing how YouTube's recommendation system works, but also of successfully striking the right balance between utilising this knowledge and maintaining the right tone with audiences. Creators can quite easily find themselves stuck between a rock and a hard place if they fail to achieve this balance, satisfying neither their audience nor "The Algorithm".

Influencer Experiences: Feeling the Algorithm

As Bucher puts it, when trying to understand algorithms as sociological phenomena, "what people experience is not the mathematical recipe as such but, rather, the moods, affects and sensations that the algorithm helps to generate" (2017: 32). This final empirical section reflects on how it *feels* the work with (or against) YouTube's algorithmic recommendation system. I address the fear induced by the ever-present possibility of algorithmic invisibility, which is exacerbated in moments of algorithmic rupture across the platform. Beyond the precarity wrought by The Algorithm on *all* creators, in this final section I turn my attention to the *algorithmic discrimination* that marginalised creators face in the influencer industry.

The Fear of Algorithmically Induced Invisibility

The overwhelming sentiments that content creators express about The Algorithm are anxiety, confusion, anger, and above all fear. For a full-time professional creator, the fear is that it will suddenly and inexplicably render them invisible to viewers and thus destroy their career. For a small aspiring creator, the fear is that they will never achieve the algorithmic visibility required for their career to take off.

Whilst content creators have never been on solid ground when it comes to YouTube's algorithms, their fears escalate during moments of algorithmic "rupture" on the platform (Duffy et al., 2021: 8), a significant incident of which was the first *Adpocalypse* in 2017. In response to reports of adverts appearing on terrorist content, as well as an anti-Semitic video posted by Felix Kjellberg (AKA PewDiePie), a number of high-profile advertisers pulled out of YouTube. In an attempt to appease advertisers, YouTube drastically tightened how it algorithmically identifies "advertiser-friendly" content, leading to a tidal wave of videos being demonetised and deselected for recommendation to viewers. Creators felt disempowered and angry that The Algorithm was making their already precarious livelihoods even more unpredictable, and heavily criticised YouTube for prioritising the interests of advertisers over the creators who provide the labour that generates value for them. As A-list creator Lilly Singh (AKA Superwoman) put it in a vlog:

> Over the past year it has all gone to hell. There's just no pattern to what is happening in essentially my business, and it is scary and it's frustrating. I don't know *if* people see my videos, I don't know *how* people see my videos, I don't know *what* channels are being promoted, I don't know *why* some channels are being promoted more than others. There's just no answers, and that's scary to me.
>
> *Singh, 2017*

There have been multiple *Adpocalypses* since 2017, as YouTube has tried to keep a lid on a succession of controversies, from the improper recommendation of content to kids, to paedophilia concerns, to hate speech (Alexander 2019a). Consequently, YouTube has struggled to balance fostering its amateur participatory culture and the interests of advertisers (Caplan and Gillespie, 2020: 9), and in recent years the platform has gradually moved away from promoting its home-grown talent in favour of Hollywood celebrities, music videos and clips from late-night shows—a safer bet for attracting advertising dollars—leaving its community of content creators feeling abandoned (Alexander 2019a). Small and aspiring creators have been disproportionately punished by these changes; there is a pervasive feeling in the London Small YouTubers community that the drawbridge has been pulled up and the algorithmic barriers to entry are insurmountable. As one creator said at the "Smaller Creators" panel at Summer in the City 2019: "They can't handle the amount of content being uploaded and so they've closed off the gates for small creators. No one small is getting recommended by The Algorithm" (Glatt, 2022).

Algorithmic Discrimination: The Marginalisation of Creators on YouTube

So far in this chapter I have discussed the heightened precarity and pressures that *all* content creators experience in the face of algorithmic recommendation systems as platformised creative workers. However, there is growing acknowledgement amongst creators, platforms, and researchers that algorithmic punishment is not evenly distributed, disproportionately impacting certain groups in line with existing social inequalities (Banet-Weiser and Glatt, 2022; Bishop, 2018; Duffy et al., 2021; Glatt, 2022; Noble, 2018).

Sociocultural and commercial inequalities across intersections of race, class, gender, ability, and sexuality persist in the influencer industry and the barriers to entry are "staggeringly high" (Duffy, 2017: 223), with minority content creators excluded from elite career opportunities on a structural level. As Nicole Ocran, Co-Founder of *The Creator Union*, said in an interview for *The Guardian*, "LGBTQ+ creators, disabled creators, plus-size creators and Black and brown influencers are constantly being asked to work for free" (Tait, 2020). Throughout data collection I heard repeatedly about systemic issues of *algorithmic discrimination*, which I define as a process whereby certain content, identities, and positionalities within the platform economy are deprioritised from recommendation, in an industry where visibility is key to success (Glatt, 2022).

The 2017 *Adpocalypse* was especially problematic for LGBTQ+ creators, despite YouTube having long positioned itself as a champion for the community. At a panel titled *Not Suitable for Advertisers* during my fieldwork at VidCon USA 2018, I witnessed an impassioned discussion about the pain and frustration that LGBTQ+ creators were experiencing with their content being automatically demonetised and age restricted, with no recourse to air their grievances with YouTube beyond tagging them on Twitter. Creators had resorted to removing any reference LGBTQ+ issues in the tags and titles of their videos, to try to avoid invisibility, but this had the adverse effect of making their videos unsearchable. One of the panellists said that she had decided to leave YouTube altogether, feeling that they no longer had her interests at heart, if indeed they ever had. This example highlights the impersonal and anonymous nature of working on social media platforms, where all but the most elite creators are left to fend for themselves with partial information about how their content is recommended or demonetised and little opportunity to communicate directly with the platforms that host their work.

Creators from more marginalised identities face greater obstacles in the pursuit of sustainable careers in this industry as a result of compounding sociocultural, technological, and commercial inequalities. This bias is baked into the very design of YouTube's algorithms, supporting arguments made by intersectional technology scholars that highlight enduring and emerging forms of intersectional discrimination on the Internet (Brock, 2011; Noble and Tynes, 2016; Noble, 2018). As Banet-Weiser and I argue, YouTube's algorithms are "designed to render some content more visible than others, and the logic of this asymmetry is based on profitability" (Glatt and Banet-Weiser, 2021: 54), a system which privileges "brand safe" creators, namely those who are white, heteronormative, middle class, and unthreatening to the neoliberal status quo. Whilst "The Algorithm" isn't understood as a friendly force in the wider influencer community-industry, for marginalised creators it is experienced as nothing short of hostile.

Conclusions

In this chapter, I have analysed "The Algorithm" as a multifaceted sociotechnical assemblage (Christin 2020) that emerged through ethnographic fieldwork in the YouTube community-industry. I conducted close readings of content creators' *discourses*, *practices*, and *experiences* to make sense of the multifaceted and situated ways that they understand and respond to YouTube's algorithms in their working lives. "The Algorithm" is variously understood as an omnipotent God, a black box to be opened, a mystery to be solved, a voracious machine, and an oppressor of marginalised groups. Above all, it is experienced as unknowable, impenetrable, mysterious, and inscrutable. Despite the diversity of my participants, I found that they universally understood The Algorithm as an antagonistic force, one which made their working lives more precarious, unpredictable, and stressful. In the influencer industry, where "[visibility] is a key vector of instability" (Duffy et al., 2021: 10), creators are obligated to bend themselves to the wills and shifts of algorithmic recommendation systems if they hope to build and sustain careers.

Some may wonder if ethnography is a useful method for investigating platforms' algorithmic recommendation systems, unable to get to the heart of how they "actually work", but I argue that attending to the lived experiences of content creators who navigate algorithms on a daily basis adds a powerful and complimentary dimension to more macro structural critiques of the asymmetries of power built into capitalist algorithmic systems (for example, Noble 2018; Pasquale 2015). As Seaver puts it, "ethnography roots these concerns in empirical soil, resisting arguments that threaten to wash away ordinary experience in a flood of abstraction" (2017: 2).

Platform companies "hold a perverse level of power in contemporary culture and society" (Duffy et al., 2021: 9), not least in their role as arbiters of the livelihoods of creative workers in the burgeoning influencer industry, and critical researchers can work to hold them to account. In this regard, research into the uneven distribution of algorithmic visibility across intersections of race, class, gender, and sexuality in the influencer industry has begun to emerge (Banet-Weiser and Glatt, 2022; Bishop, 2018; 2021; Duffy et al., 2021; Glatt, 2022), to which this chapter contributes findings regarding the *algorithmic discrimination* that my participants reported, but more is needed. I see further research into the ways in which "The Algorithm" functions particularly as a disciplinary force for marginalised content creators, and the ways in which they are able, or not, to resist such disciplining, as a key avenue for future research.

References

Abidin, C. (2015) "Communicative <3 Intimacies: Influencers and Perceived Interconnectedness," *Ada: A Journal of Gender, New Media, & Technology*, 8.

Alexander, J. (2019a) "The Golden Age of YouTube is Over," *The Verge*, 5 April, available at www.theverge.com/2019/4/5/18287318/youtube-logan-paul-pewdiepie-demonetization-adpocalypse-premium-infl

Alexander, J. (2019b) "YouTube Videos Keep Getting Longer," *The Verge*, 26 July, available at www.theverge.com/2019/7/26/8888003/youtube-video-length-contrapoints-lindsay-ellis-shelby-church-ad-revenue

Baym, N. K. (2000) *Tune In, Log on: Soaps, Fandom, and Online Community*. London: Sage.

Baym, N. K. (2018) *Playing to the Crowd: Musicians, Audiences, and the Intimate Work of Connection*. New York: NYU Press.

Bishop, S. (2018) "Anxiety, Panic and Self-optimization: Inequalities and the YouTube Algorithm," *Convergence*, 24, 69–84.

Bishop, S. (2019) "Managing Visibility on YouTube Through Algorithmic Gossip," *New Media & Society* [online first], 1–18.

Bishop, S. (2020) "Algorithmic Experts: Selling Algorithmic Lore on YouTube," *Social Media + Society*, 6(1), 1–11.

Berg, M. and Brown, A. (2020) "The Highest-Paid YouTube Stars Of 2020," *Forbes*, December 18, available at www.forbes.com/sites/maddieberg/2020/12/18/the-highest-paid-youtube-stars-of-2020/?sh=6ce0992e

Boellstorff, T. (2008) *Coming of Age in Second Life: An Anthropologist Explores the Virtually Human*. Princeton, NJ: Princeton University Press.

Brock, A. (2011) "Beyond the Pale: The Blackbird Web Browser's Critical Reception," *New Media and Society*, 13(7), 1085–1103.

Bucher, T. (2017) "The Algorithmic Imaginary: Exploring the Ordinary Affects of Facebook algorithms," *Information, Communication & Society*, 20, 30–44.

Bucher, T. (2018) *If … Then: Algorithmic Power and Politics*, Oxford: OUP.

Caplan, R. and Gillespie, T. (2020) "Tiered Governance and Demonetization: The Shifting Terms of Labor and Compensation in the Platform Economy," *Social Media + Society*, 6.

Chen, M. (2019) "A New World of Workers: Confronting the Gig Economy," *The Socialist Register 2020*, 56, 122–142.

Christin, A. (2020) "The Ethnographer and the Algorithm: Beyond the Black Box," *Theory and Society*, 49(5–6), 897–918.

Cunningham, S. and Craig, D. (2019) *Social Media Entertainment: The New Intersection of Hollywood and Silicon Valley*, New York: New York University Press.

Duffy, B. E. (2017) *(Not) Getting Paid to Do What You Love: Gender, Social Media, and Aspirational Work*, New Haven, CT: Yale University Press.

Duffy, B. E., Poell, T., and Nieborg, D. B. (2019) "Platform Practices in the Cultural Industries: Creativity, Labor, and Citizenship," *Social Media + Society*, 5(4), 1–8.

Duffy, B. E., Sannon, S., Pinch, A., and Sawey, M. (2021) "The Nested Precarities of Platformized Creative Labor," *Social Media + Society*, April 2021, 1–12.

Duffy, B. E. and Schwartz, B. (2018) "Digital 'Women's Work?': Job Recruitment Ads and the Feminization of Social Media Employment," *New Media & Society*, 20, 2972–2989.

Gill R. and Pratt, A. (2008) "In the Social Factory? Immaterial Labor, Precariousness and Cultural Work," *Theory, Culture and Society*, 25(7–8), 1–30.

Glatt, Z. (forthcoming) "'We're All Told Not to Put Our Eggs in One Basket': Uncertainty, Precarity and Cross-platform Labour in the Online Video Influencer Industry," *International Journal of Communication*, Special Issue on Uncertainty.

Glatt, Z. and Banet-Weiser, S. (2021) "Productive Ambivalence, Economies of Visibility and the Political Potential of Feminist YouTubers" in Cunningham, S. and Craig, D. (eds), *Creator Culture: Studying the Social Media Entertainment Industry*, New York: NYU Press.

Gray, M. L. and Suri, S. (2019) *Ghost Work: How to Stop Silicon Valley from Building a New Global Underclass*. Boston, MA: Houghton Mifflin Harcourt.

Hine, C. (2015) *Ethnography for the Internet: Embedded, Embodied and Everyday*, London: Bloomsbury Academic.

Hine, C. (2017) "Ethnography and the Internet: Taking Account of Emerging Technological Landscapes," *Fudan Journal of the Humanities and Social Sciences*, 10(3), 315–329.

Lange, P. (2019) *Thanks for Watching: An Anthropological Study of Video Sharing on YouTube*, Louisville: University Press of Colorado.

McRobbie, A. (2016) *Be Creative: Making a Living in the New Culture Industries*. Cambridge: Polity.

Miller, D. and Slater, D. (2000) *The Internet: An Ethnographic Approach*. Oxford: Berg.

Nardi, B. A. (2009) *My Life as a Night Elf Priest: An Anthropological Account of World of Warcraft*. Michigan: University of Michigan Press.

Noble, S. U. (2018) *Algorithms of Oppression: How Search Engines Reinforce Racism*, New York: NYU Press.

Noble, S. U. and Tynes, B. M. (2016) *The Intersectional Internet: Race, Sex, Class and Culture Online*, New York: Peter Lang Publishing.

Pasquale, F. (2015) *The Black Box Society: The Secret Algorithms That Control Money and Information*, Cambridge: Harvard University Press.

Poell, T., Nieborg, D. B., and Duffy, B. E. (2021) *Platforms and Cultural Production*. Cambridge: Polity Press.

Postill, J. and Pink, S. (2012) "Social Media Ethnography: The Digital Researcher in a Messy Web," *Media International Australia*, 145(1), 123–134.

Rosenblat, A. (2018) *Uberland: How Algorithms Are Rewriting the Rules of Work*, Oakland: University of California Press.

Seaver, N. (2017) "Algorithms as Culture: Some Tactics for the Ethnography of Algorithmic Systems," *Big Data & Society*, 4(2), 1–12.

Senft, T. M. (2008) *Camgirls: Celebrity and Community in the Age of Social Networks*, New York: Lang.

Senft, T. M. (2013) "Microcelebrity and the Branded Self," in Hartley, J., Burgess, J. and Bruns, A. (eds), *A Companion to New Media Dynamics*, Chichester: John Wiley & Sons, 346–354.

Singh, L. (2017) "We Need to Have an Honest Talk," *YouTube* (SuperwomanVlogs), 9th December, available at www.youtube.com/watch?v=KjK81YmQEuY

Stokel-Walker, C. (2018) "'Success' on YouTube Still Means a Life of Poverty," *Bloomberg*, 27 February, available at www.bloomberg.com/news/articles/2018-02-27/-success-on-youtube-still-means-a-life-of-poverty

Tait, A. (2020) "'Influencers Are Being Taken Advantage Of': The Social Media Stars Turning to Unions," *The Guardian*, 10 October, available at www.theguardian.com/media/2020/oct/10/influencers-are-being-taken-advantage-of-the-social-media-stars-turning-to-unions

40
AI DESIGN AND EVERYDAY LOGICS IN THE KALAHARI

Nicola J. Bidwell, Helen Arnold, Alan F. Blackwell,
Charlie Nqeisji, |Kun Kunta, and Martin Ujakpa

It's the rainy season in the north Kalahari and it's quiet at the lodge at the end of that long gravel road, 280 km from the nearest major Namibian town. The savannah around the waterhole, unchurned by elephants, is now abloom with wild sesame flowers. There are no tourists or other researchers inside the lodge's reception boma, unlike in the dry season, when Alan and Nic read a sheet of paper pinned to a wooden beam resting against the thatch. The printed text tells of the annual game count, and eight graphs plot the estimated animal populations over past years. At the end of each dry season local Ju|'hoansi rangers count the animals visiting 18 waterholes in a 48-hour period. Their counts are fed into scientific models with variables, such as annual rainfall, to predict species numbers across the Nyae Nyae Conservancy's 9,000 km² expanse. The graphs tell stories. These stories, though, do not thrill with the odds of encountering either a snake, after dropping a stone into a hollowed tree, or thirsty elephants while walking to school.

In the era of the algorithm, everything, including life itself, is treated as a computable object (Mbembe, 2019) and inevitably, given conservation's economic importance in Namibia, species data will figure in national engagement with the Fourth Industrial Revolution (4IR). Ju|'hoansi people, like those involved in the Nyae Nyae's annual game count,[1] might produce the raw commodity: the data used by Artificial Intelligence (AI) systems. Some already use CyberTracker[2] to record knowledge about animals that is analysed by scientists (e.g. Koot and van Beek, 2017). The analyses computed by prevalent AI systems, however, inherit from certain social and material traditions and not the imaginations and problem-solving of Ju|'hoansi people.

This chapter is about the relationship between the explainability of AI and the experiences, livelihoods and knowledge practices of marginalised groups. We present formative insights from a study in which we put some of the abstractions that are necessary to understand how AI computes relationships between variables into conversation with Ju|'hoansi people's cause-and-effect reasoning. Our project is part of a vision to design both school curricula, that introduces statistical methods for AI in locally accessible ways, and AI tools that marginalised groups can use to encode their knowledge themselves. We show how playing a game of chance contributed to an ethnographic exploration of local knowledge practices. Our approach is situated in Human-Computer Interaction (HCI), an interdisciplinary field focused on the design of technology and interactions between people and computers. Thus, we also illustrate what a practice-based

DOI: 10.4324/9781003175605-54

understanding of the abstractions used in computation brings to ethnographies of AI. Our focus on design and interaction is compatible with approaches in media anthropology that emphasise the practices of new media technologies, and the ways in which they are experienced as 'immediately cultural inflected genres of usage' (Horst and Miller, 2013: 29).

We begin by introducing anthropological studies of accountability in machine learning and data practices. Then we outline ethnographic studies in HCI that both uncover the ways that technology production reproduce colonialism in Africa and contribute to it; and illustrate some of the challenges of designing more reflexively. The rest of the chapter describes how our collaboration in the Nyae Nyae revealed qualities in cause-and-effect reasoning that mathematics curricula do not emphasise and may be important in making AI accountable to diverse knowledge practices.

Ethnographies of AI

Ethnographic research about knowledge practices in AI began in science and technology studies (STS) of the design of symbolic AI and interactive systems in the 1990s (Campagnolo, 2020). With the wide-scale application of machine learning to data about citizens, more recent ethnographies have been provoked by concerns about the opacity of algorithms and the use and curation of data.

Explainable Algorithms

Explaining the models that Machine Learning (ML) algorithms create is vital in establishing ethical global governance and legal frameworks for AI (Burrell, 2016). ML algorithms are the sets of procedures that AI systems follow in making statistical decisions on the basis of training data (Cardon et al., 2018). For instance, a classifier is a common type of algorithm that learns to automatically categorise data into a number of classes, on the basis of training examples. The decisions made by AI systems derive from statistical models that the algorithms create and refine during training as they make predictions about the data and improve the performance of these predictions. A classification algorithm, for example, effectively tests hypotheses about patterns in the data and adjusts its model of classification rules to fit the frequencies of patterns. There are many ML algorithms of varying complexity, some learn with supervision, using data labelled by humans, and others identify classes themselves. However, explaining the models created from the training data is hindered by technical illiteracy, intellectual property, intentional corporate or state secrecy (Burrell, 2016) and because even the people involved in producing ML algorithms have partial views. Not only are algorithms comprised of ensembles of, often distributed, networks that interact with each other (Campagnolo, 2020); but they formalise qualities and quantify uncertain situational things that are embedded in sociotechnical systems.

Lowrie's (2017) ethnographic study in a university department linked to 'the Russian Google' illustrates how knowledge practices in Data Science, the dominant sector that applies AI to practical problems, contribute to algorithmic opacity. To construct functioning assemblages, data scientists use statistical, mathematical and computer science methods to abstract the high-level computational mechanisms that perform predictions. However, they implement operations in code running on particular hardware architectures and improve efficiency by making many adjustments. Thus, unlike evaluating mathematical formulae or proofs or scientific experiments, data scientists assess algorithmic performance relative to the feasibility and expense of assemblages resulting from their numerous tweaks. Making algorithms legible, then, inherently changes the work of creating them and achieving transparency does not simply uncover what an algorithm comprises but, as Neyland's (2016) ethnography shows, reconfigures the social scene. Seaver (2019) found that heterogenous meanings about algorithms are produced across the social life of AI, when he observed practices and interviewed at a company, and scavenged from press releases, patent applications, conference presentations and exchanges at hackathons, on mailing lists and social media. He argues that, given opacity and the speed at which they are changed, ML algorithms do not just *express* culture but *are* culture (Seaver, 2017).

Data and the Global Souths

Joint ventures on ML, between governments, elite multi-lateral and transnational organisations including tech giants, such as Facebook and Google, have proliferated in Africa. However, while the text and images in the datasets used in training might be mined locally and labelled by low-paid humans in the Global Souths (Gray and Suri, 2019), the algorithms are created in the Global North and data transactions controlled by entities located outside of Africa (UNCTAD, 2018). Thus, many ethnographic studies about AI and the Global Souths consider the ways that power asymmetries are performed in extracting and preparing the data that is input into ML algorithms (e.g. Milan and Trere 2017; Treré, 2016).

Some anthropologists observe that private sector experts who design and implement technologies and processes that extract and prepare the data input into ML algorithms can resemble human rights practitioners and advocates (Sapignoli, 2021). Others argue that absent or inadequate privacy and data protection laws in Global South countries are exploited to test new forms of surveillance (Arora, 2020). This has prompted collating principles to guide technology designers and developers in using data (e.g. Jain and Rangaswamy, 2020). Yet, there is also concern that the practices and attitudes of users in the Global Souths are fictionalised, and interpreted through both normative values and essentialist views of selfhood and community (Arora, 2020). Certainly, increased use of big data in digital media studies (Kitchin, 2014) obscures the fabric of social relations with the generalisable, aggregated and mass (Appadurai 2016), and can relegate researchers in the Global Souths to roles as labellers of the data that powers the theories of engineers in the Global North (Wasserman, 2021). The need to develop more reflexive methods (Elish and Boyd, 2018), however, is impeded by algorithmic opacity, which prompts HCI researchers to combine ethnography with their technical literacy and design skills in more inclusive approaches to AI (e.g. Yadav, 2019; Azra and Kumar, 2021).

Ethnography, HCI and Africa

Ethnographic techniques were adopted by HCI in response to recognition that the context in which a technology will be used is not specifiable in the same way as we determine computer operations. They have become widely used to both describe the social organisation of activity for the purposes of technology design and critically analyse sociotechnical systems. As this section introduces, ethnography in HCI has not only highlighted but also contributed to the ways that technology production reproduces colonialism in Africa.

Localising Technology Production

HCI studies have explored the different ways that a paradigm of technology production, which originated in Silicon Valley, is promoted across Africa. This *universal paradigm* encompasses defining innovation, structuring problems and evaluating solutions in certain ways; using certain programming languages and design and development methodologies; and valorising certain professions, places and tools (Avle, Lindtner and Williams, 2017; Aludhilu and Bidwell, 2018). The paradigm is perpetuated by external consultation on digital policies, investment in and coordination of tech hubs, start-ups, 'dev labs' and hackathons (e.g. Csikszentmihalyi et al., 2018), and teaching in tertiary and higher education (Aludhilu and Bidwell, 2018). Stabilised by technical and historical circumstances, social infrastructures and sociotechnical assemblages and shaped by imperialist superiorities and racism the paradigm contributes to economic inequality within African nations and between Africa and elsewhere (Irani et al., 2010a; Avle and Lindtner, 2016; Irani, 2018; Arawjo, 2020).

Many HCI endeavours apply ethnographic insights to localise existing technologies to suit African settings. Some reveal that standard design constructs do not match interactions in local settings (e.g. Winschiers-Theophilus and Bidwell, 2013; Mwewa and Bidwell, 2016). Others focus on creating digital archives to store, and make shareable, *indigenous knowledge* (IK) (e.g. Stanley, Cabrero and Winschiers-Theophilus, 2017). The conceptualisation of IK emerged as a strategy to resist subjugation and produce benefits from local practices. It remains globally important to defending indigenous people's land by reference to their environmental knowledge, though is often complicated by political and historical influences that selectively authorise and valorise indigenous claims. Endeavours often use participatory approaches in attempts to address power relations (e.g. Keskinen et al., 2021). Yet, digitisation tends to frame ethnographic insights within technology production processes that direct attention to certain facts and certain ways to theorise about and manifest those facts; for instance, presenting IK as *content* that is classified according to scientific templates and rendered in certain ways (Awori, 2016). Indeed, use of ethnographic methods in designing technology to support African IK rarely explicitly accounts for the epistemologies of technology practices.

Translating Inhabitant Knowledge

Some details about how technology production shape insights about local knowledge became clear in co-author Nic's prior ethnographic studies in South Africa. Living in rural Mankosi for four years, she mediated between amaXhosa inhabitants' practices and meanings embedded in the design of communal, solar-powered, cell-phone charging stations and digital media-sharing prototypes. A small local team analysed practices in managing and using two charging stations located in two villages about 2.5 km apart. Like other inhabitants we walked between and around villages and produced meanings about the data that we generated, in interviews, station operators' written logs of the phones that inhabitants charged and observations and interactions when we fixed technical problems, within our experience of everyday life. Thus, this 'alongly' integrated knowledge (e.g. Ingold, 2011) was embodied along the paths in which the practices related to the stations were embedded. It differed from the knowledge formed in the upward integration of data generated in discrete design workshops and interviews by visiting software developers and media experts (Bidwell et al., 2013).

Designing the media-sharing prototypes that ran on communal tablets illustrates the challenges in translating knowledge embodied in inhabiting into models that are encoded in software. The prototypes embedded a model of personhood that people are individuals prior to the formation of community. This model is manifested by single-user approaches to devices and accounts (e.g. Dourish and Mainwaring 2012; Bidwell, 2016) and by the entity *person* in typical database schema. It was coherent with operators' logs of individual people who left phones to charge, passwords protecting phones, and the isiXhosa expression 'umuntu w'ubuntu', or human being conceived as an individual by, with/in self or oneself (e.g. Ntibagirirwa 2001).

However, it did not account for local emphasis on a logic that a human being is socially constituted with/in community: 'umuntu mu bantu'. In designing software Nic tried to translate this communalist logic into database models but could not explain alternative designs to local team members to reconcile ambiguities. Besides, a logic of person as prior to community, embedded in the software, did not actually interrupt inhabitants when they created and used their accounts and interacted with prototypes together with apparent social ease (Bidwell, Reitmaier and Jampo, 2014). Our difficulties in conceptualising personhood resonate with Verran's ethnographic account of building theory from Yoruba logics of number; she describes how she rendered these logics as objects yet, in ongoing daily life, 'it was scarcely possible to separate human body and numeral' (Verran, 2001:75). Nic's dichotomising was equally contrived. She produced a distinction between logics by translating communalism through a logic that is normalised in practices of database design and teaching.

Explainable AI in the Kalahari

Training and optimising ML algorithms makes the relations constructed amongst data even less explicit than building a database. However, research at the intersection of AI, probability theory and programming languages suggests that Probabilistic Programming Languages (PPL) offer potential to both teach the basics of ML and enable people to encode their knowledge themselves in computer progammes (Blackwell et al., 2019). Unfortunately, new maths curricula rarely originate within the Global Souths, which compromises their potential contribution to improving the accountability of AI. Thus, to inform approaches to curricula that can support a basic understanding of ML systems in marginalised contexts we collaborated with Ju|'hoansi people in the Nyae Nyae Conservancy.

Engaging with Ju|'hoansi People

Some 1,600 Ju|'hoansi people live in villages, of approximately 10 to 60 people, scattered across the bush, and another 1,400 live most of the time in the town of Tsumkwe. Ju|'hoan is Namibia's largest language group of the San, a culturally marginalised people with limited political representation and a Human Development Index at half of the nation's average (Legal Assistance Centre, 2014). Yet, as one of the most researched of all indigenous groups globally, Ju|'hoansi people have long sought to exploit the 'cultural economics of indigeneity' for their livelihood in the 'modern world' (Hitchcock and Biesele, 2002) by, for instance, establishing Namibia's first communal conservation scheme (Zips and Zips-Mairitsch, 2019).

Over the past decade Nic has engaged with San groups and the San Council of Namibia in different technology projects but was introduced to Ju|'hoansi people, in 2016, by Candi Miller who established links 20 years ago and co-founded the Nyae Nyae Village Schools Feeding project.[3] We stayed for a few days in a village and engaged with volunteers supporting the school and developing educational resources in Ju|'hoan. Few villages can access electricity, phone connectivity or motor transport and many inhabitants are reading-writing illiterate. Thus, the Ju|'hoansi's traditional leadership, and others with whom we maintained contact, sought support for communication between villages and our relationships deepened in projects for Ju|'hoan content-production for radio[4] (Miller, 2021), and an inter-village communication system. For instance, in field trips over six months, in 2019, co-authors Nic and Martin, both staff at a Namibian university, Candi, staff at Nyae Nyae's tribal authority and conservancy offices and inhabitants of 22 different villages designed and deployed a prototype communication system. An international team[5] developed the software but Ju|'hoansi people, including co-author |Kun, a local tech-enthusiast, installed and monitored it. Our funding application proposed that we would synchronise content on each village's device with repositories sited at six schools but, by the time we undertook design in the Nyae Nyae, children were prevented from walking to school because of the danger of encountering, elephants roaming for water in the extreme drought. Thus, we installed low-cost, solar-charging set-ups and communal phones in each of the 40 villages and software to synchronise data phone-to-phone.

A few months after launching the communication prototype Nic returned to the Nyae Nyae with co-authors who were visiting from the UK: Helen, a maths teacher, and Alan, a computer scientist with expertise in data modelling and coding language. We sought to explore how to teach the basics of probability for ML and worked closely with co-author Charlie, a Ju|'hoansi inhabitant with extensive experience of translating for researchers of different disciplines. We spoke to principals and teachers of Tsumkwe high school and the village schools, inhabitants in a village, and staff at the conservancy and tribal authority offices about mathematics curricula, how children learn in villages and everyday scenarios in which people make predictions and decisions. We had planned considerable participation in school maths classes, but the onset of COVID-19 curtailed our trip. Thus, we created games of chance and, after we left, analysed what took place when people played them. We communicated with |Kun and Charlie by email and WhatsApp about their own, and others', understandings of probability, experiences and opinions about the game and in writing this chapter.

At the Intersection of AI, Programming Languages, Probability Theory and Local Predictive Practices

We sought to explore how some of the abstractions used in ML might be included in curriculum content and supported by PPL tools in ways that are compatible with Ju|'hoansi people's predictive reasoning. A PPL is designed to describe probabilistic models and then perform inference in those models. They suit situations that would be considered 'data-poor', in relation to large-scale statistical analysis (Blackwell et al., 2019); do not necessarily require costly hardware and energy demanding processing, as generally involved in training ML algorithms (Blackwell, 2015); and can offer interactive and accessible tools (e.g. Gorinova et al., 2016, Taka et al., 2020). New programming languages can increase access to coding; for instance, Scratch, a visual language, is used to teach children to code all around the world; and various efforts have taught programming skills to indigenous youth during traditional events (e.g. Sorro et al., 2020). However, programming languages are shaped by education systems, spoken languages, written notations, terminologies and epistemological tendencies; and no efforts have tackled the culture of programming languages and algorithms (Lewis et al., 2018).

There is some consensus that PPL build on the logic of Bayesian inference (Blackwell et al., 2021), in which prediction of an unknown value begins by assigning a likelihood, a prior, to a hypothesis. A prior mathematically expresses something people already know, guess based on their experience, or estimate informed by expert advice (Morris, Oakley and Crowe., 2014). The likelihood of the prior can be adjusted after further observations, which makes the logic about using inference from data in ML more visible and may also align with the way people 'alongly integrate' to form knowledge (e.g. Ingold, 2011). Inference also resembles claims about the role of speculation in San practices of tracking animals. Liebenberg's (2013) extensive studies suggest that expert trackers, including some Ju|'hoansi, systematically observe signs, such as spoor, and speculate when signs are unclear. Trackers hypothesise about an animal's behaviour by recognising, interpreting and creating causal connections between signs, and their speculations predict novel facts to explain signs that would be otherwise meaningless. When new information emerges during a hunt that contradicts expectations, trackers construct auxiliary hypotheses to explain tracks and predict movements.

Scientists have begun to include priors based on interviews with indigenous hunters in using Bayesian inference to model animal patterns (Gryba, 2020) and maths education has deployed interactive tools to 'diagnose misconceptions' when people learn about probability (e.g. Balawi, Khalaf and Hitt, 2016). However, as far as we know, no work attempts to make the abstractions, that are fundamental to understanding how AI systems compute, accessible to indigenous groups. Indeed, Bayesian statistics are seldom taught in schools, even in the Global North, despite increased recognition of their advantages over traditional 'frequentist' statistics.

Predictive Logics: Stories and Spinner Games

Programming using a PPL involves reasoning about the relationship between two or more random variables and many approaches to teaching Bayesian statistics value conditional probability in relating observations to cause-and-effect reasoning. Thus, we designed spinner games to enable us to bring conditional probability into conversation with local reasoning.

Conditional Probability: Trees with Holes, Water and Snakes

Our spinners actually present a hybrid of Bayesian and traditional curriculum approaches to statistics and were inspired by teaching aids described by Gage and Spiegelhalter (2016), both of whom have taught in Africa. Each spinner comprises an unfolded paperclip anchored in the centre of a paper circle so it will spin when flicked. The game used three spinners, made by colouring in different sized segments so that the probability of the paperclip stopping in a coloured segment differed. One spinner represented whether or not there was hole in a tree, another whether or not the hole contained water and another whether or not that hole contained a snake. These variables arose in a scenario described by a group of 24 Ju|'hoansi men and women in a village about what children must learn in daily life.

The group discussed various themes, including learning about animal spoor and gathering food, but elaborated most on obtaining water. All villages have boreholes, however, children in Grade 3 (aged 9 to 13 years) should hear stories about finding water to be able to survive in the bush. Participants described extracting water from the tubers of a succulent plant, from puddles and trapped in hollows and crooks of tree, and one man spoke, in Ju|'hoan, of avoiding danger, "Looking for water to drink, he must take care of him selfs, maybe a snake will be there. First he must put something into the hole, to check if it is fine and then he able to drink water". It would be best, the man said, if children heard these stories both at home and school. Later, when we discussed the spinners and the scenario with the Chief, he noted the relevance to both teaching maths and helping children to take care.

Eight men and four women, aged late teens to early thirties, played the spinner game: a group at the conservancy office; a group of high-school students in Grades 9 to 11; and, |Kun and his two friends. Our account uses pseudonyms for their names. The scenario was familiar to everyone we spoke to, however some participants who played the spinner game questioned the plausibility of going to the bush alone and the probabilities of the spinners we created. One group said that many more trees with holes would contain water, in their village, than the equal probability our spinner represented; and another group that there are less snakes than our spinner suggested. Some groups also observed agency in relation to the conditions, such as first dropping a stone in the hole to check if there is a snake.

Numbers are Stories

An American teacher who had worked in Tsumkwe for a decade attributed inconsistency in Ju|'hoansi people's use of numbers to life-styles that do not prioritise accumulating things. Ju|'hoan's base-five system has words for numbers up to *g!au*, or one hand,[6] and two groups used their fingers to record the outcome of successive spins in their spinner games. The group of three men studying at high school did not use their fingers to count and spoke of difficulties translating maths to Ju|'hoan when trying to help others. After Grade 3 all teaching is in English, Namibia's national language, and a pass in English in the matriculation exam is a prerequisite for enrolling in maths and sciences at university. One high-school student spent time recalling the English mathematical terms for specific features of a circle thinking he might need to apply geometry to calculate the spinners segments. Another, Carlos, brought with him a copy of Pimentel and Wall's (2018) Grade 11 textbook, its cover bearing an endorsement by University of Cambridge International Examinations. He said, in English, 'it's hard for me to come out with … I'm actually not in deep with the thing, I'm not so understanding, I cannot just use my language'.

Young men in the final group that played the spinner game discussed, in Ju|'hoan, how they should count the outcomes of each spin. They enthusiastically drew a grid, on parcel paper we provided, that resembled the logs that rangers are taught to use in wild game counts. They labelled four columns with sketches in order: lion, snake, water, tree. The lion column remained unfilled, but they marked the others with ticks and crosses to record the outcome of each spin. After 10 sets of spins they wrote totals in ways that resembled gambling odds: "9/1" (9 spins without a snake and 1 with); "8/1" (8 without and 1 with water): "6/4" (6 trees without and 4 with a hole). Participants' engagement in the spinner game seemed to relate to the chance of danger and some were nervous about finding a snake; however Dorothy, in the conservancy group, exclaimed in English, "algebra is more scary!" and that "excitement would also come out in the storytelling" in the spinner game.

Numbers have meanings in cause-and-effect reasoning. The group that drew the grid said that the direction they walked in the bush was influenced by how many animals were in different places. In our first conversations together, Charlie had also explained that people count elephants to identify the herd, tell stories about behaviour, especially to tourists, and teach children about the need for care. His father was nearly killed by an elephant, and Charlie said a lone elephant can be aggressive in the same way, perhaps, and that he didn't want noise and people around when he is sick. Associating numbers with expectations about animal behaviour may offer a way to introduce the principle, common to PPL and Bayesian inference, that priors can be expressed mathematically. Yet, anthropomorphising in reasoning about numbers of animals also resonates with Liebenberg's (2013) observation that trackers think about what they would do if they were that animal when they speculate about its movements.

Temporal Registers

During our remote reflections, Charlie wrote a story, in English, for a new spinner game that includes factors or indicators contributing to decision-making in the Jul'hoansi community:

> Once upon a time there was some kind of famine. It was very hard and we decided to go out gathering. It was a poor rainy season and so, there were rarely bush food as the wild animals have nearly depleted all fruit bearing and underground bush food. We had to decide which direction to go to, till we eventually decided to go north as there

seemed to be signs of rain observed during the last rainy season. It was a very hot and dry day. We walked and searched, hoping to find loads of food but it wasn't going to be like that. We found only a few raisin-bush berries that were also dried out by the scorching sun and it was so tasteless and we were very thirsty and hungry out in the bush. That was the hardest day we ever experienced out in the bush. So, we had to come back and sleep with the empty tummies. From that day we decided to move away from that place to find a better place where we could have veldt food and where there are also waterholes nearby.

Causes of decisions were often bound to temporal registers. Participants in the village referred to time; such as seeing a lion print in October and whether they had seen an elephant track this year, during this week or "before yesterday". They spoke of seasons and months when teaching children in ways that convey details about conditionality and decision-making; of how dew and moisture protects crops between the rains, and the sand is dry by August. In spinner games some temporal registers may have been implicit; G|qa'o's group, for instance, noted that a hole in a tree would contain water only after rain. However many were explicit, both in English or Ju|'hoan.

To introduce the spinner game, Helen asked participants to imagine they were going to the bush *today* and then she spoke in the present tense using 'now', 'next' and so on, and a 'new day' to emphasise the return to the first spinner after completing a set of spins. However, many temporal registers were not prompted by Helen. For example, the high-school group said, in Ju|'hoan, 'This might happen one day, but not every day', or 'one day and not on another day' to describe their own experience of trees, water and snakes. The first group related each participant's set of spins to years and compared year scores, in English, with each other. "It takes 6 years to find snake", Dorothy had exclaimed, "it takes you 6 years to die!". She used her fingers as an index as she spoke of numbers of years. Participants in the third group finger-counted together as they said "today" and "tomorrow"; and, when they drew their grid, explained that the totals they had written meant they had seen a snake on "one day", and not on "nine days". Thus, as well as separate each instance of conditional probability, through a set of spins, temporal registers contributed to creating anticipation, distinguished events in storytelling, and expressed the embodiment of time.

Conclusion

Relating stories to numbers, anthropomorphising in predicting, and explicating temporality in cause-and-effect reasoning are not qualities that are unique to Ju|'hoansi people. Uncovering these qualities, however, demonstrates how physical devices and games can contribute to exploring knowledge practices ethnographically. We framed the spinner games in envisioning both content about Bayesian statistics in school curricula, and PPLs that marginalised groups might use themselves. However, physical devices and games may have wider value in conversations for the purposes of algorithmic accountability.

Conceivably, in the future, Ju|'hoan people might label data used in training ML. Conservancy rangers already use CyberTracker to log their observations of animal behaviour and ecosystems by navigating between touchscreens and selecting icons that represent their interpretation of tracks, and scientists apply statistics to the data produced. While CyberTracker records a ranger's associations between categories, within their knowledge practices, involving rangers in decisions about the statistical methods used would make analysis more accountable to their problem-solving practices. Some types of analysis might be more compatible than others with the priorities that shape trackers' imaginations in speculative tracking, such as increasing the probability of locating animals or learning more about animal behaviour from tracks (Liebenberg, 2013).

Explainability in AI requires relating the abstractions needed for a basic understanding of ML to local experience and may need to account for qualities of cause-and-effect reasoning that are currently absent in curriculum content. The use of temporal registers in Ju|'hoan participants' stories expressed experience as part of the passage of time: bodies inhabited the hot, dry day as it unfolds, finger-counting held moments that indexed to days or years. Whereas in life, moments are not separated from each other by chronological barriers (Ingold, 1993), mathematical abstractions often treat the passage of time as if we are outside of it. For instance, in teaching probability we show uncertainty by looking after dice land, but not within throws. It's a three! It's a two! It's a six! Teaching scientific methods often separates temporality from events, treating time in relations as decomposable or as an independent variable and rarely explicating time within a context. Many methods *control for* time in sampling data, such as at spatially separate waterholes over 48 hours, and then passing this data 'upwards' for analysis (e.g. Ingold, 2011) to predict game populations. Such methods abstract from the fabric of relations and yield different opportunities for learning than speculative tracking does. The expression of temporality, then, suggests that developing dynamic simulations to teach about statistics may be compatible with the different ways that people experience time when they reason about probability.

Acknowledgements

We thank all Ju|'hoansi participants in our studies, and Chief Bobo, staff of the Ju|'hoansi Tribal Authority, Nyae Nyae Conservancy and Tsumkwe secondary school, Bruce Parcher, Candi Miller, David Spiegelhalter and Breck Baldwin for advice. The Association for Progressive Communications funded the inter-village communication system and a grant from the Alborada Foundation supported the spinner games work.

Notes

1 www.nndfn.org/counting-game-essential-activities-continue-in-nyae-nyae-conservancy
2 www.cybertracker.org
3 www.candimiller.co.uk/feeding-scheme.html
4 www.candimiller.co.uk/research/thumbs-up-for-the-khuitzima
5 www.apc.org/en/huinom-project, https://videos.apc.org/u/apc/m/talking-around-elephants-sb/?fbclid=IwAR3tf0iS9Q5b_YTB0OsWwxz3ThMx-ZPMHuS96yuHpGMiksFWnJ-lvsnDziQ
6 1: n|e'e; 2: tsan; 3: n!ani; 4: #hai; 5: g!au; 6: g!au kota ka n|e'e; 7: g!au kota ka tsan; 8: g!au kota ka n!ani; 9: g!au kota ka #hai; and, 10: g!autsa.

References

Aludhilu, H. N. and Bidwell, N. J. (2018) 'Home is not Egumbo: Language, Identity and Web Design' in *Proceedings of the 2nd African Conference for Human Computer Interaction (AfriCHI'18)*. ACM.

Arawjo, I. (2020) 'To Write Code: The Cultural Fabrication of Programming Notation and Practice' in *Proceedings of the 38th Conference on Human Factors in Computing Systems (CHI'20)*. ACM.

Arora, P. (2019) 'Decolonizing Privacy Studies,' *Television & New Media* 20(4): 366–378.

Arora, P. (2020) 'All Gloom and Global Doom? Provocations on the Future of Global Media Theory,' *Global Perspectives* 1(1): 11653.

Appadurai, A. (2016) 'The Academic Digital Divide and Uneven Global Development,' *CARGC Papers* 4, available at https://repository.upenn.edu/cargc_papers/4 (accessed 29 September 2021).

Avle, S. and Lindtner, S. (2016) 'Design(ing) "Here" and "There": Tech Entrepreneurs, Global Markets, and Reflexivity in Design Processes' in *Proceedings of the 34th Conference on Human Factors in Computing Systems. (CHI'16)*. ACM, 2233–2245.

Avle, S., Lindtner, S. and Williams, K. (2017) 'How Methods Make Designers' in *Proceedings of the 2017 CHI Conference on Human Factors in Computing Systems (CHI '17)*. ACM, 472–483.

Awori, K., Vetere, F. and Smith, W. (2015) 'Transnationalism, Indigenous Knowledge and Technology: Insights from the Kenyan Diaspora' in *Proceedings of the 33rd Conference on Human Factors in Computing Systems. (CHI'15)*. ACM, 3759–3768.

Azra, I. and Kumar, N. (2021) 'AI in Global Health: The View from the Front Lines' in *Proceedings of the 39th Conference on Human Factors in Computing Systems. (CHI'21)*, ACM.

Balawi, S., Khalaf, K. and Hitt, G. W. (2016) 'Leveraging Pedagogical Innovations for Science, Technology, Engineering, and Mathematics (STEM) Education in the Middle East Context" in M. Abdulwahed, M. O. Hasna and J. E. Froyd (eds), *Advances in Engineering Education in the Middle East and North Africa*. Springer, 59–115.

Bidwell, N. J. (2016) 'Moving the Centre to Design Social Media for Rural Africa,' *AI & Society: Journal of Culture, Communication & Knowledge*, 31(1): 51–77.

Bidwell, N. J., Reitmaier, T. and Jampo, K. (2014) 'Orality, Gender & Social Audio in Rural Africa' in *Proceedings of the 11th International Conference on the Design of Cooperative Systems. (COOP'14)*. Springer.

Bidwell, N. J. and Winschiers-Theophilus, H. (2015) *Intersections between Indigenous and Traditional Knowledges and Technology Design*. Informing Science Press.

Bidwell, N. J., Winschiers-Theophilus, H., Kapuire, G. K. and Rehm, M. (2011) 'Pushing Personhood into Place: Situating Media in the Transfer of Rural Knowledge in Africa,' *International Journal of Human-Computer Studies*, 69: 618–631.

Bidwell, N. J., Siya, M., Marsden, G., Tucker, W. D., Tshemese, M., Gaven, N., Ntlangano, S., Eglinton, K. A. and Robinson, S. (2013) 'Walking and the Social Life of Solar Charging in Rural Africa,' *Transactions on Computer-Human Interaction*, 20(4): 1–33.

Bidwell, N. J., Robinson, S., Vartiainen, S., Jones, M., Lalmas, M., Marsden, G., Reitmaier, T. and Eglinton, K. (2014) 'Designing Social Media for Community Information Sharing in Rural South Africa' in *Proceedings of the Southern African Institute for Computer Scientist and Information Technologists Annual Conference (SAICSIT'14)*. ACM.

Blackwell, A. F. (2017) 'End-user Developers – What Are They Like?' in F. Paternò and V. Wulf (eds), *New Perspectives in End-User Development*. Springer, 121–135.

Blackwell, A. F. (2015) 'Interacting with an Inferred World: The Challenge of Machine Learning for Humane Computer Interaction' in *Proceedings of Critical Alternatives: The 5th Decennial Aarhus Conference*, 169–180.

Blackwell, A. F. (2014) 'Structuring the Social, Inside Software Design' in J. Leach and L. Wilson (eds), *Subversion, Conversion, Development: Cross-Cultural Knowledge Exchange and the Politics of Design*. MIT Press, 183–199.

Blackwell, A. F., Church, L., Erwig, M., Geddes, J., Gordon A. Baydin, A.G., Gram-Hansen, B, Kohn, T., Lawrence, N. Mansinghka, V., Paige, B., Petricek, T., Robinson, D., Sarkar, A. and Strickson, O. (2019) 'Usability of Probabilistic Programming Languages' in *Proceedings of the Psychology of Programming Interest Group (PPIG 2019)*.

Blackwell, Alan F., Nicola J. Bidwell, Helen L. Arnold, Charlie Nqeisji, |Kun Kunta, and Martin Mabeifam Ujakpa. (2021) 'Visualising Bayesian Probability in the Kalahari.' Proceedings of the 32nd Annual Workshop of the Psychology of Programming Interest Group. www.ppig.org/files/2021-PPIG-32nd-blackwell.pdf

Burrell, J. (2016) 'How the Machine "Thinks": Understanding Opacity in Machine Learning Algorithms,' *Big Data & Society*, 3(1): 1–12.

Campagnolo, G. M. (2020) *Social Data Science Xennials: Between Analogue and Digital Social Research*. Palgrave, 7–90.

Cardon, D., Cointet, J. P. and Mazières, A. (2018) 'Neurons Spike Back: The Invention of Inductive Machines and the Artificial Intelligence Controversy,' *Réseaux*, 211(5): 173–220.

Csikszentmihalyi, C., Mukundane, J., Rodrigues, G.F., Mwesigwa, D. and Kasprzak, M. (2018) 'The Space of Possibilities: Political Economies of Technology Innovation in Sub-Saharan Africa' in *Proceedings of the 36th Conference on Human Factors in Computing Systems (CHI'18)*. ACM, 306.

Dourish, P. and Mainwaring, S. D. (2012) 'Ubicomp's Colonial Impulse' in *Proceedings of the 14th Conference on Ubiquitous Computing (Ubicomp'13)*. ACM, 133–142.

Elish, M. C. and Boyd, D. (2018) 'Situating Methods in the Magic of Big Data and AI,' *Communication Monographs* 85(1): 57–80.

Gorinova, M. I., Sarkar, A., Blackwell, A. F. and Syme, D. (2016) 'A Live, Multiple-Representation Probabilistic Programming Environment for Novices' in *Proceedings of the 34th Conference on Human Factors in Computing Systems. (CHI'16).* ACM, 2533–2537.

Gage, J. and Spiegelhalter, D. (2016) *Teaching Probability*. Cambridge University Press.

Gray, M. L. and Suri, S. (2019) *Ghost Work: How to Stop Silicon Valley from Building a New Global Underclass.* Eamon Dolan Books.

Gryba, R. (2020) 'How Indigenous Knowledge is helping us fine-tune statistical models,' *Medium*, available at https://medium.com/ubcscience/stats-660805dd930a (accessed 29 September 2021).

Hitchcock, R. K. and Biesele, M. (2002) 'Controlling Their Destiny: Ju/'hoansi of Nyae Nyae,' *Cultural Survival Quarterly*, 26(1): 13–15.

Horst, H. and Miller, D. eds. (2013). *Digital Anthropology*. Bloomsbury.

Ingold, T. (2011) *Being Alive: Essays on Movement, Knowledge and Description*. Routledge.

Ingold, T. (1993) 'The Temporality of the Landscape,' *World Archaeology*, 25(2): 152–174.

Irani, L. (2018) 'Design Thinking: Defending Silicon Valley at the Apex of Global Labor Hierarchies,' *Catalyst: Feminism, Theory, Technoscience*, 4(1): 1–19.

Irani L., Vertesi, J., Dourish, P., Philip K. and Grinter, R. E. (2010) 'Postcolonial Computing: A Lens on Design and Development' in *Proceedings of the 28th Conference on Human Factors in Computing Systems. (CHI'10).* ACM, 1311–1320.

Jain, S. and Rangaswamy, N. (2020) 'Good Digital Identity: The Case of Aadhaar in India' in *Proceedings of the 3rd Conference on Computing and Sustainable Societies (SIGCAS'20).* ACM, 345–346.

Keskinen, P., Marley, S., Afrikaneer, H. and Winschiers-Theophilus, H. (2021) 'A Community-initiated Website Development Project: Promoting a San Community Campsite Initiative' in *Proceedings of the 3rd African Conference for Human Computer Interaction (AfriCHI'21).* ACM.

Kitchin, R. (2014) 'Big Data, New Epistemologies and Paradigm Shifts,' *Big Data & Society*, 1(1): 1–12.

Koot, S. and van Beek, W. (2017) 'Ju|'hoansi Lodging in a Namibian Conservancy: CBNRM, Tourism and Increasing Domination,' *Conservation & Society* 15(2): 136–146.

Lewis, J. E., Arista, N., Pechawis, A. and Kite, S. (2018) 'Making Kin with the Machines,' *Journal of Design and Science*, available at https://doi.org/10.21428/bfafd97b (accessed 29 September 2021).

Liebenberg, L. (2013) *The Origin of Science*. CyberTracker.

Lowrie, I. (2017) 'Algorithmic Rationality: Epistemology and Efficiency in the Data Sciences,' *Big Data & Society*, 4(1): 1–13. doi:2053951717700925

Matengu, K., Likando, G. and Haihambo, C. (2019) 'Inclusive Education in Marginalised Contexts: The San and Ovahimba Learners in Namibia' in S. Douglas (ed.), *Creating an Inclusive School Environment.* British Council, 197–208.

Mbembe, A. (2019) 'Bodies as Borders,' *From the European South*, 4: 5–18.

Milan, S. and Treré, E. (2017) *Big Data from the South: The Beginning of a Conversation We Must Have*, available at https://ssrn.com/abstract=3056958 (accessed 29 September 2021).

Miller, C. (2020) 'The Ju|'hoan of Nyae Nyae. A Case of Exclusion and Ka Jan' in J. Traxler and H. Compton (eds), *Critical Mobile Pedagogies*. Routledge.

Mwewa, L. and Bidwell, N. J. (2015) 'African Narratives in Technology Research and Design' in N. J. Bidwell and H. Winschiers-Theophilus (eds), *Intersections between Indigenous and Traditional Knowledges and Technology Design*. Informing Science Press, 353.

Morris, D. E., Oakley, J. E. and Crowe, J. A. (2014) 'A Web-based Tool for Eliciting Probability Distributions from Experts,' *Environmental Modelling & Software*, 52: 1–4.

Neyland, D. (2016) 'Bearing Account-able Witness to the Ethical Algorithmic System,' *Science, Technology & Human Values*, 41(1): 50–76.

Ntibagirirwa, S. (2001) 'A Wrong Way: From Being to Having in the African Value System,' *Protest and Engagement: South African Philosophical Studies*, 2: 65–81.

Pimentel, R. and Wall, T. (2018) *IGCSE International Mathematics Second Edition*. Cambridge University Press.

Sapignoli, M. (2021) 'The Mismeasure of the Human,' *Anthropology Today*, 37(1): 4–8.

Seaver, N. (2019) 'Knowing Algorithms' in J. Vertesi and D. Ribes (eds), *Digital STS: A Field Guide for Science & Technology Studies*. Princeton University Press, 412–422.

Seaver, N. (2017) 'Algorithms as Culture: Some Tactics for the Ethnography of Algorithmic Systems,' *Big Data & Society*, 4(2): 1–12. doi:2053951717738104

Soro, A., Wujal Wujal Aboriginal Shire Council, Taylor, J. L., Esteban M. and Brereton, M. (2020) 'Coding on Country' in *Extended Abstracts of the 38th Conference on Human Factors in Computing Systems. (CHI'20)*. ACM.

Stanley, C., Cabrero, D. G. and Winschiers-Theophilus, H. (2017) 'Challenges in Designing Cultural Heritage Crowdsourcing: Tools with Indigenous Communities' in L. Ciolfi, A. Damala., E. Hornecker, M. Lechner and L. Maye (eds), *Cultural Heritage Communities: Technologies and Challenges*. Routledge, 116–133.

Milan, S., Treré, E. and Masiero, S. (2021) *COVID-19 from the Margins. Theory on Demand*. Institute of Network Cultures.

Suzman, J. (2001) *An Assessment of the Status of the San in Namibia (Vol. 4)*. Windhoek: Legal Assistance Centre.

Taka, E., Stein, S. and Williamson, J. H. (2020) 'Increasing Interpretability of Bayesian Probabilistic Programming Models Through Interactive Visualizations,' *Frontiers in Computer Science*, 2: 1–23.

The Legal Assistance Centre (LAC) and Desert Research Foundation of Namibia (DRFN) (2014) *Reassessment of the Status of the San in Namibia (2010–2013)*.

Treré, E. (2016) 'The Dark Side of Digital Politics: Understanding the Algorithmic Manufacturing of Consent and the Hindering of Online Dissidence,' *IDSBulletin*, 47(1): 127–138.

UNCTAD: United Nations Conference on Trade and Development. (2018) *Trade and Development Report: Power, Platforms and the Free Trade Delusion*.

Verran, H. (2001) *Science and an African Logic*. University of Chicago Press.

Wasserman, H. (2021) 'New Optics on Digital Media Cultures in Africa in Re-imagining' in H. Dunn (ed.), *Media, Culture and Technology in the Global South: Reimagining Communication and Identity in Africa and the Caribbean*. Palgrave.

Winschiers-Theophilus, H. and Bidwell, N. J. (2013) 'Toward an Afro-Centric Indigenous HCI Paradigm,' *International Journal of Human-Computer Interaction*, 29(4): 243–255.

Yadav, D., Malik, P., Dabas, K. and Singh, P. (2019) 'Feed-pal: Understanding Opportunities for Chatbots in Breastfeeding Education of Women in India' in *Proceedings of the 22nd Conference on Computer-Supported Cooperative Work and Social Computing . (CSCW'19)*. ACM, 170.

Zips, W. and Zips-Mairitsch, M. (2019) 'Pricing Nature and Culture: On the Bewildering Commodification of the African Frontier – an Introduction' in Zips, W. and Zips-Mairitsch, M. (eds), *Bewildering Borders: The Economy of Conservation in Africa*. Munster: LIT Verlag, 1–34.

41
ETHNOGRAPHY OF/AND VIRTUAL REALITY

Lisa Messeri

Hushahu is the first female shaman of the Yawanawá indigenous community of the southern Brazilian Amazon. A long journey is necessary to visit her village, but she has kindly met me for the final leg of the canoe ride down the river. Sitting across from me in the boat, Hushahu, with the aid of a translator, tells me about why she wanted to become a spiritual leader and about how this hadn't previously been a life course open to women. Once on land, I get a whirlwind tour of her community and their ritual practices. As she tells me about her intense training to become a shaman, Hushahu leads me across a long bridge, intricately scaffolded of timber rising above the muddy, calm river. On the far side of the bridge, I learn of rituals that provide pathways for merging one's being with the forest. Hushahu wants to impress upon me how the forest is aware of our presence. In training to be a shaman, she was the first woman in her community to take uní (the Yawanawá word for ayahuasca) and to learn how it heals – body, mind, world. Uní allows her to see the forest's vital vibrancy – this is the message she is trying to pass on to me.

The sounds of the forests fade and my vision goes black.

I sit in the darkness for a bit, not yet wanting to take off the virtual reality headset. I lean back into the swivel chair and think about how, when I was brought to the forest's grandmother tree, as I twisted my head from side to side and up and down to take in its magnificent height and breadth, I could see fluorescent glimmers of a tree otherwise that followed my gaze. And how, as Hushahu described how uní helped her to see the forest as living, the winding paths I wandered dissolved into millions of glowing points tracing out every branch and leaf, subtly compressing or expanding as I looked around, as if I was breathing with the forest.

I take off the headset and Danielle is eager to hear my reaction. I'm at the Technicolor Experience Center (TEC) in Los Angeles, and this is the third VR piece I've seen today – having already been provided the vantage of a child huddled in a basement with her parents as bombs go off above and been positioned as a tree grown from seedling to full glory, even as the threat of deforestation nears. Nearly five months into my fieldwork with the VR community in LA, *Awavena*, directed by Australian artist Lynette Wallworth, is the most impressive piece I've seen. "Amazing, right?" asks Danielle and I can't help but agree. This was my first time meeting Danielle and visiting TEC, but I would spend several days a week here for the rest of 2018 as a scholar-in-residence, learning about the work this small team of producers and visual effects artists do to help create pieces like *Awavena* and taking part in conversations as they try to figure out how to make VR the Next Big Thing. Right now, I'm still trying to ingratiate myself with these prospective hosts. Thinking again about the grandmother tree and its fluorescent glow, I say how they should have James Cameron, director of *Avatar*, see this – half-joking but also trying to pretend that I "get" Hollywood. Even so I cringe inwardly, self-conscious of the colonial ethos in *Avatar* and wondering, in the case of *Awavena*, about the partnership between the white filmmaker and her Indigenous interlocutors. Danielle responds sincerely that they've been trying to get "Jim" to visit – Danielle's boss and head of TEC was involved on *Avatar*'s postproduction. As I leave TEC later that day having secured my residency, I feel like after months of trying I have finally been granted access to the inner sanctum – to Hollywood.

I open this chapter with two nested stories of arrival at hard-to-access places. The first, my virtual arrival at the geographically remote Yawanawá village, was facilitated through immersive virtual reality. The second, my inaugural visit to an NDA-barricaded Hollywood studio, was facilitated by many months of immersive fieldwork. Tashka, the Yawanawá chief that invited Wallworth to tell the story of Hushahu and their community, describes VR as he would uní (and how some might romanticize ethnography), "You travel to a place you have never been. Colours and sounds are intensified, you meet the ancestors, you are given a message and then you return." Hushahu, who has toured with *Awavena*, described on a panel at the World Economic Forum that VR shows "a bit of what we see, what we live, in this moment when we do this [spiritual] work" (World Economic Forum, 2018). When Tashka first tried VR – viewing an earlier piece by Wallworth at an event they both attended at Oxford University – he commented that "it opened a window like a medicine does – like a vision. It made a portal."[1] Writing of classic ethnographic texts, Clifford Geertz described how "one can and usually does feel that one is looking through a crystal window to the reality beyond" (1988: 28–29). The goal for many ethnographers and many VR creators is to offer a feeling, however fleeting, of stepping through that window or portal: of "being there."

This chapter keys into the concept of *immersion* to explore fantasies of "being there" in both virtual reality and ethnographic work, illustrating how themes long central to media anthropology remain potent for studying emerging media. I lived in LA in 2018 and conducted ethnographic research with the virtual reality community in the city. In contrast to Silicon Valley, in Silicon Beach (as some Angelenos called the small but growing tech center) VR was an object of interest not as an engineering problem but for its storytelling potential. I spent the year with high-end cinematic producers (like those at TEC) and also with start-up companies; with seasoned veterans and newer entrants; with those who were succeeding in the industry and those who struggled. I embedded at workplaces and in classrooms, and went to casual meetups and more glamorous festivals and events. My ethnography was not of the virtual worlds created by VR innovators and enthusiasts, but rather of the social worlds they inhabited in and around Los Angeles. In what follows, I find parallels between how this community thinks about VR as an immersive technology and how ethnographers reflect on their immersive methodologies. To do ethnography *of* virtual reality is to engage with what ethnography *and* virtual reality might offer each other. *Immersion* is an underspecified term in both fields. This is part of why it can be alchemically framed as a catalyst for being there and perhaps even for some grander transformation by which people might become more understanding or compassionate. Thus, I track definitions of immersion in both VR and ethnography, locate differences across immersive practices and representations, critique the fantasy that immersion can provide unmediated access to the lifeworlds of others, and conclude with a suggestion for how the anthropology of VR might unfold. Today's conversations around VR unexpectedly engage with some of anthropology's classic conversations; not only the mystique of "being there" but also the ethics of representing "the other." As media anthropology continues to bring into its fold emerging technologies, connecting these future oriented objects with the discipline's history ensures that "the new" is not merely grafted on to current conversations in the field, but connected back such that our own disciplinary assumptions continue to be unsettled, questioned, and critiqued.

Defining Immersion

Virtual reality has been enjoying a modest renaissance, triggered both by Facebook's investment in the technology and an expanded imagination of the use of the medium – from entertainment to education to training to awareness-raising. A variety of lower cost consumer headsets are available, making the technology more visible (though not yet ubiquitous) and delineating VR as a genre distinct from, for example, a virtual world accessed exclusively through a flat screen. In a VR headset, one's visual field of view is completely filled such that the user can look all around and, for some experiences, move around or interact with the scene. While a variety of aesthetic experiences can be accessed through a VR headset (from live-action documentaries like *Awavena* to animated fantasies), what unites these experiences and distinguishes the medium from others are claims that it is uniquely "immersive."

During my fieldwork, the term "immersive" was so ubiquitous as to go often undefined. It was common for someone to describe themselves as working "in immersive" without further qualification. In October 2018, however, I attended an event at TEC during which the term was removed from its black box. The event was the first annual LA Fashion Film Festival, and precisely because this was not the typical TEC (i.e., VR-enthusiastic) audience, there was a panel that was meant to help the artists and designers in attendance understand how immersive technologies might benefit their brand. Marcie Jastrow, the senior vice president of immersive media at Technicolor and the director of TEC, chaired the panel and began by explaining how "immersive media" included VR, AR (augmented reality), AI (artificial intelligence), and "sometimes blockchain." For Jastrow and those in the community with whom I worked, this grouping of digital media rolled off the tongue in 2018. It was assumed that AI, for example, was needed to create responsive experiences that achieve VR's full potential of allowing a user to explore a virtual world and interact meaningfully with its inhabitants. After Jastrow's introduction, the panelists proceeded to share their various VR/AR/AI projects and their vision for how "immersive" can change how stories are told. One of the co-directors of the festival interrupted and, looking confused, asked, "What *is* immersive?" The panelists stumbled, admitting that it is hard to define. Jastrow offered that immersive "changes the way we interact." Another panelist admitted that she doesn't even try to explain what it is; that the only way to "get it" is to put on a VR headset. In VR you have the experience that "I was there." Such an experience registers in the hippocampus, she said, and that is where memories are made. So what immersive offers, the panelist concluded, is the ability to give people memories.

In this conversation, immersion is a feature of experience created by an "immersive technology" like VR that in turn has the potential to induce collective or individual changes. Such a definition and associated claims (which I heard throughout fieldwork) loosely draws on research in perceptual and social psychology which, since the 1990s, has sought to quantify how immersive a virtual experience is or is not and the consequent social or psychological impacts. To demarcate the mechanics of a VR experience from its affect, researcher Mel Slater helpfully distinguishes between "immersion" and "presence." He defines immersion as an independent property of an experience that can be measured in terms of how effectively it triggers "the actions we know to carry out in order to perceive" (2009, 3550). Presence, on the other hand, is the *result of* immersion that creates "the 'sense of being there' in the environment depicted by the virtual reality system" (3551). Slater clarifies that this is a perceptual feeling of being there, not a cognitive belief that you have been bodily transported to a different location. "The whole point of presence," Slater writes, "is that it is the *illusion* of being there" (2018: 432). To define the outcome of immersion as an illusion of presence was not, for Slater, to undercut the technology but rather to marvel at the power of VR to consistently create such illusions even when "the reality" of the situation is known (see also Messeri 2021).

This language of being there, so familiar to the anthropologist as an index of *physical* co-location, has, for the scientific researcher, long been associated with the potential of technology to *virtually* approximate such co-location. In Marvin Minsky's agenda setting work on "telepresence," he outlined the ambition for telerobotic systems to keep workers out of dangerous situations. For these workers to do their jobs well, they had to be able to access the illusion of presence; to feel "that sense of 'being there'" (Minsky 1980: np).

Outside of specific circles of VR researchers (for whom the work of quantifying immersion and distinguishing it from presence is of central importance), the VR community in Los Angeles, as well as anthropologists and media theorists, often use immersion, presence, and "being there" interchangeably. For example, in the carefully researched and illuminating history of immersive art by Oliver Grau (a genre that extends well before and beyond VR), he writes that such media offer "a high-grade feeling of immersion, of presence (an impression suggestive of 'being there')" (2003: 7).[2] To avoid such conflation, a more acute understanding of what immersion is and how it operates is needed. How, then, might Slater's suggestion that immersion is a precondition for presence extend beyond VR and into ethnography?

Immersion in anthropology can, in drawing out the analogy, be thought of as a feature of the system – the research apparatus – that yields the epistemic authority that comes from "being there." Stefan Helmreich, in a sonic analysis of his deep sea dive in the research submersible *Alvin*, notes the multiple meanings of immersion: "as a descent into liquid, as an absorption of mind and body in some activity or interest (such as music), and – in a meaning of relevance to anthropologists – as the all-encompassing entry of a person into an unfamiliar cultural milieu" (2007: 623). Helmreich, whose critique of immersion I'll return to below, playfully writes about the liquid immersion he experienced while plunging into the depths of the ocean with his interlocutors. In enumerating different kinds of immersion, ethnography is freed from the imagination that travel is the only way for a researcher to be immersed and thus achieve presence. Digital ethnographers, for example, have described how their work is the product of immersion not in an aqueous medium nor in the physicality and locality of a cultural medium, but rather in a networked and online medium.

Patty Gray (2016) writes about doing a digital ethnography of Russian protests from a different continent. Gray (who opens her article like my own with a double scene of arrival) describes how her office was a matrix of multiple screens, allowing her to follow the protests on different media sites. In describing her work environment, she is detailing the material conditions she created to achieve, quoting one of the definitions of immersion referenced by Helmreich, "an absorption of mind and body in some activity." Thus she is able to make the lynchpin claim of ethnographic work that such immersion led to presence: "Surrounding myself with my digital devices tuned to the various platforms following the demonstrations, I found I could achieve a kind of presence in the moment" (504). And (echoing language from the VR panel described above), this feeling of "being there" was felt in her body – viscerally, emotionally – creating memories: "In many respects, I remember the demonstrations *as if* I had experienced them firsthand, as if I *had been* there in body" (506).

Keying in to the similarities between how immersion is defined by both VR researchers and anthropological fieldworkers provocatively puts the immersion of a VR experience on a continuum with the immersion of the ethnographic method. For both, immersion creates a powerful feeling of being there. But how do we understand the extent to which this feeling is, as Slater suggests, an illusion? The next section turns to the production and consumption of immersion to further tease out the role of mediation in creating the illusion of presence.

Producing and Consuming Immersion

Why is immersion so doggedly pursued in both anthropology and virtual reality? For the anthropologist, it remains central to how we generate a particular kind of knowledge. For the VR promoter, the self-evident "coolness" of being virtually elsewhere is central to articulating the value of the technology. These distinct reasons for immersion necessarily come with different expectations of who produces and consumes immersive experiences.

Gray's appeal to immersion, being there, embodiment, and memory-making comes, as she admits, from an anxiety of whether her work was "real" anthropology; did this virtual witnessing and experiencing amount to "being there"? Does she have ethnographic insight into the Russian protesters? Gray's desire to prove her immersion (and thus her presence), however, is common across online and offline ethnographies. As Geertz described, "Ethnographers need to convince us ... not merely that they themselves have truly 'been there,' but ... that had we been there we should have seen what they saw, felt what they felt, concluded what they concluded" (1988: 16). Being there, as this quote from Geertz demonstrates, is an indicator of the anthropologist's access to a particular kind of knowledge – the experiential knowledge of another place and another people.

For the VR innovator, the purpose of immersion is more varied. For a researcher like Slater, immersion is way of probing the flexibility of the human sensorium. For an entrepreneur like Jastrow, immersion is what gives VR a marketing edge. For Wallworth, the director of *Awavena*, immersion is a tool of persuasion. I met Wallworth when she came to TEC for several weeks to collaborate on a more elaborate build out of *Awavena* that was set to premier at the Venice Film Festival. Wallworth explained that she had been fortunate to show her VR pieces not only to film festival goers but to world leaders at places like the World Economic Forum and the UN. She highlighted a feature of VR immersion that I had not heard others discuss. Because the headset and earphones block out other auditory and visual stimuli, VR affords a private and distraction-free environment for the person who is watching her piece – a rare opportunity to have the complete focus of these multi-tasking individuals. Immersion, Wallworth told me, allows her to "seduce them with a powerful story" and advocate for both attitude and policy change.

Immersion, therefore, is not a monolith in its purpose and it is necessarily also varied in how it is produced and consumed. This has implications for how we understand both ethnography and VR as variously *mediated* practices. In anthropology, there are three stages at which immersion is enacted as a mode of knowledge production. First, the ethnographer in the field cultivates for themself an immersive experience, traditionally achieved by forging connections with those from whom they wish to learn. This can be accomplished through virtual networking, in person travel, or any number of hybrid and creative methods. Next, the ethnographer translates the immersive experience into a text (broadly conceived) that demonstrates both that they were immersed and the findings of their immersion. Some researchers also strive for the text itself – either momentarily or as a whole – to be immersive. Finally, there is a readerly experience of the text in which the consumer either feels immersed or believes the writer was immersed, which might influence their appraisal of the text.

When reading an ethnography, any sense of presence one might feel as a consequence of the immersiveness of the writing is, as Slater has suggested, an illusion, that is, the reader does not mistake themself for, as Geertz writes, having "truly 'been there.'" Presence, then, is mediated. The ethnographic text makes this mediation concrete and obvious, but for the ethnographer in the field there is a more visceral feeling of presence and being with others. Where an illusion remains, as will be taken up in the next section, is the extent to which, in being there, the ethnographer can claim unmediated access to one's interlocutors.

The different degrees of mediation that are apparent when considering the experience of the reader versus the ethnographer are erased in VR. At first blush, the readerly experience feels most similar to the immersion one experiences in virtual reality: an immersive experience that offers a mediated sense of presence – an illusion of being there. However, the VR consumer actively produces their experience by choosing where to look or how to move. Through such active engagement, VR claims it is offering an experience of immediacy (truly being there) by denying the mediating role of the technology in a process that media theorists Jay Bolter and Richard Grusin (1999) call remediation. The consumer of a VR experience feels as though they are having an experience of immersion in a cultural milieu rather than immersion in a text depicting that milieu. Remediation collapses the role of the ethnographer and the reader.

This denial of mediation – the refusal or inability to see that the feeling of presence that VR affords is an illusion – is central to the praise showered on the medium, especially as a medium for conveying what we might call ethnographic insight. The well-known Montreal-based VR studio, Félix and Paul, showed some of its earliest pieces (featuring nomadic communities from Kenya, Mongolia, and Malaysia) at the Margaret Mead Film Festival (see Bryant, 2016). The co-founder of this studio, Félix Lajeunesse, explained to a journalist that when a viewer feels like they are consuming media, immersion fails. Instead, Lajeunesse designs experiences that are meant to feel more immediate, in which the viewer "starts focusing on what is there, at that moment, in that instant, place, and time." The resulting immersion allows a VR experiencer to train their attention "on the human being" (quoted in Chocano, 2014). Lajeunesse is re-casting the consumer (the reader of a text) as the ethnographer. In juxtaposing how immersion is produced and consumed in VR versus ethnography, however, we can see that these are different kinds of immersion that differently (re)mediate presence. The implication of these differences – and what each domain might further learn from the other – is more apparent when examining the kinds of knowledge an immersive experience is claiming to produce.

Critiquing Immersion

As the quote from Lajeunesse suggests, there are many who believe that VR connects to our own and others' humanity. In the spring of 2018, I attended a VR mixer in LA that included a panel conversation on "The Impact of Immersive Technology." While the discussion of "impacts" was meant to include downsides or dangers, the panel mostly focused on positive impacts. One panelist asserted that VR unlocks the "best aspects of our human being." This claim is representative of a larger imaginary, widely shared by the community of VR innovators with whom I spent time, that VR could be a technology used not just for entertainment but to do good in the world. One of the first people to articulate this imaginary was LA-based journalist Nonny de la Peña. She both conceptualized "immersive journalism" (de la Peña et al., 2010) and, in 2012, created the first VR piece (about the hunger crisis in LA) to debut at a major film festival. This proof of concept excited the Hollywood community and inspired many filmmakers and documentarians (including the director of *Awavena*) to use VR to tell their non-fiction stories. Chris Milk (2015) was one such filmmaker-turned-VR-creator who, in a TED talk, made the lofty assertion (repeated ad nauseum by journalists and VR boosters) that VR was the "ultimate empathy machine."

While I witnessed some empathy fatigue during fieldwork (not an abandonment of the idea that VR can be used for good, but a weariness that it does so automatically and on its own), experiences in which the user is quite literally asked to take on the perspective of another are still being produced and showered with accolades. For example, the 2020 Emmy for "Outstanding Original Interactive Program" was awarded to *The Messy Truth VR*, described by its producers as "an empathy curriculum." In the first "episode" (which I saw at TEC when the production team came through to show an early cut to Jastrow), the user embodies a young Black boy sitting in the car with his father. Unlike *Awavena*, in which the viewer is themself, here they are a specific someone else. While the piece is live action (shot with a 360° camera), the boy's body, which the viewer can see if they look down, is a computer-generated avatar. The viewer's hand movements are tracked and appear not in one's own skin color but as this Black boy's hands might appear. In the experience, a pleasant drive and conversation between father and son is interrupted when cops pull the car over. The scene rapidly escalates and the father is pulled out of the car and the son (the VR viewer) watches through the windshield as the white police officer aggressively searches the father's body. The experience ends without resolving how violent the (fictional) event becomes. Van Jones, a CNN contributor and the producer of *The Messy Truth*, explains how VR transcends simply hearing about an injustice. "It's hard to have empathy when you haven't gone through the experience. We want to use VR to put you in a different body … Hopefully we'll understand each other a little better" (Vasquez, 2019).

Here we have anthropology's perennial strawman – the binary of self and other – reconfigured for the 21st century. Technological immersion facilitates placing my (white) self in the body of a (Black) other in order to gain an otherwise elusive understanding – an achievement previously imagined as being the product of ethnographic immersion. For a century, Branislow Malinowski's hubristic demand that ethnographers "grasp the native's point of view" has hung over the discipline. Though he presumed this could be done while maintaining a distance between self and other – after all, he does not ask the reader to "imagine yourself" as the Trobriand islander, but rather as the anthropologist – others more aggressively pursued the collapse of self and other. A 1933 appraisal of anthropology described the quintessence of the ethnographer as "the ability to forget his own culture and immerse himself sympathetically (*einfühlung*) into the primitive view point" (quoted in Helmreich 2007: 631). Here, well before VR, immersion was coupled with empathy (in the 1930s, "empathy" was not yet in wide colloquial use, but it has since become the more common translation of *einfühlung*). However, in the wake of the publication of Malinowski's diary, which revealed a very unempathetic (indeed racist and misogynist) view of the Trobriand islanders, Geertz asked his colleagues how they ought reckon with this hypocrisy and its undercutting of the ethnographic method. "What happens to *verstehen* [understanding] when *einfühlen* [empathy] disappears?" (1974: 28).[3]

From today's perspective, the question instead ought to be, "What happens to understanding when empathy, assumed to result from immersion, is unquestioningly pursued?" In taking on the perspective of the boy in *The Messy Truth*, users render his body a lifeless container for them to inhabit. My being in this boy's body erased his experience and reasserted my own privilege – my own white privilege – granted by a society that enables white people to adjudicate what is and is not just. A white person's empathy is imagined as what finally makes real the pain voiced time and again by Black men and women. In *Scenes of Subjection*, Saidiya

Hartman (1997) considers the writings of John Rankin, a white abolitionist, as he imagines himself beaten in order to demonstrate for his audience the inhumanity of slavery. Hartman describes this as "complicated, unsettling, and disturbing ... this flight of imagination and slipping into the captive's body unlatches a Pandora's box and, surprisingly, what comes to the fore is the difficulty and slipperiness of empathy" (18). She continues, "empathy in important respects confounds Rankin's efforts to identify with the enslaved because in making the slave's suffering his own, Rankin begins to feel for himself rather than for those whom this exercise in imagination presumably is designed to reach." Hartman makes the argument that Rankin's very ability to embody a Black person, despite being motivated by good intentions, only serves to reinforce "the captive body as a vessel for the uses, thoughts, and feelings of others" (19). Lisa Nakamura (2020) similarly quotes Hartman in her critique of VR empathy experiences, writing "[T]he idea [is] that you cannot trust marginalized people when they speak their own truth or describe their own suffering, but you have to experience it for yourself through digital representation, to know that it is true" (53). Grant Bollmer (2017) elaborates on the destructive capacity of "absorbing another's body and experience into one's own." He concludes that empathy "denies the existence of the Other; empathy only acknowledges the Other insofar as it can be assimilated into the same" (71).

Just as anthropology continues to revise how we represent difference, the VR community needs to reassess the harm that might come from embodying someone perceived as other as well as the imagined outcomes of such experiences. To do so requires critiquing (and demystifying) immersion by returning to questions of mediation and the illusion of presence. As previously suggested, the presence achieved through immersion in a VR experience or an ethnographic text is mediated. While a fieldworker might immerse themself such that they are present in the cultural milieu, being with others and knowing another remains a mediated experience even though it might *feel* unmediated. Helmreich's (2007) critique of immersion, which emerges from studying the knowledge practices of oceanographers that are his ethnographic others, leads him to a similar point. Scientists "do not just merge with their data" (an unmediated presence) just as "anthropologists do not just soak up culture" (630). To offer a slight rewording of Helmreich's argument, immersion obscures the boundaries and structures – the distance – that mediates knowing of either data or culture. The merging of self and other is only ever a (harmful) illusion. Ellen Strain (2003), writing at the intersection of the history of anthropology, tourism studies, and film studies, also suggests the need to reject the assumption that "being there" can ever be an unmediated experience. "Through immersion," Strain writes, particularly with Malinowski in mind, "the classical anthropologist hopes to undergo some kind of transformation, a virtual out-of-body experience that will place him in the position of the indigene, from where he may view the world as the indigene does" (31). The ethnographer (like the VR user, a medium Strain briefly discusses) might feel themself to have a direct experience of the culture, but Strain notes that even this is mediated by pre-fieldwork training. Emphasizing the mediation of presence and knowledge production cautions both ethnographer and VR creator to respect the limits of what immersion allows us to understand.

Conclusion

VR and ethnography are both in pursuit of the fantasy of "being there." Immersion transports one from the "here" of the ordinary day-to-day, to the "there" of an experience otherwise. But immersion isn't some singular thing, nor does it automatically grant epistemological or ontological insights. Articulating what immersion is, as this chapter has attempted, allows for a more measured assessment of what immersion does and what abuses perpetuated in the name of immersion ought to be prevented. Just as anthropology continues to reflexively augment its methods and representational practices, so too must the VR community.

Immersion draws ethnography *and* virtual reality into conversation, but as I worked on this chapter I troubled over what *is* (or ought be) the anthropology *of* virtual reality. To some extent, one first needs to answer "what *is* virtual reality"? In my research, I think of VR as that which draws together a heterogeneous community of researchers and creators to facilitate the articulation of diverse desires – from fantasy games to enterprise training to human betterment. But VR also might be a medium that can speak to the diverse desires of the anthropologist. VR could be used for ethnographic documentation. It could also experimentally engage with theories of the human sensorium. VR is not only of interest to the anthropologist of technology or media, but also to those working in multimodal and multisensory registers. The anthropology of virtual reality must therefore be a heterogeneous project that spans studies and applications of both production and consumption, always while connecting to anthropological themes that so vividly resonate with this technology.

An anthropology of VR treats VR as both an object of study as well as a potential tool for engagement. As Stephanie Takaragawa and colleagues have cautioned, rather than adapting without scrutiny the newest medium, anthropologists must begin by "looking at the systems that both produce the technologies being used and defining the work that can be done with them" (2019: 517). While this chapter touches upon the racial exploitation that some of the most prominent VR pieces depend on, there is more yet to be written about VR's connections with the pornography industry, ableist design practices, its military origins, and the enaction of violence not only in military simulations but in consumer games as well. During fieldwork, many folks I spent time with did not ignore these aspects of their industry, but also did not fully reckon with the implications – they were aware of the dark side of VR but optimistic about a bright future. Anthropologists have the expertise to better understand the implications of these associations. Can this anthropology of VR be done while also experimenting with how anthropology and VR can facilitate critique? A few scholars have begun doing this work, including anthropologist Mark Westmoreland who has manipulated the visual affordances of 360° video to illustrate the construction and limits of ethnographic knowledge. Westmoreland dangles the possibility of a representational medium by which, in denying the anthropologist's guarded position either behind the camera or notebook, the all-seeing immersion of 360° video "would ultimately expose all research activity 'in front of' the camera" (2020: 260). Transparency, like presence, is a potent fantasy worth pursuing even while understanding it can never be fully achieved. I hope I have offered in these musings on immersion a textual approach to the anthropology of/and virtual reality. I anticipate future media(ted) experiments.

Notes

1 The quotes from Tashka are from slides Wallworth used in a talk (ACMI, 2019). Like many Amazon communities, colonists enslaved the Yawanawá and made them work at rubber plantations from the 1940s through to the 1980s. Their traditional practices were further decimated by Christian missionaries. During the past decades of cultural revitalization, the Yawanawá have been committed to both preserving their traditional practices and participating in the global economy and attending practices of modernity (for the Yawanawá's long entanglement with global markets and flows, see Vereta Nahoum [2016]). Prior to meeting Wallworth, Tashka had co-produced a documentary about his community with Joaquin Phoenix. When he met Wallworth and saw her work, he felt VR was a better medium for capturing the spiritual practices of the Yawanawá, inviting her to tell the story of Hushahu. On fourthvr. com, a database of Indigenous VR compiled and maintained by Keziah Wallis and Miriam Ross, *Awavena* is classified as an "Indigenous partnership," meaning that Indigenous people were extensively involved in its creation even though non-Indigenous people served in key creative and technical roles.

As Wallis and Ross write in their analysis of a similar experience, such a piece might circulate through mostly Eurocentric distribution networks (at film festivals and museums) but it also demonstrates "the capacity for VR to provide new iterations of Indigenous Futurism" (Wallis and Ross 2021: 323).

2 While Grau collapses these terms, he is importantly illustrating the long history of "immersion" as a media aspiration (not simply unique to VR). See, for example, Huhtamo (1995), Friedberg (1993), Griffiths (2008), Turner (2013). Ariel Rogers (2019) draws on this history, but carefully distinguishes "immersion" from aligned terms in order to argue that the specific kind of immersion VR offers decouples the screen from the frame. If in other media experiences, the physical screen also serves as the visual frame, VR's immersion transforms the screen (embedded in the headset) into something the user controls therefore making them – not the artist – responsible for establishing the frame.

3 There have been more recent attempts to rehabilitate empathy's image in anthropology (Hollan and Throop, 2008) as well as questioning whether sympathy (which asks someone not to feel *as* another but rather as another *might*) rather than empathy might be "the ethnographer's magic" (Weston, 2018). See also Tunstall's (2013) call for those in design anthropology to move beyond empathy and toward compassion. Compassion, according to Tunstall, implies intrinsic worth whereas empathy only demands shared feelings.

References

ACMI (2019) "Shamanic Visions in VR: Lynette Wallworth Talks About Emmy Award Winning 'Awavena,'" available at: www.youtube.com/watch?v=zIM8mOYvPec (accessed January 19, 2021).

Bollmer, G. (2017) "Empathy Machines," *Media International Australia*, 165 (1): 63–76. doi: 10.1177/1329878X17726794.

Bolter, J. D. and Grusin, R. (1999) *Remediation: Understanding New Media*. Cambridge: MIT Press.

Bryant, H. (2016) "A Review of Virtual Reality Ethnographic Film, or: How We've Always Been Creating Virtual Reality," *The Geek Anthropologist*, November 17, available at: https://thegeekanthropologist.com/2016/11/17/a-review-of-virtual-reality-ethnographic-film-or-how-weve-always-been-creating-virtual-reality/ (accessed January 29, 2021).

Chocano, C. (2014) "The Last Medium," *The California Sunday Magazine*, October 5, available at: https://story.californiasunday.com/virtual-reality-hollywood (accessed January 19, 2021).

De la Peña, N., Weil, P., Liobera, J., Giannopoulos, E., Pomés, A., Spanlang, B., Friedman, D., Sanchez-Vives, M., and Slater, M. (2010) "Immersive Journalism: Immersive Virtual Reality for the First-Person Experience of News," *Presence: Teleoperators and Virtual Environments*, 19 (4): 291–301.

Friedberg, A. (1993) *Window Shopping: Cinema and the Postmodern*. Berkeley: University of California Press.

Geertz, C. (1974) "'From the Native's Point of View': On the Nature of Anthropological Understanding," *Bulletin of the American Academy of Arts and Sciences*, 28 (1): 26–45.

Geertz, C. (1988) *Works and Lives: The Anthropologist as Author*. Palo Alto, CA: Stanford University Press.

Grau, O. (2003) *Virtual Art: From Illusion to Immersion*. Cambridge: MIT Press.

Gray, P. A. (2016) "Memory, Body, and the Online Researcher: Following Russian Street Demonstrations via Social Media," *American Ethnologist*, 43 (3): 500–510. doi: https://doi.org/10.1111/amet.12342.

Griffiths, A. (2008) *Shivers Down Your Spine: Cinema, Museums, and the Immersive View*. New York: Columbia University Press.

Hartman, S. V. (1997) *Scenes of Subjection: Terror, Slavery, and Self-making in Nineteenth-century America*. Oxford: Oxford University Press.

Helmreich, S. (2007) "An Anthropologist Underwater: Immersive Soundscapes, Submarine Cyborgs, and Transductive Ethnography," *American Ethnologist*, 34 (4): 621–641.

Hollan, D. and Throop, C. J. (2008) "Whatever Happened to Empathy? Introduction," *Ethos*, 36 (4): 385–401. doi: https://doi.org/10.1111/j.1548-1352.2008.00023.x.

Huhtamo, E. (1995) "Encapsulated Bodies in Motion: Simulators and the Quest for Total Immersion," in S. Penny (ed.) *Critical Issues in Electronic Media*. New York: SUNY Press.

Messeri, L. (2021) "Realities of Illusion: Tracing an Anthropology of the Unreal from Torres Strait to Virtual Reality," *Journal of the Royal Anthropological Institute* 27: 340–359.

Milk, C. (2015) "How Virtual Reality Can Create the Ultimate Empathy Machine," *TED Conference*, March, available at www.ted.com/talks/chris_milk_how_virtual_reality_can_create_the_ultimate_empathy_machine/transcript (accessed September 26, 2019).

Minsky, M. (1980) "Telepresence," *Omni Magazine*: 45–51.

Nakamura, L. (2020) "Feeling Good about Feeling Bad: Virtuous Virtual Reality and the Automation of Racial Empathy," *Journal of Visual Culture*, 19 (1): 47–64.

Rogers, A. (2019) "'Taking the Plunge': The New Immersive Screens," in C. Buckley, R. Campe, and F. Casetti (eds), *Screen Genealogies: From Optical Device to Environmental Medium*, Amsterdam: Amsterdam University Press: 135–158.

Slater, M. (2009) "Place Illusion and Plausibility Can Lead to Realistic Behavior in Immersive Virtual Environments," *Philosophical Transactions of the Royal Society B: Biological Sciences*, 364 (1535): 3549–3557.

Slater, M. (2018) "Immersion and the Illusion of Presence in Virtual Reality," *British Journal of Psychology*, 109: 431–433.

Strain, E. (2003) *Public Places, Private Journeys: Ethnography, Entertainment, and the Tourist Gaze*. Rutgers: Rutgers University Press.

Takaragawa, S., Smith, T. L., Hennessy, K., Alvarez Astacio, P., and Chio, J. (2019) "Bad Habitus: Anthropology in the Age of the Multimodal," *American Anthropologist*, 121 (2): 517–524. doi: 10.1111/aman.13265.

Tunstall, E. (2013) "Decolonizing Design Innnovation: Design Anthropology, Critical Anthropology, and Indigenous Knowledge," in W. Gunn, T. Otto, and R. C. Smith (eds), *Design Anthropology: Theory and Practice*, New York: Bloomsbury Academic: 232–250.

Turner, F. (2013) *The Democratic Surround: Multimedia and American Liberalism from World War II to the Psychedelic Sixties*. Chicago: University of Chicago Press.

Vasquez, G. (2019) "Van Jones, Lumiere Awards Winner, The Messy Truth VR Experience," available at: www.youtube.com/watch?v=R8vhB0Dneps (accessed January 19, 2021).

Vereta Nahoum, A. (2016) "Selling 'Cultures.' The Traffic of Cultural Representations from the Yawanawa." Doctoral Dissertation. International Max Planck Research School on the Social and Political Constitution of the Economy.

Wallis, K. and Ross, M. (2021) "Fourth VR: Indigenous Virtual Reality Practice," *Convergence*, 27 (2): 313–329.

Westmoreland, M. R. (2020) "360 Video," in P. Vannini (ed.) *The Routledge International Handbook of Ethnographic Film and Video*, New York: Routledge: 256–266.

Weston, K. (2018) "The Ethnographer's Magic as Sympathetic Magic," *Social Anthropology*, 26 (1): 15–29.

World Economic Forum (2018) "Mixed Reality Behind the Scenes: Awavena," available at www.youtube.com/watch?v=ml1blLZwcEs (accessed January 19, 2021).

Yawanawá, T. (2019) "Brazil's indigenous rights movement." TEDGlobal 2014. https://www.youtube.com/watch?v=1D8_fvtGHhA (accessed 15 July, 2022).

AFTERWORD

Eric W. Rothenbuhler

WEBSTER UNIVERSITY

What a pleasure it has been to immerse myself in this valuable book. Every chapter makes a contribution and together they document a huge diversity of perspectives, cases, and research sites. I have learned much and taken away so many key points, quotations, and new references that were I to repeat them here, my little contribution would be nothing but a list.

I am most impressed and pleased to see how media anthropology has matured into a real field. Just over 20 years ago it was a newly coined name that helped us see commonalities in what had been disparate literatures. Like a gestalt shift, it was exciting; we suddenly saw things differently. It held great promise—and now, in such a short time, it is delivering.

Achievements

Here is a brief highlighting of some key accomplishments of this volume, of the chapters taken together as a whole. First, we see here a very broad sampling of media and communication situations. There are examples here of everything from television, newspapers, and recorded music, through a broad range of online and social media activities, gaming, artificial intelligence, virtual reality, and the algorithms that structure online activities, and even art and money as media. This shows a scholarly community that is pushing forward, striving to encompass the broadest definitions of its field.

Similarly, the great variety of study sites, subjects, and cases evinces both the maturity and the ambition of the field. I do not believe there is a region of the world that is not represented here and the people studied are similarly diverse, in age, gender, class, ethnicity, cultural group, and more. This is no accident, of course, but represents a commitment to inclusion and representativeness on the part of the editors, and that is a commitment widely enough shared in the field that they could deliver on it.

This diversity of media and communication situations on the one hand, and of places, people, and cases on the other, is important for simple accuracy—the world is diverse and so should our literature be—and for the quality of any knowledge claims we might make on that literature. It is only on the basis of a research literature that is truly inclusive and representative of the diversity of the world, that we can even begin to do the synthetic and comparative work that would support knowledge claims more general than the case study.

DOI: 10.4324/9781003175605-56

Reading across the studies and essays collected here, one can also see a breadth and variety of approaches, theoretical perspectives, research questions, and methods reflecting the inherent expansiveness of both anthropology and communication media themselves. First, communication and media are inherent to the human experience and so, naturally, we find them involved with, and usually central to, every aspect of being human—and most especially our lives in relationships, groups, organizations, cultures, and societies. The larger and more complex the structure, the more important the communication. Second, communication and media are fundamentally about expressing, representing, and connecting. Communication is expansive, drawing human experience outward to the other, the novel, the different. Ideas seek expression, expressions find audiences, relationships grow, networks expand.

Media anthropology mirrors this expansiveness; it has and will continue to grow, to push into ever more domains of human experience and activity. In pursuing, then, the full range of its potential topics, questions, and study sites, media anthropology must be in dialogue with an equally broad range of other research literatures. While it is a field of study, like any other, that requires specialist expertise, it also requires a broad ranging intellect and a certain pliability, a willingness to try new methods, to juggle multiple perspectives, and a readiness to think things anew. It may be a field more suited to the curious, to those whose intellect is drawn toward novelty and ambiguity, than those whose thinking seeks certainty.

Along those lines, many of the chapters here offer up new versions of what may be the most repeated lesson in the study of media and communication: It depends; things really are more complex than they appear. Most of the first generation of media effects research cumulated to an understanding that media content seldom produced direct effects, but often participated in a complex network of factors producing reinforcement or change, contingently (Klapper, 1960). Similarly in an effort to assess the effects of a communication technology per se, independent of the content it distributed, rather than settle any of the long list of questions addressed, the author proposed that there were dual effects, that the technology did both this and that, or again, contingent outcomes (Pool, 1977, 1983). Here too, in these studies, we see that things are not always what they seem, are usually more complex, and can often be inflected one way or another, depending on the details of the situation and the choices of the actors.

Fortunately, ethnographic methods, participant observation, in-depth interviewing, and the other techniques of media anthropology are attuned to capturing all this detail. It is exactly with such methods that we can get at the nuances and contingencies, the differences that make a difference in media worlds.

Comparisons

How does this volume, as a representative of the current state of media anthropology, compare with that first generation of edited volumes, by Askew and Wilk, (2002), Ginsburg, Abu-Lughod, and Larkin (2002), and Rothenbuhler and Coman (2005)?

There was an asymmetry in the interdisciplinary origins of media anthropology. While anthropologists were adding new areas of study and research questions to their portfolio, media scholars were adding new theoretical perspectives and methods to theirs. While one was expanding empirically, the other was expanding conceptually. One was carrying its discipline into new empirical territory, the other was borrowing across disciplinary lines for new explanations within their territory.

Afterword

Media anthropology of that era was dominated by proposals, questions, and debates. The seams still showed. Some of the work, especially for those of us coming from media studies, was almost a thought experiment: What could we learn if we examined televised spectacles, for example, as if they were ritual ceremonies? I am proud of that work, I think we learned a good bit. But it was not, at the beginning, mature scholarship in the same way the articles here are.

Media anthropology today, as shown by the work in this volume, is confident and mostly seamless. No one questions whether media anthropology exists; no one challenges who should be doing it, and though debates over method and perspective remain, they are aimed at progressing the field rather than policing it. There is a shared literature, set of methods, and range of perspectives here. Of course each scholar is calling on their own specialized literatures as needed for the topic at hand, using and adapting methods to fit the needs of their studies, but there is a core reference list here that is shared across a plurality of the chapters.

The most consequential changes between then and now, though, are in the world we study. Facebook was launched in 2004, YouTube in 2005, the iPhone in 2007, DVDs were still the medium of home movie watching and Blockbuster hit its peak in 2004 with over 9000 stores, Netflix was still the startup, Amazon was expanding but still primarily in online retail, known mostly for books, music, and software. Microsoft had only begun venturing beyond Windows, Office, and Explorer; video games had not escaped the console yet and were still primarily a kids market.

Those first readers in media anthropology were pulled together on the eve of the most consequential media revolution since the first generation of industrial-era communication technologies preserved sound in time, projected images through space, and connected a national geography with its urban centers via live broadcasting of news and entertainment. There can be no doubt we are living in another revolution now, with online, mobile, social, and streaming media. That revolution was unleashed by digital encoding, converting physical media to data, and that reordered technology, business and industry, and communicative engagement and experience. Interestingly it isn't yet obvious that text and culture will change as much as the rest of the system has, but we use social, mobile, and streaming media to access our news and entertainment, and to engage with each other, in very different ways than in the era of mass printed newspapers, broadcast television and radio, and wired telephones.

Quite naturally, many of the chapters here give attention to the newer digital, social, and mobile media and communicative activities of online life. Appropriately many of them use a methodological approach, digital ethnography, that had no name because it hardly existed 20 years ago. It had to be developed to fit the situation under study.

Future Dialogues

Let me suggest three areas that may attract considerably more attention and investigation.

One area ripe for attention is what we might call the phenomenology of our interactions with media technology. In regard to the cultural and psychological effects of the book, and especially the rise of the novel and popular reading, Reisman and his colleagues (1950) said that to be alone with a book was to be alone in a new way. Today it seems that to be together via social media is to be together in a new way. To be in a world with mobile phones and Google is to have a different relationship with knowledge and memory. Accessing streaming services to play any song you think of, or to watch movies and TV in places, times, and on screens of your own choosing, is a different experience than sitting down together for Sunday night TV or than a lifetime of building your own library. To follow politics on Twitter is different than sitting once a day to read a newspaper. What larger differences, socially, culturally, anthropologically, do those differences of micro-experiences make?

Second, history keeps moving. The incredible pace of technological and attendant social changes of the last 20 years will not slow quickly. But it may plateau at some point; we may find ourselves in a new relatively stable system that we cannot yet see. The telephone existed and was still diffusing for decades before reaching normality. Radio in the US took several years and multiple attempts at legal regulation before settling into a system of business, technology, and culture that still endures. We surely haven't yet seen the last new social media platform or the one that will displace all the others. We might not even know yet what the internet will become.

Yet the tumultuous 20 years we've lived through deserve historical thinking too. To take just one example, the period, age, and cohort effects of these first decades of the digital revolution are going to be very important, and very difficult to untangle. Some of the effects of these changes will be true for everyone in a given place and time; we were all in a pandemic and not only learned to use video as an everyday tool, but began to think of in-person as a special category of its own. Those are period effects. Some of the effects are very different, though, for the old and young. Life online, via social media, is a reality to live in for many of my students, but an entirely optional distraction from reality for me. Some of that difference will change over time and turn out to be an age effect, something typical of the way young people see the world. Some of those young people's experiences, though, will stay with them the rest of their lives, as the generation that was born in this time and came of age in this media world, just as I still carry the media habits I developed as a youth; that is a cohort effect.

Third, media anthropology has been devoted to the detail, the particular, to documenting the diversity of human activity and experience in media worlds. That is, as I said above, one of the values of the field and that work should continue. I hope, also, to see attempts at comparison and synthesis across cases. What are the commonalities across the tremendous diversity of our communicative situations and media activities? What are the patterns? What are the key differences on which outcomes depend?

In addition to carefully building up more general knowledge, I am an advocate for bigger, bolder statements too. Theory does not always have to be tied to what we have already observed in the world. The thought experiment has a useful place in the literature, as does the grand synthesis and big theory, and even what we might call theoretical opinion. The compelling essay is an important thing. Such work does not have to be demonstrably right or true in the usual sense to be useful and influential, if it expresses some of the same goals as our ethnographic work and resonates with what field experience has taught us. It can't be a work of fiction to succeed, but it does require style and craft. It is an expression of our art as scholars and we should appreciate each other as thinkers and writers, as well as researchers.

Conclusion

Why anthropology of media? Anthropology because no field is better situated to grasp the whole, to understand media in its context, its simultaneous individual and collective meanings, as well as its structures and constraints. Despite its colonialist roots, the best of anthropology has always been aimed to understand people in their whole context of society, culture, economy, community, and family.

Media because no understanding of any community or society can be complete without deep attention to its structures, practices, methods, and contents of communication—and when the technology and industry of media are changing, so too the nature and effects of those changes.

So what of media anthropology? The field is healthy and strong; its adherents are plentiful, their work is bountiful, and better than that, they know each other, share presumptions, and cite each other's work. They are an intellectual community. In developing new methods and coalescing around theoretical orientations and preferred topics, the field is a success. And what is most important for every field of study, there is still plenty of work to do.

References

Askew, K. and Wilk, R. R. (eds) (2002) *The Anthropology of Media: A Reader*, Malden: Blackwell Publishers.

Ginsburg, F. D., Abu-Lughod, L., and Larkin, B. (eds) (2002) *Media Worlds: Anthropology on New Terrain*. Berkeley: University of California Press.

Klapper, J. T. (1960) *The Effects of Mass Communication*. New York: The Free Press.

Pool, I. S. (1977) "Introduction" in I. S. Pool (ed) *The Social Impact of the Telephone*. Cambridge, MA: MIT Press.

Pool, I. S. (1983) *Forecasting the Telephone: A Retrospective Technology Assessment of the Telephone*. Norwood, NJ: Ablex.

Reisman, D., with Denney, R., and Glazer, N. (1950) *The Lonely Crowd*. New Haven, CT: Yale University Press.

Rothenbuhler, E. W. and Coman, M. (eds) (2005) *Media Anthropology*. Thousand Oaks, CA: Sage Publications.

APPENDIX

A broad and ambitious volume such as this one entails difficult choices in how to organize the vast wealth and breadth of material that constitute the contemporary field of media anthropology. We recognize that such a volume may be organized in myriad ways, and we provide an appendix with alternative categories that may be useful for scholarship and teaching that target particular areas of interest. The Appendix therefore lists other thematic organizations including: art; communication systems; diversity, equity and inclusion; failures; games and gaming; the Global South; labor and entrepreneurship; LGBTQ+; methods; nationalism; and visuality. It also includes a list of represented media types and countries.

Art

Chapter 11, "PhotoMedia as Anthropology: Towards a Speculative Research Method," Edgar Gómez Cruz
Chapter 27, "Inking Identity: Indigenous Nationalism in Bolivian Tattoo Art," Nell Haynes

Communication Systems

Chapter 2, "Indigenous Media: Anthropological Perspectives and Historical Notes," Philipp Budka
Chapter 5, "Technology is Wonderful Until It Isn't": Community-Based Research and the Precarity of Digital Infrastructure," Jerome Crowder, Peggy Determeyer, and Sara Rogers
Chapter 14, "Anthropology and Digital Media: Multivocal Materialities of Video Meetings and Deafness," Rebekah Cupitt
Chapter 26, "Black Gamer's Refuge: Finding Community within the Magic Circle of Whiteness," Akil Fletcher
Chapter 19, "Ethnographies of the Digitally Dispossessed," Heather Ford
Chapter 31, "Conspiracy Media Ecologies and the Case for Guerilla Anthropology," Leighton C. Peterson and Jeb J. Card
Chapter 15, "Cloudwork: Data Centre Labour and the Maintenance of Media Infrastructure," A.R.E. Taylor

Appendix

Diversity, Equity, and Inclusion

Chapter 40, "AI Design and Everyday Logics in the Kalahari," Nicola J. Bidwell, Helen Arnold, Alan F. Blackwell, Charlie Nqeisji, |Kun Kunta, and Martin Ujakpa

Chapter 5, "Technology is Wonderful Until It Isn't": Community-Based Research and the Precarity of Digital Infrastructure," Jerome Crowder, Peggy Determeyer, and Sara Rogers

Chapter 28, "Being Known and Becoming Famous in Kampala, Uganda," Brooke Schwartz Bocast

Chapter 29, "The Hall of Mirrors: Negotiating Gender on Chilean Social Media," Baird Campbell

Chapter 23, "Mediating Hopes: Social Media and Crisis in Northern Italy," Elisabetta Costa

Chapter 14, "Anthropology and Digital Media: Multivocal Materialities of Video Meetings and Deafness," Rebekah Cupitt

Chapter 26, "Black Gamer's Refuge: Finding Community within the Magic Circle of Whiteness," Akil Fletcher

Chapter 19, "Ethnographies of the Digitally Dispossessed," Heather Ford

Chapter 18, "Postcolonial Digital Collections: Instruments, Mirrors, Agents," Haidy Geismar and Katja Müller

Chapter 37, "The Algorithmic Silhouette: New Technologies and the Fashionable Body," Heather A. Horst and Sheba Mohammid

Chapter 13, "The Materiality of the Virtual in Urban Space," Jordan Kraemer

Chapter 25, "In This Together: Black Women, Collective Screening Experiences, and Space-Making as Meaning-Making," Marlaina Martin

Chapter 24, "Digital Inequality and Relatedness in India after Access," Sirpa Tenhunen

Failures

Chapter 5, "Technology is Wonderful Until It Isn't": Community-Based Research and the Precarity of Digital Infrastructure," Jerome Crowder, Peggy Determeyer, and Sara Rogers

Chapter 26, "Black Gamer's Refuge: Finding Community within the Magic Circle of Whiteness," Akil Fletcher

Chapter 18, "Postcolonial Digital Collections: Instruments, Mirrors, Agents," Haidy Geismar and Katja Müller

Chapter 6, "Media Migration," Patricia G. Lange

Games and Gaming

Chapter 10, "Producing Place through Play: An Ethnography of Location-based Gaming," Kyle Moore

Chapter 7, "The Digitally Natural: Hypomediacy and the "Really Real" in Game Design," Thomas M. Malaby

Chapter 26, "Black Gamer's Refuge: Finding Community within the Magic Circle of Whiteness," Akil Fletcher

Chapter 1, "Media Anthropology and the Digital Challenge", Mark Allen Peterson

Appendix

Global South

Chapter 40, "AI Design and Everyday Logics in the Kalahari," Nicola J. Bidwell, Helen Arnold, Alan F. Blackwell, Charlie Nqeisji, |Kun Kunta, and Martin Ujakpa
Chapter 28, "Being Known and Becoming Famous in Kampala, Uganda," Brooke Schwartz Bocast
Chapter 2, "Indigenous Media: Anthropological Perspectives and Historical Notes," Philipp Budka
Chapter 29, "The Hall of Mirrors: Negotiating Gender on Chilean Social Media," Baird Campbell
Chapter 33, "Performing Conservatism: A Study of Emerging Political Mobilisations in Latin America using 'Social Media Drama' Analysis", Raúl Castro-Pérez
Chapter 19, "Ethnographies of the Digitally Dispossessed," Heather Ford
Chapter 18, "Postcolonial Digital Collections: Instruments, Mirrors, Agents," Haidy Geismar and Katja Müller
Chapter 27, "Inking Identity: Indigenous Nationalism in Bolivian Tattoo Art," Nell Haynes
Chapter 37, "The Algorithmic Silhouette: New Technologies and the Fashionable Body," Heather A. Horst and Sheba Mohammid
Chapter 3, "A Longitudinal Study of Media in Brazil", Conrad Phillip Kottak and Richard Pace
Chapter 1, "Media Anthropology and the Digital Challenge", Mark Allen Peterson
Chapter 17, "#Everest: Visual Economies of Leisure and Labour in the Tourist Encounter," Jolynna Sinanan
Chapter 24, "Digital Inequality and Relatedness in India after Access," Sirpa Tenhunen

Labor and Entrepreneurship

Chapter 23, "Mediating Hopes: Social Media and Crisis in Northern Italy," Elisabetta Costa
Chapter 39, "Precarity, Discrimination and (In)Visibility: An Ethnography of "The Algorithm" in the YouTube Influencer Industry," Zoë Glatt
Chapter 4, ""Here, Listen to My CD-R": Music Transactions and Infrastructures in Underground Hip-Hop Touring," Anthony Kwame Harrison
Chapter 27, "Inking Identity: Indigenous Nationalism in Bolivian Tattoo Art," Nell Haynes
Chapter 10, "Producing Place through Play: An Ethnography of Location-based Gaming," Kyle Moore
Chapter 17, "#Everest: Visual Economies of Leisure and Labour in the Tourist Encounter," Jolynna Sinanan
Chapter 15, "Cloudwork: Data Centre Labour and the Maintenance of Media Infrastructure," A.R.E. Taylor

LGBTQ+

Chapter 35, "Queer and Muslim? Social Surveillance and Islamic Sexual Ethics on Twitter," Benjamin Ale-Ebrahim

Appendix

Chapter 29, "The Hall of Mirrors: Negotiating Gender on Chilean Social Media," Baird Campbell
Chapter 36, "Queer Sousveillance: Publics, Politics, and Social Media in South Korea," Alex Wolff

Methods

Chapter 12, "Content-as-Practice: Studying Digital Content with a Media Practice Approach," Christoph Bareither
Chapter 19, "Ethnographies of the Digitally Dispossessed," Heather Ford
Chapter 11, "PhotoMedia as Anthropology: Towards a Speculative Research Method," Edgar Gómez Cruz
Chapter 3, "A Longitudinal Study of Media in Brazil", Conrad Phillip Kottak and Richard Pace
Chapter 21, "Mediated Money and Social Relationships among Hong Kong Cross-boundary Students", Tom McDonald, Holy Hoi Ki Shum and Kwok Cheung Wong
Chapter 32, "Researching Political Trolls as Instruments of Political Conservatism in Turkey: A Historical Framework and Methodological Reflections on a Discourse Community", Erkan Saka

Nationalism

Chapter 27, "Inking Identity: Indigenous Nationalism in Bolivian Tattoo Art," Nell Haynes
Chapter 30, "Media Anthropology and the Crisis of Facts", Peter Hervik
Chapter 32, "Researching Political Trolls as Instruments of Political Conservatism in Turkey: A Historical Framework and Methodological Reflections on a Discourse Community", Erkan Saka
Chapter 31, "Conspiracy Media Ecologies and the Case for Guerilla Anthropology," Leighton C. Peterson and Jeb J. Card

Visuality

Chapter 28, "Being Known and Becoming Famous in Kampala, Uganda," Brooke Schwartz Bocast
Chapter 29, "The Hall of Mirrors: Negotiating Gender on Chilean Social Media," Baird Campbell
Chapter 14, "Anthropology and Digital Media: Multivocal Materialities of Video Meetings and Deafness," Rebekah Cupitt
Chapter 39, "Precarity, Discrimination and (In)Visibility: An Ethnography of "The Algorithm" in the YouTube Influencer Industry," Zoë Glatt
Chapter 27, "Inking Identity: Indigenous Nationalism in Bolivian Tattoo Art," Nell Haynes
Chapter 13, "The Materiality of the Virtual in Urban Space," Jordan Kraemer
Chapter 25, "In This Together: Black Women, Collective Screening Experiences, and Space-Making as Meaning-Making," Marlaina Martin

Appendix

Chapter 41, "Ethnography of/and Virtual Reality," Lisa Messer
Chapter 38, "Unlocking Heritage In Situ: Tourist Places and Augmented Reality in Estonia," Christian S. Ritter
Chapter 17, "#Everest: Visual Economies of Leisure and Labour in the Tourist Encounter," Jolynna Sinanan

Media types

Algorithms
- Chapter 34, "Algorithmic Violence in Everyday Life and the Role of Media Anthropology," Veronica Barassi
- Chapter 39, "Precarity, Discrimination and (In)Visibility: An Ethnography of "The Algorithm" in the YouTube Influencer Industry," Zoë Glatt
- Chapter 37, "The Algorithmic Silhouette: New Technologies and the Fashionable Body," Heather A. Horst and Sheba Mohammid

Augmented reality apps
- Chapter 38, "Unlocking Heritage In Situ: Tourist Places and Augmented Reality in Estonia," Christian S. Ritter

Billboards
- Chapter 28, "Being Known and Becoming Famous in Kampala, Uganda," Brooke Schwartz Bocast

CDs
- Chapter 4, ""Here, Listen to My CD-R": Music Transactions and Infrastructures in Underground Hip-Hop Touring," Anthony Kwame Harrison
- Chapter 5, "Technology is Wonderful Until It Isn't": Community-Based Research and the Precarity of Digital Infrastructure," Jerome Crowder, Peggy Determeyer, and Sara Rogers

Covid masks
- Chapter 11, "PhotoMedia as Anthropology: Towards a Speculative Research Method," Edgar Gómez Cruz

Discord
- Chapter 26, "Black Gamer's Refuge: Finding Community within the Magic Circle of Whiteness," Akil Fletcher

Documentary media
- Chapter 31, "Conspiracy Media Ecologies and the Case for Guerilla Anthropology," Leighton C. Peterson and Jeb J. Card

Facebook
- Chapter 22, "Narratives of Digital Intimacy: Romanian Migration and Mediated Transnational Life", Donya Alinejad and Laura Candidatu
- Chapter 12, "Content-as-Practice: Studying Digital Content with a Media Practice Approach," Christoph Bareither
- Chapter 29, "The Hall of Mirrors: Negotiating Gender on Chilean Social Media," Baird Campbell
- Chapter 33, "Performing Conservatism: A Study of Emerging Political Mobilisations in Latin America using 'Social Media Drama' Analysis" Raúl Castro-Pérez
- Chapter 23, "Mediating Hopes: Social Media and Crisis in Northern Italy," Elisabetta Costa
- Chapter 17, "#Everest: Visual Economies of Leisure and Labour in the Tourist Encounter," Jolynna Sinanan

Appendix

- Chapter 36, "Queer Sousveillance: Publics, Politics, and Social Media in South Korea," Alex Wolff

Films
- Chapter 2, "Indigenous Media: Anthropological Perspectives and Historical Notes," Philipp Budka

Film festivals
- Chapter 25, "In This Together: Black Women, Collective Screening Experiences, and Space-Making as Meaning-Making," Marlaina Martin

Gaming servers/games
- Chapter 7, "The Digitally Natural: Hypomediacy and the "Really Real" in Game Design," Thomas M. Malaby
- Chapter 10, "Producing Place through Play: An Ethnography of Location-based Gaming," Kyle Moore
- Chapter 26, "Black Gamer's Refuge: Finding Community within the Magic Circle of Whiteness," Akil Fletcher

Instagram
- Chapter 12, "Content-as-Practice: Studying Digital Content with a Media Practice Approach," Christoph Bareither
- Chapter 29, "The Hall of Mirrors: Negotiating Gender on Chilean Social Media," Baird Campbell
- Chapter 23, "Mediating Hopes: Social Media and Crisis in Northern Italy", Elisabetta Costa

Linkedin
- Chapter 23, "Mediating Hopes: Social Media and Crisis in Northern Italy", Elisabetta Costa

Mobile phones
- Chapter 17, "#Everest: Visual Economies of Leisure and Labour in the Tourist Encounter," Jolynna Sinanan
- Chapter 24, "Digital Inequality and Relatedness in India after Access," Sirpa Tenhunen

Money
- Chapter 21, "Mediated Money and Social Relationships among Hong Kong Cross-boundary Students", Tom McDonald, Holy Hoi Ki Shum and Kwok Cheung Wong

News
- Chapter 30, "Media Anthropology and the Crisis of Facts", Peter Hervik
- Chapter 1, "Media Anthropology and the Digital Challenge", Mark Allen Peterson
- Chapter 31, "Conspiracy Media Ecologies and the Case for Guerilla Anthropology", Leighton C. Peterson and Jeb J. Card

Nico Nico Douga
- Chapter 9, "Television is Not a Democracy: The Limits of Interactive Broadcast in Japan," Elizabeth A. Rodwell

Photographs
- Chapter 12, "Content-as-Practice: Studying Digital Content with a Media Practice Approach," Christoph Bareither
- Chapter 18, "Postcolonial Digital Collections: Instruments, Mirrors, Agents," Haidy Geismar and Katja Müller
- Chapter 11, "PhotoMedia as Anthropology: Towards a Speculative Research Method," Edgar Gómez Cruz

Appendix

- Chapter 17, "#Everest: Visual Economies of Leisure and Labour in the Tourist Encounter," Jolynna Sinanan

Selfies
- Chapter 12, "Content-as-Practice: Studying Digital Content with a Media Practice Approach," Christoph Bareither

Tabloid newspapers
- Chapter 28, "Being Known and Becoming Famous in Kampala, Uganda," Brooke Schwartz Bocast

Tattoos
- Chapter 27, "Inking Identity: Indigenous Nationalism in Bolivian Tattoo Art," Nell Haynes

Television
- Chapter 3, "A Longitudinal Study of Media in Brazil", Conrad Phillip Kottak and Richard Pace
- Chapter 9, "Television is Not a Democracy: The Limits of Interactive Broadcast in Japan," Elizabeth A. Rodwell

Trolls
- Chapter 32, "Researching Political Trolls as Instruments of Political Conservatism in Turkey: A Historical Framework and Methodological Reflections on a Discourse Community" Erkan Saka

Twitter
- Chapter 35, "Queer and Muslim? Social Surveillance and Islamic Sexual Ethics on Twitter," Benjamin Ale-Ebrahim
- Chapter 9, "Television is Not a Democracy: The Limits of Interactive Broadcast in Japan," Elizabeth A. Rodwell
- Chapter 36, "Queer Sousveillance: Publics, Politics, and Social Media in South Korea," Alex Wolff

Virtual assistants
- Chapter 34, "Algorithmic Violence in Everyday Life and the Role of Media Anthropology," Veronica Barassi
- Chapter 37, "The Algorithmic Silhouette: New Technologies and the Fashionable Body," Heather A. Horst and Sheba Mohammid
- Chapter 16, "Media Anthropology and Emerging Technologies: Re-working Media Presence," Sarah Pink, Yolande Strengers, Melisa Duque, Larissa Nichols, and Rex Martin

Virtual Reality
- Chapter 41, "Ethnography of/and Virtual Reality," Lisa Messeri

WeChat
- Chapter 20, "'Friends from WeChat Groups': The Practice of Friendship via Social Media among Older People in China", Xinyuan Wang

Wikipedia
- Chapter 19, "Ethnographies of the Digitally Dispossessed," Heather Ford

YouTube
- Chapter 39, "Precarity, Discrimination and (In)Visibility: An Ethnography of "The Algorithm" in the YouTube Influencer Industry," Zoë Glatt
- Chapter 6, "Media Migration," Patricia G. Lange

Zoom
- Chapter 5, "Technology is Wonderful Until It Isn't": Community-Based Research and the Precarity of Digital Infrastructure," Jerome Crowder, Peggy Determeyer, and Sara Rogers

Appendix

Countries

Australia
- Chapter 11, "PhotoMedia as Anthropology: Towards a Speculative Research Method," Edgar Gómez Cruz
- Chapter 10, "Producing Place through Play: An Ethnography of Location-based Gaming," Kyle Moore
- Chapter 16, "Media Anthropology and Emerging Technologies: Re-working Media Presence," Sarah Pink, Yolande Strengers, Melisa Duque, Larissa Nichols, and Rex Martin

Bolivia
- Chapter 27, "Inking Identity: Indigenous Nationalism in Bolivian Tattoo Art," Nell Haynes

Brazil
- Chapter 3, "A Longitudinal Study of Media in Brazil", Conrad Phillip Kottak and Richard Pace

Canada (First Nations of)
- Chapter 2, "Indigenous Media: Anthropological Perspectives and Historical Notes," Philipp Budka

Chile
- Chapter 29, "The Hall of Mirrors: Negotiating Gender on Chilean Social Media," Baird Campbell

China
- Chapter 21, "Mediated Money and Social Relationships among Hong Kong Cross-boundary Students", Tom McDonald, Holy Hoi Ki Shum and Kwok Cheung Wong
- Chapter 20, "'Friends from WeChat Groups': The Practice of Friendship via Social Media among Older People in China", Xinyuan Wang

Colombia
- Chapter 33, "Performing Conservatism: A Study of Emerging Political Mobilisations in Latin America using 'Social Media Drama' Analysis" Raúl Castro-Pérez

Denmark
- Chapter 30, "Media Anthropology and the Crisis of Facts", Peter Hervik

Estonia
- Chapter 38, "Unlocking Heritage In Situ: Tourist Places and Augmented Reality in Estonia," Christian S. Ritter

Germany
- Chapter 12, "Content-as-Practice: Studying Digital Content with a Media Practice Approach," Christoph Bareither
- Chapter 13, "The Materiality of the Virtual in Urban Space," Jordan Kraemer

India
- Chapter 19, "Ethnographies of the Digitally Dispossessed," Heather Ford
- Chapter 24, "Digital Inequality and Relatedness in India after Access," Sirpa Tenhunen
- Chapter 18, "Postcolonial Digital Collections: Instruments, Mirrors, Agents," Haidy Geismar and Katja Müller

Italy
- Chapter 23, "Mediating Hopes: Social Media and Crisis in Northern Italy" Elisabetta Costa

Japan
- Chapter 9, "Television is Not a Democracy: The Limits of Interactive Broadcast in Japan," Elizabeth A. Rodwell

Malaysia
- Chapter 8, "Media Practices and Their Social Effects," John Postill

Namibia
- Chapter 40, "AI Design and Everyday Logics in the Kalahari," Nicola J. Bidwell, Helen Arnold, Alan F. Blackwell, Charlie Nqeisji, |Kun Kunta, and Martin Ujakpa

Nepal
- Chapter 17, "#Everest: Visual Economies of Leisure and Labour in the Tourist Encounter," Jolynna Sinanan

The Netherlands
- Chapter 22, "Narratives of Digital Intimacy: Romanian Migration and Mediated Transnational Life", Donya Alinejad and Laura Candidatu

Peru
- Chapter 33, "Performing Conservatism: A Study of Emerging Political Mobilisations in Latin America using 'Social Media Drama' Analysis" Raúl Castro-Pérez

Romania
- Chapter 22, "Narratives of Digital Intimacy: Romanian Migration and Mediated Transnational Life", Donya Alinejad and Laura Candidatu

South Korea
- Chapter 36, "Queer Sousveillance: Publics, Politics, and Social Media in South Korea," Alex Wolff

Sweden
- Chapter 14, "Anthropology and Digital Media: Multivocal Materialities of Video Meetings and Deafness," Rebekah Cupitt
- Chapter 16, "Media Anthropology and Emerging Technologies: Re-working Media Presence," Sarah Pink, Yolande Strengers, Melisa Duque, Larissa Nichols, and Rex Martin

Trinidad
- Chapter 37, "The Algorithmic Silhouette: New Technologies and the Fashionable Body," Heather A. Horst and Sheba Mohammid

Turkey
- Chapter 32, "Researching Political Trolls as Instruments of Political Conservatism in Turkey: A Historical Framework and Methodological Reflections on a Discourse Community", Erkan Saka

Uganda
- Chapter 28, "Being Known and Becoming Famous in Kampala, Uganda," Brooke Schwartz Bocast

United Kingdom
- Chapter 35, "Queer and Muslim? Social Surveillance and Islamic Sexual Ethics on Twitter," Benjamin Ale-Ebrahim
- Chapter 39, "Precarity, Discrimination and (In)Visibility: An Ethnography of "The Algorithm" in the YouTube Influencer Industry," Zoë Glatt
- Chapter 15, "Cloudwork: Data Centre Labour and the Maintenance of Media Infrastructure," A.R.E. Taylor

Appendix

United States
- Chapter 4, ""Here, Listen to My CD-R": Music Transactions and Infrastructures in Underground Hip-Hop Touring," Anthony Kwame Harrison
- Chapter 5, "Technology is Wonderful Until It Isn't": Community-Based Research and the Precarity of Digital Infrastructure," Jerome Crowder, Peggy Determeyer, and Sara Rogers
- Chapter 6, "Media Migration," Patricia G. Lange
- Chapter 7, "The Digitally Natural: Hypomediacy and the "Really Real" in Game Design," Thomas M. Malaby
- Chapter 25, "In This Together: Black Women, Collective Screening Experiences, and Space-Making as Meaning-Making," Marlaina Martin
- Chapter 26, "Black Gamer's Refuge: Finding Community within the Magic Circle of Whiteness," Akil Fletcher
- Chapter 31, "Conspiracy Media Ecologies and the Case for Guerilla Anthropology", Leighton C. Peterson and Jeb J. Card
- Chapter 34, "Algorithmic Violence in Everyday Life and the Role of Media Anthropology," Veronica Barassi
- Chapter 35, "Queer and Muslim? Social Surveillance and Islamic Sexual Ethics on Twitter," Benjamin Ale-Ebrahim
- Chapter 39, "Precarity, Discrimination and (In)Visibility: An Ethnography of "The Algorithm" in the YouTube Influencer Industry," Zoë Glatt
- Chapter 37, "The Algorithmic Silhouette: New Technologies and the Fashionable Body," Heather A. Horst and Sheba Mohammid
- Chapter 13, "The Materiality of the Virtual in Urban Space," Jordan Kraemer
- Chapter 41, "Ethnography of/and Virtual Reality," Lisa Messeri

INDEX

Aadhar digital identification programme (India) 262
Ableton Live 70
Abram, S. 201
Abu Ghraib prison and eroticization of torture 435–7
Abu-Lughod, L. 35, 41, 123, 204
achievement 581–2
activism 23–4, 36–9, 99, 121, 126; indigenous media 34, 36–9, 41, 43; LGBTQ+ community sousveillance and social media in South Korea 506–7; media 23–4; political 442; social effects of media practices 125; social media drama analysis and political mobilisations in Latin America 465
actor-network theory (ANT) 175
Adams, V. 511
Adecco 333
adivaani project 265
Adivasi Academy 266
Adpocalypse 552–3
ads 95; ad-friendly content 552; excessive 94; mid-roll 550; revenue 545; targeted 481, 486
affordances 2, 26, 196, 246, 251, 290; algorithmic 179; camera 162; emotional 172; -in-practice 175; mediated 6, 306, 308, 310; photomedia 166; technological 174–6; theories 175–7, 179
Africa 2, 248, 275, 395–408; *see also* Artificial Intelligence (AI) and cause-and-effect reasoning among the Ju|'hoansi people in the Kalahari
age-based demographics 92
agency 26, 201, 339, 345, 350; indigenous media 34, 36, 38, 43
age restrictions 553
Aggasiz, L. 357
agnotology 428
Ahmed, A. 20, 339

Ahmed, S. 376
AKP regime (Turkey) 454–8, 460–1
Aktrolls (Turkey) 454–61
Alacovska, A. 337, 339
Albro, R. 386, 392 n.1
Ale-Ebrahim, B. 11
Alexa 108, 280, 483
Alexander, N. 216
'Alfie's Army' 471
algorithmic accountability 565
algorithmic affordances 179
algorithmic anxiety 547
algorithmic bias and misrecognition *see* Amazon Echo Look and algorithmic bias and misrecognition of Black bodies in Trinidad
algorithmic detectives and conspiracy theorists 548–9
algorithmic discrimination and marginalization 509, 511, 552–4
algorithmic experts or growth hackers 549
algorithmic gossip 547, 549
algorithmic hearsay and folk theories 547–9, 552
algorithmic imaginaries 548
algorithmic opacity 547, 558, 559
algorithmic optimisation versus authenticity 551–2
algorithmic profiling and datafication of children 481–90; algorithmic violence 482, 488–90; belittled and objectified, feelings of being 482, 486, 490; bureaucratic processes 482, 487–90; discrimination 487; human reductionism 485–8; inequality and marginalization 482, 485–8, 489; negotiating and resisting 486; pluriverse 483, 486; powerlessness, feelings of 484; predictive analytics 489; privacy harms 487; privileged position 482, 486; structural violence 482, 487, 489, 490; surveillance 481–5, 487; symbolic violence 482, 487, 489–90

Index

algorithmic punishment 553
algorithmic rupture 552
algorithms: classification 558; in culture 527–8; as culture 528; *see also* YouTube algorithm and influencer precarity, discrimination, and (in)visibility
Ali, K. 499
Alinejad, D. 9
Alipay 305–7, 309, 311
Althusser, L. 52
Amazon 217, 583
Amazon Alexa 108, 280, 483
Amazon Echo 481
Amazon Echo Look and algorithmic bias and misrecognition of Black bodies in Trinidad 11, 12, 519–28; algorithmic silhouettes in context 526–7; classification inaccuracy 524; closet ethnography of dress, clothing, and identity 520–1; community guidelines and censorship issues 525, 528; cultural norms and values 520; dress codes and professional identity 521, 523; gendered dimension 525, 527; professionalism of choices 522–4, 527; recommendation systems 520; respectability and reputation 521; sexuality 521, 522–4, 527; Style Check feature 522–3, 524–6; visibility and misrecognition 524–6
Amazon Mechanical Turk 216, 546
Amazon Town TV (ATTV) 51–4
Amazon Web Services (AWS) 215
Amin, K. 414
'ancient astronauts' theories 442
Anderson, B. 27, 123, 315
Android Pay 305
Ang, I. 134
anonymity 372, 457, 507
Anonymous 444
anti-abortion movement 470, 473–5
anti-censorship software 494
anti-discrimination law (South Korea) 506
anti-euthanasia movement 470–2, 475
anti-Semitism 552
Appadurai, A. 38, 216, 489
Apperley, T. 146
Apple 217
Apple Maps 108
Apple Pay 305
Application Programming Interface (API) 147
appropriation 35, 37, 41, 43, 231, 266–7, 391–2
Ara Iritija project 265
archives *see* postcolonial digital collections in museums and archives
Arnold, H. 12
AR prototype test 535
Arroyo, Father M. 472
Artificial Intelligence (AI) 2, 12, 176, 223, 282, 572; algorithmic profiling and datafication of children 484, 489; Amazon Echo Look and algorithmic bias and misrecognition 520, 524, 527; and cause-and-effect reasoning among the Ju|'hoansi people in the Kalahari 12, 557–66; conditional probability 563; data and Global Souths 559; engaging with the Ju|'hoansi 561–2; ethnographies 558; explainable AI 561; explainable algorithms 558–9; Human-Computer Interaction (HCI) 557–8, 559, 560; indigenous knowledge 560; localising technology production 559–60; numbers as stories 564; predictive logics - stories and spinner games 563; programming languages, probability theory, and local predictive practices 562–3; spinner games 564, 565; temporal registers 564–5, 566; translating inhabitant knowledge 560–1
Artivists 4 Life (A4L) 395–6, 399–405, 407
Askew, K. 427, 439
aspirational labour 548
aspirations 93–6, 231, 246, 248, 255–6, 316, 323
attack pages 277
augmented reality 146, 572; *see also* smartphone augmented reality and heritage tourist attractions in Estonia
Australia 2, 6, 7, 23, 38, 152, 235, 265; Aboriginal orality 40; Warlpiri 40; *see also* media presence in the home; photomedia
authoritarian regimes 454–6, 461–2, 468
automation 282; *see also* Amazon Echo Look and algorithmic bias and misrecognition of Black bodies in Trinidad; media presence in the home
Awavena 570–2, 574, 576, 578 n.1
Azerbaijan 509

backend channel analytic data 549
bad-faith contributions 277
Bakardjieva, M. 348
Bal, E. 315
Baldwin, J. 360
Banet-Weiser, S. 554
Banks, J. 152
Barad, K. 203
Barassi, V. 11
Barbados 521
Barber, K. 399, 406
Bareither, C. 7
Barfoed, N. 435
Barloe, J.P. 280
Barnes, S. 407
Bärtle, M. 545
Bateson, G. 19, 163
Bayesian inference 562–3, 564, 565
Baym, N.K. 551
Bazin, A. 157–8
Bean, S. 20
Beck, S. 175–6
Becker, H.S. 121

Beeman, W.O. 20
Belize 105
Bell, C. 469, 474
Bell, J. 187
Bellanova, R. 487
Benedict, R. 19
Benjamin, R. 373
Benkler, Y. 274
Berlant, L. 336, 339
Berlin *see* materiality of the virtual in urban space
Bernhardt, J.M. 86
Bhabha, H. 263–4
Bhalla, G. 264–5
Bhambra, G.K. 268 n.1
Bidwell, N. 12
big data 485, 488, 489, 494, 524, 559
Bishop, S. 547, 549
Blaagaard, B. 136
Black Experience, The (server) 371
Black gamers finding community with Magic Circle of Whiteness (MCW) 9–10, 368–77; anonymity 372; anti-Black behaviours 370, 371, 372, 375; anti-Black discrimination 368–9, 371; Black Girl Gamers (BGG) 370, 374–6, 377; Black People Discord (BPD) 370, 372, 374, 377; Black space deconstructed and overwhelmed by whiteness 370; Black Spoil Sport 370, 374–7; consumption of Black space for white play or pleasure 370; cultural logics of hetero white male gaming culture 369; Discord 370, 371–4, 375; gamified governing system 372; high-tech Blackface 372–3; levelling system 372; moderators 372–3, 376; white discrimination and harassment 370
Black Gamers (server) 371
Black Girl Gamers (BGG) 370, 377
Black People Discord (BPD) 370, 372, 374, 377
Black Spoil Sport 370, 374–7
Blackwell, A. 12
Blanchette, J.-F. 214
Blee, K. 467
Blerd Stasis (server) 371
blockchain 572
blogs/bloggers 24, 90, 94, 249, 432, 437, 448, 472, 494, 506
Boas, F. 384
Boast, R. 268 n.13
Bobo, J. 357
Bocast, B. 10
Boellstorff, T. 96, 98, 125–6, 127, 368, 485, 508
Bogost, I. 106, 109–10
Bolcatto, A. 468
Boliva *see* tattooing identity and indigenous nationalism in Bolivia
Bollmer, G. 577
Bolter, J.D. 106–7, 113, 575

Bonini, T. 459
Bosua, R. 128
bottom-up processes 8, 162, 258
Bourdieu, P. 52, 134, 136, 171, 175, 429
boyd, d. 92, 308, 465
Boyer, D. 136, 315, 340, 361, 362
Bradford, P. 221, 222
Bradshaw, S. 456, 461
brand deals 545
Brazil and television viewing 4, 20, 47–58, 92; acceptance, rejection, interpretation, and reworking (stage 2) 49; *Amazon Town TV* (ATTV) 51–4; gender roles 53; identity construction 52, 53, 55; initial contact (stage 1) 49, 54; interactive and on demand content (stage 5) 50; interpellation resistance 53–4, 58 n.3; intertextuality/extratextuality 53; liberal attitudes 50; lifelong exposure (stage 4) 49–50; Mebengokre-Kayapó TV 54–5; Prime-Time Society (PTS) 48, 51–2; product placement 53; saturation point (stage 3) 49; social merchandising 53; social status 49; sociocultural effects 49; stage model 48–50; TV and family planning 50; underground national lottery 112
Breivik, A. 434–5
Brettell, C.B. 97
British Cultural Studies 51
British Phonographic Industry – 'Home Taping is Killing Music' campaign 70
Brooklyn *see* materiality of the virtual in urban space
Brooten, L. 40
Brown, M. 392
Browne, S. 507
Bucher, T. 552
Budka, P. 4, 258
Bukowski, T. 125
bureaucratic processes 482, 487–90
Burke, H. 40
Burrell, J. 218–19, 277
Butler, J. 153, 364, 411

Cabanes, J.V.A. 461
Cabatingan, L. 521
call tree 81–2
Campana, A. 459–61
Campbell, B. 10
Campt, T.M. 360, 376
Canada 23, 265; Aboriginal Peoples Television Network (APTN) 38; First Nation communities 35, 37, 41–3; police racial profiling 494
Canclini, N.G. 382, 383, 388, 390
Candidatu, L. 9
Candy, S. 201
Canessa, A. 384
captions 177–8

Index

Cara 481
Card, J. 11
Cardullo, P. 187
Carib and Taino communities (Caribbean) 42
Carpenter, E. 37
Carruthers, S. 430
Carsten, J. 346
Cartier-Bresson, H. 162
Castells, M. 343
Castro, R. 11
Catan: World Explorers 149
Caton, S. 20
Caughey, J.L. 20
Causa Justa (Just Cause) 473
CCTV 494, 506
censorship and self-censorship 435, 494, 525, 528
centrality of media in sociality 90
Certeau, M. de 111, 171
Chakrabarty, D. 275
Chan, N.K. 509
channel page 91
Chazkel, A. 112
Chen, T. 274
Cheney, D. 430
Cheney, K. 405, 408 n.5
Chess, S. 151
Chicago School of Sociology 121
Child/Data/Citizen project 481, 482–3
children, improper recommendation of content to 553
Children's Online Privacy Protection Act (1998) 482
Chile *see* transgendering on social media in Chile
China 126, 250–1, 289, 303, 345, 348, 468, 509; Uyghur Muslim genocide 493; *see also* WeChat groups and WeChat friends in China
Chio, J. 250–1
Christensen, N.B. 251
Christiansen, C. 408 n.5
Christie, M. 265
Citron, J. 371
Clark, S. 548
class dimensions 27, 92, 428
classification algorithm 558
Claus, P. 20
clickable titles 549
clickbait 549, 551
clicks 549
click work 216
Clinton, H. 444
cloudwork *see* data centre labour and maintenance of media infrastructure
Colavito, J. 448
Coleman, E. 275, 376
Coleman, G. 456
collective screening and space-making as meaning-making 9, 355–66; alternatives of Black media screening and engagement 358–60; Black un/imagining 365–6; collective awareness and narrative-building 365; conditions, spaces, interactions, and politics of media engagement 361; co-production of meaning and screening events 360–3; corporeal and affective engagements 356; cultural backgrounds 356; distance and distancing in media histories 356–8; emotional honesty, historical revisionism, and culture-minded aesthetics 356, 365, 366; enabling distortions 357; inclusion and exclusion 363; intellectual experiences 366; interpersonal relations, commitments, and conflicts 361; media curation and usage 361; media as practice 361; misinterpretations of media consumption 361; politicized investments 358; privilege content analysis 361; radical openness 355, 366; re-conceptualisation and articulation of issues 366; reframing 361; social, intellectual, and physical engagement 356; social interests 356; social mediation 361; standardized racial dogmas 357; value added 356; visceral validation and reclaiming space, body, and affect 363–5
Colombia 466, 469, 470, 472–5
colonialism 3, 37–8, 43, 250, 260, 386–7; *see also* Oral Citations Project (Wikimedia Foundation)
Colson, E. 98
Comaroff, Jean 404
Comaroff, John 404
commercialization and competitiveness 97, 99; *see also* ads; monetisation; YouTube algorithm and influencer precarity, discrimination, and (in)visibility
community-based research and precarity of digital infrastructure 77–87; availability 80; background 78–80; call tree 81–2; community dialogue sessions 79; connectivity, literacy, etiquette and availability 84; data/privacy issues 77; expectations 83; exploring possibilities and promise of technology 82–3; fundamental infrastructures and foundational knowledge 80–2; health literacy 77–8; importance of community partnerships and promotion of digital inclusiveness 86; lessons learned 86–7; limiting of assumptions 86; medication management 77; *Mental Health and Aging* 82–3; orientation meeting 85; personalized medicine 78; pharmacogenomics 77; practice sessions 84; technology access and user issues 81–2; telehealth 78; value of technology 86; video technology 82–3; Zoom and technology literacy 84–5
community building 152, 204, 210, 370; *see also* Black gamers finding community with Magic Circle of Whiteness (MCW)
comparisons 582–3

Compass, The (Japan) 132–6, 138–41
conditionality 565
Connell, C. 393 n.6
conspiracy media ecologies in United States 11, 441–9; America's Stonehenge vandalism 442–4, 446, 449; amplification 445–6; debunking 448; fake news 441–2, 444–5; Gogmagog Affair 446–7; guerrilla archaeology, case for 446–8; indexical communities 441; mediated conspirituality 444–6; New Atheism 448; paranormal media 442, 445–6; participatory culture 441; pseudoarchaeology 442; pseudoscience 441–2; Qanon political conspiracy movement 441–2, 443–6, 447, 449; recontextualization 445; skeptic movement 448; spreadability 441, 445–6; UFO abduction stories 442, 445
consumerism 52
content-as-practice 171–80; affordances-in-practice 175; affordance theories 175–7, 179; emotional affordances 172; Holocaust memorial (Berlin) 172–4, 176–9; human actors, practical sense 174–6; materialised practice 174; methodological consequences 178–9; routinization 176–7, 179; 'sad selfie' 173–4, 176–7, 179; social media algorithms and routinised practices 176–7; technological affordances 174–6; understanding of 173–4
content creation 217
content moderation 217
content modification 552
content niche 549
content output, quantity and quality of 550
content trends and challenges 549
control 35, 43, 302, 305–8, 350, 431
Cook, M. 495–6, 501
'cool' factor 95–6
Cooper, C. 521
Cooper, W.M. 446
copyright 91, 95, 277
Corrigan, T.F. 336
corruption 56
Costa, E. 9, 175, 196, 201, 210, 258
Costanza-Chock, S. 485–6
Costera, I. 234
Cotton, C. 159
Couldry, N. 105, 119, 120, 126, 146, 171, 361, 362, 466
countering violent extremism (CVE) programs 493
COVID-19 pandemic 2, 7, 157, 164, 165, 167, 562; algorithmic profiling and datafication of children 486; Brazil 57; community-based research and precarity of digital infrastructure 77, 84–5; data centre labour and maintenance of media infrastructure 221, 224; digital inequality and relatedness in India after Internet access 344; Estonia 541; Hong Kong 304;

Italy 331, 336, 338; materiality of the virtual in urban space 185–6, 193–6; media presence in the home 233, 234; photomedia 157, 164, 165, 167; South Korea 506, 513; Turkey 458; United States 446; visual economies and Everest 247–8
Craig, D. 545
Crapanzano, V. 339
Creasap, K. 467
Creative Commons (South Africa) 274–5
Crenshaw, K. 345
Crosset, V. 459–61
Crowder, J. 5–6
crowdfunding 545
crowdsourcing 216, 549
crowdwork 546
Cruz, G. 6–7
Csordas, T. 364
cultural activism 36–8
cultural analysis 19
cultural capital 54–5
cultural factors 18–19; collective screening and space-making as meaning-making 356; indigenous media 34, 37, 38, 40, 43; location-based gaming 147; photomedia 158; postcolonial digital collections in museums and archives 259; social media drama analysis and political mobilisations in Latin America 466; tattooing identity and indigenous nationalism in Bolivia 384, 386, 388–90, 391; visual economies of leisure and labour in the tourist encounter of Everest 248; *see also* Romanian migration to Netherlands and mediated transnational life
cultural minorities 251
cultural practices 547
cultural preferences 298
culture at a distance 18
culture of evaluation 488
culture industries 21
Cunningham, S. 545
Cupitt, R. 7, 204
Curating Digital Images 172
Cutrell, E. 350
cyberattacks 427
CyberTracker 557, 565

Dahlerup, U. 434
D'Aloisio, F. 333
Danish People's Party (DPD) 427, 431, 432, 433–4
Darwin, C. 113 n.1, 125
Das, V. 20
data bundles 344
data centre labour and maintenance of media infrastructure 213–25; anticipatory maintenance 222–3; disconnection and failure events 213,

Index

222; electricity and water demands 216–17; environmental impacts 219; factory metaphor 219; Giga Tech 213–15, 220–1, 224; human error 223; maintenance of data 222–4; material, fragile, precarious infrastructure 215; onsite landscapes, ecologies and communities 216; reactive maintenance 222–3; shift work 221; transcendental media imaginary 216–17; 24/7 on-demand, real-time, and instant access pressures 215, 220–2, 224; workers 215, 217–19, 220
data discrimination 524
datafication 2
datafication of children *see* algorithmic profiling and datafication of children
data harms 487
data interface 162
Data Science 558
data sets 524, 527
data traces 483–4
data trackers 485
data transactions 559
da'wa movements 496–7
Dawkins, R. 448
Dawūd, A. 496
deafness *see* multivocal materialities of video meetings and deafness at Swedish television (SVT) Teckenspråk
Deaking University CADET Virtual Reality Training and Simulation Research Lab 231
De Beukelaer, C. 73
decolonialism 3, 258–9, 261, 262, 428; *see also* Artificial Intelligence (AI)
Deezer 459
de-identification of online photos 508, 510, 512
de la Peña, N. 575
Deliveroo 216, 546
democratisation of TV 6
demonetisation 546, 552–3
demo tapes 69–74
Den Korte Avis website (Denmark) 434
Denmark *see* racism against Muslims and neo-nationalism in Denmark
deselection of content 552, 553
Determeyer, P. 5–6
developed countries 344
developing countries 344
development communications 19–20
development theories 19
diaspora 96–7, 98, 314, 315–16, 317, 319–21; *see also* Romanian migration to Netherlands and mediated transnational life
Digital Audio Workstations 70
digital challenge 17–28; development communications 19–20; digital divide 25–6; emergence of media anthropology 21–2; functionalist foundations 17–18; imagining

communities 27; indigenous and activist media 23–4; national culture 18–19; newness of digital media 25; news and journalism 22–3; play, game and design 27–8; post-radial semiotics 26–7; symbolic systems, media as 20–1
digital collections *see* postcolonial digital collections in museums and archives
Digital Cultures Collaboratory 104
digital diaspora 96
digital directory 42
digital divide 25–6, 80, 318; *see also* digital inequality and relatedness in India after Internet access
digital exceptionalism 105
digital identity 96
Digital India campaign 260–2, 347, 352
digital inequality and relatedness in India after Internet access 9, 343–52; affordable access 351; agency and freedom of choice 350; calling function 347, 350; control of child viewing 350; digital divide 343, 345, 350–1; diversity of digital practices 346–8; economic and political empowerment 351; education, importance of for phone use 346, 351; gradations of use 345–6; identity statements/status symbols 348–9; inequalities after access 343–5; intersectionality 345; kinship relations 346, 349; music and film purchase and indirect Internet access 347–8, 350–1; recreational practices 350–1; refashioning social hierarchies 348–50; social fluidity in families 349; social hierarchies 352; social interaction 348, 352
digital infrastructure 103; *see also* data centre labour and maintenance of media infrastructure
digital intimacies 238
digitally dispossessed *see* Oral Citations Project (Wikimedia Foundation)
digital memory practices 172
digital profiling 481
digital rights 121
digital traces 164, 166, 461
digital turn 258
DiGRA (Digital Games Research Association) 105
Discord 370, 371–4, 375
discrimination 368–9, 371, 415, 487, 524, 544; *see also* Amazon Echo Look and algorithmic bias and misrecognition of Black bodies in Trinidad; LGBTQ+ community sousveillance and social media in South Korea; YouTube algorithm and influencer precarity, discrimination and (in)visibility
diversity issues 220
dndbeyond.com 112
Dodd, N. 303
Dominican Republic 303
Donner, J. 344
Doomer Girl meme 498–9
Dornfeld, B. 21

Douglas, M. 20
Dourish, P. 146, 151, 528
Downey, G. 217
Dow Schüll, N. 110
Dragsted, P. 432
Dr. Dre 72
Dresden Museum für Wölkerkunde 266
Duffy, B.E. 509, 546
Dungeons & Dragons 105–6, 113; dndbeyond.com 112
Dunne, A. 201
Duque, M. 7

East Asia 2
Eastern Europe 317, 467
Ebabil *Telegram* group 458–9
eBay 338
Egypt 339, 496–7
Einstein, A. 430
Elliot, A. 339
Elliott, M. 260
Ellis, L. 551
email 292–3
emergence of media anthropology 21–2
emerging technologies 8–9, 12; *see also* media presence in the home
Eminem 72
emojis 174, 178
emotional and affective practices theories 172
emotional affordances 172
emotional practices 177
empowerment 210
Enote, J. 268 n.13
entextualization 24
Entwistle, J. 520, 526
EPS 305
Erdoğan, R.T. 454, 457–8, 461
Escobar, A. 483, 486
Eslen-Ziya, H. 460
Espersen, S. 431
Essed, P. 436
Estonia *see* smartphone augmented reality and heritage tourist attractions in Estonia
ethical issues 146, 536, 541, 572; *see also* social surveillance and sexual ethics of Muslim LGBTQ+ community on Twitter
Ethiopia 35, 339
Europe 2, 21, 259, 344, 431, 465, 467–8, 509; *see also* Eastern Europe; Western Europe
Eurostat 318
Evans, A. 470–2
Everest *see* visual economies of leisure and labour in the tourist encounter of Everest
Everett, A. 369
everyday, memories of 467, 469
exaptation 231
explainability (AI) 566

exposure to media 48
extreme speech 437, 460
extremism 434, 438, 468

Facebook 11, 50, 92, 94, 95, 519, 559, 583; algorithmic profiling and datafication of children 482, 485, 486, 489; Black gamers finding community with Magic Circle of Whiteness (MCW) 370, 375; Brazil 56, 57; content-as-practice 172, 177; data centres 218–19; Denmark 434; Estonia 535; India 344, 346, 347; indigenous media 42; Italy 333, 334, 335, 336, 337, 338–9, 340; Japan 132, 136; Latin America 466–7, 469, 470, 471, 473; materiality of the virtual in urban space 186, 193–4; migration from MySpace 92, 93; Netherlands 320; postcolonial digital collections in museums and archives 264; social surveillance and sexual ethics of Muslim LGBTQ+ community 494, 498; South Korea 505; Uganda 403, 406–7, 408; United States 446; virtual reality immersion 572; visual economies and Everest 245–6, 247–8
facial recognition technology 524
fake news 56–7, 441–2, 444–5
fame-seeking *see* recognition and fame-seeking in Uganda
Fanon, F. 437
Farman, J. 148
fashion consumer product *see* Amazon Echo Look and algorithmic bias and misrecognition of Black bodies in Trinidad
Fat Margaret app 536–8, 539
Feaver, D. 122
Feinberg, M. 465
Félix and Paul VR studio 575
feminised labour 547
filter bubbles 524
First Nation communities in Canada 35, 37, 41–3
Fischer, S. 253
Fiverr 216
Flaherty, R.J. 360
Fletcher, A. 9–10
Flores, C.Y. 39
Flores-Saviaga, C. 455
Ford, H. 8
Fortun, K. 223
Fortun, M. 223
Foster, W.D. 357
Foucault, M. 494, 508
4chan 444
Foursquare 95
Fourth Industrial Revolution (4IR) 557
France 430
freedom of expression 436
free imagination, anarchy of 105
Freelancer 216

Freeman, C. 521
free software production 126
free speech 435
'friend circles' 188, 190
friendships *see* WeChat groups and WeChat friends in China
Frith, J. 148
fugitivity 376
Fuji Television (Japan) 132
functionalist foundations 17–18
future dialogues 583–4
future-oriented media anthropology 166–7
fuzzy logic 103

Gage, J. 563
game design and hypomediacy 6, 103–14; attenuated negotiation 111; contingency 110, 111–12; dialogic dimension 108; explicit to implicit participation 110–12; first person shooters 108; hypermediacy 107–8, 111–12, 113; ideal types 110, 114 n.3; motion-sensitive controllers 110; performative action 110; 'really real' 104, 108; remediation 105–8; ritual and the real 108–10; rules, disappearing 110–11; setup, absence of 111
Gamergate hate campaign 369
GameStop 103–4
gaming 6, 27–8; appropriate/inappropriate nature of 152–3; *see also* Black gamers finding community with Magic Circle of Whiteness (MCW); location-based gaming
Gandini, A. 459
GarageBand 70
Garcia, L.-M. 191
Gates of Vienna extreme right website 434
Geertz, C. 14, 20, 104, 108, 186, 485, 571, 574–5, 576
Gehl, R.W. 456
Geiger, S. 280
Geismar, H. 8
gender factors 27, 509; Amazon Echo Look and algorithmic bias and misrecognition of Black bodies in Trinidad 525, 527; Brazil 53; discrimination 428; Romanian migration to Netherlands and mediated transnational life 319, 321; YouTube algorithm and influencer precarity, discrimination, and (in)visibility 547; *see also* LGBTQ+ community; transgendering on social media in Chile
Georgia 339
Gerbaudo, P. 473
Germany 123, 430, 446, 484
Gershon, I. 348
Gezi Park Protests (Turkey) 455–7, 461
Ghezzi, S. 333
Gibson, J.W. 175
Giddens, A. 126, 171, 401

Giga Tech 213–15, 220–1, 224
gig economy 216, 546
Gilman, M.E. 487
Gilroy, P. 316
Gingrich, N. 431
Ginsburg, F. 35–6, 37, 38, 41, 121–3, 128, 201, 204, 315, 376, 466, 528
Gist, E.K.P. 357
Gladwell, M. 95
Glatt, Z. 12
global access rate 344
globalization 21, 40
Global Positioning System (GPS) 147
Globo (Brazil) 48, 50–1, 55
Glowaki, E.M. 86
Gmelch, G. 97
Goddard, V.A. 316, 333
Goggin, G. 148
Gogmagog Affair 446–7
Gomez, R. 95
Goodwin, W. 443
Google 236, 279–80, 485, 488, 519, 535, 559; Firebase platform 535; media content 230
Google Home voice assistant 229, 231, 234–8
Google Maps 108, 147, 149, 347, 494
Google Nest Hub Max table 234
Google Translate 345
Gould, D. 95
Graeber, D. 105–6, 487, 488, 489
Granzberg, G. 23
Grau, O. 573, 579 n.2
Gray, M. 519, 546
Gray, P. 573–4
Griffith, W.E.B. 357
Grimm, B. 392
Gripsrud, J. 139
Groot, T. 234
Ground Control Allstars tour 65, 67–8, 70–1, 72
Ground Control Records 67, 69, 72
group identities 28
group interactions and socialities 9; *see also* WeChat groups and WeChat friends in China
growth hackers 547
Grusin, R. 106–7, 113, 575
Grüter, B. 146
Guerrero, E. 357
guestlisting 191–2
Gupta, A. 489
Gyms 152

Habermas, J. 123
habitus 134, 136–7
Hacking, I. 113 n.1
Hafsteinsson, S.B. 38
Haiti 303
Halegoua, G. 148
Hall, R. 253

Hall, S. 316, 361–2, 454
Hancock, G. 442, 445
haptic interfaces 540
harassment 370, 417
Haraway, D.J. 209
Hargittai, E. 524
Harry Potter: Wizards Unite 149, 150
Hart, K. 302
Hartley, J. 136, 141
Hartman, S. 576–7
Harvey, D. 185
hashtags 174, 176
hate speech 437, 460, 553
Haynes, N. 10
Helmreich, S. 573, 577
Hepp, A. 121, 466
Hertzfeld, M. 489
Hervik, P. 10–11
Hillary, Sir D. 248–9
Himpele, J.D. 386
Hine, C. 201, 545–6
Hinote, B. 51–4
hip-hop touring *see* music transactions and infrastructures in underground hip-hop touring
Hiscock, P. 448–9
histories 4–5
Hitchins, C. 448
Hobart, M. 120, 122, 123–4, 179
Hobbis, G. 350
Hoffman, A. 487
Hogan, M. 218, 222
Holocaust memorial (Berlin) 172–4, 176–9
homogenization 47
Hong Kong *see* mediated money and social relationships among Hong Kong cross-boundary students
Hong Kong Monetary Authority (HKMA) 305
hooks, b. 355
Hop-Hop (South Korea) 505, 507
Hopkins, J. 175
Horst, H.A. 12, 99, 303
Hou, A.C.Y. 95, 96
Houdini, H. 448
Howard, P. 456, 461
Howe, C. 136
Hughes, M. 72
Hui, A. 124
Huizinga, J. 368, 369, 370, 375
Human-Computer Interaction (HCI) 557–8, 559, 560
human reductionism 485–8
Hutchby, I. 175
Hwang, K. 294
hybridity 263, 382–3, 388, 390–1, 539
hypermediacy 107–8, 111–12, 113
hypernormalization 136
hypomediacy *see* game design and hypomediacy

Iban in Malaysia 124–5
Iceland 218
Icke, D. 446
iCommons 275
ideal types (game design) 110, 114 n.3
identity 27, 204, 209, 210; Brazil and television viewing 52, 53, 55; digital 96; group 28; Romanian migration to Netherlands and mediated transnational life 315, 320; and social change 8, 10; and social formations 20; transgendering on social media in Chile 411–12; *see also* tattooing identity and indigenous nationalism in Bolivia
Identity and Awareness Talk 52
IHH (Turkey) 457
image-based practices 177
imaginaries 250, 339, 548
imaginative speculation 166–7
imagined surveillance 509
imagining communities 27
immersive journalism 575
imperialism 260
income *see* monetisation
India 8, 24, 259, 468, 489–90, 509; *see also* digital inequality and relatedness in India after Internet access; Oral Citations Project (Wikimedia Foundation); postcolonial digital collections in museums and archives
Indian Memory Project 264
Indian Ministry of Culture 260
indigenous media 23–4, 33–44; action-oriented approach 39; activism 34, 36–9, 41, 43; agency 34, 36, 38, 43; control and ownership 35, 43; cultural factors 34, 37, 38, 40, 43; First Nation communities in Canada 41–3; identities, collective and individual 36, 37, 39–40, 42, 43, 44; indigeneity and indigenizing of media technologies 39–40; inequality 36; knowledge production, circulation, and representation 43; linguistic adaptation and acculturation 37; marginalization, dispossession, and exclusion 34, 36, 41; media appropriation 35, 37, 41, 43; power 36, 43; self-determination 34, 40, 43; self-identification 34, 39; self-representation 42; sociocultural and techno-historical specifics 35; sociopolitical change 40–1
indigenous nationalism *see* tattooing identity and indigenous nationalism in Bolivia
Indonesia 20, 122, 123–4
inductive selection process 177
inequality 8, 9–10, 20, 36, 210, 340, 344, 345, 348–50; algorithmic profiling and datafication of children 482, 485–8, 489; *see also* digital inequality and relatedness in India after Internet access
influencers *see* YouTube algorithm and influencer precarity, discrimination, and (in)visibility
infoboxes 279

Index

informality 334
infrastructure: commercialized 97; culture 79; digital 103; Internet 79; issues 94; media as 5–6; opportunities 96; software 78; *see also* music transactions and infrastructures in underground hip-hop touring
Ingold, T. 159–60
Ingress 145–53
Ingress Prime 149, 150
Instagram 50, 545; algorithmic profiling and datafication of children 482; Black gamers finding community with Magic Circle of Whiteness (MCW) 375; Brazil 56, 57; Chile 415–18, 420; content-as-practice 172, 173, 176, 177; Estonia 539; Italy 332, 333, 334, 336, 337, 340; migration from Facebook 92; migration from Viners 98; social surveillance and sexual ethics of Muslim LGBTQ+ community community 494; South Korea 506, 507; visual economies and Everest 246, 249–50
integration 2
interaction 90
interactive TV broadcasting in Japan 122–42; audience positionality and professional practice 134; *Compass, The* (Japan) 132–6, 138–41; democracy issues 135–7; future of television and status of images 139–40; insular structure of TV industry 133; livestream 133; Nico Nico Douga (NND) streaming broadcast platform 132–9, 141; twenty-first century audience 134–5
intermediality 368, 376
International Monetary Fund (IMF) 398
interpersonal communication 8
interpretive approach 4, 20, 52
Interxion 221
Inuit society 121, 128, 251
invisible labour (ghost workers) 519, 528
Ipsen, G. 173
Iran 24, 339
Iranian Green Movement 494
Isika, N. 128
Israeli surveillance of Palestinian territories 494
Italy 316, 317; *see also* mediating hope amid economic crisis in Italy

Jacobson, K. 218, 222
Jakimov, T. 336–7, 339
Jamaica 248, 521
Jansen, S. 339
Japan 6, 19; *see also* interactive TV broadcasting in Japan
Jarrett, K. 217
Jasanoff, S. 280
Jastrow, M. 572, 574, 576
Jatan database (India) 262
Jazeel, T. 258
Jemelniak, D. 276

Jenkins, H. 80
Jenner, K. 410
Johnson, A. 218
Johnson, K. 527
Jones, V. 576
Ju|'hoansi people *see* Artificial Intelligence (AI) and cause-and-effect reasoning among the Ju|'hoansi people in the Kalahari
JusticeforGeorgeNYC Instagram page *194*

KADEM (Turkey) 460
Kakaotalk 506
Kanban method 535
Kandel, W. 315
karaoke songs from Hong Kong and Taiwan 122
Karp, I. 20, 408 n.9
Kayapo video-making projects (Brazil) 39, 41
KaZaA 70
Keegan, B. 455
Keewaytinook Okimakanak Kuh-ke-nah Network (KO-NET) (Canada) 34, 42, 43
Kelty, C. 126
Kennedy, J.F. 166
Khiabani, G. 494
Ki Shum, Holy Hoi 9
Kitzinger, B. 52
Kjaersgaard, P. 432–3
Kjellberg, F. (AKA PewDiePie) 552
Kleist, N. 339
Kock, C. 428
Kocurek, C.A. 369
Kottak, C.P. 4, 20, 92
Kraemer, J. 7
Krakauer, J. 249
Kubitschko, S. 120
Kuehn, K. 336
Kugle, S. 499
Kuiper, J. 187
Kunta, |K. 12
Kutcher, N. 290
Kuwahara, M. 383
Kwame Harrison, A. 5

La Ferrara, E. 51
Lajeunesse, F. 575
Lakoff, G. 430–1
Lambek, M. 399
Landry, C. 71
Landzelius, K. 41
Lange, P.G. 6, 547
large content farms and production houses 551
Larkin, B. 35, 41, 66, 70, 73, 78, 80, 105, 123, 204
Latin America *see* Brazil and television viewing; social media drama analysis and political mobilisations in Latin America; tattooing identity and indigenous nationalism in Bolivia; transgendering on social media in Chile

Lazarsfeld, P. 119
Leacock, M. 110
least developed countries 344
Leder Mackley, K. 229–31, 238
Lee, N.T. 526
Lee, S. 357
leisure and labour in the tourist encounter *see* visual economies of leisure and labour in the tourist encounter of Everest
Leonard, D. 372
Leorke, D. 147
Leung, M.W.H. 303
Lévi-Strauss, C. 20, 73, 108, 485
LGBTQ+ community 8, 553; *see also* social surveillance and sexual ethics of Muslim LGBTQ+ community on Twitter; transgendering on social media in Chile
LGBTQ+ community sousveillance and social media in South Korea 11–12, 505–13; activist groups and college organizations 506–7; anonymization 507; anti-discrimination 506, 508, 511; anti-surveillance measures 507–8; countersurveillance and anti-surveillance 507; dark sousveillance 507; de-identification of online photos 508, 510, 512; discretion practices 509; enumeration and quantification 510–13; governance effects 511; HIV/AIDS stigmatization 505; homophobia 506; interpersonal or social surveillance 506; legal, economic and social discrimination 505; legal gender change discrimination 505–6; Military Penal Code anti-sodomy law 505, 506; *nunting* 506; outing risks 506–7, 510; privacy issues 508–10; pseudonyms or nicknames 510; relational aspects of surveillance 509; self-care 510; self-performance 509; self-presentation 509; self-preservation 513; self-surveillance 509; social, economic, and legal protections, lack of 512; stigmatization, marginalization, and financial insecurity 511; survivability, endurance, and possibility 507
liberal attitudes 50
Lieback, H. 460
Liebenberg, L. 562, 564
Lim, J. 92
Lindberg, E.E. 446
Linden Lab 126
LinkedIn 223, 332, 333, 336
liquidarity 191
live-streaming 217
location-based gaming 145–54; access to and representation of public space 148; cultural issues 147; differential mobility/uneven access to movement 148, 149, 153; Enlightened or Resistance locations 150; 'farming' events 151, 152; historically significant sites 152–3; locational turn 148; location removal system 153; mapping through play 146; place-making and urban mobility 145; platformisation 145, 154; playable locative media 147–8; play as a media practice 146–7; play as place-making practice 149–50, 153–4; portals 149–50; practices, mobilities, and socialities 146; social place-making with locative media 150–1; sociocultural norms 146, 148; splintered space 148; territorialisation 150, 151
location data 506; *see also* Apple Maps; Google Maps; Global Positioning System (GPS)
location feeds 176, 177
Long Live Life Peru 470–1
Lopez, J.-A. 375
Lorenz, T. 103
Lowrie, I. 558
Lūt, Prophet 497
Luvaas, B. 164
Lynd, H. 17
Lynd, R. 17

Macdonald, S. 1, 72
MacDougall, D. 159, 166
Macha, N. 275
machine learning (ML) 12, 187, 520, 558, 559, 561, 566
MacKenzie, D.A. 201
Madan, T.N. 20
Madden, M. 487
Madianou, M. 317
Magaudda, P. 67
Mahmood, S. 496–7
Malaby, T.M. 6, 369
Malaysia 124–5, 346, 469
Malinowski, B. 73, 576, 577
Maller, C. 122
Manchester School of Anthropology 124
Mankekar, P. 21
Mann, S. 494, 502
Marcus, G.E. 376
marginalization 96, 210, 502; indigenous media 34, 36, 41; Italy 340; Kalahari 557; social surveillance and sexual ethics of Muslim LGBTQ+ community on Twitter 502; South Korea 511; *see also* Black gamers finding community with Magic Circle of Whiteness (MCW); digital inequality and relatedness in India after Internet access; media presence in the home; mediating hope amid economic crisis in Italy; transgendering on social media in Chile
Marres, N. 461
marriage equality law (South Korea) 506
Marshall, P.D. 465
Martin, M. 9
Martin, R. 7
Martine, G. 50–1

Index

Marwick, A. 494–5, 500–1
Massey, D.S. 315
mass media 18, 27, 36, 47, 185
mass migration 314
Material Display 52
materialised practices 178
materiality 5, 7, 26, 162, 216–17, 239, 255
materiality of the virtual in urban space 7, 185–97; Ausländer (foreigners) 188, 190, 196; Brooklyn 193–7; COVID-19 pandemic 185–6, 193–6; displacement 187, 193; 'friend circles' 188, 190; gentrification or yuppification 187, 188–9, 191, 193, 197; guestlisting 191–2; hipsters 188–91, 196–7; laptops 188–90, 196; mobile media in café culture 188–90; mobile self-employed people 188, 190, 196; newcomers 188; public media mutuality 190–3, 196; sociality 188–9; 'tourists' 190, 196–7; urban placemaking 186–8; virtual matter of urban space 196–7
material subjectivities 210
Mattoni, A. 126
Maurer, B. 302
Maxwell, J.C. 113 n.1
Maya Q'eqchi' video project (Guatemala) 39
Mazzarella, W. 21
Mazzolini, E. 248
Mbembe, A. 260
McCaffrey, K. 345
McDonald, T. 9, 297
McGovney-Ingram, R.L. 121
McLean Care 231
McLuhan, M. 49, 139–40, 167, 185, 602
Mead, M. 19, 163
meaning-making 209
Mebengokre-Kayapó TV (Brazil) 54–6
media anthropology degree programs 21
Media Anthropology Network 21
Media Anthropology Workshop 21
media appropriation 35, 41, 43
media convergence 27
media effects research 52
media migration from YouTube to Twitter 89–100; arrivals 98–9; aspirational aspects 93, 94, 95–6; collective conversation 97–9; collective movement 94; conceptual migration 98, 99; current situation 94; departures 98–9; deprivation or inability to tolerate one's circumstances 95; diaspora, relation to 96–7; dynamics and migration theory 93–7; emotional intensity of leaving 93; ethnographic content 91–2; forced migration 99; histories 92; individual choices 94; in-migration 98; motivations for leaving 90, 93–5; partial migration 97; radical migration 98; relocation, types of 93; return migration 97; self-actualization 95–6; transnational 90; voluntary migration 99

media practices 2; *see also* social effects of media practices
media presence in the home 229–39; 'always on' and switching off issues 235–6; applied media anthropology 238–9; case studies 235–8; command-based speech and communicational preferences 234–6, 239; content, communication, and presence 231, 233–5, 236, 238; digital intimacy 234–5; functionality 237–9; gendered characterisations of devices 235; Google Home voice assistant 229, 230, 231, 234–8; Google media content 230; hope and aspiration 231; improvisation 231, 238–9; interventional ethnography 231–3; material and sensory presence 230; privacy, security, and cost concerns 235–6; routine 231, 238–9; sensory and affective relations with technology 231; shifting modes of media and technological presence 230–1; smart home technologies 230, 231–2, 237; spatial and sensory encounters 236; trust and anxiety 231; wellbeing and independent living benefits 231–3, 239
mediated activism 36–7, 465
mediated money and social relationships among Hong Kong cross-boundary students 9, 301–12; affordances 306, 308, 310; communicative dimensions 302; consumptive relations 302, 308–11; digital money differentials 304–5; locational factors 301; methods and social context 303–4; money as media 302–3; parental nurturance and control of offspring 302, 303, 305–8; privacy from parents 307; relational factors 301; ritual communication and shared social realities 302; social impacts 303; social relationships with friends and online sellers 302, 309–10
mediated transnational life *see* Romanian migration to Netherlands and mediated transnational life
media texts, decentring of 171
mediating hope amid economic crisis in Italy 9, 331–40; income supplementation 333; job-seeking through social media 333; meaningful relationships, crafting of 337–9; new friendships 332; online branding and local forms of socialities 353–5; personal recommendations 335; precarity of employment 331–3, 334, 339–40; professional and social spheres, division of 334, 336; self-branding and self-promotion 332, 336–40; self-employment 332; social belonging and recognition 338; social connections and networking 335; sociality 340; social media and the practice of hoping 335–7, 339–40; strengthening ties with old friends and acquaintances 332; temporary jobs 333; unemployment 331–3, 335–40; wellbeing 332–3; workforce casualisation 333
mediation 26, 27; patterns 91

Index

mediatisation 2, 26, 123–5, 469; global 246; visibility and visuality 249, 255
Melanesia 350
memory chips 347
Mendoza, A. 128
merchandise sales 545
Merleau-Ponty, M. 414
Merry, S.E. 511
Merton, R. 119
Messenger 245, 254, 320
Messeri, L. 12
Messy Truth VR, The 576
Meta (Wikimedia coordination site) 272, 279
metadata 280
metrics 546, 549, 551–2
Mexico 19, 40, 446
Michaels, E. 23, 38, 40
Micheaux, O. 357
Microsoft 583
microwork platforms 216
migration *see* Romanian migration to Netherlands and mediated transnational life
Milan, S. 486
Milk, C. 576
Miller, C. 561
Miller, D. 171–2, 247, 317, 411, 421, 520, 545
Miller, R. 221
Mills, C. 428
Milo, S. 445
Minsky, M. 573
Mirzoeff, N. 160
misanthropy 435
MIT Algorithmic Justice Lab 527
moderators 372–3, 376
modernisation 18–19
Mohammid, S. 12
Molé, N. 334
monetisation 91, 94, 95, 99, 545, 547, 548
Mongolia 339
Monopoly 111
Moore, K. 6
moral empathy gap 465–6, 469, 472
Morales, E. 23, 384, 385–6, 388, 390, 393 n.5
Morgan, J. 319
Morgenthaler, A. 435–6
Morocco 339, 492
Morris, J. 248
Movimiento a Socialismo (MAS) (Bolivia) 385, 387, 388, 390
Mu, Y. 249
Muehlebach, A. 334
Mueller, G. 225
Muhammad, Prophet 496
Mukurtu project 265
Müller, K. 8
multivocal materialities of video meetings and deafness at Swedish television (SVT) Teckenspråk 7, 200–11; agency 201; 'artifacts' 204–5, 210; deafness at Swedish television (SVT) Teckenspråk 203–4; experiences 205; framing 205; intra-actions 203, 210; materialisation of D/deaf subjectivity 209; practices 205–8; processes 208–9; Swedish Sign Language (SSL) 200–1, 203–5, 207, 209–10
Munn, N. 398
Museum for Archaeology and Anthropology (Cambridge) 266
museums *see* postcolonial digital collections in museums and archives
Museum of Voice 266
Museveni, Y. 398
music duplication 70
music transactions and infrastructures in underground hip-hop touring 5, 65–75; collective belonging 74; demo tapes 69–74; DIY production 70; ethnographies 69; foundational elements of hip-hop 71; generalised exchange 73; Ground Control Allstars tour 65, 67–8, 70–1, 72; Ground Control Records 67, 69, 72; guest appearances and 'posse cuts' 72–3; infrastructural networks 71; infrastructural turn 74; infrastructures of industry, touring, and merchandise sales 67–9; Nu Gruv Alliance 65, 72; peer-to-peer (P2P) file sharing 70; self-presentations 72; social networking 71, 73; social unity 73; soft infrastructures 66, 71, 74; streaming services 70; trust, sense of 73
Muslim prayer apps interception by U.S. intelligence agencies 493
Muslims *see* political trolls and political conservatism in Turkey; racism against Muslims and neo-nationalism in Denmark; social surveillance and sexual ethics of Muslim LGBTQ+ community on Twitter
mutuality 192–3
Myanmar 40
Myerhoff, B. 466
MyKnet.org 42–3
MySpace 92

Nafus, D. 519
Nair, V. 262
Nakamura, L. 577
Namibia *see* Artificial Intelligence (AI) and cause-and-effect reasoning among the Ju|'hoansi people in the Kalahari
Napolitano, V. 164
Napster 70
Nardi, B. 368
National Archives (India) 260
nationalism 123, 260, 428, 429, 438; *see also* neonationalism; tattooing identity and indigenous nationalism in Bolivia

608

National Museum of India 260
Natsuhiko, U. 135, 137
Naver 506
Nazi Party 430
Neale, L. 95
Negroponte, N. 216
neonationalism 427, 430, 432, 437
Nepal *see* visual economies of leisure and labour in the tourist encounter of Everest
Nepal, S. 249
nerd politics 121
Netflix 2, 215, 583
Netherlands *see* Romanian migration to Netherlands and mediated transnational life
networked images 160
newness of digital media 25
news and journalism 22–3
New Zealand 152, 259, 265
NextDoor 193–4, 196
Neyland, D. 559
NHK (Japan) 139
Niantic Labs 145–53
Nichols, L. 7
Nico Nico Douga (NND) streaming broadcast platform 132–9, 141
Nieborg, D.B. 546
Nigeria 105
Nimoy, L. 443
Nintendo Wii 110
Nordic countries 430
Norgay, T. 248–9
North America 2, 18, 21
Norwich Access Group 128
novelty of a site 95
novelty of TV 92
Nqeisji, C. 12
Nu Gruv Alliance 65, 72
Nyae Nyae Conservancy (Kalahari) 557, 561–2

objectification 8
object potentials 175
Ocran, N. 553
Octopus card 305–11
Oks, M. 146
Olympics (1936) 112, 114 n.3
Ong, J.C. 461
ontological security 231
Onuoha, M. 487
Oral Citations Project (Wikimedia Foundation) 8, 272–82; acceptance, rejection, and debate 278; analysis of networks traversing articles 279–80; attack pages or copyright violations 277; authority of expertise downplayed or ignored 277; authority used to support or oppose claims 277; bad-faith contributions 277; deleted or disputed knowledge claims as entry points 281; deleted text 279; entry points via flagged erasures 277; following sources and characterisation 277–9; Funds Dissemination Committee 276; good faith collaboration 276; knowledge representation 281; links, removal of 279; new centres of power/knowledge 280–2; obstruction, refusal or demeaning of factual claims 277; page patrollers 277; platform bias 280–1; power/knowledge sources 275–7; reliable knowledge 277, 281; Reliable Sources Noticeboard 277–8; secondary sources 277–8; structured data 279–80; surr game article 273–4, 277–9, 281–2; verifiability 277; warning tags 279
Oreglia, E. 348
Ortner, S. 171
OTD Chile (Organizing Trans Diversities) 410

Pace, R. 4, 92
paedophilia concerns 553
Pakistan 20
Pandemic 110
Papua New Guinea - Kaluli tribe 109
Parson, T. 302
participatory culture 27
participatory rules 91
Partition Archive (1947) (India) 264–5
partner program 91
Parvin, N. 522, 527
Paul, J. 98
Paul, L. 98
Pauliks, K. 174, 178
PayMe (HSBC) 305
payment apps 305–11
PDF files 81
Peake, B. 79
Pearce, C. 96
Pearce, M. 526
Pelikan 458
PeoplePerHour 216
personal factors 97
personal and family ties 9
person-centric approach 429
Pertierra, A.C. 201
Peru 466, 469, 475
Peterson, L. 11, 446
Peterson, M.A. 4, 441
Peterson, R.A. 68
Philippines 461
Phillips, M. 103
PhotoMedia 166
photomedia 7, 157–68; academic methods 162; acting 168; Covid-19 pandemic 157, 164, 165, 167; facemasks, discarded 157, *157*, 162, *163*, 164, *165*, 166, 167; future-oriented media anthropology 166–7; intervention 160; method 160; noticing and connecting 164;

photography as an intervention (imagining) 160, 164–5, 166–7, 168; photography as an object (observing) 160–2, 164; photography as a method (thinking) 162–4, 168; research object 160; speculation 160, 166–7; techno-reflexivity 166, 167; use, adopt, and adapt 161; vernacular methods 161–2; visual anthropology as a practice 157–60; walking methodologies 163–4, 167
Pickren, G. 219
Pietikäinen, S. 40
piety movements 497
Pikman Bloom 149
Pimentel, R. 564
Pink, S. 7, 90, 201, 319, 459, 545
Pinochet, A. 412
'Pizzagate' 444
platformisation 27, 145, 152, 154
platform labour 187
platform urbanism 187
play, game and design 27–8
plurality of publics 465
pluriverse 483, 486
Poell, T. 546
Pohjonen, M. 456, 460
Pokémon Go 108, 145–6, 148–51, 152–3, 532
Pokéstops 152
Poletti, G. 335
police brutality, racialized 507
police brutality video recordings 494
police racial profiling 494
political activism 442
political conservatism 8, 10–11, 332, 441; *see also* political trolls and political conservatism in Turkey
political mobilizations *see* social media drama analysis and political mobilisations in Latin America
political theory 259
political trolls and political conservatism in Turkey 11, 454–62; AKP regime 454–8, 460–1; Aktrolls (pro-government) 454–61; authoritarian regime 454–6, 461–2; digital traces 461; discourse community 454–5; discursivity and troll science 460; emergency period 457; Gezi Park Protests 455–7, 461; Gulen movement 456–7; hate speech and extreme speech 460; independent and voluntary troll circles 458; Islamisation efforts 456; multi-platform, multi-method approach 456–9; reasons for study 455–6; Russian troll farms 456–7; semi-anonymity or secretive tactics 457; troll circles 457, 459; trolling as discourse community 459–61
Politiken - The Stripe (*Striben*) cartoon series (Denmark) 435
Polson, E. 148

polymedia 27, 90
Poole, D. 246–7
Population Services International (PSI) 399–407; Go-Getters program 402
portals 149–50
postcolonial digital collections in museums and archives 8, 258–69; authenticity, ownership, and circulation 266; collecting, archiving, and categorising 265; cultural appropriation 266; digital accessibility and circulation 266; digital as agent 264, 267; digital as instrument 262–3; digital as mirror or mimesis 263–4; digital objects and mimetic returns 266–7; digital projects in theory and practice 264; digital repatriation 266, 268 n.13; digitisation 260–2; historicising perspective 267; instrumentality 264, 265, 267; mimesis 264, 267; new forms of digital collecting 264–7; postcolonial theories of digital representation 262–4; power relations 258, 267; representation 258–9, 267; situating postcolonial in museums 259–60; symbolic ownership and appropriation 267
Postero, N. 386
Postill, J. 6, 36–7, 57 n.2, 134, 146, 459, 469, 545
post-radial semiotics 26–7
Poulantzas, N. 454
Powdermaker, H. 18, 215
Powell, L. 430
power 20, 23, 26, 259; asymmetries 559; digital inequality and relatedness in India after Internet access 345; dynamics 148, 152, 279–80; indigenous media 36, 43; mediated money and social relationships among Hong Kong cross-boundary students 303; postcolonial digital collections in museums and archives 258, 267; social surveillance and sexual ethics of Muslim LGBTQ on Twitter 493, 494, 495
Prabhala, A. 272–3, 279, 281
practice, media as 5, 6–7
practice approach *see* content-as-practice
practice theory 6, 52, 119–29, 127, 146, 176
Pratt, Y.P. 39
precarity of digital infrastructure *see* community-based research and precarity of digital infrastructure
precarity of employment *see* mediating hope amid economic crisis in Italy; YouTube algorithm and influencer precarity, discrimination, and (in)visibility
predictive analytics 489
Press, B. 428, 431
Prime-Time Society (PTS) (Brazil) 48, 51–2
privacy issues: community-based research and precarity of digital infrastructure 77; harms 487; LGBTQ+ community sousveillance and social media in South Korea 508–10; media presence in the home 235–6; mediated money and

social relationships among Hong Kong cross-boundary students 307; social surveillance and sexual ethics of Muslim LGBTQ+ community on Twitter 493, 500–1; WeChat groups and WeChat friends in China 290, 298–9
Probabilistic Programming Languages (PPL) 561, 563, 564, 565
Proctor, R.N. 428
product placement 53
professional content creators, rise of 545–6
profile page 91
Progress Party (Denmark) 432
Prosser, J. 414
Pro Tools 70
pseudonyms or nicknames 510
public appearances 545
public discourse 123
Puerini, J.F. 103
Purvajo-ni Aankh exhibition event 266

Q-aligned social networks 11
Qanon political conspiracy movement 11, 27, 441–2, 443–6, 447, 449
Queer Cultural Festival (South Korea) 513
Queer Film Festival (South Korea) 513
Quick Response (QR) codes 162

Rabikowska, M. 467
Raby, F. 201
race 27, 69, 92, 509
racialization 369, 427, 428, 435, 438, 507
racism 501; structural 524; *see also* Black gamers finding community with Magic Circle of Whiteness (MCW) 368, 374, 377
racism against Muslims and neo-nationalism in Denmark 10–11, 427–39; Abu Ghraib and eroticization of torture 435–7; civility and incivility concerns 431–7; 'Danish exclusionary reasoning in social media and web news commentaries' (DER) 428–9; desensitization and denial of responsibility 435; extremism 438; facts, indifference to 437–8; fractal boundaries 437–8; fractal reasoning 438; fractal scalarity 437–8; fractal spatiality 437–8; nationalism 428, 429, 438; neonationalism 427, 430, 432, 437; 1 to 8 division of power and dominance of media-driven political rights 429, 430–1; political control of media and voters 431; racialization 427, 428, 435, 438; racism 428, 429, 432–3, 436, 438; strategic ignorance 428, 431, 437–8; 'Study of Experiences and Reaction to Racialization in Denmark' (SERR) 428–30, 437; talking points 431
Rajagopal, A. 54
Ramadan, Z. 522
Rancière, J. 141
Rangaswamy, N. 350

Rankin, J. 577
Rasmussen, A.F. 431
Rathwa, N. 266
Rathwa, V. 266
Reagle, J. 276
Reckwitz, A. 171, 173, 176
recognition and fame-seeking in Uganda 10, 395–408; Artivists 4 Life (A4L) 395–6, 399–405, 407; being known 398; HIV awareness and intergenerational disease transmission 396, 398, 401, 405; modernity and morality claims 398–404, 405; Population Services International (PSI) 399–407; promiscuity and hedonism, encouragement of 396; public health awareness campaigns 396–7; publicity 395; *Red Pepper* newspaper 395, 399–400, 403–4, 406–8; sensitization projects 397–8, 400, 405; sex and development in the public sphere 398–9; 'sugar daddies' and cross-generational sex 395, 401, 403–8; tabloid press 395–7
recommendation systems 544, 547, 550, 553, 554
Redfield, R. 18
Red-Green Alliance (RGA) (Denmark) 432
Red Pepper newspaper (Uganda) 395, 399–400, 403–4, 406–8
Rees, T. 159
Reichert, R. 217
Reisman, D. 583
relatedness *see* digital inequality and relatedness in India after Internet access
relational labour 551
remediation 2, 104, 105–8, 112–13
remediation and games 105–8
repetition 176
representation, media as 5, 7–8
representational politics 279
resistance, politics of 259
(Re)start Reality app 536–7, 538, 539
Rheingold, H. 92
Richterich, A. 217
Risam, R. 258, 264
Ritter, C. 12
ritual 2; performative approach 108
robotics 223–4
Rodgers, S. 20
Rodwell, E. 6
Rogan, J. 442, 445
Rogers, A. 579 n.2
Rogers, S. 5–6
Romanian migration to Netherlands and mediated transnational life 9, 314–24; aspirations 316, 323; case background and research methodology 317–19; collective belonging 315, 317; collective imaginations 316; collective memories 314, 317; cultural formations 316–17; cultural mediation 315;

cultural memories 315; cultures of migration 315–16, 421–4; diaspora culture 314, 315–16, 319–21; diaspora formation 317; diasporic belonging 321; digital intimacies as discursive formations 316–17; gendered aspect 319, 321; identity 315, 320; imaginations 314, 317; imagined communities 315, 323; language transmission 319–21; social discourses 314; social effects 314; social mediation 315
Ross, M. 357, 578–9 n.1
Rossiter, N. 221
Rouch, J. 39
Rousseff, D. 56
routinization 121, 176–7, 179
Ruberg, B. 376
Ruchatz, J. 174, 178
Rumsfeld, D. 430
Russell, A.B. 357
Russell-Bennett, R. 95
Ryan, J. 68, 72

'sad selfie' 173–4, 176–7, 179
Safransky, S. 487
Sahapedia project 265
Sahlins, M. 73
Said, E.W. 262
Saka, E. 11, 457
Salazar, J.F. 34
Sámi people 40
Sammells, C. 391
Samsnytt (previously Avpixlat) extreme right website 434
Samsung Pay 305
San animal tracking practices (Kalahari) 562–3
sandbox-style computer games 113
saturation of TV 92
Savage, S. 455
Schatzki, T. 124, 146, 171, 173
Schieffelin, E. 14, 108–9, 110, 472
Scratch (visual language) 562
Scuro, J. 316
Seaver, N. 459, 519, 527–8, 547, 554, 559
Second Life platform 96, 125–6, 127
Secret Path app 534, 535, 536
self-actualization 90
self-construction 404, 411
self-determination 34, 40, 43
self-expression 95, 99
selfhood 399
selfies 160; *see also* 'sad selfie'
self-management 468
self-presentation 509
self-promotion 468
self-representation 42, 251, 382, 414
Senft, T. 545
Seoul Queer Culture Festival 510–12
Sewell, W.H. 121

sexism 501
sexual ethics *see* social surveillance and sexual ethics of Muslim LGBTQ+ community on Twitter
Shakhsari, S. 494
Sheehy, B. 122
Sherman, J. 519
Shibutani, T. 121
short-video-based (SVB) consumer activism 126
Shove, E. 124
Shroeder, R. 468–9
Sicart, M. 146–7, 151
Silverstein, M. 27
Simmel, G. 302
Simon, W. 430
Simonson, E. 249
Simpson, S. 548
Sinanan, J. 7–8
Sindelar, D. 461
Singer, M. 18, 466
Singh, L. (AKA Superwoman) 552
Siri 108, 280
Skype 135, 141, 320, 371
Slack 186, 193–4, 196
Slater, D. 545
Slater, M. 572–3, 575
Sloane, M. 187
smart city discourses 187
smartphone 10, 26, 86, 323, 342, 494, 519; China 289, 291–3, 295; content-as-practice 173, 176, 179; Hong Kong 302, 305–7; India 344–51; location-based gaming 147; materiality of the virtual in urban space 186, 190, 193–4; media presence in the home 230, 234; photomedia 167; social effects of media practices 123–5; visual economies in the tourist encounter (Everest) 255; *see also* digital inequality and relatedness in India after Internet access
smartphone augmented reality and heritage tourist attractions in Estonia 12, 532–41; AR prototype test 535; discovery points 535; dynamic maps 534; educational potential 532; embedded maps 535; embodying imaginings 538–40; emplacement of representation 540–1; Estonian Maritime Museum 536–8; ethical issues 536, 541; funnels and event tracking features 536; haptic interfaces 540; hybridised places 539; indirect augmented reality 537; Kanban method 535; locative media 534; making apps for tourist sites 534–6; map-based games 534; mixed reality 537–8; murals and street art 536–7, 539; pathfinder games 534; sensorial capacities 535; touristic flânerie 534–5
Smith, C. 40
Smith, S.P. 250
Snapchat 92

soap operas 19, 20, 399; *see also telenovelas*
social aspirations 248
social change and identities 8, 10
social conservatism 332, 444, 465
social effects of media practices 119–29; activist space 125; agentive (or enabling) effects 127–8; consequences 121; disabling and/or disruptive effects 128; impacts 121–2; influences 121; mediatising effects 123–5; necessity for effects 127–8; new social worlds 125; nexus of practices 124; notion of effects 121; online virtual world 125; practice theory 120; recursive public 125; social practice theory 123; social worlds 120–3, 125, 126, 127; sub worlds 121, 126; synchronic and diachronic methods 127; technological mediation 123; worlding effects 123, 125–6
social expectations 298
social factors 97
social hierarchies 26, 351, 352
social identity 52
sociality 95, 96, 98, 99, 239, 547; centrality of media 90; group 9; location-based gaming 146; materiality of the virtual in urban space 188–9; mediating hope amid economic crisis in Italy 340, 353–5
socialization 48
social life of algorithms approach 528
social media algorithms and routinised practices 176–7
social media drama analysis and political mobilisations in Latin America 11, 465–75; citizen activism 465; Colombia 466, 469, 470, 472–5; conservative mobilisation 468–70; cultural performance 466; mediatisation 469; minute of silence (ritualised action) 470–2, 475; moral empathy gap 465–6, 469, 472; morally centred social movements 467–9; participation, sense of 466; Peru 466, 469, 470–1, 475; Plantón por la vida video 474–5; pro-life march and sit-in 470–3; right-to-life of the unborn 470–5; ritualisation 469, 474
social merchandising 53
social networking 44
social network sites (SNS) 91
social pedagogy 474
social practice theory 429
social protest 121
social relatedness 351
social relationships *see* mediated money and social relationships among Hong Kong cross-boundary students
social support 95
social surveillance and sexual ethics of Muslim LGBTQ+ community on Twitter 11, 492–502; behavioural discipline 495; collective social surveillance 496; countering violent extremism (CVE) programs 493; *da'wa* movements 496–7; disciplinary power of surveillance 495; Doomer Girl meme 498–9; enjoining the right and forbidding the wrong 492, 493–7, 498, 500–2; homophobic and transphobic trolling 493, 497, 499–502; individual privacy and personal freedom, right to 493, 500–1; interpersonal forms of observational discipline 494; interpersonal and reciprocal nature of surveillance 495–6, 501; marginalization 502; misogynistic rhetoric 500; observational discipline exposing hypocrisy 502; patriarchy, oppression, and social injustice 499; power relations 493, 494; social justice-oriented approach 500; sousveillance 494–5, 501–2; state surveillance and threat of terrorism 493–4; verbal admonishment and collective accountability 497
social theory 259
sociopolitical change 40–1
Sojoyner, D.M. 376
somatic modes of attention 364
Sontag, S. 436
Souroujon, G. 468
sousveillance 494–5, 501–2; *see also* LGBTQ+ community sousveillance and social media in South Korea
South Africa 272–3, 275, 344, 560
South America 2, 509
South Korea *see* LGBTQ+ community sousveillance and social media in South Korea
Spain 123, 161, 317
speech-driven interfaces 108
Spiegelhalter, D. 563
spin doctors 431
spinner games 564–5
Spitulnik, D. 201, 204, 314–15
Spotify 2, 459
spreadability 26–7
Springer, C. 357
Sreberny, A. 494
Stafford, C. 305
stage model 48–50
Stewart, M. 34, 39
Stickam 91
Stoler, A. 264
Stovall, M. 359
Strain, E. 577
strategic ignorance 428, 431, 437–8
strategic objectification 41
Straubhaar, J. 54
Strauss, A.L. 121, 126, 127
streaming services 70
Strengers, Y. 7
Strieber, W. 443
structural inequalities 332

Index

structuralist-functionalist paradigm 18
structuration theory 126
structured organizational relationships 68
students 505; *see also* mediated money and social relationships among Hong Kong cross-boundary students
subversion 210
Suchman, L. 203
Summer in the City 546
surface ontology 520
Suri, S. 519, 546
surveillance 8, 11–12, 481; anti-surveillance 507–8; capitalism 488; imagined 509; interpersonal or social 506; relational aspects 509; self-surveillance 509; systemic 487; tech-surveillance 482–5; *see also* social surveillance and sexual ethics of Muslim LGBTQ+ community on Twitter
Sutton-Smith, B. 147
Swales, J. 454
Swartz, L. 301–3, 311
Sweden 468; *see also* multivocal materialities of video meetings and deafness at Swedish television (SVT) Teckenspråk
Switch 224
symbolic anthropology 4
symbolic systems, media as 20–1
systemic surveillance 487

Taha, M. 345
Takaragawa, S. 578
Take Back Illinois 106, *107*, 109–11
Tanner, S. 459–61
Taobao shopping platform 309
Tarantino, Q. 357
Tashka 578 n.1
TaskRabbit 216
Tasveer Ghar archive 265
tattooing identity and indigenous nationalism in Bolivia 10, 23, 381–93; abstraction and appropriation 391–2; aesthetics 386, 387, 388; content and meanings 382; cultural symbols (Ñatita with chullo and coca leaves) 388–90, 391; cultural valuation 384, 386; hybridity 382–3, 388, 390–1; identity 382–4, 386–7, 392; indigenismo 382, 386, 387; indigenous symbolism 387–91; meaning attached to style of tattoos 383; nationalisation of indigeneity 392; nationalism 386–8; politics of indigeneity 384–7; remixing 388; self-representation 382; social status 381; symbolism of indigeneity 384, 386, 390, 392; textile swallows 390–1; text tattoos 388
Taussig, M. 263
Taylor, A. 7, 218
Taylor, C. 362
Taylor, E.B. 303

Taylor, T.L. 371–2
Tea Party Movement (USA) 468
technical features 91, 99
Technicolor Experience Center (TEC) 570–2, 574
technology literacy 84–5
technomasculinity 369
techno-reflexivity 167
tech-surveillance 482–5
Telegram 458–9
telenovelas 48, 50–1
television *see* Brazil and television viewing; interactive TV broadcasting in Japan
temporal delay 174
temporalities 162
Tenhunen, S. 9
Terms and Conditions 481
terrorist content 552
text-based practices 177–8
text-centric methods 179
textual captions 174
thematic considerations 8–12
thinktanks 430
Third Wave spiritual warfare movement 446
Thomas, L. 519
Thompson, K. 248
3D virtual environments 24
thumbnails 549, 550
TikTok 99, 545
Tinder 172
top-down approach 8, 258
tourism *see* smartphone augmented reality and heritage tourist attractions in Estonia
tourist attractions *see* smartphone augmented reality and heritage tourist attractions in Estonia
T-Pain (Najm, F.R.) 368–9
Traditional Knowledge Digital Library 265
trajectories 164, 166
transgendering on social media in Chile 10, 410–21; autobiography, importance of 414; biomedical transition 411; discrimination and aggression 415; gendered subjectivity 417; Gender Identity Law (2018) 410; gender performativity theorization 411; hegemonic femininity 412; HIV/AIDS epidemic 412; identity construction 411–12; mediation and self-construction 411; moderation 420; normative femininity, rewarded and punished 415, 420; normative gender 415–17; self-representation 414; sexual harassment 417; sexualisation of femininity 415–16, 418–19; strategic visibility 411; transnormativity 412, 416; transphobia, misogyny, and stigma 418–19; underrepresentation of transfemininity online 419; visibility and recognisability 415; 'whisper network' 411
Traube, E. 20

Index

trends 121, 551
Trere, E. 126
Trinidad 509; *see also* Amazon Echo Look and algorithmic bias and misrecognition of Black bodies in Trinidad
Trump, D. 442, 444
Tumblr 506, 507
Tunstall, E. 579 n.3
Turkey 509; *see also* political trolls and political conservatism in Turkey
Turner, E. 20
Turner, T. 37–9, 41
Turner, V. 11, 20, 466, 469, 472
TV-Talk 52
Twitch 368, 375, 545
Twitter 6, 11, 50; Akgossip 457; algorithmic profiling and datafication of children 489; Black gamers finding community with Magic Circle of Whiteness (MCW) 375; Brazil 56; data centre labour and maintenance of media infrastructure 215; Japan 132–6, 138, 141; Latin America 466–7, 469, 471; South Korea 505, 506, 507; Turkey 458, 459, 460, 461; United States 443; *see also* media migration from YouTube to Twitter; social surveillance and sexual ethics of Muslim LGBTQ+ community on Twitter

Uber 216, 546
Udupa, S. 258, 456, 460
Uganda *see* recognition and fame-seeking in Uganda
Ujakpa, M. 12
UNAIDS 401
Unertl, K.M. 86
Unidos por la Vida (United for Life) 473
United Kingdom 19, 20–1, 346, 470, 483–4, 492–3
United Nations Declaration on the Rights of Indigenous Peoples 34
United Nations International Migration Report (2015) 317–18
United States 6, 17, 48, 49, 50, 348; algorithmic profiling and datafication of children 483, 490; Amazon Echo Look 522; digital intimacies 316; film industry 18, 20; hip hop 5; indigenous and activist media 23–4; legal framework 519; LGBTQ+ community 492–3, 501, 509; mass communication 121; morally centred social movements 467–8; national culture 19; news media political orientation 429; racism against Muslims and neo-nationalism 438; Syrian migrants 345; virtual reality immersion 570–1, 573; *see also* conspiracy media ecologies in United States
uploads 549
Upwork 216
urban-folk continuum 18

urban inequalities 187; *see also* materiality of the virtual in urban space; mediating hope amid economic crisis in Italy
urbanisation 18
urban space *see* materiality of the virtual in urban space
Uriasposten website (Denmark) 434
Uru Diaspora 96
user-generated content 442
user-generated maps 148
Ushahidi (Kenya) 275

van Dijk, Z. 274
Vanuatu 259
Varnelis, K. 219
Velkova, J. 218
Verran, H. 265, 561
VidCon UK & USA 546
video calls 232, 233–4, 291, 320, 348; materiality of the virtual in urban space 194, 195, 196, 197; *see also* multivocal materialities of video meetings and deafness at Swedish television (SVT) Teckenspråk; Skype; Zoom
video poker and slot machines 110
'Vietnam syndrome' 430
viewing habits 48
Vimeo 336
Vine service/Viners 98–9
virtual diaspora 96, 98
virtual reality *see* materiality of the virtual in urban space
virtual reality immersion 570–9; *Awavena* 570–2, 574, 576, 578 n.1; 'being there' 571, 573, 574, 577; critiquing and demystifying immersion 575–7; defining immersion 572–4; empathy 576–7, 579 n.3; ethics of representing 'the other' 572; immediacy 575; immersion and presence distinction 572–3; impacts 575; mediated practices 574–5, 577; methodologies 571; producing and consuming immersion 574–5; remediation 575; self and other, collapse of 576; storytelling potential 571; Technicolor Experience Center (TEC) 570–2, 574
Vishnevsky, S. 371
visibility online *see* YouTube algorithm and influencer precarity, discrimination and (in)visibility
visual economies of leisure and labour in the tourist encounter of Everest 7–8, 245–56; aesthetics for mediating aspirations 246, 248, 255–6; aspiration and achievement 248; commodification 249; cultural capital 248; deaths from summit attempts and memorials 249, 253; digital communication building and disrupting relationships 251–5; digital connectivity 249; earthquake and avalanches 247, 249, 251; environmental challenges 246; imagining and experiencing

Everest 246, 255; materiality 255; mediatisation 249, 255; narratives of solitude, spiritualism, and mountain exploration 246; obligation and reciprocity networks 246; production and circulation of images 246; visibility in global visual cultures 247–50
visual notes 161
VitalCall 234
vlogs/vloggers 6, 24, 90–1, 93–4, 97, 99, 419, 539, 546, 548, 550, 552
Vogel, E.F. 291
voice assistants *see* Amazon Alexa; Google Home voice assistant; media presence in the home; Siri
von Däniken, E. 442
Vonderau, A. 218

wadud, a. 499
Wajcman, J. 201
Wales, J. 274–5
Wallace, M. 357
Wall, T. 564
Wallis, C. 345
Wallis, K. 578–9 n.1
Wallworth, L. 570–1, 574, 578 n.1
Wang, X. 9
Ward, G.K. 40
Warde, A. 127
Warner, W.L. 17
watch time 549
Waters, J.L. 303
Watkins, S.G. 369
Wauchope, R. 448
Webex 193
WeChat groups and WeChat friends in China 9, 289–99; comradeship 291, 296, 297, 299; daily use among older generation 291–3; equity rule 294, *295*, 296; expressive group 294, 295, *295*; family groups 295; former classmates 295; former colleagues 295, 297, 299; group size 290, 293; *guanxi* rule 294, *295*, 296–8; instrumental group 294, 295–6, *295*; interpersonal ties 292, 294–5, 298–9; joke group 296; kinship and non-kinship ties 290; mediated friendship 290–1; *mianzi* (Chinese face) 294, 296–7; mixed ties 294, 295, *295*, 296–7; need rule 294, *295*; positive energy 293; privacy settings 290, 298–9; 'red envelope' group 296; same-sex, same age/generation 290; 'sent-down' group 295–6, 299; sociality rules 290, 292, 294, 297–8; types of groups 293–7; WeChat friends 289, 293; WeChat groups 289
WeChat Pay 306–8, 310–11
WeChat Wallet 305–6, 309
Weiner, J.F. 37, 38
Weismantel, M. 391
WELL (Whole Earth 'Lectronic Link) 92

Weltevred, E. 461
Westermeyer, W. 468
Western Europe 18
Western perspectives, centring of 3; *see also* postcolonial digital collections in museums and archives; racism against Muslims and neo-nationalism in Denmark
Westmoreland, M. 578
WhatsApp 50, 245, 293, 347, 458, 522, 562; content-as-practice 172; materiality of the virtual in urban space 186, 193–4, 196; mediating hope amid economic crisis in Italy 333, 335, 337; Romanian migration to Netherlands and mediated transnational life 320, 322
white supremacy 442
'Why We Post' project 290, 293
Wikidata 276, 280
Wikimedia 277, 280
Wikimedia Commons 273–5, 278–9
Wikimedia Foundation *see* Oral Citations Project (Wikimedia Foundation)
Wikimedia-l mailing list 278–9
Wikipedia 8
Wikiprojects 276
Wilk, R. 105, 122, 125
Wilken, R. 147
Willems, R. 315
Willer, R. 465
Wilson, P. 34, 39
Wilson, W. 357
Wittgenstein, L. 113 n.1
Wolff, A. 11
Wong, K.C. 9
Wood, H. 37
Woodward, S. 522
Wordpress 42
working conditions, poor 217
World Bank 385, 397, 398
World Economic Forum 427
worlding effects 123, 125–6
Worldview Shifts 52
World of Warcraft 103
Wortham, E.C. 33, 40
Wulff, M. 435–6

Yadav, A. 264
Yandex data centre (Finland) 218
Yan, Y. 291
Yang, M. 122
Yawanawá, T. 570, 571, 578 n.1
Yeşil, B. 454
Yinping, Y. 92
YouTube 2, 6, 50, 339, 583; algorithmic profiling and datafication of children 482; Brazil 57; content-as-practice 172; India 345, 348; Italy 332, 334, 338; United States 442, 446; *see also* media migration from YouTube to Twitter

YouTube algorithm and influencer precarity, discrimination and (in)visibility 12, 544–54; burnout 550; content output quantity and quality 550; demonetisation 546, 552–3; deselection of content 552, 553; discourses, practices, and experiences 544, 554; discrimination 544; elite influencers 545; feeling the algorithm 552; gaming the algorithm 549–52; gender inequalities 547; growth hackers 547; income and monetisation of content 545, 547, 548; invisibility 547, 550; metrics 546, 549, 551–2; microinfluencers 545; professional content creators 545–6; recommendation systems 544, 547, 550, 553, 554; trends 551; victories and failures 548; video length and output 550–1; views, likes, and subscribers 545; visibility 549, 551, 554

Yu, Z. 126
Yuen Thompson, B. 383
Yurchak, A. 136

Zapatista movement (Mexico) 23, 41–2
Zeffiro, A. 148
Zengyan, C. 92
Zhu, Y. 86
Zimmermann, C. 456
Zoom 78, 79, 84–5, 522; materiality of the virtual in urban space 186, 193–6, *195*
Zuboff, S. 488

Printed in the United States
by Baker & Taylor Publisher Services